Who's who

Patron
His Majesty King Charles III

President
Alan Titchmarsh CBE DL VMH

President Emerita
Dame Mary Berry

Vice-Presidents
Elizabeth Anton
Angela Azis BEM
Ann Budden
Daphne Foulsham MBE
A Martin McMillan OBE
Heather Skinner
Penny Snell CBE

Chairman
Rupert Tyler

Deputy Chairman
Sue Phipps

Hon Treasurer
Andrew Ratcliffe

Trustees
Arit Anderson
Atty Beor-Roberts
Vanessa Berridge
Raoul Curtis-Machin
Lucy Hall
Maureen Kesteven
Professor John Newton OBE
Susan Paynton
Mark Porter
Vernon Sanderson
Debbie Thomson

Chief Executive
Dr Richard Claxton

Ambassadors
Emma Bridgewater CBE
Fiona Bruce
Danny Clarke
Alan Gray
Anya Lautenbach
Joe Swift
Rachel de Thame
Jo Whiley

Chairman's message

Thanks to the generosity and dedication of our garden openers and the tireless efforts of our volunteers, I am proud to tell you that in 2025 we donated almost £3.9 million to our beneficiary charities – support that is more important than ever in these challenging times. To everyone who opened their gardens, gave their time and visited: thank you.

The National Garden Scheme thrives because of the people who support it. We are deeply grateful for the continued support of our Patron, His Majesty The King, and for the remarkable leadership of Dame Mary Berry, who stepped down as President after ten inspiring years. Her passion and wisdom have helped shape the Scheme, and we are delighted that she will remain with us as President Emerita. We now warmly welcome Alan Titchmarsh CBE DL VMH as our new President, and I know he shares our excitement for our gardens and for the future.

This year also marked another significant change: we said farewell to George Plumptre, our Chief Executive for 15 years, whose commitment was nothing short of inspirational. We thank George for his outstanding service and extend a warm welcome to Dr Richard Claxton, a former GP from Kent, who will lead us into our centenary year in 2027 and ensure that the Scheme is stronger than ever as we head into our next century.

This handbook – supported by our long-standing sponsor, Rathbones – is full of wonderful gardens waiting to be explored. Your visits make all that we do to support nursing and health charities possible, so thank you for being part of the National Garden Scheme and for helping us continue our important work.

Enjoy your visits and thank you for supporting us.

Rupert Tyler

Rupert Tyler
Chairman

Tips on using your Handbook

This book lists all the gardens opening for the National Garden Scheme. They are arranged alphabetically in county sections, each including a map, calendar of opening dates and details of each garden.

Symbols explained

NEW Gardens opening for the first time this year or re-opening after a long break.

◆ Garden also opens on non-National Garden Scheme days. (Gardens which carry this symbol contribute to the National Garden Scheme either by opening on a specific day(s) and/or by giving a guaranteed contribution.)

♿ Wheelchair access to at least the main features of the garden.

🐕 Dogs on short leads welcome.

✽ Plants usually for sale.

•)) Card payments accepted.

NPC Plant Heritage National Plant Collection.

🛏 Gardens that offer accommodation.

☕ Refreshments are available, normally at a charge.

🪑 Picnics welcome.

D Garden designed by a Fellow, Member, Pre-registered Member or Student of The Society of Garden + Landscape Designers.

🚐 Garden accessible to coaches. Coach sizes vary so please contact the garden owner or county organiser in advance to check details.

Group visits Group organisers may contact the county organiser or a garden owner direct to organise a group visit to a particular county or garden. Or you can contact the National Garden Scheme office on 01483 211535.

Children must be accompanied by an adult.

Photography is at the discretion of the garden owner; please check first. Photographs must not be used for sale or reproduction without prior permission of the owner.

Funds raised In most cases all funds raised at our open gardens come to the National Garden Scheme. However, there are some instances where income from teas or a percentage of admissions is given to another charity.

Toilet facilities are not guaranteed at all gardens.

If you cannot find the information you require from a garden owner or county organiser, call the National Garden Scheme office on 01483 211535.

✱ **RATHBONES**

Look ahead to the future you want.

We are proud to continue our sponsorship of the National Garden Scheme for 2026.

We can help you get more out of your money so you can get more out of life.

rathbones.com

Invest well. Live well.

When you invest your capital is at risk. You could lose some or all of your investment.

Rathbones is a trading name of Rathbones Investment Management Limited, which is authorised by the Prudential Regulation Authority and regulated by the Financial Conduct Authority and the Prudential Regulation Authority. Registered office: Port of Liverpool Building, Pier Head, Liverpool L3 1NW. Registered in England No. 01448919

Discover the Nation's best gardens

Every year, the National Garden Scheme opens the gates to thousands of exceptional private gardens, giving you the chance to explore these hidden gems while helping raise vital funds for nursing and health charities – all through the simple pleasures of garden visits, tea and cake.

Thanks to the incredible generosity of garden owners, volunteers, and visitors, we've donated over £77.8 million to nursing and health charities since 1927 with a record donation of £3,875,596 in 2025.

What began as a mechanism to fund district nurses has grown into the UK's most significant charitable funder of nursing. Today, we proudly support Macmillan Cancer Support, Marie Curie, Hospice UK, Parkinson's UK, The Queen's Institute of Community Nursing, Carers Trust, Maggie's and Horatio's Garden.

Year after year, your visits help us make a lasting difference to the nation's health and care.

But our purpose goes beyond opening beautiful gardens. We believe in the power of gardens to nurture both body and mind. Through our Community Garden Grants and projects promoting gardening as therapy, we bring the benefits of green spaces to more people.

We also invest in the future of horticulture – funding gardener training and offering support to those in the industry facing tough times.

With some 3,300 gardens opening across England, Wales, Northern Ireland, and the Channel Islands in 2026, there's a world of beauty waiting for you. Many gardens open on set dates, while others welcome private visits by arrangement.

So, browse this *Garden Visitor's Handbook* and start planning your next adventure. Stunning gardens, warm hospitality, and the joy of giving back – it's all here for you to discover.

Pictured: The Old Rectory, Farnborough, Wantage. Opening for the National Garden Scheme on Sunday 12 April, 10 May and Wednesday 24 June, 29 July

© Sussie Bell

YOUR GARDEN VISITS HELP CHANGE LIVES

In 2025 the National Garden Scheme donated **£3,875,596** to our beneficiaries, providing critical support to nursing and health charities.

£450,000

£450,000

£450,000

£450,000

£450,000

£475,000

SUPPORT FOR GARDENERS - £320,000
- English Heritage £125,000
- Perennial £100,000
- National Botanic Garden, Wales £26,000
- Bankside Open Spaces Trust £25,000
- Garden Museum £24,000
- Professional Gardeners' Trust £20,000

GARDENS AND HEALTH - £541,720
Charities include:
- Maggie's £125,000
- Horatio's Garden £110,000
- Army Benevolent Fund £80,000
- The Country Trust £35,000

SUPPORT FOR COMMUNITY GARDENS - £288,876

Thank you!

To find out more visit **ngs.org.uk/beneficiaries**

Charity number: 1112664

DONATE

Gardens and health: the power to do good

The National Garden Scheme has long recognised the importance of gardens to mental and physical health and wellbeing.

In 2016, the charity commissioned The King's Fund report on Gardens and Health and began an annual funding programme to support gardens and health-related projects. A year later our Gardens and Health programme was launched to continue raising awareness of the impact gardens and gardening can have on physical and mental health.

Many of the National Garden Scheme's nursing and health beneficiaries – for example Macmillan, Hospice UK, Maggie's, Marie Curie and Horatio's Garden – include gardens as part of their patient care and the charity also funds community garden projects that provide hope, routine and horticultural training and therapy to many.

This acceptance of the important role that gardens can play in our health and wellbeing continues to grow, and gardening is now one of the key pillars of social prescribing; an important component of the NHS comprehensive model of personalised care that aims to link an individual with an activity to improve their health and mental wellbeing.

"Gardening ticks many boxes," says CEO Dr Richard Claxton. "Whether it's a houseplant, a window box, an allotment or a back garden, gardening is accessible to all of us. It provides purpose, hope, routine and rewarding results. In a community context, like an allotment, therapy garden or even a garden at a GP surgery, it also generates conversation helping to reduce isolation and create a deep sense of satisfaction and purpose.

"Inactivity and isolation are major causes of ill-health, not only can they reduce life expectancy by about ten years, but they also contribute to the growing pressure on GP and hospital services. Getting people motivated, setting them on a path to new activities and opportunities is vital for the improved health and wellbeing of thousands of people."

The National Garden Scheme is fully supportive of social prescribing and champions the introduction of people to gardens and green spaces for improved health.

One example are the free visits to our gardens offered to beneficiaries including full-time and young carers. Providing carers with a well-earned, albeit short break in a beautiful garden and bringing them together with people in similar roles can be a hugely restorative. One carer who'd joined a garden visit said: "In my role as a carer there is so much of me that is lost. So even just getting up and getting dressed to go somewhere just for me was wonderful. The experience made me come alive again."

Anecdotal evidence like this is backed up by research that the National Garden Scheme has carried out over the last decade including the report we published after the Covid-19 pandemic and our more recent report on the benefits of getting into gardens in winter.

"All of our research clearly confirms what we have known since the National Garden Scheme first opened its gates in 1927; that the power of gardens to do good – both in fundraising for key nursing beneficiaries and in terms of the health benefits for those who own and visit gardens – has never been more important."

We celebrate Gardens and Health throughout the year with a dedicated Gardens and Health campaign each May championed by our highly regarded *Little Yellow Book of Gardens and Health*.

For more information visit:
www.ngs.org.uk/gardens-and-health-week

Pictured, clockwise from top: Grantee, Growing for Change, Organic Market Garden in Gwynedd is a community initiative supporting individual recovery from substance abuse or mental health issues through gardening, © Gary Phillips; Head gardener Alex and patient enjoying a gardening session in Horatio's Garden, Midlands, © Eva Nemeth; Garden visitors enjoying a group of gardens open as part of Little Missenden Gardens, Buckinghamshire, © Benjamin Mole

The impact of our donations to nursing and health

Nearly 100 years since our founding to support district nursing, the National Garden Scheme's commitment to nursing remains central. Long-term partnerships with Macmillan Cancer Support, Marie Curie, Parkinson's UK, the Queen's Institute of Community Nursing, and Hospice UK help strengthen the nursing and healthcare workforce and support the third sector as it responds to growing need.

These indispensable charities have provided vital support to the NHS, and communities across the UK, in the wake of the COVID-19 pandemic, with many still struggling to provide services in the current financial crisis.

National Garden Scheme Chief Executive Dr Richard Claxton says: "As the NHS and Social Care sectors struggle to deal with the scale of need, the sustained, long-term funding from the National Garden Scheme allows these charities to continue the provision of critical community nursing services, end of life care, and respite for families and carers across the UK."

In 2025 we donated over £3.8 million to nursing and health charities with our gardens having generated almost £78 million for our beneficiary charities since 1927.

Highlights in 2025 included marking the tenth anniversary of our support for Horatio's Garden. In that time, we have donated over £750,000 to help the charity create and care for beautiful, accessible gardens in NHS regional spinal injury centres. In 2018, we committed funding for the completion of gardens at all 11 spinal injuries units across the country and donated a further £110,000 in 2025 which contributed to the capital build of the Horatio's Garden in Sheffield. Including this one, the National Garden Scheme has now made grants to support the build of six gardens – Stoke Mandeville, Midlands, London & Southeast, Wales, and Northern Ireland.

We also celebrated fifteen years of support for The Army Benevolent Fund, marking an ongoing commitment to soldiers, former soldiers, and their families. A donation of £80,000 continued to support members of the Army family through horticultural therapy and training, outdoor activities, and access to green spaces.

Opposite: © Horatio's Garden / Eva Nemeth
Below: Young carers enjoyed a free visit to a WWT Wetland Centre as part of the National Garden Scheme's partnership with WWT. © Jonny Donvan

Our funding in 2025 also helped:

- 78,000 people affected by cancer to be reached by Maggie's centres supported by the National Garden Scheme

- Support 1,200 outpatients and 70 inpatients at Horatio's Northern Ireland

- Fund six Macmillan Nurses in their roles across England, Wales and Northern Ireland to support people living with cancer, and their families

- Provide the equivalent of 17,521 hours of hospice at home care by Marie Curie Nurses

- 10,000 people with Parkinson's to be supported by nurses funded by the National Garden Scheme

- Hospice UK invest £150,000 to enhance the quality of care, supporting hospices to deliver individualised quality care amid rapidly changing demands

- Fund the Queen's Nurse network, a national network of 3,500 nurses working in the community in England, Wales, Northern Ireland, the Channel Islands and the Isle of Man working across all community specialisms

- Fund the National Garden Scheme Nightingale Challenge, a bespoke leadership challenge for the caring services across Marie Curie

- Enable 63 carers and their families to benefit from support for essential household items, respite breaks, garden equipment, courses, and transport costs through Carers Trust

Below: Queen's nurses funded by the National Garden Scheme support patients at home across the UK.
© QICN Anna Gordon Photography

From Gardens to Great Causes Celebrating 100 Years in 2027!

For almost 100 years the National Garden Scheme has opened beautiful gardens across the country to raise millions for charity. Next year marks our Centenary, and we're planning something truly special!

 Exclusive events & garden visits

 Special offers & celebrations

 New collections from leading nurseries & garden brands

Be part of our celebrations!

Subscribe to our **FREE e-newsletter** today and follow us on social media for all the latest updates, special events, and offers.

SPECIAL OFFER

All NEW subscribers receive 15% OFF*
Sarah Raven
*min spend £20

Scan to Subscibe

Share Your Story

As part of our celebrations, we want to hear from you, our garden visitors. Whether you've visited once or 100 times, perhaps a visit changed your life, lifted your spirits, inspired your gardening or brings back happy memories, we'd love to hear from you.

Please send your stories to **stories@ngs.org.uk**

Leaving a legacy of garden visiting: a gift in your will

Imagine a future where everyone can experience the joy of garden visiting. By leaving a gift in your will to the National Garden Scheme, you can help make that vision a reality. After caring for those closest to you, a charitable gift is a deeply personal way to ensure the values you cherish live on – while inspiring others to share your passion for gardens.

Your legacy will enable the National Garden Scheme to continue discovering new gardens, opening gates to more visitors, and nurturing a lifelong love of garden visiting. Every visit helps raise vital funds for nursing and health charities, so your gift will have a lasting impact far beyond the garden gate.

Including the National Garden Scheme in your will is simple. Speak to a legal adviser to start or update your will – it's neither costly nor time-consuming. Regular reviews, every three to five years or after major life changes, ensure your wishes remain clear.

Legacies make an enormous difference. Supporters like Lynda, who donated her estate after a lifetime of garden visits, have helped us share the beauty of gardens with future generations. As her brother Martin said, "It was no surprise when Lynda told me she was donating everything to the National Garden Scheme. As an enthusiastic gardener, visiting private gardens through the National Garden Scheme was a much-loved pastime, first with our mother and later on her own".

Others, like Di's sister and brother-in-law, who loved nothing more than to visit open gardens chose to leave a gift because they wanted their passion to benefit others. Their generosity ensures that the simple pleasure of garden visiting continues to thrive.

By leaving a gift in your will, you'll help us keep gardens open, inspire new visitors, and fund essential health charities. It's a legacy that grows – and blossoms – for years to come.

Find out more about leaving a gift in your will or request a copy of our free booklet at ngs.org.uk/get-involved/giftinwill

Pass on your love of gardens with a gift in your will

Scan for more information

"Opening our garden for 20 years brought us great joy, knowing every penny supported nursing charities. As the National Garden Scheme nears its centenary, I want this legacy to thrive. Please consider leaving a gift in your will—together, we can ensure another 100 years of garden inspiration and vital nursing care." - Dame Mary Berry

For more information or to speak to a member of our team call **01483 211535**, email **giftinwill@ngs.org.uk** or visit **ngs.org.uk/giftinwill**

Share your garden and make a world of difference

Opening your garden for the National Garden Scheme is a truly rewarding experience – one that goes far beyond showcasing your horticultural achievements. It's an opportunity to share your passion, raise vital funds for nursing and health charities, and connect with a vibrant community of garden lovers. And when you open as part of a group of gardens, the joy multiplies: visitors can explore a wonderful mix of gardens, large and small, all in one day, creating a sense of community and shared celebration.

The Impact: Raising funds for great causes

For many garden owners, the greatest motivation for opening is the incredible charitable impact. Since 1927, the National Garden Scheme has donated over £77.8 million to nursing and health charities, making it the UK's largest charitable funder of nursing. In 2025 alone, we gave a record £3.8 million to beneficiaries including Macmillan Cancer Support, Marie Curie, Hospice UK, Parkinson's UK, Carers Trust, and The Queen's Institute of Community Nursing.

By opening your garden, you directly contribute to their life-changing work: helping to fund nurses, health professionals, and caseworkers who provide essential care for thousands of people living with cancer, Parkinson's, terminal illness, poor mental health, or the pressures of unpaid caring. Every ticket sold, every cup of tea and slice of cake eaten adds to this collective impact.

Joining a family of passionate gardeners

Opening your garden also connects you to a nationwide family of like-minded people who share your love of gardens. This supportive network offers camaraderie and a shared sense of purpose. The National Garden Scheme provides full guidance and public liability insurance for your opening day, giving you peace of mind.

For many, the highlight is the human connection – chatting with appreciative visitors, exchanging ideas, and seeing the joy your garden brings. It's a chance to celebrate creativity and community in a way that enriches everyone involved.

Opening your garden is a win-win: you share your beloved space, boost your own wellbeing, join a warm and supportive community, and make a tangible difference to the lives of those in need across the UK.

If friends already tell you how lovely your garden is, why not take the next step and open in 2027 – or join with neighbours and open your garden as part of a group, helping make the National Garden Scheme's centenary year truly unforgettable.

Find out more on the National Garden Scheme website: **ngs.org.uk/get-involved**

Pictured: Great Gardens, Great Cakes © Benjamin Mole

How to create your own beautiful garden without spending a fortune

Pictured: Views of the beautiful garden full of colour, that Anya created from a blank canvas

National Garden Scheme ambassador, social media creator and best-selling author, Anya Lautenbach shares her top tips on how to create your own beautiful garden fit for opening to the public and sharing with friends.

With increases in the cost of living and a squeeze on the amount of disposable income, beautiful gardens can seem like another thing that is out of reach, but creating a stunning garden in an affordable way is easier than most people think.

You can transform your outdoor space into a lovely green living room worth opening to the public and sharing with other people by thinking outside the box. It's possible to find good quality pre-owned and unique items such as tools, pots and furniture at a reasonable price on Facebook marketplace, eBay or Gumtree.

When looking for good quality items, timing is crucial! Starting your search in early spring or even late winter will make a difference, as later in the season you'll have to compete with more gardeners who will be looking for the same items as you. It's amazing what can be found by proactively asking for specific items in your local Facebook groups in January, so rather than browsing the items listed, you can ask for the items you are interested in.

Plants are expensive but if you invest in good and strong varieties, you can easily make use of plants' natural ways of reproducing and propagate them for your own garden. This will make dreamy gardens achievable at a fraction of the cost of buying more.

Propagation is a great way to save money, and it will enable you to increase your stock at a very little or no expense – with just a handful of seeds or cuttings you can create a stunning border packed with plants ready to be admired by others. Most plants are easy to propagate without a greenhouse or expensive equipment, and the process of propagation is very straightforward and does not require any special tools or experience. Depending on the plant you propagate, cuttings will turn into garden ready plants within 1-12 months.

There are many methods of propagation suitable for every season, but one of the quickest ways to fill a garden with the most amazing plants on a budget is by dividing and re-planting in different areas of your garden. Division is an incredibly simple way of reproducing plants giving you instant impact. Divided plants such as hydrangeas, dahlias, salvias or hardy geraniums establish quickly, and you can create a mature looking border full of colour and interesting textures within one year.

Even if propagation isn't for you and you prefer to buy more established plants for greater impact, there are still ways you can save money. A great and cost-effective way of acquiring plants is by buying them bare root. The most popular plants available bare root include hedges, roses, peonies and trees. They are often available from supermarkets. If you are too busy to plant your plant straight away, you can place them in a large container or dig a hole in your garden, place and cover your plants with some topsoil or compost, water well and leave for a few days or even weeks until you are ready to plant them in their final position.

The process of creating a garden on a budget can be very rewarding. Creating a garden in a more self-sufficient and sustainable way, by reusing, repurposing and propagating will not only save you a fortune, but it will also create a resilient and healthy garden, a garden for the future.

It's not about instant gratification but rather about taking pleasure in the journey. Sharing the garden you have created yourself with other people can bring you a sense of purpose, connection and satisfaction. It can even be a life changing experience.

You can find Anya on Instagram here: @anya_thegarden_fairy

Help for Horticulturalists

Perennial supports everyone working in horticulture with everyday and complex challenges.

- Confidential support
- Money and Debt advice
- Legal helpline
- Health & Wellbeing
- Life challenges e.g. bereavement
- Free online tools and more...

Find out more about our expert services or make a donation at **perennial.org.uk**

Helping people in horticulture
Perennial

A company limited by guarantee. Registered in England & Wales no: 8828584. Charity no: 1155156. Registered in Scotland, Charity no: SC040180. VAT no. 9912541 09. Gardeners' Royal Benevolent Society (trading as Perennial) is authorised and regulated by the Financial Conduct Authority under FRN: 694883.

The importance of community gardens

As part of the charity's wider Gardens and Health programme the National Garden Scheme awards grants to help community gardening projects. In 2025 we funded 114 projects with a total of £288,876, thanks to generous funding from the Julia Rausing Trust.

From social welfare and gardening projects that help the isolated, the disabled and the disenfranchised to support for community orchards, food banks and social prescribing projects at GP surgeries, the funding provides a much-needed boost to those working on or initiating community garden projects throughout England, Wales and Northern Ireland.

Danny Clarke – aka The Black Gardener – and National Garden Scheme ambassador says: "Participating in an allotment or community garden can give meaningful social connections which help to reduce loneliness and isolation. I have noticed how these spaces can bring people of all generations, cultures and backgrounds together, to happily share knowledge and traditions. It's wonderful to see the continuing generosity of the National Garden Scheme Community Garden Grants which are helping to fund these amazing spaces across the country and contributing so positively to social cohesion."

Many of the funded community projects in turn open for the National Garden Scheme completing a virtuous circle of giving and giving back. Some examples include:

The Pakistan Association Liverpool Wellbeing Garden – developed to create an inspirational space for the members to enjoy, and grow vegetables, herbs and flowers. It's been made from recycled materials, including bricks from the mosque floor. It opens as part of the Canning and Toxteth Gardens, Liverpool on 14 June 2026.

Left: Rhubarb Farm, Nottinghamshire, opens its gates through the National Garden Scheme on dates in June, July and August **Opposite:** Pakistan Association Liverpool Wellbeing Garden opens as part of the Canning and Toxteth Gardens, on Sunday 14 June

Rhubarb Farm, Nottinghamshire, a two-acre horticultural social enterprise that provides training and volunteering opportunities to ex-offenders, drug and alcohol misusers, older people, school students, people with mental and physical ill health and learning disabilities opens for the National Garden Scheme on 18 June, 16 July and 20 August 2026.

> Since the Community Garden Grants began, over £1,100,000 has been donated to more than 500 community projects. If you would like to apply for a Community Garden Grant you can find out more at ngs.org.uk/who-we-are/community-garden-grants

Host a Garden Party for a great cause!

Join the Great British Garden Party this summer and support the National Garden Scheme.

Whether it's afternoon tea, coffee morning or plant sale, every pound you raise helps vital UK nursing and health charities like Macmillan Cancer Support, Marie Curie and Hospice UK.

Sign up today and receive a free Garden Party pack with invitations, posters, recipes, and fundraising tips. Whether you raise £5 or £500, you'll make a real difference.

Sign up on our website: ngs.org.uk/gardenparty

Get involved. Host a party. Change lives.

COBRA

One of the UK's largest ranges of garden machinery

Create a lawn that is the envy of your neighbours with a brand-new lawn tractor or lawnmower from Cobra. At the heart of these powerful, feature rich machines is a choice of cut sizes and either electric, cordless or petrol engines powered by Briggs & Stratton, Honda and Loncin.

With over 65 lawnmowers in the range — including the powerful new VX petrol lawnmowers and 40VX+ cordless 4-wheeled and rear roller range, Cobra has you covered. Whatever your garden needs, Cobra has the perfect lawnmower for you.

Model Shown: Cobra RM43SP40VX

For your nearest dealer visit: **www.cobragarden.co.uk** or call: **0115 986 6646**   *Promotional prices only at participating dealers

Discover enchanting Scottish Gardens with Hebridean Island Cruises

SCOTLAND BOASTS A DIVERSE COLLECTION OF GARDENS WHICH ARE HOME TO A VAST COLLECTION OF PLANTS FROM AROUND THE WORLD, IN SPECTACULAR NATURAL SETTINGS.

Join *Hebridean Princess* or *Lord of the Highlands* on a voyage of discovery to explore the botanic beauty and rich diversity of Scotland's Highland gardens. Enjoy Scottish warmth and hospitality, bespoke experiences and unique touches coupled with indulgent luxury.

HEBRIDEAN ISLAND CRUISES

To find out more or request a brochure please call **01756 704704** or visit **www.hebridean.co.uk**

BEDFORDSHIRE

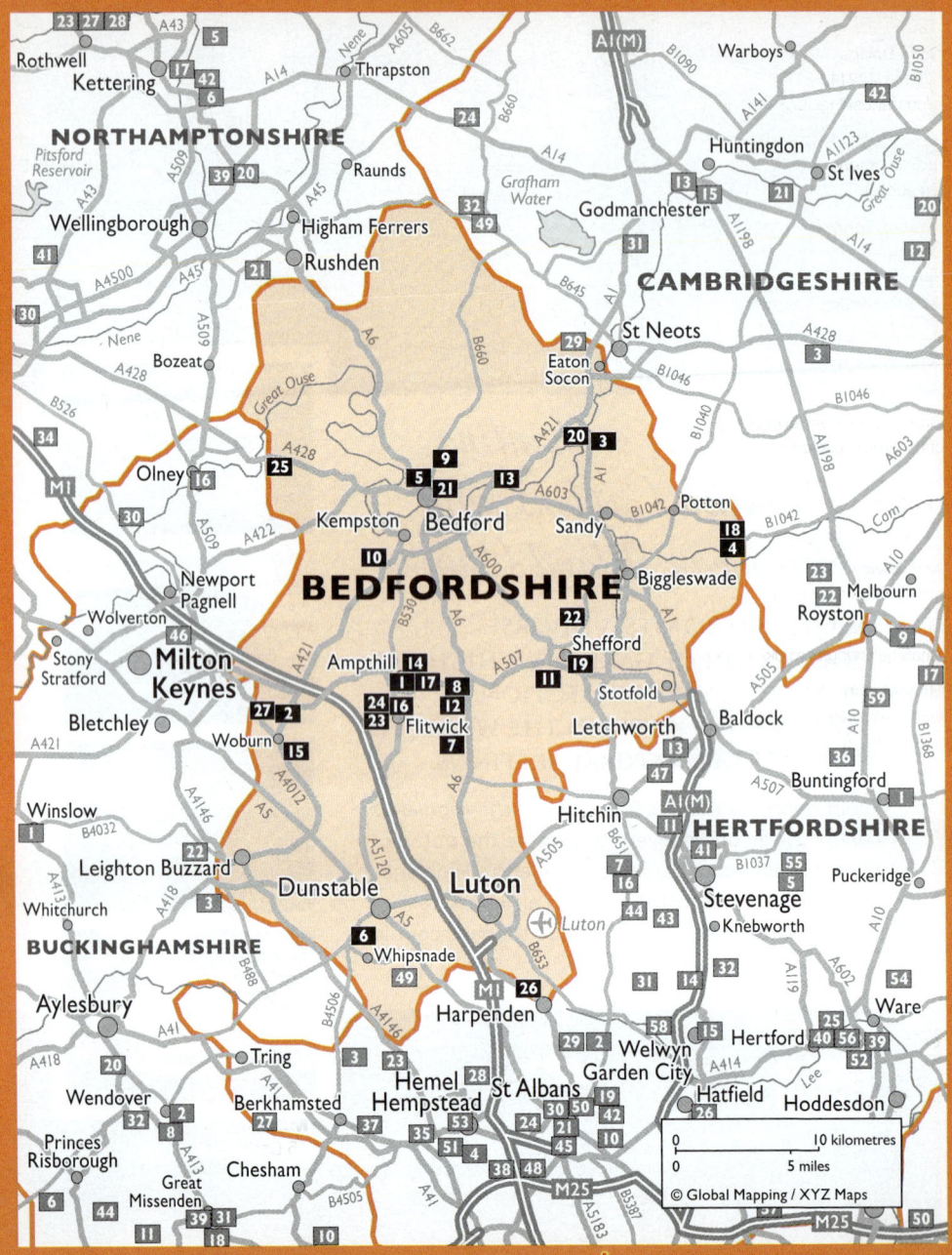

VOLUNTEERS

County Organiser
Indi Jackson
07973 857633
indi.jackson@ngs.org.uk

County Treasurer
Colin Davies
07811 022211
colin.davies@ngs.org.uk

Booklet Co-ordinator
Indi Jackson
(as above)

**Photographer &
Booklet Co-ordinator**
Venetia Barrington
venetiajanesgarden@gmail.com

Press Officer
Position Vacant

Talks
Christopher Bamforth Damp
chrisdamp@mac.com

Assistant County Organisers
Lexi Ballance
(as above)

Ann Davies
ann.davies@ngs.org.uk

Natalie Jeffs
natalie.jeffs@ngs.org.uk

Mary Mallon
mary.mallon@ngs.org.uk

Paul Randall
paul.randall@ngs.org.uk

Facebook
Indi Jackson
(as above)

@bedfordshire.ngs

OPENING DATES

All entries subject to change. For latest information check
www.ngs.org.uk
Map locator numbers are shown to the right of each garden name.

February

Snowdrop Openings

Sunday 15th
◆ King's Arms Garden 14

Saturday 21st
Townsend Farmhouse 24

Sunday 22nd
Townsend Farmhouse 24

March

Sunday 29th
8 Abbey Close 1

April

Saturday 25th
Steppingley Village Gardens 23

Sunday 26th
Steppingley Village Gardens 23

May

Saturday 2nd
22 Elmsdale Road 10

Sunday 3rd
22 Elmsdale Road 10

Monday 4th
22 Elmsdale Road 10

Sunday 10th
The Old Rectory, Wrestlingworth 18

Saturday 16th
Church Farm 7

Sunday 17th
Church Farm 7
The Old Rectory, Wrestlingworth 18

Sunday 24th
Steppingley Village Gardens 23

Monday 25th
Steppingley Village Gardens 23

Saturday 30th
40 Leighton Street 15

Sunday 31st
NEW 97 Clophill Road 8
80 West Hill 27

June

Sunday 7th
Ash Trees 2
Southill Park 22

Saturday 13th
Hollington Farm 12

Sunday 14th
Hollington Farm 12
Turvey Village Gardens 25

Saturday 20th
NEW 14 Neotsbury Road 17

Sunday 28th
Lindy Lea 16

July

Friday 3rd
Bedford Heights 5

Sunday 5th
Roxton Village Gardens 20

Saturday 18th
12 Queen Elizabeth Close 19

Sunday 19th
12 Queen Elizabeth Close 19

Sunday 26th
Brooklands 6
NEW 13 Gravenhurst Road 11

August

Saturday 1st
Beck House 4

Sunday 2nd
Beck House 4

Friday 7th
◆ The Walled Garden 26

Sunday 30th
NEW 14 Neotsbury Road 17

Monday 31st
15 Douglas Road 9

September

Sunday 6th
Howbury Hall Garden　13

October

Saturday 24th
Townsend Farmhouse　24

Sunday 25th
◆ King's Arms Garden　14

By Arrangement

Arrange a personalised garden visit with your club, or group of friends, on a date to suit you. See individual garden entries for full details.

8 Abbey Close	1
1c Bakers Lane	3
Beck House	4
Brooklands	6
Church Farm	7
NEW 14 Neotsbury Road	17
The Old Rectory, Wrestlingworth	18
12 Queen Elizabeth Close	19
1a St Augustine's Road	21

Our donation to Marie Curie this year is equivalent to 17,521 hours of hospice at home care.

Gable End, Turvey Village Gardens

THE GARDENS

1 8 ABBEY CLOSE
Ampthill, Bedford, MK45 2SH. Mrs Ann Vickers, 07776 387106. *A507 bypass to 2nd r'about for Maulden/ Flitwick. Take 1st L Abbey Ln. After passing tidy tip take 2nd R turn into Oliver St. Abbey Cl is on the bend.* **Sun 29 Mar (1.30-4.30). Adm £5, chd free. Visits also by arrangement in Apr for groups of up to 15.**
A mature, town garden with scented spring bulbs, colourful early flowering perennials, budding shrubs and trees with sprouting new leaves. A variety of evergreen shrubs also offer an interesting mix of foliage. There is a small pond providing a home to frogspawn and tadpoles. Wheelchair access onto patio, remainder of garden is gravel with narrow paths.

2 ASH TREES
Green Lane, Aspley Guise, Milton Keynes, MK17 8EN. John & Teresa. *10m from Milton Keynes & 2m from J13 M1. Green Ln is off Wood Ln. Yellow signs indicate where to turn. Some on-road parking in Wood Ln. Disabled or mobility parking only at house.* **Sun 7 June (12-5). Adm £5, chd free. Tea, coffee & cake.**
Medium sized, secluded village garden, walled in with borrowed treescape and hidden in a private lane. Herbaceous borders, shrubs, trees, bulbs, and fruit inc apricot and peach. There is a unique garden arch sculpture created for a Hampton Court show garden. Seats in quiet spots amongst the plants. Children and wheelchairs welcome as are dogs on leads. Garden is flat with reasonable access for wheelchairs and walkers.

3 1C BAKERS LANE
Tempsford, Sandy, SG19 2BJ. Juliet & David Pennington, 01767 640482, juliet.pennington01@gmail.com. *1m N of Sandy on A1 & Station Rd is on the E side. Bakers Ln is 300 yds down Station Rd on L. Parking on Station Rd & Knott's Farm Shop car park.* **Visits by arrangement 2 Feb to 29 Nov. Adm £6, chd free.**
Enchanting, wildlife friendly garden where each month of the year has something exciting to offer. Winter borders planted with colourful cornus and evergreen shrubs, underplanted here with snowdrops and hellebores. Gravel areas are carpeted with miniature cyclamen. It develops through the seasons culminating in early autumn with a spectacular show of sun-loving herbaceous plants. Plant sale of exotic and unusual plants. No refreshments but visitors are welcome to bring a picnic to enjoy in the garden. Regret, no dogs.

4 BECK HOUSE
Water End, Wrestlingworth, Sandy, SG19 2HA. Donal & Victoria McKenna, 07803 138390, tory.mckenna@btinternet.com. *Halfway between Cambridge & Bedford. From High St, Wrestlingworth turn into Water End (opp 8 & 10 High St). Garden at far end of Water End.* **Sat 1, Sun 2 Aug (2-5). Adm £8, chd free. Home-made teas. Visits also by arrangement Apr to Sept for groups of 15 to 30.**
A 2½ acre garden created over 40 years with many varied areas of interest - formal and informal areas divided by hedges and shrub borders. Features inc topiary yew avenue, circular dahlia garden (c. 40 different varieties) with small pond, parterre with English roses, herbaceous borders, courtyard garden, herb and vegetable gardens, rose and clematis pergola walk. Woodland garden. Wheelchair accessible but there are some slopes to access upper part of garden.

5 BEDFORD HEIGHTS
Brickhill Drive, Bedford, MK41 7PH. www.bedfordheights.co.uk. *Plenty of free parking is available. Our visitors car park, also called car park 1, is at the front of the building. Additional car parking is available in car park 2.* **Fri 3 July (11-3). Adm £5, chd free. Light refreshments in Graze Café.**
Originally built by Texas Instruments, a Texan theme runs throughout the building and gardens. The entrance simulates an arroyo or dry riverbed, and is filled with succulents and cacti, plus a mixture of grasses and herbaceous plants, many of which are Texan natives. There are also three courtyard gardens, where less hardy plants thrive in the almost frost-free environment.

6 BROOKLANDS
Bottom Drive, Wellhead, Dunstable, LU6 2JS. Paul Randall, 07774 742532, paul.randall3@googlemail.com. *½m W of Dunstable, very close to Dunstable Gliding Club. Main parking in the nearby field. Disabled & mobility parking in the driveway.* **Sun 26 July (11-5). Adm £6, chd free. Home-made teas. Visits also by arrangement 7 July to 31 Aug for groups of up to 15.**
A ½ acre hardy exotic garden. Many mature palms, yuccas, cycas, bananas and bamboos. Around 3000 succulent plantings, all growing in ground- very few pots. 20 varieties of Agave, the largest is now over 5ft tall. 28 Aeonium cultivars. *Echeverias, Aloes, Crassula, Haworthia* and *Sedum.* Large *Sempervivum* collection. Feature koi pool and goldfish ponds. A chalk stream borders the end of the garden. A well-maintained winding brick path runs through almost all of the garden and allows good wheelchair access.

7 CHURCH FARM
Church Road, Pulloxhill, Bedford, MK45 5HD. Sue & Keith Miles, 07941 593152. *7m from M1 J12. Parking by kind permission of The Cross Keys Pub, MK45 5HB (approx 500yds from garden). Yellow signs from the Cross Keys to Church Rd & past parish church.* **Sat 16, Sun 17 May (2-5). Adm £7, chd free. Visits also by arrangement June to Aug for groups of 10 to 20. Tour of the garden and tea or coffee with home-made cakes.**
Mixed colourful formal planting to the rear of the house leading to a gravel yard with drought tolerant borders and large topiary subjects (topiary award winner). Beyond the farmyard is a wildlife pond, kitchen garden and wildflower orchard with a rose walk. Cut flower area and countryside views. Fairy glade across meadows. Livestock may be present in adjoining fields so regret no dogs. Winner of the Henchman Choice Award for outstanding topiary 2024.

BEDFORDSHIRE

8 NEW 97 CLOPHILL ROAD
Maulden, Bedford, MK45 2AD. Stephen & Liz Harris. *What3words app: grunt.clinked.diplomas.* **Sun 31 May (11-4). Adm £5, chd free.** A mature town garden with cottage garden style planting, trees and a variety of attractive pots. Created over 35 years, it is a much loved family friendly garden, often with bits to do and quiet places to sit. Situated at the top of a hill, the garden offers views across to Maulden Woods.

9 15 DOUGLAS ROAD
Bedford, MK41 7YF. Peter & Penny Berrington. *B660 Kimbolton Rd, turn to Avon Dr, R into Tyne Cres, & Douglas Rd on R.* **Mon 31 Aug (2-5). Adm £5, chd free. Tea, coffee & cake.** This medium sized town garden has a series of outdoor rooms, separated by hedges, fences and arches. There is seating for visitors to relax and enjoy the peace and seclusion. A circular cottage garden with a central decorative fire pit, separated by plum and apple trees from vegetables and herbs grown in raised beds. The pond is home to newts, snails and midwife toads.

10 22 ELMSDALE ROAD
Wootton, Bedford, MK43 9JN. Roy & Dianne Richards. *Follow signs to Wootton, turn R at The Cock Pub, follow to Elmsdale Rd.* **Sat 2, Sun 3, Mon 4 May (12-5). Adm £6, chd free. Home-made teas.** Topiary garden greets visitors before they enter a genuine Japanese Feng Shui garden inc bonsai. Large collection of Japanese plants, koi pond, lily pond and a Japanese Tea House. The garden was created from scratch by the owners about 20 years ago and has many interesting features inc Japanese lanterns and a Kneeling Archer terracotta soldier from China.

11 NEW 13 GRAVENHURST ROAD
Campton, Shefford, SG17 5NY. Emma & Richard Connolly. *Parking on road around the church. The garden is a 2min walk.* **Sun 26 July (2-5). Adm £5, chd free. Tea, coffee & cake.** Almost ½ acre of mature gardens in three sections; a delightful small front garden with low-lying lavender hedge, a gravel garden with pond and mature borders, and a large, hidden garden with mature and new borders, fruit trees, glasshouses with raised beds, and lawns extending to a woodland area. A mix of romantic and contemporary planting and a haven for wildlife.

12 HOLLINGTON FARM
Flitton Hill, Maulden, Bedford, MK42 2BE. Susan & John Rickatson. *Between Clophill & Ampthill. Off A507, head towards Silsoe/ Flitton & then bear R. Follow yellow signs.* **Sat 13, Sun 14 June (2-5.30). Adm £7, chd free. Home-made teas. Cream teas & cakes served 2pm - 4.30pm.** Two acre country garden developed around an old farmhouse over a 30 year period. Trees and shrubs are now mature impressive specimens. Semi formal areas near the house inc a small parterre, pergola, pond and borders. In outer parts there is a small woodland planted in the 1990's and a farm wildflower meadow on Flitton Hill with views over the River Flit valley. Play areas for children. Some steps and slopes.

13 HOWBURY HALL GARDEN
Howbury Hall Estate, Renhold, Bedford, MK41 0JB. Julian Polhill & Lucy Copeman, www.howburyfarmflowers.co.uk. *Leave A421 at A428/Gt Barford exit towards Bedford. Entrance to house & gardens ½ m on R. Parking in field.* **Sun 6 Sept (2-5). Adm £7, chd free. Home-made teas.** A late Victorian garden with mature trees, sweeping lawns, herbaceous borders and a copse. The large walled garden is a working garden, where one half is dedicated to growing a large variety of vegetables and citrus, whilst the other is run as a cut flower business. Large collection dahlias in September, varieties of heritage apples and avenues of pears and apples.

14 ♦ KING'S ARMS GARDEN
Brinsmade Road, Ampthill, Bedford, MK45 2PP. Ampthill Town Council, www.ampthill-tc.gov.uk/amenities/kings-arm-garden. *Free parking for limited time in Waitrose car park. Entrance opp Market Square Cafe, down King's Arms Path, 2nd gate on the R.* **For NGS: Sun 15 Feb, Sun 25 Oct (2-4). Adm £5, chd free. Tea, coffee & cake. For other opening times and information, please visit garden website.** Small woodland garden of about 1½ acres created by plantsman, the late William Nourish. Trees, shrubs, bulbs and many interesting collections throughout the year. Since 1987, the garden has been maintained by 'The Friends of the Garden' on behalf of Ampthill Town Council. Charming woodland garden with mass plantings of snowdrops and early spring bulbs. Beautiful autumn colours in October. Wheelchair friendly path running around most of the garden.

15 40 LEIGHTON STREET
Woburn, MK17 9PH. Rita Chidley. *500yds from centre of village, L side of road. Limited on road parking outside house. Free public car park opp Woburn church.* **Sat 30 May (2-5). Adm £5, chd free. Home-made teas.** Large cottage style garden lovingly cared for by a passionate and active, 90 year old garden owner. It offers an abundance of perennials, alliums, roses, climbers, vegetables, trees and two ponds with fish. There are several 'rooms' with interesting features to explore and many quiet seating areas. Hanging baskets and a large selection of pots of unusual and tender plants.

16 LINDY LEA
Ampthill Road, Steppingley, Bedford, MK45 1AB. Roy & Linda Collins. *Next to Steppingley Hospital. Park in hospital car park.* **Sun 28 June (2-5). Adm £6, chd free. Home-made teas.** Set within an acre, this garden is a haven for wildlife with two water features, cottage garden style perennial plantings, a variety of shrubs and mature trees. There is also a vegetable garden and a sunny terrace furnished with pots and climbers. Some paths may be difficult to negotiate for wheelchair users.

BEDFORDSHIRE

17 14 NEOTSBURY ROAD NEW
Ampthill, Bedford, MK45 2SU. Natalie Baker, 07557 444549, natalieclairebaker@hotmail.com, www.thisconstantgardener.co.uk. *Turning off Oliver St. What3Words: photocopy.strapping.aunts.* **Evening opening Sat 20 June (4-9). Home-made teas. Sun 30 Aug (10-6). Adm £4, chd free. Visits also by arrangement June to Sept for groups of up to 12.**
Maintained by the owner, an RHS-qualified gardener, this cottage garden draws on naturalistic and arts and crafts styles. A winding woodchip path divides a herbaceous border from a shady, woodland-inspired one. Towering fennel, grasses, and 20+ dahlias feature, leading to a yellow writing shed framed by giant summer sunflowers. Loved by children, due to the fairytale feel.

18 THE OLD RECTORY, WRESTLINGWORTH
Church Lane, Wrestlingworth, Sandy, SG19 2EU. Josephine Hoy, 07745 848310, hoyjosephine@hotmail.co.uk. *Garden is at top of Church Ln, which is well signed, behind the church.* **Sun 10, Sun 17 May (2-5). Adm £8, chd free. Visits also by arrangement May & June.**
A four acre garden full of colour and interest. The owner has a free style of gardening sensitive to wildlife. Beds overflowing with tulips, alliums, bearded iris, peonies, poppies, geraniums and much more. Beautiful mature trees and many more planted in the last 30 years inc a large selection of *Betulas*. Gravel gardens, box hedging and clipped balls, woodland garden and wildflower meadows. Wheelchair access may be restricted to grass paths.

19 12 QUEEN ELIZABETH CLOSE
Shefford, SG17 5LE. Kasey Brock, misskaseybrock@gmail.com. *Turn off Ivel Rd into Queen Elizabeth Cl & follow to L.* **Sat 18, Sun 19 July (2-5). Adm £5, chd free. Visits also by arrangement for groups of up to 20.**
A small town garden with a jungle, rainforest feel. This garden is all about foliage with the emphasis on leaf shapes and textures; some more unusual and quirky than others. The whole garden has been designed to make you feel like you have been transported to somewhere exotic, making use of a large veranda, it can even be enjoyed in the rain.

GROUP OPENING

20 ROXTON VILLAGE GARDENS
Roxton, Bedford, MK44 3ED. *S of St Neots. At the A1, Black Cat r'about follow road signs to Roxton. Then follow signs for parking at the playing field.* **Sun 5 July (1-5). Combined adm £6, chd free. Home-made teas.**

HILL FARM HOUSE
Anna & Julian Chillingworth.

34 PARK ROAD
Paul & Margaret Gale.

Visit Roxton and see two very different gardens; An old garden replanted and landscaped over the last nine years, the other, well established over many years with an orchid house. You will see across the gardens a wide range of ornamentals, specimen trees, shrubs and vegetables being grown. Fresh home-made teas are on offer and an opportunity to visit the unique thatched C18 Congregational Chapel.

Howbury Hall Garden

BEDFORDSHIRE

21 1A ST AUGUSTINE'S ROAD
Bedford, MK40 2NB. Chris Bamforth Damp, 01234 353730, chrisdamp@mac.com. *St Augustine's Rd is on L off Kimbolton Rd as you leave the centre of Bedford.* **Visits by arrangement July to Sept. Adm £6, chd free. Home-made teas.**
A colourful town garden with herbaceous borders, climbers, a greenhouse and a pond. Planted in cottage garden style with traditional flowers, the borders overflow with late summer annuals and perennials inc salvias and rudbeckia. The pretty terrace next to the house is lined with ferns and hostas. The owners also make home-made chutneys and preserves which can be purchased on the day.

22 SOUTHILL PARK
Southill, Biggleswade, SG18 9LL. Mr & Mrs Charles Whitbread.
5m from the A1. On the outskirts of the village. What3words app: uppermost.brighter.season. **Sun 7 June (2-5). Adm £7, chd free. Cream teas.**
Southill Park first opened its gates to National Garden Scheme visitors in 1927 as one of the inaugural gardens. This is a large garden with mature trees and flowering shrubs, herbaceous borders, a formal rose garden, sunken garden, ponds and kitchen garden. It is on the south side of the 1795 Palladian house. The parkland was designed by Lancelot 'Capability' Brown. A large conservatory houses the tropical collection.

GROUP OPENING

23 STEPPINGLEY VILLAGE GARDENS
Steppingley, Bedford, MK45 5AT. *Follow signs to Steppingley, pick up yellow signs from village centre.* **Sat 25, Sun 26 Apr (2-5). Combined adm £8, chd free. Sun 24, Mon 25 May (1-5). Combined adm £10, chd free. Home-made teas at Townsend Farmhouse. Hot Dogs at Village Hall on May openings.**

21 CHURCH END
Christine & Steve Ovenden.
Open on Sun 24, Mon 25 May

THE CROFT
Stephen Cook.
Open on Sun 24, Mon 25 May

MIDDLE BARN
John & Sally Eilbeck.
Open on all dates

TOP BARN
Tim & Nicky Kemp.
Open on all dates

TOWNSEND FARMHOUSE
Hugh & Indi Jackson.
Open on all dates
(See separate entry)

Steppingley is a picturesque Bedfordshire village on the Greensand Ridge, close to Ampthill, Flitwick and Woburn. Although a few older buildings survive, most of Steppingley was built by the 7th Duke of Bedford between 1840 and 1872. Five gardens in the village offer an interesting mix of planting styles and design. Colourful displays of tulips and spring bulbs in April and cottage garden style early perennials, roses and peonies in May. There are pretty courtyards, three large wildlife ponds and several small ponds, a Victorian well, a shell grotto, glasshouses, a succulent collection, vegetable gardens and country views. The gardens are also home to chickens, ducks, moorhens, fish and much more, depending on the time of year.

24 TOWNSEND FARMHOUSE
Rectory Road, Steppingley, Bedford, MK45 5AT. Hugh & Indi Jackson. *Follow directions to Steppingley village and pick up yellow signs from village centre.* **Sat 21, Sun 22 Feb (2-4). Adm £6, chd free. Home-made teas. Evening opening Sat 24 Oct (5.30-8.30). Adm £10, chd free. Light refreshments. Home-made cakes and savouries. Opening with Steppingley Village Gardens on Sat 25, Sun 26 Apr, Sun 24, Mon 25 May.**

The Croft, Steppingley Village Gardens

Southill Park

Country garden with tree lined driveway underplanted with swathes of snowdrops and colourful early bulbs in February. Pretty cobbled courtyard with a glasshouse housing succulents and house plants. A Victorian well 30 metres deep, viewed through a glass top. Large wildlife pond and a shell grotto. A spectacular evening of lanterns, oil lamps, glass and flower rangoli in late October.
❀ ☕ 🔊

GROUP OPENING

25 TURVEY VILLAGE GARDENS
High Street, Turvey, Bedford, MK43 8EP. *Follow arrow signs from village centre. Parking in field behind Chantry House.* **Sun 14 June (1.30-5). Combined adm £9, chd free. Cream teas in Medieval church of All Saints.**

CHANTRY HOUSE
Sheila & Anthony Ormerod.

GABLE END
Chris & Wendy Knell.

7 THE GREEN
Paul & Rosemary Gentry.

MILL LODGE
Jane & Tim Brewster.

PEPPERS
Liz & Mark Upex.

The historic village of Turvey lies beside the River Great Ouse and is recorded in Domesday Book of 1086 as a parish in the Hundred of Willey. Five gardens in the village offer a varied mix of design and interest. Chantry House is a 1½ acre garden, approached by a drive bounded by mature yew and box cloud hedges where the Medieval church of All Saints overlooks the garden at this point. A south facing lawn is flanked by high rose covered walls and interspersed by herbaceous beds. 7 The Green has a wide terrace with comfortable seating and a myriad of planted pots overlooks a central lawn and flower beds. Gable End has four distinct areas with a range of planting inc fruit and vegetables. Peppers is a small, informal village garden with mixed planting aimed at attracting wildlife and achieving year-round interest. At Mill Lodge there are informal, cottage garden style borders packed with flowers, herbs and foliage plants, many pots and containers, and several fruit trees.
❀ ☕ 🔊

26 ♦ THE WALLED GARDEN
Luton, LU1 4LF. Luton Hoo Estate, 01582 721443, office@lutonhooestate.co.uk, www.lutonhooestate.co.uk. *Just outside Harpenden. From A1081 turn into West Hyde Rd. After 100 metres turn L through black gates, follow signs to Walled Garden.* **For NGS: Fri 7 Aug (11-3). Adm £7, chd free. Light refreshments at Woodyard Cafe & Brasserie. For other opening times and information, please phone, email or visit garden website.**
The five acre Luton Hoo Estate Walled Garden was designed by Capability Brown and established by noted botanist and former Prime Minister, Lord Bute, in the late 1760s. The Walled Garden partnered with the RHS and Historic Houses and is the focus of an incredible volunteer project and continues to be researched, restored, repaired and re-imagined for the enjoyment of all. Unique service buildings inc a vinery, fernery and propagation houses. Exhibition of Victorian tools. Uneven surfaces.
♿ 🐕 ❀ 🚗 ☕ 🔊

27 80 WEST HILL
Aspley Guise, Milton Keynes, MK17 8DX. James & Helen Scott, www.thegardenco.co.uk/residential/modern-sanctuary. *6m SE of Milton Keynes; close to M1 J13. Leave M1 J13. 2m W towards Woburn Sands. On West Hill, turn R onto Ln marked 80-92. No parking except for disabled visitors; please park at Cricket Club (next R on West Hill).* **Sun 31 May (12-4.30). Adm £5, chd free. Tea, coffee & cake.**
Contemporary front and rear gardens to complement a modern house within a walled garden plot. The rear garden is based on strong geometry with naturalistic planting inc several bespoke features. The front garden feels more organic, with various uses of natural stone and planting to suit some dry sunny spots as well as woodland shade. Features inc fire pit area, water feature, glasshouse, secluded seating area. There is careful use of Yorkshire stone illustrating the journey from boulder to slab. Winner of three National Awards inc a Design Excellence Award and Homes and Gardens Award for Best Small Garden (2023).
♿ 🐕 ❀ 🅿 ☕ 🔊

BERKSHIRE

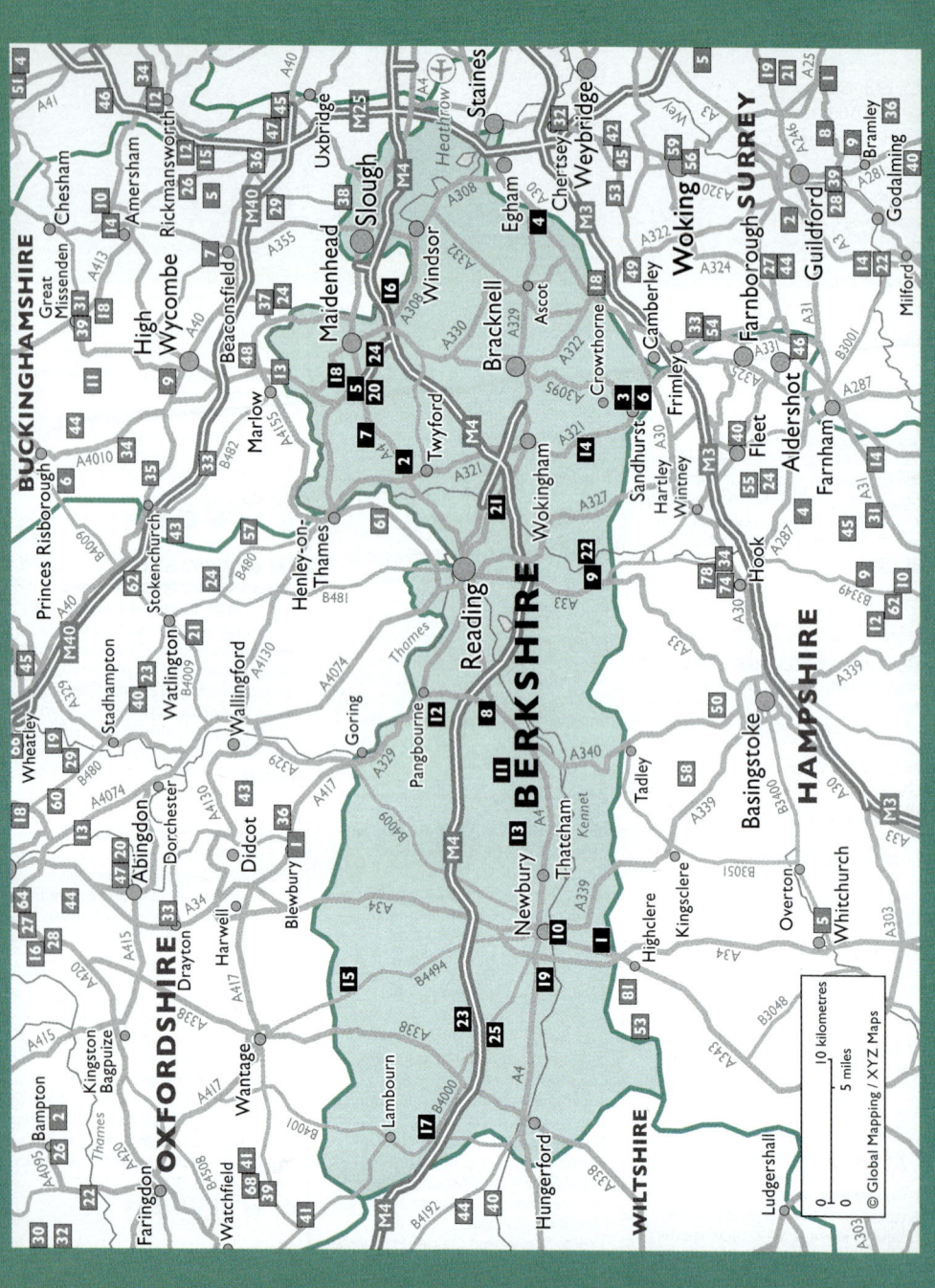

VOLUNTEERS

County Organiser
Heather Skinner
01189 737197
heather.skinner@ngs.org.uk

County Treasurer
Carolyn Clark
07701 016961
carolyn.clark@ngs.org.uk

Booklet Co-ordinator
Heather Skinner
(as above)

Assistant County Organisers
Claire Fletcher
claire.fletcher@ngs.org.uk

Carolyn Foster
07768 566482
carolyn.foster@ngs.org.uk

Rebecca Thomas
01491 628302
rebecca.thomas@ngs.org.uk

Bob Weston
01635 550240
bob.weston@ngs.org.uk

[f] @BerksNationalGardenScheme
[X] @BerksNGS
[○] @nationalgardenschemeberkshire

OPENING DATES

All entries subject to change.
For latest information check
www.ngs.org.uk
Map locator numbers
are shown to the right
of each garden name.

January

Tuesday 13th
St Timothee 18

Thursday 15th
St Timothee 18

February

Snowdrop Openings

Wednesday 4th
◆ Welford Park 23

March

Saturday 14th
Stubbings House 20

Sunday 15th
Stubbings House 20

Tuesday 17th
St Timothee 18

Thursday 19th
St Timothee 18

April

Sunday 12th
The Old Rectory, Farnborough ... 15

Wednesday 22nd
Rooksnest 17

Thursday 23rd
NEW Mulberry Cottage 13

Sunday 26th
NEW Mulberry Cottage 13

May

Saturday 9th
Stubbings House 20

Sunday 10th
6 Beverley Gardens 2
Oak Cottage 14
The Old Rectory, Farnborough ... 15
Stubbings House 20

Sunday 17th
Deepwood Stud Farm 5

Thursday 21st
Coworth Park 4
NEW The Old Stables 16

Sunday 24th
Stockcross House 19

Sunday 31st
NEW Dumbledore 7
St Timothee 18

June

Wednesday 3rd
61 Sutcliffe Avenue 21

Thursday 4th
61 Sutcliffe Avenue 21

Friday 5th
NEW The Old Stables 16

Saturday 6th
61 Sutcliffe Avenue 21

Sunday 7th
Swallowfield Village Gardens 22

Sunday 14th
NEW The Old Stables 16
Wickham House 25

Wednesday 24th
The Old Rectory, Farnborough ... 15
Rooksnest 17

Thursday 25th
St Timothee 18

Sunday 28th
Dorset Cottage 6

July

Sunday 5th
6 Beverley Gardens 2

Friday 17th
Wembury 24

Sunday 19th
King's Copse House 11

Friday 24th
6 Beverley Gardens 2

Tuesday 28th
Wembury 24

Wednesday 29th
The Old Rectory, Farnborough ... 15

August

Wednesday 5th
Wembury 24

Thursday 6th
Coworth Park 4

Sunday 23rd
6 Beverley Gardens 2
Stockcross House 19

September

Sunday 6th
Deepwood Stud Farm 5
Dorset Cottage 6

Friday 11th
NEW The Old Stables 16

November

Tuesday 3rd
St Timothee 18

Thursday 5th
St Timothee 18

By Arrangement

Arrange a personalised garden visit with your club, or group of friends, on a date to suit you. See individual garden entries for full details.

Belvedere 1
6 Beverley Gardens 2
13 Broom Acres 3
Deepwood Stud Farm 5
Dorset Cottage 6
Handpost 9
Island Cottage 10
Lower Bowden Manor 12
Rooksnest 17

The National Garden Scheme donated £3,875,596 to our nursing and health beneficiaries from money raised at gardens open in 2025.

Rooksnest

THE GARDENS

1 BELVEDERE
Garden Close Lane,
Newbury, RG14 6PP. Noushin
Garrett, 07500 925270,
noushin.garrett@gmail.com. *7m S
of M4 J13. Take A34 exit Highclere/
Wash Common, then A343 towards
Newbury. After 1m turn R into
Garden Close Ln. Car parking for
max 8 cars.* **Visits by arrangement
8 June to 15 July for groups of 15
to 25. Tea, coffee & cake.**
A garden of 2½ acres consisting of
herbaceous borders, rose garden,
fruit trees with woodland, bamboo
and rhododendron walks. A formal
parterre garden with dahlias.

2 6 BEVERLEY GARDENS
Wargrave, Reading, RG10 8ED.
Patricia Vella & Jon Black,
triciavella@gmail.com. *A4 from
Maidenhead take B477 to Wargrave.
Turn R into Silverdale Rd. A4 from
Reading take A321 into Wargrave.
Turn R at T-lights. After ¼m, turn L
into Silverdale Rd. Beverley Gardens
is on R.* **Sun 10 May, Sun 5, Fri
24 July, Sun 23 Aug (1-5). Adm
£4, chd free. Tea, coffee & cake.
Visits also by arrangement.**
The main garden has primarily
Mediterranean and exotic planting,
with paths through some of the beds,
inviting you to take a closer look. This
leads into a kitchen garden with a
greenhouse and a poultry run housing
chickens and ducks. There is a small
woodland garden with a stumpery
and fire pit. The garden has several
places to sit and relax with tea and
home-made cake. Children are very
welcome. Wheelchair access over
gravel drive in front garden, leading to
a level back garden with some bark
paths.

3 13 BROOM ACRES
Sandhurst, GU47 8PN.
Sunil Patel, 07974 403077,
garden@sunilpatel.co.uk,
www.sunilpatel.co.uk. *Between
Crowthorne & Sandhurst. From
Crowthorne/Sandhurst Rd, turn E
into Greenways, then take 1st R into
Broom Acres. Street parking.* **Visits
by arrangement 15 June to 31
Aug for groups of 15+. Hot drink
& piece of home-made cake inc.**
Adm £10, chd free.
A spellbinding ¼ acre suburban
romantic style garden with shrubbery,
exotics, specimen trees, scented
climbers, and mixed herbaceous
borders. Densely planted and
decadently flowering, a feast for all
the senses. Come for the garden,
stay for the magic, and discover
why romance remains compelling,
timeless, and enduring.

4 COWORTH PARK
Blacknest Road, Sunningdale,
Ascot, SL5 7SE. www.
dorchestercollection.com/ascot/
coworth-park. *Coworth Park is 3m
E of Ascot & is accessed from the
A329 London Rd. Visitors are invited
to arrive from 12pm & 2.30pm as the
garden tours will start promptly at
12.30pm & 3pm.* **Thur 21 May, Thur
6 Aug (12.30-5). Adm £30. Pre-
booking essential, please visit
www.ngs.org.uk for information
& booking. Two hour timed slots
at 12.30pm & 3pm. Cream tea inc
with the tour.**
A rare opportunity to enjoy a guided
tour with the Head Gardener at
Coworth Park, followed by a cream
tea in the Drawing Room. Set
amongst 240 acres of gardens,
parkland, paddocks, and woodland.
Highlights inc the beautiful terrace
and rose gardens bordered by
lavender, a sunken garden, weeping
lime trees, and a 10 acre wildflower
meadow. Cream tea inc tea or coffee,
a scone, and cake. Please email
hello@ngs.org.uk in advance with any
dietary or allergy requirements.

5 DEEPWOOD STUD FARM
Henley Road, Stubbings, nr
Maidenhead, SL6 6QW. Mr &
Mrs E Goodwin, 07878 911064,
ed.goodwin@deepwood.co. *2m
W of Maidenhead. From M4 J8/9,
take A404(M) N. At 2nd exit, take A4
towards Maidenhead. Turn L at 1st
r'about onto A4130 towards Henley.
Entrance approx 1m on R.* **Sun 17
May, Sun 6 Sept (2-5). Adm £6,
chd free. Tea, coffee & cake.
Visits also by arrangement 31 Mar
to 14 Sept for groups of 12 to 30.**
4 acres of formal and informal
gardens set within a 25 acre stud
farm. A formal rose garden with a
fountain, a walled herbaceous border
with windows through which to
admire the views and horses, two
rock gardens, and a hot plant terrace.
A small lake with a Monet style bridge
and pergola, several neo-classical
follies and statues, and a planted
woodland area with a winding path.
Partial wheelchair access.

6 DORSET COTTAGE
22 Albion Road, Sandhurst,
GU47 9BP. Sarah & Paul
Merrill, 01252 873530,
sarah.merrill@yahoo.co.uk.
*Albion Rd is N off Yorktown Rd in
Sandhurst. The turning is opp Boots
chemist. Street parking on Albion Rd
or Wellington Rd.* **Sun 28 June, Sun
6 Sept (1-5). Adm £5, chd free.
Home-made teas. Visits also by
arrangement 2 June to 28 June for
groups of 10 to 15.**
An inspirational secret garden tucked
behind a pretty red brick Victorian
cottage. Inviting paths weave around
a curving island bed, leading to long
borders packed with interesting
plants reflecting the passion of its
owner. Features inc rose and clematis
covered arches, pots filled with
tropical gems, figs, hostas, and ferns.
Towering palms, acers, and magnolia
trees offer shelter and seclusion.
Wheelchair access to most of the
garden via a grass path.

7 NEW DUMBLEDORE
Warren Row, Reading, RG10 8QS.
Mr & Mrs Guy Hindley. *5m W of
Maidenhead, 4m SE of Henley-
upon-Thames. Warren Row is off
the A4 nr Knowl Hill or the A4130 nr
Remenham. Parking in field at centre
of Warren Row, opp Green Chapel.
What3words app: birthing.stow.
drilled.* **Sun 31 May (12-4). Adm £5,
chd free. Pre-booking essential,
please visit www.ngs.org.uk for
information & booking. Home-
made teas.**
An informal garden with a mix of
colourful beds, borders, and pots,
with a focus on roses, all set against
a stunning view down the valley.
Features inc a mature *Cornus kousa*,
hydrangeas, and a wide variety of
roses, inc climbing and rambling
types growing over arches and trees.

8 ♦ ENGLEFIELD HOUSE GARDEN
Englefield, Theale, Reading, RG7 5EN. Lord & Lady Benyon, 01189 302504, peter.carson@englefield.co.uk, www.englefieldestate.co.uk. 6m W of Reading. From M4 J12, take A4 towards Newbury. At 2nd r'about, take A340 towards Pangbourne. After ½ m, the entrance is on the L. **For opening times and information, please phone, email or visit garden website.**
The 12 acre garden descends dramatically from the hill above the historic house, through woodland where mature native trees mix with rhododendrons and camellias. Drifts of spring and summer planting are followed by striking autumn colour. Stone balustrades enclose the lower terrace with lawns, roses, and mixed borders. A stream meanders through the woodland. Open every Monday from Apr-Sept (10am-6pm) and Oct-Mar (10am-4pm). Please check the Englefield Estate website for any changes before travelling. Wheelchair access to some parts of the garden.
♿ 🚗

9 HANDPOST
Basingstoke Road, Swallowfield, Reading, RG7 1PU. Faith Ramsay, 07801 239937, faith@mycountrygarden.co.uk, www.mycountrygarden.co.uk. S of Reading. From M4 J11, take A33 S. At 1st T-lights, turn L onto B3349 Basingstoke Rd. Follow road for 2¾ m; the garden is on the L, opp Barge Ln. Car sharing preferred. Parking on-site limited for up to 15 cars. **Visits by arrangement 1 May to 21 Aug for groups of 12 to 35. Adm £12, chd free. Tea or coffee & home-made cake inc.** Donation to Thrive.
A 4 acre designer's garden with many areas of interest. It features six beautiful, long herbaceous borders, attractively and densely planted in different colour sections. There is also a formal rose garden, a cutting garden, an old orchard with a grass meadow, a pretty pond, a peaceful wooded area, and a large variety of plants and trees, along with a productive fruit and vegetable patch. Regret, no dogs allowed. Largely wheelchair accessible with some gravel areas.

10 ISLAND COTTAGE
West Mills, Newbury, RG14 5HT. Karen Swaffield, karen@lockisland.com. 7m from M4 J13. Park in town centre car parks. Walk past St Nicholas Church, or between Côte Restaurant & Holland & Barrett, to the canal. Then walk 200yds to swing bridge & follow signs. Limited side road parking. **Visits by arrangement 2 June to 30 Sept for groups of 15 to 25. Adm £5, chd free. Home-made teas.**
A pretty, small waterside garden set between the River Kennet and the Kennet and Avon Canal. Interesting combinations of colour and texture, to look at rather than walk through, although visitors are welcome to do that too. A deck overlooks a sluiceway, towards a lawn and border. The garden was started from scratch in 2005, and mostly again after the floods of 2014. Trying high planters this year.

11 KING'S COPSE HOUSE
Bradfield Gate, nr Reading, RG7 6JR. Mr & Mrs J Wyatt. 11m W of Reading. M4 J12, A4 to Theale. At 2nd r'about, take 3rd exit A340 towards Pangbourne, then soon, 1st L. After 1¼ m, turn L to Bradfield Southend. In village, turn R on Hungerford Ln. After ½ m, turn L on Cock Ln. **Sun 19 July (2-5). Adm £6, chd free. Home-made teas.**
A beautiful, formally landscaped garden set in 4 acres, recently renovated to a high standard to incorporate some original and rare specimens together with new plantings. Orchard, large fish pond, secret garden, herbaceous borders, and lovely views over the Pang Valley. Walks through 40 acre SSSI ancient woodland. WWII air raid shelter.

12 LOWER BOWDEN MANOR
Bowden Green, Pangbourne, RG8 8JL. Juliette & Robert Cox-Nicol, 07552 217872, rcncities@gmail.com. 1½ m W of Pangbourne. Directions provided on booking. **Visits by arrangement 12 Jan to 27 Nov for groups of 12 to 40. Adm £15, chd free. Guided tour, tea & cake inc.**
A 7 acre designer's garden with stunning views, and where structure predominates. Specimen trees show contrasting bark and foliage. A marble 'Pan' plays to a pond with boulders and boulder shaped evergreens. Versailles planters with standard topiaries line a rill. A stumpery leads to the orchard's carpet of daffodils in April, followed later by a wave of white hydrangeas. A highlight is the variety of cornus (16), which put on a wonderful display from mid May. Some steps and gravel, but most areas accessible. Dogs welcome on leads.
♿ 🐕 🚗 ☕

13 NEW MULBERRY COTTAGE
The Slade, Bucklebury, Reading, RG7 6TE. Yvonne & Simon Sonsino. 9m W Reading, M4 J12. What3words app: fantastic.tarnished.branch. From A4, take A340 & turn L on Common Hill to South End Rd, passing through Chapel Row & Upper Bucklebury to Burdens Heath. Turn R to The Slade, until you pass houses. Limited parking signed. **Thur 23, Sun 26 Apr (10-4). Adm £5, chd free. Pre-booking essential, please visit www.ngs.org.uk for information & booking. Two hour timed slots at 10am & 2pm.**
A 1¼ acre developing cottage garden on a sunny, south facing slope, with a bourne running through. Now in its fourth yr, it inc an orchard and blossom copses underplanted with bulbs, a wildlife pond, vegetable plot, glasshouses, rose arches, and a treehouse. Features inc dry stone walls, a sun circle, and a stone garden with a rill, creating a vibrant haven for wildlife. Pottery studio open for sales. Teas, cakes and plant stall.

14 OAK COTTAGE
99B Kiln Ride, Finchampstead, Wokingham, RG40 3PD. Ms Liz Ince. 2½ m S of Wokingham. Off B3430 Nine Mile Ride, between A321 Sandhurst Rd & B3016 Finchampstead Rd. **Sun 10 May (11.30-5). Adm £5, chd free. Pre-booking essential, please visit www.ngs.org.uk for information & booking. Tea, coffee & cake. Timed slots at 11.30am, 1.30pm & 3.30pm.**
A rare opportunity to see and learn about bonsai trees, displayed by the Berkshire Bonsai Society in the lovely woodland setting of Oak Cottage Garden. The garden features many mature trees, underplanted with a collection of acers and shade-loving plants. The front garden will host a display of many varieties of bonsai.

Trees in development will also be shown, demonstrating how to prune and train bonsai. Short talks (15 mins) on growing and caring for bonsai will be held at 12.15pm, 1.45pm and 3.45pm.

15 THE OLD RECTORY, FARNBOROUGH
Wantage, OX12 8NX. **Mrs Michael Todhunter.** *4m SE of Wantage. Take B4494 from Wantage. After 4m turn L at sign for Farnborough & follow NGS signs. What3words app: diagram.advancing.emailed.* **Sun 12 Apr, Sun 10 May, Wed 24 June, Wed 29 July (2-5). Adm £7, chd free. Home-made teas.**
8 acre garden with a series of immaculately tended garden 'rooms'. Herbaceous borders, arboretum, secret garden, roses, vegetables, pool, bog gardens and woodland, with an explosion of rare and interesting plants, beautifully combined for colour and texture. Stunning views, and once home to John Betjeman (memorial window by John Piper in church). Specialist plants and home-made preserves for sale. Wheelchair access over gravel paths.

16 NEW THE OLD STABLES
1 Chestnut Park, Monkey Island Lane, Bray, SL6 2EF. **Toni Rae.** *Nr Maidenhead. M4 J8/9, take A308(M). R onto A308, then L onto B3028 to Bray. Turn R after village hall to Old Mill Ln, then Monkey Island Ln. Park at Monkey Island Hotel car park, SL6 2EE. Short walk to The Old Stables (signed).* **Thur 21 May, Fri 5 June (10.30-1); Sun 14 June (1.30-4.30); Fri 11 Sept (10.30-1). Adm £12, chd free. Pre-booking essential, please visit www.ngs.org.uk for information & booking. Tea, coffee & cake inc.**
A beautifully designed 1 acre garden divided into different areas. The formal section begins with a French style boule pit and herb garden and continues with knot gardens. A vibrant herbaceous border and two large ponds with water lilies and aquatic plants frame a sunken patio leading to an oak building. A wisteria walk leads into a naturalistic area with wildflower mounds. Wheelchair access is via a fairly narrow side gate and path, followed by smooth paths around the formal area.

17 ROOKSNEST
Ermin Street, Lambourn Woodlands, RG17 7SB. **Rooksnest Estate, 07787 085565, gardens@rooksnest.net.** *2m S of Lambourn on B4000. From M4 J14, take A338 Wantage Rd, turn 1st L onto B4000 (Ermin St). Rooksnest signed after 3m.* **Wed 22 Apr, Wed 24 June (11-3.30). Adm £6, chd free. Light refreshments. Visits also by arrangement 15 Apr to 24 June for groups of 15 to 50.**
An approx 10 acre, exceptionally fine traditional English garden. Rose garden, herbaceous garden, pond garden, herb garden, fruit, vegetable and cutting garden, and glasshouses. Many specimen trees and fine shrubs, an orchard, and terraces. Garden designed by Arabella Lennox-Boyd. Limited WC facilities. Most areas have step free wheelchair access, although surfaces consist of gravel and mown grass.

The Old Stables

18 ST TIMOTHEE

Darlings Lane, Pinkneys Green, Maidenhead, SL6 6PA. Sarah & Sal Pajwani, www.instagram.com/sarahpajwani. *1m N of Maidenhead. M4 J8/9 to A404M, 3rd exit onto A4 to Maidenhead. L at 1st r'about to A4130 Henley Rd. After ½m turn R onto Pinkneys Dr. At Pinkneys Arms pub turn L into Lee Ln. Follow NGS signs.* **Sun 31 May (11-4). Adm £7, chd free. Home-made teas. Talk & Walk events inc tea, coffee & cake start promptly at 10.30am on Tue 13, Thur 15 Jan, Tue 17, Thur 19 Mar, Thur 25 June, Tue 3, Thur 5 Nov (10.30-12.30). Adm £20, chd free. Pre-booking essential, please visit www.ngs.org.uk for information & booking.**

A 2 acre country garden planted for year-round interest with a variety of different colour themed borders each featuring a wide range of hardy perennials, bulbs, shrubs and ornamental grasses. Also inc a wildlife pond, rose terrace, olive garden, areas of long grass and beautiful mature trees, all set against the backdrop of a 1930s house. This year there will be one open day (31 May) and a series of Talk & Walk events on a variety of topics; The Winter Garden (13 Jan), The Beauty of the Wild (15 Jan, 19 Mar, 25 Jun & 5 Nov), The Joy of Spring Bulbs (17 Mar), Grasses and the Autumn Garden (3 Nov). Events start promptly with an illustrated slideshow talk and home-made teas followed by time to explore the garden.

19 STOCKCROSS HOUSE

Church Road, Stockcross, Newbury, RG20 8LP. Susan & Edward Vandyk, www.stockcrosshousegarden.co.uk. *3m W of Newbury. From M4 J13, take A34(S). After 3m, exit A4(W) towards Hungerford. At 2nd r'about, take B4000. After 1m, enter Stockcross & take 2nd L into Church Rd. Coach parking available.* **Sun 24 May, Sun 23 Aug (11-5). Adm £6, chd free. Home-made teas, with gluten free option.**

Romantic 2 acre garden set around a listed former Victorian rectory, created over the last 31 yrs. It features deep mixed borders with succession planting, and an emphasis on both height and strong complementary colour combinations. A wisteria-clad pergola, an orangery, a folly with a reflecting pond, a croquet lawn and pavilion, naturalistic planting with a pond on the lower level, a small stumpery, and a kitchen garden. Plants from garden for sale. Partial wheelchair access with some gravelled areas.

20 STUBBINGS HOUSE

Stubbings Lane, Henley Road, Maidenhead, SL6 6QL. Mr & Mrs D Good, www.stubbingsnursery.co.uk. *Located on the outskirts of Maidenhead, just mins from the M4 J8/9 & M40 J4. From A404(M) W of Maidenhead, exit at A4 r'about & follow signs to Maidenhead. At the small r'about, turn L towards Stubbings. Take the next L onto Stubbings Ln.* **Sat 14, Sun 15 Mar, Sat 9, Sun 10 May (10-4). Adm £5, chd free. Light refreshments (additional charges apply).**

Parkland garden accessed via the adjacent retail plant centre. Set around an C18 Grade II listed house (not open), which was home to Queen Wilhelmina of the Netherlands during WW2. A large lawn with a ha-ha, woodland walks, and notable trees inc historic cedars and araucaria. March brings an abundance of

Mulberry Cottage

daffodils and in May a 60 metre wall of wisteria. Attractions inc a C18 ice house and access to adjacent NT woodland. On site café offering breakfast, snacks, cream teas and seasonal lunches. Wheelchair access to a level site with firm gravel paths.

21 61 SUTCLIFFE AVENUE
Earley, Reading, RG6 7JN. Sue & Dave Wilder. *3m SE of Reading. Road: From E on Wokingham Rd (A329), pass Showcase Cinema, then turn L at Nisa (Meadow Rd), then R into Sutcliffe Ave; from W, turn R at Nisa. Train: Earley Stn, then 10 min walk.* **Wed 3, Thur 4 June (10.30-5); Sat 6 June (1-5). Adm £3.50, chd free. Tea, coffee & cake.**
A characterful, urban, wildlife friendly garden, imaginatively rewilded. The garden offers the relaxing sense of a walk in the countryside. An inviting path winds past wildflower islands, through a rose-covered arch, and leads to a pollinators' paradise garden and a small pond. Creatively recycled tree trunks and a former chicken run, now used as a fruit garden, are added features. Wheelchair access to the bottom of garden.

GROUP OPENING

22 SWALLOWFIELD VILLAGE GARDENS
Swallowfield Park, Church Road, Swallowfield, Reading, RG7 1TH. *5m S of Reading. From M4 J11, take A33 S. At 1st T-lights, turn L onto B3349, signed Swallowfield. As you enter village, follow signs to Swallowfield Park on Church Rd for parking, & to purchase tickets & maps.* **Sun 7 June (2-5.30). Combined adm £9, chd free. Home-made teas at Brambles.**

BRAMBLES
Sarah & Martyn Dadds.

5 CURLYS WAY
Carolyn & Gary Clark.

LAMBS FARMHOUSE
Eva Koskuba.

NORKETT COTTAGE
Jenny Spencer.

PRIMROSE COTTAGE
Patricia Armitage.

NEW SHEEPBRIDGE COURT
John & Denisa Goldfinch.

SWALLOWFIELD COTTAGE
Toni & Brian Carter.

Swallowfield is opening at least 7 gardens, with some located in the village itself and others nearby in the surrounding countryside. The village gardens can be reached on foot from the Swallowfield Park car park, while the gardens outside the village require a car or bicycle. Each garden is different and provides its own character and interest. Swallowfield nestles in the countryside between the Blackwater and Loddon rivers, with an abundance of wildlife and lovely views. See website for info about individual gardens. Laurels Garden centre will be selling a large selection of plants and flowers at Brambles. Wheelchair access to some gardens, however some have gravel drives, slopes and uneven ground.

23 ♦ WELFORD PARK
Welford, Newbury, RG20 8HU. Mrs J H Puxley, 01488 608691, contact@welfordpark.co.uk, www.welfordpark.co.uk. *6m NW of Newbury. M4 J13, A34(S). After 3m, exit A4(W) towards Hungerford. At 2nd r'about, take B4000. After 4m, turn R, signed Welford. Car park entrance on Newbury–Lambourn road.* **For NGS: Wed 4 Feb (11-5). Adm £11, chd £6. Soup & hot lunches available, with home-made cakes, hot & cold drinks in tent. For other opening times and information, please phone, email or visit garden website.**
One of the finest natural snowdrop woodlands in the country and a wonderful display of hellebores, Galanthus cultivars, and winter flowering shrubs throughout the extensive gardens. This is a NGS 1927 pioneer garden on the River Lambourn set around Queen Anne house (not open). Also, the stunning setting for Great British Bake Off. WC facilities. Child friendly, and dogs welcome on leads. Coach parties please book in advance. Concessions £10, chd (4-15) £6. Groups of 15+ £11 inc tea/coffee. A wheelchair friendly route has been made, please follow the signs and avoid damp areas near the river, deep wood chip paths and bridges.

24 WEMBURY
Altwood Close, Maidenhead, SL6 4PP. Carolyn Foster. *W side of Maidenhead, S of A4. Take M4 J8/9, then join A404(M) J9B. Take 3rd exit onto A4 towards Maidenhead. At 1st r'about, turn R. Take 2nd L onto Altwood Rd, then take 5th R. Follow NGS signs.* **Fri 17, Tue 28 July, Wed 5 Aug (10.30-4). Adm £4.50, chd free. Pre-booking essential, please visit www.ngs.org.uk for information & booking. Home-made teas. Two hour timed slots at 10.30am & 2pm.**
A wildlife friendly, plant lover's cottage garden with borders generously planted with bulbs, perennials, grasses, and shrubs for interest in every season. Productive vegetable garden and greenhouses. Many pots and baskets with seasonal annuals and tender perennials, especially salvias.

25 WICKHAM HOUSE
Wickham, Newbury, RG20 8HD. Mr & Mrs James D'Arcy. *7m NW of Newbury or 6m NE of Hungerford. From M4 J14: Take A338(N), signed Wantage. Approx ¾m, turn R onto B4000. Drive through Wickham. Entrance 100yds uphill on R. From Newbury: Take B4000. House on L, 75yds past Wickham speed limit sign.* **Sun 14 June (11-3). Adm £6, chd free. Home-made teas, gammon rolls & a variety of cakes.**
In a beautiful country house setting, this exceptional ½ acre walled garden was created from scratch in 2008. Designed by Robin Templar-Williams, the different rooms have distinct themes and colour schemes. A delightful arched clematis and rose walkway. A wide variety of trees, planting, pots brimming with colour, and places to sit and enjoy the views. A separate cutting and vegetable garden. Wheelchair access over gravel paths.

Our donation to the Army Benevolent Fund supported 776 individuals with horticultural related grants in 2025.

BUCKINGHAMSHIRE

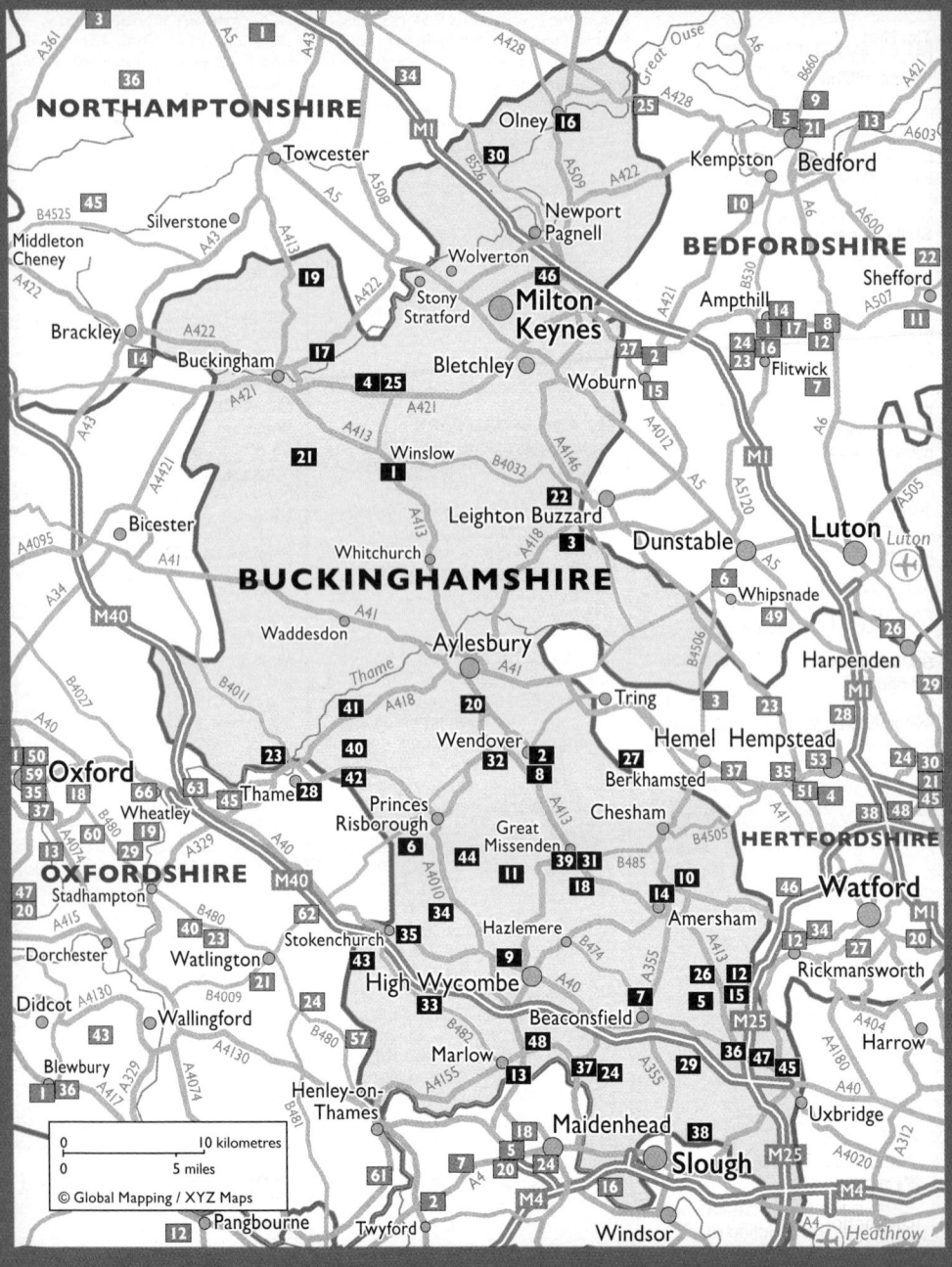

BUCKINGHAMSHIRE 43

VOLUNTEERS

County Organiser
Maggie Bateson
01494 866265
maggiebateson@gmail.com

County Treasurer
Tim Hart
01494 837328
timgc.hart@btinternet.com

Publicity
Sandra Wetherall
01494 862264
sandracwetherall@gmail.com

Social Media
Stella Vaines
07711 420621
stella@bakersclose.com

Booklet Co-ordinator
Maggie Bateson
(as above)

Talks
Clare Waters
07717 535650
clare.waters@ngs.org.uk

Assistant County Organisers
Judy Hart
01494 837328
judy.elgood@gmail.com

Mhairi Sharpley
01494 782870
mhairisharpley@btinternet.com

Stella Vaines
(as above)

Clare Waters
(as above)

@BucksNGS
@national_garden_scheme_bucks

OPENING DATES

All entries subject to change.
For latest information check
www.ngs.org.uk

Map locator numbers are shown to the right of each garden name.

March

Wednesday 11th
Turn End — 40

April

Sunday 5th
Overstroud Cottage — 31

Sunday 12th
Long Crendon Gardens — 23

Sunday 26th
Abbots House — 1

May

Wednesday 6th
Turn End — 40

Saturday 9th
8 Claremont Road — 13

Sunday 10th
8 Claremont Road — 13
♦ Stoke Poges Memorial Gardens — 38

Tuesday 12th
Red Kites — 34

Saturday 16th
8 Claremont Road — 13

Sunday 17th
8 Claremont Road — 13
The White House — 45

Monday 18th
♦ Ascott — 3

Sunday 24th
Foscote Manor — 17
Wind in the Willows — 47

Monday 25th
Glebe Farm — 19
The Plough — 32

June

Wednesday 3rd
Turn End — 40

Saturday 6th
Horatio's Garden — 20
St Michaels Convent — 36

Sunday 7th
Abbots House — 1
NEW Liscombe House — 22
Long Crendon Gardens — 23
Old Keepers — 29
Robin Hill — 35
Tythrop Park — 42

Saturday 13th
Acer Corner — 2
NEW Ashtree Cottage — 4
♦ Cowper & Newton Museum Gardens — 16
NEW Middle Shelspit Farm — 25

Sunday 14th
Acer Corner — 2
♦ Cowper & Newton Museum Gardens — 16

Thursday 18th
Cornfield Cottage — 15

Saturday 20th
Old Park Barn — 30

Sunday 21st
Old Park Barn — 30

Thursday 25th
NEW ♦ Chiltern Open Air Museum — 12
NEW ♦ Milton's Cottage — 26

July

Sunday 5th
Chiltern Forage Farm — 11
Fressingwood — 18

Wednesday 8th
The Walled Garden, Wormsley — 43

Saturday 11th
Wardrobes House — 44
NEW Willen Hospice — 46

Tuesday 14th
Red Kites — 34

Sunday 19th
Bledlow Manor — 6
18 Copperkins Lane — 14

Sunday 26th
Rackleys — 33

BUCKINGHAMSHIRE

August

Sunday 2nd
Tyringham Hall　41

Sunday 30th
◆ Nether Winchendon House　28

October

Saturday 17th
Acer Corner　2

Sunday 18th
Acer Corner　2

By Arrangement

Arrange a personalised garden visit with your club, or group of friends, on a date to suit you. See individual garden entries for full details.

Abbots House	1
Acer Corner	2
Beech House	5
Bledlow Manor	6
18 Brownswood Road	7
Cedar House	8
Chaniwa, Japanese Garden	9
Chesham Bois House	10
Kingsbridge Farm	21
Magnolia House	24
NEW Middle Shelspit Farm	25
Montana	27
Old Keepers	29
Old Park Barn	30
Overstroud Cottage	31
Red Kites	34
Robin Hill	35
The Shades	37
Touchwood	39
Turn End	40
Wind in the Willows	47
Woodlands House	48

Milton's Cottage

THE GARDENS

1 ABBOTS HOUSE
10 Church Street, Winslow, MK18 3AN. Mrs Jane Rennie, 01296 712326, jane@renniemail.com. *9m N of Aylesbury. A413 into Winslow. From town centre, take Horn St & turn R into Church St, then L fork at top. Entrance through door in wall, on Church Walk. Parking in town centre & on adjacent streets.* **Sun 26 Apr, Sun 7 June (1-5). Adm £5, chd free. Home-made teas.** Visits also by arrangement May to July for groups of 5 to 16.
Behind red brick walls lies a ¾ acre garden on four different levels, each with unique planting and atmosphere. The lower lawn with white wisteria arbour and pond; the upper lawn with rose pergola and woodland, pool area with grasses, Victorian kitchen garden, glasshouse, and wild meadow. Spring bulbs in wild areas and woodland, with many tulips in April, and remaining areas peak in June/July. There is a water feature, sculptures and many pots. Rennie's award-winning Winslow Cider is available. Partial wheelchair access due to steps leading to garden levels. Guide dogs and medical-aid dogs only.

2 ACER CORNER
10 Manor Road, Wendover, HP22 6HQ. Jo Naiman, 07958 319234, jo@acercorner.com, www.acercorner.com. *3m S of Aylesbury. Follow A413 into Wendover. Turn L at clock tower r'about onto Aylesbury Rd. Turn R at next r'about onto Wharf Rd. Continue past schools on L; garden will be on R.* **Sat 13, Sun 14 June, Sat 17, Sun 18 Oct (2-5). Adm £4.50, chd free. Home-made teas.** Visits also by arrangement 1 May to 16 Oct for groups of up to 18.
A garden designer's garden with Japanese influence and a large collection of *Acer palmatum* Japanese maples. The enclosed front garden is Japanese in style. The back garden is divided into three areas: a patio area recently redesigned in the Japanese style; a densely planted area with many acers and roses; and a corner that inc a productive greenhouse and interesting planting. There are over 70 acers in the garden.

3 ♦ ASCOTT
Ascott Estate, Wing, Leighton Buzzard, LU7 0PP. The National Trust, info@ascottestate.co.uk, www.ascottestate.co.uk. *2m SW of Leighton Buzzard, 8m NE of Aylesbury. Via A418. Buses: 150 Aylesbury to Milton Keynes, 250 Aylesbury & Milton Keynes. Access is via the visitors entrance, use postcode LU7 0ND.* **For NGS: Mon 18 May (11.30-5). Adm £12.95, chd £6.50. Adm subject to change. NT members are required to pay to enter the gardens on NGS days.** For other opening times and information, please email or visit garden website.
Combining Victorian formality with natural planting and modern design. Terraced lawns with specimen and ornamental trees and panoramic views to the Chilterns. Naturalised bulbs, mirror image herbaceous borders, and impressive topiary inc a unique box and yew sundial. Ascott House is closed on NGS Days. The Pavilion Tearoom will be open until 15 mins before closing, serving a range of hot and cold refreshments. Wheelchair access over gravel and grass pathways.

4 NEW ASHTREE COTTAGE
Nash Road, Thornborough, Buckingham, MK18 2DY. Anthony Mack. *5m from Buckingham, off the A421. From the centre of Thornborough village, take Nash Rd for approx 1m. Garden is 1m on RHS. What3words app: timidly.misty.yachting.* **Sat 13 June (1-5). Combined adm with Middle Shelspit Farm £7, chd free. Tea, coffee & cake at Middle Shelspit Farm.**
Beautiful country garden. Mature borders frame countryside valley views. The main focal point is the established Koi pond, complete with a natural bog filter. A recently constructed walled kitchen style garden ensures there is something for everyone, with vegetable beds and a flower cutting patch. Be sure to spend some time resting in the railway carriage, and don't miss the converted silo toilet! The site is largely wheelchair accessible, though some areas have uneven ground. Service and guide dogs only.

5 BEECH HOUSE
Long Wood Drive, Jordans, nr Beaconsfield, HP9 2SS. Sue & Ray Edwards, 01494 875580, raychessmad@hotmail.com. *2m NE of Beaconsfield. From A40: L to Seer Green & Jordans for approx 1m. Turn R to Jordans Way, then 1st L to Long Wood Dr. From A413: Turn into Chalfont St Giles, straight ahead until L signed Jordans, 1st L Jordans Way.* **Visits by arrangement Mar to Sept for groups of up to 50. Adm £5, chd free.**
A 2 acre garden created over the last 38 yrs, with a wide range of flowering and foliage plants in a variety of habitats for all year interest. Many different bulbs, perennials, shrubs, roses, and grasses, together with trees planted for their flowers, foliage, ornamental bark, and autumn colour give a continual display. Two meadows with a long flowering season are a popular feature with visitors. An extensive collection of plants and meadow gardens, established over 33 yrs, always attracts attention and discussion. Wheelchair access dependent upon weather conditions.

6 BLEDLOW MANOR
Off Perry Lane, Bledlow, nr Princes Risborough, HP27 9PA. Lord & Lady Carrington, 01844 273508, melaniedoughty@carington.co.uk, www.carington.co.uk/gardens. *9m NW of High Wycombe, 3m SW of Princes Risborough. ½m off B4009 in middle of Bledlow village. For SatNav use postcode HP27 9PA.* **Sun 19 July (2-5). Adm £8, chd free. Tea, coffee & cake.** Visits also by arrangement 5 May to 30 Sept for groups of 25+.
The present garden covers around 12 acres, inc the walled kitchen garden crisscrossed by paths lined with vegetables, fruit, herbs, and flowers. The sculpture garden, the replanted granary garden with a fountain and borders, as well as individual paved gardens and parterres divided by yew hedges and more. The Lyde water garden, formed out of old cress beds, is fed by numerous springs. Partial wheelchair access via steps or sloped grass to enter gardens.

7 18 BROWNSWOOD ROAD
Beaconsfield, HP9 2NU.
John & Bernadette Thompson,
07879 282191,
tbernadette60@gmail.com. *From New Town, turn R onto Ledborough Ln, then L onto Sandleswood Rd, & take 2nd R onto Brownswood Rd.* **Visits by arrangement 2 Mar to 13 Sept for groups of up to 15. Adm £4, chd free.**
A plant-filled garden, designed by Barbara Hunt. A harmonious arrangement of arcs and circles introduces a rhythm that leads through the garden. Sweeping box curves, gravel beds, brick edging, and lush planting. A restrained use of purples and reds dazzles against a grey and green background. A garden that is beautiful all year round. Spring brings lots of bulbs, and peonies are a highlight in late spring.

8 CEDAR HOUSE
Bacombe Lane, Wendover, HP22 6EQ. Sarah Nicholson, 01296 622131, sarahhnicholson@btinternet.com. *5m SE Aylesbury. From Great Missenden on the A413, proceed into Wendover. At the 1st r'about, turn L. Then turn R, over the bridge, & turn L after the crossing. Turn R at the end. Parking for 10 cars only.* **Visits by arrangement 13 Feb to 27 Sept for groups of 10+. Adm £5, chd free.**
A plantsman's garden in the Chiltern Hills, with a great variety of trees, shrubs, and plants. A sloping lawn leads to a natural swimming pond with wild flowers, inc native orchids. There is a lodge greenhouse and a good collection of half-hardy plants in pots. Local artist's sculptures can be viewed. Picnics welcome with prior request. Wheelchair access over gentle sloping lawn.

9 CHANIWA, JAPANESE GARDEN
1 Talbot Avenue, Downley, High Wycombe, HP13 5HZ. Mr Alan Mayes, 01494 451044, alan.mayes2@btopenworld.com. *From Downley T-lights off West Wycombe Rd, take Plomer Hill turn-off, then take 2nd L into Westover Rd, followed by 2nd L into Talbot Ave.* **Visits by arrangement 27 Apr to 4 Sept. Adm by donation. Tea.**
A Japanese garden, shielded from the upper garden level by Shoji screens. A winding path leads over a traditional Japanese bridge by a pond and waterfall, and invites you through a moongate to reveal a purpose built tea house. The garden is surrounded by traditional Japanese planting, inc maples, cherry blossom trees, azaleas, and rhododendrons. Ornamental grasses and bamboo complement the hard landscaping, along with a feature cloud tree and a checkerboard garden path.

10 CHESHAM BOIS HOUSE
85 Bois Lane, Chesham Bois, Amersham, HP6 6DF. Julia Plaistowe, 01494 726476, plaistowejulia@gmail.com, cheshamboishouse.co.uk. *1m N of Amersham-on-the-Hill. Follow Sycamore Rd (the main shopping centre road in Amersham), which becomes Bois Ln. Do not use SatNav once in lane, as you will be led astray.* **Visits by arrangement Mar to Aug. Adm £10, chd free, inc tea.**
A beautiful 3 acre garden with primroses, daffodils, and hellebores in early spring. It is interesting throughout most of the year, with lovely herbaceous borders, a rill with a small ornamental canal, a walled garden, an old orchard with a wildlife pond, and handsome trees, some of which are topiary. It is a peaceful oasis. Wheelchair access via gravel at front of house.

11 CHILTERN FORAGE FARM
Spring Coppice Lane, Speen, Princes Risborough, HP27 0SU. Emma Plunket, www.plunketgardens.com. *Follow signs to gate at top of the hill & park in field. Please wear trainers or walking shoes, as the ground is uneven.* **Sun 5 July (11.30-3.30). Adm £5, chd free. Tours at 11.30–12.30 & 2.30–3.30pm only (closed 12.30-2.30pm). Tea.**
Visit this rural project set in an attractive hillside location, with grassland meadows planted with fruit. Tips for foraging, encouraging wild flowers, and the creation of wildlife habitats. Spot butterflies and pollinators if the weather is calm and sunny. Enjoy a cup of tea or a cool drink under cover, and share our identification tips, survey findings, and field guides.

12 NEW ♦ CHILTERN OPEN AIR MUSEUM
Gorelands Lane, Chalfont St Giles, HP8 4AB. enquiries@coam.org.uk, www.coam.org.uk. *The Museum is located within Newland Park. Look out for the large green Newland Park boarding which marks the entrance. COAM is 100 metres along the driveway.* **For NGS: Thur 25 June (10-4). Combined adm with Milton's Cottage £7, chd free. Light refreshments.** For other opening times and information, please email or visit garden website.
The gardens at Chiltern Open Air Museum reflect the region's rich horticultural heritage. Traditional gardens inc an Arts and Crafts garden, Victorian fernery, Iron Age herb garden, and a wartime 'Dig for Victory' allotment. The site's apple and cherry orchards preserve rare varieties like D'Arcy Spice and Prestwood Black, celebrating the Chilterns' rural history.

13 8 CLAREMONT ROAD
Marlow, SL7 1BW. Andi Gallagher. *No parking at garden, but a short walk from all town car parks. From town centre, walk S on High St, turn L on Institute Rd, L on Beaufort Gardens, & R on Claremont Rd.* **Sat 9, Sun 10, Sat 16, Sun 17 May (1.30-4.30). Adm £5, chd free.**
Paintings, prints, and pots to see and buy in this small town garden, owned by an artist gardener. The unusual house was built in 2015. Gravel paths divide rectangular beds filled with herbaceous perennials, grasses, and ferns. A cow trough water feature and the owner's ceramics add surprise. A gate leads to a deliberate wild area with fruit bushes and an art studio with garden related paintings.

In 2025, our donations to Carers Trust helped them support over 1 million unpaid carers across the UK, as part of their network of local carer centres.

BUCKINGHAMSHIRE 47

18 COPPERKINS LANE
Amersham, HP6 5QF. Chris Ludlam. *1m N of Amersham. 15 min walk from Amersham Tube/Train Stn. Located off Amersham/Chesham road A416. Parking on road only, please park with consideration to neighbours.* **Sun 19 July (12-6). Adm £5, chd free. Pre-booking essential, please visit www.ngs.org.uk for information & booking. Home-made teas.**
A fabulous, compact ½ acre garden with a lawn, herbaceous borders, wild flowers, orchard, vegetable beds, playhouse, summerhouse, and pool. Originally designed as a white garden, it now inc purple, blue, and pink colours. Plenty of roses, grasses, salvia, nepeta, peonies, delphiniums, lupins, geraniums, foxgloves, alliums, lavender, astrantia, and ornamental trees, inc Davidia, plus 18 varieties of perovskia. Wheelchair access over deep gravel path, plus two sloped tiled paths on entry.

15 CORNFIELD COTTAGE
Roberts Lane, Chalfont St Peter, Gerrards Cross, SL9 0QR. Debbie & Stewart Walker. *In the hamlet of Horn Hill, 1½m from the centre of Chalfont St Peter. Take Rickmansworth Ln to Horn Hill Village Hall, then turn R onto Roberts Ln. Cornfield Cottage is 300 metres ahead on L. Limited car parking opp the house & at Horn Hill Village Hall.* **Thur 18 June (2-5). Adm £4.50, chd free. Home-made teas.**
A beautiful rural garden in a quiet country lane. The borders are planted with scented roses and bee and butterfly friendly flowers, inc honeysuckle, delphiniums, and sweet peas. Seating areas provide enjoyable views of the garden at different times of the day. A natural arch leads to a paddock with a small vegetable garden, orchard, wildflower beds, and a wood with a seasonal, spring fed pond. To reserve disabled parking (opp the house or on the drive), call 01494 268548. The entrance gate to the garden is 800mm wide.

The White House

BUCKINGHAMSHIRE

16 ◆ COWPER & NEWTON MUSEUM GARDENS
Orchard Side, Market Place, Olney, MK46 4AJ. Cowper & Newton Museum, 01234 711516, house-manager@cowperandnewtonmuseum.org.uk, www.cowperandnewtonmuseum.org.uk. *5m N of Newport Pagnell. 12m S of Wellingborough. On A509. Please park in public car park in East St.* **For NGS: Sat 13, Sun 14 June (10.30-4). Adm £4, chd free. Home-made teas.** For other opening times and information, please phone, email or visit garden website.
The tranquil Flower Garden of C18 poet William Cowper, who said, 'Gardening was, of all employments, that in which I succeeded best,' has plants introduced prior to his death in 1800, many mentioned in his writings. The Summerhouse Garden, now a Kitchen Garden, inc organically grown vegetables and flowers, as well as herb and medicinal beds, and the summerhouse Cowper called his 'verse manufactory'. Features inc lacemaking demonstrations, local artists painting and live musical entertainment. Wheelchair access on mostly hard paths.
♿ ✿ ☕ 🔊

17 FOSCOTE MANOR
Foscott, Buckingham, MK18 6AE. Kate Pryke. *Just outside Maids Moreton, NE of Buckingham. The postcode takes you to a small hamlet of cottages. For Foscote Manor, continue across the cattle grid into the fields, & you will see the gates of the Manor House.* **Sun 24 May (2-5). Adm £12, chd free. Home-made teas inc.**
A restored walled kitchen garden, with vegetables, fruit, herbs, and flowers, as the centrepiece of this 40 acre estate. The surrounding waterway is bordered by a wildflower meadow, attracting heron, egret, and kingfisher. Behind the walled garden, the back drive leads to ancient woodland, sprouting a carpet of spring bulbs, and to the lake, home to Canada geese, swans, and heron.
🐕 ☕ 🔊

18 FRESSINGWOOD
Hare Lane, Little Kingshill, Great Missenden, HP16 0EF. John & Maggie Bateson. *1m S of Great Missenden, 4m W of Amersham. From the A413 at Chiltern Hospital, turn L signed Gt & Lt Kingshill. Take 1st L into Nags Head Ln. Turn R under railway bridge, then L into New Rd & continue to Hare Ln.* **Sun 5 July (2-5.30). Adm £5, chd free. Home-made teas.**
Thoughtfully designed and structured garden with year-round colour and many interesting features inc herbaceous borders, a shrubbery with ferns, hostas, grasses and hellebores. Small formal garden, pergolas with roses and clematis. A variety of topiary and small garden rooms. A central feature incorporating water with grasses and an old olive tree. Large bonsai collection.
✿ ☕ 🔊

19 GLEBE FARM
Lillingstone Lovell, Buckingham, MK18 5BB. Mr David Hilliard, sites.google.com/site/glebefarmbarn. *Off A413, 5m N of Buckingham & 2m S of Whittlebury. From A5 at Potterspury, turn off A5 & follow signs to Lillingstone Lovell. From A413, Lillingstone Lovell is situated between Lillingstone Dayrell and Whittlebury.* **Mon 25 May (1.30-5). Adm £5, chd free. Home-made teas.**
A large cottage garden with an exuberance of colourful planting and winding gravel paths, set amongst lawns and herbaceous borders on two levels. Ponds, a wishing well, vegetable beds, a knot garden, a small walled garden, and an old tractor all feature. Everything comes together to form a beautiful garden full of surprises. Greenhouses to wander through, with seating areas and lawns to sit and relax on. Wheelchair access in some flat areas of garden.
♿ 🐕 ✿ 🛏 ☕ 🔊

20 HORATIO'S GARDEN
National Spinal Injuries Centre (NSIC), Stoke Mandeville Hospital, Mandeville Road, Stoke Mandeville, Aylesbury, HP21 8AL. www.horatiosgarden.org.uk. *The closest car park to Horatio's Garden is Car Park B at Stoke Mandeville Hospital, opp Asda (charges may apply).* **Sat 6 June (2-5). Adm £5, chd free. Tea, coffee & cake in the garden room.**
Opened in Sept 2018, Horatio's Garden at the National Spinal Injuries Centre, Stoke Mandeville Hospital is designed by Joe Swift. The fully accessible garden for patients with spinal injuries has been part funded by the NGS. The beautiful space is cleverly designed to bring the sights, sounds and scents of nature into the heart of the NHS. Everything is high quality and carefully designed to bring benefit to patients who often have lengthy stays in hospital. The garden features a contemporary garden room designed by Andrew Wells, as well as a stunning Griffin Glasshouse. We also have a wonderful wildflower meadow. Please come along and meet the lead gardener, patient experience manager, and volunteer team. Enjoy our delicious tea and home-made cake! The garden is fully accessible, having been designed specifically for patients in wheelchairs or hospital beds.
♿ ✿ 🚗 D ☕ 🔊

21 KINGSBRIDGE FARM
Steeple Claydon, MK18 2EJ. Mr & Mrs Tom Aldous, 01296 730224. *3m S of Buckingham. Halfway between Padbury & Steeple Claydon. Xrds signed to Kingsbridge Only.* **Visits by arrangement June & July for groups of 6+. Adm £7, chd free. Home-made teas in cosy, converted barn.**
A stunning, exceptional 6 acre garden, constantly evolving. The main lawn is enclosed by softly curving, colour themed herbaceous borders, with a gazebo, topiary, clipped yews, and pleached hornbeams leading to a ha-ha and the countryside beyond. A natural stream, with bog plants and nesting kingfishers, meanders serenely through shrub and woodland gardens, with many walks. A garden to visit again and again.
♿ 🐕 ✿ 🚗 ☕

22 NEW LISCOMBE HOUSE
Liscombe Park, Soulbury, Leighton Buzzard, LU7 0JN. Sir Alex & Lady Bonsor. *3m W of Leighton Buzzard. Entrance is located on the Leighton Rd (B4032). Drive through the wrought iron gates & follow signs. What3words app: first.televise.vegetable to entrance gate.* **Sun 7 June (2-5). Adm £10, chd free. Tea, coffee & cake inc.**
The gardens surrounding C17 Liscombe House (not open), revitalised with designer Jinny Blom, blend history with renewal. A walled garden, orchard, restored ponds, and courtyard garden flourish with drought resistant planting, cut flowers, topiary, and a Millennium walk. Fruit and vegetables grow within the grounds, and the historic greenhouse shelters tender plants. Teas served in a C14 chapel. Gravel carpark for disabled visitors.
♿ 🐕 ✿ 🚗 ☕ 🔊

GROUP OPENING

23 LONG CRENDON GARDENS
Long Crendon, HP18 9AN. *2m N of Thame. Park in the village, as most individual gardens do not have parking, although limited parking at 25 Elm Trees (opening in April).* **Sun 12 Apr, Sun 7 June (2-6). Combined adm £7, chd free. Home-made teas in Church House, High St (Apr) & St Mary's Church (June).**

BARRY'S CLOSE
Mr R Salmon.
Open on Sun 12 Apr

NEW 7 CARTERS LANE
Ms Helen Passingham-Hughes.
Open on Sun 12 Apr

50 CHILTON ROAD
Pete Bromley & Karen Bromley.
Open on Sun 7 June

COP CLOSE
Sandra & Tony Phipkin.
Open on all dates

25 ELM TREES
Carol & Mike Price.
Open on Sun 12 Apr

NEW 24 HIGH STREET
Mrs Wendy Thompson.
Open on Sun 7 June

MANOR HOUSE
Mr & Mrs West.
Open on Sun 12 Apr

NEW OLD COLLEGE FARMHOUSE
Mrs Anna Bernstein.
Open on Sun 12 Apr

TOMPSONS FARM
Mr & Mrs T Moynihan.
Open on Sun 7 June

NEW 19 WAINWRIGHTS
Mrs Angela Holdaway.
Open on Sun 7 June

NEW 24 WAINWRIGHTS
Mrs Margaret OMalley.
Open on Sun 7 June

Sun 12 Apr: Six different gardens, ranging in size from small to large, are laid out in a variety of different ways, some with cottage style planting, others have more formal gardens. There is spring blossom, early season flowers, water features, and wildlife friendly environments inc lakes and ponds. Throughout the gardens, there are thousands of daffodils and tulips, and some gardens offer expansive views of the Chilterns. Sun 7 Jun: Six gardens of varying sizes with borders filled with roses, shrubs, and herbaceous plants. There are many different environments inc damp gardens, vegetable plots, wildflower banks, and wildlife areas with lakes and ponds. One of the gardens was once a well loved garden, but had sadly been neglected. It is now in the process of being brought back to life by the new owners. Several gardens also have fabulous views of the Chilterns. Partial wheelchair access only at Barry's Close, Cop Close, Manor House in April, and Cop Close, Tompson's Farm, 19 Wainsrights in June.

24 MAGNOLIA HOUSE
Grange Drive, Wooburn Green, Wooburn, HP10 0QD. Elaine & Alan Ford, 07836 224855, lanforddesigns@gmail.com. *On A4094 2m SW of A40 between Bourne End & Wooburn. From Wooburn Church heading towards Maidenhead, Grange Dr is on L before r'about. From Bourne End, turn L at 2 mini r'abouts, then take 1st R.* **Visits by arrangement for groups of up to 20. Light refreshments. Contact to discuss smaller group or individual visits. Visits can be combined with The Shades, next door.**
½ acre garden with mature trees, inc a large magnolia. It features a fernery, stream, water wheel, natural pond, and a fish pond with large fish surrounded by acers. There are two greenhouses, two aviaries, and spring flowers, alliums, lilies, dahlias, and many hosta varieties. A small Japanese style area. A child friendly garden that is constantly being changed and updated. Partial wheelchair access.

25 NEW MIDDLE SHELSPIT FARM
Nash Road, Thornborough, Buckingham, MK18 2DY. Jim & Gwynne Grayson, 01296 715550, gwynnegrayson@aol.com. *5m from Buckingham, off the A421. From the centre of Thornborough village, take Nash Rd for approx 1m. Car park is signed on the RHS.* **Sat 13 June (1-5). Combined adm with Ashtree Cottage £7, chd free. Tea, coffee & cake.** Visits also by arrangement.
Our garden sits on 6 acres of old farmland offering great views. Over the last 8 yrs, many trees and shrubs have been planted. A natural stream flows into a pond with a deck to sit and rest on. A small copse of woodland is being developed, and large grass sculptures sway in the wind. The borders are full, while a pergola with a vine and wisteria provides shade on the patio, alongside a collection of acers.

26 NEW ♦ MILTON'S COTTAGE
21 Deanway, Chalfont St Giles, HP8 4JH. 01494 872313, info@miltonscottage.org, www.miltonscottage.org. *Milton's Cottage is in the centre of Chalfont St Giles, just past the village green & shops.* **For NGS: Thur 25 June (10-4). Combined adm with Chiltern Open Air Museum £7, chd free. Light refreshments at Chiltern Open Air Museum.** For other opening times and information, please phone, email or visit garden website.
Milton's Cottage is the only surviving residence of John Milton, and the place where he completed his epic masterpiece 'Paradise Lost'. It is home to a unique literary garden, planted with trees, flowers and fruits that are referenced in Milton's poetry. It is laid out as a traditional cottage garden, and is Grade II registered in its own right. Wheelchair access at the front of the garden, with a step-free path throughout, though some areas are narrow and steep.

In 2025 we awarded over £288,800 in Community Garden Grants, supporting 114 community garden projects.

27 MONTANA

Shire Lane, Cholesbury, HP23 6NA. Diana Garner, 01494 758347, montana@cholesbury.net. *3m NW of Chesham. From Chesham: Drive up The Vale to Cholesbury Common. Turn onto Cholesbury Rd by cricket club, then 1st L on Shire Ln. From Tring: Head towards Wigginton, pass Champneys, & turn down Cholesbury Rd.* **Visits by arrangement 2 Mar to 31 July for groups of up to 35. Adm £10, chd free. Home-made tea inc.**

A peaceful, large woodland garden planted by the owner with rare and unusual flowering trees, shrubs, perennials, and loads of bulbs. Shade loving herbaceous plants, a kitchen garden, and a meadow with an apiary. A gate leads to the old brickyard, now a 3 acre mixed deciduous wood with level paths, a large fernery planted in a clay pit, acers, and an avenue of thousands of daffodils. Plenty of seats to enjoy the quiet. An unmanicured garden high in the Chiltern Hills. The surrounding fields have been permanent pasture for more than 100 yrs. All visitors receive a map and plant list to use during their visit. A covered open barn for teas in both wet and dry weather. A gravel front drive leads to the garden with mainly grass or wood chipping. Most garden and woodland paths are flat and wheelchair friendly.

28 ♦ NETHER WINCHENDON HOUSE

Nether Winchendon, nr Aylesbury, HP18 0DY. Mr Robert Spencer Bernard, 01844 290101, Contactus@netherwinchendonhouse.com, www.nwhouse.co.uk. *6m SW of Aylesbury, 6m from Thame. Approx 4m from Thame on A418, turn 1st L towards Cuddington. At Xrds, turn L, then go downhill & turn R, followed by R again to parking area by the house.* **For NGS: Sun 30 Aug (2-5.30). Adm £4, chd free. Pre-booking essential, please visit www.ngs.org.uk for information & booking. Home-made teas.** For other opening times and information, please phone, email or visit garden website.

Nether Winchendon House has fine, and rare trees set in an inspiring and stunning landscape with parkland. The south lawn runs down to the River Thame. A Founder NGS Member (1927). Enchanting and romantic Mediaeval and Tudor House, one of the most romantic of the historic houses of England and listed Grade I. Dogs on leads welcome. A picturesque small village with an interesting church.

29 OLD KEEPERS

Village Lane, Hedgerley, SL2 3UY. Rob Cooper, Robcooper1612@gmail.com, www.instagram.com/oldkeepersgarden. *Parking in village hall on Kiln Ln, postcode SL2 3UU.* **Sun 7 June (12.30-4.30). Adm £5, chd free. Tea, coffee & cake.** Visits also by arrangement 12 June to 25 June for groups of 30+.

Described by visitors as 'a real gardener's garden'. A fairly new 1½ acre garden set around a Grade II listed former brickmaker's cottage (not open). The garden features borders packed with perennials, a small meadow, and a small orchard, creating a haven for wildlife. As we continue to develop the garden each year, there's always something new to discover! We designed the garden ourselves, carefully placing benches and perching spots to make the most of the beautiful views of the garden and village. It's the perfect setting to enjoy coffee and cake.

Chiltern Open Air Museum

BUCKINGHAMSHIRE 51

30 OLD PARK BARN
Dag Lane, Stoke Goldington, MK16 8NY. Emily & James Chua, 07833 118903, emilychua51@yahoo.com. *4m N of Newport Pagnell on B526. Park on High St. A short walk up Dag Ln. Accessible parking for 4 cars nr garden via Orchard Way. Please contact us for coach parking details.* **Sat 20, Sun 21 June (1.30-5). Adm £6, chd free. Tea, coffee & cake. Visits also by arrangement 8 June to 8 July for groups of 8 to 40.**
A garden of almost 3 acres, created from a rough field over 28 yrs ago. A series of terraces cut into the sloping site form the formal garden, with cross vistas, lawns, and deep borders. The aim is to provide interest throughout the year with naturalistic planting and views borrowed from the surrounding countryside. Beyond this, there is a wildlife pond, stream, grass meadow, and woodland gardens. Partial wheelchair access.

31 OVERSTROUD COTTAGE
The Dell, Frith Hill, Great Missenden, HP16 9QE. Mr & Mrs Jonathan Brooke, 01494 862701, susanmbrooke@outlook.com. *½m E Great Missenden. Turn E off A413 at Great Missenden onto B485 Frith Hill to Chesham Rd. White Gothic cottage set back in lay-by, 100yds uphill on L. Parking on R at church.* **Sun 5 Apr (2-5). Adm £4.50, chd free. Cream teas at parish church. Visits also by arrangement 14 Apr to 30 June for groups of 15 to 25.**
Artistic chalk garden on two levels. Collection of C17/C18 plants, inc auriculas, hellebores, bulbs, pulmonarias, peonies, geraniums, herbs, and succulents. Antique species and rambling roses. Potager and a lily pond. Blue and white ribbon border. The cottage was once a C17 fever house for Missenden Abbey. Features inc a garden studio with painting exhibition (share of flower painting proceeds to NGS).

32 THE PLOUGH
Chalkshire Road, Terrick, Aylesbury, HP17 0TJ. John & Sue Stewart. *2m W of Wendover. Entrance to garden & car park signed off B4009 Nash Lee Rd, 200yds E of Terrick r'about. Access to garden via the field car park.*
Mon 25 May (1-5). Adm £5, chd free. Home-made teas.
Formal garden with open views across the Chiltern countryside. Designed as a series of outdoor rooms around a listed former C18 inn (not open), inc borders, parterre, vegetable and fruit gardens, and an organic orchard with wild flowers. Delicious home-made teas in our barn, marquee, and adjacent entrance courtyard. Jams and apple juice made with fruits from the garden for sale. Cash only, please.

33 RACKLEYS
Marlow Road, Cadmore End, High Wycombe, HP14 3PP. Nick & Wendy Sargent, rackleys.co.uk. *5½m from Marlow & 9½m from Henley-upon-Thames. From Marlow: Head SE on A4155 Marlow Rd. Take 1st exit onto Dean St/Marlow Rd B482. After 5½ m, turn L. From M40 J5: Exit to Stokenchurch on A40. After ½ m, turn R onto Marlow Rd B482. After 4m, turn R.* **Sun 26 July (2-5.30). Adm £6, chd free. Tea, coffee & cake. Wine, beer & soft drinks.**
Rackleys was originally a farm built in the 1700s and has been lovingly restored into a wedding and events venue. It is set within 7 acres of stunning grounds, with sweeping views over the Chilterns. The gardens boast a wide range of flowering trees and shrubs, as well as roses, herbaceous perennials, and bulbs that provide continuous colour throughout the year. Wheelchair access to the meadow is via a grass pathway.

34 RED KITES
46 Haw Lane, Bledlow Ridge, HP14 4JJ. Mag & Les Terry, 01494 481474, lesterry747@gmail.com. *4m S of Princes Risborough. Off A4010, halfway between Princes Risborough & West Wycombe. At Hearing Dogs sign in Saunderton, turn into Haw Ln, then go ¾ m up the hill, the garden is on the L.* **Tue 12 May, Tue 14 July (2-5). Adm £6, chd free. Home-made teas £4 each (pay at gate). Visits also by arrangement 4 May to 1 Sept for groups of 20+.**
This Chiltern hillside garden of 1½ acres is planted for year-round interest and has superb views. Lovingly and beautifully maintained, it offers several different areas to relax in, each with its own character. A wildflower orchard, mixed borders, a pond, vegetables, a woodland area, and a lovely hidden garden. Many climbers in the garden change significantly through the seasons.

35 ROBIN HILL
Water End, Stokenchurch, High Wycombe, HP14 3XQ. Caroline Renshaw & Stuart Yates, 07957 394134, info@cazrenshawdesigns.co.uk, www.cazrenshawdesigns.co.uk/home/ngs. *2m from M40 J5 Stokenchurch. Turn off A40 just S of Stokenchurch towards Radnage, then take 1st R to Waterend & then follow signs.* **Sun 7 June (11-4). Adm £6, chd free. Home-made teas. Visits also by arrangement 25 May to 2 Aug for groups of 15 to 30.**
This is a garden designer's own garden at the start of the Chilterns. It features informal planting with a variety of trees, woodland-edge plants, shade borders, shrubs, perennials, and grass borders that blend into pastureland, now restored to a beautiful long-grass meadow. There is a mature cherry orchard, chickens, and a vegetable garden. The planting is constantly evolving to better suit our changing climate and enhance biodiversity. Wheelchair access in dry conditions across a mainly flat, lawned garden with no paths.

36 ST MICHAELS CONVENT
Vicarage Way, Gerrards Cross, SL9 8AT. Sisters of the Church, stmichaelsconvent.sistersofthechurch.org. *15 min walk from Gerrards Cross Stn. 10 mins from East Common buses. Parking in nearby street, limited parking at St Michael's.* **Sat 6 June (2-4). Adm by donation. Home-made teas.**
St Michael's Convent is home to the Sisters of the Church and the Society of the Precious Blood. The garden is a space for quiet reflection, to gaze upon beauty, and inc a walled garden with vegetables, a labyrinth and pond, a shady woodland dell, and a chapel. Enjoy colourful borders and beds, and mature, majestic trees. Come and see, spend time simply being!

37 THE SHADES
High Wycombe, HP10 0QD.
Pauline & Maurice Kirkpatrick, 01628 522540,
Pk@mkpdesign.com. *On A4094 2m SW of A40 between Bourne End & Wooburn. From Wooburn Church heading towards Maidenhead, Grange Dr is on L before r'about. From Bourne End, turn L at 2 mini r'abouts, then take 1st R.* **Visits by arrangement for groups of up to 20. Combined visit with Magnolia House.**
The Shades drive is approached through mature trees, with areas of shade loving plants, beds of shrubs, and herbaceous plants. The rear garden with a natural well, surrounded by plants, shrubs, roses, and acers. A green slate water feature and a scree garden with alpine plants complete the garden. Light refreshments at Magnolia House. Partial wheelchair access.

38 ♦ STOKE POGES MEMORIAL GARDENS
Church Lane, Stoke Poges, Slough, SL2 4NZ.
Buckinghamshire Council, 01753 523744, memorial.gardens@buckinghamshire.gov.uk, www.buckinghamshire.gov.uk. *1m N of Slough, 4m S of Gerrards Cross. Follow signs to Stoke Poges & from there to the Memorial Gardens. Car park opp main entrance. Disabled visitor parking in the gardens. Weekend disabled access through churchyard.* **For NGS: Sun 10 May (1-4). Adm £6, chd free. Home-made teas. For other opening times and information, please phone, email or visit garden website.**
A unique 22 acre Grade I registered garden, constructed 1934-9, with a contemporary garden extension. Rock and water gardens, a sunken Italianate colonnade, rose garden, parterres, 500 individual gated gardens, beautiful mature trees, and newly landscaped areas. Guided tours every hour. Guide dogs only.

39 TOUCHWOOD
Grimms Hill, Great Missenden, HP16 9BG. Katharine Hersee, 07801 948650,
kjhersee@gmail.com. *If coming up Grimms Hill from Great Missenden, house is after 1st LH-bend on L. If coming downhill from Prestwood, house is ¾ of the way down* Grimms Hill on RH-side. Parking for 10 cars on drive. **Visits by arrangement 18 Feb to 20 Feb for groups of 10 to 25. Adm £12, chd free. Group bookings only. Adm inc tea, coffee & cake. Advance notice required for special dietary requirements.**
A 2 acre garden containing drifts of common snowdrops, along with a few unusual ones. Strong structure provided by terracing, walls, and topiarised yew hedging. Your visit will begin with a short, illustrated talk about snowdrop varieties, before you explore the snowdrops lining a shrubbery path, woodland path, and rockery. Naturalised snowdrops also line the lawn on either side of the driveway. The visit will end with tea and cakes. Other early spring bulbs and shrubs may also be in flower, although this is seasonally dependent.

40 TURN END
Townside, Haddenham, Aylesbury, HP17 8BG. Margaret & Peter Aldington, 07887 952020, turnendestate@gmail.com, www.turnend.org.uk. *3m NE of Thame, 5m SW of Aylesbury. Exit A418 to Haddenham. Turn at Rising Sun to Townside. Street parking very limited. Please park with consideration, check website for parking. What3words app: match.sandals.transmits.* **Wed 11 Mar, Wed 6 May, Wed 3 June (1.30-3.30). Adm £6.50, chd free. Home-made teas (cash only). Visits also by arrangement 11 Mar to 3 June for groups of 10 to 20.**
Grade II registered. A series of garden rooms, each with a different planting style, envelops the architect's own Grade II* listed house (not open). A dry garden, formal box garden, sunken gardens, and mixed borders around a curving lawn, all framed by ancient walls and mature trees. Plantings inc bulbs, irises, wisteria, roses, ferns, and climbers. Courtyards with pools, pergolas, secluded seating, and a Victorian coach house.

41 TYRINGHAM HALL
Upper Church Street, Cuddington, Aylesbury, HP18 0AP. Mrs Sherry Scott MBE. *Turn R at Cuddington Xrd (Upper Church St), 100 metres to Tyringham Hall on RH-bend.* **Sun 2 Aug (2-5). Adm £5, chd free. Home-made teas.**
Medieval house that will be partly open. Large gardens with extensive lawns, a water garden with underground springs, a vegetable garden, tennis court, and swimming pool. Colourful varieties of flowers are planted throughout the garden, with mature trees offering shade where needed. There are many seating areas around the garden. Parking at garden for wheelchair visitors only.

42 TYTHROP PARK
Kingsey, HP17 8LT. Nick & Chrissie Wheeler. *2m E of Thame, 4m NW of Princes Risborough. Via A4129: At T-junction in Kingsey, turn towards Haddenham. Take L turn at the bend. Parking in field on L.* **Sun 7 June (2-5.30). Adm £8, chd free. Tea, coffee & cake.**
10 acres of garden surrounds a C17 Grade I listed manor house (not open). This large and varied garden blends traditional and contemporary styles, featuring pool borders rich in grasses with a green and white theme, walled kitchen and cutting garden with large greenhouse at its heart, box parterre, deep mixed borders, water feature, rose garden, wildflower meadow and many old trees and shrubs.

SPECIAL EVENT

43 THE WALLED GARDEN, WORMSLEY
Wormsley, Stokenchurch, High Wycombe, HP14 3YE. Wormsley Estate. *Leave M40 at J5. Turn towards Ibstone. Entrance to estate is ¼m on R. NB: 20mph speed limit on estate. Please do not drive on grass verges.* **Wed 8 July (10-3). Adm £8, chd free. Pre-booking essential, please visit www.ngs.org.uk for information & booking. Home-made teas.**
The Walled Garden at Wormsley Estate is a 2 acre garden providing flowers, vegetables and tranquil contemplative space for the family. For many years the garden was neglected until Sir Paul Getty purchased the estate in the mid 1980s. In 1991 the garden was redesigned and has changed over the years, but remains true to the original brief. Wheelchair access to grounds, but no disabled WC facilities. Disabled parking on site.

44 WARDROBES HOUSE
Woodway, Princes Risborough, HP27 0NL. Tara Leaver. *Located off the A4010, just S of Princes Risborough, on the LHS of road leading to Lacey Green, before Wardrobes Ln. No access from Wardrobes Ln. Parking in gently sloping field next to house.* **Sat 11 July (1-5). Adm £7, chd £3.50. Pre-booking essential, please visit www.ngs.org.uk for information & booking. Tea, coffee & cake.**
Located on the edge of the Chiltern Hills with far-reaching views, these 3 acre gardens surround an C18 Georgian Manor House built for the First Earl of Burlington (not open). In recent years, the gardens have been remodelled to inc formal and vegetable gardens, a classic water garden, a large greenhouse, and more informal areas. There is a variety of mature trees, inc a holm oak and yew.

45 THE WHITE HOUSE
Village Road, Denham Village, UB9 5BE. Mr & Mrs P G Courtenay-Luck. *3m NW of Uxbridge, 7m E of Beaconsfield. Signed from A40 or A412. Parking in Village Rd. The White House is in centre of village, opp St Mary's Church. Nearest train stn: Denham (Chiltern Line).* **Sun 17 May (2-5). Adm £7, chd free. Cream teas.**
A well established 6 acre formal garden in a picturesque setting. Mature trees and hedges, with the River Misbourne meandering through the lawns. Shrubberies, flower beds, a rockery, a rose garden, and an orchard. A large walled garden, along with a herb garden, vegetable plot, and Victorian greenhouses. A newly planted herbaceous border to the front garden wall. Wheelchair access with gravel entrance and paved path into gardens.

46 NEW WILLEN HOSPICE
Newport Road, Willen, Milton Keynes, MK15 9AA. Rachael Withe. *To access the hospice, drive down Milton Rd, past the church & take the next turning on the R. To access The Well, drive down Newport Rd & take the 2nd turning on the R.* **Sat 11 July (10-4). Adm £5, chd free. Light refreshments.**
The gardens at Willen Hospice span around two acres across two sites and inc lawns, wooded areas, planted beds, a working allotment, orchard and an RHS award-winning pocket garden. Set on the banks of Willen Lake, the gardens provide private and peaceful spaces for patients and their families, and are managed with an increasingly naturalistic approach to boost biodiversity. Wheelchair access at the hospice but no accessible paths in the gardens at The Well.

47 WIND IN THE WILLOWS
Moorhouse Farm Lane, Off Lower Road, Higher Denham, UB9 5EN. Ron James, 07740 177038, r.james@company-doc.co.uk. *6m E of Beaconsfield. Turn off A412 approx ½ m N of junction with A40, into Old Rectory Ln. After 1m enter Higher Denham straight ahead. Take lane next to the community centre & Wind in the Willows is the 1st house on L.* **Sun 24 May (2-4.30). Adm £6, chd free. Tea, coffee & cake. Visits also by arrangement for groups of 10+. Donation to Higher Denham Community CIO (Garden Upkeep Fund).**
A 3 acre, wildlife friendly, year-round garden comprising informal woodland and wild gardens, separated by streams. Many shrubs and trees, several variegated or uncommon, along with marginal and bog plants, and a bed of stripy roses. 'Stunning' was the word most often used by visitors. Persistent rain in 2023/24 killed some shrubs, but a large new, drier bed now houses replacements. Although unlikely to be seen on a busy day, 65 species of bird and 13 species of butterfly have been seen in and over the garden, which is also home to the now endangered water vole (Water Rat in the book Wind in the Willows), as well as frogs and toads. Wheelchair access over gravel paths and spongy lawns.

48 WOODLANDS HOUSE
Winchbottom Lane, Marlow, SL7 3RN. Jan Mash, 07928 432337, woodlandshouse-marlow@outlook.com. *Little Marlow. Winchbottom Ln is off the A4155 towards Bourne End. Single track lane, parking in field.* **Visits by arrangement July & Aug for groups of 10 to 30. Adm £12, chd free. Home-made teas inc.**
A country garden with a series of rooms, each with its own planting style: a formal box parterre with gazebo, knot garden, pool garden with grasses and perennials, Victorian style glasshouse with scented pelargoniums, a garden with raised beds of dahlias and herbs, two stumperies with hellebores and ferns, woodland and meadow walks with wonderful views, and a labyrinth. Planting is ongoing.

Chesham Bois House

© Marianne Majerus

CAMBRIDGESHIRE

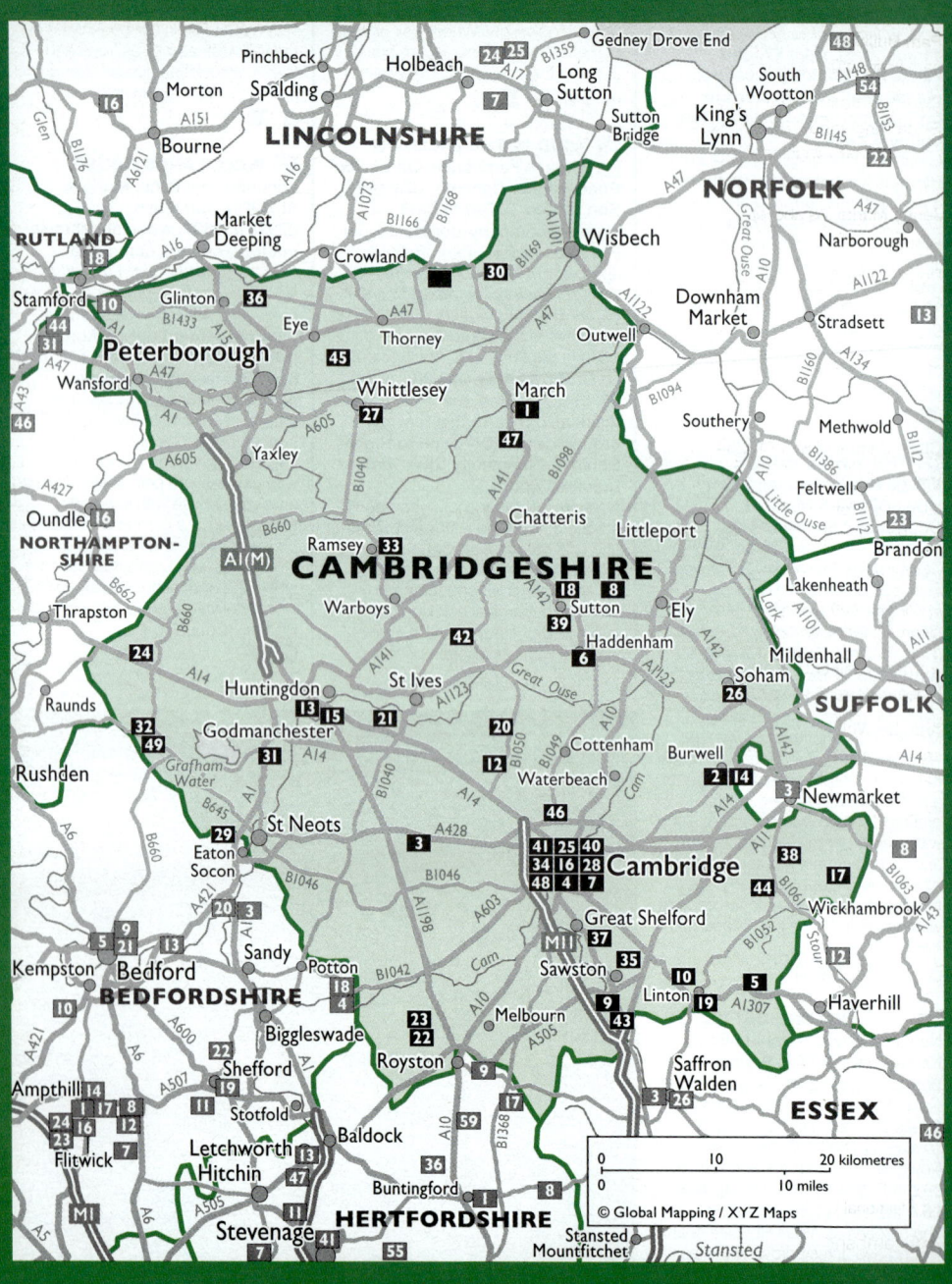

CAMBRIDGESHIRE 55

VOLUNTEERS

County Organiser
Jenny Marks 07956 049257
jenny.marks@ngs.org.uk

Deputy County Organiser
Pam Bullivant 01353 667355
pam.bullivant@ngs.org.uk

County Treasurer
Fiona Ringwood 07968 815459
fiona.ringwood@ngs.org.uk

Booklet Coordinator
Jenny Marks (As above)

Publicity
Penny Miles 07771 516458
penny.miles@ngs.org.uk

Social Media
Hetty Dean
hetty.dean@ngs.org.uk

Assistant County Organisers
Claire James 07815 719284
claire.james@ngs.org.uk

Jacqui Latten-Quinn 07941 279571
jacqui_quinn@yahoo.com

Penny Miles (As above)

Jane Pearson 07890 080303
jane.pearson@ngs.org.uk

Barbara Stalker 07800 575100
barbara.stalker@ngs.org.uk

Annette White 01638 730876
annette.white@ngs.org.uk

National Garden Scheme Cambs
cambsngs

OPENING DATES

All entries subject to change.
For latest information check
www.ngs.org.uk
Extended openings are shown
at the beginning of the month.
Map locator numbers are
shown to the right of each
garden name.

January

Every day from Monday 5th
Robinson College 34

February

Snowdrop Openings

Every day
Robinson College 34

Sunday 15th
Clover Cottage 5

Sunday 22nd
Clover Cottage 5

March

Every day
Robinson College 34

Sunday 1st
Clover Cottage 5

Saturday 14th
NEW Wellcome Genome
Campus 43

Sunday 29th
Kirtling Tower 17

April

Every day until Monday 20th
Robinson College 34

Sunday 5th
Netherhall Manor 26

Sunday 12th
Trinity Hall - Wychfield Site 41

Sunday 19th
Trinity College Fellows' Garden 40

Saturday 25th
Murray Edwards College 25

Sunday 26th
Murray Edwards College 25
41A New Road 27
Wolfson College Garden 48

May

Every Saturday and Sunday
23A Perry Road 31

Sunday 3rd
Chaucer Road Gardens 4
Netherhall Manor 26

Monday 4th
Chaucer Road Gardens 4

Sunday 10th
Stetchworth and Dullingham
Gardens 38

Sunday 17th
College Farm 6
NEW Hinchingbrooke House 13
Sutton Gardens 39

Saturday 23rd
Coveney & Wardy Hill Gardens 8

Sunday 24th
Cambourne Gardens 3
Coveney & Wardy Hill Gardens 8
Molesworth House 24
41A New Road 27
Willow Holt 45

Monday 25th
41A New Road 27
Willow Holt 45

Sunday 31st
Cottage Garden 7
Island Hall 15
Linton Gardens 19
Preachers Passing 32

June

Every Saturday and Sunday
23A Perry Road 31

Sunday 7th
Burwell Village Gardens 2
Clover Cottage 5
Duxford Gardens 9
NEW Hinchingbrooke House 13
Isaacson's 14
NEW Mill House, Brook Road 22
Mill House, Fen Road 23
The Old Rectory 30

Sunday 14th
Clover Cottage 5
Kirtling Tower 17
41A New Road 27
Sawston Gardens 35

Green End Farm

Sunday 21st
Old Farm Cottage 29
Westley Waterless Gardens 44

Saturday 27th
Leisure Land 18
NEW Sissons Barn 36
Twin Tarns 42
NEW Wits End 47
Wrights Farm 49

Sunday 28th
NEW Hinchingbrooke House 13
King's College Fellows' Garden and
Provost's Garden 16
Leisure Land 18
Stapleford Village Gardens 37
Twin Tarns 42
Wrights Farm 49

July

Every Saturday and Sunday
23A Perry Road 31

Every day from Tuesday 7th
Robinson College 34

Saturday 4th
Little Oak 20
38 Norfolk Terrace 28

Sunday 5th
Green End Farm 12
Little Oak 20
38 Norfolk Terrace 28

August

Every Saturday and Sunday
23A Perry Road 31

Every day until Thursday 13th
Robinson College 34

Sunday 2nd
Netherhall Manor 26
41A New Road 27
Preachers Passing 32

Sunday 9th
Netherhall Manor 26

Sunday 30th
41A New Road 27

Monday 31st
41A New Road 27

September

Every Saturday and Sunday
23A Perry Road 31

Every day from Wednesday 2nd
Robinson College 34

Saturday 12th
Ramsey Walled Garden 33

Sunday 13th
◆ The Manor, Hemingford Grey 21

October

Every day
Robinson College 34

Every Saturday and Sunday
Robinson College 34

November

Every day
Robinson College 34

December

Every day until Tuesday 22nd
Robinson College 34

By Arrangement

Arrange a personalised garden visit with your club, or group of friends, on a date to suit you. See individual garden entries for full details.

Beaver Lodge 1
Bustlers Cottage (Duxford Gardens) 9
Clover Cottage 5
Drovers (Coveney & Wardy Hill Gardens) 8
Farm Lodge 10
NEW Hinchingbrooke House 13
Isaacson's 14
Molesworth House 24
Netherhall Manor 26
41A New Road 27
Newnham Farmhouse (Burwell Village Gardens) 2
The Old Baptist Chapel (Sutton Gardens) 39
The Old Rectory 30
3 Roman Close (Burwell Village Gardens) 2
Twin Tarns 42
Westley Waterless Gardens 44
The Windmill 46
Wrights Farm 49

THE GARDENS

◨ BEAVER LODGE
Henson Road, March,
PE15 8BA. Mr & Mrs
Nielson-Bom, 01354 656185,
beaverbom@gmail.com. *A141 to Wisbech Rd into March. L into Westwood Ave, at end, R into Henson Rd. Garden on R opp sch playground.* **Visits by arrangement May to Sept for groups of up to 20. Adm £7.50, chd free. Light refreshments.**
An impeccable Oriental garden with more than 120 large and small bonsai trees. Discover our acers, pagodas, Oriental statues, water features and pond with koi carp; all working in harmony to create a peaceful and relaxing atmosphere. Described by visitors as an oasis of peace and tranquillity. The garden is divided into three different sections: The Mediterranian garden, pond area and a collection of acers. Seating area near waterfall finishes the scene.

GROUP OPENING

◨ BURWELL VILLAGE GARDENS
Burwell, CB25 0HB. *10m NE of Cambridge. 4m NW of Newmarket via the B1102/ B1103. 8 gardens in the village - a hearty walk around them all or bring a bike/car.* **Sun 7 June (12-5). Combined adm with Isaacson's £10, chd free. Home-made teas at Isaacson's. Home-made cakes inc gluten & nut free options.**

9 THE BRIARS
Marianne Hall & Tony Hollyer.

NEW THE CARPENTER'S LODGE
Ken & Maureen McCarthy.

3 FIELD VIEW
Richard & Nicola Farrow.

NEWNHAM FARMHOUSE
Mr & Mrs Quentin Cooke, 07802 857150,
q.cooke@ntlworld.com.
Visits also by arrangement Apr to Sept for groups of 10+. Discuss refreshments when booking.

NEW 5 ORCHARD WAY
John & Maggie Newman.

3 ROMAN CLOSE
Mrs Dove, 07437 581674,
lizdove11@icloud.com.

Visits also by arrangement 18 May to 1 Sept for groups of up to 6.

SPRING VIEW
Colin & Caroline Smith.
NPC

New this year, Carpenter's Lodge is an interesting variety of planting 'rooms', cottage, scented and gravel. 5 Orchard Way, zones of very diverse styles from Italy to Japan. 3 Roman Close, a small, pretty cottage garden, with roses, perennials and annuals. Spring View has the National Collection of Yucca, for the specialist plantsman huge diversity of form and sizes, drought tolerant planting plus other species. 9 The Briars is environmentally friendly with a pond, flowers and vegetables, featuring a living wall. Newnham Farmhouse has a walled garden surrounding a C16 thatched cottage, with over 80 Japanese acers. Packed borders and a wildflower lawn. Ponds front and back. See also Isaacsons' separate listing; a plantsman's garden of striking diversity in a series of different zones and incorporating medieval plants, in the grounds of a clunch stone house dating from 1340. 3 Field View is a new build garden with modern planting and design, borrowed vistas, wildflowers and young trees.

12 Chaucer Road, Chaucer Road Gardens

Reeves House, Stetchworth and Dullingham Gardens

GROUP OPENING

◳ CAMBOURNE GARDENS
Great Cambourne, CB23 6AH.
8m W of Cambridge on A428. From A428, take Cambourne junc into Great Cambourne. From B1198, enter village at Lower Cambourne & drive through to Great Cambourne. Follow yellow signs via either route to start at any garden. **Sun 24 May (11-5). Combined adm £7.50, chd free. Home-made teas at 13 Fenbridge.**

13 FENBRIDGE
Lucinda & Tony Williams.

88 GREENHAZE LANE
Darren & Irette Murray.

5 MAYFIELD WAY
Debbie & Mike Perry.

20 MILLER WAY
Mr Ed Savory.

43 MONKFIELD LANE
Penny Miles.

A unique and inspiring modern group, all created from new build in just a few years. This selection of five demonstrates how imagination and gardening skill can be combined in a short time to create great effects from unpromising and awkward beginnings. The grouping inc a foliage garden with collections of maple and hosta; a suntrap garden for play, socialising and colour; gardens with ponds, a vegetable plot and many other beautiful borders showing their owners' creativity and love of growing fine plants well. Cambourne is one of Cambridgeshire's newest communities, and this grouping showcases the happy, vibrant place our town has become. Excellent examples of beauty and creativity in a newly built environment.

GROUP OPENING

◳ CHAUCER ROAD GARDENS
Cambridge, CB2 7EB. *1m S of Cambridge. Off Trumpington Rd (A1309), nr Brooklands Ave junc. Parking available at MRC Psychology Dept on Chaucer Rd.* **Sun 3, Mon 4 May (2-5). Combined adm £10, chd free. Home-made teas at Upwater Lodge.**

8 CHAUCER ROAD
Tim Spiers & Camilla Worth.

12 CHAUCER ROAD
Mr & Mrs Bradley.

NEW 14 CHAUCER ROAD
Professor Maud Ellmann.

UPWATER LODGE
Mr & Mrs Pearson.

Chaucer Road Gardens are fine examples of large Edwardian gardens tucked away on the south side of Cambridge. They are all very different in size and character, some with glimpses of a bygone age. There are magnificent old trees, fine lawns, ponds and a water meadow with river frontage and rare breed sheep. Planting is varied, sometimes unusual, and in constant flux. Home-made cakes, some with garden fruit. Soay sheep. Wheelchair access consists of some gravel areas and grassy paths with fairly gentle slopes. Water meadow may be boggy.

◳ CLOVER COTTAGE
50 Streetly End, West Wickham, CB21 4RP. Paul & Shirley Shadford, 07538 569191, shirleyshadford@live.co.uk. *3m from Linton, 3m from Haverhill & 2m from Balsham. From Horseheath turn L, from Balsham turn R, thatched cottage opp triangle of grass next to old windmill.* **Sun 15, Sun 22 Feb, Sun 1 Mar (2-4). Light refreshments. Sun 7, Sun 14 June (12-4.30). Tea, coffee & cake. Adm £4, chd free. Visits also by arrangement 15 Feb to 30 June.**
In winter find a flowering cherry tree, borders of snowdrops, aconites, *Iris reticulata*, hellebores and miniature *Narcissus* throughout the packed small garden which has inspiring ideas on use of space. Pond and arbour, raised beds of fruit and vegetables. In summer arches of roses and clematis, hardy geraniums, delightful borders of English roses and herbaceous plants. Charming patio. Snowdrops, hellebores and spring flowering bulbs for sale for the winter opening. Plants also for sale in June.

◳ COLLEGE FARM
Station Road, Haddenham, Ely, CB6 3XD. Sheila & Jeremy Waller, www.primaveragallery.co.uk. *4m W of Ely. From Stretham & Wilburton, at Xrds in Haddenham, turn R. Pass the church & exactly at the bottom of the hill, turn L down narrow drive (named Madingley Way), with a mill wheel on R of the drive.* **Sun 17 May (2-5). Adm £8, chd free.**
Explore 40 acres around an intact Victorian farm. Wandering walks take you to galleries, flower beds and sculpture cattle yard. Roses, wildflowers, water plants, foxgloves and plantings of trees, hedges and fruit trees, amongst ponds and through meadows, add colour and structure. Splendid fen views, lovely water features and ancient ridge and furrow pasture land. Original farm buildings, outside and inside galleries, Interesting (not seeded) wildflowers like Jack go to bed at noon and Salsify.

◳ COTTAGE GARDEN
79 Sedgwick Street, Cambridge, CB1 3AL. Rosie Wilson. *Off Mill Rd, in Romsey, S of the railway bridge.* **Sun 31 May (2-5.30). Adm £4, chd free. Tea, coffee & cake.**
Small, long, narrow and planted in the cottage garden style with over 38 roses, some on arches and growing through trees. Particularly planned to encourage wildlife with small pond, mature trees and shrubs. Perennials and some unusual plants interspersed with sculptures.

70 inpatients and their families are being supported at the newly opened Horatio's Garden Northern Ireland, thanks to the National Garden Scheme donations.

GROUP OPENING

8 COVENEY & WARDY HILL GARDENS
Coveney, Ely, CB6 2DN. *From A142 or A10 Ely bypass, follow signs for Coveney, then for Wardy Hill. From A142 sp Witcham.* **Sat 23, Sun 24 May (1-5). Combined adm £6, chd free. Home-made teas.**

DROVERS
Mr David C Guyer, 07859 917947, guyer100@yahoo.co.uk.
Visits also by arrangement 30 Apr to 18 Sept for groups of 10 to 30.

1A THE GREEN
Mrs Kate Bullen.

NEW 3A MAIN STREET
Georgina & Graham Landick.

2 SCHOOL LANE
Mrs Jane McCartney.

SECRET GARDEN
Keith & Annette Tither.

Five medium sized gardens, in the fenland parish of Coveney overlooking Ely Cathedral. Whilst in Coveney, do visit the C13 church and award winning wildlife churchyard. The gardens, this year, are in both Coveney and Wardy Hill, with a welcoming free cuppa and cakes to buy. In Coveney there is 'The Secret Garden', with a Japanese style, giving a peaceful wander in an Oriental atmosphere; a real must. 2 School Lane, is a real plantsman's English garden, packed with interest and presented by a truly knowledgeable horticulturalist, whilst 3a Main Street is a colourful and interesting garden with tricky areas and thoughtful solutions. On the Wardy Hill Green, 1a, is a new build house and garden with a more modern feel of arbours, interesting herbaceous borders and water feature, and around the corner, Drovers is based on a Chinese pleasure garden philosophy but with English naturalist planting that wanders by a wildlife pond, beneath mature trees to a rose garden and potted terrace.

GROUP OPENING

9 DUXFORD GARDENS
Duxford, CB22 4RP. *All gardens are close to the centre of the village of Duxford. S of the A505 between M11 J10 & Sawston. Street parking. What3words app: families.cyber.gurgled.* **Sun 7 June (2-6). Combined adm £8, chd free. Home-made teas at Bustlers Cottage (cream teas) & in St Peter's Church.**

BUSTLERS COTTAGE
John & Jenny Marks, 07956 049257, jenny.marks@ngs.org.uk.
Visits also by arrangement 25 May to 13 July for groups of 10 to 30.

DUXFORD MILL
Mrs Frankie Bridgwood.

16 ICKLETON ROAD
Claire James.

THE RECTORY

3 ST JOHN'S STREET
Dr Celia Duff.

3 ST PETERS STREET
Meredith & Caroline Lloyd Evans.

31 ST PETER'S STREET
Mr David Baker.

Seven gardens of different sizes and character. The exuberant planting at 3 St Peter's St more than makes up for the small size of the garden. 31 St Peter's St, on a steep slope, is filled with surprises, and a dry rockery. Bustlers Cottage has a cottage garden inc vegetables, many trees and places to sit. Stop here for a home-made cream tea and buy some plants. The gardener at 16 Ickleton Rd is a plantaholic, unable to refuse room to an unusual plant, and has a fascinating garden as a result. At 3 St John's St, the large pond dominates a colourful garden planted with wildlife in mind, and further up the road the garden at the Rectory has a grass maze mown into the lawn. Duxford Mill is open this year, with its magnificent trees, mill race, and river, and the various different gardens within the garden - not to be missed. Wheelchair access, some gravel paths and a few steps, mostly avoidable.

10 FARM LODGE
High Street, Hildersham, Cambridge, CB21 6BU. Mrs Athene Hunt, 01223 891412, huntcam2015@gmail.com. *7m S of Cambridge. Exit 9 or 10 off M11. Off A1307, next to the Village Hall, between the river & The Pear & Olive, opp Hall Farm What3words app: replenish.cultivation.harp.* **Visits by arrangement 29 June to 30 Sept for groups of up to 25. Weekdays preferred. Adm £8, chd free. Tea, coffee & cake.**
This informal, secluded garden is just under an acre. The borders wrap around the house giving scope for planting schemes in the different aspects. There is a woodland walk, a shady dell, semi wild areas and a rustic swing hanging high from the bough of a tree. There is a kitchen garden, orchard, compost bays, and an extensive patio with a wealth of home propagated Mediterranean and unusual plants. Please contact in advance if there are mobility concerns.

12 GREEN END FARM
Over Road, Longstanton, Cambridge, CB24 3DW. Sylvia Newman, www.sngardendesign.co.uk. *8m from Cambridge. From A14 head towards Longstanton. At r'about take 2nd exit, at next r'about turn L. Garden 200 metres on L.* **Sun 5 July (11-4). Adm £6, chd free. Home-made teas. Cakes supplied by The Linton Kitchen.**
Tucked away from view, Green End Farm gardens are continually transforming. The clever design encourages both exploration and relaxation, and the garden combines traditional charm with contemporary touches. Sweeping borders are filled with a mixture of perennials and hedges and trees are used to create difference zones, chosen for colour, texture, and wildlife appeal.

The National Garden Scheme funded six Macmillan Nurses in their roles across England, Wales and Northern Ireland in 2025.

Mill House, Brook Road

13 NEW HINCHINGBROOKE HOUSE

Off Hinchingbrooke Park Road, Huntingdon, PE29 3BN. Hinchingbrooke School, 07951 189909, hbkevents@outlook.com. *In the the grounds of Hinchingbrooke House, part of Hinchingbrooke Sch. Approx 5m from A1/A14 on edge of Huntingdon town, follow directions to Hinchingbrooke hospital & turn L off Hbk Park Rd into main sch car park.* **Sun 17 May, Sun 7, Sun 28 June (11-4). Adm £5, chd free. Tea, coffee & cake.** Visits also by arrangement 17 May to 28 Aug for groups of 10 to 50. Dates limited to school holidays & weekends only. Wander the grounds of Hinchingbrooke House and discover mixed perennial borders around the historical house, inc a rose garden with parterre hedging and lily pond. Explore the large herbaceous border garden and keep a look out for specimen trees dating back to the 1700s. There is also a wooded area and views over listed boundary wall. Home-made cakes, scones and sausage rolls are available in our cafe. Wheelchair access difficult at entrance.

& ❄ 🚗 ☕ 🪑 »)

14 ISAACSON'S

6 High Street, Burwell, CB25 0HB. Drs Richard & Caroline Dyer, 01638 601742, richard@familydyer.com. *10m NE of Cambridge, 4m NW of Newmarket. Behind a tall yew hedge with topiary & grass triangle, at the S end of the village where Isaacson Rd turns off the High St. Approx 400 yds S of the church.* **Sun 7 June (12-5). Combined adm with Burwell Village Gardens £10, chd free. Home-made teas, cakes & scones available.** Visits also by arrangement 25 Apr to 28 June for groups of 12 to 30.

A plantsman's garden warmed and sheltered by the Medieval walls of a C14 house (the oldest in Burwell), richly diverse in format and planting. There are 'theatres' (auricula, pinks), hints of Snowdonia, the Mediterranean, a French potager and traditional English. Throughout there are many unusual and rare plants plus many roses, peonies and fruit trees. Around each corner a new vista surprises. Some assistance with wheelchair over bark or gravel will be required.

& 🐕 ❄ 🚗 ☕ »)

15 ISLAND HALL

Godmanchester, PE29 2BA. Grace Vane Percy, 01480 459676, enquire@islandhall.com, www.islandhall.com. *1m S of Huntingdon (A1). 15m NW of Cambridge (A14). In centre of*

41A New Road

Godmanchester next to free Mill Yard car park. **Sun 31 May (10.30-4.30). Adm £6.50, chd free. Home-made teas.**
Three acre grounds, tranquil riverside setting with mature trees. Chinese bridge over Saxon Mill Race to embowered island with wildflowers. Garden restoration begun in 1983 to mid C18 formal design, with box hedging, clipped hornbeams, parterres, topiary, beautiful vistas over the borrowed landscape of Portholme. The ornamental island has been replanted with Princeton elm avenue (*Ulmus americana*).

16 KING'S COLLEGE FELLOWS' GARDEN AND PROVOST'S GARDEN
Queen's Road, Cambridge, CB2 1ST. Provost & Scholars of King's College. *Entry by gate at King's Parade or by junc of Queen's Rd & West Rd. Parking at Lion Yard, short walk, or some pay & display places in West Rd & Queen's Rd. Ticket sales close 3.30pm.* **Sun 28 June (10-4.30). Adm £10, chd £5. Tea, coffee & cake.**
Fellows' Garden is a fine example of a Victorian garden with rare specimen trees. Rond Pont entrance leads to a small woodland walk, herbaceous and sub-tropical borders, rose pergola, kitchen garden and orchard. The Provost's Garden opens with kind permission, offering a rare glimpse of an Arts and Crafts design. Chance to view the new wildflower meadow created on the former Great Lawn. Tickets available to purchase on the day at the college shop in King's Parade. Wheelchair access to garden over gravel paths.

17 KIRTLING TOWER
Newmarket Road, Kirtling, CB8 9PA. The Lord & Lady Fairhaven. *6m SE of Newmarket. From Newmarket head towards village of Saxon St, through village to Kirtling. Turn L at the war memorial; the road is signed to Upend & the entrance is signed on the L.* **Sun 29 Mar, Sun 14 June (11-4). Adm £6, chd free. Light refreshments. Donation to Mid Anglia General Practitioner Accident Service (MAGPAS).**
Large formal gardens surrounding Kirtling Tower (not open). Large moat, ornamental Walled Garden, Cloisters Rose Garden, Cutting and Vegetable Garden. Secret Gardens, young

arboretum and pinetum. Set in 25 acres of park land with extensive views of surrounding countryside. Large swathes of *Narcissus*, *Tulipa sylvestris* and Fritillaria in spring. Craft and Plant stalls. Many of the paths and routes around the garden are grass - they are accessible by wheelchairs, but can be hard work if wet.

18 LEISURE LAND
Mepal, Ely, CB6 2AX. David & Mary Gowing. *From Ely take the A142, sp March. Stay on the A142 & cross the Mepal bridge. Turn immed R onto Engine Bank. Drive past the large brick building & turn immed L onto a single track for 800m.* **Sat 27, Sun 28 June (11-4). Adm £5, chd free.**
Nestled in the fenland landscape, Leisure Land has been developed by its owners over the last five years, creating a quiet oasis within the fenland. Eleven acres of lake, ponds and woodland to explore. Take a wander and find surprises: a fairy walk, sculptures, an area for quiet reflection and much more. Bring a friend, children, family. Take a picnic, have fun and relax in this natural environment. A delightful way to spend a summer's afternoon.

GROUP OPENING

19 LINTON GARDENS
Linton, CB21 4HS. *Turn N from the A1307 between Cambridge & Haverhill at lights into High St. On-street parking in the village (please be considerate of our neighbours), & in public car park on Coles Ln.* **Sun 31 May (2-6). Combined adm £8, chd free. Home-made teas in the Maltings Courtyard at 94 High Street, & also at St Mary's Parish Church.**

NEW BACK ROAD
David & Anne Parry-Smith.

15 BALSHAM ROAD
Lucy & Tom Wylie.

CHALKLANDS COMMUNITY GARDEN

94 HIGH STREET
Rosemary Wellings.

THE HOLLIES, 36 SYMONDS LANE
Hilary & Edwin Green.

QUEENS HOUSE
Michael & Alison Wilcockson.

30 SYMONDS LANE

NEW 36 WHEATSHEAF WAY
Emma Andrews.

Eight gardens in Linton village. Near the top of the High St, close to the junction with the A1307, is Queens House, with garden 'rooms' separated by hedging and graced by statuary. At the far end of the High St, the garden behind the Gallery Above at 94 High St is small and perfectly formed, accessed via a courtyard where teas are served, and all manner of interesting things go on. 30 Symonds Lane is a long Edwardian plot planted as a cottage garden and because of the walnut tree in the middle, the garden is at its best in late spring. The Hollies (36 Symonds Lane) is an established garden containing a surprising number of acid-loving plants and a wildflower area with mature trees as backdrop. The community garden at Chalklands is a riot of colour and joy, and a modern family garden at 15 Balsham Road shows how beauty in a garden can also accommodate a family's needs. In a 1970s estate, the established garden at 36 Wheatsheaf Way combines the beauty of roses and other flowering perennials with space for a family, and 25A Back Rd is a mature traditional English village garden with plenty of wildlife and trees. Accessible WC at church.

20 LITTLE OAK
66 Station Road, Willingham, Cambridge, CB24 5HG. Mr & Mrs Eileen Hughes, www.littleoak.org.uk/garden. *4m N of A14 J25 nr Cambridge. Easy to find on the main road in the village. Driveway parking for disabled use only What3words app: dial. spaceship.rules.* **Sat 4, Sun 5 July (12-5). Adm £5.50, chd free. Tea, coffee & cake.**
An acre garden displaying many different areas and planting schemes with a range of annual, herbaceous and perennial beds, productive kitchen garden, fruit trees and ponds. An ideal place to spend time and relax with a cup of tea and home-made cake. There is also a model railway. Main garden is wheelchair accessible.

21 ♦ THE MANOR, HEMINGFORD GREY

High Street, Hemingford Grey, PE28 9BN. Mrs D S Boston, 07984 897589, diana_boston@hotmail.com, www.greenknowe.co.uk. *4m E of Huntingdon. Off A1307. Parking for NGS opening day only, in field off double bends between Hemingford Grey & Hemingford Abbots. This will be signed. Entrance to garden via small gate off river towpath.* **For NGS: Sun 13 Sept (2-5). Adm £6, chd free. Tea, coffee & cake.** For other opening times and information, please phone, email or visit garden website.

Garden designed by author Lucy Boston, surrounds C12 manor house on which Green Knowe books based (house by appt). Three acre cottage garden with topiary, old roses, extensive collection of irises inc Dykes Medal winners and Cedric Morris var., herbaceous borders with scented plants. Meadow with mown paths. Enclosed by river, moat and wilderness. Variety of annuals for late flowering. Gravel paths throughout. Wheelchair users are encouraged to use the lawns.

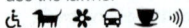

22 NEW MILL HOUSE, BROOK ROAD

Brook Road, Bassingbourn, Royston, SG8 5NS. Michael & Frances Smith. *4m N of Royston. Drive through Bassingbourn on High St, towards Litlington with sch on L. After 100yards, car park & house are 1st on R.* **Sun 7 June (11-5). Combined adm with Mill House, Fen Road £8, chd free. Home-made teas.**

Four acre traditional English garden with different areas of interest. Discover herbaceous beds, lily and rose beds and pond with a stream linked to a rock garden with water features. There are alpines, acers and dwarf conifers to see from raised seating areas which also look over open countryside. Many specimen and fruit trees as well as a lime avenue and productive vegetable garden. Mostly grass or paved areas for wheelchair access. Some gravel paths.

23 MILL HOUSE, FEN ROAD

Bassingbourn, Royston, SG8 5PQ. *2m N of Royston. On the NW outskirts of Bassingbourn. 1m from Church, on the road to Shingay. Take North End at the war memorial in the centre of Bassingbourn which is just W of the A1198 (do not take Mill Ln).* **Sun 7 June (11-5). Combined adm with Mill House, Brook Road £8, chd free.**

The garden has evolved over many years by retired garden designer owner. Divided up into interesting enclosures providing unusual formal and informal settings for many rare trees, shrubs, herbaceous plants, clematis and topiary which provides year-round interest. Wonderful elevated view over countryside and garden.

24 MOLESWORTH HOUSE

Molesworth, PE28 0QD. John & Gilly Prentis, 07771 918250, gillyprentis@gmail.com. *10m W of Huntingdon off the A14. Next to the church in Molesworth.* **Sun 24 May (2-6). Adm £5, chd free. Home-made teas. Visits also by arrangement 1 Apr to 1 July.**

Molesworth House is an old three acre rectory garden with everything that you would both expect and hope for, given its Victorian past. Every corner offers a surprise to its traditional setting, a very happy and relaxed garden - come and see for yourself. A humble gem and amazing tropical greenhouse built by the garden owner awaits your discovery. Accessible to wheelchair users, although there is some gravel.

25 MURRAY EDWARDS COLLEGE

Huntingdon Road, Cambridge, CB3 0DF. www.murrayedwards.cam.ac.uk/about-us/our-gardens. *Entry to gardens via Porters' Lodge, Buckingham Rd, off Huntingdon Rd. Parking is not available.* **Sat 25 Apr (10-4). Sun 26 Apr (10-4), open nearby Wolfson College Garden. Adm £5, chd free. Tea, coffee & cake in the Art Café. Please note: cashless payments only. Donation to Perennial.**

Informal gardens with mature trees around which the modern college was built. Gardens inc sculptures from the Women's Art Collection and herbaceous borders more recently planted for sustainability and biodiversity. Within the gardens sits the 150 year old glasshouse originally belonging to Emma Darwin, of the Darwin family. Women's Art Collection, Grade II listed College building designed by Chamberlin, Powell and Bon. Wheelchair access to the garden via paved pathways, bark and grass. Please contact in advance if a visitor has mobility concerns.

26 NETHERHALL MANOR

Tanners Lane, Soham, CB7 5AB. Timothy Clark, 01353 720269, timothy.r.clark@btinternet.com, www.netherhallmanor.com. *6m Ely, 6m Newmarket. From Newmarket: Tanners Ln 2nd R 100yds after cemetery. From Ely: Tanners Ln 2nd L after War Memorial.* **Sun 5 Apr, Sun 3 May, Sun 2, Sun 9 Aug (2-5). Adm £5, chd free. Home-made teas. Visits also by arrangement.**

An elegant English garden, touched with antiquity, and for those fond of old fashioned plants, a veritable joy. In spring, see our Tudor primroses, daffodils and hellebores as well as crown imperials and English florist tulips. Throughout summer there is a showing of Victorian pelargoniums, calceolaria and heliotropes. Margery Fish's Country Gardening and Mary McMurtrie's Country Garden Flowers, Historic Plants 1500-1900. Author's books for sale.

27 41A NEW ROAD

Whittlesey, Peterborough, PE7 1SU. Miss Emma Bates, 07766 474631, weaveremmab@gmail.com. *Follow SatNav directions for PE7 1SU. From Whittlsey, take A605 E towards Eastrea. At r'about, take 3rd exit onto B1093 then 2nd L to Inhams Rd. New Rd is 1st turning on L.* **Sun 26 Apr, Sun 24, Mon 25 May, Sun 14 June, Sun 2, Sun 30, Mon 31 Aug (12-4). Adm £3, chd free. Tea, coffee & cake. Visits also by arrangement 26 Apr to 27 Sept for groups of up to 12.**

A peaceful suburban nature garden situated on the edge of the village with fields and woodland close by. Created over several years, with wildlife the priority, the majority of the garden was overgrown with brambles. The garden is split into sections to create interest, each with a different theme. Designated a Wildlife Friendly garden by the BCN Wildlife Trust in 2025.

28 38 NORFOLK TERRACE
Cambridge, CB1 2NG. John Tordoff & Maurice Reeve. *Central Cambridge. A603 East Rd turn R into St Matthews St to Norfolk St. L into Blossom St & Norfolk Terrace is at the end.* **Sat 4, Sun 5 July (11-5). Adm £3, chd free. Light refreshments.**
This lavish Moroccan style, small paved courtyard garden, in the middle of the city, has masses of colour in raised beds and pots, backed by oriental arches. The ornamental pool defined by its patterned tiles offers the soothing splash of water. There will be a display of recent paintings by John Tordoff and handmade books by Maurice Reeve.

29 OLD FARM COTTAGE
Staploe, St Neots, PE19 5JA. Sir Graham & Lady Fry. *Approx 1m W of St Neots. Going S on Great North Rd in St Neots, turn R into Duloe Rd. Under A1 through Duloe village. Follow the road to Staploe. Last house on the L.* **Sun 21 June (1-5). Adm £5, chd free. Tea, coffee & cake.**
Terraced and formal flower beds surrounding a thatched house and leading to three acres of orchard, grassland, woodland and wetland maintained for wildlife. Present owners have planted some non-native trees, inc ornamental cherries, loquat, Metasequoia, Ginkgo, Pawlonia and monkey puzzle, extended the area of native woodland and created a wildflower meadow. Wheelchair access: Gravel, uneven ground and one steep slope.

30 THE OLD RECTORY
312 Main Road, Parson Drove, Wisbech, PE13 4LF. Helen Roberts, 07818 070641, yogahelen@talk21.com. *SW of Wisbech. From Peterborough on A47 follow signs to Parson Drove, L after Thorney Toll. From Wisbech follow the B1166 through Leverington Common.* **Sun 7 June (11-4). Adm £5, chd free. Tea, coffee & cake. Visits also by arrangement 25 May to 1 Aug for groups of 10+.**
This garden represents the personality of this Georgian house (not open), classical, formal and welcoming. A naturalistic partly walled back garden planted in the cottage style with a host of roses. There are meadows with wildflowers the grass mostly long with walking paths cut through, a gin palace, ponds and raised beds for cut flowers.

31 23A PERRY ROAD
Buckden, St Neots, PE19 5XG. David & Valerie Bunnage. *5m S of Huntingdon on A1. From A1 Buckden r'about take B661, Perry Rd approx 300yds on L.* **Every Sat and Sun 2 May to 27 Sept (2-4). Adm £5, chd free. Pre-booking essential, please visit www.ngs. org.uk for information & booking.**
Approx an acre of many garden designs inc Japanese, interlinked by gravel paths. A plantsmans garden featuring 155 acers and unusual shrubs. Quirky with interesting features and some narrow paths. Regret, not suitable for wheelchairs. WC available.

32 PREACHERS PASSING
55 Station Road, Tilbrook, Huntingdon, PE28 0JT. Keith & Rosamund Nancekievill. *Tilbrook 4½m S of J16 on A14. Station Rd in Tilbrook can be accessed from the B645 or B660. Preachers Passing faces the small bridge over the River Til at a sharp bend in Station Rd with All Saints church behind it.* **Sun 31 May, Sun 2 Aug (10.30-4.30). Adm £5, chd free. Tea, coffee & cake. Home-made ice cream and soft drinks also available.**
A ¾ acre garden fits into its pastoral setting. Near the house, parterre, courtyard and terrace offer formality; but beyond, prairie planting leads to a wildlife pond, rock gardens, meadow, stumpery, rose garden and copse. Enjoy different views from arbour, honeysuckle-covered swing or scattered benches. Deciduous trees and perennials give changing colour. There are open spaces and hidden places.

33 RAMSEY WALLED GARDEN
Wood Lane, Ramsey, Huntingdon, PE26 2XD. Ramsey Abbey Walled Garden CIO, www.ramseywalledgarden.org. *Just N of Ramsey Town Centre. Follow B1096 out of Ramsey. Just after last house on R, turn R opp cemetery. Take track to Ramsey Rural Museum. Park under trees. See map on Ramsey Walled Garden website.* **Sat 12 Sept (2-5). Adm £5, chd free. Home-made teas at Ramsey Rural Museum.**
A Victorian Walled Garden, located within the grounds of Ramsey Abbey, has been restored by volunteers and is an enchanting secret in the heart of Ramsey. Dating back to 1840, this one acre garden is dedicated to growing fruit, vegetables and flowers. Features inc a magnificent 33m glasshouse, an apple tunnel planted with Cambridgeshire varieties, a dahlia border and a collection of hardy, half hardy and rare salvias. The garden is wheelchair accessible but is 450m from the car parking area along a grass path. Motorised buggies can access the garden.

34 ROBINSON COLLEGE
Grange Road, Cambridge, CB3 9AN. Warden & Fellows, www.robinson.cam.ac.uk/about-robinson/gardens/national-gardens-scheme. *Garden at main Robinson College site, report to Porters' Lodge. On-street parking. What3words app: pinks.latest.spin.* **Daily weekdays (10-4), weekends (2-4) from Mon 5 Jan. Closed Tues 21 April - Mon 6 July, Fri 14 Aug - Tue 1 Sept, Wed 23 Dec - Thu 31 Dec. Adm £5, chd free. Pre-booking essential, please visit www.ngs.org.uk for information & booking.**
10 original Edwardian gardens linked to central wild woodland water garden focused on Bin Brook, with small lake at heart of site, giving a feeling of park and informal woodland, while keeping the sense of older more formal gardens beyond. Mature stately trees frame central wide lawn running down to the lake. Much original planting is still intact. More recent planting inc bulbs, wildflowers and trees. No picnics. Children must be accompanied at all times. Tickets must be booked on line in advance. Please collect guidebook from Porters' Lodge. In 2026 continuing building work and garden maintenance may affect part of the gardens, and occasionally parts or all of the gardens may be closed for safety reasons. Regret no dogs. Ask at Porters' Lodge for wheelchair access.

CAMBRIDGESHIRE 67

GROUP OPENING

35 SAWSTON GARDENS
Sawston, CB22 3HY. *5m SE of Cambridge. Midway between Saffron Walden & Cambridge on A1301.* **Sun 14 June (1-5). Combined adm £7, chd free. Home-made teas in Mary Challis Garden, 68 High Street. Refreshments served from 1.30-4.00pm.**

BROOK HOUSE
Ian & Mia Devereux.

34 CAMBRIDGE ROAD
Mrs Mary Hollyhead.

20 LONDON ROAD
Linda & David Ambrose.

♦ MARY CHALLIS GARDEN
A M Challis Trust Ltd, 01223 560816, chair@challistrust.org.uk, www.challistrust.org.uk.

11 MILL LANE
Tim & Rosie Phillips.

NEW PAMPISFORD PLACE
Dixon International Group.

124 WOODLAND ROAD
Mrs Helen Velioglu.

10 WYNEMARES
Mr Lee Kirby.

Eight very different inspirational gardens, new large garden Pampisford Place in adjacent Pampisford features a run of colourful planters, a newly renovated walled garden with fountain and espalier fruit trees, vegetable garden and chickens. The gardens in the village of Sawston range from small to large. Two small modern gardens are 124 Woodland Road which is an attractive well laid out and maintained garden with stunning views to the Gog Magog Hills, and 10 Wynemares presenting a colourful and creative variety of planting. Two recently redesigned long gardens are at 34 Cambridge Road which has immaculate attractive borders, vegetables and fruit, and 20 London Road which has winding gravel paths with interestingly planted borders down to a wildlife area. 11 Mill Lane is classic yet quirky and has an impressive front garden and secluded sunny rear garden. Our largest gardens are the two acre mature Mary Challis Garden with very many lovely different features, left in Trust to the village in 2006, and Brook House a 1½ acre garden in the grounds of a Grade II listed house, containing a walled kitchen garden, professionally designed borders, greenhouse, orchard and specimen trees. Nearly all parts of the gardens are accessible by wheelchair, with the exception of 20 London Road and 124 Woodland Road.

36 NEW SISSONS BARN
Thorney Road, Peakirk, Peterborough, PE6 7NT.
Ben & Laura Harris, www.sissonsbarn.co.uk. *Located just outside the village of Peakirk on the B1443. Access via Moor Rd. What3words app: gravitate.dreamer. spray.* **Sat 27 June (11-4). Adm £5, chd free. Light refreshments.**
A thoughtfully designed garden complements the elegant barn, with colourful borders, shaped lawns, and wildflower areas. Woven steel fencing separates formal and informal spaces. A whimsical willow room offers a relaxed retreat. The farmhouse garden features a hedge-lined lawn, summerhouse, mixed borders, wisteria-clad front, koi pond, rill, and sunlit terrace. Bar and light lunch available to pre-order and order on the day. Everything is on one level. There are gravel areas to cross and three steps in the Farmhouse garden.

GROUP OPENING

37 STAPLEFORD VILLAGE GARDENS
Stapleford, Cambridge, CB22 5BH. *4m S of Cambridge on A1301. What3words app: havens.disarmed. handwriting.* **Sun 28 June (1-5). Combined adm £6, chd free. Adm tickets for sale at garden gate. Regret, cash only.**

3A DUKES MEADOW
Jan & Lee Gruncell.

NEW 17 HAWTHORNE ROAD
Mr Graham Hambling.

5 PRIAMS WAY
Tony Smith.

NEW THE STONE HOUSE
Patricia Mirrlees.

So much interest in these contrasting gardens. At 5 Priams Way there is lots of colour, unusual plants, a pond and playful design. 3A Dukes Meadow is a garden with surprises at each turn, lots of sun, interesting ways of using stumps and some plants in unusual places. Colourful and engaging everywhere you look. 17 Hawthorne Rd is a garden on various levels with greenhouses containing a large collection of cacti and succulents. Lots of colour and established trees. The Stone House has a completely wild garden with very old trees, wildlife feeding stations, a pond and a mixed woodland area of young and old trees. Partial access, but there are some gravel paths, a few steps and grassy access in some gardens.

GROUP OPENING

38 STETCHWORTH AND DULLINGHAM GARDENS
Stetchworth and Dullingham, CB8 9TN. *3m S of Newmarket & 12m E of Cambridge. Stetchworth gardens & teas are all in the centre of the village. Aynsley House & The Station garden are in Dullingham.* **Sun 10 May (1.30-6). Combined adm £7, chd free. Home-made teas at St Peter's church, Stetchworth.**

NEW AYNSLEY HOUSE
Mr Rob & Dr Tamara Dimond.

THE DOVE HOUSE
Mr & Mrs T Gross.

DULLINGHAM RAILWAY STATION
Network Rail, Managed by Greater Anglia.

NEW 41 MILL LANE
Mr & Mrs Simon Crisp.

NEW REEVES HOUSE
Andrew & Dee Williamson.

NEW 53 STROLLERS WAY
Mr & Mrs Jill Pepper.

A varied group of design-led gardens. The Dove House garden wraps around a large natural carp pond with water lilies and a board walk; wisteria drapes over a pergola, and naturalised bulbs flourish under mature trees and shrubs. Reeves House features carefully planned colour combinations with modern sculptures, a vegetable garden and container planting. Aynsley House is a four acre walled garden with an avenue of cherry trees, kitchen garden, orchard, duck pond and an air-raid shelter. 53 Strollers Way is packed with mostly shade loving plants. 41 Mill Lane is a small walled garden that has gone on a journey from concrete horror to horticulture wonder, it shows what can be achieved in a small space. At Dullingham Station visitors will be transported to a charming garden in the most unlikely of places, created and cared for by a team of devoted Station Adopter volunteers, to raise the spirits of passengers on the platforms and those looking out from passing trains. Four gardens are wheelchair accessible. The Dove House has ramps and steps.

GROUP OPENING

39 SUTTON GARDENS
Sutton, Ely, CB6 2QQ. *6m W of Ely. From Ely take A142 to March, turn L at r'about to B1381 towards Earith. Parking at Brooklands Centre off The Brook & along The Row.* **Sun 17 May (1-5). Combined adm £6, chd free. Tea, coffee & cake in the Pavilion. WC available at the Pavilion.**

THE BIRCHES
Sue & Colin Frost.

61 HIGH STREET
Kate Travers & Jon Megginson, 01353 778427, katetravers@outlook.com.

THE OLD BAPTIST CHAPEL
Janet Porter & Steve Newton, 07860 332414, janet.porter@cantab.net. Visits also by arrangement 19 May to 19 July for groups of 8 to 20.

87 THE ROW
Mrs Alison Beale.

89 THE ROW
Andrew Thompson.

The Old Baptist Chapel is a garden created around a C18 building converted to a family home. It inc the adjacent burial ground. The emphasis is on year-round interest and minimal maintenance. 61 High Street is a tiny shaded garden with a host of features: interesting trees, herb and vegetable plots, water features, a greenhouse, boxes for birds, bats and bugs, and a large collection of acers. 87 The Row is a spacious family garden with pergola, herbaceous beds, shrub border, mature native trees, vegetable beds and fruit trees. 89 The Row is an informal garden on a slight slope with a variety of planted areas inc mature trees, shrubs, fernery, herbaceous, a small vegetable plot and a greenhouse. Scented plants are important throughout the garden.

4a The Row (The Birches), the garden surrounds the house and has mixed planting for year-round interest. The garden incorporates a very steep bank at the rear which demonstrates gardening on a difficult site.

40 TRINITY COLLEGE FELLOWS' GARDEN
Queen's Road, Cambridge, CB3 9AQ. Master & Fellows of Trinity College, www.trin.cam.ac.uk/about/gardens. *Short walk from city centre. At the Northampton St/ Madingley Rd end of Queen's Rd, close to Garret Hostel Ln. What3words app: foods.tables.tags.* **Sun 19 Apr (1-4). Adm £5, chd free. Tea, coffee & cake.**
Historic gardens of about eight acres with specimen trees, mixed borders, drifts of spring bulbs and informal lawns with notable influences throughout from Fellows over the years. Across chalk stream Bin Brook to Burrell's Field, some modern planting styles nestled amongst accommodation blocks in smaller intimate gardens, plus a new woodland walk and mixed fruit orchard. Members of the Gardens Team will be on hand to serve home-made cakes and drinks plus sell plants. Wheelchair access via some gravel and bark chip paths.

41 TRINITY HALL - WYCHFIELD SITE
Storey's Way, Cambridge, CB3 0DZ. The Master & Fellows, www.trinhall.cam.ac.uk/about/gardens. *1m NW of city centre. Turn into Storey's Way from Madingley Rd (A1303) & follow the yellow signs. Limited on-road parking is available.* **Sun 12 Apr (11-2). Adm £6, chd free. Home-made teas in the sports pavilion. Hot drinks, home-made cakes & savouries.**
A beautiful, large garden that complements the interesting and varied architecture. The Edwardian Wychfield House and its gardens contrast with the recent, contemporary development located off Storey's Way. Majestic trees, tulips and spring flowers on the cherry mound, shady, under-storey, woodland planting and established lawns work together to provide an inspiring garden. Tours at 12 and 1pm. Wheelchair access via gravel paths. Some steps in garden.

42 TWIN TARNS
6 Pinfold Lane, Somersham, PE28 3EQ. Michael & Frances Robinson, 07938 174536, mikerobinson987@btinternet.com. *4m NE of St Ives. Easy access from the A14. Turn onto Church St. Pinfold Ln is next to the church. Please park on Church St as access is narrow & limited.* **Sat 27, Sun 28 June (1-5). Adm £6, chd free. Cream teas.** Visits also by arrangement 1 June to 15 Sept for groups of up to 25.
One acre wildlife garden with formal borders, kitchen garden and ponds. There is a large rockery to discover and mini woodland to explore. Wander through the wildflower meadow, rose walk, character bridge and greenhouses. We also have a veranda and treehouse. The garden is adjacent to C13 village church.

43 NEW WELLCOME GENOME CAMPUS
Hinxton, Saffron Walden, CB10 1RQ. *From S: M11 J9, take A1301 towards Cambridge. 1st L at r'about, then at next r'about follow signs for Genome Campus. From N: M11 J10, E towards Saffron Walden for 1m on A505. At r'about take the 3rd exit (A1301). Cont for approx 1m.* **Sat 14 Mar (10-2). Adm £6, chd free. Pre-booking essential, please visit www.ngs.org.uk for information & booking. Light refreshments. Refreshments sales are cashless only, with the money going back into the campus.**
The Campus contains many historic features inc an C18 Hall, a former fishing lodge, pleasure garden and croquet lawn. Many references to fish reflect its former name, Trout Hall. Our orchard is a Priority One habitat, important to biodiversity. Flanking the conference centre are a meadow and fine oak specimens, and in the main lake south of the orchard are carp, reflecting the history of the Hall. When purchasing your ticket, you will be booking a place on one of four guided walks starting at 10am, 11am, 12pm and 1pm. A member of our gardening team will walk with you providing garden insights and history. Regrettably it will not be possible to wander freely in the grounds. Most of the garden is on flat ground, with minimal steps and kerbs. Grass paths in places.

CAMBRIDGESHIRE

GROUP OPENING

44 WESTLEY WATERLESS GARDENS
Westley Waterless, CB8 0RL. 07908 622292, lucycrosby.vet@gmail.com. *10m E of Cambridge, 5m S of Newmarket. All gardens are near the entrance to Church Ln. Parking along the Main St & part way up Church Ln.* **Sun 21 June (12-5). Combined adm £8, chd free. Home-made teas at Church View.** Visits also by arrangement June to Sept for groups of 5+.

CHURCH LANE HOUSE
Mrs Lucy Crosby, www.thegardencompanion.co.uk.
CHURCH VIEW
Diana Hall.
41 MAIN STREET
Maurice Biggins.

Church Lane House is just under an acre in size, comprising a wildlife pond, herbaceous borders, cut flowers, dye plants, orchard wildflower meadow, Victorian style greenhouse and kitchen garden, plus chickens, quail and bees. This is a family friendly garden with plenty of seating areas to take in the views. Church View is a country garden which inc a small flower farm. There are many old fashioned scented roses, both shrub and climbing, plus herbaceous borders, raised growing beds and two polytunnels. The garden features a wildlife pond and flowering plant-filled pots. The farm growing area changes season by season. No. 41 is a contemporary garden inspired by Piet Oudolf and Beth Chatto. Designed for wildlife, with year-round interest, inc Prairie style borders, pond, topiary and kitchen gardens. Wheelchair access is mostly on grass and some paving areas.

45 WILLOW HOLT
Willow Hall Lane, Thorney, Peterborough, PE6 0QN. Angie & Jonathan Jones, www.instagram.com/angiecjones45. *4m E of Peterborough. Turn S from A47 between Thorney and Eye. Sign post Willow Hall. Go 1.8m, we are on the R.* **Sun 24, Mon 25 May (11-5). Adm £5, chd free. Tea, coffee & cake.**
Two acres, part farm field and part old gravel diggings were combined as a building plot in 1960. In 1992 the current owners began a 30 year transformation from nettle bed and local tip to a peaceful garden of mature trees, wildflower meadow, wildlife ponds, bridges, scrap metal sculptures and a varied and impressive collection of plants and shrubs. Largely accessible for wheelchair users.

46 THE WINDMILL
10 Cambridge Road, Impington, CB24 9NU. Pippa & Steve Temple, 07775 446443, mill.impington@ntlworld.com, www.impingtonmill.org. *2½m N of Cambridge. Off A14 at J32, B1049 to Histon, L into Cambridge Rd at T-lights, follow Cambridge Rd round to R, the Windmill is approx 400yds on L.* **Visits by arrangement. Adm £10, chd free. Light refreshments inc coffee, tea, wine & nibbles. Discuss refreshments when booking.**
Over a period of 25 years, an acre and a half of wilderness has been transformed into a haven of peace and tranquillity. Gorgeous views stretching across the garden from all angles highlight differing seasonal beds with specific palettes of colour. The design follows the dictates of the Mill at the centre of the garden with an orchard (for cogs), workshops and mill specific work spaces. The Windmill (an C18 smock on C19 tower on C17 base on C16 foundations) is being restored.

47 WITS END
Knights End Road, March, PE15 0YJ. Mrs Julie Little. *Just off the A141, on L. 2nd property on L, after the Crematorium. Follow the yellow NGS signs. What3words app: scorch.panels.hubcaps.* **Sat 27 June (10.30-4). Adm £5, chd free. Tea, coffee & cake. Weather permitting: Burgers & hotdogs will be available between 12.30- 2 pm.**
A developing garden designed to welcome pollinators and birds, now thriving in its third year. Enjoy a variety of vibrant perennials, a pond with a gentle waterfall, and striking blooms like hydrangeas, rhododendrons, peonies, and bearded irises. Discover an Arctic Cabin nestled by the water and raised beds in a vegetable patch which add a productive touch to this evolving garden. There is also an ornate patio with planters. Parking close to garden entrance. Main paths are gravel. Assistance for wheelchairs available on the day.

48 WOLFSON COLLEGE GARDEN
Barton Road, Cambridge, CB3 9BB. Wolfson College. *SW Cambridge. From M11 J12, take A603 into Cambridge. Wolfson College is approx 2m from J12, on L.* **Sun 26 Apr (10-4). Adm £5, chd free. Tea, coffee & cake in the Buttery room. Open nearby Murray Edwards College.**
A 10 acre site comprised of 'rooms'. We have year-round interest and always something to see inc a small amount of themed gardens from exotic to Chinese and winter gardens, bringing plants from all over the world to create an enticing visual. We have a team of four gardeners who are able to teach visitors about what we do and hopefully inspire them. Lots of topiary to find within borders. Courtyards with fine lawns and mature trees. Sir Vivian Fuchs garden, once home to the Antarctic explorer. Herbaceous pot planting and seasonal beds. Formal mixed with the informal around beautiful buildings. Ramps and lowered curbs are on site. Disabled facilities in the porters lodge. All paths are wide enough for disabled access.

49 WRIGHTS FARM
Tilbrook Road, Kimbolton, Huntingdon, PE28 0JW. Russell & Hetty Dean, 07801 383454, hetty.dean@ngs.org.uk. *13m SW of Huntingdon. ¼m W of Kimbolton on the B645. Do not follow SatNav, not accessed from lay-by.* **Sat 27, Sun 28 June (1-5). Adm £6, chd free. Home-made teas.** Visits also by arrangement in June for groups of 10+.
A substantial garden in a rural setting taking advantage of countryside views. Varied borders with bee and butterfly friendly planting. Formal walled vegetable garden with raised beds, potting shed and greenhouses. Mediterranean style courtyard with dry garden. Newly designed and planted front garden with tropical greenhouse. Courtyard garden to annexe with raised borders and green roof seating area. Wildlife pond. Predominantly flat, but with some gravel surfaces and grass paths.

CHESHIRE & WIRRAL

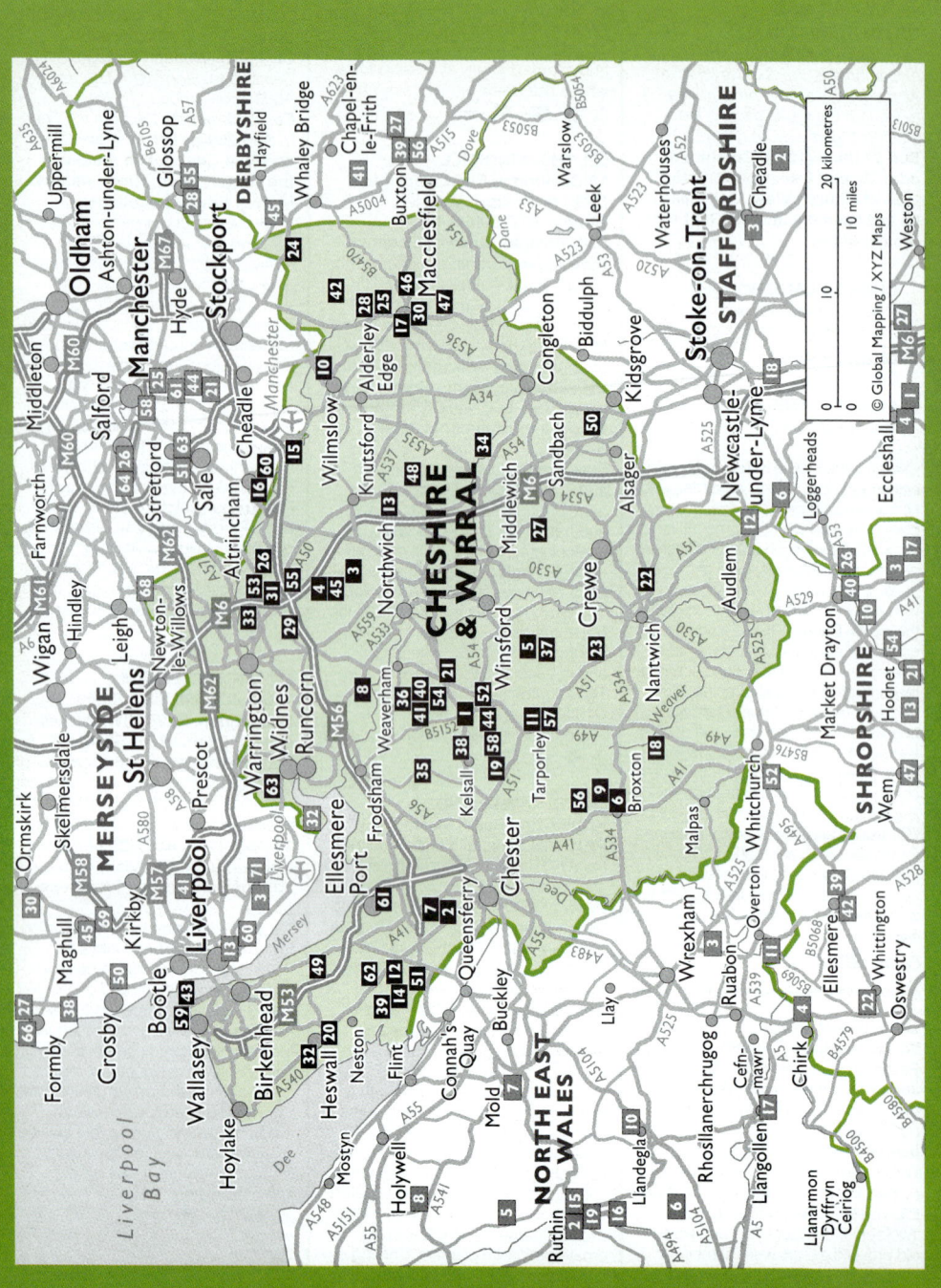

CHESHIRE & WIRRAL

VOLUNTEERS

County Organiser
Janet Bashforth
07809 030525
jan.bashforth@ngs.org.uk

County Treasurer
John Hinde
0151 353 0032
johnhinde059@gmail.com

Booklet Co-ordinator
Sharon Maher
07709 037766
sharon.maher@ngs.org.uk

Booklet Advertising
Richard Goodyear
richard.goodyear@ngs.org.uk

Social Media & Publicity
Jacquie Denyer
jacquie.denyer@ngs.org.uk

Photographer
Liz Mitchell 01260 291409
liz.mitchell@ngs.org.uk

Talks Co-ordinator
Sharon Maher (see above)

Assistant County Organisers
Sue Bryant 01619 283819
suewestlakebryant@btinternet.com

Jean Davies 01606 892383
mrsjeandavies@gmail.com

Linda Enderby 07949 496747
lmaenderby@outlook.com

Sandra Fairclough 0151 342 4645
sandrafairclough51@gmail.com

Richard Goodyear (see above)

Juliet Hill 01829 732804
t.hill573@btinternet.com

Romy Holmes 01829 732053
romy@holmes-email.co.uk

Mike Porter 07951 606906
porters@mikeandgailporter.co.uk

@National Garden Scheme
Cheshire & Wirral

OPENING DATES

All entries subject to change. For latest information check www.ngs.org.uk

Map locator numbers are shown to the right of each garden name.

February

Snowdrop Openings

Every Sunday to Sunday 15th
Briarfield   12

Sunday 22nd
Bucklow Farm   13
NEW Normans Hall   42

April

Saturday 4th
◆ Poulton Hall   49

Sunday 5th
All Fours Farm   3
◆ Poulton Hall   49

Monday 6th
All Fours Farm   3

Sunday 12th
Briarfield   12

Monday 13th
◆ Arley Hall & Gardens   4

Sunday 19th
Norley Court   41

Saturday 25th
10 Statham Avenue   53

Sunday 26th
Hill Farm   27
10 Statham Avenue   53

May

Saturday 2nd
All Fours Farm   3

Sunday 3rd
All Fours Farm   3
Laskey Farm   33
◆ Stonyford Cottage   54
Tiresford   57

Monday 4th
All Fours Farm   3
Laskey Farm   33

Thursday 7th
◆ Cholmondeley Castle Gardens   18

Friday 8th
Bolesworth Castle   9

Saturday 9th
Bolesworth Castle   9
64 Carr Wood   15
Hathaway   25

Sunday 10th
Hathaway   25

Sunday 17th
Bankhead   6
Hill Farm   27
Manley Knoll   35
Norley Court   41

Saturday 23rd
◆ Mount Pleasant   38

Sunday 24th
The Old Parsonage   45

Monday 25th
The Old Parsonage   45

Saturday 30th
10 Statham Avenue   53

Sunday 31st
10 Statham Avenue   53
Tirley Garth Gardens   58

June

Friday 5th
HMP Thorn Cross   29

Saturday 6th
NEW 7 Chesham Place   16
Laskey Farm   33
One House Walled Garden   46
◆ Peover Hall Gardens   48

Sunday 7th
NEW 7 Chesham Place   16
Deva, 3 Weaverham Road   21
24 Eastern Road   22
Laskey Farm   33
One House Walled Garden   46
◆ Peover Hall Gardens   48
Sandymere   52
Tattenhall Hall   56

Saturday 13th
NEW Harewood, Disley   24
NEW Whitby Park Community Garden   61
Willaston Grange   62

Sunday 14th
◆ Abbeywood Gardens	1
18 Dee Park Road	20
Hill Farm	27
The Homestead	31
NEW Normans Hall	42
NEW Whitby Park Community Garden	61

Wednesday 17th
18 Dee Park Road	20

Friday 19th
HMP Thorn Cross	29

Saturday 20th
All Fours Farm	3

Sunday 21st
All Fours Farm	3
2 Ashcroft Cottages	5
◆ Bluebell Cottage Gardens	8
18 Dee Park Road	20

Sunday 28th
Burton Village Gardens	14
Swineyard Hall	55

July

Friday 3rd
HMP Thorn Cross	29

Saturday 4th
NEW Marsh Farm	36
The Old Parsonage	44

Sunday 5th
Deva, 3 Weaverham Road	21
The Old Parsonage	44

Saturday 11th
Laskey Farm	33
Milford House Farm	37

Sunday 12th
Clemley House	19
Laskey Farm	33

Friday 17th
HMP Thorn Cross	29

Saturday 18th
187 Victoria Road	59

Sunday 19th
2 Ashcroft Cottages	5
Chinook Cottage	17
Norley Bank Farm	40
187 Victoria Road	59
The Wonky Garden	63

Saturday 25th
The Birches	7
NEW The Homestead	30

Sunday 26th
2 Ashcroft Cottages	5
The Birches	7
NEW The Homestead	30
Norley Bank Farm	40

Friday 31st
HMP Thorn Cross	29

August

Sunday 2nd
Hilltop Country House	28

Monday 3rd
Norley Bank Farm	40

Sunday 9th
Norley Bank Farm	40

Friday 14th
HMP Thorn Cross	29

Sunday 16th
2 Ashcroft Cottages	5
The Wonky Garden	63

Saturday 22nd
6 Oakland Vale	43

Sunday 23rd
NEW Marsh Farm	36
6 Oakland Vale	43

Friday 28th
HMP Thorn Cross	29

Sunday 30th
2 Ashcroft Cottages	5
Laskey Farm	33

Monday 31st
Laskey Farm	33

September

Saturday 5th
NEW Harewood, Disley	24

Sunday 6th
2 Ashcroft Cottages	5

Tuesday 15th
◆ Ness Botanic Gardens	39

Sunday 27th
◆ Abbeywood Gardens	1

October

Sunday 11th
Bucklow Farm	13
◆ The Lovell Quinta Arboretum	34

Saturday 17th
Parvey Lodge	47

February 2027

Sunday 28th
Bucklow Farm	13

By Arrangement

Arrange a personalised garden visit with your club, or group of friends, on a date to suit you. See individual garden entries for full details.

Adswood	2
2 Ashcroft Cottages	5
Bolesworth Castle	9
Bollin House	10
Bowmere Cottage	11
Briarfield	12
18 Dee Park Road	20
The Firs	23
166 Higher Lane	26
Hill Farm	27
The Homestead	31
Inglewood	32
Laskey Farm	33
Milford House Farm	37
Norley Bank Farm	40
Norley Court	41
The Old Parsonage	44
Parvey Lodge	47
Rosewood	51
Sandymere	52
10 Statham Avenue	53
Tattenhall Hall	56
Trustwood (Burton Village Gardens)	14
8a Warwick Drive	60
The Wonky Garden	63

310,000 people are cared for each year who are approaching the end of life or diagnosed with a terminal illness through the hospice network supported by National Garden Scheme funding.

THE GARDENS

1 ◆ ABBEYWOOD GARDENS
Chester Road, Delamere, Northwich, CW8 2HS. The Rowlinson Family, 01606 889477, info@abbeywoodestate.co.uk, www.abbeywoodestate.co.uk. *11m E of Chester. On the A556 facing Delamere Church.* **For NGS: Sun 14 June, Sun 27 Sept (9-4). Adm £7.50, chd free. Restaurant in Garden.** **For other opening times and information, please phone, email or visit garden website.** Superb setting near Delamere Forest. Total area 45 acres inc mature woodland, new woodland and new arboretum all with connecting pathways. Approx 4½ acres of gardens surrounding large Edwardian house. Vegetable garden, exotic garden, chapel garden, pool garden, woodland garden, lawned area with beds.

2 ADSWOOD
Townfield Lane, Mollington, CH1 6LB. Ken & Helen Black, 07753 683185, keneblack@outlook.com, www.kenblackclematis.com. *3m N of Chester. From Wirral take A540 towards Chester. Cross A55 at r'about, past Wheatsheaf pub, turn L into Overwood Lane. At T junction turn R into Townfield Lane. NGS sign 100 yds on the L.* **Visits by arrangement Apr to Sept for groups of 6 to 30. Adm £6, chd free. Tea, coffee & cake £4.** A cottage garden with perennials, climbers and English roses. The garden has over 150 varieties of clematis, providing colour throughout the year. There are several seating areas inc a pavilion and a summerhouse. The spring clematis have been featured on Gardeners' World. There are no steps but some of the garden paths are gravelled and the side access to the rear garden, though narrow, is wide enough for wheelchairs.
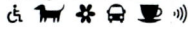

3 ALL FOURS FARM
Colliers Lane, Aston by Budworth, Northwich, CW9 6NF. Mr & Mrs Evans, www.curbishleysroses.co.uk. *M6 J19, take A556 towards Northwich. Turn immed R, past The Windmill pub. Turn R after approx 1m, follow rd, garden on L after approx 2m. Direct access available for drop off & collection for those with limited mobility.* **Sun 5, Mon 6 Apr, Sat 2, Sun 3, Mon 4 May, Sat 20, Sun 21 June (10-4). Adm £5, chd free. Tea, coffee & cake.** A traditional and well established country garden with a wide range of roses, hardy shrubs, bulbs, perennials and annuals. You will also find a small vegetable garden, pond and greenhouse as well as vintage machinery and original features from its days as a working farm. The garden is adjacent to the family's traditional rose nursery. The majority of the garden is accessible by wheelchair.

4 ◆ ARLEY HALL & GARDENS
Arley, Northwich, CW9 6NA. Viscount Ashbrook, 01565 777353, enquiries@arleyhallandgardens.com, www.arleyhallandgardens.com. *10m from Warrington. Signed from J9 & 10 (M56) & J19 & 20 (M6). Please follow the brown tourist signs or use What3words app: sheds.badminton.barn.* **For NGS: Mon 13 Apr (10-4.30). Adm £14, chd £7. Light refreshments in The Gardener's Kitchen Cafe.** **For other opening times and information, please phone, email or visit garden website.** With more than 16 acres of gardens there are many different areas to enjoy inc 8 acres of formal gardens, each with their own distinctive character, plus beyond the Chapel is The Grove, a well established arboretum and a woodland walk of a further 7 acres. Gardens are mostly wheelchair accessible (steps in some areas). Parts of the estate have cobbles which can prove difficult for manual wheelchairs.

5 2 ASHCROFT COTTAGES
Wettenhall, Winsford, CW7 4DQ. Steve & Sue Redmond, 07763 923005, sredmond24707825@aol.com. *Between Winsford & Tarporley. From Winsford follow Hall Lane for approx 2m. From Tarporley direction, follow signs for Eaton, pick up Hickhurst Lane until it meets Winsford Rd, turn L. We are 500 metres on L.* **Sun 21 June, Sun 19, Sun 26 July, Sun 16, Sun 30 Aug, Sun 6 Sept (11-5). Adm £6, chd free. Tea, coffee & cake.** **Visits also by arrangement 10 May to 30 Aug.** A ¾ acre garden full of wonder and intrigue. Come and immerse yourself amongst large herbaceous borders, mature shrubs, grasses and a large wildlife pond with waterfall. From novice to expert you'll find something new at every turn, our garden mixes both kitchen and ornamental planting with free range hens. If you want something with the wow factor this is the garden for you. Partial access for wheelchairs.

6 BANKHEAD
Old Coach Road, Barnhill, Chester, CH3 9JL. Simon & Sian Preston. *Turn L off A41 10m S of Chester into Old Coach Rd. House is on L at top of the road, just before the junction with A534.* **Sun 17 May (1-5). Adm £7, chd free. Tea, coffee & cake.** Two acres of terraced gardens developed from Victorian times with spectacular views south and west over the Dee valley towards the Welsh hills. Rose garden, herbaceous borders, large pond with Japanese style garden, rhododendrons and azaleas. Orchard and vegetable garden. Shetland ponies and chickens. Some steps to main terrace but wheelchair users can reach most areas on paths with slight inclines. Parking close to the garden for disabled access.

7 THE BIRCHES
Grove Road, Mollington, Chester, CH1 6LG. Martin Bentley & Colin Williams. *4m N of Chester. From the A540 Parkgate Rd turn onto Coal Pit Lane which leads to Grove Rd. The Birches is the 7th house on R after Redwood Riding School. What3words app: adding.move.hood.* **Sat 25, Sun 26 July (12-4.30). Adm £5, chd free. Tea, coffee & cake. Home-made jams & Mollington honey will also be available.** ¾ acre of gardens. The front night garden has white herbaceous borders. The back garden is split into 5 areas: Koi and wildlife pond garden with 200ft of herbaceous border. Meadow, grasses and tropical border garden with fernery. Orchard with hens, apiary and wildlife area. Vegetable garden. Sunken garden with stream and bog planting. Level garden with lawn or pathways to most areas.

8 ◆ BLUEBELL COTTAGE GARDENS
Lodge Lane, Dutton, WA4 4HP. Sue Beesley, 01928 713718, info@bluebellcottage.co.uk, www.bluebellcottage.co.uk. *5m NW of Northwich. From M56 (J10) take A49 to Whitchurch. After 3m turn R at T-lights towards Runcorn/Dutton on A533. Then 1st L. Signed with brown tourism signs from A533.* **For NGS: Sun 21 June (10-5). Adm £5, chd free. Tea, coffee & cake. Visitors welcome to have picnics at the nursery tables or in the meadows. Please do not take picnics into the gardens. For other opening times and information, please phone, email or visit garden website.**
South facing country garden wrapped around a cottage on a quiet rural lane in the heart of Cheshire. Packed with thousands of rare and familiar hardy herbaceous perennials, shrubs and trees. Unusual plants available at adjacent nursery. New walled garden with gorgeous brick 'moongate', greenhouse and raised vegetable beds. The opening dates coincide with the peak of flowering in the herbaceous borders. The garden is on a gentle slope with wide lawn paths. All areas are accessible. We have a wider access WC.

9 BOLESWORTH CASTLE
Tattenhall, CH3 9JJ. Mrs Anthony Barbour, 01829 782210, dcb@bolesworth.com, www.bolesworth.com. *8m S of Chester on A41. What3words: snoozing.confined.crockery. Enter via Production Gate A on Old Coach Rd & follow signs to car park. Strenuous walk from the car park over the bridge to the Rock Walk.* **Fri 8, Sat 9 May (10-5). Adm £10, chd £5. Visits also by arrangement 13 Apr to 1 May for groups of 10 to 40.**
An enchanting well planted woodland garden stretching along the sandstone ridge above Bolesworth Castle featuring large leaf, species and hybrid rhododendrons, azaleas and camellias. Explore the paths on The Rock and find the Lion & Lamb Cave with its stunning view of the Welsh Hills and the skyline of Liverpool. Continue your walk through the castle gardens and round the lake. Steep drops so children must be carefully supervised at all times. Wonderful coffee and light refreshments from The Lost Barn Coffee Roasters. Dogs to be on leads at all times (please pick up after them).

10 BOLLIN HOUSE
Hollies Lane, Wilmslow, SK9 2BW. Angela Ferguson & Gerry Lemon, 07828 207492, fergusonang@doctors.org.uk. *From Wilmslow past stn & proceed to T-junction. Turn L onto Adlington Rd. Proceed for ½ m, turn R into Hollies Ln . At the end of Hollies Ln follow yellow signage. Park on Browns Ln (other side Adlington Rd) or Hollies Ln. Parties with 5 cars or fewer can park at property.* **Visits by arrangement 15 Apr to 15 July for groups of 8 to 25. Adm £6, chd free. Tea & cake/biscuits. Cold drinks also available.**
The garden has deep borders full of perennials, a wildflower meadow and a formal area with parterres and central water feature. The perennial wildflower meadow (with mown pathways and benches), attracts lots of bees, dragonflies and other insects and butterflies. There are views over the Bollin river valley and Alderley Edge to the south and over to White Nancy in the east. Bollin House is in an idyllic location with the garden, orchard and meadow dropping into the Bollin valley. The River Bollin flows along this valley and on the opp side the fields lead up to the Alderley Edge ridge. Ramps to gravel lined paths to most of the garden. Some mown pathways in the meadow.

11 BOWMERE COTTAGE
5 Bowmere Road, Tarporley, CW6 0BS. Romy & Tom Holmes, 01829 732053, romy@holmes-email.co.uk. *10m E of Chester. From Tarporley High St (old A49) take Eaton Rd signed Eaton. After 100 metres take R fork into Bowmere Rd. Garden 100 metres on L.* **Visits by arrangement 15 June to 31 July for groups of 6 to 30. Adm £6, chd free. Home-made teas.**
A colourful and relaxing 1 acre country style garden around a Grade II listed house. The lawns are surrounded by well stocked herbaceous and shrub borders. Two plant filled courtyard gardens, a small vegetable garden, pergolas, rambling roses, clematis, hardy geraniums and hardy herbaceous plants make this a very traditional English garden.

12 BRIARFIELD
The Rake, Burton, Neston, CH64 5TL. Liz Carter, 07711 813732, carter.burton@btinternet.com, www.facebook.com/Briarfieldburton. *9m NW of Chester. Turn off A540 at Willaston-Burton Xrds T-lights & follow road for 1m to Burton village centre.* **Every Sun 1 Feb to 15 Feb (11-4). Sun 12 Apr (1-5). Home-made teas in the church along the lane. Adm £5, chd free. In Feb refreshments will be hot drinks & biscuits at the house. Opening with Burton Village Gardens on Sun 28 June. Visits also by arrangement Feb to Sept.**
Tucked under the south side of Burton Wood the garden is home to many specialist and unusual plants, some available in plant sale. This 2 acre garden is on two sites, a short walk along an unmade lane. Trees, shrubs, colourful herbaceous, bulbs, alpines and water features compete for attention. Deliberately left untidy through the winter for wildlife, the snowdrops love it. Erythronium are a feature of the garden in April. Always changing, Liz can't resist a new plant.

13 BUCKLOW FARM
Pinfold Lane, Plumley, Knutsford, WA16 9RP. Dawn & Peter Freeman. *2m S of Knutsford. M6 J19, A556 Chester. L at 2nd set of T-lights. In 1¼ m, L at concealed Xrds. 1st R. From Knutsford A5033, L at Sudlow Ln, becomes Pinfold Ln.* **Sun 22 Feb, Sun 11 Oct (12.30-4). Adm £5, chd free. Light refreshments. Non alchoholic Mulled wine, with usual tea, coffee & biscuits. 2027: Sun 28 Feb.** Donation to The Ticker Club.
Country garden with shrubs, perennial borders, rambling roses, herb garden, vegetable patch, meadow, wildlife pond/water feature and alpines. Landscaped and planted over the last 35 yrs with recorded changes. Free range hens. Carpet of snowdrops and spring bulbs. Leaf, stem, flowers and berries to show colour in autumn and winter. Cobbled yard from car park, but wheelchairs can be dropped off near gate.

Bollin House

© Liz Mitchell

GROUP OPENING

14 BURTON VILLAGE GARDENS
Burton, Neston, CH64 5SJ. *9m NW of Chester. Turn off A540 at Willaston-Burton Xrds T-lights & follow road for 1m to Burton. Parking well signed. Maps given to visitors. Buy ticket at first garden. Card reader at The Coach House.* **Sun 28 June (11-5). Combined adm £6, chd free. Home-made teas in the Sports and Social Club behind the village hall.**

BRIARFIELD
Liz Carter.
(See separate entry)

4 BURTON MANOR GARDENS
Rosemary & Anthony Hannay.

♦ **BURTON MANOR WALLED GARDEN**
Friends of Burton Manor Gardens CIO, 0151 336 6154, friendsofburtonmanorgardens.chessck.co.uk.

THE COACH HOUSE
Jane & Mike Davies.

TRUSTWOOD
Peter & Lin Friend, 0151 336 7118, Lin.friend@icloud.com.
Visits also by arrangement 3 May to 1 Aug for groups of up to 15.

The Coach House is rejoining us in 2026. With stunning views across the River Dee, the garden is full of colour and has a new water feature. Only 3 yrs old, 4 Burton Manor Gardens is a tiny gem with interesting shrubs, a herbaceous border, cheerful pots and even tomatoes in the greenhouse. Close by is Burton Manor Walled garden with period planting and a splendid vegetable garden surrounding the restored Edwardian glasshouse. Paths lead past a sunken garden and terraces to views across the Cheshire countryside. Trustwood is a relaxed country garden, a haven for wildlife with emphasis on British native trees planted along the drive, the use of insect friendly plants and wildlife ponds. Briarfield has many unusual plants, some available in the plant sale at the house. The 1½ acre main garden invites exploration not only for its variety of plants but also for the imaginative use of ceramic sculptures. Such diversity, but we are all gardening on a light sandy, slightly acid soil. Briarfield & The Coach House are too hilly for wheelchairs, with steep slopes and steps.

15 64 CARR WOOD
Hale Barns, Altrincham, WA15 0EP. Mr David Booth. *10m S of Manchester city centre. 2m from J6 M56: Take A538 to Hale Barns. L at 'triangle' by church into Wicker Lane & L at mini r'about into Chapel Lane & 1st R into Carr Wood.* **Sat 9 May (1-5). Adm £5, chd free. Home-made teas.**

⅔ acre landscaped, south facing garden overlooking Bollin valley laid out in 1959 by Clibrans of Altrincham. Gently sloping lawn, woodland walk, seating areas and terrace, extensive mixed shrub and plant borders. Ample parking on Carr Wood. Wheelchair access to terrace overlooking main garden.

16 NEW 7 CHESHAM PLACE
Bowdon, Altrincham, WA14 2JL. Mr Graham & Mrs Judith Sadler. *8m SW of Manchester. From M56 J7/8 Altrincham. Towards Altrincham on A56. After garage on R turn R at T-lights. After 1m at T-lights turn L onto Stamford Rd. Chesham Pl is 3rd on L. Parking on Stamford Rd, please do not park in Chesham Place.* **Sat 6, Sun 7 June (1-4). Adm £5, chd free. Tea, coffee & cake.**

This 1850s house and garden has been in the family for 2 generations. The garden is divided into 3 parts. The front being structured with a deep all seasons border, the middle blends traditional and contemporary seating areas overlaid with old roses. The rear has a cottage garden aesthetic with a newly established small fruit orchard with a native wildflower meadow to increase biodiversity. Small step to access garden gate. Most of garden is laid to lawn and hard ground. There are steps to access the rear part of the garden.

17 CHINOOK COTTAGE
96 Westminster Road, Macclesfield, SK10 3AJ. Miss Sara Wreford. *1m NW of Macclesfield. From Sainsburys r'about, turn L directly after Sainsburys entrance. The garden is down on the R, opp West Park/Cemetery. There is more free parking at Bollinbrook shops just further along.* **Sun 19 July (12-4.30). Adm £4, chd free. Tea, coffee & cake. Cream teas.**

A mature enclosed cottage garden of flowers, grasses, edibles and fruit trees. Patio screened by black bamboo, ferns, crocosmia, foxgloves, poppies, pieris, lychnis and many pots. Lawn surrounded by mature trees and perennials. Mediterranean themed summerhouse. Long border of rhubarb, currants and berries. Front beds inc astrantia, hollyhocks, daphne, campsis. Small greenhouse enables propagation. 2 raised beds in side garden for flowers and vegetables. Lots of seating areas to enjoy refreshments. Mainly lawn with some inclines.

18 ◆ CHOLMONDELEY CASTLE GARDENS
Cholmondeley, Malpas, SY14 8AH. The Cholmondeley Gardens Trust, 01829 720203, eo@chol-estates.co.uk, www.cholmondeleycastle.com. *4m NE of Malpas. SatNav SY14 8ET. Signed from A41 Chester-Whitchurch road & A49 Whitchurch-Tarporley road.* **For NGS: Thur 7 May (10-5). Adm £10, chd £10. Fresh coffee, lunches & cakes daily with locally sourced produce located in the heart of the Gardens.** For other opening times and information, please phone, email or visit garden website.

Discover the romantic Temple and Folly Water Gardens, Glade, Arboretum, 100m long double herbaceous border walkway Lavinia Walk, ornamental woodland upon Tower Hill and the newly created Cholmondeley Rose Garden with 250 rose varieties. Large display of daffodils, magnificent magnolias and bluebell woodland. One of the finest features of the gardens are its trees,

Normans Hall

CHESHIRE & WIRRAL

many of which are rare and unusual, with over 40 county champion trees. Partial wheelchair access.

19 CLEMLEY HOUSE
Well Lane, Duddon Common, Tarporley, CW6 0HG. Sue & Tom Makin, 07790 610586, s_makingardens@yahoo.co.uk. *8m SE of Chester, 3m W of Tarporley. A51 from Chester towards Tarporley. 1m after Tarvin turn off, at bus shelter, turn L into Willington Rd. After community centre, 2nd L into Well Lane, 3rd house.* **Sun 12 July (1-5). Adm £7, chd free. Tea, coffee & cake. Home grown organic fruits used in jams & cakes. Gluten free by prior arrangement. Cash only for teas & plants.**
2 acre organic, wildlife friendly, gold award winning cottage garden. Orchard, 2 wildlife ponds, perennial wildflower meadow, fruit and vegetable areas, rose pergola and veranda, gazebo, shepherd's hut, summerhouse, barn owl and many other nest and bat boxes. Drought tolerant gravel garden and shade garden. New wild areas. The garden is a clear example of how an oasis for wildlife can be beautiful. Vegetables and soft fruits grown without pesticides and using only natural fertilisers. Owner has qualified in garden design at Reaseheath College and worked in this field. Gravel paths may be difficult to use but most areas are flat and comprise grass paths or lawn.

20 18 DEE PARK ROAD
Dee Park Road, Wirral, CH60 3RQ. Mrs Shay & Mr Les Whitehead, 07778 309671, shaywhitehead@gmail.com. *J4 off M53. Follow signs for Brimstage, Heswall, follow to end. Turn L at r'about, take 1st L onto A540 to Chester, 1st R down Gayton Lane. Dee Park is on the bottom L.* **Sun 14, Wed 17, Sun 21 June (11-4.30). Adm £5, chd free. Tea, coffee & home-made cakes.** Visits also by arrangement in June for groups of 10+.
A long suburban garden backing onto private woodland. Mature garden laid to lawns, with mixed borders, leading on to numerous seating areas. The garden features a very unusual triple hexagonal greenhouse, which was originally purchased from the Liverpool Garden Festival site,

c1984, before taking you through to a shaded wooded area where there are numerous different types of hosta on display. Wheelchair accessible with one step to negotiate.

21 DEVA, 3 WEAVERHAM ROAD
Sandiway, Northwich, CW8 2NJ. Mr Andrew & Mrs Tracey Molyneux. *5m outside Northwich, towards Chester. Take A556 towards Chester. On entering Sandiway, pass the sandstone tower, go straight across T-lights positioning yourself ready to take the next R onto Weaverham Rd. 2nd Victorian house on L.* **Sun 7 June, Sun 5 July (10-3). Adm £5, chd free. Tea, coffee & cake.**
You are greeted at the front by a mature lavender garden, enclosed with a box hedge. To the side a walled yard with cordoned apple, pear and fig trees. Passing through a wrought iron gate a formal Victorian garden awaits with four separate beds. In the centre is a water feature created from a recommissioned factory wash station. The garden is enclosed with hawthorn hedges and features many peonies, a large china girl and a white cornus.

22 24 EASTERN ROAD
Willaston, Nantwich, CW5 7HT. Mr Roger & Mrs Rosemary Murphy. *1m E of Nantwich. From A51 Nantwich bypass follow sign into Willaston at Crewe Rd r'about. At the T junction turn R over the level Xing then immed turn L into Eastern Rd, garden is approx 100yds on R.* **Sun 7 June (11-4). Adm £5, chd free. Home-made teas.**
South facing garden evolved over the last 7yrs. Mixed herbaceous planting including various trees and assorted shrubs, also climbers, some unusual plants, raised beds, new shade loving area for 2026, seating areas, summerhouse, greenhouse with succulent collection, paths, pots and containers with a small collection of hostas plus other garden features.

23 THE FIRS
Old Chester Road, Barbridge, Nantwich, CW5 6AY. Richard & Valerie Goodyear, richard.goodyear@ngs.org.uk. *3m N of Nantwich on A51. After entering Barbridge turn R at Xrds after 100 metres. The Firs is 2nd house on L.*

Visits by arrangement 14 June to 4 Aug for groups of 10 to 30. Adm £7, chd free. Tea, coffee & cake.
Canalside garden set idyllically by a wide section of the Shropshire Union Canal with long frontage. Garden alongside canal with varied trees, shrubs and herbaceous beds, with some wild areas. All leading down to an observatory and Japanese torii gate with views across fields. Usually have nesting friendly swans with cygnets. This will be the last year of opening as the owners intend to move. Wheelchair access to main areas and to all unless the lawns are wet/soft.

24 NEW HAREWOOD, DISLEY
20 Red Lane, Disley, Stockport, SK12 2NP. Chris & Sally Robinson. *What3words app: witless.daffodils. shadowing. From Stockport head for Disley Village via the A6. At the village T-lights turn R onto Buxton Old Rd, then IMMED R again BEHIND the Ram's Head pub onto Red Lane Follow the NGS signs to find parking & disabled parking.* **Sat 13 June, Sat 5 Sept (9.30-3.30). Adm £7.50, chd free. Pre-booking essential, please visit www.ngs. org.uk for information & booking. Tea, coffee & cake. Vicar Stewart's pop up cafe can be found in the barn, offering barista coffee, home-made bakes & tea.**
The extensive gardens at Harewood in Disley surround the restored 1870s house and are a plant lover's paradise, with many rare gems. Set amidst the rolling Cheshire and Derbyshire countryside, the gardens look out over Lyme Park and Disley Dam. The gardens are set out in terraces and include an enclosed secret courtyard, a large water lily pond, a well stocked glasshouse, beautiful deep mixed borders and a woodland dell leading to an apiary. Whilst the garden is relatively young, it borrows a grounding of maturity from the many trees which define its boundaries. Harewood is a year-round garden but the month of September particularly highlights the diversity of colours in the herbaceous borders and the changing hues of the turning season. We welcome accompanied children to the garden - please keep young children supervised at all times as there are many hazards inc deep water, a ha-ha, steep steps and beehives.

25 HATHAWAY
1 Pool End Road, Tytherington, Macclesfield, SK10 2LB. Mr & Mrs Cordingley. *2m N of Macclesfield, ½m from The Tytherington Club. From Stockport follow A523 past the Butley Ash pub, at r'about turn R on A538 for Tytherington. From Knutsford follow A537 at A538, L for Tytherington. From Leek follow A523 at A537 L & 1st R A538.* **Sat 9, Sun 10 May (10-4). Adm £5, chd free. Teas, coffee, cordial & cakes.**
South-west facing garden of approx ⅕ acre, laid out in two parts. Lawn area surrounded by mature, colourful perennial borders. Rose arbour. Our small pond has now become a large one, located in the lawn, with goldfish. Larger patio. Small mature wooded area with winding paths on a lower level. Front laid to lawn with 2 main borders and feature trees. Good wheelchair access to most of garden except wood area. Owner uses a mobility scooter.

26 166 HIGHER LANE
Lymm, WA13 0RG. Trevor Holland & Marian Bingham, 07711 163411, tholland31755@yahoo.ca. *6m ESE of Warrington on E edge of Lymm, just off the A56. From M6, exit at J20, from M56 exit at J9 & follow signs to Lymm (B5158), R at T-junction onto A56 heading SE for 1½m on Higher Ln. Park on Higher Ln, garden 50yds on Whiteleggs Ln.* **Visits by arrangement 9 May to 7 Sept for groups of up to 15. Groups up to 12 can be served in the orangery when the weather is poor. Adm £5, chd free. Home-made teas. Barista coffees, sweet & savoury baked goods.**
Garden plot on Whiteleggs Ln off Higher Ln with large cedar summerhouse and orangery. Habitats and flowers for bees and wildlife. Wooded area of silver birch, maples, shrubs and pond; patio area with vine arbour and gravel garden; cottage garden with lawn and wildflower area, wisteria arbour and espalier apples. No parking on Whiteleggs Ln, please park on Higher Ln on the side of the cottages.

27 HILL FARM
Mill Lane, Moston, Sandbach, CW11 3PS. Mrs Chris & Mr Richard House, 01270 526264, housecr2002@yahoo.co.uk. *2m NW of Sandbach. From Sandbach town centre take A533 towards Middlewich. After Fox pub take next L (Mill Lane) to a canal bridge & turn L. Hill Farm 400m on R just before post box.* **Sun 26 Apr, Sun 17 May, Sun 14 June (11-5). Adm £5, chd free. Light refreshments. Visits also by arrangement 27 Apr to 5 July.**
The garden extends to approx ½ acre and is made up of a series of gardens inc a formal courtyard with a pond and vegetable garden with south facing wall. An orchard and wildflower meadow were established about 6 yrs ago. A principal feature is a woodland garden which supports a rich variety of woodland plants. This was extended in April 2020 to inc a pond and grass/herbaceous borders. A level garden, the majority of which can be accessed by wheelchair.

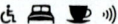

28 HILLTOP COUNTRY HOUSE
Flash Lane, Prestbury, SK10 4ED. www.yourhilltopwedding.com. *2m N of Macclesfield. A523 to Stockport. Turn R at B5090 r'about signed Bollington, after ½m turn L at Cock & Pheasant pub onto Flash Lane. At bottom of lane turn R at sign for Hilltop. What3Words checked.completed.skewed.* **Sun 2 Aug (1-4). Adm £5, chd free. Tea, coffee & cake included in admission.**
Interesting country garden of approx 4 acres set amidst 15 acres of wonderful rolling Cheshire countryside. The extensive gardens surround the C17 house and are a plant lover's paradise. Divided into smaller gardens set on different levels inc an enclosed secret parterre, wildlife areas, ponds, established mixed borders, formal herb garden and a newly planted wood. There are many mature trees which provide structure throughout. Hilltop Country House is home to a year-round garden but the month of August highlights the diversity of colours in the mixed borders. Woodland walk, herbaceous borders, dry stone walled terracing, lily ponds, gravel garden. Wisteria clad 1693 house (not open), ancient trees, orchard with magnificent views to Pennines and to the west. Partial wheelchair access to orchard, herb garden, top lawn and borders. Disabled WC.

29 HMP THORN CROSS
Arley Road, Appleton, Warrington, WA4 4RL. Jade McDonnell. *Enter through the large wooden gates opp Appleton Thorn primary school and park in the car park.* **Fri 5, Fri 19 June, Fri 3, Fri 17, Fri 31 July, Fri 14, Fri 28 Aug (10-12). Adm £5. Pre-booking essential, please visit www.ngs.org.uk for information & booking. Light refreshments.**
HMP Thorn Cross is an open prison with large sprawling grounds which we are delighted to open for the enjoyment of the public. We have an impressive range of biodiversity inc beehives, ducks, newts, birds and more! We are extremely proud of our award-winning landscape, carefully maintained by the prisoners and look forward to welcoming visitors for a unique and once in a lifetime experience. Please park in the prison car park and walk to the Farm Shop where you will be met by a member of staff. Please be there for 10am as the tour is guided, and do wear suitable footwear depending on the weather conditions on the day. Features inc pond, beehives, orchard, flower displays, planting beds, extensive woodland and herbaceous borders. Please note photo ID will be required and Visitor Passes will be provided on the day. Cameras and phones are not permitted and we regret there are no WC facilities or children allowed. After booking, please email hello@ngs.org.uk to notify us of any access requirements.

30 THE HOMESTEAD
17 Park Grove, Macclesfield, SK11 8AS. Dr Russell & Mrs Rachel Mortishire-Smith. *On the edge of Macclesfield's South Park. From the A536 (Park Lane), turn into Park Grove. At the end, pass through the stone gates into the car park of South Park. The Homestead is on the far side of the car park, through pale blue gates.* **Sat 25, Sun 26 July (11-4). Adm £5, chd free. Tea, coffee & cake.**
The Homestead's ¾ acre garden lies within Macclesfield's South Park, fronting onto Ryle's Pool with views of the parkland. Laid out in 1920, the garden is separated by hedges into several 'rooms' with seating areas, inc a sunken garden, a wild lakeside area with a restful cabin, a main lawn bordered by espaliered fruit trees and mature borders, and raised beds for growing cut flowers. Wildlife friendly.

Bolesworth Castle

31 THE HOMESTEAD
2 Fanners Lane, High Legh, Knutsford, WA16 0RZ. Janet Bashforth, 07809 030525, janbash43@sky.com. *J20 M6/J9 M56 at Lymm interchange take A50 for Knutsford, after 1m turn R into Heath Lane then 1st R into Fanners Lane. Follow parking signs.* **Sun 14 June (11-4). Adm £5, chd free.** Visits also by arrangement 1 June to 14 Aug for groups of 15 to 50.
This compact gem of a garden has been created over the last 10 yrs by a keen gardener and plantswoman. Enter past groups of liquidambar and white stemmed birch. Colour themed areas with many perennials, shrubs and trees. Past topiary and obelisks covered with many varieties of clematis and roses, enjoy the colours of the hot border. A decorative greenhouse and pond complete the picture.

♿ ❀ 🚗 ☕ 🔊

32 INGLEWOOD
4 Birchmere, Heswall, CH60 6TN. Colin & Sandra Fairclough, 07715 546406, sandrafairclough51@gmail.com. *6m S of Birkenhead. From A540 Devon Doorway/Clegg Arms r'about go through Heswall. ¼ m after Tesco, R into Quarry Rd East, 2nd L into Tower Rd North & L into Birchmere.* **Visits by arrangement 15 Apr to 8 July for groups of 12 to 30. Payment required in advance. Adm £6, chd free. Home-made teas.**
Beautiful ½ acre garden with stream, large koi pond, 'beach' with grasses, wildlife pond and bog area. Brimming with shrubs, bulbs, acers, conifers, rhododendrons, hydrangeas, herbaceous plants and hosta border. Interesting features inc hand cart, bug hotel and Indian dog gates leading to a secret garden. Lots of seating to enjoy refreshments.

♿ 🐕 ❀ ☕

33 LASKEY FARM
Laskey Lane, Thelwall, Warrington, WA4 2TF. Howard & Wendy Platt, 07785 262478, howardplatt@lockergroup.com, www.laskeyfarm.com. *2m from M6/M56. From M56/M6 follow directions to Lymm. At T-junction turn L onto the A56 in Warrington direction. Turn R onto Lymm Rd. Turn R onto Laskey Lane.* **Sun 3, Mon 4 May, Sat 6, Sun 7 June, Sat 11, Sun 12 July, Sun 30, Mon 31 Aug (11-4). Adm £6, chd £1. Home-made teas.** Visits also by arrangement 1 May to 30 Aug for groups of 20 to 50.
1½ acre garden inc herbaceous and rose borders, vegetable area, a greenhouse, parterre and a maze showcasing grasses and prairie style planting. Interconnected pools for wildlife, specimen koi and terrapins form an unusual water garden which features a swimming pond. There is a treehouse plus a number of birds and animals. Family friendly, we offer a treasure hunt, and a mini menagerie consisting of chickens, guinea fowl and guinea pigs. Most areas of the garden may be accessed by wheelchair.

♿ 🐕 ❀ 🚗 ☕ 🔊

34 ◆ THE LOVELL QUINTA ARBORETUM
Swettenham, CW12 2LF. Tatton Garden Society, 01565 831981, admin@tattongardensociety.org.uk, lovellquintaarboretum.co.uk. *4m NW of Congleton. Turn off A54 N 2m W of Congleton or turn E off A535 at Twemlow Green, NE of Holmes Chapel. Follow signs to Swettenham. Park at Swettenham Arms. What3words app: twins.sheds.keepers.* **For NGS: Sun 11 Oct (1.30-4). Adm £5, chd free. Cash only. For other opening times and information, please phone, email or visit garden website.**
This 28 acre arboretum has been established since the 1960s and contains around 2,500 trees and shrubs, some very rare. National Collections of Quercus, Pinus and Fraxinus. A large selection of oaks plus autumn flowering, fruiting and colourful trees and shrubs. Newly restored lake. Waymarked walks. Refreshments at the adjacent Swettenham Arms. With care, wheelchairs can access much of the arboretum on the mown paths.

35 MANLEY KNOLL
Manley Road, Manley, WA6 9DX. Mr & Mrs James Timpson. *3m N of Tarvin. On B5393, via Ashton & Mouldsworth. 3m S of Frodsham, via Alvanley.* **Sun 17 May (12-5). Adm £7.50, chd free. Home-made teas.**
Arts & Crafts garden created in the early 1900s. Covering 6 acres, divided into different rooms encompassing parterres, clipped yew hedging, ornamental ponds and herbaceous borders. Banks of rhododendron and azaleas frame a far-reaching view of the Cheshire Plain. Also a magical quarry/folly garden with waterfall and woodland walks.

36 NEW MARSH FARM
Marsh Lane, Crowton, Northwich, CW8 2RL. Mrs Holly Slimming, www.marshfarmflowers.co.uk. *What3words app: banana.decks.dentures. From the Hare & Hounds pub in Crowton, drive past with the pub on your R, turn R onto Bent Lane then R on to Marsh Lane.* **Sat 4 July, Sun 23 Aug (11-3). Adm £5, chd free. Tea, coffee & cake.**
An artisan flower farm on a ¼ acre plot of Cheshire countryside. Started in 2023 by Holly as an area of escapism, it has gradually grown over the last few years. Specialising in British grown seasonal cut flowers, grown sustainably without the use of pesticides and fungicides. Join us to visit a working flower farm and meander up and down the flower beds.

37 MILFORD HOUSE FARM
Long Lane, Wettenhall, Winsford, CW7 4DN. Chris & Heather Pope, 07887 760930, hclp@btinternet.com. *3m E of Tarporley. From A51 at Alpraham turn into Long Lane 2½ m to St David's Church on L. Milford House is 150 metres further on L. Park at church or limited mobility can park at house. What3words scan.craftsmen.learns.* **Sat 11 July (11-5). Adm £6, chd free. Tea, coffee & cake at St. David's Church. Gluten & dairy free, vegan options. Visits also by arrangement 15 June to 10 July for groups of 10 to 35. Refreshments £5.00. Gluten/dairy free available.**
A large country garden with lots of colour and flowers, lawn, mixed borders, white garden. New ha-ha overlooking the Zen area. Modern walled garden with a jumble of vegetables, fruit and flowers. New rose garden. Greenhouse, potting shed, wall shrubs and tender exotics, succulents, bathtub water feature and fishpond. Orchard for fruit, native, ornamental trees and wildlife pond with toads/newts. Extended Japanese garden. Gardened on organic lines to increase biodiversity and attract wildlife. Picnics in orchard. Visits by arrangement can inc woodland walks (weather dependent). Children's activities. Walled garden has gravel and flags. Accessible WC at church.

38 ◆ MOUNT PLEASANT
Yeld Lane, Kelsall, CW6 0TB. Dave Darlington & Louise Worthington, 01829 751592, louisedarlington@btinternet.com, www.mountpleasantgardens.co.uk. *8m E of Chester. Off A54 at T-lights into Kelsall. Turn into Yeld Lane opp Farmers Arms pub, 200yds on L. Do not follow SatNav directions.* **For NGS: Sat 23 May (11-4). Adm £8, chd £5. Tea, coffee & cake. For other opening times and information, please phone, email or visit garden website.**
10 acres of landscaped garden and woodland started in 1994 with impressive views over the Cheshire countryside. Steeply terraced in places. Specimen trees, rhododendrons, azaleas, conifers, mixed and herbaceous borders; 4 ponds, formal and wildlife. Vegetable garden, stumpery with tree ferns, sculptures, wildflower meadow and Japanese garden. Bog garden, tropical garden. Sculpture trail and exhibition.

39 ◆ NESS BOTANIC GARDENS
Neston Road, Ness, Neston, CH64 4AY. The University of Liverpool, 0151 795 6300, nessgdns@liverpool.ac.uk, www.liverpool.ac.uk/ness-gardens. *10m NW of Chester. Off A540. M53 J4, follow signs M56 & A5117 (signed N Wales). Turn onto A540 follow signs for Hoylake. Ness Gardens is signed locally. 487 bus takes visitors travelling from Liverpool, Birkenhead etc.* **For NGS: Tue 15 Sept (10-5). Adm £8.50, chd £4.50. For other opening times and information, please phone, email or visit garden website.**
Looking out over the dramatic views of the Dee estuary from a lofty perch on the Wirral peninsula, Ness Botanic Gardens boasts 64 acres of landscaped and natural gardens overflowing with horticultural treasures. With a delightfully peaceful atmosphere, a wide array of events taking place, plus a café and gorgeous open spaces it is a great fun-filled day out for all the family. National Collections of Sorbus and Betula. Herbaceous borders, rock garden, Mediterranean bank, potager and conservation area. Wheelchairs and scooters are available to hire but advance booking is highly recommended.

Our donation to Marie Curie this year is equivalent to 17,521 hours of hospice at home care.

40 NORLEY BANK FARM
Cow Lane, Norley, Frodsham, WA6 8PJ. Margaret & Neil Holding, 07828 913961, neil.holding@hotmail.com. *Nr Delamere forest. From the Tigers Head pub in the centre of Norley village keep the pub on L, carry straight on through the village for approx 300 metres. Cow Lane is on the R.* **Sun 19, Sun 26 July, Mon 3, Sun 9 Aug (11-5). Adm £7, chd free. Home-made teas. Some allergy free refreshments available.** Visits also by arrangement 11 July to 15 Aug for groups of 10+.
A 2 acre garden with many colourful borders and other features. A well stocked herbaceous border wraps around the farmhouse. Within an orchard are annual borders and enclosed cut flower borders which surround a greenhouse. Just beyond the house lies a vegetable garden. Walk past this to 2 wildlife ponds with a backdrop of pollinating flowers, a flower meadow and stumpery/fernery. WC available. Free range hens, donkeys and Coloured Ryeland sheep. Access in the main is possible for wheelchairs (though not the WC). There are some stone steps and a small number of narrow paths.

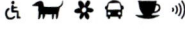

41 NORLEY COURT
Marsh Lane, Norley, Frodsham, WA6 8NY. Clare Albinson, 07717 447465, Albinsonc@hotmail.com. *20 mins E of Chester. Close to Delamere Forest. A556 - Stoneyford Ln/Cheese Hill/Cow Ln - L then R. A49 Acton Ln/Station Rd L at church next R into Marsh Ln. Norley Ct is top of hill. Parking in field at bottom of hill. Visitors with limited mobility can be dropped off at the gate or could park at the far end of the Tigers Head pub car park (5 min walk).* **Sun 19 Apr, Sun 17 May (11-5). Adm £6, chd free. Tea, coffee & cake.** Visits also by arrangement 19 Apr to 25 Oct for groups of 6 to 20. Max 13 cars can be parked close to the house.
A large spring, summer and autumn garden with wonderful views over Cheshire. Bluebell wood, rhododendrons (some perfumed), azaleas, pieris, kalmias and Embothriums. Also clematis, wisteria, roses, abutilon and jasmine. Interesting and unusual trees such as cornus, a handkerchief tree,

Judas trees, sorbus varieties, eucryphia, Katsura, an abundance of acers, a tulip tree and much more. Walled garden. Sunken gardens. Tremendous autumn colour. There is sloped access to most areas of the garden, though some are quite steep and grassed

42 NEW NORMANS HALL
Brookledge Lane, Pott Shrigley, Macclesfield, SK10 5GN. Mrs Pat McMillan. *20m S of Manchester. Off the A523 turn L at the Legh Arms onto Brookledge Lane if coming from Stockport, or R if coming from Macclesfield.* **Sun 22 Feb (11-3). Adm £8, chd free. Sun 14 June (10-4). Adm £10, chd free. Pre-booking essential, please visit www.ngs.org.uk for information & booking. Tea, coffee & cake.**
The gardens at Normans Hall are spread over 3 acres. The spring gardens consist of a snowdrop walk, a daffodil dell and a bluebell woodland. On entering our garden in summer, we have a large rill with roses at the front of the house. To the right as you come in there is a new woodland with over 100 birch trees of variety. At the rear is a selection of different herbaceous gardens.

43 6 OAKLAND VALE
New Brighton, Wallasey, CH45 1LQ. Ian Butler & Charles Stringer. *On Magazines Promenade, New Brighton. J1 M53, signs to New Brighton 'attractions' on A554. R at Morrisons r'about, up hill on A554. L at Vaughan Rd, down to river. Park before river. No cars on prom. Oakland Vale on L facing river.* **Sat 22, Sun 23 Aug (10-4). Adm £4, chd free. Tea, coffee & cake.**
A very small walled town garden densely filled with tropical and exotic style plants. Bananas, tree ferns, cordylines and bamboo along with tetrapanax and paulownia form the backdrop to more unusual 'exotic' plants and a pond. The terraced front garden overlooking the Mersey is filled with grasses, ferns, phormiums and echiums along with drought tolerant plants. Located on Magazines Promenade offering interesting river/beach walks with dockland and Liverpool views; close to Vale Park.

44 THE OLD PARSONAGE
Stable Lane, Cotebrook, Tarporley, CW6 0JL. Nick Parker & Lesley Boyle, 01829 760785, nick@nickparker.org.uk. *2m N of Tarporley on A49. From A49 turn into Utkinton Lane. After 150 yds turn L onto Stable Lane. After 150 yds turn into Cotebrook Village Hall car park situated on R. Gardens are directly opp.* **Sat 4, Sun 5 July (10.30-4.30). Adm £9, chd free. Tea, coffee & cake at Cotebrook Village Hall, directly opp the garden. WC at the hall.** Visits by arrangement May to Sept for groups of 10 to 30. Larger groups need to bring portable chairs. No undercover facilities.
A plantsperson's garden intending to give false perspective and incorporating meandering lawned and gravel paths between borders with rare and unusual plants. Wildlife and koi ponds are surrounded by aquatic planting, lilies, hostas and gunnera. A veranda and 3 gazebos feature roses and climbers. Rare breed bantam hens. A paved courtyard has many pots of lilies, dahlia and datura. Main driveway and access is gently sloping gravel. Access to the lawned area is by a steeper but manageable grassed area.

45 THE OLD PARSONAGE
Back Lane, Arley Green, Northwich, CW9 6LZ. The Hon Rowland & Mrs Flower, www.arleyhallandgardens.com. *5m NNE of Northwich. 3m NNE of Great Budworth. M6 J19 & 20 & M56 J10. Follow signs to Arley Hall & Gardens. From Arley Hall follow signs to Old Parsonage which lies across park at Arley Green (approx 1m).* **Sun 24, Mon 25 May (2-5). Adm £6, chd free. Tea, coffee & cake.**
2 acre garden in attractive and secretive rural setting in secluded part of Arley Estate, with ancient yew hedges, herbaceous and mixed borders, shrub roses, climbers, leading to woodland garden and unfenced pond with gunnera and water plants. Rhododendrons, azaleas, meconopsis, cardiocrinum, plus some interesting and unusual trees. Wheelchair access over mown grass, some slopes and bumps and rougher grass further away from the house.

46 ONE HOUSE WALLED GARDEN
off Buxton New Road, Rainow, SK11 0AD. Louise Baylis. 2½m NE of Macclesfield. Just off A537 Macclesfield to Buxton road. 2½m from Macclesfield Station. Parking in adjacent field. **Sat 6, Sun 7 June (11-4.30). Adm £5, chd free. Tea, coffee & cake.**
An historic early C18 walled kitchen garden, hidden for 60 yrs and restored by volunteers. This romantic and atmospheric garden has a wide range of vegetables, flowers and old tools. There is an orchard with friendly pigs, a wildlife area and pond, woodland walk with wildflowers, foxgloves and views, and a traditional greenhouse with ornamental and edible crops. Small plant nursery.

47 PARVEY LODGE
Parvey Lane, Sutton, Macclesfield, SK11 0HX. Mrs Tanya Walker, 07789 528093, tanya.v.walker@gmail.com. *In the heart of the village of Sutton, we are close to Fairways Garden Centre, Sutton Hall & Sutton PO.* **Sat 17 Oct (11-3). Adm £5, chd free. Tea, coffee & cake. Light refreshments. Visits also by arrangement for groups of 10+.**
A beautiful privately owned 3 acre garden with different areas to explore. Formal garden, Himalayan Cedar majestically situated at the front of the house, plenty of acer, fruit trees, shaped box hedge, tennis court lawn, lots of bulbs, rhododendron and camellia, birds and wildlife (deer). Autumn gives spectacular colour to the garden. Most of the garden is wheelchair friendly.

48 ♦ PEOVER HALL GARDENS
Over Peover, Knutsford, WA16 9HW. Mr & Mrs Brooks, 01565 654107, bookings@peoverhall.com, www.peoverhall.co.uk. *4m S of Knutsford. Do not rely on SatNav. From A50/Holmes Chapel Rd at Whipping Stocks pub turn onto Stocks Lane. Follow R onto Grotto Ln ¼m turn R onto Goostrey Ln. Main entrance on R on bend through white gates.* **For NGS: Sat 6, Sun 7 June (12-5). Adm £7, chd £4. Cream teas in the Park House Tea Room. There will be sweet treat refreshments to purchase. For other opening times and information, please phone, email or visit garden website.**
The extensive formal gardens to Peover Hall feature a series of 'garden rooms' filled with clipped box, water garden, Romanesque loggia, warm brick walls, unusual doors, secret passageways, beautiful topiary work and walled gardens, rockery, rhododendrons and pleached limes. Peover Hall, a Grade II* listed Elizabethan family house dating from 1585, provides a fine backdrop. The Grade I listed Carolean Stables, which are of significant architectural importance, will be open to view. Tours of Peover Hall will also be available over the weekend with Mr & Mrs Brooks (tours are at extra cost).

49 ♦ POULTON HALL
Poulton Lancelyn, Bebington, Wirral, CH63 9LN. The Poulton Hall Estate Trust & Poulton Hall Walled Garden Charitable Trust, 07836 590875, info@poultonhall.co.uk, www.poultonhall.co.uk. *2m S of Bebington. From M53, J4 towards Bebington; at T-lights R along Poulton Rd; house 1m on R.* **For NGS: Sat 4, Sun 5 Apr (2-5). Adm £6, chd free. Cream teas may be booked in advance. See our website for details. For other opening times and information, please phone, email or visit garden website.**
A quirky garden which children love. 3 acres, lawns fronting house, wildflower meadow. Surprise approach to walled garden, with reminders of Roger Lancelyn Green's retellings, Excalibur, Robin Hood and Jabberwock. Memorial sculpture for Richard Lancelyn Green by Sue Sharples. Rose, nursery rhyme, witch, herb and oriental gardens and Memories Reading room. Restored Excalibur garden. Level gravel paths. Separate wheelchair access (not across parking field). Disabled WC.

50 ♦ RODE HALL
Church Lane, Scholar Green, ST7 3QP. Randle & Amanda Baker Wilbraham, 01270 873237, enquiries@rodehall.co.uk, www.rodehall.co.uk. *5m SW of Congleton. Between Scholar Green (A34) & Rode Heath (A50).* **For opening times and information, please phone, email or visit garden website.**
Nesfield's terrace and rose garden with stunning view over Humphry Repton's landscape is a feature of Rode, as is the woodland garden with terraced rock garden and grotto. This area is carpeted in snowdrops in February and snowdrop walks can be booked from 1st Feb to 1st Mar on Thursdays, Fridays, Saturdays and Sundays. Other attractions inc the walk to the lake with a view of Birthday Island complete with heronry, restored ice house, working 2 acre walled kitchen garden and Italian garden. Fine display of bluebells in May and bluebell walks are also on offer. In summer we are open Weds and Bank Holiday Mons until end of Sep, 11-4pm. Courtyard Kitchen offers a wide variety of home-made cakes, breakfast and lunches.

51 ROSEWOOD
Old Hall Lane, Puddington, Neston, CH64 5SP. Mr & Mrs C E J Brabin, 0151 353 1193, angela.brabin@btinternet.com. *8m N of Chester. From A540 turn down Puddington Lane, 1½m. Park by village green. Walk 30yds to Old Hall Lane, turn L through archway into garden.* **Visits by arrangement for groups of up to 40. Adm £4, chd free. Tea.**
Year-round garden; thousands of snowdrops in Feb, camellias in autumn, winter and spring. Rhododendrons in April/May and unusual flowering trees from March to June. Autumn cyclamen in quantity from Aug to Nov. Perhaps the greatest delight to owners are 2 large *Cornus capitata*, flowering in June. Bees kept in the garden. Honey sometimes available.

52 SANDYMERE
Middlewich Road, Cotebrook, CW6 9EH. Sir John Timpson, rachel.norwood@timpson.com. *5m N of Tarporley. On A54 approx 300yds W of T-lights at Xrds of A49/A54. What3words app: tolerable.pursue.education.* **Sun 7 June (12-4). Adm £8, chd free. Home-made teas. Visits also by arrangement 18 May to 29 June for groups of 5 to 34.**
16 landscaped acres of beautiful Cheshire countryside with terraces, walled garden, extensive woodland walks and an amazing hosta garden. Turn each corner and you find another gem with lots of different water

features inc a rill built in 2014, which links the main lawn to the hostas. Look out for our new Japanese themed garden. Partial wheelchair access.

53 10 STATHAM AVENUE
Lymm, WA13 9NH. Mike & Gail Porter, 07951 606906, porters@mikeandgailporter.co.uk, www.youtube.com/watch?v=53zmVWfZa-s. *Approx 1m from J20 M6 /M56 interchange. Follow B5158 to Lymm. Take A56 Booth's Hill Rd, L towards Warrington, R on to Barsbank Lane, pass under low bridge, 50 metres turn R onto Statham Ave. No 10 is 100 metres on R. What3words app: smallest.plump.snooze.* **Sat 25, Sun 26 Apr, Sat 30, Sun 31 May (11-4). Adm £6, chd free. Homemade teas. Enjoy Gail's cakes and famous meringues with fresh fruit & cream. Visits also by arrangement 25 Apr to 29 Aug for groups of 10 to 40.**
Beautifully structured ¼ acre south facing terraced garden rising to the Bridgewater towpath. Old twisted Hazel arch opens to clay paved courtyard with roses, clematis and herbs. Rose pillars lead to lushly planted vibrant azaleas and rhododendrons in spring, pastel peonies in early summer followed by richly coloured hydrangeas and fuchsias. Tranquil, peaceful garden. Creative garden buildings. A treasure hunt/quiz to keep the children occupied. Delicious refreshments to satisfy the grown ups.

54 ◆ STONYFORD COTTAGE
Stonyford Lane, Oakmere, CW8 2TF. Janet & Tony Overland, 07816 531358, info@stonyfordcottagegardens.co.uk, www.stonyfordcottagegardens.co.uk. *5m SW of Northwich. From Northwich take A556 towards Chester. ¾ m past A49 junction turn R into Stonyford Lane. Entrance ½ m on L.* **For NGS: Sun 3 May (11-4). Adm £5, chd free. Tea, coffee & cake in our Tea Room. For other opening times and information, please phone, email or visit garden website.**
Set around a tranquil pool, this Monet style landscape has a wealth of moisture loving plants, inc iris and *Primula candelabra*. Drier areas feature unusual perennials, rarer trees and shrubs. Woodland paths meander through shade and bog plantings, along boarded walks, across wild natural areas with views over the pool to the cottage gardens. Unusual plants available at the adjacent nursery. Open Tues - Fri, Apr - Oct 10-5pm. Some gravel paths.

55 SWINEYARD HALL
Swineyard Lane, High Legh, Knutsford, WA16 0RY. Mr John & Mrs Victoria Fenton. *Between Knutsford & Lymm. Swineyard Ln is off the A50 opp the Bears Paw pub. Swineyard Hall is on L after 1km.* **Sun 28 June (11-4). Adm £5, chd free. Tea, coffee & cake.**
The gardens extend to 2 acres inc the Moat, listed as a national monument dating back to C13. Our priorities with this ongoing project have been to inc English country garden borders and specimen trees alongside the old roses, rhododendron, azaleas and horizontal willow trees. Established oak trees, hornbeam, chestnut and copper beech, to name a few, complete the scene.

7 Chesham Place

56 TATTENHALL HALL

High Street, Tattenhall, Chester, CH3 9PX. Jen & Nick Benefield, Chris Evered & Jannie Hollins, 01829 770654, janniehollins@gmail.com. *8m S of Chester off the A41. Turn L to Tattenhall, through village, turn R at Letters pub, past War Memorial on L through sandstone pillared gates. Park on road or in village car park.* **Sun 7 June (2-5.30). Adm £7, chd free. Home-made teas.** Visits also by arrangement Apr to July. We offer a guided tour of the garden for group visits.

Plant enthusiasts' garden around Jacobean house (not open). 4½ acres, wildflower meadows, interesting trees, large pond, stream, walled garden, colour themed borders, succession planting, spinney walk with shade plants, yew terrace overlooking meadow, views to hills. Glasshouse and vegetable garden. Wildlife friendly, sometimes untidy garden, interest year-round, always developing. Extensive collection of plants and trees. Historical manor farmhouse setting, Jacobean and Victorian. Partial wheelchair access due to gravel paths, cobbles and some steps.

& 🐕 ❋ 🚗 ☕))

57 TIRESFORD

Tarporley, CW6 9LY. Susanna Posnett. *Tiresford is on A49 Tarporley bypass. It is adjacent to the farm on R leaving Tarporley in the direction of Four Lane Ends* *T-lights.* **Sun 3 May (2-5). Adm £5, chd free. Home-made teas. Ice cream.**

Established 1930s garden undergoing a major restoration project to reinstate it to its former glory. Fabulous views of both Beeston and Peckforton Castles offer a wonderful backdrop in which to relax and enjoy a delicious tea. This year we hope to realise our long term plan to recreate the kitchen garden and to repair the fountain amongst the new hot borders of the sunken garden. The house has been transformed into a stylish 6 bedroom B&B. There is parking for wheelchair users next to the house and access to a disabled WC in the house.

& 🐕 ❋ ☕))

Harewood, Disley

58 TIRLEY GARTH GARDENS
Mallows Way, Willington, Tarporley, CW6 0RQ. *2m N of Tarporley. 2m S of Kelsall. Entrance 500yds from village of Utkinton. At N of Tarporley take Utkinton Road. What3words app: shift.morphing. such.* **Sun 31 May (1-5). Adm £5, chd free. Home-made teas.**
40 acre garden, terraced and landscaped, designed by Thomas Mawson who is considered the leading exponent of garden design in early C20. It is the only Grade II* Arts & Crafts garden in Cheshire that remains complete and in excellent condition. The gardens are an important example of an early C20 garden laid out in both formal and informal styles. During May the garden is bursting into flower with almost 3000 rhododendron and azalea, many 100 yrs old. Art Exhibition by local Artists.

59 187 VICTORIA ROAD
New Brighton, Wallasey, CH45 0JY. Mrs Sharon Maher & Mr Mike Costall. *Opp the side entrance to New Brighton Merseyrail train station.* **Sat 18, Sun 19 July (10-4). Adm £4, chd free. Tea, coffee & cake.**
A small, front and rear suburban garden which is nonetheless packed with plants and ideas. Roses, hostas, auriculas, a fernery and a cottage garden bed. We also have an edible garden on a roof.

60 8A WARWICK DRIVE
Hale, Altrincham, WA15 9EA. Gill & Chris Turner, 01619 803258, gillandchris_turner@hotmail.com. *M56 J6, take A538 to Altrincham. Turn L at 2nd T-lights into Park Rd. Take 2nd R into Bower Rd & turn L immed into Warwick Drive. Garden is 200yds on L, on corner of Lindop Rd.* **Visits by arrangement May to July for groups of 10 to 20. Adm inc a tour of the garden by the owner. Adm £5, chd free.**
This is a small suburban garden which is constantly evolving. Recent changes include replacing a mixed hedge with yew, making room for more planting areas, more sunlight and more plants! We design and maintain the garden ourselves for year-round interest but the front herbaceous border provides an explosion of colour in July. We will hold separate plant sales on 11 & 18 April between 10am - 2pm.

61 NEW WHITBY PARK COMMUNITY GARDEN
Whitby Park, Stanney Lane, Ellesmere Port, CH65 9AQ. Mr George Jones. *Situated within a public park on Stanney Lane in the centre of Ellesmere Port with easy access from the local area & M53 Junctions 12 & 13. Ample parking available.* **Sat 13, Sun 14 June (11-4). Adm £5, chd free. Tea, coffee & cake. Picnics can be taken in the surrounding parkland.**
A ⅓ acre, partly walled Victorian garden at the rear of the former private residence of the Grace family, a garden run by volunteers for the community. Fruit and vegetables feature heavily, and propagation plays an important part within the garden. The flower beds and shrubs are also a key feature. Produce and plants may be purchased when available. Informative guided walks will be led by a long serving volunteer and a small team within the garden. Visitors will also have full access to family friendly Whitby Park. Disabled and wheelchair access with care.

62 WILLASTON GRANGE
Hadlow Road, Willaston, CH64 2UN. Anita & Mark Mitchell. *8m outside Chester towards The Wirral. From Chester, take A540 (Chester High Rd) turning into B5151 to Willaston. Willaston Grange is 400 yards on R. From the village, take B5151 (Hadlow Road). Willaston Grange is 800 yds on L.* **Sat 13 June (12-5). Adm £6, chd free. Home-made teas.**
Sixteen years ago, Willaston Grange and gardens had been derelict for 3 years. A year of restoration work began. The gardens now extend to 6 acres with a small lake, a range of mature trees, herbaceous border, woodland and vegetable gardens, orchard and magical treehouse. The fully restored Arts & Crafts house makes for a perfect backdrop for a visit, along with afternoon teas and live music. Most areas accessible by wheelchair.

63 THE WONKY GARDEN
Ditton Community Centre, Dundalk Road, Widnes, WA8 8DF. Mrs Angela Hayler, 07976 373979, thewonkygarden@gmail.com, en-gb.facebook.com/thewonkygarden. *From the Widnes exit of the A533 turn L (Lowerhouse La) then L at the r'about. The Community Centre is ½ m up on the R. The garden entrance is on the far L of the building.* **Sun 19 July, Sun 16 Aug (11.30-3.30). Adm £5, chd free. Tea, coffee & cake. Visits also by arrangement 16 June to 26 Sept for groups of 10 to 30.**
The flower garden is our show garden, the focus for horticultural therapy/nature based activities. It has large herbaceous borders, trees and shrubs, planting focussing on the senses and wildlife. We grow masses of edibles and cut flowers in the allotment (for gifting to our community) and The Yard has a massive greenhouse, workshop, activity shelter and Friendship Garden. The garden is designed and managed by a wonderful group of volunteers and in 2025 we were awarded the prestigious King's Award for Voluntary Services. We support many community groups and individuals of all ages and abilities inc schools, colleges and work experience. Our focus is on supporting physical and mental health, isolation and loneliness. An accessible path (1½ metres wide) extends from the car park through the herbaceous and children's nature garden into the allotment and yard.

78,000 people affected by cancer were reached by Maggie's centres supported by the National Garden Scheme over the last 12 months.

CORNWALL

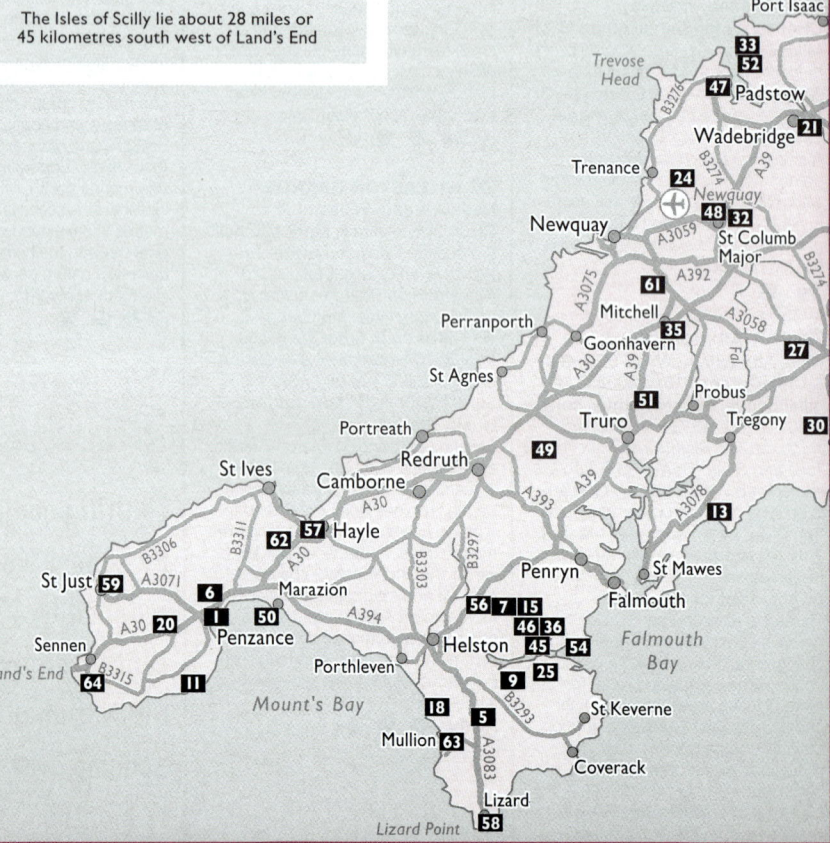

CORNWALL

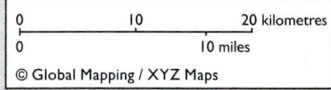

VOLUNTEERS

County Organiser
Sue Newton 07786 367610
sue.newton@ngs.org.uk

Claire Woodbine 07483 244318
claire.woodbine@ngs.org.uk

County Treasurer
Marie Tolhurst
marie.tolhurst@ngs.org.uk

Publicity
Laura Tucker
laura.tucker@ngs.org.uk

Social Media
Claire Wood 07921 153305
claire.wood@ngs.org.uk

Booklet Co-ordinator
Ian Gillbard 07969 440935
ian.gillbard@ngs.org.uk

Photographer
Keith Tucker
keith.tucker@ngs.org.uk

Visits by Arrangement
Caroline Cudmore 07484 172275
caroline.cudmore@ngs.org.uk

Assistant County Organisers
Sally Allen
sally.allen@ngs.org.uk

Kirsty Angwin
kirsty.angwin@ngs.org.uk

Kerensa Beer-Robson 07826 830068
kerensa.beer-robson@ngs.org.uk

Peter Brandreth 07745 514826
peter.brandreth@ngs.org.uk

Caroline Cudmore (see above)

Sue Gregory 07919 404333
sue.gregory@ngs.org.uk

Ian Gillbard (see above)

Sorcha Hitchcox
sorcha.hitchcox@ngs.org.uk

Libby Pidcock 01208 821305
libby.pidcock@ngs.org.uk

Graham Sykes 07719 711683
graham.sykes@ngs.org.uk

@CornwallNGS
@cornwall.ngs

OPENING DATES

All entries subject to change.
For latest information check
www.ngs.org.uk
Extended openings are shown at the beginning of the month.
Map locator numbers are shown to the right of each garden name.

March

Thursday 19th
Trevina House 65
Friday 20th
Trevina House 65
Monday 30th
Lower Tregamere 32
Tuesday 31st
Lower Tregamere 32

April

Every Wednesday from Wednesday 22nd
Polventon 44
Wednesday 1st
Lower Tregamere 32
Sunday 12th
Heycroft 21
Rose Morran 48
Thursday 16th
Trevina House 65
Friday 17th
Trevina House 65
Sunday 19th
Higher Locrenton 22
The Old School House 38
Pinsla Garden 42
Monday 20th
◆ Pencarrow 40
Saturday 25th
◆ Chygurno 11
Sunday 26th
◆ Chygurno 11
Tuesday 28th
Pinsla Garden 42
Wednesday 29th
Pinsla Garden 42

May

Every Sunday
NEW Caudworthy Park 10
Every Wednesday
Polventon 44
Saturday 2nd
Trelan 57
Sunday 3rd
East Down Barn 14
The Lodge 29
Navas Hill House 36
Monday 4th
Boconnoc 4
Wednesday 6th
NEW Lanjeth Nursery & Water Gardens 27
Thursday 7th
Pinsla Garden 42
Friday 8th
Pinsla Garden 42
Saturday 9th
◆ The Japanese Garden 24
Sunday 10th
Fan Cottage 16
Heycroft 21
Trebartha Estate Garden and Lemarne Garden 55
Thursday 14th
Trevina House 65
Friday 15th
Trevina House 65
Saturday 16th
The Old Vicarage 39
Sunday 17th
Higher Locrenton 22
Tuesday 19th
Pinsla Garden 42
Wednesday 20th
Pinsla Garden 42
Sunday 24th
NEW Bareppa 3
Lametton Mill 26
Wednesday 27th
Lametton Mill 26
Friday 29th
Bucks Head House Garden 7
Sunday 31st
Boscrowan 6

NEW Lower Tor House	31
NEW Mitchell Fruit Garden	35
Trebartha Estate Garden and Lemarne Garden	55

June

Every Sunday to Sunday 14th
NEW Caudworthy Park	10

Every Wednesday
Polventon	44

Wednesday 3rd
◆ Kestle Barton	25

Friday 5th
South Bosent	53

Saturday 6th
NEW Nellies Cottage	37
South Bosent	53
Trelan	57

Sunday 7th
NEW Nellies Cottage	37
Trevesco	63
Trevilley	64

Tuesday 9th
Pinsla Garden	42

Wednesday 10th
◆ Kestle Barton	25
Pinsla Garden	42

Thursday 11th
◆ Prideaux Place	47

Saturday 13th
Gardens Cottage	19

Sunday 14th
Alverton Cottage	1
Caervallack	9
Crugsillick Manor	13
Higher Locrenton	22

Wednesday 17th
◆ Kestle Barton	25

Thursday 18th
Trevina House	65

Friday 19th
9 Higman Close	23
South Bosent	53
Trevina House	65

Saturday 20th
9 Higman Close	23
South Bosent	53

Sunday 21st
Anvil Cottage	2
Heycroft	21
Rose Morran	48

Tuesday 23rd
Pinsla Garden	42

Wednesday 24th
◆ Kestle Barton	25
Pinsla Garden	42

Friday 26th
Bucks Head House Garden	7
Gardens Cottage	19

Saturday 27th
The Old Vicarage	39
Polruan Gardens	43
◆ Roseland House	49

Sunday 28th
Firste Park	17
Lametton Mill	26
Polruan Gardens	43
◆ Roseland House	49
NEW Sliggon Field	52

Monday 29th
NEW Sliggon Field	52

July

Wednesday 1st
◆ Kestle Barton	25
Lametton Mill	26

Friday 3rd
9 Higman Close	23
South Bosent	53

Saturday 4th
9 Higman Close	23
South Bosent	53

Sunday 5th
Pinsla Garden	42

Monday 6th
Pinsla Garden	42

Wednesday 8th
◆ Kestle Barton	25

Saturday 11th
NEW Nellies Cottage	37

Sunday 12th
Higher Locrenton	22
NEW Nellies Cottage	37

Wednesday 15th
◆ Kestle Barton	25

Thursday 16th
Trevina House	65

Friday 17th
9 Higman Close	23
South Bosent	53
Trevina House	65

Saturday 18th
◆ Chygurno	11
NEW 6 Clease Meadows	12
9 Higman Close	23
South Bosent	53

Sunday 19th
◆ Chygurno	11

Wednesday 22nd
◆ Kestle Barton	25
NEW Lanjeth Nursery & Water Gardens	27

Sunday 26th
Byeways	8
Lametton Mill	26

Wednesday 29th
◆ Kestle Barton	25
Lametton Mill	26

Friday 31st
Bucks Head House Garden	7

August

Wednesday 5th
Caervallack	9
◆ Kestle Barton	25

Friday 7th
9 Higman Close	23
South Bosent	53

Saturday 8th
9 Higman Close	23
South Bosent	53

Wednesday 12th
◆ Bonython Manor	5
◆ Kestle Barton	25

Sunday 16th
NEW Bareppa	3
Fan Cottage	16

Wednesday 19th
◆ Kestle Barton	25

Sunday 23rd
Rose Morran	48

Wednesday 26th
◆ Kestle Barton	25

Friday 28th
Bucks Head House Garden	7

Sunday 30th
Gardens Cottage	19
9 Higman Close	23
Lametton Mill	26
South Bosent	53

Monday 31st
9 Higman Close	23
South Bosent	53

September

Wednesday 2nd
◆ Kestle Barton 25
Lametton Mill 26

Saturday 5th
NEW Mitchell Fruit Garden 35

Sunday 6th
Boscrowan 6
NEW Mitchell Fruit Garden 35

Tuesday 8th
NEW Tresillian House 61

Wednesday 9th
◆ Kestle Barton 25

Wednesday 16th
◆ Kestle Barton 25
Trevina House 65

Thursday 17th
Trevina House 65

Wednesday 23rd
◆ Kestle Barton 25

Wednesday 30th
◆ Kestle Barton 25

October

Thursday 15th
Trevina House 65

Friday 16th
Trevina House 65

Sunday 18th
Trebartha Estate Garden and Lemarne Garden 55

February 2027

Sunday 21st
Heycroft 21

By Arrangement

Arrange a personalised garden visit with your club, or group of friends, on a date to suit you. See individual garden entries for full details.

Alverton Cottage 1
Boscrowan 6
Bucks Head House Garden 7
Caervallack 9
Crugsillick Manor 13
East Down Barn 14
Ethnevas Cottage 15
Fan Cottage 16
Firste Park 17
Garden Cottage 18
Gardens Cottage 19
Gwrythia 20
Heycroft 21
Higher Locrenton 22
Lametton Mill 26
NEW Little Mermaid, 27 Haddon Way 28
NEW Lower Tor House 31
Lower Tregamere 32
Malibu 33
Meanders 34
Navas Hill House 36
Pendower House 41
Polventon 44
Port Navas Chapel 45
Rose Morran 48
Secret Garden 51
Towan House 54
Trebarvah Woon 56
Trelan 57
Tremichele 58
Tremorran & The Angel 59
Tresithney 62
Trevilley 64
Trevina House 65

Gardens Cottage
© Keith Tucker

THE GARDENS

1 ALVERTON COTTAGE
Alverton Road, Penzance, TR18 4TG. David & Lizzie Puddifoot, 07985 735376, david.puddifoot@gmail.com. *Next door to YMCA. About 600 metres from Penlee car park travelling towards A30. Morrab Gardens are also close to car park.* **Sun 14 June (2-6). Adm £5, chd free. Tea, coffee & cake.** Visits also by arrangement 7 June to 5 July for groups of 10 to 20. Teas at £5.00 need to be booked in advance.
Alverton Cottage is a Grade II listed Regency house. The garden is modest in size though large for a Penzance garden, south facing and sheltered by mature trees. There is a large monkey-puzzle tree, a holm oak and many other trees. The garden was laid out in the 1860s. We have added succulents, a wildlife pond, a fernery, magnolias and have cleared and replanted since 2013. Off road disabled parking but wheelchair to garden terrace only.

2 ANVIL COTTAGE
South Hill, PL17 7LP. Barbara Clemerson. *3m NW of Callington. Head N on A388 from Callington centre. After ½ m L onto South Hill Rd (signed South Hill), straight on for 3m. Gardens on R just before St Sampson's Church.* **Sun 21 June (1.30-5). Adm £6, chd free. Tea, coffee & cake.** Refreshments served next door at Windmills. Gluten free available.
Essentially, this is a plantsman's garden. Winding paths lead through a series of themed rooms with familiar, rare and unusual plants. Steps lead up to a raised viewpoint looking west towards Caradon Hill and Bodmin Moor. Other paths take you on a circular route through a rose garden, hot beds, a tropical area and a secret garden. In the rose garden there is a new flower bed with wildlife pond.

3 NEW BAREPPA
St Winnow, Lostwithiel, PL22 0LG. Joe Flynn & Cheryl Turner. *what3words app: achieving.earlobes.drummers Take A390 to Lostwithiel, follow signs to Lerryn. 2nd St Winnow turn R next to post box. Bareppa 50 yards on L.* **Sun 24 May, Sun 16 Aug (11-3). Adm £5. Tea, coffee & cake.**
The garden contains established shrubs and trees, herbaceous borders, wildlife pond, ha-ha, lawns, fruit and vegetables and an orchard. Facing south, the garden enjoys full sun with views over to Ethy Woods. The garden is on two levels divided by the ha-ha which is the back drop to herbaceous beds for roses and climbers. Paved paths allow access to the majority of the garden and animal areas. WC with wheelchair access.

4 BOCONNOC
Lostwithiel, PL22 0RG. Fortescue Family, 01208 872507, events@boconnoc.com, www.boconnoc.com. *Off A390 between Liskeard & Lostwithiel. From East Taphouse follow signs to Boconnoc. Do not rely on SatNav, follow directions on Boconnoc website.* **Mon 4 May (2-5). Adm £8, chd free. Tea in stable yard.**
20 acres surrounded by parkland and woods with magnificent trees, flowering shrubs and stunning views. The gardens are set amongst mature trees which provide the backcloth for exotic spring flowering shrubs, woodland plants, with newly planted magnolias and a fine collection of hydrangeas. Features inc Georgian Bath House built in 1804, obelisk built in 1771, house dating from Domesday, deer park and C15 church.

5 ♦ BONYTHON MANOR
Cury Cross Lanes, Helston, TR12 7BA. Mr & Mrs Richard Nathan, 01326 240550, sbonython@gmail.com, www.bonythonmanor.co.uk. *5m S of Helston. On main A3083 Helston to Lizard Rd. Turn L at Cury Cross Lanes (Wheel Inn). Entrance 300yds on R.* **For NGS: Wed 12 Aug (2-4). Adm £13, chd £2. Tea, coffee, fruit juices and home-made cakes.** For other opening times and information, please phone, email or visit garden website.
Magnificent 20 acre colour garden inc sweeping hydrangea drive to Georgian manor (not open). Herbaceous walled garden, potager with vegetables and picking flowers; 3 lakes in valley planted with ornamental grasses, perennials and South African flowers. A 'must see' for all seasons colour.

6 BOSCROWAN
Heamoor, Penzance, TR20 8UJ. David & Elizabeth Harris, 01736 332396, elizabeth@boscrowan.co.uk, www.boscrowan.co.uk. *1m NW of Penzance. Leaving the A30 r'about signed to Heamoor, continue through Heamoor to the end & turn R into Josephs Lane. ¼ m down turn L up Bone Valley & Boscrowan turning is 200yds on L.* **Sun 31 May, Sun 6 Sept (1-5). Adm £6, chd free. Light refreshments.** Visits also by arrangement May & June.
Boscrowan sits in a sheltered valley, surrounded by mature trees. The 1½ acre garden area features herbaceous borders, a formal front garden, large pond, a willow walk, orchard and gardens in the two holiday cottages. Also an antique revolving 'Boulton and Paul' summerhouse, vegetable and flower cutting area and granite boulder garden. Emphasis on wildlife friendly plants and changing climate.

7 BUCKS HEAD HOUSE GARDEN
Trengove Cross, Constantine, TR11 5QR. Deborah Baker, 07801 444916, deborah.fwbaker@gmail.com, www.instagram.com/bucks_head_garden. *5m SW of Falmouth. A394 towards Helston, L at Edgcumbe towards Gweek/Constantine. Proceed for 0.8m then L towards Constantine. Further 0.8m, garden on L at Trengove Cross.* **Fri 29 May, Fri 26 June, Fri 31 July, Fri 28 Aug (2-4.30). Adm £6, chd free. Tea, coffee & cake.** Visits also by arrangement 8 May to 25 Sept for groups of up to 20.
Enchanting cottage and woodland gardens of native and rare trees, shrubs and perennials, encouraging biodiversity. The site of 1½ acres is on a south facing Cornish hillside with panoramic views. Protected by essential windbreak hedging, the inspiring collection of plants has been chosen to create an intriguing woodland garden and increase biodiversity. During the summer months art works will be on display.

8 BYEWAYS
Dunheved Road, Launceston, PL15 9JE. Tony Reddicliffe. *Launceston town centre. 100yds from multi-storey car park past offices of Cornish & Devon Post into Dunheved Rd, 3rd bungalow on R.* **Sun 26 July (1-5.30). Adm £5, chd free. Light refreshments.**
Small town garden developed over 14 yrs by enthusiastic amateur gardeners. Herbaceous borders, rockery. Tropicals inc bananas, gingers and senecio. Stream and water features. Roof garden. Japanese inspired tea house and courtyard. Redeveloped area features Japanese inspired planting. Sunken area with planting. Fig tree and Pawlonia flank area giving secluded seating. Living pergola. Ongoing change.

9 CAERVALLACK
St Martin, Helston, TR12 6DF. Matt Robinson & Louise McClary, 07795 560907, studiolouisemcclary@gmail.com, www.mattrobinsonarchitecture.co.uk. *5m SE of Helston. Go through Mawgan village, over 2 bridges, past Gear Farm Shop; go past turning on L, garden next farmhouse on L. Parking is in field opp entrance for June opening. Limited parking in August at house.* **Sun 14 June (1.30-4). Adm £6, chd free. Cream teas. Wed 5 Aug (10.30-5). Combined adm with Kestle Barton £8, chd free. Home-made teas on June 14th only.** Visits also by arrangement 30 Apr to 9 Sept for groups of up to 30.
2 acre romantic garden arranged into rooms, the collaboration between an artist and an architect. Colour and form of plants structured by topiary, hedging and contemporary Arts & Crafts cob walls. Grade II listed farmhouse, courtyard and ancient well. Scented roses and borders. Water features, ponds and curved steps. 54ft. covered bridge to wildflower meadow. 31 yrs in the making. Coppice and wildflower meadow; mature orchard and vegetable plot. Topiary & figurative sculpture throughout. Wheelchair access to some of the front garden (brick paths, gravel & grass), Courtyard garden & wildflower meadow. Ramp access up 2 steps to begin.

10 NEW CAUDWORTHY PARK
Maxworthy, Launceston, PL15 8LZ. Victoria Gould. *Located in the lower part of Maxworthy in between Caudworthy Bridge & Maxworthy Chapel. What3words app: throat.pebbles.awakes.* **Every Sun 3 May to 14 June (12-5). Adm £5, chd free. Light refreshments.**
A naturalistic garden with ancient and newly planted trees, ponds, hardy perennial beds, established borders and a no-dig vegetable garden. An orchard and wildflower meadows support wildlife, while rewilding areas increase biodiversity. The garden balances productive growing with sustainable, diverse habitats.

11 ♦ CHYGURNO
Lamorna, TR19 6XH. Dr & Mrs Robert Moule, 01736 732153, rmoule010@btinternet.com. *4m S of Penzance. Off B3315. Follow signs for Lamorna Cove, take the R fork in the road before the Wink pub. The garden is at the top of the hill on the L.* **For NGS: Sat 25, Sun 26 Apr, Sat 18, Sun 19 July (2-5). Adm £5, chd free.** For other opening times and information, please phone or email.
Beautiful, unique, 3 acre cliffside garden overlooking Lamorna Cove. Planting started in 1998, mainly southern hemisphere shrubs and exotics with hydrangeas, camellias and rhododendrons. Woodland area with tree ferns set against large granite outcrops. Garden terraced with steep steps and paths. Plenty of benches so you can take a rest and enjoy the wonderful views.

12 NEW 6 CLEASE MEADOWS
Camelford, PL32 9PH. Lynn Peacock. *3m S Boscastle. A39 from Wadebridge ½ m past Esso garage turn L onto Clease Rd, 1st L onto Clease Meadows, car park on the L. House 50 yds across the road.* **Sat 18 July (11-5). Adm £6, chd £2. Tea, coffee & cake.**
A garden started in 2023, cottage garden style, with wildlife pond, fernery and rewilding area with a dead hedge. A mound leads to a willow wigwam and there are meandering paths with arches throughout. A central circular brick patio is a lovely place to sit and take in the view.

13 CRUGSILLICK MANOR
Ruan High Lanes, Truro, TR2 5LJ. Dr Alison Agnew & Mr Brian Yule, 07538 218201, alisonagnew@icloud.com. *12m SE of Truro. On Roseland Peninsula. Turn off A390 Truro-St Austell road onto A3078 towards St Mawes. Approx 5m after Tregony turn 1st L after Ruan High Lanes towards Veryan, garden is 200yds on R.* **Sun 14 June (11-5). Adm £7, chd free. Tea, coffee, soft drinks, cakes & light lunches.** Visits also by arrangement May to Oct for groups of 15+.
2 acre garden, substantially re-landscaped and planted, mostly over last 15 yrs. To the side of the C17/C18 house, a wooded bank drops down to a walled kitchen garden and hot garden. In front, sweeping yew hedges and paths define oval lawns and broad mixed borders. On a lower terrace, the focus is a large pond and the planting is predominantly exotic flowering trees and shrubs. Wheelchair access to the central level of the garden, the house and cafe. Garden is on several levels connected by fairly steep sloping gravel paths.

14 EAST DOWN BARN
Menheniot, Liskeard, PL14 3QU. David & Shelley Lockett, 07803 159662, davidandshelleylockett@btinternet.com. *S side of village nr cricket ground. Turn off A38 at Hayloft restaurant/railway stn junction & head towards Menheniot village. Follow NGS signs from sharp LH bend as you enter village.* **Sun 3 May (1-4.30). Adm £4, chd free. Home-made teas.** Visits also by arrangement 1 Apr to 29 May for groups of 12 to 30.
Garden laid down between 1986-1991 with the conversion of the barn into a home and covers almost ½ acre of east sloping land with stream running north-south acting as the easterly boundary. 3 terraces before garden starts to level out at the stream. Garden won awards in the early years under the stewardship of the original owners.

15 ETHNEVAS COTTAGE
Constantine, Falmouth, TR11 5PY. Lyn Watson, 01326 340076, ethnevas@outlook.com. *6m SW of Falmouth. Nearest main roads A39, A394. Follow signs for Constantine.*

At lower village sign, at bottom of winding hill, turn off on private lane. Garden $3/4$ m up hill. **Visits by arrangement for groups of up to 20. Adm £6, chd free. Home-made teas.**
Isolated granite cottage in 2 acres. Intimate flower and vegetable garden. Bridge over stream to large pond and primrose path through semi-wild bog area. Hillside with grass paths among native and exotic trees. Many camellias and rhododendrons. Mixed shrubs and herbaceous beds, wildflower glade, spring bulbs. A garden of discovery with hidden delights.

16 FAN COTTAGE
Piggy Lane, Lerryn, Lostwithiel, PL22 0PT. Lin Briggs, robetlin@btopenworld.com. *3m from Lostwithiel. Park in council car park (free). Turn R up hill, continue past pub (approx 50yds). Turn R under Bluebell Cottage. Continue on Piggy Lane to end (approx 50yds). Fan Cottage is on R.* **Sun 10 May, Sun 16 Aug (10-5). Adm £5, chd free.** Visits also by arrangement 10 May to 16 Aug for groups of 6 to 15. Refreshments can be bought at pub or shop near car park for picnic in garden.
A 1 acre garden in a stunning setting with views over the Lerryn River. Divided into different parts there is much to interest visitors inc raised vegetable patches, fruit and apple trees, greenhouses, shrubberies and borders, a wildlife pond, and a bonsai display. Plenty of seating and places to relax. Regret no dogs. Picnics welcome or refreshments can be bought at nearby pub or shop and brought into garden for consumption. Some, but not all, of the garden is accessible by wheelchair.

17 FIRSTE PARK
Winsor Lane, Kelly Bray, Callington, PL17 8HD. Mrs Tina Monahan, 07866 997753, tina@firstepark.co.uk. *From Callington towards Kelly Bray, just before Swingletree pub, turn R into Station Rd, about $1/4$ m Firste Park is on the L top of Winsor Lane. Parking signed in adjoining field.* **Sun 28 June (11-3.30). Adm £5, chd free. Tea, coffee & cake.** Visits also by arrangement June to Sept.
1950s house with mature trees, flower gardens established about 5 yrs ago

with just over 1 acre incorporating a waterfall, pond and lawned areas. Packed with many plants and shrubs inc over 100 named roses, several varieties of hydrangeas and perfumed plants in abundance. There is an outside kitchen area, pergolas, a fruit and vegetable garden with cut flowers which we also use for dried flowers. Most of the garden is accessible but some gravel pathways.

18 GARDEN COTTAGE
Gunwalloe, Helston, TR12 7QB. Dan & Beth Tarling, 01326 241906, bethgunwalloe@gmail.com, www.instagram.com/seaview_gunwalloe/?hl=en. *Just beyond Halzephron Inn at Gunwalloe. Cream cottage with green windows.* **Visits by arrangement 1 Jan to 1 Dec. Adm £5, chd £5.**
Coastal cottage garden. Small garden with traditional cottage flowers, vegetable garden, greenhouse and meadow with far-reaching views. Collection of English terracotta pots.

19 GARDENS COTTAGE
Prideaux, St Blazey, PL24 2SS. Sue & Roger Paine, 07786 367610, sue.newton@btinternet.com, en-gb.facebook.com/gardenscottageprideaux. *1m from railway Xing on A390 in St Blazey. Turn into Prideaux Rd opp Gulf petrol station in St Blazey (signed Luxulyan). Proceed $1/2$ m. Turn R (signed Luxulyan Valley and Prideaux) & follow yellow signs.* **Sat 13 June (2-5). Home-made teas. Fri 26 June (2-5). Cream teas. Sun 30 Aug (2-5). Home-made teas. Adm £7, chd free. Selection of home-made cakes.** Visits also by arrangement 25 May to 28 Aug for groups of 10 to 30. Talk & tour offered as part of visit.
A stunning landscape and a variety of planting styles define this country garden. Formal and informal areas are enhanced with sculpture, and with its abundant herbaceous borders, dry terraces, courtyard garden, woodland glade, damp garden, beehives, orchard, fruit garden and a productive (and beautiful) kitchen garden it's a plot that feels much bigger than its one and a half acres. Check our Facebook page for special events.

20 GWRYTHIA
Sancreed, Penzance, TR20 8QS. Maggie Feeny, 07840 288916, maggiefeeny@yahoo.com, www.maggiefeeny.co.uk. *4m W of Penzance. From Penzance take A30 to Lands End, at Drift go R at Xrds to Sancreed. Go $1 1/2$ m, past Sancreed sign take 1st L up track for Gwrythia.* **Visits by arrangement 6 June to 23 Aug for groups of 8 to 20. Adm £6, chd free. No refreshments on sale, picnics welcome. Plenty of seating provided.**
A 3 acre garden with meadows, wildlife ponds, mixed ornamental borders of grasses, perennials, shrubs and roses. Walk through an established hornbeam hedge arch, into a vegetable garden, onto an artist's studio, down through a small woodland, into a meadow with large wildlife pond. Gwrythia is gardened organically, with plants chosen for both their attraction to wildlife and plant lovers alike. Maggie Feeny, an established artist and teacher, will open her beautiful meadow studio if requested during an arranged visit. You will also see her ceramics and resin sculptures dotted about the land.

21 HEYCROFT
Trevanion Road, Wadebridge, PL27 7NZ. Joanna Milner, botanyjo@gmail.com. *South side of town past the cinema. Follow yellow signs from the centre of town by the cinema. Parking is in Trevanion Park & Trevanion Close. Entrance to garden is via New Park.* **Sun 12 Apr (1-5), open nearby Rose Morran. Sun 10 May (1-5). Sun 21 June (1-5), open nearby Rose Morran. Adm £5, chd free. 2027: Sun 21 Feb.** Visits also by arrangement 14 Feb to 31 July for groups of 5 to 10. Tea, coffee and cake also by arrangement.
A small town garden divided into many different areas. Packed with many interesting features inc a pond, a very small (but proper) meadow, wisteria and fern tunnel, rockery, greenhouse, vegetable plot and some unusual plants. Developed over the last 15 yrs but still very much an ongoing project. The garden is on 2 levels with the front half only accessible by steps.

22 HIGHER LOCRENTON

St Keyne, Liskeard, PL14 4RN. Ade & Elise Allen, 01579 342301, adelise.allen@btinternet.com. Nr St Keyne Well, between Looe & Liskeard. By St Keyne Church, take the lane to St Keyne Well for ½ m. Turn L at Well. Higher Locrenton is 100 yds on R. Parking for 8 cars. **Sun 19 Apr, Sun 17 May, Sun 14 June, Sun 12 July (2-5). Adm £6, chd free. Tea, coffee & cake £3 per person. Visits also by arrangement 30 Mar to 26 Sept for groups of 8 to 25. Groups can park up to12 cars if double parked. Coaches need to park at St Keyne.** The garden is set in 2 acres on a hillside. It has been developed over the past 30 yrs and is part parkland, part 'plantsman' in style, featuring a wide variety of trees, shrubs and perennials. It is informally divided into a number of themed beds. A key aim has been to provide year-round interest in terms of atmosphere, form, colour and scent. Some parts of the garden can only be accessed via steps or somewhat steep gradients.

23 9 HIGMAN CLOSE

Dobwalls, Liskeard, PL14 4LW. Jim Stephens & Sue Martin. *3m W of Liskeard. From double mini-r'about in Dobwalls village take road to Duloe, take 2nd R onto Treheath Road, then 1st R into Higman Close.* **Fri 19, Sat 20 June, Fri 3, Sat 4, Fri 17, Sat 18 July, Fri 7, Sat 8, Sun 30, Mon 31 Aug (2-5.30). Combined adm with South Bosent £8, chd free. Home-made teas at South Bosent.** A constantly changing, multifaceted garden packed full of interesting plants but also colour, scent and form. Shady and sunny areas are exploited to the full and every effort made to create year-round interest. Sue's glasshouse is overflowing with cacti and succulents, some over 35 yrs old. All is on a scale readily relatable to small gardens. Both owners are retired horticulturalists. Regret no dogs.

24 ♦ THE JAPANESE GARDEN

St Mawgan, TR8 4ET. Natalie & Stuart Ellison, 01637 860116, info@japanesegarden.co.uk, www.japanesegarden.co.uk. *6m E of Newquay. St Mawgan village is directly below Newquay Airport. Follow brown & white road signs on A3059 & B3276.* For NGS: **Sat 9 May (10-6). Adm £6, chd £3. For other opening times and information, please phone, email or visit garden website.** Discover an oasis of tranquillity in a Japanese-style Cornish garden, set in approx 1 acre. Spectacular Japanese maples and azaleas, symbolic teahouse, koi pond, bamboo grove, stroll woodland, zen and moss gardens. A place created for contemplation and meditation. Adm free to gift shop, bonsai and plant areas. Refreshments available in the village a short walk from garden entrance. 90% wheelchair accessible, with some uneven, gravel paths.

25 ♦ KESTLE BARTON

Manaccan, Helston, TR12 6HU. Karen Townsend, 01326 231811, info@kestlebarton.co.uk, www.kestlebarton.co.uk. *10m S of Helston. Leave Helston on A3083 towards Lizard. At the r'about take 1st exit onto B3293 & follow signs towards St Keverne; after Trelowarren turn L and follow the brown signs for appprox 4m.* For NGS: **Every Wed 3 June to 29 July (10.30-5). Adm by donation. Wed 5 Aug (10.30-5). Combined adm with Caervallack £8, chd free. Every Wed 12 Aug to 30 Sept (10.30-5). Adm by donation. Modest Tea Room in garden. Cash only honesty box. Tea, coffee, cakes, ice creams, apple juice from our own orchards. For other opening times and information, please phone, email or visit garden website.** A delightful garden near Frenchmans Creek, on the Lizard, which is the setting for Kestle Barton Gallery; wildflower meadow, Cornish orchard with named varieties and a formal garden with prairie planting in blocks by James Alexander Sinclair. It is a riot of colour in summer and continues to delight well into late summer. Good wheelchair access and reasonably accessible WC. Dogs on leads welcome.

26 LAMETTON MILL

St Keyne, Liskeard, PL14 4SH. Mr Richard & Mrs Leigh Woods, 07812 103518, lamettonmill@btinternet.com, www.lamettonmill.co.uk. *The postcode is accurate, it is easier to come via Liskeard. Alternatively the St Keyne Wishing Well Halt railway stn is across the road. What3words app: access.motoring.nicknames.* **Sun 24, Wed 27 May, Sun 28 June, Wed 1, Sun 26, Wed 29 July, Sun 30 Aug, Wed 2 Sept (11-4). Adm £5, chd free. Tea, coffee & cake. Visits also by arrangement 24 May to 2 Sept for groups of 10 to 25. By arrangement adm inc tea & cake.** Nestled in the Looe Valley, the garden has been created from a wilderness. Although young it has been well planted with unusual trees and perennial plants for an abundance of colour year-round attracting bees and other pollinators. Highlights inc ITOH peonies, veronicastrums, sanguisorbas, hydrangeas and oaks, with areas planted for sun and shade. Many places to sit and enjoy the bird song.

SPECIAL EVENT

27 NEW LANJETH NURSERY & WATER GARDENS

Coombe Road, Lanjeth, St Austell, PL26 7TL. Steve Small, www.lanjeth.co.uk. *From St Austell A390 towards Newquay. A3058 through Trewoon. L to Coombe Rd & follow yellow signs. What3words app: wool.reminder.transmits.* **Wed 6 May, Wed 22 July (2-5). Adm £18, chd free. Pre-booking essential, please visit www.ngs.org.uk for information & booking. Cream teas inc in admission.** The Nursery & Water Gardens are designated as a County Wildlife Site as part of Lanjeth Heath. Stretching over 13½ acres, 130 ponds and lakes are being cleared and renovated by the current owners. Lakes and ponds are spring fed, ensuring pure ecology of each body of water where plants and wildlife flourish. As a natural wet land, water plants thrive: irises and lilies, marginals and oxygenators. A limited number of tickets are available for a private talk and tour of the gardens with one of the garden owners. The tour will start at 2pm in The Pavillion where everyone will meet for cordial/drinks. Cream tea to follow (included in the price).

CORNWALL

Secret Garden

© Keith Tucker

28 NEW LITTLE MERMAID, 27 HADDON WAY
Carlyon Bay, St Austell, PL25 3QG. Mr Peter & Mrs Tricia Howard, 07966 230222. *Directions will be provided when booking.* **Visits by arrangement 1 June to 4 Sept for groups of up to 8. Fridays only (2.30-4.30). Last adm at 3.30. Adm £5, chd free. Tea, coffee & cake.**
This new, medium sized, plant lovers garden, has been created by Tricia and Peter following their retirement from Hidden Valley Gardens near Par, which won the RHS Partner Garden of the Year in 2023. Winding paths lead through beds crammed with many treasures, inc a fern collection, dahlias and plants for pollinators. Central water feature, small pond and a bespoke greenhouse with veranda. Jeremey Hastings slate water feature in shape of Cornish Mine chimney. Many herbaceous plants. Countryside views from decking. Level access, apart from WC.

29 THE LODGE
Fletchersbridge, Bodmin, PL30 4AN. Mr Tony Ryde & Dr James Wilson. *2m E of Bodmin. From A38 at Glynn Crematorium r'about take road towards Cardinham & continue down to hamlet of Fletchersbridge. Park at Stable Art on R. Short walk to garden 1st R over river bridge.* **Sun 3 May (12-5). Adm £6, chd free. Cream teas. Also light lunches 12 noon till 2.30pm.**
3 acre riverside garden created since 1998, specialising in trees and shrubs chosen for their flowers, foliage and form, and embracing a Gothic lodge remodelled in 2016, once part of the Glynn estate. Water garden with ponds, waterfalls and abstract sculptures. Magnolias, camellias, prunus, davidias, paulownias, rhododendrons, azaleas, wisterias and bluebells abundant in early May. Wheelchair access to gravelled areas around house and along left side of garden.

30 ◆ THE LOST GARDENS OF HELIGAN
Pentewan, St Austell, PL26 6EN. Heligan Gardens Ltd, 01726 845100, heligan.reception@heligan.com, www.heligan.com. *5m S of St Austell. From St Austell take B3273 signed Mevagissey, follow signs.* **For opening times and information, please phone, email or visit garden website.**
Lose yourself in the mysterious world of The Lost Gardens where an exotic sub-tropical jungle, atmospheric Victorian pleasure grounds, an interactive wildlife project and the finest productive gardens in Britain all await your discovery. Wheelchair access to Northern gardens. Wheelchairs available at reception foc but pre booking advised due to limited number.

31 NEW LOWER TOR HOUSE

Warleggan, Mount, Bodmin, PL30 4HD. Allan Hirst, 07970 755316, allan.hirst@clmail.co.uk. *What3words app: mountain, foiled, harshest.* On A30 to Bodmin exit Warleggan, St Neot, Mount. Pass labyrinth turn R to Warleggan/Mount. We are 2nd house after cattle guard. From St Neot go to Califord Lake & turn L to Warleggan/Mount. From Mount turn at green library to go to Warleggan. **Sun 31 May (11-4). Adm £10, chd free. Tea, coffee & cake. Refreshments inc in admission.** Visits also by arrangement 3 June to 30 Sept. Wine & cheese can be provided in lieu of tea, coffee, cake.

Lower Tor House is a 20 acre oasis surrounded by Bodmin Moor with extensive walks and country wide views. The new gardens are in 2nd year of a 5 year project. Grounds include wildlife areas, pond, River Dewey, vegetable garden and access to greenhouse. There is ample seating and picnic facilities in a variety of areas. Dogs are welcome but must be kept on leads at all times. Steps and slopes limit wheelchair access to parts of garden.

♿ 🐕 ❋ ☕ 🪑

32 LOWER TREGAMERE

Tregamere, St Columb, TR9 6DN. Annette & Stuart Taylor, annette@kico.co.uk. *Approx 1m from St Columb Major. Take A30 to Indian Queens then A39 towards Wadebridge. 1½ m after Trekenning r'about turn R signed St Columb Major. After ½ m turn L signed Tregamere. Follow for ½ m. 1st L into drive after bridge.* **Mon 30, Tue 31 Mar, Wed 1 Apr (2-4). Adm £6, chd free.** Visits also by arrangement 4 May to 30 Sept for groups of up to 15.

An evolving 2½ acre garden. Bisected by a river, where English formal style juxtaposes with woodland and oriental styles. Walk through tall redwoods and past magnificent old oaks to take in many unusual trees and shrubs. Catch the cherry blossoms in late spring, the colourful acers, or the autumnal display of the Katsuras. Experience the air of tranquillity the garden evokes.

Sliggon Field

33 MALIBU
Tristram Cliff, Polzeath, Wadebridge, PL27 6TP. Nick Pickles, 07944 414006, nickdpickles@gmail.com. *Travel via Pityme/Rock/Trebetherick past Oystercatcher pub on L. Take 2nd L signed Tristram Caravan Park/ Cracking Crab Restaurant. Then L signed Tristram Cliff, up to end house. Free parking for coast & beach.* **Visits by arrangement for groups of up to 25. Hosted by keen cook a variety of refreshments/parties can be catered for. Adm £5, chd free. Cream teas, coffee, cakes & light lunches/ suppers offered by prior agreement.**
Yards away from the Coast Path, stunning views over the beach and headland, Malibu has a sheltered compact garden to the rear and a general interest front garden. A very interesting mix of features, different rockeries and strong focus on succulents, ferns and herbaceous plants. A greenhouse with many plants make this a rounded garden experience. Wheelchairs can access the front garden with ease. Rear garden can only be accessed with assistance. Ground floor WC available.

34 MEANDERS
St Nicholas Park, Lostwithiel, PL22 0BA. Chris & Sheila Marwood, 01208 872792, marwoodc1950@gmail.com. *Last house on St Nicholas Park. Off Bodmin Hill, 2nd L above Lostwithiel School. Parking at the property.* **Visits by arrangement 19 Apr to 17 May for groups of up to 10. Guided tour by owner on the legacy of the Lobb brothers. Adm £10, chd free. Tea, coffee and cake inc in adm.**
Over an acre on a south facing slope with far-reaching views. Predominantly a spring garden with maximum flowering during opening dates. Additional interest in trees and tender shrubs plus a 30ft cool glasshouse containing vireya rhododendrons and other southern hemisphere exotics. Apart from the driveway all access is via mown sloping grass with steps to half the garden.

35 NEW MITCHELL FRUIT GARDEN
Mitchell, Newquay, TR8 5BZ. Kerry Cheetham, www.mitchellfruitgarden.co.uk. *Just off the A30 at Mitchell village. Located on the slip road off the westbound carriageway. What3words app: dares.family.landowner.* **Sun 31 May (1-4). Adm £12, chd free. Pre-booking essential, please visit www.ngs.org.uk for information & booking. Sat 5, Sun 6 Sept (11-4). Adm £6, chd free. Tea, coffee & cake in the cafe (with % of proceeds to NGS).**
Nestled in the heart of Cornwall, our 1 acre sub-tropical garden is only 2 years old. Created by award winning garden designer, Kim Parish, in a former field, large beds are densely planted with an array of exotic specimens alongside more well known perennials, creating a sea of colour from late spring through to autumn. The fruit farm also offers a sunflower field, PYO soft fruits and cafe. On Sun 31 May, visitors can pre-book to join a special tour with expert talks starting at 1pm. Discover the fruit growing, cut flower beds and polytunnels. Followed by the art of rose growing with the Cornish Rose Company who share the site. Then visit the sub-tropical garden. Disabled parking spaces. Wide, but uneven paths around the site. Fruit tunnels not wheelchair accessible.

36 NAVAS HILL HOUSE
Bosanath Valley, Mawnan Smith, Falmouth, TR11 5LL. Aline & Richard Turner, 01326 251233, alineturner@btinternet.com. *1½m from Trebah & Glendurgan Gardens. Head through Mawnan Smith, past Trebah & Glendurgan Gardens then follow yellow signs. We suggest that you do not follow SatNav which tells you to turn R before Mawnan Smith.* **Sun 3 May (2-5). Adm £6, chd free. 'All you can eat' cream teas with home-made cake & scones served on the terrace £6. Visits also by arrangement 4 May to 16 May for groups of up to 25.**
8½ acre elevated valley garden with paddocks, woodland, kitchen garden and ornamental areas. The ornamental garden consists of 3 plantsman areas with specialist trees and shrubs, walled rose garden, water features and rockery. Young and established wooded areas with bluebells, camellia walks and 2 plantations of 10 yr old large leafed rhododendrons. Seating areas with views across wooded valley. There is plenty of parking at the property. There is usually some sort of musical entertainment around the tea area at about 3.30pm. Partial wheelchair access, some gravel and grass paths.

37 NEW NELLIES COTTAGE
Portlooe, Looe, PL13 2HY. Sandy Horton & James Howe. *Nr West Looe. A387 to Looe, turn R at sign Talland & Portlooe, bear L then 1st L past Portlooe Barton Farm (on R) then R down private rd OR from Harbour up West Looe Hill until road levels & turn L down private road.* **Sat 6, Sun 7 June, Sat 11, Sun 12 July (10.30-5.30). Adm £5, chd free. Tea, coffee & cake.**
A 2 acre sheltered south facing garden located in a 4 acre site inc woodland and mill pond ½ m from the sea. We started to create the terraced sloping garden on a bramble covered site around 2010 and it was a steep learning curve - it is a garden where lessons can be learnt! Owners' studio open (glass and painting).

38 THE OLD SCHOOL HOUSE
Averys Green, Cardinham, Bodmin, PL30 4EA. Mike & Libby Pidcock. *Edge of Cardinham village. A30 to Cardinham. Xrds in village towards church on R. Pass cemetery, and tennis court on L, 3rd house on R after tennis court. Parking Parish Hall opp church or at tennis court.* **Sun 19 Apr (11-5). Adm £5, chd free. Light refreshments. Open nearby Pinsla Garden.**
Cottage garden created in the grounds of a Victorian school by a passionate and enthusiastic gardener over 40 yrs. Not so much by design, but led by a love of plants and trying anything: herbaceous, annuals, bulbs, shrubs, trees, fruit cage, espalier apples, cut flower patch and some veg. Wildflower area, wildlife ponds, bird feeding stations, jungle corner, quirky containers. Plenty of seating.

39 THE OLD VICARAGE
Talland, PL13 2JA. Rachel James & Iain Doubleday, 07966 195378, oldvicaragetalland@gmail.com, instagram.com/oldvicaragetalland. Situated next to Talland Church & opp Talland Barton Farm. From Looe follow A387 towards Polperro for 1¼m & take L turn signed 'The Bay' & 'Tencreek'. Follow winding road for 1¼m. Entrance on L, just before Talland Church. **Sat 16 May, Sat 27 June (1-5). Adm £6, chd free. Tea, coffee & cake.**
Vibrant 4 acre south-facing coastal garden, with varied stunning vistas of Talland Bay, the ancient Talland Church and surrounding hills. Mature Monterey pines lead directly to the SW Coast Path. Restoring this historic churchyard garden has been an ongoing labour of love since 2018. Paths and some steep steps wind through terraced gardens, with seating to rest and enjoy the wonderful views. Special features inc large magnolia and copper beech, a small vineyard, and recreational facilities inc a tennis lawn, pétanque, and sand pit for younger children. New orchard in the churchyard garden. Main garden area around the house is accessed over gravel paths, with an accessible WC.

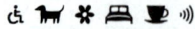

40 ♦ PENCARROW
Washaway, Bodmin, PL30 3AG. Molesworth-St Aubyn Family, 01208 841369, info@pencarrow.co.uk, www.pencarrow.co.uk. 4m NW of Bodmin. Signed off A389 & B3266. Free parking. **For NGS: Mon 20 Apr (10-5). Adm £11, chd free. Cream teas. The Peacock Cafe will be open all day. For other opening times and information, please phone, email or visit garden website.**
50 acres of tranquil, family-owned Grade II* listed gardens. Superb specimen conifers, azaleas, magnolias and camellias galore. Many varieties of rhododendron give a blaze of spring colour; blue hydrangeas line the mile-long carriage drive throughout the summer. Discover the Iron Age hill fort, lake, Italian gardens and granite rock garden. Dogs welcome, café and children's play area. Gravel paths, some steep slopes.

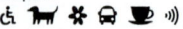

41 PENDOWER HOUSE
Lanteglos-by-Fowey, PL23 1NJ. Roger Lamb, 07860 391959, rl@rogerlamb.com. Nr Polruan off B3359 from East Taphouse. 2m from Fowey if using the Bodinnick ferry. Parking in NT Lantivet Bay car park. Yellow signs from B3359. **Visits by arrangement 15 June to 15 July for groups of up to 36. Adm £5, chd free.**
Set in the heart of Daphne du Maurier country in its own valley this established garden, surrounding a Georgian rectory, is now undergoing a revival having been wild and neglected for some years. It has formal herbaceous terraces, a cottage garden, orchard, ponds, streams and a C19 shrub garden with a fine collection of azaleas, camellias and rhododendrons plus rare mature specimen trees.

42 PINSLA GARDEN
Glynn, nr Cardinham, Bodmin, PL30 4AY. Mark & Claire Woodbine, www.pinslagarden.wordpress.com. 3½m E of Bodmin. From A30 or Bodmin take A38 towards Plymouth, 1st L at r'about, go past Crematorium & Cardinham Woods turning. Continue towards Cardinham village, up steep hill, 2m on R. **Sun 19 Apr (11-5), open nearby The Old School House. Tue 28, Wed 29 Apr, Thur 7, Fri 8, Tue 19, Wed 20 May, Tue 9, Wed 10, Tue 23, Wed 24 June, Sun 5, Mon 6 July (11-5). Adm £6, chd free.**
Surround yourself with deep nature. Pinsla is a tranquil cottage garden buzzing with insects enjoying the sheltered sunny edge of a wild wood. Lose yourself in an experimental tapestry of naturalistic growing and self seeding. There are lots of unusual planting combinations, cloud pruning, intricate paths, garden art and a stone circle. Sorry, no teas, but do bring a picnic, or use cafe close by. Partial wheelchair access as paths are bumpy, gravelled or narrow.

GROUP OPENING

43 POLRUAN GARDENS
Polruan, PL23 1PZ. Mrs Sue Rowe, sjsherwood2@gmail.com. A390 to East Taphouse. B3359 towards Looe. B3359 - Lanreath R to Lanteglos Highway. By old telephone box turn L at Whitecross. Park at St Saviour's pay car park (PL23 1PZ). Car or foot ferries from Fowey. Tickets, map, teas in Village Hall. **Sat 27, Sun 28 June (1-5). Combined adm £6, chd free. Cream teas.**
Polruan Gardens is a group of over 8 gardens dotted around our small, very hilly village. All have stunning views of the River Fowey estuary or sea. Our gardens show various styles of coastal planting and terracing to suit steep slopes and occasionally lots of steps! Woodland, ponds, roses, herbaceous borders, rhododendrons, summer planting, picnic areas and even a funicular railway and art studio.

44 POLVENTON
Fletchers Bridge, Bodmin, PL30 4AN. Mr & Mrs D Watson, 07816 967340. 2m E of Bodmin. From A30 > A38 Plymouth. At r'bout 1st L past Crematorium, stone bridge, sharp R bend, ignore L Cardinham Woods, continue 500yd Fletchers Bridge. Before Stable Arts, acute R turn. Polventon100yd on L. **Every Wed 22 Apr to 24 June (11-5). Adm £6, chd free. Pre-booking essential, please visit www.ngs.org.uk for information & booking. Tea, coffee & cake. Visits also by arrangement 22 Apr to 24 June for groups of up to 15.**
Interesting 1¼ acres bordered by woodland. A working garden with mixed and cut flower borders, hydrangea walk, stream and waterfall, bog garden fed by natural springs, mature rhododendrons, camellias and azaleas, bluebells, adolescent Japanese acers, ornamental and specimen shrubs, a peaceful woodland glade. Sloping areas, narrow paths, stout shoes recommended.

45 PORT NAVAS CHAPEL
Port Navas, Constantine, Falmouth, TR11 5RQ. Keith Wilkins & Linda World, 01326 341206, keithwilkins47@gmail.com. 2m E of Constantine, nr Falmouth. From the direction of Constantine village, we are the 2nd driveway on R after the 'Port Navas' village sign. **Visits by arrangement for groups of up to 25. Adm £6, chd free. Refreshments by prior arrangement.**
Japanese style garden set in ¾ acre of woodland, next to the old Methodist

Chapel, with ornamental ponds and waterfalls, rock formations, Tsukubai water feature, granite lanterns, woodland stream with bridges, geodesic dome and Zen garden. New additions and extensions are being added all the time, particularly Japanese garden features. We usually issue a quiz list to guests to find items around the garden. Wheelchair access to driveway and sloping grass areas, giving access to most areas of the garden.

46 ♦ POTAGER GARDEN
High Cross, Constantine, Falmouth, TR11 5RF. Mr Mark Harris, 01326 341258, enquiries@potagergarden.org, www.potagergarden.org. *5m SW of Falmouth. From Falmouth, follow signs to Constantine. From Helston, drive through Constantine & continue towards Falmouth.* **For opening times and information, please phone, email or visit garden website.**
Potager has emerged from the bramble choked wilderness of an abandoned plant nursery. With mature trees which were once nursery stock and lush herbaceous planting interspersed with fruit and vegetables Potager Garden aims to demonstrate the beauty of productive organic gardening. There are games to play, hammocks to laze in and boules and badminton to enjoy. Potager café serving vegetarian food all day.

47 ♦ PRIDEAUX PLACE
Tregirls Lane, Padstow, PL28 8RP. Mrs Elisabeth Prideaux-Brune, 01841 532411, office@prideauxplace.co.uk, prideauxplace.co.uk. *½m W of Padstow centre. Off A389 Wadebridge to Padstow road. Follow brown historic house signs.* **For NGS: Thur 11 June (10.30-4.30). Adm £5, chd free. Fully licensed cafe offering light lunches, cream teas etc. For other opening times and information, please phone, email or visit garden website.**
A garden of vistas, overlooking its ancient deer park and Camel Estuary to Bodmin Moor and beyond. The gardens suffered badly after the Second World War, but today's exciting and extensive restoration programme is well underway, bringing the gardens back to their former glory.

Mitchell Fruit Garden

48 ROSE MORRAN
Talskiddy, St Columb, TR9 6EB. Peter & Jenny Brandreth, 07711 517159, jennybrandreth@yahoo.com. *2 m N of St Columb Major. From A39 take Talskiddy/St Eval turn. Then take 2nd R signed Talskiddy & follow yellow NGS signs.* **Sun 12 Apr, Sun 21 June, Sun 23 Aug (2-5). Adm £6, chd free. Tea, coffee & cake. Visits also by arrangement 11 Apr to 30 Aug for groups of 12 to 30.**
Colour, shape and texture define this North Cornwall garden. The property and gardens extend to about an acre, with lawn, wild areas and Cornish hedges completing the 2 acre plot. Landscaped and planted over 12 yrs there is a mix of shrubs and trees interplanted with perennials to ensure year-round display. Vegetable beds and a polytunnel with tender plants make this a rounded garden visit. There are level areas to view and the whole garden is accessible via grass slopes but some are quite steep. There is one step to the inside WC.

49 ◆ ROSELAND HOUSE
Chacewater, TR4 8QB. Mr & Mrs Pridham, 01872 560451, charlie@roselandhouse.co.uk, www.roselandhouse.co.uk. *4m W of Truro. Park in village car park (100yds) or on surrounding roads.* **For NGS: Sat 27, Sun 28 June (1-5). Adm £5, chd free. Tea, coffee & cake.** For other opening times and information, please phone, email or visit garden website.
The 1 acre garden is a mass of summer colour in late June and July when the National collection of *Clematis viticella cvs* is in flower. Other climbing plants abound lending foliage, flower and scent. Situated in the garden is a specialist climbing plant nursery which along with a Victorian conservatory and greenhouse is open. The garden features two ponds and lots of seating areas. Some slopes.

SPECIAL EVENT

50 ◆ ST MICHAEL'S MOUNT
Marazion, TR17 0HS. James & Mary St Levan, 01736 887822, enquiries@stmichaelsmount.co.uk, www.stmichaelsmount.co.uk. *2½ m E of Penzance. ½m from shore at Marazion by Causeway.* For opening times and information, please phone, email or visit garden website or visit www.ngs.org for details of special pop-up opening date.
Infuse your senses with colour and scent in the unique sub-tropical gardens basking in the mild climate and salty breeze. Clinging to granite slopes the terraced beds tier steeply to the ocean's edge, boasting tender exotics from places such as Mexico, the Canary Islands and South Africa. This year the St Aubyn Family will be opening the gardens again, but pre-booking is essential. Please visit St Michael's Mount website for details of pop-up opening and the link to book online. Last entry to the garden is 4pm. Aeoniums, aloes and agave rear out of the bedrock, succulents appear from the flower beds basking in the sun. Salvias, tulbaghia and pelargoniums provide binding threads through the East and West Terraces and the Walled Gardens hold their own surprises.

51 SECRET GARDEN
Tresithick, Trispen, Truro, TR4 9AU. Alan & Caroline Rounsevell, 07890 738688, alangardencare. arg.arg@gmail.com. *A39 from Truro. Exit Trispen/St Erme & turn immed R. Follow signs to end of the road & yellow signs to lane leading to garden. What3words app: trickster.slumped. bitter.* **Visits by arrangement 4 July to 30 Aug for groups of up to 20. Adm £6, chd free.**
Lovingly created during lockdown, transformed from a rubbish dump! An upcycled garden hidden within enclosed walls of an old farm building. Colourful tropical planting of bananas, cannas, agapanthus etc propagated on site. Sunken stone fire-pit, Mediterranean bistro kitchen, unique pergolas. Nearby raised beds for fruit and vegetable and overflowing polytunnel. Wide flat paths suitable for wheelchairs.

52 NEW SLIGGON FIELD
Trebetherick, Wadebridge, PL27 6SB. Mr Julian Webb. *From Wadebridge to Trebetherick via Rock. In Trebetherick look for village shop on R, then after a small parade of shops the private drive to garden is 200yds on R. Parking limited in garden. Park outside shops or on L and short walk downhill.* **Sun 28, Mon 29 June (11-5). Adm £6, chd free. Light refreshments.**
The garden has several distinct areas and is set out on different levels which are all connected by a network of gravel pathways. The garden features herbaceous borders, a copse, lawns, mature bushes, tree ferns, raised beds for vegetables, a wild area and wood ferns.

53 SOUTH BOSENT
Liskeard, PL14 4LX. Adrienne Lloyd & Trish Wilson. *2½ m W of Liskeard. From r'about at junction of A390 & A38 take exit to Dobwalls. At mini-r'about, R to Duloe, after 1¼ m at Xrds turn R. Garden on L after ¼ m.* **Fri 5, Sat 6 June (2-5.30). Adm £5, chd free. Fri 19, Sat 20 June, Fri 3, Sat 4, Fri 17, Sat 18 July, Fri 7, Sat 8, Sun 30, Mon 31 Aug (2-5.30). Combined adm with 9 Higman Close £8, chd free. Home-made teas.**
This garden has been developed from farmland. The aim is to create a combination of interesting plants coupled with habitat for wildlife over a total of 9½ acres. There are several garden areas, woodland gardens, a meadow, ponds of varying sizes, inc a rill and waterfall. In spring, the bluebell wood trail runs alongside the stream. Main garden area accessible. No wheelchair access to bluebell wood due to steps.

54 TOWAN HOUSE
Old Church Road, Mawnan Smith, Falmouth, TR11 5HX. Mr Dave & Mrs Tessa Thomson, 01326 250378, tandd.thomson@ btinternet.com. *Approx 5m from Falmouth. On entering Mawnan Smith, fork L at the Red Lion pub. When you see the gate to Nansidwell, turn R into Old Church Rd. Follow NGS signs.* **Visits by arrangement 14 June to 13 Sept for groups of 5 to 20. Adm £6, chd free. Home-made teas.**
Towan House is a coastal garden with some unusual plants and views to St Mawes, St Anthony Head lighthouse and beyond with easy access to the SW coast path overlooking Falmouth Bay. It is approximately ¼ acre and divided into 2 gardens, one exposed to the north and east winds, the other sheltered allowing tropical plants to flourish such as Hedychium, fuchsias and cannas.

55 TREBARTHA ESTATE GARDEN AND LEMARNE GARDEN

Trebartha, nr North Hill, Launceston, PL15 7PD. **The Latham Family.** *6m SW of Launceston. Near junction of B3254 & B3257. What3words app: breathing.blown.zoomed. No coaches.* **Sun 10, Sun 31 May (2-5); Sun 18 Oct (1-4). Adm £10, chd free. Home-made teas.** Historic landscape gardens featuring streams, cascades, rocks and woodlands, with fine veteran and champion trees, bluebells, ornamental walled garden; also visit Lemarne garden en route. Allow at least an hour for a circular walk. Some steep and rough paths, which can be slippery when wet. Stout footwear advised.

56 TREBARVAH WOON

Seworgan, Constantine, Falmouth, TR11 5QN. **Paul & Vicky Bryant, 07407 415080, pandvbryant@msn.com.** *Off A394 between Falmouth & Helston. Access from A394. From Falmouth take L signed Constantine & Gweek after Edgecumbe, turning R to Seworgan after 1½m. From Helston take R marked Seworgan & Laity. Off Trebarvah Farm track.* **Visits by arrangement 8 May to 15 Aug for groups of up to 10. Visits on Mon, Tue, Wed, Fri & Sat. Tea, coffee, cake & scones.** A steeply sloping upper valley garden of just over 1 acre. The Helford stream forms a long lower boundary some of which is managed. The site is terraced and planted at several levels inc small cottage garden by conservatory. Azaleas, camellias, rhododendrons and magnolias enjoy the poor acid soil. The garden also contains vegetable beds, a wild area, a pond and a small wood.

57 TRELAN

Wharf Road, Lelant, St Ives, TR26 3DU. **Nick Williams, 07817 425157, nick@nickgwilliams.com.** *Close to St Uny Church, Lelant. Trelan Gardens are off Wharf Rd which leads to a car park on Dynamite Quay. Car park signed at the end of Wharf Rd & the gardens are 100m down on R.* **Sat 2 May, Sat 6 June (2-5). Adm £6, chd free. Tea, coffee & cake. Visits also by** arrangement 2 May to 30 Aug for groups of 8 to 20.

Trelan has a distinctly tropical feel. There is a swimming pond surrounded by lush vegetation, an Italianate sunken garden, a fern garden, numerous young trees and countless *Echium pininana*. There's also an echium root sculpture 'The avenue of tortured souls' and lots of pathways. It is a feast for the eyes!

58 TREMICHELE

Housel Bay, The Lizard, Helston, TR12 7PG. **Mike & Helen Painton, 01326 290108, paintonfam@btinternet.com.** *On the Lizard peninsular approx 10m from Helston. Follow directions to Lizard village. Park on the village green, parking is by voluntary contribution. Walk along Beacon Terrace & follow signs for Housel Bay Hotel.* **Visits by arrangement Apr to July for groups of up to 15. Adm £5, chd free. Light refreshments. Tea, coffee, cold drinks, home-made cake & cookies.**

A coastal garden, created in 2016, of approx 1 acre overlooking the Atlantic and the Lizard Lighthouse. It is a steep sloping garden divided into 3 terraces accessed by slopes or steps. A productive kitchen garden, with raised beds and fruit trees. Greenhouse and cold frames. A wildflower meadow with access to the coast path. Banks have a mix of planting inc hardy exotics.

59 TREMORRAN & THE ANGEL

Truthwall, St Just, Penzance, TR19 7QJ. **Annie & Martin Henry Holland, 07768 166309, missanniehenry@hotmail.com, www.tremorran.co.uk/tremorran-and-the-angel-gallery.html.** *Situated on the iconic B3306 coast road Lands End to St Ives ½m outside of St Just. Opp the Botallack sign. What3words app: column.crabmeat.remit.* **Visits by arrangement 1 Apr to 21 Sept for groups of up to 20. Adm £10, chd free. Home-made teas. Coffee & biscuits in the morning, tea & cake in the afternoon.**

Set in the grounds of Tremorran, a mine captain's house built in the early 1900s. A maze of paths lead to many 'rooms' furnished with seating and sculptures. A sloping pebble beach around the wildlife pond is planted with a variety of grasses and sea holly. Well-stocked borders contain trees, established shrubs, hydrangeas, rhododendrons, and herbaceous plants. Artist Studios & Gallery. Walk the Labyrinth and Sacred Stone Circle.

SPECIAL EVENT

60 ♦ TRESCO ABBEY GARDENS

Tresco, TR24 0QQ. **Mr R A Dorrien-Smith, 01720 424108, gardencafe@tresco.co.uk, www.tresco.co.uk.** *28m SW Lands End. You can fly to neighbouring St. Mary's from Lands End, Newquay or Exeter. You can also travel by helicopter to St Marys or Tresco or travel to St Marys by ferry from Penzance.* **For opening times and information, please phone, email or visit garden website or visit www.ngs.org for details of special pop-up opening date.**

Meander a myriad of winding paths through flowers of the King Protea and the handsome Lobster Claw, great blue spires of Echium, brilliant Furcraea, Strelitzia and shocking-pink drifts of Pelargonium. World renowned Tresco Abbey Garden is home to plants from every Mediterranean climate zone, flourishing just 28 miles off the coast of Cornwall. Augustus Smith established Tresco Abbey Garden in the C19 around the ruins of a Benedictine Abbey. Today, the garden is a sanctuary for some 2,000 specimens from across the southern hemisphere and subtropics, from Brazil to New Zealand; Myanmar to South Africa. Please visit www.ngs.org.uk for details of special pop-up event which will be pre booked tickets only. Garden café and shop usually open 10am - 4pm daily March till October. See garden website for updates.

Our donation in 2025 has enabled Parkinson's UK to fund 2 new nursing posts this year directly supporting people with Parkinson's.

Trelan

SPECIAL EVENT

61 NEW **TRESILLIAN HOUSE**
Kestle Mill, TR8 4PS. Duana Pearson - Head Gardener. *2m SE of Newquay. Opp Dairyland on A3058.* **Tue 8 Sept (2-5). Adm £18, chd free. Pre-booking essential, please visit www.ngs.org.uk for information & booking. Cream teas in The Barn inc in admission.** Tresillian gardens surround the house within 22 acres of lawns, woodlands, orchards, an ornamental lake, paths through camellia woods and a fine walled organic kitchen garden. Our speciality kitchen garden crops are uniquely grown by lunar cycle Moon Gardening. Historic National Collection of Cornish Heritage apple cultivars in main orchard; over 100 trees of 54 varieties, planted in early 1990s. A limited number of tickets are available for a talk and guided tour by Head Gardener, Duana Pearson. Please meet at 2pm. The tour will take in the walled gardens and surrounding estate. Cream teas served in the barn afterwards (inc in admission).

62 TRESITHNEY
Bowl Rock, Lelant, St Ives, TR26 3JE. Caroline Marwood, 07515 339400, carolinemarwood@me.com, www.facebook.com/Tresithney. *At Bowl Rock just off The Old Coach Rd between the A3074 & B3311. A garden on The St Michael's Way footpath between Carbis Bay & Trencrom Hill. Turn at Bowl Rock, between Lelant & St Ives. Marked with flag.* **Visits by arrangement May to July. Adm includes cream tea & depends on numbers agreed on booking.**
This is a unique 'Walking Garden' on the ancient St Michael's Way. The garden is approx 1½ acres with a variety of distinct areas, inc a rose garden, potager, fernery, orchard and wild areas. With beautiful views up to Trencrom Hill, an Iron Age Hill Fort. Artist studio will also be open. Partial wheelchair access by using main path through centre of garden.

63 TREVESCO
7 Commons Close, Mullion, Helston, TR12 7HY. Colin Read. *Situated on the W side of Mullion on the road to Poldhu Cove & Cury. ¼m from village centre car parks.* **Sun 7 June (11-4). Adm £5, chd free. Tea, coffee & cake.**
This ¼ acre garden has been established over 16 yrs in a subtropical style with rare unusual plants. Many tender plants have been established without winter protection very successfully due to local climate. These inc agaves, aloe, puya, aeoniums and different varieties of palm tree. There is also a pond and one feature olive tree. Also there is a separate fruit and vegetable garden.

64 TREVILLEY
Sennen, Penzance, TR19 7AH. Patrick Gale & Aidan Hicks, 07970 060401, trevilley@btinternet.com, www.galewarning.org/trevilley. *For walkers, Trevilley lies on the footpath from Trevescan to Polgigga & Nanjizal. On Open Day follow the signs into our parking field. If visiting by arrangement, check with us re parking. There may be scope to park coaches in Trevescan.* **Sun 7 June (1-5.30). Adm £6, chd free. Tea, coffee & cake. Visits also by arrangement in June for groups of 6+.**
As featured on BBC Gardeners' World, this eccentric, romantic and constantly evolving garden, as befits the intense creativity of its owners, has been carved out of an expanse of concrete farmyard over 20 yrs. Featuring an elaborate network of decorative cobbling, pools, container garden, vegetable garden, shade garden, the largely subtropical mowhay garden and both owners' studios, but arguably its glory is the westernmost walled rose garden in England. The garden visit can form the climax of enjoying the circular coast path walk from Land's End to Nanjizal and back across the fields. Visitors may leave their cars with us while they take a walk across the fields to Nanjizal or Trevescan (where there is sometimes a cafe). Dogs are welcome on leads.

65 TREVINA HOUSE
St Neot, Liskeard, PL14 6NR. Kevin & Sue Wright, 07428 102104, kevin@trevina.com, www.facebook.com/TrevinaInCornwall. *1m N of St Neot. From A38 turn off at Halfwayhouse pub. Head up hill to Goonzion Downs. Bear L & keep straight on towards Colliford Lake. From A30 take Colliford Lake/St Neot turning. Head towards St Neot.* **Thur 19, Fri 20 Mar, Thur 16, Fri 17 Apr, Thur 14, Fri 15 May, Thur 18, Fri 19 June, Thur 16, Fri 17 July, Wed 16, Thur 17 Sept, Thur 15, Fri 16 Oct (10.30-5). Adm £6, chd free. Visits also by arrangement. Please car share where possible as narrow access and limited parking.**
The gardens at Trevina are both old and new. From a Victorian cottage garden with original cobbled paths to rewilded woodland. A stream fed trout pond occupies the site of a medieval fish pond and the site of a Cornish Round. The gardens have colour and interest year-round, from the first snowdrops, bluebells, apple blossom and ripe apples in October. There is a traditional kitchen garden and organic orchard with spring bulbs. Wildflower meadow in season, woodland walks and bluebells in season.

Our 2025 donation to the Queen's Institute of Community Nursing now helps support over 3,500 Queen's Nurses working in the community in England, Wales, Northern Ireland, the Channel Islands and the Isle of Man.

CUMBRIA

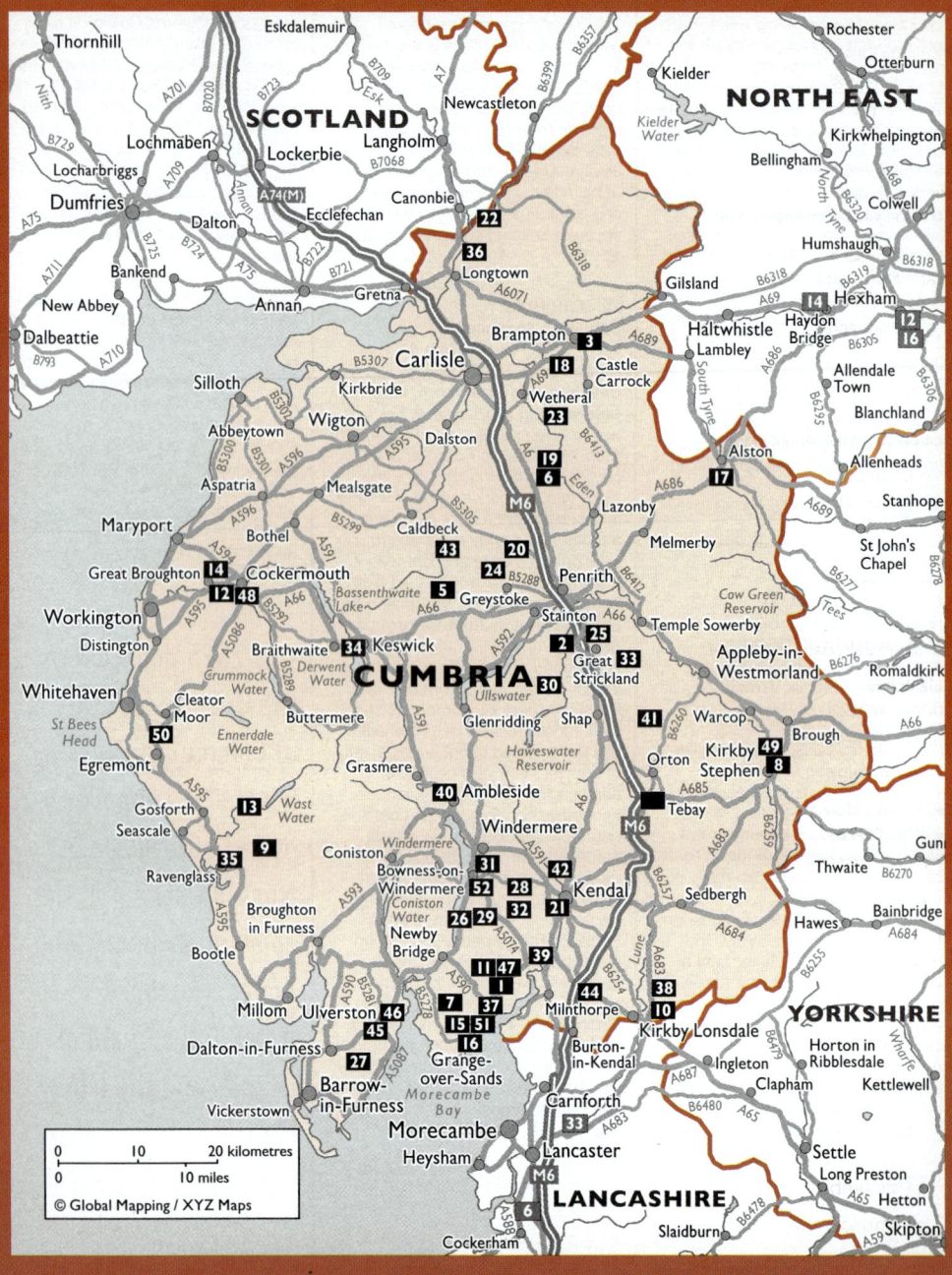

CUMBRIA

VOLUNTEERS

County Organiser
Cate Bowman
01228 573903
cate.bowman@ngs.org.uk

County Treasurer
Belinda Quigley
07738 005388
belinda.quigley@ngs.org.uk

Publicity – Social Media
Gráinne Jakobson
01946 813017
grainne.jakobson@ngs.org.uk

Booklet Co-ordinator
Cate Bowman
01228 573903
cate.bowman@ngs.org.uk

Assistant County Organisers
Carole Berryman
07808 974877
carole.berryman@outlook.com

Christine Davidson
07966 524302
christine.davidson@ngs.org.uk

Bruno Gouillon
01539 532317
brunog45@hotmail.com

Gráinne Jakobson (as above)

Liz Jolley
07948 472923
liz.jolley@ngs.org.uk

Belinda Quigley (as above)

Alannah Rylands
01697 320413
alannah.rylands@ngs.org.uk

@CumbriaNGS
@ngscumbria

OPENING DATES

All entries subject to change.
For latest information check
www.ngs.org.uk
Map locator numbers are shown to the right of each garden name.

March

Saturday 7th
◆ Swarthmoor Hall — 45

Sunday 8th
◆ Swarthmoor Hall — 45

Monday 30th
◆ Rydal Mount and Gardens — 40

Tuesday 31st
◆ Rydal Mount and Gardens — 40

April

Wednesday 1st
◆ Rydal Mount and Gardens — 40

Thursday 16th
NEW Netherwood Hotel — 37

Sunday 26th
Summerdale House — 44

May

Sunday 3rd
Low Fell West — 29

Monday 4th
Low Fell West — 29

Friday 8th
Low Crag — 28

Saturday 9th
Low Crag — 28

Sunday 10th
Low Crag — 28

Sunday 17th
Hazel Cottage — 19
NEW Leypits — 26
Matson Ground — 31

Wednesday 20th
Johnby Hall — 24

Saturday 23rd
Coombe Eden — 6
Galesyke — 13

Sunday 24th
Coombe Eden — 6
Galesyke — 13

Sunday 31st
Brampton East Gardens — 3

June

Monday 1st
◆ Rydal Mount and Gardens — 40

Tuesday 2nd
◆ Rydal Mount and Gardens — 40

Wednesday 3rd
◆ Rydal Mount and Gardens — 40

Saturday 6th
NEW Hylands House — 21

Sunday 7th
Hayton Village Gardens — 18
◆ Hutton-In-The-Forest — 20
Yewbarrow House — 51

Saturday 13th
◆ Swarthmoor Hall — 45

Sunday 14th
Hazel Cottage — 19
NEW Low Rough Hill — 30
◆ Swarthmoor Hall — 45

Wednesday 17th
Johnby Hall — 24

Saturday 20th
NEW ◆ Morland House Gardens — 33

Sunday 21st
Askham Hall — 2
Fernhill Coach House — 11
Ivy House — 23
Stewart Hill Cottage — 43
Vicarage House East — 47
Yews — 52

Wednesday 24th
NEW ◆ Morland House Gardens — 33

Saturday 27th
NEW Glaramara — 14
NEW The Mount — 34
The White House — 48

Sunday 28th
Grange over Sands Hidden Gardens — 16
NEW The Mount — 34
Ulverston Town & Country Gardens — 46

CUMBRIA

July

Saturday 4th
Crumble Cottages 7
Esk Bank 9

Sunday 5th
Crumble Cottages 7
Esk Bank 9
Hazel Cottage 19
NEW Little Urswick Village Gardens 27
Yewbarrow House 51

Thursday 9th
Larch Cottage Nurseries 25

Saturday 11th
Park House 38
School House 41
Woodend House 50

Sunday 12th
NEW Inch Farm 22
Park House 38
Woodend House 50

Sunday 19th
Winton Park 49

Saturday 25th
Eden Place 8

Sunday 26th
Eden Place 8

August

Every day from Sunday 16th to Sunday 23rd
Fell Yeat 10

Sunday 2nd
Yewbarrow House 51

Thursday 6th
Larch Cottage Nurseries 25

Saturday 8th
Galesyke 13

Sunday 9th
Abi and Tom's Garden Plants 1
Galesyke 13
Ivy House 23

Saturday 22nd
Middle Blakebank 32

Sunday 30th
Fell Yeat 10

Monday 31st
Fell Yeat 10
♦ Netherby Hall 36

September

Thursday 3rd
Larch Cottage Nurseries 25

Sunday 6th
Yewbarrow House 51

Saturday 12th
NEW Hylands House 21

By Arrangement

Arrange a personalised garden visit with your club, or group of friends, on a date to suit you. See individual garden entries for full details.

Chapelside 5
Crumble Cottages 7
Esk Bank 9
Foinhaven 12
Galesyke 13
Grange Fell Allotments 15
Grange over Sands Hidden Gardens 16
NEW Hartside Nursery Garden 17
Johnby Hall 24
Low Fell West 29
Matson Ground 31
NEW Muncaster Mill 35
Rose Croft 39
Sprint Mill 42
Stewart Hill Cottage 43
Woodend House 50
Yewbarrow House 51

Hylands House

CUMBRIA 107

THE GARDENS

1 ABI AND TOM'S GARDEN PLANTS
Halecat Garden Nursery, Witherslack, Grange-over-Sands, LA11 6RT. Abi & Tom Attwood, www.abiandtom.co.uk. 20 mins from Kendal. From A590 turn N to Witherslack. Follow brown tourist signs to Halecat. Rail Grange-Over-Sands 5m, Bus X6 2m, NCR 70. **Sun 9 Aug (10-5). Adm £5, chd free. Home-made teas.**

The 1 acre nursery garden is a fusion of traditional horticultural values with modern approaches to the display, growing and use of plant material. Our full range of perennials can be seen growing alongside one another in themed borders in the very shady damp corners or south facing hot spots. The propagating areas, stock beds and family garden, normally closed to visitors, will be open on the NGS day. More than 1,000 different herbaceous perennials are grown in the nursery, many that are excellent for wildlife. For other opening times and information please visit our website. We are on a sloping site that has no steps but steep inclines in places.

2 ASKHAM HALL
Askham, Penrith, CA10 2PF. Charles Lowther, 01931 712350, hello@askhamhall.co.uk, www.askhamhall.co.uk. 5m S of Penrith. Turn off A6 for Lowther & Askham. **Sun 21 June (11.30-7). Adm £8, chd free. Light refreshments.**

Askham Hall is a Pele Tower incorporating C14, C16 and early C18 elements in a courtyard plan. Opened in 2013 with luxury accommodation, a restaurant, outdoor heated pool and wedding barn. Splendid formal garden with terraces of herbaceous borders and topiary, dating back to C17. Meadow area with trees and pond, kitchen gardens and animal trails. Café serving wood-fired pizzas, cakes, hot and cold drinks with indoor and outdoor seating.

GROUP OPENING

3 BRAMPTON EAST GARDENS
Brampton, CA8 1EX. Bridget Barling. Gardens located at the eastern side of Brampton, between the Co-op & the top of Station Rd. Parking around The Sands & Lanercost Rd area of Brampton. Community garden & Sands Terrace are to the W of The Sands. A map will be provided on entry to the first garden. **Sun 31 May (1-4). Combined adm £5, chd free. Home-made teas at Huffnpuff. Visitors can picnic at the Community Garden, weather permitting. The Sands grassed area can also be used for picnics which also has a roofed shelter.**

HUFFNPUFF
CA8 1EX. Bridget Barling.

IVY COTTAGE
CA8 1UB. Mrs Sally Nelson.

LOVER'S LANE COMMUNITY GARDEN
CA8 1TN. www.facebook.com/Loverslanecommunitygarden.

6 SANDS COTTAGES
CA8 1UQ. Ms Jane Streames.

NEW 8 TREE GARDENS
CA8 1TZ. Angie Tomlinson.

10 TREE GARDENS
CA8 1TZ. Bill Parkin.

11 TREE GARDENS
CA8 1TZ. Shelagh Smith.

WOODLANDS
CA8 1EX. Mr & Mrs Potter.

A selection of gardens of differing sizes and styles. Huffnpuff was built in 2019 so is a fairly new garden on a steep south facing slope, currently developing. Sands Cottages, Back Lane, are 3 small, but very different hidden gardens. 8, 10 & 11 Tree Gardens are 3 neighbouring gardens with their own characters, all different in style maturity and design. These small gardens are mainly on a slope, with different priorities. The Community Garden is a productive vegetable and soft fruit garden, with 40 members, which anyone can join. Woodlands is a large garden on a steep hill with ponds and a stream and wildlife habitat being an important feature. Ivy Cottage is an interesting and varied garden with wilder areas and some more formal areas. Mecanopsis will hopefully be in flower. All gardens have wildlife areas and planting designed to feed insects and wildlife.

5 CHAPELSIDE
Mungrisdale, Penrith, CA11 0XR. Tricia & Robin Acland, 01768 779672. 12m W of Penrith. On A66 take minor road N signed Mungrisdale. After 2m, sharp bends, garden on L after tiny church on R. Use church car park at foot of our short drive. **Visits by arrangement 15 May to 28 June for groups of 5 to 20. Adm £5, chd free.**

1 acre, windy garden below fell, round C18 farmhouse and outbuildings. Fine views. Tiny stream, large pond. Herbaceous, gravel, alpine and shade areas, bulbs in grass. Wide range of plants, many unusual. Relaxed planting regime, lively plant combinations. Run on organic lines. Art constructions in and out, local stone used creatively. There may be plants for sale.

In 2025, National Garden Scheme funding helped Perennial support 950 unique callers to their helpline looking for advice and information.

6 COOMBE EDEN
Armathwaite, Carlisle, CA4 9PQ. Belinda & Mike Quigley. *8m SE of Carlisle. Turn off A6 just S of High Hesket signed Armathwaite. Continue to bottom of hill where garden can be found on R turn for Lazonby.* **Sat 23, Sun 24 May (12-5). Adm £5, chd free. Home-made teas.**
A country garden of over 1 acre, with a contemporary feel, surrounding a C18/19 converted farmhouse. A beck runs through the lower garden with a Japanese style bridge, rhododendrons and hosta beds. Choice trees can be seen throughout inc Japanese acers, snake bark maples, white birches, flowering dogwoods and rowans. A long herbaceous border and paths lead to a formal garden and vegetable patch. Views of Settle to Carlisle railway embankments. (Station at Armathwaite 1m).

7 CRUMBLE COTTAGES
Beckside, Cartmel, LA11 7SP. Sarah Byrne & Stewart Cowe, 015395 34405, sarah@crumblecottages.co.uk, www.crumblecottages.co.uk. *What3words app: jolly.alike.mixers. 1m from Cartmel then follow yellow signs. Search Crumble Cottages Cartmel on google maps you will see the pin.* **Sat 4, Sun 5 July (11-5). Adm £7.50, chd free. Light refreshments.** Visits also by arrangement Apr to Sept for groups of 10+.
Cottage gardens using a variety of different colour schemes with topiary surround our C17 listed Cumbrian Longhouse. The remaining 4 acres are divided into a water garden with ponds and rewilded areas designed to improve biodiversity, kitchen gardens using companion planting within listed bee bole wall, large polytunnel, wildflower meadows, butterfly borders, cut flower beds and woodland walks. Wheelchair access to ornamental areas by house and outlying areas of garden but only by a wheelchair that can cope with slightly uneven ground.

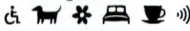

8 EDEN PLACE
Kirkby Stephen, CA17 4AP. J S Parrot Trust. *¼m N of Kirkby Stephen. Take the A685 Kirkby Stephen to Brough road. Cross the bridge & take R turn. Eden Place is 200 yds on R.* **Sat 25, Sun 26 July (10-4). Adm £5, chd free. Tea, coffee & cake.**
3 acre garden with many large perennial borders and island beds enclosed by tall hedges. Part of the garden is made over to aviaries with exotic birds, some are free-flying.

9 ESK BANK
Eskdale Green, Holmrook, CA19 1UE. Pooja & Adrian Norton, 07947 146737, esk.bank@btinternet.com. *Take the A595 to Holmrook, turn off on the road to Eskdale Green. Park at the Green Station. By train to Ravenglass for Eskdale, then take La'al Ratty steam train to the Green Station.* **Sat 4 July (10.30-5); Sun 5 July (10.30-4.30). Adm £5, chd free.** Visits also by arrangement 6 June to 29 Aug for groups of 10 to 30.
Nestled in Eskdale, the ¾ acre cottage style garden is on a south-facing slope with 360 panoramic views of the valley. There is a mix of perennial beds and herbaceous borders with many roses and shrubs inc rhododendrons, magnolia and azaleas. There is a summerhouse and a large kitchen garden with a greenhouse. The sloping lawns have an orchard, wildflower borders and a small pond. Public WC available in Eskdale Green village next to shop.

10 FELL YEAT
Casterton, Kirkby Lonsdale, LA6 2JW. Mr C. Benson. *1m E of Casterton village. On the road to Bull Pot. Leave A65 at Devils Bridge, follow A683 for 1m, take the R fork to High Casterton at golf course, straight across at 2 sets of Xrds, house on L, ¼m from no-through-rd sign.* **Daily Sun 16 Aug to Sun 23 Aug (11-4). Sun 30, Mon 31 Aug (11-4). Adm £4, chd free.**
Relaxed, natural 1 acre garden, the largest part of which was started 35 yrs ago. Planted with many unusual trees, shrubs and large collection of hydrangeas. Increasingly emphasis is on encouraging wildlife and creating a wilder feel. A wonderful breeding ground for owls, sparrowhawks and buzzards. Enjoy the meandering paths, fernery, maturing stumpery and new grotto house with rocks and ferns. Adjoining nursery specialising in ferns, hostas, hydrangeas and many unusual plants.

11 FERNHILL COACH HOUSE
Bleacragg Road, Witherslack, Grange-over-Sands, LA11 6RX. Adele & Mike Walford. *Country road, ½m beyond Halecat & Abi and Tom's Garden Plants. From A590 turn N to Witherslack. Follow brown signs to Halecat, continue along Bleacragg Rd for ½m. Fernhill on L. Rail to Grange-over-sands Bus X6 - 2m walk, NCR 70. Roads & parking are not suitable for coaches.* **Sun 21 June (11-4). Combined adm with Vicarage House East £5, chd free. Tea, coffee & cake at Vicarage House East. Tea, coffee, apple juice, scones & biscuits at Fernhill.**
Cottage garden; mixed borders, vegetables, greenhouse, orchard, small ponds, roses. Organic and biodiverse. We propagate cottage garden plants and grow and sell heritage and northern fruit trees and produce apple juice. Witherslack Orchard Group apple and damson juice. Numerous apple trees for sale. Wheelchair access to flower garden only. Paths are uneven and on sloping ground.

12 FOINHAVEN
Brigham, Cockermouth, CA13 0SY. Bill Wheeler, 01900 827921, junebill1@gmail.com. *2m W Cockermouth. Leave Cockermouth on A5086 & turn R at r'about on A66. 1st L for Brigham, Foinaven 100y on L after 30mph sign.* Visits by arrangement Apr to Sept for groups of up to 10. **Adm £4, chd free. Light refreshments.**
Cottage style, small garden in a village location. Densely planted around a chalet bungalow on sloping, half acre site. Wide range of small trees, shrubs and perennials. Pond, bog garden, rockeries and camomile lawn. Parking on site. Partial wheelchair access.

13 GALESYKE
Wasdale, CA20 1ET. Christine McKinley, 01946 726267, mckinley2112@sky.com. *In Wasdale valley, between Nether Wasdale village & the lake. From Gosforth, follow signs to Nether Wasdale & then to lake, approx 5m. From Santon Bridge follow signs to Wasdale then to lake, approx 2¼m.* **Sat 23, Sun 24 May, Sat 8, Sun 9 Aug (10-5). Adm £6, chd free. Cream teas.** Visits also by arrangement 15 May to 1 Sept.

4 acre garden combining formal areas, shrubberies and woodland, dissected by the River Irt which can be crossed by a suspension bridge. In spring the garden is vibrant with azaleas and rhododendrons, in summer by an impressive collection of colourful hydrangeas. Set in the heart of the Wasdale valley the garden has an unforgettable backdrop of the Screes and the high Lakeland fells. There is a magnificent Victorian sandstone sundial in the garden.

14 NEW GLARAMARA
Dovenby, Cockermouth, CA13 0PN. **Margaret & Frank Armstrong.** *2m NW of Cockermouth. From Cockermouth take A594 towards Maryport turn L opp Ship Inn, Dovenby. 3rd turn on R the barn conversion at the top of shared drive. Foot access only, disabled drop off possible.* **Sat 27 June (12-5.30). Combined adm with The White House £6, chd free. Home-made teas at The White House.**
A relaxed nature and family friendly garden in a village setting with mixed borders of herbaceous perennials and shrubs planted for year-round interest. A football pitch sized lawn, children welcome for a kick about! A granite set courtyard area with small beds, pots and planters along with farm troughs, grindstone and some seating. All easily accessible. Ramp into courtyard area. Gentle slope on to lawn.

15 GRANGE FELL ALLOTMENTS
Fell Road, Grange-over-Sands, LA11 6HB. **Mr Bruno Gouillon, 01539 532317, brunog45@hotmail.com.** *Opp Grange Fell Golf Club. Rail 1.3m, Bus 1m X6, NCR 70.* **Visits by arrangement May to Sept. Adm £7, chd free. Tea, coffee & cake.**
The allotments are managed by Grange Town Council. Opened in 2010, 30 plots are now rented out and offer a wide selection of gardening styles and techniques. The majority of plots grow a mixture of vegetables, fruit trees and flowers. There are a few communal areas where local fruit tree varieties have been donated by plot holders with herbaceous borders and annuals.

The National Garden Scheme donated £3,875,596 to our nursing and health beneficiaries from money raised at gardens open in 2025.

Low Crag

Grange Fell Allotments

GROUP OPENING

16 GRANGE OVER SANDS HIDDEN GARDENS
Grange-over-Sands, LA11 7AF. Bruno Gouillon, 01539 532317, brunog45@hotmail.com. *Off Kents Bank Rd, 3 gardens on Cart Lane then last garden up Carter Rd for Shrublands. Rail 1.4m; Bus X6; NCR 70.* **Sun 28 June (11-4). Combined adm £5.50, chd free. Tea, coffee & cake.** Visits also by arrangement May to Sept. Donation to St Mary's Hospice.

21 CART LANE
Veronica Cameron.

ELDER COTTAGE
Bruno Gouillon & Andrew Fairey.

HAWTHORNE COTTAGE
Mrs Carroll Ashton.

SHRUBLANDS
Jon & Avril Trevorrow.

Four very different gardens hidden down narrow lanes off the road south out of Grange. Off Kents Bank Road, the 3 gardens on Cart Lane all back onto the railway embankment, providing shelter from the wind but also creating a frost pocket. The garden at 21 Cart Lane is a series of rooms designed to create an element of surprise with fruit and vegetables in raised beds. Elder Cottage is an organised riot of fruit trees, vegetables, shrubby perennials and herbaceous plants. Productive and peaceful. Hawthorne Cottage has been redesigned and replanted over the last 2 yrs to create a garden with colour and interest. Up the hill on Carter Rd, Shrublands is a ¾ acre garden situated on a hillside overlooking Morecambe Bay. Visitors with mobility issues can access Shrublands and 21 Cart Ln, but can only view Elder Cottage from the roadside and Hawthorne Cottage from the gate.

17 NEW HARTSIDE NURSERY GARDEN
Penrith Road, Alston, CA9 3BL. Mr Neil & Mrs Sue Huntley, 01434 381372, enquiries@plantswithaltitude.co.uk, www.plantswithaltitude.co.uk. *1m SW of Alston. Nursery entrance is on L of A686. Park in nursery car park & walk down to garden & plant sales area. This is quite a steep slope so contact us if you have limited mobility.* **Visits by arrangement 15 Mar to 18 Oct for groups of up to 30. Limited wheelchair access. Adm £5, chd free.**
An established garden in the North Pennines. Situated at over 1000 feet the garden features mountain plants primulas, saxifrages, woodland plants, erythroniums, trilliums and ferns plus a number of roscoeas. The season starts with snowdrops and continues with a wide range of unusual plants. As autumn approaches the garden includes a range of gentians, Japanese saxifrages and roscoea. Crevice garden, troughs and raised beds.

GROUP OPENING

18 HAYTON VILLAGE GARDENS
Hayton, Brampton, CA8 9HR. www.facebook.com/NGSopengardens/?locale=en_GB. 5m E of M6, J43 at Carlisle towards Hexham. Signed: Hayton ½m S of A69. 3m W of Brampton. Please park one side only & leave space for less able nr Stone Inn. Tickets/map sold at Kinrara opp Stone Inn & in East & West (cash preferred). Gardens extend over ½ mile What3words app: romance.cooked.tango. **Sun 7 June (12-5). Combined adm £5, chd free. Tea, coffee & cake in Hayton Village Primary School. Also cold refreshments in one of the gardens outside if suitable. Village green available for picnics. Meals, drinks & WCs at The Stone Inn.**

BRACKENHOW
CA8 9HR. Susan Tranter.

CURLEW COTTAGE
CA8 9HN. Frances & David Scales.

THE GARTH
CA8 9HR. Linda Mages & Frank O'Connor.

HEMPGARTH
CA8 9HR. Sheila & David Heslop.

KINRARA
CA8 9HR. Tim & Alison Brown.

MILLBROOK
CA8 9HT. Monica Carruthers.

TOWNFOOT HOUSE
CA8 9HR. Alison Springall.

TOWNHEAD COTTAGE
CA8 9JQ. Chris & Pam Haynes.

WEST GARTH COTTAGE
CA8 9HL. Debbie Jenkins, www.westgarth-cottage-gardens.co.uk.

Easily accessible, delightful village with a village green growing one of the oldest walnut trees in the country. Remnants of damson orchards grown for the dyeing industry. Close to Hadrian's Wall. A picturesque valley of 9 quality gardens of very varied sizes and styles, mostly around old stone cottages. Smaller and larger cottage gardens, courtyards and containers, woodland walks, exuberant borders, frogs, pools, colour and texture throughout. Spring bulbs, azaleas and wisteria precede roses, clematis and perennials. Artworks at a number of gardens from sculpture, paintings, metalwork or constructions of garden finds: some for sale. Cash preferred. Pleases note furthest gardens at Townhead require a half mile walk (and back) with no pavement, or extra driving. Suggest that less mobile arrive early for ease of parking. Kinrara, owned by architect/artists with multiple garden design experience, may open on additional dates in 2026 (visit www.ngs.org.uk for pop-up dates). West Garth Cottage is owned by a professional artist/designer. Each often has artwork for sale. Hayton Choir will perform at Millbrook at 2pm. Accessibility ranges from full to none.

19 HAZEL COTTAGE
Armathwaite, Carlisle, CA4 9PG. Mr D Ryland & Mr J Thexton. *8m SE of Carlisle. Turn off A6 just S of High Hesket signed Armathwaite, after 2m house facing you at T-junction. 1¼m walk from Armathwaite train stn.* **Sun 17 May, Sun 14 June, Sun 5 July (12-5). Adm £5, chd free. Tea, coffee & cake.**
Flower arrangers and plantsman's garden extending to approx 5 acres. Inc mature herbaceous borders, pergola, ponds and planting of disused railway siding providing home to wildlife. Many variegated and unusual plants. Varied areas, planted for all seasons, south facing, some gentle slopes, ever changing. Partial access for wheelchair users, small steps to WC area. Main garden planted on gentle slope.

20 ♦ HUTTON-IN-THE-FOREST
Penrith, CA11 9TH. Lord & Lady Inglewood, 01768 484449, info@hutton-in-the-forest.co.uk, www.hutton-in-the-forest.co.uk. *6m NW of Penrith. On B5305, 2m from exit 41 of M6 towards Wigton.* **For NGS: Sun 7 June (10-5). Adm £11, chd free. Delicious home-made cakes & scones, light lunches & teas served in the Cloisters tearoom. For other opening times and information, please phone, email or visit garden website.**
Hutton-in-the-Forest is surrounded on two sides by distinctive yew topiary and grass terraces which to the south lead to C18 lake and cascade. 1730s walled garden is full of old fruit trees, tulips in spring, roses and an extensive collection of herbaceous plants in summer. Our gravel paths can make it difficult to push a wheelchair in places.

21 NEW HYLANDS HOUSE
Brigsteer Road, Kendal, LA9 5DY. Emma Cowan, 07919 818585, emma@hylandshouse.co.uk, www.hylandsholidaylets.co.uk. *Walkable from Kendal Town. Take the A590 towards Kendal from Jct 36, then take the Kendal South turn towards the town centre. Pass the Parish Church & turn L up Gillingate. Brigsteer Rd is at the top of the hill on L.* **Sat 6 June, Sat 12 Sept (10-4). Adm £5, chd free. Tea, coffee & cake.**
Hylands is an Arts & Crafts house and garden built in 1910. Tucked back from the road the gardens cover 2½ acres with varied areas, including formally laid out gardens, a wildlife pond, wilder areas, an exotic area, woodland walk, kitchen garden, orchard, as well as some extraordinary sculptures. Organically managed the garden restoration began in 2020.

22 NEW INCH FARM
Longtown, Carlisle, CA6 5PP. Peter & Linda O'Shea, 07880 310747, theinchfarm@gmail.com, inchfarm.co.uk. *4m NE of Longtown. From J44 of M6 follow A7 to Longtown, turn R at the Spar supermarket on to Netherby road to Kirk Andrews Moat. Turn L at signpost for Inch. Follow road to the end. What3words app: purse.compose.spin.* **Sun 12 July (11-4.30). Adm £5, chd free. Tea, coffee & cake.**
Interesting garden created from scratch since 2018, situated beside the River Liddle and viaduct. Using natural features of wood and stone to create colourful beds of perennials and shrubs, chosen to survive wetter winters. A stream runs to a natural pond, and a pergola with stone steps, which divides the fruit and vegetable garden, leads to a steep bank and riverside walk with seating. The main garden is accessible. There is a very gentle slope.

23 IVY HOUSE
Cumwhitton, CA8 9EX. Martin Johns & Ian Forrest. *6m E of Carlisle. At the bridge at Warwick Bridge on A69 take turning to Great Corby & Cumwhitton. Through Great Corby & woodland until you reach a T-junction. Turn R into village.* **Sun 21 June, Sun 9 Aug (1-5). Adm £5, chd free. Light refreshments.**
Approx 2 acres of sloping fellside garden with meandering paths leading to a series of 'rooms': inc pond, fern garden, Acer terrace, shrubberies, herbaceous borders and grass and herb gardens. Copse with meadow leading down to beck. Trees, shrubs, ferns, grasses, bamboos, evergreens and perennials planted with emphasis on variety of texture and colour. Sadly unsuitable for wheelchairs due to steep slopes. WC available.

24 JOHNBY HALL
Johnby, Penrith, CA11 0UU. Henry & Anna Howard, 01768 483257, bookings@johnbyhall.com, www.johnbyhall.com. *Greystoke, Penrith. From Greystoke village green follow signs to Johnby, forking L as you leave the village. Gateway signed Johnby Hall after 1m on the L.* **Evening opening Wed 20 May, Wed 17 June (6-8). Adm £10, chd free. Pre-booking essential, please visit www.ngs.org.uk for information & booking. Light refreshments. Tea, coffee & cakes or biscuits. Visits also by arrangement 18 May to 9 July. Limit of 15 cars per group and car sharing is encouraged.**
Large, very informal and natural mature garden around an ancient manor house. Intriguing courtyards are full of wild flowers and old roses; the 1683 walled garden is now an orchard. Wildflower lawns and meadows in summer, a bluebell walk through the beginnings of a pinetum with some unusual young specimens, and a field of free-range rare-breed pigs.

25 LARCH COTTAGE NURSERIES
Melkinthorpe, Penrith, CA10 2DR. Peter Stott, www.larchcottage.co.uk. *4m S of Penrith. From N leave M6 J40 take A6 S. From S leave M6 J39 take A6 N signed off A6.* **Thur 9 July, Thur 6 Aug, Thur 3 Sept (1-4). Adm £5,** chd free. Refreshments available in our restaurant, La Casa Verde.
A unique nursery and garden designed and built over the past 40 yrs. The gardens inc lawns, flowing perennial borders, rare and unusual shrubs, trees, a small orchard and a kitchen garden. A natural stream runs into a small lake, a haven for wildlife and birds. At the head of the lake stands a small frescoed chapel designed and built by the owner for family use (open on NGS open days). Japanese dry garden, pond, Italianesque columned garden for shade plants. Glass walled kitchen garden. Italianesque tumbled down walls act as a backdrop for the borders, showcasing rare and unusual shrubs, trees and stock plants. Accessible to wheelchair users although the paths are rocky in places.

26 NEW LEYPITS
Birks Road, Tower Wood, Windermere, LA23 3PH. Carol Carthy. *Midway between Newby Bridge & Bowness next to the Park Cliffe caravan site. Approach on A590 then A592 from Newby Bridge only. Birks Rd on the R after approx 3m signed Park Cliff caravan site. Park at Great Tower Scout Camp - ¼m walk to garden and steep on return journey.* **Sun 17 May (2-6). Adm £5, chd free. Tea, coffee & cake.**
This 1½ acres garden has been created over the last 12 yrs from an impenetrable overgrown woodland by its lady owner. It is a garden of trees, rock and water which has been replanted with many choice rhododendrons, azaleas, hydrangeas and woodland plants whilst trying to keep its wild atmosphere. Long distance views towards Lake Windermere and the Lakeland fells have been rediscovered.

GROUP OPENING

27 NEW LITTLE URSWICK VILLAGE GARDENS
Ulverston, LA12 0PL. *4m W of Ulverston. A590 from Ulverston approx 2m to Little Urswick. Parking, tickets & maps at Recreation Hall, LA12 0TA.* **Sun 5 July (11-4). Combined adm £5, chd free. Home-made teas at Little Urswick Recreation Hall.**

NEW BURNSMEAD FARM
LA12 0PN. Richard & Anne Kenyon.

NEW CORNAA
LA12 0PN. Mike & Bev Williams.

NEW CRAG FIELD
LA12 0PR. Joe & Christine Peacock.

NEW EAST VIEW
LA12 0PN. Simon & Sally Barton.

NEW 9 GREENBANK GARDENS
LA12 0RN. Mr & Mrs K Morris.

NEW 15 GREENBANK GARDENS
LA12 0RN. Anne Atkinson.

NEW 21 GREENBANK GARDENS
Inez Rixom.

NEW REDMAYNE HALL
LA12 0PL. Jennie Werry.

Situated on the southwest peninsular of Cumbria close to Morecambe Bay and the Cumbrian fells, these 8 gardens are all within walking distance of each other. They range in size and diversity, from more modern bungalows with formal planting and entertaining areas to ones with established trees and shrubs, all with far-reaching views. Visitors will encounter an eco friendly garden with beehives and an established mulberry tree, a Victorian orangery that was rescued from going into landfill, an ancient farmhouse with very mature trees and herbaceous borders and a very private rear garden with a lily pond. A creatively designed garden has vegetables and herbaceous plants side by side, plus a garden created by two cycling enthusiasts with some original pieces throughout. An abundance of fruit trees herbaceous borders, roses and vegetable plots are to be found amongst the gardens.

28 LOW CRAG
Crook, Kendal, LA8 8LE. Chris Dodd & Liz Jolley. *Halfway between Kendal (3m) & Windermere (4m). From Kendal turn off B5284 just before Sun Inn. Pass Ellerbeck Farm on R, continue ¼m. Low Crag is 3rd drive on L at Footpath sign. For parking follow signs.* **Fri 8, Sat 9, Sun 10 May (9-6). Adm £5, chd free. Tea, coffee & cake.**
A relaxed 2 acre nature-friendly garden using organic principles

Morland House Gardens

and set around former farmhouse and barns. The more formal garden features yew hedge, herbaceous planting, arboretum, orchard, vegetable and herb garden. This transitions to compost area, pond, damson hedges, meadows, some scythed, and the greater landscape of the Lyth Valley. Long views with seating and viewpoints.

29 LOW FELL WEST
Crosthwaite, Kendal, LA8 8JG. Barbie Handley, 07423 055928, barbie@handleyfamily.co.uk. *4½ m S of Bowness. Off A5074, turn W just S of Damson Dene Hotel. Follow lane for ½ m.* **Sun 3, Mon 4 May (11-5). Adm £5, chd free. Light refreshments.** Visits also by arrangement for individuals and groups of up to 30.

This 2 acre woodland garden in the tranquil Winster valley has extensive views to the Pennines. The four season garden, restored since 2003, inc expanses of rock planted sympathetically with grasses, unusual trees and shrubs, climaxing for autumn colour. There are native hedges and areas of plant rich meadows. A woodland area houses a gypsy caravan and there is direct access to Cumbria Wildlife Trust's Barkbooth Reserve of Oak woodland, bluebells and open fellside. Wheelchair access to much of the garden, but some rough paths and steep slopes.

30 NEW LOW ROUGH HILL
Askham, Penrith, CA10 2QL. Mrs Jo Blythe. *8m from Penrith & 6m from Shap up on the fell between Helton & Bampton. Follow yellow signs from the phone box in Bampton & the road junction after Helton.* **Sun 14 June (2-5). Adm £4, chd free. Home-made teas.** Low Rough Hill was an upland farm and the only plant it boasted was a honeysuckle before being sold in 2018. Now a traditional cottage garden with borders and shrubs, stone walls, ponds, a small kitchen garden and behind a stone barn a stunning rose garden in a sheltered south facing spot. The current owners took over the mantel in 2023 and the 1½ acre garden goes from strength to strength. Gravel & cobble driveway and the garden is quite slopey in places but as long as the wheelchair can cope with that most of the garden is accessible.

31 MATSON GROUND
Windermere, LA23 2NH.
Matson Ground Estate
Co Ltd, 07831 831918,
sam@matsonground.co.uk. ⅔ m
E of Bowness. Turn N off B5284
signed Heathwaite. From E 100yds
after Windermere Golf Club, from
W 400yds after Windy Hall Rd. Rail
2½ mi; Bus 1m, 6, 599, 755, 800;
NCR 6 (1m). **Sun 17 May (11.30-3).
Adm £6.50, chd free. Home-made
teas.** Visits also by arrangement
12 Jan to 11 Dec for groups of 5+.
2 acres of mature, south facing
gardens. A good mix of formal and
informal planting inc topiary features,
herbaceous and shrub borders,
wildflower areas, stream leading
to a large pond and developing
arboretum. Rose garden, rockery,
topiary terrace borders, ha-ha.
Productive, walled kitchen garden
c1862, a wide assortment of fruit,
vegetables, cut flowers, cobnuts and
herbs. Greenhouse.

32 MIDDLE BLAKEBANK
Underbarrow, Kendal, LA8 8HP.
Christian Burrell & Stuart
McGill, www.instagram.com/
blakebankfarmhouse. *Lyth
valley between Underbarrow &
Crosthwaite. From Underbarrow
take A5074 to Crosthwaite. The
garden is on Broom Lane, a turning
between Crosthwaite & Underbarrow
signed Red Scar & Broom Farm.
What3words app: hampers.speedily.
budget.* **Sat 22 Aug (11-4). Adm
£5, chd free. Tea, coffee & cake.**
With meticulously considered
grounds that inc formal planting
areas, abundant borders, a wondrous
orchard and a wildflower meadow,
you will be sure to discover colour,
texture, and creativity in whichever
direction you look. Developed and
nurtured by the previous owners,
the gardens are now chaotically
maintained by two, out-of-their depth
novice gardeners.

33 NEW ♦ MORLAND HOUSE GARDENS
Morland, Penrith, CA10 3AZ.
The William Joseph Markham
Bare Trust, 01931 234714, julia.
evans@morlandhouse.net,
www.morlandhouse.net. *8m SE
of Penrith & 7m NW of Appleby-in-
Westmorland. What3words app:
prospered.extend.stow From the A6
S of Eamont Bridge, take the turning
to Cliburn. From the A66, just S of
Temple Sowerby, take the turning to
Morland. Then follow NGS signs.* **For
NGS: Sat 20, Wed 24 June (10.30-
5). Adm £5, chd free.** Pre-booking
essential, please visit www.ngs.
org.uk for information & booking.
Refreshments are self-service by
donation and will be in the Old
School at entrance. Variety of
teas, coffee, juice & home-made
cakes. For other opening times
and information, please phone,
email or visit garden website.
A 4 acre garden and wildlife haven of
historic interest. Formal lawns flanked
by ancient yews and a long herbaceous
border lead to smaller lawns, espaliered
apples and a rose garden with terraces
below. Lower level beck walk and
quarry garden are by guided tour.
Limited tickets online only for entry and
tour at 10.30, 12.30 & 2.30.

34 NEW THE MOUNT
Portinscale, Keswick,
CA12 5RD. Caroline Howarth &
Clive Penkett, 07900 251351,
info@themountkeswick.co.uk,
www.themountkeswick.co.uk.
*From A66 take exit signed Grange &
Portinscale. Drive past Farmers Arms
on L and look out for artistic sign
for The Mount Guesthouse (L) well
before The Chalet cafe. What3words
app: intention.garden.symphonic.*
**Sat 27, Sun 28 June (11-5).
Adm £5, chd free.** Pre-booking
essential, please visit www.ngs.
org.uk for information & booking.
Tea, coffee & cake.
Nature is given the upper-hand in this
small cottage garden with self-seeded
foxgloves, verbascum and fennel
accentuating the design of beautiful
garden spaces, lovingly created by
tall grasses, rose swags and water-
troughs. This allows visitors of all
kinds their own hidden space and
sanctuary, from birds and hedgehogs
(and the odd weed) to holiday-makers
enjoying their breakfast in the garden.

35 NEW MUNCASTER MILL
Ravenglass, CA18 1ST. Christine
Hoye-Turner, 07936 107401,
millgarden18@gmail.com. *On A595
¾ m N of the turning for Ravenglass.
As A595 crosses the RAER 'Ratty
Railway' turn in by the millstones
marked Muncaster Mill.* **Visits by
arrangement 15 June to 13 Sept.
Adm £5, chd free. Tea, coffee &
cake.**
Almost 2 acres of garden created
since 2003. Naturalistic in style with
a number of ponds, trees, shrubs,
cornus, rhododendrons, azaleas,
rambler roses and hydrangea.
Seasonal perennials and spring bulbs
to give interest throughout the year.
'La Ratty' steam train runs alongside
garden. The garden has areas that
are often wet, with steep slopes, and
sturdy shoes are recommended.

36 ♦ NETHERBY HALL
Longtown, Carlisle, CA6 5PR.
Mr Gerald & Mrs Margo
Smith, 01228 792732,
events@netherbyhall.co.uk,
netherbyhall.co.uk. *2m N of
Longtown. Take Junction 44 from
the M6 & follow the A7 to Longtown.
Take Netherby Rd & follow it for
about 2m. Netherby Hall is on L.* **For
NGS: Mon 31 Aug (10-4). Adm £6,
chd free.** For other opening times
and information, please phone,
email or visit garden website.
Netherby Hall Garden is 36 acres,
consisting of a 1½ acre walled
kitchen garden which produces
fruit, vegetables and herbs for
the Pentonbridge Inn restaurant.
Herbaceous borders and traditional
kidney beds are set amongst
wonderful lawns, woodlands with
many fine specimen trees, azaleas
and rhododendrons, all within a
designed landscape bordering the
River Esk. Ample parking. Carriage
paths allow easy access around the
Victorian pleasure grounds & walled
garden.

37 NEW NETHERWOOD HOTEL
Lindale Road, Grange-Over-
Sands, LA11 6ET. Bruna
Remesso, 01539 532552,
enquiries@netherwood-hotel.
co.uk, www.facebook.com/
netherwoodhotelandspa. *From
Kendal direction, take the A590
towards Barrow in Furness. At
the r'about at Meathop, follow the
B5277 towards Lindale. Go through
the village & carry on towards
Grange-O-Sands. Signs to the hotel
will be on R. The entrance is well
signed & easy to access.* **Thur 16
Apr (11-2). Adm £5, chd free. Tea,
coffee & cake.**
Lovely gardens over 3 terraces. Made
up of herbaceous borders, seasonally
planted flower beds which are framed
by mix of yew and cherry laurel
topiary. The grounds are rich with

wildlife and are maintained with nature in mind. The Hotel has several parking areas and visitors are welcome to use their facilities during their visit on the Open Day. The main terrace is wheelchair friendly.

38 PARK HOUSE
Barbon, Kirkby Lonsdale,
LA6 2LG. Mr & Mrs P Pattison.
2½ m N of Kirkby Lonsdale. Off A683 Kirkby Lonsdale to Sedburgh road. Follow signs into Barbon Village. **Sat 11, Sun 12 July (10.30-4.30). Adm £5, chd free. Home-made teas.**
Romantic Manor House (not open). Extensive vistas. Formal tranquil pond encased in yew hedging. Meadow with meandering pathways, water garden filled with bulbs and ferns. Formal lawn, gravel pathways, cottage borders with hues of soft pinks and purples, shady border, kitchen garden. An evolving garden to follow.

39 ROSE CROFT
Levens, Kendal, LA8 8PH.
Enid Fraser, 07976 977018,
fraserenid@gmail.com. *Approx 9 mins from J36 on M6; 4 mins from A590 r'about. From J36 take A590 toward Barrow. R turn to Levens; at pub, turn down sharp L. Follow road to garden on L. About 1 min drive, telegraph pole by house just before PV Dobsons.* **Visits by arrangement 1 June to 13 Sept for groups of up to 25. Adm £5, chd free. Tea, coffee & cake.**
This 'secret' garden's richness in herbaceous plants, grasses, shrubs and trees belies the twin challenges of thin topsoil and an acutely sloping site. With grand views across the Lyth valley, steps and pathways carry down to lower-level lawns, streamside summerhouse and wild flowers. Long season of interest with designed elements providing bountiful displays well into late summer.

40 ♦ RYDAL MOUNT AND GARDENS
Rydal, Ambleside, LA22 9LU.
Helen Green, 01539 433002,
info@rydalmount.co.uk,
www.rydalmount.co.uk. *Rydal Mount is located between Ambleside & Grasmere. Accessible by bus to Rydal, on foot from Ambleside, or by car. The car park is adjacent to the main entrance on Rydal Hill, just off the A591.* **For NGS: Mon 30, Tue 31 Mar, Wed 1 Apr, Mon 1, Tue 2, Wed 3 June (10.30-4). Adm £6.50, chd free. For other opening times and information, please phone, email or visit garden website.**
Rydal Mount is the historic home of the Wordsworth family. The poet, William Wordsworth, was a talented landscape gardener as well as a poet, and the Rydal Mount garden is the largest example of his design. The garden stretches over 5 acres, including terraces that Wordsworth built, informal herbaceous borders, trees planted by the poet, and a wonderful range of traditional lakeland plants.

41 SCHOOL HOUSE
Silver Street, Crosby Ravensworth, Penrith, CA10 3JA. Judith & Nigel Harrison. *Exit M6, J39 drive N to Shap on A6 & take the R turn at the Shap Chippy signed to Crosby Ravensworth, at T junction in the village turn L and park by church then follow signs to walk to garden.* **Sat 11 July (1-5). Adm £5, chd free. Home-made teas.**
A fairly newly created medium sized cottage garden next to the River Lyvennet in a village setting. Next to the house is a formal garden of lawn, herbaceous borders and box hedging. Then we have a small orchard, and vegetable beds. A wilder area contains a meadow, a natural spring fed pond and a ditch as a flood mitigation measure. We also have a number of green roofs and a riverbank sitting area.

Our donation to the Army Benevolent Fund supported 776 individuals with horticultural related grants in 2025.

Netherwood Hotel

42 SPRINT MILL
Burneside, Kendal, LA8 9AQ. Edward & Romola Acland, 01539 725168, 07806 065602, mail@sprintmill.uk. *2m N of Kendal. From Burneside follow signs towards Skelsmergh for ½m, then L into drive. From A6, about 1m N of Kendal follow signs towards Burneside, then R into drive. What3words app: segregate. petty.error.* **Visits by arrangement. Pls visit www.ngs.org.uk for details of pop up openings. Refreshments are self-service by donation. Variety of teas, good coffee & home-made cakes.**
Unorthodox organically run garden, the wild and natural alongside provision of owners' fruit, vegetables and firewood. Idyllic riverside setting, 5 acres to explore inc wooded riverbank with hand-crafted seats. Large vegetable and soft fruit area, following no dig and permaculture principles. Hand tools prevail. Historic water mill with original turbine. The 3 storey building houses owner's art studio and personal museum, inc collection of old hand tools associated with rural crafts. Goats, hens, ducks, rope swing, very family friendly. Short walk to our flower-rich hay meadows. Access for wheelchairs to some parts of both garden and mill.

43 STEWART HILL COTTAGE
Hesket Newmarket, CA7 8HX. Mrs D Scott, 01768 484841, ardrannoch@hotmail.com. *7m W of Penrith. From S leave A66 at the turning to Hutton Roof. Carry on through Berrier. After Berrier take 3rd turning on R & we are 2nd dwelling on R.* **Sun 21 June (2-5). Adm £7, chd free. Home-made teas. Visits also by arrangement. Donation to Community Action Nepal.**
20 yr old garden comprising mainly roses, courtyard, organic vegetable garden ornamental pool and croquet lawn. Wild swimming pool and boules pitch.

In 2025 we awarded over £288,800 in Community Garden Grants, supporting 114 community garden projects.

44 SUMMERDALE HOUSE
Cow Brow, Nook, Lupton, LA6 1PE. David & Gail Sheals, www.summerdalegardennursery.co.uk/the-garden-1. *7m S of Kendal, 5m W of Kirkby Lonsdale. From J36 M6 take A65 towards Kirkby Lonsdale, at Nook take sharp R turn Farleton. Location not signed on highway. For GPS use both house name and postcode LA6 1PE.* **Sun 26 Apr (11-4.30). Adm £6, chd free. Home-made teas.**
1½ acre part-walled country garden set around C18 former vicarage. Several defined areas have been created by hedges, each with its own theme and linked by intricate cobbled pathways. Relaxed natural planting in a formal structure. Rural setting with fine views across to Farleton Fell. Large collection of auriculas with displays during the season.

45 ♦ SWARTHMOOR HALL
Swarthmoor Hall Lane, Ulverston, LA12 0JQ. 01229 583204, info@swarthmoorhall.co.uk, www.swarthmoorhall.co.uk. *1m SW of Ulverston. Follow A590 to Ulverston. Turn off at junction to Ulverston railway stn & follow brown/blue tourist signs to Hall. Station 0.9m, 20 mins on foot. NCR70 & 700 (1m).* **For NGS: Sat 7, Sun 8 Mar (11-3); Sat 13, Sun 14 June (11-4). Adm £3, chd free. Light refreshments. For other opening times and information, please phone, email or visit garden website.**
Traditional English country garden surrounding a Grade II* C17 hall, the cradle of Quakerism where it began in 1652. Cottage style gardens, woodland garden, quiet garden dedicated to peaceful contemplation, ornamental vegetable garden and wildflower meadow with fabulous crocus display in late February/March. Only 5 minutes from main road, but an oasis of peace and tranquillity. Please check the website for opening times for the historic Hall and Gardens. Our on site café offers a range of hot and cold drinks, fabulous cakes and scones, ice creams and other snacks. There is wheelchair access around most of the site including into all of the garden areas.

GROUP OPENING

46 ULVERSTON TOWN & COUNTRY GARDENS
Oubas Hill, Ulverston, LA12 7LA. *4 gardens within 1m of the centre of Ulverston. Ulverston is on the A590, with 1 garden on the A590 as you approach from the east. Public transport is avail to Ulverston (Rail & buses 6 & X6) but a circuit of the 4 gardens is 4½m.* **Sun 28 June (11-5). Combined adm £5, chd free. Light refreshments at Hamilton Grove, Urswick Rd & Beckside Bungalow.**

NEW BECKSIDE BUNGALOW
LA12 7BN. Mr Martin & Mrs Anthea Hebblethwaite.

104 BIRCHWOOD DRIVE
LA12 9NY. Jane Parker.

HAMILTON GROVE
LA12 7LB. Helen & Martin Cooper.

NEW 23 URSWICK ROAD
LA12 9LG. Mrs Caroline Spence.

4 very different gardens. Birchwood Drive shows inspired use of a small corner plot: joyful front garden, pavement side garden with fruit, vegetables, flowers and grasses; a delightful secret garden, a place to sit in peace. Urswick Road has a large front garden and 200 ft level back garden divided into woodland, flower and vegetable/fruit sub-gardens. A plantsman's paradise. Beckside Bungalow is on 5 levels with perennial shrubs, climbers, annual flower borders and vegetable/fruit area. It rises up with growing views over the town and to the Pennines. Hamilton Grove is a ½ acre garden sloping down from a terrace with a wow-factor view of the garden, fields and distant Pennines. A mixture of formality and informal perennial and annual herbaceous planting down to a dry canal feeder. Tree planting and shaping has minimised the effect of the slope. The terrace has a collection of scented-leaf pelargonium. Ulverston is an historic market town, with its 1½ m canal to Morecambe Bay and lighthouse monument to Sir John Barrow, its other famous son being Stan Laurel (museum in Town).

47 VICARAGE HOUSE EAST
Witherslack, Grange-over-Sands, LA11 6RS. Steve & Jackie Ratcliffe.
Turn off A590 at Witherslack junction, past Derby Arms pub. In village turn L on to Church Rd (following brown signs to Halecat Garden Nursery) & stay on road for 1m. Pass Dean Barwick School. **Sun 21 June (11-4). Combined adm with Fernhill Coach House £5, chd free. Tea, coffee & cake.**
A secret haven, surrounded by stone walling and woodland, the backbone of which is a wildlife pond and walled garden. A series of connecting rooms create a sequence of gardens, each with their own distinctive character. Inc a flower and herbaceous formal garden planted by colour schemes, a vegetable garden, orchard with mown paths, a woodland garden with hellebores and a hosta collection. Pls park on road between Dean Barwick School and the church. Those who are less able can access via drive adj to Church Green.

48 THE WHITE HOUSE
Brigham Road, Cockermouth, CA13 0AX. Jean & John Jowsey.
From Penrith turn R into C'mouth off A66 at Travel Lodge r'about. 3rd turn L into Brigham Rd. 40 metres along on L follow lane up to house. (NB foot access only up lane-no cars please). **Sat 27 June (12-5.30). Combined adm with Glaramara £6, chd free. Home-made teas.**
The garden is a large urban plot slowly developed over the last 20 yrs, parts of which date back to Victorian times. High walls on most sides have provided shelter along with a pergola. Mixed borders of herbaceous perennials, shrubs and trees, a formal pond, a fruit and vegetable area, small orchard, a stable yard with pots, planters and potting shed, a greenhouse and covered seating areas. Most areas are easily accessed but paths along pergola may prove difficult. A ramp provides access into the lower fruit and vegetable garden.

49 WINTON PARK
Appleby Road, Kirkby Stephen, CA17 4PG. Mr Anthony Kilvington, www.wintonparkgardens.co.uk.
2m N of Kirkby Stephen. On A685 turn L signed Gt Musgrave/Warcop (B6259). After approx 1m turn L as signed. **Sun 19 July (11-4). Adm £6, chd free. Light refreshments.**

5 acre country garden bordered by the banks of the River Eden with stunning views. Many fine conifers, acers and rhododendrons, herbaceous borders, hostas, ferns, grasses, heathers and several hundred roses. Four formal ponds plus rock pool. Partial wheelchair access.

50 WOODEND HOUSE
Woodend, Egremont, CA22 2TA. Grainne & Richard Jakobson, 019468 13017, gmjakobson22@gmail.com. *2m S of Whitehaven. Take A595 from Whitehaven towards Egremont. On leaving Bigrigg take 1st turn L. Go down the hill. Garden is at the bottom of the road opp Woodend Farm.* **Sat 11, Sun 12 July (11-5). Adm £5, chd free. Home-made teas. Visits also by arrangement 1 July to 25 Aug for groups of 6 to 15.**
A beautiful garden tucked away in a small hamlet. Meandering gravel paths lead around the garden with imaginative, colourful planting and quirky features. Take a look around a productive, organic potager using no-dig methods, wildlife pond, mini spring and summer meadows and sit in the pretty summerhouse. Designed to be beautiful year-round and wildlife friendly. The gravel drive and paths are difficult for wheelchairs but more mobile visitors can access the main seating areas in the rear garden.

51 YEWBARROW HOUSE
Hampsfell Road, Grange-over-Sands, LA11 6BE. Jonathan & Margaret Denby, 07733 322394, jonathan@bestlakesbreaks.co.uk, www.yewbarrowhouse.co.uk. *¼m from town centre. Proceed along Hampsfell Rd passing a house called Yewbarrow to brow of hill then turn L onto a lane signed 'Charney Wood/Yewbarrow Wood' & sharp L again. Rail 0.7m, Bus X6, NCR 70.* **Sun 7 June, Sun 5 July, Sun 2 Aug, Sun 6 Sept (11-4). Adm £6, chd free. Light refreshments. Visits also by arrangement May to Sept for groups of 10 to 40.**
More Cornwall than Cumbria, according to Country Life, a colourful 4 acre garden filled with exotic and rare plants, with dramatic views over Morecambe Bay. Outstanding features inc the Orangery, the Japanese garden with infinity pool, the Italian terraces and the restored Victorian kitchen garden. Dahlias, cannas and colourful exotica are a speciality. Find us on YouTube-https://youtu.be/A8L1CtRJtCE?si=Rmt4NTwId_eEmHkG.

52 YEWS
Storrs Park, Bowness-on-Windermere, LA23 3JR.
Sir Christopher & Lady Scott, www.yewsestate.com. *1.4m S of Bowness-on-Windermere. On A5074 about 0.3m N of Blackwell, The Arts & Crafts House. Rail Windermere 3m, What3words app: ballots.speak.fractions.* **Sun 21 June (11-4.30). Adm £6.50, chd free. Home-made teas.** Donation to International Dendrology Society.
7 acre garden overlooking Windermere which has undergone extensive redevelopment since 2018. Formal gardens designed by Mawson and Avray Tipping inc sunken borders, rose garden and croquet lawn. Newly planted woodland walk, bog garden and renovated Yew maze. Naturalistic planting, areas left for wildlife and many fine trees. New kitchen garden built 2022 and original Messenger glasshouse. There is some level access to formal areas of the garden but only via gravel paths.

In 2025, our donations to Carers Trust helped them support over 1 million unpaid carers across the UK, as part of their network of local carer centres.

DERBYSHIRE

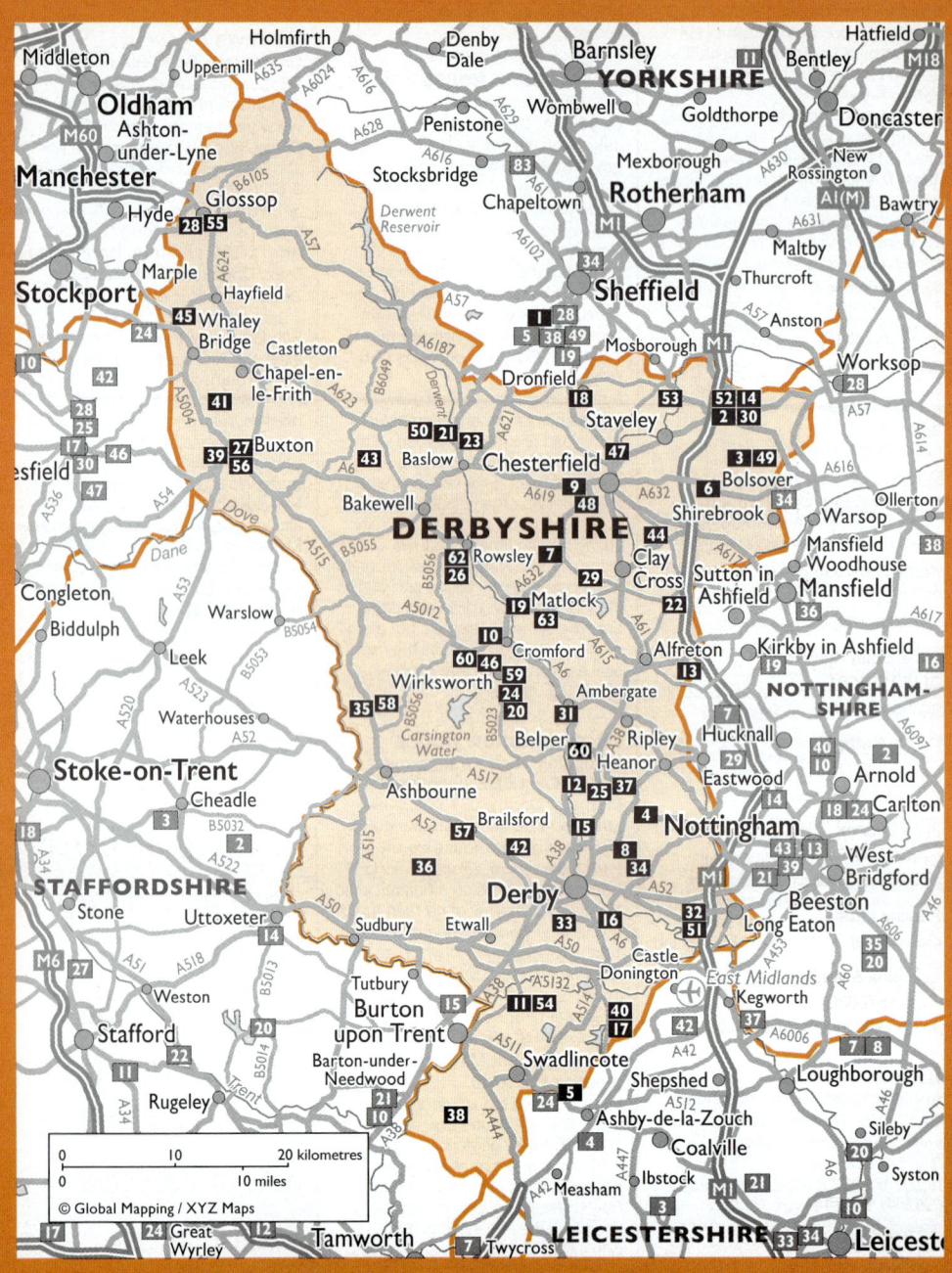

VOLUNTEERS

County Organiser
Hildegard Wiesehofer
07809 883393
hildegard@ngs.org.uk

County Treasurer
Anne Wilkinson
07831 598396
annelwilkinson@btinternet.com

Social Media
Tracy & Bill Reid
07932 977314
billandtracyreid@ngs.org.uk

Booklet Co-ordinators
Dave & Valerie Booth
07891 436632
valerie.booth1955@gmail.com

Group Visit Co-ordinator
Pauline Little
01283 702267
plittle@hotmail.co.uk

Assistant County Organisers
Dave & Valerie Booth
(See above)

Kathy Fairweather
07779 412702
kathy.fairweather@ngs.org.uk

Gill & Colin Hancock
01159 301061
gillandcolinhancock@gmail.com

Paul & Kathy Harvey
01629 822218
pandk.harvey@ngs.org.uk

Jane Lennox
07939 012634
jane@lennoxonline.net

Pauline Little
(See above)

Christine & Vernon Sanderson
01246 570830
christine.r.sanderson@uwclub.net

@ngsderbyshire
@derbyshirengs

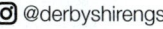

OPENING DATES

All entries subject to change.
For latest information check
www.ngs.org.uk
Map locator numbers are shown to the right of each garden name.

February

Snowdrop Openings

Saturday 7th
The Old Vicarage 46

Sunday 8th
The Old Vicarage 46

Saturday 14th
The Dower House 17

Sunday 15th
The Dower House 17

Saturday 28th
Meveril Lodge 41

March

Sunday 1st
Coxbench Hall 15
Meveril Lodge 41

Sunday 8th
Fern Bank 20

Saturday 21st
Chevin Brae 12

Sunday 29th
36 Edge Road 19

April

Monday 6th
Greenacres 25
Repton NGS Village Gardens 54

Sunday 12th
The Paddock 47

Saturday 18th
◆ Cascades Gardens 10

Sunday 19th
Dronfield Hall Barn 18

Wednesday 22nd
NEW ◆ Bolsover Castle 6

Sunday 26th
Barlborough Gardens 2
Holmlea 31

May

Monday 4th
Repton NGS Village Gardens 54

Wednesday 6th
◆ Renishaw Hall & Gardens 53

Saturday 9th
NEW Ivy House 32

Sunday 10th
Fir Croft 21
NEW Ivy House 32
27 Wash Green 59

Saturday 16th
334 Belper Road 4
2 Haddon View 26
The Old Vicarage 46

Sunday 17th
2 Haddon View 26
Locko Park 34
The Old Vicarage 46

Wednesday 20th
Fir Croft 21

Saturday 23rd
12 Ansell Road 1
◆ Cascades Gardens 10
Longford Hall Farm 36
Moorfields 44

Sunday 24th
12 Ansell Road 1
Longford Hall Farm 36
Moorfields 44
60 Poplar Road 51

Monday 25th
12 Ansell Road 1
◆ Tissington Hall 58

June

Wednesday 3rd
Fir Croft 21
Repton NGS Village Gardens 54

Thursday 4th
The Hollies 30

Saturday 6th
The Dower House 17
Ford Lodge 22
The Smithy 56

Sunday 7th
334 Belper Road 4
88 Church Street West 13
The Dower House 17
Ford Lodge 22
Gorsey Bank Gardens 24
The Smithy 56

Wednesday 10th
The Hollies 30

Saturday 13th
The Barn Chalico Farm 3
◆ Cascades Gardens 10
Holmlea 31
NEW The Lodge, Tissington Gates 35
◆ Melbourne Hall Gardens 40
Pear Tree Cottage 49

Sunday 14th
The Barn Chalico Farm 3
Fir Croft 21
Holmlea 31
◆ Melbourne Hall Gardens 40
◆ Meynell Langley Trials Garden 42
Pear Tree Cottage 49

Wednesday 17th
◆ Bluebell Arboretum and Nursery 5

Saturday 20th
NEW Southcot, The Green 57

Sunday 21st
NEW Southcot, The Green 57

Wednesday 24th
NEW Pingle Cottage 50

Saturday 27th
Gorse Cottage 23

Sunday 28th
Gorse Cottage 23
High Roost 28
Hill Cottage 29
Slatelands House 55

July

Wednesday 1st
◆ Renishaw Hall & Gardens 53

Saturday 4th
12 Ansell Road 1
NEW The Lodge, Tissington Gates 35
Meveril Lodge 41

Sunday 5th
12 Ansell Road 1
8 Curzon Lane 16
Meveril Lodge 41
60 Poplar Road 51
Yew Tree Bungalow 63

Monday 6th
◆ Tissington Hall 58

Saturday 11th
Barlborough Gardens 2
Longford Hall Farm 36

Sunday 12th
Barlborough Gardens 2
Longford Hall Farm 36
◆ Meynell Langley Trials Garden 42
The Paddock 47

Wednesday 15th
◆ Bluebell Arboretum and Nursery 5

Saturday 18th
◆ Cascades Gardens 10
NEW Hawthornden 27
Marlborough Cottage 39
New Mills School 45

Sunday 19th
8 Curzon Lane 16
NEW Hawthornden 27
58A Main Street 38
Marlborough Cottage 39
49 Middle Row 43
New Mills School 45

Saturday 25th
2 Haddon View 26
NEW The Lodge, Tissington Gates 35
26 Windmill Rise 61
Woodend Cottage 62

Sunday 26th
2 Haddon View 26
26 Windmill Rise 61
Woodend Cottage 62

August

Saturday 1st
Byways 9

Sunday 2nd
Byways 9
Greenacres 25
9 Main Street 37

Sunday 9th
Clarendon 14
8 Curzon Lane 16
Raiswells House 52

Sunday 16th
36 Edge Road 19
◆ Meynell Langley Trials Garden 42
Yew Tree Bungalow 63

Bolsover Castle

DERBYSHIRE

Monday 17th	
♦ Tissington Hall	58
Wednesday 19th	
♦ Bluebell Arboretum and Nursery	5
Saturday 22nd	
Chevin Brae	12
Sunday 23rd	
27 Wash Green	59
Monday 24th	
♦ Tissington Hall	58
Saturday 29th	
12 Ansell Road	1
12 Water Lane	60
Sunday 30th	
12 Ansell Road	1
The Hollies	30
12 Water Lane	60
Monday 31st	
12 Ansell Road	1
Repton NGS Village Gardens	54
♦ Tissington Hall	58

September

Saturday 5th	
The Old Vicarage	46
Sunday 6th	
Broomfield Hall	8
Coxbench Hall	15
♦ Meynell Langley Trials Garden	42
The Old Vicarage	46
Saturday 12th	
Holmlea	31
Sunday 13th	
Holmlea	31

By Arrangement

Arrange a personalised garden visit with your club, or group of friends, on a date to suit you. See individual garden entries for full details.

12 Ansell Road	1
Askew Cottage (Repton NGS Village Gardens)	54
334 Belper Road	4
Brierley Farm	7
Byways	9

10 Chestnut Way (Repton NGS Village Gardens)	54
Chevin Brae	12
88 Church Street West	13
Coxbench Hall	15
8 Curzon Lane	16
The Dower House	17
Greenacres	25
High Roost	28
34 High Street (Repton NGS Village Gardens)	54
Hill Cottage	29
The Hollies	30
Holmlea	31
Littleover Lane Allotments	33
9 Main Street	37
58A Main Street	38
Meveril Lodge	41
Moorfields	44
The Old Vicarage	46
The Paddock	47
Park Hall	48
22 Pinfold Close (Repton NGS Village Gardens)	54
60 Poplar Road	51
The Smithy	56
27 Wash Green	59
12 Water Lane	60
Yew Tree Bungalow	63

THE GARDENS

1 12 ANSELL ROAD

Ecclesall, Sheffield, S11 7PE. Dave Darwent, 01246 413667, poptasticdave@me.com. *Approx 3m SW of City Centre. Travel to Ringinglow Rd (88 bus), then Edale Rd (opp Ecclesall CofE Primary Sch). 3rd R - garden is on L ¾ way down.* **Sat 23, Sun 24, Mon 25 May, Sat 4, Sun 5 July, Sat 29, Sun 30, Mon 31 Aug (12-5). Adm £4, chd free. Light refreshments inc vegan & GF options. Visits also by arrangement 1 Apr to 23 Aug for groups of up to 15. Adm price inc tea, coffee and cake for by arrangement visits.**
98 yrs after being created outside the then newly built house, this suburban garden remains in the same family and is largely unchanged from 1928. This year, some areas are being rejuvenated, inc the main rose bed and the lawns. Between 2026 and 2028, a programme of rejuvenation is under way to restore some tired elements of the garden to their former vigour.

✿ ☕))

GROUP OPENING

2 BARLBOROUGH GARDENS

Clowne Road, Barlborough, Chesterfield, S43 4EH. Christine Sanderson, 07956 203184, christine.r.sanderson@uwclub.net, www.facebook.com/barlboroughgardens. *7m NE of Chesterfield. Off A619 between Chesterfield & Worksop. ½m E M1, J30. Follow signs for Barlborough then yellow NGS signs. At De Rhodes Arms r'about take 3rd exit onto Clowne Rd S43 4EH - where 2 gardens located.* **Sun 26 Apr (11.30-4.30). Combined adm £5, chd free. Sat 11, Sun 12 July (11.30-4.30). Combined adm £7, chd free. Tea, coffee & cake.**

90 BOUGHTON LANE
S43 4QF. Angela and Ian Cross.
Open on Sat 11, Sun 12 July
GREYSTONES BARN
S43 4EN. Kathryn and John Hardwick.
Open on Sat 11, Sun 12 July
THE HOLLIES
Vernon, Christine and Fleur Sanderson.
Open on all dates
(See separate entry)
LINDWAY
S43 4TR. Thomas Pettinger.
Open on all dates
THE RED BRICK HOUSE
S43 4TS. Steven and Ashlyn Miller.
Open on Sat 11, Sun 12 July

Barlborough is an ancient village, steeped in history, perched on the top of yellow limestone scarp in the furthest North East corner of Derbyshire. The July weekend garden opening coincides with the 'Big Barlborough Festival' with lots of additional exhibitions and activities taking place. St James The Greater Church, an ancient place of worship will be open to visitors both afternoons of the July opening weekend. Five colourful gardens of different sizes and styles will be opening their garden gates. A map detailing the location of all five gardens will be issued with adm ticket. More information can be found by visiting the Barlborough Gardens

121

Facebook page. Packets of feed can be purchased at 90 Boughton Lane to feed the poultry. Partial wheelchair access at The Hollies, 90 Boughton Lane and Greystones Barn.

3 THE BARN CHALICO FARM
Elmton, Worksop, S80 4LS. **Mrs Anne Merrick.** *2m from Creswell, 3m from Clowne, 5m from J30, M1. From M1 J30 take A616 to Newark. Follow approx 4m. Turn R at Elmton signpost. At junc turn R, the village centre is in ½m.* **Sat 13, Sun 14 June (1-5). Combined adm with Pear Tree Cottage £6, chd free. Cream teas at the Old Schoolroom next to the church. Soft drinks available.**
A new garden in keeping with the Arts & Crafts style. The beds have been raised for ease of maintenance with easy access pathways throughout. An orchard of fruit trees has been planted, a woodland garden created and pre-existing wildflower meadow has been maintained. Village trail with interpretation boards.

4 334 BELPER ROAD
Stanley Common, DE7 6FY. **Gill & Colin Hancock,** 01159 301061, gillandcolinhancock@gmail.com. *7m N of Derby. 3m W of Ilkeston. On A609, ¾m from Rose & Crown Xrds (A608). Please park in field up farm drive.* **Sat 16 May, Sun 7 June (12-4). Adm £5, chd free.** Visits also by arrangement 11 Apr to 27 June for groups of up to 30. Refreshments inc in adm price for by arrangement visits.
Beautiful country garden with many attractive features inc a laburnum tunnel, rose and wisteria domes, old workmen's hut, wildlife pond. Take a walk through the 10 acres of woodland and glades to a ½ acre lake. Organic vegetable garden. See the lovely wisteria pergola in May and wild orchids and rose meadow in June. Plenty of seating to enjoy home-made cakes. Children welcome with plenty of activities to keep them entertained. Abundant wildlife.

5 ♦ BLUEBELL ARBORETUM AND NURSERY
Annwell Lane, Smisby, Ashby-de-la-Zouch, LE65 2TA. **Robert Vernon,** 01530 413700, sales@bluebellnursery.com, www.bluebellnursery.com. *1m NW of Ashby-de-la-Zouch. Arboretum is clearly signed in Annwell Ln (follow brown signs), ¼m S, through village of Smisby off B5006, between Ticknall & Ashby-de-la-Zouch. Free parking.* **For NGS: Wed 17 June, Wed 15 July, Wed 19 Aug (9-4). Adm £6, chd free.** For other opening times and information, please phone, email or visit garden website.
Beautiful 9 acre woodland garden with a large collection of rare trees and shrubs. Interest throughout the year with spring flowers, cool leafy areas in summer and sensational autumn colour. Many information posters describing the more obscure plants. Adjacent specialist tree and shrub nursery. Please be aware this is not a wood full of bluebells, despite the name. The woodland garden is fully labelled and the staff can answer questions or talk at length about any of the trees or shrubs on display. Please wear sturdy, waterproof footwear during or after wet weather. Full wheelchair access however grass paths can become inaccessible after heavy rain.

49 Middle Row

DERBYSHIRE

6 BOLSOVER CASTLE [NEW]
Castle Street, Bolsover, Chesterfield, S44 6PR. English Heritage. *Located in the town of Bolsover, 6m E of Chesterfield on A632. If you are travelling to the castle via the M1, leave at J29a.* **For NGS: Evening opening Wed 22 Apr (5.30-7). Adm £20, chd free. Pre-booking essential, please email fundraising@english-heritage.org.uk or visit www.english-heritage.org.uk/visit/places/bolsover-castle/events for information & booking. Light refreshments inc in adm price.** For other opening times and information, please email or visit garden website.

Meet the Head Gardener and members of their team for an exclusive evening tour. Bolsover Castle is an extraordinary C17 aristocratic retreat. Explore the Fountain Garden with its C17 Venus fountain, framed by period planting and fan-trained fruit trees; wander the restored wall walk for sweeping views of the Vale of Scarsdale. Tickets will be available to buy from the English Heritage website from 1st March 2026.

☕

7 BRIERLEY FARM
Mill Lane, Brockhurst, Ashover, Chesterfield, S45 0HS. Anne & David Wilkinson, 07831 598396, annelwilkinson@btinternet.com. *6m SW of Chesterfield, 4m NE of Matlock, 1½m NW of Ashover. From the A632 turn W into Alicehead Rd, L into Swinger Ln, 2nd L into Brockhurst Ln & R into Mill Ln. Brierley Farm is the only house on the L.* **Visits by arrangement 8 June to 28 Aug for groups of 15 to 30. Afternoons only. Adm £10. Home-made teas on request; please ask for pricing.**

This hillside site features two acres of garden and lawns and three acres of woodland with paths - a bridge over the dividing stream connects the two. There are three linked ponds and raised stone-walled beds featuring seasonal planting from early spring through the summer and into the autumn.

8 BROOMFIELD HALL
Morley, Ilkeston, DE7 6DN. Derby College Group, www.facebook.com/BroomfieldPlantCentre. *4m N of Derby. 6m S of Heanor on A608, N of Derby.* **Sun 6 Sept (10-4). Adm £5, chd free. Tea, coffee & cake at a volunteer-led pop-up café.**

25 acres of constantly developing educational Victorian gardens/woodlands maintained by volunteers and students. Herbaceous borders, walled garden, themed gardens, rose garden, potager, prairie plantings, Japanese garden, tropical garden, winter garden and plant centre. Cacti, carnivorous, bonsai, fuchsia specialists and craft stalls. A gem of Derbyshire. Most of garden is accessible to wheelchair users and assistance is available if needed.

9 BYWAYS
7A Brookfield Avenue, Brookside, Chesterfield, S40 3NX. Terry & Eileen Kelly, 07414 827813, telkel1@aol.com. *1½m W of Chesterfield. Follow A619 from Chesterfield towards Baslow. Please park carefully in Brookfield School Car Park, or neighbouring roads. Brookfield Ave is 2nd on R.* **Sat 1, Sun 2 Aug (11.30-4.30). Adm £4, chd free. Light refreshments inc gluten free option. Visits also by arrangement 17 July to 14 Aug for groups of 10 to 25. Donation to Ashgate Hospice.**

Three times winners of the Best Back Garden over 80 sqm, and also twice winners of Best Front Garden, Best Container Garden and Best Hanging Basket in Chesterfield in Bloom. Well established perennial borders inc helenium, monardas, phlox, grasses, acers. Rockery and many planters containing acers, pelargoniums, ferns and hostas. Large shady pergola with acers, hostas and ferns.

10 CASCADES GARDENS ◆
Clatterway, Bonsall, Matlock, DE4 2AH. Alan & Alesia Clements, 07585 808067, cascadesgardens@gmail.com, www.cascadesgardens.com. *3m SW of Matlock. From Cromford A6 T-lights turn to Wirksworth. Turn R along Via Gellia, signed Buxton & Bonsall. After 1m turn R up hill towards Bonsall. Garden entrance at top of hill. Park in village car park.* **For NGS: Sat 18 Apr, Sat 23 May, Sat 13 June, Sat 18 July (12-3). Adm £8, chd £4. Home-made teas. For other opening times and information, please email or visit garden website.**

The Meditation Garden and Bonsai centre: Fascinating 4 acre peaceful garden in spectacular natural surroundings with woodland, cliffs, stream, pond and an old limestone quarry. Inspired by Japanese gardens and Buddhist philosophy, secluded garden rooms for relaxation and reflection. Beautiful landscape with a wide collection of unusual perennials, conifers, shrubs and trees. Mostly wheelchair accessible. Gravel paths, some steep slopes.

11 10 CHESTNUT WAY
Repton, DE65 6FQ. Pauline Little, 07842 500673, plittle@hotmail.co.uk. *6m S of Derby. From A38/A50, S of Derby, follow signs to Willington, then Repton. In Repton turn R at r'about. Chestnut Way is ¼m up hill, on L.* **Visits by arrangement for groups of 5 to 30. Soup available for winter openings. Adm £10, chd free. Light refreshments.**

A large and wonderfully diverse garden with lots of separate areas of interest and thoughtful planting throughout. The unusual sculptures and renowned home-made teas make for a memorable visit. Overflowing borders and a surprise round every corner. Come in May for the best selection of plants for sale from the garden. Special interest in woodland/shade plants and composting. Level garden, good solid paths to main areas. Some grass/bark paths. Can be wet in winter, come prepared.

---

70 inpatients and their families are being supported at the newly opened Horatio's Garden Northern Ireland, thanks to the National Garden Scheme donations.

2 CHEVIN BRAE
Chevin Road, Milford, Belper, DE56 0QH. Dr David Moreton, 07778 004374, davidmoretonchevinbrae@gmail.com. 1½m S of Belper. Coming from S on A6 turn L at Strutt Arms & cont up Chevin Rd. Park on Chevin Rd. After 300yds follow arrow to L up Morrells Ln. After 300yds Chevin Brae on L with silver garage. **Sat 21 Mar, Sat 22 Aug (1-5). Adm £3, chd free. Home-made teas inc cakes, pastries and biscuits which are also home-made. Many feature fruit and jam from the garden.** Visits also by arrangement 2 Feb to 1 Oct for groups of up to 16. Adm inc refreshments for by arrangement visits.

A large garden, with swathes of daffodils in the orchard during spring. Extensive wildflower planting along edge of wood features aconites, snowdrops, wood anemones, fritillaries and dog's tooth violets. Other parts of garden will have hellebores and early camellias. In the summer, the large flower borders and rose trellises give much colour, and the vegetable and fruit gardens are at their peak.

3 88 CHURCH STREET WEST
Pinxton, NG16 6PU. Rosemary Ahmed, 07842 141210. *Pinxton is approx 1m from M1 J28. At motorway island take B6019 to Alfreton & take the 1st L Pinxton Ln which turns into Alfreton Rd, the garden is signposted from there.* **Sun 7 June (12-4.30). Adm £4, chd free. Light refreshments inc home-made cakes.** Visits also by arrangement 20 Apr to 20 Sept for groups of 5 to 20.

Plantwoman's garden, developed over 25 yrs to inc collections of hardy geraniums, agaves, ferns, persicaria and grasses. The garden has a quirky mix of salvage items. A wild lawn, small rockery, upcycled garden room with mature grapevine, mixed borders and a large patio with displays of succulents. The garden is on several levels and has steep steps.

4 CLARENDON
28 Clowne Road, Barlborough, Chesterfield, S43 4EN. Neil & Lorraine Jones. *7m NE of Chesterfield. 7m W of Worksop, off J30 of M1. Clarendon and Raiswell House are within easy walking distance of each other; with 2 pubs in between.* **Sun 9 Aug (11.30-4.30). Combined adm with Raiswells House £5, chd free.**

A bay tree archway leads to the first of many seating areas, underneath a specimen Cedar. This leads to a triangular shaped front lawn and an artificial stream. A pathway of York stones then takes you down the side of the house to a very secluded rear garden full of specimen conifers, evergreen shrubs and acers. Plenty of comfortable seating to enjoy the vistas and the summer sunshine. Secret walkways meander around the perimeter of the garden leading to a gazebo, a pond with bridge and waterfall, a playhouse, a pear archway, vegetable planters and a greenhouse. Brass band playing during the afternoon. Partial wheelchair access.

5 COXBENCH HALL
Alfreton Road, Coxbench, Derby, DE21 5BB. Coxbench Hall Ltd, 01332 880200, office@coxbench-hall.co.uk, www.coxbench-hall.co.uk. *4m N of Derby close to A38. After going through Little Eaton, turn L onto Alfreton Rd for 1m, Coxbench Hall is on L next to Fox & Hounds pub between Little Eaton & Holbrook. From A38 take Kilburn turn & go towards Little Eaton.* **Sun 1 Mar (10-11.30am); Sun 6 Sept (2.30-4.30). Adm £4, chd free. Tea, coffee & cake inc home-made diabetic, dairy free and gluten free cakes.** Visits also by arrangement Mar to Sept for groups of up to 15. Refreshments available at an additional cost.

Former ancestral Georgian Home of the Meynell family, the gardens focus on sustainability, organic and wildlife friendly themes. There is a tropical style garden, ponds, hostas, fruits, C18 potting shed, veteran yew tree and hillside terraced garden of wildflowers and trees with a curved stone path incorporating reclaimed sleepers. A stoned path by the upper woodland overlooks the gardens below. The wheelchair accessible gardens are developed to inspire the senses of the residents via different colours, textures and fragrances of plants. Block paved path around the edges of the main lawn. Regret no wheelchair access to woodland area.

6 8 CURZON LANE
Alvaston, Derby, DE24 8QS. John & Marian Gray, 01332 601596, maz@curzongarden.com, www.curzongarden.com. *2m SE of Derby city centre. From city centre take A6 (London Rd) towards Alvaston. Curzon Ln on L, approx ½m before Alvaston shops.* **Sun 5, Sun 19 July, Sun 9 Aug (12.30-4.30). Adm £4, chd free. Tea, coffee & cake.** Visits also by arrangement July & Aug for groups of 10 to 30.

Mature garden with lawns, borders packed full with perennials, shrubs and small trees, tropical planting and hot border. Ornamental and wildlife ponds, greenhouse with different varieties of tomato, cucumber, peppers and chillies. Well-stocked vegetable plot. Gravel area and large patio with container planting.

7 THE DOWER HOUSE
Church Square, Melbourne, DE73 8JH. William & Griselda Kerr, 07799 883777, griseldakerr@btinternet.com. *6m S of Derby. 5m W of J23A M1. 4m N of J13 M42. When in Church Sq, turn R just before the church by a blue sign giving service times. Gates are 50 yds ahead.* **Sat 14, Sun 15 Feb (10-3.30); Sat 6, Sun 7 June (10-4.30). Adm £8, chd free. Tea, coffee & cake.** Visits also by arrangement 1 Apr to 30 Oct for groups of 10 to 50. All tours guided. No indoor tearoom; refreshments if weather allows.

Beautiful view of Melbourne Pool from balustraded terrace of 1829 house. Garden drops steeply by paths, arbour or steps down a bank of some 60 shrubs, to lawn with herbaceous borders. Numerous paths lead to different areas of the garden, providing varied planting opportunities inc a bog garden, glade, shrubbery, grasses, herb and kitchen garden, rose tunnel, orchard and small woodland. Hidden paths and different areas entice children to explore the garden to find various hidden animals such as a bronze crocodile and stone dragons. Children must be supervised by an adult at all times due to the proximity of water. Wheelchair access is to top level of the garden only. Shoes with a good grip are essential as slopes are steep. There is no parking within 50 yds.

DERBYSHIRE 125

18 DRONFIELD HALL BARN
High Street, Dronfield,
S18 1PX. Dronfield Heritage
Trust, 07814 140034,
admin@dronfieldhallbarn.org,
www.dronfieldhallbarn.org.
*Dronfield High St, 5m S Sheffield,
5m Chesterfield, 5 min walk Dronfield
Stn. The Barn is located in the
centre of Dronfield. Please follow
the 'Garden Open for Charity' signs.
Two accessible spaces off (High St).
Free, unlimited parking at Sainsburys
(S18 1NW) to the rear.* **Sun 19 Apr
(10.30-4.30). Adm £4, chd free.
Light refreshments.**
Beautifully restored over 10 yrs by
Dronfield Heritage Trust volunteers,
the gardens surround the 1430
Grade II* listed medieval barn. In
April, visitors will enjoy a wide variety
of tulips across the borders, in pots
and species tulips in the rockeries.
Year-round interest inc native trees,
a medieval herb garden, and shade-
loving perennials. Spring bulbs.
Garden tour and talk. The garden and
barn are on one level, however the
main garden is situated on a slope.
There is a hard standing path that
runs top to bottom.

19 36 EDGE ROAD
Matlock, DE4 3NH. Mr David Pass.
*Matlock town centre. From the rear
M&S town centre car park, go up
Imperial Rd for about 150 metres.
Garden is on corner of Imperial Rd/
Edge Rd. Use the Edge Rd access.*
**Sun 29 Mar, Sun 16 Aug (10-4).
Adm £5, chd free. Tea, coffee &
cake.**
Matlock town centre garden of approx
1 acre. Beautifully designed and
landscaped. Herbaceous borders,
Japanese garden, wildlife pond,
mature trees, woodland walk, formal
borders and many points of interest.
Spectacular views of Riber Castle and
the Derwent Valley. This garden is a
real hidden gem.

20 FERN BANK
38 Gorsey Bank, Wirksworth,
Matlock, DE4 4AD. Scott
Thompson and Beccy Owen. *13m
N of Derby. 5m S of Matlock. From
Duffield on B5023. R onto Water
Ln immed after mini r'about, signed
Hannage Brook Medical Centre.
From Cromford on B5036/B5023
3rd L after pelican crossing. Parking
on Water Ln/Hannage Way.* **Sun
8 Mar (11-4). Adm £4, chd free.
Light refreshments. Opening with
Gorsey Bank Gardens on Sun 7
June.**
Set in a former small gritstone quarry,
this hillside garden is surrounded
by woodland and grazing farmland.
The garden is largely terraced, with
winding pathways, overlooked by
a magnificent gingko tree. This is a
wildlife friendly cottage style garden
in a unique setting. Spring highlights
inc snowdrops, daffodils, hellebores
and various spring flowering shrubs.
Please do not park beyond the
railway level crossing. It is a steep
uphill walk on tarmac to Fern Bank,
but the garden and spectacular views
are worth the effort.

21 FIR CROFT
Froggatt Road, Calver, S32 3ZD.
Dr S B Furness. *4m N of Bakewell.
At junc of B6001 with A625 (formerly
B6054), adj to Froggatt Edge
Garage.* **Sun 10, Wed 20 May, Wed
3, Sun 14 June (1-4). Adm by
donation.**
World renowned plantsman's garden,
large screes and rockery. 3000
alpines, dwarf conifers and rare native
plants, many not seen anywhere
else. Spectacular tufa wall with rare
alpines, ponds, lilies and cascade
system. 2 National Collections;
Sempervivium and Jovibarba. Peak
District endangered plant collection
pending (2026).Celebrating 40
consecutive years of NGS openings
by the same owner. Wheelchair
access to part of garden only.

♿ ❀ NPC

22 FORD LODGE
Winkpenny Lane, Tibshelf,
Alfreton, DE55 5RG. Richard and
Jean Briley. *7m S of Chesterfield.
Off B6014, Tibshelf High St. Turn at
the RS Fitness Studios and follow
yellow signs. Off street parking is
available in RS Fitness Studios Car
park by kind permission of RS.* **Sat
6, Sun 7 June (1-5). Adm £4, chd
free. Tea, coffee & cake.**
Various 'garden rooms,' ranging from
a formal area to our water themed,
cottage and Mediterranean garden.
There is a wide range of plants, from
roses through to Abyssinian bananas
and various grasses. Plenty of seating
areas from which to enjoy the relaxing
atmosphere whilst listening to the
sound of the stream and perhaps
enjoy afternoon tea and home-made
cakes, many of which are gluten free.

23 GORSE COTTAGE
Bar Road, Curbar, Hope Valley,
S32 3YB. Mrs Caralyn Denver. *Off
A623 in Curbar. Below Baslow &
Curbar Edges. 6m N of Bakewell,
3m to Chatsworth. Turn off A623
at Bridge Inn onto Bar Road. The
garden is ½m up the hill. Parking by
church or on lane. Limited disabled
parking.* **Sat 27, Sun 28 June
(11-4.30). Adm £4, chd free. Tea,
coffee & cake inc gluten free
options.**
Delightful cottage garden bounded
by mature trees, rhododendrons and
far-reaching views to Chatsworth.
Features inc a shady spring garden,
mixed perennial borders, secret
summerhouse, south facing patio
and pond, home to newts and
dragonflies. Beyond the hedge find
a hidden seat to enjoy the kitchen
garden, greenhouse and fruit trees,
lovingly tended by the grandchildren.
Wheelchair access to the patio, which
overlooks part of the garden.

♿ 🐕 ❀ ☕ 🔊

310,000 people are cared for each year who are approaching the end of life or diagnosed with a terminal illness through the hospice network supported by National Garden Scheme funding.

GROUP OPENING

24 GORSEY BANK GARDENS
Wirksworth, Matlock, DE4 4AB. Miss Philippa Cooper. At the southern edge of Wirksworth. From Duffield on B5023. R onto Water Ln immed after mini r'about, signed Hannage Brook Medical Centre. From Cromford on B5036/B5023 3rd L after pelican crossing. Parking on L off Hannage Way. **Sun 7 June (11-4). Combined adm £7, chd free. Light refreshments at Fern Bank. Home-made sandwiches and cake at Watts House.**

2 BROOKLANDS AVENUE
DE4 4AB. Miss Philippa Cooper.

FERN BANK
Scott Thompson and Beccy Owen.
(See separate entry)

MILL COTTAGE
DE4 4AD. Kirstie and Andy Lyne.

WATTS HOUSE
DE4 4AR. Sue and Robert Watts.

A charming hillside hamlet at the southern edge of the historic market town of Wirksworth, set in the beautiful Derbyshire Dales. This group features four gardens which demonstrate contrasting design responses to challenging terrain with a wide variety of planting; 2 Brooklands Ave has been developed since 2019, using a naturalistic planting style, with many interesting and unusual plants. Fern Bank is a hidden gem set in a small former quarry, surrounded by farmland, with beautiful views. Mill Cottage is a secluded cottage style garden with mill stream and architectural features, with seating areas to enjoy the different aspects. Watts House is a delightful tranquil garden. The four gardens are within comfortable walking distance, although it is a steep uphill walk on tarmac to Mill Cottage and Fern Bank, but the gardens and spectacular views are well worth the effort. The walk to Watts House is relatively flat. Ticket sales at 2 Brooklands Avenue. Flights of steps in all the gardens. Watts House features Robert's sculptures, some previously exhibited at RHS Chatsworth.

25 GREENACRES
Makeney Road, Holbrook, Belper, DE56 0TF. Veronica Holtom, 07749 277927, veronica.cooke1@icloud.com. 5m N of Derby. Approach via Makeney Rd using the private drive for Holbrook Hall Care Home. Disabled visitors park at the house; other visitors park at Holbrook St Michael's football club car park. **Mon 6 Apr, Sun 2 Aug (1-5). Adm £6, chd free. Tea, coffee & cake. Visits also by arrangement 1 Apr to 27 Sept for groups of 10 to 35.** Spectacular large garden in rural Derbyshire, wonderful uninterrupted countryside views. Stroll among pines, weeping birches, acers, oaks and beeches. Mature camellias, shrubs, hellebores and spring bulbs. Beautiful mixed beds and borders, ornamental grasses, lily pond, cascades and rock garden. Colourful patio plants, sweeping lawns, strategic seating areas and walkways. A peaceful haven. There are a few avoidable steps, and the majority of the site is fairly level.

26 2 HADDON VIEW
Birchover Road, Stanton-in-the-Peak, Matlock, DE4 2LR. Steve Tompkins. 5m S of Bakewell. At top of hill in Stanton-in-Peak on road to Birchover. Turn off A6 at Rowsley, or at the B5056, and follow signs. **Sat 16, Sun 17 May (11-4). Adm £4, chd free. Sat 25, Sun 26 July (11-4). Combined adm with Woodend Cottage £5, chd free. Tea, coffee & cake.**
In May, rhododendrons and azaleas make a lovely spring display. They surround the summerhouse and are part of the herbaceous borders. Marsh marigolds and bog bean encircle the four ponds. In July, the classic herbaceous borders are in full bloom. 50 pots are a great display and red, white and pink water lilies adorn the four ponds. Glorious views over Haddon Hall and towards Bakewell.

27 NEW HAWTHORNDEN
150 Lightwood Road, Buxton, SK17 6RW. Mr Frank Brennan. N of Buxton town centre, on E side of Lightwood Rd, down from junc with Corbar Rd. Hawthornden and Marlborough Cottage are 500m apart. All payments to be made at Marlborough Cottage. From Marlborough Cottage, turn L. At end of Corbar Rd, turn R. Hawthornden is No.150. **Sat 18, Sun 19 July (10.30-4.30). Combined adm with Marlborough Cottage £7, chd free.**
A varied garden with an extensive lawn leading into woodland over 1½ acres. Planted with hardy shrubs and perennials the lush gardens have several wildlife ponds and lead down to a brook. Backing on to Peak District farmland, the gardens are a jam-packed transition from formal to wild - great for children to explore.

28 HIGH ROOST
27 Storthmeadow Road, Simmondley, Glossop, SK13 6UZ. Peter & Christina Harris, 01457 863888, harrispeter448@gmail.com. ¾m SW of Glossop. From Glossop A57 to Manchester, L at 2nd r'about, up Simmondley Ln nr top R turn. From Marple A626 to Glossop, in Ch'worth R up Town Ln past Hare & Hound pub 2nd L. **Sun 28 June (12-4). Adm £5, chd free. Tea, coffee & cake. Visits also by arrangement 25 May to 12 July for groups of up to 30. Donation to Donkey Sanctuary.**
Garden on terraced slopes, views over fields and hills. Winding paths, archways and steps explore different garden rooms packed with plants, designed to attract wildlife. Alpine bed, gravel gardens; vegetable garden, water features, statuary, troughs and planters. A garden which needs exploring to discover its secrets tucked away in hidden corners. Features inc a craft stall, children's garden quiz and lucky dip.

29 HILL COTTAGE
Ashover Road, Littlemoor, Ashover, nr Chesterfield, S45 0BL. Jane Tomlinson & Tim Walls, 07946 388185, lavenderhen@aol.com. 1.8m from Ashover village, 6.3m from Chesterfield & 6.1m from Matlock. Hill Cottage is on Ashover Rd (also known as Stubben Edge Ln). Opp the end of Eastwood Ln. **Sun 28 June (10.30-4). Adm £4, chd free. Tea, coffee & cake. Visits also by arrangement 29 June to 31 July for groups of up to 15.**
Hill Cottage is a lovely example of an English country cottage garden. Whilst small, the garden has full mixed borders packed with colour

and fragrance, around a heart shaped lawn. Hostas, dahlias and a wide variety of perennials and annuals grown in pots. The gravel garden is a recent addition. Also a greenhouse full of chillies, tomatoes and scented pelargoniums and a small Potager. Far-reaching views over a pastoral landscape to Ogston reservoir.

30 THE HOLLIES
87 Clowne Road, Barlborough, Chesterfield, S43 4EH. Vernon, Christine and Fleur Sanderson, 07956 203184, christine.r.sanderson@uwclub.net, www.facebook.com/barlboroughgardens. *7m NE of Chesterfield. Off A619 midway between Chesterfield & Worksop. ½m E M1, J30. Follow signs for Barlborough then yellow NGS signs. At De Rhodes Arms r'about take 3rd exit onto Clowne Rd. Garden at far end on L. Please drive past to park further along Clowne Rd and walk back.* **Thur 4, Wed 10 June (1.30-4.30). Cream teas. Sun 30 Aug (11.30-4.30). Tea, coffee & cake. Adm £4, chd free. Opening with Barlborough Gardens on Sun 26 Apr, Sat 11, Sun 12 July. Visits also by arrangement May to Aug for groups of 10 to 30.**
The Hollies maximises the unusual garden layout and ine shade area, patio garden with Moroccan corner, cottage border plus fruit trees. A wide selection of home-made cakes on offer inc gluten free, sugar free, dairy free and vegan options. Home-made preserves for sale. Extensive view across arable farmland. An area of the garden, influenced by the Majorelle Garden in Marrakech, was achieved using upcycled items together with appropriate planting. This garden project was featured on an episode of "Love Your Garden". Partial wheelchair access - gravel paths on either side of the house lead to the patio area.

31 HOLMLEA
Derby Road, Ambergate, Belper, DE56 2EJ. Bill & Tracy Reid, 07932 977314, billandtracy.reid@gmail.com. *On the A6 in Ambergate - between Belper & Matlock. 9m N of Derby, 6m S of Matlock. Easy access from M1 J28. On A6 next to Bridge House Cafe. Additional Parking at Anila Restaurant opp Hurt Arms. Short walk from Ambergate Stn.* **Sun 26 Apr, Sat 13, Sun 14 June, Sat 12, Sun 13 Sept (11-4). Adm £5, chd free. Home-made teas in 'The Pavilion'. Refreshments self-service with honesty box. Gluten free and vegan options. Visits also by arrangement 15 June to 3 July for groups of 10+.**
Explore the 1½ acre garden, described by many visitors as unique. Wide variety of plants grown in different situations. Large kitchen garden inc cut flower patch, beautiful riverside walk and canal lock water feature. Visitors are invited in April for apple blossom, June for roses and pop-up garden railway and September for late season colour. Children very welcome. Adjacent to Shining Cliff Woods, SSI. Wheelchair route around main features of the garden. Unfortunately the Riverside Walk is not suitable for wheelchairs.

32 NEW IVY HOUSE
56 Longmoor Lane, Breaston, Derby, DE72 3BB. Mrs Sue Hayward, www.facebook.com/IvyHouseBreastonNGS. *From M1 and A52 Exit J25 for Long Eaton, Turn R at the mini island, Turn R on bend for Longmoor Ln, under motorway bridge. Ivy House is on the LHS. What3words app: mint.bubble.loves.* **Sat 9, Sun 10 May (10-4). Adm £5, chd free. Tea, coffee & cake.**
Contemporary meets a traditional romantic garden; Overarching trees and paths leading to areas each with a different focus to discover. The owner is a professional garden designer and two-time Chelsea Gold Medal winner, with a passion for unusual shrubs and flowering trees. Small water features add character throughout. Wildlife friendly. Visitors can enjoy tea and cake in the quirky garden bothy. Features inc a pond garden, orchard, cutting garden, meadow. fernery and a 'gnomery'. Most main features accessible. Access to terrace via main entrance. Alternative entrance for wheelchair to main garden and tea area but rough ground.

33 LITTLEOVER LANE ALLOTMENTS
19 Littleover Lane, Normanton, Derby, DE23 6JF. 07746 114678, info@littleoverlaneallotments.org.uk, www.littleoverlaneallotments.org.uk. *On Littleover Ln opp the junc with Foremark Ave. Off the Derby Outer Ring Rd (A5111). At the Normanton Park r'about turn into Stenson Rd then R into Littleover Ln. The main gates are on the L as you travel down the road.* **Visits by arrangement 3 Mar to 30 Oct. Refreshments provided.**
A quiet oasis just off Derby's Outer Ring Road, hidden away in a residential area. A private site of nearly 12 acres, established in 1920, cultivated in a variety of ways, inc organic, no dig and potager style. Come and chat with plot holders about their edibles and ornamentals. Many exotic and Heritage varieties cultivated. Later in the year produce can be available to sample. The many allotments showcase a wide variety of gardening styles and provide you with inspiration for your own garden. Disabled parking is available on site. All avenues are stoned, but the extensive site is on a slope and so some areas not easily accessible.

34 LOCKO PARK
Locko Road, Spondon, Derby, DE21 7BW. Lucy Palmer, www.lockopark.co.uk. *6m NE of Derby. From A52 Borrowash bypass, 2m N via B6001, turn to Spondon. SatNav use DE21 7BW Via Locko Rd. What3words app: shady.cheeks.judge.* **Sun 17 May (2-5). Adm £7, chd free. Tea, coffee & cake.**
An original 1927 open garden for the National Garden Scheme. A large garden, consisting of a pleasure garden and a rose garden. Extensive grounds featuring rhododendrons. House (not open) by Smith of Warwick with Victorian additions. Chapel (open) built by Charles II, with original ceiling. Tulip tree in the arboretum purported to be the largest in the Midlands. Large collection of rhododendron and azalea.

The National Garden Scheme funded six Macmillan Nurses in their roles across England, Wales and Northern Ireland in 2025.

128 DERBYSHIRE

35 NEW THE LODGE, TISSINGTON GATES
Tissington, Ashbourne, DE6 1NH. Clare Greenwood & Patrick Poitevin. *4m N of Ashbourne. On A515 Ashbourne to Buxton. Roadside parking by The Lodge & along The Avenue. Additional parking available in the village & in the Tissington Trail car park.* **Sat 13 June, Sat 4, Sat 25 July (11.30-4). Adm £4, chd free. Home-made teas.**
Once hidden behind a wall of trees, the ½ acre garden is in a process of transformation. Now with 360° views of the countryside, you'll see a variety of traditional cottage garden plants inc roses, foxgloves and poppies among other more recent additions (many grown on from seed). There's also a vegetable plot, greenhouse, young orchard and an astronomical observatory with an 11 inch telescope. On a sunny day, there's the opportunity to safely view the sun and observe its incredible solar activity through specialist telescopes.

36 LONGFORD HALL FARM
Longford, Ashbourne, DE6 3DS. Liz Wolfenden, www.longfordhallfarmholidaycottages.co.uk. *From A52 take turn to Hollington. At T-junc (Long Ln) turn R & follow signs. Use drive with Longford Hall Farm sign at the entrance.* **Sat 23, Sun 24 May, Sat 11, Sun 12 July (1.30-5). Adm £5, chd free. Home-made teas.**
The garden consists of a large front garden, where shrubs such as hydrangeas, roses, ferns, grasses and hosta beds surround a modern pond and fountain. There is also a large pond with pontoon and a stumpery. The rear walled garden has traditional herbaceous borders and a modern rill feature. Most of the garden is on one level.

37 9 MAIN STREET
Horsley Woodhouse, Ilkeston, DE7 6AU. Ms Alison Napier, 01332 881629, ibhillib@btinternet.com. *3m SW of Heanor. 6m N of Derby. Turn off A608 Derby to Heanor Rd at Smalley, towards Belper, (A609). Garden on A609, 1m from Smalley turning.* **Sun 2 Aug (1.30-4.30). Adm £4, chd free. Cream teas. Soft drinks on request. Visits also by arrangement 16 May to 6 Sept for groups of 10 to 50.**
⅓ acre hilltop garden with lovely farmland views. Terracing, borders, lawns and pergola create space for an informal layout with planting for colour effect. Features inc large wildlife pond with water lilies, bog garden and small formal pool. Emphasis on carefully selected herbaceous perennials mixed with shrubs and old fashioned roses. Gravel garden for sun loving plants and scree garden, both developed from former drive. Wide collection of homegrown plants for sale - please bring your own carrier bag. All parts of the garden accessible to wheelchairs. Wheelchair adapted WC.

38 58A MAIN STREET
Rosliston, Swadlincote, DE12 8JW. Paul Marbrow, 07596 629886, paulmarbrow@hotmail.co.uk. *Rosliston. If exiting the M42, J11 onto the A444 to Overseal follow signs Linton then Rosliston. From A38, exit to Walton-on-Trent, then follow Rosliston signs. Brown signs for Rosliston Forestry will help.* **Sun 19 July (12.30-5.30). Adm £5, chd free. Light refreshments. Visits also by arrangement 18 June to 7 Aug for groups of 5 to 30.**
¾ acre garden formed from a once open field over the last few years. The garden has developed into themed areas and is changing and maturing. Japanese, arid beach, bamboo grove with ferns, water gardens etc. The 100m² indoor garden for cacti, exotic and tender plants, is now becoming established as a mini Eden. Areas are easily accessible, although some are only for the sure of foot, advice signs will be situated on unsuitable routes.

39 MARLBOROUGH COTTAGE
25 Corbar Road, Buxton, SK17 6RQ. Sandra and Graham Jowett. *Short distance N of Buxton Town Centre, off A5004 Manchester Rd. At junc with Marlborough R. 500 metres from Hathornden. Turn L as from Cottage to end of Corbar Rd. At Lightwood Rd turn R and Hawthornden is 6th on L. Free parking at both gardens.* **Sat 18, Sun 19 July (10.30-4.30). Combined adm with Hawthornden £7, chd free.**
Victorian gardener's cottage close to the centre of Georgian Buxton. ⅕ of an acre organic garden, reclaimed in the last seven years. It is 400m above sea level, surrounded by mature trees and is a tranquil haven for wildlife. Has front and rear borders, herbs and a variety of containers and ornaments. Also a small wildlife pond, wildflowers, vegetable beds, soft fruit and a greenhouse.

40 ♦ MELBOURNE HALL GARDENS
Church Square, Melbourne, Derby, DE73 8EN. Melbourne Gardens Charity, 01332 862502, info@melbournehall.com, www.melbournehall.com. *6m S of Derby. At Melbourne Market Place turn into Church St, go down to Church Sq. Garden entrance across visitor centre next to Melbourne Hall tearoom.* **For NGS: Sat 13, Sun 14 June (1-5). Adm £10, chd £5. For other opening times and information, please phone, email or visit garden website.**
A 17 acre historic garden with an abundance of rare trees and shrubs. Woodland and waterside planting with extensive herbaceous borders. Meconopsis, candelabra primulas, various Styrax and Cornus kousa. Other garden features inc Bakewells wrought iron arbour, a yew tunnel and fine C18 statuary and water features. Discover 300 yr old trees, waterside planting, feature hedges and herbaceous borders. Don't forget to visit the pigs, alpacas, goats and various other animals in their garden enclosures. Gravel paths, uneven surface in places, some steep slopes.

41 MEVERIL LODGE
Lesser Lane, Combs, High Peak, SK23 9UZ. Mrs Sally Williams, 07952 741640, williams.sally@live.co.uk. *5m S of Buxton. From B5470 Chapel-en-le-Frith, head to Combs village & Beehive Inn on R, turn L then R down Lesser Ln for ½ m. Parking limited at property, advised to park in village. What3words app: boat.appealing.hoot.* **Sat 28 Feb, Sun 1 Mar (11-3); Sat 4, Sun 5 July (11-5). Adm £6, chd free. Tea, coffee & cake inc gluten free and vegan options. Home-made soup and cheese scones at snowdrop opening. Visits also by arrangement 25 Feb to 31 Aug for groups of 10+. Short talk about the development of the garden its interesting plants.**

A recently developed 1½ acre rural garden surrounded by a stream, divided into areas themed by colour and season, with an emphasis on scented plants. White, summer, dark, hot, silver garden areas, and wildflower streamside walk, winter interest borders and kitchen garden. The garden has snowdrops, hellebores, roses and unusual trees and shrubs. Display of National Plant Collection of Peperomia. The paths around the garden are graveled, but mainly flat. The woodland streamside walk and hot gardens are not accessible by wheelchair.

& ✿ NPC ☕))

42 ♦ MEYNELL LANGLEY TRIALS GARDEN

Lodge Lane (off Flagshaw Lane), Kirk Langley, Ashbourne, DE6 4NT. Robert & Karen Walker, 01332 824358, enquiries@meynellgardens.com, www.meynellgardens.com. *4m W of Derby, nr Kedleston Hall. Head W out of Derby on A52. At Kirk Langley turn R onto Flagshaw Ln (signed to Kedleston Hall) then R onto Lodge Ln. Follow Meynell Langley Gardens signs.* **For NGS: Sun 14 June, Sun 12 July, Sun 16 Aug, Sun 6 Sept (10-4). Adm £5, chd free.** For other opening times and information, please phone, email or visit garden website.

A plant persons paradise with over 200 floral baskets and containers together with herbaceous perennial borders, fishpond and wildlife ponds, in total covering about an acre. 24 raised beds for vegetables and a greenhouse for tomatoes, cucumbers etc. The purpose of the garden is to trial and test the garden worthiness of plants grown at the adjacent nursery. Adjacent tearooms serving lunches and refreshments daily. Plant sales from adjacent nursery. Level ground, firm grass and some hard paths.

&   ☕))

43 49 MIDDLE ROW

Cressbrook, Buxton, SK17 8SX. Ms Jane Money and Mr Chris Gilbert. *4m NW of Bakewell. Midway between Litton and Monsal Head. Garden by phone box at top of village. Parking: Layby near Church 250 metre walk or limited roadside. Avoid white lines. What3words app: desire.aura.excavate.* **Sun 19 July (1-5). Adm £4. Tea, coffee & cake in the Cressbrook Club (next door). Gluten free and vegan options available.**

Steep, terraced, south facing, hillside garden in small, historic mill village, with glorious views over Monsal Dale. Formal side garden with Summerhouse, rose hedge and wisteria arch leads to surprise view over rockery, large, colourful herbaceous border and, further down, small herbaceous borders, two small ponds and wildlife area. Lower garden is accessed by steep steps with no handrail.

☕))

44 MOORFIELDS

261 Chesterfield Road, Temple Normanton, Chesterfield, S42 5DE. Peter, Janet & Stephen Wright, 01246 852306, peterwright100@hotmail.com. *4m SE of Chesterfield. From Chesterfield take A617 for 2m, turn on to B6039 through Temple Normanton, taking R fork signed Tibshelf, B6039. Garden ¼m on R.* **Sat 23, Sun 24 May (1-5). Adm £4, chd free. Light refreshments inc gluten free options.** Visits also by arrangement May & June for groups of 12+.

Two adjoining gardens, each planted for seasonal colour, which during the late spring and early summer feature perennials inc alliums, lupins, camassia and bearded irises. The larger garden has mature, mixed island beds and borders, a gravel garden to the front, a small wildflower area, large wildlife pond, orchard, soft fruit beds and vegetable garden. Open aspect with extensive views to mid Derbyshire.

✿

Hawthornden

45 NEW MILLS SCHOOL
Church Lane, New Mills, High Peak, SK22 4NR. Mr Craig Pickering. *12m NNW of Buxton. From A6 take A6105 signed New Mills, Hayfield. At CofE Church turn L onto Church Ln. Sch on L. Parking on site.* **Sat 18, Sun 19 July (2-5). Adm £4, chd free. Tea, coffee & cake in School Library.**
Mixed herbaceous perennials and shrub borders, with mature trees, lawns and gravel border situated in the semi-rural setting of the High Peak inc a Grade II listed building with four themed quads. The school was awarded highly commended in the School Garden 2019 RHS Tatton Show and won the Best High School Garden and the People's Choice Award. Ramps allow wheelchair access to most of outside.

46 THE OLD VICARAGE
The Fields, Middleton by Wirksworth, Matlock, DE4 4NH. Jane Irwing, 01629 825010, irwingjane@gmail.com. *Behind church on Main St & nr school. Travelling N on A6 from Derby turn L at Cromford, at top of hill turn R onto Porter Ln, at T-lights, turn R onto Main St. Park on Main St near DWT. Walk through churchyard. No parking at house.* **Sat 7, Sun 8 Feb (11-3). Light refreshments at the house. Sat 16, Sun 17 May (11-5); Sat 5, Sun 6 Sept (11-4). Home-made teas at the house. Adm £5, chd free. For February opening home made soup will be available. Visits also by arrangement 1 Mar to 20 Sept for groups of 5 to 20.**
Glorious garden with mixed flowering borders and mature trees in gentle valley with fantastic views to Black Rocks. All-season interest. Acid loving plants such as camellias and rhododendrons are grown in pots in courtyard garden. Tender ferns and exotic plants grown in fernery. Beyond is the orchard, fruit garden, vegetable patch and greenhouse, the home of honey bees, doves and hens. A garden designed to create a variety of different spaces in which to enjoy planting combinations from wide views over the countryside to enclosed and intimate places.

47 THE PADDOCK
12 Manknell Rd, Whittington Moor, Chesterfield, S41 8LZ. Mel & Wendy Taylor, 01246 451001, debijt9276@gmail.com. *2m N of Chesterfield. Whittington Moor just off A61 between Sheffield & Chesterfield. Parking at Victoria Working Mens Club, garden signed from here.* **Sun 12 Apr, Sun 12 July (11-5). Adm £4, chd free. Tea, coffee & cake. Visits also by arrangement Apr to Sept.**
½ acre garden incorporating small formal garden, stream and koi filled pond. Stone path over bridge, up some steps, past small copse, across the stream at the top and back down again. Past herbaceous border towards a pergola where cream teas can be enjoyed.

48 PARK HALL
Walton Back Lane, Walton, Chesterfield, S42 7LT. Kim Staniforth, 07785 784439, kim.staniforth@btinternet.com. *2m SW of Chesterfield centre. From town on A619 L into Somersall Ln. On A632 R into Acorn Ridge. Park on field side only of Walton Back Ln.* **Visits by arrangement Apr to July for groups of 10+. Adm £7, chd free.**
Romantic two acre plantsman's garden, in a stunningly beautiful setting surrounding C17 house (not open) four main rooms, terraced garden, parkland area with forest trees, croquet lawn, sunken garden with arbours, pergolas, pleached hedge, topiary, statuary, roses, rhododendrons, camellias, several water features. Two steps down to gain access to garden.

49 PEAR TREE COTTAGE
Elmton, Worksop, S80 4LS. Geoff & Janet Cutts. *2m from Creswell, 3m from Clowne, 5m from J30, M1. From M1 J30 take A616 to Newark. Follow approx 4m. Turn R at Elmton signpost. At junc turn R, the village centre is in ½ m. Garden opp The Elm Tree Inn.* **Sat 13, Sun 14 June (1-5). Combined adm with The Barn Chalico Farm £6, chd free. Cream teas at the Old School Room next to the church. Soft drinks available at The Barn Chalico Farm. Cakes for sale at Pear Tree Cottage.**
The owners have lived at Pear Tree Cottage for 49 years. Their aim has been to make a garden in the cottage style that is easy to maintain. A small vegetable patch shares the front garden as the back is just a lovely view over the local countryside. Small areas have different themes. There are fairies and other areas where plants are allowed to take over. Original water colour paintings for sale in The Little Gallery located at the garden.

50 NEW PINGLE COTTAGE
The Fold, Stoney Middleton, Hope Valley, S32 4TJ. Sally Shaw. *6m N of Bakewell, 1m E of Eyam, 3m NW of Chatsworth. Minutes from the A623 between Chapel-en-le-Frith and Chesterfield. Please park in the lay-bys on the A623, or considerately in the village. No parking at house.* **Wed 24 June (10.30-4). Adm £4, chd free. Home-made teas.**
0.7 acre garden, renovated over the last 4 yrs from neglect, but still a work in progress. Open, sloping garden with stunning views over the local Derbyshire Edges and down the wooded valley. Several planted beds inc a rubble bed and a prairie bed. Large productive area for vegetables and fruit. 2 patios, a large greenhouse, a pond. Tender plants in pots.

51 60 POPLAR ROAD
Breaston, Derby, DE72 3BH. Mrs Frances O'Brien, 079466 25745, frances.obrien60@googlemail.com. *Situated between Derby and Nottingham. From M1 J25, leave exit for Long Eaton onto Bostocks Ln. At mini r'about turn R then 1st R onto Longmoor Ln. After ½ m, turn L onto Poplar Rd. 1st house on L.* **Sun 24 May, Sun 5 July (1-5). Adm £6, chd free. Tea, coffee & cake. Visits also by arrangement 18 May to 12 July.**
Rambling roses and clematis climb through flowering fruit and conifer trees. Small flowering cornus and cersis trees. Ornamental ponds with mature fish. Plants with nectar rich flowers for bees and pollinators. Perennial wildflower meadow. Natural pond for spawning newts and frogs. Beehives, wood stack for hedgehogs, mice and insects. Gardens with sculpture and glass art surround house. Accessible in most parts of garden. Ground is mainly lawn with access points to some areas rather narrow.

DERBYSHIRE 131

52 RAISWELLS HOUSE
Park Street, Barlborough, Chesterfield, S43 4ES. Mr Andrew & Mrs Rosie Dale. *7m NE of Chesterfield. 7m W of Worksop, off J30 of M1. Clarendon and Raiswells House are within easy walking distance of each other, with 2 pubs in between.* **Sun 9 Aug (11.30-4.30). Combined adm with Clarendon £5, chd free. Light refreshments.**
A spacious ½ acre garden surrounded by fields and a woodland backdrop, designed to give a peaceful, calm, relaxing aura. Large borders are full of architectural foliage, trees, ferns, giant Agapanthus plants and a rose arch. There are 5 seating areas, all with dawn to dusk lighting, to enjoy different views of the garden. The summerhouse offers shade from the sunshine or shelter from the showers. Within the garden you will find a formal topiary courtyard and a koi pond. Brass band playing at Clarendon during the afternoon and with light refreshments available at Raiswells House. Partial access for wheelchairs.

53 ◆ RENISHAW HALL & GARDENS
Renishaw Park, Eckington, Sheffield, S21 3WB. Alexandra Hayward, 01246 432310, enquiries@renishaw-hall.co.uk, www.facebook.com/RenishawHall. *8m from Sheffield city centre. 2m from J30 on M1, well sign posted from J30 r'about. What3words app: bungalows.relished.staining.* **For NGS: Wed 6 May, Wed 1 July (10.30-4.30). Adm £12, chd £6. Takeaway kiosk at the Gardens entrance plus at Renishaw's Café within the stables courtyard.** For other opening times and information, please phone, email or visit garden website.
Renishaw Hall and Gardens boasts seven acres of stunning gardens created by Sir George Sitwell in 1885. The Italianate gardens feature various rooms with extravagant herbaceous borders. Rose gardens, rare trees and shrubs, National Collection of Yucca and Echium, sculptures, woodland walks and lakes create a magical and engaging garden experience. The National Garden Scheme openings coincide with the bluebells being in flower on Wed 6 May and the roses blooming on Wed 1 July. Afternoon Teas available in the Courtyard Café - prebooking is required. Please visit the website to book: www.renishaw-hall.co.uk. Mobility scooter and wheelchairs available to hire free of charge. Pre-booking strongly advised. Wheelchair route and map around the formal gardens.

GROUP OPENING

54 REPTON NGS VILLAGE GARDENS
Repton, Derby, DE65 6FR. Pauline Little. *6m S of Derby. From A38, A50 junction, S of Derby follow signs to Willington then Repton. Off Repton High St turn L into Pinfold Ln, Pinfold Cl 1st L.* **Mon 6 Apr, Mon 4 May, Wed 3 June (12-5). Combined adm £8, chd free. Mon 31 Aug (12-5). Combined adm £5, chd free.**

ASKEW COTTAGE
DE65 6FZ. Louise Hardwick, 07970 411748, louise.hardwick@hotmail.co.uk, www.hardwickgardendesign.co.uk.
Open on Mon 6 Apr, Mon 4 May, Wed 3 June
Visits also by arrangement 5 May to 30 Sept for groups of 5 to 30.

10 CHESTNUT WAY
DE65 6FQ. Pauline Little. 07842 500673, plittle@hotmail.co.uk
Open on Mon 6 Apr, Mon 4 May, Wed 3 June
Visits by arrangement for groups of 5 to 30.

34 HIGH STREET
DE65 6GD. Adrian and Natalie Argyle, 01283 701277, nargyle@argylefrics.co.uk.
Open on all dates
Visits also by arrangement 4 May to 4 Sept for groups of up to 25.

22 PINFOLD CLOSE
DE65 6FR. Mr & Mrs O Jowett, 01283 701964, helen.jowett23@gmail.com.
Open on all dates
Visits also by arrangement 4 May to 31 Aug.

REPTON ALLOTMENTS
DE65 6FX.
Open on Mon 6 Apr, Mon 4 May, Wed 3 June

NEW SERENDIPITY
DE65 6FP. Mr & Mrs Chris Chilton.
Open on Mon 6 Apr, Mon 4 May, Wed 3 June

Repton is a thriving village dating back to Anglo Saxon times. The village gardens are all very different, ranging from the very small to very large, several of them have new features for 2026. A new garden Serendipity is a shady woodland retreat best in Spring. Askew Cottage is a professionally designed garden and has many structural features linked together by curving paths and is undergoing changes in the winter. 34 High Street is a traditional old-established garden at the rear of one of the historic village properties. 10 Chestnut Way is a plantaholic's garden which is always very popular. 22 Pinfold Close is a small garden but is packed full with a special interest in tropical plants and has an orchid house and conservatory. The award winning Repton Allotments is a small set of allotments currently undergoing a revival with community area, with 2 polytunnels and attractive views across Derbyshire. Please check which gardens are open on the date you plan to visit. Plenty of seating throughout. Some gardens have grass or gravel paths but most areas wheelchair accessible.

55 SLATELANDS HOUSE
Slatelands Road, Glossop, SK13 6LH. Mr Ian Laybourn. *Slatelands Rd has a barrier across causing minimal parking if accessing from Pikes Ln/Hollincross Ln side. More parking when accessing from Turnlee Rd/Earls Way side. (signposted 50yds walk to house).* **Sun 28 June (12-4). Adm £5, chd free. Tea, coffee & cake inc gluten free options, all home-baked. Free tea & coffee refills. Soft drinks available.**
Victorian mill-owner's stone residence built on rising ground. Sloped bank from road is terraced stone retaining low-maintenance ilex balls, wild grasses with geraniums flowing down between. Front lawn, patios and plantings at house level. Rising rear ground comprises stone walls, terraced beds, lawns, patio and a waterfall, all set amidst rich plantings of warm colours and just a touch of whimsy. Craft sale Steep cobbled drive from road to house level for teas/cakes and seating area. Side plantings and rear are viewable, but then steps go further up.

56 THE SMITHY
Church Street, Buxton, SK17 6HD.
Roddie & Kate MacLean,
01298 78276, director@creative-heritage.net. *200 metres S of Buxton Market Place, in Higher Buxton. Located on access-only Church St, which cuts corner between B5059 & A515. Walk S from Buxton Market Place car park. Take slight R off A515, between Scriveners Bookshop & The Swan Inn.* **Sat 6, Sun 7 June (10-5). Adm £4, chd free. Visits also by arrangement 30 May to 26 July for groups of up to 20.**
Small oasis of calm in the town centre, designed by its architect-owners. Pretty colour-themed borders and dappled tree cover. Many visitors comment about how the owners have optimised the use of the space without appearing to cram it all in. Herbaceous borders, wildlife pond, octagonal greenhouse, raised vegetable beds and several different seating areas for eating outdoors. Garden with many levels; steps at entrance and around the garden.
🔊

57 NEW SOUTHCOT, THE GREEN
Church Lane, Brailsford, Ashbourne, DE6 3BX. Mrs Carolyn Keeling. *4m S of Ashbourne on A52. From Ashbourne take the A52 to Brailsford. After 4m turn R into The Green, signposted 'Thurvaston and Brailsford Church' After 50yds turn L into estate. What3words app: apart.revived.lunching.* **Sat 20, Sun 21 June (11-5). Adm £4, chd free. Home-made teas inc gluten free and vegan cakes available.**
⅓ acre wildlife friendly garden on 2 levels with lawns, colourful perennial planted borders and raised vegetable beds. A cobbled path winds through a shady border to rose swags with clematis and roses intertwined. Shallow steps lead down to a lower level of more informal planting and a large natural pond containing crested newt. Pergolas supporting hops, sweet peas and roses add height to borders. Stunning wisteria on 3 walls of the house flowers in May and a second smaller, darker flowering in September. Children's Quiz. Please don't park in the small estate. Please park carefully on The Green. Most of the garden is accessible for people with mobility issues, inc wheelchairs. Limited parking at the house for Disabled access only.
♿ 🐕 ✿ ☕ 🔊

58 ♦ TISSINGTON HALL
Tissington, Ashbourne, DE6 1RA. Sir Richard & Lady FitzHerbert, 01335 352200, sirrichard@tissingtonhall.co.uk, www.tissingtonhall.co.uk. *4m N of Ashbourne. E of A515 on Ashbourne to Buxton Rd in centre of Tissington.*

27 Wash Green

For NGS: Mon 25 May, Mon 6 July, Mon 17, Mon 24, Mon 31 Aug (12-3). Adm £9, chd £5. Cream teas at award winning Herbert's Fine English Tearooms. Tel 01335 350501. For other opening times and information, please phone, email or visit garden website.
Large garden surrounding Tissington Hall in the ancient village of Tissington. Celebrating 89 yrs in the National Garden Scheme, with stunning rose garden on west terrace, herbaceous borders and five acres of rounds. Features inc Tissington Craft Fairs at the Village Hall and Onawick Candle workshop also open in the village. Wheelchair access advice from ticket seller. Please seek staff and they shall park you nearer the gardens.

59 27 WASH GREEN
Wirksworth, Matlock, DE4 4FD. Paul & Kathy Harvey, 07811 395679, pandk.harvey@ngs.org.uk, www.facebook.com/27washgreen.
⅓ m E of Wirksworth centre. From Wirksworth centre, follow B5035 towards Whatstandwell. Cauldwell St leads over railway bridge to Wash Green, 200 metres up steep hill on L. Park in town or uphill from garden entry. **Sun 10 May, Sun 23 Aug (11-4). Adm £5, chd free. Tea, coffee & cake inc gluten free options. Visits also by arrangement Apr to Sept for groups of 10 to 30.**
Beautiful large garden, with outstanding views of historic Wirksworth town, and the surrounding Ecclesbourne valley. Inner walled area has topiary, pergola and mixed borders. The larger part of the garden has sweeping lawns, large beds planted for year-round colour, wildlife pond with summerhouse, bog garden, areas of woodland and specimen trees. Also productive fruit and vegetable garden. Drop off at property entry for wheelchair access. The inner garden has flat paths with good views of whole garden.

60 12 WATER LANE
Middleton-by-Wirksworth, Matlock, DE4 4LY. Hildegard Wiesehofer, 07809 883393, wiesehofer@btinternet.com.
Approx 2½ m SW of Matlock. 1½ m NW of Wirksworth, 8m from Ashbourne. From Derby: At A6 & B5023 intersection take Wirksworth Rd. Follow NGS signs. From Ashbourne: take Matlock Rd to Middleton. Follow NGS signs. Park on main road. Limited parking in Water Ln. **Sat 29 Aug (10.30-4.30); Sun 30 Aug (10.30-4). Adm £5, chd free. Tea, coffee & cake inc gluten free options. Visits also by arrangement 4 May to 28 Aug for groups of 12 to 25. Garden tour outlining geological and historical background of the cottage.**
Small, eclectic hillside cottage garden on different levels, created as a series of rooms. Each room has been designed to capture the stunning views over Derbyshire and Nottinghamshire. Mini woodland walk, ponds, eastern and 'infinity' garden. Emphasis is on holistic, sustainable and organic principles. Glorious views and short distance from many Derbyshire Dales attractions, inc Matlock Bath, Black Rock, High Peak Trail, Middleton Top Visitor Centre and Engine House.

61 26 WINDMILL RISE
Belper, DE56 1GQ. Kathy Fairweather. *From Belper Market Place take Chesterfield Rd towards Heage. Top of hill, 1st R Marsh Ln, 1st R Windmill Ln, 1st R Windmill Rise. Limited parking on Windmill Rise - disabled mainly.* **Sat 25, Sun 26 July (11-4). Adm £4, chd free. Light refreshments inc gluten free and vegan options. A wide range of savoury and sweet refreshments, all home-made.**
Behind a deceptively ordinary façade, lies a real surprise. A lush oasis, much larger than expected, with an amazing collection of rare and unusual plants. A truly plant lovers' organic garden divided into sections: woodland, Japanese, secret garden, cottage, edible, ponds and small stream. Many seating areas, inc a summerhouse in which to enjoy a variety of refreshments. Live music by local artist, weather permitting.

62 WOODEND COTTAGE
Main Road, Stanton-In-The-Peak, Matlock, DE4 2LX. Will Chandler. *5m S of Bakewell. At top of hill in Stanton-in-Peak on road to Birchover. Turn off A6 at Rowsley, or at the B5056, and follow signs.* **Sat 25, Sun 26 July (11-4). Combined adm with 2 Haddon View £5, chd free. Tea, coffee & cake at 2 Haddon View. Woodend Cottage will have a pop-up pub serving draught ale straight from the barrel, from a local brewery.**
The owner has made unique stone buildings on a strip of land on the roadside opposite his house, inc a tiny stone shelter with a fireplace and chimney. Narrow paths weave amongst the plants and stonework. The hidden rear garden has diverse planting, a vegetable plot and a "pop-up" pub.

63 YEW TREE BUNGALOW
Thatchers Lane, Tansley, Matlock, DE4 5FD. Jayne Conquest, 07745 093177, jayne.conquest62@gmail.com. *2m E of Matlock, off A615 in Tansley. On A615, 2nd R after Tavern at Tansley. Parking available in Charles Gregory & Sons Timber yard car park opp Tavern Inn.* **Sun 5 July, Sun 16 Aug (11.30-4). Adm £5, chd free. Home-made teas. Visits also by arrangement 6 July to 14 Aug for groups of 6 to 30.**
Plantswoman's ½ acre cottage style garden on a slope created by the present owners over 40 yrs. Many mixed borders planted with many choice and unusual trees, shrubs, herbaceous perennial, bulbs and annuals to provide year-round interest. Several seats to view different aspects of the garden. Shady area planted with a wide range of ferns. Vegetable and fruit garden. The garden is sloping but most of garden can be seen from the patio.

78,000 people affected by cancer were reached by Maggie's centres supported by the National Garden Scheme over the last 12 months.

DEVON

DEVON 135

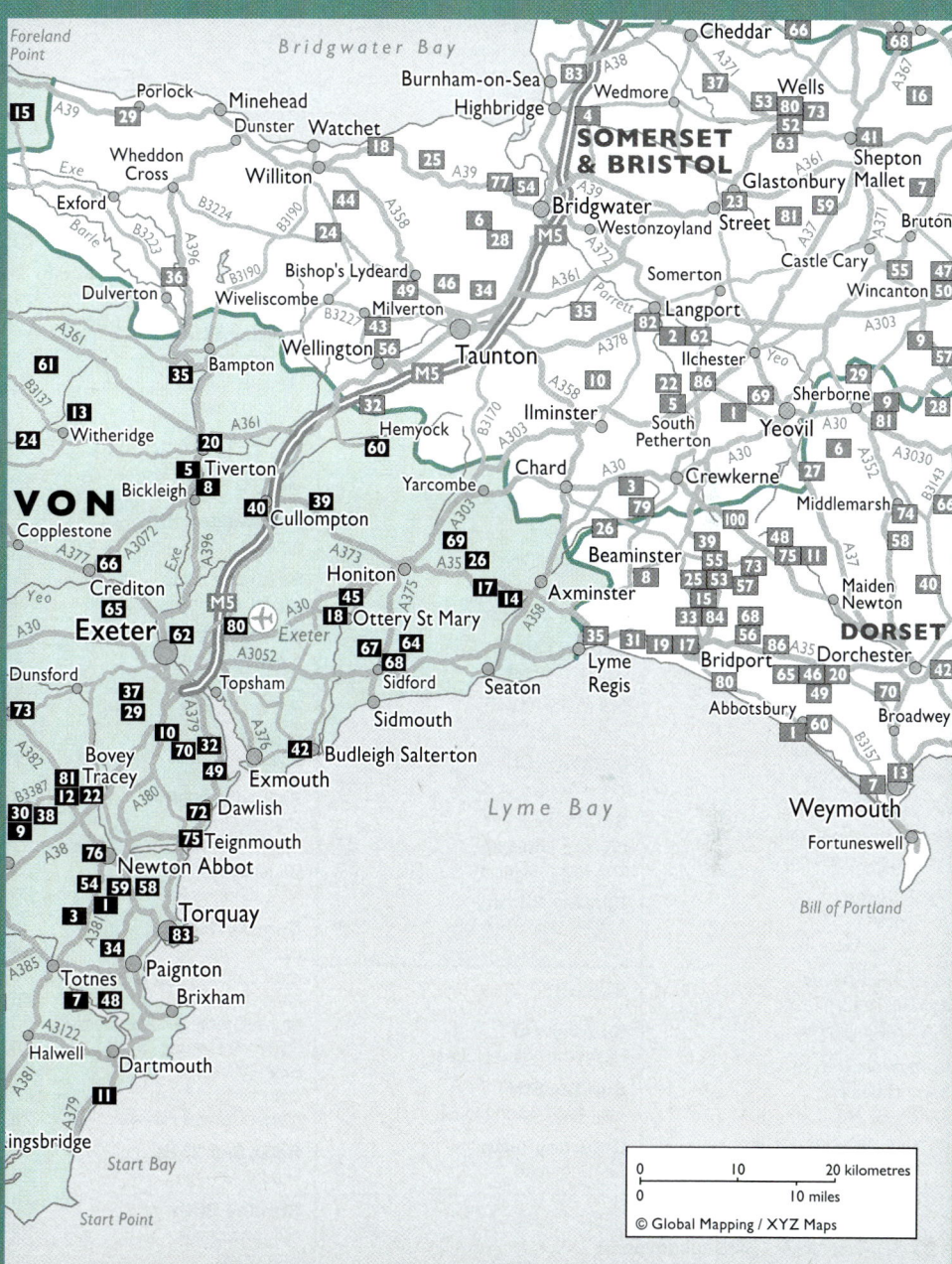

# VOLUNTEERS

County Organiser & Dartmoor
Miranda Allhusen 01647 440296
Miranda@allhusen.co.uk

County Treasurer
Nigel Hall 07802 923352
nigel.hall@ngs.org.uk

Publicity
Chris Britton 01626 899106
chris.britton@ngs.org.uk

Booklet Co-ordinator
Anne Sercombe 01626 923170
anne.sercombe@ngs.org.uk

Social Media
Neil Littleales 07722 321838
littleales@ngs.org.uk

Talks
Neil & Kerry Littleales
(as above and below)
Julia Tremlett 07715 718040
juliatremlett16@gmail.com

Assistant County Organisers

Central Devon
Rosie Moore 01837 847737,
devonrosie@yahoo.com

East Devon
Penny Walmsley 01404 831275
walyp_uk@yahoo.co.uk

Exeter
Jenny Phillips 01392 254076
jennypips25@hotmail.co.uk

Exmoor
Angela Percival 01598 741243
lalindevon@yahoo.co.uk

North Devon
Jo Hynes
hynesjo@gmail.com

North East Devon
Jill Hall 07860 643322
jill22hall@gmail.com

North West Devon
Kerry Littleales
07727 657246
kerry.littleales@ngs.org.uk

South Hams
Position Vacant

South West Devon
Pamela Millward 01803 782981
neilandpam72@gmail.com

Torbay
Jenny Saunders 07789 425994
Jennymsaunders@aol.com

OPENING DATES

All entries subject to change.
For latest information check
www.ngs.org.uk
Map locator numbers are
shown to the right of each
garden name.

February

Snowdrop Openings

Friday 6th	
Higher Cherubeer	33
Thursday 12th	
Little Ash Bungalow	45
Friday 13th	
Higher Cherubeer	33
Saturday 14th	
The Mount, Delamore	51
Sunday 15th	
The Mount, Delamore	51
Saturday 21st	
Higher Cherubeer	33
The Mount, Delamore	51
Sunday 22nd	
The Mount, Delamore	51

March

Sunday 1st	
East Worlington House	24
Sunday 8th	
East Worlington House	24
Saturday 14th	
Samlingstead	63

Sunday 15th	
Haldon Grange	29
Sunday 22nd	
Haldon Grange	29
Sunday 29th	
Bickham House	10
Chevithorne Barton	20
Haldon Grange	29
Heathercombe	31
Little Dinworthy	46
Upper Gorwell House	78

April

Friday 3rd	
Spring Lodge	70
Saturday 4th	
Haldon Grange	29
Sunday 5th	
Andrew's Corner	4
Haldon Grange	29
1 Pilton Lawn	57
Monday 6th	
Andrew's Corner	4
Haldon Grange	29
Wednesday 8th	
Ashley Court	5
Saturday 11th	
Haldon Grange	29
Sunday 12th	
Andrew's Corner	4
Bickham House	10
Haldon Grange	29
Friday 17th	
Sidbury Manor	67
Saturday 18th	
Haldon Grange	29
Musselbrook Cottage Garden	53
Regency House	60
NEW Shobrooke Park Gardens	66
Sunday 19th	
Haldon Grange	29
Kia-Ora Farm & Gardens	40
Little Dinworthy	46
Musselbrook Cottage Garden	53
Regency House	60
Sidbury Manor	67
South Wood Farm	69
Upper Gorwell House	78
Saturday 25th	
Haldon Grange	29
Sunday 26th	
Haldon Grange	29
Sherwood	65

@Devon NGS   @ngsdevon

DEVON 137

May

Saturday 2nd
Bagtor Mill Gardens	9
◆ Goren Farm	26
Greatcombe	27
Haldon Grange	29
Heathercombe	31
Journey's End	38

Sunday 3rd
Andrew's Corner	4
Bagtor Mill Gardens	9
Bickham House	10
Brendon Gardens	15
Chevithorne Barton	20
◆ Goren Farm	26
Greatcombe	27
Haldon Grange	29
Heathercombe	31
Journey's End	38
Kia-Ora Farm & Gardens	40

Monday 4th
Andrew's Corner	4
Brendon Gardens	15
◆ Goren Farm	26
Greatcombe	27
Haldon Grange	29
Journey's End	38
Kia-Ora Farm & Gardens	40

Tuesday 5th
◆ Goren Farm	26

Wednesday 6th
◆ Goren Farm	26

Thursday 7th
◆ Goren Farm	26

Friday 8th
Avenue Cottage	7
◆ Goren Farm	26
Sutton Mead	73

Saturday 9th
Avenue Cottage	7
◆ Goren Farm	26
Haldon Grange	29
Haytor Gardens	30
Heathercombe	31
Musselbrook Cottage Garden	53
Sutton Mead	73

Sunday 10th
◆ Goren Farm	26
Haldon Grange	29
Haytor Gardens	30
Heathercombe	31
Musselbrook Cottage Garden	53
Sutton Mead	73

Monday 11th
◆ Goren Farm	26

Tuesday 12th
◆ Goren Farm	26
◆ Hotel Endsleigh	36

Wednesday 13th
◆ Goren Farm	26

Thursday 14th
◆ Goren Farm	26

Friday 15th
◆ Goren Farm	26

Saturday 16th
Bradford Tracy House	13
◆ Goren Farm	26
Haldon Grange	29
Heathercombe	31

Sunday 17th
Bradford Tracy House	13
◆ Goren Farm	26
Haldon Grange	29
Heathercombe	31
Little Dinworthy	46
Upper Gorwell House	78

Monday 18th
◆ Goren Farm	26

Tuesday 19th
◆ Goren Farm	26
Heathercombe	31

Wednesday 20th
Ashridge Court	6
◆ Goren Farm	26
Heathercombe	31

Thursday 21st
Ashridge Court	6
◆ Goren Farm	26
Heathercombe	31

Friday 22nd
◆ Goren Farm	26
Heathercombe	31

Saturday 23rd
◆ Goren Farm	26
Greatcombe	27
Haldon Grange	29
Heathercombe	31
Journey's End	38
Mowhay	52
1 Pilton Lawn	57
NEW Wylam House	83

Sunday 24th
◆ Cadhay	18
◆ Goren Farm	26
Greatcombe	27
Haldon Grange	29
Heathercombe	31
Journey's End	38
Kia-Ora Farm & Gardens	40
Mowhay	52

NEW Wylam House	83

Monday 25th
◆ Cadhay	18
◆ Goren Farm	26
Greatcombe	27
Haldon Grange	29
Journey's End	38
Kia-Ora Farm & Gardens	40
Mowhay	52

Tuesday 26th
◆ Goren Farm	26
Heathercombe	31

Wednesday 27th
◆ Goren Farm	26
Heathercombe	31

Thursday 28th
◆ Goren Farm	26
Heathercombe	31

Friday 29th
◆ Goren Farm	26
Heathercombe	31

Saturday 30th
Abbotskerswell Gardens	1
◆ Goren Farm	26
Haldon Grange	29
Heathercombe	31
Kentisbeare House	39
Regency House	60

Sunday 31st
Abbotskerswell Gardens	1
Bickham House	10
Chevithorne Barton	20
◆ Goren Farm	26
Haldon Grange	29
Heathercombe	31
Regency House	60

June

Monday 1st
◆ Goren Farm	26

Tuesday 2nd
◆ Goren Farm	26

Wednesday 3rd
◆ Goren Farm	26

Thursday 4th
◆ Goren Farm	26

Friday 5th
East Woodlands Farmhouse	23
◆ Goren Farm	26

Saturday 6th
Dunley House	22
East Woodlands Farmhouse	23
◆ Goren Farm	26

DEVON

Haldon Grange	29
Heathercombe	31
Higher Orchard Cottage	34
The Old Rectory	55
Rosebarn Gardens	62
South Wood Farm	69
7 West Clyst Barnyard	80

Sunday 7th
Dunley House	22
East Woodlands Farmhouse	23
◆ Goren Farm	26
Haldon Grange	29
Heathercombe	31
Higher Orchard Cottage	34
Kia-Ora Farm & Gardens	40
The Old Rectory	55
Regency House	60
Rosebarn Gardens	62
Sherwood	65
South Wood Farm	69
7 West Clyst Barnyard	80

Monday 8th
◆ Goren Farm	26
Regency House	60

Tuesday 9th
◆ Goren Farm	26

Wednesday 10th
Ashley Court	5
◆ Goren Farm	26

Thursday 11th
◆ Goren Farm	26

Friday 12th
◆ Goren Farm	26

Saturday 13th
◆ Docton Mill	21
Ermecot House	25
◆ Goren Farm	26
NEW Growing Well Garden	28
Heathercombe	31
Mowhay	52
Musselbrook Cottage Garden	53
Ogwell Gardens	54
Teignmouth Gardens	75

Sunday 14th
Ermecot House	25
◆ Goren Farm	26
NEW Growing Well Garden	28
Heathercombe	31
High Garden	32
◆ Mothecombe House	50
Mowhay	52
Musselbrook Cottage Garden	53
Ogwell Gardens	54
Teignmouth Gardens	75

Monday 15th
◆ Goren Farm	26

Tuesday 16th
◆ Goren Farm	26

Wednesday 17th
◆ Goren Farm	26

Thursday 18th
◆ Goren Farm	26

Friday 19th
◆ Goren Farm	26
Sidbury Mill	68

Saturday 20th
Chagford Community Gardens	19
◆ Goren Farm	26
Heathercombe	31
2 Middlewood	49
Parracombe Gardens	56
The Priory	59

Sunday 21st
Bickham House	10
Chagford Community Gardens	19
◆ Goren Farm	26
Heathercombe	31
Kia-Ora Farm & Gardens	40
2 Middlewood	49
Parracombe Gardens	56
The Priory	59
Sidbury Mill	68
Upper Gorwell House	78

Monday 22nd
◆ Goren Farm	26

Tuesday 23rd
◆ Goren Farm	26

Wednesday 24th
◆ Goren Farm	26

Thursday 25th
◆ Goren Farm	26

Friday 26th
◆ Goren Farm	26

Saturday 27th
◆ Goren Farm	26

Sunday 28th
Linden Rise	44

July

Friday 3rd
Idestone Barton	37

Saturday 4th
Backswood Farm	8
Bovey Tracey Gardens	12
Brendon Gardens	15
Greatcombe	27
Idestone Barton	37
NEW Wembury Walled Garden	79
Willow Glade Farm	82

Sunday 5th
Backswood Farm	8
Bickham House	10
Bovey Tracey Gardens	12
Brendon Gardens	15
Greatcombe	27
Kia-Ora Farm & Gardens	40
NEW Wembury Walled Garden	79
Willow Glade Farm	82

Friday 10th
2 Middlewood	49

Saturday 11th
Am Brook Meadow	3
Journey's End	38
Samlingstead	63

Sunday 12th
Am Brook Meadow	3
Journey's End	38
2 Middlewood	49

Saturday 18th
Larcombe Farmhouse	41
Musselbrook Cottage Garden	53
Rose Ash House	61

Sunday 19th
Kia-Ora Farm & Gardens	40
Larcombe Farmhouse	41
Musselbrook Cottage Garden	53
Rose Ash House	61
Upper Gorwell House	78

Saturday 25th
Greatcombe	27
1 Pilton Lawn	57

Sunday 26th
Avenue Cottage	7
Bickham House	10
Greatcombe	27

August

Sunday 2nd
Kia-Ora Farm & Gardens	40
Middle Well	48

Saturday 8th
Lewis Cottage	43
Mowhay	52

Sunday 9th
Bickham House	10
Lewis Cottage	43
Mowhay	52

Monday 10th
Lewis Cottage	43

Tuesday 11th
Lewis Cottage	43

Wednesday 12th
Lewis Cottage   43
Thursday 13th
Lewis Cottage   43
Friday 14th
Lewis Cottage   43
Saturday 15th
Lewis Cottage   43
Sunday 16th
Kia-Ora Farm & Gardens   40
Lewis Cottage   43
Sunday 23rd
Bickham House   10
Little Ash Bungalow   45
Sunday 30th
◆ Cadhay   18
Kia-Ora Farm & Gardens   40
Monday 31st
◆ Cadhay   18
Kia-Ora Farm & Gardens   40

September

Friday 4th
Sutton Mead   73
Saturday 5th
NEW Honeywell   35
Sutton Mead   73

Sunday 6th
NEW Honeywell   35
Sutton Mead   73
Sunday 13th
Kia-Ora Farm & Gardens   40
Upper Gorwell House   78
Sunday 27th
Kia-Ora Farm & Gardens   40

October

Saturday 17th
Dunley House   22
Sunday 18th
Dunley House   22
Regency House   60
Monday 19th
Regency House   60
Sunday 25th
Chevithorne Barton   20
Sherwood   65

November

Friday 6th
Ashridge Court   6
Saturday 7th
Ashridge Court   6

February 2027

Wednesday 3rd
Little Ash Bungalow   45
Friday 5th
Higher Cherubeer   33
Thursday 11th
Little Ash Bungalow   45
Saturday 20th
Higher Cherubeer   33

By Arrangement

Arrange a personalised garden visit with your club, or group of friends, on a date to suit you. See individual garden entries for full details.

32 Allenstyle Drive   2
Andrew's Corner   4
Ashridge Court   6
Avenue Cottage   7
Bickham House   10
Brambly Wood (Haytor Gardens)   30
Breach   14
Brendon Barton (Brendon Gardens)   15
Brendon Gardens   15
The Bridge Mill   16
East Woodlands Farmhouse   23
Haldon Grange   29
Hall Farm (Brendon Gardens)   15
Heathercombe   31
Higher Cherubeer   33
Higher Orchard Cottage   34
Higher Tippacott Farm (Brendon Gardens)   15
Kia-Ora Farm & Gardens   40
Lee Ford   42
Lewis Cottage   43
Little Ash Bungalow   45
Middle Well   48
Mowhay   52
Musselbrook Cottage Garden   53
The Old Rectory   55
Regency House   60
Samlingstead   63
Sand Farmhouse   64
Sherwood   65
Spring Lodge   70
Stone Farm   71
Stonelands House   72
Sutton Mead   73
Tamar House   74
Torview   76
Truants Cottage   77
Whitstone Farm   81

Greatcombe

THE GARDENS

GROUP OPENING

1 ABBOTSKERSWELL GARDENS
Abbotskerswell, TQ12 5PN. *2m SW of Newton Abbot town centre. A381 Newton Abbot/Totnes rd. Sharp L turn from Newton Abbot, R from Totnes. Field parking at Fairfield. Maps & tickets valid for both days avail from 1pm at all gardens & at Church House.* **Sat 30, Sun 31 May (1-5). Combined adm £8, chd free. Tea, coffee & cake at Church House in the village from 2pm. Picnics in the field at Fairfield.**

ABBOTSFORD
Wendy & Phil Grierson.

ABBOTSKERSWELL ALLOTMENTS

1 ABBOTSWELL COTTAGES
Jane Taylor.

FAIRFIELD
Brian Mackness.

4 LAKELAND
Ali & Dave Peters.

PINE TREES LODGE
Gary & Richard.

7 WILTON WAY
Mr Vernon & Mrs Cindy Stunt.

16 WILTON WAY
Katy & Chris Yates.

For 2026 Abbotskerswell offers seven gardens, ranging from small to large, plus the village allotments. The gardens offer a wide range of planting styles and innovative landscaping. Cottage gardens, terracing, wildflower areas, specialist plants and an arboretum. Ideas for every type and size of garden. Visitors are welcome to picnic in the field or arboretum at Fairfield. Wheelchair access to some of the gardens. Partial access to most others.

&. ❀ 🚗 ☕ 🧺 ᴗ))

2 32 ALLENSTYLE DRIVE
Yelland, Barnstaple, EX31 3DZ. Steve & Dawn Morgan, 07587 185911, fourhungrycats@gmail.com, www. devonsubtropicalgarden.rocks. *5m W of Barnstaple. From Barnstaple take B3233 towards Instow. Through Bickington & Fremington. L at Yelland sign into Allenstyle Rd. 1st R into Allenstyle Dr. Light blue bungalow. From Bideford go past Instow on B3233.* **Visits by arrangement 8 Aug to 14 Sept for groups of up to 30. Tea.**
Our garden, on heavy clay, is 30m x 15m and is packed full of all our favourite plants. See our collections of bananas, gingers, cannas, colocasias, delicate and scented tropical and hardy passion flowers as well as rudbeckias, perennial sunflowers, a wildlife pond and a large cedar greenhouse. Relax and inhale the heady scents of the garden and rest awhile in the many seating areas.

3 AM BROOK MEADOW
Torbryan, Ipplepen, Newton Abbot, TQ12 5UP. Jennie & Jethro Marles. *5m from Newton Abbot on A381. Leaving A381 at Causeway Cross go through Ipplepen village, heading towards Broadhempston. Stay on Orley Rd for ¾ m. At Poole Cross turn L signed Totnes, then turn 2nd L into field parking.* **Sat 11, Sun 12 July (2-6). Adm £7, chd free. Home-made teas.**
Country garden developed over past 20 years to encourage wildlife. Perennial native wildflower meadows, large ponds with ducks and swans, streams and wild areas covering 10 acres are accessible by gravel and grass pathways. Formal courtyard garden with water features and herbaceous borders and prairie style planting together with poultry and bees close by. Appeared on Gardeners' World Aug 2024. Wheelchair access to most gravel path areas is good, but grass pathways in wildflower meadow are weather dependent.

4 ANDREW'S CORNER
Skaigh Lane, Belstone, EX20 1RD. Robin & Edwina Hill, 01837 840332, edwinarobinhill@outlook.com, www.andrewscorner.garden. *3m E of Okehampton. Signed to Belstone from A30. In village turn L, signed Skaigh. Follow NGS signs. Garden approx ½ m on R. Visitors may be dropped off at house, parking in nearby field.* **Sun 5, Mon 6, Sun 12 Apr, Sun 3, Mon 4 May (2-5). Adm £6, chd free. Home-made teas. Visits also by arrangement 1 Feb to 1 June. Refreshments may be available according to group size and time of day.**
Take a walk on the wild side in this tranquil moorland garden. Join garden owner Robin as he explains the evolution of the garden which has been open for over 50 years. April openings highlight magnolias, trillium and the lovely erythroniums. Early May the maples, rhododendrons and unusual shrubs provide interest. Late May brings the Snowdrop Tree, Chilean Firebush and the spectacular blue poppies. Wheelchair access difficult when wet.

&. 🐕 ❀ ☕ ᴗ))

5 ASHLEY COURT
Ashley, Tiverton, EX16 5PD. Tara Fraser & Nigel Jones, 07768 878015, hello@ ashleycourtdevon.co.uk, www.ashleycourtdevon.co.uk. *1m S of Tiverton on the Bickleigh road (A396). Turn off the A396 to Ashley & then immed L. Take the drive to the L of Ashley Court Lodge Cottage (don't go up Ashley Back Lane where the SatNav will direct you).* **Wed 8 Apr, Wed 10 June (1-5). Adm £6, chd free. Tea, coffee & cake. Speciality teas inc many delicious vegan recipes & cakes containing fruits & vegetables from the walled kitchen garden.**
Ashley Court is a small Regency country house with an historically interesting walled kitchen garden currently undergoing restoration. It is unusually situated in a deep valley and has a frost window and the remains of several glasshouses and cold frames. View the apple loft, root stores, stable buildings, woodland walk and lawns, borders and beautiful mature trees. A walk through discovery and history. The walled garden probably pre-dates the 1805 house as there was previously an older Ashley Court on the other side of the garden. Peculiar features such as a curved garden wall and the frost window make it unusual.

6 ASHRIDGE COURT
North Tawton, EX20 2DH. Chris & Carolyn Richards, 01837 880192, info@ashridge-court.co.uk, www.ashridge-court.co.uk. *Just outside North Tawton. From town centre take Market St between Town Hall & chemist past church. Continue for 1½ m, turn L into Ashridge Court. What3words app: truffles.producing. pleasing.* **Wed 20, Thur 21 May, Fri 6, Sat 7 Nov (11-4). Adm £6, chd free. Light refreshments made from locally sourced produce inc beef**

from Estate. Selection of home-made cakes & hot drinks. **Visits also by arrangement 1 May to 1 Nov.** Main garden of 6 acres dates from early 1900s, walled garden significantly older. Stunning range of mature conifers, an Arts and Crafts circular garden room featuring Japanese maples. From Ashridge Great Barn steps to woodland walk via tree ferns, newly planted flowering trees and shrubs, stumpery, walled garden and upper arboretum all in various stages of restoration by current owners. Limited mobility parking available. Wheelchair access to top part of garden. Separate parking area for disabled access to teas and WC.

&

7 AVENUE COTTAGE

Ashprington, Totnes, TQ9 7UT. Mr Richard Pitts & Mr David Sykes, 01803 732769, richard. pitts@btinternet.com, www.avenuecottage.com. *3m SE of Totnes. A381 Totnes to Kingsbridge for 1m; L for Ashprington, into village then L by pub. Garden ¼m on R after Sharpham Estate sign.* **Fri 8, Sat 9 May, Sun 26 July (10.30-4.30). Adm £5, chd free. Pre-booking essential, please visit www.ngs.org.uk for information & booking. Home-made teas. Visits also by arrangement Apr to Sept for groups of up to 25.**

11 acre woodland valley garden containing many rare and unusual trees and shrubs with views over the River Dart AONB. Azaleas, hydrangeas and magnolias are a speciality. A spring rising in the garden under a massive rhododendron feeds two ponds and a small stream running through a meadow with mown paths. Openings require pre-booking due to limited parking. If coming on foot, visitors can pay at the gate.

Stone Farm

8 BACKSWOOD FARM
Bickleigh, Tiverton, EX16 8RA. Andrew Hughes, 07860 609609, info@tradingsites.net, www.backswood.co.uk. *2m SE of Tiverton. Take A396 off the A361. Turn L to Butterleigh opp Tesco, L at mini r'about, after 150 yds turn R up Exeter Hill for 2m then 1st R to Bickleigh. After 500 yds turn 1st R into farm entrance.* **Sat 4, Sun 5 July (2-5). Adm £6, chd free. Tea, coffee & cake.**
Created with the natural environment at its heart, this evolving 2 acre nature garden provides uniquely designed homes for wildlife. Wander through the flower meadow visiting individually designed rooms with many structures, water features and pools. Seating areas afford stunning views towards Exmoor and Dartmoor. Both native and herbaceous plants have been chosen to benefit insect and bird life. Dogs on leads. WC available.

GROUP OPENING

9 BAGTOR MILL GARDENS
Ilsington, Newton Abbot, TQ13 9RT. Mark Wills. *Coming from Haytor at Smokey Cross take the road to Bickington & at Birchanger Cross turn R to Bagtor. Coming from Liverton/Ilsington carry on towards Haytor until Smokey Cross & turn L.* **Sat 2, Sun 3 May (10-4). Combined adm £6, chd free.**

BAGTOR MILL
Mark Wills.

LEMON COTTAGE
Phil & Jamie Richards.

Bagtor Mill is a C17 corn mill beside the River Lemon surrounded by a wildlife garden with rhododendrons, camellias, ponds, bluebells and massive gunnera. The 21 acres of ancient woodland that joins the garden in a steep valley follow the old packhorse track made by charcoal burners. Opposite is Lemon Cottage with a spring-fed pond, a Japanese-inspired garden and 14 acres of woodland with views across Dartmoor. While the main paths are accessible, not all paths in both gardens are.

10 BICKHAM HOUSE
Kenn, Exeter, EX6 7XL. Julia Tremlett, 07715 718040, juliatremlett16@gmail.com. *6m S of Exeter, 1m off A38. Leave A38 at Kennford Services, follow signs to Kenn, 1st R in village, follow lane for ¾m to end of no through rd. Only use SatNav once you are in the village of Kenn.* **Sun 29 Mar, Sun 12 Apr, Sun 3, Sun 31 May, Sun 21 June, Sun 5, Sun 26 July, Sun 9, Sun 23 Aug (2-5). Adm £7, chd free. Home-made teas. Visits also by arrangement 30 Mar to 31 Aug. Small coaches only.**
6 acres with large lawn and colour-themed borders. Mature trees inc huge tulip tree. Formal courtyard garden with olive tree. 1 acre walled garden with profusion of vegetables and flowers. Palm tree avenue leading to millennium summerhouse. Late summer colour with dahlias, crocosmia, agapanthus etc. Cactus and succulent greenhouse.

Shobrooke Park Gardens

© Brian and Nina Chapple

Pelargonium collection. Lakeside walk. WC, disabled access.

11 ♦ BLACKPOOL GARDENS
Dartmouth, TQ6 0RG. Sir Geoffrey Newman, 01803 771801, beach@blackpoolsands.co.uk, www.blackpoolsands.co.uk. *3m SW of Dartmouth. From Dartmouth follow brown signs to Blackpool Sands on A379. Entry tickets, parking, WCs & refreshments available at Blackpool Sands. Regret no dogs.* **For opening times and information, please phone, email or visit garden website.** Carefully restored C19 subtropical plantsman's garden with collection of mature and newly planted tender and unusual trees and shrubs; carpet of spring flowers. Paths and steps lead gradually uphill and above the Captain's Seat offering fine coastal views. Recent plantings follow the southern hemisphere theme with callistemons, pittosporums, acacias and buddlejas.

GROUP OPENING

12 BOVEY TRACEY GARDENS
Bovey Tracey, TQ13 9LZ. *6m N of Newton Abbot. Take A382 to Bovey Tracey. Parking on local roads. Follow the yellow signs and purchase ticket from any garden.* **Sat 4, Sun 5 July (1.30-5.30). Combined adm £6, chd free. Cream teas at 3 Redwoods, next door to No 2.**

GREEN HEDGES
TQ13 9LZ. Alan & Linda Jackson.
2 REDWOODS
TQ13 9YG. Mrs Julia Mooney.
NEW **14 ST PAUL'S CLOSE**
TQ13 9JD. Steve & Sue Nickels.

Nestling in the Dartmoor foothills, Bovey Tracey offers a wide range of gardens. Green Hedges is packed full of interest: colourful borders, shade plants, organic vegetables, greenhouses and a small stream. 14 St Paul's Close is a small, but well structured garden offering both shade and sunny aspects. 2 Redwoods has mature trees, a Dartmoor leat, a fernery, a sunny gravel garden and acid loving shrubs. Delicious cream teas will be served next door, at 3 Redwoods. Partial wheelchair access.

13 BRADFORD TRACY HOUSE
Witheridge, Tiverton, EX16 8QG. Elizabeth Wilkinson. *20 mins from Tiverton. The postcode will get you to the Bradford Tracy Lodge a thatched cottage at the bottom of the drive which has 2 bouncing hares on the top. NGS direction signs from Witheridge & Rackenford.* **Sat 16, Sun 17 May (1.30-5). Adm £6, chd free. Tea & home-made cakes served takeaway style to enjoy in the garden or inside.**
A pleasure garden set around a Regency hunting lodge combining flowers with grasses, shrubs and huge trees in a natural and joyful space. It is planted for productivity and sustainability giving harvests of wonderful flowers, fruits, herbs and vegetables (and weeds!). There are beautiful views over the lake, forest walks, deep blowsy borders, an ancient wisteria and an oriental treehouse garden.

14 BREACH
Shute Road, Kilmington, Axminster, EX13 7ST. Judith Chapman & BJ Lewis, 01297 35159, jachapman16@btinternet.com. *1½ m W of Axminster off A35. Turn L off the A35 at the War Memorial, continue up Shute Rd, past farm on R & after 150m, Breach is a short walk along a byway to the L. Parking is on Shute Rd.* **Visits by arrangement 8 Apr to 23 Oct for groups of 15+. Home-made teas.**
Over 3 acres with many mature trees and some unusual trees planted recently, such as Hoheria and Nyssa. Herbaceous borders, shrubberies, vegetable/fruit area. Bog garden using natural spring and 2 ponds attract dragonflies. Disused shale tennis court has orchids and is being developed as wildflower area. Soil mainly acidic and a band of specimen rhododendrons was planted 13 yrs ago. Development continues. Partial wheelchair access.

GROUP OPENING

15 BRENDON GARDENS
Brendon, Lynton, EX35 6PU. 01598 741343, lalindevon@yahoo.co.uk. *Within and on the edge of Brendon village. 1m S of A39 N Devon coast road between Porlock & Lynton.* **Sun 3, Mon 4 May, Sat 4, Sun 5 July (12-5). Combined adm £6, chd free. Light lunches: home-made quiches with varied salad. Home-made cakes, inc gluten free & cream teas. WC. Visits also by arrangement Apr to Sept.**

BARN FARM
Andrew & Debra Hodges.
BRENDON BARTON
Nigel & Maria Floyd, lalindevon@yahoo.co.uk.
Visits also by arrangement Apr to Sept.
HALL FARM
Karen Wall, 01598 741604, kwall741604@btinternet.com.
Visits also by arrangement Apr to Sept.
HIGHER TIPPACOTT FARM
Angela & Malcolm Percival, 01598 741343, lalindevon@yahoo.co.uk.
Visits also by arrangement Apr to Sept.

Stunning part of Exmoor National Park. Close to coast and excellent walking along river and over moorland. Barn Farm: Stylish courtyard garden on 2 levels incorporating walls and old stone buildings. Roses, shrubs and other cottage garden flowers and vegetables. Adjoining paddock with pond, copse and young orchard of Devon varieties. Brendon Barton: Dramatic garden with big stones and interesting agricultural bygones. Seating areas, lawn and water. Interesting planting inc many spring bulbs within this unique structure. Hall Farm: C16 longhouse set in 2 acres of tranquil mature gardens, with lake and wild area beyond. Idyllic setting with views. Rare Whitebred Shorthorn cattle, rheas and chickens. Higher Tippacott Farm: 950ft alt on moor, facing south overlooking its own valley with stream and pond. Interesting planting on many interconnecting levels with lawns. Young fruit trees in meadow. Vegetable patch with sea glimpse. Lovely views along valley and up to high moorland. Plants, books and bric a brac for sale at Higher Tippacott Farm. Display of vintage telephones and toys. Tombola.

16 THE BRIDGE MILL
Mill Rd, Bridgerule,
Holsworthy, EX22 7EL. Rosie
& Alan Beat, 01288 381341,
rosie@thebridgemill.org.uk,
www.thebridgemill.org.uk. *In
Bridgerule village on R Tamar between
Bude & Holsworthy. Between the
chapel by river bridge & church at
top of hill. The mill is at bottom of
hill opp Short & Abbott agricultural
engineers. See website for detailed
directions.* **Visits by arrangement
11 May to 30 June for groups of
15+. Visit inc tour of historic mill,
wildflower walk & garden areas.
Adm £5, chd free. Home-made
teas in the garden if the weather is
fine, or in the stable if wet. Home-
made cakes with organic tea/
coffee. Gluten free cakes & dairy
alternatives available.**
One acre organic gardens around
working water mill. Cottage garden
style planting; herb garden with
medicinal and dye plants; productive
fruit and vegetable garden, and wild
woodland. The water garden by the
river Tamar is being redeveloped
after tree felling by beavers and
ash die-back. The historic water
mill was restored to working order
in April 2012 and in 2017 Alan was
awarded a plaque by the Society for
the Protection of Ancient Buildings
for his sympathetic restoration of the
buildings. Wheelchair access to the
ground floor of the mill and most of
the gardens plus accessible WC and
baby change facilities.

17 ♦ BURROW FARM GARDENS
Dalwood, Axminster, EX13 7ET.
Mary & John Benger,
07903 527940, enquiries@
burrowfarmgardens.co.uk,
www.burrowfarmgardens.co.uk.
*3½ m W of Axminster. From A35 turn
N at Taunton Xrds then follow brown
signs. What3words app: guidebook.
fetches.fortress.* **For opening times
and information, please phone,
email or visit garden website.**
This beautiful 13 acre garden has
unusual trees, shrubs and herbaceous
plants. Traditional summerhouse
looks towards lake and ancient oak
woodland with rhododendrons and
azaleas. Early spring interest and
superb autumn colour. The more
formal Millennium garden features
a rill. Anniversary garden featuring
late summer perennials and grasses.
Café, nursery and gift shop with range
of garden ironwork. Various events

inc spring and summer plant fair and
open air theatre held at garden each
year. Visit events page on website for
more details.

18 ♦ CADHAY
Ottery St Mary, EX11 1QT. Rupert
Thistlethwayte, 01404 813511,
information@cadhay.org.uk,
www.cadhay.org.uk. *1m NW of
Ottery St Mary. On B3176 between
Ottery St Mary & Fairmile. From E exit
A30 at Iron Bridge. From W exit A30
at Patteson's Cross, follow brown
signs for Cadhay.* **For NGS: Sun 24,
Mon 25 May, Sun 30, Mon 31 Aug
(2-5). Adm £6, chd free. Cream
teas. For other opening times and
information, please phone, email or
visit garden website.**
Tranquil 2 acre setting for Tudor
manor house. 2 medieval fish ponds
surrounded by rhododendrons,
gunnera, hostas and flag iris. Roses,
clematis, lilies and hellebores
surround walled water garden. 120ft
herbaceous border walk informally
planted. Magnificent display of dahlias
throughout. Walled kitchen gardens
have been turned into allotments and
old apple store is now a tearoom.
Gravel paths.

19 CHAGFORD COMMUNITY GARDENS
Chagford, TQ13 8BW. Mr Nicky
Scott. *What3words app: clinking.
vegans.scarecrow. From High St,
past Church, bear L, fork R lane to
Long Stay/Health Centre car park,
continue R by foot along lane, take
1st R to Community Allotments
gate, or via Jubilee Fields (no dogs
through play area).* **Sat 20, Sun 21
June (10-4). Adm £5, chd free.
Tea, coffee & cake.**
Community plot in heart of village
with starter beds for people on
waiting list for allotments. Wide range
of medicinal and culinary herbs,
vegetables, mature fruit trees, beds
of unusual perennial plants. Focus on
native wild flowers, seed collection,
health benefits. Wildlife pond,
greenhouse, composting area, sheds
and covered seating area. Stunning
views; adjacent leat with water from
Dartmoor. Seeds for sale. Wheelchair
access possible, some inclines,
limited disabled parking on site.

20 CHEVITHORNE BARTON
Chevithorne, Tiverton,
EX16 7QB. Head Gardener,
chevithornebarton.co.uk. *3m NE
of Tiverton. Follow yellow signs from
A361 & A396.* **Sun 29 Mar, Sun
3, Sun 31 May, Sun 25 Oct (1-5).
Adm £6, chd free. Tea, coffee &
cake.** Donation to Plant Heritage.
Walled garden, summer borders
and Robinsonian inspired woodland
of rare trees and shrubs. In
spring the garden features a large
collection of magnolias, camellias,
and rhododendrons with grass
paths meandering through a sea of
bluebells, and grass meadows. Home
to National Collection of Quercus
(Oaks). Lots of autumn colour.

21 ♦ DOCTON MILL
Lymebridge, Hartland,
EX39 6EA. Lana & John
Borrett, 07507 586144,
docton.mill@btconnect.com,
www.doctonmill.co.uk. *8m W
of Clovelly. Follow brown tourist
signs on A39 nr Clovelly. Avoid
using Satnav when close and avoid
going through Tosberry & Edistone.*
**For NGS: Sat 13 June (11-5).
Adm £7, chd free. Cream teas
& light lunches available all
day. For other opening times and
information, please phone, email or
visit garden website.**
Situated in a stunning valley location.
The garden surrounds the original mill
pond and the microclimate created
within the wooded valley enables
tender species to flourish. Recent
planting of herbaceous, stream and
summer garden give variety through
the season.

22 DUNLEY HOUSE
Bovey Tracey, TQ13 9PW. Mr &
Mrs F Gilbert. *2m E of Bovey Tracey
on road to Hennock. From A38
going W turn off slip road R towards
Chudleigh Knighton on B3344, in
village follow yellow signs to Dunley
House. From A38 going E turn off on
Chudleigh K slip road L and follow
signs.* **Sat 6, Sun 7 June, Sat 17,
Sun 18 Oct (2-5). Adm £6, chd
free. Home-made teas.**
Nine acre garden set among mature
oaks, sequoiadendrons and a huge
liquidambar started from a wilderness
in mid eighties. Rhododendrons,
camellias and over 40 different
magnolias. Arboretum, walled garden
with borders and fruit and vegetables,

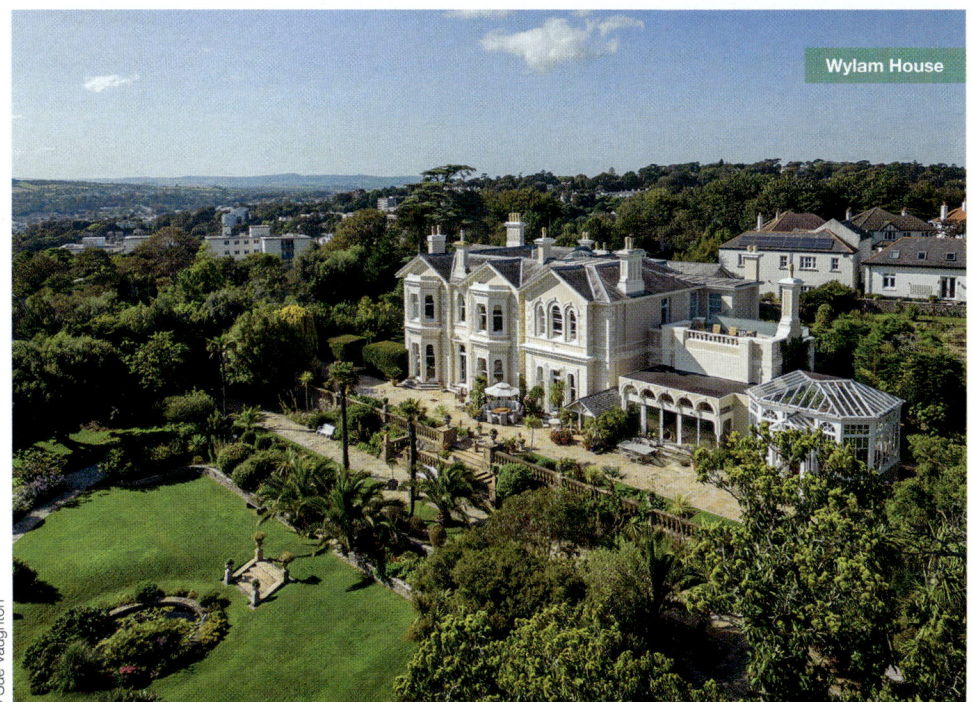

Wylam House

rose garden and new enclosed garden with lily pond. Large pond renovated in 2016 with new plantings. Woodland walk around perimeter of property.

&. 🐕 ✤ ☕))

23 EAST WOODLANDS FARMHOUSE
Alverdiscott, Newton Tracey, Barnstaple, EX31 3PP.
Ed & Heather Holt,
heatherholtexmoor@gmail.com.
5m NE of Great Torrington, 5m S of Barnstaple, off B3232. From Great Torrington turn R into single track rd before Alverdiscott OR from Barnstaple turn L after Alverdiscott. 1m down road R fork at Newlands house. What3words: Dorms.pets. pets. **Fri 5, Sat 6 June (10.30-4); Sun 7 June (2-4). Adm £6, chd free. Tea, coffee & cake. Gluten free cakes available. Visits also by arrangement 11 May to 28 Aug.**
East Woodlands is a beautiful RHS inspired and designed garden full of rooms packed with plants, shrubs and trees. Enjoy the spectacular bamboos, flowing grasses alongside rose, Mediterranean, Japanese, cottage and bog gardens (unfenced pond), all set in an acre looking out over N Devon countryside. Occasional live music. Lots of seating areas. Wheelchair access through most of gardens over 20mm gravel chip pathways.

&. ✤ ☕))

24 EAST WORLINGTON HOUSE
East Worlington, Witheridge, Crediton, EX17 4TS. Barnabas & Campie Hurst-Bannister. *In centre of E Worlington, 2m W of Witheridge. From Witheridge Square R to E Worlington. After 1½ m R at T-junction in Drayford, then L to Worlington. After ½ m L at T-junction. 200 yds on L. Parking nearby, disabled parking at house.* **Sun 1, Sun 8 Mar (1.30-5). Adm £6, chd free. Cream teas in thatched parish hall next to house.**
Thousands of purple crocuses feature in this 2 acre garden, set in a lovely position with views down the valley to Little Dart river. These spectacular crocuses have spread over many years through the garden and into the neighbouring churchyard. Walks from the garden across the river and into the woods. Dogs on leads please.

&. 🐕 ☕))

25 ERMECOT HOUSE
Ermington, Ivybridge, PL21 0LH. Dr Charlotte Grezo. *2m S of Ivybridge & just E of Ermington. Approach from A3121. From E take small lane on R immed after Ermington House Residential Home, from W take small lane on L immed after bridge over River Erme. What3words download.skid.feared.* **Sat 13, Sun 14 June (12-5). Adm £6, chd free. Tea, coffee & cake.**
3½ acres of gardens and meadows located between the Erme and the Ludbrook. It is managed to encourage wildlife and pollinators. It includes a walled garden planted with roses and herbaceous borders, a remodelled vegetable and herb garden, a mature orchard, and river and meadow walks with views over the Ludbrook, which runs through it. A rose covered pergola runs the length of the walled garden. Lovely trees stand in the lawns and along the river bank. No smoking garden. Children to be supervised at all times. Art Exhibition with artwork and paintings by local artists and a guest artist featuring local landscapes and places.

✤ ☕))

Growing Well Garden

26 ◆ GOREN FARM
Broadhayes, Stockland, Honiton, EX14 9EN. Julian Pady, 01404 881335, info@goren.co.uk, www.goren.co.uk. *6m E of Honiton, 6m W of Axminster. Go to Stockland television mast. Head 400 metres N signed from Broadhayes Cross. Follow NGS signs & brown Goren Meadows signs.* **For NGS: Evening openings Sat 2 May to Fri 5 June (5-9). Adm by donation. Sat 6, Sun 7 June (11-5). Adm £8, chd £4. Cream teas. Evening openings Mon 8 June to Sat 27 June (5-9). Adm by donation. Cream teas only available in evening if pre booked, picnics are welcome at any time. For other opening times and information, please phone, email or visit garden website.** Fifty acres of natural species-rich wildflower meadows. Easy access footpaths. Dozens of varieties of wild flowers and grasses. Thousands of orchids from early June and butterflies in July. Georgian house with stunning views of Blackdown Hills. Late season, when the meadows are setting seed ready to be mown, butterflies, beetles and many other insects are in abundance on the wildflower seed heads. Nature trail with species information signs and picnic tables. Visit the cider museum, walled vegetable garden and greenhouse. Various music events are held throughout the summer. Café open serving cream teas and light lunches during daytime opening hours. Partial wheelchair access to meadows. Dogs welcome on a lead only, please clean up after your pet.

& 🐕 ✿ 🛏 ☕ 🪑 »)

27 GREATCOMBE
Greatcombe Gardens & Gallery, Holne, Ashburton, TQ13 7SP. Robbie & Sarah Richardson, 07725 314887, sarah@greatcombe.com, www.facebook.com/greatcombegardens. *4m from either Ashburton or Buckfastleigh. 4m NW Ashburton via Holne Bridge & Holne village. 4m NE Buckfastleigh via Scorriton. Narrow lanes. Large car park adjacent to garden.* **May: Sat 2, Sun 3, Mon 4, Sat 23, Sun 24, Mon 25. July: Sat 4, Sun 5, Sat 25, Sun 26 (1-5). Adm £6, chd free. Home-made teas.** A hidden gem, providing both inspiration and tranquillity. The garden offers a wide range of plants and planting schemes adding interest around every corner. Featuring flowering shrubs, mature trees, herbaceous borders, colourful pots, a moorland stream, acers and unusual hydrangeas. 'Enchanting, magical place, a real asset to the NGS, fabulous home-made teas' (visitor comment). Plant nursery, artist's studio, metal plant supports in all sizes.

🐕 ✿ ☕ »)

28 NEW GROWING WELL GARDEN
Bow Medical Practice, Iter Cross, Bow, Crediton, EX17 6FB. Dr Susan Taheri, growingwellgarden.co.uk. *E of Bow village on A3072. 7m W of Crediton, from Exeter take A377 to Copplestone then A3072 to Bow. From A30 take A3124 towards North Tawton then R to A3072.* **Sat 13, Sun 14 June (11-4). Adm £6, chd free. Tea, coffee & cake.** Based at an NHS GP surgery, an allotment style garden provides a calm space for prescribed therapeutic gardening activities to improve

physical and mental wellbeing in a friendly, inclusive, community environment supported by volunteers where everyone can enjoy nature. Formal layout balanced with informal planting. Fruit, flowers and vegetables grown mostly from seed, using no-dig method. Plant sales to Growing Well Garden project, cash only. Access with care, mostly level ground, weather dependent.

&. ✿ ☕))

29 HALDON GRANGE
Dunchideock, Exeter, EX6 7YE. Ted Phythian, 01392 832349, judithphythian@yahoo.com, youtu.be/G0gluYoWncA. *5m SW of Exeter. From A30 through Ide village to Dunchideock 5m. L to Lord Haldon, Haldon Grange is next L. From A38 (S) turn L on top of Haldon Hill follow Dunchideock signs, R at village centre to Lord Haldon.* Sun 15, Sun 22, Sun 29 Mar, Sat 4, Sun 5, Mon 6, Sat 11, Sun 12, Sat 18, Sun 19, Sat 25 Sun 26 Apr, Sat 2, Sun 3, Mon 4, Sat 9, Sun 10, Sat 16, Sun 17, Sat 23, Sun 24, Mon 25, Sat 30, Sun 31 May, Sat 6, Sun 7 June (1-5). Adm £6, chd £3. Tea, coffee & cake. Our visitors are welcome to bring a picnic. **Visits also by arrangement 22 Mar to 14 June for groups of 10+.**
Peaceful, well established 19 acre garden, parts dating back to 1770s. This hidden gem boasts one of the largest collections of rhododendrons, azaleas, magnolias and camellias. Interspersed with mature and rare trees and complemented by a lake and cascading ponds. 6 acre arboretum, large lilac circle, wisteria pergola with views over Woodbury completes this family run treasure. Plant sale, teas and home bakes (cash only) open at other times. On site car parking. WC available, alcohol wipes and hand gel provided. Strictly no dogs. Wheelchair access to main parts of garden.

&. ✿ ☕

GROUP OPENING

30 HAYTOR GARDENS
Haytor, Newton Abbot, TQ13 9XT. *300m from Haytor on road to Ilsington. From Bovey Tracey, turn L at red phone box. After approx 300 metres Brambly Wood signed on R. Garden 50 metres. Haytor House next to this turning. Parking 200 metres further down the road*

in field on L. Sat 9, Sun 10 May (11-5). **Combined adm £8, chd free. Home-made teas at both gardens.**

BRAMBLY WOOD
Lindsay & Laurie Davidson, lindsay.davidson2012@me.com. **Visits also by arrangement 11 May to 31 Aug for groups of 10 to 30.**

HAYTOR HOUSE
Judy Gordon Jones & Hilary Townsend.

Two very different gardens on the edge of `Dartmoor with views across to Torbay and the Teign estuary. New borders and plants have been added to the 1 acre garden at Brambly Wood where the mature rhododendrons, azaleas and camellias are a delight in May. There are many herbaceous borders, a fruit and vegetable cage with raised beds, and tranquil seating areas throughout. You are welcome to browse our studios showing artisan pottery, textiles and art work. The ¼ acre garden at Haytor House was designed along more classical lines as a project for horticultural students in the 1930s and provides distinctive planting within partitioned areas. An inner walled garden with a folly leads to 3 further garden 'rooms' with a lily pond, raised beds, mixed herbaceous borders and large shrubs and acers among its many features.

🐕 ✿ ☕))

---

31 HEATHERCOMBE
Manaton, nr Bovey Tracey, TQ13 9XE. Claude & Margaret Pike Woodlands Trust, 01626 354404, gardens@pike.me.uk, www.heathercombe.com. *7m NW of Bovey Tracey. From Bovey Tracey take scenic B3387 to Haytor/ Widecombe. 1.7m past Haytor Rocks (before Widecombe Hill) turn R to Hound Tor & Manaton. 1.4m past Hound Tor turn L at Heatree Cross to Heathercombe.* Sun 29 Mar, Sat 2, Sun 3, Sat 9, Sun 10 May (1.30-5.30). Every Tue to Sun 16 May to 31 May (1.30-5.30). Sat 6, Sun 7, Sat 13, Sun 14, Sat 20, Sun 21 June (11-6). Adm £6, chd free. Self service tea & coffee. Please bring cash. Picnics welcome. **Visits also by arrangement. Donation to Rowcroft Hospice.**
Secluded valley with beautiful shrubs

and trees in a natural setting of streams, ponds, daffodils, a profusion of bluebells, wild flowers, ferns, mosses and lichens. Large collection of colourful rhododendrons, azaleas and interesting flowering trees and shrubs. Orchard and cottage gardens. Over 2 miles of shrub and woodland walks with many benches and summerhouses to sit and enjoy the sights and sounds of nature. Dogs welcome. Disabled reserved parking close to tea room & WC.

&. 🐕 ☕ 🪑

32 HIGH GARDEN
Chiverstone Lane, Kenton, Exeter, EX6 8NJ. Chris & Sharon Britton, www.highgardennurserykenton. wordpress.com. *5m S of Exeter on A379 Dawlish Rd. Leaving Kenton towards Exeter, L into Chiverstone Lane, 50yds along lane.* Sun 14 June (2-5.30). Adm £5, chd free. Home-made cakes.
Stunning garden of over 4 acres. Huge range of trees, shrubs, perennials, grasses, climbers and exotics planted over past 19 yrs. Great use of foliage gives texture and substance as well as offsetting the floral display. 70 metre summer herbaceous border. Over 40 individual mixed beds surrounded by meandering grass walkways. Cut flower and vegetable gardens. Tropical border. Slightly sloping site but the few steps can be avoided.

&. 🐕 ☕))

33 HIGHER CHERUBEER
Dolton, Winkleigh, EX19 8PP. Jo & Tom Hynes, hynesjo@gmail.com. *2m E of Dolton. From the A3124 between Winkleigh & Dolton turn S towards Stafford Moor Fisheries, take 1st R signed Dolton, garden 500m on L.* Fri 6, Fri 13, Sat 21 Feb (2-5). Adm £6, chd free. Home-made teas. 2027: Fri 5, Sat 20 Feb. **Visits also by arrangement for groups of 10+. Group visits in Feb, April, May, June, Sept & Oct.**
1¾ acre country garden with gravelled courtyard and paths, raised beds, alpine house, lawns, herbaceous borders, woodland beds with naturalised cyclamen and snowdrops, kitchen garden with large greenhouse and orchard. Winter openings for National Collection of Cyclamen species, hellebores and over 400 snowdrop varieties. Millwood Plants will be selling snowdrops and other winter flowers.

&. ✿ 🚗 [NPC] ☕))

34 HIGHER ORCHARD COTTAGE

Aptor, Marldon, Paignton, TQ3 1SQ. Mrs Jenny Saunders, 07789 425994, jennymsaunders@aol.com, www.facebook.com/HigherOrchardCottage. *1m SW of Marldon. A380 Torquay to Paignton. At Churscombe Cross r'about R for Marldon, L towards Berry Pomeroy, take 2nd R into Farthing Lane. Follow for exactly 1m. Turn R at NGS sign & follow signs for parking.* **Sat 6, Sun 7 June (11-5). Adm £6, chd free. Tea, coffee & cake. Visits also by arrangement 30 Apr to 30 Sept for groups of up to 20. Group size restricted due to limited parking. Refreshments can be arranged.**
Two acre garden with generous colourful herbaceous borders, wildlife pond, specimen trees and shrubs, productive vegetable beds. Grass path walks through wildflower meadows in lovely countryside, art and craft installations by local artists and crafters.

35 HONEYWELL NEW

Stoodleigh, Tiverton, EX16 9QA. Paula Moore. *4 m W of Tiverton. Honeywell is not on google maps. Look for NGS yellow signs from the Stoodleigh Inn approx 1m from Honeywell. What3words: reddish, downfield, slope.* **Sat 5, Sun 6 Sept (11-5). Adm £6, chd free. Home-made teas. Shelter available.**
Over 5 yrs we have lovingly transformed the site of an old farmyard, planting with changing climate, our altitude and winds in mind. Many large grasses, interplanted with perennials grown for their flowers and foliage. Grasses give structure, shape and importantly movement. Reclaimed materials have been cleverly used in "the shack", a shelter to enjoy refreshments and stunning views to Exmoor.

36 ♦ HOTEL ENDSLEIGH

Milton Abbot, Tavistock, PL19 0PQ. Olga Polizzi, 01822 870000, hotelendsleigh@thepolizzicollection.com, thepolizzicollection.com/hotel-endsleigh/garden. *7m NW of Tavistock, midway between Tavistock & Launceston. From Tavistock, take B3362 to Launceston. 7m to Milton Abbot then 1st L, opp school. From Launceston & A30, B3362 to Tavistock. At Milton Abbot turn R opp school.* **For NGS: Tue 12 May (11-3). Adm £10, chd free. For other opening times and information, please phone, email or visit garden website.**
Set in 108 acres, Endsleigh was the last garden designed by Humphry Repton in 1814. Today the visitor can enjoy Repton's vision for the gardens with its streams, rills, pools and cascades splashing through valleys of Champion Trees. Closer to the house, a 'cottage orne' style hunting lodge, you will find a 100 metre herbaceous border, rose arch, yew walk, and Shell House.

37 IDESTONE BARTON

Dunchideock, Exeter, EX2 9UE. Mr & Mrs James Studholme. *SW of Exeter near the village of Ide. From Ide take rd to Dunchideock. After 500 metres fork R (signed Idestone). Take 1st L after 1m. Follow over Xrds and down steep sided S bend. Car park signed on R What3words: Posed Drum Wakes.* **Fri 3, Sat 4 July (12-5.30). Adm £5, chd free. Tea, coffee & cake.**
Romantic 6 acre country garden in unspoilt countryside only 3m from Exeter. Built on 5 different levels, with several distinctive rooms, garden features yew-hedged kitchen garden, croquet lawn, rose terrace, orchard, swimming pond, wildflower meadow and arboretum.

38 JOURNEY'S END

Green Lane, Ilsington, Newton Abbot, TQ13 9RB. Brian & Sheree Sedgbeer. *½m from HayTor Dartmoor. From Bovey Tracey take the road towards HayTor, go past Ullacombe Farm Shop. Turn 1st L into Green Lane, 300 metres on the L well signed. What3words ///nightcap.fresh.binder.* **Sat 2, Sun 3, Mon 4, Sat 23, Sun 24, Mon 25 May, Sat 11, Sun 12 July (10-4). Adm £6, chd free. Tea, coffee & cake.**
Our 2 acre wildlife garden gives us such joy seeing the constant activity and the huge variety of wildlife active on the native grasses, the many wild flowers, shrubs, herbaceous plants, pond etc that provide a food source. Also the brash piles, the wildlife homes we have erected so all creatures have a home here at Journey's End, our self build award winning home. Wildlife photographic exhibition.

39 KENTISBEARE HOUSE

Kentisbeare, Cullompton, EX15 2BR. Nicholas & Sarah Allan. *2m E of M5 J28 (Cullompton). Turn off A373 at Post Cross signed Kentisbeare. After ½m past cricket field & main drive on R, entrance to car park is through next gate on R.* **Sat 30 May (10.30-4.30). Adm £6, chd free. Home-made teas.**
Surrounding the listed former Kentisbeare rectory, the gardens have been redesigned and planted by the present owners in recent years with various planting themes that complement the surrounding countryside. Formal beds, lake walk, kitchen garden and glasshouse, wildflower meadow, orchard. Diverse and interesting collection of trees, shrubs and woodland plants.

40 KIA-ORA FARM & GARDENS

Knowle Lane, Cullompton, EX15 1PZ. Mrs M B Disney, 01884 32347, rosie@kia-orafarm.co.uk. *On W side of Cullompton & 6m SE of Tiverton. M5 J28, through town centre to r'about, 3rd exit R, top of Swallow Way turn L into Knowle Lane, garden beside Cullompton Rugby Club What3Words - snored.playfully.marzipan.* **Sun 19 Apr, Sun 3, Mon 4, Sun 24, Mon 25 May, Sun 7, Sun 21 June, Sun 5, Sun 19 July, Sun 2, Sun 16, Sun 30, Mon 31 Aug, Sun 13, Sun 27 Sept (2-5.30). Adm £5, chd free. Home-made teas. Teas, plants & sales not for NGS. Visits also by arrangement Apr to Sept for groups of 20+. State for NGS when booking.**
Charming, peaceful 10 acre garden with lawns, lakes and ponds. Water features with swans, ducks and other wildlife. Mature trees, shrubs, rhododendrons, azaleas, heathers, roses, herbaceous borders and rockeries. Interesting garden for all ages and surprises around every corner! To finish off, sit back and enjoy a traditional home-made tea and cakes.

41 LARCOMBE FARMHOUSE

Diptford, Totnes, TQ9 7PD. Jim & Mandy Hanbury. *3m from A38. Turn off at Marley Head between South Brent & Buckfastleigh. Head towards Diptford & Morleigh. From Totnes 4m on Plymouth & Avonwick Rd turn L onto Diptford road & follow*

signs. **Sat 18, Sun 19 July (11-4). Adm £6, chd free. Pre-booking essential, please visit www.ngs. org.uk for information & booking. Tea, coffee & cake.**
A beautiful south facing cottage garden in the rural hamlet of Larcombe. In July expect to see an abundance of traditional cottage florals, roses and hydrangea in an undulating garden of about an acre with a stream running through it. Find some peaceful seating areas and enjoy exploring the features of this tranquil space. Walkers and cyclists welcome without pre booking.

42 LEE FORD
Knowle Village, Budleigh Salterton, EX9 7AJ. Mr & Mrs N Lindsay-Fynn, 01395 445894, crescent@leeford.co.uk, www.leeford.co.uk. $3\frac{1}{2}$ m E of Exmouth. For SatNav use postcode EX9 6AL. **Visits by arrangement Apr to Sept for groups of 10 to 26. Adm £7.50, chd free. Home-made teas. Discounted entry for 10 or more £7. Morning coffee & biscuits, morning & afternoon teas with selection of cakes or cream teas served in conservatory.** Donation to Lindsay-Fynn Trust.
Extensive, formal and woodland garden, largely developed in 1950s, but recently much extended with mass displays of camellias, rhododendrons and azaleas, inc many rare varieties. Traditional walled garden filled with fruit and vegetables, herb garden, bog garden, hydrangea collection, greenhouses for ornamentals, conservatory with pot plants inc pelargoniums, bougainvilleas and coleus. Direct access to pedestrian route and National Cycle Network Route 2 which follows old railway linking Exmouth to Budleigh Salterton. Woodland and formal garden are an ideal destination for cycle clubs or rambling groups. Formal gardens are lawn with paths. Moderately steep slope to woodland garden on tarmac drive with gravel paths in woodland.

43 LEWIS COTTAGE
Spreyton, nr Crediton, EX17 5AA. Mr & Mrs M Pell and Mr R Orton, 07773 785939, rworton@mac.com, www.lewiscottageplants.co.uk. 5m NE of Spreyton, 8m W of Crediton. From Hillerton X keep stone X to your R. Drive approx $1\frac{1}{2}$ m, Lewis Cottage on L, drive down farm track. From Crediton follow A377 N. Turn L at Barnstaple X junction, then 2m from Colebrooke Church. **Daily Sat 8 Aug to Sun 16 Aug (12-5.30). Adm £5.50, chd free. Home-made teas. Visits also by arrangement June to Sept for groups of 12 to 24.**
4 acre garden located on SW facing slope in rural mid Devon. Evolved primarily over last 30 yrs, harnessing and working with the natural landscape. Using informal planting and natural structures to create a garden that reflects the souls of those who garden in it. It is an incredibly personal space that is a joy to share. Lower half of garden under restoration; some parts may not always be accessible. Spring camassia cricket pitch, rose garden, large natural dew pond, woodland walks, bog garden, hornbeam rondel, winter garden, hot and cool herbaceous borders, fruit and vegetable garden, outdoor poetry reading room and plant nursery selling plants mostly propagated from the garden.

44 LINDEN RISE
Chapel Lane, Combe Martin, Ilfracombe, EX34 0HJ. Jenny Sheppard. In Combe Martin High St turn R, uphill, at old PO onto Chapel Lane, Linden Rise is on R opp Hollands Park where parking is available. **Sun 28 June (2-5). Adm £5, chd free. Light lunches. Tea, coffee & cake.**
In an area of outstanding natural beauty with countryside and sea views, $1\frac{1}{2}$ acre garden of lawns, mature trees and shrubs, pergola, decorative ponds, small orchard and seasonal flower borders. Raffle with 1st prize: weekend in a holiday home. Art exhibition by local artist. Musician playing. Cake gift stall. Wheelchair access to most areas.

45 LITTLE ASH BUNGALOW
Fenny Bridges, Honiton, EX14 3BL. Helen & Brian Brown, 07833 247927, helenlittleash@hotmail.com, www.facebook.com/littleashgarden. 3m W of Honiton. Leave A30 at 1st turn off from Honiton 1m, Patteson's Cross from Exeter $\frac{1}{2}$ m & follow NGS signs. **Thur 12 Feb (10-3). Pre-booking essential, please visit www.ngs.org.uk for information & booking. Sun 23 Aug (1-5). Adm £5, chd free. Tea, coffee & cake. 2027: Wed 3, Thur 11 Feb. Visits also by arrangement May to Sept for groups of 10+. Coaches welcome.**
Country garden of $1\frac{1}{2}$ acres, packed with different and unusual bulbs, herbaceous perennials, trees, and shrubs. Designed for year-round interest, wildlife and owners' pleasure. Naturalistic planting in colour coordinated borders, underplanted with 400+ snowdrop varieties. Natural stream, pond and damp woodland area, mini wildlife meadows and raised gravel/alpine garden, various metal sculptures. Grass paths.

46 LITTLE DINWORTHY
Bradworthy, Holsworthy, EX22 7QX. Melanie & Simon Osborne, www.LittleDinworthy.co.uk. 3m NW of Bradworthy. In Bradworthy Square, head towards Meddon/Hartland on North Rd. Take 2nd L to Dinworthy at North Moor X, & follow NGS signs. Lane entrance to Little Dinworthy will be on R. **Sun 29 Mar, Sun 19 Apr, Sun 17 May (11-4). Adm £7, chd £2. Home-made teas. Children's woodland trail included in entry.**
A wildlife garden and lake with young 22 yr old woodland. A developing garden with magnolias, flowering cherries and a variety of different specimen trees. Wild flowers abound encouraging multiple species in the many natural habitats. Around the house, box and yew topiary add a touch of fun and solidity to the profusion of growth. Meadow walks and children's woodland trail. Suitable footwear is recommended due to wet grass and some muddy paths. Dogs welcome on leads in garden and woodland. Tearoom in the stone studio barn with wood burner and WC.

Our donation to Marie Curie this year is equivalent to 17,521 hours of hospice at home care.

47 ♦ LUKESLAND
Harford, Ivybridge, PL21 0JF.
Mrs R Howell and Mr & Mrs
J Howell, 07906 480362,
lorna.lukesland@gmail.com,
www.lukesland.co.uk. 10m E of
Plymouth. Turn off A38 at Ivybridge.
1½m N on Harford road, E side
of Erme valley. Beware of using
SatNavs as these can be very
misleading. **For opening times and
information, please phone, email or
visit garden website.**
24 acres of flowering shrubs, wild
flowers and rare trees with pinetum
in Dartmoor National Park. Beautiful
setting of small valley around
Addicombe Brook with lakes,
numerous waterfalls and pools.
Extensive and impressive collections
of camellias, rhododendrons,
azaleas and acers; also spectacular
Magnolia campbellii and huge *Davidia
involucrata*. Superb spring and
autumn colour. Open Suns, Weds
and BH (11-5) 15 March - 7 June and
4 Oct -15 November. Adm £9.00,
under 16s free. Group tours available
by appointment. Discount for parties
of 25+. Children's trail.

48 MIDDLE WELL
Waddeton Road, Stoke Gabriel,
Totnes, TQ9 6RL. Neil & Pamela
Millward, 01803 782981,
neilandpam72@gmail.com. *A385
Totnes towards Paignton. Turn off
A385 at Parkers Arms, Collaton St.
Mary. After 1m, turn L at Four Cross.
What3words app gong.starch.
hindering. Parking at Sandridge
Barton Winery on main open day.*
**Sun 2 Aug (11-5). Adm £6, chd
free. Home-made teas. Visits
also by arrangement Apr to Nov.
Large coaches need to park 300m
away. Small coaches may drop off
at gate.**
Tranquil 2 acre garden, plus
woodland, stream and rill, containing
a wealth of interesting plants chosen
for colour, form and long season of
interest. Many seats from which to
enjoy the sound of water. Interesting
structural features (rill, summerhouse,
pergola, cobbling, slate bridge).
Heady mix of perennials, shrubs,
bulbs, climbers and specimen
trees. Striking architectural features
complemented by painterly planting,
late colour, vegetable garden. Child
friendly. Please visit www.ngs.org.
uk for possible May pop-up opening.
Mostly accessible by wheelchair.

49 2 MIDDLEWOOD
Cockwood, Exeter, EX6 8RN. Cliff
& Chris Curd. *1m S of Starcross.
A379 from Dawlish, R at Cofton
Cross, passing Cofton Holidays.
Middlewood ½m on R. A379 from
Exeter, turn L at Cockwood Harbour.
Turn R & pass The Ship. Park on
Church Rd, not in Middlewood.*
**Sat 20, Sun 21 June, Fri 10, Sun
12 July (1-5.30). Adm £6, chd
free. Cream teas. Plain scones
& drinks without food also
available.**
Entered via a courtyard is this former
market garden on a north facing
slope. Steep, uneven paths. View
over the Exe. Food production and
wildlife garden. Self-sufficiency
ethos; greenhouse, polytunnel, fruit
cage, raised vegetable beds, wild
area, ponds, beehive. Productive
fruit bushes and trees inc many
exotics. Steep access path means
not wheelchair accessible and only
the courtyard is accessible to those
with mobility challenges. Called
'inspirational' by visitors. The Anchor
Inn at Cockwood harbour 300 yds.
Cofton Country Holidays with superb
pool and restaurant open to the
public ½m away.

50 ♦ MOTHECOMBE HOUSE
Mothecombe, Holbeton, Plymouth,
PL8 1LA. Mr & Mrs J Mildmay-
White, jmw@flete.co.uk, flete.
co.uk/mothecombe-gardens.
*12m E of Plymouth. From A379
between Yealmpton & Modbury
turn S for Holbeton. Continue 2m
to Mothecombe.* **For NGS: Sun 14
June (11-5). Adm £6, chd free.
Home-made teas in the garden.
For other opening times and
information, please email or visit
garden website.**
Queen Anne House (not open) with
Lutyens additions and terraces set
in private estate hamlet. Walled
gardens, orchard with spring bulbs
and magnolias, camellia walk leading
through bluebell woods to streams
and pond. Mothecombe Garden is
managed for wildlife and pollinators.
Bee garden with 250 lavenders in
16 varieties. New project to manage
adjacent 6 acre meadow as a
traditional wildflower pasture. Sandy
beach at bottom of garden, unusual
shaped large *Liriodendron tulipifera*.
Lunches avail at The Schoolhouse,
Mothecombe village. Gravel paths,
two slopes.

51 THE MOUNT, DELAMORE
Cornwood, Ivybridge, PL21 9QP.
Mr & Mrs Gavin Dollard. *Between
Ivybridge & Yelverton. Pls park in car
park for Delamore Park Offices not in
village. From Ivybridge turn L at Xrds
in Cornwood village, keep pub on
L, follow wall on R to sharp R bend,
turn R.* **Sat 14, Sun 15, Sat 21, Sun
22 Feb (10.30-3.30). Adm £7.50,
chd free.**
Welcome one of the first signs of
spring by wandering through swathes
of thousands of snowdrops in this
lovely wood. Closer to the village
than to Delamore Gardens, paths
meander through a sea of these lovely
plants, some of which are unique to
Delamore and which were sold as
posies to Covent Garden market as
late as 2002. The Cornwood Inn in
the village is now community owned.
Main house and garden open for
sculpture exhibition every day in May.

52 MOWHAY
Merton, nr Great Torrington,
EX20 3DS. Kerry & Neil
Littleales, 07727 657246,
kerrylittleales@outlook.com,
www.makingmowhay.co.uk. *10
mins S of Great Torrington. Access
via the A386. From Torrington or
Hatherleigh enter Merton village &
follow yellow parking signs. Walk
up the hill following yellow signs
(approx 5 mins). What3words app:
risen.navigate.rural.* **Sat 23, Sun
24, Mon 25 May (11-4). Sat 13,
Sun 14 June (11-4), open nearby
Musselbrook Cottage Garden.
Sat 8, Sun 9 Aug (11-4). Adm
£6, chd free. Home-made teas.
During May soup & a roll may
be on offer on colder days.
Gluten free available. Visits also
by arrangement 26 May to 7 Aug
for groups of 10+. £10 adm inc
refreshments & guided tour.**
A ¾ acre countryside garden
developed over 4 yrs. Planted
abundantly and vibrantly - the garden
paths take a colourful journey through
various areas. Visit the white garden,
bonsai collection, rose terrace and
fish pond, the lower beds with small
waterfall, orchard, vegetable patch,
wildlife pond, cozy garden room and
The Wizard Walk! All with an eye
to reusing and recycling wherever
possible. A selection of coasters,
pictures and other crafted products
will be on sale. Grass paths, some
gravel and a gentle slope. Previous
visitors have navigated the majority

of the garden with assistance in a couple of areas.
& ⛬ 🚗 ☕ 🔊

53 MUSSELBROOK COTTAGE GARDEN
Sheepwash, Beaworthy, EX21 5PE. Richard Coward, 01409 231677, coward.richard@sky.com. *1.3m N of Sheepwash. SatNav may be misleading. A3072 to Highampton then 1.3m after Sheepwash L on track signed Lake Farm. A386 S of Merton take road to Petrockstow. Up hill opp, much later L. After 350 yds turn R down track signed Lake Farm.* Sat 18, Sun 19 Apr, Sat 9, Sun 10 May (11-4.30). Sat 13, Sun 14 June (11-4.30), open nearby Mowhay. Sat 18, Sun 19 July (11-4.30). Adm £6, chd free. Visits also by arrangement 26 Apr to 3 May for groups of 6 to 15. Visitors are welcome to bring picnics.
One acre naturalistic/ wildlife/ plantsman's/sensory garden (autism friendly) on sloping site. Year-round interest with rare and unusual plants. 13 ponds (koi and lilies), stream, Japanese garden, Mediterranean garden, wildflower meadow, massed bulbs. Hundreds of ericaceous plants inc camellias, magnolias, rhododendrons, acers, hydrangeas. Grasses/bamboo. Clock golf. Small aquatic/general nursery. A mattock and serrated edged spade essential for digging our rocky soil. Nursery can be visited by appointment.
✿ 🪑

Wembury Walled Garden

GROUP OPENING

54 OGWELL GARDENS
Ogwell, TQ12 6AH. *1½m SW of Newton Abbot. Tickets available at all of the gardens, but cashless payments can only be made at Rydon Brake, Rectory Road, TQ12 6AH where teas & cake are also served. A map of the gardens will be provided.* Sat 13, Sun 14 June (11-4). Combined adm £8, chd free. Home-made teas at Rydon Brake, Rectory Road, TQ12 6AH.

BUTTERCOMBE COTTAGE
Helen Clarke.

HOLBEAM MILL
Mr Nick Holdsworth.

RYDON BRAKE
Paul & Pauline Wynter.

4 SUNNY HOLLOW
Paul & Anthea Martin.

NEW SWALLOWFIELD
Paul & Sally Tyler.

WILLOW TREE HOUSE
Dan & Katy Farrell-Wright.

WYNDHAM CROFT
Shani & Richard Broome.

The Ogwell group offers seven gardens of varying styles, inc small cottage gardens, an historic mill and those focused on encouraging wildlife, one with a swimming pond and striking planting, and large gardens with ponds, a bonsai collection and other attractions. Regret that not all gardens are wheelchair accessible.
☕ 🔊

55 THE OLD RECTORY
Ashreigney, Chulmleigh, EX18 7NB. Jill & Gerrit Lemmens, 07482 533593, Jill.leppard@hotmail.co.uk. *Located 100 yds from Bush Corner (red Post Box) on the road between Ashreigney & Chulmleigh. Take directions from Bush Corner to a public bridleway via a lane; the Old Rectory is the LH fork after 100 yds.* Sat 6, Sun 7 June (11-4). Adm £5, chd free. Tea, coffee & cake. Savoury scones, gluten free & vegan options available. Visits also by arrangement May to Sept for groups of 6 to 26.
One acre wildlife friendly garden incorporating traditional herbaceous borders with colour themes and seasonal interest, with pond and water features, wildflower meadow, glasshouse, raised vegetable beds; a developing arboretum of recently planted trees, foxglove and fern area and small jungle. Set within tranquil and rural mid Devon with adjoining fields and woodland.
⛬ ✿ ☕ 🪑 🔊

GROUP OPENING

56 PARRACOMBE GARDENS
Parracombe, EX31 4QL. *Off A39 between Blackmore Gate & Lynton. Follow signs for car parking. Card payments taken at the Pavilion Stores & Cafe, cash only at gardens.* **Sat 20, Sun 21 June (12-5). Combined adm £6, chd free. Tea, coffee & cake in the Pavilion Stores & Café.**

CHURCH COTTAGE
Jo & Harry Harrison.
Open on all dates

LAUREL HOUSE
Lesley & John Brownlee.
Open on Sun 21 June

LITTLECLOSE
Julia & Jeremy Holtom.
Open on all dates

NEW PARK VIEW
Phillippa Hughes and Keith Palmer.
Open on all dates

NEW PARRACOMBE C OF E (VC) PRIMARY
Devon County Council.
Open on all dates

SOUTH HILL HOUSE
Alison Smith & Dave Austin.
Open on all dates

Set in the historic Exmoor village of Parracombe, with its Norman motte & bailey castle and St Petrock's, an ancient Grade I listed C12 church (guided tours available). Church Cottage has informal cottage style beds, a large vegetable/cut flower area and an orchard. Laurel House is a small gem of a garden, packed with successional planting and landscape features. Littleclose has a terraced garden, roses, an orchard and a lovely view of the motte & bailey castle. Park View's small secret garden is planted with herbaceous perennials and bulbs and a pond encourages wildlife. South Hill House has a walled front garden and a cobbled courtyard leading to the rear garden, with its herbaceous borders and mature trees, set beside the river Heddon. Parracombe village primary school will showcase flowers and vegetables grown by the pupils. Teas/light lunches and WC at Pavilion Community Stores and Café. Lunches available at the Fox & Goose (booking advised 01598 763219).

57 1 PILTON LAWN
Pilton, Barnstaple, EX31 4AA.
Louise Southworth. *Once in Raleigh Rd, take the 1st L, then immed R. Garden is at the end of this road. Free parking in Raleigh Rd, with some limited parking in parts of Pilton Lawn.* **Sun 5 Apr, Sat 23 May, Sat 25 July (10.30-8). Adm £5, chd free. Light refreshments. Cakes, snacks & drinks.**
This modest yet deceptively spacious garden, brings the indoors out, providing a relaxed and chilled vibe. Cornish slab pathways take you around the garden and features inc 'Alice' the boat! Carefully considered planting creates privacy and year-round interest. Enjoy refreshments served from the hand built shack bar and relax in the seating areas amidst the varied range of plants. Wheelchair access will allow the use of the shack bar and socialising area.

58 ♦ PLANT WORLD
St Marychurch Road, Newton Abbot, TQ12 4SE. Ray Brown, 01803 872939, info@plant-world-seeds.com, www.plant-world-gardens.co.uk. *2m SE of Newton Abbot. 1½m from Penn Inn turn-off on A380. Follow brown tourist signs at end of A380 dual carriageway from Exeter.* **For opening times and information, please phone, email or visit garden website.**
Four acres of landscaped gardens with fabulous views, called Devon's 'Little Outdoor Eden'. Representing 5 continents, they feature an extensive collection of rare and exotic plants from around the world. With attractions for all ages in the gardens. Rare and unusual plant nursery. Attractive viewpoint café and picnic area. Special meal deals for coach parties. Please email for details. Open daily April to end September 9.30am–4.30pm.

59 THE PRIORY
Priory Road, Abbotskerswell, Newton Abbot, TQ12 5PP. Priory residents. *Between Newton Abbot & Abbotskerswell. 2m SW of Newton Abbot town centre. A381 Newton Abbot/Totnes Rd, sharp L turn from NA, sharp R turn from Totnes. At mini-r'about in village centre turn L into Priory Rd & follow the signs.* **Sat 20, Sun 21 June (1-5). Adm £7, chd free. Tea, coffee & cake.**
The Priory is a Grade II* listed building, originally a manor house extended in Victorian times as a home for an Augustinian order of nuns, now a retirement complex of 44 apartments and cottages. The grounds extend to approx 5 acres and inc numerous flower borders, a wildflower meadow, an area of woodland with some interesting specimen trees, cottage gardens and lovely views. Small Mediterranean garden and area of individually owned raised beds and greenhouses. Wheelchair access difficult in woodland and meadow areas.

60 REGENCY HOUSE
Hemyock, EX15 3RQ. Mrs Jenny Parsons, 07772 998982, jenny.parsons@btinternet.com, www.regencyhousehemyock.co.uk. *8m N of Honiton. M5 J26/27. At Catherine Wheel pub in Hemyock take Dunkeswell-Honiton Rd. Entrance ½m on R. Please do not drive on the long grass alongside the drive. Good parking, disabled parking (only) at house.* **Sat 18, Sun 19 Apr, Sat 30, Sun 31 May, Sun 7, Mon 8 June, Sun 18, Mon 19 Oct (2-5). Adm £8, chd free. Home-made teas. Visits also by arrangement 1 Apr to 30 Oct for groups of 10 to 30.**
5 acre plantsman's garden approached across a little ford. Many interesting and unusual trees and shrubs. Visitors can try their hand at identifying plants with the very comprehensive and amusing plant list. Plenty of space to eat your own picnic. Walled vegetable and fruit garden, lake, ponds, bog plantings and sweeping lawns. Horses, Dexter cattle and Jacob sheep. A tranquil space to relax in. Gently sloping gravel paths give wheelchair access to the walled garden, lawns, borders and terrace, where teas are served.

61 ROSE ASH HOUSE
Rose Ash, South Molton, EX36 4RB. Caro & Murray Hammick. *5m S of South Molton. Centre of Rose Ash, head W from thatched cottage (signed to Romansleigh) follow NGS signs. After 150 yards park in field on L. Follow signs to garden. Parking might change if VERY wet.* **Sat 18, Sun 19 July (11-4). Adm £5, chd free. Cream teas, soft drinks, cakes etc. will be available.**

Several acres of informal garden around old manor house, next to the village green and church, with views to Dartmoor and Exmoor. Fun mixed borders, rose arbour, shrubs, interesting trees, uncut grassland and vegetable garden. Martyn Rix, plant hunter extraordinaire, will hopefully be on hand to identify any plants you bring. Melinda Hilliard, a garden design consultant, can assist with garden planning. Reasonable wheelchair access to the whole garden - there are few steep slopes or steps.

GROUP OPENING

62 ROSEBARN GARDENS
Exeter, EX4 6DY. *Situated in N of the City off Pennsylvania Rd & Rosebarn Lane nr the University. Rosebarn Ave can be reached on the 'K' bus from the City Centre.* **Sat 6, Sun 7 June (1-5). Combined adm £6, chd free. Home-made teas.**

7 ROSEBARN AVENUE
Steve & Sue Bloomfield.

16 ROSEBARN AVENUE
Chris & Jane Read, www.facebook.com/ SixteenRosebarnAvenue.

25 ROSEBARN AVENUE
Jenny & Mike Phillips.

73 ROSEBARN LANE
Gerry & Lizzy Sones.

Featuring four gardens on a short walking circuit. No 7 is a traditional 1950s garden with flower borders, pond, wild area and a recently redesigned and planted front garden. No16 was redesigned in 2022. This landscaped garden features a kitchen garden, pond, summerhouse, herbaceous beds and native trees. No 25 is a typical townhouse garden featuring perennial borders, plant house, potting shed, vegetable plot and mature apple trees. No 73 has an interesting landscaped front garden and a tranquil mature back garden divided into 'rooms', a large pond and many specimen trees.

63 SAMLINGSTEAD
Near Roadway Corner, Woolacombe, EX34 7HL. Roland & Marion Grzybek, 01271 870886, roland135@msn.com. *1m outside Woolacombe. Stay on A361 all the way to Woolacombe. Passing through town head up Chalacombe Hill, L at T-junction, garden 150 metres on L.* **Sat 14 Mar, Sat 11 July (10.30-3.30). Adm £5, chd free. Cream teas in 'The Swallows' a purpose built out-building. Hot sausage rolls (meat & vegetarian), cakes, tea, coffee & soft drinks. Visits also by arrangement 2 Mar to 30 Sept.**
Garden is within 2 mins of N Devon coastline and Woolacombe AONB. 6 distinct areas; cottage garden at front, patio garden to one side, swallows garden at rear, meadow garden, orchard and field (500 metres walk with newly planted hedgerow). Slightly sloping ground so whilst wheelchair access is available to most parts of garden certain areas may require assistance.

64 SAND FARMHOUSE
Roncombe Lane, Sidbury, Sidmouth, EX10 0QN. Mrs Denise Lyon, 07975 647760, deniselyon@icloud.com, www. greenstudiogardendesign.com. *On the beautiful Roncombe Valley in the E Devon AONB. Recommended approach is from Sidbury Village end. We are 200m past Sand House. From Honiton, your app may take you L at the Hare & Hounds but ignore it & carry on down the hill.* **Visits by arrangement 1 May to 5 Oct for groups of 5 to 20. £10 adm inc home-made cake & a drink.**
A wonderful vantage point over a hidden valley, this long, sloping, beautiful ⅓ acre garden has been designed to delight. With long established trees such as *Cedrus deodora* and *Sequoiadendron giganteum* (we think...come and help us decide!) together with many newer trees and lush, varied planting, you might agree with my Dad: 'These borders are better than RHS Wisley!'.

65 SHERWOOD
Newton St Cyres, Exeter, EX5 5BT. Nicola Chambers, 07702 895435, nikkinew2012@yahoo.com, www. facebook.com/SherwoodGardensDevon. *2m SE of Crediton. Off A377 Exeter to Barnstaple road, ¾m Crediton side of Newton St Cyres, signed*

DEVON 153

Sherwood, entrance to drive in 1¾m. Do not follow SatNav once on lane, don't fork R, just drive straight & keep going. **Sun 26 Apr, Sun 7 June, Sun 25 Oct (1-5). Adm £8, chd £3. Pre-booking essential, please visit www.ngs. org.uk for information & booking. Home-made teas. Visits also by arrangement 1 Jan to 30 Dec for groups of 5 to 60. Picnics welcome. Regret no dogs.**
23 acres with 2 steep wooded valleys. Wild flowers, spring bulbs, especially daffodils; extensive collections of magnolias, camellias, rhododendrons, Knaphill azaleas, berberis, heathers, maples, cotoneasters, buddleias, hydrangeas, cornus and epimedium. Suitable footwear required due to areas of steep terrain.

66 NEW SHOBROOKE PARK GARDENS
Crediton, EX17 1DG. Dr & Mrs J R Shelley, www.shobrookepark.com. *1m NE of Crediton, off the A3072 Tiverton road.* **Sat 18 Apr (10.30-5). Adm £5, chd free. Picnics welcome.**
15 acre woodland garden laid out in mid C19 with extensive Portland Stone terraces and views over the 200 acre park with ponds.

67 SIDBURY MANOR
Sidmouth, EX10 0QE. George Cave, www.sidburymanor.com. *1m NW of Sidbury. Sidbury village is on A375, S of Honiton, N of Sidmouth.* **Fri 17, Sun 19 Apr (2-5). Adm £7, chd free. Cream teas.**
Built in the 1870s by the owner's family, the Victorian manor house is set within the E Devon AONB. It comes complete with 20 acres of garden inc substantial walled gardens, extensive arboretum containing many fine trees and shrubs, a number of champion trees, and areas devoted to magnolias, rhododendrons and camellias plus an abundance of daffodils. Partial wheelchair access.

Cadhay

68 SIDBURY MILL
Burnt Oak, Sidbury, Sidmouth, EX10 0RE. **Helen Munday.** *On the A375 at the southern end of Sidbury village. From Honiton take A375 towards Sidmouth. In Sidbury pass the church on the L & continue for ½ m. Sidbury Mill on L. From Sidmouth take A375 towards Honiton. Sidbury Mill brown signs on R.* **Fri 19, Sun 21 June (11-4). Adm £5, chd free. Tea, coffee, cold drinks, sweet & savoury treats. Seating outside as well as under cover.**

The gardens and grounds of Sidbury Mill extend to 6 acres. As well as diversity of plants and trees, it is a haven for wildlife. The gardens range from a perennial, rose and shrub garden, a greenhouse and vegetable patch, to mature woodland through which the River Sid flows. A 'woodland walk' encompasses many elements of the gardens through which the visitor will appreciate the plants and wildlife. The needs of a water mill are a great influence on the gardens and grounds of Sidbury Mill, including the river and various leats. The water wheel is an integral part of the back garden. Sidbury Mill is one of the last working water mills in the south-west, milling wheat grown in our nearby field. In the garden floral borders, greenhouse etc are accessible via a ramp, gravel path and small step. The woodland walk is mainly flat with grass paths.

69 SOUTH WOOD FARM
Cotleigh, Honiton, EX14 9HU. **Professor Clive Potter.** *3m NE of Honiton. From Honiton head N on A30, take 1st R past Otter Valley Field Kitchen layby. Follow for 1m. Go straight over Xrds and take first L. Entrance after 1m on R.* **Sun 19 Apr (1-5). Adm £10, chd free. Pre-booking essential, please visit www.ngs.org.uk for information & booking. Sat 6, Sun 7 June (2-5). Adm £7, chd free. Tea, coffee & cake.**

Designed by renowned Arne Maynard around C17 thatched farmhouse, country garden exemplifying how contemporary design can be integrated into a traditional setting. Herbaceous borders, roses, yew topiary, knot garden, wildflower meadows, wildlife ponds, orchards, lean-to greenhouses and a mouthwatering kitchen garden create an unforgettable sense of place. For the April date, tickets are limited to 100 and must be pre booked. A stunning array of tulips and spring bulbs feature throughout the garden. Gravel pathways, cobbles and steps.

70 SPRING LODGE
Kenton, Exeter, EX6 8EY. **David & Ann Blandford,** 07905 506641, **Bland62@yahoo.com.** *Between Lyson & Oxton. Head for Lyson then Oxton.* **Fri 3 Apr (10-4). Adm £5, chd £1. Pre-booking essential, please visit www.ngs.org.uk for information & booking. Teas, coffee, soft drinks, cakes & biscuits.** **Visits also by arrangement Apr to Aug for groups of 5 to 20.**

Originally part of the Georgian pleasure gardens to Oxton House, the garden at Spring Lodge boasts a hermit's cave, dramatic cliffs and a stream which runs under the house. Built in the quarry of the big house this ½ acre garden is on many levels, with picturesque vistas and lush planting. Pre booking essential due to restricted parking.

DEVON 155

71 STONE FARM
Alverdiscott Road, Bideford,
EX39 4PN. Mr & Mrs Ray
Auvray, 01237 421420,
rayauvray@icloud.com. 1½m
from Bideford towards Alverdiscott.
From Bideford cross river using Old
Bridge & turn L onto Barnstaple St.
2nd R onto Manteo Way & 1st L at
r'about. **Visits by arrangement
May to Sept for groups of 10+.
Individuals/small groups pls
check NGS website for details of
pop up openings. Adm £5, chd
free. Tea, coffee & cake.**
Two acre country garden managed
by head gardener, Fiona Thompson,
with striking herbaceous borders, dry
stone wall terracing, white garden,
Japanese themed garden, and "hot"
garden. Extensive vegetable gardens
with polytunnels and greenhouse and
our ⅓ acre walled garden. Orchard
with traditional apple, pear and plum
trees. New woodland meadow area
and herb garden. Some gravel paths
but wheelchair access to whole
garden with some help.

72 STONELANDS HOUSE
Stonelands Bridge, Dawlish,
EX7 9BL. Mr Kerim Derhalli
(Owner) Mr Saul Walker (Head
Gardener), 07815 807832,
saulwalkerstonelands@outlook.
com. *Outskirts of NW Dawlish.
From A380 take junction for B3192
& follow signs for Teignmouth, after
2m L at Xrds onto Luscombe Hill,
further 2m, main gate on L.* **Visits
by arrangement Apr to June for
groups of 10 to 20. Tues-Thurs
weekdays only. Adm £7, chd
free. Tea, coffee & cake. Pls
book refreshments through Head
Gardener, separate payment on
the day.**
Beautiful 12 acre pleasure garden
surrounding early C19 property
designed by John Nash. Many
mature specimen trees, shrubs and
rhododendrons, large formal lawn,
recently landscaped herbaceous
beds, vegetable garden, woodland
garden, orchard with wildflower
meadow and riverside walk.
An atmospheric and delightful
horticultural secret. Wheelchair
access to lower area of gardens.
Paths through woodland, meadow
and riverside walk may be unsuitable
for wheelchairs.

73 SUTTON MEAD
Moretonhampsread,
TQ13 8PW. Edward & Miranda
Allhusen, 01647 440296,
miranda@allhusen.co.uk, www.
facebook.com/suttonmeadgarden.
*12m from Exeter, Newton Abbot
& Okehampton. ½m N of
Moretonhampstead on A382.* **Fri 8,
Sat 9, Sun 10 May, Fri 4, Sat 5,
Sun 6 Sept (12-5). Adm £6, chd
free. Home-made teas. Hot soup
& savoury scones. Visits also by
arrangement.**
A large garden with splendid views of
Dartmoor. Remote yet only a dozen
miles from Exeter, Okehampton
and Newton Abbot. A constantly
colourful garden. May features
numerous varieties of rhododendron,
azalea and late spring bulbs and in
September hydrangeas, dahlias,
agapanthus and much more. Mature
orchard, productive vegetable
garden, substantial tree planting,
croquet lawn. Wander through
tranquil woodland. Lawns surround
a granite lined pond with a seat at
the water's edge. Elsewhere unusual
planting, grasses, bog garden, granite
walls, rill fed pond, secluded seating
and an unusual concrete gothic
greenhouse all contribute to a garden
of variety that has been developed
and constructed over 48 yrs by the
current owners. Plants from the
garden for sale and teas are a must.
Dogs on leads welcome.

74 TAMAR HOUSE
Bridgerule, Holsworthy, EX22 7EJ.
Mr Paul Rutherford, 07711 564072,
ozoneeng@aol.com. *11 mins W of
Holsworthy. Tamar House is opp the
Bridge Inn, Bridgerule. What3words
app: somewhere.hotspots.tank.*
**Visits by arrangement June to
Sept for groups of up to 8. Open
7 days a week. Adm £5, chd free.**
This small Japanese style garden
inc many Japanese acer palmatum
shrubs surrounded by rocks, gravel
pathways, bamboo and many other
plants indigenous to the Nippon
Islands. The garden is divided into
rooms which inc a dry garden, water
features, a koi pond area, a moss
garden, a specimen bonsai area,
a Shinto shrine and raised decking
looking out over the Tamar River. The
owner of the garden has spent many
years in Japan and in 2021 started
to build a Zen garden based around
wabi sabi which can be defined as
"beauty in imperfection" remembering
that nothing lasts, nothing is finished,
and nothing is perfect.

GROUP OPENING

75 TEIGNMOUTH GARDENS
Bitton Park Road, Teignmouth,
TQ14 9DF. *6m E of Newton Abbot,
16m S of Exeter. Please park in the
car park for Bitton House (charges
apply). Tickets for all gardens can be
bought at The Orangery. A map will
be provided.* **Sat 13, Sun 14 June
(1-5). Combined adm £6, chd free.
Teas available in Teignmouth's
many cafes.**

21 GORWAY
TQ14 8PX. Mrs Christine
Richman.

26 HAZELDOWN ROAD
TQ14 8QR. Mrs Ann Sadler.

THE ORANGERY
TQ14 9DF. The Friends of
Teignmouth Orangery.

21 WOODLAND AVENUE
TQ14 8UU. Larissa Letwyn.

Four gardens, inc the beautifully
restored Orangery, are opening in
the picturesque coastal town of
Teignmouth. A wide range of garden
styles and sizes can be explored this
year from very small but inspiring
manicured gardens to large wildlife
havens and clifftop exotic. Features
inc courtyards, greenhouses,
pollinator friendly planting, exotic
plants, streams and ponds, fruit and
vegetable beds and some stunning
sea views. Tickets are valid for both
days. Partial wheelchair access at
some gardens.

Our donation in 2025 has enabled Parkinson's UK to fund 2 new nursing posts this year directly supporting people with Parkinson's.

76 TORVIEW
44 Highweek Village, Newton Abbot, TQ12 1QQ. Ms Penny Hammond, 01626 368948, penny.hammond2@btinternet.com.
On N of Newton Abbot accessed via A38. From Plymouth: A38 to Goodstone, A383 past Hele Park & L onto Mile End Rd. From Exeter: A38 to Drumbridges then A382 past Forches Cross & take next R. Please park in nearby streets. **Visits by arrangement Apr to Sept for groups of 10 to 25. Refreshments inc in adm. Adm £10, chd free. Tea, coffee & cake.**
Owned by two semi-retired horticulturists: Mediterranean formal front garden with wisteria clad Georgian house and small alpine house. Rear courtyard with tree ferns, pots/troughs, lean-to 7 metre conservatory with tender plants and climbers. Steps to 30x20 metre walled garden - flowers, vegetables and trained fruit. Shade tunnel of woodland plants. Many rare and unusual plants.

77 TRUANTS COTTAGE
Zeal Monachorum, Crediton, EX17 6DF. Jackie Watson, 07979 267009, Jacquelinewatsondevon@gmail.com. *Village between Crediton & Okehampton. From A3072, turn L after church in village centre. Truants on R near bottom of hill. From Bow, just after R turn to Waie Inn, go a few yards up hill, on L. Parking at Waie Inn. Further details can be emailed on request.* **Visits by arrangement 4 May to 31 July for groups of up to 12. Weekdays only. Adm £5, chd free. Cream teas.**
Listed thatched cottage with pretty garden in village conservation area. ⅓ acre inc variety of roses, colourful mixed herbaceous borders, lawns, wild grasses, wildlife pond with lilies, spring bluebells and range of specimen trees. View of garden 'rooms' from patio. Cream teas in garden or indoors. Limited parking in drive, also at nearby Waie Inn (lunch/dinner available).

78 UPPER GORWELL HOUSE
Goodleigh Road, Barnstaple, EX32 7JP. Dr J A Marston, www.gorwellhousegarden.co.uk. *¾ m E of Barnstaple centre on Bratton Fleming road. Drive entrance between 2 lodges on L coming uphill (Bear St) approx ¾ m from Barnstaple centre. Take R fork at end of long drive. New garden entrance to R of house up steep slope.* **Sun 29 Mar, Sun 19 Apr, Sun 17 May, Sun 21 June, Sun 19 July, Sun 13 Sept (2-6). Adm £7.50, chd free. Cream teas. Picnics welcome.**
Created mostly since 1979, this 4 acre garden overlooking the Taw estuary has a benign microclimate which allows many rare and tender plants to grow and thrive, both in the open and in the walled garden. Several strategically placed follies complement the enclosures and vistas within the garden. Mostly wheelchair access but some very steep slopes at first to get into garden.

79 NEW WEMBURY WALLED GARDEN
Wembury, Plymouth, PL9 0EF. Penny Hammond & Sue Minter. *Outskirts of Wembury village. East of Plymouth, from the A379 follow road signs to Wembury via Elburton.* **Sat 4, Sun 5 July (11-5). Adm £6, chd free. Tea, coffee & cake.**
Originally the productive garden for Wembury House, the Walled Garden dates from 1780. About an acre with an attached old orchard currently being restored and developed by the tenants (owners of Torview). Beds of flowers grown for cutting, vegetables and soft fruit. An exotic garden, wildlife pond and wildflower meadows. Roses, irises and mixed borders. 2 historic glasshouses, one by the Messenger Company contains peach and nectarine trees and a grapevine. The second is a Foster & Pearson house, now in a state of dereliction, with an attached pineapple pit which has been modernised and is used for cropping. Citrus collection. Some slopes but fairly gentle, more challenging in wet conditions - mostly grass paths.

80 7 WEST CLYST BARNYARD
West Clyst, Exeter, EX1 3TR. Ethel Hillier. *From Pinhoe take B3181 towards Broadclyst. At Westclyst T-lights continue straight past speed camera 1st R onto Private Road over M5 bridge, R into West Clyst Barnyard.* **Sat 6, Sun 7 June (1.30-5). Adm £5, chd free.**
Over an acre of garden set in a medieval barnyard, with wildflower meadow (wild orchids in June) created with hay from an ancient site, a formal garden with shrubs and perennial borders, fruit trees, wildlife pond, bog garden, fruit cage and vegetable patch and all surrounded by farmland. Visitors are welcome to bring a picnic and relax in the meadow. Arts and crafts for sale. Gardens and paddock accessible on same level, disabled visitors can be driven to gate of No 7 but then please park in the car park.

81 WHITSTONE FARM
Whitstone Lane, Bovey Tracey, TQ13 9NA. Katie & Alan Bunn, 01626 832258, klbbovey@gmail.com. *½ m N of Bovey Tracey. From A382 turn opp golf club, after ⅓ m turn at swinging sign 'Private road leading to Whitstone'. Follow NGS signs.* **Visits by arrangement Mar to Oct for groups of up to 25. Mini buses, not coaches can access the narrow lane. Car sharing recommended. Adm £7, chd free. Tea, coffee & cake. Gluten free option. Donation to Plant Heritage.**
Nearly 4 acres of steep hillside garden with stunning views of Haytor and Dartmoor. Snowdrops start in January followed by bluebells throughout the garden. Arboretum planted 45 yrs ago, over 200 trees from all over the world inc magnolias, camellias, acers, alders, betula, davidias and sorbus. Always colour in the garden and wonderful tree bark. Major plantings of rhododendrons and hydrangeas. Late flowering Eucryphias (National Collection). Display of architectural and metal sculptures and ornaments. Partial access to lower terraces for wheelchair users.

82 WILLOW GLADE FARM
Ashwater, Beaworthy, EX21 5DL. Mr K & Mrs M Drowne. *1.2m off A3079 nr Halwill Junction. From A3072, turn towards Okehampton at Dunsland Cross, onto the A3079. Turn R at Morecombe Cross, in 1m Willow Glade is on R. What3words app: manhole.really.worms.* **Sat 4 July (10.30-4); Sun 5 July (10.30-4.30). Adm £5, chd free. Tea, coffee & cake.**
An environmentally friendly, sustainable 5 acre smallholding using traditional methods and elements of permaculture and no dig. The formal layout belies the beauty of beds filled with edibles and companion planting

DEVON 157

Bradford Tracy House

bringing colour, height and diversity to the garden. Explore paths through a small woodland walk, wildlife pond, orchard and wildflower meadow. Willow crafts will also be on display.

🐕 ✻ ☕ 🪑))

83 NEW **WYLAM HOUSE**
Haldon Road, Torquay,
TQ1 2LX. Mr & Mrs George
Berg, 07836 684595,
Info@wylamhouse.com,
www.wylamhouse.com. *From Imperial Hotel head up the hill on Parkhill Rd. Cross over Meadfoot Sea Rd to Higher Woodfield Rd to reach a sharp hairpin turn on R onto Middle Lincombe Rd, then immed L onto Ridgeway Rd which leads to Haldon Rd. Wylam is black gates on R.* **Sat 23, Sun 24 May (11-4.30). Adm £6, chd free. Tea, coffee & cake.**
A mid C19 Italianate Villa, built in 1861, with 2 acres of semi-formal decorative gardens. The gardens are south-facing and slope away from the back of the house. At 300ft above sea level they overlook Torbay and have commanding magnificent views. The garden is laid out to lawns and flower beds, with a large central ornamental pond, and a late Victorian listed rose garden. Upper region of the gardens accessible by wheelchair.

♿ 🐕 🚗 🅿 ☕ 🪑))

> In 2025, National Garden Scheme funding helped Perennial support 950 unique callers to their helpline looking for advice and information.

DORSET

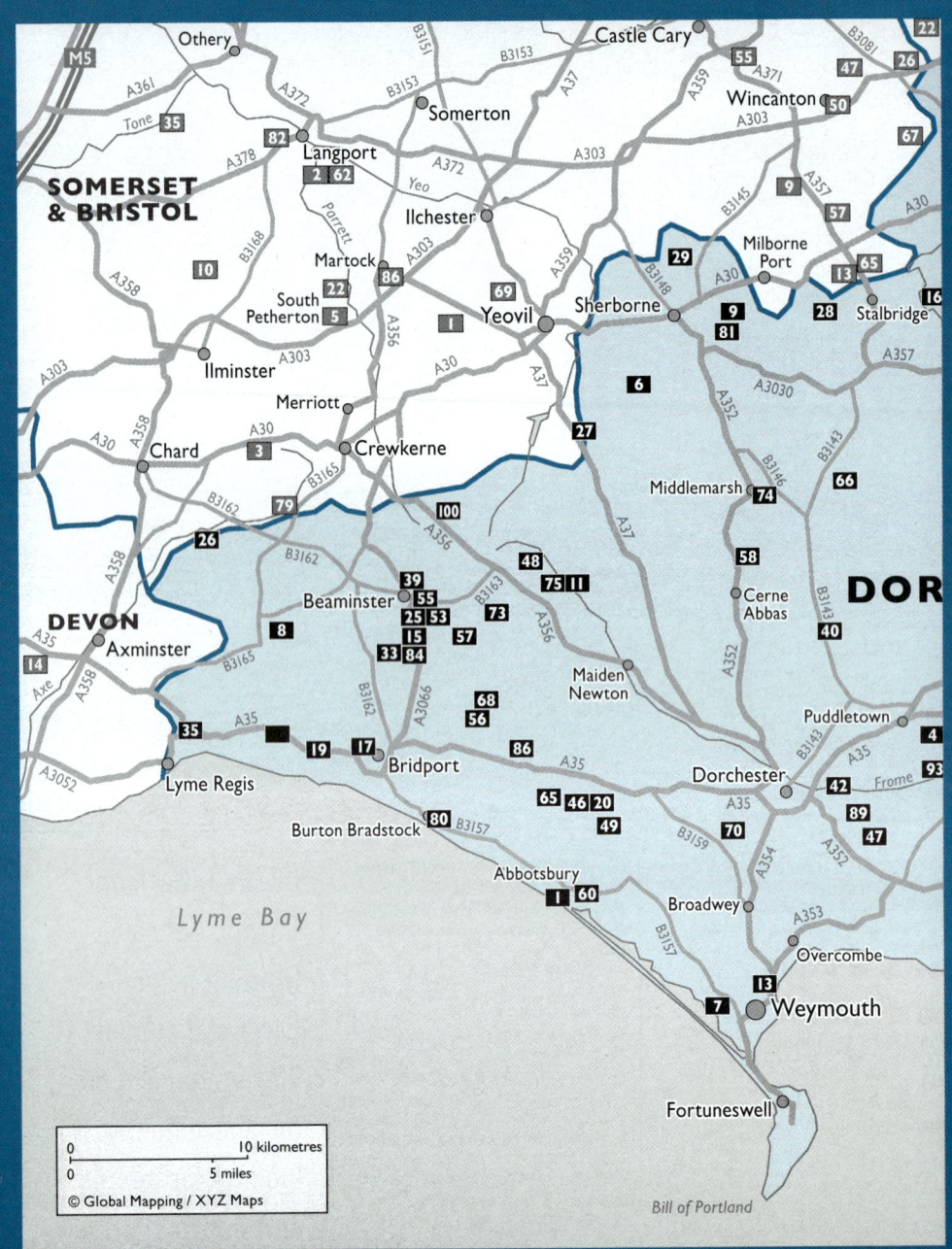

DORSET 159

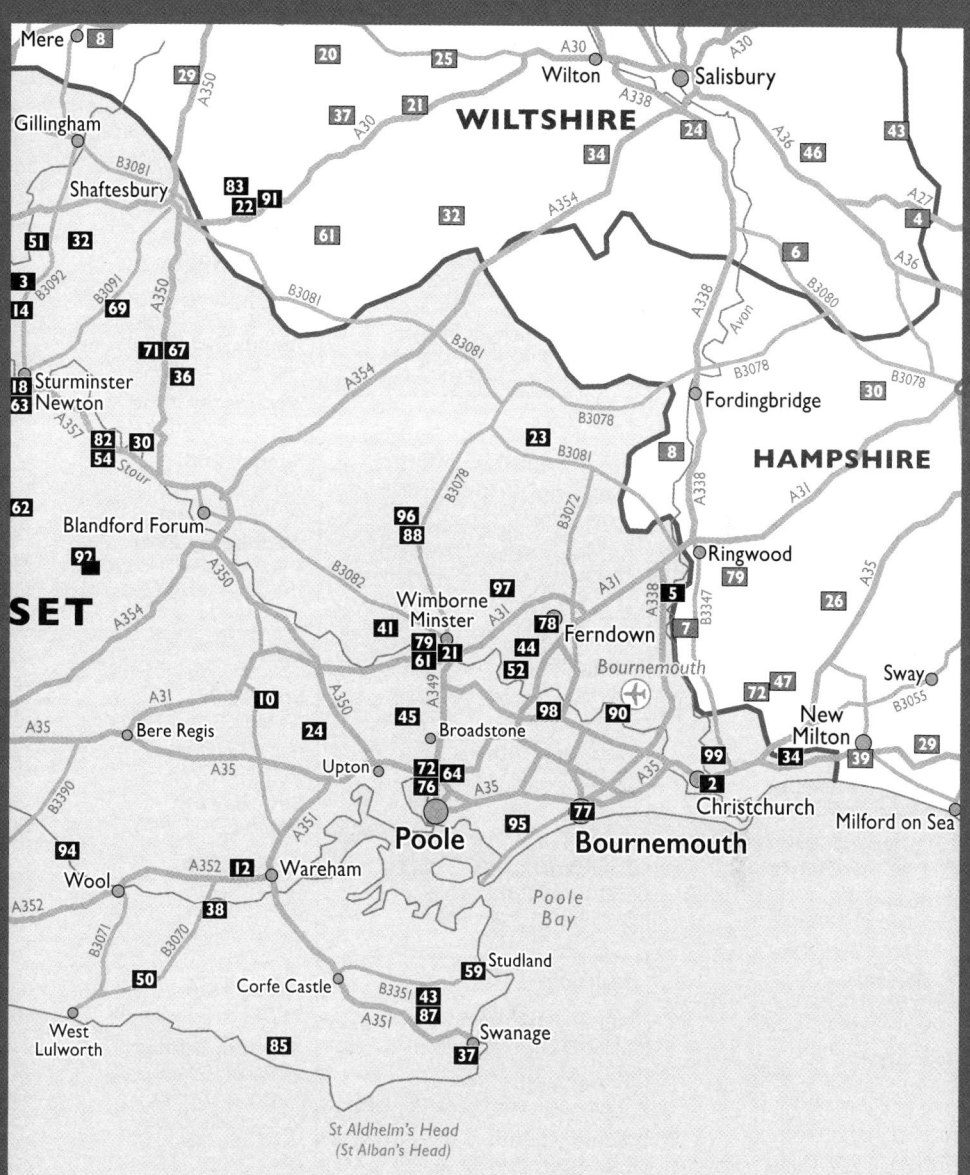

VOLUNTEERS

County Organiser
Pip Davidson 07765 404248
pip.davidson@ngs.org.uk

County Treasurer
Roger Morgan 07368 886402
roger.morgan@ngs.org.uk

Publicity
Sue Thomas 07968 819996
sue.thomas@ngs.org.uk

Social Media
Tony Leonard 07711 643445
tony.leonard@ngs.org.uk

Booklet Editor
Pamela Johnson 01258 472098
pamela.johnson@ngs.org.uk

Photographer (West Dorset)
Christopher Middleton
07771 596458
christophermiddleton@mac.com

Photographer (East Dorset)
Tony Leonard (see above)

Assistant County Organisers
North
Jules Attlee 07837 289964
julesattlee@icloud.com

Joanna Mains 01747 839831
mainsmanor@tiscali.co.uk

Central
Caroline Hart 07932 812720
caroline.hart@ngs.org.uk

Tony Leonard (see above)

East
Mary Angus 01202 872789
mary@gladestock.co.uk

Phil Broomfield 07810 646123
phil.broomfield@ngs.org.uk

South East
Mari Larthe 07990 977333
mari.larthe@ngs.org.uk

West Central
Suzie Baker 07786 695150
suzie.baker@ngs.org.uk

South Central
Emily Cave 01308 482266
emily.cave@ngs.org.uk

Hilary Over 01258 456773
hilary.over@ngs.org.uk

@National Gardens Scheme Dorset
@ngsdorset

West
Trish Neale 01308 863790
trish.neale@ngs.org.uk

South West
Felicity Perkin 01297 480930
felicity.perkin@ngs.org.uk

OPENING DATES

All entries subject to change.
For latest information check
www.ngs.org.uk
Extended openings are shown at the beginning of the month.

Map locator numbers are shown to the right of each garden name.

February

Snowdrop Openings
Friday 6th
10 Ryan Close   78
Saturday 7th
10 Ryan Close   78
Sunday 8th
10 Ryan Close   78
Friday 13th
The Old Vicarage   69
10 Ryan Close   78
Saturday 14th
10 Ryan Close   78
Sunday 15th
The Old Vicarage   69
10 Ryan Close   78
Saturday 28th
Manor Farm, Hampreston   52

March

Sunday 1st
Manor Farm, Hampreston   52
Friday 20th
◆ Athelhampton House Gardens   4
Sunday 22nd
Myrtle Cottage   62

April

Monday 6th
◆ Edmondsham House   23
Wednesday 8th
◆ Edmondsham House   23
Saturday 11th
Chideock Manor   19
Ivy House Garden   40
Sunday 12th
Chideock Manor   19
Ivy House Garden   40
Wednesday 15th
◆ Edmondsham House   23
Sunday 19th
Broomhill   11
Frankham Farm   27
Tuesday 21st
Horn Park   39
Wednesday 22nd
◆ Edmondsham House   23
Sunday 26th
The Old Rectory, Litton Cheney   65
Western Gardens   95
Wednesday 29th
◆ Edmondsham House   23
The Old Rectory, Litton Cheney   65

May

Sunday 3rd
Annalal's Gallery   2
22 Avon Avenue   5
10 Ryan Close   78
Saturday 9th
Falconers   24
Sunday 10th
Falconers   24
NEW 39 Pergin Crescent   72
The Secret Garden at Serles House   79
Friday 15th
24 Carlton Road North   13
Saturday 16th
24 Carlton Road North   13
Ivy House Garden   40
22 Lancaster Drive   45
Myrtle Cottage   62

DORSET

Sunday 17th
Bembury Farm 6
24 Carlton Road North 13
Ivy House Garden 40
22 Lancaster Drive 45
Little Benville House 48
Myrtle Cottage 62
Pugin Hall 75
The Secret Garden at Serles House 79

Monday 18th
24 Carlton Road North 13
Deans Court 21

Tuesday 19th
Deans Court 21

Friday 22nd
Mappercombe Manor 56
Pipsford Farm 73

Saturday 23rd
The Old Vicarage 68

Sunday 24th
Annalal's Gallery 2
♦ Careys Secret Garden 12
NEW 64 Hinton Wood Avenue 34
The Manor House, Beaminster 55
Mappercombe Manor 56
The Old Vicarage 68
Tumblins 92

Monday 25th
NEW 64 Hinton Wood Avenue 34
The Manor House, Beaminster 55

Sunday 31st
Charles Chesshire Garden & Nursery 17

June

Thursday 4th
Slape Manor 84

Saturday 6th
NEW Bloxworth Lodge 10
Oakdale Library Gardens 64

Sunday 7th
22 Avon Avenue 5
Black Shed 9
The Chantry 15
Chantry Farm 16
Frankham Farm 27
Hingsdon 33
10 Ryan Close 78
NEW Whitemoor Farm 97

Tuesday 9th
♦ Holme for Gardens 38
NEW Smedmore House 85

Wednesday 10th
Knitson Old Farmhouse 43
The Stables 87

Thursday 11th
Bettiscombe Manor 8
Knitson Old Farmhouse 43
Shute House 83
The Stables 87

Friday 12th
The Old School House 67
Penmead Farm 71

Saturday 13th
Chideock Manor 19

Sunday 14th
Broomhill 11
Chideock Manor 19
Hanford School 30
Manor Farm, Hampreston 52
The Old School House 67
NEW 3 Park Farm Close 70
Penmead Farm 71
NEW 39 Pergin Crescent 72
Pugin Hall 75
Shillingstone Gardens 82
Tulip Tree 91
Tumblins 92
Utopia 93

Wednesday 17th
NEW The Treehouse 90

Thursday 18th
Farrs 25

Saturday 20th
The Hollow, Blandford Forum 36
Muddy Patches 60

Sunday 21st
Annalal's Gallery 2
♦ Athelhampton House Gardens 4
NEW Cherry Cottage 18
The Hollow, Blandford Forum 36
Langebride House 46
Muddy Patches 60
NEW Newton Cottage 63
Wyke Farm 100

Tuesday 23rd
♦ Littlebredy Walled Gardens 49

Wednesday 24th
The Hollow, Blandford Forum 36

Saturday 27th
NEW 64 Hinton Wood Avenue 34
The Manor House, Beaminster 55
20 Wicket Road 98

Sunday 28th
Donhead Hall 22
NEW 64 Hinton Wood Avenue 34
The Manor House, Beaminster 55

20 Wicket Road 98
NEW 3 Willow Hamlet 99

Tuesday 30th
♦ Littlebredy Walled Gardens 49

July

Every Wednesday
The Hollow, Swanage 37

Friday 3rd
Stafford House 89

Saturday 4th
8 Manor Gardens 53

Sunday 5th
8 Manor Gardens 53
The Old Rectory, Litton Cheney 65
NEW 3 Park Farm Close 70
NEW Shadrack Dairy Farm 80

Thursday 9th
Lulworth Castle House 50

Sunday 12th
22 Avon Avenue 5
♦ Hogchester Farm 35
Manor Farm, Hampreston 52

Saturday 18th
The Potting Shed 74

Sunday 19th
Broomhill 11
Hilltop 32

Saturday 25th
Glenholme Herbs 29

Sunday 26th
Black Shed 9
Glenholme Herbs 29
Hilltop 32
Tumblins 92
NEW 3 Willow Hamlet 99

Monday 27th
Annalal's Gallery 2

Wednesday 29th
Knitson Old Farmhouse 43
The Stables 87

Thursday 30th
Knitson Old Farmhouse 43
The Stables 87

August

Every Wednesday
The Hollow, Swanage 37

Saturday 1st
NEW Manor Farm, Stour Provost 51

DORSET

Sunday 2nd
Hilltop 32
NEW Manor Farm, Stour
Provost 51
Manor Farm, Hampreston 52
The Old Rectory, Pulham 66

Thursday 6th
Broomhill 11
The Old Rectory, Pulham 66

Sunday 9th
22 Avon Avenue 5
Charles Chesshire Garden &
Nursery 17
Hilltop 32

Saturday 15th
1C Rectory Road 76

Sunday 16th
Hilltop 32
1C Rectory Road 76

Thursday 20th
Farrs 25

Sunday 23rd
Annalal's Gallery 2
Staddlestones 88

Saturday 29th
Ardhurst 3

Sunday 30th
Ardhurst 3
NEW 3 Willow Hamlet 99

September

Tuesday 1st
◆ Knoll Gardens 44

Friday 4th
◆ Bennetts Water Gardens 7

Sunday 6th
Manor Farm, Hampreston 52
Morval 59

Friday 11th
◆ Museum of East Dorset 61

Sunday 13th
Annalal's Gallery 2

Friday 18th
◆ Knoll Gardens 44

Wednesday 23rd
◆ Athelhampton House Gardens 4

October

Wednesday 7th
◆ Edmondsham House 23

Sunday 11th
Frankham Farm 27

Wednesday 14th
◆ Edmondsham House 23

Friday 16th
◆ Museum of East Dorset 61

Wednesday 21st
◆ Edmondsham House 23

Wednesday 28th
◆ Edmondsham House 23

November

Friday 20th
◆ Museum of East Dorset 61

December

Sunday 6th
Annalal's Gallery 2

Monday 21st
◆ Athelhampton House Gardens 4

By Arrangement

Arrange a personalised garden visit with your club, or group of friends, on a date to suit you. See individual garden entries for full details.

Bembury Farm 6
Broomhill 11
Carraway Barn 14
Chantry Farm 16
Corner Cottage 20
Frith House 28
The Hollow, Swanage 37
Knitson Old Farmhouse 43
Lewell Lodge 47
NEW Manor Farm, Stour
Provost 51
Manor House 54
Muddy Patches 60
Myrtle Cottage 62
NEW Newton Cottage 63
The Old Rectory, Litton Cheney 65
The Old Rectory, Pulham 66
The Old Vicarage 69
Russell-Cotes Art Gallery &
Museum 77
Slape Manor 84
South Eggardon House 86
Staddlestones 88
Tumblins 92
Utopia 93
Western Gardens 95
White House 96
NEW 3 Willow Hamlet 99

Hingsdon

© Christopher Middleton

THE GARDENS

1 ♦ ABBOTSBURY SUBTROPICAL GARDENS
Abbotsbury, Weymouth, DT3 4LA. Ilchester Estates, 01305 871387, info@abbotsbury-tourism.co.uk, www.abbotsburygardens.co.uk. *8m W of Weymouth. From B3157 Weymouth-Bridport, 200yds W of Abbotsbury village.* **For opening times and information, please phone, email or visit garden website.**
30 acres, started in 1760 and considerably extended in C19. Much recent replanting. The maritime microclimate enables this Mediterranean and southern hemisphere garden to grow rare and tender plants. National Collection of Hoherias (flowering Aug in NZ garden). Woodland valley with ponds, stream and hillside walk to view the Jurassic Coast. Open all year except for Christmas week. Partial wheelchair access, some very steep paths and rolled gravel but we have a selected wheelchair route with sections of tarmac hard surface.

2 ANNALAL'S GALLERY
25 Millhams Street, Christchurch, BH23 1DN. Anna & Lal Sims, www.annasims.co.uk. *Town centre. Park in Saxon Square PCP - exit to Millhams St via alley at side of church.* **Sun 3, Sun 24 May, Sun 21 June, Mon 27 July, Sun 23 Aug, Sun 13 Sept, Sun 6 Dec (2-4). Adm £3.50, chd free.**
Enchanting 180 yr old cottage, home of two Royal Academy artists. 32ft x 12½ ft garden on 3 patio levels. Pencil gate leads to colourful scented Victorian walled garden. Sculptures and paintings hide among the flowers and shrubs. Unusual studio and garden room. Mural of a life-size greyhound makes the cottage easy to find and adds a smile to people's faces.

3 ARDHURST
Nash Lane, Marnhull, Sturminster Newton, DT10 1JZ. Mr & Mrs Ed Highnam. *3m N of Sturminster Newton. From A30 E Stour, B3092 3m to Marnhull, Crown Inn on R. Turn R down Church Hill, follow NGS yellow signs. From Sturminster Newton, 3m into Marnhull, turn L down Church Hill. Parking in field indicated.* **Sat 29, Sun 30 Aug (1-5.30). Adm £7, chd free. Home-made teas.**
This garden is organic and has been 10 yrs in the making. A plantsman's garden with deep perennial borders, large netted vegetable area, water harvesting, and all work in progress. A riot of colour with salvias, grasses and hot plants in Aug/Sept. Every plant for pollination and year-round interest. Tall grasses and varied fruit trees. New round border of soft planting in 2023. Greenhouse and butternut squash scrambling through and up the hedges! Parking in driveway for wheelchair access only. Driveway is rough & assistance will be needed. Rest of garden laid to lawn, patio at rear for shade.
&

Our 2025 donation to the Queen's Institute of Community Nursing now helps support over 3,500 Queen's Nurses working in the community in England, Wales, Northern Ireland, the Channel Islands and the Isle of Man.

4 ◆ ATHELHAMPTON HOUSE GARDENS
Athelhampton, Dorchester, DT2 7LG. Giles Keating, 01305 848363, hello@athelhampton.house, www.athelhampton.co.uk. *Between Poole & Dorchester just off the A35. 5m E of Dorchester well signed off A35 trunk road at Puddletown. Easily reached from A31 Ringwood, & A354 Blandford Forum.* **For NGS: Fri 20 Mar, Sun 21 June, Wed 23 Sept (10-5); Mon 21 Dec (10-3.30). Adm £12.50, chd free. Light refreshments in the Coach House at Athelhampton. Coffee, lunches & afternoon tea. Entry ticket is for the garden only, at a lower price than normal. Tickets for the house sold separately. For other opening times and information, please phone, email or visit garden website.**
The award-winning gardens at Athelhampton surround the Tudor manor house and date from 1891. The Great Court with 12 giant yew topiary pyramids is overlooked by two terraced pavilions. This glorious Grade I architectural garden is full of vistas with spectacular planting, ponds with fountains and the River Piddle flowing past. Wheelchair map to guide you around the gardens. There are accessible toilets in the Visitor Centre. Please see our Accessibility Guide on our website.

5 22 AVON AVENUE
Avon Castle, Ringwood, BH24 2BH. Terry & Dawn Heaver, dawnandterry@yahoo.com. *Past Ringwood from E A31 turn L after garage, L again into Matchams Ln, Avon Castle 1m on L. A31 from W turn R into Boundary Ln, then L into Matchams Ln, Avon Ave ½ m on R.* **Sun 3 May, Sun 7 June, Sun 12 July, Sun 9 Aug (12-5). Adm £5, chd free. Tea, coffee & home-made cakes.**
Japanese themed water garden featuring granite sculptures, ponds, waterfalls, azaleas, rhododendrons, cloud topiary and a collection of goldfish and water lilies. Children must be under parental supervision due to large, deep water pond. Regret no dogs.
❋ ☕

6 BEMBURY FARM
Bembury Lane, Thornford, Sherborne, DT9 6QF. Sir John & Lady Garnier, 01935 873551, dodie.garnier32@gmail.com. *Bottom of Bembury Lane, N of Thornford village. 6m E of Yeovil, 3m W of Sherborne on Yetminster road. Follow signs in village. Parking in field.* **Sun 17 May (1-5). Adm £8, chd free. Light refreshments.** Visits also by arrangement May to Sept for groups of 10 to 40.
Created and developed since 1996 this peaceful garden has lawns and large herbaceous borders informally planted with interesting perennials around unusual trees, shrubs and roses. Large collection of clematis; also a pretty woodland walk, wildflower corner, lily pond, oak circle, yew hedges with peacock, clipped hornbeam round kitchen garden and plenty of seating to sit and reflect.
♿ 🐕 ❋ ☕ 🎵

7 ◆ BENNETTS WATER GARDENS
Putton Lane, Chickerell, Weymouth, DT3 4AF. James Bennett, 01305 785150, info@bennettswatergardens.com, www.bennettswatergardens.com. *2m W of Weymouth Harbour on the B3157 to Bridport. Follow the brown signs for 'Water Gardens'. From the A35 at Dorchester take the A354 S to Weymouth & Portland, then take the B3157 W towards Chickerell.* **For NGS: Fri 4 Sept (10-4). Adm £10, chd £4. Home-made lunches, cakes & cream teas.** For other opening times and information, please phone, email or visit garden website. Donation to Plant Heritage.
A tranquil, beautifully landscaped garden spread over about 8 acres. It is particularly celebrated for its extensive collection of water lilies. The site holds the National Plant Collection of Nymphaea with a Claude Monet style Japanese bridge, tropical house, woodland walks and Museum. Regret no dogs. Partial wheelchair access but during periods of sustained wet weather the gardens are closed to wheelchair users. Pls contact us for further advice.
♿ ❋ 🚗 NPC ☕  🎵

SPECIAL EVENT

8 BETTISCOMBE MANOR
Bettiscombe, Bridport, DT6 5NU. Mr Jasper Conran. *Follow signs for Bettiscombe, park at village hall.* **Thur 11 June (10-5). Adm £60, chd free. Pre-booking essential, please visit www.ngs.org.uk for information & booking. Light refreshments in the village hall. Salmon & cucumber sandwiches, strawberries, pastries, cakes, tea, coffee, champagne & elderflower presse.**
Designer Jasper Conran has given one of England's loveliest smaller houses, Bettiscombe Manor, a garden to match, with orchards, mellow brick enclosures, and broad beds flanking an unforgettable view of the Vale, looking down to the sea. The garden has a magical quality, it is informally planted and flower-filled, reflecting the designer's predilection for constantly evolving and creative planting. A limited number of tickets have been made available for this exclusive special event, kindly hosted by Jasper's Head Gardener. It includes a talk on the gardens and how they have evolved to empathetically embrace and work within the surrounding landscape. The talk will also provide a background to how the garden has been created, as well as its ongoing development and provide further detail on what is growing in the garden currently.

9 BLACK SHED
Blackmarsh Farm, Dodds Cross, Sherborne, DT9 4JX. Paul & Helen Stickland, www.blackshed.flowers/blog. *From Sherborne, follow A30 towards Shaftesbury. Black Shed approx 1m E at Blackmarsh Farm, on L, next to The Toy Barn. Large car park shared with The Toy Barn.* **Sun 7 June, Sun 26 July (1-5). Adm £5, chd free. Home-made teas.**
Over 200 colourful and productive flower beds growing a sophisticated selection of cut flowers and foliage to supply florists and the public for weddings, events and occasions throughout the seasons. Traditional garden favourites, delphiniums, larkspur, foxgloves, scabious and dahlias alongside more unusual perennials, foliage plants and grasses, creating a stunning and unique display. A warm welcome and

generous advice on creating your own cut flower garden is offered. Easy access from gravel car park. Wide grass pathways enabling access for wheelchairs. Gently sloping site.

10 NEW BLOXWORTH LODGE
Charborough Park, Wareham, BH20 7EE. **Mr David & Mrs Emma Fletcher.** *Upon arrival in Bloxworth, with the thatched brick bus shelter on your L, we are the 2nd house on R, a large white house down a driveway. Parking in nearby field.* **Sat 6 June (11-4). Adm £7, chd free. Tea, coffee & cake.**
A large garden with lawns and smaller garden areas surrounding the house. The gardens inc a north-facing garden created 3 yrs ago, a small woodland garden, south-facing gravel gardens, wall trained roses, an orchard, vegetable garden and a pool garden with roses. The gardens feature a naturalistic planting style with many areas to sit and enjoy the surroundings. Parking avail in the backyard for wheelchair access.

11 BROOMHILL
Rampisham, Dorchester, DT2 0PT. **David & Carol Parry, 07775 806875, carol.parry2@btopenworld.com.** *11m NW of Dorchester. From Dorchester A37 Yeovil, 9m L Evershot. From Yeovil A37 Dorchester, 7m R Evershot. Follow signs. From Crewkerne A356, 1½ m after Rampisham Garage L Rampisham. Follow signs.* **Sun 19 Apr (2-5). Adm £5, chd free. Sun 14 June (1-5). Combined adm with Pugin Hall £10, chd free. Sun 19 July, Thur 6 Aug (2-5). Adm £5, chd free. Home-made teas.** Visits also by arrangement 1 June to 7 Aug for groups of 10+. We can provide a light lunch if required.
A former farmyard transformed into a delightful, tranquil garden set in 2 acres. Clipped box, island beds and borders planted with shrubs, roses, grasses, masses of unusual perennials and choice annuals to give vibrancy and colour into the autumn. Lawns and paths lead to a less formal area with large wildlife pond, meadow, shaded areas and bog garden. Orchard, vegetable and cutting garden. Gravel entrance, the rest is grass, some gentle slopes.

Horn Park

12 ♦ CAREYS SECRET GARDEN
Wareham, BH20 7PG. www.careyssecretgarden.co.uk. *We send the exact location once you have booked a ticket. The garden is within a 3m radius of Wareham, (5 min drive from the train stn). 11m from Poole & 19m from Dorchester.* **For NGS: Sun 24 May (10-3). Adm £9.50, chd £3.75. Pre-booking essential, please phone 07927 132148 or visit www.careyssecretgarden.co.uk for information & booking. Tea, coffee & cake in the Secret Coffee Shop within the walled garden. For other opening times and information, please phone or visit garden website.**
Behind a 150 yr old wall, situated just outside of Wareham, sits 3 ½ acres in the midst of transformation. Left untouched for more than 40 yrs, this garden is now flourishing again, with a focus on permaculture and rewilding. Awarded 'Winner of Winners' at Dorset Tourism Awards 2024 as well as Gold for the Ethical, Responsible, and Sustainable Tourism Award. Those with mobility issues are welcome to contact us in advance and we can tailor your visit to your needs accordingly.

13 24 CARLTON ROAD NORTH
Weymouth, DT4 7PY. Anne & Rob Tracey. *8m S of Dorchester. A354 from Dorchester, almost opp Rembrandt Hotel R into Carlton Rd North. From Town Centre follow esplanade towards A354 Dorchester, L into Carlton Rd North.* **Fri 15, Sat 16, Sun 17, Mon 18 May (2-5). Adm £4, chd free. Tea, coffee & home-made cake.**
Town garden near the sea. Long garden on several levels. Steps and narrow sloping paths lead to beds and borders filled with trees, shrubs and herbaceous plants inc many unusual varieties. A garden which continues to evolve and reflect an interest in texture, shape and colour. Wildlife is encouraged. Raised beds in front garden create a space for vegetable growing.

14 CARRAWAY BARN
Carraway Lane, Marnhull, Sturminster Newton, DT10 1NJ. Catherine & Mark Turner, 07905 960281, Carrawaybarn.ngs@gmail.com. *From Shaftesbury A30 & B3092. ½ m after The Crown turn R into Carraway Ln. From Sturminster Newton B3092 2.8m turn L into Carraway Ln. Bear R behind 1st house, until in large courtyard.* **Visits by arrangement June & July for groups of 8 to 40. Adm £10, chd free. Home-made teas.**
Set in 2 acres, around C19 former barn. In recent years, a natural swimming pond, large shrub border, waterfall, late summer borders and pergola have been created. Shady woodland walks, a white border of hydrangeas, hostas and ferns lead to the beautiful established walled garden, where deep borders are planted with roses, peonies, alliums, geraniums and topiary, encircling a water lily pond. Partial wheelchair access; gravelled courtyard and walled garden, gently sloping lawns.

15 THE CHANTRY
Chantry Street, Netherbury, Bridport, DT6 5NB. Peter Higginson. *1m S of Beaminster, follow signs for Netherbury. Garden is in centre near church.* **Sun 7 June (2-6). Combined adm with Hingsdon £8, chd free. Teas available at Hingsdon.**
Set in the middle of the village and within stone walls and hedges, a 1 acre established traditional garden of lawns, trees, shrubs and colourful mixed borders on a gently sloping site, with a formal pond and some new planting.

16 CHANTRY FARM
Phillips Hill, Marnhull, Sturminster Newton, DT10 1NU. Ivan & Sue Shenkman, 07767 455089, sueshenkman@mac.com. *Between Shaftesbury & Sherborne. From the A30 turn W at East Stour to Marnhull on the B3092. After the Crown pub turn 2nd R onto New St. After 1m at the L bend Chantry Farm is on the R. What3words app: sample. somewhere.send.* **Sun 7 June (1-5). Adm £8, chd free. Home-made teas. Visits also by arrangement May to Sept for groups of 10 to 40.**
Chantry Farm offers a series of gardens surrounding the C16 farmhouse and three renovated barns. Designed by Justin Spink there are colourful long borders, walled gardens, swimming pool area, cutting and vegetable gardens. Espalier fruit trees, pleached hornbeam and weeping pears divide the areas. Fields with mown paths and beautiful views. Seating and wheelchair access. Wonderful views, marble bowl water feature, home-made cakes.

17 CHARLES CHESSHIRE GARDEN & NURSERY
Sheepwash Barn, Symondsbury, Bridport, DT6 6HH. Charles Chesshire, www.charleschesshire.co.uk. *1m W of Bridport. From A35, head through Symondsbury past Shear Plot on R, down hill & the garden is on R, or from Bridport take Symondsbury Estate road to Mill Lane & the garden is on L.* **Sun 31 May, Sun 9 Aug (1-5). Adm £5, chd free. Tea, coffee & cake.**
Set in heavenly Dorset countryside, the ½ acre garden is composed of an intricate web of gravel paths weaving between deep and colourful borders to create an intimate experience for the extensive collection of new and unusual plants. At the heart of the garden is a Japanese styled koshi-kake 'waiting room', surrounded by the cool greens of dwarf pines, grasses and ferns.

18 NEW CHERRY COTTAGE
Orchard Close, Sturminster Newton, DT10 2HN. Mr Derek & Mrs Penny Pycroft. *What3words app: spend.strides.dusters. ½ m SW Sturminster Newton, off the A357, opp bottom of Glue Hill. Limited parking. Public car parks 15 min walk in Sturminster Newton or follow parking signs on the day.* **Sun 21 June (12-5.30). Combined adm with Newton Cottage £10, chd free.**
Modern country garden. Sunny gravel areas with Mediterranean planting, lawns and mixed borders. Large paved terrace overlooks an informal lawn. Silver birch, flowering shrubs, grasses, perennials and bulbs mix happily together in densely planted borders. Abundant roses and clematis clothe the fences. Garden designed by artist Pamela Johnson, whose garden next door is also open on the same day. Most of the garden can be accessed without steps but gravel paths may be difficult for wheelchairs.

19 CHIDEOCK MANOR
Chideock, Bridport, DT6 6LF. Mr & Mrs Howard Coates, www.chideockmanorgarden.co.uk. *2m W of Bridport on A35. In centre of village turn N at church. The Manor is ¼m along this road on R.* **Sat 11, Sun 12 Apr, Sat 13, Sun 14 June (2-5). Adm £10, chd free. Home-made teas.**
12 acres of formal and informal gardens. Bog garden beside stream and series of ponds. Yew hedges and mature trees. Lime and crab apple walks, herbaceous borders, colourful rose and clematis arches, fernery and nuttery. Walled vegetable garden and orchard. Woodland and lakeside walks. Fine views and much variety. Partial wheelchair access.

20 CORNER COTTAGE
Long Bredy, Dorchester, DT2 9HU. Susan & Colin Dyer, 01308 482882 or 07311 631960, sej_dyer@hotmail.co.uk. *7m E of Bridport. 8m W of Dorchester. W on A35 from Dorchester, turn L approx 4m from Winterbourne Abbas. 7m E on A35 from Bridport, turn R. Follow road down & turn L at T-junction. Drive along stone wall & turn L up drive to park.* **Visits by arrangement 23 June to 14 July for groups of up to 10. Home-made teas.**
⅓ of an acre of a structured cottage style garden inc a productive, attractive kitchen garden, small orchard and deep flower and shrub borders. Well-placed seating areas invite enjoyment of different aspects of the garden and its surroundings. Clipped box, perennials, roses and clematis feature. The aim is to have food, scent and colour on every day of the year.

21 DEANS COURT
Deans Court Lane, Wimborne Minster, BH21 1EE. Sir William Hanham, 01202 849314, info@deanscourt.org, www.deanscourt.org. *Pedestrian entrance (no parking) is via Deans Court Ln. Vehicle entrance (with parking) is via Poole Rd (BH21 1QF).* **Mon 18, Tue 19 May (11-4). Adm £8, chd free. Home-baked cakes & light lunches available in our Café on Deans Court Lane.**
13 acres of peaceful, partly wild gardens in ancient monastic setting with mature specimen trees,

Saxon fish pond, herb garden and orchard beside River Allen close to town centre. First Soil Association accredited garden, within C18 serpentine walls. The Permaculture system has been introduced here with chemical free produce. For disabled access, please contact us in advance of visiting to help us understand your specific needs and work out the best plan. Follow signs within grounds for disabled parking closer to gardens. Deeper gravel on some paths. See website extended description re access.

22 DONHEAD HALL
Donhead St Mary, Shaftesbury, SP7 9DS. Paul & Penny Brewer. *4m E of Shaftesbury. A30 towards Shaftesbury. In Ludwell turn R opp brown sign to Tollard Royal. Follow road for ¾m & bear R at T-junction. Donhead Hall 50 yds on L on corner of Watery Lane, cream gates.* **Sun 28 June (1-4). Adm £8, chd free. Home-made teas.**
Walled garden overlooking deer park. The house and garden are built into the side of a hill with uninterrupted views to Cranborne Chase. Martin Lane Fox designed the terracing and advised on the landscaping of the gardens which are on 4 different levels. Large mixed borders and specimen trees, kitchen garden with glasshouses.

23 ♦ EDMONDSHAM HOUSE
Edmondsham, Wimborne, BH21 5RE. Mrs Julia Smith, 01725 517207, julia.edmondsham@homeuser.net. *9m NE of Wimborne. 9m W of Ringwood. Between Cranborne & Verwood. Edmondsham off B3081. Wheelchair access & disabled parking at west front door.* **For NGS: Mon 6 Apr (2-5). Every Wed 8 Apr to 29 Apr (2-5). Every Wed 7 Oct to 28 Oct (2-5). Adm £5, chd £2. Cash only. Tea, coffee, cake & soft drinks available 3.30pm to 4pm in Edmondsham House on Weds only.** For other opening times and information, please phone or email. Donation to Prama Care.
Six acres of mature gardens and grounds with trees, rare shrubs, spring bulbs and shaped hedges surrounding C16/C18 house, giving much to explore inc C12 church adjacent to garden. Large Victorian

walled garden is productive and managed organically (since 1984) using 'no dig' vegetable beds. Wide herbaceous borders planted for seasonal colour. Traditional potting shed, cob wall, sunken greenhouse. Coaches by appointment only. Some grass and gravel paths.

24 FALCONERS
89 High Street, Lytchett Matravers, Poole, BH16 6BJ. David Dent. *6m W from Poole. Garden is past village hall at end of High St, on L. No parking at the garden, please park considerately in the village.* **Sat 9, Sun 10 May (10.30-4.30). Adm £5, chd free. Tea, coffee & cake.**
Behind the gate of 150 yr old Falconers Cottage lies a ¼ acre mature garden with some interesting plants. The character cottage and garden have been cared for and enhanced by the current custodians. As you wander round the many aspects, inc pond, herbaceous bed, climbers and vegetable plot, you will find restful areas to sit and enjoy this garden in spring. Regret unsuitable for wheelchairs.

The National Garden Scheme donated £3,875,596 to our nursing and health beneficiaries from money raised at gardens open in 2025.

South Eggardon House

SPECIAL EVENT

25 FARRS
3 Whitcombe Rd, Beaminster, DT8 3NB. Mr & Mrs John Makepeace, www.johnmakepeacefurniture.com. *Southern edge of Beaminster. On B3163. Car parking in the Square or Yarn Barton Car Park, or side streets of Beaminster.* **Thur 18 June, Thur 20 Aug (2-4.30). Adm £40, chd free. Pre-booking essential, please visit www.ngs.org.uk for information & booking. Cream teas in the house or garden, weather dependent. Donation to Victoria & Albert Foundation.**
Enjoy several distinctive walled gardens, rolling lawns, sculpture and giant topiary around one of Beaminster's historic town houses. John's inspirational grass garden and Jennie's very contrasting garden with an oak fruit cage; a riot of colour. Glasshouse, straw bale studio and orchard. Remarkable trees, planked and seasoning in open sided barn for future furniture commissions. A limited number of tickets have been made available for these two special afternoon openings, hosted by John and Jennie Makepeace. There will be a warm welcome from John at 2pm in the main rooms of the house, with a talk on his furniture design and recent commissions. Jennie will then give a guided walk around the gardens followed by a cream tea. Some gravel paths, alternative wheelchair route through orchard.

26 ◆ FORDE ABBEY GARDENS
Forde Abbey, Chard, TA20 4LU. Mr & Mrs Julian Kennard, 01460 221290, info@fordeabbey.co.uk, www.fordeabbey.co.uk. *4m SE of Chard. Signed off A30 Chard-Crewkerne & A358 Chard-Axminster. Also from Broadwindsor B3164.* **For opening times and information, please phone, email or visit garden website.**
Thirty acres of gardens with mature shrubs, magnificent arboretum of champion trees, ponds, herbaceous borders, rockery, bog garden, working walled kitchen garden and wildflower meadows. England's tallest powered fountain. Other features inc crocus lawns, tulip displays, ponds and plant fairs. Gardens open on weekends in Feb, daily from 1st Mar - 31st Oct and Wed - Sun from 1st Nov - 21st Dec. House from 1st April - 31st Oct, Tues to Fri, Sun and BH Mon. Some parts of the garden are accessible by a wheelchair. Please ask at the Gift Shop for best wheelchair route.

27 FRANKHAM FARM
Ryme Intrinseca, Sherborne, DT9 6JT. Susan Ross MBE, 07594 427365, neilandsusanross@gmail.com. *3m S of Yeovil. Just off A37 - turn next to Hamish's farm shop signed to Ryme Intrinseca, go over small bridge and up hill, drive is on L.* **Sun 19 Apr, Sun 7 June, Sun 11 Oct (12-5). Adm £7, chd free. BBQ, vegetarian soup, home-made cakes by village bakers.**
3½ acre garden, created since 1960 by the late Jo Earle for year-round interest. This large and lovely garden is filled with a wide variety of well grown plants, unusual labelled shrubs and trees. Productive vegetable

garden. Clematis and other climbers. Spring bulbs through to autumn colour, particularly oaks. Dogs welcome in selected woodland areas. Ramp avail for the 2 steps to the garden. WCs inc disabled.

28 FRITH HOUSE
Stalbridge, DT10 2SD. Mr & Mrs Patrick Sclater, 07778 785293, rosalynsclater@frith.farm. *4m E of Sherborne. Between Milborne Port & Stalbridge. From A30 1m, follow sign to Stalbridge. From Stalbridge 2m & turn W by PO.* **Visits by arrangement May & June for groups of 12 to 40. Weekday visits only. Adm £10, chd free. Home-made teas inc in admission.**
Approached down a long drive with fine views, 5 acres of garden around Edwardian house and self-contained hamlet. Range of mature trees, lakes and flower borders. House terrace edged by rose border and featuring Lutyensesque wall fountain and game larder. Well-stocked kitchen gardens. Woodland walks with masses of bluebells in spring. Garden with pretty walks set amidst working farm. Accessible gravel paths.

29 GLENHOLME HERBS
Penmore Road, Sandford Orcas, Sherborne, DT9 4SE. Maxine & Rob Kellaway, www.glenholmeherbs.co.uk. *3m N of Sherborne. Pls see directions on our website & type Glenholme Herbs in Google maps to find us as the postcode will take you to the wrong location.* **Sat 25, Sun 26 July (10-4). Adm £5, chd free. Home-made teas.**
Paths meander through large, colourful beds inspired by Piet Oudolf. Featuring a wide selection of herbs and salvias along with grasses, verbena and echinacea. Planted with wildlife in mind and alive with pollinators. The garden also features a beautiful natural swimming pond. A mixture of grass and firm gravel paths.

30 HANFORD SCHOOL
Child Okeford, Blandford Forum, DT11 8HN. Sherborne Schools Group, www.hanfordschool.co.uk. *From Blandford take A350 to Shaftesbury; 2m after Stourpaine turn L for Hanford. From Shaftesbury take A350 to Poole; after Iwerne Courtney turn R to Hanford. NGS signage from A350 & A357.* **Sun 14 June (11-3). Adm £5, chd free. Teas, coffees & light refreshments served from our 'horsebox', with tables & chairs on the main lawn to sit and enjoy the views.**
One of the few schools in England with a working kitchen garden growing quantities of seasonal vegetables, fruit and flowers for the table. The rolling lawns host sports matches, gymnastics, dance and plays while ancient cedars and the 1650s Chapel look on. Teas on the lawn with beautiful views. What a place to go to school or visit. Several steps/ramp to main house. No wheelchair access to WC.

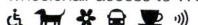

32 HILLTOP
Woodville, Stour Provost, Gillingham, SP8 5LY. Josse & Brian Emerson, www.hilltopgarden.co.uk. *7m N of Sturminster Newton, 5m W of Shaftesbury. On B3092 turn E at Stour Provost Xrds, signed Woodville. After 1¼m thatched cottage on R. On A30, 4m W of Shaftesbury, turn S opp Kings Arms. 2nd turning on R signed Woodville, 100 yds on L.* **Every Sun 19 July to 16 Aug (2-6). Adm £4.50, chd free. Tea, coffee & cake.**
Summer at Hilltop is a gorgeous riot of colour and scent, the old thatched cottage barely visible amongst the flowers. Unusual annuals and perennials grow alongside the traditional and familiar, boldly combining to make a spectacular display, attracting an abundance of wildlife. Plenty of sunny seating, or shady under the majestic oak. Very peaceful. Distant rural views. Unique, gothic garden loo.

33 HINGSDON
Netherbury, Bridport, DT6 5NQ. Anne Peck. *Between Bridport & Beaminster. 1½m from A3066 or 1m from B3162 signed to Netherbury.* **Sun 7 June (2-6). Combined adm with The Chantry £8, chd free. Home-made teas at Hingsdon only (not at The Chantry).**
Hingsdon is a hilltop garden of about 2 acres with spectacular panoramic views. There are many unusual shrubs, mostly planted within the last 15 yrs, a mixed border of two halves (cool and hot), rose garden and a large kitchen garden. There is also a small arboretum with an idiosyncratic collection of over 90 trees. The main garden is accessible, although sloping, but the arboretum is too steep for wheelchair access. The kitchen garden has steps.

34 NEW 64 HINTON WOOD AVENUE
Highcliffe, Christchurch, BH23 5AJ. Mrs Glynda Morrison. *3½m E from Christchurch. From Christchurch Bypass onto A35, past Sainsbury's on L. Turn R at Hinton Stn sign, over bridge into Hinton Wood Ave. Park in Holmhurst Ave on L.* **Sun 24, Mon 25 May, Sat 27, Sun 28 June (1-5). Adm £5, chd free. Home-made teas.**
A small cottage garden inc approx 30 roses, delphiniums, lupins, heuchera and agapanthus. A water feature under shade with hostas, astilbe ferns, tetrapanax and other shade loving plants. Greenhouse with vegetables and seedlings. Our garden is west facing, allowing a mixture of shade loving plants as well as a lovely assortment of cottage garden flowers. Wheelchairs can enter paved driveway, through gate to courtyard leading to main garden. All paved and flat surfaces.

Our donation to the Army Benevolent Fund supported 776 individuals with horticultural related grants in 2025.

35 ♦ HOGCHESTER FARM
Axminster Road, Charmouth, Bridport, DT6 6BY. Mr Rob Powell, 07714 291846, rob@hogchester.com. *A35 Charmouth Rd, follow dual carriageway & take turning at signs for Hogchester Farm.* **For NGS: Sun 12 July (9-6). Adm £5, chd £2. Coffee shack serving drinks, cream teas & light refreshments.** For other opening times and information, please phone or email.
Hogchester Farm is a collaboration between those seeking connection with nature and themselves through conservation therapy and the arts. The 75 acre old dairy farm has been largely gifted to nature which has helped to preserve the overflowing abundance of natural life. Having worked closely with the Dorset Wildlife Trust, Hogchester Farm has been able to preserve wild meadows and wilding areas which are filled with local flora and fauna inc wild orchids, foxgloves and primroses. The farm offers something for everyone, making a great family day out. There will be a talk on the history of Hogchester wildflower meadows and meadows conservation at 2pm.

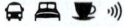

36 THE HOLLOW, BLANDFORD FORUM
Tower Hill, Iwerne Minster, Blandford Forum, DT11 8NJ. Sue Le Prevost. *Between Blandford & Shaftesbury. Follow signs on A350 to Iwerne Minster. Turn off at Talbot Inn, cont straight to The Chalk, bear R along Watery Lane for parking in Parish Field on R. 5 min uphill walk to house.* **Sat 20, Sun 21, Wed 24 June (2-5). Adm £5, chd free. Home-made cakes & gluten-free available.**
Hillside cottage garden built on chalk, about ⅓ acre with an interesting variety of plants in borders that line the numerous sloping pathways. Water features for wildlife and well placed seating areas to sit back and enjoy the views. Productive fruit and vegetable garden in converted paddock with raised beds and greenhouses. A high maintenance garden which is constantly evolving. Use of different methods to plant steep banks.

37 THE HOLLOW, SWANAGE
25 Newton Road, Swanage, BH19 2EA. Suzanne Nutbeem, 01929 423662, gdnsuzanne@gmail.com. *½ m S of Swanage town centre. From town follow signs to Durlston Country Park. At top of hill turn R at red post box into Bon Accord Rd. 4th turn R into Newton Rd.* **Every Wed 1 July to 26 Aug (2-5). Adm £5, chd free.** Visits also by arrangement 3 July to 25 Aug.
Wander in a dramatic sunken former stone quarry, a surprising garden at the top of a hill above the seaside town of Swanage. Stone terraces with many unusual shrubs and grasses form beautiful patterns of colour and foliage attracting butterflies and bees. Pieces of mediaeval London Bridge lurk in the walls. Steps have elegant handrails. WC available. Exceptionally wide range of plants inc cacti and air plants.

38 ♦ HOLME FOR GARDENS
West Holme Farm, Wareham, BH20 6AQ. Simon Goldsack, 01929 554716, simon@holmefg.co.uk, www.holmefg.co.uk. *2m SW Wareham. Easy to find on the B3070 road to Lulworth 2m out of Wareham.* **For NGS: Tue 9 June (9-5). Adm £8, chd free. Light refreshments in the Orchard Café.** For other opening times and information, please phone, email or visit garden website. Donation to Plant Heritage.
Set within the picturesque Isle of Purbeck, award-winning Holme for Gardens is a family run treasure, with beautifully landscaped gardens, a well-stocked garden centre with friendly knowledgeable staff, gift shop plus our light and airy Orchard Café and conservatory. The 15 acre garden delights the visitor with bold landscape features, colourful borders and achieves a wide diversity of wildlife through floral diversity. Grass paths are kept in good order and soil is well drained so wheelchair access is reasonable except immediately after heavy rain.

39 HORN PARK
Tunnel Road, Beaminster, DT8 3HB. Mr & Mrs David Ashcroft. *1½ m N of Beaminster. On A3066 from Beaminster, L before tunnel (see signs).* **Tue 21 Apr (2.30-4.30). Adm £6, chd free. Home-made teas.**
Large plantsman's garden with magnificent views over Dorset countryside towards the sea. Many rare and mature plants and shrubs in terrraced, herbaceous, rock and water gardens. Woodland garden and walks in woods. Many beautiful roses. Wildflower meadow with 164 varieties of grasses and flowers inc orchids.

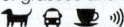

40 IVY HOUSE GARDEN
Piddletrenthide, DT2 7QF. Bridget Bowen. *9m N of Dorchester. On B3143. In middle of Piddletrenthide village nr The Piddle Inn.* **Sat 11, Sun 12 Apr, Sat 16, Sun 17 May (2-5). Adm £5, chd free. Tea, coffee & cake.**
A steep and challenging ½ acre garden with fine views, on a south facing site in the beautiful Piddle valley. Wildlife friendly garden with mixed borders, ponds, greenhouses and a polytunnel and large 'No-dig' vegetable and fruit garden. The 'rewilded' upper slopes offer peace and quiet. Daffodils, tulips and hellebores in quantity for spring openings. Come prepared for steep terrain and a warm welcome! Run on organic lines with plants to attract birds, bees and other insects. Insect friendly plants usually for sale. Honey and home-made jams available. Beekeeper present to answer queries. We hope to have live music in the garden

41 ♦ KINGSTON LACY
Wimborne Minster, BH21 4EA. National Trust, 01202 883402, kingstonlacy@nationaltrust. org.uk, www.nationaltrust.org.uk/kingston-lacy. *2½ m W of Wimborne Minster. On Wimborne-Blandford road B3082.* **For opening times and information, please phone, email or visit garden website.**
35 acres of formal garden, incorporating parterre and sunken garden planted with Edwardian schemes during spring and summer. 5 acre kitchen garden and allotments. Victorian fernery containing over 35 varieties. Rose garden, mixed herbaceous borders, vast formal lawns and Japanese garden restored to Henrietta Bankes' creation of 1910. National Collection of Convallaria and *Anemone nemorosa*. Snowdrops, blossom, bluebells, autumn colour

and Christmas light display. Deep gravel on some paths but lawns suitable for wheelchairs. Slope to visitor reception and South Lawn. Dogs allowed in some areas of woodland.

42 ◆ KINGSTON MAURWARD GARDENS AND ANIMAL PARK
Kingston Maurward, Dorchester, DT2 8PY. Kingston Maurward College, 01305 215003, enquiries@coastland.ac.uk, animal-park.kmc.ac.uk/the-gardens. *1m E of Dorchester off A35. Follow brown Tourist Information signs.* **For opening times and information, please phone, email or visit garden website.** Stepping into the grounds you will be greeted with 35 impressive acres of formal gardens. During the late spring and summer months, our National Collection of penstemons and salvias display a lustrous rainbow of purples, pinks, blues and whites, leading you on through the ample hedges and stonework balustrades. An added treat is the Elizabethan walled garden, offering a new vision of enchantment. Open early Jan to mid Dec. Hours will vary in winter depending on conditions - check garden website or call before visiting. Partial wheelchair access only, gravel paths, steps and steep slopes. Map provided at entry, highlighting the most suitable routes.

43 KNITSON OLD FARMHOUSE
Corfe Castle, Wareham, BH20 5JB. Rachel Helfer, 01929 421681, rjehelfer@gmail.com. *Purbeck. Between Corfe Castle & Swanage. Follow the A351 3m E from Corfe Castle. Turn L signed Knitson. After 1m fork R. We are on L after ¼ m.* **Wed 10, Thur 11 June, Wed 29, Thur 30 July (12-5). Combined adm with The Stables £8, chd free. Home-made light refreshments. Visits also by arrangement Mar to Oct for groups of up to 20.**
Mature cottage garden nestled under chalk downland. Herbaceous borders, rockeries, climbers and shrubs, evolved and designed over 60 yrs for year-round colour. Wildlife friendly, sustainable kitchen garden inc 20+ different fruits for self-sufficiency. Historical stone artefacts, ancient trees and shrubs are part of the integral design. Plants are selected for drought tolerance and hardiness.

100+ shrubs, both new and some over 100 yrs old. Vegetables year-round sustain a healthy lifestyle. Points of historical interest inc an ancient side-handled quern, Roman padstones, and a C15 farmhouse. Garden is on a slope, main lawn and tea area are level but there are uneven, sloping paths.

SPECIAL EVENT
44 ◆ KNOLL GARDENS
Stapehill Road, Wimborne, BH21 7ND. Mr Neil Lucas, 01202 873931, enquiries@knollgardens.co.uk, www.knollgardens.co.uk. *2½ m W of Ferndown. Brown tourist signs from all directions, inc from A31. Car park on site.* **For NGS: Tue 1 Sept (2-4.30). Adm £25, chd free. Pre-booking essential, please visit www.ngs.org.uk for information & booking. Tea, coffee & cake included in adm. Fri 18 Sept (10-5). Adm £8.95, chd £6.95. Self-service refreshment facilities. For other opening times and information, please phone, email or visit garden website.**
A wonderfully calming garden with naturalistic plantings of ornamental grasses interspersed with an array of flowering perennials. Grand specimen trees and beautiful shrubs offer shady spots to take in the open vistas of the prairie style gardens, benefiting both wildlife and environment. On Tues 1st Sept owner, Neil Lucas, will be offering a guided tour of the gardens (tickets must be pre-booked). The tour will focus on the garden's changing seasonal highlights, from some of the spectacular individual plants to mass plantings of Knoll's acclaimed grasses. Some slopes. Various surfaces inc gravel, paving, grass and bark.

45 22 LANCASTER DRIVE
Broadstone, BH18 9EL. Karen Wiltshire. *2 mins from Broadstone village centre. From B3074 Higher Blandford Rd, take first L onto Springdale Rd, 2nd R onto Springdale Ave, then head straight on to Lancaster Dr, the house will be on the R. Park on Lancaster Dr.* **Sat 16, Sun 17 May (11-5). Adm £5, chd free. Tea, coffee & cake.**
Hidden in the heart of Broadstone,

this 360ft woodland garden blends timeless oaks, a natural spring and seasonal acers with spaces for calm and reflection. A gravel garden with spring-fed water features and a sleek porcelain terrace invite quiet moments, while the owner's handmade pottery adds a personal, artistic touch to this sanctuary for wildlife.

46 LANGEBRIDE HOUSE
Long Bredy, DT2 9HU. Emma Orr. *8m W of Dorchester. S off A35, midway between Dorchester & Bridport. Well signed. 1st gateway on L in village.* **Sun 21 June (1-5). Adm £6, chd £3. Home-made teas.**
A lovely mature garden, designed in the 1960s, surround this large old rectory in a secluded spot in the stunning Bride Valley. Layered lawns, dissected by yew hedges, and dominated by some impressive and distinctive trees give a tranquil feel to this well spread-out garden. With herbaceous borders, a large hydrangea bed, a walled garden, orchard and rockery it has a little of everything. Partial wheelchair access if wet weather.

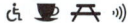

47 LEWELL LODGE
West Knighton, Dorchester, DT2 8RP. Rose & Charles Joly, 07711 643445, tony.leonard@ngs.org.uk. *3m SE of Dorchester. Turn off A35 onto A352 towards Wareham, take West Stafford bypass, turn R for West Knighton at T junction. ¾ m turn R up drive after village sign.* **Visits by arrangement Apr to Sept for groups of 10+.**
Elegant 2 acre classic English garden designed by present owners over last 25 yrs, surrounding Gothic Revival house. Double herbaceous borders enclosed by yew hedges with old fashioned roses. Shrub beds edged with box and large pyramided hornbeam hedge. Crab apple tunnel, box parterre and pleached hornbeam avenue. Large walled garden, many mature trees and woodland walk. Garden is level but parking is on gravel and there are gravel pathways.

Muddy Patches

48 LITTLE BENVILLE HOUSE
Benville Lane, Corscombe, Dorchester, DT2 0NN. Jo & Gavin Bacon. 2½m (6mins) from Evershot village on Benville Lane. Benville may be approached from A37, via Evershot village. House is on L ½m after Benville Bridge. Alternatively from A356, Dorchester to Crewkerne road, 1m down on R. **Sun 17 May (1-5). Combined adm with Pugin Hall £10, chd free. Home-made teas.**
Contemporary garden, with landscape interventions by Harris Bugg Studio within a varied ecological AONB and historic landscape off Benville Lane, mentioned in Thomas Hardy's Tess. Within the curtilage there are new herbaceous borders, woodland planting, walled vegetable and cutting garden, cloud pruned topiary, ha-ha, ornamental and productive trees and moat which is a listed Ancient Monument. Bring a tennis racquet and appropriate footwear and try the tennis court and enjoy the view.

49 ◆ LITTLEBREDY WALLED GARDENS
Littlebredy, DT2 9HL. The Walled Garden Workshop, 01305 898055, secretary@wgw.org.uk, www.littlebredy.com. *8m W of Dorchester. 10m E of Bridport. 1½m S of A35. NGS days: park on village green then walk 300yds. For the less mobile (and on normal open days) use gardens car park.* **For NGS: Tue 23, Tue 30 June (2-5.30). Adm £6, chd free. Home-made teas.** For other opening times and information, please phone, email or visit garden website.
1 acre walled garden on south facing slopes of Bride River valley. Herbaceous borders, riverside rose walk, lavender beds and potager vegetable and cut flower gardens. Partial wheelchair access, some steep grass slopes. For disabled parking please follow signs to main entrance car park next to the walled garden.

SPECIAL EVENT

50 LULWORTH CASTLE HOUSE
Lulworth Park, East Lulworth, Wareham, BH20 5QS. James & Sara Weld. *In the village of E Lulworth enter through the main entrance to Lulworth Castle and Park & follow the signs.* **Thur 9 July (10.30-1). Adm £25, chd free. Pre-booking essential, please visit www.ngs.org.uk for information & booking. Light refreshments at the Weld Arms, set menu available for visitors.**
Large coastal garden next to Lulworth Castle with views to the sea. Pleasure grounds surround a walled garden filled with roses and perennials, behind which sits a working kitchen garden. In front of the house the scented walk leads to a wildflower meadow, lavender labyrinth and Islamic garden with rills and fountains. A new wild white garden has been created over the past winter. A limited number of tickets have been made available for this special one-day event. Meet at the front of the house on the main drive at 10.30.After tea and coffee, with biscuits or pastries, there will be an introductory talk on the gardens followed by a guided tour. After visiting the garden a set menu lunch will be made available at the nearby Weld Arms from 1pm (not inc in adm price). To make a booking visit: https://theweldarms.co.uk or telephone: 01929 400211.

&

51 NEW MANOR FARM
Stour Provost, Gillingham, SP8 5SA. Mrs Maili Hemans, 07836 626053. *4m S of Gillingham. Turn R off B3092 in Stour Provost (coming from Gillingham) in to Church Lane. Manor Farm is the 1st driveway on R. What3words app: upcoming.incensed. topmost.* **Sat 1, Sun 2 Aug (1.30-5). Adm £7, chd free. Home-made teas.** Visits also by arrangement in Aug for groups of 10 to 20.
The garden has been created on a site that surrounds the C15 farmhouse. The planting consists of deep herbaceous borders, set against the old stone walls. Old existing fruit trees have been incorporated in the design. A natural swimming pond was added in 2024. Formal hedging and a huge amount of bulbs were added to the front area of the garden in 2021 and 2025.

&

52 MANOR FARM, HAMPRESTON
Wimborne, BH21 7LX. Guy & Anne Trehane. *2½ m E of Wimborne, 2½ m W of Ferndown. From Canford Bottom r'about on A31, take exit B3073 Ham Lane. ½ m turn R at Hampreston Xrds. House at bottom of village.* **Sat 28 Feb (10-1); Sun 1 Mar (1-4). Light refreshments. Sun 14 June, Sun 12 July, Sun 2 Aug, Sun 6 Sept (1-5). Home-made teas. Adm £7, chd free.**
Traditional farmhouse garden designed and cared for by 3 generations of the Trehane family for over a 100 years. Garden is noted for its herbaceous borders and rose beds within box and yew hedges. Mature shrubbery, water and bog garden. Excellent plants as usual for sale at openings inc hellebores in March.

&

53 8 MANOR GARDENS
North Street, Beaminster, DT8 3EE. Nigel & Julie Cowderoy. *4 mins walk N from town square. Walk along North St from the square. Turn 1st R. Garden is at top of close. Parking in square, public car park & on street parking nearby.* **Sat 4, Sun 5 July (2-5). Adm £5, chd free.**
Beautiful Mediterranean style tranquil, terraced riverside garden, developed over the last few years demonstrating possibilities for harnessing a sloping garden. Various growing zones could provide inspiration for any domestic garden on a south facing slope. Colourful, dense planting with both hardy and exotic plants. Uneven, narrow pathways in some areas.

54 MANOR HOUSE
Blandford Road, Shillingstone, Blandford Forum, DT11 0SF. Tom & Claire Downes, 07748 616496, clare@downesfamily.co.uk. *Entrance off A357.* **Visits by arrangement May to July for groups of 10 to 25. Adm £8. Home-made teas.**
Large garden with old brick walls providing backdrop for perennial borders, kitchen garden with ornamental fruit cages and handsome raised beds.

&

55 THE MANOR HOUSE, BEAMINSTER
North Street, Beaminster, DT8 3DZ. Christine Wood. *200yds N of town square. Please park in the square or public car park, we are a 5 mins walk along North St from the Square. Limited disabled parking on site.* **Sun 24, Mon 25 May, Sat 27, Sun 28 June (11-5). Adm £10, chd free. Home-made teas in the Coach House garden.**
Set in the heart of Beaminster, 16 acres of stunning parkland with mature specimen trees, lake and cascade. The Manor House looks forward again to welcoming old and new visitors to enjoy this peaceful garden, a haven for wildlife with a woodland walk, wildflower meadow and walled garden 'serendipity'. Ornamental ducks, black swans, pigmy goats, alpaca,chickens. Partial wheelchair access.

56 MAPPERCOMBE MANOR
Nettlecombe, Bridport, DT6 3SS. Arthur Crutchley. *4m NE of Bridport. From A3066 turn E signed W Milton & Powerstock. After 3m leave Powerstock on your L, bear R at Marquis of Lorne pub, entrance drive 150yds ahead.* **Fri 22, Sun 24 May (1-5). Adm £8, chd free. Home-made teas.**
Elegant Manor House that was originally a monks' rest house with stew pond and dovecote. South facing gardens on 4 levels with ancient monastic route and sweeping views. Approx 4 acres of gardens with well-planted borders, inc echiums, salvias and euphorbia. Apart from stonework and mature trees, garden mostly replanted in last 25 yrs. Many old roses and a haven for bees and butterflies. Dogs on leads. Partial wheelchair access, gravel and stone paths, steps. 150 yd walk from car park, limited parking by house.

In 2025 we awarded over £288,800 in Community Garden Grants, supporting 114 community garden projects.

57 ♦ MAPPERTON HOUSE, GARDENS & WILDLANDS
Mapperton, Beaminster, DT8 3NR. Earl & Countess of Sandwich, 01308 862645, office@mapperton.com, www.mapperton.com. *6m N of Bridport. Off A356/A3066. 2m SE of Beaminster off B3163.* **For opening times and information, please phone, email or visit garden website.** Italianate terraced valley gardens overlooked by the Tudor/Jacobean manor house, Mapperton Gardens is centred around the octagonal pool. Framed by a formal structure of bold hedging, clipped topiary, grottoes and stone statues, the design is softened by nature and planting. The gilded orangery looks out towards the lower terrace to reveal a C17 summerhouse, spring-fed ponds and wild garden. The Arboretum and woodland walks unfold with magnolias, redwoods and dogwoods, with sweeping valley views. For groups of 10 or more, a tour of the Gardens can be booked with Mapperton's Head Gardener for an additional £5 per person (not for NGS). For group bookings email groups@mappterton.com. 2026 will also feature a tree guide for the Arboretum. Visitors to Mapperton House will be able to see the American Heiress Exhibition as part of the House tour. New for 2026, dogs are now allowed on a short lead in the formal gardens.

58 ♦ MINTERNE GARDEN
Minterne House, Minterne Magna, Dorchester, DT2 7AU. Lord Digby, 01300 341370, enquiries@minterne.co.uk, www.minterne.co.uk. *2m N of Cerne Abbas. On A352 Dorchester-Sherborne road.* **For opening times and information, please phone, email or visit garden website.** As seen on BBC Gardeners' World and voted one of the 10 prettiest gardens in England by The Times. Famed for their display of historic rhododendrons, azaleas, Japanese cherries and magnolias in April/May when the garden is at its peak. Small lakes, streams and cascades offer new vistas at each turn around the 1m horseshoe shaped gardens covering 23 acres. The season ends with spectacular autumn colour. Snowdrops in Feb. Spring bulbs, blossom and bluebells in April. Easter trails for children. Over 200 acers provide spectacular autumn colour in Sept/Oct, inc Halloween trails for children. Fireworks at end of October.

59 MORVAL
Ferry Road, Studland, Swanage, BH19 3AQ. Rohini Finch. *From Swanage & Purbeck direction the garden is 250m beyond the shop on Ferry road. From the Ferry the garden is 250m beyond the Knoll Beach Hotel. Follow yellow NGS signs, car park in field opp.* **Sun 6 Sept (12-5). Adm £8, chd £4. Home-made teas.**
Large 3 acre coastal garden that has recently undergone extensive renovation. Deep, informal, mixed borders surround the front lawn, planted in a contemporary style and containing many unusual plants. The roof garden commands stunning views to a long elegant back garden and Studland Bay. Rear garden borders are filled with unusual shrubs and trees giving way to garden heath. Both front and back garden are easily accessible with wheelchairs. Steps to roof garden which is not accessible.

60 MUDDY PATCHES
West Street, Abbotsbury, Weymouth, DT3 4JT. P Ellis, Muddypatches@gmail.com, www.facebook.com/muddypatchesabbotsbury. *From Bridport take the B3157 coastal road to Abbottsbury. On entering Abbotsbury, Muddy Patches is on West St on the R. What3words app: business.unspoiled.slap.* **Sat 20, Sun 21 June (10-4). Adm £4, chd £2. Tea, coffee & cake.** Visits also by arrangement.
A beautiful village garden set in the glorious Dorset countryside with amazing views of the rolling hills and the historic St Catherine's Chapel. Enjoy a stroll around the gardens and see the amazing range of native and tropical plants, explore our wildlife area, visit the fairies in their garden or enjoy a delicious lunch, cake or ice cream. On site free parking available.

61 ♦ MUSEUM OF EAST DORSET
23-29 High Street, Wimborne Minster, BH21 1HR. Museum of East Dorset, 01202 882533, info@museumofeastdorset.co.uk, www.museumofeastdorset.co.uk. *Behind the Museum Building, with direct access via Crown Mead by the Library. Wimborne is just off A31. From W take B3078, from E take B3073 towards town centre. From Poole & Bournemouth enter town from S on A341. Although there is no on site parking there are several public car parks with a 5 min walk of the museum.* **For NGS: Evening opening Fri 11 Sept, Fri 16 Oct, Fri 20 Nov (6-8.30). Adm £15, chd free. Pre-booking essential, please visit www.ngs.org.uk for information & booking. Light refreshments in the Museum Tea Room, wine & soft drinks. For other opening times and information, please phone, email or visit garden website.**
Behind the Museum of East Dorset is a tranquil walled garden tucked away in the centre of Wimborne. Colourful herbaceous borders and heritage orchard trees line the path which stretches 100 metres down to the mill stream. This year we have 3 evening garden lectures taking place at the Museum. Please visit www.ngs.org.uk for details. Wheelchair access through Tea Room entrance via a labelled side door and not the main entrance.

62 MYRTLE COTTAGE
Woolland, Blandford Forum, DT11 0ES. Brian & Lynn Baker, 01258 817432, brian.baker15@btinternet.com. *7m W of Blandford Forum. Situated at the base of Bulbarrow Hill, pass the church on your L, pass the turning to Ibberton on the R. Myrtle Cottage is on the R after the Elwood Centre.* **Sun 22 Mar (10-5); Sat 16, Sun 17 May (10-5.30). Adm £5, chd free. Tea, coffee & cake.** Visits also by arrangement Mar to Sept.
A small to medium size segmented cottage garden, sympathetic to wildlife with a wildflower meadow and pond, part flower, part fruit and vegetable, a mix for everyone. Interesting hostas in pots and numerous chilli plant varieties grown from seed in the greenhouse. Snake's head fritillaries are a feature in March.

63 NEW NEWTON COTTAGE
Orchard Close, Newton, Sturminster Newton, DT10 2HN. Pamela Johnson & Gethyn Davies, 01258 472098, pamelastur@outlook.com. *What3words app: spend.strides. dusters. ½m SW Sturminster Newton, off the A357, opp bottom of Glue Hill. Limited parking. Public car parks 15 min walk in Sturminster Newton or follow parking signs on the day.* **Sun 21 June (12-5.30). Combined adm with Cherry Cottage £10, chd free. Home-made teas. Visits also by arrangement Feb to Sept.**
Sunny gravel gardens, a large informal lawn and woodland trees complement the views of fields and pastures. Familiar plants are used in a naturalistic style with carefully edited self-seeding invaders. It's visited by a wide variety of wildlife, not all beneficial! This is the inspiration for Pamela's artwork which will be on display in the studio along with a selection of Gethyn's paintings. Both Gethyn and Pamela are professional artists and Pamela is also a retired garden designer. Fantastic plant sale and delicious home-made cakes. Most of the garden can be accessed without steps, but some gravel paths may be difficult for wheelchairs.

& ✻ ☕))

64 OAKDALE LIBRARY GARDENS
Wimborne Road, Poole, BH15 3EF. Oakdale Library Gardens Association, www.facebook.com/Oakdalelibrarygardens. *Corner of Wimborne Rd & Dorchester Rd. Number 25/26 bus towards Canford Heath. Bus stop directly adjacent to Library. Free parking on site.* **Sat 6 June (10-1). Adm by donation. Light refreshments on NGS open days only.**
Award winning gardens comprising of the 'Bookerie' Reading and Rhyme time garden where wildlife is welcomed with bee friendly planting, an insect mansion and pond. Also a Commemorative Garden, a nautical themed garden, herb garden and children's adventure trail. The gardens have been designed and maintained by volunteers. Featured in '111 places in Poole that you shouldn't miss ' by Katherine Bebo. The Bookerie is only open during Library opening hours. Other gardens open at all times. Plant sales on NGS open days. Full wheelchair access in all the gardens except the children's adventure trail.

& 🐕 ✻ ☕

65 THE OLD RECTORY, LITTON CHENEY
Litton Cheney, Dorchester, DT2 9AH. Richard & Emily Cave, 01308 482266, emilycave@rosacheney.com. *9m W of Dorchester. 1m S of A35, 6m E of Bridport. Park in village and follow signs.* **Sun 26, Wed 29 Apr, Sun 5 July (11-5). Adm £8, chd free. Tea, coffee & cake. Visits also by arrangement 26 Apr to 30 Sept for groups of up to 20.**
Steep paths lead to beguiling 4 acres of natural woodland with many springs, streams, 2 pools, one a natural swimming pool planted with native plants. Formal front garden, designed by Arne Maynard, with pleached crabtree border, topiary and soft planting inc tulips, peonies, roses and verbascums. Walled garden with informal planting, kitchen garden, orchard with spring blossom and 350 rose bushes for a cut flower business.

🐕 ☕ 🪑))

66 THE OLD RECTORY, PULHAM
Dorchester, DT2 7EA. Mr & Mrs N Elliott, 01258 817595, gilly.elliott@hotmail.com, www.instagram.com/theoldrectory_pulham. *13m N of Dorchester. 8m SE of Sherborne. On B3143 turn E at Xrds in Pulham. Signed Cannings Court.* **Sun 2, Thur 6 Aug (2-5). Adm £10, chd free. Tea, coffee & cake. Visits also by arrangement 15 May to 15 Sept for groups of 5 to 50.**
4 acres of formal and informal gardens surrounding C18 rectory with splendid views. Yew pyramid allées and hedges, circular herbaceous borders with late summer colour. Exuberantly planted terrace, purple and white beds. Box parterres, mature trees, pond, sheets of daffodils, tulips, glorious churchyard, ha-ha, pleached hornbeam circle. Enchanting flower filled bog garden with stream and islands. 10 acres of woodland walks. Mostly wheelchair accessible.

& 🐕 ✻ 🚗 ☕))

67 THE OLD SCHOOL HOUSE
The Street, Sutton Waldron, Blandford Forum, DT11 8NZ. David Milanes. *7m N of Blandford. Turn into Sutton Waldron from A350, continue for 300 yds, 1st house on L in The Street. Entrance past house through gates in wall.* **Fri 12 June (3-6); Sun 14 June (2-6). Adm £5, chd free. Open nearby Penmead Farm. Home-made teas at Old School House on 12th June and at Penmead Farm on 14th June.**
Village garden of almost an acre laid out in last 13 yrs with hornbeam hedges creating 'rooms' inc orchard, secret garden and pergola walkway. Raised bed for growing vegetables. Strong framework of existing large trees, beds are mostly planted with roses and herbaceous plants. Pleached hornbeam screen. A designer's garden with interesting semi-tender plants close to the house with benches to sit and relax on. Level lawns.

& 🐕 ✻ ☕))

68 THE OLD VICARAGE
Powerstock, Bridport, DT6 3TE. Jo Willett & Stuart Rock. *4.7m NE of Bridport. From Bridport or Beaminster follow signs for Powerstock off A3066. Drive into centre of village. Parking up School Hill above church. House is 5 mins walk. What3words app: crunches.fork.sampling.* **Sat 23, Sun 24 May (12-5). Adm £5, chd free. Tea, coffee, elderflower juice & cake at Old Vicarage Coach House.**
A classic English garden of 1½ acres with many rooms and several notable features. Extensively replanted over the past 5 yrs with a variety of herbaceous borders, grasses, a rose terrace and a tulip and dahlia square under a crab apple canopy. It also features a rare 'maiden' ancient mulberry, a 'font garden' (with Victorian font), vegetable garden, pond, orangery, orchard and croquet lawn. Front garden accessible. Gravel path to back.

& ✻ 🚗 ☕))

In 2025, our donations to Carers Trust helped them support over 1 million unpaid carers across the UK, as part of their network of local carer centres.

DORSET 175

Newton Cottage

69 THE OLD VICARAGE
East Orchard, Shaftesbury, SP7 0BA. Miss Tina Wright, 01747 811744, tina_lon@msn.com. 4½m S of Shaftesbury, 3½m N of Sturminster Newton. On B3091 between 90° bend & layby with defibrillator red phone box. Parking is on the opp corner towards Hartgrove. Car park will be open from around 1pm to 1.30pm for opening at 2pm. **Fri 13, Sun 15 Feb (2-5). Adm £5, chd free. Home-made teas in garden with lots of places to shelter if it is wet.** Visits also by arrangement 5 Jan to 20 Dec.
1.7 acre established garden and wildlife garden, with hundreds of different snowdrops, crocus and many other bulbs and winter flowering shrubs. A stream meanders down to a pond and there are lovely reflections in the swimming pond, the first to be built in Dorset. The wildlife garden has been planted with several unusual trees. Plus a 1.3 acre field under development but almost completed. Special features inc grotto, old Victorian man pushing his lawn mower (which his owner purchased brand new in 1866). Pond dipping, swing and other children's attractions. Cakes inc gluten free, and vegans are also catered for. Not suitable for wheelchairs if very wet.

70 NEW 3 PARK FARM CLOSE
Martinstown, Dorchester, DT2 9TW. Phil & Roelie Newman. 3m SW of Dorchester. From the Dorchester A35 bypass at the Monkey Jump r'about (W of Poundbury) follow signs to Martinstown. We are at the E edge of the village up a gravel drive. Postcode in SatNav works. **Sun 14 June, Sun 5 July (1-5). Adm £5, chd free. Home-made teas.**
A quirky child friendly 1 acre garden with distinct sections. Lower section consists of a large scale model canal with operational locks and a 1:20 model village. Visitors may operate boat and locks. The middle section has 2 large ponds surrounded by a 'beach' area, trees, shrubs and flower beds. The top section consists of a large wildflower maze and vegetable patch. Treasure trail for kids. Parking in driveway for wheelchair access. Some assistance might be needed to get up small slope. For other parking follow signs.

71 PENMEAD FARM
The Street, Sutton Waldron, Blandford Forum, DT11 8PF. Matthew & Claire Cripps. $5\frac{1}{2}$ m S of Shaftesbury. From A350 turn into Sutton Waldron. Drive through the village & entrance is approx $\frac{1}{4}$ m on R after the road bridge which straddles the stream. **Fri 12 June (3-7). Wine. Sun 14 June (2-6). Home-made teas. Adm £5, chd free. Open nearby The Old School House. Wine & light refreshments from 5.30 pm on Friday opening.**
Situated on the site of an old brick works the property is bordered by over 30 mature oak trees. The garden comprises a woodland and stream (Fontmell Brook) walk, meadows, substantial vegetable garden, orchard, spring fed pond and small semi walled garden. Being on clay soil roses thrive. Views to Pen Hill and Fontmell Down. Some sloping paths and can be wet under foot. Accessible bar steep slope down to stream and some gravel paths.

72 NEW 39 PERGIN CRESCENT
Poole, BH17 7AL. Mr Steve & Mrs Allison Mason. Pergin Cres is situated at the eastern end of Upton Rd. **Sun 10 May, Sun 14 June (2-5). Adm £4, chd free. Cream teas.**
This 1950s property is situated on the outskirts of Poole with a front garden of appro 850sq metres and a rear garden of approx 112sq metres. Planting is mainly perennial to provide year-round interest. Two trees provide cover for the many birds that visit. More seasonal planting tends to be in tubs and pots. There is a small patio and small fish pond with a dozen attractive shubunkins.

73 PIPSFORD FARM
Beaminster, DT8 3NT. Charlie & Bee Tuke. 2m SE of Beaminster off B3163, 7m N of Bridport. Postcode & SatNav bring you to the main front drive entrance, clearly signed. **Fri 22 May (2-5). Adm £10, chd free. Pre-booking essential, please visit www.ngs.org.uk for information & booking.**
3 acres of formal and informal gardens. Ponds surrounded by mature specimen trees, acers, hydrangeas, ferns and bamboo. Bog garden, with raised walkway. Walled garden with herbaceous beds, pond, pergola covered in apples and productive beds bordered by Ilex crenata. Cut flower area with paths to greenhouses and fruit cage, surrounded by mature yew hedges.

74 THE POTTING SHED
Middlemarsh, Sherborne, DT9 5QN. Andrew & Michele Cole, www.therapygarden.co.uk. 7m S of Sherborne, 11m N of Dorchester on the A352 in Middlemarsh. 300 yrds S of The Hunters Moon pub. **Sat 18 July (10-4). Adm £5, chd free. Cream teas. Gluten free & vegan scones, freshly picked herbal teas & home-made jams.**
The Potting Shed opened its doors in April 2023. This new 2 acre Wellbeing Nursery and Therapy Garden has been created from scratch to enhance relaxation and tranquillity. The community garden has been planted organically to encourage all forms of wildlife. There is an acre of wildflower meadow, plant nursery and tea garden to explore. It truly is a special place to relax, unwind and be inspired. Partial wheelchair access, small area of gravel, remainder paved and hard paths plus grass.

75 PUGIN HALL
Rampisham, nr Dorchester, DT2 0PR. Tim & Ali Wright. Near centre of village. NW of Dorchester. From Dorchester A37 Yeovil, 9m L Evershot, follow signs. From Crewkerne A356, take 1st L to Rampisham, Pugin Hall is on L after $\frac{1}{2}$ m. Parking at Village Hall. **Sun 17 May (1-5). Combined adm with Little Benville House £10, chd free. Sun 14 June (1-5). Combined adm with Broomhill £10, chd free. Home-made teas.**
Pugin Hall was once Rampisham Rectory, designed in 1847 by Augustus Pugin, who also helped to design the interior of the Houses of Parliament. A Grade I listed building, it is surrounded by $4\frac{1}{2}$ acres of garden, including a large front lawn with rhododendrons, a walled garden filled with topiary and soft floral planting and an orchard. The walled garden is planted with shrubs, roses, clematis, masses of unusual perennials, and Japanese anemones against a backdrop of espalier fruit trees and box hedging with spirals. Pugin Hall is the only intact Pugin designed building currently in private ownership and is considered to be the most complete example of domestic architecture designed by him. The plan of the house encompasses Pugin's characteristic pinwheel design: an arrangement of rooms whose axis rotate about a central hall and lends itself well to the varying effects of light and shade within.

76 1C RECTORY ROAD
Poole, BH15 3BH. Dave Hutchings. 5 mins from Poole town centre. The bungalow is behind the main houses on the road down a pedestrian access drive. **Sat 15, Sun 16 Aug (11-4). Adm £5, chd free. Tea, coffee & cake.**
An unusual character house and garden. With a passion for maximalist design the house and garden has been designed and built by the owner over the last 7 yrs. Both garden and house are full of objet d'art spanning centuries, there's curiosities to see in every corner.

77 RUSSELL-COTES ART GALLERY & MUSEUM
East Cliff, Bournemouth, BH1 3AA. Phil Broomfield, 07810 646123, russellcotes@bcpcouncil.gov.uk, www.russellcotes.com. On Bournemouth's East Cliff Promenade. Next to the Royal Bath Hotel, 2 mins walk from Bournemouth Pier. The closest car park is Bath Road South. Parking also available on the cliff top. **Visits by arrangement Apr to Oct for groups of 6 to 15. Adm £3, chd free.**
Enjoy a private garden tour of this sub-tropical garden sited on the cliff top, overlooking the sea, full of a wide variety of plants from around the globe. East Cliff Hall was the home of Sir Merton and Lady Annie Russell-Cotes. The garden was restored allowing for modern access with areas retaining the original 1901 design conceived by the founders, such as the ivy clad grotto and Japanese influence. The Russell-Cotes Café serves a delicious range of light lunches, teas, coffees, and cakes. Some gravel paths and no wheelchair access to terrace.

78 10 RYAN CLOSE
Ferndown, BH22 9TP. Mrs Jane Norris. *From Tescos in Ferndown, up Church Rd to T-lights. Proceed across Wimborne Rd East into Ameysford Rd, 2nd R into Ryan Close, then immed R into even numbers.* **Fri 6, Sat 7, Sun 8, Fri 13, Sat 14, Sun 15 Feb (11-3). Adm £5. Light refreshments. Sun 3 May, Sun 7 June (2-5). Adm £3.50, chd free. Home-made teas. Soup & cake during snowdrop season (refreshments & plant sales cash only).**
In February 150 varieties of snowdrops carefully named in baskets. In early summer this plantswoman's garden is filled with a remarkable selection of mostly perennial plants, making a vibrant display all year. The beds are densely planted to suppress weeds, with alliums hardy geraniums and tulips in May followed by salvias in June. Hellebores for sale on Sun 8 Feb only.

79 THE SECRET GARDEN AT SERLES HOUSE
47 Victoria Road, Wimborne, BH21 1EN. Chris & Bridget Ryan. *Centre of Wimborne. On B3082 W of town, very near hospital. Westfield car park 300yds. Off road parking close by.* **Sun 10, Sun 17 May (12.30-4.30). Adm £5, chd free. Tea, coffee, cake & sandwiches. Donation to MIND.**
The former home of the late Ian Willis, who lived here for just under 40 yrs. Alan Titchmarsh described this amusingly creative garden as 'one of the best 10 private gardens in Britain'. The ingenious use of unusual plants complements the imaginative treasure trove of garden objets d'art. Wheelchair access to garden only. Narrow steps may prohibit wide wheelchairs.

80 SHADRACK DAIRY FARM NEW
Mill Street, Burton Bradstock, DT6 4QZ. Miss Alexandra Wilson-Jones. *In the village of Burton Bradstock. Turn into Mill St by the Three Horseshoes pub. The entrance is opp the PO, there are 3 milk churns outside. Please note there is no parking avail on the site.* **Sun 5 July (10-6). Adm £4, chd free. Tea, coffee & cake.**
A relatively new garden on a challenging site in the yard of a former dairy farm. The sense of the farmyard is maintained, whilst incorporating plants to introduce form, structure and colour. This is mainly with the use of pots and containers. There are also areas of more natural planting, designed as zones, such as a wildflower orchard, arid succulent area, and Mediterranean garden.

81 ◆ SHERBORNE CASTLE
New Rd, Sherborne, DT9 5NR. Mr E Wingfield Digby, www.sherbornecastle.com. *½ m E of Sherborne. On New Rd B3145. Follow brown signs from A30 & A352.* **For opening times and information, please visit garden website.**
Sherborne Castle Gardens offers a stunning blend of history and natural beauty. Spanning 42 acres, the 'Capability' Brown gardens feature manicured lawns, serene lake, and vibrant flower beds. With scenic walking paths, ancient trees, and views of the majestic castle, it's a peaceful haven for nature and history lovers. Partial wheelchair access, gravel paths, steep slopes, steps.

GROUP OPENING

82 SHILLINGSTONE GARDENS
Shillingstone, DT11 0SF. Caroline Salt. *4m W of Blandford Forum. The village lies on the A357 between Blandford Forum & Sturminster Newton. Parking at Shillingstone House, additional parking & WC at Church Centre.* **Sun 14 June (10-4). Combined adm £7, chd free. Light refreshments at Shillingstone Church Centre, Main Rd, Shillingstone DT11 0SW.**

CHERRY COTTAGE
Lal & Gloria Ratnayake.

SHILLINGSTONE HOUSE
Michael & Caroline Salt.

Both gardens are in the centre of this pretty village which lies close to the River Stour with Hambledon Hill as a backdrop. The larger garden has some magnificent trees, traditional borders, old brick walls supporting multiple rambling roses and an old fashioned walled kitchen garden mixing vegetables, fruit and flowers. Nearby a cottage garden packed with exotic plants, Bonsai, pond, fruit and herbs and beds of perenials and annuals. Wheelchair access to Shillingstone House garden only.

SPECIAL EVENT

83 SHUTE HOUSE
Donhead St Mary, Shaftesbury, SP7 9DG. John & Suzy Lewis. *2½ m E of Shaftesbury. 2m from the Dorset & Wiltshire border, follow navigation using postcode, house on L in centre of village, parking in field.* **Thur 11 June (2-4.30). Adm £25, chd free. Pre-booking essential, please visit www.ngs.org.uk for information & booking. Home-made teas.**
Sir Geoffrey Jellicoe, one of our finest landscape architects, was commissioned in 1969 to create a water garden for Lady Anne and Captain Michael Tree. The result was Shute House Gardens; his favourite and some say his finest work. The River Nadder rises at the top of the garden and is diverted into canals, waterfalls, rills and mysterious pools through a series of atmospheric garden 'rooms'. A limited number of tickets have been made available for this special one day event, which includes a talk and private guided tour with the garden owner, Suzy Lewis followed by tea and cake. Please note the refreshments will be served in two sittings; one before and one after the garden tour. The first 20 tickets sold will take the tour first followed by refreshments. Wheelchair access to the main front garden, although pathways and the woodland walkway would limit access to certain parts of the garden.

SPECIAL EVENT

84 SLAPE MANOR
Netherbury, Bridport, DT6 5LH. Paul Mulholland & Tarsha Finney, 07534 676148, info@slapemanor.com. *1m S of Beaminster. Turn W off A3066 to Netherbury. House ½ m S of Netherbury on back road to Bridport signed Waytown.* **Evening opening Thur 4 June (4-9.30). Adm £50. Pre-booking essential, please visit www.ngs.org.uk for information & booking. The visit will include a glass of local sparkling wine, oysters, charcuterie & cheeses. There will

also be live music. Visits also by arrangement 1 Feb to 1 Dec for groups of 8 to 20.
A limited number of tickets have been made available for this exclusive special event. Please meet on the main front drive to the house by the porch where garden owners Tarsha & Paul will welcome you. After giving the background to their thinking behind the ongoing development of the gardens, Head Gardener, Hannah Gardner will then give a talk and guided tour around the gardens. The gardens have been transformed in recent years with formal and informal planting in many areas, with an ever-evolving empathetic approach which aims to work naturalistically within the surrounding landscape. Mostly flat with some sloping paths and steps. Ground is often wet and boggy.

Shillingstone House
© Christopher Middleton

SPECIAL EVENT

85 NEW SMEDMORE HOUSE
Kimmeridge, BH20 5PG.
Dr Philip Mansel,
www.smedmorehouse.com.
7m S of Wareham. Turn W off A351 (Wareham-Swanage) at sign to Kimmeridge, turn L before Kimmeridge village, continue up drive. **Tue 9 June (2-5). Adm £50, chd free. Pre-booking essential, please visit www.ngs.org.uk for information & booking. Home-made teas.**
Two acres of romantically disordered gardens, including walled flower gardens, Mediterranean garden and herb courtyard. Extensive lawn on the side of the house with deep herbaceous borders including display of hydrangeas, interesting plants and shrubs. A giant Holm oak marks the path that takes you through woods and fields, past sphinxes, urns and obelisks and down to the sea at Kimmeridge Bay. This event is kindly hosted by Dr Philip Mansel. Philip and his gardener will give a talk and guided tour of the principle rooms of the house and areas of the garden. Dr Mansel is a renowned historian, copies of his book "King of the World" about Louis 14th of France will be on sale (cash only).

86 SOUTH EGGARDON HOUSE
Askerswell, Dorchester, DT2 9EP.
Buffy Sacher, 07920 520280,
buffysacher@gmail.com. *From Dorchester on A35 turn R for Askerswell. Through village at T junction. Go straight over. From Bridport on A35 take 1st turning to Askerswell. Pass Spyway Inn on R. Turn next L.* **Visits by arrangement for groups of 8 to 30. Adm £15, chd free. Light refreshments.**
5 acres of formal and informal gardens designed around a 2000 yr old yew tree and lake. Water garden with streams, pond and lake. Woodland walk, orchard, wild garden, large herbaceous borders filled with roses and perennials. Ornamental kitchen garden.

87 THE STABLES
Knitson, Corfe Castle, Wareham, BH20 5JB. Rebecca Charron.
Situated in a hamlet, 3m E of Corfe Castle. Follow the A351 3m E from Corfe Castle. Turn L signed Knitson onto single track road. After 1m fork R. We are on L after ¼ m. What3words app: currently. accordion.panicking. **Wed 10, Thur 11 June, Wed 29, Thur 30 July (12-5). Combined adm with Knitson Old Farmhouse £8, chd free. Light refreshments.**
Much loved garden planted in a contemporary style with deep borders filled with easy care colourful perennials interspersed with shrubs. The garden was established in 2016 on flat compacted sand that had been a horse dressage arena. The aim was to plant a garden full of flowers in a naturalistic style enabling it to fit into the surrounding landscape. In addition to the main garden, we have a working kitchen garden. Wildflower and grass areas and a water storage pond at the top of the adjoining field. There is a small area of 5 year old planted trees on the north side of the garden. Parking close to garden with gravel yard then short uphill slope to main garden area.

88 STADDLESTONES
14 Witchampton Mill, Witchampton, Wimborne, BH21 5DE. Annette & Richard Lockwood, 01258 841405, richardglockwood@yahoo.co.uk.
5m N of Wimborne off B3078. Follow signs through village & park in sports field, 7 mins walk to garden. Limited disabled parking nr garden. **Sun 23 Aug (2-5). Adm £6, chd free. Home-made teas. Visits also by arrangement 1 May to 14 Sept.**
A beautiful setting for a cottage garden with colour themed borders, pleached limes and hidden gems, leading over a chalk stream to a shady area which has some unusual plants. Plenty of areas just to sit and enjoy the wildlife. Wire bird sculptures by local artist. Wheelchair access to first half of garden.

SPECIAL EVENT

89 STAFFORD HOUSE
West Stafford, Dorchester,
DT2 8AD. Lord & Lady Fellowes.
2m E of Dorchester in Frome Valley. Follow signs to West Stafford from the West, 1st house on L before you get to the village, green park railings and gate. **Fri 3 July (10-12.30). Adm £25, chd free. Pre-booking essential, please visit www.ngs.org.uk for information & booking. Home-made elevenses inc cake & biscuits in a gardening theme.**
The gardens at Stafford House inc a river walk and tree planting in the style of early C19 Picturesque. Humphry Repton prepared landscape proposals for the garden and the designs were later implemented, they were also included in his famous Red Books. A limited number of tickets have been made available for this private morning opening, hosted by Lord and Lady Fellowes. The head gardener, Pip Poulton, will give a talk and guided tour of the gardens and grounds inc ongoing empathetic recent renovations. Special home-made elevenses will be served on the main terrace or underneath the turkey oak tree planted in 1633. There will then be the opportunity to explore the grounds and gardens, finishing at approx 12.30pm.

90 NEW THE TREEHOUSE
Merritown Lane, Hurn,
Christchurch, BH23 6DT. Miss Francesca Potton, www.facebook.com/diverseabilitiesplus.
Continue 1m down the road from Bournemouth Airport (towards Parley) turning L & L again into the shared car park, continuing down until you reach the Diverse Abilities sign. **Wed 17 June (10-4). Adm £5, chd free. Tea, coffee & cake.**
Our fully accessible sensory garden is a tranquil haven for children and adults supported by Diverse Abilities. It features insect-loving plants, vibrant allium and echinacea, soft lamb's ear and bunny tail grass, and fragrant, edible choices like lavender, creeping thyme and *Salvia elegans*, designed to delight every sense safely and beautifully. The garden is fully accessible in all areas.

91 TULIP TREE
Donhead St Mary, Shaftesbury,
SP7 9DL. Rodney & Penny Short.
4m E of Shaftesbury. A30 towards Shaftesbury. In Ludwell turn R opp brown sign to Tollard Royal. Follow road for ¾m & bear R at T-junction. Bear R at next fork. Pass Chapel on R. Tulip Tree is next L. **Sun 14 June (2-5). Adm £5, chd free. Home-made teas.**
Two acres of paddock with mown paths behind house and 1acre of garden around house dominated by 120 yr old *Liriodendron tulipifera* which originates from N America, and the Northofagus trees from S America. Both are unusual plantings for a farmhouse garden in Dorset. The garden is divided into separate areas by mature hedges and old stone walls. The patio and rose garden are recent additions. Parking is on hard-standing in paddock. Specified disabled parking near the house. Sloping path from top to bottom lawn.

92 TUMBLINS
Bulbarrow Lane, Winterborne Stickland, Blandford Forum,
DT11 0ED. John & Claire Scott, 01258 880841,
claire@historystore.ltd.uk. *6m W of Blandford Forum. At Blandford Forum follow signs to Brewery. 2nd r'about turn L, 2nd R to Winterborne Stickland. At village turn R for Bulbarrow, then turn L for Bulbarrow. Turn L for Winterborne Houghton.* **Sun 24 May, Sun 14 June, Sun 26 July (10.30-4.30). Adm £5, chd free. Coffee & biscuits avail in the morning, light lunches & afternoon tea & cakes from midday.** Visits also by arrangement 1 May to 1 Oct.
3 acre hilltop garden with extensive views. Swimming lake, orchards, kitchen garden, mixed borders and unusual trees inc, *Wolemia nobolis*, *Ginko biloba* and Monterey pine. Roses and hydrangeas thrive. The swimming lake is surrounded by a mass planting of hemerocallis providing a wall of orange in the summer. The mini arboretum and fernery are different to other parts of the garden and the gravel garden has a more tropical feeling planted with palms, banana, bromeliads and tetrapanax. The garden is accessible for wheelchairs, though sloping and the gravel garden may be difficult.

93 UTOPIA
Tincleton, Dorchester,
DT2 8QP. Nick & Sharon Spiller, 07970 971983,
sharspiller@hotmail.co.uk. *4m SE of Dorchester. Take signs to Tincleton from Dorchester, Puddletown. Pick up garden signs in the village. Drop off only at garden.* **Sun 14 June (1-5). Adm £6, chd £4. Light refreshments.** Visits also by arrangement 29 May to 13 June for groups of up to 20.
Approx ½ acre of secluded, peaceful garden made up of several rooms inspired by different themes. Inspiration is taken from Mediterranean and Italian gardens, woodland space and water gardens. Seating is scattered throughout to enable you to sit and enjoy the different spaces and take advantage of both sun and shade. Parking available within a 10 min walk or park in village.

94 ♦ THE WALLED GARDEN
Moreton, Dorchester,
DT2 8RH. 01929 405685, info@walledgardenmoreton.co.uk, walledgardenmoreton.co.uk. *In the village of Moreton, near Crossways. Look for the brown signs out on the main road.* **For opening times and information, please phone, email or visit garden website.**
The Walled Garden is a beautiful 5 acre landscaped formal garden in the village of Moreton. The village is close to the historic market town of Dorchester and situated on the River Frome. A wide variety of perennial plants sit in the borders, which have been styled in original Georgian and Victorian designs. Sculpture from various local artists, family area and play park, animal area, and plant shop, plus on site café.

95 WESTERN GARDENS
24A Western Ave, Branksome Park, Poole, BH13 7AN. Mr Peter Jackson, 01202 708388,
pjbranpark@gmail.com. *3m W of Bournemouth. From S end Wessex Way (A338) at gyratory take The Avenue, 2nd exit. At T-lights turn R into Western Rd then at bottom of hill L. At church turn R into Western Ave.* **Sun 26 Apr (2-5). Adm £7, chd free. Home-made teas.** Visits also by arrangement 12 Apr to 10 May for groups of 20+.

Created over 50 yrs the award winning garden offers enormous variety with rose, courtyard and woodland gardens, herbaceous borders and cherry tree and camellia walk. Lush foliage and vibrant flowers give year-round colour and interest enhanced by wood sculpture and topiary. 'This secluded and magical 1 acre garden captures the spirit of warmer climes and begs for repeated visits' (Gardening Which?). Plants, home-made jams and chutneys for sale. Wheelchair access to ¾ garden.

96 WHITE HOUSE
Newtown, Witchampton, Wimborne, BH21 5AU. Mr Tim Read, 01258 840438, tim@witchampton.org. *5m N of Wimborne off B3078. Travel through village of Witchampton towards Newtown for 800m. Pass Crichel House's castellated gates on L. White House is a modern house sitting back from road on L after further 300m.* **Visits by arrangement 1 May to 1 Sept for groups of 8 to 15. Adm £8, chd free. Home-made teas.**
1½ acre garden set on different levels, with a Mediterranean feel, planted to encourage wildlife and pollinators. Wildflower border, pond surrounded by moisture loving plants, prairie planting of grasses and perennials, orchard. Chainsaw sculptures of birds of prey. Reasonable wheelchair access to all but the top level of the garden.

97 NEW WHITEMOOR FARM
Whitemoor, Holt, Wimborne, BH21 7DA. Mr Graham & Mrs Kim Bell. *3m N of Wimborne. 1m from Barley Mow Inn to Broomhill Xrds, signpost to Whitemoor ¼ m on L.* **Sun 7 June (1-5). Adm £6, chd free. Tea, coffee & cake served at cabin by pond.**
Approx 4 acre informal country garden, surrounded by ancient oaks and hedgerows. Range of mixed borders with mature shrubs, perennials, bulbs and grasses. Large ornamental pond within lovely planting of Japanese maples contrasting with hot, dry areas. There is a Mediterranean pool terrace, orchard, newly dug lake and small woodland area. Mainly flat with lawns, gravel and wood chip paths.

98 20 WICKET ROAD
Kinson, Bournemouth, BH10 5LT. Carron Bowen (& Peter Hellawell). *300 metres SE of Kinson Green. From Kinson Green (The Hub/Library): follow Wimborne Rd (A341) towards Northbourne. Turn R after shops into Kitscroft Rd, R again into Bramley Rd; Wicket Rd is second L. No 20 is on the L.* **Sat 27, Sun 28 June (2-5). Adm £5, chd free. Tea, coffee & cake.**
Built around a modern terrace, this small suburban garden (just 18 x 13 metres) sits on an awkward shaped plot, over a bed of clay. Set down from its neighbours, it developed a habit of flooding. But you'd never know. 'Borrow, hint, reveal, distract, attract, conceal' – the design uses every trick in the gardening handbook to create a truly memorable space. Exhibition of the garden's history, some unusual plants, a unique 'quay' (for storing run-off water as part of a hidden drainage system) and an array of small-scale features. Access is via the garage through a narrow doorway (26"). However, once in the garden, paths are wide with step-free route to most areas.

99 NEW 3 WILLOW HAMLET
68-69 Whitehayes Road, Burton, Christchurch, BH23 7PA. Mrs Suzanne Langley, 07796 876898, selangley@mail.com. *7m from Bournemouth. Look for signs off Whitehayes Rd.* **Sun 28 June, Sun 26 July, Sun 30 Aug (12-4). Adm £5, chd free. Cream teas.** Visits also by arrangement 28 June to 25 July.
A vibrant garden with rich seasonal colour, extensive range of plants to cascading hanging baskets. Paths weave through borders to a pergola framed in wisteria and climbers, while mature trees and woodland planting shelter wildlife. Thoughtful seating areas invite visitors to pause, admire the views, and enjoy the garden's changing character. Paintings and sculptures throughout the garden. The garden opens onto a working art studio and gallery and paintings will be for sale.

SPECIAL EVENT

100 WYKE FARM
Chedington, Beaminster, DT8 3HX. Alex & Robert Appleby, www.wykefarm.com. *Take the turning from the A356, opp The Winyards Gap Inn, away from Chedington, signed to Halstock. Drive 1m down the lane and we are the 1st farm entrance on the L.* **Sun 21 June (2.30-4). Adm £25, chd free. Pre-booking essential, please visit www.ngs.org.uk for information & booking. Home-made teas in the white courtyard garden.**
The owners of Wyke Farm, Robert and Alex Appleby, are both fanatical about rewilding, environmental conservation and preservation of the natural habitat. They have lived at Wyke Farm for almost 20 yrs and in this time have worked hard to sympathetically restore the land to inc a substantial wildflower meadow at the front of the house, and a large lake and woodland area. There are herbaceous borders and lawns around the house and a rose garden that leads to the woodland garden, then a more formal courtyard garden that leads through the barn to a kitchen garden. A limited number of tickets have been made available for this special rewilding event. Meet at the front of the house on the main drive for an introductory talk and guided tour with Ecologist, Tom Brereton, who has supported the Applebys on their work at Wyke Farm. The paths are gravel.

70 inpatients and their families are being supported at the newly opened Horatio's Garden Northern Ireland, thanks to the National Garden Scheme donations.

ESSEX

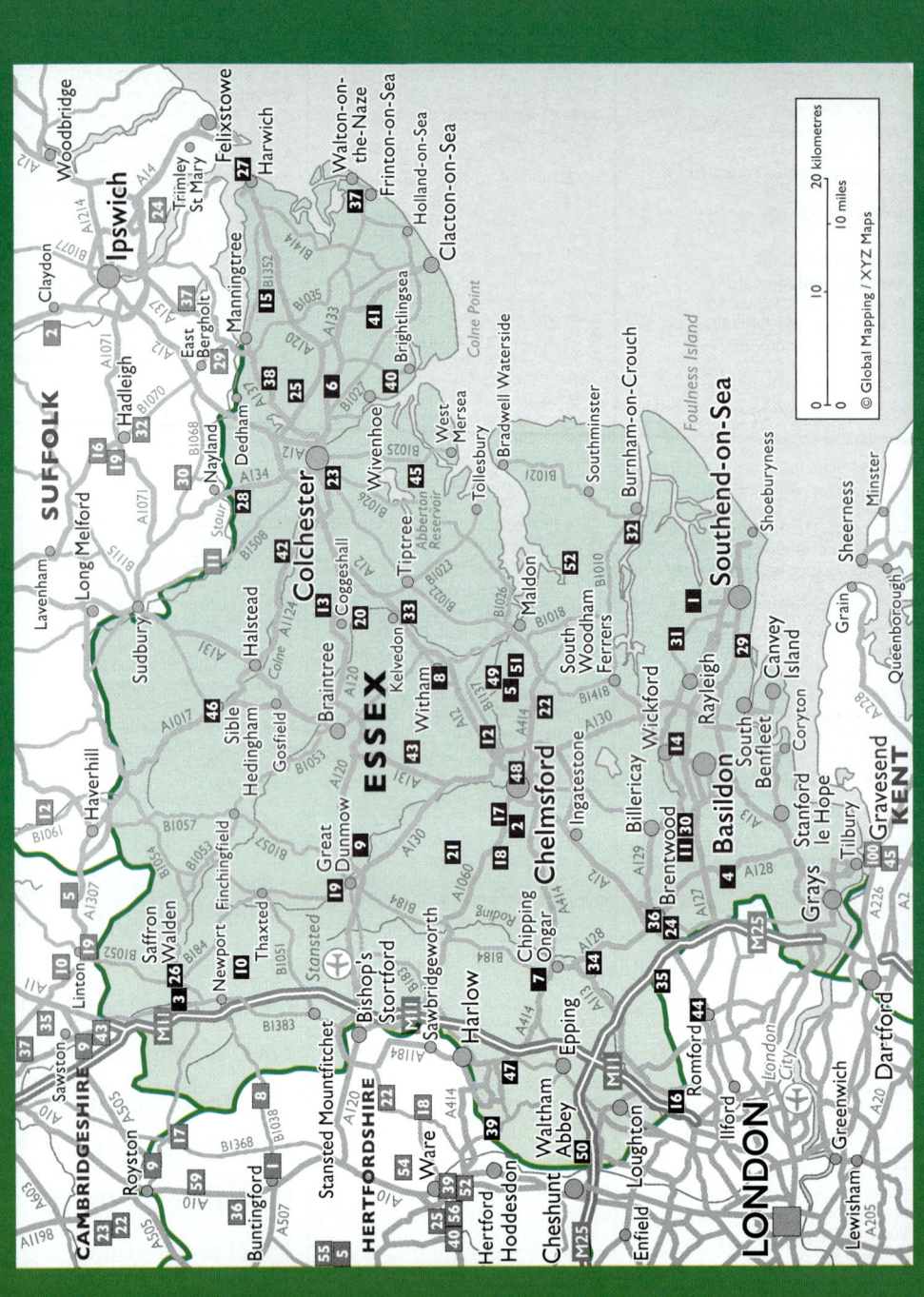

VOLUNTEERS

County Organiser
Victoria Kennedy 07801 039688
victoria.kennedy@ngs.org.uk

County Treasurer
Liz Grant 07852 383352
liz.grant@ngs.org.uk

Publicity & Social Media Co-ordinator
Debbie Thomson
07759 226579
debbie.thomson@ngs.org.uk

Social Media
Natasha Matthews
07962 120856
natasha.gallop@ngs.org.uk

By Arrangement Visit Co-ordinator
Alan Gamblin 07720 446797
alan.gamblin@ngs.org.uk

Booklet Co-ordinator
Tracey Field 07754 383764
tracey.field@ngs.org.uk

Assistant County Organisers
Tricia Brett 01255 870415
tricia.brett@ngs.org.uk

Avril & Roger Cole-Jones
01245 225726
randacj@gmail.com

Barbara Lewis 07508 011131
barbara.lewis@ngs.org.uk

Sharon Holdsworth
07721 528739
sharon.holdsworth@ngs.org.uk

Frances Vincent 07766 707379
frances.vincent@ngs.org.uk

Talks
Richard Wollaston 01245 231428
richard.wollaston@ngs.org.uk

County Photographer
Caroline Cassell 07973 551196
caroline.cassell@ngs.org.uk

@EssexNGS   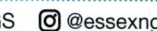 @essexngs

OPENING DATES

All entries subject to change.
For latest information check
www.ngs.org.uk
Extended openings are shown at the beginning of the month.
Map locator numbers are shown to the right of each garden name.

February

Snowdrop Openings

Saturday 7th
Horkesley Hall 28

Sunday 8th
◆ Green Island 25

Wednesday 11th
Horkesley Hall 28

Thursday 12th
Dragons 18

Friday 13th
Ulting Wick 49

Wednesday 18th
Dragons 18

Saturday 21st
Brookfield 12

Sunday 22nd
Brookfield 12
Grove Lodge 26

March

Sunday 8th
Anglia Ruskin University Writtle 2
Grove Lodge 26

Tuesday 17th
Ulting Wick 49

April

Every Thursday and Friday
Feeringbury Manor 20

Sunday 12th
2 Cedar Avenue 14

Tuesday 14th
◆ Beth Chatto's Plants & Gardens 6

Saturday 18th
NEW Kelvedon Hall, Brentwood 34

Sunday 19th
Ulting Wick 49

Friday 24th
Ulting Wick 49

Saturday 25th
◆ Green Island 25

May

Every Thursday and Friday
Feeringbury Manor 20

Sunday 3rd
Furzelea 22

Saturday 9th
Bassetts 5

Sunday 10th
NEW Ivy Cottage 30
The Old Rectory 43

Sunday 17th
The Gates 24
May Cottage 37
Oak Farm 42
1 Whitehouse Cottages 51

Sunday 24th
The Mount 39

Saturday 30th
NEW Bramble House 9
Mayfield Farm 38

Sunday 31st
NEW Bramble House 9
Oak Farm 42
Waltham Abbey Gardens 50

June

Every Thursday
Barnards Farm 4

Every Thursday and Friday
Feeringbury Manor 20

Saturday 6th
The Garden Studio 23
Isabella's Garden 29
NEW 46 Sandford Road 48

Sunday 7th
Blake Hall 7
Furzelea 22
The Garden Studio 23
Isabella's Garden 29

184 ESSEX

Wednesday 10th
8 Dene Court ... 17

Saturday 13th
NEW Broctons Farmhouse ... 10
Moverons ... 40

Sunday 14th
The Delves ... 16
Fudlers Hall ... 21
Grove Lodge ... 26
Moverons ... 40
Oak Farm ... 42

Thursday 18th
◆ Audley End House ... 3
1 Brook Cottage ... 11
NEW Ivy Cottage ... 30

Friday 19th
1 Brook Cottage ... 11
NEW Ivy Cottage ... 30

Saturday 20th
Allways ... 1
1 Brook Cottage ... 11

Sunday 21st
Chippins ... 15

Tuesday 23rd
8 Dene Court ... 17

Saturday 27th
18 Pettits Boulevard ... 44

Sunday 28th
Barnards Farm ... 4
2 Cedar Avenue ... 14
18 Pettits Boulevard ... 44

July

Every Thursday and Friday
Feeringbury Manor ... 20

Saturday 4th
69 Rundells - The Secret Garden ... 47

Sunday 5th
The Mount ... 39

Wednesday 8th
8 Dene Court ... 17
Long House Plants ... 35

Thursday 9th
Ulting Wick ... 49

Sunday 12th
Harwich Gardens ... 27

Sunday 19th
Oak Farm ... 42
1 Whitehouse Cottages ... 51

Friday 24th
8 Dene Court ... 17

Saturday 25th
Isabella's Garden ... 29

Sunday 26th
Isabella's Garden ... 29

Beth Chatto Garden

© Gary Morriscoe

The Mount

August

Wednesday 5th
Long House Plants　　　　　　35

Thursday 6th
8 Dene Court　　　　　　　　17

Saturday 22nd
8 Dene Court　　　　　　　　17
Kamala　　　　　　　　　　　31

Sunday 23rd
Kamala　　　　　　　　　　　31

Sunday 30th
Ulting Wick　　　　　　　　　49

September

Every Thursday and Friday
Feeringbury Manor　　　　　　20

Wednesday 2nd
Long House Plants　　　　　　35

Friday 4th
Ulting Wick　　　　　　　　　49

Saturday 5th
18 Pettits Boulevard　　　　　44

Sunday 6th
Oak Farm　　　　　　　　　　42
18 Pettits Boulevard　　　　　44

Sunday 13th
Furzelea　　　　　　　　　　22

Sunday 27th
NEW Broctons Farmhouse　　10

October

Every Thursday and Friday to Friday 16th
Feeringbury Manor　　　　　　20

Saturday 3rd
NEW Bramble House　　　　　9

Sunday 4th
NEW Bramble House　　　　　9
Elmbridge Mill　　　　　　　　19

Sunday 11th
♦ Green Island　　　　　　　25

Wednesday 14th
♦ Beth Chatto's Plants & Gardens　　　　　　　　　　6

By Arrangement

Arrange a personalised garden visit with your club, or group of friends, on a date to suit you. See individual garden entries for full details.

Bassetts　　　　　　　　　　　5
Blunts Hall　　　　　　　　　　8
1 Brook Cottage　　　　　　　11
Bucklers Farmhouse　　　　　13
2 Cedar Avenue　　　　　　　14
Chippins　　　　　　　　　　15

The Delves　　　　　　　　　16
8 Dene Court　　　　　　　　17
Feeringbury Manor　　　　　　20
Furzelea　　　　　　　　　　22
Grove Lodge　　　　　　　　26
Horkesley Hall　　　　　　　　28
Isabella's Garden　　　　　　　29
NEW Ivy Cottage　　　　　　　30
Keeway　　　　　　　　　　　32
Kelvedon Hall　　　　　　　　33
Loxley House　　　　　　　　36
May Cottage　　　　　　　　37
Mayfield Farm　　　　　　　　38
The Mount　　　　　　　　　39
Moverons　　　　　　　　　　40
Moynes Farm　　　　　　　　41
Oak Farm　　　　　　　　　　42
NEW Ransomes　　　　　　　45
Rookwoods　　　　　　　　　46
69 Rundells - The Secret Garden　　　　　　　　　　47
Silver Birches (Waltham Abbey Gardens)　　　　　　　　　　50
Ulting Wick　　　　　　　　　49
NEW 27 Worcester Close　　　52

THE GARDENS

1 ALLWAYS
14 St Andrews Road, Rochford, SS4 1NP. Ms Liz Grant. *Traverse down St Andrews Rd. The blue house can be found 100m on the R.* **Sat 20 June (11-4). Adm £6, chd free. Tea, coffee & cake.**
A cottage style garden of a Grade II listed 1930's home. A mature wisteria greets visitors on the front of the cottage. The rear garden has an area of lawn flanked by perennial borders with a viburnum arch leading to an attractive pond with Monet style bridge, pebbled beach area and a mature Indian Bean tree. A wildlife pond and bog garden was created in 2022 in the woodland area. After recently discovering some old steps leading down to the diverted River Roach, a new woodland area was opened in 2024.

2 ANGLIA RUSKIN UNIVERSITY WRITTLE
Lordship Road, Writtle, Chelmsford, CM1 3RR. Anglia Ruskin University Writtle, www.aru.ac.uk. *4m W of Chelmsford. Off A414, near Writtle village. Parking available on the main campus (student car park) clearly sign posted.* **Sun 8 Mar (10-3.30). Adm £5, chd free.**
Anglia Ruskin University Writtle has 15 acres of informal lawns with naturalised bulbs and wildflowers. Large tree collection, mixed shrubs, herbaceous border, dry/ Mediterranean borders, seasonal bedding and landscaped glasshouses. All gardens have been designed and built by our students studying a wide range of horticultural courses. Wheelchair access: some gravel, majority of areas accessible to all. Well behaved dogs on leads please.
&

3 ◆ AUDLEY END HOUSE
Off London Road, Saffron Walden, CB11 4JF. English Heritage, www.english-heritage.org.uk/visit/places/audley-end-house-and-gardens/events. *1m W of Saffron Walden on B1383 (M11 exit 8 or 10).* **For NGS: Evening opening Thur 18 June (5.30-7.30). Adm £20, chd free. Pre-booking essential, please email fundraising@english-heritage.org.uk or visit www.english-heritage.org.uk/visit/places/audley-end-house-and-gardens/events for information & booking. Light refreshments. For other opening times and information, please email or visit garden website.**
Audley End is a spectacular early C17 mansion set in an outstanding landscaped park. Stroll through a landscape designed and influenced by Capability Brown, later enhanced by William Sawry Gilpin. Highlights inc the intricately patterned Parterre laid out in 1832, restored in 1988, with shrubs, perennials, and annuals, plus an atmospheric organic Walled Kitchen Garden.

4 BARNARDS FARM
Brentwood Road, West Horndon, CM13 3FY. Bernard & Sylvia Holmes & The Christabella Charitable Trust, 07504 210405, vanessa@barnardsfarm.eu, www.barnardsfarm.eu. *5m S of Brentwood. On A128 1½ m S of A127 Halfway House flyover. From junc cont S on A128 under the railway bridge. Garden on R just past bridge. What3words app: tulip.folds.statue.* **Every Thur 4 June to 25 June (11-4.30). Sun 28 June (1-5.30). Adm £10, chd free. Light refreshments.**
So much to explore: Climb the Belvedere for the wider view and take the train for a woodland adventure. Summer beds and borders, ponds, lakes and streams, walled vegetable plot. 'Japanese garden', sculptures grand and quirky enhance and delight. Barnards Miniature Railway rides (BMR): Separate charges apply. Sunday extras: Bernard's Sculpture tour 2.30pm. Car collection. 1920s Cycle shop. Archery. Model T Ford Rides. Season Tickets cost £40. Aviators welcome (PPO). Picnics welcome. Wheelchair accessible WC. Golf Buggy tours available. An accessible carriage for wheelchair available on the railway. Guide dogs welcome.
&

5 BASSETTS
Bassetts Lane, Little Baddow, Chelmsford, CM3 4BZ. Mrs Margaret Chalmers, 07940 179572, magschalmers@btinternet.com. *1m down, Tofts Chase becomes Bassetts Ln. Yellow house on L, wooden gates, red brick wall. From Spring Elms Ln go down Bassetts Ln, L at the bottom of the hill. Cont for ¼ m.* **Sat 9 May (10-5). Adm £5, chd free. Visits also by arrangement 8 June to 16 Oct.**
A two acre garden, tennis court, swimming pool surrounding an early C17 house (not open) with plants for year-round interest set on gently sloping ground with lovely distant views of the Essex countryside. Shrub borders and mature ornamental trees, an orchard and two natural ponds. Many places to sit and relax. No refreshments but bring a picnic and enjoy the views. Please check wheelchair access with garden owner.
&

6 ◆ BETH CHATTO'S PLANTS & GARDENS
Elmstead Market, Colchester, CO7 7DB. Beth Chatto's Plants & Gardens, 01206 822007, customer@bethchatto.co.uk, www.bethchatto.co.uk. *¼ m E of Elmstead Market. On A133 Colchester to Clacton Rd in village of Elmstead Market.* **For NGS: Tue 14 Apr, Wed 14 Oct (10-4). Adm £15, chd free. Light refreshments at Chatto's Tearoom inc sandwiches, paninis, soup, salads, cakes, hot & cold beverages. For other opening times and information, please phone, email or visit garden website.**
Internationally famous gardens, inc dry, damp, shade, reservoir and woodland areas. The result of over 60 years of hard work and application of the huge body of plant knowledge possessed by Beth Chatto and her husband Andrew. Visitors cannot fail to be affected by the peace and beauty of the garden. Beth is renowned internationally for her books, her gardens and her influence on the world of gardening and plants. Picnic area in the adjacent field. Regret, no cash. Card payments only. Disabled WC and parking. Wheelchair access around all of the gardens on gravel or grass.

7 BLAKE HALL
Bobbingworth, CM5 0DG. Mr & Mrs H Capel Cure, www.blakehall.co.uk. *10m W of Chelmsford. Just off A414 between Four Wantz r'about in Ongar & Talbot r'about in N Weald. Signed on A414.* **Sun 7 June (10.30-4). Adm £6,**

chd free. Home-made teas in barn.
25 acres of mature gardens within the historic setting of Blake Hall (not open). Arboretum with broad variety of specimen and spectacular ancient trees, a ha-ha and original ice house. Lawns overlooking countryside. With its beautiful rose garden, stunning herbaceous border and magnificent rambling roses, June is a wonderful time of the year to visit the gardens at Blake Hall. Some gravel paths.

8 BLUNTS HALL
Blunts Hall Drive, Witham, CM8 1LX. Alan & Lesley Gamblin, 07720 446797, alan.gamblin@ngs.org.uk, www.bluntshallgarden.co.uk. Blunts Hall Dr is off of Blunts Hall Rd. **Visits by arrangement 5 May to 14 Aug for groups of 15 to 40. Adm £12, chd free. Cream teas. Discuss refreshments when booking.**
Restored three acre Victorian garden. Courtyard garden and terrace leading down to lawns with re-instated parterre surrounded by herbaceous borders. Orchard with old and new fruit trees and vegetable plot. Listed Ancient Monument. Woodland walk around spring-fed pond. Fernery. Steps lead down to front lawns recently planted with a yew avenue. Specimen trees.

9 NEW BRAMBLE HOUSE
Pound Hill, Little Dunmow, Dunmow, CM6 3HR. Mr & Mrs Joice. *12m N of Chelmsford. B1256 from Gt Dunmow/Braintree. Turn at Felsted/Lt Dunmow. Gdn is opp village sign. From Chelmsford via Felsted to Lt Dunmow take L after painted sign & park. What3words app: wolves.porridge.amaze.* **Sat 30, Sun 31 May, Sat 3, Sun 4 Oct (10-4). Adm £5, chd free. Tea, coffee & cake.**
This rural garden features a recently redesigned, south facing front courtyard. Herbaceous mixed borders with spring bulbs and autumnal colour. A large enclosed vegetable garden with potting shed and cold frames. A wildflower bank and woodland areas, mature trees, natural hedges and chemical free lawns. A redundant swimming pool area has been turned into a petanque pitch and gazebo. Petanque pitch for playing boules. Limited parking on driveway. Flat access to most of the garden on grass, gravel and paving. Steps to front garden and back patio.

10 NEW BROCTONS FARMHOUSE
Rook End Lane, Debden, Saffron Walden, CB11 3LR. Polly & Charles Turner. *4½ m from Saffron Walden, 12m from Bishops Stortford. Take B1383 to Newport, towards Debden. From Bishops Stortford take B1004 to Newport towards Debden. Cont on Debden Rd through village. Turn R onto Rook End Ln Broctons Farmhouse is on your R.* **Sat 13 June, Sun 27 Sept (11-4). Adm £6, chd free. Tea, coffee & cake.**
Discover 2¾ acre English country garden surrounding a Grade II listed farmhouse. Developed for year-round interest featuring a range of interesting plants divided by yew hedging. Features inc a hot garden with slate ball water feature, perennial grass garden, herbaceous garden, terrace, mini orchard, a tree lined walk to a Alitex greenhouse with cutting and vegetable beds. A large pond and plenty of seating throughout adds to the tranquility of this beautiful and inspiring garden. Wheelchair access to the vast majority of the garden.

11 1 BROOK COTTAGE
Laindon Common Road, Little Burstead, Billericay, CM12 9TA. Mr James Slocombe & Dr Benjamin Cooper, 07861 207667, jaslocombe@gmail.com, www.1brookcottage.com. *1m S of Billericay & 1m N of A127 (Basildon) Parking 200m from garden. Blue badge holders & those that need accessible parking, contact owner 24hrs in advance for priority parking. What3words app: rally.submit.beast.* **Thur 18, Fri 19 June (12-4). Combined adm with Ivy Cottage £13, chd free. Tea, coffee & cake. Evening opening Sat 20 June (6-9.30). Adm £7.50, chd free. Wine. Evening opening: BBQ, soft & alcoholic drinks available. Visits also by arrangement May to Sept.**
Traditional cottage front and back gardens, plus 3½ acre curtilage of meadow and woodland. Garden combines variety, colours and textures: find a profusion of roses, peonies, lilies and classic blooms interspersed with more exotic plants and flowers. Wander to find an amphitheatre, A-frame 'treehouse', campfire circle, summerhouse, vegetables and vines. Grounds invite exploration and contemplation. Particularly attractive for landscape/nature artists (easels welcome) and picnics.

12 BROOKFIELD
Church Road, Boreham, Chelmsford, CM3 3EB. Bob & Linda Taylor. *4m NE Chelmsford. Take B1137 Boreham village, turn R into Church Rd at Lion Inn. In approx ¼ m turning on R after The Chase marked 58-76 Church Rd. Pedestrians & disabled access only - please park nearby & walk down.* **Sat 21, Sun 22 Feb (11-4). Adm £5, chd free. Light refreshments.**
The gardens and meadow at Brookfield cover over three acres. Open only in February this year for snowdrops, crocus etc in the meadow and woodland areas. Wheelchair access to main part of garden. Partial access to meadow.

13 BUCKLERS FARMHOUSE
Buckleys Lane, Coggeshall, Colchester, CO6 1SB. Ann Bartleet, 01376 561505, ann@bartleet.co.uk. *1½ m E of Coggeshall. 1m N of A120 via Salmons Ln.* **Visits by arrangement 20 Apr to 12 June for groups of 15 to 35. Adm inc a talk and tour by the owner. Home-made teas in the traditional Essex barn or outdoors.**
Traditional country garden, with blowsy borders, yew hedges, topiary and a little knot garden. A very tranquil, magical place, with two ponds and a pool. In the spring we have about 1,000 tulips. Later, there is a terrace full of succulents, almost no room for sitting! This two acre garden has been created by the owners over the last 60 years. Half of the garden is wheelchair accessible.

The National Garden Scheme funded six Macmillan Nurses in their roles across England, Wales and Northern Ireland in 2025.

14 2 CEDAR AVENUE
Wickford, SS12 9DT. Chris Cheswright & Michael Bodman, 07910 585684, cheswright@blueyonder.co.uk. *Off Nevendon Rd, 5 mins from Wickford High St. From Basildon on A132 turn 1st exit onto Nevendon Rd at BP r'bout, R onto Park Dr, 2nd R Cedar Ave.* **Sun 12 Apr, Sun 28 June (11-4). Adm £6, chd free. Tea, coffee & cake.** Visits also by arrangement Apr to Aug for groups of 10 to 25. A large town garden with a dry front garden, pots arranged on a large patio. Large range of trees, shrubs, grasses and perennials. In spring species tulips, *Narcissus*, *Camassias* and other spring flowers adorn the garden. Later in the year hostas, carnivorous plants, tropical style plants and a large variety of hardy plants are on display outdoors and in four greenhouses. Areas for wildlife and a pond. Access via side of house. The majority of the garden is wheelchair accessible via a flat lawn area, although some paths are uneven.

& ❋ ☕ ⋅))

15 CHIPPINS
Heath Road, Bradfield, CO11 2UZ. Kit & Ceri Leese, 01255 870730, ceriandkit@gmail.com. *3m E of Manningtree. Take A137 from Manningtree Stn turn L opp garage. Take 1st R towards Clacton. At Radio Mast turn L into Bradfield cont through village. Bungalow opp primary sch on R.* **Sun 21 June (11-4). Adm £5, chd free.** Visits also by arrangement 23 May to 31 July for groups of 5 to 30. Afternoon tea with home-made cakes is available for small parties. Artist and plantaholic's paradise packed with interest. Hostas in huge pots. Plenty of places to sit and enjoy wildlife. Meandering stream and small ponds. An explosion of colour with daylilies, rambling roses, salvias, canna and dahlias. An abundance of tubs and hanging baskets in front garden. Studio and etching press in conservatory with paintings on show. Studio and press in conservatory with paintings on show. Kit is a landscape artist and printmaker, pictures always on display.

& ❋ 🚗 ☕ ⋅))

16 THE DELVES
37 Turpins Lane, Chigwell, IG8 8AZ. Fabrice Aru & Martin Thurston, 07932 137373, martin.thurston@talktalk.net. *Between Woodford & Epping. Chigwell, 2m from N Circular Rd at Woodford. Follow the signs for Chigwell (A113) through Woodford Bridge into Manor Rd & turn L. Bus 275 & W14 go past garden.* **Sun 14 June (11-6). Adm £5, chd free.** Visits also by arrangement 16 May to 11 Oct for groups of up to 8. An unexpected hidden, magical, part-walled garden showing how much can be achieved in a small space. An oasis of calm with densely planted rich, lush foliage, tree ferns, hostas, topiary and an abundance of well maintained shrubs complemented by a small pond and three water features designed for year-round interest. Please note that only 10 visitors can be accommodated in the garden at a time.

Green Island

© Gary Morrisroe

17 8 DENE COURT
Chignall Road, Chelmsford, CM1 2JQ. Mrs Sheila Chapman, 01245 266156. *W of Chelmsford (Parkway). Take A1060 Roxwell Rd for 1m. Turn R at T-lights into Chignall Rd. Dene Court 3rd exit on R. Parking in Chignall Rd.* **Wed 10, Tue 23 June, Wed 8, Fri 24 July, Thur 6, Sat 22 Aug (12-4). Adm £4, chd free.** Visits also by arrangement 1 June to 15 Sept for groups of 12 to 40.
Beautifully maintained and designed as a compact garden. Owner is well-known RHS gold medal-winning exhibitor (now retired). Circular lawn, long pergola and walls festooned with roses and climbers. Large selection of unusual clematis. Densely-planted colour coordinated perennials add interest from June to Sept in this immaculate garden.

18 DRAGONS
Boyton Cross, Chelmsford, CM1 4LS. Mrs Margot Grice. *3m W of Chelmsford. On A1060. ½m W of The Hare Pub.* **Thur 12, Wed 18 Feb (11-3). Adm £5, chd free.** Pre-booking essential, please visit www.ngs.org.uk for information & booking. Tea, coffee & cake.
Galanthus are a passion. A plantswoman's ¾ acre garden, planted to encourage wildlife. Sumptuous colour-themed borders with striking plant combinations, featuring specimen plants, fernery, clematis and grasses. Meandering paths lead to ponds, patio, scree garden and small vegetable garden. Two summerhouses, one overlooking stream and farmland.

19 ELMBRIDGE MILL
Little Easton, Dunmow, CM6 2HZ. Cilla Swan. *N of Great Dunmow, B184.* **Sun 4 Oct (12-4). Adm £5, chd free. Tea, coffee & cake.**
A beautiful, tranquil and romantic, country garden full of topiary, unusual plants and specimen trees. Elmbridge Mill (not open) with mill stream, one side flowing under the house, and the River Chelmer on the other. Explore the orchard, productive vegetable garden and walk down to the mill pond. Beautiful autumn colours.

20 FEERINGBURY MANOR
Coggeshall Road, Feering, CO5 9RB. Mr & Mrs Giles Coode-Adams, 01376 561946, seca@btinternet.com. *Between Feering & Coggeshall, on Coggeshall Rd, 1m from Feering village.* **Every Thur and Fri 2 Apr to 31 July (10-4). Every Thur and Fri 3 Sept to 16 Oct (10-4). Adm £6, chd free.** Visits also by arrangement for groups of up to 30. Donation to Feering Church.
There is always plenty to see in this peaceful 10 acre garden with two ponds and River Blackwater. Jewelled lawn in early April then spectacular blossom lead on to a huge number of different and colourful herbaceous plants, many unusual, culminating in a purple explosion of michaelmas daisies in late September. No wheelchair access to arboretum due to steep slope.

21 FUDLERS HALL
Fox Road, Mashbury, CM1 4TJ. Mr & Mrs A J Meacock. *7m NW of Chelmsford. Chelmsford take A1060, R into Chignal Rd. ½m turn L to Chignal St James. Approx 5m, 2nd R into Fox Rd signed Gt Waltham. Fudlers From Gt Waltham. Take Barrack Ln for 3m.* **Sun 14 June (2-5). Adm £6, chd free. Home-made teas.**
Award winning, romantic two acre garden surrounding C17 farmhouse with lovely views. Many long herbaceous borders, ropes and pergolas festooned with rambling, perfumed, old fashioned roses. The entire garden has been designed and planted by the current owners over 45 years and is now a quintessential example of an English country garden. Wonderful views across Chelmer Valley. Two new flower beds, many roses. 500 year old yew tree. Wheelchair access: gravel farmyard and 30ft path to gardens, all of which is level lawn.

22 FURZELEA
Bicknacre Road, Danbury, CM3 4JR. Avril & Roger Cole-Jones, 01245 225572, randacj@gmail.com. *4m E of Chelmsford, 4m W of Maldon. S off A414 in Danbury follow yellow signs. At village centre, go S onto Mayes Ln 1st R past Cricketers Pub. Turn L & NT car park immed on L, garden on R 50metres. Check NGS website* before visiting. **Sun 3 May, Sun 7 June, Sun 13 Sept (11-5). Adm £6, chd free. Tea, coffee & cake. Gluten free available.** Visits also by arrangement 13 Apr to 30 Sept for groups of 15 to 50.
Country garden of just under an acre designed, planted and maintained by the owners over time to showcase the seasons with colour, scent, and form. Paths lead through archways and box hedging to lawns and flower beds amassed with seasonal planting of shrubs, roses, and herbaceous perennials, bulbs and dahlias. Tulips, salvias and grasses of particular interest along with many unusual plants. Black and White Garden plus exotics add to the visitors interest. Short walk to Danbury Country Park and Lakes and short drive to RHS Hyde Hall Plants and metal plant supports are for sale.

23 THE GARDEN STUDIO
30 Gladwin Road, Colchester, CO2 7HS. Andrea Parsons MSGD & Kevin Looker, www.andreaparsons.co.uk. *1m from Colchester centre. There is plenty of street parking.* **Sat 6, Sun 7 June (10-5). Adm £5, chd free. Tea, coffee & cake.**
A beautiful south facing garden evolved over the years from family garden to studio garden. A backdrop of large trees in the neighbouring gardens frames the view and beech hedges and clipped yew makes the garden feel more extensive than it is. A stunning art studio exhibiting both Andrea's artwork and her award winning garden designs is hidden amongst the rich planting and lovely seating areas. With five Chelsea Flower Show medals to her name Andrea will be available to discuss design ideas and answer questions about visitors own gardens.

Our donation to Marie Curie this year is equivalent to 17,521 hours of hospice at home care.

24 THE GATES
London Road Cemetery, London Road, Brentwood, CM14 4QW. Ms Mary Yiannoullou, www.frontlinepartnership.org. *Enter the Cemetery (opp Tesco Express). Drive to the rear of the cemetery, our garden is on L. Limited parking within but plenty on the surrounding roads.* **Sun 17 May (11-3). Adm £4, chd free. Light refreshments at tea hut with covered seating and indoor shop. A selection of home-made cakes, bacon rolls and a veggie option.**

A horticultural project that offers adults with a learning disability an opportunity to develop new skills within a horticultural setting. You will be able to visit our greenhouses, allotments, various gardens and seating areas, The Dell and our tearoom/classroom. There will be a large variety of plants, produce and craft for sale. Our ethos is reclaim and recycle. Everything on site has been sustainably built, modified and planted by the team. In addition to the permanent structures, we have numerous gardens, seating areas, wildlife friendly spaces, water features, art installations and creative ideas around the site. Good wheelchair access via slopes and ramps to the majority of the site.

25 ◆ GREEN ISLAND
Park Road, Ardleigh, CO7 7SP. Fiona Edmond, 01206 230455, greenislandgardens@gmail.com, www.greenislandgardens.co.uk. *3m NE of Colchester. From Ardleigh village centre, take B1029 towards Great Bromley. Park Rd is 2nd on R after level X-ing. Garden is last on L.* **For NGS: Sun 8 Feb, Sat 25 Apr, Sun 11 Oct (11-4). Adm £10, chd £3.50. Light lunches and refreshments available in the tearoom. Picnics welcome in the car park area only.** For other opening times and information, please phone, email or visit garden website. Donation to Plant Heritage.

A garden for all seasons, highlights inc bluebells, azaleas, autumn colour, winter *Hamamelis* and snowdrops. A plantsman's paradise. Carved within 20 acre mature woodland are huge island beds, Japanese garden, terrace, gravel, seaside and water gardens, all packed with rare and unusual plants. Flat and easy walking or pushing wheelchairs. Ramps at entrance and tearoom. Disabled parking and WC.

26 GROVE LODGE
3 Chater's Hill, Saffron Walden, CB10 2AB. Chris Shennan, 01799 522271, cds.2022@icloud.com. *Approx 10 mins walk from town centre. Facing the Common on E side, about 100yds from the turf maze. Note: Chater's Hill is one way.* **Sun 22 Feb, Sun 8 Mar, Sun 14 June (2-5). Adm £6, chd free. Home-made teas. Visits also by arrangement 2 Jan to 22 Dec.**

A large walled garden close to the town centre with unusually high biodiversity (e.g. 20 species of butterfly recorded) close to the turf maze and Norman castle. Semi woodland on light free draining chalk soil allows bulbs, hellebores and winter flowering shrubs to thrive. Two ponds, topiary and orchard blend some formality with informal areas where wildlife thrives. A profusion of winter aconites, snowdrops, other bulbs and spring blossom. Lots of seating from which to enjoy the garden. Wheelchair access via fairly steep drive leading to terrace from which the garden may be viewed.

GROUP OPENING

27 HARWICH GARDENS
Harwich, CO12 3NH. *Centre of Old Harwich. Car park on Wellington Rd (CO12 3DT) within 50 metres of St Helens Green. Street parking available.* **Sun 12 July (11-4). Combined adm £5, chd free. Light refreshments inc tea, coffee and cake at 8 St Helens Green.**

63 CHURCH STREET
Sue & Richard Watts.

38 HARBOUR CRESCENT
Alan & Sue Edgar.

42 KINGS QUAY STREET
Mrs Elizabeth Crame.

QUAYSIDE COURT
Dave Burton.

8 ST HELENS GREEN
Frances Vincent.

All different gardens are within walking distance in the historical town of Harwich with their own special identity. 8 St Helens Green, just 100 metres from the sea, is a small town garden with roses, dahlias, hydrangeas and agapanthus mixed with perennials and many pots. 38 Harbour Crescent has an eastern theme. A long narrow garden that gives the impression of a much larger secluded garden. Filled with trees, shrubs, water features and many seating areas. Quayside Court, a community garden, unusually boasts a sunken garden hidden from view at the end of the car park which features a wall mural, pond, vegetable patch, roses and climbers. New additions inc a pergola and greenhouse. 42 Kings Quay Street courtyard garden is behind a Grade II listed house. Raised brick beds incorporate established plants such as a grape vine, David Austin roses, tree peony and a combination of edible and ornamental plants. 63 Church Street is a long, narrow walled courtyard with shrubs, climbers, perennials and a small vegetable plot packed into the garden. All feature historical elements or historic views. There will be an art display at 8 St Helens Green with commission to the National Garden Scheme on any purchases.

28 HORKESLEY HALL
Vinesse Road, Little Horkesley, Colchester, CO6 4DB. Mr & Mrs Johnny Eddis, 07808 599290, horkesleyhall@hotmail.com, www.airbnb.co.uk/rooms/10354093. *6m N of Colchester City Centre. 2m W of A134, 10 mins from A12. On Vinesse Rd, look for the grass triangle with tree, turn into Lt Horkesley Church car park. Go to gates beyond church. What3words app: incline.long.utensil.* **Sat 7 Feb (1-4); Wed 11 Feb (11-4). Adm £6, chd free. Home-made teas in St Peter & St Paul's Church. Soups, home-made cakes, bacon rolls & hot drinks. Visits also by arrangement for groups of 8 to 20.**

Traditional English garden of several acres of romantic family garden surrounding classical house overlooking two lakes. Major 20ft balancing stones sculpture, topiary and exceptional trees. A developing snowdrop collection and winter walk with an excellent plant stall and wonderful teas in the warm church next to the house. Owls can invariably be heard close by later in the afternoon. This garden inspired the foundation of Parasol-UK which is proud to donate a percentage of all parasol sales to the National Garden Scheme as an official partner. Partial wheelchair access in areas with easy access to refreshments. Some gravel paths and slopes.

29 ISABELLA'S GARDEN
42 Theobalds Road, Leigh-on-Sea, SS9 2NE. Mrs Elizabeth Isabella Ling-Locke, 07366 766986, ling_locke@yahoo.co.uk. *From London, take A13 towards Southend on Sea. As you pass 'Welcome to Leigh-on-Sea' sign, turn R at T-lights onto Thames Dr, then L onto Western Rd. Carry on 0.6m then R onto Theobalds Rd.* **Sat 6, Sun 7 June, Sat 25, Sun 26 July (12-4.30). Adm £6, chd free. Cream teas. Wide range of home-made cakes and cream teas inc gluten free and vegan options. Visits also by arrangement June & July for groups of 12 to 40. By arrangement visits adm inc refreshments.**
This enchanting town garden is bursting with a profusion of colour from early spring through to the autumn months. Roses, clematis, agapanthus, herbaceous plants, alpines, pots with unusual succulents and cacti fill every corner of this garden. There is a wildlife pond, water features as well as many other garden features which are to be found hiding within the shrubbery and throughout the garden. This garden is situated in Leigh on Sea, and just a five min walk from the cockle sheds of Old Leigh and Leigh railway station. Step free access to the majority of the garden. There are steps near the house.

30 NEW IVY COTTAGE
Laindon Common Road, Little Burstead, Billericay, CM12 9TB. Peter & Christabel Strong, 07948 350511, christabelstrong@icloud.com. *1m S of Billericay, 1m N of A127/Basildon. Parking 200m from garden. Blue badge holders or those that need accessible parking, contact owner 24hrs in advance for priority parking. What3words app: force. shall.outer.* **Sun 10 May (12-4). Adm £7.50, chd free. Thur 18, Fri 19 June (12-4). Combined adm with 1 Brook Cottage £13, chd free. Tea, coffee & cake on combined openings, refreshments served at 1 Brook Cottage. Visits also by arrangement for groups of 6 to 16. Possible to also combine with 1 Brook Cottage.**
Cottage garden presenting a mixture of herbaceous, annual and climbing plants in a garden of 1½ acres. With borrowed views and mature (250 yrs+) trees, providing a tranquil space to enjoy wildlife attracted by a large water lily pond. A haven for birds, butterflies and bees. Herbaceous borders, a dry garden and dell make this a garden to quietly reflect, take photographs or have a picnic. Particularly attractive for landscape and nature artists (easels welcome) and picnics.

18 Pettits Boulevard

Ivy Cottage

31 KAMALA
262 Main Road, Hawkwell, Hockley, SS5 4NW. Karen Mann. *3m NE of Rayleigh. From A127 at Rayleigh Weir take B1013 towards Hockley. Garden on L after White Hart Pub & village green.* **Sat 22, Sun 23 Aug (11-4). Adm £6, chd free. Tea, coffee & cake.**
Spectacular herbaceous borders which sing with colour as displays of salvia are surpassed by dahlia drifts. Gingers, *Brugmansia*, various bananas, bamboos and *Canna* add an exotic note. Grasses sway above the blooms, giving movement. Rest in the rose clad pergola while listening to the two Amazon parrots in the aviary. The garden features an RHS accredited dahlia named 'Jake Mann'. Trees and shrubs inc acers, *Catalpa aurea*, *Cercis* 'Forest Pansy' and a large unusual *Sinocalycanthus* (Chinese Allspice) a stunning, rare plant with fantastic flowers.

☕ 🔊

32 KEEWAY
Ferry Road, Creeksea, nr Burnham-on-Crouch, CM0 8PL. John & Sue Ketteley, 01621 782083, sueketteley@hotmail.com. *2m W of Burnham-on-Crouch. B1010 to Burnham on Crouch. At town sign take 1st R into Ferry Rd signed Creeksea & Burnham Golf Club. NGS sign at gate.* **Visits by arrangement June & July for groups of 10+. Plants for sale. Adm £10, chd free. Tea, coffee & cake.**
Large, mature country garden with stunning views over the River Crouch. Formal terraces surround the house with steps leading to sweeping lawns, mixed borders packed full of bulbs and perennials, formal rose and herb garden with interesting water feature. Further afield there are wilder areas, paddocks and lake. A productive greenhouse, vegetable and cutting gardens complete the picture.

33 KELVEDON HALL
Kelvedon Hall Lane, Kelvedon, Colchester, CO5 9BN. Mr & Mrs Jack Inglis, 07973 795955, v_inglis@btinternet.com, www.instagram.com/kelvedonhallgarden. *Nr Colchester. Take Maldon Rd towards Great Braxted from Kelvedon High St. Go over R Blackwater bridge & bridge over A12. At T-junc turn R onto Kelvedon Rd. Take 1st L, sign for KH, a single gravel road ³⁄₄ m.* **Visits by arrangement 1 Apr to 26 June for groups of 18 to 40. Adm £12.50, chd free. Home-made teas in the Courtyard Garden or the Pool Walled Garden (weather permitting). Please discuss refreshments when booking.**
Varied six acre garden surrounding a gorgeous C18 house. A blend of formal and informal spaces interspersed with modern sculpture. Pleached hornbeam, yew and box topiary provide structure. A courtyard walled garden juxtaposes a modern walled pool garden, both providing season long displays. Herbaceous borders offset an abundance of roses around the house. Lily covered ponds with a wet garden.

34 NEW KELVEDON HALL, BRENTWOOD
Kelvedon Hall Lane, Kelvedon Hatch, Brentwood, CM14 5TN. Mrs Katie Channon. *7m from Shenfield stn. Large white arch with gatehouses. From Brentwood on A128: on L after the Secret Nuclear Bunker. From Ongar or London on A128: on R after the garden centre. What3words app: stared.riders.oufit.* **Sat 18 Apr (10.30-4). Adm £7, chd free. Tea, coffee & cake.**
An extraordinary ancient untouched woodland with self seeded bluebells,

beautiful trees left to grow wild with a path carefully opened around the entire wood. A unique swimming pool put in by Chips Channon and a bordered back garden.

35 LONG HOUSE PLANTS

Church Road, Noak Hill, Romford, RM4 1LD. Tim Carter, www.longhouseplants.com. *3½m NW of J28, M25. Take A1023 Brentwood. At 1st T-lights, turn L to S Weald. After ⅘m turn L at T-junc. Travel 1⅗m & turn L, over M25. ½m turn R into Church Rd, nursery opp church. Disabled Car Parking. Please note: these directions avoid ULEZ.* **Wed 8 July, Wed 5 Aug, Wed 2 Sept (11-4). Adm £7, chd £3. Tea, coffee & cake.**

A beautiful garden- yes, but one with a purpose. Long House Plants has been producing homegrown plants for 20 years and here is a chance to see where it all begins. With wide paths and plenty of seats carefully placed to enjoy the plants and views. It has been thoughtfully designed so that the collections of plants look great together through all seasons. Paths are suitable for wheelchairs and mobility scooters. Disabled WC in nursery. Two cobbled areas not suitable but alternative routes.

36 LOXLEY HOUSE

49 Robin Hood Road, Brentwood, CM15 9EL. Robert & Helen Smith, 07740 124034, owfc@talktalk.net. *1m N of Brentwood town centre. On A128 N towards Ongar turn R at mini r'about onto Doddinghurst Rd. Take the 1st road on L into Robin Hood Rd. 2 houses before the bend on L.* **Visits by arrangement 1 May to 13 Sept for groups of 10 to 30. Adm £10, chd free. Tea, coffee & cake.**

On entering you will be surprised and delighted by this town garden. A colourful patio with pots and containers. Steps up onto a lawn with circular beds surrounded by hedges, herbaceous borders, trees and climbers. Two water features, one a Japanese theme and another with ferns in a quiet seating area. The garden is planted to offer colour throughout the seasons.

37 MAY COTTAGE

19 Walton Road, Kirby-Le-Soken, Frinton-on-Sea, CO13 0DU. Julie Abbey, 07885 875822, jools.abbey@hotmail.com. *Garden is on B1034. 2m before Walton on Naze. ¼m after Red Lion pub & on the same side of road.* **Sun 17 May (11-4). Adm £5, chd free. Tea, coffee & cake. Visits also by arrangement 18 May to 31 May for groups of 6+.**

Over the years this garden has been transformed from a blank canvas to a cottage garden with a wide variety of planting often grown from cuttings and an eclectic mix of artefacts. From the lawn, leads a path to the bakers oven, a small structure that is over 100 years old and is a writing room. There are three ponds and a stream, summerhouse and greenhouse.

38 MAYFIELD FARM

Hungerdown Lane, Ardleigh, CO7 7LZ. Ed Fairey & Jennifer Hughes, 01206 230883, jen@faireyassociates.co.uk. *3½m NE of Colchester. From Ardleigh village centre cont on the A137 to Manningtree. 3rd R, Tile Barn Ln. R again Hungerdown Ln. 500yds garden on R.* **Sat 30 May (10-4). Adm £12, chd free. Tea, coffee & cake. Visits also by arrangement Apr to Aug for groups of 15 to 40.**

Mayfield Farm is a seven acre garden which only a few years ago was largely a field, with a huge glasshouse and polytunnels. Now filled with many beautiful beds and borders, we have also created a secret garden and planted yew hedging for topiary. Over a 100,000 bulbs have been planted in the garden during the past few years to create a wonderful spring display. Always a new and exciting project being undertaken. Mostly flat but areas of gravel, grass and paddock for parking.

39 THE MOUNT

Epping Road, Roydon, Harlow, CM19 5HT. David & Liz Davison, 07711 231555, david.t.davison@gmail.com. *300 metres W of the junc with High Street. From Harlow, pass the High Street on your R. 300metres you will see yellow signs on R. From the stn, turn R at T-Junc. 300 metres on R.* **Sun 24 May, Sun 5 July (11-6). Adm £7, chd free. Tea, coffee & cake. Visits also by arrangement for groups of 15+. Adm £10 inc refreshments.**

The garden is set in a total of eight acres. Three acres of formal gardens and five acres woodland planted in 2003. The formal gardens are divided into nine separate areas. The lawns are edged with mixed planting for different seasons from snowdrops, spring bulb displays through the summer plants and shrubs. There are many surprising statues and sculptures throughout the grounds. Fully accessible for wheelchairs and scooter users. There are two steps to WC. Regret no WC access for wheelchair users.

40 MOVERONS

Brightlingsea, CO7 0SB. Lesley & Payne Gunfield, lesleyorrock@me.com. *7m SE of Colchester. On B1029 to Brightlingsea turn R at the old church signed Moverons Farm. Follow lane & garden signs for approx 1m.* **Sat 13, Sun 14 June (10-5). Adm £6, chd free. Home-made teas. Visits also by arrangement 29 May to 30 Sept for groups of 10+.**

Tranquil four acre garden in touch with its surroundings and stunning estuary views. A wide variety of planting in mixed borders to suit different growing conditions. Large natural ponds, plenty of seating areas, unusual water feature, sculpture and art exhibition. Sit in our barn for rainy day teas. Magnificent trees some over 300 years old give this garden real presence. Most of the garden is wheelchair accessible via grass and gravel paths. There are some steps and bark paths.

41 MOYNES FARM

Wick Road, Great Bentley, Colchester, CO7 8RA. Veronica Strucelj & Jim Carr, 07538 604947, verostrucelj@icloud.com. *NE Essex. 9m SE from Colchester towards Clacton on Sea. 2m from Great Bentley, between Aingers Green & Weeley Heath.* **Visits by arrangement June to Sept for groups of 10 to 30. Light refreshments.**

A traditional, large country garden and four acre woodland with walks. Vibrant planting, mature trees, shrubs and perennials. A formal courtyard area with box parterre maze, rose garden, wildlife pond and parkland.

194 ESSEX

42 OAK FARM
Vernons Road, Wakes Colne, Colchester, CO6 2AH. Ann & Peter Chillingworth, 01206 240230, chillingworthpeter23@gmail.com. *6m NW of Colchester. Vernons Rd off A1124, halfway between Ford St & Chappel. From Colchester, 3rd R after t-lights at Ford St bridge; Oak Farm is 200m up on R. From Halstead, 2nd L after Chappel viaduct.* **Sun 17, Sun 31 May, Sun 14 June, Sun 19 July, Sun 6 Sept (2-4.30). Adm £5, chd free. Home-made teas.** Visits also by arrangement 11 May to 11 Sept for groups of 10 to 25.
Informal farmhouse garden of about an acre on an exposed site. Garden designed to make most of stunning views across Colne Valley to south and west, framed to north by listed house and farmyard. Trees, shrubs, borders, roses and secret garden at best in early and mid summer. Prairie garden, salvias and dahlias come into their own in late summer to early autumn. Wheelchair access to most of the garden. Steps in places.

43 THE OLD RECTORY
Boreham Road, Great Leighs, Chelmsford, CM3 1PP. Pauline & Neil Leigh-Collyer. *Approx ½ m outside the village of Great Leighs. From Boreham village (J19 off A12) turn into Waltham Rd & travel about 5m, Garden on L. From Great Leighs travel on Boreham Rd for ¾ m, garden on R.* **Sun 10 May (12-4.30). Adm £7.50, chd free. Tea, coffee & cake.**
Wander around four acres of mature gardens surrounded by open countryside. Aspects inc herbaceous borders, a delightful courtyard, lake, fountain and sweeping lawns. Wander through arched walkways and discover many specimen trees. Beautiful wisteria climbing along the house. Many seating areas to enjoy alternative vistas. Extensive car parking available on grass off the main road. Picnics allowed. Main areas accessible for wheelchairs. Some areas limited by gravel paths and steps.

44 18 PETTITS BOULEVARD
Rise Park, Romford, RM1 4PL. Peter & Lynn Nutley. *From M25 take A12 towards London, turn R at Pettits Ln junc then R again into Pettits Blvd or Romford Stn. 103 or 499 bus to Romford Fire Stn & yellow signs.* **Sat 27, Sun 28 June, Sat 5, Sun 6 Sept (1-5). Adm £5, chd free.**
The garden is on three levels with an ornamental pond, patio area with shrubs and perennials, many in pots. Large eucalyptus tree leads to a woodland themed area with many ferns and hostas. There are agricultural implements and garden ornaments giving a unique and quirky feel to the garden. Tranquil seating areas situated throughout.

45 NEW RANSOMES
Wigborough Road, Peldon, Colchester, CO5 7RA. Andrew & Nicky Ellis, 07768 986611, andrew@essexguesthouse.co.uk, www.essexguesthouse.co.uk. *7m S of Colchester. On the Wigborough Rd on the outskirts of Peldon (3rd house on R as you enter the village). What3words app: storming.lakes.breakfast.* **Visits by arrangement 1 May to 11 Sept for groups of 10 to 30. Discuss refreshments when booking. Car sharing needed for larger groups. Adm £10, chd free. Home-made teas.**
A two acre country garden with a focus on biodiversity. The colourful cottage garden leads to a meadow and young tree shelter belt. Wildflower meadows, dead hedging, log piles and a large lily pond create a haven for wildlife. An orchard, soft-fruit garden, an apiary and a productive vegetable garden with greenhouse and potting shed provide both homegrown produce and a plant nursery for the garden.

46 ROOKWOODS
Yeldham Road, Sible Hedingham, CO9 3QG. Peter & Sandra Robinson, 07770 957111, sandy1989@btinternet.com, www.rookwoodsgarden.com. *8m NW of Halstead. From Haverhill/ A1017: take 1st R after 30mph sign. From Braintree: turn L before the 40mph sign, leaving the village.* **Visits by arrangement May to Sept for groups of up to 25. Adm £7, chd free. Home-made teas.**
Arriving at the garden there is no need to walk far. You can linger over tea, under a dreamy wisteria canopy while enjoying views across the garden. If a good walk appeals, there is not only the herbaceous borders to walk through, a beautiful meadow leads to an eight acre oak wood and there are grassy paths mown though the rest of the garden shaded by a variety of mature and teenage trees. Wheelchair access over gravel drive.

47 69 RUNDELLS - THE SECRET GARDEN
Harlow, CM18 7HD. Mr & Mrs K Naunton, 07981 882448, k_naunton@hotmail.com. *3m from M11 J7. A414 exit T-lights take L exit Southern Way, mini r'about 1st exit Trotters Rd leading into Commonside Rd, after shops on L, 3rd L into Rundells.* **Sat 4 July (2-5). Adm £4, chd free. Tea, coffee & cake.** Visits also by arrangement June to Aug for groups of up to 20.
69 Rundells is a very colourful, small town garden packed with a wide variety of shrubs, perennials, herbaceous and bedding plants in over 200 assorted containers. Hard landscaping on different levels has a summerhouse, water features and various seating areas to sit and take in the garden. A small fairy garden has been added to give interest for younger visitors. The garden is next to a large allotment and this is open to view with lots of interesting features inc a bee apiary. Honey and other produce for sale (conditions permitting).

48 NEW 46 SANDFORD ROAD
Chelmsford, CM2 6DQ. Mrs Anne Eisenberg. *1m N of Chelmsford City Centre. Sandford Rd adjoins Chelmer Village retail park, just off the A138. The property is ¼ m from the A138 junc. What3words app: slower.giant.audio.* **Sat 6 June (10-4). Adm £5, chd free. Tea, coffee & cake. Soft drinks, and gluten-free biscuits and cakes will also be available.**
The garden is densely planted with a strong Japanese influence. There are three areas: deck and patio with large grapevine over a pergola. Acers, roses and grasses in pots. Middle section has bamboos, roses and acers and the final section is accessed via a bridge over a koi pond with gunnera, darmera. Also a pergola and ferns. It is wildlife friendly, so wildflowers and some weeds are encouraged.

49 ULTING WICK
Crouchmans Farm Road, Ulting, Maldon, CM9 6QX. Mr & Mrs B Burrough, 07984 614947, philippa.burrough@btinternet.com, www.ultingwickgarden.co.uk. *3m NW of Maldon. Take R turn to Ulting off B1019 as you exit Hatfield Peverel by a green. Garden on R after 2m. Please note: Garden still accessible through roadworks on Maldon Rd. Please ignore closure signs.* **Fri 13 Feb (2-5). Adm £15. Pre-booking essential, please visit www.ngs.org.uk for information & booking. Tue 17 Mar (11-4). Adm £10. Pre-booking essential, please visit www.ngs.org.uk for information & booking. Sun 19, Fri 24 Apr, Thurs 9 July, Sun 30 Aug, Fri 4 Sept (2-5). Adm £7.50, chd free. Home-made teas. For March opening, home-made soup & rolls will be offered alongside cakes. Visits also by arrangement 16 Feb to 1 Oct for groups of 15+. Tea, coffee & home-made cake is provided. Donation to All Saints Ulting Church.**
Listed black barns provide backdrop for vibrant and exuberant planting in eight acres. Snowdrops, narcissus, tulips, flowing innovative spring planting, herbaceous borders, pond, mature weeping willows, kitchen garden, dramatic late summer beds with zingy, tender, exotic plant combinations. Drought tolerant perennial and mini annual wildflower meadows. Woodland. Many plants propagated in-house. Unusual plants for sale. Beautiful walks along the River Chelmer from the garden. Walk and Talk by Head Gardener in February and March. This garden is proud to have provided plants for the National Garden Scheme's Show Garden at Chelsea Flower Show 2024. Some gravel around the house but main areas of interest are accessible for wheelchairs.

&♿ 🐎 ❀ 🚗 ☕

GROUP OPENING

50 WALTHAM ABBEY GARDENS
Waltham Abbey, EN9 1LG. *M25, J26 to Waltham Abbey. At T-lights by McD turn R to r'about. Take 2nd exit to next r'about. Take 3rd exit (A112) to T-lights. L to Monkswood Av.* **Sun 31 May (11.30-5). Combined adm £7, chd free. Tea, coffee & cake at Silver Birches. Regret, cash only.**

THE CHIMES, 3-4 CHURCH STREET
Caroline Moores.

NEW 34 MONKSWOOD AVENUE
Diane & Bill Munro.

76 MONKSWOOD AVENUE
Dan Gallagher.

SILVER BIRCHES
Frank & Linda Jewson, 01992 714047, frank.jewson@btconnect.com. **Visits also by arrangement May to Sept for groups of 10 to 20.**

Come and visit our four gardens in the historic town of Waltham Abbey. Silver Birches, Quendon Drive has three lawns surrounded by mixed borders with mature shrubs and trees. The pond is home to much wildlife. Take a short stroll in the hidden woodland walk before enjoying tea and home-made cake. At 76 Monkswood Avenue, there are mixed borders, a greenhouse and wildlife pond. You may also be tempted to purchase one of the many Victorian chimney pots which add another dimension for displaying plants in the garden and are available for purchase in the wildlife friendly front garden. At 34 Monkswood Avenue you will be greeted by a very pretty front garden, the lawn surrounded by colourful planting, make your way through to the garden at the rear and enjoy the bee friendly planting and shrubs here. The fourth garden, The Chimes, a Grade II listed house (not open) built in 1537 has brick-edged raised borders around a gravel area and planted with perennials and shrubs. There is partial wheelchair access to one part of the garden at Silver Birches and similarly at The Chimes.

♿ ❀ ☕ 🎵

51 1 WHITEHOUSE COTTAGES
Blue Mill Lane, Woodham Walter, CM9 6LR. Mrs Shelley Rand. *Between Maldon & Danbury, short drive from A12. A414 through Danbury. Signs to Woodham Walter, turn L go past The Anchor. Cont through village. R into Blue Mill Ln. Parking in the top paddock & drop-off point near garden.* **Sun 17 May, Sun 19 July (10.30-3). Adm £5, chd free. Home-made teas.**
Nestled betwixt farmland in rural Essex, is our small secret garden, that has a wonderful charm to it. Bordered by three acres of paddocks with grazing horses, a little plot of loveliness wraps around our Victorian cottage, roses and grape smother the porch in June. A meandering lawn takes you through beds and borders softly planted with a cottage feel, a haven for wildlife and people alike. Dean Harris, a local artist blacksmith, will have a pop-up forge, making and selling metal garden accessories.

☕ 🎵

52 NEW 27 WORCESTER CLOSE
Mayland, Chelmsford, CM3 6TD. Michael & Sandra Rust, 07765 304313, rust.s@sky.com. *7m W of Maldon. Entering Mayland pass the Gulf Garage on R, turn next L into Nipsells Chase, then take the 5th L turn to Orchard Dr 1st R to Worcester Close.* **Visits by arrangement 4 June to 30 July for groups of 12 to 15. Adm £10. Tea, coffee & cake.**
Truly a plantsman's garden; Crammed full of an amazing collection of hardy perennials, many rare and unusual species which can be viewed from a meandering slate path round the colourful borders.

❀ ☕

310,000 people are cared for each year who are approaching the end of life or diagnosed with a terminal illness through the hospice network supported by National Garden Scheme funding.

GLOUCESTERSHIRE

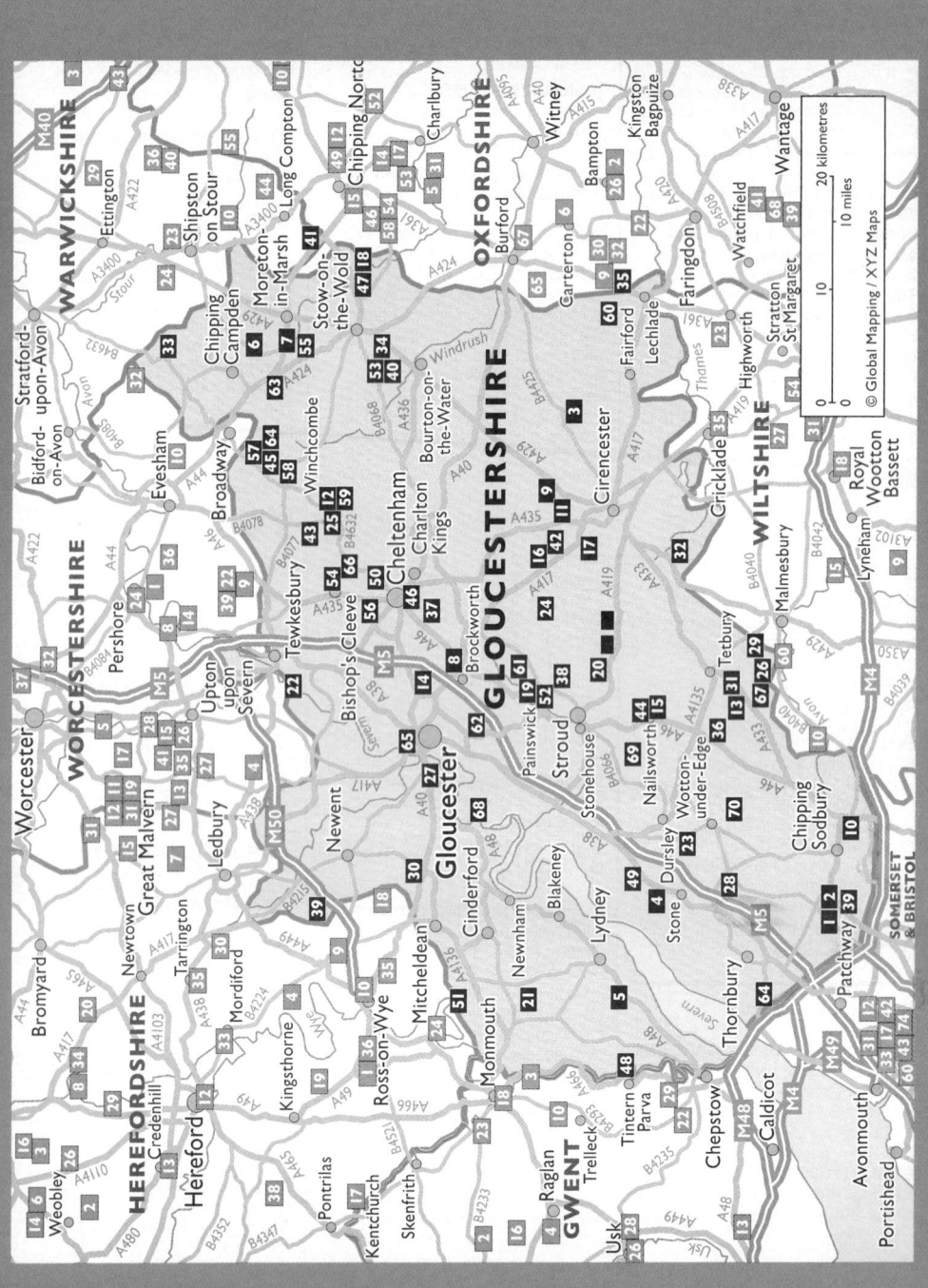

GLOUCESTERSHIRE 197

VOLUNTEERS

County Organiser
Vanessa Berridge
01242 609535
vanessa.berridge@ngs.org.uk

County Treasurer
Pam Sissons
01242 573942
pam.sissons@ngs.org.uk

Social Media
Mandy Bradshaw
01242 512491
mandy.bradshaw@ngs.org.uk

Alex Boulton
alex.boulton@ngs.org.uk

Publicity
Ruth Chivers
01452 767604
ruth.chivers@ngs.org.uk

Booklet Co-ordinator
Vanessa Graham 07595 880261
vanessa.graham@ngs.org.uk

By Arrangement Co-ordinator
Simone Seward 01242 573733
simone.seward@ngs.org.uk

Assistant County Organisers
Yvonne Bennetts 01242 463151
yvonne.bennetts@ngs.org.uk

Ali James 07780 000828
ali.james@ngs.org.uk

Valerie Kent 01993 823294
valerie.kent@ngs.org.uk

Immy Lee 07801 816340
immy.lee@ngs.org.uk

Sally Oates 01285 841320
sally.oates@ngs.org.uk

Jeanette Parker 01454 299699
jeanette_parker@hotmail.co.uk

Rose Parrott 07853 164924
rosemary.parrott@ngs.org.uk

Liz Ramsay 01242 672676
liz.ramsay@ngs.org.uk

@gloucestershirengs
@ngs_gloucestershire

OPENING DATES

All entries subject to change.
For latest information check
www.ngs.org.uk
Map locator numbers are shown to the right of each garden name.

January
Sunday 25th
Home Farm 30

February
Snowdrop Openings
Sunday 8th
Home Farm 30
Trench Hill 61
Saturday 14th
Cotswold Farm 16
Sunday 15th
Cotswold Farm 16
Trench Hill 61
Sunday 22nd
Algars Manor 1
Algars Mill 2

March
Sunday 15th
Trench Hill 61

April
Sunday 5th
◆ Highnam Court 27
Trench Hill 61
Monday 6th
Trench Hill 61
Saturday 11th
Prior's Piece 50
Tuesday 14th
Kemble House 32
Wednesday 15th
Daylesford House 18
Lords of the Manor Hotel 40
Friday 17th
◆ Sudeley Castle Gardens 59

Sunday 19th
◆ Upton Wold 63
Monday 20th
◆ Kiftsgate Court 33
Tuesday 21st
Wortley House 70
Sunday 26th
Algars Manor 1
Algars Mill 2
The Gate 25
Thursday 30th
Charlton Down House 13

May
Sunday 3rd
Eastcombe and Bussage Gardens 20
◆ Highnam Court 27
NEW The Old Bakehouse 45
Trench Hill 61
NEW Warren Farmhouse 64
Monday 4th
Eastcombe and Bussage Gardens 20
Trench Hill 61
Wednesday 13th
Downton House 19
Thursday 14th
Downton House 19
Saturday 16th
NEW Besom Cottage 5
◆ Cerney House Gardens 11
Charingworth Court 12
Sunday 17th
NEW Besom Cottage 5
Charingworth Court 12
◆ Stanway Fountain & Water Garden 58
Friday 22nd
Camers 10
Saturday 23rd
Little Orchard 38
Sunday 24th
Little Orchard 38
Pasture Farm 47
Monday 25th
Pasture Farm 47
Saturday 30th
Cotswold Farm 16
Sunday 31st
Cotswold Farm 16
Tuffley Gardens 62

GLOUCESTERSHIRE

June

Wednesday 3rd
Trench Hill   61

Friday 5th
NEW Rose Farm   54
Westaway   66

Saturday 6th
Forthampton Court   22
The Patch   48

Sunday 7th
Calmsden Manor   9
Forthampton Court   22
The Glebe House   26
Hodges Barn   29
Park House   46
The Patch   48
Weir Reach   65

Monday 8th
◆ Berkeley Castle   4
The Glebe House   26
Hodges Barn   29

Wednesday 10th
Arlington and Bibury Gardens   3
Oak House   43
Rockcliffe   53
Trench Hill   61
Weir Reach   65

Saturday 13th
1 Cobden Villas   15
Oak House   43
Ohio   44
Pond Cottage   49

Sunday 14th
Arlington and Bibury Gardens   3
1 Cobden Villas   15
Pond Cottage   49
Stanton Village Gardens   57

Tuesday 16th
Wortley House   70

Wednesday 17th
Lords of the Manor Hotel   40
Trench Hill   61

Thursday 18th
Charlton Down House   13
Richmond Villages Painswick   52

Saturday 20th
◆ Sezincote   55

Sunday 21st
Blockley Gardens   6
Leckhampton Court Hospice   37
Moor Wood   42

Wednesday 24th
Lasborough Park   36
Trench Hill   61

Sunday 28th
◆ Cerney House Gardens   11
NEW Churchdown Gardens   14
Kirkham Farm   34
Langford Downs Farm   35
Little Orchard Kempley Dymock   39

July

Thursday 2nd
Charlton Down House   13

Sunday 5th
Woodchester Park House   69

Wednesday 8th
Rockcliffe   53

Saturday 11th
HMP Leyhill   28
NEW Rose Farm   54
Westaway   66

Sunday 12th
Trench Hill   61

Wednesday 15th
The Stables   56

Thursday 16th
Charlton Down House   13
Richmond Villages Painswick   52

Friday 17th
◆ The Garden at Miserden   24

Thursday 23rd
Charlton Down House   13

August

Sunday 2nd
◆ Highnam Court   27

Wednesday 5th
◆ Thyme   60

Sunday 9th
◆ Westonbirt School Gardens   67

Monday 10th
◆ Kiftsgate Court   33

Thursday 13th
Charlton Down House   13
Richmond Villages Painswick   52

Sunday 16th
NEW Frog Lane Flower Farm & Netherfields   23
◆ Stanway Fountain & Water Garden   58

Thursday 20th
Charlton Down House   13

Sunday 23rd
◆ Bourton House Garden   7

Wednesday 26th
Lasborough Park   36

Thursday 27th
Charlton Down House   13

Sunday 30th
Trench Hill   61

Monday 31st
Trench Hill   61

September

Saturday 5th
Cotswold Farm   16

Sunday 6th
Brockworth Court   8
Cotswold Farm   16

Wednesday 16th
Lords of the Manor Hotel   40

Sunday 20th
The Manor   41

February 2027

Sunday 7th
Trench Hill   61

Saturday 13th
Cotswold Farm   16

Sunday 14th
Cotswold Farm   16
Trench Hill   61

78,000 people affected by cancer were reached by Maggie's centres supported by the National Garden Scheme over the last 12 months.

GLOUCESTERSHIRE

By Arrangement

Arrange a personalised garden visit with your club, or group of friends, on a date to suit you. See individual garden entries for full details.

Awkward Hill Cottage (Arlington and Bibury Gardens)	3
Brockworth Court	8
Camers	10
Charingworth Court	12
Charlton Down House	13
Cotswold Farm	16
Daglingworth House	17
20 Forsdene Walk	21
The Gate	25
Hookshouse Pottery	31
Kemble House	32
Little Orchard	38
Moor Wood	42
Oak House	43
Pasture Farm	47
The Patch	48
Pond Cottage	49
Radnors	51
Trench Hill	61
Wicks Green Farm	68

Besom Cottage

THE GARDENS

1 ALGARS MANOR
Station Rd, Iron Acton, BS37 9TB. Mrs B Naish. *9m N of Bristol, 3m W of Yate/Chipping Sodbury. Turn S off Iron Acton bypass B4059, past village green & White Hart pub, 200yds, then over level Xing. No access from Frampton Cotterell via lane; ignore SatNav. Parking at Algars Manor.* **Sun 22 Feb (1-4). Tea. Sun 26 Apr (1-5). Home-made teas. Combined adm with Algars Mill £7, chd free. February: Tea & biscuits at Algars Mill. April: Home-made cakes & teas at Algars Manor.**
2 acres of woodland garden beside River Frome, mill stream, native plants mixed with collections of 60 magnolias and 70 camellias, rhododendrons, azaleas, eucalyptus and other unusual trees and shrubs. Daffodils, snowdrops and other early spring flowers.

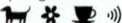

2 ALGARS MILL
Frampton End Rd, Iron Acton, Bristol, BS37 9TD. Mr & Mrs John Wright. *9m N of Bristol, 3m W of Yate/Chipping Sodbury. (For directions see Algars Manor).* **Sun 22 Feb (1-4). Tea. Sun 26 Apr (1-5). Home-made teas. Combined adm with Algars Manor £7, chd free. February: Tea & biscuits at Algars Mill. April: Home-made cakes & teas at Algars Manor.**
2 acre woodland garden bisected by River Frome; spring bulbs; shrubs; very early spring feature (Feb-Mar) of wild Newent daffodils. 300-400yr-old mill house (not open) through which millrace still runs.

GROUP OPENING

3 ARLINGTON AND BIBURY GARDENS
Arlington, Cirencester, GL7 5ND. Victoria Summerley. *15 mins NE of Cirencester. Please park at Pudding Hill Barn as no parking at Long Cottage or Awkward Hill Cottage. Access is via country lane leading off the B4425 (the main road through Bibury). 10 min walk between gardens. The lane to Awkward Hill Cottage is steep.* **Wed 10 June (3-7); Sun 14 June (10-2). Combined adm £12.50, chd free. Pre-booking essential if coming by car, please visit www.ngs.org.uk for information & booking. Home-made teas in the Schoolroom of the Baptist Church. WC available. Home-made cakes.**

AWKWARD HILL COTTAGE
Mrs Victoria Summerley,
07718 384269,
v.summerley@hotmail.com,
www.awkwardhill.co.uk.
Visits also by arrangement 20 May to 11 July for groups of 10 to 30.

LONG COTTAGE
Heather & Craig Chapman.

PUDDING HILL BARN
Karen Gray & Marcus Child.

Pudding Hill Barn is a large country garden, sloping down to the River Coln, with more formal planting around the house, and meadow and woodland walks. The Trout Hut sits on a vantage point above the river, and there are chickens. Long Cottage is a courtyard cottage garden, crammed

Westonbirt Gardens

with ingenious ideas that make the most of the space. Awkward Hill Cottage is a country garden with a pond, a gravel garden, mixed borders and shade planting. Pre booking only if coming by car. Visitors on foot can pay on the gate.

4 ♦ BERKELEY CASTLE
Berkeley, GL13 9PJ. Charles Berkeley, 01453 810303, info@berkeley-castle.com, www.berkeley-castle.com. *Halfway between Bristol & Gloucester, 10mins from J13 &14 of M5. Follow signs to Berkeley from A38 & B4066. Visitor entrance L off Canonbury Street, just before town centre.* **For NGS: Mon 8 June (10.30-5). Adm £8, chd £4. Light refreshments in the Kitchen Garden Restaurant.** For other opening times and information, please phone, email or visit garden website.
Unique historic garden of a keen plantsman, with far-reaching views across the River Severn. Gardens contain many rare plants which thrive in the warm microclimate against the stone walls of this medieval castle. Woodland, historic trees and stunning terraced borders. Adm price does not inc entrance into the castle.

5 NEW BESOM COTTAGE
Lower Common, Aylburton, Lydney, GL15 6DU. Ms Jo Johnson. *3m SW of Lydney town centre. A48, Chepstow to Lydney road, turn off, signed Aylburton Common. Besom Cottage is ¾m from the main road, the 3rd property past the chapel on the L. What3words app: commoners. export.list.* **Sat 16, Sun 17 May (1-5). Adm £5, chd free. Home-made teas.**
Landscape architect's garden created from a former pub car park. Tiered with large, local boulders and planted with ornamental and native planting surrounding a circular lawn. Features inc an ornamental pond, stumpery, woodland fern garden and garden art. The garden falls from the road to a stream with stepped paths. A separate vegetable garden and orchard are part of the property.

GROUP OPENING

6 BLOCKLEY GARDENS
Blockley, Moreton-in-Marsh, GL56 9DB. Rupert & Mandy Williams-Ellis. *3m NW of Moreton-in-Marsh. Just off the A44 Morton-in-Marsh to Evesham road.* **Sun 21 June (1-6). Combined adm £10, chd free. Home-made teas at St George's Hall and the Allotments.**

BLOCKLEY ALLOTMENTS
Blockley and District Allotment Association, blockleyallotments. wixsite.com/blockleyallotments.

CHURCH GATES
Mrs Brenda Salmon.

CLAREMONT HOUSE
Linda & Berns Russ.

GARDEN HOUSE
Nick & Ginny Williams-Ellis.

THE OLD SILK MILL
Mr D Martell.

SNUGBOROUGH MILL
Rupert & Mandy Williams-Ellis.

WOODRUFF
Paul & Maggie Adams.

This popular historic Cotswold hillside village has a great variety of high quality, well-stocked gardens - large and small, old and new. The delightful spring fed Blockley Brook flows right through the village and some of the gardens, inc former water mills and millponds. From some gardens there are wonderful rural views. Children welcome, but close supervision is essential.

7 ♦ BOURTON HOUSE GARDEN
Bourton-on-the-Hill, GL56 9AE. Mrs R Quintus, 01386 700754, info@bourtonhouse.com, www.bourtonhouse.com. *2m W of Moreton-in-Marsh on A44.* **For NGS: Sun 23 Aug (10-5). Adm £10, chd free. Light refreshments & home-made cakes in Grade I Listed C17 tithe barn.** For other opening times and information, please phone, email or visit garden website.
Award-winning, 3 acre garden featuring imaginative topiary, wide herbaceous borders with many rare, unusual and exotic plants, water features, unique shade house and many creatively planted pots.

Fabulous at any time of year, but magnificent in summer months and early autumn. Walk around a 7 acre pasture, with free printed guide to specimen trees available. 70% access for wheelchairs. Disabled WC.
&. ✤ ⛟ ☕ »)

8 BROCKWORTH COURT
Court Road, Brockworth, GL3 4QU. Tim & Bridget Wiltshire, 01452 862938, timwiltshire@hotmail.co.uk. *6m E of Gloucester. 6m W of Cheltenham. Adj St Georges Church on Court Rd. From A46 turn into Mill Lane, turn R, L, R at T junctions. From Ermin St, turn into Ermin Park, then R at r'about then L at next r'about.* **Sun 6 Sept (2-5.30). Adm £6, chd free. Home-made teas. Visits also by arrangement Apr to Oct for groups of 10 to 30. Guided tours of the historic house inc.**
This intense yet informal tapestry style garden beautifully complements the period manor house which it surrounds. Organic, naturalistic, with informal cottage style planting areas that seamlessly blend together. Natural fish pond, with Monet bridge leading to small island with thatched Fiji house. Kitchen garden once cultivated by monks. Views to Crickley and Coopers Hill. Adjacent Norman church (open). Historic tithe barn, manor house visited by Henry VIII and Anne Boleyn in 1535. Partial wheelchair access.
&. ⛟ ☕

9 CALMSDEN MANOR
Calmsden, Cirencester, GL7 5ET. Mr M & Mrs J Tufnell. *5m N of Cirencester. Turn to Calmsden off A429 at The Stump pub. On entering the village Manor gates are straight ahead of you.* **Sun 7 June (2.30-6.30). Adm £10, chd free. Tea, coffee & cake.**
With borders originally designed by Mary Keen, Calmsden Manor is a well loved garden. A treat for plant lovers, design enthusiasts, vegetable growers or those simply looking for a lovely day out. Inc herbaceous borders, a small arboretum, wild grass and flower meadow, and a walled garden.

10 CAMERS
Badminton Road, Old Sodbury, Bristol, BS37 6RG. **Mr & Mrs Michael Denman**, 01454 327929, jodenman@btinternet.com, www.camers.org. *2m E of Chipping Sodbury. Entrance in Chapel Lane off A432 at Dog Inn. Enter through the field gate & drive to the top of the fields to park next to the garden.* **Fri 22 May (2-5.30). Adm £7, chd free. Light refreshments. Visits also by arrangement 1 May to 18 Sept for groups of 20+. Refreshments on request.**
Elizabethan farmhouse (not open) set in 4 acres of constantly developing garden and woodland with spectacular views over Severn Vale. Garden full of surprises, formal and informal areas planted with wide range of species to provide year-round interest. Parterre, topiary, Japanese garden, bog and prairie areas, white and hot gardens, woodland walks. Some steep slopes.

SPECIAL EVENT
11 ♦ CERNEY HOUSE GARDENS
North Cerney, Cirencester, GL7 7BX. **Mr N W Angus & Dr J Angus**, 07759 481802, cerneyhouse@gmail.com, www.cerneygardens.com. *4m NW of Cirencester. On A435 Cheltenham road turn L opp Bathurst Arms, follow road past church up hill, then go straight towards pillared gates on R (signed Cerney House).* **For NGS: Evening opening Sat 16 May (5-8). Adm £17.50. Pre-booking essential, please visit www.ngs.org.uk for information & booking. Sun 28 June (10-7). Adm £7, chd £1. Tea, coffee & cake in The Bothy Tearoom. Evening event includes refreshments, wine & nibbles. For other opening times and information, please phone, email or visit garden website.**
A romantic English garden for all seasons. There is a secluded Victorian walled garden featuring herbaceous borders overflowing with colour. In the summer the magnificent display of rambling roses come to life. On Saturday 16 May a special ticketed event will start promptly at 5 pm in the Bothy. Mr Nicholas & Dr Janet Angus will give an introduction about the house, gardens and the relationship with the National Garden Scheme. You will then have the freedom of the garden. Walled garden accessible for electric wheelchairs. Gravel paths and inclines will not suit manual wheelchairs.

12 CHARINGWORTH COURT
Broadway Road, Winchcombe, GL54 5JN. **Susan & Richard Wakeford**, 07791 353779, susanwakeford@gmail.com, www.charingworthcourtcotswoldsgarden.com. *8m NE of Cheltenham. 400 metres N of Winchcombe town centre on B4632. Limited parking along Broadway Rd. Town car parks in Bull Lane, Chandos St (short stay) and all day parking (£1) in Back Lane. Map on garden website.* **Sat 16, Sun 17 May (11-5.30). Adm £6, chd free. Tea, coffee & cake. Visits also by arrangement 1 May to 19 July for groups of 10 to 30.**
Artistically and lovingly created 1½ acre garden surrounding restored Georgian/Tudor house (not open). Relaxed country style with Japanese influences, large pond, sculpture and a walled vegetable/flower garden, all created over 30 yrs from a blank canvas. Mature copper beech trees, Cedar of Lebanon and Wellingtonia; and younger trees replacing an earlier excess of *Cupressus leylandii*. Partial access due to gravel paths which can be challenging but several areas accessible without steps. Pls ring to book disabled parking.

13 CHARLTON DOWN HOUSE
Charlton Down, Tetbury, GL8 8TZ. **Neil & Julie Record**, cdh.groupbookings@gmail.com. *From Tetbury, take A433 towards Bath for 1½ m; turn R (north) just before the Hare & Hounds, then R again after 200yds into Hookshouse Lane. Charlton Down House is 600yds on R.* **Thur 30 Apr, Thur 18 June, Thur 2, Thur 16, Thur 23 July, Thur 13, Thur 20, Thur 27 Aug (1-5). Adm £7, chd free. Home-made teas. Cash preferred for refreshments. Visits also by arrangement 20 Apr to 28 Aug for groups of 25 to 35.**
Extensive country house gardens in 180 acre equestrian estate. Formal terraces, perennial borders, walled topiary garden, enclosed cut flower garden and large glasshouse. Jubilee copse. Rescue animals. Ample parking. Largely flat terrain; most garden areas accessible but regret we do not have specific disabled WC.

GROUP OPENING

14 NEW CHURCHDOWN GARDENS
Churchdown, Gloucester, GL3 2HP. **Mrs Shirley Sills.** *Between A46 Shurdington Rd Cheltenham and B4063 off the Golden Valley towards Gloucester. Free car park in village centre next to 2 Chapel Hay Close. Card payments at Melville Rd & Chapel Hay Close.* **Sun 28 June (12-5). Combined adm £6, chd free.**

2 CHAPEL HAY CLOSE
Mrs Shirley Sills.

NEW DUART HOUSE
Carolyn Edwards.

NEW 5 FAR SANDFIELD
Sue Watters.

NEW 86 MELVILLE ROAD
Juliet & David Pearce.

Four village gardens in Churchdown, each with its own very distinctive style and brimming with ideas to inspire and delight: Chapel Hay is a plantswoman's garden with year-round interest created within the last 4 yrs. Featuring perennials, shrubs, trees, climbers, gravel area and water features. Duart House occupies ⅓ acre with a beautiful kitchen garden, conservatory, succulents, shrubs perennials, roses and pond. Far Sandfield is a small garden featuring scented plants and a wall fountain. 86 Melville Road is a suburban garden featuring vine covered pergola, trees, ferns, grasses, perennials and Art Studio.

15 1 COBDEN VILLAS
Meadow Bank, Walkley Wood, Nailsworth, GL6 0RT. **Sue Ratcliffe.** *Parking in Nailsworth town centre with a 10 min walk to Shortwood Rd, L at the Britannia pub onto Horsley Rd; R onto Pike Lane. There is very limited on road parking in Pike Lane/Meadow Bank.* **Sat 13 June (10-4), open nearby Ohio. Sun 14 June (10-4). Adm £5, chd free. Tea, coffee & cold drinks.**
This organic and wildlife friendly hillside garden is divided into distinct areas. A small mixed woodland area provides separation from the adjacent lane with underplanting of shade loving native and unusual plants. Terraced beds and borders adopt cottage garden planting ethos with

extensive ground cover and shrubs. A rill and small pond provides a home for frogs and dragonflies. Regret this garden is not suitable for children.

16 COTSWOLD FARM
Duntisbourne Abbots, Cirencester, GL7 7JS. John & Sarah Birchall, 07845 122165, garden@birchall.org.uk, www.cotswoldfarmgardens.org.uk. *5m NW of Cirencester off old A417. From Cirencester L signed Duntisbourne Abbots Services, R & R underpass. Drive ahead. From Gloucester L signed Duntisbourne Abbots Services. Pass Services. Drive L.* **Sat 14, Sun 15 Feb (11-3). Light refreshments. Sat 30, Sun 31 May, Sat 5, Sun 6 Sept (2-5). Home-made teas. Adm £7.50, chd free. 2027: Sat 13, Sun 14 Feb. Visits also by arrangement.**
This beautiful Arts & Crafts garden overlooks a quiet valley on descending levels with terraces designed by Norman Jewson in the1930s. Enclosed by Cotswold stone walls and yew hedges, the garden has year-round interest inc a snowdrop collection with over 80 varieties. The terraces, shrub garden, herbaceous borders and bog garden are full of scent and colour from spring to autumn. Rare orchid walks. Picnics welcome.

17 DAGLINGWORTH HOUSE
Daglingworth, Cirencester, GL7 7AG. David & Henrietta Howard, 07970 122122, ettajhoward@gmail.com. *3m NW of Cirencester off A417/419. House with blue gate beside church in centre of Daglingworth, at end of No Through Road.* **Visits by arrangement 1 Apr to 11 Sept for groups of 5 to 25. (Refreshments should be booked in advance). Adm £8, chd free. Tea, coffee & cake.**
Over the last 30 yrs we have created a 3 acre classical garden with a humorous contemporary twist. There is a grotto, a temple, a walled garden, woodland, small grass and meadow gardens, and a sunken garden. Pools, a mirror canal, a cascade, topiary shapes, good hedging and sculptures. Pretty village setting next to Saxon church.

18 DAYLESFORD HOUSE
Daylesford, GL56 0YG. Lord & Lady Bamford. *5m W of Chipping Norton. Off A436 between Stow-on-the-Wold & Chipping Norton. What3words app: greet.kettles.briskly.* **Wed 15 Apr (1-5). Adm £11, chd free. Home-made teas.**
Magnificent C18 landscape grounds created in 1790 for Warren Hastings, greatly restored and enhanced by present owners under organic regime. Lakeside and woodland walks within natural wildflower meadows. Large formal walled garden, centred around orchid, peach and working glasshouses. Trellised rose garden. Collection of citrus within period orangery. Secret garden, pavilion, formal pools. Very large garden with substantial distances. The owners of Daylesford House have specifically requested that photographs are NOT taken in their garden or grounds. No dogs allowed except guide dogs. Partial wheelchair access.

19 DOWNTON HOUSE
Gloucester St, Painswick, GL6 6QN. Jane Kilpatrick. *4m N of Stroud. Entry to garden is via Hollyhock Lane only. NO cars in Lane. Park in Stamages Lane Car Park off A46 below church, or in Churchill Way, 1st L off Gloucester St B4073.* **Wed 13, Thur 14 May (10.30-3.30). Adm £6, chd free. Home-made teas in the garden.**
Plant enthusiast and author's walled ⅓ acre garden in heart of historic Painswick. Planted for year-round foliage colour and interest with particular focus on plants that thrive on thin limey soil in a changing climate. Garden features unusual trees, shrubs and peonies associated with owner's interest in plant introductions from China. Exedra Nursery from Painswick Rococo Garden will be selling plants. Steep ramp provides access to path and paved area.

GROUP OPENING

20 EASTCOMBE AND BUSSAGE GARDENS
Eastcombe, Stroud, GL6 7EB. *3m E of Stroud. What3words app: sprinter.grudge.cloth. Maps/tickets & cashless payments at Redwood GL68AZ & Hawkley Cottage GL67DQ. Cash only at Eastcombe* Village Hall GL67EB & 20 Farmcote Close GL67EG. *On street parking only. Tickets valid for both days.* **Sun 3, Mon 4 May (1-5.30). Combined adm £10, chd free. Tea, coffee & cake at Eastcombe Village Hall (cash only) from 1pm-5pm both days. Ice creams at Hawkley Cottage.**

CADSONBURY
Natalie & Glen Beswetherick.

17 FARMCOTE CLOSE
John & Sheila Coyle.

20 FARMCOTE CLOSE
Ian & Dawn Sim.

21 FARMCOTE CLOSE
Robert & Marion Bryant.

HAMPTON VIEW
Geraldine & Mike Carter.

HAWKLEY COTTAGE
Helen & Gerwin Westendorp.

12 HIDCOTE CLOSE
Mr K Walker.

HIGHLANDS
Helen & Bob Watkinson.

1 JASMINE COTTAGE
Mrs June Gardiner.

LINDENS
John & Ann Cooper.

MOUNT PLEASANT
Mrs G Peyton.

REDWOOD
Heather Collins.

50 STONECOTE RIDGE
Julie & Robin Marsland.

VALLEY VIEW
Mrs Rebecca Benneyworth.

WHITE HOUSE
Jane & Dave Gandy.

WOODVIEW COTTAGE
Julian & Eileen Horn-Smith.

Medium and small gardens in a variety of styles and settings within these picturesque hilltop villages, with their spectacular views of the Toadsmoor Valley. In addition, one large garden is located in the bottom of the valley, approachable only on foot as are some of the other gardens in Eastcombe. Full descriptions of each garden and those with wheelchair access can be found on the National Garden Scheme website. Please show any pre-booked tickets at ticket venues where you will be given a trail map. WC at village hall and Hawkley Cottage. Plants for sale at village hall and some gardens.

Charingworth Court

21 20 FORSDENE WALK
Coalway, Coleford, GL16 7JZ.
Pamela Buckland, 01594 837179.
From Coleford take Lydney/ Chepstow Rd at T-lights. L after police station ½ m up hill turn L at Xrds then 2nd R (Old Road) straight on at minor Xrds then L into Forsdene Walk. **Visits by arrangement 1 May to 19 July for groups of up to 15. Regrettably not suitable for children or dogs. Adm £4. Tea, coffee & cake. Cash only.**
Corner garden full of design ideas to maximise smaller spaces in interlocking colour themed rooms, some on different levels, packed with perennials and grasses. A shady pergola for ferns and hostas. A small man-made stream. Low maintenance gravelled areas with trees, shrubs and self-sown perennials, plus pots in abundance.

22 FORTHAMPTON COURT
Forthampton, Tewkesbury, GL19 4RD. Alan & Anabel Mackinnon. *W of Tewkesbury. From Tewkesbury A438 to Ledbury. After 2m turn L to Forthampton. At Xrds go L towards Chaceley. Go 1m turn L at Xrds.* **Sat 6, Sun 7 June (12.30-4.30). Adm £8, chd free. Home-made teas.**
Charming and varied garden surrounding N Gloucestershire medieval manor house (not open) within sight of Tewkesbury Abbey. Inc borders, lawns, roses and magnificent Victorian vegetable garden. Disabled drop off at entrance, some gravel paths and uneven areas.

23 NEW FROG LANE FLOWER FARM & NETHERFIELDS
North Nibley, Dursley, GL11 6DJ. Margie Hoffnung, www. froglaneflowerfarm.co.uk. *What3words app: commutes. expressed.revives takes you to Old Vicarage Car Park gates. In N Nibley opp the Black Horse pub go down The Street. When you reach the church take R fork (Frog Lane). FLFF is through Old Vicarage gates immed past church on L.* **Sun 16 Aug (11-4). Adm £6, chd free. Tea, coffee & cake at Netherfields, next door.**
Spectacularly situated on the edge of the Cotswolds escarpment, with panoramic views over the R Severn towards the Black Mountains, visible on a clear day. We grow and propagate seasonal, chemical-free cut flowers/foliage and never use floral foam/materials that cannot be recycled/reused. Visitors can also explore the adjacent garden of Netherfields below FLFF where teas will be served. Large selection of unusual flowers/foliage grown for cutting; plantswoman's garden adjacent with wildflower meadow, hazel tunnel, established borders. Wheelchair access possible with a helper but pls note the entire flower farm slopes gently and access to Netherfields is also sloping the entire way.

24 ♦ THE GARDEN AT MISERDEN
Miserden, Stroud, GL6 7JA. Mr Nicholas Wills, 01285 821303, hello@miserden.org, www.miserden.org. *6m NW of Cirencester. Leave A417 for Birdlip, drive through Whiteway & follow signs for Miserden.* **For NGS: Fri 17 July (10-5). Adm £12, chd free.** For other opening times and information, please phone, email or visit garden website.
A timeless walled garden designed in the C17 with a wonderful sense of peace and tranquillity. Known for its magnificent mixed borders and Lutyens' Yew Walk and quaint grass steps; there is also an ancient mulberry tree, enchanting arboretum and stunning views across the Golden Valley. Routes around the garden are gravel or grass; there are alternative routes to those that have steps. Disabled WC at the café.

25 THE GATE
80 North Street, Winchcombe, GL54 5PS. Vanessa Berridge & Chris Evans, 01242 609535, vanessa.berridge@ngs.org.uk. *Winchcombe is on B4632 midway between Cheltenham & Broadway. Parking behind Library in Back Lane, 50 yds from The Gate. Entry to garden via Cowl Lane.* **Sun 26 Apr (1-5). Adm £4.50, chd free. Home-made teas. Visits also by arrangement 27 Apr to 31 July for groups of 5 to 20.**
Compact cottage style garden planted with a colourful display of tulips in spring, also with perennials, annuals and climbers in the walled courtyard of C17 former coaching inn. Also a separate, productive, walled kitchen garden with espaliers and other fruit trees. Wheelchair access to most areas of the garden; other areas are partially visible from negotiable paths.

26 THE GLEBE HOUSE
Church Lane, Shipton Moyne, Tetbury, GL8 8PW. Mr & Mrs Richard Boggis-Rolfe. *2½ m S of Tetbury. Next to church in Shipton Moyne. What3words app: spoil. prune.snuggle.* **Sun 7, Mon 8 June (1-5). Adm £8, chd free. Tea, coffee & cake at both gardens. Tickets to each garden £8 at their gates. Open nearby Hodges Barn.**
The gardens and grounds of the former Rectory are about 4 acres. Double herbaceous border, walled kitchen and flower garden, ornamental statuary and water features, swimming pool garden, greenhouses and a paddock with goats, chickens and ponies. Path through the orchard to a copse with a small folly. Walks round the pond and stream to Hodges Barn or to another folly with views of the Church. Gravel and mown paths to each part of the garden and disabled parking in the stable yard by prior arrangement.

Our 2025 donation to the Queen's Institute of Community Nursing now helps support over 3,500 Queen's Nurses working in the community in England, Wales, Northern Ireland, the Channel Islands and the Isle of Man.

27 ◆ HIGHNAM COURT
Highnam, Gloucester, GL2 8DP. Mr R J Head, www.HighnamCourt.co.uk. *2m W of Gloucester. On A40/A48 junction from Gloucester to Ross or Chepstow. At this r'about take exit at 3 o'clock if coming from Gloucester direction. Do NOT go into Highnam village.* **For NGS: Sun 5 Apr, Sun 3 May, Sun 2 Aug (11-4.30). Adm £6, chd free. Home-made teas. For other opening times and information, please visit garden website. Donation to other charities.**
40 acres of Victorian landscaped gardens surrounding magnificent Grade I* listed house (not open), built in 1658 for William Cooke, the son of Sir Robert Cooke, following damage to the original structure in the English Civil War. The gardens were set out by the artist, Thomas Gambier Parry, and have been lovingly restored by the current owner, Roger Head. The gardens are home to lakes, shrubberies, a wildflower meadow, multiple rose gardens (5000+ roses), knot gardens, an oriental garden, a newly constructed white garden, a kitchen garden, multiple wood carvings and a listed Pulhamite water garden with grottos and fernery. In the orangery, you can see a selection of rare air plants and carnivorous plants.

28 HMP LEYHILL
Leyhill, Wotton-Under-Edge, GL12 8BT. Mark Nutley.  *1m off the M5 Junction 14. The Gardens are located within HMP Leyhill clearly signed. Please park in the Visitor's Car Park & make your way to the Visitors Entrance where a member of staff will meet you.* **Sat 11 July (9.30-3.30). Adm £10. Pre-booking essential, please visit www.ngs.org.uk for information & booking. Tea, coffee & cake.**
Visitors will be taken on a guided group tour of the gardens. Extensive perennial borders and annual beds lead to an alpine rockery. Meandering via an incline path are further annual beds, a memorial bed plus established trees and extensive lawns. There is a large commercial horticulture section growing salad crops, fruits and vegetables together with a plant nursery. A small conservation area with a bug hotel and a pond with waterfall make for an attractive and welcome visit. Please be on time for your allocated time slot as the tour is guided. Photo ID will be required for entry and cameras and phones are not permitted. WC facilities are available. Please note over 18s only. Partial wheelchair access.

29 HODGES BARN
Shipton Moyne, Tetbury, GL8 8PR. Mr & Mrs N Hornby, www.hodgesbarn.com. *3m S of Tetbury. On Malmesbury side of village. What3words app: gashes.crinkled.horn.* **Sun 7, Mon 8 June (1-5). Adm £8, chd free. Home-made teas at the Pool House. Open nearby The Glebe House. Tickets to each garden £8 at their gates.**
Very unusual C15 dovecote converted into family home. Cotswold stone walls host climbing and rambling roses, clematis, vines, hydrangeas and together with yew, rose and tapestry hedges create formality around house. Mixed shrub and herbaceous borders, old fashioned rose border, water garden, woodland garden planted with cherries and magnolias. Vegetable and picking flower garden.

30 HOME FARM
Newent Lane, Huntley, GL19 3HQ. Mrs T Freeman. *4m S of Newent. On B4216 ½m off A40 in Huntley travelling towards Newent.* **Sun 25 Jan, Sun 8 Feb (11-4). Adm £4.50, chd free. Online booking or cash on the day.**
Set in elevated position with exceptional views. 1m walk through woods and fields to show carpets of spring flowers. Enclosed garden with fern walk, sundial and heather bed. White and mixed shrub borders. Stout footwear advisable as though the woods have woodchip paths the pasture to get from copse to copse is steep in places. The local garden centre has a very good cafe serving light lunches and home-made cakes to accompany tea or coffee.

31 HOOKSHOUSE POTTERY
Hookshouse Lane, Tetbury, GL8 8TZ. Lise & Christopher White, 07703 288615, lise.hookshouse@gmail.com, www.hookshousepottery.co.uk. *2½m SW of Tetbury. Follow signs from A433 at Hare & Hounds Hotel,* *Westonbirt. Alternatively take A4135 out of Tetbury towards Dursley & follow signs after ½m on L.* **Visits by arrangement 15 May to 15 July for groups of 15 to 35. Adm £7, chd free. Refreshments by request.**
Garden offers a combination of long perspectives and intimate corners. Planting inc wide variety of perennials, with emphasis on colour interest throughout the seasons. Herbaceous borders, woodland garden and flower meadow, water garden containing treatment ponds (unfenced) and flowform cascades. Sculptural features. Kitchen garden with raised beds, orchard. Run on organic principles. Pottery showroom with hand thrown woodfired pots inc frost proof garden pots. Mostly wheelchair accessible.

32 KEMBLE HOUSE
Kemble, Cirencester, GL7 6AD. Jill Kingston, 07798 830287, kingsjill50@gmail.com. *3m from Cirencester. Approaching Kemble on the A429 from Cirencester, turn L onto School Rd then R onto Church Rd, pass Kemble Church on L. Kemble House is the next house on L.* **Tue 14 Apr (2-5). Adm £7.50, chd free. Visits also by arrangement 5 Mar to 30 May.**
A landscaped garden with many tall lime trees. Herbaceous borders line the lawns. The main one in front of the house is a grass tennis court that was laid in the 1880s. There is a walled garden with many fruit trees and two rose gardens. Two paddocks surround the property with Hebridean sheep. Wheelchair access possible, gravel pathways and some steps.

33 ◆ KIFTSGATE COURT
Chipping Campden, GL55 6LN. Mr & Mrs J G Chambers, 01386 438777, kiftsgte@aol.com, www.kiftsgate.co.uk. *4m NE of Chipping Campden. Opp Hidcote NT Garden.* **For NGS: Mon 20 Apr (2-6); Mon 10 Aug (12-6). Adm £12.50, chd £5. Home-made teas. Light lunches in August. For other opening times and information, please phone, email or visit garden website.**
Magnificent situation and views, many unusual plants and shrubs, tree peonies, hydrangeas, abutilons, species and old-fashioned roses inc largest rose in England, *Rosa filipes* 'Kiftsgate'.

34 KIRKHAM FARM

Upper Slaughter, Cheltenham, GL54 2JS. **Mr & Mrs John Wills.** *On road between Lower Slaughter & Lower Swell. Opp farm buildings on roadside. 1½ m W of Fosseway A429 & SW of Stow on the Wold.* **Sun 28 June (11-5). Adm £7, chd free. Home-made teas.**
A country garden overlooking lovely views with several mixed borders that always have a succession of colour. Gravel gardens, trees and shrubs and a hidden pool garden, raised beds, cutting beds and a developing wildflower bank give plenty of interest. Teas are served in our beautifully restored stone barn. The majority of the garden is accessible.

35 LANGFORD DOWNS FARM

Langford Downs Farm, nr Lechlade, GL7 3QL. **Mr & Mrs Gavin MacEchern, 07778 355115, caroline@macechern.com.** *South of Burford. Access from A361 via layby behind copse - 6m from Burford towards Lechlade on the R OR 2m from Lechlade towards Burford on the L (NOT in Langford).* **Sun 28 June (1-5). Adm £7, chd free. Home-made teas. Cash only.**
Cotswold house and good sized garden created in 2009, with extensive tree planting, and mixed tree, shrub and herbaceous borders. Traditional hedges comprising arches and windows and crab apple espalier. Extensive cut flower and vegetable garden, interesting courtyard with raised nursery beds. Cotswold pond with natural spring, bug hotels, magic garden and lots of quirky things to see and find! Private visits also by arrangement (non NGS). All areas wheelchair friendly.

SPECIAL EVENT

36 LASBOROUGH PARK

Lasborough, Tetbury, GL8 8UF. **Sir Hans Rausing.** *6m W of Tetbury. Continue along the driveway from A46 passing the church, farm & Manor house on L. Keep going along the road passing through the gates, over the cattle grid & drive towards Lasborough.* **Wed 24 June, Wed 26 Aug (10-4). Adm £25. Pre-booking essential, please visit www.ngs.org.uk for information & booking. Home-made teas included after the tour.**
12 acre garden inc formal lawns, shrub, roses and herbaceous borders, topiary, woodland garden and parterre garden. The walled garden is designed to display borders, fruit, vegetables and cut flowers. The planting throughout the garden reflects the fruits of a long collaboration between the owner and Tom Stuart-Smith. A limited number of tickets have been made available for a morning or afternoon guided tour on 2 different days by Head Gardener, Brian Corr. Brian is former Head of Gardens to the King's Foundation. Each tour will take approx 2 hours and will start at 10am and 2pm.

Duart House, Churchdown Gardens

37 LECKHAMPTON COURT HOSPICE

Church Road, Leckhampton, Cheltenham, GL53 0QJ. www.sueryder.org/care-centres/hospices/leckhampton-court-hospice. *2m SW of Cheltenham. From Church Rd take driveway by church signed Sue Ryder Leckhampton Court Hospice & follow parking signs.* **Sun 21 June (11-4). Adm £6, chd free. Tea, coffee & cake. Visitors welcome to picnic on our back lawn (bring your own chairs & picnic blankets).**
Set in Grade II* listed medieval estate, the informal gardens at Leckhampton Court Hospice surround the buildings. Courtyard garden and new feature gardens designed by Peter Dowle, RHS Chelsea gold medal winner. Highlights inc woodland walk around lake, new embankment garden (funded by the National Garden Scheme) and terrace with magnificent views across Cheltenham towards Malvern. Numerous protected mature trees and lawns. Features inc a golden maple tree planted by His Majesty King Charles III to commemorate his 70th birthday, a kitchen garden supplying fresh vegetables for patients and a new bluebell wood (spring only). Wheelchair access in some areas: from back of reception to Sir Charles Irving terrace; woodland walk; main courtyard.

38 LITTLE ORCHARD

Slad, Stroud, GL6 7QD. Rod & Terry Clifford, 07967 253420, terryclifford.tlc@gmail.com. *2m from Stroud, 10m from Cheltenham. Last property in Slad village from Stroud, on L before leaving 30mph speed limit travelling to Birdlip on B4070. SatNav may not bring you directly to property. Parking on verge opp.* **Sat 23, Sun 24 May (11-4). Adm £5, chd free. Tea, coffee & cake. Cider tasting available. Visits also by arrangement May to Sept for groups of 5 to 30.**
One acre garden created from wilderness on a challenging, steeply sloping site using many reclaimed materials, stonework and statuary. Multiple terraces and garden 'rooms' enhanced with different planting styles and water features to complement the natural surroundings. Many seating areas with stunning views. Children's Trail. Cidery offering tastings. Exhibition and sale of local artists' work. Wheelchair access possible to some areas of the garden but challenging due to the severity of slopes and steps. Please phone for further details.

39 LITTLE ORCHARD, KEMPLEY DYMOCK

Kempley, Dymock, GL18 2BU. Ros Flook. *7m from Ross-on-Wye, 8m from Ledbury. From Ross M50, J3. L B4221, then R for Kempley. After 2½m, follow NGS signs for parking & garden. From Ledbury B4126, 5m turn R B4125, after120 metres turn L onto Kempley Rd for 2m, follow NGS signs.* **Sun 28 June (1-5). Adm £5, chd free. Tea, coffee & cake.**
4 acre wildlife friendly garden with views borrowed from open countryside. Mature native and specimen trees together with ornamental borders, rose garden and cottage gardens can all be explored from the large connecting lawns. Year-round interest: ponds, productive apple orchard, woodland, wildflower meadows, ancient horse chestnut. Seasonal floral interest from annual and perennial planting. Limited disabled parking at house. Wheelchair access restricted to garden areas nearest the house, regret WC not wheelchair accessible.

40 LORDS OF THE MANOR HOTEL

Upper Slaughter, Cheltenham, GL54 2JD. Mike Dron (Head Gardener), 01451 820243, reservations@lordsofthemanor.com, www.lordsofthemanor.com. *2m W of Bourton-on-the-Water. From Fosse way follow signs for the Slaughters from close to Bourton-on-the-Water (toward Stow). From B4077 (Stanway Hill road) coming from Tewkesbury direction, follow signs 2m after Ford village.* **Wed 15 Apr, Wed 17 June, Wed 16 Sept (10-3). Adm £8, chd £5. Light refreshments are available from the hotel, from light lunches to afternoon tea. Pre-booking is essential for afternoon tea.**
Classic Cotswold country garden with a very English blend of semi-formal and informal, merging beautifully with the surrounding landscape. Beautiful walled garden, established wildflower meadow, the River Eye. The herb garden and stunning bog garden were originally designed by Julie Toll around 2012.

41 THE MANOR

Little Compton, GL56 0RZ. Reed Learning. *½m from A44 or 2m from A3400. Follow signs to Little Compton, then yellow NGS signs.* **Sun 20 Sept (1-5). Adm £6, chd free. Home-made teas in churchyard next door.**
Arts & Crafts garden surrounding Jacobean manor house. Large plant collection, with deer park, meadow and arboreta. Croquet, golf, and tennis free to play. Children, picnics, and dogs very welcome. Arts and Crafts layout, water features, extensive mixed planting and styles, formal lawns, hedges and topiary, unique enclosed setting, sculptures, deer and sheep. Orchard & flower garden (small part of the formal gardens) not accessible by wheelchair. Disabled drop-off at entrance.

42 MOOR WOOD

Woodmancote, GL7 7EB. Mr & Mrs Henry Robinson, 07973 688240, henry@moorwoodhouse.co.uk, www.moorwoodroses.co.uk. *3½m NW of Cirencester. Turn L off A435 to Cheltenham at N Cerney, signed Woodmancote 1¼m; entrance in village on L beside lodge with white gates.* **Sun 21 June (2-6). Adm £7.50, chd free. Home-made teas. Visits also by arrangement 14 Jan to 30 June for groups of 5 to 28. Includes a tour by Henry Robinson.**
Two acres of shrub, orchard and wildflower gardens in beautiful isolated valley setting. Holder of National Collection of Rambler Roses. June 10th to 30th is usually the best time for the roses.

NPC

43 OAK HOUSE

Greenway Lane, Gretton, Cheltenham, GL54 5ER. Paul & Sue Hughes, 01242 603990, ppphug@gmail.com. *In centre of Gretton. Signed Gretton from B4077, approx 3m from A46 Teddington Hands r'about. Greenway Lane 300 metres R past railway bridge. Parking on main road with short walk to garden.* **Wed 10, Sat 13 June (2-5). Adm £5, chd free. Tea, coffee & cake. Cash only. Visits also by arrangement Apr to July for groups of up to 20.**
One acre secret garden divided into rooms. Gradually developed over the last 30 yrs. Many places to sit

and enjoy the scent of honeysuckle, philadelphus and over 50 varieties of roses. Wildflower meadow, gazebo and summerhouse. Formal lily pond and small wildlife pond. Some quirky features. You may even see a fairy.

44 OHIO
Star Hill, Forest Green, Nailsworth, GL6 0NJ. Tracy Gwyer. *4m S of Stroud. From the centre of Nailsworth go up Spring Hill from the r'about then R into Moffatt Rd. Parking is limited in Star Hill so park locally & walk down Star Hill to the garden.* **Sat 13 June (10-4). Adm £5, chd free. Tea, coffee & cake. Open nearby 1 Cobden Villas.**
Medium sized garden on a slope with far reaching views with 2 wildlife ponds, plus dedicated areas for wildlife. Herbaceous borders packed with colour from perennials, bulbs, grasses, roses and shrubs. Patios with many colourfully planted containers and pots. Plenty of seating areas throughout taking in the fabulous views.

45 NEW THE OLD BAKEHOUSE
High Street Stanton, Broadway, WR12 7NE. Pamela Horton. *Opp village cross in Stanton Village. Stanton is off B4632 Winchcombe to Broadway Rd. Take road towards The Mount Inn at T junction in village. The Old Bakehouse is 60 metres on R hand side of High St.* **Sun 3 May (1-6). Combined adm with Warren Farmhouse £10, chd free. Tea, coffee & cake at Warren Farmhouse garden next door. Adm inc a drink & a piece of cake.**
2 acre country garden with lawns, mature trees, natural stream, shrubs and seasonal flowers. Vegetable growing area and orchard beyond. C12 St Michael & All Angels Church also open in Church Lane, a short walk away. All gravel paths, driveway the most difficult, but once in the garden gravel is more impacted which is easier. No problem for electric wheelchairs.

46 PARK HOUSE
Thirlestaine Road, Cheltenham, GL53 7AS. Yoko Mathers. *Off A40 through Cheltenham. Street parking nearby. Enter garden through side gate.* **Sun 7 June (1-4.30). Adm £5,**
chd free. Cream teas.
Award-winning ¼ acre rear garden of a Cheltenham Regency town house inc a striking new Japanese 'Karesansui' Garden. Stones and rocks cascade into a gravel pond. Acers, ornamental pine trees and a sheltered 'Machiai' sitting bench complete the scene. Specimen trees are grouped in the lawn. Inviting summerhouse with wisteria walkway. Shrubs and wide herbaceous border frame the garden.

47 PASTURE FARM
Upper Oddington, GL56 0XG. Mrs John Lloyd, 07850 154095, ljmlloyd@yahoo.com. *3m W of Stow-on-the-Wold. Just off A436, midway between Upper & Lower Oddington.* **Sun 24, Mon 25 May (11-5). Adm £8, chd free. Tea, coffee & cake. Visits also by arrangement 7 June to 1 Sept.**
Informal country garden developed over 40 yrs by current owners. Mixed borders, topiary, orchard and many species of trees. Gravel garden and rambling roses in 'the ruins'. A concrete garden and wildflower area leads to vegetable patch. Large spring-fed pond with ducks. Also bantams, chickens, black Welsh sheep and Kunekune pigs. Public footpath across 2 small fields arrives at C11 church, St Nicholas, with doom paintings, set in ancient woodlands. Truly worth a visit (See Simon Jenkins' Book of Churches). Mostly wheelchair accessible.

48 THE PATCH
Hollywell Lane, Brockweir, Chepstow, NP16 7PJ. Mrs Immy Lee, 07801 816340, immylee1@hotmail.com, www.thepatchbrockweir.com. *6½m N of Chepstow & 10½m S of Monmouth, off A466, across Brockweir Bridge. From Monmouth & Chepstow direction follow SatNav to Brockweir Bridge, then yellow signs. From Coleford/ Gloucester direction follow SatNav out of St. Briavels, then yellow signs.* **Sat 6, Sun 7 June (1-5). Adm £5, chd free. Home-made teas. Visits also by arrangement 8 June to 28 June for groups of 5 to 25.**
Rural ¼ acre garden with stunning views across the Wye Valley. The maturing planting of 60+ roses, shrubs, grasses and perennials in a modern English Garden style provides year-round interest. The established borders are linked by meandering grass paths and small seating areas in different parts of the garden. Partial wheelchair access.

49 POND COTTAGE
Breadstone, Berkeley, GL13 9HG. Nicky Fussell, nickyfussell@aol.com. *8m S of M5 J13; 6m N of M5 J14; 1½m from A38; 3m NE of Berkeley. After entering Breadstone village from the A38, Pond Cottage is on R immed after Breadstone Care Home. What3words: upgrading.cubic. adhesive. Nearest railway stn Cam & Dursley 4.4m.* **Sat 13, Sun 14 June (11.30-4.30). Adm £6.50, chd free. Home-made cakes with gluten-free & vegan options, choice of tea or coffee £5. Visits also by arrangement 25 May to 30 Sept for groups of 15 to 50. Group visits are for adults only. Home-made cakes with tea/coffee £5.**
Opened in 2025, Pond Cottage, a converted C19 former farm building, sits within 3 acres of gardens comprising 2 acres of meadow with trees and an old orchard contrasting with a formal acre of mixed borders, Mediterranean courtyard and wildlife pond. A key feature of the garden are varieties of roses, over 100 plants in all, that ensures colour throughout the season.

50 PRIOR'S PIECE
Mill Street, Prestbury, Cheltenham, GL52 3BQ. Mrs D Taylor. *2m NE of Cheltenham. Take B4632 from Cheltenham to Prestbury or from Winchcombe to Prestbury following signs to Cheltenham.* **Sat 11 Apr (1-5). Adm £5.50, chd free. Tea, coffee & cake.**
Semi-formal garden with lawns and box hedges. Many interesting trees and shrubs inc an enormous magnolia, ginkgos, acers, lilac and Portuguese laurel. In the grounds is an historic dovecote leading to a beautiful part of the garden which is a secluded area of tranquillity. The garden is surrounded by mature trees, historic buildings and views of the church. Wheelchair access possible but may require assistance on the gravel areas.

51 RADNORS
Wheatstone Lane, Lydbrook, GL17 9DP. Mrs Mary Wood, 01594 861690/07473 959068, woodmary37@gmail.com. *In the Wye Valley on the edge of the Forest of Dean. From Lydbrook, go down through village towards the River Wye. At the T junction turn L into Stowfield Rd. Wheatstone Ln (300 metres) is 1st turning L after the white cottages. Radnors is at end of lane.* **Visits by arrangement 17 Mar to 30 Sept for groups of 5 to 20. Adm £5, chd free. Home-made cakes with tea, coffee or fruit juice.**
5 acre hillside woodland garden in AONB on bank above the River Wye. Focus on wildlife, naturalistic planting and weeds that are left for specific insects/birds. It has many paths, a wooded area, wildflower area, ponds, flower beds and borders, lawns, stumpery, fernery, vegetable beds and white garden. Of particular interest is the path along a disused railway line, the July lilies and summer/autumn dahlias.

52 RICHMOND VILLAGES PAINSWICK
Stroud Road, Painswick, Stroud, GL6 6UL. Richmond Villages/Bupa, www.richmond-villages.com. *5m E of Stroud. South of Painswick village on the A46, take R turn into retirement village car park.* **Thur 18 June, Thur 16 July, Thur 13 Aug (10-3). Adm £5, chd free. Tea, coffee & cake in Cafe, & restaurant meals available if booked in advance. Cash only.**
Situated on the southern slopes of Painswick, this 4 acre retirement

Cotswold Farm

© Mandy Bradshaw

village boasts formal lawns and borders planted for year-round interest. A varied mix of herbaceous perennials and shrubs, with many areas of interest inc a wildflower meadow, fruit trees and herbs that combine to attract an abundance of wildlife. There are gentle slopes in the wildflower meadow and around some areas of the village.

53 ROCKCLIFFE
Upper Slaughter, Cheltenham, GL54 2JW. Mr & Mrs Simon Keswick, www.rockcliffegarden.co.uk. *2m from Stow-on-the-Wold. 1½m from Lower Swell on B4068 towards Cheltenham. Leave Stow-on-the-Wold on B4068 through Lower Swell. Continue on B4068 for 1½m. Rockcliffe is well signed on R.* **Wed 10 June, Wed 8 July (10-5). Adm £8, chd free. Teas available. Donation to Kate's Home Nursing.** Large traditional English garden of 8 acres inc pink garden, white and blue garden, herbaceous borders, rose terrace, large walled kitchen garden and greenhouses. Pathway of topiary birds leading up through orchard to stone dovecote. Regret no dogs. There are 2 wide stone steps through gate, otherwise good wheelchair access.

54 NEW ROSE FARM
Stockwell Lane, Woodmancote, Cheltenham, GL52 9QE. Richard Basnett & Tamsin Hyde. *5m NW of Cheltenham. Off the B4632 Cheltenham to Winchcombe road turn to Woodmancote. 1.1m to Stockwell Lane. Turn R, Rose Farm on R after Beverley Gardens. Park in Hillside Gardens/Close or Apple Tree pub.* **Fri 5 June, Sat 11 July (11-4). Adm £4, chd free. Open nearby Westaway.** Compact garden surrounding listed former farmhouse and historic outbuildings. Herbaceous and mixed borders, wildflower meadows, wildlife pond, potager and vegetable garden. Historic cider mill. Contemporary garden sculptures. Artist's studio with exhibition and sale of contemporary art and sculptures. Apple Tree pub is 100 metres from house and offers lunch and refreshments. Nearby Westaway also offers tea, coffee and cakes. Level access to main garden and artist's studio. Steps to front garden.

55 ♦ SEZINCOTE
Moreton-in-Marsh, GL56 9AW. Mrs D Peake, 01386 700444, enquiries@sezincote.com, www.sezincote.co.uk. *3m SW of Moreton-in-Marsh. From Moreton-in-Marsh turn W along A44 towards Evesham; in 1½m (just before Bourton-on-the-Hill) turn L, by stone lodge with white gate opp Batsford Arboretum.* **For NGS: Sat 20 June (2-5). Adm £9, chd free. Home-made teas. Refreshment monies not for NGS. For other opening times and information, please phone, email or visit garden website.** Exotic, oriental water garden by Repton and Daniell, with lake, pools and meandering stream, banked with massed perennials. Large semi-circular orangery, formal Indian garden, fountain, temple and unusual trees of vast size in lawn and wooded park setting. House in Indian manner designed by Samuel Pepys Cockerell.

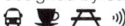

56 THE STABLES
Hyde Lane, Cheltenham, GL51 9QN. Linda Marsh. *10 mins from M5 J10. From J10 take A4019. At r'about turn L into Kingsditch Lane. Pass under rail bridge into Hyde Lane. Take first L parking opp entrance & parking at playing fields car park & in Swindon Village.* **Wed 15 July (12-4). Adm £6, chd free.** The garden extends to 0.6 acre on the original stables site and is surrounded by fields. Inspired by the work of Piet Oudolf and featured on Gardeners' World in 2024, the garden consists of large perennial beds which merge into the surrounding landscape. It has been developed over the last 5 yrs from a bare site and includes a recently planted 1 acre wildflower meadow.

GROUP OPENING

57 STANTON VILLAGE GARDENS
Stanton, nr Broadway, WR12 7NE. Susan Hughes, susanhughes2023@hotmail.com. *3m S of Broadway. Off B4632, between Broadway (3m) & Winchcombe (6m).* **Sun 14 June (1-6). Combined adm £10, chd free. Home-made teas in several gardens around the village. Donation to Village charities.**

A selection of gardens open in this picturesque, unspoilt Cotswold village. Many houses border the street with long gardens hidden behind. Gardens vary from those with colourful herbaceous borders, established trees, shrubs and vegetable gardens to tiny cottage gardens. Some also have attractive natural water features fed by the stream which runs through the village. Regret gardens not suitable for wheelchair users Church also open. The Mount Inn is open for lunch. An NGS visit not to be missed in this gem of a Cotswold village

58 ♦ STANWAY FOUNTAIN & WATER GARDEN
Stanway, Cheltenham, GL54 5PQ. The Earl of Wemyss & March, 01386 584528, office@stanwayhouse.co.uk, www.stanwayfountain.co.uk. *9m NE of Cheltenham. 1m E of B4632 Cheltenham to Broadway road on B4077 Toddington to Stow-on-the-Wold road.* **For NGS: Sun 17 May, Sun 16 Aug (2-5). Adm £7, chd £3. Home-made teas in Stanway Tearoom. For NGS day admission is to garden only. For other opening times and information, please phone, email or visit garden website.** 20 acres of planted landscape in early C18 formal setting. The restored canal, upper pond and fountain have recreated one of the most interesting Baroque water gardens in Britain. Striking C16 manor with gatehouse, tithe barn and church. The garden features Britain's highest fountain at 300ft, and it is the world's highest gravity fountain. It runs at 2.45pm and 4.00pm for 30 mins each time. Partial wheelchair access in garden, some flat areas, able to view fountain and some of garden.

Our donation in 2025 has enabled Parkinson's UK to fund 2 new nursing posts this year directly supporting people with Parkinson's.

59 ♦ SUDELEY CASTLE GARDENS

Winchcombe, GL54 5JD. Lady Ashcombe, 01242 604244, enquiries@sudeley.org.uk, www.sudeleycastle.co.uk. 8m NE Cheltenham, 10m from M5 J9. SatNavs use GL54 5LP. Free parking. **For NGS: Fri 17 Apr (10-3). Adm £10, chd £5. Light refreshments at The Pavilion. Admission is for the garden only.** **For other opening times and information, please phone, email or visit garden website.**
At Sudeley Castle Gardens you can explore 10 award-winning gardens, including The Queen's Garden, filled with many varieties of roses in the Tudor Parterre fashion. Our gardens reflect the 1000 years of the castle's history with its own unique style and design. Sudeley Castle remains the only private castle in England to have a Queen buried within the grounds - Queen Katherine Parr, the last and surviving wife of King Henry VIII – who lived and died in the castle. A circular route around the gardens is wheelchair accessible although some visitors may require assistance from their companion.

60 ♦ THYME

Southrop Estate, Southrop, Lechlade, GL7 3PW. Caryn Hibbert, 01367 850174, enquiries@thyme.co.uk, www.instagram.com/Thyme.England. Pls follow the signs through the village of Southrop towards Lechlade & to our estate drive. Disabled parking avail close to the garden **For NGS: Wed 5 Aug (11-4). Adm £10, chd free. Tea, coffee & cake. There are 2 restaurants on site that visitors can book, the Ox Barn & The Swan at Southrop.** **For other opening times and information, please phone, email or visit garden website.**
Situated on the edge of water meadows, Thyme's carefully managed kitchen gardens ensure abundance from the land, while protecting and maintaining the fertile alluvial soil. The garden is productive for much of the year, and features a herb garden, cutting gardens and polytunnels to extend the seasons. We grow a large variety of flavoursome and unusual varieties to supply our restaurants. Pls note this is a farm environment and some of the pathways are uneven

61 TRENCH HILL

Sheepscombe, GL6 6TZ. Celia & Dave Hargrave, 01452 814306, celia.hargrave@outlook.com. 1½m E of Painswick between the A46 & Sheepscombe. From Cheltenham A46 take 1st turn signed Sheepscombe, follow for approx 1½m passing Tocknells. Or from the Butcher's Arms in Sheepscombe (with it on R) leave village and take lane signed for Cranham. **Sun 8, Sun 15 Feb (11-4); Sun 15 Mar, Sun 5, Mon 6 Apr, Sun 3, Mon 4 May (11-6). Every Wed 3 June to 24 June (2-6). Sun 12 July, Sun 30, Mon 31 Aug (11-6). Adm £5, chd free. Home-made teas. Decaf, gluten, dairy free & vegan usually available. 2027: Sun 7, Sun 14 Feb.** Visits also by arrangement 16 Feb to 14 Sept for groups of up to 30. Any group wishing to arrive on a coach must speak to owners first.
Approx 3 acres set in a small woodland with panoramic views. Variety of herbaceous and mixed borders, rose garden, tulips, extensive vegetable plots, wildflower areas, plantings of spring bulbs with thousands of snowdrops and hellebores, woodland walk, two small ponds, waterfall and larger conservation pond. Interesting wooden sculptures, many within the garden. Cultivated using organic principles. Children's play area. Mostly wheelchair accessible but some steps and slopes.

GROUP OPENING

62 TUFFLEY GARDENS

Tuffley Lane, Gloucester, GL4 0DT. Martyn & Jenny Parker. 3m S Gloucester. Follow arrows from St. Barnabas r'about. Cash tickets & maps from 24 Tuffley Lane. On road parking. **Sun 31 May (11-4). Combined adm £7, chd £1. Teas available.**
A number of mature suburban gardens of all sizes and styles. Old favourites plus new openers. Lots of colourful flowers, shrubs, trees, baskets and tubs. Circular route of approx one mile. Close to Robinswood Hill Country Park, 250 acres of open countryside and viewpoint, pleasant walks and waymarked trails. Some gardens have partial wheelchair access.

63 ♦ UPTON WOLD

Moreton-in-Marsh, GL56 9TR. Mr & Mrs I R S Bond, 07801 930666, uptonwold@icloud.com, www.uptonwold.co.uk. 4½m W of Moreton-in-Marsh on A44. From Moreton/Stow ½m past A424 turn R to road into fields then L at mini Xrds. From Evesham 1m past B4081 C/Campden Xrds turn L at end of stone wall to road into fields then as above. **For NGS: Sun 19 Apr (10-5). Adm £15, chd free. Home-made teas.** **For other opening times and information, please phone, email or visit garden website.**
The Hidden Garden of the Cotswolds, Upton Wold has commanding views, yew hedges, herbaceous walks, vegetable, pond and woodland gardens, and a labyrinth. An abundance of unusual plants, shrubs and trees. National Collections of Juglans and Pterocarya. A garden of interest to any garden and plant lover. Snowdrop walks from 7 Feb to 8 March. Details on website.

64 NEW WARREN FARMHOUSE

High Street, Stanton, Broadway, WR12 7NE. Jacqueline Tucker. What3words:- grazed sidelined sock. Stanton is off B4632 Winchcombe to Broadway Rd. Take road towards The Mount Inn at T junction in village. Warren Farmhouse is 70 metres on R hand side of High St. **Sun 3 May (1-6). Combined adm with The Old Bakehouse £10, chd free. Tea, coffee or soft drink & cake inc in entry price. Any extras charged separately.**
Originally a strip farm, this is a zoned garden. The main family lawn and borders are planted for year-round interest. A secluded courtyard and formal fountain pond exists by the house. Vegetable beds and fruit cages lead to a spring interest woodland garden beyond which Soay sheep graze in a paddock. Fruit trees and woodland colonise the ridge and furrow hillside beyond.

65 WEIR REACH
The Rudge, Maisemore, Gloucester, GL2 8HY. **Sheila & Mark Wardle.** *3m NW of Gloucester. Turn into The Rudge by White Hart pub. Parking 100yds from garden.* **Sun 7, Wed 10 June (11-5). Adm £5, chd free. Tea, coffee & cake.**
Country garden by River Severn. Approx 2 acres with herbaceous beds and mixed borders plus productive fruit and vegetable gardens. Clematis, roses and acers, stone ornaments, small sculptures, bonsai collection. Planted rockery with waterfall and stream connect 2 ponds. Large specimen koi pond borders patio. Meadow with specimen trees leading to river and country views.

66 WESTAWAY
Stockwell Lane, Cleeve Hill, Cheltenham, GL52 3PU. **Liz & Ian Ramsay.** *5m NW of Cheltenham. Off the B4632 Cheltenham to Winchcombe road at Cleeve Hill. Parking in the lay-bys at the top of Stockwell Ln on B4632. Follow arrows to garden.* **Fri 5 June, Sat 11 July (11-4). Adm £6, chd free. Home-made teas. Open nearby Rose Farm.**
Hillside 1½ acre garden situated on the Cotswold escarpment with spectacular views. Interesting solutions to the challenges of gardening on a gradient, reflecting the local topography. Mixed shrub and herbaceous borders, bog garden, orchard, small arboretum and several wildflower areas. Landscaping inc extensive terracing with grass banks. Not suitable for visitors with limited mobility.

67 ◆ WESTONBIRT SCHOOL GARDENS
Tetbury, GL8 8QG. Holfords of Westonbirt Trust, 01666 881373, jbaker@holfordtrust.com, www.holfordtrust.com. *3m SW of Tetbury. Enter through main school gates on A433 - some SatNavs will send you via a side entrance where there will be no access - main school gates only please.* **For NGS: Sun 9 Aug (11-4). Adm £7.50, chd free. Tea, coffee, soft drinks, water & biscuits available throughout the day. Please note that picnics are not permitted in the gardens. For other opening times and information, please phone, email or visit garden website.**

The former private garden of Robert Holford, founder of Westonbirt Arboretum, the gardens and parkland cover 28 acres. Formal Victorian gardens inc walled Italian garden now restored with early herbaceous borders and exotic border. Rustic walks, lake now fully restored, statuary and grotto. Rare, exotic trees and shrubs. Beautiful views of Westonbirt House which is open for guided tours to see fascinating Victorian interior on designated days of the year. Gravelled paths in some areas, grass in others and wheelchair users are limited to downstairs part of the house due to evacuation protocols.

68 WICKS GREEN FARM
Wicks Green, Longney, Gloucester, GL2 3SP. **Dianne Evans, 07894 133104, dianne@evanlee.co.uk.** *What3words app: broom.almost.messy. From A38 turn into Castle Lane, over Epney Bridge, R to Longney, turn L into Chatter St, follow the lane for 1m. Wicks Green Farm will be signed with parking opp on hardstanding.* **Visits by arrangement Apr to Oct for groups of 6 to 24. Adm £5, chd free. Tea, coffee & cake. Also home-made chutneys & pickles, seasonal garden produce. Cash only.**
Set in 1½ acres, Wicks Green Farm is surrounded by countryside, has flower borders, vegetable garden, a spring fed pond and orchard; some of the pear trees are very old local varieties. The orchard with apple, pear, and plum trees is beautiful in blossom. The garden is planted for colour year-round. The old bakehouse has been re-purposed for garden entertaining. This year we are introducing our alpacas which you can walk/feed at an additional charge.

69 WOODCHESTER PARK HOUSE
Nympsfield, Stonehouse, GL10 3UN. **Robin & Veronica Bidwell.** *Nr Nailsworth. Off the road joining Nailsworth & Nympsfield (Tinkley Ln). Approx 3m from Nailsworth, turn R down next turning after the NT Tinkley Gate.* **Sun 5 July (12-5). Adm £7, chd free. Tea, coffee & cake.**
This partially walled garden of approx 3 acres incorporates extensive herbaceous borders, a yew walk, a rose covered belvedere overlooking a large pond, a woodland garden, rose walk, vegetable garden and terrace. Wide variety of plants and settings. Wheelchair access to most parts of the garden but there are steep slopes to be negotiated.

70 WORTLEY HOUSE
Wortley, Wotton-under-Edge, GL12 7QP. **Simon & Jessica Dickinson.** *On Wortley Road 1m S of Wotton-under-Edge. Grand entrance on L as you enter Wortley coming from Wotton-Under-Edge.* **Tue 21 Apr, Tue 16 June (2-5). Adm £15, chd free. Pre-booking essential, please visit www.ngs.org.uk for information & booking. Home-made teas inc in adm.**
A diverse garden of over 20 acres created during the last 30 yrs by the current owners. Includes a walled garden, pleached lime avenues, nut walk, potager, ponds, Italian garden, arbour, shrubberies and wildflower meadows. Strategically placed follies, urns and statues enhance extraordinary vistas. Wheelchair access to most areas, a golf buggy also available.

In 2025, National Garden Scheme funding helped Perennial support 950 unique callers to their helpline looking for advice and information.

HAMPSHIRE

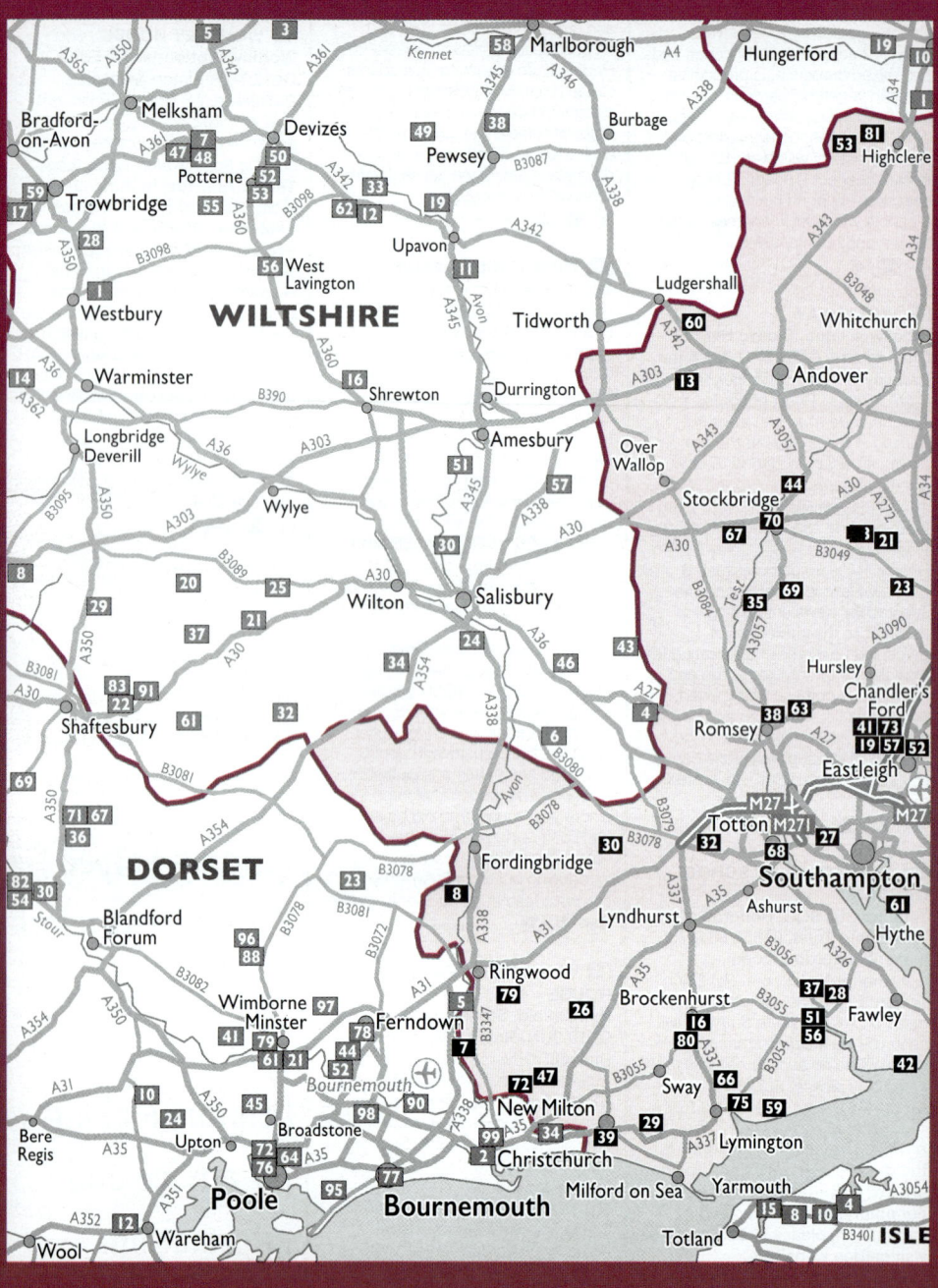

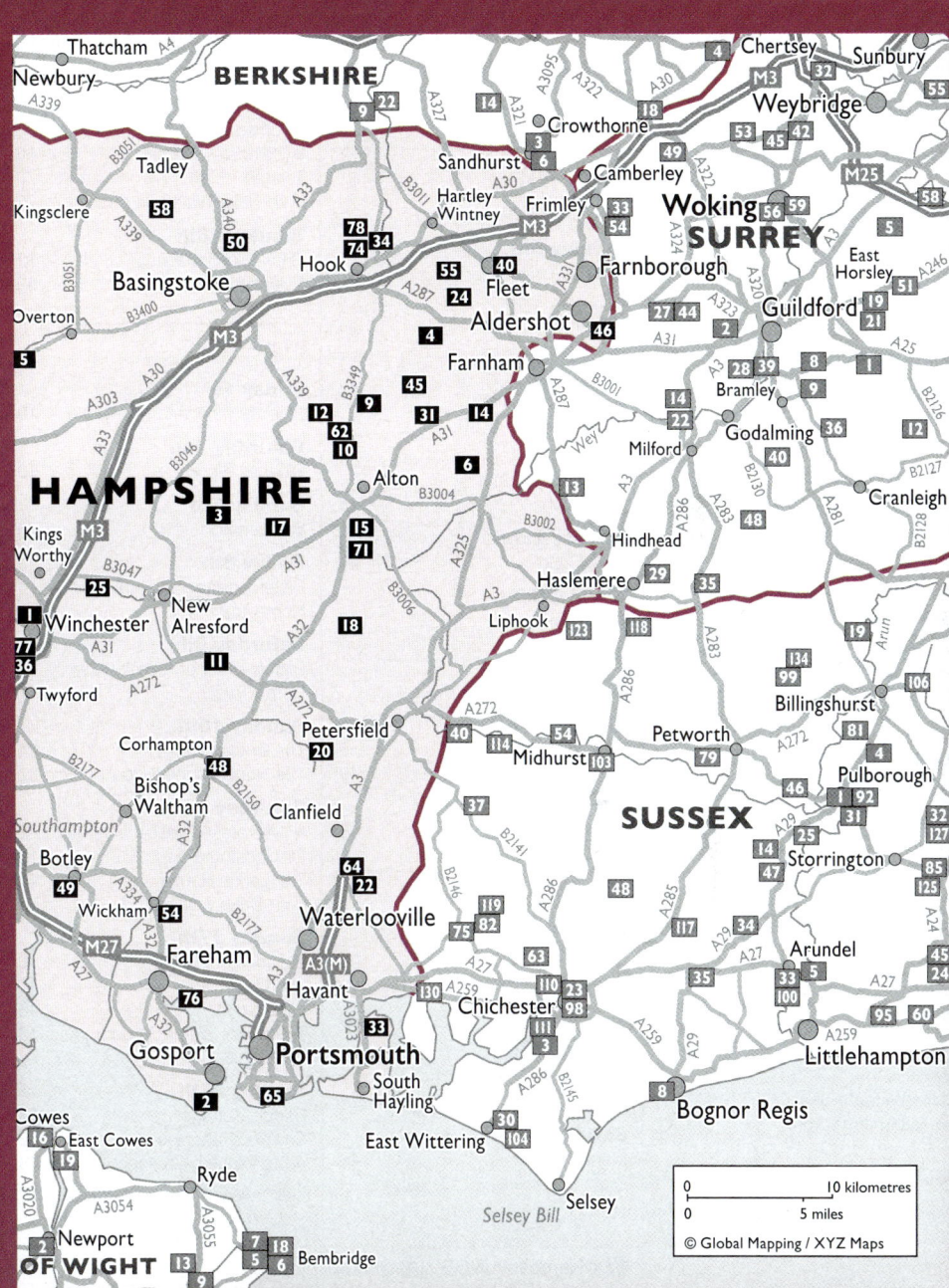

VOLUNTEERS

County Organiser
Mark Porter 07814 958210
markstephenporter@gmail.com

County Treasurer
Fred Fratter 01962 776243
fred@fratter.co.uk

Publicity
Pat Beagley 01256 764772
pat.beagley@ngs.org.uk

Social Media - Facebook
Mary Hayter 07512 639772
mary.hayter@ngs.org.uk

Booklet Co-ordinator
Mark Porter (as above)

Assistant County Organisers
Kim Donald kd581@aol.com

Central
Sue Cox 01962 732043
suealex13@gmail.com

Central West
Kate Cann 01794 389105
kategcann@gmail.com

East
Louise Moreton 07943 837993
louise.moreton@ngs.org.uk

North
Cynthia Oldale 01420 520438
c.k.oldale@btinternet.com

North East
Lizzie Powell 07799 031044
lizziepowellbroadhatch@gmail.com

North West
Adam Vetere 01635 268267
adam.vetere@ngs.org.uk

South
Barbara Sykes 02380 254521
barandhugh@aol.com

South West
Elizabeth Walker 01590 677215
elizabethwalker13@gmail.com

West
Jane Wingate-Saul 01725 519413
jw-saul@hotmail.com

OPENING DATES

All entries subject to change.
For latest information check
www.ngs.org.uk
Map locator numbers are shown to the right of each garden name.

February

Snowdrop Openings

Sunday 8th
Bramdean House 11
Sunday 15th
Little Court 43
Monday 16th
Little Court 43
Wednesday 18th
The Down House 25
Thursday 19th
The Down House 25
Sunday 22nd
Little Court 43
Monday 23rd
Little Court 43

March

Sunday 15th
Bere Mill 5
Little Court 43
Tuesday 17th
◆ Chawton House 15

April

Friday 3rd
Crawley Gardens 21
Sunday 5th
Pylewell Park 59
Monday 6th
Beechenwood Farm 4
Crawley Gardens 21
Saturday 11th
Manor Lodge 49

Sunday 12th
Lepe House Gardens 42
Manor Lodge 49
Old Thatch & The Millennium Barn 55
Saturday 18th
Lord Wandsworth College 45
Twin Oaks Water Garden 73
Sunday 19th
Lord Wandsworth College 45
Southsea Gardens 65
◆ Spinners Garden 66
Terstan 70
Twin Oaks Water Garden 73
Sunday 26th
Brick Kiln Cottage 12
Pylewell Park 59

May

Friday 1st
Bluebell Wood 10
Saturday 2nd
Bluebell Wood 10
Sunday 3rd
Walhampton 75
Friday 8th
Bisterne Manor & Stable Family Home Trust 7
Saturday 9th
Bisterne Manor & Stable Family Home Trust 7
Sunday 10th
The Dower House 24
The House in the Wood 37
Saturday 16th
◆ Alverstoke Crescent Garden 2
21 Chestnut Road 16
The Laurel House 41
Twin Oaks Water Garden 73
Sunday 17th
21 Chestnut Road 16
The Laurel House 41
Little Court 43
Twin Oaks Water Garden 73
Tylney Hall Hotel 74
Sunday 24th
Bridge Cottage 13
Shalden Park House 62
4 Stannington Crescent 68

f @HampshireNGS **◉** @hampshirengs

HAMPSHIRE

Monday 25th
Beechenwood Farm 4
Bere Mill 5
Bridge Cottage 13

Friday 29th
Winchester College 77

Saturday 30th
Ferns Lodge 29
Ladybower 40
Spitfire House 67
Winchester College 77

Sunday 31st
NEW Armsworth Hill Farm 3
Ferns Lodge 29
Ladybower 40
Spitfire House 67
4 Stannington Crescent 68

June

Wednesday 3rd
NEW Armsworth Hill Farm 3

Saturday 6th
Froyle Gardens 31
1 Povey's Cottage 58

Sunday 7th
Froyle Gardens 31
♦ The Hospital of St Cross 36
The Montagu Arms Hotel 51
1 Povey's Cottage 58
South View House 64
Southsea Gardens 65

Wednesday 10th
1 Povey's Cottage 58

Thursday 11th
Stockbridge Gardens 69

Friday 12th
Redenham Park House 60

Saturday 13th
21 Chestnut Road 16
NEW The Hoe 32
5 Oakfields 52
Twin Oaks Water Garden 73
Woodend Gardens 79

Sunday 14th
Binsted Place 6
21 Chestnut Road 16
Fritham Lodge 30
NEW The Hoe 32
5 Oakfields 52
Old Thatch & The Millennium Barn 55
Stockbridge Gardens 69
The Thatched Cottage 71
Twin Oaks Water Garden 73
Woodend Gardens 79

Saturday 20th
NEW Horsebridge Station House 35
Kingfishers Care Home 39
The Old Rectory, Wickham 54

Sunday 21st
Broadhatch House 14
NEW Horsebridge Station House 35
The Old Rectory, Wickham 54
Pines Corner Wildlife Garden 57
Terstan 70

Monday 22nd
Broadhatch House 14

Tuesday 23rd
Broadhatch House 14

Thursday 25th
Mill House 50

Sunday 28th
Bramdean House 11
Longstock Park Water Garden 44
Mill House 50
Pines Corner Wildlife Garden 57
Tylney Hall Hotel 74

July

Saturday 4th
26 Lower Newport Road 46
15 Rothschild Close 61

Sunday 5th
Bere Mill 5
26 Lower Newport Road 46
Wicor Primary School Community Garden 76

Sunday 12th
1 Wogsbarne Cottages 78

Monday 13th
1 Wogsbarne Cottages 78

Friday 17th
Fairweather's Nursery 28
Woolton House 81

Saturday 18th
Fairweather's Nursery 28
Hook Cross Allotments 34
8 Tucks Close 72

Sunday 19th
NEW Abbotts Barton Care Home 1
Bleak Hill Nursery & Garden 8
Hook Cross Allotments 34
8 Tucks Close 72

Monday 20th
Bleak Hill Nursery & Garden 8

Thursday 23rd
The Down House 25

Sunday 26th
Terstan 70

August

Saturday 1st
Manor House 48
Twin Oaks Water Garden 73

Sunday 2nd
Manor House 48
South View House 64
Twin Oaks Water Garden 73

Saturday 8th
21 Chestnut Road 16
Church House 17

Sunday 9th
Bleak Hill Nursery & Garden 8
21 Chestnut Road 16
Church House 17
The Homestead 33

Monday 10th
Bleak Hill Nursery & Garden 8

Saturday 22nd
Twin Oaks Water Garden 73

Sunday 23rd
Twin Oaks Water Garden 73

Sunday 30th
Blounce House 9
The Thatched Cottage 71

Monday 31st
Bere Mill 5
Bleak Hill Nursery & Garden 8
The Thatched Cottage 71

September

Saturday 5th
The Laurel House 41
15 Rothschild Close 61

Sunday 6th
The Laurel House 41
15 Rothschild Close 61
Terstan 70
Woodpeckers Care Home 80

Sunday 13th
Bramdean House 11

Friday 18th
Woolton House 81

February 2027

Sunday 14th
Little Court ... 43

Monday 15th
Little Court ... 43

Sunday 21st
Little Court ... 43

Monday 22nd
Little Court ... 43

By Arrangement

Arrange a personalised garden visit with your club, or group of friends, on a date to suit you. See individual garden entries for full details.

Bere Mill	5
Binsted Place	6
Blounce House	9
Brick Kiln Cottage	12
Broadhatch House	14
Church House	17
Colemore House Gardens	18
The Cottage	19
The Court House	20
Crookley Pool	22
The Deane House	23
The Down House	25
Durmast House	26
Endhouse	27
Ferns Lodge	29
The Homestead	33
The Island	38
Lepe House Gardens	42
Little Court	43
The Old Rectory	53
1 Povey's Cottage	58
15 Rothschild Close	61
Spitfire House	67
Terstan	70
The Thatched Cottage	71
Trout Cottage (Stockbridge Gardens)	69
8 Tucks Close	72
Twin Oaks Water Garden	73
Tylney Hall Hotel	74

Woodpeckers Care Home

THE GARDENS

1 NEW ABBOTTS BARTON CARE HOME
Worthy Road, Winchester, SO23 7HB. Chris Marsh, Colten Care, www.coltencare.co.uk/abbotts-barton/your-garden. What3words app: garden.blooming.peace. From M3 (S or N): Exit J9 for Winchester. Follow signs for A272/A31 Winchester. Continue onto Easton Ln, then turn L onto Worthy Rd. We are on the RHS, just past junction with Park Rd. **Sun 19 July (11-4). Adm £5, chd free. Tea, coffee & cake.**
Our care home's cottage garden offers tranquillity with circular walking routes past vibrant roses and perennial borders. Wildflower areas attract pollinators, while a greenhouse nurtures plants. A water feature soothes, grape vines shade the pergola, and winding paths through blooms invite quiet reflection and a connection with nature.

2 ♦ ALVERSTOKE CRESCENT GARDEN
Crescent Road, Gosport, PO12 2DH. Gosport Borough Council, www.alverstokecrescentgarden.co.uk. 1m S of Gosport. From A32 & Gosport follow signs for Stokes Bay. Continue alongside bay to small r'about, turn L into Anglesey Rd. Crescent Garden signed 50yds on R. **For NGS: Sat 16 May (10-4). Adm by donation. Home-made teas.** For other opening times and information, please visit garden website.
Restored Regency ornamental garden designed to enhance fine crescent (Thomas Ellis Owen 1828). Trees, walks and flowers lovingly maintained by community and council partnership. A garden of considerable local historic interest highlighted by impressive restoration and creative planting. Adjacent to St Mark's churchyard, worth seeing together. Heritage, history and horticulture, a fascinating package. Green Flag Award 2025.

3 NEW ARMSWORTH HILL FARM
Old Alresford, Alresford, SO24 9RJ. Mr James & Mrs Caroline Masterton. *From the B3406 just N of Old Alresford, turn off towards Armsworth & Upper Wield. Continue for 2m, then turn L at the Armsworth Hill sign, & L again over the cattle grid up the drive.* **Sun 31 May, Wed 3 June (2-5.30). Adm £6, chd free. Tea, coffee & cake.**
A newly designed and planted 4 acre garden in unspoilt countryside with views to the South Downs. Yew hedges and brick and flint walls divide a quartet of flower beds planted with David Austin roses, herbaceous perennials, young trees and a sunken garden. Enjoy a camassia meadow, cutting garden, formal lawns and an area of woodland with mown paths. Wheelchair access via gravel drive.

4 BEECHENWOOD FARM
Hillside, Odiham, Hook, RG29 1JA. Mr & Mrs M Heber-Percy. *5m SE of Hook. Turn S into King St from Odiham High St. Turn L after cricket ground for Hillside. Take 2nd R after 1½m, modern house ½m.* **Mon 6 Apr, Mon 25 May (2-5). Adm £5, chd free. Home-made teas.**
Opening for over 40 yrs, this 2 acre garden with many parts. Lawn meandering through woodland with drifts of spring bulbs. Rose pergola with steps, pots with spring bulbs and later aeoniums. Fritillary and cowslip meadow. Walled herb garden with pool and exuberant planting. Orchard inc white garden and hot border. Greenhouse and vegetable garden. Rock garden extending to grasses, ferns and bamboos. Shady walk to belvedere. 8 acre copse of native species with grassed rides. Assistance available with gravel drive and avoidable shallow steps.

5 BERE MILL
London Road, Whitchurch, RG28 7NH. Rupert & Elizabeth Nabarro OBE, 07703 161074, rupertnab@gmail.com, www.beremillfarm.co.uk/garden. *9m E of Andover, 12m N of Winchester. Take B3400 from centre of Whitchurch, turn R at Bere Mill Butchery sign at top of hill (approx ½ m). Visitors with disability or limited mobility park adjacent to butchery.* **Sun 15 Mar, Mon 25 May, Sun 5 July, Mon 31 Aug (1-5). Adm £8, chd free. Tea & cakes in Bere Mill West Barn.** Visits also by arrangement 31 Jan to 30 Nov for groups of 20 to 99. Fixed charge of £450 for any group size.
On an isolated stretch of the upper River Test, gardens have been built incrementally over 30 yrs with bulbs, herbaceous and Mediterranean borders, magnolia, irises, and tree peonies, along with summer and autumn borders. A traditional orchard and two small arboretums, one specialising in Japanese planting. The garden stretches into the landscape and forms part of a renaturing project. The garden aims to complement the natural beauty of the site and to incorporate elements of oriental garden design and practice. Unfenced and unguarded rivers and streams. Wheelchair access good unless very wet.

6 BINSTED PLACE
River Hill, Binsted Road, Binsted, Alton, GU34 4PQ. Max & Catherine Hadfield, 01420 23146, 07774 908416, catherine.hadfield1@icloud.com. *At eastern edge of Binsted village on Binsted Rd. 1m from Xrd at Blacknest. 1½m from A325. Parking limited, but on-road parking outside the property. The drive is one-way only, so enter carefully.* **Sun 14 June (1-6). Adm £6, chd free. Home-made teas inc.** Visits also by arrangement 25 May to 20 Sept for groups of 20 to 30. Not available during August.
Binsted Place, a C17 farmhouse with attractive local stone outbuildings, is surrounded by a series of garden rooms covering approx 1½ acres, enclosed by yew hedges and old walls. It is very traditional in style and inc many roses, pergolas, herbaceous borders, lily pond and a productive vegetable garden and orchards. Level, step free wheelchair access to most of the garden.

Our donation to the Army Benevolent Fund supported 776 individuals with horticultural related grants in 2025.

HAMPSHIRE 219

7 BISTERNE MANOR & STABLE FAMILY HOME TRUST
Bisterne, Ringwood, BH24 3BN. Leo & Becca Mills, www.bisterneestate.com/history. What3words app: searcher.movements.juggled, then follow yellow signs. **Fri 8, Sat 9 May (10-6). Adm £10, chd free. Tea, coffee & cake.**
Two spectacular gardens in one visit, united by history. The first is a formal and kitchen garden linked to C16 Bisterne Manor (not open). The second, located next to the manor, is a beautiful garden adjoining the Stable Family Home Trust, which supports adults with learning disabilities. Together, they form a beautiful 4 acre setting on the edge of the New Forest. Wheelchair access to a level garden with wide gravel paths.

8 BLEAK HILL NURSERY & GARDEN
Braemoor, Bleak Hill, Harbridge, Ringwood, BH24 3PX. Tracy & John Netherway, www.bleakhillplants.co.uk. 2½m S of Fordingbridge. Turn off A338 at Ibsley. Go through Harbridge village to T-junction at top of hill, turn R for ¼m. **Sun 19 July (2-5); Mon 20 July (11-3); Sun 9 Aug (2-5); Mon 10 Aug (11-3); Mon 31 Aug (2-5). Adm £5, chd free. Home-made teas. No refreshments on 20 July & 10 Aug, welcome to bring a picnic. Cash only.**
Enjoy this ¾ acre garden, pass through the moongates to reveal the billowing borders contrasting against a seaside scene with painted beach huts and a boat on the gravel. Herbaceous borders complemented by a spectacular tropical border fill the garden with colour wrapping around a pond and small stream. Greenhouses with cacti and sarracenias. Vegetable patch and small wildflower meadow. Small adjacent nursery.

9 BLOUNCE HOUSE
Blounce, South Warnborough, Hook, RG29 1RX. Tom & Gay Bartlam, 07788 911184, tomb@thbartlam.co.uk. 4m N of Alton. In hamlet of Blounce, 1m S of South Warnborough on B3349 from Odiham to Alton. **Sun 30 Aug (1-4). Adm £6, chd free. Tea, coffee & cake.** Visits also by arrangement 8 June to 11 Sept for groups of 10 to 30.

A 2 acre garden surrounding a classic Queen Anne house (not open). Mixed planting to give interest from spring to late autumn. Herbaceous borders with a variety of colour themes. In late summer an emphasis on dahlias, salvias and grasses.

10 BLUEBELL WOOD
Stancombe Lane, Bavins, New Odiham Road, Alton, GU34 5SX. Mrs Jennifer Ospici, www.bavins.co.uk. On the corner of Stancombe Ln & the B3349, 2½m N of Alton. **Fri 1, Sat 2 May (11-4). Adm £10, chd free. Light refreshments.**
Unique 100 acre ancient bluebell woodland. If you are a keen walker you will have much to explore on the long meandering paths and rides dotted with secluded seats. The wood is very challenging for those with mobility problems. Refreshments will be served in an original rustic building and inc soups using natural woodland ingredients.

11 BRAMDEAN HOUSE
Bramdean, Alresford, SO24 0JU. Mr & Mrs E Wakefield, garden@bramdeanhouse.com, www.instagram.com/bramdean_house_garden. 4m S of Alresford, 9m E of Winchester, & 9m W of Petersfield. In centre of village on A272. Entrance opp sign to the church. Parking is signed across the road from entrance. **Sun 8 Feb (1.30-3.30); Sun 28 June (12.30-3.30); Sun 13 Sept (1.30-3.30). Adm £7, chd free. Tea, coffee & cake. Donation to Bramdean Church.**
Beautiful 5 acre garden best known for its mirror image herbaceous borders, a 1 acre walled garden, carpets of spring bulbs, and a large, unusual collection of plants and shrubs giving year-round interest. Features inc fine snowdrops, a large collection of old fashioned sweet peas, an expansive collection of nerines, a boxwood castle and the nation's tallest sunflower 'Giraffe'. Private visits also by arrangement for groups of 5+ (non-NGS). The garden is on a slope and mainly grass. Some paths require narrower than standard wheelchair for access. Assistance dogs only.

12 BRICK KILN COTTAGE
The Avenue, Herriard, nr Alton, RG25 2PR. Barbara Jeremiah & Kay Linnell, 01256 381301, barbara@klca.co.uk. 4m NE of Alton, nr Lasham Gliding Club. A339 Basingstoke to Alton, 7m out of Basingstoke turn L along The Avenue, past Lasham Gliding Club on R, then past Back Ln on L & take next track on L, one field later. **Sun 26 Apr (11.30-3.30). Adm £5, chd free. Home-made teas.** Visits also by arrangement 27 Apr to 8 May for groups of 10 to 30.
A 2 acre bluebell woodland garden with a perimeter woodland path inc treehouse, pebble garden, billabong, ferny hollow, bug palace, waterpool, shepherd's hut and a traditional cottage garden filled with herbs. The garden is maintained using eco-friendly methods as a haven for wild animals, butterflies, birds, bees and English bluebells. Children's reading area and games. A haven in the trees. Gallery of textiles. This year the bluebell day will inc music.

13 BRIDGE COTTAGE
Amport, Andover, SP11 8AY. John & Jenny Van de Pette. 3m SW of Andover. Leave the A303 at East Cholderton from E or Thruxton village from W. Follow signs to Amport. Parking in a field by Amport village green. What3words app: stress.threaded.dialects. **Sun 24, Mon 25 May (2-5.30). Adm £6, chd free. Home-made teas.**
This 2 acre garden is a haven for wildlife, developed over 24 yrs by the current owners. A lake is edged with glorious herbaceous borders. A trout stream with water voles and kingfishers. Organic vegetable garden, fruit cage, small mixed orchard and arboretum with unusual trees. Superb plant sale. Treasure hunt for children. Paths in the vegetable garden are not suitable for wheelchairs.

14 BROADHATCH HOUSE
Bentley, Farnham, GU10 5JJ. Bruce & Lizzie Powell, 07799 031044, lizziepowellbroadhatch@gmail.com. 4m NE of Alton. Turn off A31 (Bentley bypass) through village, then L up School Ln. R to Perrylands, after 300yds drive on R. What3words app: driveways.shelters.absorbs. **Sun 21, Mon 22, Tue 23 June**

(2-5). **Adm £7.50, chd free.** Visits also by arrangement 11 May to 30 June.

A 3½ acre garden set in lovely Hampshire countryside with views to Alice Holt. Divided into different areas by yew hedges and walled garden. Focussing on as long a season as possible on heavy clay. Features inc two reflective pools to help break up lawn areas, lots of flower borders and beds, mature trees, working greenhouses, and a vegetable garden. Wheelchair access with gravel paths and steps in some areas.

15 ♦ CHAWTON HOUSE

Chawton, Alton, GU34 1SJ. Chawton House, 01420 541010, info@chawtonhouse.org, www.chawtonhouse.org. *2m S of Alton. In Chawton village take the Gosport Rd opp Jane Austen House towards St Nicholas Church. Chawton House is at the end of the road on the L. Parking nearby & in village.* **For NGS: Tue 17 Mar (10-3.30). Adm £8, chd free. Light refreshments.** For other opening times and information, please phone, email or visit garden website.

Daffodils and spring flowering bulbs are scattered through this 15 acre listed English landscape garden. Sweeping lawns, a wilderness, terraces and shrubbery walks surround the Elizabethan manor house. The walled garden designed by Edward Knight inc a rose garden, flower borders, orchard, kitchen garden, and herb garden based on 'A Curious Herbal' (1737-39) by Elizabeth Blackwell. Hot and cold drinks, wine, light lunches, cream teas, home-made cakes and local ice creams available in our tea shed on the main drive and in The Old Kitchen Tearoom at the house.

16 21 CHESTNUT ROAD

Brockenhurst, SO42 7RF. Iain & Mary Hayter, www.21-chestnut-rdgardens.co.uk. *New Forest. Please use village car park a short walk away. Limited parking for those less mobile in road. Leave M27 J2, follow Heavy Lorry Route. Mainline station less than 10 min walk.* **Sat 16, Sun 17 May, Sat 13, Sun 14 June, Sat 8, Sun 9 Aug (11.30-5). Adm £5, chd free. Home-made teas.**

A ⅓ acre in a central village location. A cottage garden which can be described as fully matured with areas that are either delicate and subtle or intense, with aromas to tingle the senses using a true colour palate fit for the connoisseur with earthy and floral notes, rich and fruity like a vintage wine, all served with home-made cakes. Open for the NGS for over 20 yrs, it's a place to relax.

The National Garden Scheme donated £3,875,596 to our nursing and health beneficiaries from money raised at gardens open in 2025.

Bisterne Manor & Stable Family Home Trust

17 CHURCH HOUSE
Trinity Hill, Medstead, Alton, GU34 5LT. Mr Paul & Mrs Alice Beresford, 01420 562592, pauljames2309@gmail.com. 5m WSW of Alton. From A31 Four Marks follow signs to Medstead for 1½ m to village centre, turn R into Church Ln/Trinity Hill. From N on A339, R at Bentworth Xrds & continue via Bentworth to Medstead. **Sat 8 Aug (2-5.30); Sun 9 Aug (2-5). Adm £8, chd £2. Tea, coffee & cake.** Visits also by arrangement 1 May to 18 Sept for groups of 10 to 60. Discuss light lunches or evening visits with wine & canapés when booking.
A colourful 1 acre garden, set within a wide variety of mature trees and shrubs. Long, sweeping, colour themed mixed borders give lots of ideas for planting in sun and shade. Contrasting features and textures throughout the garden are enhanced by interesting sculptures. Espaliered fruit trees, a woodland area, small greenhouse and roses in different settings all contribute to this much loved garden. For further information see Facebook, search Church House Garden Medstead. Wheelchair access via gravel drive to flat lawned garden. No access to some paths and patio.

18 COLEMORE HOUSE GARDENS
Colemore, Alton, GU34 3RX. Mr & Mrs Simon de Zoete, 01420 588202, simondezoete@gmail.com. 4m S of Alton, off A32. Approach from N on A32, turn L into Shell Ln, ¼ m S of East Tisted. Go under bridge, keep L until you see Colemore Church. Park on verge of church. **Visits by arrangement May to July for groups of 10 to 40. Adm £10, chd free. Light refreshments.**
4 acres in lovely unspoilt countryside, featuring rooms containing many unusual plants and different aspects with a spectacular arched rose walk, water rill, mirror pond, herbaceous and shrub borders. Newly designed by David Austin roses, an octagonal garden with 25 different varieties. Explore the interesting arboretum, grass gardens and thatched pavilion. Every yr the owners seek improvement and the introduction of new, interesting and rare plants. Propagated plants for sale, many of which can be found in the garden. Some are unusual and not readily available elsewhere. During private visits, a conducted tour is offered, along with an explanation of future plans, rationale, and objectives.

19 THE COTTAGE
16 Lakewood Road, Chandler's Ford, Eastleigh, SO53 1ES. Hugh & Barbara Sykes, 02380 254521, barandhugh@aol.com. Leave M3 J12, follow signs to Chandler's Ford. At King Rufus on Winchester Rd, turn R into Merdon Ave, then 3rd road on L. **Visits by arrangement Mar to May for groups of 5+. Adm £5.50, chd free. Home-made teas.**
¾ acre garden. Colourful in spring with azaleas, rhododendrons, camellias, trilliums and erythroniums under old oaks and pines. Herbaceous cottage style borders with unusual plants for year-round interest. Bog garden, ponds, kitchen garden. Enjoy the birdsong with over 35 bird species noted. Wildlife areas. Our 40th year sharing the garden with visitors. Garden croquet, natural Easter egg decorating demonstrations and talks about bees can be inc in visits. NGS sundial for opening for 30 yrs. 'A lovely tranquil garden', Anne Swithinbank. Hampshire Wildlife Trust Wildlife Garden Award. Honey from our beehives for sale.

20 THE COURT HOUSE
East Meon, Petersfield, GU32 1NJ. George & Clare Bartlett, 07747 827751, clarebartlett@doctors.org.uk. 5m W of Petersfield. What3words app: pegs.cheaper.presumes. Signed from A32 in West Meon to East Meon. Entrance on R 200yds past East Meon church. From A3 at Petersfield take A272, L at Langrish to East Meon, entrance on L after 2m. **Visits by arrangement 15 June to 18 Sept for groups of 10 to 30. Adm £10, chd free. Light refreshments.**
A 2 acre garden, surrounding a medieval manor house (not open), laid out in the 'Arts and Crafts' style with separate areas divided by yew hedges and stone walls. The established herbaceous borders contain some unusual plants providing interest throughout the summer. Steps lead to a lower level with reflecting pool and progressively less formal planting. 1 acre vineyard. Gravel path and two shallow steps to herbaceous borders. Additional steps dividing other areas of the garden.

GROUP OPENING

21 CRAWLEY GARDENS
Crawley, Winchester, SO21 2PR. 5m NW of Winchester. Between B3049 (Winchester - Stockbridge) & A272 (Winchester - Andover). Parking throughout village. **Fri 3, Mon 6 Apr (2-5.30). Combined adm £8, chd free. Home-made teas in the village hall.**

LITTLE COURT
Mrs A R Elkington.
(See separate entry)

PAIGE COTTAGE
Mr & Mrs T W Parker.

Crawley is a charming period village nestled in chalk downland, featuring thatched cottages, a C14 church, and a village pond. The gardens offer seasonal interest with both traditional and contemporary approaches to landscape and planting. Little Court is a 3 acre country garden with beautiful country views, carpets of spring bulbs, herbaceous borders, and a large meadow. Paige Cottage is a 1 acre traditional English garden surrounding a period thatched cottage (not open), with bulbs, wild flowers, and old climbing roses. Plants from the garden for sale at Little Court.

22 CROOKLEY POOL
Blendworth Lane, Horndean, PO8 0AB. Mr & Mrs Simon Privett, 02392 592662, jennyprivett@icloud.com. 5m S of Petersfield, 2m E of Waterlooville, off the A3. From Horndean up Blendworth Ln between bakery & hairdresser. Entrance 200yds before church on L with white railings. **Visits by arrangement 9 May to 28 Sept for groups of 15+. Adm £10, chd free. Tea, coffee & cake.**
Here the plants choose where to grow. Californian tree poppies elbow valerian aside to crowd round the old pool. This 2 acre artist and plantsman's garden is full of colour over a long season. A large collection of salvias thrive here. Tomatoes share the greenhouse with exotics. Hellebores bloom under the trees, and a 100 yr old wisteria rampages along pergolas and walls. Wildflower meadow in the orchard.

23 THE DEANE HOUSE
Sparsholt, Winchester,
SO21 2LR. Mr & Mrs Richard
Morse, 07774 863004,
chrissiemorse7@gmail.com.
3½ m NW of Winchester. Off A3049
Stockbridge Rd, onto Woodman Ln,
signed Sparsholt. Turn L at cream
house on L with green gables & go
to top of drive. Plenty of parking. Do
not follow SatNav. What3words app:
grapevine.socket.skips. **Visits by
arrangement 16 Mar to 11 Sept
for groups of 10+. Tea, coffee
& cake or lunches. Prosecco &
canapés for evening visits.**
A beautiful 4 acre rural garden,
overlooking Woodman vineyard,
nestled on a gentle south facing
slope, landscaped to draw the eye
from one gentle terraced lawn to
another with borders merging into
the surrounding countryside and
vines. Featuring a good selection of
specimen trees, a walled garden,
prairie planting and herbaceous
borders. Millennium avenue of tulip
trees. Water features and sculptures.
Tour of Woodman vineyard can be
arranged. Sorry, no dogs. Although
the garden is on the side of a hill there
is always a path to avoid steps.

24 THE DOWER HOUSE
Church Lane, Dogmersfield, Hook,
RG27 8TA. Anne-Marie & Richard
Revell. 3½ m E of Hook. Turn N off
A287. For SatNav please use RG27
8SZ. **Sun 10 May (2-4.30). Adm £6,
chd free. Home-made teas.**
6 acres inc bluebell wood with
large and spectacular collection of
rhododendrons, azaleas, magnolias
and other flowering trees and shrubs;
set in parkland with fine views over 20
acre lake.

25 THE DOWN HOUSE
Itchen Abbas, SO21 1AX. Jackie
& Mark Porter, 07814 958810,
markstephenporter@gmail.com.
5m E of Winchester on B3047. 5th
house on R after the Itchen Abbas
village sign, if coming on B3047
from Kings Worthy. 500 metres on
L after The Plough pub if coming on
B3047 from Alresford. **Wed 18, Thur
19 Feb (1-4.30). Adm £12, chd
free. Home-made teas inc. Pre-
booking essential, please visit
www.ngs.org.uk for information &
booking. Thur 23 July (2-5). Adm
£8, chd free. Home-made teas.
Visits also by arrangement 16 Feb
to 27 Feb for groups of 10+.**
A 2 acre garden laid out in rooms
overlooking the Itchen Valley, adjoining
the Pilgrim's Way. In winter come and
see garden structure, snowdrops,
aconites and crocus, plus borders of
dogwoods, willow stems and white
birches. In summer, a terrace of
agapanthus and succulents, pleached
hornbeams, rope-lined fountain
garden, formal box-edged potager,
a new wildlife pond and sustainable
garden, yew-lined avenue and walks
in adjoining meadows.

26 DURMAST HOUSE
Bennetts Lane, Burley, BH24 4AT.
Mr P E G Daubeney, 01425 402132,
philip@daubeney.co.uk,
www.durmasthouse.co.uk. 5m SE
of Ringwood. Off Burley to Lyndhurst
road, nr White Buck Hotel, C10 road.
**Visits by arrangement 1 Apr to 1
Aug for groups of 10 to 50. Adm
£8, chd free. Talk & tour of the
garden inc. Self service tea & cake.**
Designed by Gertrude Jekyll, Durmast
has contrasting hot and cool colour
borders, a formal rose garden edged
with lavender, and a long herbaceous
border. Many old trees inc cedar
and Douglas firs, a Victorian rockery,
and an orchard filled with beautiful
spring bulbs. Features inc rare
azaleas; Fama, Princeps, and Gloria
Mundi from Ghent and rose bowers
with rare French roses; Eleanor
Berkeley, Psyche and Reine Olga de
Wurtemberg. Wheelchair access on
stone and gravel paths.

27 ENDHOUSE
6 Wimpson Gardens,
Southampton, SO16 9ES.
Kevin Liles, 02380 777590,
mendip51@icloud.com. West
Southampton. Exit M271 at J1
toward Lordshill. At 2nd r'about,
turn R into Romsey Rd towards
Shirley. After ½ m turn R at Xrds into
Wimpson Ln, 3rd on R Crabwood
Rd (additional parking). Wimpson
Gardens 4th on R. **Visits by
arrangement 18 May to 10 July
for groups of 15 to 25. Adm £9,
chd free. Home-made teas inc.**
Endhouse is a tranquil urban oasis
of linked gardens, inc a secret rose
garden. It has won Southampton's
Best Private Garden award six
times and features statuary, studio
ceramics, specimen palms, tree
ferns, and acers. Mixed borders and
ornamental greenhouse grow a wide
range of herbaceous plants, roses,
and salad crops. Comfortable seating
and quality refreshments make it a
popular visit for many groups.

28 FAIRWEATHER'S NURSERY
Hilltop, Beaulieu, SO42 7YR.
Patrick Fairweather, 01590 612113,
info@fairweathers.co.uk,
www.fairweathers.co.uk. Hilltop
Nursery. 1½ m NE of Beaulieu village
on B3054. Please leave plenty of time,
the guided tour will start promptly at
11am. **Fri 17, Sat 18 July (11-12.30).
Adm £10, chd free. Pre-booking
essential, please visit www.ngs.
org.uk for information & booking.
Light refreshments.**
Fairweather's hold a specialist
collection of over 400 agapanthus
grown in pots and display beds, inc
AGM award-winning agapanthus
trialled by the RHS. Patrick
Fairweather will give a guided
tour of the nursery at 11am with a
demonstration of how to get the best
from agapanthus and companion
planting. Open nearby Patrick's Patch
at Fairweather's Garden Centre, High
Street, Beaulieu. Wheelchair access
over gravel paths.

29 FERNS LODGE
Cottagers Lane, Hordle,
Lymington, SO41 0FE.
Sue Grant, 07860 521501,
sue.grant@fernslodge.co.uk,
www.fernslodge.co.uk. Approx
5½ m W of Lymington. From Silver
St turn into Woodcock Ln, 100
metres to Cottagers Ln, parking in
field opp garden. From A337 turn
into Everton Rd & drive approx
1½ m, Cottagers Ln on R. **Sat 30,
Sun 31 May (2-5). Adm £10, chd
free. Home-made teas inc. Visits
also by arrangement in June for
groups of 10 to 50. Please discuss
refreshment options on booking.**
Bustling 4 acre wildlife garden filled
with scent, colour and mature trees.
½ acre cottage garden around
owners Victorian lodge, full of forget-
me-nots, foxgloves, clematis, roses,
agapanthus, and salvia. Brick paths
wind through with plentiful seating,
perfect for tea. The large garden is
being gradually restored with new
planting inc tree ferns, two cedar
greenhouses, and fine 3D art. New
potting shed being built. Wheelchair
access to many areas.

30 FRITHAM LODGE
Fritham, SO43 7HH. Sir Chris & Lady Powell. 6m N of Lyndhurst. 3m NW of M27 J1 (Cadnam). Follow signs to Fritham. **Sun 14 June (2-4). Adm £5, chd free. Home-made teas.**
A walled garden of 1 acre in the heart of the New Forest, set within 18 acres surrounding a house that was originally a Charles I hunting lodge (not open). Herbaceous and blue and white mixed borders, pergolas and ponds. A box hedge enclosed parterre of roses, fruit and vegetables. Visitors will enjoy the ponies, donkeys, sheep and old breed hens on their meadow walk to the woodland and stream.

GROUP OPENING

31 FROYLE GARDENS
Lower Froyle, Froyle, GU34 4LG. www.froyleopengardens.org.uk. Located midway between Alton & Farnham, just off the A31. Access to Froyle from A31 between Alton & Farnham at Bentley, or at Hen & Chicken Inn. Park at Recreation Ground in Lower Froyle, GU34 4LG. Map provided. Additional signed parking in Upper Froyle. **Sat 6, Sun 7 June (1.30-6). Combined adm £10, chd free. Home-made teas in the village hall & picnics welcome on the recreation ground in Lower Froyle.**

ALDERSEY HOUSE
Nigel & Julie Southern.

DAY COTTAGE
Nick & Corinna Whines, www.daycottage.co.uk.

2 HIGHWAY COTTAGE
Faith Richards & Gordon Mitchell.

OLD BREWERY HOUSE
Vivienne & John Sexton.

OLD STABLE BARN
Polly & Simon Marshall.

1 TURNPIKE COTTAGES
Ms Pam Walls.

2 TURNPIKE COTTAGES
Bruce Collinson.

WALBURY
Ernie & Brenda Milam.

WELL LANE CORNER
Mark & Sue Lelliott.

A warm welcome awaits as Froyle Gardens open their gates once again, enabling visitors to enjoy a wide variety of types of garden, all of which have undergone further development since last yr and will be looking splendid. Froyle 'The Village of Saints' has many old and interesting buildings. Our gardens harmonise well with the surrounding landscape and most have spectacular views. The gardens themselves are diverse with rich planting. You will see greenhouses, water features, vegetables, roses, clematis and wildflower meadows. Lots of ideas to take away with you, along with plants to buy and delicious teas served in the village hall. Close by is a playground with a zip wire where children can let off steam. There is also an exhibition of richly embroidered historic vestments in the Church in Upper Froyle (separate donation). The gardens are well spread out so wear comfortable shoes! No wheelchair access to Day Cottage, Old Stable Barn and 1 Turnpike Cottages. Gravel drive at 2 Highway Cottage.

32 NEW THE HOE
Winsor Road, Winsor, Southampton, SO40 2HJ. Heidi Burnett. From M27 J1, take A31 to Cadnam, for 200yds, then A336 for 600yds. Turn L into Winsor Rd; the garden is on the R. Parking opp at James Farm. **Sat 13, Sun 14 June (12.30-5.30). Adm £4, chd free. Tea, coffee & cake.**
This Grade II listed C16 thatched cottage (not open) nestles within a small informal garden. Long borders with perennials, shrubs and herbs jostle together with rose pillars and rope framing the front garden, which also has chickens and a self-built shepherd's hut. The back garden has a brick patio with a C16 well, formal pond, David Austin rose garden with an arbour, a potting shed, and a greenhouse.

33 THE HOMESTEAD
Northney Road, Hayling Island, PO11 0NF. Stan & Mary Pike, 07792 575020, jhomestead@aol.com. 3m S of Havant. From A27 Havant & Hayling Island r'about, travel S over Langstone Bridge & turn immed L into Northney Rd. Car park entrance on R after Langstone Hotel. **Sun 9 Aug (1.30-5). Adm £5, chd free. Home-made teas. Visits also by arrangement July to Sept for groups of 12+.**
1¼ acre garden surrounded by working farmland with views to Butser Hill and Chichester Harbour. Trees, shrubs, colourful herbaceous borders and small walled garden with herbs, vegetables and trained fruit trees. Large pond and woodland walk with shade loving plants. A quiet and peaceful atmosphere with plenty of seats to enjoy the vistas within the garden. An extensive range of plants for sale. Visitors can also visit the adjoining flower farm. Wheelchair access with some gravel paths.

34 HOOK CROSS ALLOTMENTS
Reading Road, Hook, RG27 9DB. Hook Allotment Association. Northern edge of Hook village on B3349, Reading Rd. 900 metres N of A30 r'about. Concealed entrance track is on RHS at foot of hill opp a farm entrance, straight after turns to B & M Fencing & Searle's Ln. **Sat 18, Sun 19 July (1-5). Adm £5, chd free. Tea, coffee & cake.**
5¼ acre community run allotments overlooking Hook village. Explore more than 100 plots showcasing a variety of vegetables, fruit, and flower growing styles, plus a community orchard, wildflower meadow and banks, and wildlife friendly gardening information. Talk with plot holders about growing your own, vote for your favourite scarecrow, and learn about soil health with guest display from Soil Ecology Laboratory.

35 NEW HORSEBRIDGE STATION HOUSE
Horsebridge, Kings Somborne, Stockbridge, SO20 6PU. Mrs Val Charrington. W of Winchester. From the A3057 from Stockbridge or Romsey, turn at sign to Horsebridge nr Kings Somborne. The drive to the station is directly opp the John O'Gaunt pub. Limited parking at station & Test Way car park. **Sat 20, Sun 21 June (2-5). Adm £5, chd free.**
The gardens at Horsebridge are set against the backdrop of the restored 1865 railway station, featuring full-length platforms, carriages, signals, and a signal box. Set in nearly two acres of extensive lawns and flower beds, the garden is surrounded by farmland and water meadows, near the River Test, covering the original sidings. The lawns and platforms are accessible by wheelchair. Disabled parking on lawn.

36 ♦ THE HOSPITAL OF ST CROSS
St Cross Road, Winchester, SO23 9SD. The Hospital of St Cross & Almshouse of Noble Poverty, 01962 878218, office@hospitalofstcross.co.uk, www.hospitalofstcross.co.uk. ½m S of Winchester. From City Centre: B3335 (Southgate St/St Cross Rd) S. Turn L immed before The Bell Inn. To walk: Approx 20 mins via river path S from Cathedral & College. From M3 J11: St Cross Rd, turn R at Bell Inn. **For NGS: Sun 7 June (1-5). Adm £5, chd free. Tea, coffee & cake.** For other opening times and information, please phone, email or visit garden website.
The Medieval Hospital of St Cross nestles in water meadows beside the River Itchen and is one of England's oldest almshouses. The tranquil, walled 'Compton Garden', created in the late C17 by Bishop Compton, contains beautiful sculptural herbaceous borders, old-fashioned roses, and magnificent trees, along with a large carp and lily pond. The Hundred Men's Hall Tearoom and the Porter's Lodge Gift Shop will be open. Wheelchair access with uneven surfaces in places.

37 THE HOUSE IN THE WOOD
Beaulieu, SO42 7YN. Victoria Roberts. New Forest. 8m NE of Lymington. Leaving the entrance to Beaulieu Motor Museum on R (B3056), take next R signed Ipley Cross. Take 2nd gravel drive on RH-bend, approx ½m. **Sun 10 May (1.30-5). Adm £6, chd free. Cream teas.**
Peaceful 12 acre woodland garden with continuing progress and improvement. Very much a spring garden with tall, glorious mature azaleas and rhododendrons in every shade of pink, orange, red and white, interspersed with acers and other woodland wonders. A magical garden to get lost in with many twisting paths leading downhill to a pond. Used in the war to train the Special Operations Executive.

38 THE ISLAND
Greatbridge, Romsey, SO51 0HP. Mr & Mrs Christopher Saunders-Davies, 01794 512100, ssd@littleroundtop.co.uk. 1m N of Romsey on A3057. Entrance at bridge. Follow drive 100yds. Car park on RHS. **Visits by arrangement June to Aug for groups of 15 to 20. Morning visits only. Bookings can be made from 1 April. Adm £15. Light refreshments.**
6 acres both sides of the River Test. Fine display of daffodils, tulips, spring flowering trees and summer bedding. The main garden has herbaceous and annual borders, fruit trees, rose pergola, lavender walk and extensive lawns. An arboretum planted in the 1930s by Sir Harold Hillier contains three ponds, shrubs and specimen trees providing interest throughout the yr. No dogs allowed.

39 KINGFISHERS CARE HOME
The Meadows, New Milton, BH25 7FJ. Chris Marsh, Colten Care, www.coltencare.co.uk/kingfishers/your-garden. New Forest. W on A337 from Lymington to New Milton. L opp fish & chip shop down Southern Rd, 1st R into The Meadows. Park in allocated car parking spaces or on Southern Rd. **Sat 20 June (11-4). Adm £5, chd free. Tea, coffee & cake.**
This colourful care home garden offers the visitor wide, winding paths leading to many points of interest: herbaceous borders, a lavender avenue, pergola, greenhouse, vegetable patch, and, most recently, a fascinating water feature. Residents are actively involved in planning, propagating plants, and creating habitats for local wildlife, inc bug houses. This easily accessible garden has something for everyone to enjoy.

40 LADYBOWER
47 Connaught Road, Fleet, GU51 3LR. Muriel Pratt. Central Fleet. Exit J4A of M3 & follow directions to Fleet, pass train station & turn L at 2nd T-lights on to Kings Rd, Connaught Rd is 3rd on the R. Parking at Ark Veterinary Surgery, 41 Connaught Rd (50 metres). **Sat 30, Sun 31 May (2-5). Adm £5, chd free. Home-made teas inc gluten free option.**
This garden, covering over ¼ of an acre, was created 10 yrs ago. Spread across three terraces it has a large acer bed, several herbaceous borders, and a large pond surrounded by rockery. Still evolving, it offers a peaceful oasis in the centre of a thriving market town. Floral displays from roses, rhododendrons, and salvias, with an additional collection of hostas. Wheelchair access over flat patio and slopes to two of the three terraces. Parking on drive by prior arrangement, please call 07743 899494.

41 THE LAUREL HOUSE
4 Beechwood Crescent, Chandler's Ford, Eastleigh, SO53 5PA. Gill Ellaway. Leave M3 J12, follow signs to Romsey. Follow Hocombe Rd to Xrds. Turn L onto Hursley Rd. Turn 4th R into Beechwood Cres. **Sat 16, Sun 17 May, Sat 5, Sun 6 Sept (1-5). Adm £5, chd free. Home-made teas & gluten free option.**
An enchanting ⅔ acre, garden designer's garden, developed over 35 yrs has matured into a vibrant tapestry of colour, texture and scent. Woodland walks feature dry-shade plants, while hot beds bloom in late summer. Wildlife thrives with ponds, bird boxes and wood piles. Sustainable practices like composting enrich the soil. This garden offers a tranquil retreat, full of inspiration year-round. Mostly wheelchair accessible. One step to the top garden level (ramp available). Bark paths in the woodland area may be unsuitable.

42 LEPE HOUSE GARDENS
Lepe, Exbury, Southampton, SO45 1AD. Michael & Emma Page, emma.page@lepe.org.uk, www.lepe.org.uk. New Forest. ½m from Lepe Country Park, 2m from Exbury Gardens. Entrance to drive through gates on S-side of Lepe Rd. What3words for: belong.nurses.highlight. **Sun 12 Apr (1.30-4.30). Adm £10, chd free. Tea, coffee & cake inc.** Visits also by arrangement 15 Apr to 12 June for groups of 15 to 30. Adm £15, chd free, inc refreshments & a guided tour by owner & head gardener.
This 14 acre spring woodland garden was laid out in 1893. An embarkation point for D-Day, the lighthouse in the garden now marks the entrance to the Beaulieu River with stunning views. Features inc walled garden with camellias, coastal walk overlooking the Solent, woodland with mature magnolias, rhododendrons, arboretum with drifts of spring bulbs, wildlife ponds, and formal areas inc wishing well.

HAMPSHIRE

43 LITTLE COURT
Crawley, Winchester, SO21 2PU.
Mrs A R Elkington, 01962 776365,
elkslc@btinternet.com. *5m NW
of Winchester. Crawley village lies
between B3049 (Winchester -
Stockbridge) & A272 (Winchester
- Andover), 400yds from either pond
or church.* **Sun 15, Mon 16, Sun
22, Mon 23 Feb (2-4.30); Sun 15
Mar, Sun 17 May (2-5.30). Adm
£6, chd free. Home-made teas
in the village hall. 2027: Sun 14,
Mon 15, Sun 21, Mon 22 Feb.
Opening with Crawley Gardens
on Fri 3, Mon 6 Apr. Visits also by
arrangement 14 Feb to 5 July.**
A sheltered, naturalistic garden
with year-round interest, especially
memorable in spring. Mature
and exuberant, with a large plant
collection and a traditional walled
kitchen garden. There are many
butterflies in the wildflower meadow.
Rustic seats throughout, good views,
and described as 'an oasis of peace
and tranquillity.' Sorry, no dogs. Plants
grown from the garden for sale. Cold
drinks in the garden on hot days.

44 LONGSTOCK PARK WATER GARDEN
Leckford, Stockbridge, SO20 6EH.
Leckford Estate Ltd, part
of John Lewis Partnership,
www.leckfordestate.co.uk. *4m S
of Andover. From Leckford village
on A3057 towards Andover, cross
the river bridge & take 1st turning L
signed Longstock. What3words app:
drags.deduced.input.* **Sun 28 June
(10-4). Adm £10, chd free.**
A famous water garden with extensive
collection of aquatic and bog plants,
set within 7 acres of woodland with
rhododendrons and azaleas. A walk
through the park leads to the National
Collections of *Buddleja* and *Clematis
viticella*, as well as an arboretum and
herbaceous border at Longstock Park
Nursery. Refreshments at Longstock
Park Farm Shop and Nursery.
Assistance dogs only.

45 LORD WANDSWORTH COLLEGE
Long Sutton, Hook, RG29 1TB.
Lord Wandsworth College. *3m S of
Odiham. SatNav will direct you to the
College's main gates. From there,
our visitor car park is clearly signed.*
**Sat 18, Sun 19 Apr (11-3). Adm £4,
chd free. Tea, coffee, soft drinks
& home-made cakes.**
Lord Wandsworth College is set in
1200 acres of rolling farmland and
wooded valleys. The main college
campus is set around formal lawns
with mature paper bark maples, cedar
trees, cherry trees, and magnolias.
The herbaceous borders are planted
with an array of tulips, daffodils, and
alliums. A South African inspired
border runs the full length of the new
Science Centre.

46 26 LOWER NEWPORT ROAD
Aldershot, GU12 4QD. Pete &
Angie Myles. *Nr to Aldershot
junction of the A331. Parking is
usually arranged with the factory
opp 'Jondo' & The Salvation Army.
Signage will be in place on the day, if
available. We are located 100 metres
away from the McDonald's drive
through.* **Sat 4, Sun 5 July (10.30-
4). Adm £3, chd free. Tea, coffee
& cake.**
A T-shaped town garden full of ideas,
divided into four distinct sections: a
semi-enclosed patio area with pots
and water feature; a free-form lawn
with a tree fern, perennials, bulbs,
shrubs, and over 200 varieties of
hosta; a secret garden with a 20ft x
6ft raised pond, an exotic planting
backdrop, and African carvings; and
a potager garden with vegetables,
roses, cannas, and plant storage.

47 ♦ MAC PENNYS WOODLAND GARDEN & NURSERY
154 Burley Road, Bransgore,
Christchurch, BH23 8DB. Mr &
Mrs T M Lowndes, 01425 672348,
office@macpennys.co.uk,
www.macpennys.co.uk. *6m SE of
Ringwood, 5m NE of Christchurch.
From Crown Pub Xrd in Bransgore
take Burley Rd, following sign for
Thorney Hill & Burley. Entrance
½m on R.* **For opening times and
information, please phone, email or
visit garden website.**
4 acre woodland garden originating
from worked out gravel pits in the
1950s, offering interest year-round,
but particularly in spring and autumn.
Attached to a large nursery that
offers for sale a wide selection of
homegrown trees, shrubs, conifers,
perennials, hedging plants, fruit trees
and bushes. Tearoom offering locally
made cakes, afternoon tea (pre-
booking required) and light lunches,
using locally sourced produce
wherever possible. Nursery closed
Christmas through to the New Year.

Partial wheelchair access on grass
and gravel paths. Can be bumpy with
tree roots and, muddy in winter.

48 MANOR HOUSE
Church Lane, Exton, SO32 3NU.
Tina Blackmore. *Off A32, just N of
Corhampton. Pass The Shoe Inn on
your L, go to the end of the road to
a T-junction, turn R & Manor House
is immed on the L, just below the
church.* **Sat 1, Sun 2 Aug (2-4).
Adm £6, chd free. Home-made
teas.**
An enchanting, 1 acre mature walled
garden set in the Meon Valley. Yew
hedges and flint walls divide the
garden into rooms. Herbaceous
borders feature colourful cottage
favourites inc delphiniums, roses,
geraniums, gaura, and verbena.
The white garden is planted with
hydrangeas and roses. A highly
productive walled vegetable garden,
a parterre with a fountain, and
woodland and meadow with wild
flowers. Featured in the August
2026 issue of The English Garden
magazine.

49 MANOR LODGE
Brook Lane, Botley, Southampton,
SO30 2ER. Gary & Janine Stone.
*6m E of Southampton. From A334
W of Botley, turn into Brook Ln.
Manor Lodge is ½m on R. Signed
parking in Brook Ln, then 8 min walk
to garden. Limited on-site parking
for disabled drivers; drop-off only for
disabled passengers.* **Sat 11, Sun
12 Apr (2-5). Adm £5, chd free.
Tea, coffee & cake, inc gluten-
free option.**
1½ acre garden of an enthusiastic
plantswoman. A garden still in
evolution with established areas and
new projects to give fresh interest
each yr. Informal and formal planting,
dry/gravel and wet areas, sunny
and shady beds, kitchen garden
and greenhouse, woodland and
wildflower meadow walks. There are
large established trees and newer
specimen shrubs and trees. Planting
combinations for year-round interest.
Largely flat with hard paving, but
some gravel and grass to access all
areas.

HAMPSHIRE 227

50 MILL HOUSE
Vyne Road, Sherborne St John, Basingstoke, RG24 9HU. Harry & Devika Clarke. *2m N of Basingstoke. From Basingstoke take the A340 N. 400 metres beyond the hospital, turn R for Sherborne St John. Go through, past a red phone box & 400 metres up a hill. As it crests, on L, take track to Mill House.* **Thur 25, Sun 28 June (2-5.30). Adm £6, chd free. Tea, coffee & cake.**
Set in a private valley, the 3 acres of domestic fruit, vegetables, wild flowers and casual planting are arranged around a power generating watermill. Sustainability and low maintenance lie at its heart, to fit with modern life. Open views, set with mature trees and livestock, give a tranquil sense of space, with moving and static water framed in an undulating landscape. Partial wheelchair access. Park in car park and follow disabled access signs.
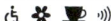

51 THE MONTAGU ARMS HOTEL
Palace Lane, Beaulieu, Brockenhurst, SO42 7ZL. Mrs Suzy Bench, 01590 612324, reception@montaguarmshotel.co.uk, montaguarmshotel.co.uk. *On the southeastern edge of the New Forest, in the centre of Beaulieu Village. What3words app: respects.tightest.barman.* **Sun 7 June (10-4). Adm £6, chd free. Tea, coffee & cake.**
With winding pathways, lush green lawns and vibrant flower beds, our English country garden is a sanctuary for the senses, whatever the season. Visit our productive kitchen garden and greenhouse. Inhale the sweet scent of roses, lilies, sweet peas and honeysuckle that perfume the air as you wander through the garden. Enjoy our many birds as they eagerly hunt for worms in our rich soil. Join Matt, the Head Gardener, for his popular guided tours.

52 5 OAKFIELDS
Allbrook, Eastleigh, SO50 4RP. Martin & Margaret Ward. *7m S of Winchester. M3 J12, follow signs to Eastleigh. 3rd exit at r'about into Woodside Ave, 2nd R into Bosville, 2nd R onto Boyatt Ln, 1st R to Porchester Rise & 1st L into Oakfields.* **Sat 13, Sun 14 June (2-5). Adm £5, chd free. Tea, coffee & cake.**
A ⅓ acre garden is full of interesting and unusual plants, with predominantly woodland beds and rambling roses cascading from birch trees. Two interconnected ponds with rockery and a cascade accommodate moisture loving plants. The woodland areas are planted with camellias, hydrangeas, and azaleas, underplanted with a wide range of shade loving, unusual plants and ferns. Wheelchair access over hard paths and some gravel.

Lord Wandsworth College

53 THE OLD RECTORY
East Woodhay, Newbury, RG20 0AL. David & Victoria Wormsley, 07801 418976, victoria@wormsley.net. *6m SW of Newbury. Turn off A343 between Newbury & Highclere to Woolton Hill. Turn L to East End, continue ¾ m beyond East End. Turn R, garden opp St Martin's Church.* **Visits by arrangement 1 May to 16 Oct for groups of 20+. Adm £13, chd free. Tea & home-made cake inc.**
A classic English country garden of about 2 acres surrounding a Regency former rectory (not open). Formal lawns and terrace provide tranquil views over parkland. A large walled garden with topiary and roses, full of interesting herbaceous plants and climbers for successional interest. Also a Mediterranean pool garden, orchard, wildflower meadow and fruit garden. Explore and enjoy.

54 THE OLD RECTORY, WICKHAM
Southwick Road, Wickham, Fareham, PO17 6HR. Neville Craig. *2m N of M27 on A32 to Alton. E from village for 300 metres off A32, then turn onto B2177 to Southwick. 1st house on R before bend.* **Sat 20, Sun 21 June (2-5). Adm £8, chd free. Home-made teas.**
5 acres surround the house, built c1700 and later gifted to the Winchester Diocese. Since 2000, the current owners have developed the garden in the style of Capability Brown, featuring attractive displays of roses, hydrangeas, herbaceous plants, shrubberies, and trees. Specimen tree planting is ongoing. Four interconnected ponds, along with an acre of rewilding meadow and uncut hedges, encourage all nature. Live music by pianist Nick Blunn.

GROUP OPENING

55 OLD THATCH & THE MILLENNIUM BARN
Sprats Hatch Lane, Winchfield, Hook, RG27 8DD. Jillian Ede, www.old-thatch.co.uk. *3m W of Fleet. 1½ m E of Winchfield stn, follow NGS signs. Sprats Hatch Ln opp Barley Mow pub. Onsite parking at Old Thatch inc disabled parking & other parking in adjacent field. Public car park at Barley Mow slipway ½ m away. If weather is wet, check garden* website. **Sun 12 Apr, Sun 14 June (2-6). Combined adm £5, chd free. Tea, coffee & cake. Pimms if hot & mulled wine if cool.**

THE MILLENNIUM BARN
Mr & Mrs G Carter.

OLD THATCH
Jill Ede.

Who could resist visiting Old Thatch, a chocolate box thatched cottage (not open), featured on film and TV, a smallholding with a 5 acre garden and woodland alongside the Basingstoke Canal (unfenced). A succession of spring bulbs, a profusion of wild flowers, perennials and homegrown annuals pollinated by our own bees and fertilised by the donkeys, who await your visit. Over 30 named clematis and rose cultivars. Children enjoy our garden quiz, adults enjoy tea and home-made cakes. Arrive by narrow boat! Trips on 'John Pinkerton' may stop at Old Thatch on NGS days www.basingstoke-canal.org.uk. Also Accessible Boating shuttle from Barley Mow wharf, approx every 45 mins (entrance to garden is an additional charge). Signed parking for Blue Badge holders: please use entrance by the red telephone box. Paved paths and grass slopes give access to the whole garden.

56 ♦ PATRICK'S PATCH
Fairweather's Garden Centre, High Street, Beaulieu, SO42 7YB. Patrick Fairweather, 01590 612307, info@fairweathers.co.uk, www.fairweathers.co.uk. *SE of New Forest at head of Beaulieu River. Leave M27 at J2 & follow signs for Beaulieu Motor Museum. Go up the one-way High St & park in Fairweather's car park on the L.* **For opening times and information, please phone, email or visit garden website.**
Patrick's Patch is a thriving kitchen garden opposite Fairweather's Garden Centre in Beaulieu, brimming with vegetables, fruit and herbs. Cared for by volunteers and schoolchildren, it is both productive and educational, offering a welcoming space where visitors can enjoy seasonal planting, wildlife and the simple pleasure of gardening. Open daily, free entry, donation welcome. Refreshments available at Steff's Kitchen. Wheelchair access on gravelled site.

57 PINES CORNER WILDLIFE GARDEN
78 Kingsway, Chandler's Ford, Eastleigh, SO53 1FJ. J & S Page. *At M3 J12 follow signs to Chandler's Ford onto Winchester Rd, then 1st R & 2nd L into Kingsway. Entry via side gates on Lake Rd (1st R). What3words app: groups.nodded. snake.* **Sun 21, Sun 28 June (2-5). Adm £4, chd free. Tea, coffee & cake (cash preferred).**
Mid-size suburban garden designed for nature with native flowers and shrubs, and maintained for the ecosystem. Meadow and flowering lawn, hedgerows, dragonfly ponds, bee hotels, and log piles. It is a garden for those curious about our native nature and wilder gardening. Optional tour and nature corner to show and explain what is here, why and how we garden. Hiltingbury Lakes nearby.

58 1 POVEY'S COTTAGE
Stoney Heath, Baughurst, Tadley, RG26 5SN. Jonathan & Sheila Richards, 01256 850633, smrichards3012@icloud.com, www.facebook.com/onepoveyscottage. *Between villages of Ramsdell & Baughurst, 10 min drive from Basingstoke. Take A339 out of Basingstoke, direction Newbury. Turn R off A339 towards Ramsdell, then 4m to Stoney Heath. Pass under overhead power cables, take next L into unmade road & Povey's is 1st on the R.* **Sat 6, Sun 7, Wed 10 June (1-5). Adm £5, chd free. Home-made teas. Visits also by arrangement June to Aug for groups of 10 to 25.**
Informal herbaceous borders, trees and shrubs, a small orchard area, two greenhouses, fruit cage, productive vegetable garden, and a wildflower meadow area. Beehives in one corner of the garden and chickens in another corner. A feature of the garden is an unusual natural swimming pond, surrounded by water lilies, frequently visited by diving swallows and dragonflies. Plants and home-made 'Bee' pottery for sale. Wheelchair access across flat grassed areas, but no hard pathways.

HAMPSHIRE

59 PYLEWELL PARK
South Baddesley, Lymington, SO41 5SJ. Lady Elizabeth Teynham. *Coast road 2m E of Lymington. From Lymington follow signs for Car Ferry to Isle of Wight, continue for 2m to South Baddesley.* **Sun 5, Sun 26 Apr (2-5). Adm £5, chd free.**
A large parkland garden laid out in 1890. Enjoy a walk along the extensive informal grass and moss paths down to the lakes. These are bordered by fine rhododendron, magnolia and azalea trees. Wild daffodils bloom in March and carpets of bluebells in late April and May. The large lakes feature giant gunnera and are home to magnificent swans. Distant views across the Solent to the Isle of Wight. Pylewell House and surrounding garden is private. Glasshouses, swimming pool and other outbuildings are not open to visitors. Lovely day out for families and dogs. Bring your own tea or picnic and wear suitable footwear for muddy areas. Gumboots may be essential in wet conditions.

60 REDENHAM PARK HOUSE
Redenham Park, Andover, SP11 9AQ. Lady Clark. *Approx 1½m from Weyhill on the A342 Andover to Ludgershall road.* **Fri 12 June (10-1). Adm £6, chd £2.50. Home-made teas, cream teas & savouries at pool house.**
Redenham Park built in 1784. The garden sits behind the house (not open). The formal rose garden is planted with white flowered roses. Steps lead up to the main herbaceous borders, which peak in late summer. A calm green interlude, a gate opens into gardens with espaliered pears, apples, mass of scented roses, shrubs and perennial planting surrounds the swimming pool. A door opens onto a kitchen garden.

61 15 ROTHSCHILD CLOSE
Southampton, SO19 9TE. Steve Campion, 07968 512773, Spcampion10@gmail.com. *3m from M27 J8. From M27 J8 follow A3025 towards Woolston. After cemetery r'about L to Weston, next r'about 2nd exit Rothschild Cl.* **Sat 4 July, Sat 5 Sept (11-4); Sun 6 Sept (11-3). Adm £4, chd free. Pre-booking essential, please visit www.ngs.org.uk for information & booking. Home-made teas.** Visits also by arrangement July to Sept for groups of up to 8.
Small, 8 metre x 8 metre, modern city garden incorporating family living with lush tropical foliage. A large range of unusual tropical style plants inc tree ferns, bananas, cannas, gingers and dahlias. The garden has flourished over the last 9 yrs into a tropical oasis with many plants grown from seeds and cuttings. Tropical plant enthusiasts do come to have a cuppa in the jungle! Adjacent to the River Solent and Royal Victoria Country Park.

62 SHALDEN PARK HOUSE
The Avenue, Shalden, Alton, GU34 4DS. Mr & Mrs M Campbell. *4½m NW of Alton. B3349 from Alton or M3 J5 onto B3349. Turn W at Kapadokya Restaurant (formerly The Golden Pot pub) signed Herriard, Lasham, Shalden. Entrance ½m on L. Disabled parking on entry.* **Sun 24 May (2-5). Adm £5, chd free. Tea, coffee & cake.**
Shalden Park House welcomes you to our 4 acre garden to enjoy a stroll through the arboretum, herbaceous borders, rose garden, kitchen garden and wildlife pond. Refreshments will be served from the pool terrace.

63 ◆ SIR HAROLD HILLIER GARDENS
Jermyns Lane, Ampfield, Romsey, SO51 0QA. Hampshire County Council, 01794 368787, info.hilliers@hants.gov.uk, www.hants.gov.uk/hilliergardens. *2m NE of Romsey. Follow brown tourist signs off M3 J11, or off M27 J2, or A3057 Romsey to Andover.* **For opening times and information, please phone, email or visit garden website.**
Established by the plantsman Sir Harold Hillier, this 180 acre garden holds a unique collection of 12,000 different hardy plants from across the world. It inc the famous Winter Garden, Magnolia Avenue, Centenary Border, Himalayan Valley, Gurkha Memorial Garden, Magnolia Avenue, spring woodlands, Hydrangea Walk, fabulous autumn colour, 14 National Collections and over 600 champion trees. The Centenary Border is one of the longest double mixed border in the country, a feast from early summer to autumn. Celebrated Winter Garden is one of the largest in Europe. Electric scooters and wheelchairs for hire (please pre-book). Accessible WC and parking. Registered assistance dogs only.

64 SOUTH VIEW HOUSE
60 South Road, Horndean, Waterlooville, PO8 0EP. James & Victoria Greenshields, www.instagram.com/southview_house_exotic_garden. *Between Horndean & Clanfield. From N A3 towards Horndean, R at T-junction to r'about. From S A3, B2149 to Horndean, continue on A3 N to r'about, 1st exit onto Downwood Way, 3rd L into South Rd. House is 3rd on R. Roadside parking.* **Sun 7 June, Sun 2 Aug (1-5). Adm £4, chd free. Tea, coffee & cake.**
A lush ½ acre tropical style garden in Hampshire featuring rare palms and themed zones inc a jungle clearing with fire pit, an arid section with drought tolerant exotics, courtyard garden, two themed ponds, and woodland area. The front garden blends cottage charm with bold exotic flair, creating a unique fusion of traditional and tropical styles. Wheelchair access to garden via a gravel drive on a gentle slope.

GROUP OPENING

65 SOUTHSEA GARDENS
Southsea, Portsmouth, PO4 0PR. Ian & Liz Craig, 07415 889648, ian.craig1@mac.com. *Parking in Craneswater School, St Ronan's Rd, off Albert Rd. Follow signs from Albert Rd or Canoe Lake on seafront.* **Sun 19 Apr, Sun 7 June (1.30-5). Combined adm £8, chd free. Home-made teas at 28 St Ronan's Avenue.**

35 GAINS ROAD
Leeann Roots.

67 GAINS ROAD
Lyn & Ian Payne.

2 KENILWORTH VILLAS
Mr Richard & Mrs Wendy Collins.

28 ST RONAN'S AVENUE
Ian & Liz Craig, www.28stronansavenue.co.uk.

Four gardens near to Southsea promenade are examples of what can be done in an urban setting. 35 and 67 Gains Road are small gardens designed and planted with artistic flair by the owners, inc ferns, bamboo,

and sculpture. The creative gardeners are keen plantspeople and have made the very most of the limited space in both front and rear gardens with planting of an exceptional standard. 28 St Ronan's Avenue is divided into different areas inc a wildflower meadow and pond. Planting is a mixture of traditional and tender plants inc puya, agaves, echeveria, echiums, tree and tree ferns. Tulips feature in April and alliums in May and June. Recycled items are used to create sculptures. 2 Kenilworth Villas, on Kenilworth Road, showcases bearded irises in May/June. Trees have been planted for privacy and as a wind break. Planting is a mixture of herbaceous perennials, climbers, shrubs, spring bulbs, bananas, and dahlias in late summer.

---

66 ♦ SPINNERS GARDEN
School Lane, Pilley, Lymington, SO41 5QE. Andrew & Vicky Roberts, 07545 432090, info@spinnersgarden.co.uk, www.spinnersgarden.co.uk. *New Forest. 1½m N of Lymington off A337.* **For NGS: Sun 19 Apr (1.30-5). Adm £6, chd free. Cream teas.** For other opening times and information, please phone, email or visit garden website.
Peaceful woodland garden overlooking the Lymington valley with many rare and unusual plants. Drifts of trilliums, erythroniums and anemones light up the woodland floor in early spring. The garden continues to be developed with new plants added to the collections and the layout changed to enhance the views over a pond and small arboretum. The house was rebuilt in 2014 to reflect its garden setting. Andy will take groups of 15 on tours of the hillside with its woodland wonders and draw attention to the treats at their feet.

67 SPITFIRE HOUSE
Chattis Hill, Stockbridge, SO20 6JS. Tessa & Clive Redshaw, 07711 547543, tessa@redshaw.co.uk. *2m from Stockbridge. Follow the A30 W from Stockbridge for 2m. Go past the Broughton/Chattis Hill Xrds, do not follow SatNav into Spitfire Ln, take next R to the Wallops & then immed R again to Spitfire House.* **Sat 30 May (2-5); Sun 31 May (12-3).**

Adm £5, chd free. Home-made teas on 30 May only. Picnics welcome on 31 May. Visits also by arrangement in June for groups of up to 32.
A country garden situated high on chalk downland. On the site of a WW11 Spitfire assembly factory with Spitfire tethering rings still visible. This garden has wildlife at its heart and inc fruit and vegetables, a small orchard, wildlife pond, woodland planting and large areas of wildflower meadow. Wander across the downs to be rewarded with extensive views. Wheelchair access with areas of gravel and a slope leading up to wildflower meadow.

68 4 STANNINGTON CRESCENT
Totton, Southampton, SO40 3QB. Brian & Julia Graham. *From M271 at r'about take 2nd exit, continue over causeway then L for Totton. At Totton central r'about take 2nd exit, Salisbury Rd. Stannington Cres 1st R immed after the Memorial car park.* **Sun 24, Sun 31 May (1.30-5). Adm £4, chd free. Tea, coffee & cake.**
1930s town house (not open) in 100ft x 50ft plot. A garden of two parts reflecting Brian's passion for nature and Julia's wish for a 'normal' garden. Wildlife area with pond, grasshopper bank and small wild grass meadow. Hedgehog boxes, bat box, numerous bird boxes and bug hotels to encourage wildlife. Mature wisteria, ferns and mixed planting borders.

GROUP OPENING

69 STOCKBRIDGE GARDENS
Stockbridge, SO20 6EX. *9m W of Winchester. On A30, at the junction of A3057 & B3049. All gardens & parking on High St.* **Thur 11, Sun 14 June (1-5). Combined adm £10, chd free.**

FISHMORE HOUSE
Clare & Richard Hills.

THE OLD RECTORY
Robin Colenso & Chrissie Quayle.

SHEPHERDS HOUSE
Kim & Frances Candler.

TROUT COTTAGE
Mrs Sally Milligan, sally@sallymilligan.co.uk. Visits also by arrangement 15 June to 31 July for groups of 10+.

Four gardens will open this yr in Stockbridge, each offering a variety of styles and character. Trout Cottage is a small walled garden, inspiring those with small spaces and little time to achieve tranquillity and beauty. Showcasing around 180 plants flowering for almost 10 months of the yr. The Old Rectory has a partially walled garden with a formal pond, fountain, and planting near the house, plus a streamside walk under trees, extensive new planting, and a woodland area. Shepherds House on Winton Hill features herbaceous borders, a kitchen garden, and a belvedere overlooking the pond. Fishmore House is a 8 yr old garden on a ¾ acre plot, with the key elements of design being planting, water, and a borrowed landscape. It is fully accessible, with bound gravel paths and no steps, and surrounded by the River Test, with seating to enjoy the views and large, sweeping herbaceous borders. Wheelchair access to all gardens. Gravel path at Shepherds House.

70 TERSTAN
Longstock, Stockbridge, SO20 6DW. Penny Burnfield, paburnfield@gmail.com, www.pennyburnfield.wordpress.com. *¾m N of Stockbridge. From Stockbridge (A30) turn N to Longstock at bridge. Garden ¾m on R.* **Sun 19 Apr, Sun 21 June, Sun 26 July, Sun 6 Sept (2-5). Adm £5, chd free. Home-made teas.** Visits also by arrangement Apr to Sept for groups of 10+.
A garden for all seasons, developed over 55 yrs into a profusely planted, contemporary cottage garden in peaceful surroundings. There is a constantly changing display in pots, starting with tulips and continuing with many unusual plants. Features inc gravel garden, water features, cutting garden, showman's caravan and live music. Wheelchair access with some gravel paths and steps.

In 2025 we awarded over £288,800 in Community Garden Grants, supporting 114 community garden projects.

71 THE THATCHED COTTAGE

Church Road, Upper Farringdon, Alton, GU34 3EG. David & Cally Horton, 01420 587922, dwhorton@btinternet.com. *3m S of Alton off A32. From A32, take road to Upper Farringdon. At top of the hill turn L into Church Rd, follow round corner, past Masseys Folly (large red brick building) & we are the 1st house on the R.* **Sun 14 June, Sun 30, Mon 31 Aug (2-5.30). Adm £7, chd free. Tea, coffee & cake.** Visits also by arrangement 15 June to 27 Aug for groups of 10 to 40. Donation to Cardiac Rehab.

Hidden behind a C16 thatched cottage is an enticing 1½ acre garden. Colourful pots welcome you onto the terrace and two call ducks on the pond. Mature beds burst with cottage garden plants and shrubs. Raised beds are filled with vegetables. Walk through the newly built pergola covered in roses and clematis to a gypsy caravan which sits in a peaceful area of shrub roses and mature specimen trees. Fully accessible by wheelchair after a short gravel drive.

72 8 TUCKS CLOSE

Bransgore, Christchurch, BH23 8ND. Bob Sawyer, 01425 673605, xglbob@aol.com. *5m NE of Christchurch. 3m from Christchurch on A35, turn towards Bransgore at the Cat & Fiddle for 2m past shops & follow yellow signs. From B3347 follow Derritt Ln for 2m then turn R onto Brookside.* **Sat 18, Sun 19 July (11-5). Adm £4, chd free.** Visits also by arrangement June & July for groups of up to 15.

A small garden (12 metre x 12 metre) that is full of interest and ideas showing what can be achieved in a small space. Borders have mature trees and shrubs underplanted with perennials, half-hardy plants such as hedychium and annuals add to the overall effect. A gravel area has replaced the lawn making room for a different range of plants. Borders have been updated this autumn with plants for hot weather. Teas and light lunches available at Macpennys Woodland Garden and Nurseries nearby.

73 TWIN OAKS WATER GARDEN

13 Oakwood Road, Chandler's Ford, Eastleigh, SO53 1LW. Syd & Sue Hutchinson, 07876 715046, syd@sydh.co.uk, www.facebook.com/twinoaksngs. *Leave M3 J12. Follow signs to Chandlers Ford onto Winchester Rd. After ½ m turn R into Hiltingbury Rd. After approx ½ m turn L into Oakwood Rd.* **Sat 18, Sun 19 Apr, Sat 16, Sun 17 May, Sat 13, Sun 14 June, Sat 1, Sun 2, Sat 22, Sun 23 Aug (1-5). Adm £5.50, chd free. Tea, coffee & cake inc gluten free option.** Visits also by arrangement 7 Apr to 24 Aug for groups of 12 to 30. Min charge £72.

Suburban water garden. Enjoy spring colour from azaleas, rhododendrons and bulbs, then summer colour from perennials, water lilies and tropical plants. A lawn meanders between informal beds and ponds, and bridges lead to a tranquil pergola seating area overlooking a wildlife pond. A rockery is skirted by a stream and a waterfall tumbles into a large lily pond, home to dragonflies. Tropical aviary. Short gravel drive suitable for mobility scooters and wide-tyred wheelchairs, leading to a step-free garden.

74 TYLNEY HALL HOTEL

Ridge Lane, Rotherwick, RG27 9AZ. Elite Hotels, 01256 764881, sales@tylneyhall.com, www.tylneyhall.co.uk. *3m NW of Hook. From M3 J5 via A287 & Newnham, M4 J11 via B3349 & Rotherwick.* **Sun 17 May, Sun 28 June (10-4). Adm £7.50, chd free. Tea, coffee & cake in the Chestnut Suite from 12pm.** Visits also by arrangement.

A large garden of 66 acres with

South View House

beautiful vista, extensive woodlands, and fine avenues of wellingtonias. Features inc rhododendrons, azaleas, an Italian garden, lakes, a large water and rock garden, and dry stone walls originally designed with assistance of Gertrude Jekyll. Partial wheelchair access.

75 WALHAMPTON
Beaulieu Road, Walhampton, Lymington, SO41 5ZG. Walhampton School Trust Ltd. *1m E of Lymington. From Lymington follow signs to Beaulieu (B3054) for 1m & turn R into main entrance at 1st school sign, 200yds after top of hill.* **Sun 3 May (2-6). Adm £6, chd free. Tea, coffee & cake.** Donation to St John's Church, Boldre. Glorious walks through large C18 landscape garden surrounding magnificent mansion (now a school). Visitors will discover three lakes, serpentine canal, climbable prospect mount, period former banana house and later an orangery and plantsman's glade. Italian terrace by Peto with magnificent views to the Isle of Wight. Drives and colonnade by Mawson and delightful statue of Mercury with his bow. David Hill will give a talk at the Mercury fountain, followed by a guided tour, approx every 70 mins from 2.15pm to about 5.45pm. Wheelchair access with some gravel paths and slopes.

76 WICOR PRIMARY SCHOOL COMMUNITY GARDEN
Portchester, Fareham, PO16 9DL. Louise Moreton, www.wicor.hants.sch.uk. *Halfway between Portsmouth & Fareham on A27. Turn S at Seagull pub r'about into Cornaway Ln, 1st R into Hatherley Dr. Entrance to school is almost opp. Parking on site, pay at main gate.* **Sun 5 July (12-4). Adm £4, chd free. Home-made teas.** As shown on BBC Gardeners' World in 2017. Beautiful school gardens tended by pupils, staff and community gardeners. Wander along Darwin's path to see the coastal garden, Jurassic garden, orchard, tropical bed, stumpery, wildlife areas, allotments and apiary, plus one of the few camera obscuras in the south of England. Wheelchair access to all areas over flat ground.

77 WINCHESTER COLLEGE
College Street, Winchester, SO23 9NA. The College, www.instagram.com/winchestercollegeheritage. *Entrance to the College is via the Porters' Lodge on College St, a short walk from Winchester city centre. There is very limited parking nr the College.* **Fri 29, Sat 30 May (11-4). Adm £10, chd free. Tea, coffee & cake in the Warden's Garden.** The historic gardens of Winchester College inc a traditional college 'quad', a quiet sitting garden for the old College sick house, the tranquil gardens of the College's war memorial, and the Warden's Garden with its herbaceous borders, woodland, and a private section of one of the world's most famous chalk streams.

78 1 WOGSBARNE COTTAGES
Rotherwick, RG27 9BL. Miss S & Mr R Whistler. *2½m N of Hook. M3 J5, M4 J11, A30 or A33 via B3349.* **Sun 12, Mon 13 July (2-5). Adm £5, chd free. Home-made teas.** Small traditional cottage garden with a 'roses around the door' look, much photographed for calendars, jigsaws and magazines. Mixed flower beds and borders. Vegetables grown in abundance. Ornamental pond and alpine garden. Views over open countryside to be enjoyed whilst you take afternoon tea on the lawn. Over 40 yrs of opening for NGS. Wheelchair access with some gravel paths.

GROUP OPENING

79 WOODEND GARDENS
Woodend Road, Crow, Ringwood, BH24 3DG. *2½m to Ringwood. Take the Christchurch Rd (B3347) from Ringwood, after ⅓m turn L onto Moortown Ln (signed Burley), after 1m Woodend Rd is on the L. Last house in road.* **Sat 13, Sun 14 June (11-4.30). Combined adm £10, chd free. Tea, coffee & cake.**

HOLLYHURST
Mary Reddyhoff.
TROLLS MEAD
Sheila Lister.

Trolls Mead is a 1 acre garden with interest throughout the yr, whether newly planted, in full bloom, or left in its natural state with seed heads to create an architectural display or simply for the birds to appreciate. The wooded area and lake is still under construction but all are welcome to explore. The bottom meadow with its mown paths has SSSI status with natural wild flowers inc wild orchids. Hollyhurst is a 2 acre site of mature trees, shrubs and herbaceous perennials, which are generally resistant to deer, has been created on a freely draining acid soil. Ponds and small sculptures augment the vistas.

80 WOODPECKERS CARE HOME
Sway Road, Brockenhurst, SO42 7RX. Chris Marsh, Colten Care, www.coltencare.co.uk/woodpeckers/your-garden. *New Forest. Signed from A337 Lymington to Brockenhurst Rd. Sway Rd to Brockenhurst centre. L then R past petrol stn, Woodpeckers on R.* **Sun 6 Sept (11-4). Adm £5, chd free. Tea, coffee & cake.** Vibrant plantings of dahlias, crocosmias, and rudbeckias around the residents' lounge provide an unusual distraction for both residents and visitors. In late summer, the courtyard, orchard, and woodland look especially beautiful, with views across neighbouring fields where New Forest ponies and deer roam. Spot the disguised bug house and a striking wooden chainsaw sculpture.

81 WOOLTON HOUSE
Woolton Hill, Newbury, RG20 9TZ. Rosamond Brown. *8m S of Newbury. From A343 take road to Woolton Hill, keep L at Xrds. Continue through village, turn L on 1st lane after short downhill & sign to Woolton Hill Sports Ground (Fullers Ln) & immed R on 1st driveway.* **Fri 17 July, Fri 18 Sept (2-5). Adm £8, chd free. Home-made teas.** Spectacular, contemporary walled garden set in 4 acres, designed by Pascal Cribier with influence of Mondrian and planted in blues and yellows, interspersed with vegetables. Unique red and green 'tramline' garden. Red courtyard picking garden and walled sedum and cactus garden. Rose garden with majestic pond. Stunning use of colour and texture.

HEREFORDSHIRE

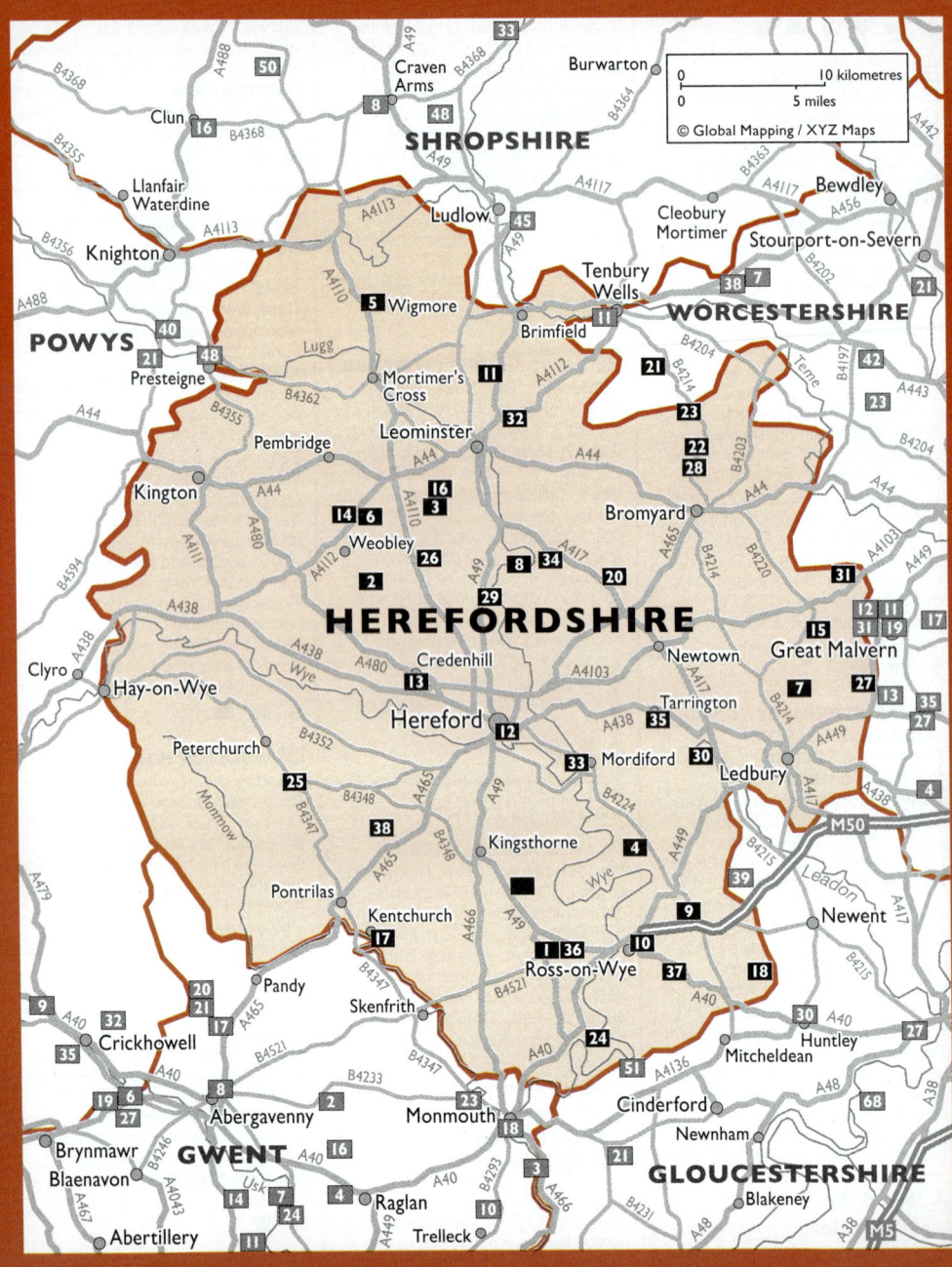

VOLUNTEERS

County Organiser
Lavinia Sole
07880 550235
lavinia.sole@ngs.org.uk

County Treasurer
Gigi Luscombe
01497 831791
gigi.luscombe@ngs.org.uk

Booklet Coordinator
Chris Meakins
01544 370215
christine.meakins@btinternet.com

Booklet Distribution
Lavinia Sole (As above)

Social Media
Position vacant

Photographer
Denise Davies
07947 562389
ddavies175@btinternet.com

Talks
Angela O'Connell
07970 265754
angela.oconnell@icloud.com

Graham O'Connell
07788 239750
graham.oconnell22@gmail.com

Assistant County Organisers
Angela O'Connell
(as above)

Graham O'Connell
(as above)

Penny Usher
01568 589824
pennyusher@btinternet.com

@NGSHerefordshire

OPENING DATES

All entries subject to change.
For latest information check
www.ngs.org.uk

Extended openings are shown at the beginning of the month.

Map locator numbers are shown to the right of each garden name.

January

Every Thursday from Thursday 22nd
Ivy Croft   16

February

Snowdrop Openings

Every Thursday
Ivy Croft   16

Sunday 22nd
Bury Court Farmhouse   5

Saturday 28th
Wainfield   36

March

Sunday 1st
Wainfield   36

Thursday 5th
Ivy Croft   16

Sunday 15th
Bury Court Farmhouse   5
Coddington Vineyard   7

Saturday 21st
◆ Ralph Court Gardens   28

Sunday 22nd
◆ Ralph Court Gardens   28
Whitfield   38

Wednesday 25th
Ivy Croft   16

Saturday 28th
Wainfield   36

Sunday 29th
Wainfield   36

Monday 30th
◆ Moors Meadow Gardens   22

April

Every Wednesday
Ivy Croft   16

Wednesday 1st
◆ Stockton Bury Gardens   32

Friday 3rd
Coddington Vineyard   7

Saturday 4th
Coddington Vineyard   7

Saturday 11th
Netherwood Manor   23

Sunday 12th
Lower House Farm   21
Netherwood Manor   23

Friday 17th
Aulden Farm   3
Ivy Croft   16

Saturday 18th
Aulden Farm   3
Ivy Croft   16

Sunday 19th
Aulden Farm   3
Bury Court Farmhouse   5
Ivy Croft   16

Monday 20th
◆ Moors Meadow Gardens   22

Thursday 23rd
Lower Hope   20

Saturday 25th
Wainfield   36

Sunday 26th
Wainfield   36

May

Every Wednesday
Ivy Croft   16

Sunday 3rd
Dinmore Gardens   8
Lower House Farm   21

Monday 4th
Dinmore Gardens   8

Sunday 10th
Archways   1

Friday 15th
◆ Hereford Cathedral Gardens   12

Saturday 16th
Netherwood Manor   23

Sunday 17th
Bury Court Farmhouse 5
Netherwood Manor 23
The Nutshell 24

Monday 18th
♦ Moors Meadow Gardens 22

Thursday 21st
Lower Hope 20

Saturday 23rd
Wainfield 36

Sunday 24th
Arrow Cottage 2
Wainfield 36

Monday 25th
Arrow Cottage 2
Coddington Vineyard 7

Sunday 31st
Sheepcote 30
NEW Tankard Walls 34

June

Every Wednesday
Ivy Croft 16

Thursday 4th
Kentchurch Court 17

Friday 5th
Kentchurch Court 17

Sunday 7th
Brockhampton Cottage 4
Grendon Court 9
NEW The Knapp 18
Lower House Farm 21

Saturday 13th
Netherwood Manor 23
The Old House 25

Sunday 14th
Bury Court Farmhouse 5
Netherwood Manor 23
The Old House 25
Whitfield 38

Monday 15th
♦ Moors Meadow Gardens 22

Friday 19th
♦ The Picton Garden 27

Sunday 21st
The Hurst 15

July

Every Wednesday
Ivy Croft 16

Saturday 4th
Greytree Cottage 10

Sunday 5th
Greytree Cottage 10

Thursday 9th
Coddington Vineyard 7

Saturday 11th
♦ Ralph Court Gardens 28

Sunday 12th
♦ Ralph Court Gardens 28

Monday 13th
♦ Moors Meadow Gardens 22

Saturday 18th
Ivy Croft 16

Sunday 19th
Bury Court Farmhouse 5
Ivy Croft 16

Friday 24th
♦ The Picton Garden 27

Thursday 30th
Lower Hope 20

August

Every Wednesday
Ivy Croft 16

Monday 3rd
♦ Moors Meadow Gardens 22

Saturday 8th
The Vine 35

Sunday 16th
Bury Court Farmhouse 5

September

Every Wednesday
Ivy Croft 16

Saturday 5th
Herefordshire Growing Point 13

Sunday 6th
Herefordshire Growing Point 13
NEW The Knapp 18

Sunday 13th
Bury Court Farmhouse 5

Saturday 19th
Ivy Croft 16

Sunday 20th
Ivy Croft 16
NEW Tankard Walls 34

Monday 21st
NEW Tankard Walls 34

Saturday 26th
♦ Ralph Court Gardens 28

Sunday 27th
♦ Ralph Court Gardens 28

October

Every Wednesday to Wednesday 14th
Ivy Croft 16

Sunday 4th
Bury Court Farmhouse 5

Monday 26th
♦ Moors Meadow Gardens 22

November

Saturday 21st
♦ Ralph Court Gardens 28

Sunday 22nd
♦ Ralph Court Gardens 28

By Arrangement

Arrange a personalised garden visit with your club, or group of friends, on a date to suit you. See individual garden entries for full details.

Aulden Farm 3
Bury Court Farmhouse 5
Castle Moat House 6
Coddington Vineyard 7
Hares Orchard 11
Hillcroft at Dilwyn 14
Ivy Croft 16
Lower House Farm 21
The Old House 25
NEW Orchard End 26
Revilo 29
Shuttifield Cottage 31
Stone Barn 33
Wainfield 36
Weston Hall 37

HEREFORDSHIRE 237

Archways

THE GARDENS

1 ARCHWAYS
St Owens Cross, Hereford, HR2 8LG. Mrs Christine Mayne. *3m N of Ross-on-Wye. From A49 take B4521 to Abergaveny. Garden 400 yds on L. Travelling E on B4521 from Abergaveny or N on the B4137 from the A40 look for sign at the x-roads by New Inn pub.* **Sun 10 May (10-4.30). Adm £4, chd free. Light refreshments. Tea, coffee, cordials & cakes available.**
Discover a vibrant spring display. Explore the Japanese garden with dwarf rhododendrons, azaleas and candelabra primulas. Wander through the meadow of camassias and irises as well as a woodland filled with bluebells, tulips and daffodils. There are borders and containers bursting with Dutch and bearded iris. Don't miss the stunning wisteria arch. Level access to most of the garden via normal size gate entrance.

2 ARROW COTTAGE
Ledgemoor, Weobley, HR4 8RN. Jim & Annie Manchester. *From Weobley, turn R at the The Unicorn. Ledgemoor is signposted for 1m on L. Then follow yellow NGS signs. Postcode brings you to the house.* **Sun 24, Mon 25 May (11-5). Adm £5, chd free. Tea, coffee & cake.**
A relaxed country garden with unusual trees, statuary and many sitting areas. Interesting walkways lead you to a stream with colourful planting, rill and wildlife pond. Wander through a hosta garden and woodland garden. There is a also a large, productive, no dig vegetable garden full of seasonal bounty. Wheelchair access but with uneven ground and some steps.

3 AULDEN FARM
Aulden, Leominster, HR6 0JT. Alun & Jill Whitehead, 01568 720129, web@auldenfarm.co.uk, www.auldenfarm.co.uk. *4m SW of Leominster. From Leominster take Ivington/Upper Hill Rd, ¾m after Ivington church turn R signed Aulden. From A4110 signed Ivington, take 2nd R signed Aulden.* **Fri 17, Sat 18, Sun 19 Apr (11-5). Adm £5, chd free. Home-made teas. Open nearby Ivy Croft. Home-made ice cream also available. Visits also by arrangement June to Aug.**
Informal country garden, thankfully never at its Sunday best. Three acres planted with wildlife in mind. Emphasis on structure and form, with a hint of quirkiness, a garden to explore with eclectic planting. Irises thrive around a natural pond, shady beds and open borders, seats abound, feels mature but ever evolving. Our own ice cream and home-burnt cakes available: Lemon Chisel a specialty.

4 BROCKHAMPTON COTTAGE
Brockhampton, HR1 4TQ. Peter Clay & Catherine Connolly. *8m SW of Hereford. 5m N of Ross-on-Wye on B4224. In Brockhampton take road signed to B Court nursing home, pass N Home after ¾m, go down hill & turn L. Car park 500yds downhill on L in orchard.* **Sun 7 June (11-4). Adm £7.50, chd free. Open nearby Grendon Court. Picnics welcome by the lake.**
Created from scratch in 1999 by the owner and Tom Stuart-Smith, this beautiful hilltop garden looks south and west over unspoilt countryside. Enjoy a woodland garden, five acre wildflower meadow, a Perry pear orchard and in valley below: lake, stream and arboretum. Extensive borders are planted with drifts of perennials in the modern romantic style. Steep walk from car park. Teas at Grendon Court. Visit Grendon Court (11-4) after your visit to us. This garden is proud to have provided plants for the National Garden Scheme's Show Garden at Chelsea Flower Show 2024.

5 BURY COURT FARMHOUSE
Ford Street, Wigmore, Leominster, HR6 9UP. Margaret & Les Barclay, 01568 770618, l.barclay@zoho.com. *10m from Leominster, 10m from Knighton, 8m from Ludlow. On A4110 from Leominster, at Wigmore turn R just after shop & garage. Garden is on the R. Park on road (accessible parking in courtyard).* **Sun 22 Feb, Sun 15 Mar, Sun 19 Apr, Sun 17 May, Sun 14 June, Sun 19 July, Sun 16 Aug, Sun 13 Sept, Sun 4 Oct (2-5). Adm £5, chd free. Home-made teas. Visits also by arrangement 11 Feb to 14 Oct for groups of up to 20. Adm inc refreshments.**
A ¾ acre garden surrounds the 1820s stone farmhouse (not open). The courtyard contains a pond, mixed borders, fruit trees and shrubs, with steps up to a terrace which leads to lawn and vegetable plot. The main garden (semi-walled) is on two levels with mixed borders, greenhouse, pond, mini-orchard, many spring flowers, and wildlife areas. Year-round colour. Mostly accessible for wheelchairs by arrangement.

6 CASTLE MOAT HOUSE
Dilwyn, Hereford, HR4 8HZ. Mr & Mrs Voogd, 07717 781662, mjvoogd@outlook.com. *6m W of Leominster. On A44, take exit A4112 to Dilwyn. Garden by the village green.* **Visits by arrangement May to Aug for groups of 10 to 30. Cream teas. Discuss refreshments when booking.**
A two acre plot consisting of a more formal cottage garden that wraps around the house. The remaining area is a tranquil wild garden with paths to a Medieval castle motte, part filled moat and Medieval fish and fowl ponds. A haven for wildlife and people alike. The garden contains some steep banks and deep water, with limited access to motte, moat and ponds.

7 CODDINGTON VINEYARD
Coddington, HR8 1JJ. Sharon & Peter Maiden, 01531 641817, sgmaiden@yahoo.co.uk, www.coddingtonvineyard.co.uk. *4m NE of Ledbury. From Ledbury to Malvern A449, follow brown signs to Coddington Vineyard.* **Sun 15 Mar, Fri 3, Sat 4 Apr (11-3); Mon 25 May (11-4). Adm £5, chd free. Tea, coffee & cake. Evening opening Thur 9 July (5-9). Adm £6, chd free. Wine. Apple juice & home-made produce may be on sale. Visits also by arrangement 30 Mar to 12 Oct for groups of 10+.**
Five acres inc two acre vineyard, listed farmhouse, and cider mill. Garden with terraces, wildflower meadow, woodland with massed spring bulbs, large pond with stream garden masses of primula, hellebores and snowdrops, *Hamamelis and Parottia*. Azaleas followed by roses and perennials. Developing year on year, planting for autumn colour Vineyard with three varieties of grapes. In spring, the gardens are a mass of bulbs. Lots to see all year.

GROUP OPENING

8 DINMORE GARDENS
Dinmore, Hereford, HR1 3JR. *8m N of Hereford, 8m S of Leominster. From Hereford on A49, turn R at bottom of Dinmore Hill towards Bodenham, gardens 1m on L. From Leominster on A49, L onto A417, 2m turn R & through Bodenham, following NGS signs to garden.* **Sun 3, Mon 4 May (11-4). Combined adm £7.50, chd free. Home-made teas at Southbourne garden.**

HILL HOUSE
Stuart Hackwell & Rachel Burton.
PINE LODGE
Frank Ryding.
SOUTHBOURNE
Graham & Lavinia Sole.

Three neighbouring gardens with panoramic views over Bodenham Lakes to the Malvern Hills and Black Mountains. Hill House: a two acre garden on the lower slopes of Dinmore Hill, bordering the Bodenham Lake Nature Reserve. Pine Lodge: Two and a ½ acres of woodland featuring most of Britain's native trees (Goblins are thought to live here!). Southbourne: A two acre, terraced garden with herbaceous beds, shrubs, pond and ornamental woodland. Tickets sold at Southbourne.

9 GRENDON COURT
Upton Bishop, Ross-on-Wye, HR9 7QP. Mark & Kate Edwards. *3m NE of Ross-on-Wye. M50 J3. Hereford B4224 Moody Cow Pub, 1m open gate on R. From Ross. A40, B449, Xrds R Upton Bishop. 100yds on L by cream cottage.* **Sun 7 June (11-4). Adm £7.50, chd free. Home-made teas. Open nearby Brockhampton Cottage. Picnics welcome in car park field.**
A contemporary garden designed by Tom Stuart-Smith. Planted on two levels, a clever collection of mass-planted perennials and grasses of different heights, textures and colour give all year interest. The upper walled garden with a sea of flowering grasses makes a highlight. Wheelchair access possible but some gravel.

10 GREYTREE COTTAGE
Brampton Road, Greytree, Ross-on-Wye, HR9 7HY. Elaine & Simon Leney. *N outskirts of Ross on Wye. From town centre take Greytree Rd into Homs Rd into Greytree. Please park here or in 2nd Ave. Walk to entrance in 1st Ave, HR9 7HX (no parking here). What3words app: enhances.impresses.various.* **Sat 4, Sun 5 July (10-4). Adm £5, chd free. Tea, coffee & cake.**
A ¾ acre garden with views to the Black Mountains. Gardened with wildlife and nature in mind, inc large pond, wildlife habitats and large bug hotel. Over 120 native trees planted in formal and informal groupings. Traditional sunny and shady herbaceous and prairie borders alongside small container vegetable garden. Large oak gazebo and deck adjacent to pond where refreshments will be served.

11 HARES ORCHARD
Moreton Eye, Leominster, HR6 0DP. Sue Evans & Guy Poulton, 01568 614501, s.evans.gp@btinternet.com. *A49 Ashton turn to Moreton Eye, Luston. Garden is 1m on L. What3words app: betrayed.trapdoor.requested.* **Visits by arrangement May & June for groups of 10 to 20. Adm inc refreshments which can be discussed at booking. Adm £15, chd free. Home-made teas.**
Three acre wildflower meadow with many plant species inc rare orchids. Owner led tour with plant identification. Old tennis court converted to gravel garden with raised vegetable beds and water feature. Explore the large greenhouse and view remnant of Stourport/Leominster canal. Flower beds and pond with candelabra primula and bog plants.

12 ◆ HEREFORD CATHEDRAL GARDENS
Hereford, HR1 2NG. Dean of Hereford Cathedral, 01432 374202, tickets@herefordcathedral.org, www.herefordcathedral.org/events. *Centre of Hereford, just off the Cathedral Close. The ticket desk is in the cathedral car park, please approach the desk to sign in with staff.* **For NGS: Fri 15 May (10-3.30). Adm £7, chd free.** For other opening times and information, please phone, email or visit garden website.
Explore the Chapter House garden, Cloister garden, the Canon's garden with plants with ecclesiastical connections and roses. See the lower end of the private Dean's garden with fruit trees and a view of the River Wye. This event is an open session where visitors can explore the gardens at their own pace, with gardeners and guides based within the gardens to share the history of the site. Partial wheelchair access. For more information please visit website or contact the team in advance: events@herefordcathedral.org.

13 HEREFORDSHIRE GROWING POINT
Trenchard Avenue, Credenhill, Hereford, HR4 7DX. www.growingpoint.org.uk. *Look out for signs to Headway Hereford; Our garden is around the back. Volunteers will be here to guide you. Parking at the front and rear of Headway House.* **Sat 5, Sun 6 Sept (10-4). Adm £5, chd free. Tea, coffee & cake.**
A purposefully designed therapy garden, for those living with mental and physical challenges to gain the benefits of therapeutic horticulture. A fully accessible garden featuring a range of mixed plantings, to facilitate activities to promote mental wellbeing. The garden has a sensory area, vegetable garden and a small wildflower area. There is also an outdoor teaching area. Polytunnel bursting with life and greenhouse. Art work displayed throughout garden. Fully wheelchair accessible.

In 2025, our donations to Carers Trust helped them support over 1 million unpaid carers across the UK, as part of their network of local carer centres.

14 HILLCROFT AT DILWYN
Dilwyn, Hereford, HR4 8JF.
Rhonda Wood & Steven Brown, 07949 116413,
rhondagiffin@aol.com. *6m W of Leominster on A44. Turn R opp turning for Dilwyn village. Then immed take L fork & follow lane for ½m. Limited parking on drive.* **Visits by arrangement 5 May to 31 May for groups of up to 15. Limited parking. Adm £5, chd free. Discuss refreshments when booking.**
The garden is approx 1.3 acres with an organic vegetable plot and polytunnel. Main garden has lawn with perennial beds either side containing small shrubs and trees. Paths reveal a wooded area to the rear containing magnolias, camellias, rhododendrons, eucalyptus and other large trees. Informal and relaxed planting. Visit the on site pottery studio - Steven Brown Ceramics.

15 THE HURST
Bosbury Road, Cradley, Malvern, WR13 5LT. Clare Gogerty. *16m E of Hereford, 11m W of Worcester. 'The Hurst' is situated directly on the Bosbury Rd. From the junc of A4103 & B4220, garden is 0.7m towards Bosbury on the L. On-road parking.* **Sun 21 June (1-4.30). Adm £5, chd free. Home-made teas.**
A 1½ acre garden based on the five elements: fire, water, earth, air and spirit, which is the subject of the garden owner's book 'Your Magical Garden'. At the heart of the garden is a cosmic spiral made from turf with a reflecting steel bowl at its centre. Borders are coloured themed to tie in with the elements. It is also a productive smallholding with an orchard, vegetable beds, hens and sheep. Gently sloping gravel and grass track to lower area. Orchard not suitable for wheelchairs.

16 IVY CROFT
Ivington Green, Leominster, HR6 0JN. Roger Norman, 01568 720344, ivycroft@homecall.co.uk, www.ivycroftgarden.co.uk. *3m SW of Leominster. From Leominster take Ryelands Rd to Ivington. Turn R at church, garden ¾m on R. From A4110 signed Ivington, garden 1¾m on L.* **Every Thur 22 Jan to 5 Mar (10-4). Every Wed 25 Mar to 14 Oct (10-4). Fri 17, Sat 18, Sun 19 Apr (11-5), open nearby Aulden Farm. Sat 18, Sun 19 July, Sat 19, Sun 20 Sept (11-4). Adm £5, chd free. Tea, coffee & cake.** Visits also by arrangement.
Now 30 years old, the garden shows signs of maturity, inc some surprising trees. A very wide range of plants is displayed, blending with countryside and providing habitat for wildlife. The cottage is surrounded by borders, snowdrops, raised beds, trained pear trees and containers for all year interest. Paths lead to the wider garden inc mixed borders, vegetables framed with espalier apples. Partial wheelchair access.

17 KENTCHURCH COURT
Kentchurch, HR2 0DB.
Mr J Lucas-Scudamore, www.kentchurchcourt.co.uk. *12m SW of Hereford. From Hereford A465 towards Abergavanny, at Pontrilas turn L signed Kentchurch. After 2m fork L, after Bridge Inn. Garden opp church.* **Thur 4, Fri 5 June (11-4). Adm £7.50, chd free. Home-made teas. Refreshments also at The Bridge Inn.**
Kentchurch Court is situated close to the Welsh border. Formal garden and traditional vegetable garden redesigned with colour, scent and easy access. Walled garden and herbaceous borders, rhododendrons and wildflower walk. Extensive collection of mature trees and shrubs. Stream with habitat for spawning trout and views into deer park at the heart of the estate. First opened for the NGS in 1927. Wheelchair access over some slopes and shallow gravel.

18 NEW THE KNAPP
Aston Ingham, Ross-On-Wye, HR9 7LS. Mrs Julia Askew. *From S, Lea A40 or N Kilcot B4221 turn onto the B4222 to Aston Ingham Village Hall. Park at Hall. 300m to garden. Regret, no parking at garden. What3words app: pulps.seasick. justifies.* **Sun 7 June, Sun 6 Sept (11-4). Adm £5, chd free. Home-made teas in the Aston Ingham village hall.**
Country garden of an acre, started nine years ago with wildlife in mind. Discover a pond, hazel copses and wildflower meadow. Features also inc naturalistic prairie planting with abundant grasses and perennials. Cottage garden borders filled with colour and roses. Explore our kitchen garden with orchard and polytunnel.

20 LOWER HOPE
Lower Hope Estate, Ullingswick, Hereford, HR1 3JF. Mrs Sylvia Richards, www.lowerhopegardens.co.uk. *5m S of Bromyard. A465 N from Hereford, after 6m turn L at Burley Gate on A417 towards Leominster. After approx 2m take 3rd R to Lower Hope/Pencombe. After ½m garden on L, enter via car park. Disabled parking available.* **Thur 23 Apr, Thur 21 May, Thur 30 July (2-5). Adm £7.50, chd £2. Tea, coffee & cake.**
Outstanding five acre garden with wonderful seasonal variations. Impeccable lawns with herbaceous borders, rose gardens, white garden, Mediterranean, Italian and Japanese gardens. Natural streams, man-made waterfalls, bog gardens. Woodland with azaleas and rhododendrons with lime avenue to lake with wildflowers and bulbs. Glasshouses with exotic plants and seasonal breeding butterflies. Regret, tickets bought on the gate will be cash only payments. Wheelchair access to most areas.

21 LOWER HOUSE FARM
Vine Lane, Sutton, Tenbury Wells, WR15 8RL. Mrs Anne Durston Smith, 07891 928412, adskyre@outlook.com, www.kyre-equestrian.co.uk. *3m SE of Tenbury Wells; 8m NW of Bromyard. From Tenbury take A4214 to Bromyard. After approx 3m turn R into Vine Ln, then R fork to Lower House Farm.* **Sun 12 Apr, Sun 3 May, Sun 7 June (11-4). Adm £5, chd free. Home-made teas.** Visits also by arrangement 6 Apr to 30 Sept for groups of 10+.
Award-winning country garden surrounding C16 farmhouse (not open) on working farm. Herbaceous borders, roses, box-parterre, productive kitchen and cutting garden, spring garden, ha-ha allowing wonderful views. Wildlife pond. Walkers and dogs can enjoy numerous footpaths across the farm land. There is spectacular autumn colour and dahlias.

22 ◆ MOORS MEADOW GARDENS

Collington, Bromyard, HR7 4LZ. Ros Bissell, 01885 410318, moorsmeadow@hotmail.co.uk, www.moorsmeadow.co.uk. *4m N of Bromyard, on B4214. ½ m up lane follow yellow arrows.* **For NGS: Mon 30 Mar, Mon 20 Apr, Mon 18 May, Mon 15 June, Mon 13 July, Mon 3 Aug, Mon 26 Oct (10-5). Adm £9, chd £2. For other opening times and information, please phone, email or visit garden website.** Multi award winning, inspirational seven acre organic hillside garden with a vast amount of species, many rarely seen; emphasis on working with nature, a wildlife haven. Intriguing features and sculptures, a delight for the garden novice as well as the serious plantsman. Wander through fernery, grass garden, extensive shrubberies, herbaceous beds, meadow, dingle, pools and kitchen garden. Unique home-crafted sculptures. Winner of BBC Hereford and Worcester Make a Difference Green Award- Highly Commended (2025).
◁))

The National Garden Scheme funded six Macmillan Nurses in their roles across England, Wales and Northern Ireland in 2025.

Stockton Bury Gardens

23 NETHERWOOD MANOR
Stoke Bliss, Tenbury Wells, WR15 8RT. **Earl & Countess of Darnley**, 01885 410321, bookings@netherwoodestate.co.uk, www.netherwoodestate.co.uk, www.instagram.com/netherwoodestate. *5m N of Bromyard. Halfway between Bromyard & Tenbury Wells on B4214. Signed from road. What3words app: incisions.acrobats. dirt.* **Sat 11, Sun 12 Apr, Sat 16, Sun 17 May, Sat 13, Sun 14 June (10-4). Adm £8, chd free. Home-made teas.**
Well established three acre garden centred on Medieval dovecote, with historic parkland backdrop. Several distinct areas, each with own interest, inc walled garden with herbaceous borders, 'wilderness' garden, gravel garden and ponds (unfenced). Wide variety of unusual shrubs and trees and plenty of interest throughout spring and summer.

24 THE NUTSHELL
Goodrich, Ross-on-Wye, HR9 6HG. **Louise Short.** *Halfway between Ross on Wye & Monmouth, close to the A40 & the Cross Keys pub.* **Sun 17 May (9.30-3.30). Adm £5, chd free. Tea, coffee & cake. Bacon rolls before midday.**
The Nutshell is a cottage garden in approx ½ acre, created from scratch over the last 25 years. The garden is made up of different areas separated by herbaceous borders and rose arches. There is a lovely selection of plants used inc many peonies and an extensive collection of hostas. The owner has a keen interest in propagation with two polytunnels of plants available to purchase.

25 THE OLD HOUSE
Vowchurch, Hereford, HR2 0RB. **Mr & Mrs K Waistell**, 07733 811284, kipcarwaistell@hotmail.com. *Pass Vowchurch church on L & cross the bridge. Parking in field on L. Entrance 100yds after bridge. Walk back over bridge to enter churchyard. Cross over to gap in hedge.* **Sat 13, Sun 14 June (12-5). Adm £5, chd free. Tea, coffee & cake. Visits also by arrangement 2 May to 30 Aug for groups of up to 20. Refreshments are an additional £3.**
Medium-sized riverside garden of a Grade II listed timber-framed house built 1565, with a variety of trees, shrubs and borders, and vintage cars to see too. Visit the adjoining unusual parish church, with an exhibition relating to Alice in Wonderland- a former vicar was Lewis Carroll's brother. Teas and WC available at Village Hall opposite Church. Wheelchair access via footpath and drive.

Orchard End

HEREFORDSHIRE 243

26 NEW ORCHARD END
Bush Bank, Hereford, HR4 8EN. Bill & Jenny Baker, 07517 215004, wjbaker52@googlemail.com. *Between Hereford & Leominster. On A4110 go N through Canon Pyon or S through Knapton. Take rd to Upper Hill opp Bush Inn. We are 1st on L past the 40mph sign. What3words app: equivocal.mental.brass.* **Visits by arrangement May to July for groups of 5 to 12. Limited parking available onsite. Adm £5, chd free. Tea, coffee & cake. Soft drinks available for children.**
One acre garden on heavy clay with 60+ acers, 80+ hostas and beds of grasses and shrubs. We also have fruit and ornamental trees and a small but productive vegetable plot. We are still developing the layout and planting - there's always something to pull up or put in - and we enjoy swapping ideas and advice. There are several seating areas to enjoy a cup of tea and a cake. Parts accessed via reasonably flat lawns. Some slight gradients.

27 ♦ THE PICTON GARDEN
Old Court Nurseries, Walwyn Road, Colwall, WR13 6QE. Paul, Meriel & Helen Picton, 01684 540416, info@oldcourtnurseries.co.uk, www.oldcourtnurseries.co.uk. *3m W of Malvern. On B4218 (Walwyn Rd) N of Colwall Stone. Turn off A449 from Ledbury or Malvern onto the B4218 for Colwall.* **For NGS: Evening opening Fri 19 June, Fri 24 July (5-8). Adm £6, chd free. Light refreshments. Wine from Coddington Vineyard as well as a choice of soft drinks will be served.** For other opening times and information, please phone, email or visit garden website. Donation to Plant Heritage.
A 1½ acre garden west of Malvern Hills. Bulbs and a multitude of woodland plants bloom in spring. Interesting perennials and shrubs in August. September and early October see a colourful border display of the National Plant Collection of Michaelmas daisies, backed by autumn coloured trees. Many unusual plants to be seen, inc more than 100 different ferns and over 300 varieties of snowdrop. Wheelchair access via gravel paths. All fairly level and no steps.

28 ♦ RALPH COURT GARDENS
Edwyn Ralph, Bromyard, Hereford, HR7 4LU. Mr & Mrs Morgan, 01885 483225, ralphcourtgardens@aol.com, www.ralphcourtgardens.co.uk. *1m from Bromyard Centre. From Bromyard follow the Tenbury road for approx 1m. On entering the village of Edwyn Ralph, take 1st turn on R towards the church. We are the 1st property on R.* **For NGS: Sat 21, Sun 22 Mar, Sat 11, Sun 12 July, Sat 26, Sun 27 Sept, Sat 21, Sun 22 Nov (10-5). Adm £16, chd £10. Our restaurant overlooks the Malvern Hills and offers a wide range of food from light snacks, home-made cakes & lunches.** For other opening times and information, please phone, email or visit garden website. All tickets must be purchased through the garden website or at the gate.
Discover 15 amazing gardens set in the grounds of a gothic rectory. A family orientated garden with a twist, incorporating an Italian Piazza, an African Jungle, Dragon Pool, Alice in Wonderland and the elves in their conifer forest and our new section Dinosaur World. These are just a few of the themes within this stunning garden. Overlooking the Malvern Hills 120 seater Licensed Restaurant. All the gardens are professionally landscaped, showcasing a wide variety of both common and rare plant species. No matter the season, visitors can expect vibrant colours and engaging displays within the gardens. Many water features and many child friendly themes inc our new Dinosaur World. All areas ramped for wheelchair and pushchair access.

29 REVILO
Wellington, Hereford, HR4 8AZ. Mrs Shirley Edgar, 01432 830189, shirleyskinner@btinternet.com. *6m N of Hereford. On A49 from Hereford turn L into Wellington village, pass church on R. After barn on L, turn L up driveway in front of The Harbour, to furthest bungalow.* **Visits by arrangement 11 Apr to 12 Sept for groups of 8 to 25. Adm £4, chd free. Home-made teas.**
A ⅓ acre flower arranger's garden, surrounding a bungalow. Features inc mixed borders, a gravel garden, meadow and woodland areas. Discover the scented garden, late summer bed, gravelled herb garden and kitchen garden. Wheelchair access to all central areas of the garden from the car park area.

30 SHEEPCOTE
Putley, Ledbury, HR8 2RD. Tim & Julie Beaumont. *5m W of Ledbury. Garden is off the A438 Hereford to Ledbury Rd. Passenger drop off; parking 200yds.* **Sun 31 May (1-5). Adm £5, chd free. Tea, coffee & cake.**
A ⅓ acre garden taken in hand from 2011 retaining many quality plants, shrubs and trees from earlier gardeners. Topiary holly, box, hawthorn, privet and yew formalise the varied plantings around the croquet lawn and gravel garden. Discover beds with heathers, azaleas, lavender surrounded by herbaceous perennials and bulbs. There are also small ponds and a kitchen garden with raised beds to explore. Art exhibition by Anya Beaumont will be taking place on the day. Anya is a visual artist working across mediums. The physical environment and its influence have been a significant factor in her practice. If any pieces are sold, a percentage will be given as a donation to the National Garden Scheme.

31 SHUTTIFIELD COTTAGE
Birchwood, Storridge, Malvern, WR13 5HA. Mr & Mrs David Judge, 01886 884243, judge.shutti@btinternet.com. *15m E of Hereford. Coming from Hereford turn L off A4103 at Storridge opp the church to Birchwood. After 1¼m L down tarmac drive signposted to Shuttifield Cottage (150 yards).* **Visits by arrangement 1 Apr to 20 Sept for groups of 10+. Requests for spontaneous visits for small numbers are welcome. Adm £5, chd free. Home-made teas. Visitors may bring picnics.**
Superb position and views. Unexpected three acre plantsman's garden with extensive herbaceous borders, unusual trees, shrubs, and perennials for all year interest. Anemones, magnolias, bluebells, rhododendrons, azaleas and camelias in the spring. Large old rose garden with many spectacular climbers. Small deer park, and walks in a 20 acre wood containing wildlife ponds and wildflowers.

32 ♦ STOCKTON BURY GARDENS
Kimbolton, HR6 0HA. Raymond G Treasure, 07880 712649, twstocktonbury@outlook.com, www.stocktonbury.co.uk. *2m NE of Leominster. From Leominster to Ludlow on A49 turn R onto A4112. Gardens 300yds on R.* **For NGS: Wed 1 Apr (11-4.30). Adm £10.50, chd £6.50. Tea, coffee & cake in Tithe Barn Café. We also offer soft drinks, wine, cider & beer. There is also a full menu of seasonal hot & cold lunches available.** For other opening times and information, please phone, email or visit garden website.
Four acre garden with colour and interest from April until the end of September. Many rare and unusual set amongst Medieval buildings. Features inc pigeon house, tithe barn, grotto, cider press, Roman hoard, pools, secret garden, garden museum and rill, all surrounded by countryside views. Partial wheelchair access. An able bodied companion is advisable for wheelchair users.

33 STONE BARN
Church Lane, Hampton Bishop, Hereford, HR1 4JY. Mary-Ann Robinson & Colin Campbell, 01432 870436. *From Hereford take B4224 towards Fownhope for 3m. After Bunch of Carrots pub take 3rd turn on L. Follow signs to garden and parking.* **Visits by arrangement in June for groups of 8 to 30. Adm inc refreshments. Coach parking at Village Hall. Adm £7.50. Home-made teas.**
Developed over 30 years from a farmyard and field with lovely views. Different sections with interesting shrubs, two ponds, a vegetable parterre and flower garden room. A pagoda and orchard with *Magnolia grandiflora, Davidia involucrata*, clematis and several varieties of *Cornus*. Mainly flat lawns and gravel paths.

34 NEW TANKARD WALLS
Woodhouse Lane, Bodenham, Hereford, HR1 3LB. Joannah Weightman & David Cutler. *From A49 turn onto A417 at Hope Under Dinmore. 2m after Hampton Court, cont past petrol stn on R to Bodenham Parish Hall. Park at Parish Hall. Short walk to garden. Last house on R before farm.*

Sun 31 May (11-5). Adm £7, chd £2. Sun 20, Mon 21 Sept (1-4). Adm £6, chd £2. Tea, coffee & cake.
Flowing round a classical 1930s house, built for Elinor Parr of Croft Castle, this beautiful garden is reaching maturity. Two acres of agricultural land transformed, with specimen trees besides a sweeping driveway, deep mixed borders around the croquet lawn, terraces, rose garden, woodland, topiary, orchard and a wonderful lily pond. Listen for larks from the gazebo and enjoy the long view. All areas are wheelchair/mobility scooter accessible.

35 THE VINE
School Lane, Tarrington, HR1 4EX. Richard & Tonya Price. *Between Hereford & Ledbury on A438. In Tarrington village, S of the A438. Park as directed. Disabled parking only at house.* **Sat 8 Aug (2.30-6). Adm £6, chd free. Cream teas.**
Mature, traditional garden in peaceful setting with stunning views of the surrounding countryside. Consisting of various rooms with mixed and herbaceous borders. Secret garden in blue, yellow, white, croquet lawn with C18 summerhouse, temple garden with ponds, herb and nosegay garden, kitchen garden around greenhouse on the paddock. *Cornus* avenues with obelisk and willow bower.

36 WAINFIELD
Peterstow, Ross-on-Wye, HR9 6LJ. Nick & Sue Helme, 01989 730663, sue_longtown@yahoo.co.uk. *From the A49 between Ross-on-Wye & Hereford. Take the B4521 to Skenfrith/Abergavenny. Wainfeild is 50yds on R.* **Sat 28 Feb, Sun 1, Sat 28, Sun 29 Mar, Sat 25, Sun 26 Apr, Sat 23, Sun 24 May (10-4). Adm £5, chd free. Tea, coffee & cake.** Visits also by arrangement 27 Feb to 30 June for groups of 15+.
Three acre informal garden inc areas for wildlife. Discover our rose garden, beautiful magnolias and Cornus as well as a pond with waterfall. Plenty of early spring bulbs, followed by tulips and bluebells. Delightful canopied Hosta Walk with ferns under an old mulberry. Lush summer planting and a fruit walk with cowslips all set in an open area of interesting and unusual

trees and sculptures. Wheelchair access via grass and gravel paths.

37 WESTON HALL
Weston-under-Penyard, Ross-on-Wye, HR9 7NS. Mr P Aldrich-Blake, 01989 562597, aldrichblake@btinternet.com. *1m E of Ross-on-Wye. On A40 towards Gloucester, shortly after 40 mph sign for Weston-under-Penyard.* **Visits by arrangement Apr to Sept for groups of 10 to 30. Adm £6, chd free. Light refreshments.**
Six acres surrounding Elizabethan house (not open). Large walled garden with herbaceous borders, vegetables and fruit, overlooked by Millennium folly. Lawns and mature and recently planted trees and shrubs, with many unusual varieties. Orchard, ornamental ponds and lake. Four generations in the family, but still evolving year on year. Wheelchair access to walled garden only.

38 WHITFIELD
Wormbridge, HR2 9BA. Mr & Mrs Edward Clive, www.whitfield-hereford.com/gardens. *8m SW of Hereford. The entrance gates are off the A465, Hereford to Abergavenny road, ½ m N of Wormbridge. Postcode for SatNav HR2 9DG.* **Sun 22 Mar, Sun 14 June (2-5). Adm £5.50, chd free. Home-made teas.**
The Whitfield Estate has been a supporter of the National Garden Scheme for over 50 years with extensive parkland and woodland walks. Our woodland has a grove of coastal redwood trees planted in 1851. Wildflowers, ponds, walled garden, many flowering magnolias (species and hybrids). We also have a wonderful ginkgo tree planted in1780. Partial access for wheelchair users: some gravel paths and steep slopes. Dogs on leads welcome.

Our donation to Marie Curie this year is equivalent to 17,521 hours of hospice at home care.

HERTFORDSHIRE

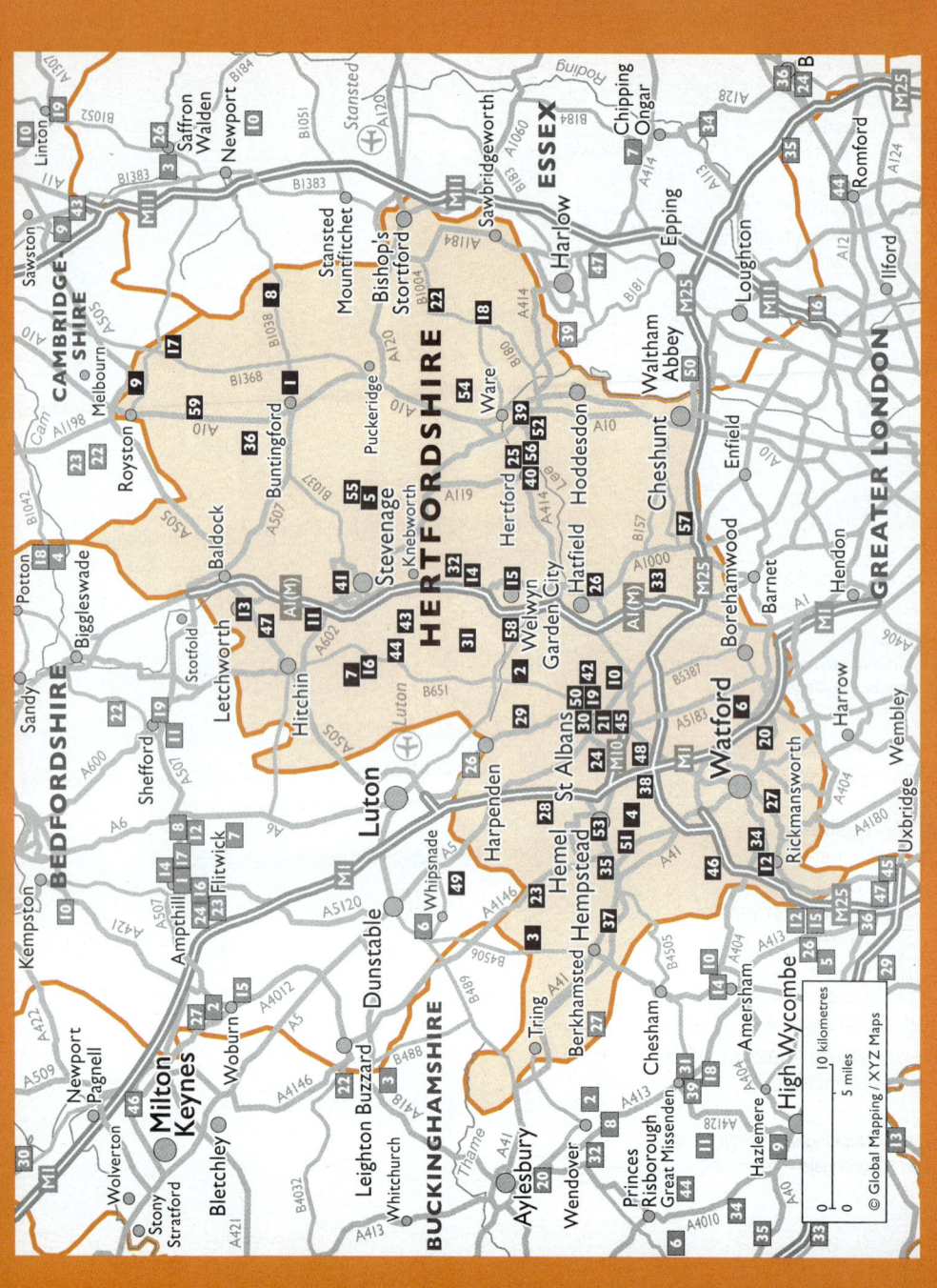

VOLUNTEERS

County Organisers
Bella Stuart-Smith 07710 099132
bella.stuart-smith@ngs.org.uk

Kate Stuart-Smith 07551 923217
kate.stuart-smith@ngs.org.uk

County Treasurer
Peter Barrett 01442 393508
peter.barrett@ngs.org.uk

Publicity
Shubha Allard
shubha.allard@ngs.org.uk

Photography
Lucy Standen 07933 261347
lucy.standen@ngs.org.uk

Julie Meakins 07899 985324
meakinsjulie@gmail.com

Gary Morrisroe 07787 297082
gary.morrisroe@ngs.org.uk

Photography & Story Telling
Anna Marie Felice 07500 306273
annamarie.felice@gmail.com

Social Media - Facebook
Anastasia Rezanova
anastasia.rezanova@ngs.org.uk

Social Media - Twitter
Mark Lammin 07966 625559
mark.lammin@ngs.org.uk

Radio
Lucy Swift
lucy.swift@ngs.org.uk

Talks
Katy Cheetham
katy.cheetham@ngs.org.uk

Booklet Coordinator
Janie Nicholas 07973 802929
janie.nicholas@ngs.org.uk

New Garden Enquiries
Julie Wise 07759 462330
julie.wise@ngs.org.uk

Tessa Birch 07721682481
tessa.birch@ngs.org.uk

Communications Officer
Lorna Nightinghale 07725 767655
lorna.nightingale@ngs.org.uk

Assistant County Organisers
Parul Bhatt
parul.bhatt@ngs.org.uk

Karen Blain
karen.blain@ngs.org.uk

Kate de Boinville
kdeboinville@gmail.com

Rebecca Fincham
rebecca.fincham@ngs.org.uk

Kerrie Lloyd-Dawson 07736 442883
kerrie.lloyddawson@ngs.org.uk

Ashleigh Lock 07510 057531
ashleigh.lock@ngs.org.uk

Sarah Marsh 07813 083126
sarah.marsh@ngs.org.uk

OPENING DATES

All entries subject to change.
For latest information check
www.ngs.org.uk
Extended openings are shown
at the beginning of the month.
Map locator numbers are
shown to the right of each
garden name.

January

Friday 30th
8 Gosselin Road 25

Saturday 31st
Walkern Hall 55

February

Snowdrop Openings

Sunday 1st
Walkern Hall 55

Wednesday 4th
8 Gosselin Road 25

Friday 6th
1 Elia Cottage 18
8 Gosselin Road 25

Sunday 8th
1 Elia Cottage 18

Tuesday 10th
◆ Benington Lordship 5

Sunday 15th
10 Cross Street 13
Serendi 47

Tuesday 17th
10 Cross Street 13
Serendi 47

March

Saturday 21st
◆ Hatfield House West Garden 26

Sunday 22nd
◆ Benington Lordship 5

Saturday 28th
Walkern Hall 55

Sunday 29th
Walkern Hall 55

April

Sunday 12th
Alswick Hall 1

Friday 17th
NEW Bhaktivedanta Manor 6

Sunday 19th
The Old Rectory, Cottered 36
◆ St Paul's Walden Bury 44

May

**Every day from Saturday 9th
to Sunday 17th**
42 Falconer Road 20

Sunday 10th
◆ St Paul's Walden Bury 44

Monday 11th
◆ Ashridge House Gardens 3

Tuesday 12th
◆ Ashridge House Gardens 3

Wednesday 13th
◆ Ashridge House Gardens 3
Rustling End Cottage 43

Friday 15th
Rustling End Cottage 43

 @HertfordshireNGS    @HertfordshirNGS    @hertsngs

HERTFORDSHIRE

Saturday 16th
The Manor House, Ayot St
Lawrence   31

Sunday 17th
The Manor House, Ayot St
Lawrence   31
NEW Porthill House   40

Saturday 23rd
42 Falconer Road   20

Sunday 24th
Amwell Cottage   2
42 Falconer Road   20

Monday 25th
43 Mardley Hill   32

Friday 29th
Danesbury Fernery   14
16 Langley Crescent   30

Saturday 30th
Danesbury Fernery   14
16 Langley Crescent   30
NEW 24 Rose Walk   42
Sunnyside Rural Trust - Hemel
Hempstead   51

Sunday 31st
15 Gade Valley Cottages   23
The Pines   39
NEW White Horse Cottage   59

June

Tuesday 2nd
Gorhambury House   24

Saturday 6th
The Cherry Tree   11
NEW Holtsmere End Farm   28

Sunday 7th
Brent Pelham Hall   8
♦ St Paul's Walden Bury   44
Sarratt Community Garden   46
Serge Hill Gardens   48
Warrenwood   57

Sunday 14th
Brambley Hedge   7
Burloes Hall   9
NEW Dinsley Field   16
Gable House   22
Pie Corner   38
Shortgrove Manor Farm   49

Friday 19th
NEW Bhaktivedanta Manor   6

Sunday 21st
Dovehouse Shott   17
Thundridge Hill House   54

Friday 26th
28 Fishpool Street   21

Sunday 28th
28 Fishpool Street   21
St Stephens Avenue Gardens   45
9 Tannsfield Drive   53

July

Sunday 5th
15 Gade Valley Cottages   23

Friday 17th
Meadowgate   33

Saturday 18th
NEW 203 Northridge Way   35

Sunday 19th
Meadowgate   33

Sunday 26th
35 Digswell Road   15

August

Sunday 2nd
9 Tannsfield Drive   53

Friday 7th
Walled Garden, 1 Farquhar Street   56

Sunday 9th
Walled Garden, 1 Farquhar Street   56

Friday 14th
NEW Bhaktivedanta Manor   6

Saturday 15th
NEW 46 Belmont Road   4

Sunday 16th
NEW 46 Belmont Road   4

Wednesday 19th
8 Gosselin Road   25

Sunday 30th
8 Kingcroft Road   29
St Stephens Avenue Gardens   45

Monday 31st
8 Kingcroft Road   29

September

Saturday 5th
102 Cambridge Road   10

Sunday 6th
Burloes Hall   9
102 Cambridge Road   10
Serendi   47

Sunday 27th
The Pines   39

October

Friday 9th
NEW Sweet Briar Flower Farm   52

By Arrangement

Arrange a personalised garden visit with your club, or group of friends, on a date to suit you. See individual garden entries for full details.

NEW Bhaktivedanta Manor   6
102 Cambridge Road   10
The Cherry Tree   11
38 The Clump   12
10 Cross Street   13
35 Digswell Road   15
1 Elia Cottage   18
49 Ellis Fields   19
42 Falconer Road   20
Hertfordshire's Tiny Tropical Garden   27
Morning Light   34
Patchwork   37
Pie Corner   38
The Pines   39
NEW 4 Rectory Croft   41
Serendi   47
NEW Soil Squad   50
9 Tannsfield Drive   53
Thundridge Hill House   54
Waterend House   58

310,000 people are cared for each year who are approaching the end of life or diagnosed with a terminal illness through the hospice network supported by National Garden Scheme funding.

THE GARDENS

1 ALSWICK HALL
Hare Street Road, Buntingford, SG9 0AA. Mike & Annie Johnson, www.alswickhall.com/gardens. *1m from Buntingford on B1038. From the S take A10 to Buntingford, drive into town & take B1038 (after the Co-op) E towards Hare St Village. Alswick Hall is 1m on R.* **Sun 12 Apr (12-4). Adm £8, chd free. Light refreshments. Lunch, licensed bar, teas & home-made cakes.**
Listed Tudor House with five acres of landscaped gardens set in unspoiled farmland. Two well established natural ponds with rockeries. Sweeping large herbaceous borders, unusual mature shrubs, a woodland walk and wildflower meadow with drifts of snakeshead fritillarias. In spring, there is a fantastic selection of daffodils, tulips, camassias and crown imperials. A plant stall and various interesting and unusual trade stands. Good access for wheelchair users with lawns and wood chip paths. Slight undulations in places.

2 AMWELL COTTAGE
Amwell Lane, Wheathampstead, AL4 8EA. Colin & Kate Birss, www.instagram.com/amwellcottage. *½ m S of Wheathampstead. From St Helen's Church, Wheathampstead turn up Brewhouse Hill. At top L fork (Amwell Ln), 300yds down lane, park in field opp.* **Sun 24 May (2-5). Adm £6, chd free. Home-made teas.**
Informal garden of approx 2½ acres around C17 cottage. Large orchard of mature trees, with billows of cow parsley in spring, laid out with paths. Extensive lawns with borders, framed by tall yew hedges and old brick walls. Daffodils early in the year. Many roses in beds, borders and a tunnel. Stone seats with views, woodland pond, greenhouse, vegetable garden with raised beds and fire-pit area. Wheelchair access via gravel drive.

3 ♦ ASHRIDGE HOUSE GARDENS
Berkhamsted, HP4 1NS. EF Corporate Education Ltd, www.ashridgehouse.org.uk. *4m N of Berkhamsted. 1m S of Little Gaddesden. What3words app: fenced.liquid.reverses.* **For NGS:**
Mon 11, Tue 12, Wed 13 May (9-4). Adm £8, chd free. Light refreshments at Bakehouse Café. Bakehouse Cafe only accepts payments by card. Dine inside or out in the courtyard, for both light refreshments & substantial meals. For other opening times and information, please visit garden website.
The Grade II* gardens were designed by Humphry Repton, in 1813, and modified by Sir Jeffry Wyatville. The 190 acres inc formal gardens, a large lawn area leading to avenues of trees and arboretum. In May, the highlights of the garden are the azaleas and spring bulb and bedding displays. Free garden introduction talks available on the day. Once a monastic site, then home to Henry VIII and his children. One of Repton's finest gardens with influences from the Bridgewater dynasty, comprising colourful formal bedding, a rosary, shrubberies and breathtaking views. NB: Rhododendron Avenue is undergoing major restoration in 2026. The main garden features, cafe and toilets are accessible via wheelchair.
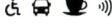

4 NEW 46 BELMONT ROAD
Hemel Hempstead, HP3 9NY. John & Christina Jones. *Approx 1m E of Hemel Hempstead town centre. From A414 St Albans Rd take r'about for Bennett's End Rd. 1st R at St Albans Hill past Snow Centre. Take 2nd turn on L onto Risedale Rd then 1st R onto Belmont Rd.* **Sat 15, Sun 16 Aug (12-5). Adm £4.50, chd free. Tea, coffee & cake.**
Discover a hidden tropical oasis now open to the public for the first time. Lush planting inc bananas, palms, bamboo, cannas, Tetrapanax and more. Relax on spacious decking, spot wildlife by the pond, or unwind in the summerhouse. Meet Belmont, our 6ft wooden bear, ready to welcome you. A calm, leafy escape awaits.
☕ 🔊

5 ♦ BENINGTON LORDSHIP
Stevenage, SG2 7BS. Mr & Mrs R Bott, 01438 869668, garden@beningtonlordship.co.uk, www.beningtonlordship.co.uk. *4m E of Stevenage. In Benington Village, next to church. Signs off A602.* **For NGS: Tue 10 Feb (11-4). Cream teas in the tearoom. Sun 22 Mar (2-5). Tea, coffee & cake in the tearoom. Adm £9, chd £4. For other opening times and**
information, please phone, email or visit garden website.
A seven acre site with ruin of C12 Norman keep and C19 neo Norman folly. Highlights inc spectacular snowdrops and spring bulbs; formal rose garden; walled kitchen garden with vegetables, gravel garden and wildflower meadow; orchard with perennial meadow; lake; naturalistic planting of main border with wildlife friendly and drought tolerant plants; unspoilt panoramic views over surrounding parkland. The garden is on a slope and paths are uneven. There is only partial wheelchair access. Accessible WC available in parish hall or church.
♿ 🚗 ☕ 🔊

6 NEW BHAKTIVEDANTA MANOR
Dharam Marg, Hilfield Lane Aldenham, Watford, WD25 8EZ. parag.mungale@gmail.com, www.krishnatemple.com/visit/#attractions. *Leave M1 at J5 take A41 towards Watford. Follow brown signs to Hare Krishna Temple. Park in Car Park A.* **Fri 17 Apr, Fri 19 June, Fri 14 Aug (11-3). Adm £5, chd free. Pre-booking essential, please visit www.ngs.org.uk for information & booking. Light refreshments. Lunches usually served at 1:30pm. Visits also by arrangement for groups of 10 to 30.**
A chance to visit the unique and beautiful gardens surrounding Bhaktivedanta Manor at the Hare Krishna Temple. Our gardens consist of the peaceful George Harrison Garden- dedicated to the late Beatle, a woodland, and a rose garden. Visitors can enjoy a guided tour and meet the Head Gardener. You will also get the chance to meet our cows at the Farm. A hot lunch is inc in your booking.
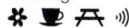

70 inpatients and their families are being supported at the newly opened Horatio's Garden Northern Ireland, thanks to the National Garden Scheme donations.

7 BRAMBLEY HEDGE
1 Chequers Lane, Preston, Hitchin, SG4 7TX. **Lynda & Steve Woodward.** *3m S of Hitchin. From A602, Three Moorhens r'about take exit to Gosmore, pass through Gosmore & cont for 2m into Preston. Chequers Ln is 1st on R, by white fence.* **Sun 14 June (1-5.30). Combined adm with Dinsley Field £7, chd free. Home-made teas.**
Brambley Hedge covers an area of approx ¼ acre. The front garden is mainly set to shrubs and small trees. The rear garden is sections or 'rooms' planted in a cottage style, with around 40 varieties of roses, popular and some less common perennials. There is also a vegetable plot and numerous pots for annuals. The owner is a keen amateur wood turner and some of his work will be on show. The paths are mainly flat and level, some may be slightly narrow.

8 BRENT PELHAM HALL
Brent Pelham, Buntingford, SG9 0HF. **Alex & Mike Carrell.** *From Buntingford take the B1038 E for 5m. From Clavering take the B1038 W for 3m.* **Sun 7 June (1-4). Adm £8, chd free. Tea, coffee & cake in the Estate Office.**
Surrounding a beautiful Grade I listed property, the gardens consist of 12 acres of formal gardens, redesigned in 2007 by the renowned landscaper Kim Wilkie. With two walled gardens, a potager, walled kitchen garden, greenhouses, orchard and a new double herbaceous border, there is lots to discover. The further 14 acres of parkland boast lakes and wildflower meadows. Small vintage car collection on show. Access by wheelchair to most areas of the garden, inc paths of paving, gravel and grass.

9 BURLOES HALL
Newmarket Road, Royston, SG8 9NE. **Lady Newman,** www.burloeshallweddings.co.uk. *1m N of Royston. From M11/A505 turn L on Newmarket Rd. 200yds 1st turning on L Burloes Hall or B1329 from Barley to Royston, turning on L signed Burloes Farm.* **Sun 14 June, Sun 6 Sept (11-5). Adm £7, chd free. Tea, coffee & cake.**
The garden was designed and created in the 1900's. Extensive planting by Gill Chamberlain of Garden Rescue Limited from 2007 to the present day.

Formal gardens with deep colourful mixed herbaceous borders. Bountiful Nepeta and white roses. Handsome beech trees and mature yew hedges with extensive lawns.

10 102 CAMBRIDGE ROAD
St Albans, AL1 5LG. **Anastasia & Keith,** keith.a.robertson@gmail.com. *Nr Ashley Rd end of Cambridge Rd in The Camp neighbourhood on E side of city. S of A1057 (Hatfield Rd). Take the A1057 from A1(M) J3. Take A1081 from M25 J22.* **Sat 5, Sun 6 Sept (2-5.30). Adm £5, chd free. Tea, coffee & cake. Visits also by arrangement 27 July to 18 Oct for groups of 10 to 25. Donation to Alzheimer's Research UK.**
Contemporary space sympathetically redesigned in 2017 to keep many of the existing plants, trees and shrubs from a 1930s semi's garden. Modern take on the classic garden in two halves: ornamental and vegetable. All year interest gabion borders packed with perennials and annuals, central bed featuring a pond and a mature Japanese maple. All vegetables, annuals, and some perennials, grown from seed. Dogs and photography welcome. A growing collection of Aeoniums.

11 THE CHERRY TREE
Stevenage Road, Little Wymondley, Hitchin, SG4 7HY. **Patrick & Jane Woollard,** 07952 655613, cherrywy@btinternet.com. *½ m W of A1M J8. Follow sign to Little Wymondley; under railway bridge & house is R at central island flower bed opp Bucks Head Pub. Parking in adjacent roads.* **Sat 6 June (11-5). Adm £5, chd free. Tea, coffee & cake. Visits also by arrangement 25 Apr to 31 July for groups of 6 to 12.**
The garden has been recently updated. This is a colourful space on several levels containing shrubs, trees and climbers enabling the garden to be viewed from different aspects. Much of the planting, inc exotics of which many are perfumed, is in containers that are re-sited in various positions throughout the seasons. A heated greenhouse and summerhouse maintain tender plants in winter.

12 38 THE CLUMP
Rickmansworth, WD3 4BQ. **Rupert & Fiona Wheeler,** 01923 776858, rupert_wheeler@sky.com. *1m W of Rickmansworth. From M25 J18, drive towards Rickmansworth for about 350yds. Turn R into The Clump. No. 38 is about 350yds on the R.* **Visits by arrangement May to Sept for groups of 5 to 20. Adm £7, chd free. Light refreshments.**
A plantsman's garden containing unusual trees and shrubs on the edge of a wood. The shrubs and trees in the middle garden surround a pond and create an air of relaxing tranquillity. The rear garden is the setting for modern sculptures. There is also a collection of cacti.

13 10 CROSS STREET
Letchworth Garden City, SG6 4UD. **Renata & Colin Hume,** 01462 678340, renata@cyclamengardens.com, www.cyclamengardens.com. *Nr town centre. From A1(M) J9 signed Letchworth, across 2 r'abouts, R at 3rd, across next 3 r'abouts L into Nevells Rd, 1st R into Cross St.* **Sun 15, Tue 17 Feb (1-4.30). Combined adm with Serendi £8, chd free. Tea, coffee & home-made cookies. Visits also by arrangement Mar to Oct for groups of up to 30.**
A garden with mature fruit trees is planted for interest throughout the year. The structure of the garden evolved around three circles- two grass lawns and a wildlife pond. Mixed borders connect the different levels of the garden. Winter flowering shrubs and spring bulbs.

14 DANESBURY FERNERY
North Ride, Welwyn, AL6 9RD. **Welwyn Hatfield Borough Council,** www.danesburyfernery.org.uk. *Exit A1M J6 signed to Welwyn Village & follow yellow signs. 1½ m from J6. Danesbury Fernery is in Danesbury Nature Reserve. Street parking available nearby.* **Evening opening Fri 29, Sat 30 May (5.30-8). Adm £4, chd free. Wine.**
A hidden dell garden full of flowering perennials, gorgeous ferns and a chalk bank brimming with wildflowers, many rare. Gravel paths meander over a rustic bridge with an imaginative 'river' below which then lead you to a Victorian grotto and waterfall made from Pulhamite

HERTFORDSHIRE 251

(artificial rock) built in 1860.

15 35 DIGSWELL ROAD
Welwyn Garden City,
AL8 7PB. Adrian & Clare de Baat, 07914 115860, adrian.debaat@ntlworld.com, www.adriansgarden.org. ½ m N of Welwyn Garden City centre. From the Campus r'about in city centre take N exit just past Campus West into Digswell Rd. Over the White Bridge, 200yds on L. **Sun 26 July (2-5.30). Adm £5, chd free. Tea, coffee & cake. Visits also by arrangement** July to Oct for groups of 10 to 20. Adm inc tea, coffee & cake.
Town garden of around a ⅓ acre with naturalistic planting inspired by the Dutch garden designer, Piet Oudolf. The garden has perennial borders plus a small meadow packed with herbaceous plants and grasses. The contemporary planting gives way to the exotic, inc a succulent bed and under mature trees, a lush jungle garden inc bamboos, bananas, palms and tree ferns. Grass paths and gentle slopes to all areas of the garden.

16 NEW DINSLEY FIELD
School Lane, Preston, Hitchin, SG4 7UE. Wendy & Richard Woods. *3m S of Hitchin. From A602, Three Moorhens r'about, take exit to Gosmore. Pass through Gosmore & cont 2m into Preston. Cont past Red Lion pub on R, along School Ln. House past Village Hall on R.* **Sun 14 June (1-5.30). Combined adm with Brambley Hedge £7, chd free. Cold drinks & ices. Home-made teas available at Brambley Hedge.**
An acre garden featuring sweeping herbaceous borders surrounding a large lawn; woodland area of mature and specimen trees (inc a weeping willow and spectacular Chinese dogwood); ponds (home to newts and an abundance of wildlife); alpine and herb gardens; fruit cage, greenhouse and raised vegetable beds; vintage style orangery housing an established grapevine. Patio areas with seating.

17 DOVEHOUSE SHOTT
Smiths End Lane, Barley, Royston, SG8 8LL. Stephen & Justine Marsh. *The drive starts beside The Hoops.* **Sun 21 June (11-5). Adm £7, chd free. Home-made teas.**
A lovely cottage garden with quirky features owned by the producer of Pinkster Gin and Blooming Natural. Masses of lupins and other perennials in the borders, a kitchen garden, orchard, lavender walks, roses and a wildlife meadow. Step free access to most areas.

Waterend House

1 ELIA COTTAGE
Nether Street, Widford, Ware, SG12 8TH. Margaret & Hugh O'Reilly, 01279 843324, hughoreilly56@yahoo.co.uk. *B1004 from Ware towards Much Hadham. Travel down dip towards Much Hadham, at X-road take R into Nether St. 8m W of Bishop's Stortford on B1004 through Much Hadham at Widford sign turn L. B180 from Stanstead Abbots.* **Fri 6, Sun 8 Feb (12.30-4.30). Adm £5, chd free. Light refreshments. Visits also by arrangement Mar to Sept.**
A ⅓ acre romantic garden. Snowdrops, hellebores and crocus welcome visitors in spring. Followed in June by clematis and roses. Pond, cascade water features, stream with Monet style bridge. Plenty of seats, two summerhouses. New ½ acre nature meadow opposite. Fairy Hunt for children – weather permitting.

2 49 ELLIS FIELDS
St Albans, AL3 6BG. Karen Blain, ef.opengarden@outlook.com. *Situated at the far end of Ellis Fields.* **Visits by arrangement 1 May to 1 Oct. Light refreshments.**
A small tranquil urban garden, with both front and back gardens for viewing. Different structural evergreen plants and seasonal planting. There are lots of bee and bird friendly summer flowers, and copious numbers of hydrangeas. Painted wooden arches and pathways lead you to raised decked seating areas to enjoy the plants. Wheelchair access via a side gate. The garden should be mostly accessible to all. There are two short steps to slightly higher levels.

3 42 FALCONER ROAD
Bushey, Watford, WD23 3AD. Mrs Suzette Fuller, 07714 294170, suzettesdesign@outlook.com. *M1 J5 follow signs for Bushey. From London A40 via Stanmore towards Watford. From Watford via Bushey Arches, through to Bushey High St, turn L into Falconer Rd, opp St James church.* **Daily Sat 9 May to Sun 17 May (12-6). Sat 23, Sun 24 May (12-6). Adm £6, chd free. Visits also by arrangement June & July for groups of 5 to 10.**
Enchanting, magical and unusual Victorian style space. Bird cages and chimney pots feature, plus a walk through conservatory with many plants.

4 28 FISHPOOL STREET
St Albans, AL3 4RT. Jenny & Antony Jay, www.instagram.com/jenjay.fishpool. *No. 28 is at the Cathedral end of Fishpool St. Entrance to the garden is through the Lower Red Lion car park.* **Evening opening Fri 26 June (5.30-7.30). Sun 28 June (2-5). Home-made teas. Adm £8, chd free.**
This secret garden is in town centre St Albans close to the Cathedral and on entering it one gets an immediate feeling of peace and tranquillity. It features a C17 Grade II Tripe House and 70 year old box and yew topiary. The garden is divided into several rooms with different planting schemes and colour combinations. Each room flows into the next taking you on a journey of discovery.

5 GABLE HOUSE
Church Lane, Much Hadham, SG10 6DH. Tessa & Keith Birch. *Follow signs to the church. Cont around the R bend & past several white cottages. Gable House driveway is immed on R. Please park in the High St.* **Sun 14 June (11-4). Adm £5, chd free. Home-made teas.**
Nestled in the village, a stunning walled garden of just under an acre. Surrounding the house, the garden encompasses both the formal and naturalistic with structural evergreens and sweeping abundant borders. The planting displays an emphasis on strong colour and varied texture. Sustainably managed, features inc a wildlife pond, a woodland walk, a beehive and an ornamental vegetable garden. Level garden with easy wheelchair access.

6 15 GADE VALLEY COTTAGES
Dagnall Road, Great Gaddesden, Hemel Hempstead, HP1 3BW. Bryan Trueman. *3m N of Hemel Hempstead. Follow B440 N from Hemel Hempstead & through Water End. Go past turning for Great Gaddesden on L. Park in village hall car park on R. Gade Valley Cottages on R (short walk).* **Sun 31 May, Sun 5 July (1.30-5). Adm £5, chd free. Home-made teas.**
Medium sized sloping rural garden. Patio, lawn, borders and pond. Paths lead through a woodland area emerging by wildlife pond and sunny border. A choice of seating offers views across the beautiful Gade Valley or quiet shady contemplation with sounds of rustling bamboos and bubbling water. Many acers, hostas and ferns in shady areas. *Hemerocallis*, iris, *Crocosmia* and *Phlox* found in sun.

7 GORHAMBURY HOUSE
Gorhambury, St Albans, AL3 6AH. Viscount & Viscountess Grimston, www.gorhamburyestate.co.uk. *Please use AL3 6AE in SatNav to take you to the correct gate. Parking will be in a field close to the house.* **Tue 2 June (9.30-3.30). Adm £12. Pre-booking essential, please visit www.ngs.org.uk for information & booking. Tea, coffee & cake.**
Gorhambury House garden was laid out in the 1820s and has evolved over the generations. The current owners have engaged Tom Stuart-Smith to do the design and planting plans and this blends with the older elements that are still in place. In June there are some wonderful rhododendrons, camellias, flowering shrubs and trees as well as formal lawns, wildflower meadows and historic topiary. Gravel paths and grass with a wheelchair accessible WC.

8 8 GOSSELIN ROAD
Bengeo, Hertford, SG14 3LG. Annie Godfrey & Steve Machin, www.daisyroots.com. *Take B158 from Hertford signed to Bengeo. Gosselin Rd 2nd R after White Lion Pub.* **Fri 30 Jan, Wed 4, Fri 6 Feb, Wed 19 Aug (1-4). Adm £5.**
As owners of local nursery, Daisy Roots, this garden acts as trial ground and show case for perennials and ornamental grasses grown there. Over 300 varieties of snowdrop in February, deep borders packed with perennials and grasses later in the year. Small front garden with lots of foliage interest. Regret, no dogs.

9 ♦ HATFIELD HOUSE WEST GARDEN
Hatfield, AL9 5HX. The Marquess & Marchioness of Salisbury, 01707 287010, visitors@hatfield-house.co.uk, www.hatfield-house.co.uk. *Pedestrian entrance to Hatfield Park is opp Hatfield train stn. From here you can obtain directions to the*

HERTFORDSHIRE 253

Holtsmere End Farm

gardens. Free parking is available. **For NGS: Sat 21 Mar (10.30-4). Adm £16, chd £8. For other opening times and information, please phone, email or visit garden website. Donation to a charity to be nominated by Lady Salisbury.**
Visitors can enjoy the spring bulbs in the lime walk, sundial garden and view the famous Old Palace garden, childhood home of Queen Elizabeth I. The adjoining woodland garden is at its best in spring with masses of naturalised daffodils and bluebells. Visitors can enjoy refreshments at the Coach House Kitchen Restaurant which serves a variety of delicious foods throughout the day. There is a good route for wheelchairs around the West Garden and a plan can be picked up at the garden kiosk.

27 HERTFORDSHIRE'S TINY TROPICAL GARDEN
12 Longmans Close, Byewaters, Watford, WD18 8WP. Mark Lammin, 07966 625559, mark.lammin@ngs.org.uk, www.instagram.com/hertstinytropicalgarden. *Leave M25 J18 (A404) & follow Rickmansworth/Croxley Green then A412 to Watford. Follow signs for Watford & Croxley Business Parks & then NGS signs. Parking on neighbouring roads.* **Visits by arrangement 4 July to 30 Aug for groups of up to 10. Adm £10, chd free. Tea, coffee & cake.**
See how dazzling colour, scent, lush tropical foliage, trickling water and clever use of pots in a densely planted small garden can transport you to the tropics. Stately bananas and canna rub shoulders with delicate lily and roses amongst a large variety of begonia, hibiscus, ferns and houseplants in a tropical theme more often associated with warmer climes. Beautiful walks along the Grand Union Canal and on the Croxley Green Boundary Walk (signposted). Croxley Common Moor is a very short level stroll away with 113 acres of open moorland, woods and river, as well as the impressive Buddleia Walk.

28 NEW HOLTSMERE END FARM
Holtsmere End Lane, Redbourn, St Albans, AL3 7AW. Gerald & Virginia Corbett. *Im N of Hemel Hempstead. Take the B487 out of HH towards Redbourn. Turn L up Holtsmere End Ln. After 1m turn L in front of HE Manor. After 100 yds arrive at garden.* **Sat 6 June (2-5). Adm £6, chd free. Home-made teas.**
A one acre garden divided into "rooms" around a period farmhouse. Discover a listed barn and other old farm buildings as well as a front lawn surrounded by peony and other flower beds. There is also a Coode Adams rose trellis, croquet lawn, walnut tree lawn, and a productive kitchen garden. Also explore a two acre paddock and orchard. Enjoy 80 different varieties of roses.

29 8 KINGCROFT ROAD
Southdown, Harpenden, AL5 1EJ. Zia Allaway, www.ziaallaway.com. 1½m S of Harpenden town centre. From Harpenden take the St Albans Rd A1081 S. At 1st r'about turn L onto Southdown Rd. Cont straight over 3 r'abouts to Grove Rd. Take the 3rd turning on R to Coleswood Rd. Take 1st turning on L. **Evening opening Sun 30 Aug (5-8). Wine. Mon 31 Aug (2.30-5.30). Home-made teas. Adm £5, chd free.**
Beautiful mature town garden designed by garden writer and horticulturist in a contemporary informal style, with small pond and pebbled beach area, gravel garden, a wide range of summer bulbs, herbaceous perennials and shrubs, mature trees, shady borders, greenhouse, and inspirational container displays. A small courtyard features flower filled window boxes and fruit in raised beds.

30 16 LANGLEY CRESCENT
St Albans, AL3 5RS. Jonathan Redmayne. ½m S of St Albans city centre. M25 J21a, follow B4630. At mini r'about by King Harry Pub turn L. At next r'about turn R along A4147, then R at mini r'about. Langley Cres is 2nd L. **Evening opening Fri 29 May (5-8). Wine. Sat 30 May (2.30-5.30). Tea, coffee & cake. Adm £5, chd free.**
A compact walled garden set on a slope with a wide range of unusual herbaceous perennials, shrubs and trees, both edible and ornamental, and a gentle ambience. The rear garden is divided into two parts; the lower section comprises extensive herbaceous beds inc a collection of Phlomis and leads to a secluded area for quiet contemplation beside a wildlife pond surrounded by rambling roses. Fruit trees, herbaceous borders for pollinators, glasshouse and plant propagation areas. Wheelchair access to most areas of the garden. Garden is on a slope.

31 THE MANOR HOUSE, AYOT ST LAWRENCE
Welwyn, AL6 9BP. 4m W of Welwyn. 20 mins J4 A1M. Take B653 Wheathampstead. Turn into Codicote Rd follow signs to Shaws Corner. Parking in field, short walk to garden. A disabled drop-off point is available at the end of the drive. **Sat 16, Sun 17 May (11-5). Adm £9, chd free. Home-made teas. Home-made cakes, scones, coffee & cold drinks available.**
A six acre garden set in mature landscape around Elizabethan Manor House (not open). A one acre walled garden inc glasshouses, fruit and vegetables, double herbaceous borders, rose and herb beds. Herbaceous perennial island beds, topiary specimens. Parterre and temple pond garden surround the house. Gates and water features by Arc Angel. Garden designed by Julie Toll. Produce for sale. The drop off point is 5min walk from the garden. There are steps in part of the garden but the majority of the garden is suited to wheelchair access.

32 43 MARDLEY HILL
Welwyn, AL6 0TT. Kerrie Lloyd Dawson & Pete Stevens, www.agardenlessordinary.blogspot.co.uk. 5m N of Welwyn Garden City. On B197 between Welwyn & Woolmer Green, on crest of Mardley Hill by bus stop. Please consider our neighbours and other road users when parking. **Mon 25 May (12-5). Adm £5, chd free. Home-made teas.**
An unexpected garden created by plantaholics and packed with unusual plants. Focus on foliage and long season of interest. Various areas: alpine bed; sunny border; deep shade; white-stemmed birches and woodland planting; naturalistic stream, pond and bog; chicken house and potted vegetables; potted exotics. Seating areas on different levels. This garden is proud to have provided plants for the National Garden Scheme's Show Garden at Chelsea Flower Show 2024.

33 MEADOWGATE
36 Bluebridge Road, Brookmans Park, Hatfield, AL9 7SA. Alison Anscombe. 4m S of Hatfield, 3½m N of M25 J23. ½m from BP train stn. From Hatfield: 2.2m S on A1000, R to Dixons Hill Rd, L to Station

203 Northridge Way

Rd, to Bluebridge Rd. From M25 J23: 1.8m N on Swanland Rd, R to Warrengate Rd, R to Hawkshead Ln. From BP Train station: ½m walk. **Evening opening Fri 17 July (6-8). Wine. Sun 19 July (1.30-5). Tea, coffee & cake. Adm £6, chd free.**
A garden designer's own medium size garden enclosed by mature beech hedging. Patio borders feature roses, lavender, achillea, hydrangeas, brunnera, silver birch and colourful pots. Steps with topiary yew to lawn. Island beds full of grasses and colourful perennials, with the emphasis on colour, form, texture and movement. A relaxing patio at the back features a pond and more planting. Wheelchair access to the large patio and planting beds only due to steps. The main garden planting can still be mostly seen from the patio.

34 MORNING LIGHT
7 Armitage Close, Loudwater, Rickmansworth, WD3 4HL. Roger & Patt Trigg, 01923 774293, roger@triggmail.org.uk. *From M25 J18 take A404 towards Rickmansworth. After ¾m turn L into Loudwater Ln, follow bends, then turn R at T-junc & R again into Armitage Close. Limited parking for cars.* **Visits by arrangement Apr to Sept for groups of up to 20. Adm £5, chd free. Tea, coffee & cake. An extensive plant sale will be held on Sun 24 May, 12-4 pm.**
A south facing plantsman's garden, densely planted with hardy and tender perennials and shrubs. *Astilbes* and phlox feature along with island beds, a pond, chipped wood paths. Tall perennials can be viewed from the raised deck. Large conservatory stocked with sub-tropicals.

35 NEW 203 NORTHRIDGE WAY
Hemel Hempstead, HP1 2AU. **Lois Horbury.** *From Hemel train stn (London Rd), turn R onto Fishery Rd. At the next r'about turn L onto Northridge Way. Parking next to church on R after ½m. Garden opp car park.* **Sat 18 July (1-5). Adm £5, chd free. Tea, coffee & cake.**
A productive garden on four levels, full of fruit trees (inc peach and apricot) and vegetable beds filled with vegetables all grown from seed. The garden is divided into 'rooms' at various heights giving wonderful and varied views with peaceful secluded sanctuaries to sit and relax. A hand built brick pizza oven provides a wonderful backdrop for cana lilies, sunflowers and cosmos. Well established hardy banana area, raised brick decking area with a variety of tropical plants.

36 THE OLD RECTORY, COTTERED
The Old Rectory, Cottered, nr Buntingford, SG9 9QP. **Debbie Taussig.** *Between Baldock & Buntingford. On A507 in the centre of Cottered. Garden is on L travelling from Baldock. After the Bull pub & opp recreation ground.* **Sun 19 Apr (1.30-5). Adm £7, chd free. Tea, coffee & cake.**
This five acre garden is a garden of many parts and surrounds the house, a former rectory. Discover our herbaceous garden, rose garden, and an ornamental kitchen and cutting garden. Wander through a perennial meadow, winter garden, bog garden and woodland. There are formal lavender beds and an orchard with wildflowers. Explore the lake with an island and two further ponds.

37 PATCHWORK
22 Hall Park Gate, Berkhamsted, HP4 2NJ. **Jean & Peter Block, 01442 864731, patchwork2@btinternet.com.** *3m W of Hemel Hempstead. Entering E side of Berkhamsted on A4251, turn L 200yds after 40mph sign.* **Visits by arrangement Apr to Sept for groups of 5 to 20. Adm £7, chd free. Tea, coffee & biscuits available on request. Discuss refreshments when booking.**
A ¼ acre garden with lots of year-round colour, interest and perfume. Sloping site containing rockeries, two small ponds, herbaceous borders, island beds with bulbs in spring and dahlias in summer, roses, fuchsias, hostas, begonias, patio pots and tubs galore - all set against a background of trees and shrubs of varying colours.

38 PIE CORNER
Millhouse Lane, Bedmond, Abbots Langley, WD5 0SG. **Bella & Jeremy Stuart-Smith, 07710 099132, piebella1@gmail.com, www.instagram.com/piecornergarden.** *Near Watford, Hemel Hempstead & St Albans. In centre of Bedmond,* Millhouse Ln is opp the shops. Entry is 50m down Millhouse Ln. Parking in field. Alternative parking in village car park, short walk away. What3words app: cloud.owners.invest. **Sun 14 June (2-5). Adm £7, chd free. Home-made teas. Visits also by arrangement May to July for groups of 15+. Contact owner for prices & refreshment details.**
A garden designed to complement the modern classical house. Formal borders near the house, pond, views across a large lawn, punctuated with wildflowers to the valley beyond. More informal shrub plantings with bulbs edge the woodland. A dry gravel garden leads through more meadow to vegetable garden. Blossom, wild garlic, bluebells in spring. Wisteria, roses, flowering shrubs and herbaceous follow. Includes azaleas and rhododendrons, and towering climbing wilder roses. Robust wheelchairs can access most areas on grass or gravel paths except the formal pond where there are steps. There are some steep grassy slopes.

39 THE PINES
58 Hoe Lane, Ware, SG12 9NZ. **Peter Laing, 07852 454393, peteralaing@hotmail.com.** *Approx ½m S of Ware centre. At S (top) end of Hoe Ln, close to entrance to Hertford Rugby Club (car parking) & opp Pinewood Sch. Look for prominent white gateposts with lions.* **Sun 31 May, Sun 27 Sept (2-5). Adm £5, chd free. Tea, coffee & cake. Visits also by arrangement May to Sept.**
Plantsman's garden with many unusual plants, created by present owner over 35 years. An acre, on an east to west axis so much shade, sandy soil over chalk but can grow ericaceous plants. Front garden formal with fountain. Main garden mature trees, herbaceous borders and island beds. Features inc gravel garden, pergola and obelisk with moss rose "William Lobb". Among many specimen trees, the rare Kashmir cypress.

40 NEW PORTHILL HOUSE
Redwoods, Bengeo, Hertford, SG14 3BT. Alex & Sophie Gurr. *Exit A1(M) J4 & head towards Hertford. At r'about take 1st exit to A119; next r'about take 2nd exit & follow for 0.3m. Turn L onto Old Cross & follow until Port Hill. Garden at the end of Redwoods.* **Sun 17 May (11-4). Adm £6, chd free. Tea, coffee & cake.**
The garden at Porthill House is approx 1½ acres in size and framed by high brick walls and mature trees, inc a redwood believed to be over 300 years old. The large central lawn drops down from the house to give an extended view over the whole garden. Gravel paths lead all around, alongside deep, mature borders, through areas of formal topiary to a small orchard and wildflower area. Accessible but drive and pathways are deep gravel so may be hard work to traverse.

41 NEW 4 RECTORY CROFT
Rectory Lane, Stevenage, SG1 4BY. Mrs Wendy Martindale, 07803 888162, wendyhome@mpm-eng.co.uk. *1m from J8 of A1. Leave A1 at J8 & take A602 Stevenage. At 1st r'about, turn L onto Coreys Mill Ln, Lister Hosp on L. At the T-junc, turn R (B197), take next L onto Rectory Ln.* **Visits by arrangement Apr to Oct for groups of up to 20. Adm £6, chd free. Tea, coffee & cake.**
Garden developed and maintained since 2019, inc a patio that wraps around the house. A large lawn is surrounded by a variety of herbaceous borders individualised by colour, shade, ericaceous soil and wildflowers. The garden also inc climbers, trees, roses and a herb bed. The mixture of shrubs and perennials inc salvias, rudbeckia, skimmia, hellebores. The patio extends around the house with a built in slope to avoid steps and would enable wheelchair access to much of the garden.

42 NEW 24 ROSE WALK
St Albans, AL4 9AF. Mrs Alexandra Butler. *In Marshallswick area of St Albans. Off Sandpit Ln. What3words app: tips.chimp.stump.* **Sat 30 May (1.30-5.30). Adm £5, chd free. Home-made teas.**
A newly designed, family garden offering year-round enjoyment. Featuring mature trees, new plants, a pond, and a vegetable patch, it boasts multiple seating areas and focal points. A path leads to a physiotherapy room which is surrounded by plants which provide structure, texture, colour, and scent, to create a restorative and accessible space, fostering wellbeing and connection with nature. The whole garden is accessible by wheelchair with access from the side gate of the house.

43 RUSTLING END COTTAGE
Rustling End, Codicote, SG4 8TD. Julie & Tim Wise, www.rustlingend.com. *1m N of Codicote. From B656 turn L into '3 Houses Ln' then R to Rustling End. House 2nd on L. What3words app: help.sling.thinks.* **Wed 13 May (2-5). Home-made teas. Evening opening Fri 15 May (5.30-8). Wine. Adm £6, chd free.**
Meander through our wildflower meadow to a cottage garden with contemporary planting. Behind lumpy hedges explore a garden managed for wildlife. Natural planting provides an environment for birds, small mammals and insects. Our terrace features drought tolerant low maintenance plants. A flowery mead surrounds the formal pond and an abundant floral vegetable garden provides produce for the summer. Hens in residence. No Mow May lawn meadow.

44 ♦ ST PAUL'S WALDEN BURY
Whitwell, Hitchin, SG4 8BP. The Bowes Lyon family, stpaulswalden@gmail.com, www.stpaulswaldenbury.co.uk. *5m S of Hitchin. On B651; ½m N of Whitwell village. From London leave A1(M) J6 for Welwyn (not Welwyn Garden City). Pick up signs to Codicote, then Whitwell.* **For NGS: Sun 19 Apr, Sun 10 May, Sun 7 June (2-6). Adm £8, chd free. Home-made teas.** For other opening times and information, please email or visit garden website. Donation to St Paul's Walden Charity.
Spectacular formal woodland garden, Grade I listed, laid out 1720, covering over 50 acres. Long rides lined with beech hedges lead to temples, statues, lake and a terraced theatre. Seasonal displays of daffodils, camelias, irises, magnolias, rhododendrons, lilies. Wildflowers encouraged - cowslips, bluebells. This was the childhood home of the late Queen Mother. Children welcome. Dogs on leads. Good wheelchair access to part of the garden.

GROUP OPENING

45 ST STEPHENS AVENUE GARDENS
St Albans, AL3 4AD. www.instagram.com/heather.osborne20. *1m S of St Albans City Centre. From A414 take A5183 Watling St. At mini r'about by St Stephens Church/King Harry Pub take B4630 Watford Rd. St Stephens Ave is 1st R.* **Sun 28 June, Sun 30 Aug (2.30-5.30). Combined adm £8, chd free. Tea, coffee & cake.**

20 ST STEPHENS AVENUE
Heather Osborne.

30 ST STEPHENS AVENUE
Carol & Roger Harlow.

Only five doors apart, these two town gardens have been developed in totally different but equally inspiring ways- from an innovative drought tolerant front garden full of achilleas, eryngiums and self seeding perennials, to paths winding through plant packed borders with specimen trees, flowering shrubs and climbers in a series of 'rooms'. Our June opening at no 20 features roses, clematis and geraniums; in August, dahlias, asters, salvias and late season perennials come to the fore. Seasonal patio containers, hostas, wildlife pond, seating in sun and shade, home-made cakes and teas served in the conservatory, WC. The gravelled front at no 30 leads round to a sunken garden used as an outdoor kitchen to enjoy the fruits of a productive allotment. Clipped box, beech and hornbeam in the back garden provide a cool backdrop for the strong colours of the double herbaceous borders. A gate beneath an apple arch frames the view to the park beyond. Plants for sale at June opening only.

46 SARRATT COMMUNITY GARDEN
The Green, Sarratt, Rickmansworth, WD3 6AT. Flo Garvey, www.facebook.com/sarrattcommunitygarden. *Directly behind Sarratt Post Office Stores, in the centre of Sarratt Village. Parking available in village, though walking and cycling are encouraged.* **Sun 7 June (11-4). Adm £5, chd free. Tea, coffee & cake.**
A thriving, productive community garden, growing fruit, vegetables and cut flowers for local people. This garden is run on organic principles, with a passion for the environment and education. There will be refreshments available, and there is space to sit for around 30 people.

47 SERENDI
22 Hitchin Road, Letchworth Garden City, SG6 3LT. Valerie, 07548 776809, valerie.aitken22@gmail.com, www.instagram.com/serendigarden. *1m from city centre. A1M J9 signed Letchworth on A505. At 2nd r'about take 1st exit Hitchin A505. Straight over T-lights. Garden 1m on R.* **Sun 15, Tue 17 Feb (1-4.30). Combined adm with 10 Cross Street £8, chd free. Sun 6 Sept (1-4.30). Adm £5, chd free. Home-made teas. Visits also by arrangement 18 Feb to 13 Sept for groups of 10 to 30.**
A well designed garden, with many areas for sitting and all year-round interest and colour. Spring bulbs, snowdrops, ferns, allium, tulips, hostas and containers. Later perennials, roses, clematis, delightful dahlias, a developing exotic area, a gravel area and new knot garden. A greenhouse for over wintering, a Griffin glasshouse with *Tibochina, Clivia, Aeonium, Pelargoniums*, cacti and more. Wheelchair access via gravel entrance, driveway and paths.

GROUP OPENING

48 SERGE HILL GARDENS
Serge Hill Lane, Bedmond, WD5 0RT. www.tomstuartsmith.co.uk. ½ m E of Bedmond. *Go to Bedmond & take Serge Hill Ln, where you will be directed past the lodge & down the drive. Parking is in a large field.* **Sun 7 June (1-5). Combined adm £18, chd free. Pre-booking essential, please visit www.ngs.org.uk for information & booking. Home-made teas.**

THE BARN
Sue & Tom Stuart-Smith, www.tomstuartsmith.co.uk/our-work/toms-garden.

THE PLANT LIBRARY
Tom & Sue Stuart-Smith, www.sergehillproject.co.uk.

SERGE HILL
Kate Stuart-Smith, www.instagram.com/katestuartsmith.

Three large country gardens a short walk from each other. Tom and Sue Stuart-Smith's garden at The Barn has an enclosed courtyard with tanks of water, herbaceous perennials and shrubs tolerant of generally dry conditions. To the north there are views over the five acre wildflower meadow. The West Garden is a series of different gardens overflowing with bulbs, herbaceous perennials, and shrubs. There is also an exotic prairie planted from seed in 2011. The Plant Library is a collection of over 1000 herbaceous plants first planted in 2021. Next door at Serge Hill, there is a lovely walled garden with a large Foster and Pearson greenhouse, orderly rows of vegetables, and disorderly self-seeded annuals and perennials. The walls are crowded with climbers and shrubs. From here you emerge to a meadow, a mixed border and a wonderful view over the ha-ha to the park and woods beyond. Follow the gardens on Instagram: @tomstuartsmith @suestuartsmith @katestuartsmith @tomstuartsmithstudio.

49 SHORTGROVE MANOR FARM
Dovehouse Lane, Kensworth, Dunstable, LU6 2PQ. Helen & David Barlow. *Between Kensworth & Whipsnade. If using SatNav, please do not follow the postcode. Entrance is on Buckwood Ln. What3words app: jeeps.best.legal.* **Sun 14 June (11-4). Adm £8, chd free. Tea, coffee & cake in the Pool House.**
A 6½ acre garden set in mature landscape around a Grade II listed C15 Farmhouse. Formal gardens inc a sunken garden with pond, rose covered pergola, terraces, fountain, Orangery and topiary specimens. There is also a wild area and derelict orchard. Shortgrove Manor Farm is home to The National Citrus Collection. The citrus are on display outside during the summer months.

50 NEW SOIL SQUAD
Sandridge Road Allotments, 24-26 Marshall Avenue, St Albans, AL3 6BL. Mrs Vicky Gutteridge, 07780 996181, hello@soilsquad.uk, www.soilsquad.uk. *15 mins from M25 & M1. Situated between 24 & 26 Marshall Ave. Follow the long drive to the green metal gates. Enter & park; Soil Squad is immed on L. What3words app: garage.venue.emerge.* **Visits by arrangement 4 May to 17 July for groups of 5 to 10. Tea, coffee & cake.**
Soil Squad's Community Composting Hub turns food waste into living compost for gardens and allotments. We showcase hot and cold composting, maturation bays, Johnson–Su bioreactors and leaf mould. We focus on planet, plant and people health, Soil Squad is for anyone keen to enrich both their soil and wellbeing. The Wilderhood Watch Allotment is also open, designed for wildlife and productivity. Wilderhood allotment will also be open for visitors to explore. Wheelchair accessible. Paths are woodchip.

78,000 people affected by cancer were reached by Maggie's centres supported by the National Garden Scheme over the last 12 months.

51 SUNNYSIDE RURAL TRUST - HEMEL HEMPSTEAD
Two Waters Road, Hemel Hempstead, HP3 9BY. Sunnyside Rural Trust Charity, www.sunnysideruraltrust.org.uk. *5mins from the A41, Hemel Hempstead exit. The entrance & car park to Sunnyside - Hemel Hempstead are found off the Two Waters Rd, behind the K2 restaurant. More parking is available at Durrants Hill Rd, HP3 9TH.* **Sat 30 May (10-4). Adm £5, chd free. Tea, coffee & cake at the Sunnyside Up Cafe & Farmshop.**
Sunnyside Hemel Hempstead is the base for the charity's Green Flag awarded plant nursery. We work with people with learning disabilities to grow peat-free perennial and annual bedding for domestic and commercial clients. On site, you'll find Arit Anderson's peat-free Hampton Court show garden 2024, alongside our Tranquillity Garden and allotments. A select range of perennial, bedding and herb plants will be available for sale. Enjoy our on site cafe and farm shop, where you can purchase Sunnyside produce, inc apple juice, jam, and chutneys. A wide range of hot beverages, home-made cakes and lunches are also available. Assisted wheelchair access where there are woodland and grass paths.

52 NEW SWEET BRIAR FLOWER FARM
London Road, Hertford, SG13 7NT. Nicola Stuart O'Brien, sweetbriarflowerfarm.co.uk. *Exit M25 J25 & head towards Hertford on A10. After 7m take slip road to A414. At Foxholes r'about take 1st exit onto London Rd. take 1st L onto Foxholes Farm Dr.* **Fri 9 Oct (11-5). Adm £5, chd free. Light refreshments at Foxholes café.**
Our ethos is to grow in harmony with the seasons, without chemicals, producing natural, scented traditional flowers. At Sweet Briar we are smitten by the beauty of English flowers. Pick your own will be available. Please bring a bucket and snips.

53 9 TANNSFIELD DRIVE
Hemel Hempstead, HP2 5LG. Peter & Gaynor Barrett, 01442 393508, peteslittlepatch@virginmedia.com, www.peteslittlepatch.co.uk. *Approx. 1m NE of Hemel Hempstead town centre & 2m W of J8 on M1. From M1 J8, cross r'about to A414 to Hemel Hempstead. Under footbridge, cross r'about then 1st R across dual c'way to Leverstock Green Rd. On to High St Green. L into Ellingham Rd then follow signs.* **Sun 28 June, Sun 2 Aug (1.30-4.30). Adm £4, chd free. Home-made teas. Visits also by arrangement 29 June to 8 Aug for groups of 10 to 15. Adm £8 inc refreshments.**
A town garden to surprise the visitor. Dense planting with the ever-present sound of trickling water creates an intimate and welcoming oasis of calm. By taking the narrow paths, each of which divides, thereby continually offering a choice of direction, the visitor will be able to find several different routes around the garden where they can come across the many features the garden has to offer.

54 THUNDRIDGE HILL HOUSE
Cold Christmas Lane, Ware, SG12 0UE. Christopher & Susie Melluish, 01920 462500,

Gorhambury House

c.melluish@btopenworld.com. *2m NE of Ware. ¾m from Maltons off the A10 down Cold Christmas Ln, crossing the bypass.* **Sun 21 June (2-5.30). Adm £6, chd free. Cream teas. Visits also by arrangement May to Sept for groups of 20 to 40.**
Well established garden of approx 2½ acres; good variety of plants, shrubs and roses, attractive hedges. Visitors often ask for the unusual yellow bed, 'A most popular garden to visit'. Wonderful views in and out of the garden especially down to the Rib Valley to Youngsbury and the ruined Tower of St Mary and All Hallows church. Youngsbury was visited briefly by Lancelot Capability Brown. A level garden with paved, gravel and grass areas.

55 WALKERN HALL
Walkern, Stevenage, SG2 7JA. Mrs Kate de Boinville. *4m E of Stevenage. Turn L at War Memorial as you leave Walkern, heading S for Benington (immed after small bridge). Garden 1m up hill on R.* **Sat 31 Jan, Sun 1 Feb, Sat 28, Sun 29 Mar (12-4). Adm £6, chd free. Home-made teas. Warming home-made soup, tea, coffee & cakes.**
Walkern Hall is essentially a winter woodland garden. Set in eight acres, the carpet of snowdrops and aconites is a constant source of wonder in winter. This Medieval hunting park is known more for its established trees such as the tulip trees and a magnificent London plane tree which dominates the garden. In March there a stunning display of daffodils and other spring bulbs. There is wheelchair access but quite a lot of gravel and a cobbled courtyard. No disabled WC.

56 WALLED GARDEN, 1 FARQUHAR STREET
Bengeo, Hertford, SG14 3BN. Stacey & Carrick Lambert, www.pollenplantingdesign.co.uk. *½m from Hertford town centre in the conservation area of Bengeo. Cont out of town up Port Hill & take 1st L into Cross Rd. Turn L at the end & along to the garden on L.* **Fri 7 Aug (6-8.30am). Wine. Sun 9 Aug (12-5). Tea, coffee & cake. Adm £5, chd free. Refreshments provided by Isabel Hospice on Sun 9 Aug.**
A passionate plant persons town garden set within Victorian walls,
incorporating full curvaceous borders of select herbaceous and woody plants which surround an ever decreasing central lawned area. Many plants are homegrown within the greenhouse with wildlife in mind and adorn the borders year-round whilst the mature trees surrounding the garden, welcome many birds. Wheelchair access via gravel paths.

57 WARRENWOOD
39 Firs Wood Close, Potters Bar, EN6 4BY. Val & Peter Mackie. *Potters Bar, High St (A1000) fork R towards Cuffley, along the Causeway. Immed before the T-lights, R down Coopers Ln Rd. ½m on L Firs Wood Close.* **Sun 7 June (11-5). Adm £6, chd free. Tea, coffee & cake.**
Situated within Northaw Park, a three acre garden made up of a woodland area, a field inc a wildflower meadow and a more formal ½ acre around the house. Raised vegetable beds and Victorian greenhouse. Choice of seating areas inc a breeze house, sunken fire pit area and colourful patio benches under the pergola covered with wisteria. Tranquil views up to Northaw village.

58 WATEREND HOUSE
Waterend Lane, Wheathampstead, St Albans, AL4 8EP. Mr & Mrs J Nall-Cain, 07736 880810, sj@nallcain.com, www.instagram.com/waterendhousegarden. *2m E of Wheathampstead. Approx 10 mins from J4 of A1M. Take B653 to Wheathampstead, past Crooked Chimney Pub, after ½m turn R into Waterend Ln. Cross river, house is immed on R. Parking in the lane next to the house.* **Visits by arrangement 16 Feb to 27 July for groups of 20 to 25. Enjoy a tour of the garden and hear about its history. Adm £14. Home-made teas. Adm inc refreshments.**
A hidden garden of four acres sets off an elegant Jacobean Manor House (not open). Steep grass slopes and fine views of glorious countryside. Large quantities of spring bulbs, formal flint-walled garden. Roses, peonies and irises in summer. Formal beds and lots of colour throughout the year. Mature specimen trees, ponds, formal vegetable garden and chickens. Personalised tour of garden inc. A meditation garden surrounded by a gallery of hornbeam. Take a peak at a row of elephants. A woodland
path lined with hellebores. The owner will take you on a personalised tour of the garden and explain the history of the garden, the house and the surrounding area. Hilly garden. Wheelchair access to lower gardens only.

59 NEW WHITE HORSE COTTAGE
Reed End, Therfield, Royston, SG8 9RL. *From S: A10 towards Royston turning L immed after cafe. From N: A10 towards Buntingford turning R just before cafe. Follow the lane for ½m to the thatched cottage on R. Limited parking on gravel driveway & lane. What3words app: chill.backpacks.ignore.* **Sun 31 May (10-4). Adm £4, chd free. Pre-booking essential, please visit www.ngs.org.uk for information & booking. Home-made teas.**
Romantic cottage garden of under an acre surrounding a C16 listed thatched cottage. Developed by the owners over eight years with formal and informal spaces and creative use of an unusual shaped plot. Emphasis on wildlife and pollinators, the garden is planted with roses, lavender, clematis, hostas, shrubs and herbaceous perennials providing year-round colour and scent, set among countryside views.

Our donation in 2025 has enabled Parkinson's UK to fund 2 new nursing posts this year directly supporting people with Parkinson's.

ISLE OF WIGHT

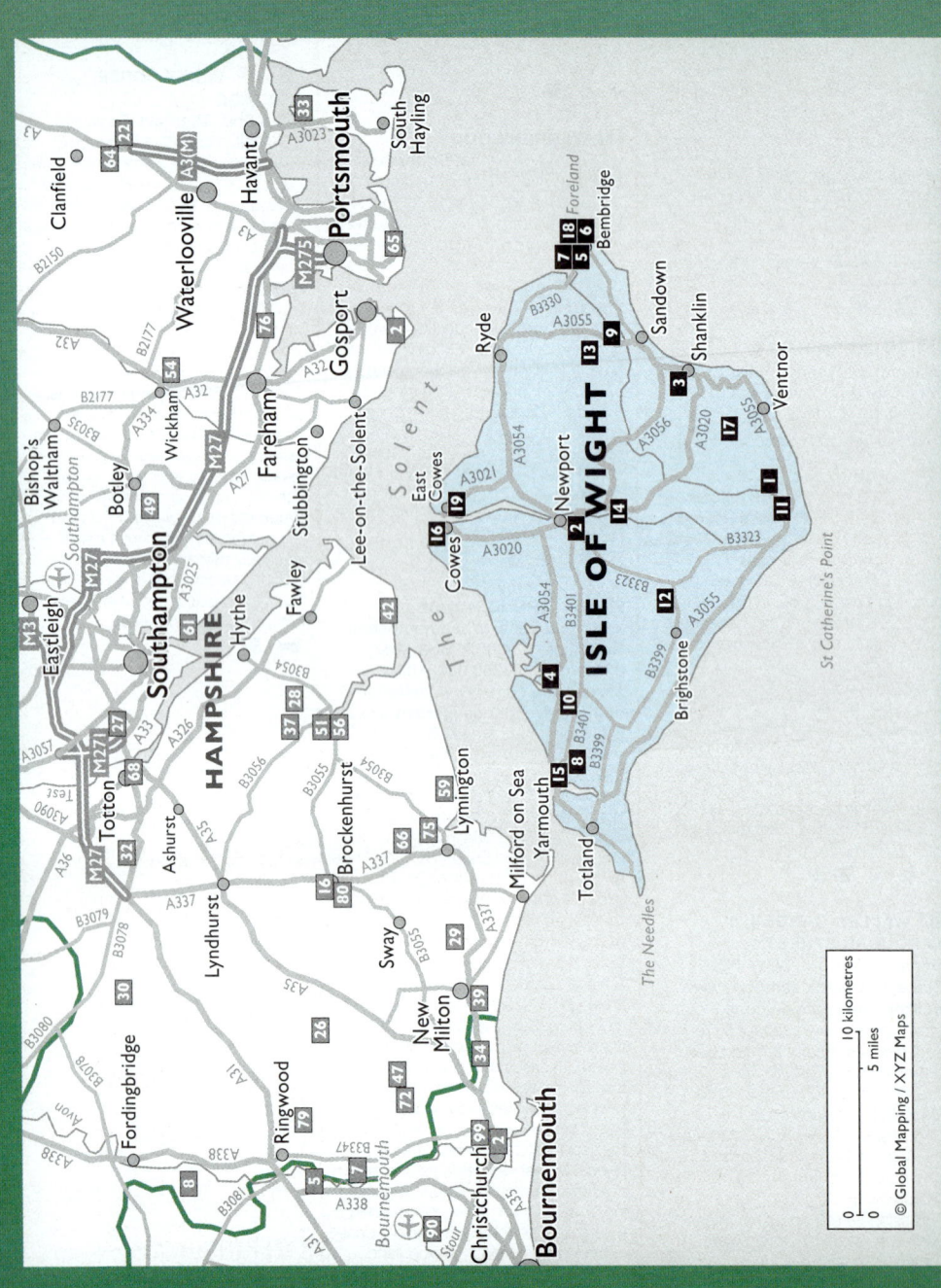

ISLE OF WIGHT

VOLUNTEERS

County Organiser
Jane Bland 01983 874592
jane.bland@ngs.org.uk

County Treasurer
Sally Parker 01983 612495
sally.parker@ngs.org.uk

Booklet Co-ordinator
Jane Bland (as above)

Booklet Advertising
Joanna Truman 01983 873822
joanna_truman@btinternet.com

Assistant County Organisers
Sally Parker
(as above)

Joanna Truman
(as above)

@iow_ngs

OPENING DATES

All entries subject to change.
For latest information check
www.ngs.org.uk
Map locator numbers are
shown to the right of each
garden name.

May

Sunday 17th
Goldings 8
Thorley Manor 15

Sunday 24th
Northcourt Manor Gardens 12

Sunday 31st
Morton Manor 9

June

Saturday 6th
East Cliff 7
Niton Gardens 11
Rookley Gardens 14

Sunday 7th
Niton Gardens 11
Rookley Gardens 14

Saturday 13th
NEW Wroxall Village Gardens 17

Saturday 20th
Ashknowle House 1

Sunday 21st
Ashknowle House 1
Darts 5
Yew Tree Lodge 18

July

Sunday 19th
♦ Nunwell House 13

Sunday 26th
Dove Cottage 6

August

Saturday 1st
1 Union Road 16

By Arrangement

Arrange a personalised garden visit
with your club, or group of friends,
on a date to suit you. See individual
garden entries for full details.

NEW 17 Chatfield Lodge	2
NEW Claverhouse	3
Crab Cottage	4
Morton Manor	9
Ningwood Manor	10
Northcourt Manor Gardens	12
Talsa (Niton Gardens)	11
1 Union Road	16
163 York Avenue	19

Oakdene, Rookley Gardens

© Lucy Hooper

THE GARDENS

1 ASHKNOWLE HOUSE
Ashknowle Lane, Whitwell,
Ventnor, PO38 2PP. Mr & Mrs K
Fradgley. *4m W of Ventnor. Take the
Whitwell Rd from Ventnor or Godshill.
Turn into unmade lane next to Old
Rectory, ignore the no motor vehicles
sign. Field parking. Disabled parking
at house.* **Sat 20, Sun 21 June (12-4). Adm £5, chd free. Home-made teas.**
The mature garden of this Victorian
house (not open) has great diversity
inc woodland walks, water features,
colourful beds and borders. The
large, well maintained kitchen garden
is highly productive and boasts a
wide range of fruit and vegetables
grown in cages, tunnels, glasshouses
and raised beds. Diversely planted
and highly productive orchard inc
protected cropping of strawberries,
peaches and apricots. Propagation
areas for trees, shrubs and crops.

2 NEW 17 CHATFIELD LODGE
Newport, PO30 1XR. Clive
Eason, 07970 536904,
c.eason@outlook.com. *17 Chatfield
Lodge is located in a cul-de-sac
just off Watergate Rd.* **Visits by
arrangement 10 Apr to 10 Oct for
groups of 5 to 10. Adm £7, chd
free. Home-made teas.**
This subtropical garden is an
unexpected find, especially given the
more traditional front garden, which
features mainly lavender and salvias.
The garden contains over 100 tree
ferns, some reaching up to 12ft in
height, alongside many palms and a
patio filled with subtropical plants that
resemble a Costa Rican rainforest.
The tree ferns have been planted to
reflect a Tasmanian rainforest.

3 NEW CLAVERHOUSE
Shanklin, PO37 7EL.
Glenys Lloyd-Williams,
enjoyaplay@outlook.com. *A 1960s
bungalow at the top of a small close
off Whitecross Ln. From Ryde or
Newport via Merrie Gardens r'about,
take 6th L into Whitecross Ln, then
R into Scotchells Cl. Bus 2, alight
Green Ln or bus 8, alight Morrisons.
Parking for 3 cars on drive.* **Visits by
arrangement 15 June to 14 Sept
for groups of up to 10. Individuals
are also very welcome!. Adm £5.**
Tea, coffee & cake.
Small sloping garden. Get ideas to
add interest, variety, and reduce the
impact of an incline. Just 60ft x 40ft,
with raised and traditional beds filled
with shrubs, annuals, and perennials,
plus climbers, pots, and troughs.
Each bed has its own character or
colour theme. Also, a selection of soft
fruit and trees, a raised vegetable plot,
and a wild area. A chalet, colourful
shed, swing seat, and water butts.

4 CRAB COTTAGE
Mill Road, Shalfleet, PO30 4NE.
Mr & Mrs Scott, 07768 065756,
susch11@icloud.com. *4½ m E of
Yarmouth. At New Inn, Shalfleet, turn
into Mill Rd. Continue 400yds to end
of metalled road, drive onto unmade
road through NT gates. After 100yds
pass Crab Cottage on L. Park opp
on grass.* **Visits by arrangement
Apr to Sept. Adm £5, chd free.**
Tea, coffee & cake.
1¼ acres on gravelly soil. Part
glorious views across croquet lawn
over Newtown Creek and Solent,
leading through wildflower meadow
to hidden water lily pond, secluded
lawn and woodland walk. Part walled
garden protected from westerlies with
mixed borders, leading to terraced
sunken garden with ornamental pool
and pavilion, planted with exotics,
tender shrubs and herbaceous
perennials. Wheelchair access over
gravel and uneven grass paths.

5 DARTS
Darts Lane, Bembridge,
PO35 5YH. Joanna Truman. *Up the
hill from Bembridge Harbour, then
turn L after the Co-op down Love Ln.
Take 1st L; the house is painted grey.*
**Sun 21 June (12.30-5). Combined
adm with Yew Tree Lodge £7,
chd free.**
A classic walled garden featuring
roses, climbers, shrubs, two large
raised vegetable beds, and a running
water feature. Access to garden via
two raised steps, and three additional
steps to reach top garden.

6 DOVE COTTAGE
Swains Lane, Bembridge,
PO35 5ST. Mr James & Mrs Alex
Hearn. *Head E on Lane End Rd,
passing Lane End Court Shops on
L. Take 3rd turning on L onto Swains
Ln. Dove Cottage is on R.* **Sun 26
July (12-4). Adm £6, chd free.**
An enclosed garden with lawn and
woodland area. A central path leads
through the woodland setting which
has mature variegated shrubs and
perennials, leading to the swimming
pool area and tennis court.

7 EAST CLIFF
Love Lane, Bembridge, PO35 5NH.
Kate & Ian Cheshire. *Disabled
parking only. Please do not drive
down Love Ln, as access is limited
& there is no parking. Kindly park in
the local area.* **Sat 6 June (2.30-5).
Adm £8, chd free. Home-made
teas. Cash preferred on the day.
Last admission 4.30pm.**
The property is situated on a
cliff overlooking the Solent. The
garden, designed by Arabella
Lennox-Boyd, spans approx 8
acres. When designing the garden,
Arabella took into consideration the
cliffside location, the wind, and sea
air, selecting plants suited to the
environment. Her inspired design
features a series of distinct and
beautiful garden areas. Come and
take a look! Well behaved dogs
welcome on leads.

8 GOLDINGS
Thorley Street, Thorley, Yarmouth,
PO41 0SN. John & Dee Sichel. *E
of Yarmouth. Follow directions for
Thorley from Yarmouth/Newport
road or from Wilmingham Ln. Then
follow NGS signs. Parking shared
with Thorley Manor.* **Sun 17 May (2-5). Combined adm with Thorley
Manor £5, chd free. Teas.**
A country garden with many focuses
of interest. A newly planted orchard
already producing cider apples
in large amounts. A small, but
productive vegetable garden and
a well maintained lawn with shrub
borders and roses. A microclimate
has been created by the adjustment
of levels to create a series of terraced
areas for planting.

9 MORTON MANOR
Morton Manor Road, Brading,
Sandown, PO36 0EP. Mr & Mrs G
Godliman, 07768 605900, patricia.
godliman@yahoo.co.uk. *Off A3055,
5m S of Ryde, just out of Brading. At
Yarbridge T-lights turn into The Mall.
Take next L into Morton Manor Rd.*
**Sun 31 May (11-4). Adm £5, chd
free. Light refreshments. Visits**

East Cliff

also by arrangement Apr to Sept. A colourful garden of great plant variety. Mature trees inc many acers with a wide variety of leaf colour. Early in the season a display of rhododendrons, azaleas and camellias and later many perenials, hydrangeas and hibiscus. Ponds, sweeping lawns, roses set on a sunny terrace and much more to see in this extensive garden surrounding a picturesque C16 manor house (not open). Wheelchair access over gravel driveway.

10 NINGWOOD MANOR
Station Road, Ningwood, nr Newport, PO30 4NJ. Nicholas & Claire Oulton, 07738 737482, claireoulton@gmail.com. Nr Shalfleet. From Newport, turn L opp the Horse & Groom pub. Ningwood Manor is 300-400yds on the L. Please use 2nd set of gates. **Visits by arrangement 11 May to 15 Aug for groups of up to 25. Adm £6, chd free. Tea, coffee & cake.**
A 3 acre landscaped country garden, divided into several areas: a walled courtyard, croquet lawn, white garden, and kitchen garden. They flow into each other, each with their own gentle colour schemes. The exception is the croquet lawn garden, which is a riot of colour, mixing oranges, reds, yellows and pinks. Much new planting has taken place over the past few yrs. The owners have several new projects underway, so the garden is a work in progress. Features inc a vegetable garden with raised beds and a small summerhouse, part of which is alleged to be Georgian. Please note the ground is very uneven, visitors must take care.

GROUP OPENING

11 NITON GARDENS
Church Street, Niton, PO38 2BX. 5m W of Ventnor. Parking in village & car park in Allotment Rd (off Rectory Rd). Tickets & maps available from the library (open days only), entrance on Star Inn Rd. Parking for Niton Undercliff in St Catherine's Rd. **Sat 6, Sun 7 June (12.30-5). Combined adm £8, chd free. Home-made teas at Buddle Homestead (cash only).**

NEW BUDDLE HOMESTEAD
Jay Lowein.

HOLLY BANK
Lynda & Nigel Paice.

NEW HYDEAWAY
Beryl & Ian Webster.

PUCKASTER CORNER
Mary & Ian McCallum.

NEW RANDOM STONES
Jane Barnett.

NEW SUNDIAL COTTAGE
Jon & Melanie Boileau Goad.

TALSA
Tom Pritchard, 07447 000088, wightscape@gmail.com.
Visits also by arrangement 2 May to 27 Sept.

TILLINGTON VILLA
Paul & Catherine Miller.

Niton is a charming village with a strong community spirit, home to two lovely churches, two pubs (one with a smuggling past), a PO, shops, supermarket, library, school, and recreation grounds. Nestled in beautiful countryside at the southern tip of the island, where there is also a lighthouse and harbour. The gardens are located in the heart of the village and in the Undercliff, surrounded by scenic walks and bridleways. Varied in style and size, they offer colour, fragrance, and interest, from cottage and country gardens to vegetable plots and wildlife havens. We hope you enjoy them all. Details of wheelchair access will be on the map from the library (open days only). Cashless payments only at the library.

Talsa, Niton Gardens

12 NORTHCOURT MANOR GARDENS
Main Road, Shorwell, Newport, PO30 3JG. Mr & Mrs J Harrison, 01983 740415, john@northcourt.info, www.northcourt.info. *4m SW of Newport. On entering Shorwell from Newport, entrance at bottom of hill on R. If entering from other directions head through village in direction of Newport. Garden on the L, on bend after passing the church.* **Sun 24 May (12-5). Adm £7, chd free. Home-made teas.** Visits also by arrangement 21 Mar to 31 Oct for groups of 5 to 45. Introductory talk & tour (additional charge).
A 15 acre garden surrounding a large C17 manor house (not open). A boardwalk through the jungle garden, a stream and bog garden, and a large variety of plants enjoying the different microclimates. A large collection of camellias and magnolias, woodland walks, a tree collection, salvias and subtropical plantings for autumn drama. A productive 1 acre walled kitchen garden, numerous shrub roses, and a formal parterre. Features inc a picturesque wooded valley around the house, bathhouse and snail mount leading to terraces. A plantsman's garden.

13 ◆ NUNWELL HOUSE
Coach Lane, Brading, PO36 0JQ. Mr & Mrs S Bonsey, info@nunwellhouse.co.uk, www.nunwellhouse.co.uk. *3m S of Ryde. Signed off A3055 as you arrive at Brading from Ryde & turn into Coach Ln.* **For NGS: Sun 19 July (1-4.30). Adm £5, chd free. Home-made teas. For other opening times and information, please email or visit garden website.**
Six acres of tranquil and beautifully set formal and shrub gardens. Exceptional Solent views over historic parkland and Brading Haven from the terraces. Small arboretum and herbaceous borders. The house, developed over five centuries, is full of architectural interest.

GROUP OPENING

14 ROOKLEY GARDENS
Rookley, Newport, PO30 3BJ.
4m S of Newport. From the main Newport to Sandown road, take turning for Rookley at Blackwater. No. 3 bus stops outside Oakdene. **Sat 6, Sun 7 June (10.30-4). Combined adm £6, chd free. Home-made teas at Oakdene.**

OAKDENE
Mr Tim Marshall.
OLD SCHOOL COTTAGE
Mr Nigel Palmer.
THE OLD STABLES
Mrs Susan Waldron.

A varied group of gardens in Rookley village, each unique in size, design, and interest. Set within a well-kept, vibrant community, features range from grassy paths lined with colourful borders and places to rest, to beautiful designs displaying a riot of colour, shape, and form. Visitors will also find fruit and vegetables, wild flowers, and bees.

15 THORLEY MANOR
Thorley, Yarmouth, PO41 0SJ. Mr & Mrs Blest. 1m E of Yarmouth. From Bouldnor take Wilmingham Ln, house ½m on L. **Sun 17 May (2-5). Combined adm with Goldings £5, chd free. Teas at Goldings.** Mature informal gardens of over 3 acres surrounding manor house (not open). Garden set out in a number of walled rooms, perennial and colourful self-seeding borders, shrub borders, lawns, large old trees and an unusual island lawn, all seamlessly blending into the surrounding farmland. The delightful cottage garden of Goldings is open, a short walk away.

16 1 UNION ROAD
Cowes, PO31 7TW. Mr & Mrs B Hicks, georgeous1@gmail.com. Old Town. Take the Cowes Rd (A3020) as far as Northwood T-lights (by the car garage). Bear L & follow signs for Northwood House. Parking at Northwood House, PO31 8AZ, then 3 min walk. **Sat 1 Aug (11-5). Adm £6, chd free. Home-made teas. Visits also by arrangement 1 May to 25 Sept for groups of 5 to 50.**

A south facing town garden with views of the Solent and plenty of sea air. Planting is tropical and takes full advantage of the many hours of sunshine. A combination of unusual plants from drier and arid environments with lush planting in the zones towards the bottom of the garden. Specimen trees and a beautiful walled garden area. A pond featuring wildlife and Mediterranean planting. The working area of the garden features grapevines and olive, apple, fig, citrus and walnut trees. A living agapanthus wall and finally, a herb wall within the outdoor kitchen. Garden designed by Helen Elks-Smith in 2019. Refreshments are made using produce grown in the garden and at the allotment.

GROUP OPENING

17 NEW WROXALL VILLAGE GARDENS
34 Clarence Road, High Street, Wroxall, PO38 3DP. 2m N of Ventnor on B3327. Enter village from N, past the Parish Church, turn L into Station Rd & park in car park or nearby roads. The Methodist church is down the main road on L as you head towards the shop. **Sat 13 June (1.30-4.30). Combined adm £3, chd free. Home-made teas at St Johns Church.**

BLUEBELL COTTAGE
Mr Ken & Mrs Lynn Orchard.
NEW 34 CLARENCE ROAD
Terri Darnbrook.
NEW WROXALL METHODIST CHURCH
Rev Lin Francis.
NEW 15 YARBOROUGH ROAD
Jill Poole.

Nestled in the heart of the small village of Wroxall, you will find a collection of gardens, each different in style, inc traditional cottage, productive, and modern planting. Some have been created from a blank canvas, while others have been cared for over many yrs. One garden features a natural spring that flows through several of the gardens that open. All are within comfortable walking distance. The church is accessible via a long ramp with easy access to the refreshment area and throughout the garden.

18 YEW TREE LODGE
Love Lane, Bembridge, PO35 5NH. Jane Bland. On the Bembridge circular one-way system, take 1st L after Co-op into Love Ln. Darts is on the L, Yew Tree Lodge is facing you when Love Ln turns sharply to the R. **Sun 21 June (12.30-5). Combined adm with Darts £7, chd free. Home-made teas.**
Yew Tree Lodge is flanked by mature oak trees and well established gardens, its main axis being north south. It is divided into separate areas which take into account available natural light and soil type. I have been gardening here for over 10 yrs, during this time the garden has altered a great deal. As well as flowering plants there is a vegetable garden, fruit cages and a cool greenhouse. Wheelchair access over paved path connecting the front and back gardens, and paved access to decking area.

19 163 YORK AVENUE
East Cowes, PO32 6BD. Mr Roy Dorland, 07768 107779, roydorland@hotmail.com. Approach East Cowes through Whippingham by the A3021. Pass Barton Manor on R & continue past Osborne House on R. York Ave on L. Ample roadside parking on LHS. **Visits by arrangement 23 May to 2 Aug for groups of 15 to 30. Adm £5, chd free. Home-made teas.**
Situated near Osborne House, this large colourful garden is packed with unusual hardy perennials and many lovely trees and shrubs. On the terrace is a large date palm, and beyond the main garden there are tropical plants and ferns. You then pass through a gate into a secret garden. There are plenty of seats with tables throughout this relaxing garden.

In 2025, National Garden Scheme funding helped Perennial support 950 unique callers to their helpline looking for advice and information.

KENT

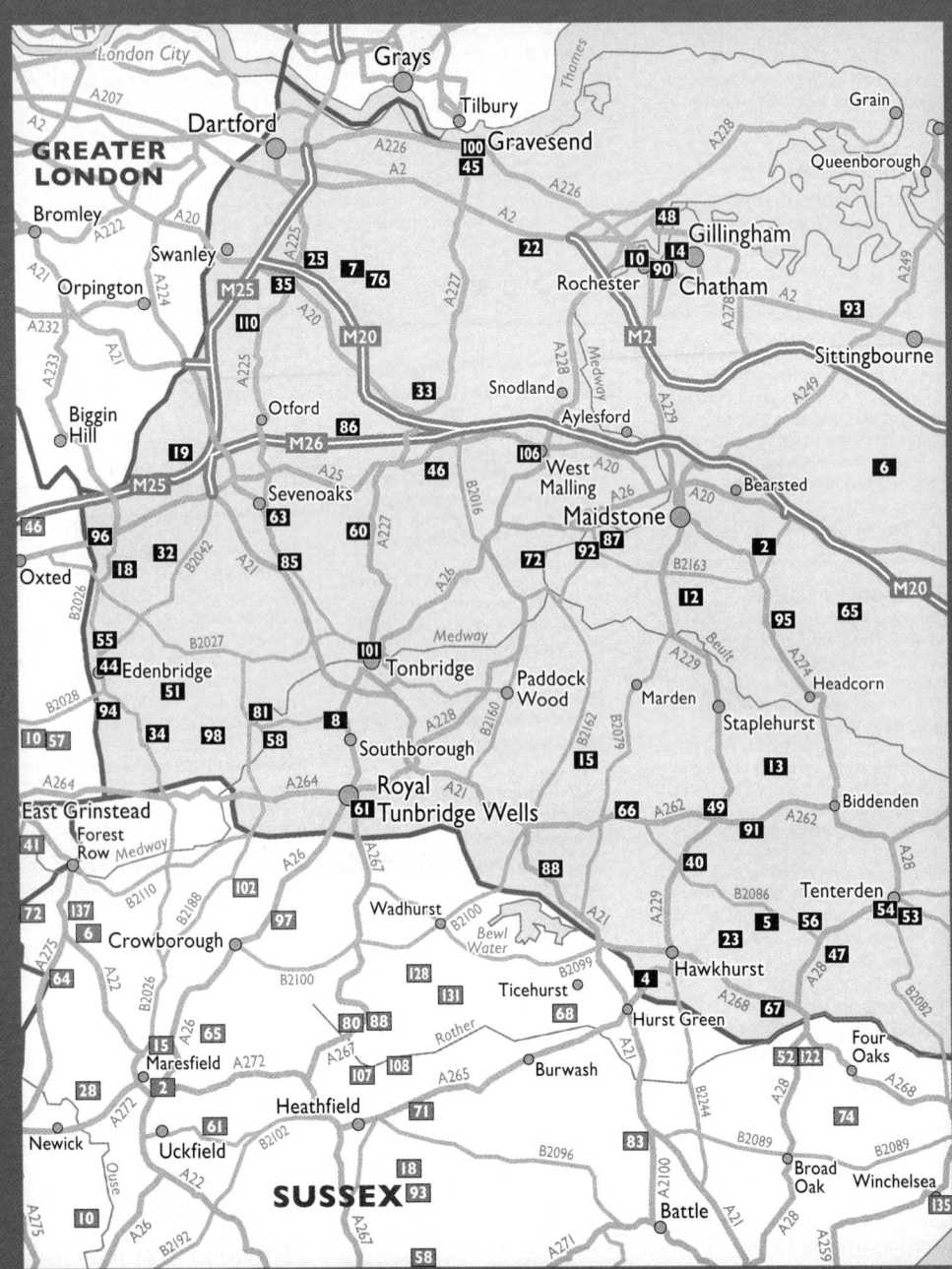

KENT 267

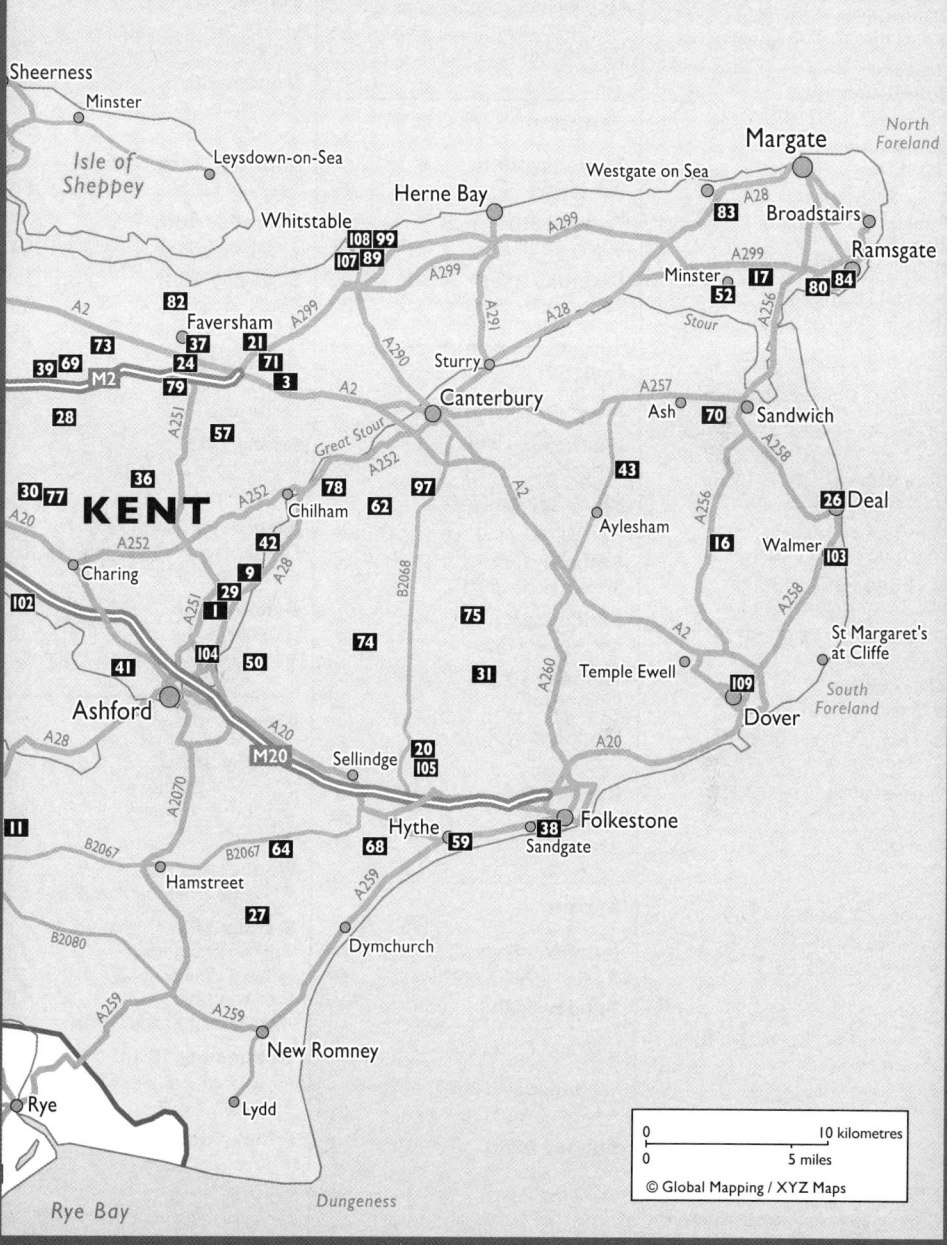

VOLUNTEERS

County Organiser
Nicola Denoon Duncan
01233 758600
nicola.denoonduncan@ngs.org.uk

County Treasurer
Andrew McClintock
01732 838605
andrew.mcclintock@ngs.org.uk

Publicity
Susie Challen
susie.challen@ngs.org.uk

Booklet Advertising
Nicola Denoon Duncan
(see above)

Booklet Co-ordinator
Ingrid Morgan
ingrid@morganhitchcock.co.uk

Booklet Distribution
Diana Morrish
07831 432528
diana.morrish@ngs.org.uk

Assistant County Organisers

Jacqueline Anthony 01892 518879
jacquelineanthony7@gmail.com

Clare Barham 01580 241386
clarebarham@holepark.com

Pam Bridges 07999 525516
pam.bridges@ngs.org.uk

Mary Bruce 01795 531124
mary.bruce@ngs.org.uk

Trudie Easton 07867 851779
trudie.easton@ngs.org.uk,

Andy Garland
andy.garland@bbc.co.uk

Sue Harris 07582 718658
sue.harris@powell-cottonmuseum.org

Virginia Latham 01303 862881
virginia.latham@ngs.org.uk

Sian Lewis
sian.lewis@ngs.org.uk

Jane Streatfeild 01342 850362
janestreatfeild@btinternet.com

Nicola Talbot 01342 850526
nicola@falconhurst.co.uk

@KentNGS

@nationalgardenschemekent

OPENING DATES

All entries subject to change.
For latest information check
www.ngs.org.uk

Map locator numbers are
shown to the right of each
garden name.

January

Thursday 29th
Spring Platt　95

Friday 30th
Spring Platt　95

Saturday 31st
Copton Ash　24

February

Snowdrop Openings

Wednesday 4th
Spring Platt　95

Thursday 5th
Spring Platt　95

Saturday 7th
Knowle Hill Farm　65

Sunday 8th
Knowle Hill Farm　65

Tuesday 10th
Spring Platt　95

Wednesday 11th
Spring Platt　95

Sunday 15th
Copton Ash　24
◆ Doddington Place　28

March

Sunday 1st
◆ Great Comp Garden　46

Sunday 15th
Copton Ash　24
◆ Doddington Place　28

Wednesday 18th
◆ Hever Castle & Gardens　51

Sunday 22nd
Godmersham Park　42
Stonewall Park　98

Sunday 29th
◆ Mount Ephraim Gardens　71

Monday 30th
◆ Ightham Mote　60

April

Sunday 5th
Copton Ash　24
Nettlestead Place　72

Monday 6th
◆ Cobham Hall　22
Copton Ash　24

Saturday 11th
The Knoll Farm　64

Thursday 16th
Tonbridge School　101

Saturday 18th
Bishopscourt　10
◆ Godinton House & Gardens　41

Sunday 19th
Bilting House　9
Nettlestead Place　72

Friday 24th
Oak Cottage and Swallowfields Nursery　74

Saturday 25th
Oak Cottage and Swallowfields Nursery　74

Sunday 26th
Balmoral Cottage　5
◆ Boughton Monchelsea Place　12

May

Sunday 3rd
1 Brickwall Cottages　13
NEW Lympne Castle　68
Stonewall Park　98

Wednesday 6th
◆ Riverhill Himalayan Gardens　85

Sunday 10th
1 Brickwall Cottages　13
Ladham House　66
The Orangery　78
Whitstable Joy Lane Gardens　107

Wednesday 13th
◆ Hole Park　56
◆ Scotney Castle　88

Friday 15th
◆ Squerryes Court　96

Sunday 17th
Bilting House　9

Thursday 21st
NEW Hartridge House 49

Friday 22nd
NEW Hartridge House 49

Saturday 23rd
Avalon 3
Balmoral Cottage 5
Hurst House 58
NEW Snakesbury 93

Sunday 24th
Avalon 3
Balmoral Cottage 5
Old Bladbean Stud 75
NEW Snakesbury 93
Tankerton Gardens 99

Monday 25th
Falconhurst 34

Tuesday 26th
NEW Wedgwood House 104

Thursday 28th
Oak Cottage and Swallowfields Nursery 74
NEW Wedgwood House 104

Friday 29th
Oak Cottage and Swallowfields Nursery 74

Saturday 30th
NEW 1 Beeches Farm Cottages 7
Bishopscourt 10
Finch's 39
♦ Godinton House & Gardens 41
Hythe Gardens 59
Windy Ridge 109

Sunday 31st
Hythe Gardens 59
West Malling Early Summer Gardens 106

June

Wednesday 3rd
Great Maytham Hall 47

Saturday 6th
Brompton Village Gardens 14
The Coach House 21
Court Lodge 25
4 Southview Cottages 94

Sunday 7th
Brompton Village Gardens 14
The Coach House 21
Old Bladbean Stud 75
Whitstable Town Gardens 108

Monday 8th
Norton Court 73

Tuesday 9th
Norton Court 73

Wednesday 10th
♦ Hole Park 56
Marshborough Farmhouse 70

Saturday 13th
Elham Gardens 31
95 High Street 53
99 High Street 54
Ivy Chimneys 61

Sunday 14th
Downs Court 29
Elham Gardens 31
Godmersham Park 42
95 High Street 53
99 High Street 54
NEW Link Hill House 67
St Clere 86

Thursday 18th
♦ Goodnestone Park Gardens 43
♦ Riverhill Himalayan Gardens 85

Friday 19th
NEW Farningham Mill 35
♦ Godinton House & Gardens 41

Saturday 20th
NEW Farningham Mill 35
NEW Fernleas 38
NEW St Helens Lodge 87

Sunday 21st
♦ Chevening 19
Downs Court 29
Farriers Cottage 36
Old Bladbean Stud 75
♦ The World Garden at Lullingstone Castle 110

Saturday 27th
Sir John Hawkins Hospital 90

Sunday 28th
Bidborough Gardens 8
Deal Town Gardens 26
Faversham Open Gardens 37
NEW Link Hill House 67
Sir John Hawkins Hospital 90

Tuesday 30th
♦ Walmer Castle 103

July

Friday 3rd
Hoppickers East 57

Saturday 4th
Chapel Farmhouse 16
Hoppickers East 57

Lynsted Community Kitchen Garden 69
4 Southview Cottages 94

Sunday 5th
Chapel Farmhouse 16
Goddards Green 40
Gravesend Garden for Wildlife 45
Old Bladbean Stud 75
NEW Pegwell & West Cliff Gardens 80
Smiths Hall 92
Thames House 100

Saturday 11th
Hammond Place 48
Stable House 97

Sunday 12th
Hammond Place 48
Stable House 97

Tuesday 14th
Avalon 3

Friday 17th
NEW Wedgwood House 104

Saturday 18th
NEW 2 Herons Brook 50
Knowle Hill Farm 65

Sunday 19th
1 Barnfield Cottages 6
♦ Boughton Monchelsea Place 12
NEW 2 Herons Brook 50
Knowle Hill Farm 65
Old Bladbean Stud 75
♦ Quex Gardens 83

Thursday 23rd
♦ Knole 63

Friday 24th
Hoppickers East 57

Saturday 25th
Hoppickers East 57
The Orangery 78

Sunday 26th
The Orangery 78

August

Saturday 1st
Avalon 3
4 Southview Cottages 94

Sunday 2nd
Avalon 3

Saturday 15th
1 Barnfield Cottages 6

Sunday 16th
1 Barnfield Cottages 6
Chapel House Estate 17
Marshborough Farmhouse 70

Saturday 22nd
Avalon 3
NEW St Helens Lodge 87

Sunday 23rd
Avalon 3

Saturday 29th
NEW 71a High Street 52

Sunday 30th
NEW 71a High Street 52

September

Wednesday 2nd
♦ Emmetts Garden 32

Friday 4th
Hoppickers East 57

Saturday 5th
Hoppickers East 57

Sunday 6th
1 Barnfield Cottages 6
♦ Boldshaves 11
The Copper House 23
Ramsgate Gardens 84
Thames House 100

Wednesday 9th
♦ Chartwell 18

Saturday 12th
NEW 71a High Street 52

Sunday 13th
♦ Doddington Place 28
NEW 71a High Street 52
♦ Sissinghurst Castle Garden 91

Wednesday 16th
♦ Penshurst Place & Gardens 81

Friday 18th
♦ Godinton House & Gardens 41

Thursday 24th
♦ Goodnestone Park Gardens 43
♦ Mount Ephraim Gardens 71

October

Sunday 4th
♦ Hole Park 56

Sunday 25th
♦ Great Comp Garden 46

February 2027

Saturday 6th
Knowle Hill Farm 65

Sunday 7th
Knowle Hill Farm 65

By Arrangement

Arrange a personalised garden visit with your club, or group of friends, on a date to suit you. See individual garden entries for full details.

Applecote 1
Arnold Yoke 2
Avalon 3
Badgers 4
1 Barnfield Cottages 6
NEW 1 Beeches Farm Cottages 7
Boundes End (Bidborough Gardens) 8
1 Brickwall Cottages 13
Cacketts Farmhouse 15
Churchfield 20
The Coach House 21
The Copper House 23
Copton Ash 24
Dean House 27
Downs Court 29
Eagleswood 30
Fairseat Manor 33
Goddards Green 40
NEW 18 Grange Close 44
Gravesend Garden for Wildlife 45
2 Highfields Road 55
Kenfield Hall 62
The Knoll Farm 64
Knowle Hill Farm 65
NEW Link Hill House 67
Norton Court 73
The Old Rectory, Fawkham 76
The Old Rectory, Otterden 77
Ouden 79
Pheasant Barn 82
45 Seymour Avenue 89
4 Southview Cottages 94
Thames House 100
Tram Hatch 102
West Court Lodge 105

Faversham Open Gardens

Victoria Lodge, Pegwell & West Cliff Gardens

THE GARDENS

◻ APPLECOTE
Pilgrims Way, Boughton Aluph, Ashford, TN25 4EX. Jenny and Angus Fraser, 07778 881346, jennyafraser@btinternet.com. 3m N of Ashford. At corner of Boughton Aluph village green take Pilgrims Way for 500 metres and turn 1st L into Brewhouse Ln. 2nd entrance on R 200 metres up lane. **Visits by arrangement 4 May to 18 June for groups of up to 15. Adm £10, chd free. Tea, coffee & cake inc in adm price.**
Mature romantic garden created in an old chalk pit, comprising a gravel garden, parterre, middle garden of mixed planting beds connected by a rose arch to a wilder area, and vegetable garden. The garden abounds with topiary, roses, flowering shrubs and perennials suited to the very dry soil. The garden is steeply banked on two sides with paths for viewing from above.

◻ ARNOLD YOKE
Back Street, Leeds, Maidstone, ME17 1TF. Richard & Patricia Stileman, 07968 787950, richstileman@btinternet.com. *3m E of Maidstone.* From M20 J8 take A20 Lenham R to B2163 to Leeds. Through Leeds R into Horseshoes Ln, 1st R into Back St. House ¾ m on L. From A274 follow B2163 to Langley L into Horseshoes Ln 1st R Back St. **Visits by arrangement 11 May to 18 Sept for groups of 10 to 24. Adm £12. Home-made teas inc in adm price.**
13 yrs in the making, this one acre garden bordering a C15 Hall House features extensive yew and box hedging, a paradise garden with water feature, a rock garden and many mixed borders. Extensive planting of small trees of special interest. Borders planted to offer interest from March to October. Wheelchair access from the car park and around most parts of the garden.
& ☕

◻ AVALON
57 Stoney Road, Dunkirk, ME13 9TN. Mrs Croll, avalongarden8@gmail.com. *4m E of Faversham, 5m W of Canterbury,*

2½ m E of J7 M2. M2 J7 or A2 E of Faversham take A299, 1st L, Staplestreet, then L, R past Mt Ephraim, turn L, R. From A2 Canterbury, turn off Dunkirk, bottom hill turn R, Staplestreet then R, R. Park in side roads. **Sat 23, Sun 24 May, Tue 14 July, Sat 1, Sun 2, Sat 22, Sun 23 Aug (10.30-4). Adm £7, chd free. Tea, coffee & cake. Visits also by arrangement 25 May to 6 Sept for groups of 5 to 20.**
½ acre edge of woodland garden, for all seasons, on north west slope, something round every corner, views of surrounding countryside. Collections of roses, hostas and ferns plus rhododendrons, shrubs, trees, vegetables, fruit, unusual plants and flowers. Planted by feeling, making it a reflective space and plant lovers' garden. Plenty of seating for taking in the garden and resting from lots of steps. Wide variety of plants and planting zones from woodland to open areas and productive beds, adapting to changing climate and dryer conditions. Friendly chickens. Borrowed countryside landscape and views across Thames estuary.

4 BADGERS
Bokes Farm, Horns Hill, Hawkhurst, Cranbrook, TN18 4XG. Bronwyn Cowdery, 01580 754178, cowderyfamily@btinternet.com. On the border of Kent & E Sussex. In centre of Hawkhurst, follow A229 in the direction of Hurst Green. Pass 'The Wealden Advertiser'. At sharp L bend turn R up Horns Hill. Drive slowly up Horns Hill. **Visits by arrangement 21 Aug to 16 Sept for groups of 6 to 25. Adm £10, chd free. Tea, coffee & cake.**
The garden comes into its own from end of August, when the Tropical Garden is in full growth. There is also a walled Italian style garden, small Japanese area and woodland with ponds and a waterfall. The Tropical Garden has a wide variety of Palms, Bananas, Gingers, Eucomis and Dahlias and has a network of paths threading through for you to explore and immerse yourself in the tropics.

5 BALMORAL COTTAGE
The Green, Benenden, Cranbrook, TN17 4DL. Charlotte Molesworth. Few 100yds down unmade track to the W of St George's Church, Benenden. **Sun 26 Apr, Sat 23, Sun 24 May (12-5). Adm £10, chd free.**
Lovingly nurtured for over 40 yrs, this romantic garden features sculptural topiary, lush mixed borders, and an organic vegetable plot. Designed with care for nesting birds and small mammals, it reflects the artistry of a dedicated plantswoman and offers a rare, harmonious blend of beauty and wildlife. Featuring sculptural topiary As seen on Monty Don's British Gardens.

6 1 BARNFIELD COTTAGES
The Street, Wormshill, Sittingbourne, ME9 0TU. Mr Ian Bond-Webster, 07982 659718, ibondwebster@gmail.com. Between Maidstone and Sittingbourne on North Downs. Top Hollingbourne Hill turn R, at the next Xrds turn L. From A2 at Sittingbourne, Highsted Rd, then Highsted Valley, R fork up Bottom Pond Rd. 2m to Wormshill, follow signs. **Sun 19 July, Sat 15, Sun 16 Aug, Sun 6 Sept (12-5). Adm £6, chd free. Tea, coffee & cake. Visits also by arrangement 4 June to 30 Sept for groups of up to 20.**
A med sized 4 yr old garden divided into two areas. The main area consists of herbaceous borders and island beds, planted with unusual perennials and grasses, both tender and hardy to give year-round colour and interest. The second area is chiefly devoted to vegetables and fruit with flowering shrubs to provide interest.

7 NEW 1 BEECHES FARM COTTAGES
Canada Farm Road, South Darenth, Dartford, DA2 9LA. Frances Moore, 07776 222271, francesmoore8@gmail.com. From Valley Rd turn on to Scudders Hill or From Pinden (Green St, Green Rd) turn on to Canada Farm Rd. **Sat 30 May (11-4). Adm £6, chd free. Tea & coffee inc in adm price (small charge for cake). Visits also by arrangement 5 June to 4 July for groups of up to 12.**
Tranquil haven for people and wildlife. Plantaholic's garden in a peaceful rural setting with many unusual plants. Organically managed, rich variety of perennials, grasses, heritage vegetables and National Collection of Tulbaghia. Undercover seating for tea and home-made cake, ample parking in field, picnic area. Interesting plants for sale.

GROUP OPENING

8 BIDBOROUGH GARDENS
Bidborough, Tunbridge Wells, TN4 0XB. Carole & Mike Marks. 3m N of Tunbridge Wells, between Tonbridge & Tunbridge Wells W off A26. Take B2176 Bidborough Ridge signed to Penshurst. Take 1st L into Darnley Dr, then 1st R into St Lawrence Ave. (Boundes End, 2 St Lawrence Ave). **Sun 28 June (1-5). Combined adm £10, chd free. Home-made teas at Boundes End inc gluten & dairy free options. Donation to Hospice in the Weald.**

BOUNDES END
Carole & Mike Marks, 01892 542233, carole.marks@btinternet.com, www.boundesendgarden.co.uk. Visits also by arrangement 22 June to 30 Aug for groups of 5 to 25. Refreshments inc in adm price.

4 THE CRESCENT
Mrs Ann Tyler.

DARNLEY LODGE
Frances & Carl Stick.

SHEERDROP
Mr John Perry.

The Bidborough gardens (collect garden list from Boundes End, 2 St Lawrence Avenue) are in a small village at the heart of which are The Kentish Hare pub (book in advance), the church, village store and primary school. Partial wheelchair access, some gardens have steps.

9 BILTING HOUSE
nr Ashford, TN25 4HA. Mr John Erle-Drax. A28, 5m E from Ashford, 9m S from Canterbury. Wye 1½ m. **Sun 19 Apr, Sun 17 May (1.30-5.30). Adm £8, chd free. Cream teas.**
Six acre garden with ha-ha set in beautiful part of Stour Valley. Wide variety of rhododendrons, azaleas and ornamental shrubs. Woodland walk with spring bulbs. Mature arboretum with recent planting of specimen trees. Rose garden and herbaceous borders.

10 BISHOPSCOURT
24 St Margaret's Street, Rochester, ME1 1TS. Central Rochester, nr castle & cathedral. On St Margaret's St at junction with Vines Ln. **Sat 18 Apr, Sat 30 May (11-2). Adm £6, chd free. Home-made teas.**
Bishopscourt has been home to the Bishops of Rochester since 1920. The 1½ acre walled garden has been continuously developed for over a decade and provides a secluded oasis. The garden comprises of lawns, meadow, mature trees, hedging, rose garden, gravel garden, mixed herbaceous borders, glasshouse, vegetable garden and a raised 'lookout' offering views of the castle and the river.

11 ◆ BOLDSHAVES
Woodchurch, nr Ashford, TN26 3RA. Mr & Mrs Peregrine Massey, 01233 860283, masseypd@hotmail.co.uk, www.boldshaves.co.uk. Between Woodchurch & High Halden off Redbrook St. From centre Woodchurch, church on L & pubs on R, 2nd L down Susan's Hill, ½ m 1st R then L after 100yds to Boldshaves. Straight on past oast on L. **For NGS: Sun 6 Sept (2-6). Adm £10, chd**

Farningham Mill

free. **Home-made teas.** For other opening times and information, please phone, email or visit garden website. Donation to Childhood First.

7 acre garden developed over past 30 yrs, partly terraced, south-facing, with wide range of ornamental trees and shrubs, walled garden, Italian garden, Diamond Jubilee garden, Camellia Dell, herbaceous borders (inc flame bed, red borders and rainbow border), vegetable garden, woodland and ponds; wildlife haven renowned for nightingales and butterflies. Home of the Wealden Literary Festival. Grass paths and slope.

12 ♦ BOUGHTON MONCHELSEA PLACE

Church Hill, Boughton Monchelsea, Maidstone, ME17 4BU. Mr & Mrs Dominic Kendrick, 07952 878166, mk@boughtonplace.co.uk, www.boughtonplace.co.uk. *4m SE of Maidstone. For SatNav use ME17 4HP. What3words app: couch.blocks.picked. From Maidstone follow A229 S for $3\frac{1}{2}$ m to T-lights at Linton Xrds, turn L onto B2163, house 1m on R or take J8 off M20 & follow Leeds Castle signs to B2163, house $5\frac{1}{2}$ m on L.* **For NGS: Sun 26 Apr, Sun 19 July (2-5.30). Adm £7.50. Tea, coffee & cake. Cash only.** For other opening times and information, please phone, email or visit garden website.

150 acre estate mainly park and woodland, spectacular views over own deer park and the Weald. Grade I manor house (not open). Courtyard herb garden, intimate walled gardens, box hedges, herbaceous borders, orchard. Planting is romantic rather than manicured. Terrace with panoramic views, bluebell woods, wisteria tunnel, David Austin roses, traditional greenhouse and kitchen garden. Visit St Peter's church next door to see the huge stained glass Millennium Window designed by renowned local artist Graham Clark and the tranquil rose garden overlooking the deer park of Boughton Place. Steep steps and narrow paths make the garden unsuitable for wheelchairs and disabled visitors.

13 1 BRICKWALL COTTAGES

Frittenden, Cranbrook, TN17 2DH. Mrs Sue Martin, 01580 852425, suemartin41@icloud.com, www.geumcollection.co.uk. *6m NW of Tenterden. E of A229 between Cranbrook & Staplehurst. W of A274 between Biddenden & Headcorn. Park in village & walk along footpath opp school. What3words app: forgiven.downsize.scrub.* **Sun 3, Sun 10 May (2-5.30). Adm £7, chd free. Home-made teas.** Visits also by arrangement 27 Apr to 18 May for groups of up to 25. Donation to Plant Heritage.

The garden is a secluded oasis in the centre of the village. It is filled with a wide range of plants, inc many trees, shrubs, perennials and over 100 geums which make up the National Collection. In an effort to attract more wildlife some areas of grass have been left unmown, and a new butterfly and moth 'meadow' was created during lockdown to replace the main nursery area. Some paths are narrow and wheelchairs may not be able to reach far end of garden.

GROUP OPENING

14 BROMPTON VILLAGE GARDENS

Garden Street and Prospect Row, Brompton, Gillingham, ME7 5AL. Jennifer Jones. *Close to Chatham Historic Dockyard and RSME Barracks. Between Chatham & Gillingham A231 - Dock Rd next to Historic Dockyard. At r'about take A231 Wood St, opp. RSME Barracks enter Mansion Row, 1st R Garden St. Parking in village.* **Sat 6, Sun 7 June (2-5). Combined adm £7, chd free. Tea, coffee & cake at 26 Garden Street.**

26 GARDEN STREET
Mrs Lissie Larkin.

7 PROSPECT ROW
Ms Elaine Fowler.

14 PROSPECT ROW
Nic and Patrick Fysh.

16 PROSPECT ROW
Jennifer Jones.

19 PROSPECT ROW
Karen and Neil Fabian Burgess.

5 small town gardens redesigned by their owners in recent years, giving different ideas for use of space and planting. Opening in 2 adjacent streets in historic Brompton. 16 Prospect Row is a plantswoman's garden, rich in planting that encourages wildlife and features unusual varieties. 19 Prospect Row was redesigned from a garden for small children, into an elegant Italianate style garden. 7 Prospect Row was completely redesigned from scratch several years ago after extensive building works and planting is now maturing into an elegant colourful garden with a variety of plants complemented by seating areas. 26 Garden Street is a colourful English country garden full of classic planting with summerhouse and relaxed seating areas. 14 Prospect Row is being reopened by the grandson of the previous owner. Together with his wife and young family, he is adapting the garden into a family friendly space while maintaining the elegance of the original garden.
❊ ☕ 🌼)))

15 CACKETTS FARMHOUSE
Haymans Hill, Horsmonden, TN12 8BX. Mr & Mrs Lance Morrish, 07831 432528, diana.morrish@hotmail.co.uk. Take B2162 from Horsmonden towards Marden. 1st R into Haymans Hill, 200yds 1st L, drive immed to R of Little Cacketts/H Engineering. What3words app: noun.dramatic.verse. **Visits by arrangement 1 June to 17 July for groups of 10 to 30. Adm £12, chd free. Cream teas inc in adm price.**
1½ acre tranquil garden surrounding C17 farmhouse (not open). Walled garden with a magnificent wisteria, bog garden, stream and ponds, woodland garden with unusual plants, bug hotel. Four acre hayfield with self planted wild flowers, an extra three acres of wild flowers planted last year. Small area in the main garden with many orchids. Two topiary elephants.
♿ 🐕 🏠 ☕

16 CHAPEL FARMHOUSE
Lower Street, Tilmanstone, Deal, CT14 0HY. Nigel Watts and Tanuja Pandit. *4m N of Dover. Exit A256 at Tilmanstone r'about then immed R to Dover Rd. Garden is 100yds down Chapel Rd on the L past the Plough and Harrow. Limited parking on Chapel Rd, more on Dover Rd.* **Sat 4, Sun 5 July (1-6). Adm £6, chd free. Tea, coffee & cake.**
Recently established small garden designed by Kristina Clode on three sides of a semi-detached listed farmhouse. It is divided into a number of separate spaces inc a courtyard style front garden, a Japanese style garden with pond, a formal lawn area, deep herbaceous borders, a meadow with fruit trees and a formal vegetable garden. Emphasis on sustainability and friendliness to wildlife. Wheelchair access via rear gate.
♿ ❊ 📀 ☕ 🌼)))

17 CHAPEL HOUSE ESTATE
Thorne Hill, Ramsgate, CT12 5DS. Chapel House Estate, www.chapelhouseestate.co.uk. What3words app: restriction.dynasties.usages. *From Canterbury A253 towards Ramsgate, from Sandwich A256 towards Ramsgate. At Sevenscore r'about take slip road turn R, Cottington Rd, follow Chapel House Estate signs.* **Sun 16 Aug (1-5). Adm £6, chd free. Tea, coffee & cake in the Thorne Barn. The on-site restaurant will be open, but tables must be pre-booked through garden website.**
Nestled in the Kent countryside, Chapel House Estate's gardens blend wild beauty with thoughtful design. Explore the tranquil Apple Orchard, vibrant wildflower meadows, and abundant kitchen gardens that supply the estate's restaurant. Landscaped lawns, serene courtyards, and sweeping views make this a truly enchanting escape. A 35 acre private estate featuring Arts and Crafts style gardens, a wild apple orchard, and the historic C13 Chapel House. A helipad is located just beyond the orchard. Please note: uneven paving and steps may present difficulties for some visitors.
🐕 ❊ ☕ 🌼)))

18 ♦ CHARTWELL
Mapleton Road, Westerham, TN16 1PS. National Trust, 01732 868381, chartwell@nationaltrust.org.uk, www.nationaltrust.org.uk/chartwell. *4m N of Edenbridge, 2m S of Westerham. Fork L off B2026 after 1½m.* **For NGS: Wed 9 Sept (10-5). Adm £10, chd £5. Light refreshments.** For other opening times and information, please phone, email or visit garden website.
Informal gardens on hillside with glorious views over Weald of Kent. Water features and lakes together with red brick wall built by Sir Winston Churchill, former owner of Chartwell. Lady Churchill's rose garden. Avenue of golden roses runs down the centre of a must see productive kitchen garden. Hard paths to Lady Churchill's rose garden and the terrace.
♿ 🐕 ❊ ☕ 🏠 🌼)))

19 ♦ CHEVENING
nr Sevenoaks, TN14 6HG. The Board of Trustees of the Chevening Estate, 01732 744809, info@cheveninggardens.com, www.cheveninggardens.com. *4m NW of Sevenoaks. Turn N off A25 at Sundridge T-lights on to B2211; at Chevening Xrds 1½m turn L.* **For NGS: Sun 21 June (2-5). Adm £12, chd £1. Home-made teas. Local ice-cream.** For other opening times and information, please phone, email or visit garden website.
The pleasure grounds of the Earls Stanhope at Chevening House are today characterised by lawns and wooded walks around an ornamental lake. First laid out between 1690 and 1720 in the French formal style, in the 1770s a more informal English design was introduced. In the early C19 lawns, parterres and a maze were established, a lake was created from the ornamental canal and basin, and many specimen trees were planted to shade woodland walks. Expert-guided group tours of the park and gardens can sometimes be arranged with the Estate Office when the house is unoccupied. Gentle slopes and gravel paths throughout.
♿ 🐕 ❊ ☕ 🏠)))

20 CHURCHFIELD
Pilgrims Way, Postling, Hythe, CT21 4EY. Chris & Nikki Clark, 01303 863558/07415 263413, coulclark@hotmail.com. *2m NW of Hythe. From M20 J11 turn S onto A20. 1st L after ½m on bend take road signed Lyminge. 1st L into Postling. What3words app: patch.toolbar.bookmark.* **Visits by arrangement Apr to Sept for**

groups of up to 35. Combined with West Court Lodge.
At the base of the Downs, springs rising in this garden form the source of the East Stour. Two large ponds are home to wildfowl and fish and the banks have been planted with drifts of primula, large leaved herbaceous bamboo and ferns. The rest of the five acre garden is a Kent cobnut platt and vegetable garden, large grass areas and naturally planted borders and woodland. Postling Church open for visitors. Footpaths onto the North Downs with extensive views. Areas around water may be slippery. Children must be carefully supervised.

21 THE COACH HOUSE
Kemsdale Road, Hernhill, Faversham, ME13 9JP. Alison & Philip West, 07801 824867, alison.west@kemsdale.plus.com. *3m E of Faversham. At J7 of M2 take A299, signed Margate. After 600 metres take 1st exit signed Hernhill, take 1st L over dual carriageway to T-junc, turn R & follow yellow NGS signs.* **Sat 6 June (11-5). Sun 7 June (11-5), open nearby Whitstable Town Gardens. Adm £7, chd free. Cream teas.** Visits also by arrangement 20 May to 30 Sept. Refreshments available for by arrangement visits at £5pp.
The ¾ acre garden has views over surrounding fruit-producing farmland. Sloping terraced site and island beds with year-round interest, a pond room, herbaceous borders containing bulbs, shrubs, perennials and a tropical bed. The different areas are connected by flowing curved paths. Unusual planting on light sandy soil where wildlife is encouraged. Some garden accessible to wheelchairs but some slopes. Seating available in all areas.

22 ◆ COBHAM HALL
Brewers Road, Cobham, DA12 3BL. Commercial Manager: Louis Glynn-Williams, 01474 823371, commercial@cobhamhall.com, www.cobhamhall.com. *3m W of Rochester, 8m E of M25 J2. Entrance drive is off Brewers Rd, 50 metres E from Cobham/Shorne A2 junc. Closest train stn: Sole St (2.8m) or Ebbsfleet International (6.8m). What3words app: brush.bigger.spoken.* **For NGS: Mon 6 Apr (2-5). Adm £6.50, chd free. Cream**

teas in the Gilt Hall. **For other opening times and information, please phone, email or visit garden website.**
Landscaped for the 4th Earl of Darnley by Humphrey Repton, the gardens inc extensive tree planting, The Gothic Dairy, The Pump House and some of the classical garden buildings are also being renovated for all our visitors. The grounds yield many delights for the lover of nature, especially in spring, when the gardens and woods are resplendent with daffodils, narcissi and a myriad of rare bulbs. Film location for the TV series 'The Crown'. Gravel and slab paths throughout the gardens. Land uneven with many slopes. Please call in advance for assistance.

23 THE COPPER HOUSE
Hinksden Road, Benenden, Cranbrook, TN17 4LE. Eleanor Cochrane, 07710 614962, eleanor.cochrane@btinternet.com. *Located close to Hinksden Dairy.* **Sun 6 Sept (2-4). Adm £10, chd free. Pre-booking essential, please visit www.ngs.org.uk for information & booking. Cream teas.** Visits also by arrangement 1 June to 4 Sept for groups of up to 15. Min group charge of £100.
A modern flower garden planted to provide continuous interest and colour throughout the season. Mixed planting of annuals, perennials, bulbs and shrubs. Small wildflower meadow and orchard. Small hazel nuttery underplanted with shade loving plants. Three small ponds to encourage wildlife. Woodland ponds. Contemporary house and garden intimately connected with the wider landscape. A palate of rich purples, magenta, blues and dusky maroons cut through with shards of bleached grass.

24 COPTON ASH
105 Ashford Road, Faversham, ME13 8XW. Drs Tim & Gillian Ingram, 01795 535919, coptonash@yahoo.co.uk, www.coptonash.co.uk. *½m S of A2. On A251 Faversham to Ashford road. Opp E bound J6 with M2. Parking possible beyond Aldi in Tettenhall Way. A251 single yellow lines are Mon to Fri restrictions, so available at weekends.* **Sat 31 Jan (12-4). Sun 15 Feb, Sun 15 Mar (12-4), open nearby Doddington**

Place. **Sun 5, Mon 6 Apr (12-5). Adm £5, chd free. Home-made teas.** Visits also by arrangement Feb to June for groups of up to 30.
Garden grown out of a love and fascination with plants. Contains wide collection inc many rarities. Special interest in woodland flowers, snowdrops and hellebores with flowering trees and shrubs of spring. Evolving meadow with winter and spring bulbs. Refreshed Mediterranean plantings to adapt to a warming climate. Raised beds with choice alpines and bulbs. Alpine and dryland plant nursery. Gravel drive, shallow step by house and some narrow grass paths.

25 COURT LODGE
Horton Road, Horton Kirby, Dartford, DA4 9BN. Louise Cannon and Tristan Ward. *9m N of Sevenoaks, 5m S of Dartford. In Horton Kirby village off Horton Rd: white gates, next to St Mary's Church. Please look out for parking and entrance signs. Farningham Rd nearest railway stn. What3words app: divisions.lists.opera.* **Sat 6 June (2-5.30). Adm £8, chd free. Home-made teas.**
Beautifully situated on the River Darenth, beyond the old farmyard and C18 dovecote, are gardens evolved over 4 generations. Mature trees and an elegant lawn lead down to the river. Behind old yew hedges lie a secluded white garden, kitchen garden, a renovated rose walk, and bee loving mixed borders. There is a walled Italian Garden and also a wild bank across the river. Lots to enjoy.

Our 2025 donation to the Queen's Institute of Community Nursing now helps support over 3,500 Queen's Nurses working in the community in England, Wales, Northern Ireland, the Channel Islands and the Isle of Man.

Fernleas

GROUP OPENING

26 DEAL TOWN GARDENS
Deal, CT14 6EB. *Deal Town centre. Signs from all town car parks. Maps & tickets at the first garden visited. Cash only.* **Sun 28 June (10-4). Combined adm £5, chd free.**

61 COLLEGE ROAD
Andrew Tucker.

4 GEORGE ALLEY
Lyn Freeman & Barry Popple.

16 ST ANDREW'S ROAD
Martin Parkes & Paul Green.

88 WEST STREET
Lyn & Peter Buller.

Start from any town car park (signs from here). 88 West Street: A non-water herbaceous garden with perennials, shrubs, clematis and roses and shade garden. 4 George Alley: A pretty alley leads to a secret garden with courtyard, leading to a vibrant cottage garden with summerhouse. 61 College Rd: Small garden filled with colour and a profusion of plants. 16 St Andrew's Road: A tropical themed walled urban garden with sun-drenched borders, lawn and family seating area.

27 DEAN HOUSE
Newchurch, Romney Marsh, TN29 0DL. Jaqui Bamford, 07480 150684, jaquibamford@gmail.com. *Between the village of Newchurch & New Romney. Bilsington Xrds SE towards New Romney. 2.9m to S bend. Garden R after bend. New Romney leave A259 NE on St Marys Rd 3.7m. Garden on L. What3words app: finest.cuts.processes.* **Visits by arrangement 15 June to 16 Aug. Adm £5, chd free. Tea, coffee & cake.**
Country garden, formerly a farmyard, with mature trees, shady areas, wildlife pond, log cabin, container garden areas, sun-drenched gravel and herbaceous borders designed for pollinators. Extensive views across Romney Marsh. Visitors can also explore 5 acres of land to which the garden leads to see a re-wilding project in its early years. Large collection of cannas, cacti, succulents and aeoniums. Photos of the garden and surrounding area in different seasons are on display throughout the garden. Wheelchair must be operable on flat gravel and grass areas. Some paths will not be accessible.

28 ♦ DODDINGTON PLACE
Church Lane, Doddington, Sittingbourne, ME9 0BB. Mr & Mrs Richard Oldfield, 01795 717050, enquiries@doddingtonplacegardens.co.uk, www.doddingtonplacegardens.co.uk. *6m SE of Sittingbourne. From A20 turn N opp Lenham or from A2 turn S at Teynham or Ospringe (Faversham), all 4m.* **For NGS: Sun 15 Feb (11-4); Sun 15 Mar (11-5), open nearby Copton Ash. Sun 13 Sept (11-5). Adm £14, chd £4. Tea, coffee & cake.** For other opening times and information, please phone, email or visit garden website.
10 acre garden, wide views; trees and cloud clipped yew hedges; woodland garden with azaleas and rhododendrons; Edwardian rock garden; formal garden with mixed borders. A flint and brick late C20 gothic folly; a disused pinnacle from the southeast tower of Rochester Cathedral at the end of the Wellington Walk and a Wobbly Tower recently installed above the sunk garden. Snowdrops in February. The garden proudly provided plants for the National Garden Scheme's Gold Medal Show Garden at Chelsea Flower Show in 2024 designed by Tom Stuart Smith. Wheelchair access possible to majority of gardens except rock garden.

KENT

29 DOWNS COURT
Church Lane, Boughton Aluph, Ashford, TN25 4EU. Mr Bay Green, 07984 558945, bay@baygee.com. *4m NE of Ashford. From A28 Ashford or Canterbury, after Wye Xrds take next turn NW to Boughton Aluph Church signed Church Ln. Fork R at pillar box, garden only drive on R. Park in field. Disabled parking in drive.* **Sun 14, Sun 21 June (2-5). Adm £8, chd free. Visits also by arrangement 30 May to 5 July.**
3 acre downland garden on alkaline soil with fine trees, mature yew and box hedges, mixed borders. Shrub roses and rose arch pathway, small parterre. Sweeping lawns and lovely views over surrounding countryside.

30 EAGLESWOOD
Slade Road, Warren Street, Lenham, ME17 2EG. Mike & Edith Darvill, 01622 858702, mike.darvill@btinternet.com. *Approx 12m E of Maidstone. E on A20 nr Lenham, L into Hubbards Hill for approx 1m then 2nd L into Slade Rd. Garden 150yds on R.* **Visits by arrangement 14 Mar to 22 Nov for groups of 5 to 40. Adm £6, chd free. Tea, coffee & cake.**
A 2 acre garden for plant enthusiasts, featuring a wide range of trees and shrubs (many rare and unusual), herbaceous material and woodland plants grown to give year-round interest particularly in spring with magnolias/camellias and autumn colour.

GROUP OPENING

31 ELHAM GARDENS
High Street, Elham, CT4 6TD. www.elhamgardeningsociety.org.uk. *10m S of Canterbury, 6m N of Hythe. Enter Elham from Lyminge (off A20) or Barham (off A2). Car parking in various street locations and weather permitting, as signed, in the sch grounds and The Triangle field opposite in New Rd.* **Sat 13, Sun 14 June (12-4.30). Combined adm £10, chd free. Home-made teas in the Old Vicarage Garden (2-4pm).**
Elham has a thriving community of keen amateur gardeners, many of whom will open their delightful gardens again, along with others opening their beautiful and interesting gardens for the first time, providing a wide range of style and size. This picturesque village provides an idyllic setting with its beautiful Grade I listed St Mary's church at its centre, situated in glorious countryside within the Elham Valley Area of Outstanding Natural Beauty. The Elham Food & Craft Festival will be in The Square and St Mary's Church between 11am - 2pm on Sunday 14 June. There will be a plant stall in the Old Vicarage Garden.

32 ♦ EMMETTS GARDEN
Ide Hill, Sevenoaks, TN14 6BA. National Trust, 01732 751507, emmetts@nationaltrust.org.uk, www.nationaltrust.org.uk/emmetts-garden. *5m SW of Sevenoaks. 1½m S of A25 on Sundridge-Ide Hill Rd. 1½m N of Ide Hill off B2042.* **For NGS: Wed 2 Sept (10-5). Adm £10, chd £5. Light refreshments in the Stables tearoom. For other opening times and information, please phone, email or visit garden website.**
5 acre hillside garden, with the highest tree top in Kent, noted for its fine collection of rare trees and flowering shrubs. The garden is particularly fine in spring, while a rose garden, rock garden and extensive planting of acers for autumn colour extend the interest throughout the season. Hard paths to the tearoom and WCs. Some steep slopes. Volunteer driven buggy available for lifts up steepest hill.

33 FAIRSEAT MANOR
Vigo Road, Fairseat, Sevenoaks, TN15 7LU. Robert and Anne-Marie Nelson, 01732 822256, anne.marie.nelson@btinternet.com. *Opp the pond in Fairseat village.* **Visits by arrangement 9 Feb to 14 Mar for groups of up to 15. Adm £7, chd free. Light refreshments.**
2 acre mature garden on top of the North Downs. Extensive spring bulbs with many varieties of snowdrops. Rose and perennial borders, sunken garden with pond, and meadows. All accessible, with one step to sunken pond garden.

34 FALCONHURST
Cowden Pound Road, Markbeech, Edenbridge, TN8 5NR. Mr & Mrs Charles Talbot, www.falconhurst.co.uk. *3m SE of Edenbridge. B2026 at Queens Arms pub turn E to Markbeech. 2nd drive on R before Markbeech village.* **Mon 25 May (11-4). Adm £8.50, chd free.**
Country garden with fabulous views devised and cared for by the same family for 170 yrs. Deep mixed borders with old roses, peonies, shrubs and a wide variety of herbaceous and annual plants, ruin garden, walled garden, cutting garden, interesting mature trees and shrubs, kitchen garden, woodland areas. Disabled parking by the house.

35 NEW FARNINGHAM MILL
High Street, Farningham, Dartford, DA4 0DG. Farningham Mill. *J3 M25 follow A20 to Farningham. 2nd r'about 3rd exit. At T-Junc L into High St, Farningham Mill is 2nd gate on R before the bridge and opp The Lion Hotel. What3words app: brands.stuck.traps.* **Fri 19, Sat 20 June (10-5). Adm £5, chd free. Tea, coffee & cake.**
C18 walled garden restored over the last 10 yrs. Gravel paths bordered by herbaceous beds of flowering shrubs and cottage garden flowers; roses, hydrangeas, delphiniums and lavender. Sit for a while among herb borders and planters or stroll further into the original orchard, a 2 acre oasis of calm bordered by the Darent, a precious chalk stream, where children can enjoy a nature-trail.

36 FARRIERS COTTAGE
Throwley Forstal, Faversham, ME13 0PJ. Mr Simon Joy. *5m SW of Faversham. Leave A251 at sign for Belles Forstal & Throwley. 1st R into Workhouse Rd, L at the end then 1st R into Almshouse Rd. Farriers Cottage is on L of the Forstal What3Words app: crowd.dunk.question.* **Sun 21 June (1-4.30). Adm £6, chd free. Tea, coffee & cake.**
Four acres of garden and meadows, hidden from sight behind the narrow garden entrance from the village Forstal. The formal flower garden behind the house moves through yew hedges into the kitchen garden and then, under a hornbeam arch, through two orchards to the wildlife pond and series of four small meadows which are managed to provide habitat for pollinators and other insects. No hard paving or walkways, so can be tricky in wet weather, but all areas of the garden, orchard and meadow on level ground with no steps.

GROUP OPENING

37 FAVERSHAM OPEN GARDENS
Market Place, Faversham, ME13 7AG. www.instagram.com/favershamopengardens. *Central Faversham and surrounding area.* **Sun 28 June (10-4). Combined adm £8, chd free. Some gardens offer refreshments (details in ticket/handbook).**
Faversham Open Gardens and Garden Market Day is a community-led event showcasing over 25 small and larger town gardens. The Garden Market (10am - 4pm) is selling plants and other gardening items. Enjoy the contrasts between the different gardens, from plant lovers' plots to 'outdoor rooms', family spaces, tiny courtyards, allotments, wildlife-friendly gardens, community projects and more. Those opening their gardens may not always be expert gardeners but they all love their gardens enough to share them for the day. Faversham's historic architecture makes this a special day out - it is famous for its pubs and cafes. Access to all gardens is by ticket/handbook, which lists each garden and its address. Buy from the Faversham Open Gardens stall in Market Place (ME13 7AG) from 10am on the day. Tickets bought via the NGS website must be shown at the stall to receive an entry ticket/handbook. Pre-booked tickets can be collected from the Visitor Information Centre from 28th June. The Garden Market runs in the historic Market Place and features a large number of garden-related stalls and leading nurseries selling plants, local pottery, gardenalia, garden books and more. Some gardens are accessible by wheelchair, details can be found in the ticket/handbook.

38 NEW FERNLEAS
Radnor Cliff Crescent, Folkestone, CT20 2JQ. Mr Steve & Mrs Ann Blunt. *Sandgate village. What3words app: happy.swimsuits.shelving. From Folkestone to Sandgate on A259, turn L onto Radnor Cliff Cres.* **Sat 20 June (11-4). Adm £6, chd free. Tea, coffee & cake.**
A seaside garden with views out to France and Dungeness. The garden comprises a patio, gravel garden with coastal planting, a lawn with perennial borders, roses and a lavender lined path leading to a wildflower bank and a terraced kitchen garden. To the rear of the house is woodland rising up the hillside towards the Leas. There is a path through the trees with some steep steps with handrails.

39 FINCH'S
Kingsdown, Sittingbourne, ME9 0RA. Leonie and Nick Britcher. *4m SE of Sittingbourne, 6m W of Faversham. Entry and parking for the garden will be via a gate into the field on Ludgate Ln. What3words app: visa.gains.candle.* **Sat 30 May (11-4). Adm £6.50, chd free. Tea, coffee & cake.**
Gardening for wildlife in the North Kent Downs. The garden at Finch's was redesigned by the current owners when they purchased the property in 2021. Areas to explore inc formal garden, kitchen garden, nuttery, wildflower meadow, large wildlife pond and 1½ acre woodland planted in 2021. Lots of benches to sit, relax and enjoy the garden.

40 GODDARDS GREEN
Angley Road, Cranbrook, TN17 3LR. John & Linde Wotton, 07768 500552, jpwotton@gmail.com, www.goddardsgreengarden.com. *½m SW of Cranbrook. On W of Angley Rd. A229 at junc with High St, opp War Memorial.* **Sun 5 July (12-4). Adm £7, chd free. Home-made teas. Prior notice needed of dietary restrictions. Visits also by arrangement Apr to July for groups of 10 to 50.**
Gardens of about 7 acres, surrounding beautiful 500+yr old clothier's hall (not open), laid out in 1920s and redesigned since 1992 to combine traditional and modern planting schemes. Fountain and rill, water garden, fern garden, mixed borders of bulbs, perennials, shrubs, trees and exotics; birch grove, grass border, pond, kitchen garden, meadows, arboretum and mature orchard; 2 wild acres. Some slopes and steps, but most areas (not WC) are wheelchair accessible. Disabled parking near the house.

41 ♦ GODINTON HOUSE & GARDENS
Godinton Lane, Ashford, TN23 3BP. The Godinton House Preservation Trust, 01233 643854, info@godintonhouse.co.uk, www.godintonhouse.co.uk. *1½m W of Ashford. M20 J9 to Ashford. Take A20 towards Charing & Lenham, then follow brown tourist signs.* **For NGS: Sat 18 Apr, Sat 30 May, Fri 19 June, Fri 18 Sept (12.30-5.30). Adm £11, chd £2.50. Cream teas. Ticket office serves takeaway refreshments. Please check garden website for tearoom opening times. For other opening times and information, please phone, email or visit garden website.**
Godinton Gardens, predominantly designed by Sir Reginald Blomfield in 1896, span twelve tranquil acres enclosed by vast yew hedges. These historic gardens feature terraced lawns, herbaceous borders, a rose garden, ponds, a large walled garden, wild garden, Italian garden, and glasshouses, blending timeless design with seasonal beauty. Partial wheelchair access to most of the gardens.

42 GODMERSHAM PARK
Godmersham, CT4 7DT. Mrs Fiona Sunley. *5m NE of Ashford. Off A28, midway between Canterbury & Ashford What3words app: shams.universe.clutches.* **Sun 22 Mar, Sun 14 June (1-5). Adm £9, chd free. Tea, coffee & cake in the Orangery.**
24 acres of restored wilderness and formal gardens set around C18 mansion (not open). Topiary, rose garden, herbaceous borders, walled kitchen garden and recently restored Italian and swimming pool gardens. Daffodils in spring and roses in June. Historical association with Jane Austen. Also visit the Heritage Centre. Deep gravel paths.

43 ♦ GOODNESTONE PARK GARDENS
The Street, Goodnestone, Canterbury, CT3 1PL. Julian Fitzwalter, 01304 840107, office@goodnestone.com, www.goodnestonepark.co.uk. *6m SE of Canterbury. Village lies S of B2046 from A2 to Wingham. Brown tourist signs off B2046. Use CT3 1PJ for SatNav.* **For NGS: Thur 18 June, Thur 24 Sept (11-4). Adm £10, chd £4. Light refreshments at The Old Dairy Café: 01304 695098. For other opening times and information, please phone, email or visit garden website.**

Dean House

One of Kent's outstanding gardens and the favourite of many visitors. 14 acres with views over parkland. Something special year-round, with famous walled gardens, outstanding trees and woodland garden with cornus collection and hydrangeas later. Also a contemporary gravel garden and new area of tropical planting. Access to the gardens and the café from the car park is level; a sloping path leads to the walled gardens.

44 NEW 18 GRANGE CLOSE
Edenbridge, TN8 5LT. **Sheila Parish**, 01732 866245, sheila.parish@btinternet.com. *Near East Grinstead and Lingfield approx 3m. Suggest use of SatNav TN8 5LT. Grange Cl is a cul-de-sac close to Edenbridge town, so parking can be restricted at times.* **Visits by arrangement 16 May to 13 June for groups of 5 to 8. Adm £5, chd free.**

A compact Japanese style front and back garden, lovingly cultivated over 20 years. It features mature bonsai trees, a tranquil pond, a traditional bridge, and a soothing water feature, creating a peaceful and authentic atmosphere.

45 GRAVESEND GARDEN FOR WILDLIFE
68 South Hill Road, Windmill Hill, Gravesend, DA12 1JZ. **Judith Hathrill**, 07810 550991, judith.hathrill@live.com. *On Windmill Hill. From A2 take A227 towards Gravesend. At T-lights with Cross Ln turn R then L at next T-lights, following NGS signs. Park in Sandy Bank Rd or Rouge Ln. What3words app: causes.answer.just.* **Sun 5 July (2-5). Adm £5, chd free. Home-made teas.** Visits also by arrangement June & July for groups of up to 16. Refreshments can be inc in adm price if required.

This small cottage style garden is packed with native wildflowers, perennials, annuals, herbs, grasses, ferns, trees and shrubs to attract and sustain wildlife throughout the year. Container grown vegetables, 3 ponds and a lawn with seating for teas. Photographic display in summerhouse. New this year, extended and replanted terraced garden with small meadow areas. Information and leaflets about gardening for wildlife always available. Plants available for sale are chosen to encourage and support wildlife in the garden.

46 ♦ GREAT COMP GARDEN
Comp Lane, Platt, Borough Green, Sevenoaks, TN15 8QS. **Great Comp**, 01732 885094, office@greatcompgarden.co.uk, www.greatcompgarden.co.uk. *7m E of Sevenoaks. 2m from Borough Green Station. Accessible from M20 & M26 motorways. A20 at Wrotham Heath, take Seven Mile Ln, B2016; at 1st Xrds turn R; garden on L ½ m.* **For NGS: Sun 1 Mar, Sun 25 Oct (10-5). Adm £12, chd £4.** For other opening times and information, please phone, email or visit garden website.

Skillfully designed 7 acre garden of exceptional beauty. Spacious setting with maintained lawns and paths lead visitors through plantsman's collection of trees, shrubs, heathers and herbaceous plants. Early C17 house (not open). Magnolias, hellebores and snowflakes (Leucojum), hamamelis and winter flowering heathers are a great feature in the spring. A great variety of perennials in summer inc salvias, dahlias and crocosmias. Tearoom open daily for morning coffee, home-made lunches and cream teas. Disabled WC available.

47 GREAT MAYTHAM HALL
Maytham Road, Rolvenden, Tenterden, TN17 4NE. The Sunley Group. *4m from Tenterden. Maytham Rd off A28 at Rolvenden Church, ½m from village on R. Designated parking for visitors.* **Wed 3 June (12-3.30). Adm £9, chd free.**
Lutyens designed gardens famous for having inspired Frances Hodgson Burnett to write The Secret Garden (pre Lutyens). Parkland, woodland with bluebells. Walled garden with herbaceous beds and rose pergola. Pond garden with mixed shrubbery and herbaceous borders. Interesting specimen trees. Large lawned area, rose terrace with far-reaching views.

48 HAMMOND PLACE
High Street, Upnor, Rochester, ME2 4XG. Paul & Helle Dorrington. *3m NE of Strood or at A2. J1 take A289 to Grain at r'about follow signs to Gillingham. After 2nd r'about take 1st L following signs to Upnor & Upnor Castle. Park in free car park & continue by foot to the High St.* **Sat 11, Sun 12 July (10-4). Adm £6, chd free. Tea, coffee & cake.**
A small garden in a historically interesting village growing an eclectic mix of flowers, fruit and vegetables around a Scandinavian style house. Features inc greenhouse, pond and a Sauna Hut.
❋ ☕ ⏺))

49 NEW HARTRIDGE HOUSE
Starvenden Lane, Sissinghurst, Cranbrook, TN17 2AN. Simon Jay and Kerstin Nilsson Jay. *Cranbrook Common, near Sissinghurst. From Wilsley Pound r'bt take A229 N. Approx 1m, turn L just after Murco garage.* **Thur 21, Fri 22 May (11-4). Adm £7.50, chd free. Tea, coffee & cake inc soft drinks.**
Listed garden originally established by Col Charles Grey, founder of RHS Harlow Carr, at the beginning of the C20. The lower garden comprises original rhododendrons and azaleas, while the upper garden was recently planted by the current owners with herbaceous borders framed by the original yew hedging. The gardens are surrounded by woodlands, inc a lime walk and a small lake.

50 NEW 2 HERONS BROOK
Naccolt, Brook, Ashford, TN25 5NX. Jennifer Hill. *What3words app: polices.blaring. kitchen. Parking in field opposite.* **Sat 18, Sun 19 July (11-4). Adm £6, chd free.**
This smallish garden is a vibrant paradise full of colour and life. The greenhouse shelters succulents, fruit trees, herbs, salad crops and exotics, while around it dahlias, grapes, berries and tomatoes flourish. Overflowing pots and lush flower beds add stunning colour with a welcoming dining area perfect for relaxation in an abundant retreat. Wheelchair access to main garden via short uneven drive.
&. ❋ ⏺))

51 ♦ HEVER CASTLE & GARDENS
Edenbridge, TN8 7NG. Hever Castle Ltd, 01732 865224, info@hevercastle.co.uk, www.hevercastle.co.uk. *3m SE of Edenbridge. Between Sevenoaks & East Grinstead off B2026. Signed from J5 & J6 of M25, A21, A264.* **For NGS: Wed 18 Mar (10.30-6). Please check garden website for 2026 admission prices.** For other opening times and information, please phone, email or visit garden website.
Romantic double-moated castle, the childhood home of Anne Boleyn, set in 150 acres of formal and natural landscape. Topiary, Tudor herb garden, magnificent Italian garden with classical statuary, sculpture and fountains. 38 acre lake, yew and water mazes. Spring is a wonderful time to view the gardens as spectacular carpets of daffodils welcome visitors and tulips are in full bloom. Partial wheelchair access.
&. 🐕 ❋ 🚗 🚌 ☕ 🧺

52 NEW 71A HIGH STREET
Minster, Ramsgate, CT12 4AB. Callum Philpott. *At the top of the high street in Minster.* **Sat 29, Sun 30 Aug, Sat 12, Sun 13 Sept (10-4.30). Adm £5, chd free.**
A small but exciting garden packed full of interesting exotic and rare plants from around the world. Winding paths take you in a journey from lush jungles to dry deserts and everything in between! Nestled on the high street in Minster the garden is a true plant lovers paradise with an eclectic array of flora and ingenious ideas to make every bit of space count.
❋

53 95 HIGH STREET
Tenterden, TN30 6LB. Judy & Chris Older. *Enter via Bridewell Car Park. Parking free on sundays. Drive to far end, venue on R.* **Sat 13, Sun 14 June (12-5). Combined adm with 99 High Street £6, chd free.**
Small town house garden divided into 3 rooms. Developed since June 2021 from a blank canvas, now well-stocked with perennials and summer flowers to capacity. Colourful and traditional. Plenty of seating. Wheelchair access via 99 High Street.
&. 🐕 ❋

54 99 HIGH STREET
Tenterden, TN30 6LB. Mrs Veryan Rahr. *Entrance via far end of Bridewell Ln Car Park. Entrance through No. 95 High Street garden.* **Sat 13, Sun 14 June (12-5). Combined adm with 95 High Street £6, chd free.**
Small, narrow garden with long brick path and divided into 'rooms', with seating areas. Mainly shaded with interesting planting developed over the last 25 yrs. Narrow paths.
&. 🐕

55 2 HIGHFIELDS ROAD
Edenbridge, TN8 6JN. Auralucia Brook, auraluciabrook@hotmail.com. *Marlpit Hill / Edenbridge. From the main road B2026, turn into Swan Ln. Turn into Highfields Rd. 2nd house on L.* **Visits by arrangement 11 July to 26 July for groups of up to 15. Adm £5.**
The garden is a multi-season, in the hope of attracting wildlife, birds, amphibians, and, of course, humans. A large collection of plants, upcycled pots, abundant ornaments. It has won 1st and 2nd prizes for few years in the local district. Enjoy the sounds, scents, textures, secrecy, relaxation, and diversity in a very small space and an unusual, unique garden.

56 ♦ HOLE PARK
Benenden Road, Rolvenden, Cranbrook, TN17 4JB. Mr & Mrs Edward Barham, 01580 241344, info@holepark.com, www.holepark.com. *4m SW of Tenterden. Midway between Rolvenden & Benenden on B2086. Follow brown tourist signs from Rolvenden. What3words app: sized. sticking.bypasses.* **For NGS: Wed 13 May, Wed 10 June, Sun 4 Oct (11-6). Adm £12.50, chd £2.50.**

Light refreshments. Picnics are permitted only in the designated picnic site and car park, please. The Coach House cafe is open for light lunches and teas 11am-5pm. For other opening times and information, please phone, email or visit garden website.
Proud to stand amongst the group of gardens which first opened in 1927 soon after it was laid out by the owners great-grandfather. The 15 acre garden is surrounded by parkland and contains fine yew hedges, large lawns with specimen trees, walled gardens, pools and mixed borders combined with bulbs, rhododendrons and azaleas. Massed bluebells in woodland walk, standard wisterias, orchids in flower meadow and glorious autumn colours make this a garden for all seasons. Redesigned and newly planted walled garden with oval path and deep herbaceous beds a particular feature. Wheelchairs are available and may be reserved. Please email info@holepark.com.

57 HOPPICKERS EAST
Hogbens Hill, Selling, Faversham, ME13 9QZ. Katherine Pickering. *Signs from Hogbens Hill. From A251 signed Selling 1m, then NGS signs.* **Fri 3 July (11-4). Sat 4 July (11-4), open nearby Lynsted Community Kitchen Garden. Fri 24, Sat 25 July, Fri 4, Sat 5 Sept (11-4). Adm £5, chd free.**
6 yr old ¼ acre garden. Emphasis on pollinators and other insects. No dig principles. Lots of colour all summer from colour coordinated mixed borders. Collection of dahlias and hostas. Many old cottage garden favourites and a few new ones. Flat grass paths.

58 HURST HOUSE
Poundsbridge Lane, Penshurst, Tonbridge, TN11 8AG. AJ Lampitt. *A21 S, exit onto A26 to Bidborough. Cont for 0.8m, turn R onto B2176. Cont for 2.7m then turn L onto Poundsbridge Ln. Take 1st R onto single track lane. What3words app: collected.unlisted.coconuts.* **Sat 23 May (10-4). Adm £10, chd free. Tea, coffee & cake.**
A Victorian walled garden under restoration since 2021, with restored 1902 Thomas Messenger vinery and glasshouse, a beautiful formal garden with far-reaching views, filled with perennials, roses and other unusual plants, an orchard and ponds. The wildflower meadow is an ongoing project and a native woodland was planted in 2022 with a Woodland Trust grant. Features inc natural swimming pond, formal rose garden, secluded Mediterranean garden, rockery and woodland walk. Wheelchair access inside the walled garden.

GROUP OPENING

59 HYTHE GARDENS
Hythe, CT21 5UF. *Three gardens on hillside above Hythe town and one near the sea. Transport required to visit most gardens: Topgallant: 5 North Rd CT21 5UF. Eaton Lands Allotment, Castle Rd. CT21 5EZ. 20 Spanton Crescent CT21 4SF. Lisbon Cottage, Park Rd CT21 6EU.* **Sat 30, Sun 31 May (12-5.30). Combined adm £8, chd free. Home-made teas at Topgallant, CT21 5UF.**

NEW GABRIELLE'S ALLOTMENT
LISBON COTTAGE
Heidi Bailey.
20 SPANTON CRESCENT
Nikki Griffith, www.nikkigriffithart.co.uk.
TOPGALLANT
Mary Sampson.

Four gardens in the lovely town of Hythe. On the hillside near St Leonards church is Topgallant - a green and shady Sculptors garden which will be doing teas. Above that is an interesting allotment at Eaton Lands, Castle Road. Sea views, and differing ways of dealing with the sloping hillside are also afforded by 20 Spanton Crescent. Lisbon Cottage is a smaller designer garden nearer the sea. All the gardens give an insight to seaside gardening. An insight into the joys and sorrows of gardening by the coast. Planting for succession, sun, wind and wildlife.

60 ◆ IGHTHAM MOTE
Mote Road, Ivy Hatch, Sevenoaks, TN15 0NT. National Trust, 01732 810378, ighthammote@ nationaltrust.org.uk, www.nationaltrust.org.uk/ightham-mote. *Nr Ivy Hatch: 6m E of Sevenoaks; 6m N of Tonbridge; 4m SW of Borough Green. E from Sevenoaks on A25 follow brown sign R along Coach Rd. W from Borough Green on A25 follow brown sign L along Coach Rd. N from Tonbridge on A227 follow brown sign L along High Cross Rd.* **For NGS: Mon 30 Mar (10-5). Adm £19, chd £9.50. Light refreshments in the Mote Café.** For other opening times and information, please phone, email or visit garden website.
Lovely 14 acre garden surrounding a picturesque medieval moated manor house c1320, open for NGS since 1927. Herbaceous borders, lawns, C18 cascade, fountain pools, courtyards and cutting garden provide formal interest; while the informal lakes, stream, pleasure grounds, stumpery/fernery and orchard complete the sense of charm and tranquillity, along with the recently reinstated walled garden. Please check NT website for access details (map available).

61 IVY CHIMNEYS
28 Mount Sion, Tunbridge Wells, TN1 1TW. Laurence & Christine Smith. *At the end of Tunbridge Wells High St, with Pizza Express on the corner, turn L up Mount Sion. Ivy Chimneys is a red brick Queen Anne house at the top of the hill on the R.* **Sat 13 June (11.30-5). Adm £5, chd free.**
Town centre garden with herbaceous borders and masses of roses set on three levels of lawns, all enclosed in an old walled garden. Large vegetable/cutting garden and herb garden. New small rock garden with ferns and grasses. The property is Queen Anne and one of the oldest houses in Tunbridge Wells. Car Parking in public car parks near the Pantiles. High Street cafes and restaurants nearby.

The National Garden Scheme donated £3,875,596 to our nursing and health beneficiaries from money raised at gardens open in 2025.

Norton Court

© Susie Challen

62 KENFIELD HALL
Kenfield, Petham, Canterbury, CT4 5RN. Barnaby & Camilla Swire, kenfieldhallgarden@gmail.com. *Petham nr Canterbury. Kenfield Rd off Chartham Downs Road. What3words app: tricky.cornfield.kings.* **Visits by arrangement 1 May to 1 Sept for groups of 10+. Contact Tom Waddy, head gardener, by email to arrange. Adm £10, chd free.**
An evolving, 8 acre historic and organic garden set in a peaceful AONB with fantastic views of the surrounding landscape. The site includes mature trees, C18 formal sunken garden as well as a Japanese garden incorporating a naturally managed pool with diverse wildlife. There are also herbaceous beds, spring bulbs, a wildflower meadow and vegetable garden with cut flowers.

63 ◆ KNOLE
National Trust Knole, Sevenoaks, TN15 0RP. Lord Robert Sackville-West. *1½ m SE of Sevenoaks. Leave M25 at J5 (A21). Park entrance S of Sevenoaks town centre off A225 Tonbridge Rd (opp St Nicholas Church). For SatNav use TN13 1HX. Additional parking charges apply.* **For NGS: Thur 23 July (11-3.30). Adm £5, chd £2.50. Pre-booking essential, please phone 01732 462100, email knole@nationaltrust.org.uk or visit www.nationaltrust.org.uk/knole for information & booking. Opening in addition to NT adm charges.** For other opening times and information, please phone, email or visit garden website.
Lord Sackville's private garden at Knole is a magical space, featuring sprawling lawns, a walled garden, an untamed wilderness area and a medieval orchard. Follow signage on site for the entrance to the garden. Doors will open to reveal the secluded lawns of the 26 acre garden and stunning views of the house. Last entry at 3.30pm and closes at 4pm. Please book in advance using Knole's website. Refreshments are available in the Brewhouse Café. Bookshop and shop in Green Court. Food and drink, inc picnics are not allowed in Lord Sackville's private garden. Wheelchair access via the bookshop. Paths are mostly gravel so may be difficult for manual wheelchair users. Assistance dogs only in the garden.

64 THE KNOLL FARM
Giggers Green Road, Aldington, Ashford, TN25 7BY. Lord & Lady Aldington, ca@aldingtonlow.com. *Above the Royal Military Canal on the Aldington Dymchurch road. The postcode leads to Goldenhurst, the drive entrance is opp and further down hill. What3words app: commutes.long.gathers.* **Sat 11 Apr (11-4). Adm £10, chd free. Visits also by arrangement 13**

Apr to 1 June for groups of up to 20. Limited car parking space. Donation to Bonnington Church. Avenue of 70 hornbeams,10 acres of woodland garden featuring bluebells, primroses, anemones, over130 camellias, Acer japonica, rhododendrons, and a growing collection of specimen pines and oaks; formal elements; and far-reaching views across Romney Marsh. Paths throughout but the whole garden is on a slope.

65 KNOWLE HILL FARM
Ulcombe, Maidstone, ME17 1ES. Andrew & Elizabeth Cairns, 07860 177101, elizabeth@ knowlehillfarm.co.uk, www. knowlehillfarmgarden.co.uk. *7m SE of Maidstone. From M20 J8 follow A20 towards Lenham for 2m. Turn R to Ulcombe. After 1½m, L at X'rds, after ½m 2nd R into Windmill Hill. Past Pepper Box Pub, ½m 1st L to Knowle Hill.* **Sat 7, Sun 8 Feb (11-3.30); Sat 18, Sun 19 July (2-5). Adm £6, chd free. Home-made teas. 2027: Sat 6, Sun 7 Feb. Visits also by arrangement 26 Jan to 30 Sept.**
2 acre garden created over 40 yrs on south facing slope below the Greensand Ridge. Spectacular views. Snowdrops and hellebores, many tender plants, china roses, agapanthus, salvias and grasses flourish on light soil. Box hedges and topiary lend structure. Lavender ribbons hum with bees. Pool enclosed in small walled white garden. Spring bulbs followed by cowslips flower early in the grass. Due to the narrow lanes leading to the garden, access for large coaches is limited. Partial wheelchair access due to steep slopes.

66 LADHAM HOUSE
Ladham Road, Goudhurst, TN17 1DB. Paul and Jill Thompson. *8m E of Tunbridge Wells. On NE of Goudhurst, off A262. Through village towards Cranbrook, turn L at The Goudhurst Inn. 2nd R into Ladham Rd, main gates approx 500yds on L.* **Sun 10 May (2-5). Adm £8, chd free. Tea, coffee & cake.**
10 acres of garden with many interesting plants, trees and shrubs, inc rhododendrons, camellias, azaleas and magnolias. A beautiful rose garden, arboretum, an Edwardian sunken rockery, ponds, a spectacular 60 metre twin border, a vegetable garden and a woodland walk. Car display.

67 NEW LINK HILL HOUSE
Rye Road, Sandhurst, Cranbrook, TN18 5PQ. Mr Pritchard, linkhillgarden@gmail.com. *1m E of Sandhurst. Follow signs, house is next to Lomas Ln.* **Sun 14, Sun 28 June (11-4). Adm £5, chd free. Pre-booking essential, please visit www.ngs.org. uk for information & booking. Tea, coffee & cake.** Visits also by arrangement May & June for groups of up to 10.
A walled garden brought back to life totalling about ⅓ of an acre. Planted with a playful scheme of roses, perennials and a hot border along the south facing side. A testament to the love of roses the garden really at it's best when these stars are in season. A small orchard of young fruit trees along with a gravel garden in its infancy. Planted by amateur gardeners and busy parents to bring joy.

68 NEW LYMPNE CASTLE
The Street, Lympne, Hythe, CT21 4LQ. Lympne Castle Management Ltd. *A few miles from J11 off the M20, approx 1½ hours from central London What3words app: bespoke.arranges.teach.* **Sun 3 May (12-6). Adm £10, chd free. Tea, coffee & cake in the castle bar.**
Gardens set around a medieval castle, a historic landmark in Lympne, Kent. Visit the newly built Italianate style garden comprising of ancient wisteria and topiaries. The courtyard garden features extensive spring bulb displays and the formal lawn terraces with herbaceous borders has amazing views over the Romney Marsh and English Channel. This garden features a mix of natural beauty and tranquil spaces. Visit the refurbished orchard garden, with raised vegetable garden for homegrown produce and climbing roses. The newly built ornamental garden features a water fountain and lily pond, pergolas with grapevines to offer shade and beautiful topiaries. Surrounding the castle, you will find a bluebell woodland and a small annual meadow. Other features inc ancient mulberry trees, woven hazel archways, magnolia grandiflora and mature cordyline australis. Partial wheelchair access. Courtyard entrance, castle and orchard gardens accessible, however terrace and ornamental garden have steps.

69 LYNSTED COMMUNITY KITCHEN GARDEN
Lynsted Park, Lynsted, Sittingbourne, ME9 0JH. Mrs V R Ross Russell, www. lynstedkitchengarden.com. *15min drive from Faversham or Sittingbourne. Nearest Train - Teynham stn. Postcode ME9 0JH brings you to the start Lynsted Park's drive, please follow signs from there.* **Sat 4 July (11-4). Adm £7, chd free. Home-made teas. Open nearby Hoppickers East.**
½ acre community garden set up and run by local people, who grow organic fruit and vegetables together, sharing all aspects of sowing, growing and harvesting. Use the 'No Dig' approach with soil health, sustainable water management and composting being key elements. Bees kept on site, and ongoing efforts are being made to enhance the biodiversity of the garden. Lynsted Community Kitchen Garden is set in a 7 acre field that is largely left wild but with small areas mown that can be used to sit down and picnic. The garden is sited in a field. In wet ground conditions, we would not advise wheelchairs.

70 MARSHBOROUGH FARMHOUSE
Farm Lane, Marshborough, Sandwich, CT13 0PJ. David & Sarah Ash. *1½m W of Sandwich, ½m S of Ash. From Ash take R fork to Woodnesborough. After 1m Marshborough sign. L into Farm Ln at white thatched cottage, garden 100yds on L. Parking in farmyard.* **Wed 10 June, Sun 16 Aug (12-5). Adm £7, chd free. Home-made teas.**
Interesting 2½ acre plantsman's garden, developed enthusiastically over 27 yrs by the owners. Paths and lawns lead to many unusual shrubs, trees and perennials in island beds, borders, rockery and raised dry garden creating year-round colour and interest. Tender pot plants, succulents, pond and water features. Over 70 varieties of Salvia both hardy and tender.

71 ♦ MOUNT EPHRAIM GARDENS

Hernhill, Faversham, ME13 9TX. Mr Dawes, 01227 751496, info@mountephraimgardens.co.uk, www.mountephraimgardens.co.uk. *3m E of Faversham. From end of M2, then A299 take slip road 1st L to Hernhill, signed to gardens.* **For NGS: Sun 29 Mar, Thur 24 Sept (11-4). Adm £10, chd £4. Home-made teas in West Wing tearoom.** For other opening times and information, please phone, email or visit garden website.

A privately-owned family home set in 10 acres of terraced Edwardian gardens with stunning views over the Kent countryside. Highlights inc a Japanese rock and water garden, arboretum, unusual topiary and a spectacular grass maze plus many mature trees, shrubs and spring bulbs. Partial wheelchair access; top part manageable, but steep slope. Disabled WC. Full access to tea room.

72 NETTLESTEAD PLACE

Nettlestead, Maidstone, ME18 5HA. Mr & Mrs Roy Tucker, www.nettlestead-place.co.uk. *6m W/SW of Maidstone. S off A26 onto B2015 then 1m on L, Nettlestead Court Farm after Nettlestead Church.* **Sun 5, Sun 19 Apr (1.30-4.30). Adm £10, chd free. Home-made teas.**

C13 manor house in 10 acre plantsman's garden. Large formal rose garden. Large herbaceous garden of island beds with rose and clematis walkway leading to a garden of succulents. Fine collection of trees and shrubs; sunken pond garden, maze of thuja, terraces, bamboos, camellias, glen garden, acer and daffodil lawns. Young pinetum adjacent to garden. Sculptures featured throughout. Beautiful countryside views. Gravel and grass paths. Most of garden accessible (but not sunken pond garden). Steep bank and lower area accessible with some difficulty.

73 NORTON COURT

Teynham, Sittingbourne, ME9 9JU. Tim & Sophia Steel, 07798 804544, sophia@nortoncourt.net. *Off A2 between Teynham & Faversham. L off A2 at Esso garage into Norton Ln; next L into Provender Ln; L signed Church for car park What3words app: comedians.stews.unearthly.* **Mon 8, Tue 9 June (2-5). Adm £15, chd free. Home-made teas inc in adm price.** Visits also by arrangement 15 May to 17 July for groups of 15 to 30.

10 acre garden within parkland setting. Mature trees, topiary, wide lawns and clipped yew hedges. Orchard with mown paths through wildflowers. Walled garden with mixed borders and climbing roses. Pine tree walk. Formal box and lavender parterre. Treehouse in the Sequoia. Church open, adjacent to garden. Flat ground except for 2 steps where ramp is provided.

74 OAK COTTAGE AND SWALLOWFIELDS NURSERY

Elmsted, Ashford, TN25 5JT. Martin & Rachael Castle. *6m NW of Hythe. From Stone St (B2068) turn W opp the Stelling Minnis turning. Follow signs to Elmsted. Turn L at Elmsted village sign. Limited parking at house, further parking at Church (7min walk).* **Fri 24, Sat 25 Apr, Thur 28, Fri 29 May (11-4). Adm £6, chd free. Home-made teas.**

Get off the beaten track and discover this beautiful ½ acre cottage garden in the heart of the Kent countryside. This plantsman's garden is filled with unusual and interesting perennials. Curving lawns framed by abundantly planted borders. There is a small specialist nursery packed with herbaceous perennials. Greenhouses containing species pelargonium and Salvia collections.

75 OLD BLADBEAN STUD

Bladbean, Canterbury, CT4 6NA. Carol Bruce, www.oldbladbeanstud.co.uk. *9m S of Canterbury. From B2068, follow signs into Stelling Minnis, turn R onto Bossingham Rd, then follow yellow NGS signs through single track lanes.* **Sun 24 May, Sun 7, Sun 21 June, Sun 5, Sun 19 July (2-6). Adm £7, chd free. Cream teas.**

Romantic walled rose garden with 90+ old fashioned rose varieties, tranquil yellow and white garden, square garden with a tapestry of self sowing perennials and Victorian style greenhouse, 300ft long colour schemed symmetrical double borders and an organic fruit garden. Maintained entirely by the owner, the gardens were designed to be managed as an ornamental ecosystem. Subject of the owner's new book: In Nature's Slipstream, published by DK in spring 2026.

76 THE OLD RECTORY, FAWKHAM

Valley Road, Fawkham, Longfield, DA3 8LX. Karin & Christopher Proudfoot, 01474 707513, keproudfoot@gmail.com. *1m S of Longfield. Midway between A2 & A20, on Valley Rd 1½ m N of Fawkham Green, 0.3m S of Fawkham church, opp sign for Gay Dawn Farm/Corinthian Sports Club. Parking on drive only. Not suitable for coaches.* Visits by arrangement 2 Feb to 27 Feb for groups of up to 20. Small numbers welcome but may be combined to make up a larger group. **Adm £10, chd free. Tea, coffee & cake inc in adm price.**

1½ acres with impressive display of long-established naturalised snowdrops and winter aconites; also collection of over 130 named snowdrops. Garden developed around the snowdrops over 40 yrs, inc hellebores, pulmonarias and other early bulbs and flowers, with foliage perennials, shrubs and trees, also natural woodland. Gentle slope, gravel drive, some narrow paths.

77 THE OLD RECTORY, OTTERDEN

Bunce Court Road, Faversham, ME13 0BY. Mrs Gry Iverslien, 07734 538272, gry@iverslien.com. *North Downs. Postcode takes you to Bunce Ct. Garden is 600 yrds further on just past Cold Harbour Ln.* **Visits by arrangement Apr to Sept for groups of 10 to 30. Restricted parking. Car share advised. Adm £10, chd free. Tea, coffee & cake inc in adm.**

A stunning 4 acre woodland garden full of seasonal beauty. Wander among majestic rhododendrons and camellias, carpets of spring bulbs, a formal rose garden, cutting garden and vibrant hydrangea beds. A large wildlife pond, varied specimen trees, and colourful pots of tulips, narcissus and other spring flowers complete the charm.

78 THE ORANGERY
Mystole, Chartham, Canterbury, CT4 7DB. Rex Stickland & Anne Prasse. *5m SW of Canterbury. Turn off A28 to Shalmsford St. In 1½m at Xrds turn R downhill. Continue & ignore drive on L (Mystole House only). At sharp R bend in 600yds turn L into drive.* **Sun 10 May, Sat 25, Sun 26 July (1-5). Adm £7, chd free. Tea, coffee & cake.**
1½ acre gardens around C18 orangery, now a house (not open). Magnificent extensive herbaceous border and impressive walled wisteria. Large walled garden with a wide variety of shrubs, mixed borders and unusual specimen trees. Water features and intriguing collection of modern sculptures in natural surroundings. Splendid views from the terrace over ha-ha to the lovely Chartham Downs. Ramps to garden.

79 OUDEN
Brogdale Road, Ospringe, Faversham, ME13 8XY. Frances & Paul Moskovits, 07715 985729, paulandfranmoskovits@live.co.uk. *Close to Faversham. From A2 in Faversham turn S along Brogdale Rd for ¾m, Ouden is on R. Parking on roadside.* **Visits by arrangement in July for groups of up to 15. Adm £6, chd free. Tea, coffee & cake.**
A variety of mature shrubs and trees form the backbone of this ¼ acre plot. The front garden features a shrubbery and cottage planting. The rear garden has a well-stocked colourful long border leading to two greenhouses. Exotic planting intermingles with traditional garden favourites. Small paths allow time for a closer look. Situated close to Belmont House & Gardens, The National Fruit Collection at Brogdale Farm and market town of Faversham.

GROUP OPENING

80 NEW PEGWELL & WEST CLIFF GARDENS
Ramsgate, CT11 0JB. Jane Hills. *Pegwell Rd is off London Rd. West Cliff Rd is a few metres from the r'bout where London Rd meets Grange Rd. Tickets at 31 Pegwell Road.* **Sun 5 July (10-5). Combined adm £7, chd free. Home-made teas. Afternoon tea also available.**

NEW **31 PEGWELL ROAD**
Jane Hills Kinsella.
NEW **PRIORY VILLA**
Mrs Shirley Flynn.
NEW **VICTORIA LODGE**
Ms Judith Castle.

Visit three distinctly different gardens all found on the west side of Ramsgate town. (10-15 minute walk) Tickets sold at 31 Pegwell Rd. These coastal properties enjoy the microclimate allowing echiums, bougainvillea, oleander, canna, succulents and aeoniums to thrive throughout the entire year. 31 has houseplants which connect the house to the garden plus a unique water feature and over 200 pots. Priory Villa has over 150 roses, a stunning greenhouse and interesting sculptures. Victoria Lodge has lots of history, beautiful seating areas and Koi Carp. All three gardens have tree ferns.

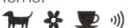

81 ♦ PENSHURST PLACE & GARDENS
Penshurst, TN11 8DG. Lord & Lady De L'Isle, 01892 870307, contactus@penshurstplace.com, www.penshurstplace.com. *6m NW of Tunbridge Wells. SW of Tonbridge on B2176, signed from A26 N of Tunbridge Wells.* **For NGS: Wed 16 Sept (10-5). Adm £15, chd £9. Light refreshments at The Porcupine Pantry.** For other opening times and information, please phone, email or visit garden website.
11 acres of garden dating back to C14. The garden is divided into a series of rooms by over a mile of yew hedge. Profusion of spring bulbs, formal rose garden and famous peony border. Woodland trail and arboretum. Year-round interest. Toy museum. Some parts not paved and uneven in places. 2 wheelchairs available to hire.

82 PHEASANT BARN
Church Road, Oare, ME13 0QB. Paul & Su Vaight, 07843 739301, suvaight46@gmail.com. *2m NW of Faversham. Entering Oare from Faversham, turn R at Three Mariners pub towards Harty Ferry. Garden 400yds on R, before church. Parking on roadside.* **Visits by arrangement 5 June to 5 July for groups of up to 20. Adm £8, chd free.**
Series of smallish gardens around award-winning converted farm buildings in beautiful situation overlooking Oare Creek. Main garden is nectar rich planting in formal design with a contemporary twist inspired by local landscape. Also vegetable garden, dry garden, water features, mowed paths in wildflower meadow, fruit trees, late summer perennial beds and grass labyrinth. Kent Wildlife Trust Oare Marshes Bird Reserve within 1 mile. Two village inns serving lunches/dinners, booking recommended.

83 ♦ QUEX GARDENS
Quex Park, Birchington, CT7 0BH. Powell-Cotton Museum, 01843 842168, enquiries@powell-cottonmuseum.org, www.powell-cottonmuseum.org. *3m W of Margate. Follow signs for Quex Park from A299 then A28 towards Margate, turn R into B2048 Park Ln. Quex Park is on L.* **For NGS: Sun 19 July (11-4). Adm £7.50, chd £5. Light refreshments in Felicity's Café & Quex Barn. Many light refreshments available around the estate.** For other opening times and information, please phone, email or visit garden website.
10 acres of woodland and gardens with fine specimen trees unusual on Thanet, spring bulbs, wisteria, shrub borders, old figs and mulberries, herbaceous borders. Victorian walled garden with cucumber house, long glasshouses, cactus house, fruiting trees. Peacocks, dovecote, chickens, bees, woodland walk, wildlife pond, children's maze, croquet lawn, picnic grove, lawns and fountains. Head Gardener and team will be available on the day for a chat and to answer questions. Concession tickets can be purchased at the door. Garden almost entirely flat with tarmac paths. Sunken garden has sloping lawns to the central pond.

Our donation to the Army Benevolent Fund supported 776 individuals with horticultural related grants in 2025.

GROUP OPENING

84 RAMSGATE GARDENS
Ramsgate, CT11 9PX. Anne-Marie Nixey. *Enter Ramsgate on A299, then A255. At r'about 2nd exit London Rd. Less than 1m to r'about, L onto Grange Rd or straight ahead down West Cliff Rd.* **Sun 6 Sept (12-5). Combined adm £5, chd free. Tea, coffee & cake.**

104 GRANGE ROAD
Anne-Marie Nixey.

6 VALE SQUARE
Stephen Davies.

10 VALE SQUARE
Mr Graham & Mrs Alyson Brett.

Evolving gardens in the beautiful, yet windy, coastal town of Ramsgate showing different sized plots and how to make unique gardens out of them. Varied planting from traditional roses and bedding plants to a range of vegetables and fruit trees, as well as use of recycled and sustainable materials and incorporating traditional family areas. Vale Square Gardens highlight what can be achieved in front gardens too. Wheelchair access is available at Vale Square front gardens, as well as a small part of Grange Road garden.

85 ◆ RIVERHILL HIMALAYAN GARDENS
Riverhill, Sevenoaks, TN15 0RR. The Rogers Family, 01732 459777, info@riverhillgardens.co.uk, www.riverhillgardens.co.uk. *2m S of Sevenoaks on A225. Leave A21 at A225 & follow signs for Riverhill Himalayan Gardens.* **For NGS: Wed 6 May, Thur 18 June (10-5). Adm £14, chd £7.50. Light refreshments at the Cafe, Malabar. For other opening times and information, please phone, email or visit garden website.**
Beautiful hillside garden, privately owned by the Rogers family since 1840. Spectacular rhododendrons, azaleas and fine specimen trees. Edwardian Rock Garden with extensive fern collection, Rose Walk and Walled Garden with sculptural terracing. Bluebell walks. Extensive views across the Weald of Kent. Hedge maze, adventure playground and den building. Café serves speciality coffee, light lunches and cakes. Plant sales and quirky shed shop selling beautiful gifts and original garden ornaments. Disabled parking. Easy access to café, shop and tea terrace. Accessible WC.

86 ST CLERE
Kemsing, Sevenoaks, TN15 6NL. Mr Simon & Mrs Eliza Ecclestone, www.stclere.co.uk. *6m NE of Sevenoaks. 1m E of Seal on A25, turn L signed Heaverham. In Heaverham turn R signed Wrotham. In 75yds straight ahead marked Private Rd; 1st L to house. Main entrance What3words app: trail. inner.valid.* **Sun 14 June (2-5). Adm £7.50, chd free. Tea, coffee & cake in the Garden Room. Tea and cake provided by local primary school.**
4 acre garden, full of interest. Formal terraces surrounding C17 mansion (not open), with beautiful views of the Kent countryside. Herbaceous and shrub borders, productive kitchen and herb gardens, lawns and rare trees. Some gravel paths and small steps.

87 NEW ST HELENS LODGE
Lower Road, East Farleigh, Maidstone, ME15 0JT. Mr and Mrs Michael Stubbs. *3m W of maidstone. Black house opp bus stop with E Farleigh pictorial village sign in front garden. Sign only visible if coming from W Farleigh / Teston direction.* **Sat 20 June, Sat 22 Aug (12-5). Adm £9, chd free. Tea, coffee & cake inc in adm price.**
Garden on three levels. Inc a white garden with paving and steps to lawn and raised pond, mixed borders and a late summer border. Fruit tunnel to a greenhouse, summerhouse, secret garden and raised vegetable beds. Secluded seating areas with pretty views of the garden. Limited parking on drive for people with mobility problems. All other parking in Lower Road towards West Farleigh.

88 ◆ SCOTNEY CASTLE
Lamberhurst, TN3 8JN. National Trust, 01892 893020, scotneycastle@nationaltrust.org.uk, www.nationaltrust.org.uk/scotneycastle. *6m SE of Tunbridge Wells. On A21 London - Hastings, brown tourist signs. Bus: (Mon to Fri) 256 Tunbridge Wells to Wadhurst Autocar service via Lamberhurst alight Lamberhurst Green.* **For NGS: Wed 13 May (10-5). Adm £19, chd £9.50. Light refreshments in the Courtyard tearoom. For other opening times and information, please phone, email or visit garden website.**
The medieval moated Old Scotney Castle lies in a peaceful wooded valley on the Kent/Sussex border. In the 1830s its owner, Edward Hussey III, set about building a new house, partially demolishing the Old Castle to create a romantic ruin, the centrepiece of his visionary landscape. Manual wheelchairs and individual mobility scooters are available to borrow. Booking recommended for mobility scooters by calling 01892 893820.

89 45 SEYMOUR AVENUE
Whitstable, CT5 1SA. Kevin Tooher, 07962 972882, sirplantalot@outlook.com. *Near the centre of Whitstable town & 400yds from Whitstable stn. Take Thanet Way off A299 towards Whitstable. 2nd r'about, L into Millstrood Rd, bottom of hill R into Old Bridge Rd, Station car park on L & Seymour Ave on R.* **Visits by arrangement. Adm £6, chd free. Visits weekends only in June, daily in July, and weekdays only in September and October.**
Larger than usual town centre garden - about 1/4 acre with wide range of unusual plants grown on heavy wet clay with lots of exotics growing in containers, troughs and pots. Main driveway gravel but mostly wheelchair accessible. Chip bark paths in the garden.

90 SIR JOHN HAWKINS HOSPITAL
High Street, Chatham, ME4 4EW. The Governors of Sir John Hawkins Hospital, www.hawkinshospital.org.uk. *On the N side of Chatham High St, on the border between Rochester & Chatham. Leave A2 at J1 & follow signs to Rochester. Pass Rochester Stn & turn L at main junc T-lights, travelling E towards Chatham.* **Sat 27, Sun 28 June (11-5). Adm £3, chd free. Cream teas. Farm House Teas and light refreshments served all day.**
Built on the site of Kettle Hard - part of Bishop Gundulph's Hospital of St Bartholomew, the Almshouse is a

square of Georgian houses dating from the 1790s. A delightful small secluded garden overlooks the River Medway, full of vibrant and colourful planting. A lawn with cottage style borders leads to the riverside and a miniature gnome village captivates small children. Disabled access via stairlift, wheelchair to be carried separately.

91 ◆ SISSINGHURST CASTLE GARDEN

Biddenden Road, Sissinghurst, Cranbrook, TN17 2AB. National Trust, 01580 710700, sissinghurst@nationaltrust.org.uk, www.nationaltrust.org.uk/sissinghurst-castle-garden. *2m NE of Cranbrook, 1m E of Sissinghurst on Biddenden Rd (A262), see our website for more information.* **For NGS: Sun 13 Sept (11-5.30). Adm £19, chd £9.50. Light refreshments in Coffee Shop and Granary Restaurant. Picnics on designated area in Vegetable Garden.** For other opening times and information, please phone, email or visit garden website. Historic, poetic, iconic; a refuge dedicated to beauty. Vita Sackville-West and Harold Nicolson fell in love with Sissinghurst Castle and created a world renowned garden. More than a garden, visitors can also find an Elizabethan tower, see changing exhibitions, enjoy estate walks and can picnic in the vegetable garden. Food, drink and animals are not allowed in the formal garden. Free welcome talks and estate walks leaflets. Café, restaurant, gift, secondhand book and plant shops are open from 10am-5.30pm. Some areas unsuitable for wheelchair access due to narrow paths and steps. An accessible map is available from visitor reception.

92 SMITHS HALL

Lower Road, West Farleigh, ME15 0PE. Stephen and Natasha Norman. *3m W of Maidstone. From A26 Tonbridge to Maidstone, turn S 3m W of Maidstone down B2163 over stone bridge. At T-junc turn R onto Lower Rd B2010. Pass Tickled Trout pub, bear L 100yds up Ewell Ln to car park.* **Sun 5 July (11-5). Adm £10, chd free. Home-made teas.** Donation to Heart of Kent Hospice.

Delightful 3 acre gardens surrounding a beautiful 1719 Queen Anne House (not open). Lose yourself in numerous themed rooms: sunken garden with pond and fountain, deep herbaceous borders, many roses (300) in formal rose garden and rose walk. Pleasant woodland walk starting at tulip tree avenue. A new feature this year is an extensive planting of a Tuscan wildflower meadow. Some gravel paths.

St Helens Lodge

93 NEW SNAKESBURY
Iwade Road, Newington, Sittingbourne, ME9 7JY. Mr Gareth Bedford. *1m NE of Newington. From the A2 in Newington, drive down Church Ln. At the bottom of Church Ln turn R into Iwade Rd. Look for the yellow signs. What3words app: headlines.fortnight.monkeys.* **Sat 23, Sun 24 May (11-4). Adm £7, chd free. Tea, coffee & cake.**
Snakesbury has a wide range of interest from formal borders to new woodland. In a plot of five acres, garden areas include a white garden, a shrub garden, long borders, a small orchard, a walled kitchen garden, ponds and a field which is gradually being planted up as woodland. Wild in areas and with a huge range of plants inc some rarely-seen ornamental trees and shrubs. Wheelchair access is highly dependent on the weather due to grass paths.

94 4 SOUTHVIEW COTTAGES
Marsh Green Road, Marsh Green, Edenbridge, TN8 5QG. Deon Swanepoel and David Paddon, 07940 782819, swanpad@live.co.uk. *B2028 between Edenbridge and Dormansland. From Edenbridge, take B2026 S towards Hartfield, then turn R onto B2028 towards Dormansland. Approx ½m to garden. Turn R and park by the church.* **Sat 6 June, Sat 4 July, Sat 1 Aug (11-5). Adm £5, chd free. Tea, coffee & cake. Visits also by arrangement May to Aug for groups of 8 to 16.**
A compact 'secret' garden of multiple spaces. Entrance courtyard with a green wall, glass conservatory, rear terrace catching the sun, central circular seating area, shaded tropical areas, and working space, divided by a zig-zagging freestanding espaliered beech hedge that frames the path that draws you through the garden and leads you to the different spaces. The owners have created a localised microclimate supporting tropical planting.

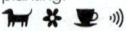

95 SPRING PLATT
Boyton Court Road, Sutton Valence, Maidstone, ME17 3BY. Mr & Mrs John Millen. *5m SE of Maidstone. From A274 nr Sutton Valence follow yellow NGS signs.* **Thur 29, Fri 30 Jan, Wed 4, Thur 5, Tue 10, Wed 11 Feb (10.30-3).**
Adm £5, chd free. Pre-booking essential, please phone 01622 843383, email j.millen@talktalk.net or visit www.kentsnowdrops.com for information & booking. Light refreshments inc home-made soup and bread. Teas and coffees.
1 acre garden with panoramic views of the Weald. Approx 500 different varieties of snowdrops in raised sleeper beds but many more now planted in grass around the garden with spring flowers in borders. Large vegetable garden, 4 greenhouses, natural spring fed water feature and a croquet lawn. Citrus fruit trees now in large Alpine House.

96 ♦ SQUERRYES COURT
Squerryes, Westerham, TN16 1SJ. Henry Warde, www.squerryes.co.uk. *½m W of Westerham. Signed from A25.* **For NGS: Fri 15 May (11-5). Adm £8, chd free.** Home-made teas. For other opening times and information, please visit garden website.
15 acres of garden, lake and woodland surrounding beautiful C17 manor house (not open). Lovely throughout the seasons from the spring bulbs to later-flowering borders. Cenotaph commemorating General Wolfe. C18 dovecote. Lawns, yew hedges, ancient trees, parterres, azaleas and roses.

97 STABLE HOUSE
Heppington, Lower Hardres, Canterbury, CT4 7AN. Charlie & Lucy Markes. *2m S of Canterbury off Faussett Hill. 2m S of Canterbury, off B2068 at Faussett Hill, Lower Hardres. 1st R after Bridge Rd if coming from Canterbury, 400m after Granville pub on the L if coming towards Canterbury.* **Sat 11, Sun 12 July (10-2). Adm £6, chd free. Tea, coffee & cake.**
5 acre mature wildflower meadow with winding mown paths adjoining 2 acres of relaxed, informal interlinked gardens. These surround converted Edwardian stable block in lovely setting with views across vineyards towards the North Downs. Gravel garden, vegetable garden and walkthrough garden room beneath clocktower. Disabled parking by arrangement close to garden. Tel - 07831 615998. Not all areas wheelchair accessible.

98 STONEWALL PARK
Chiddingstone Hoath, Edenbridge, TN8 7DG. Mr & Mrs Fleming. *4m SE of Edenbridge. Via B2026. ½ way between Markbeech & Penshurst. Plenty of parking (on the lawn) which will be signed. Entrance at the Truggers Ln end. What3words app: hint.irrigate.holly.* **Sun 22 Mar, Sun 3 May (2-5). Adm £7, chd free. Tea, coffee & cake.** Donation to MSA & St Mary's Church, Chiddingstone.
Vast amounts of C19 self-seeded daffodils which lead down to a romantic woodland garden in a historic setting. In May, bluebells take over the daffodils in abundance. Winding, mossy paths lead you to a range of interesting trees, sandstone outcrops and lakes, featuring stunning species of rhododendrons, magnolias and azaleas. Please wear boots and bring walking sticks as the paths can be slippery and muddy during the spring months. The paths are quite steep so care is needed going down towards the lakes.

GROUP OPENING

99 TANKERTON GARDENS
Tankerton, CT5 1NS. *1m E of Whitstable. All 5 gardens are in central Tankerton. No more than 15min walk between gardens.* **Sun 24 May (10-5). Combined adm £7, chd free. Tea, coffee & cake.**

61 GRAYSTONE ROAD
Ms Lisa Chapman.

25 OAKWOOD DRIVE
Ms Joanna Janicka.

NEW 2 QUEENS ROAD
Mr Matthew Langford.

96 QUEENS ROAD
Ms Wendy Cunningham.

50 SUMMERFIELD AVENUE
Janet Maxwell.

A group of diverse gardens inc an artists gravel garden, plantswoman's garden, flowers for cutting, kitchen garden and chickens. Beautifully thought through with plenty of innovative and some, cost saving, ideas. Close to cafes and WC facilities.

100 THAMES HOUSE
29 Royal Pier Road, Gravesend, DA12 2BD. Dr Daniel Curran, 07753 605607. *Gravesend Heritage Quarter. Last house on L along Royal Pier Rd, past the Clarendon Hotel, and up a short set of steps from the pavement. What3words app: prime. posts.behind.* **Sun 5 July, Sun 6 Sept (1-5). Adm £5, chd free. Tea, coffee & cake. Visits also by arrangement 1 May to 1 Sept for groups of 8+.**
Three different outdoor spaces connected by steps. The main terrace, with views over the Thames River, and the small western "white" terrace with fish pond, are classically planted to sit harmoniously with the listed building which dominates these areas. The third larger space is the main garden, a modern styled walled garden with lawn, mixed borders, fruit trees and contemporary seating areas.

101 TONBRIDGE SCHOOL
High Street, Tonbridge, TN9 1JP. The Governors. *Maps & guides available for visitors. At N end of Tonbridge High St. Parking signed off London Rd (B245 Tonbridge-Hildenborough) in the Tonbridge Sports Centre car park.* **Thur 16 Apr (9-3.30). Adm £7.50, chd free. Cream teas inc home-made scones. Gluten free options available. Coffee and soft drinks.**
In front of and behind Tonbridge School you will find five gardens that you can visit. These are: The Boars Head, The Garden of Remembrance, Smythe Library Garden, Skinners Library Garden, and the Barton Science Centre Garden. It is hoped that the Chapel will be open for visits. The school gardens provide vibrant outdoor teaching and relaxation areas for boys and staff. Guided tours throughout the day given by Stephen Harmer, Head Gardener. WCs on site. Please note that Skinners Library path is uneven.

102 TRAM HATCH
Barnfield Road, Charing Heath, Ashford, TN27 0BN. Mrs P Scrivens, 07835 758388, Info@tramhatch.com, www.tramhatch.com. *10m NW of Ashford. A20 towards Pluckley, over m'way, 1st R to Barnfield. At end, L past Barnfield, Tram Hatch ahead.*

Visits by arrangement 7 Apr to 16 Sept for groups of 10 to 30. Adm £7.50, chd free.
Meander your way off the beaten track to a mature 3 acre garden changing through the seasons. You will enjoy a garden laid out in rooms. Large selection of trees, vegetable, rose and gravel gardens, colourful containers. River Stour and the Angel of the South enhance your visit. Please come and enjoy, then relax in the lovely garden room for tea. Great River Stour plus other water features. Large variety of trees, garden split into rooms each different and large vegetable garden. The garden is totally flat, apart from a very small area which can be viewed from the lane.

103 ♦ WALMER CASTLE
Kingsdown Road, Walmer, Deal, CT14 7LJ. English Heritage. *On coast S of Walmer, on A258; J13 of M20 or from M2 to Deal.* **For NGS: Evening opening Tue 30 June (5.30-7). Adm £20, chd free. Pre-booking essential, please email fundraising@english-heritage.org.uk or visit www.english-heritage.org.uk/visit/places/walmer-castle-and-gardens/events for information & booking. Light refreshments. For other opening times and information, please email or visit garden website.**
Highlights inc the elegantly planted kitchen garden and glasshouses, the dramatic Queen Mother's Garden designed by Penelope Hobhouse, a Jungle Moat with rare and unique exotic plants, and the sweeping herbaceous Broadwalk with its distinctive 'Cloud Hedge'. Also, the large collection of dahlias are expected to be in full bloom.

104 NEW WEDGWOOD HOUSE
The Grove, Kennington, Ashford, TN24 9HA. Mr Nicholas & Mrs Karen Fowler. *The Grove is off The St in Old Kennington. 2m N of Ashford. The St, off A28, (opp Stubbs), 1st L into The Grove. Parking in the street.* **Tue 26, Thur 28 May, Fri 17 July (12-4). Adm £7.50. Pre-booking essential, please visit www.ngs.org.uk for information & booking. Tea, coffee & cake inc in adm.**
A medium-sized mature suburban garden surrounding a traditional Kent house. Several mixed borders, some colour themed, inc grasses, roses, gravel Mediterranean areas and a wild section with Hugel mound. A large walled patio displays containers showcasing differing leaf shape, colour and texture. Several seating areas around the garden. Enjoy tea and cake in the large Victorian greenhouse.

105 WEST COURT LODGE
Postling Court, The Street, Postling, nr Hythe, CT21 4EX. Mr & Mrs John Pattrick, 07814 419638, pattrickmalliet@gmail.com. *2m NW of Hythe. From M20 J11 turn S onto A20. Immed 1st L. After ½m on bend take road signed Lyminge. 1st L into Postling.* **Visits by arrangement Apr to Sept for groups of up to 35. Combined with Churchfield. Tea, coffee & cake in Postling village hall.**
South facing one acre walled garden at the foot of the North Downs, designed in two parts: main lawn with large sunny borders and a romantic woodland glade planted with shadow loving plants and spring bulbs, small wildlife pond. Lovely C11 church will be open next to the gardens.

In 2025, our donations to Carers Trust helped them support over 1 million unpaid carers across the UK, as part of their network of local carer centres.

2 Herons Brook

GROUP OPENING

106 WEST MALLING EARLY SUMMER GARDENS
West Malling, ME19 6LW. *On A20, nr J4 of M20. Park (Ryarsh Ln & Stn) in West Malling. Please start your visit either at Brome House or Went House. Parking available at New Barns Cottages. A map of the locations will be provided.* **Sun 31 May (12-5). Combined adm £10, chd free. Home-made teas at New Barns Cottages only.**

ABBEY BREWERY COTTAGE
Dr David & Mrs Lynda Nunn.

BROME HOUSE
John Pfeil & Shirley Briggs.

NEW BARNS COTTAGES
Mr & Mrs Anthony Drake.

26 OFFHAM ROAD
Mary and David Herrington.

TOWN HILL COTTAGE
Veronica and Peter Cosier.

WENT HOUSE
Alan & Mary Gibbins.

West Malling is an attractive small market town with some fine buildings. Enjoy six lovely gardens that are entirely different from each other and cannot be seen from the road. Brome House and Went House have large gardens with specimen trees, old roses, mixed borders, attractive kitchen gardens and garden features inc a coach house, Roman temple, fountain and parterre. Town Hill Cottage is a walled town garden with mature and interesting planting. Abbey Brewery Cottage is a recent jewel-like example of garden restoration and development. 26 Offham Road is a charming, closely planted, small town garden. New Barns Cottages is an extensive cottage and woodland garden threequarters of a mile from West Malling High Street, in iconic Kent countryside. Numerous cameos, viewing platform, photos of the garden's evolution.

GROUP OPENING

107 WHITSTABLE JOY LANE GARDENS
Whitstable, CT5 4LT. www.facebook.com/ whitstableopengardens. *Off A299, or A290. Down Borstal Hill, L by garage into Joy Ln. Tickets and map from 19 Joy Ln.* **Sun 10 May (10-4). Combined adm £7, chd free. Tea, coffee & cake.**
Enjoy a day visiting a dozen or so eclectic gardens along Joy Lane and neighbourhood by the sea. From Arts & Crafts villas to mid century bungalows, some productive, others wildlife friendly, large or compact, we garden on heavy clay, are prone to northerly winds and hope to inspire those new to gardening with our ingenuity and style. To find out more: visit Whitstable Gardens on Facebook. Plant stalls at 19 Joy Lane.

GROUP OPENING

108 WHITSTABLE TOWN GARDENS
Whitstable, CT5 1DD. www.facebook.com/ whitstableopengardens. *Tickets & map at: Stream Walk (CT5 1HJ), Umbrella Centre (CT5 1DD) & The Guinea 31 Island Wall (CT5 1EW).* **Sun 7 June (10-5). Combined adm £7, chd free. Light refreshments at Whitstable Umbrella Centre.**
The magic of Whitstable's gardens lies not in acres of land, but in the ingenuity of town gardeners making the most of their spaces. Here, small plots, hidden corners and the challenges of a seaside climate spark creativity and invention. Gravel, walls, rooftops and shingle are all turned to advantage, with gardeners finding surprising ways to bring colour, texture and life into the town. Some gardens brim with roses and climbers, others create calm through artful planting, while community spaces show what can be achieved when people come together. Exploring them is a celebration of diversity, imagination and the sheer pleasure of plants. No two gardens are alike, yet together they reflect the character and creativity of Whitstable itself. Tickets and map at: Stream Walk (CT5 1HJ), Umbrella Centre (CT5 1DD) and The Guinea 31 Island Wall (CT5 1EW). Refreshments at Stream Walk Community Garden and Whitstable Umbrella Centre. Plant sale at The Guinea No 31 Island Wall.

109 WINDY RIDGE
Dover Road, Guston, Dover, CT15 5EH. Canon David & Mrs Marianne Slater. *1m N of Dover. From Dover Castle take Guston Rd next to Coach Park follow for ¾m, Windy Ridge on L side. Please use Car Park on opp side, signposted. What3words app: charm.slim.rope.* **Sat 30 May (1-5). Adm £6, chd free. Home-made teas.**
Well established series of separate areas in ⅓ acre plot developed since 2008. Shrubs, herbaceous borders, lawns, pergola with wisteria, trees in pots, productive raised beds, soft and top fruit. Self sufficient in water (in most years) with extensive rain harvesting, gravity fed to vegetable area. Paths mostly smooth but narrow in places with some low steps to some seating areas.

110 ♦ THE WORLD GARDEN AT LULLINGSTONE CASTLE
Eynsford, DA4 0JA. Mrs Guy Hart Dyke, 01322 862114, info@lullingstonecastle.co.uk, www.lullingstonecastle.co.uk. *1m from Eynsford. Over Ford Bridge in Eynsford Village. Follow signs to Roman Villa. Keep Roman Villa immed on R then follow Private Rd to Gatehouse. What3words app: slowly.simple.defend.* **For NGS: Sun 21 June (11-5). Adm £12.50, chd free. Light refreshments. For other opening times and information, please phone, email or visit garden website.**
The World Garden is located within the two acre, C18 Walled Garden in the stunning grounds of Lullingstone Castle, where heritage meets cutting-edge horticulture. The garden is laid out in the shape of a miniature map of the world. Thousands of species are represented, all planted out in their respective beds. The World Garden Nursery offers a host of horticultural and homegrown delights, to reflect the unusual and varied planting of the garden. Wheelchairs available upon request.

LANCASHIRE
Merseyside, Greater Manchester

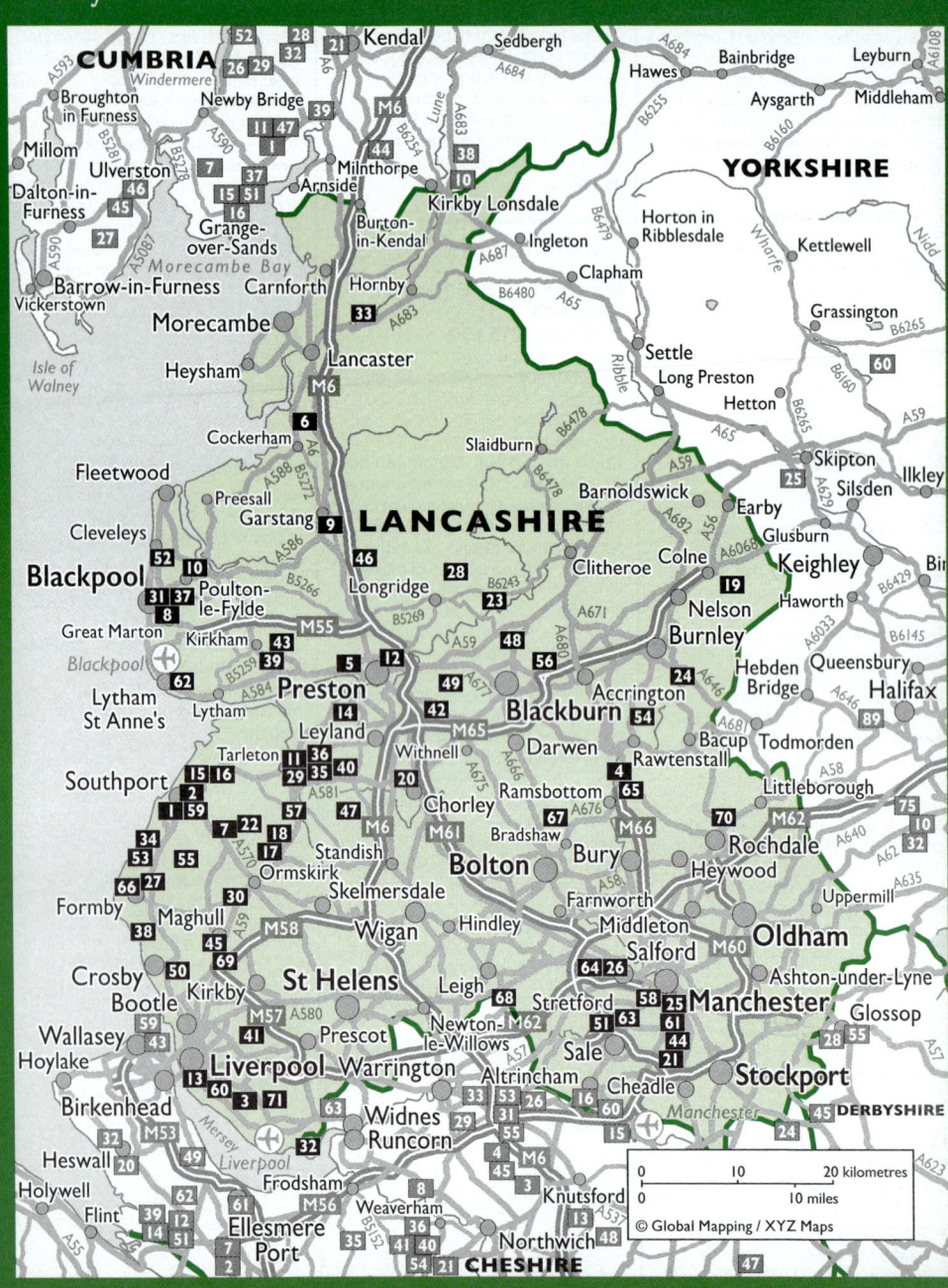

LANCASHIRE

VOLUNTEERS

County Organiser
Marian & Brian Jones
01695 574628
marianandbrian.jones@ngs.org.uk

County Treasurer
Peter Curl
01704 893713
peter.curl@ngs.org.uk

Publicity
Christine Ruth
07740 438994
caruthchris@aol.com

Social Media
Carolyn Waite
07437 527599
carolyn.waite@ngs.org.uk

Booklet Co-ordinator
Brian Jones
(see above)

Booklet Distribution
Marian Jones (see above)

Visits by Arrangement
Marian Jones (see above)

Talks Co-ordinator
Sue Beacon
077092 43986
sbeacon303@gmail.com

Photographer
Norman Rigby
01704 840329
norman.rigby@ngs.org.uk

Assistant County Organisers
Sue Beacon (see above)

Julie Clark 07775 360860
julie.clark.works@gmail.com

Sandra Curl 01704 893713
peter.curl@btinternet.com

Margaret & Geoff Fletcher
01704 567742
margaret.fletcher@ngs.org.uk

Gill & Danny O'Donoghue
07919 216868
gillanddanny.odonoghue@ngs.org.uk

Margaret Richardson 07867 848218
marg254@btinternet.com

Carolyn Waite (see above)

@NGSLancs @NGSLancs @NGSLancs

OPENING DATES

All entries subject to change. For latest information check
www.ngs.org.uk

Map locator numbers are shown to the right of each garden name.

February

Snowdrop Openings

Sunday 8th	
Weeping Ash Garden	68
Sunday 15th	
Weeping Ash Garden	68

May

Saturday 9th	
3 Tower End	66
Sunday 10th	
3 Tower End	66
Saturday 16th	
Halton Park House	33
Sunday 17th	
Halton Park House	33
12 Willow Hey	69
Woolton Village Gardens	71
Saturday 23rd	
Matshead Lodge	46
Sunday 24th	
Bretherton Gardens	11
Drummersdale Crossing Cottage	22
NEW 18 Scarisbrick New Road	59
Saturday 30th	
The Hawes	34
Mill Barn	49
Sunday 31st	
Ainsdale & Birkdale Gardens	1
NEW 52 Crabtree Lane	17
◆ Hazelwood	36
Kington Cottage	43
Mill Barn	49

June

Friday 5th	
NEW 319 Chapel Lane	14
Saturday 6th	
NEW Aspley's Barn	6
NEW Blackpool Carers Centre	8
Hale Village Gardens	32
Mill Barn	49
33 Pershore Grove	53
NEW Rufford Gardens Trail	57
Sunday 7th	
NEW Aspley's Barn	6
NEW Blackpool Carers Centre	8
NEW 319 Chapel Lane	14
NEW 13 Cleveleys Avenue	15
NEW 15 Cleveleys Avenue	16
Hale Village Gardens	32
Mill Barn	49
NEW Rufford Gardens Trail	57
Sefton Park Gardens	60
Wednesday 10th	
HMP Kirkham	39
Saturday 13th	
NEW Elizabeth Gaskell's Garden	25
Ellesmere Park Gardens	26
Holly House	40
Sunday 14th	
Allerton & Grassendale Gardens	3
NEW 173 Bescar Lane	7
Bretherton Gardens	11
Canning and Toxteth Gardens	13
Didsbury Village Gardens	21
Hightown Gardens	38
Wednesday 17th	
HMP Kirkham	39
Saturday 20th	
Dyneley Hall	24
NEW Grow Blackpool @The Grange	31
Sunday 21st	
Dutton Hall	23
Monday 22nd	
NEW Cancerhelp	12
Tuesday 23rd	
NEW Cancerhelp	12
Wednesday 24th	
NEW Cancerhelp	12
Thursday 25th	
NEW Cancerhelp	12
Friday 26th	
NEW Cancerhelp	12

Saturday 27th
NEW Cancerhelp	12
Dyneley Hall	24
Giles Farm	28
◆ Turton Tower Herbaceous Garden	67

Sunday 28th
Arevinti	4
NEW Cancerhelp	12
NEW Formby Gardens	27
Giles Farm	28
Glynwood House	29
Gorse Hill Nature Reserve	30
Kington Cottage	43
18 Moor Drive	50
NEW Topmill Park	65

July

Saturday 4th
Dyneley Hall	24
Jack Green Cottage	42

Sunday 5th
79 Crabtree Lane	18
Jack Green Cottage	42

Saturday 11th
NEW 84 Breck Road	10
Dyneley Hall	24
NEW Mellor & Clayton-le-Dale Gardens	48
204 Norbreck Road	52

Sunday 12th
Ainsdale & Birkdale Gardens	1
NEW 84 Breck Road	10
Mawdesley Gardens	47
NEW Mellor & Clayton-le-Dale Gardens	48
Moss Park Allotments	51
204 Norbreck Road	52

Saturday 18th
18 Highcross Hill	37
NEW Shepherd Road Allotments	62

Sunday 19th
Allerton & Grassendale Gardens	3
Bretherton Gardens	11
Derian House Children's Hospice	20
18 Highcross Hill	37
Maghull Station	45
St Wilfrid's Community Garden	58
32 Wood Hey Grove	70

Saturday 25th
The Quaker Meeting House	54

Sunday 26th
3 Alexandra Mews	2
30 Bonds Lane	9
Glynwood House	29
Kington Cottage	43
The Quaker Meeting House	54
Southlands	63

August

Sunday 2nd
Arevinti	4
Maggie's, Manchester	44
The Shakespearean Garden, Platt Fields Park	61
NEW Topmill Park	65
Weeping Ash Garden	68

Saturday 15th
Rishton Tropical Garden	56
28 Stafford Road	64

Sunday 16th
Rishton Tropical Garden	56
Sefton Park Gardens	60

Saturday 22nd
Ashton Walled Community Gardens	5

Sunday 23rd
NEW 12 Huntsman Wood	41

Sunday 30th
Allerton & Grassendale Gardens	3
Hazel Cottage	35

September

Saturday 5th
28 Stafford Road	64

By Arrangement

Arrange a personalised garden visit with your club, or group of friends, on a date to suit you. See individual garden entries for full details.

Arevinti	4
Ashton Walled Community Gardens	5
NEW Cancerhelp	12
79 Crabtree Lane	18
Dent Hall	19
Giles Farm	28
3 Harrock View (Mawdesley Gardens)	47
Hazel Cottage	35
18 Highcross Hill	37
Kington Cottage	43
Mill Barn	49
18 Moor Drive	50
Moss Park Allotments	51
204 Norbreck Road	52
33 Pershore Grove	53
Rainbag Cottage	55
St Wilfrid's Community Garden	58
14 Saxon Road (Ainsdale & Birkdale Gardens)	1
Southlands	63
28 Stafford Road	64
32 Wood Hey Grove	70

The Hawes

THE GARDENS

GROUP OPENING

1 AINSDALE & BIRKDALE GARDENS
14 Saxon Road, Southport, PR8 2AX. Mrs Margaret Fletcher. ¼ m S of Southport. Gardens signed from A565. **Sun 31 May, Sun 12 July (11-5). Combined adm £6, chd free. Tea, coffee & cake at 12 & 14 Saxon Rd, 5 Cromer Rd & 34 Dunbar Crescent.**

NEW 81 BURNLEY ROAD
PR8 3LP. Julie Prole.
Open on Sun 31 May

NEW 5 CROMER ROAD
PR8 2NH. Helen Rose Carroll.
Open on all dates

NEW 34 DUNBAR CRESCENT
PR8 3AB. Deborah Hirshman & Roy Yule.
Open on Sun 12 July

12 SAXON ROAD
PR8 2AX. Karen & Douglas Traynor.
Open on Sun 31 May

14 SAXON ROAD
PR8 2AX. Margaret & Geoff Fletcher, 01704 567742, margaret.fletcher@ngs.org.uk.
Open on all dates
Visits also by arrangement 1 June to 2 Aug for groups of 10 to 30.

A group formed to showcase some of the beautiful gardens to visit around the Victorian seaside town of Southport. They range in size and design from a walled garden featuring tender perennials to a mature tranquil ever evolving garden. Three new gardens provide good examples of cottage gardening, entertaining spaces and a developing garden full of surprises. Gardens illustrate successful growing of shrubs and perennials in sandy soils.

2 3 ALEXANDRA MEWS
Queens Road, Southport, PR9 9JH. Ian Whitaker. ½ m N of Southport. M6 J26 join M58 for Liverpool, M58 J3 A570 to Ormskirk & then Southport. Turn R onto A565 over r'about 2nd exit, 2nd R onto Alexandra Rd. Garden is at the next junction. **Sun 26 July (10-5). Adm £3.50, chd free. Tea, coffee & cake.**

Large corner plot with deep colourful cottage style beds transformed from an area totally covered in slate. A small wildlife pond overflows into a bog garden and there are two pergolas with climbing roses, honeysuckle and jasmine. Small enclosed seating area, another seating area in sunny position. Summerhouse and plans for a large water feature. Most of the garden is wheelchair accessible. There are some uneven paths.

GROUP OPENING

3 ALLERTON & GRASSENDALE GARDENS
80 Elm Hall Avenue, Liverpool, L18 5JA. Andrew Thomson. 3m S from end of M62. Follow Queens Drive S then follow NGS signage **Sun 14 June, Sun 19 July (11-4). Combined adm £5, chd free. Sun 30 Aug (11-4). Combined adm £4, chd free. Light refreshments at at 80 Elm Hall Drive & Stanlowe View on 14th June & at 146 Mather Ave on 19th July & 30th Aug.**

NEW CALDERSTONES NATURE RESERVE
L18 3JB. Friends of Harthill & Calderstones Park (with land use agreement from Liverpool City Council), www.facebook.com/groups/343882162667503.
Open on Sun 19 July

NEW 80 ELM HALL DRIVE
L18 5JA. Mr Andrew Thomson.
Open on Sun 14 June, Sun 19 July

33 GREENHILL ROAD
L18 6JJ. Tony Rose.
Open on Sun 19 July, Sun 30 Aug

146 MATHER AVENUE
L18 7HB. Barbara Peers.
Open on Sun 19 July, Sun 30 Aug

NEW 9 STANLOWE VIEW
L19 0PX. Pauline & Allastair Davey.
Open on Sun 14 June

The highly acclaimed Calderstones Park Nature Reserve, as featured on Gardeners' World, joins the Allerton and Grassendale group this year for their July opening. And a new large suburban garden joins for the June date. The other private and distinctive Liverpool gardens each have their own special charm, with rare exotics in one, colour themed borders in another, fruit and food production elsewhere.

4 AREVINTI
1 School Court, Ramsbottom, Bury, BL0 0SD. Lavinia Tod, 01706 822474, arevintgarden@gmail.com. 4m N of Bury. Exit at J1 turn R onto A56 signed Ramsbottom continue straight until yellow signs. **Sun 28 June, Sun 2 Aug (11-4). Combined adm with Topmill Park £5, chd free. Sandwiches or quiche with side salad served in our garden room. Visits also by arrangement 8 May to 30 Sept for groups of 6 to 20.**

The garden is enhanced by views of the West Pennine moors. We have four garden rooms, oriental, Italian, English and gravel style gardens, all enhanced with statues, water features, herbaceous perennials and sedum roofs. A talk on the weavers uprising, which remembers the 200 year anniversary, will be held at Porritts tomb at 1pm and 3pm. There is a garden quiz and a fairy house with miniature garden. Miniature railway will be running during the day.

70 inpatients and their families are being supported at the newly opened Horatio's Garden Northern Ireland, thanks to the National Garden Scheme donations.

5 ASHTON WALLED COMMUNITY GARDENS

Pedders Lane, Ashton-on-Ribble, Preston, PR2 1HL. Let's Grow Preston, 07535 836281, letsgrowpreston@gmail.com, www.letsgrowpreston.org. W of Preston. From M6 J30 head towards Preston, turn R onto Blackpool Rd, continue for 3½ m, turn L onto Pedders Lane & next R onto the park. Entrance to walled garden is 50 metres on L. **Sat 22 Aug (10-3). Adm £5, chd free. Tea, coffee & cake. Vegan & gluten free options.** Visits also by arrangement 1 Mar to 1 Sept. We are happy to provide tours through the garden spaces.

Formal raised beds within a walled garden, a peace garden and an edible garden. The formal part of the garden uses plants predominantly from just 3 families; rose, geranium and aster. It is punctuated by grasses and has been designed to demonstrate how diverse and varied plants can be from just the one family. Practical demonstrations and talking tour about the work that Let's Grow Preston does within the PR postcode. This includes improving mental and physical wellbeing, and working with the 41 food hubs of Preston. Flat ground with ramps where necessary to enable access for all. Disabled WC.

6 NEW ASPLEY'S BARN

Main Road, Thurnham, Lancaster, LA2 0DP. Dr Nicholas Walmsley. 4m S of Lancaster. From Lancaster take A588 from Pointer r'about to Thurnham. Parking at Throstle Croft on R. From S, take B5272 to Cockerham then continue N on A598 to Thurnham. Parking at Throstle Croft on L. **Sat 6, Sun 7 June (11-4). Adm £4, chd free. Tea, coffee & cake.**

The ¾ acre garden features 2 large ponds, a variety of mature trees and shrubs together with mixed planting. The open south-facing space of the main lawn offers sunny herbaceous borders and terraced planting whilst 4 separate and interlinked lawns are surrounded by large trees, mature shrubs, hostas, ferns and other shade lovers offering a tranquil and secluded feel.

7 NEW 173 BESCAR LANE

Scarisbrick, Ormskirk, L40 9QR. Graeme & Sarah Mitchell. 4m NW of Ormskirk. What3words app: witless.final.rumble From Ormskirk take A570 to Southport. After 4m turn R onto B5242, Bescar Brow Lane. In ½ m turn L onto Bescar Lane. 2nd property on the R. **Sun 14 June (10.30-4). Adm £4, chd free. Tea, coffee & cake.**

A delightful cottage style garden set in the lovely rural village of Scarisbrick. Main garden comprises wildlife and ornamental ponds with colourful herbaceous borders. The former paddock is home to a polytunnel, cut flower bed and herb garden. Small orchard and wildlife friendly area with mown paths. Various seating areas inc a wisteria covered pergola and beautifully planted vintage containers. Cobbled driveway, slight incline into main garden.

Glynwood House

8 NEW BLACKPOOL CARERS CENTRE
147 Newton Drive, Blackpool, FY3 8LZ. blackpoolcarers.org. ½ m W of Blackpool town centre. On site parking for blue badge holders. Blackpool Carers Centre is located at Beaverbrooks House; easily found on Newton Drive. What3words app: sizes.flown.glow. **Sat 6, Sun 7 June (11-4). Adm £5, chd free. Home-made teas.**
The garden was designed by landscape architect, Laurence Mitchell, to meet the needs of unpaid carers, some as young as five. It features a woodland storytelling space, a bug hotel, raised beds, orchard and plenty of areas for outdoor play alongside the mature, protected trees. 2026 marks the 10th anniversary since our centre was transformed by DIY SOS, Children in Need and the Beaverbrooks Charitable Trust.

9 30 BONDS LANE
Garstang, Preston, PR3 1ZB. Mr Alan & Mrs Liz Pearson. ½ m S of Garstang town centre. From the South follow the B6430 N from the A6 (signed Garstang). From the North follow the B6430 S through the town & follow the signs for Preston. Parking adjacent to the property. **Sun 26 July (11-5). Adm £5, chd free. Tea, coffee & cake.**
A 90 yr old garden, which has been in the hands of the current owners for 30 yrs. To the front are formal lawns and beds of annuals with topiary and a side bed of perennials and gatepost features To the rear are 3 lawned areas with one now being left as meadow and orchard. A varied planting throughout with a lot of hostas, a year-round garden with many features, seating and vistas. A steep gradient to the drive otherwise mainly accessible.

10 NEW 84 BRECK ROAD
Poulton-Le-Fylde, FY6 7HT. Mrs Lesley Middleton. M55 J3 towards Fleetwood on A585\586. L at T- lights signed Poulton Plaiz (Garstang Rd). L at 2nd T- lights on to Moorland Rd. Parking towards end. Corner house with entrance on Moorland Rd. **Sat 11, Sun 12 July (11-4). Adm £4, chd free. Tea, coffee & cake.**
A wrap around garden on corner plot. Inc shady areas, wildlife pond, mature shrubs, herbaceous perennials, alliums, verbena, circium and hostas. Courtyard area with pots. Town Crier to open garden at 11am on Sat 11 July. Live Ukelele band at 2 pm both days, weather permitting. Cash only for refreshments.

GROUP OPENING

11 BRETHERTON GARDENS
Bretherton, Leyland, PR26 9AN. 8m SW of Preston. Between Southport and Preston, from A59, take B5247 towards Chorley for 1m. Gardens signed from South Rd (B5247). Maps and tickets at all gardens. **Sun 24 May, Sun 14 June, Sun 19 July (12-5). Combined adm £6, chd free. Home-made teas at Bretherton Congregational Church from 12 noon.**

HAZEL COTTAGE, 6 SOUTH VIEW
PR26 9AN. John & Kris Jolley. (See separate entry)

LANESIDE, 10 BAMFORDS FOLD
PR26 9AL. Robert & Ann Alty.

OWL BARN
PR26 9AD. Richard & Barbara Farbon.

PALATINE, 6 BAMFORDS FOLD
PR26 9AL. Alison Ryan.

A group of contrasting gardens spaced across an attractive award-winning village with a conservation area. Hazel Cottage's former Victorian orchard plot has evolved into a series of themed spaces while the adjoining land has a natural pond, meadow and developing native woodland. Owl Barn has herbaceous borders filled with cottage garden and hardy plants, a productive kitchen garden with fruit, vegetables and cut flowers. There are two ponds with water features and secluded seating areas. Palatine is a garden of 3 contrasting spaces started in 2019 around a modern bungalow to attract wildlife and give year-round interest. In the same cul-de-sac, Laneside is still a work in progress. The garden is on 3 sides of the bungalow, with mature shrubs and trees, a rose garden, perennials and a small fruit growing area. Also an inherited woodland walk which is a current project. Home-made preserves for sale. Full wheelchair access at Palatine, other gardens have narrow paths or gravel limiting accessibility.

12 NEW CANCERHELP
Vine House, 22 Cromwell Road, Ribbleton, Preston, PR2 6YB. Mrs Jeanette Smalley, 01772 793344, info@cancerhelppreston. co.uk, www.facebook.com/cancerhelpprestonltd. 5mins from junction 31 of the M6. On the corner of Langdale Rd & Cromwell Rd. The Centre has signage in the corner of the borders at the intersection of the 2 roads. What3words app: Sticks. tools.noted. **Daily Mon 22 June to Sun 28 June (10-5). Adm by donation. Light refreshments. Teas, coffees, cordials & cakes available.** Visits also by arrangement June & July for groups of up to 10.
Work on our 'Sanctuary' garden began in 2025, thanks to the generosity of the National Garden Scheme's Garden for Health funding programme. This special garden, with subtle planting will provide a space for comfort and reflection. Opening for the National Garden Scheme in 2026 will be a symbol of hope, growth and renewal in supporting clients on their journey. There will be an opportunity to chat to the CancerHelp Team about how the garden has been integrated into the services that we provide. The garden has been designed for wheelchair access and there are routes into the garden avoiding steps.

In 2025 we awarded over £288,800 in Community Garden Grants, supporting 114 community garden projects.

GROUP OPENING

13 CANNING AND TOXTETH GARDENS
27 Canning Street, Liverpool, L8 7NN. *Georgian Quarter. Parking close to gardens on Hope St (Pay) also Mulgrave St & Granby St (Free)* **Sun 14 June (1-5). Combined adm £6, chd free. Light refreshments.**

27 CANNING STREET
L8 7NN. Mrs Waltraud Boxall.

 **45 CANNING STREET**
L8 7NN. Mr Bob & Mrs Abi Pointing.

EL JARDIN DE LA NUESTRA SENORA
30 Catharine St, Liverpool, L8 7NL. R.C. Archdiocese of Liverpool.

GRANBY BACK ALLEY GARDEN
37-39 Cairns Street, Liverpool, L8 2UW.

GRANBY WINTER GARDEN
37-39 Cairns Street, Liverpool, L8 2UW. Granby Four Streets CLT, www.granby4streetsclt.co.uk.

GRAPES COMMUNITY FOOD GARDEN
Windsor Street, Liverpool, L8 1XE. Squash Liverpool, squashliverpool.co.uk.

PAKISTAN ASSOCIATION LIVERPOOL WELLBEING GARDEN
68A Mulgrave Street, Liverpool, L8 2TF. Pakistan Association Liverpool.

THE SQUASH CAFE GARDEN
112 - 114 Windsor Street, Liverpool, L8 8EQ. Squash Liverpool, squashliverpool.co.uk.

An elegant garden in the Georgian quarter joins the range of gardens from the grand Georgian terraces, to the restored Victorian streets. They include Granby Winter Garden and the back alley garden recently featured on Gardeners' World. The winter garden was created out of derelict houses, in an area being beautifully regenerated thanks to the efforts of local people. They join the unusual classically designed Spanish garden of St Philip Neri church. El Jardin de la Nuestra Senora was created on a bomb site after WW2. The church's exquisite Byzantine interior, designed by PS Gilby, will also

be open. In contrast to the Georgian Quarter classicism are the vibrant Grapes Community Food Garden and Squash Cafe garden in Windsor Street, plus the Wellbeing garden of the Liverpool Pakistan Association. It is a fascinating group, all within the historic heart of Liverpool, with many architecturally important buildings including Liverpool's Anglican cathedral, the largest cathedral in Europe.

✤ 🍵 •))

14 **319 CHAPEL LANE**
New Longton, Preston, PR4 4AB. Mr Stephen & Mrs Karen Brooke. *4m S of Preston & 4m from M6 (J29) & M65 (J1). From the M6/M65 Motorways follow the signs for the Lancashire Police HQ. From A59 follow signs for New Longton. What3words app: traps.rust.town.* **Fri 5 June (2-7); Sun 7 June (11-5). Adm £5, chd free. Home-made teas.**

Newly established in 2022, this long, flat garden backs onto a communal field and recreation area. Designed to support birds and wildlife, the garden features include a large wildlife pond with bog garden, raised produce beds, a wide herbaceous border for pollinators, and seating areas with summerhouse. Gravel drive and Victorian outhouses support clematis and trailing vegetables. Access to a large dog walking area via garden gate.

🐕 🍵 •))

15 NEW **13 CLEVELEYS AVENUE**
Southport, PR9 9SS. Susan Rhodes. *3m N of Southport. Pls park on Cleveleys Rd not the Ave. What3words app: parade.eaten.sweep. Signed from Marshside Rd.* **Sun 7 June (11-5). Combined adm with 15 Cleveleys Avenue £5, chd free. Tea, coffee & cake.**

Set among Marshide's shrimpers' cottages, this sunny garden has winding gravel paths, borders of shrubs, trees and wildflowers, and a water feature beneath a covered seating area. A large studio and terrace add a contemporary touch. The owner favours a natural, gently evolving style, creating a welcoming space full of charm, wildlife and discovery. Flat garden, couple of steps at the end which leads to the garden studio.

♿ 🍵

16 NEW **15 CLEVELEYS AVENUE**
Marshside, Southport, PR9 9SS. Meryl Pickstone-Blundell. *3m N of Southport. What3words app: parade.eaten.sweep. Pls park on Cleveleys Rd not the Ave. Signed from Marshside Rd* **Sun 7 June (11-5). Combined adm with 13 Cleveleys Avenue £5, chd free. Tea, coffee & cake.**

A 7 yr retirement project from a novice gardener, creating 3 distinguishable garden sections. A garden which has an evergreen winter framework and planting, which changes to provide seasonal interest and colour. Interspersed with a variety of potted plants are water features and an eclectic selection of ornaments and sheds! There is only one small step leading to the main garden.

♿ 🍵

17 **52 CRABTREE LANE**
Burscough, Ormskirk, L40 0RN. Mrs Elizabeth Crabtree. *3m NE of Ormskirk. What3words app: perky.kickbacks.unroll. Take A59 Preston-Liverpool Rd L onto Higgins Lane, R onto Crabtree Lane. Parking available at Slipway Pub. Walk over the canal bridge, down the towpath to the house.* **Sun 31 May (11-4). Adm £5, chd free. Tea, coffee & cake.**

A long, rural garden with flowing, informal planting: a patio adjoined by wide borders, a lawn beneath a large weeping willow, formal Koi pond, and an orchard with free-roaming chickens. Our 3 acre field supports our smallholding with beehives, a goat, sheep, and hens. There are polytunnels, raised beds, a wildlife pond, and areas for soft fruit, vegetables and cut flowers.

✤ 🍵 •))

18 79 CRABTREE LANE
Burscough, L40 0RW. Sandra & Peter Curl, 01704 893713, peter.curl@btinternet.com, www.youtube.com/watch?v=CW7S8nB_iX8. *3m NE of Ormskirk. A59 Preston - Liverpool Rd. From N before bridge R into Redcat Lane signed for Martin Mere. From S over 2nd bridge L into Redcat Lane after ³⁄₄ m L into Crabtree Lane.* **Sun 5 July (11-4). Adm £5, chd free. Home-made teas.** Visits also by arrangement June to Aug. Includes an introductory talk on how the garden developed.

85 Ribchester Road, Mellor & Clayton-le-Dale Gardens

¾ acre year-round plantsperson's garden with many rare and unusual plants. Herbaceous borders and island beds, pond, rockery, grasses and autumn hot bed. Many stone features built with reclaimed materials. Shrubs and rhododendrons, Koi pond and waterfall, hosta and fern walk. Gravel garden with Mediterranean plants. Patio surrounded by shrubs and raised alpine bed. Trees give areas for shade loving plants. Many beds replanted recently. Many stone buildings and features. Flat grass paths.

19 DENT HALL
Colne Road, Trawden, Colne, BB8 8NX. Chris Whitaker-Webb & Joanne Smith, 01282 861892, denthall@tiscali.co.uk. *10 min from end of M65. Turn L at end of M65. Follow A6068 for 2m; just after 3rd r'about turn R down B6250. After 1½m, in front of church, turn R, signed Carry Bridge. Keep R, follow road up hill, garden on R after 300yds.* **Visits by arrangement 1 June to 13 Sept for groups of 10+. Adm £7.50, chd free. Home-made teas.**

Nestled in the oldest part of Trawden villlage and rolling Lancashire countryside, this mature and evolving country garden surrounds a 400 yr old grade II listed property (not open); featuring a parterre, lawns, herbaceous borders, shrubbery, wildlife pond with bridge to seating area and a hidden summerhouse in a woodland area. Plentiful seating throughout. Some uneven paths and gradients.

20 DERIAN HOUSE CHILDREN'S HOSPICE
Chancery Road, Chorley, PR7 1DH. www.derianhouse.co.uk. *Astley Village, Chorley. From B5252 pass Chorley Hospital on L, at r'about 1st exit to Chancery Lane. Hospice on L after 0.4m. What3words app: bridge.gossiping. exotic.* **Sun 19 July (10-4). Adm £3, chd free. Tea, coffee & cake.**

Derian House cares for more than 400 seriously ill babies, children, young people and their families from across the North West. The gardens at the hospice offer tranquil outdoor spaces for children and their families to spend precious time together. Family activities, home-made cakes and plant sale. Gardens and refreshments area are wheelchair friendly, accessible parking and WC facilities also available.

GROUP OPENING

21 DIDSBURY VILLAGE GARDENS
Manchester, M20 3GZ. *5m S of city centre. From M60 J5 follow signs to Northenden. Turn R at T-lights onto Barlow Moor Rd to Didsbury. From M56 follow A34 to Didsbury.* **Sun 14 June (12-5). Combined adm £7, chd free. Home-made teas at 3 Pine Road, M20 6UY. Tickets from 68 Brooklawn Drive or any of the gardens.**

68 BROOKLAWN DRIVE
M20 3GZ. Anne & Jim Britt, www.annebrittdesign.com.

3 THE DRIVE
M20 6HZ. Peter Clare & Sarah Keedy, www.peterclaregardendesign.co.uk.

1 OSBORNE STREET
M20 2QZ. Richard & Teresa Pearce-Regan.

40 PARRS WOOD AVENUE
M20 5ND. Tom Johnson.

NEW 3 PINE ROAD
M20 6UY. Mrs Fiona & Mr Ian Hall.

38 WILLOUGHBY AVENUE
M20 6AS. Simon Hickey.

This year we have 6 very beautiful and individual gardens to visit in the attractive suburb of Didsbury. There is so much to see and inspire in these gardens, from our traditional cottage gardens complete with a wrought iron verandah, new huge water bowl, with alliums, roses, clematis and topiary, to the soft lines of a very natural wildlife friendly garden buzzing with insects. If you have shady conditions you could learn so much from one of the best shady gardens that you'll find in a suburban setting and many tips on creating beautiful planterly privacy. Our gardens offer a diverse range of water features and inspirational, stylish and wildlife friendly planting ideas - all within our relatively small garden spaces which are a feast to the eye and full of detail to imitate at home. Wheelchair access to some gardens.

3 Harrock View, Mawdesley Gardens

22 DRUMMERSDALE CROSSING COTTAGE
Wholesome Lane, Scarisbrick, Ormskirk, L40 9SW. Mrs Janet & Mr Mike Hinton. *500 yds SE of Bescar Ln Railway Stn. There is no parking at the garden. Postcode L40 9RB will take you to parking in adjacent meadow. Follow yellow signs from Drummersdale Lane. What3words app: wedge.flock. blemishes. OS Grid SD 399 144.* **Sun 24 May (11-4). Adm £4, chd free. Home-made cakes, cream teas inc vegan options.**
Beautiful ½ acre country garden with open views to adjacent farmland. Various trees and shrubs inc mature rhododendrons and wisteria. Herbaceous perennial beds. Wildlife ponds, summerhouse with viewing window overlooking beehives. Shaded areas with ferns and hostas. Polytunnel with a variety of fruit, vegetables and vine. Meadow, orchard and woodland walks. Vegetable patch and wildflower areas are under development.

23 DUTTON HALL
Gallows Lane, Ribchester, PR3 3XX. Mr & Mrs A H Penny, www.duttonhall.co.uk. *2m NE of Ribchester. Signed from B6243 & B6245 Directions on website also. What3words app: copying.botanists. mostly.* **Sun 21 June (1-5). Adm £7.50, chd free. Home-made teas. Donation to Plant Heritage.**
An increasing range of unusual trees and shrubs have been added to the existing collection of old fashioned roses, inc rare and unusual varieties and Plant Heritage National Collection of Pemberton Hybrid Musk roses. Formal garden at front with backdrop of C17 house (not open). Analemmatic Sundial, pond, meadow areas all with extensive views over Ribble valley. Wildlife trail. Plant Heritage plant stall with unusual varieties for sale.

24 DYNELEY HALL
Buck Clough Lane, Cliviger, Burnley, BB11 3RE. Peregrine Towneley. *What3words app: breed. future.chief. From Todmorden follow A646 for 7m passing under low bridge. After 30 yds turn L. From Burnley follow A646 for 1½m. Approaching low bridge turn R. Then follow yellow signs.* **Every Sat 20 June to 11 July (11-3). Adm £6, chd free. Tea, coffee & cake.**
2½ acre Pennine woodland garden. Herbaceous borders. Rhododendrons, azaleas, tree peonies, old-fashioned roses, shrubs and a collection of rare and interesting trees. Dyneley garden was designed by the influential English garden designer James Russell in the 1960s. The garden has evolved to include influences from the Italian gardens of 'Ninfa' and has stunning views to the wider landscape. Partial wheelchair access to some areas of the garden due to changes in levels and uneven paths.

25 NEW ELIZABETH GASKELL'S GARDEN
84 Plymouth Grove, Manchester, M13 9LW. Ms Sally Jastrzebski-Lloyd, elizabethgaskellhouse. co.uk/about-elizabeth-gaskells-house/the-garden. *1m from Manchester city centre & main railway stations. Elizabeth Gaskell's House is located on the A5184, nr to Manchester Royal Infirmary Follow brown signs from the A6 & A34. Free on street parking or NCP parking at hospital.* **Sat 13 June (11-4). Adm £5, chd free. Tea, coffee & cake.**
Elizabeth Gaskell's garden opened in 2014 after extensive research and restoration work and is now an urban oasis one mile from the city centre. With a layout based on an 1850s map volunteers have recreated the garden using period plants and those referenced in Elizabeth Gaskell's writings. The garden has twice received the Britain in Bloom Gold award. The Whitworth & Pankhurst Centre is nearby. With wide, flat pathways the garden is fully accessible with step free access throughout. Accessible WC also available.

The National Garden Scheme funded six Macmillan Nurses in their roles across England, Wales and Northern Ireland in 2025.

GROUP OPENING

26 ELLESMERE PARK GARDENS
35 Ellesmere Road, Eccles, Manchester, M30 9FE. Enid Noronha. *4m S from central Manchester. At M602 junction turn L onto Gilda Brook Rd, then R onto Half Edge Ln. Follow round to Monton Rd & turn R onto Stafford Rd. At the top turn L onto Ellesmere Rd then R x2 for 11 Westminster Rd.* **Sat 13 June (11.30-4). Combined adm £7, chd free. Tea, coffee & cake at 35 Ellesmere Rd, hot dogs at 20 Stafford Rd & tea & biscuits at 11 Westminster Rd.**

35 ELLESMERE ROAD
M30 9FE. Enid Noronha.

20 STAFFORD ROAD
M30 9HW. Mrs Paula Gibson.

11 WESTMINSTER ROAD
M30 9HF. George & Lynne Meakin.

The group consists of 3 diverse suburban gardens in adjoining streets in Eccles. 35 Ellesmere Road is a cottage style garden with walkways, palisade, greenhouse and raised beds with vegetables and herbs. Lawns with box hedges. Mature fruit and other trees. At 11 Westminster Road there is a pretty front garden with topiary chickens, well-stocked with perennials, mature trees, and box hedging. The garden is divided by a trellis and rose arch which separates the flower beds and lawn from the fruit growing area, and there are a large number of fuchsias grown in pots. Finally at 20 Stafford Road the garden features mature trees and shrubs alongside many recent additions. An ongoing project involves upcycling items the garden owners find interesting. The owners like to put bold colours and statements in wherever they can to enable colour year-round, a large wildlife pond has been added and a pergola with climbing plants. Some areas with only partial wheelchair access.

LANCASHIRE

GROUP OPENING

27 NEW FORMBY GARDENS
33 Brewery Lane, Formby, L37 7DY. Sue & Dave Hughes. *7m S of Southport. Gardens signed from A565 Formby bypass. Maps and tickets at all gardens.* **Sun 28 June (11-3). Combined adm £5, chd free. Tea, coffee & cake at Brewery Lane & Moss Side, where a live band will be playing.**

33 BREWERY LANE
L37 7DY. Sue & Dave Hughes.

BRIDGE INN COMMUNITY FARM
L37 0AF. bridgeinnfarm.org.uk.

4 BUTTERMERE CLOSE
L37 2YB. Marilyn & Alan Tippett.

1 A MOSS SIDE
L37 3JY. John & Dina Nixon

NEW 7 PINEWOOD AVENUE
L37 2HY. Lucy McIver.

A new group for 2026 featuring 4 gardens and a community farm. Each garden has its own features and themes. 33 Brewery Lane has a paved terrace, colour themed raised beds and lawns. The productive area has raised beds of vegetables and cut flowers raised from seed. 4 Buttermere Close is made on shallow, sandy soil with a mixture of shrubs and perennials, many of special interest and adapted to a coastal site. A small pond for wildlife and a gravel garden being established. 1A Moss Side has front, back and courtyard gardens encircling the house. Large beech trees, various young and mature fruit trees, vegetables, soft fruit and herbs in raised beds. Greenhouses, ponds and rockery. 7 Pinewood Avenue is a garden with shrubs, perennials, wildlife pond, wildflower area, raised beds for cut flowers and vegetables. The garden attracts lots of birds. Bridge Inn Community Farm is a beautiful 4 acre smallholding with plants, flowers, trees and ponds and views looking out over the countryside. The Farm provides education and work based activities for adults with special educational needs.

♿ 🐕 ❀ ☕ ♪

28 GILES FARM
Four Acre Lane, Thornley, Preston, PR3 2TD. Kirsten & Phil Brown, 07925 603246, phil.brown32@aol.com. *3m NE of Longridge. Pass through Longridge & follow signs for Chipping. After 2m turn R at the old school up Hope Lane. Turn L at the top & continue to the farm where there is ample parking.* **Sat 27, Sun 28 June (12-5). Adm £6, chd free. Tea, coffee & cake. A wide selection of home-made cakes & sandwiches.** Visits also by arrangement 29 June to 17 July for groups of 20 to 40. Guided tour with hand drawn map inc for groups followed by refreshments.
Nestled high on the side of Longridge Fell, with beautiful long-reaching views across the Ribble valley, the gardens surround the old farmhouse and buildings. The gardens are ever evolving and inc an acre of perennial wildflower meadows, wildlife ponds, woodland areas and cottage gardens. There are plentiful areas to sit and take in the views. There are steps and uneven surfaces in the gardens.

🐕 ❀ ☕ ♪

29 GLYNWOOD HOUSE
Eyes Lane, Bretherton, Leyland, PR26 9AS. Terry & Sue Riding. *5m W of Leyland. Turn onto Eyes Lane by Bretherton War Memorial. After 50 yds take the R fork, after 100 yds follow the road around to the L. Glynwood House is a further 200 yds on L.* **Sun 28 June, Sun 26 July (11-5). Adm £4, chd free. Picnics welcome, with plenty of seating in the garden. There is also a wide range of refreshments at the Old Corn Mill Café a 4 min drive away.**
Set in a peaceful rural location with spectacular views. Highlights of this ¾ acre plant lovers' garden include themed mixed borders with many rare and unusual plants, a wildlife pond with cascade water feature and meandering paths through a woodland shaded area. A patio garden, surrounded by a large pergola, features a kinetic sycamore seed sculpture. Many places to sit, relax and enjoy the views. Previous runner-up in the Daily Mail National Garden competition and past regional finalist in the NGS 'Nations Favourite Garden' vote. Wheelchair access to all areas apart from woodland paths.

♿ 🐕 ❀ 🚗 🪑 ♪

30 GORSE HILL NATURE RESERVE
Holly Lane, Aughton, Ormskirk, L39 7HB. Jonathan Atkins (Reserve Manager), www.gorsehillnaturereserve.co.uk. *1½ m S of Ormskirk. A59 from L'pool past Royal Oak pub take 1st L Gaw Hill Lane turn R Holly Lane. From Preston follow A59 across T-lights at A570 J & at r'about. After Xing lights turn R Gaw Hill Lane turn R Holly Lane.* **Sun 28 June (12-4). Adm £4, chd free. Tea, coffee & cake. Our Gorse Hill Heritage Orchard apple juice is also available.**
Paths lead you through our mixed broadleaf and coniferous 6 acre woodland taking you past a wildlife pond and boardwalk flanked with wild flowers. Mown grassy paths through our 5 acre wildflower meadow allow you to stroll through and enjoy the wild flowers, butterflies and bees. Our polytunnel and heritage orchard are also open for self guided walks. Stunning views across the Lancashire Plain.

🐕 ❀ ☕ ♪

31 NEW GROW BLACKPOOL @THE GRANGE
Dinmore Avenue, Blackpool, FY3 7RW. Angela Nagorski. *1m E of Blackpool town centre. Based at the @TheGrange Community Centre, Bathurst Ave, Grange Park. Car parking adjacent to the building. What3words app: ledge.guitar.cover.* **Sat 20 June (11-3). Adm £4, chd free. Tea, coffee & cake.**
A productive garden with areas that are given over to growing fruit, vegetables and herbs. Two large polytunnels, raised beds and areas of seating are placed alongside an accessible modern space. Dead hedges have been created to provide supportive habitat for wildlife and organic materials are composted on site.

♿ 🐕 ❀ ☕ 🪑 ♪

GROUP OPENING

32 HALE VILLAGE GARDENS
2 Pheasant Field, Hale Village, Liverpool, L24 5SD. Roger & Tania Craine. *6m S of M62 J6. Take A5300, A562 towards L'pool, then A561 & then L for Hale. From S L'pool head for the airport then L sign for Hale. The 82A bus from Widnes/Runcorn to L'pool has village stops.* **Sat 6, Sun 7 June (1-5). Combined adm £5, chd free. Home-made teas at 2 Pheasant Field & 33 Hale Rd.**

LANCASHIRE 303

4 CHURCH ROAD
L24 4BA. Ms Chris Chesters.

54 CHURCH ROAD
L24 4BA. Norma & Ray Roe.

66 CHURCH ROAD
L24 4BA. Liz Kelly-Hines & David Hines.

2 PHEASANT FIELD
L24 5SD. Roger & Tania Craine.

WHITECROFT, 33 HALE ROAD
L24 5RB. Donna & Bob Richards.

The delightful village of Hale is set in rural South Merseyside between Widnes and Liverpool Airport. It is home to the cottage, sculpture and grave of the famous giant known as the Childe of Hale. Five gardens of various sizes have been developed by their present owners. There are 2 gardens (a large skilfully landscaped one and a beautiful contemporary one) to the west of the village and 3 delightful gardens in Church Rd to the east of the village.

33 HALTON PARK HOUSE
Halton Park, Halton, Lancaster, LA2 6PD. Mr & Mrs Duncan Bowring. *7min drive from both J34 & 35 M6. On Park Lane, approx 1½m from Halton or Caton. Park Lane accessed either from Low Rd or High Rd out of Halton. From Low Rd turn into Park Lane through pillars over cattle grid.* **Sat 16, Sun 17 May (11-4). Adm £6, chd free. BBQ over lunch time. Home-made cakes and cream teas.**
Approx 6 acres of garden, with gravel paths leading through large mixed herbaceous borders, terraces, orchard with developing wildflower meadow and terraced vegetable beds. Wildlife pond and woodland walk in dell area, extensive lawns, large greenhouse and herb garden. Plenty of places to sit and rest to enjoy the view. Gravel paths (some sloping) give access to viewing points over the majority of the garden. Hard standing around the house.

34 THE HAWES
Sandringham Road, Ainsdale, Southport, PR8 2NZ. Niall & Joan Roy. *5m S of Southport. From A565, at r'about turn R into Station Rd through Ainsdale Village. Take 1st R after level crossing and drive to far end of Sandringham Rd.*

Sat 30 May (11-4). Adm £5, chd free. Light refreshments.
A 6 acre woodland garden plus numerous lawns and borders with stunning summer colour as well as several water features. The formal garden is designed with an arts and crafts theme. A long woodland walk leads you through rhododendron and pinewoods where you may glance shy red squirrels. The garden has several wilding areas.

35 HAZEL COTTAGE
6 South View, Bretherton, Leyland, PR26 9AN. John & Kris Jolley, 01772 600896, 07791 210481, jolley@johnjolley.plus.com. **Evening opening Sun 30 Aug (4-8). Adm £4, chd free. Prosecco & soft drinks available. Opening with Bretherton Gardens on Sun 24 May, Sun 14 June, Sun 19 July. Visits also by arrangement May to Sept for groups of 10 to 30.**
Wildlife and plant lovers' garden developed from Victorian cottage plot and adjoining field. Series of themed spaces to delight the senses and the mind. Courtyard, ponds, mixed borders, kitchen garden, perennial meadow, orchard, developing woodland, many places to sit and relax.

36 ◆ HAZELWOOD
North Road, Bretherton, Leyland, PR26 9AY. Jacqueline Iddon & Thompson Dagnall, 01772 601433, jacquelineiddon@gmail.com, www.jacquelineiddon.co.uk. *8m SW of Preston. Between Southport and Preston, from A59, take B5247 for 1m then L onto B5248. Garden signed from North Rd.* **For NGS: Sun 31 May (1-4). Adm £4, chd free. Cream teas. For other opening times and information, please phone, email or visit garden website.**
1½ acre garden and hardy plant nursery, gravel garden with pots and seating area, shrubs, herbaceous borders, stream-fed pond with woodland walk. New Alpine House, cutting and vegetable garden. Oak-framed summerhouse, log cabin sculpture gallery fronted by cottage garden beds. Talk/demonstration by Jacqueline Iddon 'Right Plant Right Place' at 2 pm. Extensive sculpture collection, the work of Thompson Dagnall, Printmaking Studio with prints and cards by Tilly Dagnall.

Majority of the garden is accessible to wheelchairs.

37 18 HIGHCROSS HILL
Poulton-le-Fylde, FY6 8BT. Simon & Julie Clark, 07775 360860, julie.clark.works@gmail.com. *3m W of Blackpool Tower. What3words app: holds.entry.tuned. M55 J3 A585/A586 to Poulton. At 4th lights turn L; Hardhorn Rd. Then R; Longhouse Lane & L onto High Cross Rd. Garden is off Staining Old Rd. Parking on High Cross Hill for those with limited mobility.* **Sat 18, Sun 19 July (11-4). Adm £4, chd free. Tea, coffee & cake. Visits also by arrangement 1 June to 28 Aug for groups of 5 to 12.**
Relaxed garden on sloping plot accessed via 10 steps. Colour-themed perennials; fig, apple and plum trees. Some raised beds and gravel border. Retreat into the cosy 'orb' with your cake. Live music at 2pm.

GROUP OPENING

38 HIGHTOWN GARDENS
Mark Road, Hightown, Liverpool, L38 0BG. Barbara Jones. *11m N of Liverpool & 11m S of Southport. M57/58 join A5758 Brooms Cross at r'about 2nd exit A565. At lights L onto B5193/Orrell Hill Lane. Turn R Moss Lane. Turn L onto Alt Rd, then R (over bridge) Kerslake Way & follow NGS signs at r'about.* **Sun 14 June (12-4). Combined adm £6, chd free. Tea, coffee & cake at 7 Mark Rd.**

11 BLUNDELL AVENUE
L38 9ED. Karen Rimmer.

7 MARK ROAD
L38 0BG. Barbara & Derek Jones.

WEST BANK, SCHOOL ROAD
L38 0BN. Barbara MacArthur.

A welcoming group of gardens in the village of Hightown. Visit a plantswoman's quirky garden full of surprises, a recently-built, contemporary garden with pond feature and a small garden with a modern touch that's full of colour. There is wheelchair access to West Bank in School Road and the Mark Road garden.

39 HMP KIRKHAM
Freckleton Road, Kirkham, Preston, PR4 2RN. Diane Clare. *The prison is located off the A583 (Freckleton Rd). Visitors should park at the farm shop which is 1st R as you turn off Freckleton Rd for the prison. Overspill parking also avail in general visitor car park.* **Wed 10, Wed 17 June (10-12). Adm £10. Pre-booking essential, please visit www.ngs.org.uk for information & booking. Light refreshments at the farm shop near the entrance.**
The prison has 150 acres of farm and grounds maintained by prisoners learning horticultural and agricultural skills. The site has gardens with herbaceous borders, lawns, heritage orchard, allotments, greenhouses, wildflower meadow, wellness garden, wildlife and fish ponds and extensive woodland. You will be accompanied by the farm manager who will give a guided tour of the farm and grounds. Good mobility essential as the walks are on uneven ground and mini buses are used to take visitors up to the farm. Produce, inc fruit, veg, plants and meat from rare breeds, is sold through the farm shop. Please note we will need names of all visitors plus NI numbers ahead of your visit.

40 HOLLY HOUSE
289 Moor Road, Croston, Leyland, PR26 9HP. Mrs Elaine Raper. *Situated on the A581, approx 200 metres past the Highfield pub if coming from Leyland area.* **Sat 13 June (11-5). Adm £4, chd free. Home-made teas.**
Large garden, approx an acre of perennial beds with mature trees. Pond with decking area leading to wooded area beyond with rill. Two wisteria clad pergolas, parterre with adjacent gazebo. Mostly accessible to the main parts of the garden. Wood behind pond not accessible for wheelchairs.

41 12 HUNTSMAN WOOD
West Derby, Liverpool, L12 0HY. Mr Graham Moore. *By Croxteth Country Park on a private housing estate 5 mins from Queens Drive, the main artery road running through Liverpool. Some on street parking & more on Coachman's Drive.* **Sun 23 Aug (11-4). Adm £3.50, chd free. Tea, coffee & cake.**
An exotic and tropical garden with impressive and mature specimens of tree ferns, palms, banana plants and other plant rarities. There is a large koi pond and a rockery with a waterfall. The garden has various pathways leading to different parts of the garden. There are two patios with plenty of seating. Not all parts of the garden are wheelchair accessible due to the narrow pathways.

42 JACK GREEN COTTAGE
Mill House Lane, Brindle, Chorley, PR6 8NS. Aurelia & Peter McCann. *5m N Chorley. From Chorley A6 turn R at r'about on B5256 Westwood Rd then L at r'about on B5256 Sandy Lane through Brindle for 2m, then L on Hill House Lane for ¾m. Turn L on Oram Rd for 200yd.* **Sat 4, Sun 5 July (11-4). Adm £5, chd free. Tea, coffee & cake.**
This 2¾ acre garden has been lovingly restored, developed and improved in the last 15 yrs. With long borders of cottage style plants, Japanese style garden, herb garden, orchards, soft fruit bed and vegetable plots, there is a surprise around every corner. Secluded BBQ area, Victorian-style greenhouse, a recycled bottle greenhouse and a willow tunnel are but few of the delights awaiting you. Not all areas suitable for wheelchair users & should ideally be accompanied as some parts of the garden may be difficult to navigate.

43 KINGTON COTTAGE
Kirkham Road, Treales, Preston, PR4 3SD. Mrs Linda Kidd, 01772 683005. *M55 J3. Take A585 to Kirkham, exit Preston St, L into Carr Lane to Treales village. Cottage on L.* **Sun 31 May, Sun 28 June, Sun 26 July (10-4). Adm £4, chd free. Tea, coffee & cake. Visits also by arrangement 31 May to 31 Aug for groups of 8 to 25.**
Nestling in the beautiful village of Treales this generously sized Japanese garden has many authentic and unique Japanese features, alongside its 2 ponds linked by a stream. The stroll garden leads down to the tea house garden. The planting and the meandering pathways blend together to create a tranquil meditative garden in which to relax. New additions complete four Japanese garden styles. Bonsai display at the July opening. Wheelchair access to some areas, uneven paths.

44 MAGGIE'S, MANCHESTER
Kinnaird Road, Manchester, M20 4QL. Laura Birch, www.maggies.org/our-centres/maggies-manchester. *At the end of Kinnaird Rd which is off Wilmslow Rd opp the Christie Hospital.* **Sun 2 Aug (12-4). Adm £5, chd free. Light refreshments.**
The architecture of Maggie's Manchester, designed by world-renowned architect Lord Foster, is complemented by gardens designed by Dan Pearson, Best in Show winner at Chelsea Flower Show. Combining a rich mix of spaces, inc the working glasshouse and vegetable garden, the garden provides a place for both activity and contemplation. The colours and sensory experience of nature becomes part of the Centre through micro gardens and internal courtyards, which relate to the different spaces within the building. Wheelchair access to most of the garden from the front entrance.

45 MAGHULL STATION
Station Road, Maghull, Liverpool, L31 3DE. Merseyrail. *7 m N of Liverpool. Follow A59 into Maghull turning R at 2nd set of T-lights (opp Maghull Town Hall) Follow road over canal bridge & station is approx ½ m.* **Sun 19 July (11-4.30). Adm £3, chd free. Coffee bar on site serving light refreshments hot & cold.**
Filled with colourful herbaceous plants, shrubs, rockery, hanging baskets, troughs and large planters tumbling with a wide variety of bedding plants - a wonderful sight for commuters arriving in Maghull plus a hidden surprise garden. Winners of RHS North West In Bloom Best Station in 2021 and the best in Britain in the World Cup of Stations competition 2024. Our Hornby train made from waste products sits in its own beautifully planted cottage garden. Hidden pathways with their own secrets Unusual plants. Disabled parking spaces available.

46 MATSHEAD LODGE
Brock Side, Bilsborrow, Preston, PR3 0GL. Sheila & Nick Baines. *2m N of Bilsborrow. Parking at Barton Grange Garden Centre on A6 (permission granted). Cross A6 to car sales yard follow public footpath over railway bridge along river & foot bridge to NGS signage. Parking in*

lay-bys on Lydiate Lane & Claughton, 5 mins walk Accessible parking at garden. **Sat 23 May (10.30-4). Adm £7, chd free. Tea, coffee & cake.** Set in approx 2 acres, a garden of mixed herbaceous borders, with shrubs, orchard and loose stone paths. Hidden away on the banks of river Brock featuring Japanese area, and ponds. The walk from Barton Grange to the garden takes approx 10mins after crossing the A6. Accessible parking only at the garden reached down a narrow single track lane.

GROUP OPENING

47 MAWDESLEY GARDENS
Bentley Lane, Mawdesley, Ormskirk, L40 3AD. Jill & Mark Brindle. *10 mins from M6 J27. From M6 J27 take 1st exit, past Crow Orchard petrol station.* Turn R onto Moss Ln. After ¾m turn R onto Courage Low Ln. Turn L onto Bentley Lane. Garden is on R after Ridley Lane. Card payments taken at Anderton Mill Cottage & Harrock View. **Sun 12 July (11-4.30). Combined adm £5, chd free. Tea, coffee & cake at 10 Anderton's Mill & Harrock View.**

ANDERTON MILL COTTAGE
L40 3AD. Jill & Mark Brindle.

10 ANDERTON'S MILL
L40 3TW. Heather & Alan Beezley.

FERNDALE
L40 2RA. Bob & Margaret Mercer.

3 HARROCK VIEW
PR7 5PZ. Tony & Janet Trafford, 07809 656388, tony.trafford@norlec.com.
Visits also by arrangement 14 June to 16 Aug for groups of 25 to 40.

A group of 4 gardens in and around Mawdesley, a pretty rural village between Chorley and Ormskirk. Each garden has something different to offer, from cottage gardens, shaded areas, carnivorous plants, handcrafted metalworks, colourful container plantings, idyllic views of neighbouring countryside, exotic planting and even animal sculptures. Of course there are home-made cakes and refreshments to be had along the way! Some gardens are partially accessible to wheelchair users.

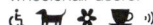

Our donation to Marie Curie this year is equivalent to 17,521 hours of hospice at home care.

Rishton Tropical Garden

LANCASHIRE

GROUP OPENING

48 NEW MELLOR & CLAYTON-LE-DALE GARDENS
85 Ribchester Road, Clayton Le Dale, Blackburn, BB1 9HT. Liz Seed. *1m N of Blackburn. Take B6245 off A59 ¾m opp St Peters. What3words app: Ribchester Rd - divisions.wipe.manage, Holly Cottage - swept.youth.verse, Whinney Lane Barn - feeds.stem.spared.* **Sat 11, Sun 12 July (11-4). Combined adm £6, chd free. Tea, coffee & cake at 85 Ribchester Road & Whinney Lane Barn.**

NEW HOLLY COTTAGE
BB2 7EJ. Lyndsay Vause.

85 RIBCHESTER ROAD
BB1 9HT. Mrs Elizabeth Seed.

NEW WHINNEY LANE BARN
BB2 7EH. Rachel Heys.

On the edge of the Ribble valley, this group of 3 contrasting gardens offers a delightful mix of character, creativity, and horticultural inspiration. From clever planting and varied landscaping to wildlife havens and charming entertaining spaces, each garden has something unique to enjoy. 85 Ribchester Road features colourful herbaceous borders, ironwork arches, a pergola, and both formal and wildlife ponds, perfect for reflection and biodiversity. Holly Cottage includes a meadow pond with stunning views, raised vegetable beds, composting area, secluded seating, and an enclosed cottage garden full of perennials and edibles. Whinney Lane Barn is a classic cottage garden with dahlias, a cutting garden and a sunken outdoor space for refreshments amid the blooms. Some paths are grassy/uneven or have steps, so not all areas are wheelchair accessible.

49 MILL BARN
Goosefoot Close, Samlesbury, Preston, PR5 0SS. Chris Mortimer, 07742 924124, chris@millbarn.net. *6m E of Preston. From M6 J31 2½m on A59/A677 B/burn. Turn S. Nabs Head Ln, then Goosefoot Ln.* **Sat 30, Sun 31 May, Sat 6, Sun 7 June (11-5). Adm £5, chd free. Home-made teas. Picnics welcome. Visits also by arrangement May to July for groups of 5 to 30.**
The unique and quirky garden at Mill Barn is a delight, or rather a series of delights. Along the River Darwen, through the tiny secret grotto, past the suspension bridge and view of the fairytale tower, visitors can stroll past folly, sculptures, lily pond, and lawns, enjoy the naturally planted flower beds, then enter the secret garden and through it the pathways of the wooded hillside beyond. A garden developed on the site of old mills gives a fascinating layout which evolves at many levels. The garden jungle provides a smorgasbord of flowers to attract insects throughout the season. Children enjoy the garden very much. Partial wheelchair access.

50 18 MOOR DRIVE
Crosby, Liverpool, L23 2UP. Mrs Vicki Hall, 07963 983286. *12m S of Southport & 7m N of Liverpool close to Crosby village. A565 from Southport. Formby bypass becomes Southport Rd. Continues onto Moor Lane. Turn into Moor Drive, turn R at junction, then R into cul-de-sac. House on L at the bottom of the cul-de-sac.* **Sun 28 June (11-4). Adm £3.50, chd free. Tea, coffee, soft drinks & home-made cakes will be available. Visits also by arrangement 1 July to 14 July for groups of up to 30. Street parking only.**
Wonderfully planted, picturesque urban garden with numerous trees, shrubs and climbers developed over several years. Emphasis on encouraging wildlife and organic gardening practices. Lawned areas, mixed perennial planting, small vegetable garden with crop rotation. Greenhouse. Ornamental and wildlife ponds. Seating areas surrounded by scented climbers and roses. Several frogs and a tortoise live here. Crosby beach is a short drive away, where it is possible to visit the art installation 'Another Place' by renowned sculptor Anthony Gormley. Good access to front garden, seating areas and most of rear garden. Some uneven pebble paths around greenhouse area.

51 MOSS PARK ALLOTMENTS
Lesley Road, Stretford, Manchester, M32 9EE. Peter Bazley, 07738 761220, peterdb56@hotmail.com. *3m SW of Manchester. From M60 J7 (Manchester), A56 (Manchester), A5181 Barton Rd, L onto B5213 Urmston Lane, ½m L onto Lesley Rd signed Stretford Cricket Club. Parking at 2nd gate.* **Sun 12 July (11-4). Adm £5, chd free. Tea, coffee & cake. Gorgeous array of home-made cakes. Visits also by arrangement June to Aug.**
Moss Park is a stunning, award winning allotment site in Stretford, Manchester. Wide grass paths flanked by pretty flower borders give way to a large variety of well-tended plots bursting with ideas to try at home, from insect hotels to unusual fruits and vegetables. Take tea and cake on the lawn outside the quirky society clubhouse that looks like a beamed country pub. WC facilities. Partial wheelchair access but most plots can be viewed from grass runways.

52 204 NORBRECK ROAD
Thornton-Cleveleys, FY5 1RE. Mrs Nicola & Mr David Barnett, allotmentcat@sky.com. *5m N of Blackpool. Short drive from the M55. J3 towards Fleetwood. Follow A585 to Norcross r'about. At Norcross take 2nd exit to Warren Dr. Follow Warren Dr to Norbreck Rd. Parking on road. What3words app: zebra.truly.heads.* **Sat 11 July (10-4); Sun 12 July (11-3). Adm £4, chd free. Self service tea, coffee, cake & biscuits. Visits also by arrangement in July for groups of 5 to 20.**
A colourful garden with deep planted borders of mixed perennial planting, bedding, shrubs and trees. Lots of containers and pots. Blackpool in Bloom runner up. Large Hosta collection in pots and planted out. Plenty of seating areas. Two small frog ponds. There are 2 small steps down in to the garden. Accessible to top paved area with views down the garden.

53 33 PERSHORE GROVE
Ainsdale, Southport, PR8 2SY. Mr Francis Proctor, 07866 667066, francisandbarbara33@gmail.com. *4.9m S of Southport. Disabled parking on the garden driveway. Other parking please use Westminster Drive.* **Sat 6 June (11-5). Adm £5, chd free. Tea, coffee & cake. Visits also by arrangement 19 May to 18 Oct for groups of 10 to 20.**
Small garden, inc a bridge, romantic ruin and man made caves with many

LANCASHIRE 307

entertaining features, 30 years in the construction. Use of recycled building materials. Entrance to caves may not be suitable for those with mobility issues.

54 THE QUAKER MEETING HOUSE
13 Co Operation Street, Crawshawbooth, Rossendale, BB4 8AG. Mr Philip Whitehead, www.crawshawboothquakers. org.uk. *2m N of Rawtenstall, off the A682. Turn L at zebra crossing from Rawtenstall. Enter walled garden opp Masons Arms pub.* **Sat 25 July (11-5); Sun 26 July (1-5). Adm £3, chd free. Tea, coffee & cake.** Our walled garden is situated at a Quaker C18 2* listed Meeting House and burial ground. The garden, which has manicured lawns and borders with three benches, reflects an atmosphere of peace and tranquillity with a colourful display of plants, shrubs and trees. An accessible WC is available at the left side of the building beneath the cottage.

55 RAINBAG COTTAGE
Carr Moss Lane, Halsall, Ormskirk, L39 8RZ. Sue & Mick Beacon, 07709 243986, sbeacon303@gmail.com. *8m NW of Ormskirk. What3words app: doll.talkative.hamsters. A570 from Ormskirk to Southport after 4m, L into Gorsuch Lane A5147. After 1½m pass church R into Carr Moss Ln which becomes single track, house sign on L after 2m.* **Visits by arrangement 1 May to 7 June for groups of 10 to 30. Includes talk about the history of Rainbag Cottage & garden tour. Tea, coffee & cake.**
A magical ½ acre cottage garden in a rural setting with open views to the surrounding countryside. Oriental themed stroll garden with wildlife ponds and moongate. Herbaceous borders, woodland walk, raised beds with vegetables and cut flowers. Small flower meadow, fruit trees, greenhouse, wormery and bug pad Focus on encouraging wildlife. Various seating areas. Fairies, scarecrows and an angel live here.

56 RISHTON TROPICAL GARDEN
52 Tomlinson Place, Rishton, Blackburn, BB1 4AZ. Mr Tez Donnelly, www.facebook.com/LancsTropicalGarden. *Junction 7 M65, then Clitheroe exit on the r'about, then turn L to Rishton. Turn R into Parker St, then L into Wheatfield St. Please note there is no parking at the address.* **Sat 15, Sun 16 Aug (12-4). Adm £4, chd free. Tea, coffee & delicious home-made cakes.**
A tropical style new build garden around 3 sides of the house. With lots of unusual lush exotic style plants, such as bananas, palm trees, cannas, gingers, tree ferns and a massive tetrapanax. New plants and beds added for 2026. Many of the unusual plants available for sale. The garden is located next to the Leeds Liverpool canal.

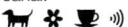

GROUP OPENING

57 NEW RUFFORD GARDENS TRAIL
Flash Lane, Rufford, Ormskirk, L40 1SW. Mr John & Mrs Jane Hoban. *7m NE of Ormskirk. via Liverpool Rd S A59. Please park in village hall car park situated on Flash Lane.* **Sat 6 June (10-4). Combined adm £7, chd free. Sun 7 June (10-4). Combined adm £5, chd free. Home-made teas. Home-made teas at Oaklands on Saturday & Rufford Cricket Club (adjacent to 31 Cousins Lane) on Sunday.**

31 COUSINS LANE
L40 1TN. Brenda & Roy Caslake.
Open on all dates

OAKLANDS
L40 1SW. Mr John & Mrs Jane Hoban, www.facebook.com/OurOaklands.
Open on all dates

NEW 16 WHITEFIELD CLOSE
L40 1US. Mrs Wendy Fairclough.
Open on Sat 6 June

3 lovely and very diverse gardens in the pretty rural village of Rufford. A beautiful, well established woodland garden with mature trees, several water features and seating areas flanked with ferns and hostas. A country cottage garden with lovely mixed borders and secluded corners punctuated with open views of the village cricket ground. New to the group is a shady garden loosely designed on a Fibonacci spiral with a backdrop of whispering Aspen. All of the gardens are wildlife friendly and planted to encourage pollinators. So enjoy the tranquil atmosphere of these lovely gardens while you relax and treat yourself to a cuppa along with a slice of delicious home-made cake! Wheelchair access at Oaklands is via pathways through woodland. Some of these paths may be uneven.

58 ST WILFRID'S COMMUNITY GARDEN
Royce Road, Manchester, M15 5BJ. Jackie Garvey, 01618 061265, firmstart@firmstart.co.uk, www.firmstart.co.uk. *From Stretford Rd (A5067) turn R into Chorlton Rd then R into Royce Rd. From Princess Rd turn. L into Old Birley St, follow onto Royce Rd; from Mancunian Way take A506 at Cambridge St Junction, follow round round to R (as it becomes Cavendish St) then Stretford Rd. What3words app: brain.slip.models.* **Sun 19 July (10-3). Adm £5, chd free. Tea, coffee & cake. On-site vegan bakery will provide refreshments.** Visits also by arrangement 19 July to 1 Aug. The Community Garden is a hidden gem tucked away in the car park of St Wilfrid's Enterprise Centre, a vibrant and tranquil retreat. The garden's design is a beautiful mosaic of varied plantings, with a strong emphasis on colour. Winding pathways lead visitors through an array of flower beds towards the former Grade II listed St Wilfrid's Church, designed by renowned architect AW Pugin (1842). Many of the local community were married or christened in this Pugin-designed church which visitors can explore at the opening (many original features remain). Small on site car park and street parking nearby.

Our donation in 2025 has enabled Parkinson's UK to fund 2 new nursing posts this year directly supporting people with Parkinson's.

308 LANCASHIRE

59 NEW **18 SCARISBRICK NEW ROAD**
Southport, PR8 6PY. Carmel Malley. ½m from Southport town centre on A570. Garden signed from Eastbank St r'about and from Kew r'about. On street parking on Sefton St. **Sun 24 May (1-4). Adm £3, chd free. Tea, coffee & cake.**
A ¼ acre town garden, with front and back gardens, featuring a beautiful selection of shrubs and perennials. The garden is in a state of transition to accommodate more flowering plants. The garden features sandstone boulders, wisteria, lilac, laburnum and a water feature. There is also a large lawn and seating area.

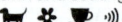

GROUP OPENING

60 SEFTON PARK GARDENS
Liverpool, L17 1AS. *From end of M62 take A5058 Queens Drive S through Allerton to Sefton Park. Circle the park and use postcodes.* Maps available at all gardens. **Sun 7 June, Sun 16 Aug (1-5). Combined adm £5, chd free. Refreshments in June at Prince Alfred Rd & Park Mount. Refreshments in August at Fern Grove & Sefton Park Allotments.**

6 CROXTETH GROVE
L8 0RX. Stuart Speeden.
Open on Sun 16 Aug

FERN GROVE COMMUNITY GARDEN
L8 0RY. Liverpool City Council, ferngrovegarden.weebly.com.
Open on Sun 16 Aug

NEW **36 NORTH SUDLEY ROAD**
L17 0BG. Michael & Rosie Grisenthwaite.
Open on all dates

PARKMOUNT
L17 3BP. Jeremy Nicholls.
Open on Sun 7 June

37 PRINCE ALFRED ROAD
L15 8HH. Jane Hammett.
Open on Sun 7 June

SEFTON PARK ALLOTMENTS
Greenbank Drive, Liverpool, L17 1AS. Sefton Park Allotments Society.
Open on Sun 16 Aug

SEFTON VILLA
L8 3SD. Patricia Williams.
Open on Sun 7 June

A new private garden at 36 North Sudley Rd with a large collection of rare and unusual roses joins 3 beautifully planted gardens to open in early June for roses and early summer displays. And in mid August the new garden shows off its seasonal perennial display, alongside the produce and dahlias at Sefton Park Allotments, Fern Grove Community Garden and the delightfully planted garden in Croxteth Grove. In August look out for the SSAFA armed forces charity plot and the children's plot at Sefton Park Allotments, children's activities at Fern Grove Community Garden, and classical music 2-4pm at Sefton Park Allotments.

Calderstones Nature Reserve, Allerton & Grassendale Gardens

61 THE SHAKESPEAREAN GARDEN, PLATT FIELDS PARK
Manchester, M14 6LA. Manchester City Council, www.facebook.com/ShakespeareanGarden. *Off Wilmslow Rd, down Mabfield Rd. There is a car park in the park nr the Mabfield Rd entrance; if that is full there is street parking near the park entrance.* **Sun 2 Aug (11-5). Adm £5, chd free. Tea, coffee & cake. WC at the Lakeside Centre nr the car park, approx 5-10 mins walk from the garden.**

The concept of a Shakespearean Garden was first developed in Victorian England with the idea of creating a garden with some, or all, of the trees and flowers mentioned in the Bard's works. With strong links to the suffrage movement and Edwardian society our garden opened in 1922 and was rescued from near obscurity by volunteers 4 yrs ago. There is an Elizabethan style parterre and a human sunclock. At our summer Open Day there will be information boards around the garden and a lovely nature trail inc various forms of hibernacula hidden amongst the banks. We list our annual Xmas event details on our FB page in Nov. There are 2 entrances into the garden; one down steps, but the entrance on the E side is sloped. There are wide paths inside the garden.

62 NEW SHEPHERD ROAD ALLOTMENTS
Shepherd Road, Lytham St. Annes, FY8 3SW. Mrs Ruth Williams. *From St Annes Sq head E on B5233. Straight ahead through 2 sets of T-lights then turn 2nd R onto Shepherd Rd. Park on road at Hope Street Park then a short walk. What3words app: under.email.period.* **Sat 18 July (10-3). Adm £5, chd free. Light refreshments. Tea, coffee, soft drinks & cake.**

An amazing and award-winning haven away from the hustle of life, featured on BBC Gardeners' World in 2024, with over 170 plots growing a wide variety of fruit and vegetables, flowers and trees. A rough track leads you around the site where many of the plots can be viewed, or stroll along the grassy paths to find tucked-away gems like the wildlife area and the orchard. Make time to have refreshments outside the cabin. Partial wheelchair access. The track around the plot is not tarmac and quite rough.

63 SOUTHLANDS
12 Sandy Lane, Stretford, M32 9DA. Maureen Sawyer & Duncan Watmough, 0161 283 9425, moe@southlands12.com, www.southlands12.com. *3m S of Manchester. Sandy Lane (B5213) is situated off A5181 (A56) ¼m from M60 J7.* **Sun 26 July (12-6). Adm £5, chd free. Home-made teas. Cake-away service (take a slice of your favourite cake home). Visits also by arrangement 1 June to 30 Aug for groups of up to 30. Adm price for groups inc refreshments.**

This beautiful, unique and organic multi-award winning artist's town garden inc a Mediterranean, ornamental and tranquil woodland garden. Stunning herbaceous borders and a kitchen potager with large greenhouse add to its continued appeal. Fabulous container plantings throughout. Described as 'A work of Art' 'Absolutely stunning' and 'An English garden at its very best'. Artist's work on display on open days and shown to private parties if requested.

64 28 STAFFORD ROAD
Ellesmere Park, Monton, Manchester, M30 9HW. Tracey & Tony, 07834 452180, shepsurf@gmail.com, www.instagram.com/monton_garden/7tseNHyl. *M602 Eccles exit, take the 1st exit then at the lights, turn L. Follow the road for 1m heading towards Monton, go over small r'about, next R is Stafford Rd.* **Sat 15 Aug (10-4.30); Sat 5 Sept (12-4.30). Adm £5, chd free. Tea, coffee & cake. Visits also by arrangement 1 June to 14 Sept for groups of 8+.**

A large garden in Manchester with borders full of woodland jungle plants. Mature bamboos, inc a magnificent *Borinda papyrifera*, large palm trees and a collection of rare, hardy plants from around the world inc a number of hardy Schefflera plants. Search for Tony's YouTube channel at 'montongarden'. There is a small gravel area over which a wheelchair will have to pass.

65 NEW TOPMILL PARK
Bye Road, Ramsbottom, Bury, BL0 0HH. Mr David Wolfenden. *From Manchester on M66 at J1 take A56 to Ramsbottom, follow A56 for 2m then turn R onto Bye Rd From Rochdale follow A56 to Bury at Edenfield Junction continue on A56 for 1m then turn L onto Bye Rd. Limited parking for 6-8 cars at bottom of Bye Rd* **Sun 28 June, Sun 2 Aug (10.30-4). Combined adm with Arevinti £5, chd free. Tea, coffee, soft drinks & baked goods (home made scones, clotted cream & jam).**

The park was originally the site of a mill long since demolished. The overgrown site was reclaimed by local residents during lock down to create a community park. Many plants, shrubs and trees were donated by friends and neighbours, transforming the area into a quiet tranquil wildlife haven. We have bees and an allotment where plants are grown for the park and sold to raise funds for the park. Small bake sale. Tombola.

66 3 TOWER END
Victoria Road, Formby, Liverpool, L37 1LP. Phil & Sue Allison. *6m S of Southport off A565 Formby by pass. At r'about 3rd exit to Ryeground Ln. Follow NGS signs to Victoria Rd cul-de-sack. 0.6m on R. Blue badge holders can park on yellow lines. Otherwise park on Harington Rd Estate on L. The garden is a 10 minute walk from Freshfield Station or Harington Road Estate.* **Sat 9, Sun 10 May (11-5). Adm £6.50, chd free. Tea, coffee & cake.**

Nearly an acre of vistas and walkways in a pine woodland setting off the NT Nature Reserve. Different styles of garden incorporating many water and stone features, folly, topiary, fernery, rock and gravel garden. Japanese style area. Patios with seating. Large variety of trees, shrubs, rhododendrons, wisteria, acers and conifers, all linked by paths, steps and lawns. Created by former owners of Lady Green Garden Centre.

Grapes Community Food Garden, Canning and Toxteth Gardens

67 ♦ TURTON TOWER HERBACEOUS GARDEN
Tower Drive, Turton, Bolton, BL7 0HG. Nancy Walsh, nancy.walsh@hotmail.co.uk, www.turtontower-kitchengarden.co.uk. 1½ m from Edgworth. Turton Tower is signed off the B6391 between Bolton & Edgworth. **For NGS: Sat 27 June (10.30-4). Adm £4, chd free.** For other opening times and information, please email or visit garden website.
The garden is set in the historic Turton Tower grounds and was originally the kitchen garden in Victorian times. A group of volunteers have restored and created the garden over the last 16 yrs. The garden today consists of raised vegetable beds and soft fruit areas but most of the garden is divided into smaller feature gardens. Turton Tower's history is reflected in its Tudor and Victorian beds. More contemporary gardens are The White Garden and Japanese Garden. There are also 2 long herbaceous borders with a large variety of perennials. We have an interesting variety of ferns and shade loving plants in our stumperies. Our new garden is a wildlife garden and pond surrounding the ruined Bothy. Plants, cards and jam will be for sale. The paths are wheelchair friendly but in some places are moderately sloped.

68 WEEPING ASH GARDEN
Bents Garden & Home, Warrington Road, Glazebury, WA3 5NS. John Bent, www.bents.co.uk. 15m W of Manchester. Next to Bents Garden & Home, just off the A580 East Lancs Rd at Greyhound r'about nr Leigh. Follow brown 'Garden Centre' signs. **Sun 8, Sun 15 Feb, Sun 2 Aug (10-4). Adm by donation.**
Created by retired nurseryman and photographer John Bent, Weeping Ash is a garden of year-round interest with a beautiful display of early snowdrops. Broad sweeps of colour lend elegance to this stunning garden which is much larger than it initially seems with hidden paths and wooded areas creating a sense of natural growth. Bents Garden & Home offers a choice of dining destinations inc The Fresh Approach Restaurant, Caffe nel Verde and a number of al fresco dining options as well as an extensive homegrown plant collection.

69 12 WILLOW HEY
Maghull, Liverpool, L31 3DL. Dr Mike & Mrs Di Pearson. From A59, aim for Maghull Railway Stn & cross the level Xing. Willow Hey is 1st on R & our house is at the 1st corner with a bright yellow door. Limited parking on road. **Sun 17 May (10.30-4). Adm £6, chd free. Tea, coffee & cake.** Cafe at nearby Maghull station.
Developed over 40 yrs the garden is ⅔ of an acre with many interesting features and a wide range of plants shrubs and over 60 different trees, inc many unusual and rare specimens. Features inc a beautiful limestone water feature, alpine beds, an orchard and canal bank. Designed for year-round colour, in May expect wisteria, Buddleia alternifolia, cornus, azaleas, rhododendrons and more. Most areas can be accessed with care and a sturdy 'pusher'.

70 32 WOOD HEY GROVE
Syke, Rochdale, OL12 9UA. Graham & Janine Bullas, 07957 829462, g.bullas@ntlworld.com. Around 2m N of Rochdale town centre. Follow the A671 (Whitworth Rd) out of Rochdale towards Burnley & turn R at the 2nd r'about (Fieldhouse Ln) At the next junction turn L & Wood Hey Grove will be 1m on L. **Sun 19 July (11-4). Adm £4, chd free. Tea, coffee & cake. Home-made focaccia & cakes available to eat on the day or takeaway.** Visits also by arrangement 20 July to 20 Sept for groups of 5 to 10. Refreshments available.
The garden was Graham's retirement landscape project and continues to evolve 14 yrs on. The planting only really started when Janine also retired 7 yrs ago and the garden is now taking shape. The hard landscaping is a mix of complex curves over 4 levels with paved patios, hardwood decking, lawns, trees and herbaceous borders complementing the overall scheme. We offer home-made bread, cakes and craft items for sale on the day. The steps within the garden would prevent access to the whole plot but most of the garden is visible due to the slope of the garden.

GROUP OPENING

71 WOOLTON VILLAGE GARDENS
Hillside Drive, Woolton, Liverpool, L25 5NR. 6m SE of Liverpool city centre. Gardens are best accessed by car or bus (75, 78, 81, 89). Nearest train: Hunts Cross (1.7m) Parking is easiest on Hillside Drive. **Sun 17 May (12-5). Combined adm £5, chd free. Tea, coffee & cake at Nos 4 & 23 Hillside Drive.**

GREEN RIDGES, RUNNYMEDE CLOSE
L25 5JU. Sarah & Michael Beresford.

23 HILLSIDE DRIVE
L25 5NR. Bruce & Fiona Pennie.

15 LYNTON GREEN
L25 6JB. Gill & Danny O'Donoghue, www.instagram.com/thegardeninbloomuk.

MERRICK, 4 HILLSIDE DRIVE
L25 5NS. Kerry & Tony Marson.

Four suburban gardens located in the beautiful historic village of Woolton featuring C17 buildings that act as a backdrop to the public space plant displays maintained by Woolton in Bloom, for whom the gardens also open. The gardens feature herbaceous borders, water features, tropical plants, greenhouses, kitchen garden, and garden sculptures.

310,000 people are cared for each year who are approaching the end of life or diagnosed with a terminal illness through the hospice network supported by National Garden Scheme funding.

LEICESTERSHIRE & RUTLAND

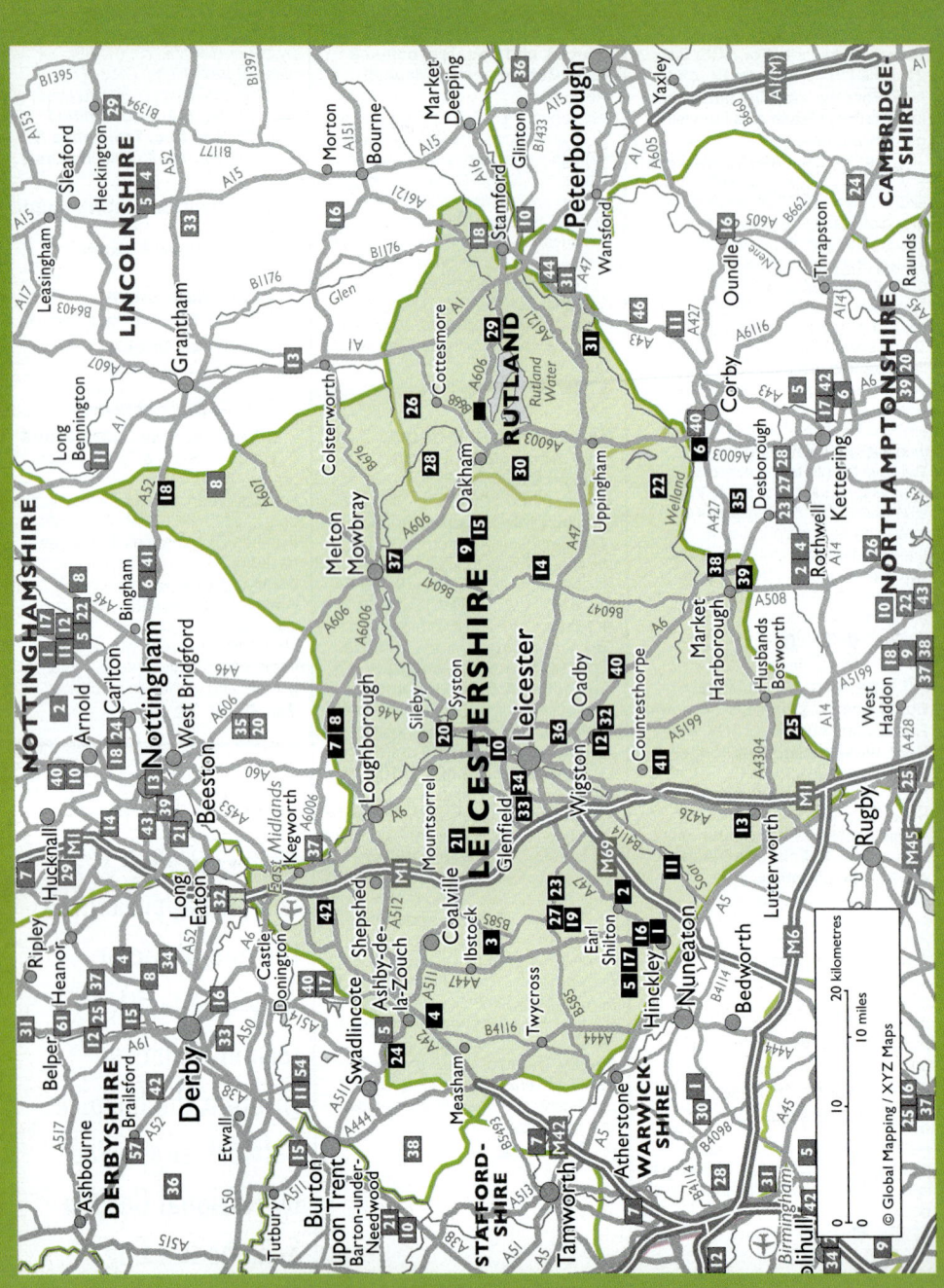

VOLUNTEERS

Leicestershire

County Organiser
Alison Blythe 01664 481997
alison.blythe@ngs.org.uk

County Treasurer
Di Beste 07917 003908
di.beste@ngs.org.uk

Publicity
Carol Bartlett 07879 891097
carol.bartlett@ngs.org.uk

Booklet Co-ordinator
(Leicestershire & Rutland)
Carole Troake 07580 500261
carole.troake@ngs.org.uk

Social Media
Zoe Lewin 07810 800 007
zoe.lewin@ngs.org.uk

Photographer
Rosie Furniss 07837 793321
rosie.furniss@ngs.org.uk

Talks
Karen Gimson 07930 246974
k.gimson@btinternet.com

John Fraser 07502 015663
jmf9216@gmail.com

Group Visit Co-ordinator
Judith Boston 07740 945332
judith.boston@ngs.org.uk

Rutland

County Organisers
Sally Killick 07799 064565
sally.killick@ngs.org.uk

Lucy Hurst 07958 534778
lucy.hurst@ngs.org.uk

County Treasurer
Val Carroll 07598 235679
val.carroll@ngs.org.uk

Publicity
Lucy Hurst (see above)

Social Media
Nicola Oakey 07516 663358
nicola.oakey@ngs.org.uk

Assistant County Organiser
Chris Carroll 07708 972562
chris.carroll@ngs.org.uk

OPENING DATES

All entries subject to change.
For latest information check
www.ngs.org.uk

Extended openings are shown at the beginning of the month.

Map locator numbers are shown to the right of each garden name.

February

Snowdrop Openings

Sunday 15th
The Acers 1
Oak Cottage 24

Saturday 21st
Hedgehog Hall 14
Westview 40

Sunday 22nd
Hedgehog Hall 14
Westview 40

March

Sunday 8th
Tresillian House 37

April

Sunday 12th
Oak Cottage 24

Sunday 26th
Dairy Cottage 11
The Old Hall 26
Westbrooke House 39

May

Sunday 3rd
Tresillian House 37
Tudor House 38

Sunday 10th
Burrough Hall 9

Saturday 16th
NEW Bigbury House 5
8 Hinckley Road 17

Sunday 17th
NEW Bigbury House 5
8 Hinckley Road 17
The Old Vicarage, Whissendine 28

Saturday 23rd
Westview 40

Monday 25th
Westview 40

June

Every Wednesday
Stoke Albany House 35

Saturday 6th
NEW 164 Battram Road 3
28 Gladstone Street 12
The New Barn 23

Sunday 7th
28 Gladstone Street 12
The New Barn 23
Redhill Lodge 31
NEW Stoneygate and
  Knighton Gardens 36
Westbrooke House 39

Thursday 11th
Nevill Holt Hall 22

Friday 12th
Nevill Holt Hall 22

Saturday 13th
88 Brook Street 7
109 Brook Street 8
NEW The Cottage 10
NEW Hinckley Gardens 16
NEW The Lodge Brascote 19
Nevill Holt Hall 22
The Old Rectory 27

Sunday 14th
88 Brook Street 7
109 Brook Street 8
NEW The Cottage 10
NEW Hinckley Gardens 16
NEW The Lodge Brascote 19
Nevill Holt Hall 22
The Old Rectory 27
Prebendal House 29

@NGSLeicestershire
@leicestershire_ngs

@rutlandngs
@rutlandngs

Friday 19th
Brickfield House 6

Sunday 21st
NEW 10 High Street 15
Tresillian House 37

Saturday 27th
Oak Tree House 25
The Secret Garden, Glenfield Hospital 34

Sunday 28th
Oak Tree House 25
The Secret Garden, Glenfield Hospital 34

July

Every Wednesday
Stoke Albany House 35

Saturday 4th
Manor House 20

Sunday 5th
Manor House 20

Sunday 12th
Green Wicket Farm 13
Quaintree Hall 30
Willoughby Gardens 41

Wednesday 15th
Green Wicket Farm 13

Saturday 18th
NEW Bigbury House 5
8 Hinckley Road 17
St Wolstan's House 32

Sunday 19th
NEW Bigbury House 5
8 Hinckley Road 17
St Wolstan's House 32

Sunday 26th
NEW Beau Briar 4

August

Sunday 2nd
Honeytrees Tropical Garden 18

Saturday 8th
8 Saintbury Road 33

Sunday 9th
8 Saintbury Road 33

Sunday 16th
Honeytrees Tropical Garden 18

Sunday 23rd
15 The Woodcroft 42

Sunday 30th
Honeytrees Tropical Garden 18
Tresillian House 37

September

Sunday 13th
Redhill Lodge 31

October

Sunday 25th
Tresillian House 37

By Arrangement

Arrange a personalised garden visit with your club, or group of friends, on a date to suit you. See individual garden entries for full details.

The Acers 1
Barracca 2
Brickfield House 6
88 Brook Street 7
109 Brook Street 8
Dairy Cottage 11
Farmway (Willoughby Gardens) 41
Green Wicket Farm 13
Honeytrees Tropical Garden 18
Manor House 20
Mountain Ash 21
Redhill Lodge 31
Stoke Albany House 35
Tresillian House 37
Westview 40
15 The Woodcroft 42

The Lodge, Brascote

THE GARDENS

1 THE ACERS
10 The Rills, Hinckley, LE10 1NA. Mr Dave Baggott, 01455 617237, davebaggott18@hotmail.com. *10 mins from J1 of M69. Off B4668 out of Hinckley. Turn into Dean Rd then 1st R into The Rills. Last house on R.* **Sun 15 Feb (10.30-4). Adm £5, chd free. Tea, coffee & cake. Visits also by arrangement 15 Feb to 31 Oct for groups of up to 20.**
Medium sized garden with a Japanese theme inc a zen garden, Japanese tea house, koi pond, more than 20 different varieties of acers, many choice alpines, trilliums, cyclamen, erythroniums, cornus, hamamelis and dwarf conifers. Approx 200 different varieties of snowdrops in spring. Large greenhouse.

2 BARRACCA
Ivydene Close, Earl Shilton, LE9 7NR. Mr John & Mrs Sue Osborn, 01455 842609, susan. osborn1@btinternet.com. *10m W of Leicester. From A47 after entering Earl Shilton, Ivydene Cl is 4th on L from Leicester side of A47.* **Visits by arrangement 15 Feb to 19 July for groups of up to 45. Discuss refreshments when booking. Adm £10, chd free. Tea, coffee & cake inc in adm price.**
1 acre garden with lots of different areas, silver birch walk, wildlife pond with seating, apple tree garden, Mediterranean planted area and lawns surrounded with herbaceous plants and shrubs. Patio area with climbing roses and wisteria. There is also a utility garden with greenhouses, vegetables in beds, herbs and perennial flower beds, lawn and fruit cage. Part of the old gardens owned by the Cotton family used to open approx 9 acres to the public in the 1920's. Partial wheelchair access.

3 NEW 164 BATTRAM ROAD
Ellistown, Coalville, LE67 1GB. Mr & Mrs Bowyer. *Battram village, 2m from Ellistown, Leics. 10 mins from M1 J22. Towards Coalville, L towards Ellistown, L towards Bagworth. ½ way down Battram Rd on R. Parking available at Battram woods car park.* **Sat 6 June (10-4).**
Adm £5, chd free. Tea, coffee & cake.
A rural country garden on a quiet road to Battram Woods with curved borders heavily planted with shrubs and perennials. Just to name a few: a Robinia 'Lace Lady', Viburnum, Thalictrum, Eremurus, Oriental poppies and roses. Further highlights inc a *Cornus alternifolia* 'Argentea', a natural pond, and a circular seating area offering views of the National Forest. Wheelchair users may require assistance to cross some gravel areas.

4 NEW BEAU BRIAR
Packington, Ashby-De-La-Zouch, LE65 1WR. Rosemary Woodhouse and Richard Badcock. *2m from J12 A42. Follow signs for Measham then 1st L for Packington. Follow road to give way sign then turn L to Normanton Rd. Garden on L. Roadside Parking.* **Sun 26 July (12-5). Adm £5, chd free. Tea, coffee & cake.**
A large level mature garden in a central location within the village. This is a garden for gardeners interested in plants with colour and variety everywhere. There are north and south facing borders with a good mix of sun and shady areas, sumptuous pot planting, and a lovely vine laden pergola shading the main terrace. There is a fine collection of acers both in the borders and in pots. Level site with good wheelchair access.

5 NEW BIGBURY HOUSE
Higham Lane, Stoke Golding, Nuneaton, CV13 6EX. Mr Paul & Mrs Emily Grice. *3m NW of Hinckley. Approach from any direction to the village then follow NGS signs. Bigbury house is on Higham Ln as you approach from Station Rd. Please park roadside on Station Rd (avoid traffic calming area).* **Sat 16, Sun 17 May, Sat 18, Sun 19 July (12-4). Combined adm with 8 Hinckley Road £6, chd free. Tea, coffee & cake.**
A new build house enjoying a high position looking towards the Ashby canal with beautiful views. The ¼ acre rear sloping garden has had extensive landscaping to create multi level areas providing seating and lawned areas with well-stocked borders of mainly herbaceous plants grown from seed or splitting to create all year-round interest and colour.

Wheelchair access to patio area which provides a view of the lower tiers of the garden.

6 BRICKFIELD HOUSE
Rockingham Road, Cottingham, Market Harborough, LE16 8XS. Simon & Nicki Harker, 07775 672403, nickiharker@gmail.com. *SatNav will take you into Cottingham Village but garden is ½ m from Cottingham on Rockingham Rd/B670 towards Rockingham.* **Fri 19 June (12-4). Adm £5, chd free. Tea, coffee & cake. Visits also by arrangement 9 June to 18 June for groups of up to 25.**
Lovely views overlooking the Welland Valley, this 2 acre garden has been developed from a sloping brickyard rubbish plot over 37 yrs. There is a kitchen garden, orchard, herbaceous borders filled with roses, perennials and shrubs, paths and many pots, filled with succulents, herbs and colourful annuals.

7 88 BROOK STREET
Wymeswold, LE12 6TU. Adrian & Ita Cooke, 01509 880155, itacooke@btinternet.com. *4m NE of Loughborough. From A6006 Wymeswold turn S by church onto Stockwell, then E along Brook St. Roadside parking on Brook St.* **Sat 13, Sun 14 June (2-5). Combined adm with 109 Brook Street £7, chd free. Tea, coffee & cake at 109 Brook Street. Visits also by arrangement 30 May to 28 June for groups of 10 to 40.**
The garden is set on a hillside with lovely views across the village. It comprises a cottage style garden; then a series of water features inc a stream and a 'champagne' pond; and finally a vegetable plot, small orchard and wildflower meadow. Artistic touches run throughout and local artwork is featured. The ponds attract great crested and common newts, frogs, toads and grass snakes.

78,000 people affected by cancer were reached by Maggie's centres supported by the National Garden Scheme over the last 12 months.

8 109 BROOK STREET
Wymeswold, LE12 6TT. Maggie & Steve Johnson, 07973 692931, steve@brookend.org, www.brookend.org. *4m NE of Loughborough. From A6006 Wymeswold turn S onto Stockwell, then E along Brook St. Roadside parking along Brook St. Steep drive with limited disabled parking at house.* **Sat 13, Sun 14 June (2-5). Combined adm with 88 Brook Street £7, chd free. Tea, coffee & cake inc gluten free and vegetarian options.** Visits also by arrangement 30 May to 28 June for groups of 10 to 40. Option to visit one garden or two. Price will inc refreshments.
South facing, ¾ acre, gently sloping garden with views over open countryside. Modern garden with mature features. Patio with roses and clematis, wildlife and fish ponds, mixed borders, vegetable garden, orchard, hot garden and woodland garden. Something for everyone. Optional tour of rain water harvesting. Some gravel paths. For wheelchair access, drive to top of driveway and ask for assistance.

9 BURROUGH HALL
Somerby Road, Burrough on the Hill, Melton Mowbray, LE14 2QZ. Richard & Alice Cunningham. *Somerby Rd, Burrough on the Hill. Close to B6047. 10 mins from A606. 20 mins from Melton Mowbray.* **Sun 10 May (2-5). Adm £6, chd free. Tea, coffee & cake.**
Burrough Hall was built in 1867 as a classic Leicestershire hunting lodge. The garden, framed by mature trees and shrubs, was extensively redesigned by garden designer George Carter in 2007. The garden continues to develop. This family garden designed for all generations to enjoy is surrounded by magnificent views across High Leicestershire. In addition to the garden there will be a small collection of vintage and classic cars on display. Gravel paths and lawn.

10 NEW THE COTTAGE

School Lane, Birstall, Leicester, LE4 4EA. Jessie Morris and Dan Longman. *N Leicester City 3½ m from centre. From N, enter Birstall on A6 L'borough Rd at Wanlip r'about, follow A6 S ½ m, School Ln is a L turn. From S, enter Birtstall on A6 Red Hill Cir r'about, A6 N ¼ m, School Ln is R turn.* **Sat 13, Sun 14 June (11-4). Adm £4, chd free. Tea, coffee & cake.**
Medium sized town garden wrapped around a C16 cottage surrounded by mature evergreens planted with alliums, hostas, ferns, callas, salvias, hardy geraniums, climbers, roses and much more. The back garden has wide herbaceous borders with drifts of pastel and silver cottage garden perennials, a rock edged pond with a waterfall, a chicken run, a greenhouse, vegetable beds and a patio packed with pots.

11 DAIRY COTTAGE
15 Sharnford Road, Sapcote, LE9 4JN. Mrs Norah Robinson-Smith, 01455 272398, nrobinsons@yahoo.co.uk. *9m SW of Leicester. Sharnford Rd joins Leicester Rd in Sapcote to B4114 Coventry Rd. Follow NGS signs.* **Sun 26 Apr (11-4). Adm £3, chd free. Home-made teas inc cakes.** Visits also by arrangement 14 June to 2 Aug.
Peaceful garden with places to sit and enjoy the old cottage setting. The garden is over ½ an acre which inc a walled cottage garden, stumpery, potager, fernery and woodland walk. The planting consists of many unusual shrubs and trees and over 90 clematis, climbing roses and colourful herbaceous borders. An ideal garden for plant collectors. May need to access over a gravel drive.

12 28 GLADSTONE STREET
Wigston Magna, LE18 1AE. Chris & Janet Huscroft. *4m S of Leicester. Off Wigston by-pass (A5199) follow signs off McDonalds r'about.* **Sat 6, Sun 7 June (11-5). Adm £3.50, chd free. Home-made teas.**
The mature 70'x15' town garden is divided into rooms and bisected by a pond with a bridge. It is brimming with unusual hardy perennials, inc collections of ferns and hostas, also Miniature Hosta Theatre. David Austin roses chosen for their scent feature throughout, inc a 30' rose arch. A shade house with unusual hardy plants and regular changes to planting. Pond relined and refurbished in 2025. Parts of the garden can be viewed, narrow paths and step limit full access.

13 GREEN WICKET FARM
Ullesthorpe Road, Bitteswell, Lutterworth, LE17 4LR. Mrs Anna Smith, 01455 552646, greenfarmbitt@hotmail.com. *2m NW of Lutterworth J20 M1. From Lutterworth follow signs through Bitteswell towards Ullesthorpe. Garden situated behind Bitteswell Cricket Club. Use this as a landmark rather than relying on SatNav.* **Sun 12, Wed 15 July (2-5). Adm £5, chd free. Light refreshments.** Visits also by arrangement 1 July to 16 Aug for groups of up to 25.
A fairly formal garden on an exposed site surrounded by open fields. Mature trees enclosing the many varied plants chosen to give all round year interest. Many unusual hardy plants grown along side good reliable old favourites present a range of colour themed borders. Grass and gravel paths allow access to the whole garden. Disabled parking areas.

14 HEDGEHOG HALL
3 Loddington Road, Tilton on the Hill, LE7 9DE. Janet & Andrew Rowe. *8m W of Oakham. 2m N of A47 on B6047 between Melton & Market Harborough. Follow yellow NGS signs in Tilton towards Loddington. Disabled parking on road outside the White House 20yds past the entrance.* **Sat 21, Sun 22 Feb (11-4). Adm £5, chd free. Light refreshments in St Peters Church, Tilton. Open nearby Westview.**
½ acre organically managed plant lover's garden. Beautiful shade and woodland areas, with a large collection of approx 350 different snowdrops. All set on the north facing terraces along with many unusual hellebores, trilliums, euphorbias, ferns, cyclamen, pulmonaria and many rare bulbs. Many highly perfumed winter flowering shrubs inc daphne, viburnum, sarcococca and hamamelis. Regret, no wheelchair access to terraced borders.

15 NEW 10 HIGH STREET
Somerby, Melton Mowbray, LE14 2PZ. Chris & Angela Fisher. *From Oakham or Melton, turn into village. Garden is on R on corner & behind stone walls. Parking is on the road leading to church. Limited extra parking further into village.* **Sun 21 June (11-4). Adm £5, chd free.**

Tea, coffee & cake in the church. A 10 yr project to turn a medium size plot dominated by car parking and conifers into a garden. Terraced herbaceous borders, edged by an entirely self-seeded dry gravel garden lead to a courtyard with reflecting pool and terrace. Kitchen garden, raised beds, greenhouse, small orchard and island beds. Pond with bog garden, and fern rockery lead to a sunken patio overlooking the horse pond.

GROUP OPENING

16 NEW **HINCKLEY GARDENS**
Ashby Road, Hinckley, LE10 1SW.
Mrs Lynda Blower. *SW Leics near to the border with Warks, with access off the M69 or A5. From Hinckley town centre on the B4667.* *All 3 houses in close proximity with plenty of off road parking.* **Sat 13, Sun 14 June (11-4). Combined adm £6, chd free. Tea, coffee & cake at 182 Ashby Road; Tea coffee and sandwiches at 133 Ashby Road.**

NEW **133 ASHBY ROAD**
Mrs Michele Spencer.

182 ASHBY ROAD
Ms Lynda Blower.

NEW **2 WENDOVER DRIVE**
Mr & Mrs Jerry and Sherry Bettington.

3 gardens which provide different interests to visitors. Wendover Drive is a well manicured estate garden which inc a variety of hostas and ferns complemented by perennials and annuals for colour. 182 Ashby Road, a 120ft cottage style garden packed with lots of colourful perennials and many salvage collectables-cited around the garden. 133 Ashby Road, is a 300ft relaxed town garden with mature trees, rhododendrons, hostas, ferns, wildlife pond and folly.

In 2025, National Garden Scheme funding helped Perennial support 950 unique callers to their helpline looking for advice and information.

164 Battram Road

17 8 HINCKLEY ROAD
Stoke Golding, Nuneaton, CV13 6DU. John & Stephanie Fraser. *3m NW of Hinckley. Approach from any direction into village then follow NGS signs. Please park roadside with due consideration to other residents properties.* **Sat 16, Sun 17 May, Sat 18, Sun 19 July (12-4). Combined adm with Bigbury House £6, chd free. Tea, coffee & cake.**
A small SSW garden with water features and small hosta 'theatre' to add interest to the colourful and some unusual perennials inc climbers to supplement the trees and shrubs in May and July. Garden established and recently re-established by current owner to provide seating for a variety of views of the garden. Many perennials in the garden are represented in the plants for sale. Wheelchair access to garden room patio which provides a view of the lower part of the garden.

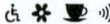

18 HONEYTREES TROPICAL GARDEN
85 Grantham Road, Bottesford, NG13 0EG. Julia Madgwick & Mike Ford, 07966 445794, Julia_madgwick@hotmail.com, www.facebook.com/HoneytreesTropicalGarden. *6m NW of Grantham. 7m E of Bingham on A52. Turn into village. Garden is on L on slip road behind hedge going out of village towards Grantham. Parking on grass opp property.* **Sun 2, Sun 16, Sun 30 Aug (11-4). Adm £5, chd free. Home-made teas.** Visits also by arrangement 1 July to 5 Sept for groups of 10+.
Tropical and exotic with a hint of jungle! Raised borders with different themes from lush foliage to arid cacti. Exotic planting as you enter the garden gives way on a gentle incline to surprises, inc glasshouses dedicated to various climatic zones interspersed with more exotic planting, ponds and a stream. Representation of over 20 yrs plant hunting. Treehouse and viewing platform to view tree ferns from above whilst being among the canopy of the trees. Fernery dedicated to exotic and rare ferns from around the world. There are some steps and ramps. Gravel and bark in certain areas but wheelchair access to most parts of the garden.

19 NEW THE LODGE BRASCOTE

Brascote, Newbold Verdon, Leicester, LE9 9LE. Mrs Anne Constable. *12m W of Leicester. L immed after the large village sign Newbold Verdon. Follow the signs to Brascote. The Lodge is the white house situated on L of sharp bend. Parking available opp house.* **Sat 13 June (11-6); Sun 14 June (10-4). Combined adm with The Old Rectory £8, chd free. Tea, coffee & cake.**

Burrough Hall

A large country garden with themed borders, inc moon, pink wedding, bronze and a recently planted golden border to celebrate 50 yrs of gardening. There is a small prairie area and 4 ponds. A kitchen garden and several old varieties of fruit trees. Around the garden and in the greenhouse you will find plants that have originated in China. There is an avenue of old Chestnut trees. The garden is accessed via a paved drive. Wheelchair access is possible with care over lawned areas.

20 MANOR HOUSE
70 Main Street, Cossington, Leicester, LE7 4UW. Harry Longman & Alison Armstrong, 07939 148618, harry.longman@gmail.com. *Soar Valley, between Leicester and Loughborough. Take Platts Ln on S approach to Cossington (NOT from house on Main St). Gateway on N side of lane 400 metres from Syston Rd. Turn at - What3words app: pampering.progress.challenge.* **Sat 4, Sun 5 July (11-6). Adm £6, chd free. Tea, coffee & cake. Visits also by arrangement for groups of 8 to 24. Refreshments inc in adm price for group visits.**
Entering from the field, rhododendrons beneath a great oak welcome you to Lovers' Walk, drawing you past feathery acers to the main lawn, where to the scent of azalea you take in a treescape of scale. Pendent limes, pines, birches and cedars feature, above them all a great copper beech. Move on to the mixed borders where roses, cistus and iris will delight you among the dozens of species planted. Space to walk and take in huge trees. Mixed borders for the plant enthusiast, encouraging wildlife of all sizes. Huge swings for kids of all ages. Easily accessible by cycle route 6 and Leicestershire Round footpath. The ground from the car park and around the garden is flat, but mainly grass, so is fine for wheelchairs in dry weather but may be soft if wet.

21 MOUNTAIN ASH
140 Ulverscroft Lane, Newtown Linford, LE6 0AJ. Mike & Liz Newcombe, 01530 242178, mjnew12@gmail.com. *7m SW of Loughborough, 7m NW of Leicester, 1m NW of Newtown Linford. Head ½m N, through Newtown Linford, along Main St towards Sharpley Hill, fork L into Ulverscroft Ln & Mountain Ash, is about ½m along on the L. Parking is along the opp verge.* **Visits by arrangement 15 Apr to 28 Aug for groups of 15 to 50. Adm £11, chd free. Tea, coffee & cake inc in adm price.**
2 acre garden with stunning views across Charnwood countryside. Near the house are patios, lawns, water feature, flower and shrub beds, fruit trees, soft fruit cage, greenhouses and vegetable plots. Lawns slope down to gravel garden, large wildlife pond and areas of woodland with walks through many species of trees. Over 50 garden statues and ornaments. Many places to sit and relax.

22 NEVILL HOLT HALL
Drayton Road, Nevill Holt, Market Harborough, LE16 8EG. Mr David Ross, www.nevillholtfestival.com. *5m NE of Market Haborough. Signed off B664 at Medbourne.* **Thur 11, Fri 12, Sat 13 June (10-9); Sun 14 June (10-7). Adm £10, chd free. Tea, coffee & cake in restaurant marquee. Meals and a fully stocked bar also available. Donation to Nevill Holt Community Arts.**
Nevill Holt Hall dates from the C13. Spacious and well proportioned, 10 acres of gardens are designed by Chelsea gold medal winner Rupert Golby. Highlights inc 3 distinctive walled gardens and generous herbaceous borders showing off an ancient Cedar of Lebanon. Nevill Holt Festival runs for 3 weeks in June. Full details and tickets will be available from January at www.nevillholtfestival.com. Walk-up tickets may be available on the day of the NGS opening, subject to availability. Adm £6 after 6pm.

23 THE NEW BARN
92 Newbold Road, Desford, LE9 9GS. A Nichols & R Pullin. *8m from J21 M1 & 12m from J22 M1.* **Sat 6, Sun 7 June (11-4). Adm £5, chd free. Tea, coffee & cake. Donation to Plant Heritage.**
A sloping ¾ acre plantsman's garden. Entering via a side gate visitors will discover different levels and spaces which enable them to enjoy the design and unusual plants throughout the garden. This is a well established garden that inc the National Collection of over 80 Geranium Phaeum cultivars planted to demonstrate their versatility and garden worthiness.

24 OAK COTTAGE
Well Lane, Blackfordby, Swadlincote, DE11 8AG. Colin & Jenny Carr. *Blackfordby, just over 1m from (& between) Ashby-de-la-Zouch or Swadlincote. From Ashby-de-la-Zouch take Moira Rd, turn R on Blackfordby Ln. As you enter Blackfordby, turn L to Butt Ln & quickly R to Strawberry Ln. Park up, then it is a 2 min walk to Well Ln entrance.* **Sun 15 Feb, Sun 12 Apr (10-4). Adm £5, chd free. Tea, coffee & cake.**
½ acre garden set around Blackfordby's 'hidden' listed thatched cottage, which itself is more than 300 yrs old. 3.4 acres of paddocks, front and rear gardens to explore with extensive displays of snowdrops (inc a named collection) as well as hellebores throughout. Later in spring the display changes to Snakes Heads and mature magnolias. The lower paddock has been planted with 450 native trees as part of the National Forest Freewoods scheme, with a drainage pond created at its base. The central swathe is being developed with wildflowers. At the top of the rear garden there is a chicken run, old and new orchards and a peach house.

25 OAK TREE HOUSE
North Road, South Kilworth, LE17 6DU. Pamela & Martin Shave. *15m S of Leicester. From M1 J20, take A4304 towards Market Harborough. At North Kilworth turn R, signed South Kilworth. Garden on L after approx 1m.* **Sat 27 June (11-5); Sun 28 June (10.30-1.30). Adm £5, chd free. Tea, coffee & cake.**
⅔ acre beautiful country garden full of colour, formal design, softened by cottage style planting. Modern sculptures. Large herbaceous borders, vegetable plots, pond, greenhouse, shady area, colour-themed borders. Extensive collections in over 300 pots, home to everything from alpines to trees. Trees with attractive bark. Many clematis and roses. Dramatic arched pergola. Constantly changing garden. Access to patio and greenhouse via steps.

26 THE OLD HALL

Main Street, Market Overton, LE15 7PL. Mr & Mrs Timothy Hart. *6m N of Oakham; 5m from A1 via Thistleton. 10m E from Melton Mowbray.* **Sun 26 Apr (2-5). Adm £7, chd free. Home-made teas with Hambleton Bakery Cakes.**

Set on a southerly ridge. Stone walls and yew hedges divide the garden into enclosed areas with herbaceous borders, shrubs, long walks and young and mature trees. There are interesting plants flowering most of the time. In 2020 a Japanese Tea House was added at the bottom of the garden. Partial wheelchair access. Gravel and mown paths. Return to house is steep. It is, however, possible to just sit on the terrace.

27 THE OLD RECTORY

Main Street, Newbold Verdon, Leicester, LE9 9NN. Gianni and Kate De Fraja. *10m W of Leicester. On the village Main St, just before the turning for the church. Bus stop 'Old White Swan' on lines 153. What3words app: hedge.areas.videos.* **Sat 13 June (11-6); Sun 14 June (10-4). Combined adm with The Lodge Brascote £8, chd free. Tea, coffee & cake.**

The garden surrounds the Georgian Old Rectory. It contains many species of trees, ranging in age from centuries-old to very young saplings. In June, the roses are at their best, and there are new hydrangeas. Hostas and the woods around the gravel paths are good throughout the season. There is a new, large circular bed, which the owners started planting in January 2025. The garden is accessed via a gravel drive. Wheelchair access is possible with some attention.

28 THE OLD VICARAGE, WHISSENDINE

2 Station Road, Whissendine, LE15 7HG. Prof Peter & Dr Sarah Furness, www.rutlandlordlieutenant.org/garden. *Up hill from St Andrew's church, 1st L in Station Rd.* **Sun 17 May (2-5). Adm £6, chd free. Home-made teas in St Andrew's Church, Whissendine (next door).**

2/3 acre garden, terrace with topiary, formal fountain courtyard and raised beds backed by gothic orangery. Herbaceous borders surround main lawn, hidden white walk. Wisteria tunnel to raised vegetable beds and large ornate greenhouse, beehives, Gothic hen house plus rare breed hens. Features inc pebble mosaics and woodwork. The gravel drive is hard work for wheelchair users. Some areas are accessible only by steps.

29 PREBENDAL HOUSE

Crocket Lane, Empingham, LE15 8PW. Matthew & Rebecca Eatough. *5m E of Oakham. Facing the church on Church St, through large gates on R.* **Sun 14 June (1.30-5). Adm £7, chd free. Home-made teas.**

A garden reimagined one year on. After an entire garden redesign with new planting and landscaping finishing in June 2025, the garden is maturing and settling into its new rhythm. A C18 walled garden with extensive flower and vegetable beds, herbaceous borders and glasshouse. Another notable feature is the lavender bank and garden pavilion. Mostly wheelchair friendly over gravel.

30 QUAINTREE HALL

Cedar Street, Braunston, LE15 8QS. Mrs Caroline Lomas. *Braunston, nr Oakham. 2m W of Oakham, in the centre of the village of Braunston, off Cedar St.* **Sun 12 July (12-5). Adm £5, chd free. Home-made teas.**

An established garden surrounding the medieval hall house (not open) inc a formal box parterre to the front of the house, a spring garden, a formal walled garden with yew hedges, a newly-replanted late summer garden and terraced courtyard garden with conservatory. A wide selection of interesting plants can be enjoyed, each carefully selected for colour and aspect by the knowledgeable garden owner. Thistleton Herb Nursery will have a stand selling many of the plants in the garden. The gravel drive can cause difficulty for wheelchairs but all steps can be avoided.

31 REDHILL LODGE

Seaton Road, Barrowden, Oakham, LE15 8EN. Richard & Susan Moffitt, 07894 064789, s.moffitt@yahoo.co.uk, www.m360design.co.uk. *1m from village of Barrowden along Seaton Rd.* **Sun 7 June, Sun 13 Sept (10-3). Adm £6, chd free. Light refreshments. Visits also by arrangement for groups of 10+.**

A bold contemporary garden on varying levels with panoramic views. Year-round interest is seen in the evergreen structure, landform, and water features in the form of a stone rill and a natural swimming pond. Planting is vibrant and varied. Formal rose gardens and herbaceous borders alongside naturalistic prairie style planting. Slate and steel sculptures add a further modern twist.

32 ST WOLSTAN'S HOUSE

Church Nook, Wigston Magna, LE18 3RA. Mr Kevin De-Voy & Mr Stephen Walker. *On corner of Church Nook & Bull Head St opp St Wistan's church. No parking at garden. Public car parks, all within 5min walk on Frederick St, Junction Rd & Paddock St.* **Sat 18, Sun 19 July (11-5). Adm £5, chd free. Home-made teas.**

Approx 1/2 acre garden divided into garden rooms with formal and informal planting featuring specimen *Sequoia sempervirens* and *Cedrus libani*. Inc formal white garden, rose garden, sunken Italian garden with Triton fountain, lawned area surrounded by mixed border and paths with rose and wisteria pergola and laburnum arch, Edwardian conservatory, terracotta garden and well garden with raised beds.

33 8 SAINTBURY ROAD

Glenfield, Leicester, LE3 8EL. Martin and Rosie Furniss. *3m NW of Leicester. Off Faire Rd which is opp County Hall on the A50. 2m from A50 and A46 interchange.* **Sat 8, Sun 9 Aug (11-4). Adm £4, chd free. Tea, coffee & cake inc home-made cookies.**

A medium sized town garden with two deep borders crammed with shrubs, climbers, perennials and annuals inc cannas, salvias, geraniums and hostas. However, with over 20 varieties, its colourful dahlias which steal the show. Container plants with a tropical feel surround a patio water feature. An arch leads to the rear with vegetable boxes, a greenhouse, flower nooks and yet more dahlias.

34 THE SECRET GARDEN, GLENFIELD HOSPITAL

Groby Road, Leicester, LE3 9QP. **Karen James.** *Upon arrival to the Glenfield Hospital, please follow the blue directional signage.* **Sat 27, Sun 28 June (10.30-3). Adm £3.50, chd free. Light refreshments in the Secret Garden cafe.**
Set within the grounds of the Glenfield Hospital, the Secret Garden is 1 acre in size, hidden behind the walls of a Victorian Walled garden which has been lovingly designed and restored for the benefit of all those who visit it and in consideration of the rich history and heritage of the garden and the wider Leicester Frith site. All main pathways are wheelchair accessible.

35 STOKE ALBANY HOUSE

Desborough Road, Stoke Albany, Market Harborough, LE16 8PT. Mr & Mrs A M Vinton, 01858 535227, jamescoop867@gmail.com, www.stokealbanyhouse.co.uk. *4m E of Market Harborough. Via A427 to Corby, turn to Stoke Albany, R at the White Horse (B669) garden ½ m on the L.* **Every Wed 3 June to 29 July (2-4.30). Adm £6, chd free.** Visits also by arrangement 3 June to 29 July. Donation to Marie Curie Cancer Care.
4 acre country house garden; fine trees and shrubs with wide herbaceous borders and sweeping striped lawn. Good display of bulbs in spring, roses June and July. Walled grey garden; nepeta walk arched with roses, parterre with box and roses. Mediterranean garden. Heated greenhouse, potager with topiary, water feature garden and sculptures.

149A Avenue Road, Stoneygate and Knighton Gardens

LEICESTERSHIRE & RUTLAND

GROUP OPENING

36 NEW STONEYGATE AND KNIGHTON GARDENS
Leicester, LE2 1LW. Ms Alison Simpson. *3m S of Leicester city centre. Gardens are within a 2m radius in S Leicester. Street parking at all addresses except 20 Ripon St which has residents only parking.* **Sun 7 June (12-5). Combined adm £6, chd free. Tea, coffee & cake in the church.**

NEW **149A AVENUE ROAD**
John North and Dr Angela Holland.

NEW **BISHOP'S LODGE**
Dr Lynn Snow.

NEW **119 CARISBROOKE ROAD**
Richard Johnson and Mariette Clare.

NEW **20 RIPON STREET**
Ms Alison Simpson.

NEW **154 SHANKLIN DRIVE**
Karl and Tina Charnley.

NEW **30 SPRINGFIELD ROAD**
Ms Barbara Matthews.

Six very different and interesting small and medium gardens displaying a variety of planting styles with a range of early summer flowering. 20 Ripon Street is a small terraced courtyard garden with ornamental trees, shady planting, perennials and climbers and a pond. The Bishop's Lodge, the garden of the Bishop, has a contemplative feel with a large lawn with multi layered plant borders. 30 Springfield Road is a gravel based garden with an extensive range of climbers, dry and traditional planting. 149a Avenue Road has intensively planted squares with climber, shrubs and perennials and a fern border accessed through a paved courtyard. 119 Carisbrooke Road is planted to encourage wildlife through its extensive perennials border and wild grass aspects. 154 Shanklin Drive is planted as a Mediterranean style garden with rows of lavender adjoining and gravel insert planting. There is also an ornamental pond.

37 TRESILLIAN HOUSE
67 Dalby Road, Melton Mowbray, LE13 0BQ. Mrs Alison Blythe, 01664 481997, alisonblythe@tresillianhouse.com, www.tresillianhouse.com. *½m S of Melton Mowbray centre. Situated on B6047 Dalby Rd, S of Melton town centre. (Melton to Gt Dalby/Market Harborough rd). Parking on site.* **Sun 8 Mar, Sun 3 May, Sun 21 June, Sun 30 Aug, Sun 25 Oct (11-4). Adm £5.50, chd free. Light refreshments in Log Cabin.** Visits also by arrangement 1 Apr to 21 Sept for groups of 6 to 35. Small coaches (up to 30) can park on site. Larger coaches park down road. Donation to Rotary Club of Melton Mowbray.
¾ acre garden re-established by current owner. Beautiful blue cedar

The Cottage

trees, specimen tulip tree. Variety of trees, plants and bushes reinstated. Original bog garden and natural pond. Koi pond; glass garden room holds exhibitions and recitals. Vegetable plot. Cowslips and bulbs in springtime. Wide variety of shrubs, plants and flowers. Quiet and tranquil oasis. Small Art Exhibition by local artists. The natural pond has been replanted by pond specialists, Wild Water Ponds. Live traditional jazz June and August. Keep warm in October with stew and dumplings or soup. Slate paths, steep in places but manageable.

38 TUDOR HOUSE
Manor Road, Great Bowden, Market Harborough, LE16 7HE. Tim and Liz Blades. *1m from Market Harborough train stn. From A6 r'about, take exit for Great Bowden. Cont for ½ m. Turn R at Xrds onto Main St. Cont on Main St, past the Red Lion pub, then turn R onto Manor Rd. Garden is 90yds on L.* **Sun 3 May (11-4). Adm £5, chd free. Tea, coffee & cake.**
One acre family garden featuring woodland, spring bulbs, lawns, greenhouse, pond, fire pit, sculptures and the owners' impulse plant purchases. A new vegetable patch and fruit cage were hastily established before the garden opened last year; come and see the progress and witness the battle with dry shade and perennial weeds after last summer's drought.

39 WESTBROOKE HOUSE
52 Scotland Road, Little Bowden, Market Harborough, LE16 8AX. Bryan & Joanne Drew. *½ m S Market Harborough. From Northampton Rd follow NGS arrows & park in public car park or on nearby roads - not on the road directly opp the entrance. No parking at property.* **Sun 26 Apr, Sun 7 June (10-4). Adm £6, chd free. Tea, coffee & cake.**
Westbrooke House is a late Victorian property built in 1887. The gardens comprise 6 acres in total and are approached through a tree lined driveway of mature limes and giant redwoods. Key features are walled flower garden, walled kitchen garden, fernery, lower garden, wildlife pond, spring garden, lawns, woodland paths and a meadow with a wildflower area, ha-ha and hornbeam avenue.

40 WESTVIEW
1 St Thomas's Road, Great Glen, Leicester, LE8 9EH. Gill & John Hadland, 01162 592170, gillhadland1@gmail.com. *7m S of Leicester. Take either r'about from A6 into village centre then follow NGS signs. Please park in Oaks Rd.* **Sat 21 Feb (11-4), open nearby Hedgehog Hall. Sun 22 Feb (11-4); Sat 23, Mon 25 May (11-5). Adm £4, chd free. Home-made teas. Home-made soup & rolls available at the Feb openings.** Visits also by arrangement Feb to Sept for groups of 5 to 20.
A small, organically managed walled cottage garden with year-round interest. Rare and unusual plants, many grown from seed. Courtyard garden with stone troughs and containers, alpines, herbaceous borders, woodland areas with unusual ferns, small wildlife pond, greenhouse, vegetables, fruit and herbs. Collection of Snowdrops. Recycled materials used to make quirky garden ornaments and water feature. Restored Victorian outhouse functions as a garden office and houses a collection of old garden tools and ephemera.

GROUP OPENING

41 WILLOUGHBY GARDENS
Willoughby Waterleys, LE8 6UD. *9m S of Leicester. From A426 heading N turn R at Dunton Bassett lights. Follow signs to Willoughby. From Blaby follow signs to Countesthorpe. 2m S to Willoughby.* **Sun 12 July (11-5). Combined adm £6, chd free. Light refreshments in the Village Hall.**

FARMWAY
Eileen Spencer, 07795 058582, eileenfarmway9@msn.com.
Visits also by arrangement 1 July to 23 Aug for groups of up to 20.

HIGH MEADOW
Phil & Eva Day.

JOHN'S WOOD
Jill Harris and Clare Frankham.

3 ORCHARD ROAD
Diane Brearley.

Willoughby Waterleys lies in the South Leicestershire countryside. 4 gardens will be open. John's Wood is a 1½ acre nature reserve planted to encourage wildlife. Farmway is a plant lovers garden with many unusual plants in colour themed borders. 3 Orchard Road is a small south facing garden packed with interesting features. High Meadow has been evolving over 16 yrs. Inc mixed planting and ornamental vegetable garden.

42 15 THE WOODCROFT
Diseworth, Derby, DE74 2QT. Nick Hollick, 07736 672585, nicknollick@me.com. *Exit M1 J23a, follow signs for A453 to East Midlands Airport. Continue for 2m, take exit to Diseworth onto Grimes Gate. Continue through village then R onto The Green. 2nd R onto The Woodcroft.* **Sun 23 Aug (11-4). Adm £4.50, chd free. Home-made teas.** Visits also by arrangement 7 Feb to 27 Sept for groups of 6 to 20.
⅓ acre garden developed by the owner over 46 yrs with mature choice trees and shrubs, old and modern shrub roses, fern garden, wildlife garden, drifts of snowdrops and colour themed mixed herbaceous borders. Gazebo overlooking large wildlife pond, seating throughout the garden. Sand bed planned for 2026 for borderline hardy plants. Three steps from the upper terrace to the main garden accessible to wheelchairs with assistance.

Our 2025 donation to the Queen's Institute of Community Nursing now helps support over 3,500 Queen's Nurses working in the community in England, Wales, Northern Ireland, the Channel Islands and the Isle of Man.

LINCOLNSHIRE

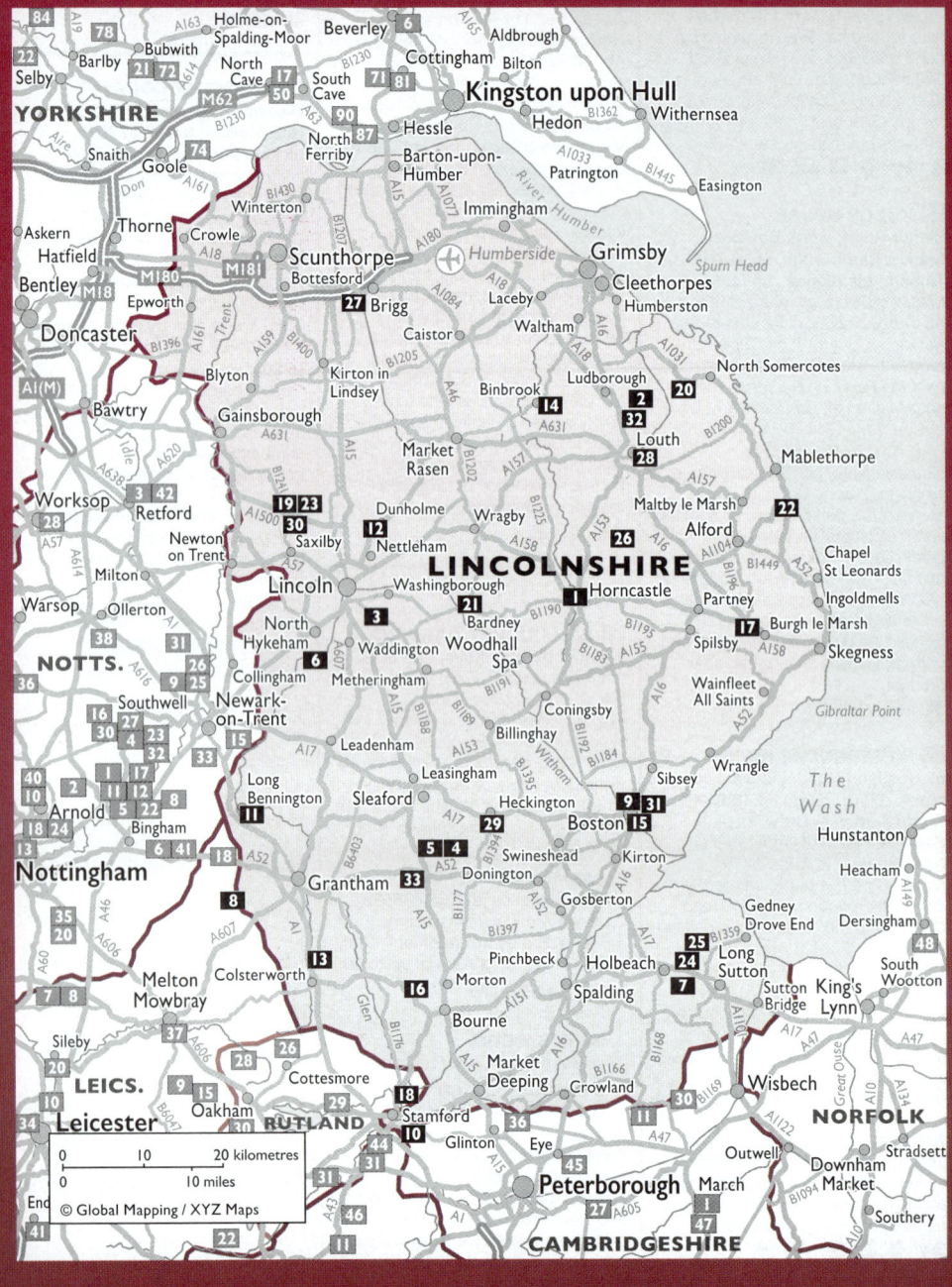

VOLUNTEERS

County Organiser
Lesley Wykes
01673 860356
lesley.wykes@ngs.org.uk

County Treasurer
Kate Richardson
07496 550516
kate.richardson@ngs.org.uk

Social Media
Diane Puncheon
01427 800008
diane.puncheon@ngs.org.uk

Publicity
Tricia Elliott
01427 788517
t.elliott575@gmail.com

Booklet Co-Ordinator
Linda Dawes
07854 661155
linda.dawes@ngs.org.uk

Talks Co-ordinator
Neil Timm
01472 398092
neilfernnursery@gmail.com

Assistant County Organisers
Karen Bourne
07860 504047
karen@karenwrightpr.com

Heather Charles
07496 329471
heather.charles@ngs.org.uk

Sylvia Ravenhall
01507 526014
sylvan@btinternet.com

@LincolnshireNGS

OPENING DATES

All entries subject to change.
For latest information check
www.ngs.org.uk
Extended openings are shown at the beginning of each month.
Map locator numbers are shown to the right of each garden name.

February

Snowdrop Openings
Sunday 15th
Woodlands   32

March

Sunday 29th
The Old Vicarage   24

April

Friday 3rd
◆ Easton Walled Gardens   13

Sunday 5th
Ashfield House   3
Woodlands   32

Saturday 11th
◆ Burghley House Private South
Gardens   10

Sunday 12th
◆ Burghley House Private South
Gardens   10

Sunday 19th
23 Accommodation Road   1

Sunday 26th
23 Accommodation Road   1
Dunholme Lodge   12

May

Sunday 3rd
23 Accommodation Road   1
NEW Oxcombe Manor   26
Woodlands   32

Saturday 9th
◆ Belvoir Castle   8

Sunday 10th
◆ Belvoir Castle   8

Tuesday 12th
NEW ◆ Grimsthorpe Castle   16

Sunday 17th
The Old Vicarage   24
Old White House   25

Saturday 23rd
Aswarby House   4
Aswarby Park   5
NEW Scawby Hall   27

June

Saturday 6th
Willoughby Road Allotments   31
NEW Woodside Farmhouse   33

Sunday 7th
◆ Auburn Hall   6
49 Church Street   11
Woodlands   32
NEW Woodside Farmhouse   33

Sunday 14th
Home Farm   18
Shangrila   29

Sunday 21st
The Fern Nursery and Bowling
Club   14

Tuesday 23rd
NEW ◆ Grimsthorpe Castle   16

Thursday 25th
The Ash   2

Saturday 27th
The Ash   2

Sunday 28th
The Ash   2
Dunholme Lodge   12
Walnut Lodge   30

July

Sunday 5th
NEW Ivy Cottage   19
NEW Mere House   23
The Old Vicarage   24
NEW Oxcombe Manor   26

Saturday 18th
Battleford Hall   7

Sunday 19th
Battleford Hall   7
NEW The Manor   21

Sunday 26th
◆ Gunby Hall and Gardens   17

August

Every Thursday and Sunday
The Secret Garden of Louth 28

Sunday 2nd
Woodlands 32

Saturday 8th
The Fern Nursery and Bowling Club 14

Sunday 9th
Fydell House 15

Sunday 16th
Boston Exotic Garden 9

September

Sunday 20th
Woodlands 32

By Arrangement

Arrange a personalised garden visit with your club, or group of friends, on a date to suit you. See individual garden entries for full details.

Ashfield House 3
Boston Exotic Garden 9
Fydell House 15
Home Farm 18
Ludney House Farm 20
Marigold Cottage 22
The Old Vicarage 24
The Secret Garden of Louth 28

Mere House

THE GARDENS

1 23 ACCOMMODATION ROAD
Horncastle, LN9 5AS. Mr & Mrs D Chapman. *From turning off Lincoln Rd A158, onto Accommodation Rd we are situated approx 600yds on R. Roadside parking.* **Sun 19, Sun 26 Apr, Sun 3 May (11-4). Adm £3.50, chd free.**
A medium sized garden to wander around and discover different plants; A range of tall and dwarf bearded iris, Auricula theatres showing off lovely doubles and there are also a range of fruit trees and bushes. Sitting in the garden, which is designed to have small rooms showing off flowers, you can relax and take it all in. Talk to the owners and discover garden plaques throughout. Mixture of plants and garden wall plaques to purchase finishes an enjoyable experience. Partial wheelchair access to decking area.

2 THE ASH
Main Road, Covenham St Bartholomew, Louth, LN11 0PF. Angela & Mervyn Aylett. *N of Louth. From A16 go E on Pear Tree Ln. At the x-roads turn R to Covenham St. Bartholomew. Cont into the village, garden is on the R. What3words app: rides.bronze.circulate.* **Thur 25, Sat 27, Sun 28 June (10-3). Adm £5, chd free. Light refreshments in the village hall.**
What is now the garden was a field when we moved here in 2021. Work commenced in the October and today the garden is full of shrubs, trees, cutting garden and vegetable patch. This, along with the pond, has brought a great amount wildlife to the garden and is a constant source of joy. The development of the garden has been totally based on no dig principles, which has proved a great success.

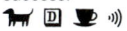

3 ASHFIELD HOUSE
Lincoln Road, Branston, Lincoln, LN4 1NS. John & Judi Tinsley, 07977 505682, john@tinsleyfarms.co.uk. *3m S of Lincoln on B1188. N outskirts of Branston on the B1188 Lincoln Rd. Signed 'Tinsley Farms - Ashfield'. Nr bus stop, follow signs down drive.* **Sun 5 Apr (11-4). Adm £6, chd free. Light refreshments. Visits also by arrangement Apr to Oct.**
Discover 140 flowering cherries and 30 magnolias. Many thousands of spring bulbs, sweeping lawns and lake. Beautiful naturally landscaped garden with some superb mature trees as well as a fascinating arboretum. One of the best flowering cherry displays in the area. Fairly level garden. Wheelchair access via grass paths.

4 ASWARBY HOUSE
Aswarby, Sleaford, NG34 8SE. Penny & James Herdman. *Past church on R of road. 300yds from the gates of Aswarby Park. Plenty of parking available on the roadside.* **Sat 23 May (2-5). Combined adm with Aswarby Park £10, chd free. Home-made teas in Aswarby Park.**
Garden of one acre planted in the grounds of a handsome C18 house and coachhouse. It has a partial walled garden, wildflower meadow surrounded by ornamental grasses and a 30 metre long herbaceous border. With two box parterres, and woodland shrubs, it has stunning views over ancient ridge and furrow grassland. This garden would complement your visit to Aswarby Park.

5 ASWARBY PARK
Aswarby, Sleaford, NG34 8SD. Mr & Mrs George Playne, www.aswarbyestate.co.uk. *5m S of Sleaford on A15. Take signs to Aswarby. Entrance is straight ahead by church through black gates.* **Sat 23 May (2-5). Combined adm with Aswarby House £10, chd free. Home-made teas.**
Formal and woodland garden in a parkland setting of approx 20 acres. Yew trees form a backdrop to borders and lawns surrounding the house, formally a converted stable block. The walled garden incorporating a greenhouse with a Muscat grapevine which is over 300 years old. Other attractions inc a unique rose walk, a cutting garden created in 2022 and a wildflower bed in 2023. Partial wheelchair access on gravel paths and drives.

6 ♦ AUBOURN HALL
Harmston Road, Aubourn, Lincoln, LN5 9DZ. Mr & Mrs Christopher Nevile, 01522 788224, office@aubournestate.co.uk, www.aubournestate.co.uk. *7m SW of Lincoln. Signed off A607 at Harmston & off A46 at Thorpe on the Hill.* **For NGS: Sun 7 June (12-4). Adm £8.50, chd free. Home-made refreshments. For other opening times and information, please phone, email or visit garden website.**
The peaceful and secluded 12 acre garden that surrounds Aubourn Hall is a dramatic reimagining of a space previously untended. It features a Golden Garden, rose garden, prairie garden, a stumpery and a 13 ring grass labyrinth. The southern part of the garden is divided into rooms while the Big Lawn occupies the space to the west and leads into the woodland gardens and ponds behind the house. Partial wheelchair access.

7 BATTLEFORD HALL
Bensgate Road (formerly Proudfoot Lane), Fleet, Holbeach, Spalding, PE12 8NL. Mr & Mrs J. Holmes. *Access via main gates from Bensgate (formerly Proudfoot Ln). A former old rectory found next to St. Mary Magdalene Church. Fleet, approx 3m E from Holbeach.* **Sat 18, Sun 19 July (11-4). Adm £7, chd free. Tea, coffee & cake.**
' A new garden on old bones'. A Victorian garden with formal clipped hedging, rose parterres alongside colourful borders and a walled herbalist garden. A canopy of mature trees, comprising of Ginkgo Biloba, Mulberry, London plane and Cedar of Lebanon. A new area of 'jungle' planting with banana trees, bamboo and Tetrapanax papyrifer.

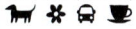

The National Garden Scheme donated £3,875,596 to our nursing and health beneficiaries from money raised at gardens open in 2025.

8 ♦ BELVOIR CASTLE
Belvoir, Grantham, NG32 1PE. The Duke & Duchess of Rutland, 01476 871001, info@belvoircastle.com, www.belvoircastle.com. *9m W of Grantham. Follow brown heritage signs for Belvoir Castle on A52, A1, A607.* **For NGS: Sat 9, Sun 10 May (9.30-5). Adm £10, chd £6. Last entry to the garden at 4.30pm. For other opening times and information, please phone, email or visit garden website.**
The striking Regency castle sits proudly overlooking the beautiful Vale of Belvoir and is surrounded by Capability Brown landscape. The plans to the ten hectares of pleasure gardens originally designed by Harold Peto have only recently been rediscovered with all the classic hallmarks of the designer. The roses in the garden today are the design of Emma, the current Duchess of Rutland. Flat shoes essential and steep climb to Castle. Aviary Tearoom serving a range of home-cooked lunches and afternoon teas. Bistro cafe and farm shop selling a range of fresh produce available at Belvoir's Retail Village. Adventure playground and nature walks through the Capability Brown designed parkland. Historic Castle tours available. Only rose garden accessible by wheelchair. Steep slopes and steps in places.
& 🚗 ☕ 🪵 »)

9 BOSTON EXOTIC GARDEN
40 Allington Garden, Boston, PE21 9DW. Nigel Smith, 07932 626266, bostonexoticgarden@gmail.com. *1m NE of Boston town centre. From Boston take A16 towards Spilsby. Take 3rd L into Hospital Ln then 2nd R into Linden Way. 1st L is Allington Garden. What3words app: hatch.awake.magic.* **Sun 16 Aug (11-4). Adm £5, chd free. Tea, coffee & cake. Visits also by arrangement 1 Aug to 30 Aug for groups of up to 20.**
Built from a blank canvas since 2017, this 42m x 12m garden has been transformed into an exotic garden full of interesting tropical plants with huge lush foliage. Various forms of banana plants, *Canna* and *Brugmansia*. Many of the plants are tender so need protection over winter. Various paths to explore. Small wildlife pond. There are two steps up to main lawn from large patio area. A ramp will be available. There are a few narrow paths.
& ✱ ☕ »)

10 ♦ BURGHLEY HOUSE PRIVATE SOUTH GARDENS
Stamford, PE9 3JY. Burghley House Preservation Trust, 01780 752451, burghley@burghley.co.uk, www.burghley.co.uk. *1m E of Stamford. From Stamford follow signs to Burghley via B1443.* **For NGS: Sat 11, Sun 12 Apr (10-4). Adm £12, chd £9.50. Pre-booking essential, please visit www.ngs. org.uk for information & booking. For other opening times and information, please phone, email or visit garden website.**
The Private South Gardens at Burghley House will open for the NGS with spectacular spring bulbs in a park like setting with magnificent trees. Relish the opportunity to enjoy Capability Brown's famous lake and summerhouse. Entry via Garden Kiosks. Adm charge is a special pre-book price only via NGS website. Visitors paying at the gate on the day will be charged a Gardens ticket price. Wheelchair access via gravel paths.
& ✱ 🚗 ☕ »)

11 49 CHURCH STREET
Long Bennington, Newark, NG23 5ES. Di Ablewhite, www.withamsidehouse.com. *Equidistant between Grantham and Newark, just off the A1. Enter Church St opp the sch. Garden is halfway down on the L. 2 large brick pillars at the top of the drive. What3words app: mini.waistcoat.delighted.* **Sun 7 June (11-4). Adm £5, chd free. Tea, coffee & cake.**
A beautiful riverside garden with fabulous open views. We have mature trees, topiary, borders and several relaxing seating areas in different styles. The house and garden are also used as a photoshoot location. Fairly wheelchair friendly, but some gravel areas and low steps.
& 🐕 ✱ ☕ »)

12 DUNHOLME LODGE
Dunholme, Lincoln, LN2 3QA. Hugh & Lesley Wykes. *4m NE of Lincoln. Turn off A46 towards Welton at the r'about. After ½m turn L up long private road.* **Sun 26 Apr, Sun 28 June (11-5). Adm £5.50, chd free. Home-made teas.**
A WWII airfield site and farm. Garden developed over 35 years comprising five acres of trees, shrubs, mixed borders, spring bulbs, roses, wildflower area, large wildlife pond, vegetable patch and topiary. War memorial and pop-up museum, craft stalls, vintage vehicles and music. Most areas wheelchair accessible but some loose stone and gravel and some grass.
& 🐕 ✱ 🚗 ☕ »)

13 ♦ EASTON WALLED GARDENS
Easton, NG33 5AP. Sir Fred & Lady Cholmeley, 01476 530063, info@eastonwalledgardens. co.uk, www.visiteaston.co.uk. *7m S of Grantham. 1m from A1, off B6403.* **For NGS: Fri 3 Apr (11-4). Adm £12.50, chd £5. For other opening times and information, please phone, email or visit garden website.**
A 400 year old, restored 12 acre garden set in the heart of Lincolnshire. Home to snowdrops, sweetpeas, roses and meadows. The River Witham meanders through the gardens, teeming with wildlife. Other garden highlights inc a yew tunnel, turf maze and cut flower gardens. The Applestore Tearoom and Coffee Room offers hot and cold drinks, light savoury snacks, home-made cakes. Regret no wheelchair access to lower gardens but tearoom, shop, upper gardens and facilities are all accessible.
& ✱ 🚗 🛏 ☕ »)

14 THE FERN NURSERY AND BOWLING CLUB
Grimsby Road, Binbrook, Market Rasen, LN8 6DH. Neil Timm, www.fernnursery.co.uk. *On B1203 from Market Rasen. On the Grimsby road from Binbrook Square, 400m.* **Sun 21 June, Sat 8 Aug (11-4). Adm £4, chd free. Tea, coffee & cake in the bowling pavilion. Refreshments provided by Binbrook Bowling Club.**
A wildlife garden with a natural stream running through which supplies a pond and water features. Discover rock features, acid beds and a sheltered winter garden with a sundial; a small wood with the main fern collection. There is a nursery and bowling green where a game is often played. Large shrubs, a bank of drought tolerant plants and herbaceous perennials, seats, a gazebo, and bridge Artwork at 'Scaliwags' garden just off the bowling green also open to view. Partial wheelchairs access, gravel paths.
& 🐕 ✱ 🚗 ☕

15 FYDELL HOUSE

South Square, Boston, PE21 6HU. Boston Preservation Trust, 01205 351520, info@fydellhouse.org.uk, www.facebook.com/fydellhouse. *Through the Market Sq, past Boots. One way street by Guildhall. There are 3 car parks within 200yds of the house. Disabled parking in council car park opp the house.* **Sun 9 Aug (10-4). Adm £4, chd free. Light refreshments.** **Visits also by arrangement.**

Within three original red brick walls a formal garden has been created in 1995. Yew buttresses, arbours and four parterres use Dutch themes. The borders contain herbaceous plants and shrubs. The north facing border holds shade loving plants. There is a mulberry and walnut tree. The astrolabe was installed in 1997. A Victorian rockery is built from slag from ironworks in Boston. Ramps to front door and widened paths in the garden.

16 NEW ♦ GRIMSTHORPE CASTLE

Grimsthorpe, Bourne, PE10 0LY. Grimsthorpe & Drummond Castle Trust, 01778 591205, visit@grimsthorpe.co.uk, www.grimsthorpe.co.uk. *3m NW of Bourne. 8m E of A1 on A151 from Colsterworth junc. Main entrance gates indicated by brown tourist sign.* **For NGS: Tue 12 May, Tue 23 June (10-5). Adm £10, chd £6. Tea, coffee & cake at Coach House Tearoom.** **For other opening times and information, please phone, email or visit garden website.**

The Grade I listed gardens encompass nearly 70 acres and inc large formal lawns, fine topiary and formal hedges, ornamental and productive kitchen garden, large herbaceous borders, rose parterre and woodland walks with spring bulb displays. Visitors can explore the surrounding 3000 acre estate that encompasses a Capability Brown landscape, in addition to the tranquil and relaxing gardens. Home-made light lunches, hot and cold drinks, cakes and snacks from our Tea Trailer (10-4). Farm shop, adventure playground, historic house and park trails. Gravel paths and disabled ramps.

In 2025, our donations to Carers Trust helped them support over 1 million unpaid carers across the UK, as part of their network of local carer centres.

Ivy Cottage

Easton Walled Gardens

17 ♦ GUNBY HALL AND GARDENS
Spilsby, PE23 5SS. National Trust, 01754 892998, gunbyhall@nationaltrust.org.uk, www.nationaltrust.org.uk/gunby-hall. 2½m NW of Burgh-le-Marsh. 7m W of Skegness. On A158. Signed off Gunby r'about. **For NGS: Sun 26 July (10-4). Adm £7, chd £3.50. Tea, coffee & cake in the Gunby tearoom. For other opening times and information, please phone, email or visit garden website.**
Eight acres of formal and walled gardens. Old roses, herbaceous borders, herb garden and kitchen garden with fruit trees and vegetables. Greenhouses and sweeping lawns. Tennyson's Haunt of Ancient Peace. Enjoy a sweet treat from the tearoom, or visit one of many craft and trade stalls in the courtyard. House and Garden Adm: £12 Adult, £6 Child. Wheelchair access in gardens. Mobility scooter available. Gunby's dedicated wheelchair for ground floor of house. There are steps into the house.

18 HOME FARM
Little Casterton Road, Ryhall, Stamford, PE9 4HA. Steve & Karen Bourne, 07771 804466, sjbourne@outlook.com. 1½m N of Stamford. Just off the A6121 Stamford to Bourne Rd. 1½m N of Stamford. At mini-r'about turn towards Little Casterton & Tolethorpe Hall. Car park 50yds on L. **Sun 14 June (11-5). Adm £6, chd free. Home-made teas.** Visits also by arrangement in June for groups of 15 to 50.
A large farmhouse garden featuring more than 120 old English rose varieties. Herbaceous beds with delphiniums, salvias, grasses, and another planted in hot reds and yellows with alstroemeria, *Geum* and sunflowers. A terrace with far-reaching views surrounded by lavender and a wildflower area with pathways, woodland walk, large fruit cage, apple orchard and vegetable garden. Most areas accessible by wheelchair.

19 NEW IVY COTTAGE
Stow Road, Sturton By Stow, Lincoln, LN1 2BZ. Martin & Jill Fish, www.martinfish.com. 10m NW of Lincoln between Sturton & Stow. House on R. Postcode stops short of garden. Parking for both gardens at Mere House opp. Limited blue badge parking at Ivy Cottage. What3words app: engage.tycoons.refrained. **Sun 5 July (11-4). Combined adm with Mere House £10, chd free. Tea, coffee & cake at Mere House. Adm inc refreshments.**
Ivy Cottage garden has been redesigned and planted over the past three years. The 0.3 acre garden features a summerhouse, patio and mixed borders with a selection of trees, shrubs, roses and perennials giving all year-round interest. A large greenhouse with edible crops and a display of ornamental plants. The productive kitchen garden features raised vegetable beds, herbs and trained fruit.

20 LUDNEY HOUSE FARM
Ludney, Louth, LN11 7JU.
Jayne Bullas, 07733 018710,
jayne@theoldgatehouse.com.
Between Grainthorpe & Conisholme we are on the main road. There is a paddock for parking. **Visits by arrangement 1 May to 13 Sept for groups of 10 to 30. Adm £10, chd free. Tea, coffee & cake. Adm inc refreshments.**
A beautiful large garden, lovingly developed over the last 25 years with several areas of formal and informal planting inc a pond which attracts a wonderful variety of wildlife. There is an excellent mix of trees, shrubs, perennials, rose garden and wildflower area. There are plenty of seats positioned around to sit and enjoy a cuppa and piece of cake. Wheelchair access to most of garden.

21 NEW THE MANOR
Church Lane, Bardney, Lincoln, LN3 5TZ. Mrs Samantha Cook, www.bardneymanorwalledgarden.com. *Drive on Church Ln, past graveyard on L. Turn L after red dog bin & into the drive. What3words app: tasters.interviewer.wiped.* **Sun 19 July (11-4). Adm £7, chd free. Tea, coffee & cake.**
Set in the heart of rural Lincolnshire, Bardney Manor Walled Gardens offer a rare opportunity to step back in time and experience the charm of a English kitchen garden being lovingly restored for the modern day. Enclosed by high brick walls, the garden provides shelter and creates a unique microclimate that allows fruit, vegetables and flowers and herbs to thrive. Wheelchair access to all areas of the garden.

22 MARIGOLD COTTAGE
Hotchin Road, Sutton-on-Sea, LN12 2NP. Stephanie Lee & John Raby, 07853466554, marigoldlee@icloud.com, www.rabylee.uk/marigold. *16m N of Skegness on A52. 7m E of Alford on A1111. 3m S of Mablethorpe on A52. Turn off A52 on High St at Cornerhouse Cafe. Follow road past playing field on R. Road turns away from the dunes. House 2nd on L.* **Visits by arrangement May to Aug for groups of 10+. Adm by donation. Home-made teas.**
Slide open the Japanese gate to find secret shaded paths. You will be taken aback by the abundance of planting combinations. There are pergolas covered in climbers, raised beds, a large kitchen garden and everywhere places to rest and absorb the ambience. Stephanie is always on hand to share her love of gardening and expertise. Not forgetting, substantial plant sales propagated from the garden. New hosta theatre and heuchera installation. Most of garden is wheelchair accessible along flat, paved paths.

23 NEW MERE HOUSE
Stow Road, Sturton by Stow, Lincoln, LN1 2BZ. Nigel & Alice Gray. *10m NW of Lincoln between Sturton & Stow. 1m from centre of Sturton village heading to Stow, house on L. NB: Postcode will not bring you far enough out of Sturton village. What3words app: roadblock.validated.obliging.* **Sun 5 July (11-4). Combined adm with Ivy Cottage £10, chd free. Tea, coffee & cake. Adm inc refreshments.**
Approx 1½ acres of established garden planted for the first time in 1975, redesigned in 1996, 2011, renewed over the last year. There is also a cutting garden, pleached hedges, vegetable garden and orchard. Work in continual progress includes long herbaceous border and new border for the dryer conditions. The garden is wheelchair accessible, some grass paths.

24 THE OLD VICARAGE
Low Road, Holbeach Hurn, PE12 8JN. Mrs Liz Dixon-Spain, lizdixonspain@gmail.com. *2m NE of Holbeach. Turn off A17 N to Holbeach Hurn. 1st R at war memorial into Low Rd. Old Vicarage is on R approx 400yds. Parking in grass paddock.* **Sun 29 Mar (12-3.30). Adm £5, chd free. Sun 17 May (1-5). Combined adm with Old White House £8, chd free. Refreshments served at Old White House. Sun 5 July (1-5). Adm £5, chd free. Visits also by arrangement 22 Mar to 27 Sept for groups of 5 to 30.**
A two acre garden with 160 year old tulip, plane and beech trees: borders of shrubs, roses, herbaceous plants. Snowdrops, early bulbs, hellebores in woodland. Shrub roses and herb garden in old paddock area, surrounded by informal borders with pond, bog garden, wildflowers, grasses and bulbs. Small fruit and vegetable garden. Grass and flower meadow. Garden managed environmentally for 35 years. Wheelchair access via gravel drive. Some hard paths but mostly grass.

25 OLD WHITE HOUSE
Baileys Lane, Holbeach Hurn, PE12 8JP. Mrs A Worth. *2m N of Holbeach. Turn off A17 N to Holbeach Hurn, follow signs to village, cont through, turn R after Rose & Crown pub at Baileys Ln.* **Sun 17 May (1-5). Combined adm with The Old Vicarage £8, chd free. Home-made teas and cakes.**
A mature garden of 1½ acres featuring herbaceous borders, roses, patterned garden, herb garden and walled kitchen garden. Large catalpa, tulip tree that flowers, ginko and other specimen trees.

26 NEW OXCOMBE MANOR
Oxcombe, Horncastle, LN9 6LU. Mr Edward Gorst, www.oxcombepottery.co.uk. *From the Bluestone Heath Rd turn into road signposted 'Oxcombe'. What3words app: tinsel.mouse.corrects.* **Sun 3 May, Sun 5 July (11.30-5.30). Adm £7, chd free. Tea, coffee & cake.**
Oxcombe lies in a secluded picturesque valley of the Lincolnshire Wolds, with a manor house, traditional farmstead and parish church among a kitchen garden, orchard, lawns, woodland and flower beds. Today it offers a tranquil retreat for developing potters and artists. The gardens are cared for but not manicured, beginning a new chapter with fresh projects planned under new tenure. Visitors can enjoy the gardens while trying pottery taster sessions, browse local produce stalls, and relax with tea and home-made cakes. Explore the historic All Saints Church, wander a short woodland trail, and discover the Visitor Centre with its history of the Lincolnshire Wolds and Oxcombe. Main gardens are wheelchair accessible, excluding some small sections. There is a wheelchair accessible toilet located 100m from the gardens.

27 NEW SCAWBY HALL
Vicarage Lane, Scawby, Brigg, DN20 9LX. Mr & Mrs Sutton Nelthorpe, www.scawbyhall.com. *The car park may be reached by heading through the gates for Scawby Hall at the intersection of Vicarage Ln & Messingham Ln.* **Sat 23 May (11-4). Adm £6, chd free. Tea, coffee & cake in the church.**
The kitchen garden at Scawby Hall was developed during the Victorian era and maintains the original framework of four quadrants with box hedging edged with espaliered fruit trees. Brilliant peony display in late spring and dahlias in late summer. Traditional garden with productive vegetable patch with some modern additions such as a beautiful pleached copper beech circle and grass collection. Paths are lined with woodchip.

28 THE SECRET GARDEN OF LOUTH
68 Watts Lane, Louth, LN11 9DG. Jenny & Rodger Grasham ½ m S *of Louth town centre. For SatNav & to avoid Watts Ln use postcode LN119DJ. Mount Pleasant Ave, leads straight up to our house.* **Every Thur and Sun 2 Aug to 30 Aug (11-4). Adm £5, chd free. Pre-booking essential, please phone 07977 318145, email sallysing@hotmail.co.uk or visit www.facebook.com/thesecretgardenoflouth for information & booking. Tea, coffee & cake.** Visits also by arrangement 2 Aug to 30 Aug for groups of 10+.
Blank canvas of ⅕ acre in early 90s. Developed into lush, colourful, exotic plant packed haven. A whole new world on entering from street. Exotic borders, raised exotic island, long hot border, pond and stumpery. Intimate seating areas throughout. Can children find where the frogs are hiding? Butterflies and bees but how many different types? Feed the fish, find Cedric the spider, Simon the snake, Colin the Crocodile and more. Main areas wheelchair accessible with care. Narrow paths. Not suitable for mobility scooters.

29 SHANGRILA
Little Hale Road, Great Hale, Sleaford, NG34 9LH. Marilyn Cooke & John Knight. *On B1394 between Heckington & Helpringham.*

Sun 14 June (11-5). Adm £4.50, chd free. Tea, coffee & cake.
Approx three acre garden with sweeping lawns, long herbaceous borders and colour themed island beds. Discover the hosta collection, and relax in the seating area by the lavender beds. Features also inc topiary, acer collection and a Japanese zen garden. Wheelchair access to all areas.

30 WALNUT LODGE
Bransby, Lincoln, LN1 2PH. David Lunt. *7m NW of Lincoln. From Saxilby on A57 take B1241 to Sturton. From the A1500 look for the yellow sign to Bransby 3m E of Sturton. Please park in Bransby Horses staff car park.* **Sun 28 June (10-4). Adm £5, chd free. Tea, coffee & cake.**
Rural garden of ½ acres established by the owners over the past ten years on clay. Herbaceous borders extending to 60m. Mature trees comprise limes, walnut and false acacia. Raised vegetable garden. Outstanding views to the Lincoln cliff to the east. The charity Bransby Horses, is located in the village and the visitor centre is well worth a visit.

31 WILLOUGHBY ROAD ALLOTMENTS
Willoughby Road, Boston, PE21 9HN. Willoughby Road Allotments Association, www.willoughbyroadallotments.com. *Entrance is adjacent to 109 Willoughby Rd. Street parking only.* **Sat 6 June (11.30-3.30). Adm £4, chd free. Light refreshments.**
Set in five acres the allotments comprise 60 plots growing fine vegetables, fruit, flowers and herbs. There is a small orchard and wildflower area and a community space adjacent. Discover artwork created by Bex Simon and there is a small cafe open to the public on site. We work with schools, social prescribing and community groups. Community area with kitchen and disabled WC. Large polytunnel with raised beds inside and out. The allotments are completely wheelchair accessible and good for mobility scooters.

32 WOODLANDS
Peppin Lane, Fotherby, Louth, LN11 0UW. Ann & Bob Armstrong, www.woodlandsplants.co.uk. *2m N of Louth off A16 signed Fotherby. Please park on R verge opp allotments & walk approx 350 yds to garden. If full, please park considerately in the village. No parking at garden.* **Sun 15 Feb (10.30-3.30); Sun 5 Apr, Sun 3 May, Sun 7 June, Sun 2 Aug, Sun 20 Sept (10.30-4.30). Adm £5, chd free. Home-made teas. For our Feb opening we are offering home-made soup to warm visitors.**
Renowned for its rich planting of shaded beds, but plenty to interest sun lovers too, especially salvias. A good selection available in the RHS listed nursery. The new crevice garden is developing nicely and once again we are holding a winter opening featuring drifts of snowdrops and aconites amongst winter flowering shrubs and a small, but expanding collection of named snowdrops. Award winning professional artist's studio open to visitors. National collection of *Codonopsis* with Plant Heritage status. Wheelchair access possible with care. Some parking at the house for those with limited mobility.

33 NEW WOODSIDE FARMHOUSE
Newton, Sleaford, NG34 0EE. Mrs Anne Walton. *8m S of Sleaford. Taking the turn for Newton from the A52. Once in the village turn R at the T-junc. Look for car parking signs on R next to the old pub.* **Sat 6, Sun 7 June (10.30-4.30). Adm £5, chd free. Tea, coffee & cake.**
Wrapping around a C17 Lincolnshire Longhouse, the garden has been 16 years in the making. From a derelict house and plot, the garden has evolved to provide space for living, working, exercising, cherishing plants and relaxing. With water, a large netted vegetable plot, apple orchard, wild patch, chicken accommodation and formal contemporary area, there is much to explore.

LONDON

VOLUNTEERS

County Organiser
Penny Snell
01932 864532
pennysnellflowers@btinternet.com

County Treasurer
Marion Smart
marion.smart@ngs.org.uk

Publicity
Sonya Pinto
07779 609715
sonya.pinto@ngs.org.uk

Booklet Co-ordinator
Sue Phipps
07771 767196
sue.phipps@ngs.org.uk

Booklet Distributor
Joey Clover
joey.clover@ngs.org.uk

Social Media
Holly Eastlake
Karen Hepworth
Tayla McLuskie
Lena Robinson
LondonSocialMedia@ngs.org.uk

Assistant County Organisers

Central London
Eveline Carn
07831 136069
evelinecbcarn@icloud.com

Croydon & outer S London
Position vacant
For details please contact Penny Snell (as left)

Dulwich & surrounding area
Clive Pankhurst
07941 536934
alternative.ramblings@gmail.com

E London
Teresa Farnham
07761 476651
farnhamz@yahoo.co.uk

Finchley & Barnet
Debra & Tim Craighead
07415 166617
dcraighead@icloud.com

Greenwich & surrounding area
Hugh Hallard
07886 833756
hugh.hallard@ngs.org.uk

Hackney
Philip Lightowlers
07910 850276
plighto@gmail.com

Hampstead
Joan Arnold
07850 764543
joan.arnold40@gmail.com

Islington
Vanessa Easlea
020 7700 7335
vanessa.easlea@ngs.org.uk

Northwood, Pinner, Ruislip & Harrow
Brenda White
020 8863 5877
brenda.white@ngs.org.uk

NW London
Susan Bennett & Earl Hyde
020 8883 8540
suebearlh@yahoo.co.uk

Outer NW London
James Duncan Mattoon
07504 565612

Outer W London & Clapham
Sarah Corvi
07803 111968
sarah.corvi@ngs.org.uk

SE London
Janine Wookey
07711 279636
j.wookey@btinternet.com

SW London
Joey Clover (as above)

W London, Barnes & Chiswick
Siobhan McCammon
07952 889866
siobhan.mccammon@gmail.com

@LondonNGS
@londonngs

40 Bronson Road

LONDON GARDENS LISTED BY POSTCODE

Inner London Postcodes

E and EC London
69 Antill Road, E3
26 College Gardens, E4
6 Eglington Road, E4
36 Garfield Road, E4
Lower Clapton Gardens, E5
Forest Gate Community Garden, E7
42 Latimer Road, E7
84 Lavender Grove, E8
London Fields Gardens, E8
St Joseph's Hospice, E8
37 Harold Road, E11
Wanstead Gardens, E11
Aldersbrook & Lakehouse Gardens, E12
28a Worcester Road, E17
83 Cowslip Road, E18
85 Cowslip Road, E18
25 Mulberry Way, E18
The Inner and Middle Temple Gardens, EC4

N and NW London
Arlington Square Gardens, N1
Barnsbury Group, N1
Canonbury Gardens, N1
De Beauvoir Gardens, N1
57 Huntingdon Street, N1
King Henry's Walk Garden, N1
5 Northampton Park, N1
19 St Peter's Street, N1
6 Thornhill Road, N1
36 Thornhill Square, N1
66 Abbots Gardens, N2
7 Deansway, N2
24 Twyford Avenue, N2
32 Highbury Hill, N5
32 Highbury Place, N5
Olden Community Garden, N5
33 Hampstead Lane, N6
OmVed Gardens, N6
48 Hungerford Road, N7
11 Park Avenue North, N8
77a Muswell Road, N10
Princes Avenue Gardens, N10
5 St Regis Close, N10
25 Springfield Avenue, N10
Golf Course Allotments, N11
25 Arlington, N12
Holtwhites Bakery & Deli, N13
15 Norcott Road, N16
36 Ashley Road, N19
21 Oakleigh Park South, N20
Ally Pally Allotments, N22
Chitts Hill Allotment & Garden Society, N22
Railway Cottages, N22
36 Park Village East, NW1
Royal College of Physicians, Garden of Medicinal Plants, NW1
93 Tanfield Avenue, NW2
Adelaide Community Garden Club, NW3
1A Primrose Gardens, NW3
The Mysteries of Light Rosary Garden, NW5
85 Corringham Road, NW11
92 Hampstead Way, NW11
100 Hampstead Way, NW11

SE and SW London
Garden Barge Square at Tower Bridge Moorings, SE1
The Garden Museum, SE1
Lambeth Palace, SE1
The Rockingham Garden Estate, SE1
71 Coldharbour Lane, SE5
24 Grove Park, SE5
16 Sears Street, SE5
Eltham Palace and Gardens, SE9
The Gatehouse, SE9
Woodlands, SE9
41 Southbrook Road, SE12
13 Waite Davies Road, SE12
15 Waite Davies Road, SE12
Blackheath Gardens, SE13
Choumert Square, SE15
Court Lane Group, SE21
38 Lovelace Road, SE21
12 Dovedale Road, SE22
14 Dovedale Road, SE22
209 Friern Road, SE22
4 Piermont Green, SE22
86 Underhill Road, SE22
86A Underhill Road, SE22
58 Cranston Road, SE23
Forest Hill Garden Group, SE23
39 Wood Vale, SE23
75 Bampton Road, SE23
5 Burbage Road, SE24
South London Botanical Institute, SE24
Stoney Hill House, SE26
Cadogan Place South Garden, SW1
Eccleston Square, SW1
Spencer House, SW1
51 The Chase, SW4
52 The Chase, SW4
Royal Trinity Hospice, SW4
152a Victoria Rise, SW4
The Hurlingham Club, SW6
25 Stirling Road, SW9
103 Thurleigh Road, SW12
49 Lonsdale Road, SW13
68 Nowell Road, SW13
1 Fife Road, SW14
40 Chartfield Avenue, SW15
100 Knollys Road, SW16
31 Ryecroft Road, SW16
40 Bronson Road, SW20
35 Burstow Road, SW20
Paddock Allotments & Leisure Gardens, SW20

W and WC London
Rooftopvegplot, W1
Warren Mews, W1
St George's Fields, W2
Acton Gardens, W3
Zen Garden at Japanese Buddhist Centre, W3
Chiswick Mall Gardens, W4
Maggie's West London, W6
27 St Peters Square, W6
1 York Close, W7
Edwardes Square, W8
57 St Quintin Avenue, W10
Arundel & Elgin Gardens, W11
Arundel & Ladbroke Gardens, W11
Lloyd Square, WC1X

Outer London postcodes

59 The Chase, BR1
59 Ashburton Avenue, CR0
The Exchange Erith, DA8
Oak Farm/Homestead, EN2
Theobald's Farmhouse, EN2
Fernveil Gardens, EN4
West Lodge Park, EN4
190 Barnet Road, EN5
3 Old Fold Close, EN5
Bryan's Jungle, EN8
42 Risingholme Road, HA3
31 Arlington Drive, HA4
4 Manningtree Road, HA4
Long Cottage, HA5
1 Dorset Court, HA6
Frith Lodge, HA6
Horatio's Garden, HA7
53 Lady Aylesford Avenue, HA7
26 Hillcroft Crescent, HA9
19 Rokeby Gardens, IG8
4 Oaklea Passage, KT1
7 Woodbines Avenue, KT1
The Watergardens, KT2
15 Catherine Road, KT6
Hampton Court Palace, KT8
Juniper House, KT8
5 Pemberton Road, KT8
Stud Nursery Community Garden, KT8
61 Wolsey Road, KT8
239A Hook Road, KT9
40 Ember Lane, KT10
9 Imber Park Road, KT10
The Bungalows, RM6
Maggie's at The Royal Marsden, SM2
100 Colne Road, TW2
116 Whitton Road, TW3
Sussex Cottage, TW3
47A Wheatley Road, TW7
Kew Green Gardens, TW9
Marksbury Avenue Gardens, TW9
119 Mortlake Road, TW9
31 West Park Road, TW9
Petersham House, TW10
93 Clarence Road, TW11
26 Teddington Park Road, TW11
Hampton House, TW12
16 Links View Road, TW12
Little Cranham, TW12
9 Warwick Close, TW12
Dragon's Dream, UB8
Church Gardens, UB9

OPENING DATES

All entries subject to change. For latest information check
www.ngs.org.uk

April

Sunday 12th
🆕 The Gatehouse, SE9
39 Wood Vale, SE23
Tuesday 14th
51 The Chase, SW4
Wednesday 15th
39 Wood Vale, SE23
Friday 17th
Maggie's at The Royal Marsden, SM2
Saturday 18th
🆕 ♦ Eltham Palace and Gardens, SE9
Sunday 19th
51 The Chase, SW4
Edwardes Square, W8
Frith Lodge, HA6
84 Lavender Grove, E2
Olden Community Garden, N5
Petersham House, TW10
Royal Trinity Hospice, SW4
Thursday 23rd
♦ Hampton Court Palace, KT8
Friday 24th
♦ The Garden Museum, SE1
Sunday 26th
Arundel & Ladbroke Gardens, W11
The Watergardens, KT2

May

Sunday 3rd
7 Deansway, N2
42 Risingholme Road, HA3
Monday 4th
King Henry's Walk Garden, N1

Saturday 9th
The Hurlingham Club, SW6
Sunday 10th
Eccleston Square, SW1
Garden Barge Square at Tower Bridge Moorings, SE1
Oak Farm/Homestead, EN2
3 Old Fold Close, EN5
Princes Avenue Gardens, N10
Thursday 14th
57 Huntingdon Street, N1
Sunday 17th
Arundel & Elgin Gardens, W11
Blackheath Gardens, SE13
40 Ember Lane, KT10
🆕 Forest Gate Community Garden, E7
Forest Hill Garden Group, SE23
92 Hampstead Way, NW11
100 Hampstead Way, NW11
9 Imber Park Road, KT10
Kew Green Gardens, TW9
🆕 100 Knollys Road, SW16
🆕 49 Lonsdale Road, SW13
🆕 68 Nowell Road, SW13
27 St Peters Square, W6
Stoney Hill House, SE26
36 Thornhill Square, N1
West Lodge Park, EN4
Thursday 21st
Lambeth Palace, SE1
Saturday 23rd
Cadogan Place South Garden, SW1
16 Links View Road, TW12
🆕 St George's Fields, W2
Sunday 24th
36 Ashley Road, N19
75 Bampton Road, SE23
Kew Green Gardens, TW9

16 Links View Road, TW12
4 Piermont Green, SE22
41 Southbrook Road, SE12
Sussex Cottage, TW3
86 Underhill Road, SE22
86A Underhill Road, SE22
13 Waite Davies Road, SE12
15 Waite Davies Road, SE12
116 Whitton Road, TW3
Monday 25th
36 Ashley Road, N19
Thursday 28th
57 Huntingdon Street, N1
The Inner and Middle Temple Gardens, EC4
1A Primrose Gardens, NW3
Friday 29th
Chiswick Mall Gardens, W4
🆕 103 Thurleigh Road, SW12
Saturday 30th
59 Ashburton Avenue, CR0
1A Primrose Gardens, NW3
St Joseph's Hospice, E8
🆕 103 Thurleigh Road, SW12
Sunday 31st
40 Bronson Road, SW20
🆕 Canonbury Gardens, N1
Chiswick Mall Gardens, W4
De Beauvoir Gardens, N1
Dragon's Dream, UB8
🆕 100 Knollys Road, SW16
Maggie's West London, W6
🆕 OmVed Gardens, N6
1A Primrose Gardens, NW3
🆕 103 Thurleigh Road, SW12
Wanstead Gardens, E11

June

Saturday 6th
Zen Garden at Japanese Buddhist Centre, W3
Sunday 7th
66 Abbots Gardens, N2
Acton Gardens, W3
31 Arlington Drive, HA4
190 Barnet Road, EN5
Barnsbury Group, N1
51 The Chase, SW4
Choumert Square, SE15
Court Lane Group, SE21
1 Fife Road, SW14
Horatio's Garden, HA7
London Fields Gardens, E8
Marksbury Avenue Gardens, TW9
36 Park Village East, NW1
South London Botanical Institute, SE24
25 Springfield Avenue, N10
152a Victoria Rise, SW4
61 Wolsey Road, KT8
Zen Garden at Japanese Buddhist Centre, W3
Friday 12th
239A Hook Road, KT9
Saturday 13th
The Mysteries of Light Rosary Garden, NW5
Sunday 14th
15 Catherine Road, KT6
🆕 59 The Chase, BR1
26 College Gardens, E4
🆕 85 Corringham Road, NW11
🆕 12 Dovedale Road, SE22
🆕 14 Dovedale Road, SE22
🆕 6 Eglington Road, E4
37 Harold Road, E11
🆕 32 Highbury Hill, N5
32 Highbury Place, N5
🆕 100 Knollys Road, SW16
Lloyd Square, WC1X
Long Cottage, HA5
Lower Clapton Gardens, E5
77a Muswell Road, N10

LONDON 339

21 Oakleigh Park South, N20
Royal Trinity Hospice, SW4
5 St Regis Close, N10
Stud Nursery Community Garden, KT8
7 Woodbines Avenue, KT1

Wednesday 17th
NEW The Exchange Erith, DA8

Saturday 20th
Hampton House, TW12
NEW Little Cranham, TW12
6 Thornhill Road, N1
Zen Garden at Japanese Buddhist Centre, W3

Sunday 21st
Arlington Square Gardens, N1
33 Hampstead Lane, N6
38 Lovelace Road, SE21
31 Ryecroft Road, SW16
19 St Peter's Street, N1
Warren Mews, W1
Zen Garden at Japanese Buddhist Centre, W3

Friday 26th
5 Pemberton Road, KT8

Saturday 27th
NEW 25 Arlington, N12
NEW Fernveil Gardens, EN4
5 Northampton Park, N1
Paddock Allotments & Leisure Gardens, SW20

Sunday 28th
♦ Church Gardens, UB9
NEW 1 Dorset Court, HA6

Monday 29th
Royal College of Physicians, Garden of Medicinal Plants, NW1

July

Saturday 4th
26 Hillcroft Crescent, HA9

Sunday 5th
Aldersbrook & Lakehouse Gardens, E12
Ally Pally Allotments, N22
69 Antill Road, E3
83 Cowslip Road, E18

85 Cowslip Road, E18
26 Hillcroft Crescent, HA9
Holtwhites Bakery & Deli, N13
NEW Juniper House, KT8
Railway Cottages, N22
NEW The Rockingham Garden Estate, SE1
57 St Quintin Avenue, W10
16 Sears Street, SE5

Saturday 11th
35 Burstow Road, SW20
Rooftopvegplot, W1
26 Teddington Park Road, TW11

Sunday 12th
71 Coldharbour Lane, SE5
36 Garfield Road, E4
119 Mortlake Road, TW9
25 Mulberry Way, E18
Rooftopvegplot, W1
93 Tanfield Avenue, NW2
31 West Park Road, TW9

Saturday 18th
The Bungalows, RM6

Sunday 19th
Bryan's Jungle, EN8
The Bungalows, RM6
NEW Chitts Hill Allotment & Garden Society, N22
93 Clarence Road, TW11
42 Latimer Road, E7
19 Rokeby Gardens, IG8
57 St Quintin Avenue, W10
25 Stirling Road, SW9
Theobald's Farmhouse, EN2
24 Twyford Avenue, N2

Sunday 26th
100 Colne Road, TW2
58 Cranston Road, SE23

August

Saturday 1st
NEW 47A Wheatley Road, TW7

Sunday 2nd
NEW 4 Oaklea Passage, KT1
5 St Regis Close, N10
NEW Woodlands, SE9

Saturday 8th
The Bungalows, RM6
53 Lady Aylesford Avenue, HA7

Sunday 9th
The Bungalows, RM6
51 The Chase, SW4
52 The Chase, SW4
4 Manningtree Road, HA4

Sunday 16th
NEW 209 Friern Road, SE22
11 Park Avenue North, N8
9 Warwick Close, TW12

Saturday 22nd
The Bungalows, RM6
1 York Close, W7

Sunday 23rd
The Bungalows, RM6
1 York Close, W7

Sunday 30th
42 Risingholme Road, HA3

September

Sunday 6th
Golf Course Allotments, N11
24 Grove Park, SE5

Saturday 12th
NEW 48 Hungerford Road, N7

Sunday 13th
NEW Adelaide Community Garden Club, NW3
NEW 48 Hungerford Road, N7
Royal Trinity Hospice, SW4

Sunday 27th
Bryan's Jungle, EN8

October

Sunday 25th
The Watergardens, KT2
West Lodge Park, EN4

By Arrangement

Arrange a personalised garden visit with your club, or group of friends, on a date to suit you. See individual garden entries for full details.

NEW 25 Arlington, N12
Arundel & Ladbroke Gardens, W11
36 Ashley Road, N19
75 Bampton Road, SE23
190 Barnet Road, EN5
Bryan's Jungle, EN8
5 Burbage Road, SE24
40 Chartfield Avenue, SW15
51 The Chase, SW4
52 The Chase, SW4
100 Colne Road, TW2
7 Deansway, N2
NEW 6 Eglington Road, E4
NEW Fernveil Gardens, EN4
33 Hampstead Lane, N6
Hampton House, TW12
26 Hillcroft Crescent, HA9
NEW 48 Hungerford Road, N7
57 Huntingdon Street, N1
84 Lavender Grove, E8
Long Cottage, HA5
119 Mortlake Road, TW9
The Mysteries of Light Rosary Garden, NW5
15 Norcott Road, N16
5 Northampton Park, N1
21 Oakleigh Park South, N20
1A Primrose Gardens, NW3
42 Risingholme Road, HA3
27 St Peters Square, W6
57 St Quintin Avenue, W10
5 St Regis Close, N10
93 Tanfield Avenue, NW2
24 Twyford Avenue, N2
West Lodge Park, EN4
28a Worcester Road, E17

THE GARDENS

66 ABBOTS GARDENS, N2
East Finchley, East Finchley, N2 0JH. Stephen & Ruth Kersley, www.instagram.com/garden_at_66. *8 min walk from rear exit of East Finchley tube stn (Northern line). Take Causeway to East End Rd, then 2nd L into Abbots Gardens. Buses: 143 stops at Abbots Gardens, 102, 263, & 234 all go to High Rd, N2.* **Sun 7 June (2-6). Adm £5, chd free. Home-made teas.** A combination of dramatic grasses and fused glass creates a calming atmosphere. Mosaics surround a water feature that is home to fish. Fused glass amphorae, feathers, and leaves catch the eye amongst grasses, ornamental shrubs, and perennials. A rose-bedecked archway leads to a quiet space with a vegetable plot, silver birches, and a slate pebble fountain. Stephen studied garden design at Capel Manor College; Ruth is a stained glass artist. Also, take a look at the lovely front garden at No. 8 Abbots Gardens, created by Stephen.

GROUP OPENING

ACTON GARDENS, W3
Acton, W3 8JE. *A 5 min walk from Acton Town Tube stn & 15 mins from South Acton Overground stn.* **Sun 7 June (2-6). Combined adm £8, chd free. Tea at 41 Mill Hill Road only.**

118B AVENUE ROAD
Gareth Sinclair.

29 HEATHFIELD ROAD
Alister Thorpe & Lucy Kirkpatrick, www.instagram.com/alistergthorpe.

41 MILL HILL ROAD
Marcia Hurst.

An interesting selection of three different gardens: 29 Heathfield Road is a small but enchanting woodland garden designed by Stefano Marinaz, surrounding an Arts & Crafts house (not open). It features meandering slate-chip paths, many grasses, and is packed with small garden ideas. 118B Avenue Road was built on rubble, this garden has distinct areas providing habitat for wildlife, inc a pond, beehives, and a bog garden. 41 Mill Hill Road is a plantaholic's garden full of colour and shape, with a new extension featuring a gravel garden and pond.

NEW ADELAIDE COMMUNITY GARDEN CLUB, NW3
Eton Road behind 68 Adelaide Road, NW3 3PX. Adelaide Community Garden Club Ltd, onthehill.info/2025/02/adelaide-community-garden-club. *Nr Primrose Hill, Chalk Farm & Belsize Park. What3words app: times.result.discouraged. 300 metres from Chalk Farm Tube Stn (towards Swiss Cottage), nr Primrose Hill. Buses 31 & C11. Free parking on Sundays. Entrance via gate on Eton Rd at junction with Fellows Rd, behind 68 Adelaide Rd.* **Sun 13 Sept (1.30-5.30). Adm £5, chd free. Tea, coffee, cake & lunches on the lawn, under gazebos.**
Discover Primrose Hill's secret community garden, nearly 50 yrs old. A tapestry of 43 small allotment plots, communal greenhouses, lawns and flower beds, beehives, and a woodland with a pond. Highlights inc: expert tropical vegetable gardening, a labelled medicinal herb border, an exhibition of paintings and prints of the garden in the greenhouse gallery, plant sale, and sale of liquid manure. The main path has no steps or ramps but is uneven in places. Side paths are narrow. The composting WC is not wheelchair accessible.

&

GROUP OPENING

ALDERSBROOK & LAKEHOUSE GARDENS, E12
16 Wanstead Park Avenue, Wanstead, E12 5ES. *From Wanstead Underground Stn on Wanstead High St, take bus 101 towards Beckton. Alternatively, from Manor Park Stn, take bus 101 towards Wanstead.* **Sun 5 July (1-5). Combined adm £8, chd free. Tea, coffee & cake at 16 Wanstead Park Avenue. Open nearby 85 Cowslip Road.**

19 BELGRAVE ROAD
Gill Usher.

NEW 152 BELGRAVE ROAD
Sarah Jeffrey.

39 DOVER ROAD
Brenda Keer.

4 EMPRESS AVENUE
Ruth Martin.

16 WANSTEAD PARK AVENUE
Ruth & Andrew Seager.

Five town gardens are situated in the Aldersbrook and Lakehouse Estates between Wanstead Park and Wanstead Flats. 19 Belgrave Road is a diverse garden, eclectic and bursting at the seams with trees and plants. Gill, a ceramicist, uses the plants in her garden studio. 152 Belgrave Road a new 'no waste' large family garden utilising all the waste from the house renovation to create an environmentally conscious drought tolerant garden. 39 Dover Road retains its original Edwardian layout, with mature trees inc a female *Ginkgo biloba*. At 4 Empress Avenue a largish garden is divided in two with a cutting bed, soft fruit and wildlife areas inc pond and two mixed borders. 16 Wanstead Park Avenue is a cottage garden with mixed planting, a micro meadow, a tiny pond, and grey water irrigation.

ALLY PALLY ALLOTMENTS, N22
Alexandra Palace Way, N22 7BB. Peter Campbell. *Entry gate in fence nr footpath to Springfield Ave & Alexandra Palace Garden Centre. Follow NGS signs. Bus: W3 to Alexandra Palace Garden Centre. Parking nearby in Duke's Ave, N10. Blue Badge holder parking in The Grove. No parking onsite.* **Sun 5 July (1-4). Adm £5, chd free. Home-made teas. Open nearby Railway Cottages.**
Situated on a south facing hillside alongside Alexandra Park, this 140 plot allotment site has the feel of an urban village, with spectacular views towards central London and, on a clear day, the North Downs. Its diverse community of gardeners grows fruit, vegetables, and flowers, with an emphasis on promoting biodiversity. Clearly marked trails will enable you to explore the site and meet plot holders. Plants, produce, and used tools on sale. A card reader available for teas and produce.

---

69 ANTILL ROAD, E3
Bow, E3 5BT. Mr William Dowden. *Short walk from Mile End tube or buses 277, 339, 425 & D6 on Grove Rd.* **Sun 5 July (1-7). Adm £5, chd free. Tea.**
A tropically inspired garden with

16 Sears Street

a range of trees and shrubs. The garden is divided into rooms which show off the elegance of hydrangeas and roses and the lushness of palms, yews and acers. There are several water features and an elegant gazebo. A tranquil place in which to relax with friends and family.

NEW 25 ARLINGTON, N12
North Finchley, N12 7JR. Shweta Mehta, 07773 332892, shweta1605@gmail.com. *10 min walk from Woodside Park Stn (Northern Line). From Woodside Park tube stn, turn R on Holden Rd, then L on Tillingham Way, R on Southover, & L to Arlington. Bus: 326 to Chiddingfold stop. Keep on Southover; top of Southover, turn L to Arlington.* **Sat 27 June (1-6). Adm £5, chd free.** Visits also by arrangement 15 June to 15 Sept for groups of 10 to 15.
This stunning contemporary cottage garden, created over the last 6 yrs, is filled with scented roses. It features generous perennial borders, roses, shrubs, and interesting trees. There are several seating areas designed to catch the sun throughout the day. The garden also boasts a striking marble water feature, Archimedes wheel, which inspired the overall design.

31 ARLINGTON DRIVE, HA4
Ruislip, HA4 7RJ. John & Yasuko O'Gorman. *Tube: Ruislip, then bus H13 to Arlington Dr (opp Millar & Carter), or 15 min walk up Bury St. Please note: No parking on Arlington Dr. Ample parking on roads south of Arlington Dr.* **Sun 7 June (2-5). Adm £5, chd free. Tea, coffee & cake.**
A cottage garden at heart, with a wonderful oriental influence. Traditional cottage garden favourites are combined with Japanese plants, reflecting Yasuko's passion for plants and trees of her native Japan. Acers, tree peonies, rhododendrons, and flowering cherries are underplanted with hostas, ferns, hellebores, and perennials to create a lush, exotic scheme, with an emphasis on structure and texture.

GROUP OPENING

ARLINGTON SQUARE GARDENS, N1
N1 7DP. *South Islington. Off New North Rd via Arlington Ave or Linton St. Buses: 21, 76, 141. 15 min walk from Angel tube. LTNs operate in this area. Free parking on Sundays.* **Sun 21 June (2-5.30). Combined adm £10, chd free.**

4 ARLINGTON AVENUE
Helen Nowicka.

15 ARLINGTON AVENUE
Armin Eiber & Richard Armit.

26 ARLINGTON AVENUE
Thomas Blaikie, www.instagram.com/thomas_blaikie.

21 ARLINGTON SQUARE
Alison Rice.

25 ARLINGTON SQUARE
Michael Foley.

30 ARLINGTON SQUARE
James & Maria Hewson.

5 REES STREET
Gordon McArthur & Paul Thompson-McArthur.

Seven early Victorian terraced houses share similarly sized small gardens and conditions, but each has a very different style. From a garden designer's exotic contemporary space to an organic wildlife haven, there is something for every gardener, whether green-fingered or a complete beginner. You'll find exotic and unusual plants, gorgeous flowers, lawn paths, hard landscaping, composting, rewilding, thrifty upcycling, fruit and vegetables, herbs, beehives, and even a wildlife pond. These gardens reflect the diverse tastes and interests of friends who met through community gardening, helping to transform and maintain Arlington Square from a drab, rundown space into an award-winning, beautiful, and plant-rich public garden. Like the seven private gardens, it offers a calm oasis just minutes from the bustle of the City of London. Entrance to all the gardens involves steps, with the only step-free exception being Arlington Square public garden.

ARUNDEL & ELGIN GARDENS, W11

Kensington Park Road, Notting Hill, W11 2JD. Residents of Arundel Gardens & Elgin Crescent, www.instagram.com/arundelelgin. *Entrance opp 174 Kensington Park Rd. Nearest tube stns within walking distance: Ladbroke Grove (5 mins), Notting Hill Gate (15 mins), Holland Park (15 mins). Buses: 52, 452, 23, & 228 all stop opp garden entrance.* **Sun 17 May (2-6). Adm £5, chd free. Home-made teas.**

A friendly and informal garden square. One of the best preserved gardens of the Ladbroke Estate with mature and rare trees, plants, and shrubs, laid out according to the original Victorian design of 1862. The larger garden inc a topiary hedge, a rare mulberry tree, a pergola, and benches from which vistas can be enjoyed. The central hedged garden is an oasis of tranquillity, with extensive and colourful herbaceous borders. All looked after by Gardener, Paul Walsh. Play areas for young children.

ARUNDEL & LADBROKE GARDENS, W11

Kensington Park Road, Notting Hill, W11 2EP. Arundel & Ladbroke Gardens Committee, anna.aylmerlloyd@gmail.com, www.arundelladbrokegardens.co.uk. *Entrance on Kensington Park Rd, between Ladbroke & Arundel Gardens. Tube stns: Notting Hill Gate or Ladbroke Grove. Buses: 23, 52, 228, & 452. Alight at stop for Portobello Market/Arundel Gardens.* **Sun 26 Apr (2-6). Adm £5, chd free.** Visits also by arrangement 30 Apr to 30 Sept for groups of up to 25.

This private communal garden is one of the few that retains its attractive mid-Victorian design of lawns and winding paths. A woodland garden at its peak in spring, with rhododendrons, flowering dogwoods, early roses, bulbs, ferns, and rare exotics. Picnics welcome, and local bakeries and food shops nearby. Playground for small children. Wheelchair access with a few steps and gravel paths to negotiate.

59 ASHBURTON AVENUE, CR0

Croydon, CR0 7JG. Paul Cooper & Neil Miller. *South London. What3words app: ground.manliness.badly.* **Sat 30 May (1-4.30). Adm £6, chd free. Tea, coffee & cake.**

Stroll around a ⅓ acre enclosed suburban garden whilst enjoying imaginative planting in flowing borders. Explore a mixture of cottage garden and hardy tropical plants, and discover rarities you might not expect to see growing outdoors in the UK. Collections of *Impatiens sodenii*, heliotropes, agaves and mangaves, the National Dispersed Collection of Ajuga, and the proposed National Collection of Knautia. Features inc a wildlife pond, beehives, a 12' x 8' greenhouse, a herb garden, and several seating areas. Level wheelchair access to main garden.

36 ASHLEY ROAD, N19

Crouch Hill, N19 3AF. Alan Swann & Ahmed Farooqui, swann.alan@googlemail.com, www.instagram.com/space36garden. *Between Stroud Green & Crouch End. Tube: Archway or Finsbury Park. Overground: Crouch Hill. Buses: 210 or 41 from Archway to Hornsey Rise; W7 from Finsbury Park to Heathville Rd. Car: Free parking on Ashley Rd at weekends.* **Sun 24, Mon 25 May (2-6). Adm £5, chd free. Tea, coffee & cake.** Visits also by arrangement 15 May to 31 Aug for groups of up to 35.

A lush town garden, rich in texture, colour, and form, with a number of microhabitats inc ferneries, a bog garden, lily and wildlife ponds, rockeries, alpine troughs, and bespoke vertical planters. At its best in May, when Japanese maples display a great variety of shapes and colours, ferns unfurl fresh, vibrant fronds over the stream, and climbers burst into flower on the balcony and pergola. Young ferns and plants propagated from the garden for sale. Pop-up café offering a variety of cakes, biscuits, gluten free and vegan options, as well as traditional home-brewed ginger beer. Seating areas around the garden.

75 BAMPTON ROAD, SE23

Forest Hill, SE23 2AX. Max Vickers, 07532 324510, max@maxvickers.uk. *7 min walk from Forest Hill Stn; nearest bus stop is on Perry Vale.* **Sun 24 May (2-5). Adm £5, chd free. Pre-booking essential, please visit www.ngs.org.uk for information & booking. Cream teas.** Visits also by arrangement 2 Mar to 30 Nov for groups of up to 20.

A designer's small garden, set in a tranquil, tree lined oasis behind a modernist terrace near Forest Hill Station. The garden is defined by strong architectural features, like espaliered crab apples, yew and box topiary, and steel water tanks. Planting is dense and lush in early summer, with peonies, grasses, and hostas, building to an exuberant autumn display.

190 BARNET ROAD, EN5

The Upcycled Garden, Arkley, Barnet, London, EN5 3LF. Hilde Wainstein, 07949 764007, hildewainstein@hotmail.co.uk. *1m S of A1, 2m N of High Barnet tube stn. Garden located at corner of A411 Barnet Rd & Meadowbanks cul-de-sac. Nearest tube stn: High Barnet, then 107 bus to Glebe Ln stop. Ample unrestricted roadside parking. Do not park half on pavement.* **Sun 7 June (1.30-5.30). Adm £5, chd free. Home-made teas & gluten free options.** Visits also by arrangement 18 May to 30 Aug for groups of 5 to 30.

Walled garden, 90ft x 36ft, with a modern design and year-round interest. A handmade copper pipe trellis divides the space into contrasting areas. Herbaceous planting and bulbs drift around trees, shrubs, and a pond. A kitchen garden with soft fruit and vegetables. Upcycled containers, recycled objects, and home-made sculptures. Gravel garden areas are never watered. Mostly organic. Home-made jams, plants all propagated from the garden, and a range of seeds collected in autumn 2025 are for sale. Wheelchair access, with single steps within the garden.

> *Our donation to the Army Benevolent Fund supported 776 individuals with horticultural related grants in 2025.*

LONDON 343

GROUP OPENING
BARNSBURY GROUP, N1
N1 1BX. *Barnsbury, N1. Tube: King's Cross, Caledonian Rd, or Angel. Train: Caledonian Rd & Barnsbury (Mildmay line). Buses: 17, 91, 259 to Caledonian Rd, or 4, 19, 30, 38, 43 to St Mary's Church, Upper St, for Lonsdale Sq.* **Sun 7 June (2-6). Combined adm £12, chd free. Individual garden £4 each. Home-made teas at 57 Huntingdon Street.**

◆ **BARNSBURY WOOD**
London Borough of Islington, ecologycentre@islington.gov.uk.

57 HUNTINGDON STREET
Julian Williams.
(See separate entry)

2 LONSDALE SQUARE
Jenny Kingsley.

NEW **5 THORNHILL GROVE**
Ms V Easlea.

Discover four contrasting spaces in Barnsbury's Georgian squares. 57 Huntingdon Street is a secluded garden with birches, ferns, perennials, grasses, and container ponds that encourage wildlife. 2 Lonsdale Square is a charming, small cobblestoned garden with herbaceous beds and apple trees, structured with euonymus and yew hedges. Climbing roses and star jasmine add a delicious scent, while planters overflow with lavender and pansies. 5 Thornhill Grove is a secluded, brick-paved walled garden with perennials, various climbing and species roses, select shrubs, and shade planting. Barnsbury Wood is London's smallest nature reserve, a hidden gem and one of Islington's few sites of semi-mature woodland. It's a tranquil oasis of wild flowers and massive trees, just minutes from Caledonian Road. Wildlife information available. These gardens reveal what can be achieved with the right plants in the right conditions, surmounting difficulties of dry walls and shade. Steep steps; limited wheelchair and buggy access.

GROUP OPENING
BLACKHEATH GARDENS, SE13
Blackheath, SE13 7EA. *SE London. Gardens located between Lewisham town centre, the Heath, & Blackheath village. Trains to Lewisham & Blackheath stns. It is a 10-15 min walk between gardens. Limited free street parking on Sundays.* **Sun 17 May (2-6). Combined adm £10, chd free. Entry to one garden £5. Home-made teas.**

NEW **46 DARTMOUTH ROW**
Jane Howlett.

28 GRANVILLE PARK
Joanna Herald.

49 LEE ROAD
Jane Glynn & Colin Kingsnorth.

Three lovely and varied gardens set amongst the gentle hills and winding roads of historic Blackheath. 28 Granville Park is the family home of a garden designer for over 30 yrs. This gently contoured hillside garden features a variety of garden rooms, extensive landscaping, mixed planting, and an abundance of colour. 46 Dartmouth Row is a newly reshaped garden with wildlife at its heart, inc a wildflower meadow, pond, and a shed with a living green roof, alongside traditional roses and perennials. At 49 Lee Road, you will find a generous oasis of calm encompassing over an acre of garden. Benches sit beneath rambling roses overlooking sweeps of formal lawns and flower beds. Paths through silver birches and grasses reveal a treehouse clad with roses and clematis. The prolific vegetable garden is a sight to see!

40 BRONSON ROAD, SW20
West Wimbledon, SW20 8DY. Sara Faulkner. *7 min walk from Wimbledon Chase Stn; 13 min walk from Raynes Park Stn. Free on street parking on weekends.* **Sun 31 May (12-5). Adm £5. Pre-booking essential, please visit www.ngs.org.uk for information & booking.**
This very small, prize-winning garden, winner of BBC Gardeners' World Garden of the Year 2024, 'Judges' Choice', is approx 60 square metres and designed for year-round interest. There are three distinct areas filled with perennials, shrubs, climbers,

pollinator friendly flowers, and vintage or reclaimed furniture and pots. The summerhouse is a repurposed cabin that makes a lovely lounge and art studio. There is a canopy of small trees, mainly fruit trees, creating privacy and shelter for the seating areas.

BRYAN'S JUNGLE, EN8
3 King Edward Road, Waltham Cross, EN8 7HZ. Bryan Hewitt, bryan.hewitt@me.com. *Nr Enfield, via Bullsmoor Ln. Advise travel by train to Waltham Cross Stn or bus to Waltham Cross Bus Stn, then 7 min walk. By car, 10 mins from M25 J25. Parking cannot be guaranteed. Look out for big yellow arrows on the day.* **Sun 19 July, Sun 27 Sept (11-5). Adm £4, chd free. Light refreshments. Pre-booking preferred or cash only on the day. Visits also by arrangement 1 June to 15 Oct for groups of 10 to 15.**
Ideal for visitors with a special interest in tropical plants. Small courtyard garden transformed into 'Bryan's Jungle', with many exotic trees and shrubs inspired by Matthew Kettle's tropical garden in Lake Worth, Florida. Walls clad with a collection of vintage advertising signs. Statuary and architectural salvage lurk in shady alleys. Every corner tells a story. Bryan worked as gardener/historian at Myddelton House for 34 yrs, gleaning extensive knowledge. Horticultural advice can be sought.

THE BUNGALOWS, RM6
2 Kenneth Road, Romford, RM6 6QR. John Seaman. *Close to Chadwell Heath stn if arriving by train. Free on street parking.* **Sat 18, Sun 19 July, Sat 8, Sun 9, Sat 22, Sun 23 Aug (10-5). Adm £4.50, chd free. Tea.**
A new garden featuring a wide range of exotic style planting, inc canna, ginger, and bananas amongst many other plants. It is rich in colour, shape, and form, and inc several ponds with frogs. The evolving garden has no grass; instead, it is covered with wood chips and filled with good ideas for small gardens.

5 BURBAGE ROAD, SE24

Herne Hill, SE24 9HJ. Crawford & Rosemary Lindsay, 020 7274 5610, rl@rosemarylindsay.com, www.rosemarylindsay.com. *Nr Herne Hill stn. Nr junction with Half Moon Ln. Herne Hill & N Dulwich train stns, 5 min walk. Buses: 3, 37, 40, 68, 196, 468.* **Visits by arrangement Mar to June.**
The garden of a member of the Society of Botanical Artists and a regular writer for Hortus journal. 150ft x 40ft, with large and varied range of plants, inc many unusual. Herbaceous borders for sun and shade, climbing plants, pots, terraces, and lawns. Immaculate topiary. Gravel areas to reduce watering. All box has been removed due to blight and moth damage, and replaced with suitable alternatives to maintain a similar look. A garden that offers delight from spring to summer.

35 BURSTOW ROAD, SW20

Wimbledon, SW20 8ST. Martin & Primavera Moretti. *Wimbledon/Raynes Park. 15 min walk from Wimbledon tube. 15 min bus, plus 5 min walk from South Wimbledon. Limited free parking on Burstow Rd.* **Sat 11 July (11-4). Adm £5, chd free. Tea, coffee, soft drinks & cakes inc gluten free options.**
A small suburban garden packed with herbaceous perennials and seasonal bedding displays. Features inc an ornamental fish pond, a small wildlife pond and herb garden. A good example of what can be achieved in a small space with a bit of love and attention.

☕ ⁍))

CADOGAN PLACE SOUTH GARDEN, SW1

93 Sloane Street, Knightsbridge, SW1X 9RX. The Cadogan Estate, www.cadogan.co.uk. *Directly opp Cadogan House, 93 Sloane St, SW1X 9PD.* **Sat 23 May (10-4). Adm £5, chd free.**
Many surprises, unusual trees and shrubs, are hidden behind the railings of this large London square. The first square to be developed by architect Henry Holland for Lord Cadogan at the end of the C18, and was then called the London Botanic Garden. Mulberry trees, planted for silk production at the end of the C17, then cherry trees, wisteria pergola, and bulbs are outstanding in spring. Beautiful 300 yr old black mulberry tree (originally planted to produce silk, but incorrect variety!). Area of drought resistant, pollinator plants. This was once the home of the Royal Botanic Garden. Now featuring a bug hotel, children's playground, and four wildlife ponds.

&. 🪑 ⁍))

GROUP OPENING

NEW **CANONBURY GARDENS, N1**
Alwyne Villas & Alwyne Road, Islington, N1 2HG. *Canonbury. Car: LTN Low Traffic Neighbourhood (road cameras). Parking nearby. Tube: Highbury & Islington or Angel. Train: Great Northern, Essex Road. Buses: To Town Hall, Upper St, or St Paul's Rd, 10 min walk.* **Sun 31 May (12.30-5). Combined adm £10, chd free. Home-made teas.**

NEW	3 ALWYNE ROAD
NEW	4B ALWYNE ROAD
NEW	10 ALWYNE VILLAS
NEW	19 ALWYNE VILLAS
NEW	29 CANONBURY GROVE
NEW	48 CANONBURY PARK NORTH

Unique opportunity to visit six private gardens in this leafy and pretty part of historic Islington, along the New River Walk. These gardens only open under the NGS. Planted sympathetically to support biodiversity. There are beehives at 19 Alwyne Villas (avoid if allergic). Enjoy the topiary fish outside 29 Canonbury Park North, the well planted contrasts of 10 Alwyne Villas and 4b Alwyne Road, and discover how individual owners enjoy their spaces and reflect their personalities. Each garden has been adapted to its urban setting with pots, espaliered fruit trees, and colour palettes from calm whites to the hot. All gardens are within a 10 min walk of each other, making for a fabulous afternoon outing. Maps and signage will be provided, inc a walk along the New River. Plants for sale at certain gardens. Dogs are welcome on leads. Please note: Entrance to most gardens involve steep steps and uneven, narrow paths. Some have ponds. No wheelchair access.

15 CATHERINE ROAD, KT6

Surbiton, KT6 4HA. Malcolm Simpson & Stefan Gross. *10 min walk from Surbiton Stn. Public transport recommended. Limited free parking in immediate area at weekends.* **Sun 14 June (12-5). Combined adm with 7 Woodbines Avenue £8, chd free. Tea & cakes at 7 Woodbines Avenue.**
A well-loved town garden, approx 40ft by 70ft, features deep borders of shrubs and perennial planting, sculptures, a small folly, and a walled area. A stroll along the river leads you to 7 Woodbines Avenue, where visitors can enjoy the gardens along the Queen's Promenade, partly restored by volunteers.

40 CHARTFIELD AVENUE, SW15

Putney, SW15 6HG. Sally, WhatsApp message 07809 731430. *10 min walk from Putney train stn & 15 mins from East Putney tube stn. Buses: 14, 37, 39, 85, & 93 stop at end of Chartfield Ave on Putney Hill. Some free parking at weekends.* **Visits by arrangement Apr to Nov. Art clubs & groups of artists are welcome. Refreshments on request.**
Famous for its Mediterranean feel, this layered garden features clipped hedges, topiary, and pleached hornbeam on the terrace, contrasting with a riot of grasses and perennials around the main circular pathway. Tumbling climbers cover pergolas, with vast borders and shady seating areas. 15 yrs in the making, with over 30 new trees, it is particularly delightful in spring and autumn. The garden inc gravel and kitchen gardens, and an ongoing experiment with a 'no-lawn' strategy. Small and large groups are welcome. Meet one of the garden's designers by arrangement. The Potting Shed pop-up bar/café is open on request.

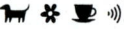

51 THE CHASE, SW4

SW4 0NP. Mr Charles Rutherfoord & Mr Rupert Tyler, 07841 418399, charles@charlesrutherfoord.net, www.charlesrutherfoord.net. *Off Clapham Common Northside. Tube: Clapham Common. Buses: 137, 452, 77, 87, 345, 37.* **Evening opening Tue 14 Apr (5-8). Adm £5, chd free. Sun 19 Apr (11-5). Adm £5, chd free. Open nearby Royal Trinity Hospice. Sun 7 June (11-5). Adm £5, chd free. Open nearby**

152a Victoria Rise. Sun 9 Aug (11-5). Combined adm with 52 The Chase £8.50, chd free. Entry to one garden: Adult £5, chd free on 9 Aug only. Light refreshments. Visits also by arrangement 15 Mar to 30 Oct for groups of up to 30.
Charles, past Chairman of Society of Garden Designers, and Rupert, Chairman of NGS and Garden Museum have created the garden over 40 yrs. Spectacular in spring when 2500 tulips bloom among camellias, irises and tree peonies. Scented front garden. Rupert's geodetic dome shelters seedlings, succulents and the subtropical. Roses, brugmansia, hibiscus and dahlias later in the season. New vegetable garden added in 2023.

52 THE CHASE, SW4
Clapham, SW4 0NH. desistevens@hotmail.com. *Off Clapham Common Northside. Tube: Clapham Common. Buses: 137, 452, 77, 87, 345, 37.* **Sun 9 Aug (11-5). Combined adm with 51 The Chase £8.50, chd free. Entry to one garden: Adult £5, chd free. Light refreshments at 51 The Chase.** Visits also by arrangement 16 Mar to 1 Sept for groups of 5 to 10.
52 The Chase is a newly created garden which inc existing and established planting. Garden designer Charles Rutherfoord worked closely with the owners to make a space of calm and quiet reflection as well as for entertaining. Old climbing roses and well established camellias fuse with acers and hydrangeas. A stunning cascade links the terraced beds of tree ferns, hostas, and Musa. Darley stone and Gault brick paviours add to the sense of sanctuary and harmony. Not suitable for those unsteady on their feet.

NEW 59 THE CHASE, BR1
Bromley, BR1 3DE. James & Jo Wyatt. *9m SE of Charing Cross. What3words app: layers.strain.trains.* **Easy to find. Sun 14 June (1-5). Adm £5, chd free. Tea, coffee & cake.**
The garden begins on a decked terrace with seasonal pots. A short flight of fairly steep steps, without a handrail, leads to a formal lawn area framed by clipped yews, half-standard Portuguese laurels (*Prunus lusitanica* 'Myrtifolia'),

and, at the centre, a sculptural Niwaki (*Ilex crenata*). Further steps up reveal a cottage style garden with abundant borders, colour, and seating areas.

GROUP OPENING

CHISWICK MALL GARDENS, W4
Chiswick Mall, Chiswick, W4 2PF. *By car: Hogarth r'about turn down Church St or A4 (W), turn L to Eyot Gardens. Tube: Stamford Brook or Turnham Green, walk under A4 to river. Buses: 110, 190, 267, H91.* **Evening opening Fri 29 May (6-8). Wine. Sun 31 May (1.30-5.30). Combined adm £15, chd free. Fri: Tickets & wine at Miller's Court only. Sun: Tickets can be purchased at any garden, no refreshments available.**

CEDAR HOUSE
Stephanie & Philippe Camu.
Open on all dates

FIELD HOUSE
Rupert King,
www.fieldhousegarden.co.uk.
Open on all dates

MILLER'S COURT
Miller's Court Tenants Ltd.
Open on all dates

THE OLD VICARAGE
Eleanor Fein.
Open on Sun 31 May

ST JOHN'S
George Spalton KC & Jemma Spalton.
Open on Sun 31 May

ST PETERS WHARF
Barbara Brown.
Open on all dates

SWAN HOUSE
Mr & Mrs George Nissen.
Open on all dates

Gardens on or near the Thames in historic Old Chiswick. You will visit a riverside garden in an artist's community, several large walled gardens, and a communal garden on the riverbank with well-planted borders and lovely views.

NEW CHITTS HILL ALLOTMENT & GARDEN SOCIETY, N22
81- 83 Wolves Lane, N22 5JD. Chitts Hill Allotment & Garden Society, www.instagram.com/chittshillallotment. *North London. Entrance next to St Cuthbert's Church, opp Maryland Rd. Tube: Wood Green (Piccadilly line). Bus: W4 (stop: Sylvan Ave). Parking in nearby streets. No parking on site.* **Sun 19 July (12-5). Adm £5, chd free. Home-made teas.**
Allotment Site: 260 plots; established 1913. Designated Local Wildlife Site featuring mature oak trees, edible and ornamental plants, wildlife ponds, a wellbeing garden, communal composting area, and a trading shed. Culturally diverse, showcasing a wide range of gardening techniques, inc food forest and hügelkultur. Refreshments and plant sale (cashless). Trail map of open plots. Site tours. Dogs welcome on leads. Wheelchair access to main paths, Community Hub, wellbeing garden, and WC. Some uneven paths.

CHOUMERT SQUARE, SE15
Off Choumert Grove, Peckham, SE15 4RE. The Residents. *Close to Choumert Grove car park. Off Choumert Grove. Trains to Peckham Rye from London Victoria, London Bridge, London Blackfriars, & Clapham Junction. Buses: 12, 36, 37, 63, 78, 171, 312, 345. Choumert Grove car park free on Sundays.* **Sun 7 June (1-6). Adm £5, chd free. Savoury items, home-made teas & Pimms.** Donation to St Christopher's Hospice.
About 46 mini cottage gardens with maxi planting in a Shangri-la situation that the media has described as a 'floral canyon' leading to a small communal secret garden. The day is primarily about gardens and sharing with others our residents' love of this little corner of the inner city. It is also renowned for its demonstrable community spirit and a variety of stalls and attractions. Wheelchair access: one small step to a raised paved area in the communal garden.

♦ CHURCH GARDENS, UB9
Church Hill, Harefield, Uxbridge, UB9 6DU. Patrick & Kay McHugh, 01895 823539, churchgardensharefield@gmail.com, www.churchgardens.co.uk. *From Harefield village, continue for ¼m down Church Hill. From A40 Uxbridge junction, follow signs to Harefield. Turn off Church Hill towards St Mary's Church.* **For NGS: Sun 28 June (11-5). Adm £7.50, chd £3. Light refreshments. Pre-booking preferred, please visit www.churchgardens.co.uk for information. For other opening times and information, please phone, email or visit garden website.**
Harefield's own secret garden. C17 Renaissance walled gardens on the outskirts of Harefield, featuring a geometrically designed organic kitchen garden, 60 metre long herbaceous borders, fruit cage, alpines, herb garden, vine mount, an orchard with a large wildlife pond, a fern mount, forest garden, and a rare arcaded wall dating back to the early 1600s. A unique opportunity to view an ongoing restoration project. Lunches served between 12-3pm and a selection of home-made cakes and drinks available throughout the day.

93 CLARENCE ROAD, TW11
Teddington, TW11 0BN. Kate Brittin. *10 min walk from Teddington Stn. Limited free parking in the street.* **Sun 19 July (11-4). Adm £6, chd free. Tea, coffee & cake.**
The owner of this garden is a plant enthusiast and passionate about wildlife. Connected by pathways and a central lawn, the garden inc: a kitchen garden with vegetable beds, soft fruit, and espalier apples and pears; a gravel courtyard garden with a potting shed and greenhouse; a formal natural swimming pond and summerhouse; herbaceous borders and a small fernery; chickens and bees; and a veranda and conservatory.

71 COLDHARBOUR LANE, SE5
SE5 9NS. Mr Joshua May, www.instagram.com/theurban_gardener. *Camberwell. Close to both Denmark Hill & Loughborough Junction train stns.* **Sun 12 July (2-5). Adm £4, chd free. Tea, coffee & cake.**
A front garden designed to brighten up a neighbouring bus stop, and a small (7 x 5 metre) cottage back garden planted to attract bees and butterflies. Featuring rambling, climbing, and shrub roses, along with a variety of native and exotic plants. Aiming for continuous flowers, from winter Scillonian narcissi to autumn dahlias.

26 COLLEGE GARDENS, E4
Chingford, E4 7LG. Lynnette Parvez. *2m from Walthamstow. A 15 min walk from Chingford train stn. Take bus 97 from Walthamstow Central tube stn, alight at College Gardens, then short walk downhill.* **Sun 14 June (2-5). Adm £4, chd free. Tea, coffee & cake.**
Large suburban garden of approx two-thirds of an acre. A sun terrace leads to established borders featuring a variety of climbing and shrub roses. Beyond this lies a wildlife pond and lawn, and a small woodland walk with spring plants and wildlife. At the far end, there are raised vegetable beds and colour themed island beds.

100 COLNE ROAD, TW2
Twickenham, TW2 6QE. Karen Grosch, 020 8893 3660, info@whettonandgrosch.co.uk, www.instagram.com/karensroofgarden. *5 min walk from Twickenham Green. 12 min walk from Twickenham or Strawberry Hill train stns. From Richmond train & tube stn, take bus 406 or H22 & alight at Twickenham Green, then short walk. By road, turn off Staines Rd if coming from M25/M3 & A416.* **Sun 26 July (11-6). Adm £7.50. Pre-booking essential, please visit www.ngs.org.uk for information & booking. Light refreshments. Visits also by arrangement 21 June to 2 Aug for groups of 5 to 6. For larger groups conatct owner as weight limitations apply.**
Enchanting first floor roof garden above 1850s workers cottage with converted 1950s studios, and artist workshops to the rear. Access via wide spiral staircase to sheltered garden 9 x 8 metres, intensively planted and fully containerised. Trees, shrubs, climbers, subtle annual perennial plant combinations and new 7 x 10 metre rear extensive roof area with biodiverse mix of sedums and wild flowers. Not suitable for those who are unsteady on their feet.

NEW 85 CORRINGHAM ROAD, NW11
Hampstead Garden Suburb, NW11 7DL. Mrs Claire Hilton. *Golders Green. Short walk from Golders Green Underground Stn up Rotherwick Rd onto Corringham Rd & from Hampstead Heath Extension across Hampstead Way into Corringham Rd.* **Sun 14 June (2-5.30). Adm £5, chd free. Tea, coffee & home-made cake.**
The front garden is planted with shrubs and trees, together with some herbaceous perennials. The pretty back garden is divided into three 'garden rooms' and features a mix of shrubs, herbaceous perennials, and small trees, all arranged in a cottage garden style.

GROUP OPENING

COURT LANE GROUP, SE21
SE21 7EA. *SE London. Buses: P4, 12, 40, 176, 185 to Dulwich Library 37. Train stn: North Dulwich, then 12 min walk. Ample free parking in Court Ln.* **Sun 7 June (2-5.30). Combined adm £10, chd free. Tea & cakes at 122 Court Lane. Light refreshments at 164 Court Lane.**

122 COURT LANE
Jean & Charles Cary-Elwes.

164 COURT LANE
James & Katie Dawes.

No. 164 was recently redesigned to create a more personal and intimate space, with several specific zones. A modern terrace and seating area lead onto a lawn with abundant borders and a beautiful mature oak. A rose arch connects to the vegetable beds and greenhouse. No. 122 has a countryside feel, backing onto Dulwich Park, with colourful herbaceous borders and a variety of unusual plants. Live jazz on the terrace, a children's trail, plant sale and a wormery demonstration at No.122.

83 COWSLIP ROAD, E18

South Woodford, E18 1JN. Fiona Grant. *5 min walk from South Woodford tube stn (Central line) & close to the A406 exit at Charlie Brown's r'about. Buses 123 & W12 stop nearby.* **Sun 5 July (2-6). Combined adm with 85 Cowslip Road £6, chd free. Tea, coffee & cake.**

An 80ft long, wildlife friendly garden arranged on two levels at the rear of a Victorian semi. The patio features a selection of containers and a step down to the lawn, passing a pond filled with wildlife. Flower beds are packed with an eclectic mix of perennials. There is ample seating on the patio, with additional seating in the delightful adjacent garden. Wheelchair access via side of house to patio. Steps down to main garden.

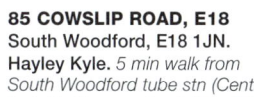

85 COWSLIP ROAD, E18

South Woodford, E18 1JN. Hayley Kyle. *5 min walk from South Woodford tube stn (Central line). Parking on street.* **Sun 5 July (2-6). Combined adm with 83 Cowslip Road £6, chd free. Light refreshments. Chilled drinks.**

Family friendly garden with a spacious patio and decking area, featuring a variety of colourful perennials in established flower beds. I love experimenting to see what grows, encouraged and guided by my wonderful neighbour, which is why I'm opening with her!

58 CRANSTON ROAD, SE23

Forest Hill, SE23 2HB. Mr Sam Jarvis & Mr Andres Sampedro. *12 min walk from nearest train stns: Forest Hill or Honor Oak. Nearest bus stops: Stanstead Rd/Colfe Rd (routes 185, 122), Kilmorie Rd (185, 171), or Brockley Rise/Cranston Rd (122, 171).* **Sun 26 July (12-5). Adm £4.50, chd free. Teas, cakes, tortilla & sangria.**

An exotic style plant lover's garden features a modern landscaped path and carefully curated subtropical planting. Vivid evergreens inc palms, cordyline, loquat, and cycad provide structure and year-round interest. Tree ferns, bananas, and tetrapanax add to the striking foliage, while cannas, dahlias, and agapanthus offer vibrant pops of colour against the black painted boundaries.

GROUP OPENING

DE BEAUVOIR GARDENS, N1

100 Downham Road, Hackney, N1 5BE. *Old Street Tube, then bus 76 or 141 to Downham Rd stop. 10 min walk from Northchurch Rd (buses 38, 73, 56, 341, & 476). 9 min walk from Haggerston Stn.* **Sun 31 May (2-6). Combined adm £10, chd free. Home-made teas at 100 Downham Road & 82B Mortimer Road.**

100 DOWNHAM ROAD
Ms Cecilia Darker.

64 LAWFORD ROAD

NEW 82B MORTIMER ROAD
Elizabeth Haines.

21 NORTHCHURCH TERRACE
Nancy Korman.

NEW 66 SOUTHGATE ROAD
Mr Ben Thomson.

10 UFTON GROVE
Ms Lynn Brooks.

Six gardens to explore in De Beauvoir, a leafy enclave of Victorian villas near to Islington and Dalston. The area boasts some of Hackney's keenest gardeners and a thriving gardening club. New this year is 66 Southgate Road a chic and contemporary professionally designed town garden, as is 10 Ufton Grove which also has an abundance of water features, carp pond and interesting sculptures. Also new is 82B Mortimer Road, which features a large lawn surrounded by mature borders with olive trees, a weeping willow, and camellias. 21 Northchurch Terrace is a walled garden with a formal pond and deep borders which have recently been replanted. 100 Downham Road features two green roofs, a pond with a miniature Giverny style bridge and cosy seating areas giving different viewpoints. 64 Lawford Road is a small cottage style garden packed with old-fashioned roses, espaliered apples and scented plants.

93 Clarence Road

7 DEANSWAY, N2
East Finchley, N2 0NF. Joan Arnold & Tom Heinersdorff, 07850 764543, joan.arnold40@gmail.com. *Hampstead Garden Suburb. From East Finchley tube stn take exit along the Causeway to East End Rd, then L down Deansway. From Bishops Ave, head N up Deansway towards East End Rd, close to the top. Bus 143 to Abbots Gardens.* **Sun 3 May (12.30-5.30). Adm £5, chd free. Home-made teas. Gluten free cakes. Borscht served from 12.30pm. Visits also by arrangement Mar to July for groups of 10 to 30.**
A garden of stories, statues, shapes, and structures surrounded by trees and hedges. Bird friendly and cottage style, with scented roses, clematis, mature shrubs, a weeping mulberry, and abundant planting. Containers, spring bulbs, and grapevine provide year-round colour. A secret, shady and wild woodland area with ferns and a tiny water feature continues to be developed. Refreshments and plants for sale (cash or card). Wheelchair access through side passage to patio. Assistance may be required with three shallow steps to the lawn and main garden.

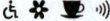

NEW 1 DORSET COURT, HA6
48 Hilliard Road, Northwood, HA6 1SD. Dawn Blaker. *Please park on Hilliard Rd.* **Sun 28 June (2-5). Adm £5. Pre-booking essential, please visit www.ngs.org.uk for information & booking. Tea, coffee & cake.**
A delightful, small, walled garden filled with plants, with white as the main theme for the planting. The garden is set out in the style of a classic town garden, featuring wall trained apple trees, statuary, a lawn, and large planters. There is excellent use of climbing plants, as well as beautifully planted beds.

NEW 12 DOVEDALE ROAD, SE22
East Dulwich, SE22 0NF. Mrs Sharon Molla. *Small garden on Dovedale Rd, off Colyton Rd. Bus stops for routes 63 & 363 are very nearby, at the bottom of Honor Oak Rd. The nearest stations are Peckham Rye & Honor Oak Park.* **Sun 14 June (2-5). Combined adm with 14 Dovedale Road £7, chd free. Light refreshments.**
Though small, this garden has three distinct parts, with weaving paths adding interest. A wooded rear area is filled with choisya, a 20 yr old white *Magnolia grandiflora*, a mature olive, and a yellow-berried pyracantha. The centre has shrubs and perennials, with roses, ceanothus, *Fuchsia* 'Hawkshead', and hydrangeas. By the house, the sunny third zone with pot plants that enjoy warmth, alongside soft grasses.

NEW 14 DOVEDALE ROAD, SE22
East Dulwich, SE22 0NF. Ms Jane Chopping. *Small garden in Dovedale Rd, off Colyton Rd. Bus stops for routes 63 & 363 are very nearby, at the bottom of Honor Oak Rd. The nearest stations are Peckham Rye & Honor Oak Park.* **Sun 14 June (2-5). Combined adm with 12 Dovedale Road £7, chd free.**
A charming and lovingly tended small garden, passed down through three generations of a family, retains a classic period look. It features two camellias, ceanothus in spring, followed by a vigorous climbing rose, hydrangea, and heucheras enclosed by a collection of tall, mature shrubs in summer, which provide a haven for birds. This is a garden that, at a glance, has a gentle feeling of nostalgia.

🔊

DRAGON'S DREAM, UB8
Grove Lane, Uxbridge, UB8 3RG. Chris & Meng Pocock. *The garden is in a small lane very close to Hillingdon Hospital. Limited parking available next door, otherwise, park in Royal Ln nearby. Buses: U1, U3, U4, U5, U7.* **Sun 31 May (2-5). Adm £5, chd free. Tea, coffee, home-made cakes, & Malaysian curry puffs.**
This is an unusual and secluded garden with two contrasting sections, divided by a brick shed that is completely covered by a rampant wisteria, climbing hydrangea, and rose. Other highlights inc a rare dawn redwood tree and a huge *Gunnera manicata*. Additional features inc a Romneya poppy, ferns, rose and herb beds, tree peonies, acers, and a pond.

ECCLESTON SQUARE, SW1
Pimlico, SW1V 1NP. The Residents of Eccleston Square, www.ecclestonsquaregardens.com. *Off Belgrave Rd, nr Victoria stn. Parking allowed on Sundays.* **Sun 10 May (2-5). Adm £5, chd free. Home-made teas.**
Planned and developed by Thomas Cubitt in the 1830s, the 3 acre garden square is subdivided into sections with noteworthy collections of roses, camellias, ferns and tree peonies. The garden holds the National Collection of Ceanothus comprising over 70 species and cultivars, some of which are now rare. Notable important additions of unusual and tender plants are being grown and tested.

♿ ❀ NPC ☕ 🔊

EDWARDES SQUARE, W8
South Edwardes Square, Kensington, W8 6HL. Edwardes Square Garden Committee, www.edwardes-square-garden.co.uk. *Tube: Kensington High St & Earls Court. Buses: 9, 10, 27, 28, 31, 49 & 74 to Odeon Cinema. Entrance in South Edwardes Square.* **Sun 19 Apr (12-5). Adm £5, chd £1. Tea, coffee & cake.**
One of London's prettiest secluded garden squares, covering 3½ acres. Laid out differently from other squares, with serpentine paths designed by Agostino Agliothe, an Italian artist and decorator who lived at No. 15 from 1814 to 1820. This quiet oasis is a wonderful mixture of rolling lawns, mature trees, and imaginative planting. Children's play area. WC. Near Holland Park, only a 5 min walk. Walking distance to Kensington Gardens. Wheelchair access through main gate, South Edwardes Square.

NEW 6 EGLINGTON ROAD, E4
Chingford, E4 7AN. Paula Bright, 07768 843208, paulakbright@gmail.com. *2m from Walthamstow. 7 min walk from Chingford train & bus stns. Street parking.* **Sun 14 June (2-5). Adm £5. Open nearby 26 College Gardens. Visits also by arrangement 3 May to 4 Sept for groups of 5 to 18. Evenings visits only from 4.30pm.**
'The Secret Garden': a little oasis of calm, with something to enchant around every corner. The garden of this 1920s property was redesigned and created in 2019. From the terrace with

containers of bamboo, wisteria, and laurel, steps lead to raised beds filled with lavender, roses, clematis, dahlias, and shrubs. These provide a haven for birds, bees, and butterflies, while a water feature soothes the senses.

NEW ♦ ELTHAM PALACE AND GARDENS, SE9
Court Yard, Eltham, SE9 5QE. English Heritage. *Located off Court Rd, SE9. From J3 of the M25, take A20 to Eltham. TfL bus services 124, 126, 160, or 161 stop nearby, then a short walk. Mottingham Stn is ½ m (about a 10 min walk) from Eltham Palace.* **Evening opening Sat 18 Apr (5.30-7). Adm £20, chd free. Pre-booking essential, please email fundraising@ english-heritage.org.uk or visit www.english-heritage.org.uk/ visit/places/eltham-palace-and-gardens/events for information & booking. Light refreshments. For other opening times and information, please email or visit garden website.**
Meet the Head Gardener for a tour of Eltham Palace Gardens. Highlights inc tree peonies beginning to flower in the garden rooms, along with hellebores, scented shrubs, and early bulbs mingling throughout the Rock Garden and medieval moat. Spring tulip displays add further interest to the Tudor remains, all under the watchful eye of the C15 Great Hall, making for a peaceful, sensory evening stroll.

40 EMBER LANE, KT10
Esher, KT10 8EP. Sarah & Franck Corvi. *½ m from centre of Esher. From the A307, turn into Station Rd which becomes Ember Ln.* **Sun 17 May (1-5). Combined adm with 9 Imber Park Road £7, chd free. Home-made teas.**
A contemporary family garden designed and maintained by the owners with distinct areas for outdoor living. A 70ft east facing plot where the lawn has been mostly removed to make space for the owner's love of plants and several ornamental trees which provide privacy.

SPECIAL EVENT

NEW THE EXCHANGE ERITH, DA8
The Old Library, Walnut Tree Road, Erith, DA8 1RA. Ms Sarah Batten, www.theexchangeerith.com. *South East London. Take Elizabeth line to Abbey Wood, then change to Southeastern, two stops to Erith. The journey from London Bridge to Erith Stn takes 35 mins. From Erith Stn, a 4 min walk, follow signs to Town Centre.* **Evening opening Wed 17 June (6-8.30). Adm £50. Pre-booking essential, please visit www.ngs.org.uk for information & booking. Light refreshments.**
Special Event: An evening with Sarah Price. Meet award-winning garden designer Sarah Price and learn about the garden she has conceived for The Exchange Erith, an exemplar of experimental horticulture and community learning, inspired by local heritage. Explore the garden and join Sarah for an illustrated lecture and panel discussion. Wine and sandwiches inc. Pre-booking is essential. The garden is wheelchair accessible.

NEW FERNVEIL GARDENS, EN4
56 Park Road, New Barnet, Barnet, EN4 9QF. Tim Forster & John Chesebro, 07941 261957, tim4ster@hotmail.com. *15 min walk from Cockfosters Tube up Mt Pleasant, 2nd L on Edgeworthy Rd, then L onto Park Rd. Or take the 384 bus from New Barnet train stn; it passes the house.* **Sat 27 June (12-5). Adm £5, chd free. Tea, coffee & cake. Gluten free options. Visits also by arrangement May to Oct for groups of up to 20. Saturdays only (10-4).**
Fernveil Gardens offers a 65 metre wander around arid beds, tropical plants, a fernery, and woodland, ending in a bamboo forest and a Mongolian yurt. It was created in 2020 during lockdown, and this vibrant 4 yr old garden is now thriving and ready for you to enjoy. Discover a carnivorous plant greenhouse, a pond with fish and frogs, large wood sculpture, and seating areas.

1 FIFE ROAD, SW14
East Sheen, Mortlake, SW14 7EW. Mr & Mrs J Morgan. *Bus routes 33, 337 stops are a 15 min walk away on Upper Richmond Rd. Mortlake Train Stn SWT approx 20 mins away. Please note we are at the Christchurch Rd end of Fife Rd. On street parking.* **Sun 7 June (1-5). Adm £5, chd free. Home-made teas.**
Dominated by two large cedar trees, the garden has undergone some changes since a redesign in 2013. A maturing oak tree stands in the wild garden alongside fruit trees and a 'dead hedge'. A productive vegetable garden and greenhouse is managed using a no-dig regime. The lawn is maintained for No Mow May, and the borders feature perennials and shrubs. A sunny terrace lies close to the house.

310,000 people are cared for each year who are approaching the end of life or diagnosed with a terminal illness through the hospice network supported by National Garden Scheme funding.

FOREST GATE COMMUNITY GARDEN, E7 (NEW)

136 Earlham Grove, Forest Gate, E7 9AD. Forest Gate Community Garden CIO, www.fgcommunitygarden.org. *Easily accessible via the Elizabeth or Suffragette lines. From Forest Gate Stn, turn R & take the 1st R. We are on the corner of Earlham Grove & Sprowston Rd. Free street parking.* **Sun 17 May (10-4). Adm £3, chd free. Light refreshments.**

Full of ideas for re-use and sustainability, FGCG provides a haven for people and wildlife just minutes from a busy town centre. A beautiful outdoor community space for events and learning features a wildlife pond teeming with tadpoles, a buddleia arch, a shelter, an art space, and planters dedicated to botanist Dr John Fothergill. Our focus is increasingly on pollinators and native species. Wheelchair access to most of the garden via paths made of either rubber matting over bark chips or paving.

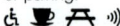

GROUP OPENING

FOREST HILL GARDEN GROUP, SE23

28 Horniman Drive, Forest Hill, SE23 3BP. *Off South Circular Rd (A205), behind Horniman Museum & Gardens. Forest Hill Stn, 10 min walk. Buses 176, 185, 197, & 356 go to Horniman Museum. Bus P4 goes to Ewelme Rd. Buses 63 & 363 go to Therapia Rd. Bus P12 goes to Netherby Rd.* **Sun 17 May (1-5). Combined adm £10, chd free. Home-made teas & gluten free option. Donation to St Christopher's Hospice.**

THE COACH HOUSE, 3 THE HERMITAGE
SE23 3QD. Pat Rae.

HILLTOP, 28 HORNIMAN DRIVE
SE23 3BP. Frankie Locke.

35 NETHERBY ROAD
SE23 3AL. Mr & Mrs K MacLennan.

Walk up from the station or bus stops, perhaps through the award-winning Horniman Gardens and discover three very different gardens. A charming garden filled with fruit trees lower down will take you back to a time when this area was rich in orchards. See the sculptures in an artist's walled courtyard garden around a C18 coach house, where pots of all sizes are planted for year-round interest. Then, sample savouries and cakes with your tea on the lawn of a country style garden designed for children as well as gardeners, featuring a large chicken run, raised vegetable beds, a greenhouse, fruit cage, and meadow. Plants and refreshments for sale at Hilltop, 28 Horniman Drive. Sorry, no wheelchair access to gardens, as they inc slopes and steps.

27 St Peters Square

NEW 209 FRIERN ROAD, SE22
East Dulwich, SE22 0BD. Richard Watts, www.gardenhouselondon.co.uk. *We are just off Lordship Ln, nr Dulwich Library, on Friern Rd, between Ethrow St & Goodrich Rd. What3words app: fully.lows.gasp.* **Sun 16 Aug (1-4). Adm £5, chd free. Tea, coffee & cake.**

Our terraced house is enfolded in gardens that wrap around the house and take us on a journey through a series of four interlinked spaces. With exuberant, relaxed planting, and hills and valleys that keep us close to each bloom, we think of ourselves as having a garden with a house in it, rather than the other way around. Come and explore. Get lost. Journey further than you think possible. Hidden pockets and spaces, elevated sections, and meandering paths. Secret depths that feel a world away from the street.

FRITH LODGE, HA6
Sandy Lane, Northwood, HA6 3ES. Mr & Mrs Doig. *From Watford Rd, head along Sandy Ln towards Seven Acres. The garden is approx 300 metres on the R. The entrance gate can be found using the What3words app: film.audio.beside.* **Sun 19 Apr (2-5). Adm £5, chd free. Tea, coffee & cake.**

A garden of approx 1 acre at the former gate lodge of the Eastbury Park Estate (now Northwood HQ). Dominated by mature oak trees, the current owners have sought to cut back overgrown ponticum and laurel, to establish a diverse garden with year-round interest. The garden has extensive lawns, some sloping, with alternative access to lower areas. The garden uses block planting to great effect. Step-free access to main patio and a graded ramp to the lower part of garden. Limited Blue Badge parking on main drive.

GARDEN BARGE SQUARE AT TOWER BRIDGE MOORINGS, SE1
31 Mill Street, SE1 2AX. Mr Nick Lacey. *5 min walk from Tower Bridge. Mill St off Jamaica Rd, between London Bridge & Bermondsey stns, Tower Hill also nearby. Buses: 47, 188, 381, RV1.* **Sun 10 May (2-5). Adm £5, chd free. Home-made teas.**

Series of seven floating barge gardens connected by walkways and bridges. Gardens have an eclectic range of plants for year-round seasonal interest. Marine environment: suitable shoes and care needed. Small children must be closely supervised.

◆ THE GARDEN MUSEUM, SE1
5 Lambeth Palace Road, SE1 7LB. The Garden Museum. *Lambeth side of Lambeth Bridge. Tube: Lambeth North, Vauxhall, Waterloo. Buses: 507 Red Arrow from Victoria or Waterloo stns, also 3, 77, 344, C10.* **For NGS: Evening opening Fri 24 Apr (6-8). Adm £25, chd free. Pre-booking essential, please phone 020 7401 8865, email info@gardenmuseum.org.uk or visit www.gardenmuseum.org.uk for information & booking. Wine. Enjoy an exclusive evening of music, crafts, & a garden tour with Matt Collins, Head Gardener, plus the chance to view the 'John Bradbury Blake' exhibition. For other opening times and information, please phone, email or visit garden website.**

At the heart of The Garden Museum is a courtyard garden, designed by Dan Pearson as an 'Eden' of rare plants inspired by John Tradescant's journeys as a plant collector. Alongside it, visitors can enjoy a thriving community garden, as well as displays of historic gardening tools and artworks created by artist–gardeners. The museum and garden are accessible for wheelchairs.

36 GARFIELD ROAD, E4
Chingford, E4 7DG. Clare & Steve Francis. *Access to garden via back gate located on Cart Ln. 5 min walk from both Chingford train & bus stns, & 2 mins from Station Rd. Off street parking in surrounding streets, & no restrictions on Sundays. What3words app: privately.trio.tinsel.* **Sun 12 July (2-5). Adm £4, chd free. Sorry, no refreshments available.**

A charming, tranquil oasis just off the busy high street. The garden is packed with pots containing a variety of perennial and herbaceous plants, screening bamboos, and climbers. It was designed 2 yrs ago, using pots to create walkways and features that maximise the available space. A partly demolished garage has been cleverly converted into a cabana style seating area. There are lots of curios, dotted about the garden for added interest.

꜆))

NEW THE GATEHOUSE, SE9
Court Yard, Eltham, SE9 5QE. Mr & Mrs Barnes. *Next to Eltham Palace. Entrance beside the Court Yard entrance to Eltham Palace. A 15 min walk from either Eltham or Mottingham stns. Buses: 132, 160, 161, 28, 321.* **Sun 12 Apr (10.30-5). Adm £6, chd free. Tea, coffee & cake.**

One of London's largest private gardens, The Gatehouse comprises grounds originally part of Eltham Palace. Restored by current owners over the past 25 yrs, this large walled garden features both formal and informal areas, with a variety of shrubs, spring planting, sculptures, and a Tudor inspired rose garden. Mature trees offer quiet, shady spots for sitting peacefully and enjoying refreshments. Wheelchair access via a ramped entrance and step-free access.

GOLF COURSE ALLOTMENTS, N11
Winton Avenue, N11 2AR. GCAA Haringey, www.golfcourseallotments.co.uk. *Junction of Winton Ave & Blake Rd. Tube: Bounds Green. Buses: 102, 184, 299 to Sunshine Garden Centre, Durnsford Rd. Walk through park to Bidwell Gardens. Straight up Winton Ave. New LTN on Blake Rd, beware cameras. No parking on site.* **Sun 6 Sept (1-4.30). Adm £5, chd free. Home-made teas & light lunches (cashless payments encouraged).**

Large, long established allotment with over 200 plots, some organic. Maintained by a culturally diverse community, growing a wide variety of fruit, vegetables, and flowers, all enjoyed by bees. Discover picturesque corners, quirky sheds, and tours of the best plots. Admire prize-winning exhibits at the Autumn Show. Plot 147: a jewel not to be missed! A visit feels like a holiday in the countryside. Healthy, fresh allotment produce, chutneys, jams and honey for sale. Wheelchair access to main paths only. Gravel and uneven surfaces. WC inc disabled.

24 GROVE PARK, SE5
Camberwell, SE5 8LH. Clive Pankhurst, www.alternative-planting.blogspot.com. *Chadwick Rd end of Grove Park. Peckham Rye or Denmark Hill stns, both 10 min walk. Good street parking.* **Sun 6 Sept (11.30-4.30). Adm £5, chd free. Home-made teas.**
Discover an exotic garden bursting with the vibrant energy of late summer. A bold, immersive space inspired by travels through Southeast Asia. This huge hidden garden, created from derelict land, gives unexpected size. It delivers the 'wow' factor, with many amazed by both its size, dramatic foliage, and jungle-like atmosphere. Renowned for delicious home-made cake and plant sale.

33 HAMPSTEAD LANE, N6
Highgate, N6 4RT. Michelle Berriedale-Johnson, 07476 994645, michelle@salonmusic.co.uk, walksonhampsteadheath.co.uk. *From Highgate go W down Hampstead Ln to just before you reach Bishopswood Rd/Highgate School playing fields, or just past playing fields & Bishopswood Rd if going on bus routes 210 & 310.* **Sun 21 June (12.30-6). Adm £5, chd free. Tea, coffee, cake & cream teas. Adm inc a cup of tea.** Visits also by arrangement June & July for groups of up to 10.
Lush south facing walled garden bounded by Hampstead Heath with mature trees, no-mow lawn, and shady patios under a mirrored trellis. Features inc a herbaceous border, fern garden, hot dry banks and a pond. A wild area with compost and wood store can be seen under the apple tree. A 'growing garden' for SEND children, featuring raised vegetable beds, fruit bushes, a herb garden, vines, and a pond. The group working on the garden will be on site to explain the project and its progress. Two steps up to the entrance patio, but accessible with a ramp.

92 HAMPSTEAD WAY, NW11
Hampstead Garden Suburb, NW11 7XY. Ann & Tom Lissauer. *In square set back on Hampstead Way, between Finchley Rd & Meadway. 15 min walk from Golders Green stn. Buses 13, 102 & 460 on Finchley Rd, stop at Temple Fortune Ln & walk down Hampstead Way to*

the square. **Sun 17 May (1.30-5.30). Combined adm with 100 Hampstead Way £10, chd free. Tea, coffee & cake on the square between the two gardens.**
An informal garden, interesting year-round, combines wildlife friendly planting with a passion for plants. Different areas provide a variety of habitats, inc a wildlife pond. Where there used to be lawns, there are now meadows with mown paths and wild flowers. Shaded and sunny beds offer opportunities to grow a wide range of interesting plants.

100 HAMPSTEAD WAY, NW11
Hampstead Garden Suburb, NW11 7XY. S & J Fogel. *North West London. In square set back on Hampstead Way, between Finchley Rd & Meadway. Buses 13, 102, & 460 on Finchley Rd; get off at Temple Fortune Ln & walk down Hampstead Way to the square. Nearest tube stn: Golders Green.* **Sun 17 May (1.30-5.30). Combined adm with 92 Hampstead Way £10, chd free. Tea, coffee & cake on the square between the two gardens.**
Corner cottage garden with a variety of viewing perspectives, featuring sculpture and planting in recycled objects (pallets, sinks, dustbins, a mattress on wheels, wine boxes, poles, and chimneys). The garden comprises several rooms, inc a formal parterre, wooded area, walkway, small meadow, and formal lawn. Silver medalist in the London Gardens Society's 'Large Garden with Help' category in 2023 and 2024.

SPECIAL EVENT

♦ HAMPTON COURT PALACE, KT8
East Molesey, KT8 9AU. Historic Royal Palaces, www.hrp.org.uk. *Follow brown tourist signs on all major routes. Junction of A308 with A309 at foot of Hampton Court Bridge. Traffic is heavy around Hampton Court. Please leave plenty of time, the tour will start promptly at 6pm & will not be able to wait.* **For NGS: Evening opening Thur 23 Apr (6-8). Adm £20, chd free. Pre-booking essential, please visit www.ngs.org.uk for information & booking. Wine.** For other opening times and information, please visit garden website. Donation to Historic Royal Palaces.

Take the opportunity to join a special National Garden Scheme private tour after the wonderful historic gardens have closed to the public. Spring walk during the tulip festival. Wheelchair access over some unbound gravel paths.

HAMPTON HOUSE, TW12
90 High Street, Hampton, TW12 2SW. Mrs Gillie Hamshere, 07810 463826, 138wpj@gmail.com. *$1/3$ m from Hampton Open Air Pool. N.B. Not Hampton Hill.* **Sat 20 June (12-5). Combined adm with Little Cranham £8, chd free. Tea, coffee & cake.** Visits also by arrangement 12 Apr to 28 June for groups of 8 to 20.
Step off the High Street into this secluded garden of half an acre that stretches from an elegant Queen Anne house (not open) to its border with Bushy Park. A long herbaceous border, large lawn and well established trees inc a pair of 200 yr old yew, as well as mulberry and cherry trees. A wonderful vista from the terrace enjoys the borrowed landscape of Bushy Park. Several dog themed garden statutory.

37 HAROLD ROAD, E11
Leytonstone, E11 4QX. Dr Matthew Jones Chesters. *Tube: Leytonstone, exit L subway, 5 min walk. Train: Leytonstone High Road, 5 min walk. Buses: 257 & W14. Parking at stn or limited on street.* **Sun 14 June (1-5). Adm £5, chd free. Tea, coffee & cake.**
A charming 50ft x 60ft corner garden, designed for beauty and bounty. Seven fruit trees anchor fragrant climbers, woodland plants, and shade loving edibles, while fastigiate trees frame raised vegetable beds and a rockery. A long lawn flows between roses, perennials, and prairie planting. The family lawn and patio feature a raised pond, palms, and rhubarb. Planting is designed to produce fruit, fragrance, and lovely memories. A garden map with planting plans is provided. Tea and fruit drinks are inc, and home-made cakes, muffins, and preserves are for sale.

NEW 32 HIGHBURY HILL, N5
Highbury, N5 1AL. What3words app: retail.others.toast. Tube & Train: Holloway Road, Arsenal, Highbury & Islington. Buses: From Holloway Rd 263, 43, or from Highbury Barn 19, 4, then walk. **Sun 14 June (2-5.30). Adm £5, chd free. Open nearby 32 Highbury Place.**
A large garden, originally designed by Matthew Wilson, comprises a central lawn bordered by mixed beds featuring hydrangeas, irises, alliums, dogwoods, grasses, and roses. Structure is provided by buttressed yews, pergolas, and Yorkstone pathways and terraces. At the back is a potager style garden, where there are pleached apple and pear trees, raspberries, herbs, and dahlias. Access via a wide gate with step-free access into garden. Shallow steps lead down to lawn and some terraces.

32 HIGHBURY PLACE, N5
Islington, N5 1QP. Michael & Caroline Kuhn. *Highbury Fields. Tube & Train: Highbury & Islington. Buses: 4, 19, 30, 43, 271, 393 to Highbury Corner. 3 min walk up Highbury Place, opp the stn.* **Sun 14 June (2-5.30). Adm £5, chd free. Home-made teas. Open nearby 32 Highbury Hill.**
An 80ft garden behind a C18 terraced house (not open). An upper York stone terrace leads to a larger terrace, surrounded by overfilled beds with cottage garden style planting. Further steps lead to a lawn beside a rill and a lower terrace. A willow tree dominates the garden, accompanied by amelanchiers, fruit trees, dwarf acers, a winter flowering cherry, and magnolia.

26 HILLCROFT CRESCENT, HA9
Wembley Park, HA9 8EE. Gary & Suha Holmyard, 07773 691331, garyh@lawyer.com. *½ m from Wembley Park Stn. If held on Wembley event day, we can provide free parking permits. Turn R out of Wembley Park Stn & walk down Wembley Park Dr, then turn L into Manor Dr. Hillcroft Cres is 2nd road on R.* **Sat 4, Sun 5 July (11.30-4.30). Adm £5, chd free. Home-made teas. Visits also by arrangement 1 June to 24 July for groups of 10 to 40. Please book as far in advance as possible.**
Small cottage front garden with arched entrance featuring a cloud tree, wisteria, yucca, canna, hydrangeas, roses, and lilies. Rear garden approx 70 x 80ft, with summerhouse, arbours, and water features. Planting inc a 'pagoda fig tree', apple, pear, olive, banana, and soft fruits. Ten distinct flower beds, each with its own particular interest, with feature plants, unusual shrubs, and exotics. Plenty of seating throughout the garden. Wheelchair access through side gate via driveway.

HOLTWHITES BAKERY & DELI, N13
66 Aldermans Hill, N13 4PP. Kate Smith, www.holtwhitesbakery.co.uk. *North London. A few mins walk from Palmers Green train stn. Turn R as you exit the stn, & you will find us on the corner of Aldermans Hill & Grovelands Rd, opp Broomfield Park.* **Sun 5 July (1.30-5.30). Adm £3.50, chd free. Tea, coffee & cake.**
Our walled courtyard garden opened in spring 2023 with an exuberant burst of colour, to welcome our customers and a host of pollinators. The garden reflects our ethos of sharing food and space with the wider community: edible plants weave through light, naturalistic planting, contrasting with formally trained roses. Evolving with wildlife in mind, providing water and creative habitat structures. All profits from refreshment sales will be donated to the NGS. Visitors are encouraged to explore historic Broomfield Park, directly opposite the garden, with its lakes, wildlife, orchard, conservatory, and magnificent views. Wheelchair access to the lower level of the courtyard garden, café and WC.

239A HOOK ROAD, KT9
Chessington, KT9 1EQ. Mr & Mrs D St Romaine, www.gardenphotolibrary.com. *4m S of Kingston. A3 from London, turn L at Hook underpass onto A243. Garden 300yds on L. Parking opp in park or on road, no restrictions at night. Buses K4, 71, 465 from Kingston & Surbiton to North Star pub.* **Evening opening Fri 12 June (7-10). Adm £6.50, chd free. Wine.**
Abundant, romantic planting within a semi-formal layout. A central path of standard hollies, urns and box balls leads to a water feature with fish. Rectangular beds with rose covered obelisks form a grid either side of the central axis, allowing planting to be viewed from all sides. Sun and shade borders, shrubs and perennials. Raised vegetable bed and garden room. Lighting enhances the evening atmosphere. Wheelchair access with one low step.

HORATIO'S GARDEN, HA7
Royal National Orthopaedic Hospital, Brockley Hill, Stanmore, HA7 4LP. Horatio's Garden, www.horatiosgarden.org.uk. *Public transport from Stanmore Tube Stn to the hospital. There is also a taxi rank outside the stn. Parking: Use main car park (10 min walk). Do not use Aspire parking. Disabled parking available.* **Sun 7 June (1-4). Adm £5, chd free. Tea, coffee & cake. Vegan & gluten free options.**
Opened in September 2020, Horatio's Garden London & South East, located at the Royal National Orthopaedic Hospital in Stanmore, is designed by Tom Stuart-Smith. The garden is on one level, with smooth paths throughout, ensuring it is easily accessible to patients in beds and wheelchairs. Essential design features inc a social space, private areas for patients to seek solitude or share with family and friends, the calming sound of flowing water, a garden room, and a greenhouse. June is the perfect time to see the garden bursting into summer colour. The whole site is designed for wheelchairs. The route from the car park is an uphill walk of approx 5-10 mins.

In 2025 we awarded over £288,800 in Community Garden Grants, supporting 114 community garden projects.

NEW 48 HUNGERFORD ROAD, N7

N7 9LP. Natasha Gomperts, 07806 600041, n.gomperts@gmail.com. *Caledonian Road tube or Mildmay line plus bus. Buses: 29, 253, 274, 17, 390. Street parking possible, check Arsenal match days. What3words app: owners.crowned. begin.* **Sat 12 Sept (2.30-5.30); Sun 13 Sept (2-5). Adm £5, chd free. Light refreshments. Visits also by arrangement.**
Evolved over 20 yrs, this large, bi-level Victorian garden, set on London clay, features varied formations of colour and foliage each year. Tall trees loom over generous beds, rampant with flowering shrubs, roses, perennials, and bulbs. Climbers adorn the perimeter, creating elegant vistas that showcase striking modernist sculptures, stonework, and a very unusual extension. All main garden features are visible from the wheelchair accessible main lawn. Please note: A low step at front gate.
& 💭))

57 HUNTINGDON STREET, N1

Barnsbury, Islington, N1 1BX. Julian Williams, 07759 053001, julianandroman@me.com. *Train: Caledonian Rd & Barnsbury. Tube: King's Cross, Highbury & Islington, or Caledonian Rd. Buses: Caledonian Rd: 17, 91, 259, 274. Hemingford Rd: 153 from Angel.* **Evening opening Thur 14, Thur 28 May (6-8). Adm £5, chd free. Wine. Opening with Barnsbury Group on Sun 7 June.** Visits also by arrangement May to July for groups of up to 12.
A secluded woodland garden room beneath an ash canopy, framed by a timber palisade supporting roses, hydrangeas, and clematis. An understorey of silver birch and hazel provides a setting for shade loving ferns, perennials, grasses, and a bog garden, and is framed by two container ponds, reclaimed brick pathways, and bench seating. New for 2026: a water feature by sculptor Andrew Revell.
💭))

THE HURLINGHAM CLUB, SW6

Ranelagh Gardens, SW6 3PR. The Members of the Hurlingham Club, www.hurlinghamclub.org.uk. *Main gate at E end of Ranelagh Gardens. Tube: Putney Bridge (110yds). Local roads have restricted access. No parking on site.* **Sat 9 May (10-4). Adm £7, chd free. Tea, coffee & cake. Card payments only, no cash accepted.**
Rare opportunity to visit this 42 acre jewel with many mature trees, 2 acre lake with water fowl, expansive lawns and a river walk. Capability Brown and Humphry Repton were involved with landscaping. The gardens offer a diverse range of planting and spaces in a classic English country gardens style. The riverbank walk along the Thames is a haven for wildlife and flying pollinators. Light refreshments on site weather depending. Free-but-ticketed guided tour at 11am, tickets available at welcome tent. Wheelchair and pushchair access across the site, however smaller paths in borders are often laid to woodchip and not as accessible.
& 💭))

9 IMBER PARK ROAD, KT10

Esher, KT10 8JB. Jane & John McNicholas. *½m from centre of Esher. From the A307, turn into Station Rd, which becomes Ember Ln. Go past Esher train stn on R. Take 3rd road on R into Imber Park Rd.* **Sun 17 May (1-5). Combined adm with 40 Ember Lane £7, chd free. Home-made teas.**
An established cottage style garden, always evolving, designed and maintained by the owners who are passionate about gardening and collecting plants. The garden is south facing with well-stocked, large, colourful herbaceous borders containing a wide variety of perennials, evergreen and deciduous shrubs, a winding lawn area and a small garden retreat.
❀ 💭))

SPECIAL EVENT

THE INNER AND MIDDLE TEMPLE GARDENS, EC4

Crown Office Row, Inner Temple, EC4Y 7HL. The Honourable Societies of the Inner & Middle Temples, www.innertemple.org.uk/www.middletemple.org.uk. *Entrance: Main Garden Gate on Crown Office Row, access via Tudor*

69 Antill Road

St Gate or Middle Temple Ln Gate. Please note the tour starts promptly at 11.30am. **Thur 28 May (11.30-3). Adm £65. Pre-booking essential, please visit www.ngs.org.uk for information & booking. Adm inc conducted tour of the gardens by Head Gardeners & light lunch in Middle Temple Hall.**
Inner Temple Garden is a haven of tranquillity and beauty with sweeping lawns, unusual trees and charming woodland areas. The well known herbaceous border shows off inspiring plant combinations from early spring through to autumn. The award-winning gardens of Middle Temple are comprised of a series of courtyards and a main garden which extends from the Medieval Hall to the Embankment. Please note this event is not suitable for children. Please email hello@ngs.org.uk in advance of any dietary requirements and if wheelchair access is required.

NEW JUNIPER HOUSE, KT8
8a Beauchamp Road,
East Molesey, KT8 0PA.
John & Jane Crafts,
juniperhousebb@gmail.com, www.bedandbreakfasthamptoncourt.co.uk. *Just 3 mins from East Molesey's main High St via Walton Rd. 20 min walk from Hampton Court Stn. 5 min walk from 411 Manor Rd bus stop (Tesco). Free on-road parking.* **Sun 5 July (2-5). Adm £5, chd free. Home-made teas.**
A large town garden, home to a wide variety of plants, many of which have been collected and nurtured over many years. In July, penstemons, hibiscus, and clematis may be in flower. Other features of interest inc the rear courtyard and greenhouse, a nursery area, and the original Edwardian outhouses. There is also a herb bed and a kitchen garden behind the pool house, where vegetables are grown for our B&B.

GROUP OPENING

KEW GREEN GARDENS, TW9
Kew, TW9 3AH. *NW side of Kew Green. Tube: Kew Gardens. Train stn: Kew Bridge. Buses: 65, 110. Entrance via riverside.* **Sun 17 May (2-5). Combined adm £8, chd free. Evening opening Sun 24 May (5.30-7.30). Combined adm £10, chd free. Tea, coffee & cake in St Anne's Church (17 May). Wine (24 May).**

69 KEW GREEN
John & Virginia Godfrey.

71 KEW GREEN
Mr & Mrs Jan Pethick.

73 KEW GREEN
Sir Donald & Lady Elizabeth Insall.

The long gardens run for 100yds from the back of historic houses on Kew Green down to the Thames towpath. Together, they cover nearly 1 acre, and, in addition to the style and structures of the individual gardens, they can be seen as one large space, exceptional within London. The borders between the gardens are mostly relatively low, and the trees and large shrubs in each contribute to viewing the whole, while roses and clematis climb between gardens, adding colour to two adjacent gardens at the same time.

KING HENRY'S WALK GARDEN, N1
11C King Henry's Walk, N1 4NX. Friends of King Henry's Walk Garden, www.khwgarden.org.uk. *Mildmay in Islington, nr Dalston Junction. Buses: 30, 38, 56, 141. Located behind adventure playground on King Henry's Walk, off Balls Pond Rd.* **Mon 4 May (2-4.30). Adm £5, chd free. Tea, coffee & cake. Donation to Friends of KHW Garden.**
Vibrant ornamental planting welcomes visitors to this hidden oasis, leading into a verdant community garden with a secluded woodland area, beehives, a wildlife pond, wall-trained fruit trees, and plots used by local residents to grow their own fruit and vegetables. Live music. Disabled access WC.

NEW 100 KNOLLYS ROAD, SW16
Streatham Hill, SW16 2JU. Clair Stretton. *What3words app: repay.risks.kicks. Accessible from Tulse Hill, West Norwood & Streatham Hill stns, all within a 15 min walk. Halfway down the road, from the Streatham Hill or West Norwood approach.* **Sun 17, Sun 31 May, Sun 14 June (2-5). Adm £5, chd free. Pre-booking essential, please visit www.ngs.org.uk for information & booking. Tea, coffee & cake.**

A unique hillside garden, in development since 2021. Divided into sections, this south facing garden contains many pollinator friendly plants and habitats, with an emphasis on recycling. A small gully winds down the path to channel rainwater, alongside a tiered, planted concrete terrace and fruit and vegetable beds. The space has been designed to be magical for children. International Garden Photographer of the Year 2025, Max A. Rush, will have work on display and will be available to chat at the top of the garden.

53 LADY AYLESFORD AVENUE, HA7
Stanmore, HA7 4FG. Jadon. *About a 15 min walk from Stanmore Stn, off Uxbridge Rd, close to St John's Church. H12, 340, & 324 bus stops are a 5 min walk from the garden. Limited free parking nearby.* **Sat 8 Aug (12-5). Adm £5. Tea, coffee & cake.**
A compact tropical fusion garden developed over the past 7 yrs. The garden is set in a development of the Battle of Britain RAF base. This delightful gem of a corner garden with water features and a stunning display of plants and flowers, shows what can be achieved, even in a small space. Colours and textures blend effortlessly to create a harmonious space, with exceptional attention to detail.

70 inpatients and their families are being supported at the newly opened Horatio's Garden Northern Ireland, thanks to the National Garden Scheme donations.

LAMBETH PALACE
Lambeth Palace Library, 15
Lambeth Palace Road, London SE1
7JT. The Church Commissioners,
www.archbishopofcanterbury.org.
*Entrance opp Evelina Children's
Hospital. Stn: Waterloo. Tube:
Westminster, Vauxhall all 10 min
walk. Buses: 3, C10, 77, 344.*
**Thur 21 May (4-7). Adm £6, chd
free. Pre-booking essential,
please visit ngs.org.uk for
information & booking. Self-serve
tea & coffee in the library.**
Lambeth Palace has one of the
oldest and largest private gardens in
London. Occupied by Archbishops
of Canterbury since 1197. Parkland
style garden features mature trees,
woodland and native planting, a
formal rose terrace, summer gravel
border, labyrinth, scented chapel
garden and active beehives. In the
Library (opened 2021), there will
be a display on the history of the
garden created around Lambeth
Palace. Library staff will be available
to discuss archive material (sign-up
on arrival). Garden tours available.
Please note: Gates will open at 4pm,
last entry is 6pm and garden closes at
7pm. Wheelchair access with ramped
path to rose terrace. Disabled WC.
Assistance dogs only.

42 LATIMER ROAD, E7
Forest Gate, E7 0LQ. Janet Daniels.
*8 mins walk from Forest Gate or
Wanstead Park stns. From Forest Gate
cross to Sebert Rd, then 3rd road on
L.* **Sun 19 July (11-4). Adm £4, chd
free. Tea, coffee & cake.**
Passionate plant collector's garden
in two separate areas. The first area
(90ft x 15ft) features an abundance
of baskets, climbers, shrubs, fruit
trees, and ponds. Step down into a
large secret garden (70ft x 30ft) with
exuberant borders, a wildlife pond
with gunnera, and a mulberry tree.
Discover unusual and exotic plants
along with other quirky features.
Wildlife friendly. Plants for sale.

84 LAVENDER GROVE, E8
Hackney, E8 3LS. Anne
Pauleau, 07930 550414,
a.pauleau@hotmail.co.uk. *Walk
from Haggerston or London Fields
train stns. The nearest bus stop is
the 394 in Lansdowne Dr, just round
the corner. LTNs operate in this area.*
**Sun 19 Apr (2-5). Adm £5, chd
free. Home-made teas. Opening**
**with London Fields Gardens
on Sun 7 June.** Visits also by
arrangement 8 Apr to 24 Sept for
groups of 5 to 20.
Courtyard garden with tropical
backdrop of bamboos and palms,
foil to clipped shrubs leading to
wilder area, the cottage garden with
mingling roses, lilies, alliums, grasses,
clematis, poppies, star jasmine and
jasmine. A very highly scented garden
with rampant ramblers and billowing
vegetation enchanting all senses.
Tulips and daffodils herald spring.
Fiery crocosmias and dahlias trumpet
late summer. Children's quiz offered
with prize on completion.

16 LINKS VIEW ROAD, TW12
Hampton Hill, TW12 1LA. Guy &
Virginia Lewis. *South West London, nr
Richmond & Kingston upon Thames. 5
min walk from Fulwell Stn. On 281, 267,
285 & R70 bus routes.* **Sat 23, Sun 24
May (2.30-4.30). Adm £5, chd free.
Home-made teas.**
A surprising garden featuring acers,
hostas, a fern collection, and
other unusual shade loving plants.
Many climbing roses, clematis, a
herbaceous border, and pots of
exotic plants. A rockery and a folly
with a shell grotto and a waterfall
leading to a small pond and bog
garden. A lawn and a formal pond.
A wild area with chickens and a
summerhouse. A greenhouse with
a succulent collection. A veranda
with a pelargonium collection. One
very friendly dog. Plants for sale inc
many succulents, and greenhouse/
conservatory plants, species
pelargoniums, and a variety of
plectranthus. Wheelchair access with
assistance.

NEW **LITTLE CRANHAM, TW12**
88 High Street, Hampton,
TW12 2SW. Mrs Lettie Gingell.
*Walk down long drive next to No. 90.
No driveway access for cars.* **Sat 20
June (12-5). Combined adm with
Hampton House £8, chd free. Tea,
coffee & cake.**
A hidden garden with rural views, laid
to lawn with flower beds, a pond, and
a decking area. Outstanding views of
Bushy Park and beyond complement
the peace and quiet of this large open
space, tucked behind the High Street.
Fully enclosed by walls and fences,
it provides a sunny, tranquil spot to
spend time and relax. The garden is a
work in progress, with areas still to be
developed. A garden with scope for
change, with new areas being added
constantly.

LLOYD SQUARE, WC1X
WC1X 9BA. Lloyd Square Garden
Committee. *Off Amwell St.* **Sun 14
June (2.30-6). Adm £5, chd free.
Home-made teas.**
The distinctive pedimented façades of
the houses around the square provide
a backdrop to this secluded private
London square, in the middle of the
Lloyd Baker Estate. Although the
Victorian layout with its pergolas and
arbours has been maintained, mature
sheltering trees and recent informal
border planting create a natural space
and a calm haven. Wheelchair access
is possible across lawns and gravel
pathways.

GROUP OPENING

LONDON FIELDS GARDENS, E8
Hackney, E8 3JW. *London Fields.
LTNs operate in this area. 7 min
walk from 149, 242, 243 bus stop,
Middleton Rd. 10 mins from 30,
38, 55 stops on Dalston Ln. 7 mins
from Haggerston train stn or 10 min
walk through London Fields from
Mare St buses.* **Sun 7 June (2-6).
Combined adm £10, chd free.
Home-made teas.**

NEW **33 ALBION DRIVE**
Dr Mary Glover.

84 LAVENDER GROVE
Anne Pauleau.
(See separate entry)

53 MAPLEDENE ROAD
Tigger with Paul Cullinan.

55 MAPLEDENE ROAD
Amanda Hayes & Tony Mott.

84 MIDDLETON ROAD
Penny Fowler.

A fascinating and very diverse
collection of gardens in London
Fields, all within easy walking
distance of each other. New this year
is 33 Albion Drive, a gravel garden
designed specifically for birds and
bees. At 84 Lavender Grove, there
are twin south facing gardens: a
courtyard with a tropical backdrop
and a highly scented, romantic
cottage garden. At 84 Middleton
Road lies an unusually large secret
garden where you can wander down
meandering woodland paths and

forget you are in London. The other two are north facing, with much the same space but totally different styles. 53 Mapledene Road is an established plantaholic's garden in five sections, with not a spare unplanted inch. 55 Mapledene Road has a Moorish-inspired terrace leading to a wildlife garden with plants chosen to attract birds, bees, and butterflies. A fabulous afternoon to see five such contrasting gardens.

LONG COTTAGE, HA5
54 High View, Pinner, HA5 3PB.
David & Prue Ruback,
07775 643055. *15 min walk from Pinner Tube Stn (Metropolitan line). High View runs between West End Ln & Cuckoo Hill.* **Sun 14 June (2-5.30). Adm £5, chd free. Tea, coffee & cake. Visits also by arrangement May to Sept.**
A photographer's garden. A large, colourful suburban garden enclosed by trees and various types of bamboo. The lawn with raised beds and several tranquil seating areas offering alternative vistas. A patio displays a range of potted plants, providing a spectrum of colour. Planting inc a variety of shrubs, roses, clematis, and perennials, all designed to showcase colour, leaf design, and texture. Features inc quirky artifacts, interesting vistas, and acrylic floral images. Access via side entrance. One shallow step; remainder of the garden is easily accessible.

NEW **49 LONSDALE ROAD, SW13**
Barnes, SW13 9JR. Paul Wuensche. *West London. Large house opp school playing fields about 200 metres W of Hammersmith bridge.* **Sun 17 May (12.30-5). Combined adm with 68 Nowell Road £10, chd free. Tea, coffee & cake.**
Large London garden that has undergone extensive development over the last 6 yrs. Its most notable features inc two very large deodars and a monkey puzzle tree, which cast a lot of shade. The main shrubs in spring should be wisteria and rhododendron, along with formal areas and two different ponds. Stone and tile work take inspiration from the East Ruston Old Vicarage Garden in Norfolk.

---

38 LOVELACE ROAD, SE21
Dulwich, SE21 8JX. José & Deepti Ramos Turnes. *Trains: Victoria to West Dulwich stn (12 mins), or London Bridge/Blackfriars to Tulse Hill stn (18 mins). Buses: 2, 3, & 68, then a short 10 min walk.* **Sun 21 June (11.30-5). Adm £5, chd free. Light refreshments.**
This charming garden welcomes you with an elegant all-white front, while the rear gives the illusion of endless space. Curving borders overflow with a mix of roses, delphiniums, foxgloves, and unusual plants for both sun and shade, complemented by a tranquil, hosta-lined stream. Mature Japanese acers, a Holm oak, and fruit trees provide structure and colour, adding depth to this hidden oasis. A lovely selection of delicious home-made cakes and savoury snacks will be available, alongside tea, coffee, and soft drinks.

GROUP OPENING

LOWER CLAPTON GARDENS, E5
Lower Clapton, E5 0RL. *12 min walk from Hackney Central, Hackney Downs or Homerton stns. Buses 38, 55, 106, 242, 253, 254 or 425, alight Lower Clapton Rd or Powerscroft Rd. Street parking.* **Sun 14 June (2-6). Combined adm £7, chd free. Home-made teas at 75 Mayola Road.**

8 ALMACK ROAD
Philip Lightowlers.

10 ALMACK ROAD
Mr Ben Myhill.

75 MAYOLA ROAD
Ms Christine Taylor.

Lower Clapton is an area of mid-Victorian terraces sloping down to the River Lea. These gardens reflect their owner's tastes and interests. 75 Mayola Road has a woodland walk, a vegetable patch and Caribbean style shed. 10 Almack Road is a long garden with architectural plants like trachycarpus palms and cordylines, a large pond and much Yorkstone and London brick. Next door at No. 8 is a similar space but divided into two rooms, one cool and peaceful the other with hot colours, succulents and greenhouse.

MAGGIE'S AT THE ROYAL MARSDEN, SM2
2 Oakleaf Avenue,
Sutton, SM2 5GP.
maggies.org/royalmarsden. *Bright red building based on the grounds of the Royal Marsden Hospital in Sutton. Maggie's is on corner of Cotswold Rd & Oakleaf Ave via The Royal Marsden Hospital entrance. Belmont train stn, 10min walk uphill. Buses: 80, 420, 280, S1. Parking in pay-on-exit patient car park.* **Fri 17 Apr (1-5). Adm £4, chd free. Tea, coffee & cake.**
The garden surrounding the centre is designed by the world-famous Dutch Landscape Architect Piet Oudolf, who envisioned a dynamic landscape. The garden is divided into four interconnected zones. Piet has carefully chosen the plants according to how much sun each zone receives. We have the shaded, woodland, spring and summer zones, creating a powerful experience for the eyes. Wheelchair access over raised paths.

MAGGIE'S WEST LONDON, W6
Charing Cross Hospital, Fulham Palace Road, Hammersmith, W6 8RF. Maggie's West London, www.instagram.com/maggies.west.london. *Follow Fulham Palace Rd from Hammersmith stn towards Charing Cross Hospital. The centre is on the corner of the hospital grounds of St Dunstan's Rd, and is painted tomato-orange.* **Sun 31 May (10-1). Adm £5, chd free. Tea, coffee & cake.**
The garden at Maggie's West London was designed by Dan Pearson OBE in 2008. It is now a well established space offering therapy and peace to those affected by cancer each year. The gardens surround the vivid orange walls of the centre. The path leading to the centre meanders through scented beds and mature trees. Visitors have access to various courtyards with a wonderful array of flora, grapevines and even a mature pink silk mimosa. Maggie's West London won the RIBA Stirling Prize for the best building designed by a British architect when first built. Wheelchair access to ground floor gardens and courtyards. Roof gardens not accessible.

4 MANNINGTREE ROAD, HA4
Ruislip, HA4 0ES. Costas Lambropoulos & Roberto Haddon. *Manningtree Rd is just off Victoria Rd, a 10–15 min walk from South Ruislip Tube Stn.* **Sun 9 Aug (2-6). Adm £5, chd free. Light refreshments.**
A compact garden with an exotic feel, combining hardy architectural plants with more tender varieties. A feeling of a small oasis, featuring plants such as *Musa basjoo*, *Ensete ventricosum* 'Montbeliardii', and a tree fern. Potted Mediterranean plants on the patio inc a fig tree, jasmines, and two olive trees. Cakes, savouries, home-made jams and biscuits for sale.

GROUP OPENING

MARKSBURY AVENUE GARDENS, TW9
Richmond, TW9 4JE. *Approx 10 min walk from Kew Gardens tube stn. Exit westbound platform onto North Rd. Take 3rd L into Atwood Ave. Marksbury Ave is 1st R. Buses 190, 419 or R68 stop at S end of road.* **Sun 7 June (2-5). Combined adm £7, chd free. Tea, coffee & cake in The Barn Church (corner of Marksbury Ave & Atwood Ave).**

26 MARKSBURY AVENUE
Sue Frisby.

59 MARKSBURY AVENUE
Clarissa & Michael Fletcher.

60 MARKSBURY AVENUE
Gay Lyle.

62 MARKSBURY AVENUE
Sarah Halaka & Andy Ciechan.

Although of similar size, these four neighbouring gardens in Kew are all very different. At No. 26 you will find many New Zealand natives. Fruit trees abound, with plums, figs, apples, red and black currants, apricots, mulberry, feijoa, loquat and citrus, alongside a delicate chamomile lawn. Over the road at No. 59, the garden has evolved largely through its own propagation and self-seeding. Shade is provided by a variety of ornamental trees, which lead to a lower patio and a small vegetable patch. No. 60 is a typical town garden where visitors can enjoy a fine display of patio roses, flowering shrubs and climbers, inc numerous varieties of clematis displayed around a curved lawn. Next door at No. 62 is a family garden,

created from scratch in 2018, with a brick edged lawn and yew topiary cones for structure.

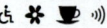

119 MORTLAKE ROAD, TW9
Kew, TW9 4AW. Karen Penney, Karenpenney@sky.com. *What3words app: drop.bravo.charm. Nearest tube/overground stn: Kew Gardens. Bus route R68. Parking in West Park Ave (free on Sundays) or Kew Retail Park car park (max 4 hrs).* **Sun 12 July (2-6). Adm £5, chd free. Tea, coffee & cake.** Visits also by arrangement 4 May to 10 July for groups of 6 to 25.
Thoughtful combinations of form and colour create a stunning summer display. The deep beds are colour themed and packed with a wide range of perennials. A lush 'fernarium' gives way to pastel cottage planting. On the garden's sunny side, a riot of colour bursts from an impressive 'hot' border. With something new around every corner, this garden shows the potential of an ordinary sized town garden. Pollinator and butterfly friendly.

25 MULBERRY WAY, E18
South Woodford, E18 1EB. Mrs Laura Piercy-Farley. *Just 200 metres from the A406, M11 J4. 100 metres from South Woodford Underground Stn (Central line), westbound exit. Cross the pedestrian crossing & turn L. Garden is 100 metres on R, opp the public car park.* **Sun 12 July (2-5). Adm £6, chd free. Light refreshments, home-made cakes, Pimm's & wine.**
A Victorian terraced house in London with a dog friendly, Italian style patio garden. The garden has a tranquil white theme, with a preference for white hydrangeas. It offers year-round interest with box hedges, bay trees, evergreen shrubs, and climbers. There are places to sit, lounge, eat, and relax.

77A MUSWELL ROAD, N10
N10 2BS. Ms Jennifer Granville. *Off Colney Hatch Ln. From Highgate Tube, take 134 or 43 bus to Queens Ave stop. From Bounds Green Tube, take 102 or 144 bus to Roseberry Rd stop. Free on street parking on Muswell Rd.* **Sun 14 June (2-6). Adm £5, chd free. Home-made teas. Open nearby 5 St Regis Close.**

The garden is 6 yrs old and inspired by the bedtime story 'The Little Green Gate', that opens onto Fairy Land, told to the owner by her grandfather. The garden comprises three linked decks, all providing a different mood and experience, with a rose arch, wildlife pond, and several green gates. Bugs are encouraged, with architect designed bug hotel, fairies sometimes stay too. Tea, coffee, juice, home-made cakes, biscuits, and ice cream for kids (and grown-ups!). Sorry, no wheelchair access.

THE MYSTERIES OF LIGHT ROSARY GARDEN, NW5
St Dominic's Priory (the Rosary Shrine), Southampton Road, Kentish Town, NW5 4LB. Raffaella Morini on behalf of the Church & Priory, 07778 526434, garden@raffaellamorini.com, rosaryshrine.co.uk/rosary-shrine/visit-the-shrine/garden. *Entrance to the garden is via Alan Cheales Way, on the RHS of the church, next to the school.* **Sat 13 June (1-5). Adm £5, chd free. Tea, coffee & cake.** Visits also by arrangement May to Sept.
A walled garden behind the Priory Church of Our Lady of the Rosary and St Dominic, commissioned by the Dominican Friars as a spiritual and meditative space representing the 'Mysteries of Light' of the Holy Rosary. A sandstone path marks out a Rosary with black granite beads, surrounded by flowers traditionally associated with the Virgin Mary: roses, lilies, iris, periwinkle, and columbine. The garden is fully accessible, with stone path and a wheelchair friendly gravel path.

15 NORCOTT ROAD, N16
Stoke Newington, N16 7BJ. Amanda Welch, 020 8806 5723, amandashetlandwelch@gmail.com. *Buses: 67, 73, 76, 106, 149, 243, 393, 476, 488. Clapton & Rectory Road train stns. LTNs operate in this area.* **Visits by arrangement 12 Jan to 30 Nov. Min charge per visit £20 so bring at least two friends. Adm £6, chd free. Tea, coffee & cake.**
Large walled garden with aged fruit trees, a pond, and an abundance of herbaceous plants, a kind of cottage garden but in London. Open by arrangement only. Fix your date and time with the owner. You are welcome

to stay as long as you like; there is plenty of space to sit and enjoy tea and cake. Plants are available depending on the season, and the garden can be enjoyed at any time of year.

5 NORTHAMPTON PARK, N1
N1 2PP. Andrew Bernhardt & Anne Brogan, 07805 399010, bernhardt8@gmail.com. *Backing on to St Paul's Shrubbery, Islington. 5 min walk from Canonbury train stn, 10 mins from Highbury & Islington tube stn (Victoria line). Buses: 73, 30, 56, 341, 476.* **Sat 27 June (1.30-6). Adm £5, chd free. Wine, Prosecco & strawberries. Visits also by arrangement 1 May to 1 Oct for groups of up to 20. No refreshments.**
The transformation of a 'rescue garden': this once neglected, south facing walled garden, dating from the 1840s, now regularly opens. Reopened in 2025 after a complete redesign, we have blended traditional and tropical planting to highlight colour, sunlight, and space. By spring 2026, we hope the garden will begin to show its new character. WC available.

NEW **68 NOWELL ROAD, SW13**
Barnes, SW13 9BS. Marlene Samuels. *What3words app: tune.miles.speaks.* **Sun 17 May (12.30-5). Combined adm with 49 Lonsdale Road £10, chd free. Tea, coffee & cake.**
A cosy suburban garden, full of warm colours to celebrate the arrival of spring, with impactful mature shrubs, in the heart of Barnes. Weigelas and hydrangeas take pride of place in the late spring, along with a variety of rhododendrons and camellias. A clever use of space allows for generous planting, large pergola and a raised L-shaped pond. Sculpture by local artist. A short walk from the River Thames, this garden is open in combination with 49 Lonsdale Road which provides a wonderful borrowed view.

OAK FARM/HOMESTEAD, EN2
Cattlegate Road, Crews Hill, Enfield, EN2 9DS. Genine & Martin Newport. *Walk from Crews Hill Stn (turn L onto main road; entrance opp Warmadams). Freedom Pass & Oyster Card valid. Follow NGS arrows. Exit J24 or J25 of M25. Within ULEZ zone. On site parking (entrance on Cattlegate Rd, signed 'Homestead').* **Sun 10 May (12-4). Adm £6, chd free. Home-made teas served in the barn.**
In the heart of Crews Hill's nurseries lies our 3 acre garden and meadow. Reclaimed over 35 yrs from a former pig farm, it now features relaxed planting and a haven for wildlife. A walled garden leads to a vegetable plot, greenhouse, and orchard with a woodland walk. In September, the garden is carpeted with abundant cyclamen. An arboretum and lovely country views. Wheelchair access over grass.

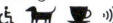

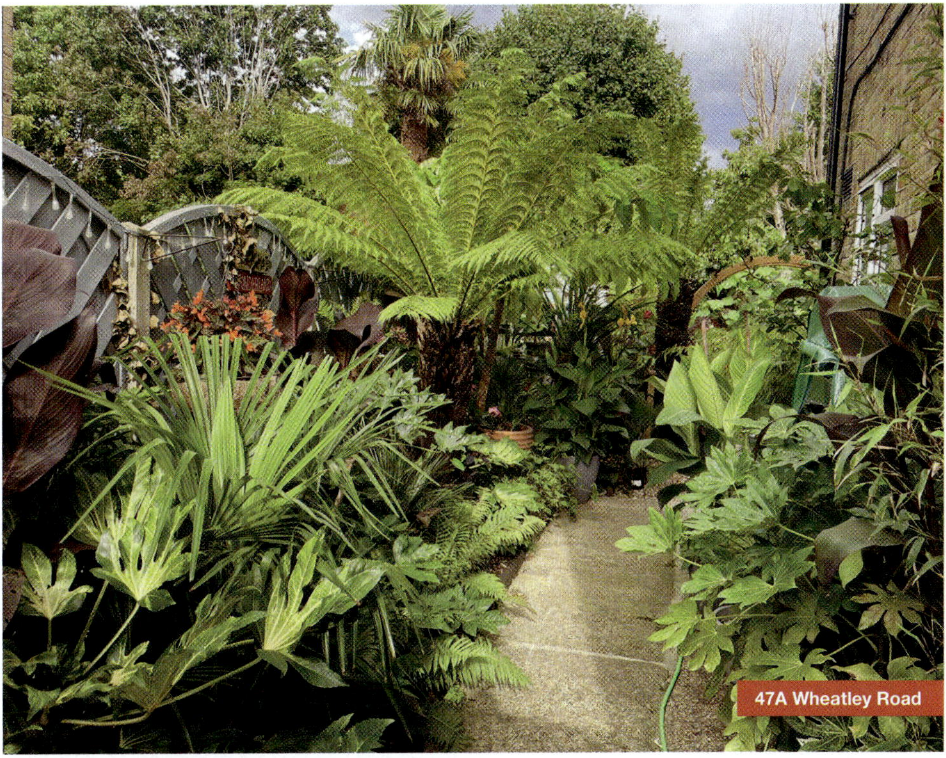
47A Wheatley Road

4 OAKLEA PASSAGE, KT1
Kingston Upon Thames, KT1 2AJ. Sheila Cheek. *Located behind Kingston College. Parking is limited on Milner Rd. Take the K2, K3, 71, or 281 bus from Surbiton & get off at Kingston College.* **Sun 2 Aug (2-5). Adm £5, chd free. Home-made teas.**
Hidden behind tall buildings is an unexpected cottage garden delight. The front garden of this Grade II listed cottage features two mature silver birches, a lawn, and flower borders. New fruit trees and an oak pergola covered with wisteria and solanum lead to a secluded, sunny rear garden with a large terrace, gazebo, pond, and herbaceous beds bursting with colour from hydrangeas, salvias, and gauras. For wheelchair access directions, please contact owner on 07717 670810.

21 OAKLEIGH PARK SOUTH, N20
Springhill, N20 9JS. Carol & Robin Tullo, 07909 901731/07930 480707, robin.tullo@btinternet.com. *Totteridge & Whetstone tube stn (Northern line): 15 min walk or take 251 bus. Oakleigh Park train stn: 10 min walk. Also buses 34 & 125 from High Rd. Plenty of street parking.* **Sun 14 June (2-6). Adm £5, chd free. Home-made teas. Visits also by arrangement 4 May to 26 July for groups of 10 to 25.**
A mature garden over 200ft, with a lawn framed by a magnificent 100 yr old ash tree with its tree seat. A path leads to a large pond area, fed by a natural spring within landscaped terraced paving. Beyond this lies a herb and vegetable area, an orchard with bulbs and wild flowers, and the working part of the garden. A mix of sunny borders, pond marginals, and shaded woodland areas, with plenty of seating. Accessible entrance to garden, with level wheelchair access to terrace and lawn. Path to pond area, but raised levels beyond.

3 OLD FOLD CLOSE, EN5
Barnet, EN5 4QL. Amanda Magill. *1m S of M25 J24 in Hadley Highstone. Follow signs for Old Fold Manor Golf Course. Note: Entrance to garden only via Old Fold Ln, opp Hadley Common. Bus: 234, 326, & 384 to Barnet High St (10 min walk). Train: Great Northern to Hadley Wood Stn. Tube: High Barnet Stn,* Northern line (20 min walk). **Sun 10 May (2-5). Adm £5, chd free. Tea, coffee & cake.**
A foliage centred garden with weaving caramel coloured paths, featuring bronze coloured metal art installations throughout. Beth Chatto inspired dry beds dominate the upper part of the garden, while a shrub surrounded woodland zone occupies the centre. A grassy mound, rockery, and Japanese themed area lie closest to the back gate, which opens out to an extensive rockery in the garage area. Hadley Common 1 min walk for picnics.

OLDEN COMMUNITY GARDEN, N5
Whistler Street (opp No. 22), N5 1NH. London Borough of Islington, www.oldengarden.org. *Islington. Walk from Highbury & Islington, Arsenal or Holloway Rd tube stns, or Drayton Park train stn, or from bus stops on Holloway Rd, along Drayton Park to Whistler St.* **Sun 19 Apr (2-5). Adm £5, chd free. Home-made teas.**
A 2 acre secret oasis of biodiversity on a railway embankment. Spring bulbs and blossom flourish. A lawn, herbaceous garden, wildflower meadow, wildlife pond, and 1 acre woodland delight visitors. We also have an orchard, vegetable beds, and a new butterfly garden. We compost green waste, use harvested water, and build dead hedges. Visitors enjoy walks in the woodland, and tea on the patio or in the garden house. Wheelchair access to all areas of top terrace. Accessible WC.

OMVED GARDENS, N6
1 Townsend Yard, Highgate, N6 5JF. Karen Leason, omvedgardens.com. *From Highgate Stn, exit onto Archway Rd, turn L on Southwood Ln, then continue to Townsend Yard on R. Buses 143, 210, 271 stop nearby. What3words app: lungs.limit.bronze.* **Sun 31 May (11-3). Adm £10, chd free. Pre-booking essential, please visit www.ngs.org.uk for information & booking. Light refreshments.**
OmVed Gardens in North London is a garden, exhibition, events, and learning space exploring food, ecology, and creativity for climate resilience. The garden features a native flower meadow, an organic kitchen garden, an amphitheatre showcasing a Paul Mount sculpture, a sunlit greenhouse, a seed library, a barn and kitchen with terrace, and a rooftop edible garden. No wheelchair access through kitchen garden and roof garden. Accessible WC in barn.

PADDOCK ALLOTMENTS & LEISURE GARDENS, SW20
51 Heath Drive, Raynes Park, SW20 9BE. Paddock Horticultural Society. *Buses 57, 131, 200 to Raynes Park stn, then 10 min walk or bus 163. Bus 152 to Bushey Rd, 7 min walk. Bus 413, 5 min walk from Cannon Hill Ln. Street parking.* **Sat 27 June (12-5). Adm £4, chd free. Light refreshments.**
An allotment site not to be missed, over 150 plots set in 5½ acres. Our tenants come from diverse communities growing a wide range of flowers, fruit and vegetables. Some plots are purely organic, others resemble English country gardens. Winner of London in Bloom Best Allotment on four occasions. Plants and produce for sale. Ploughman's lunch available. Wheelchair access over mainly level paved and grass paths.

11 PARK AVENUE NORTH, N8
Crouch End, N8 7RU. Steven Buckley & Liz Roberts. *Between Crouch End & Muswell Hill. Buses: 144, W3, W7. Tube: Finsbury Park or Turnpike Lane. Train: Hornsey or Alexandra Palace.* **Sun 16 Aug (11.30-5.30). Adm £5, chd free. Pre-booking essential, please visit www.ngs.org.uk for information & booking. Home-made teas.**
An award-winning exotic garden, featured on Gardeners' World (episode 23, 2025) and in the RHS The Garden magazine (July 2024). Dramatic foliage, spiky and lush, dominates with the focus on palms, cycads, aloes, agaves, dioons, dasylirions, aeoniums, tree ferns, nolinas, bamboos, yuccas, bananas, cacti, puyas and succulents. Trees include orange, peach, *Cussonia spicata* and Szechuan pepper.

36 PARK VILLAGE EAST, NW1
Camden Town, NW1 7PZ. Christy Rogers. *Tube: Mornington Cres or Camden Town, 7 min walk. Opp railway, just S of Mornington St*

bridge. Free parking on Sundays. **Sun 7 June (2-6). Adm £6, chd free. Home-made teas.**
A large, peaceful garden behind a sympathetically modernised John Nash house. Relandscaped in 2014, retaining the original mature sycamores and adding hornbeam hedges dividing a woodland area and orchard from a central large lawn, a mixed herbaceous border, and a rose bank with a seating area. Children enjoy an artificial grass slide. Musical entertainment is provided by young musicians. Wheelchair access via grass ramp down from driveway to main garden (steeper than wheelchair regulations).

5 PEMBERTON ROAD, KT8
East Molesey, KT8 9LG. Armi Maddison. *Please enter the garden down the side path to R of house.* **Evening opening Fri 26 June (7-9). Adm £5, chd free. Wine.**
An artist's sheltered and secluded gravel garden, designed alongside our house build in 2015. It features many grasses and pink, blue, and white plantings, with occasional pops of bright colour. A galvanised drinking trough with bulrushes and water lilies, together with a large mature central acer tree, combines with several seating areas to extend the living space into this fabulous outdoor room. The no5workshops studio will also be open on the day, with 10% of proceeds going to the NGS. My work is inspired by the garden, with many plants and leaf shapes grown for my botanical printmaking.

PETERSHAM HOUSE, TW10
Petersham Road, Petersham, Richmond, TW10 7AA. Francesco & Gael Boglione, www.petershamnurseries.com. *Stn: Richmond, bus 65 to Dysart. Entry to garden off Petersham Rd, through Petersham Nurseries. Parking very limited on Church Ln.* **Sun 19 Apr (11-4). Adm £7.50, chd free.**
Broad lawn with large topiary and generously planted herbaceous borders. Adjoins Petersham Nurseries with extensive plant sales, shop and café serving lunch, tea and cake (no reservations required). Wheelchair access possible through a separate entrance.

4 PIERMONT GREEN, SE22
East Dulwich, SE22 0LP. Janine Wookey. *A triangle of green space facing Peckham Rye, at Honor Oak Rd end. Stns: Peckham Rye & Honor Oak. Buses: 63 & 363 (pass the door); & 12 stops a few yards away. No parking on green, but free parking on nearby side streets.* **Sun 24 May (1-5). Adm £5, chd free. Home-made teas. Open nearby 86 Underhill Road.**
This L-shaped garden, partly enclosed by a Victorian wall, has an old fashioned woodland feel, with roses, a lovely spreading mulberry, and viburnum trees overlooked by ginkgo and purple elder. Global warming allows a banana grove to flourish alongside fig, lemon, pear, and plum. A low maintenance gravel area offers aeoniums and a pretty mallow, *Althaea cannabina*. By the house, bright pots give a Mediterranean feel. The foxglove tree draws attention, particularly when in flower in the spring. Limited wheelchair access with a couple of front steps to negotiate.

1A PRIMROSE GARDENS, NW3
Hampstead, NW3 4UJ. Debra & Tim Craighead, dcraighead@me.com. *Belsize Park. Convenient from Belsize Park & Chalk Farm tube stns (5 mins), or Swiss Cottage (12 mins). Also, buses 1, 268, & C11. Free parking on Sundays.* **Evening opening Thur 28, Sat 30 May (6-8). Adm £8. Wine. Sun 31 May (2.30-5.30). Adm £5, chd free. Home-made teas.** Visits also by arrangement 22 May to 20 Sept for groups of 10 to 35. Optional talk & tour to adjacent Regents Park gardens.
A hidden oasis in the heart of Belsize Park, cool and relaxing. Planted with various microclimates for surrounding buildings, walls, and the desire for privacy. Mirrors help create a sense of intrigue. Densely planted for texture and revolving seasonality, with tree ferns, foxgloves, clematis, ferns, salvias, and lilies. A restricted colour palette of white, purple, and pops of orange/russet throughout the yr. Bird friendly, with a sedum rooftop that attracts bees and butterflies.

GROUP OPENING

PRINCES AVENUE GARDENS, N10
Muswell Hill, N10 3LS. *Buses: 43 & 134 from Highgate Tube Stn; also W7, 102, 144, 234, & 299. Princes Ave opp M&S in Muswell Hill Broadway & The Village Green pub in Fortis Green Rd.* **Sun 10 May (12-5). Combined adm £6, chd free. Tea, coffee & cake. Gluten free & vegan options.**

17 PRINCES AVENUE
Patsy Bailey & John Rance.

28 PRINCES AVENUE
Lucinda Oppenheimer.

In a beautiful Edwardian avenue in the heart of the Muswell Hill Conservation Area, two peaceful traditional gardens lie just off the bustling Broadway, perfect for relaxing and entertaining. The gardens are very different: 17 Princes Avenue is south facing but shaded by large surrounding trees, inc a ginkgo. It features a superb display of hostas and ferns. 28 Princes Avenue, opp, is north facing. Mature trees, shrubs, and beautifully planted mixed borders give a feeling of calm, with acers, fruit trees, and a rose arch. A trampoline lurks in a secret corner. Live music at 17 Princes Avenue by the Secret Life Sax Quartet at 2.30pm and 3.30pm. There is a small step at 17 Princes Avenue; help available on request.

GROUP OPENING

RAILWAY COTTAGES, N22
2 Dorset Road, N22 7SL. *Nr Alexandra Palace. Tube: Wood Green, 10 min walk. Train: Alexandra Palace, 3 mins. Buses: W3, 184, 3 mins. Free parking in local streets on Sundays.* **Sun 5 July (2-5). Combined adm £5, chd free. Home-made cakes & cold drinks. Open nearby Ally Pally Allotments.**

2 DORSET ROAD
Jane Stevens.

4 DORSET ROAD
Mark Longworth.

14 DORSET ROAD
Cathy Brogan.

22 DORSET ROAD
Mike & Noreen Ainger.

24A DORSET ROAD
Eddie & Jane Wessman.

Tucked away from the bustle of Wood Green, near Alexandra Palace, a row of historic railway cottages takes visitors back in time. Five front gardens, as featured on Gardeners' World in March 2025, will open to the public. At No. 2, clipped hedges contrast with climbing roses, honeysuckle, abutilon, grasses, ferns, and a fig tree. No. 14 is an informal, organic, bee-friendly haven, planted with fragrant herbs, flowers, and shrubs. No. 22 is nurtured by the grandson of the original railway worker resident, a lovely place to sit, relax, and enjoy the varied planting. By contrast, 24A is a potager style cottage garden, with raised beds overflowing with vegetables and flowers. Home-made cakes and soft drinks will be on sale, along with the chance to browse our popular plant stall. A large green beside Dorset Road is perfect for a picnic.

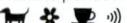

42 RISINGHOLME ROAD, HA3
Harrow, HA3 7ER. Brenda White, 0208 863 5877, brenda.white@ngs.org.uk. *Wealdstone & Harrow Weald. Buses: 258, 340,182,140 Salvatorian College/St Joseph's Catholic Church, Wealdstone. Tube/train: Harrow & Wealdstone Stn (10 min walk or bus). Road opp the Salvatorian College.* **Sun 3 May, Sun 30 Aug (2-5). Adm £5, chd free. Tea, coffee & cake.** Visits also by arrangement 4 May to 30 Sept for groups of 5 to 20.
A stunning, paved 120ft long garden packed with plants, divided into themed areas inc a raised bed vegetable garden, a large aviary, a beehive, and a summerhouse. A shady garden that makes the most of every space!

NEW THE ROCKINGHAM GARDEN ESTATE, SE1
Harper Road, Bermondsey, SE1 6AG. Ian Zanardelli. *From Elephant & Castle, walk E along New Kent Rd. Take 3rd L onto Harper Rd. The Welcome Garden is 100 metres ahead on L. Nearest bus stop: Rodney Pl (routes 1, 53, 63, 172, 188, 363, 415, 453).* **Sun 5 July (10-4). Adm £5, chd free. Cold brew tea, coffee & home-made edible delights in the Welcome Garden.**
Discover the Rockingham Garden Estate: An urban countryfile. For the past 13 yrs, our community has been hard at work transforming a council estate into a green urban oasis. We have established gardens, nature zones, wildlife ponds, an apiary, and orchards. We have planted 1km of hedgerow and over 50,000 wildflower bulbs to develop new biodiversity corridors. We are the future. Come see us grow! Site of Important Nature Conservation (SINC) Designation. A gentle slope leads to Welcome Gate, with mostly level grass and gravel surfaces. Pathways provide good access across the rest of the estate.

19 ROKEBY GARDENS, IG8
Woodford Green, IG8 9HT. Pauline Gunn. *From Churchill statue in Woodford Green, take 1st L turn onto Forest Approach & continue straight across Xrds. At top of hill, turn L into Rokeby Gardens. Please*

51 The Chase

park on one side of the road. **Sun 19 July (2-5). Adm £4, chd free. Tea, coffee, soft drinks & home-made cakes.**

A calming, colourful town garden, measuring 75ft by 25ft, features a Koi pond and a raised bed with a north facing border. Convivial seating areas offer different views of the garden when entertaining. Cottage style planting inc perpetual flowering roses purchased from RHS flower shows, along with fuchsia, brunnera, hosta, primula, and phlox. Pots of roses and fruit add seasonal interest.

ROOFTOPVEGPLOT, W1
122 Great Titchfield Street, W1W 6ST. Miss Wendy Shillam, 07597 438666, coffeeinthesquare@me.com. *Westminster. Located on the flat roof of a private house, on the 5th floor. Ring the doorbell labelled 'Wendy Shillam & Michael Smith' to gain entry to the building.* **Sat 11, Sun 12 July (11-5). Adm £6, chd free. Pre-booking essential, please visit www.ngs.org.uk for information & booking. Home-made teas.**

A nutritional garden with views across London, where fruit and vegetables grow amongst complementary flowers in six inches of soil, in raised beds on a flat roof. Trellises and greenhouse tomatoes. Afternoon teas and morning coffees, with home-made cakes and scones for sale. Wendy is currently writing a book titled Dark Matter, about the benefits of brown flours and the nutritional elements in cereals. She will be happy to share a few recipes from the book.

ROYAL COLLEGE OF PHYSICIANS, GARDEN OF MEDICINAL PLANTS, NW1
11 St Andrews Place, Regents Park, NW1 4LE. Royal College of Physicians of London, garden.rcplondon.ac.uk. *Tubes: Great Portland St & Regent's Park. Garden is one block N of stn exits, on Outer Circle opp SE corner of Regent's Park. There is no access via Peto Place.* **Mon 29 June (12-4). Adm £6, chd free. Tea, coffee & cake.**

We have almost 1000 different plants connected to the role of plants in medicine, both today and in the past. These inc plants named after physicians, plants used to make modern medicines, those with long standing traditional uses, plants used in medical traditions from all the continents of the world, and plants featured in the College's first Pharmacopoeia Londinensis of 1618. Guided tours will be offered throughout the day by physicians, explaining the uses of the plants, their histories, and other stories. Books about the plants in the medicinal garden will be on sale, alongside free leaflets. All plants are labelled with their botanical names. Entry to garden is at far end of St Andrew's Place. Accessible paths around the garden with some slopes. Wheelchair lift for WC. No parking on site.

ROYAL TRINITY HOSPICE, SW4
30 Clapham Common North Side, SW4 0RN. Royal Trinity Hospice, www.royaltrinityhospice.london/our-gardens. *1⅓m from Clapham Junction. 8 min walk from Clapham Common tube. Buses: 35, 37, 345,137, 249 & 322 (137 stops outside).* **Sun 19 Apr (11-4), open nearby 51 The Chase. Sun 14 June, Sun 13 Sept (11-4). Adm £5, chd free. Light refreshments.**

Our front gardens feature perennials, shrubs and trees inc wisteria on the front of the buildings. The rear landscaped gardens have lawns with herbaceous borders either side of a path that leads to the Koi pond. Plenty of year-round colour from bulbs, herbs, annuals, perennials, roses, shrubs and trees. We have a large glasshouse to grow plants and vegetables from seed. Interesting sculpture by George Rickey called Four Open Squares Horizontal Tapered in the pond. Wheelchair access via ramps and pathways.

31 RYECROFT ROAD, SW16
Streatham, SW16 3EW. Chrissy Silver, www.instagram.com/chrissysgarden2024. *Nr Crown Point. Mainline: Streatham & West Norwood stns. Buses: 68, 196, 249, 417, & 468, all to Crown Point.* **Evening opening Sun 21 June (6-10). Adm £8, chd free. Wine.**

Large, sunny garden with an open aspect and far-reaching views towards the North Downs from the roof terrace. A herbaceous border around a large lawn, cut flower bed, a small woodland area, and a rockery with Mediterranean planting. Old-fashioned roses both at the front and back of the garden. Lovely old Yorkstone and slate paths help divide the garden into smaller, cosier areas.

NEW ### ST GEORGE'S FIELDS, W2
The Estate Office, Albion Street, Westminster, W2 2YE. St George's Fields, www.stgeorgesfields.org.uk. *Opp the N side of Hyde Park. The entrance to St George's Fields is via two large vehicle & pedestrian gates, located nr the junction of Connaught St & Albion St. What3words app: count.season.race.* **Sat 23 May (11-2). Adm £6, chd free. Pre-booking essential, please visit www.ngs.org.uk for information & booking.**

Described as an 'oasis in Central London', St George's Fields is a gated, low density housing concept designed for convenient city living. This unique community of 300 flats is set within 2½ acres of private, tranquil woodland gardens, which separate each of the early 1970s buildings. The unique ziggurat pyramid style buildings incorporate five levels of large balconies, each with hanging gardens.

ST JOSEPH'S HOSPICE, E8
Mare Street, Hackney, E8 4SA. St Joseph's Hospice, www.stjh.org.uk/about-us/our-gardens. *South end of Mare St, nr Broadway Market. South of King Edward's Rd. Buses 254, 106, 388, 26. Use King Edward's Rd bus stop coming S from Hackney Central & Victoria Park Rd bus stop coming N from Bethnal Green (Central line).* **Sat 30 May (10-4). Adm £3, chd free. Tea, coffee & cake.**

The formal gardens at St Joseph's Hospice are a healing space. Made up of seven distinct garden spaces, each with secluded seating, intended to promote important end of life conversations with friends and family. When you visit at the end of May, you will find an abundance of roses in full bloom as the impressive wisteria fades away. Wheelchair access to gardens, although there are some slopes. Wheelchair accessible WC.

27 ST PETERS SQUARE, W6
British Grove, W6 9NW.
Oliver & Gabrielle Leigh-Wood, 07810 677478,
oliverleighwood@hotmail.com.
London. Tube to Stamford Brook, exit stn & turn S down Goldhawk Rd. At T-lights continue ahead into British Grove. Entrance to garden at 50 British Grove, 100yds on L. **Sun 17 May (2-6). Adm £8, chd free. Home-made teas.** Visits also by arrangement 1 May to 1 June.
This long, secret space, is a plantsman's eclectic semi-tamed wilderness. Created over the last 12 yrs it contains lots of camellias, magnolias and fruit trees. Much of the hard landscaping is from skips and the whole garden is full of other people's unconsidered trifles of fancy inc a folly and summerhouse.

19 ST PETER'S STREET, N1
Islington, N1 8JD. Adrian Gunning. Angel, Islington. Tube: Angel. Buses: 19, 30, 43, 38, 4 all to Islington Green. **Sun 21 June (2.30-5.30). Adm £5, chd free. Open nearby Arlington Square Gardens.**
A charming, secluded town garden featuring climbing roses, trees, shrubs, climbers, a pond, a patio with containers, and a gazebo with a trompe l'oeil mural.

57 ST QUINTIN AVENUE, W10
North Kensington, London, W10 6NZ. Mr H Groffman, 020 8969 8292. *Less than 1m from Ladbroke Grove or White City tube stns. Buses: 7, 70, & 220 all go to North Pole Rd.* **Sun 5, Sun 19 July (2-6). Adm £5, chd £2.50. Tea, coffee & cake.** Visits also by arrangement 5 July to 23 Aug.
Award-winning 30 x 40ft garden, now in its 40th consecutive yr of opening for the NGS! A diverse selection of plants, inc shrubs chosen for their foliage effects. Patio with colour themed bedding. Clever use of mirrors and plant associations. Good selection of climbers and wall shrubs. This yr's special display commemorates the centenary of the birth of Britain's longest reigning monarch, HM Queen Elizabeth II.

5 ST REGIS CLOSE, N10
Alexandra Park Road, Muswell Hill, N10 2DE. Mrs S Bennett & Mr E Hyde, 020 8883 8540, suebearlh@yahoo.co.uk. *Take 2nd L onto Alexandra Park Rd when coming from Colney Hatch Ln. Buses 102 & 299 from Bounds Green Tube to St Andrew's Church, or 102 from East Finchley. Buses 43 & 143 stop on Colney Hatch Ln. A short walk, follow NGS signs. Parking on side roads, inc coaches.* **Sun 14 June (2-6.30), open nearby 77a Muswell Road. Sun 2 Aug (2-6.30). Adm £5, chd free. Home-made teas, gluten free option & herbal teas (cash preferred).** Visits also by arrangement 1 May to 18 Oct for groups of 10 to 60. Short talk on history of the garden.
Cornucopia of sensual delights. Artist's garden famous for architectural features and delicious cakes. Baroque temple, pagodas, Raku tiled mirrored wall conceals plant nursery. American Gothic shed overlooks Liberace terrace and stairway to heaven. Maureen Lipman's favourite garden; combines colour, humour, trompe l'oeil with wildlife friendly ponds, waterfalls, weeping willow, lawns and abundant planting. A unique experience awaits! Unusual architectural features inc Oriental tea house overlooking carp pond. Mega plant sale and open studio with ceramics and cards (cash preferred). Wheelchair access not suitable for everyone, please check with owners for details.

16 SEARS STREET, SE5
SE5 7JL. Jonathan Gregson, www.backyardbotanics.co.uk. *5 min walk from Bowyer Place (Stop N, Camberwell Rd) for buses from Elephant & Castle, or Wyndham Rd bus stop from Denmark Hill. A TfL cycle hire docking station on corner of Camberwell Rd & Albany Rd.* **Sun 5 July (11-4.30). Adm £5, chd free. Tea, coffee & cake.**
Described as a 'backyard botanic garden', this small city garden crams in plants from more than 200 plant families, making it one of the most botanically diverse in London. Created by a plant addict, it has spaces dedicated to different regions of the world. Bananas, monkey puzzle trees, and ferns native to the rainforests of Borneo jostle for space with traditional roses, lilies, and foxgloves.

SOUTH LONDON BOTANICAL INSTITUTE, SE24
323 Norwood Road, SE24 9AQ. South London Botanical Institute, www.slbi.org.uk. *Mainline: Tulse Hill. Buses from Brixton: 2, 415, 68, 196, 322 & 468.* **Sun 7 June (2-5). Adm by donation. Light refreshments.** Donation to South London Botanical Institute.
London's smallest botanical garden. Highlights inc unusual bulbs, ferns, flowering trees, and roses. Wild flowers flourish beside medicinal herbs. Scented, native, and woodland plants are featured, growing among rare trees and shrubs. There is also a collection of succulents in our greenhouse.

41 SOUTHBROOK ROAD, SE12
Lee, SE12 8LJ. Barbara Polanski. *Southbrook Rd is located off A205, South Circular, which is accessed via Burnt Ash Rd. Train: Lee & Hither Green stns, both a 10 min walk. Bus: P273, 202. Please enter via side access & look out for the yellow balloons!* **Sun 24 May (1-5.30). Adm £5, chd free. Home-made teas. Open nearby 13 & 15 Waite Davies Road.**
Developed over 25 yrs, this garden features a formal layout with wide, mixed herbaceous borders full of colour, surrounded by mature trees that frame sunny lawns, an immaculate central box parterre, and an Indian pergola. Ancient pear trees are festooned in June with large clouds of white Kiftsgate and Rambling Rector roses. Discover fish and damselflies in two lily ponds. Orangery, gazebo, and wall fountain. Many sheltered places to sit and relax. Enjoy refreshments in a small classical garden building, with interior wall paintings and almost hidden by roses climbing high into the trees. Side access for standard wheelchairs. Gravel driveway with one step.

◆ SPENCER HOUSE, SW1
27 St James' Place, Westminster, SW1A 1NR. RIT Capital Partners, www.spencerhouse.co.uk. *From Green Park tube stn, exit on S side, walk down Queen's Walk, turn L through narrow alleyway. Turn R & Spencer House will be in front of you.* **For opening times and information, please visit garden website.**
Originally designed in the C18 by Henry Holland, the garden was among the grandest in the West

End. Restored in 1990 under the Chairmanship of Lord Rothschild, the garden now evokes its original layout with planting suggested by early C19 nursery lists and supplemented with native wild flowers for biodiversity.

25 SPRINGFIELD AVENUE, N10
Muswell Hill, N10 3SU. Heather Hampson & Nigel Ragg. *Centre of Muswell Hill. From main r'about in Muswell Hill, head down Muswell Hill towards Crouch End. Springfield Ave is 1st on L. No. 25 is opp the steps to Grosvenor Gardens.* **Sun 7 June (2-6). Adm £5, chd free. Home-made teas.**
Be pleasantly surprised by this city garden! Magical, packed with colour, fragrance, rambling roses, and quirky ideas to stimulate conversation and imagination. A visual delight, with three terraces, each with an individual atmosphere, leading to a summerhouse set against a backdrop of mature trees. Plenty of spots to sit and enjoy scrumptious tea and cakes. A good plant sale. The summerhouse is a place to rest and view the owner's artworks, which are for sale in aid of the NGS. Please note that this is a steep garden, with different levels and uneven steps.

25 STIRLING ROAD, SW9
Stockwell, SW9 9EF. Francis & Barry. *Equidistant from Clapham North & Stockwell tube stns. Free parking on Sundays on Stirling Rd.* **Sun 19 July (10.30-5.30). Adm £5. Pre-booking essential, please visit www.ngs.org.uk for information & booking. Home-made teas.**
Gardeners' World: Garden of the Year Finalist 2025. This small but perfectly formed tropical oasis is set in a south west facing plot. It features elements of a woodland forest, with a variety of ferns hidden in its nooks and crannies. Visitors are drawn to an array of large, lush green foliage and bright, bold flowers in this exotic, jungle style garden, along with a water feature and seating areas.

STONEY HILL HOUSE, SE26
Rock Hill, SE26 6SW. Cinzia & Adam Greaves. *Off Sydenham Hill. Nearest train stns: Sydenham, Gipsy Hill or Sydenham Hill. Buses to Crystal Palace: 202 or 363 via Sydenham Hill. House at end of cul-de-sac on L when coming from Sydenham Hill.* **Sun 17 May (2-6). Adm £8, chd free. Home-made teas. Soft drinks & Prosecco.**
Garden and woodland of approx 1 acre, providing a secluded, secret green oasis in the city. Paths meander through mature rhododendron, oak, yew and holly trees, offset by pieces of contemporary sculpture. The garden is on a slope, and a number of viewpoints set at different heights provide varied perspectives. The planting in the top part of the garden is fluid, and flows seamlessly into the woodland. Swings and a treehouse provide entertainment for children and adults alike! Dogs welcome on a lead only. Wheelchair access to the main lawn is via a series of ten shallow steps or a grassy slope alongside them. Paths in the woods are uneven.

STUD NURSERY COMMUNITY GARDEN, KT8
Home Park (Kingston Gate entrance), Hampton Court Road, Kingston Upon Thames, KT8 9DB. Historic Royal Palaces, balancesupport.org.uk/horticultural-services. *Within Home Park, Hampton Court Palace. Enter from Kingston Gate at the bottom of Kingston Bridge (located on Hampton Court Rd, KT1 4AE). To entrance, What3words app: look.sketch.custom.* **Sun 14 June (11-3). Adm £5, chd free. Tea, coffee & cake.**
Stud Nursery is a community garden for adults with learning disabilities. We support around 40 clients each week to get involved with gardening, growing vegetables, propagating plants, and cooking garden-to-table produce. Our Edwardian walled garden of nearly 1 acre is a wonderful resource, with three glasshouses, several raised beds, vegetable garden, wildlife habitat, and chickens.

SUSSEX COTTAGE, TW3
128 Whitton Road, Hounslow, TW3 2EP. John Meinke. *Hounslow Stn, 5 min walk. Bus 281 passes outside. Unrestricted parking on local roads.* **Sun 24 May (1-5). Combined adm with 116 Whitton Road £8, chd free. Home-made teas.**
A surprising garden with a number of unique features, many of which date back to the 1920s. The garden is on several levels, and features a stone bridge, pond and air raid shelter.

There are many well established trees which gives the garden a private, woodland feel. Traditional planting with a focus on supporting biodiversity.

93 TANFIELD AVENUE, NW2
Neasden, NW2 7SB. Mr James Duncan Mattoon, 07504 565612. *Nr Dollis Hill, Willesden & Wembley. Nearest stn: Neasden (Jubilee line), then 10 min walk; or various bus routes to Neasden Parade or Tanfield Ave.* **Sun 12 July (2-6). Adm £5, chd free. Home-made teas. Visits also by arrangement 1 June to 1 Sept for groups of up to 20.**
An intensely exotic Mediterranean and subtropical paradise garden! A sunny deck with implausible planting and panoramic views of Harrow and Wembley plunges into an incredibly exotic, densely planted oasis of delight, with two further seating areas engulfed by flowers such as acacia, abutilon, eryngium, hedychium, plumbago, salvias, and hundreds more in vigorous competition. Birds and bees love it! The previous garden was Tropical Kensal Rise (Doyle Gardens), featured on BBC2's Open Gardens and in the Sunday Telegraph. This garden has been featured in Garden Week and Garden Answers magazine. Steep steps lead down to the main garden.

26 TEDDINGTON PARK ROAD, TW11
Teddington, TW11 8ND. Fiona & Roy Trosh. *South West London, between Twickenham & Kingston. 10 min walk from Teddington Stn & town centre, 15 min walk from Strawberry Hill Stn. 33 & R68 bus routes. Very limited parking locally.* **Sat 11 July (12-5). Adm £4, chd free. Pre-booking essential, please visit www.ngs.org.uk for information & booking. Cold drinks, light refreshments & cake.**
Suburban garden, approx 60ft in length, partially redesigned by RHS Chelsea Gold Medal-winning designer Tom Massey, whom we asked to create a design to replace our lawn while retaining the existing mature borders. The garden inc a stream and pond, stepping stones instead of paths, relaxed and informal planting, and a stunning tree support for a leaning willow tree, which incorporates a swing.

THEOBALD'S FARMHOUSE, EN2
Burnt Farm Ride, Crews Hill, Enfield, EN2 9DY. Alison Green, www.theobaldsfarmhousegarden.com. *N Enfield, ¼m inside M25 J24 or J25. Under ½m from Crews Hill Stn. From Crews Hill Stn, head downhill along Cattlegate Rd to sharp bend by Jollye's. Turn L into Burnt Farm Ride. From Enfield, turn R at the bend. Garden is 200yds along road on R.* **Sun 19 July (1-5.30). Adm £20, chd £10. Pre-booking essential, please visit www.ngs.org.uk for information & booking. Timed slots at 1pm, 2.30pm & 4pm. Adm inc tea, coffee, soft drinks, cakes & gluten free option on covered terrace.**
Award-winning, 2 acre organic Arts and Crafts garden created by designer owner Alison Green. The 1650s property has 14 distinct gardens, with colour themed borders, a knot garden, spiral landform, topiary, water gardens, wildflower meadows, woodlands, and a vegetable garden. This organic garden inc unusual exotics, annuals, and biennials, for all yr interest and supporting pollinators. Alison will give a short talk hourly. Visits also by arrangement (non-NGS); please email alison.g.green@talk21.com. Most areas are accessible, though there is gravel and shallow steps. Stepped entrance to non-disabled WC with handrail.

6 THORNHILL ROAD, N1
Islington, N1 1HW. Janis Higgie. *Barnsbury. Tube: Angel or Highbury & Islington. Train: Caledonian & Barnsbury. Bus: to Liverpool Rd.* **Sat 20 June (11-5). Adm £4, chd free. Tea, coffee & cake.**
150ft Islington garden, designed and planted over the last 30 yrs. This fully accessible family garden draws inspiration from the owner's antipodean roots. A brick path leads visitors past lawns, raised beds, a water feature, a fire bowl, and a creative mix of plants from around the world, inc kowhai and hoheria trees, along with many shade-tolerant plants. This garden has a lot, even the kitchen sink! Completely wheelchair friendly.

36 THORNHILL SQUARE, N1
Barnsbury, N1 1BE. Anna & Christopher McKane. *Tube: King's Cross, Caledonian Rd or Angel. Overground: Caledonian Rd & Barnsbury. Buses: 17, 91, 259 to Caledonian Rd.* **Sun 17 May (2-5.30). Adm £5, chd free. Home-made teas.**
A 120ft country garden in the centre of town has informal herbaceous borders packed with unusual plants and soft coloured roses. The garden has been developed over more than 40 yrs and inc unusual mature trees. Bonsai trees are arrayed on the patio. Effort has been made to work out what plants will survive dry shade. Gold Award, Best Hidden Gem, Islington In Bloom 2024.

NEW 103 THURLEIGH ROAD, SW12
Balham, SW12 8TY. Mr & Mrs Charles MacKinnon. *Nearest stns: Wandsworth Common (BR) & Clapham South (Tube). What3words app: like.shift.serve. Enter via the garden gate to R of house.* **Evening opening Fri 29 May (5.30-8). Adm £10, chd £5. Sat 30 May (11-6); Sun 31 May (11.30-4.30). Adm £5, chd free. Wine (29 May). Tea & home-made cakes (30 & 31 May).**
The property (not open) features an 80ft x 90ft (26 metres x 22 metres) walled garden surrounded by lime trees, with an adjoining courtyard and parterre measuring 20 metres x 13 metres. A significant redesign was completed in 2025, incorporating a large planted gravel area. Wheelchair access requires crossing 5 metres of loose gravel before reaching the lawn.

24 TWYFORD AVENUE, N2
N2 9NJ. Rachel Lindsay & Jeremy Pratt, 07930 632902, jeremypr@blueyonder.co.uk. *Twyford Ave runs parallel to Fortis Green, between East Finchley & Muswell Hill. Tube: Northern line to East Finchley. Buses to East Finchley: 102, 143, 234, 263. Buses to Muswell Hill: 43, 134, 144, 234. Buses 102 & 234 stop at end of road. Garden signed from Fortis Green.* **Sun 19 July (2-6). Adm £5, chd free. Home-made teas. Visits also by arrangement 20 July to 24 July.**
A very sunny, 120ft south facing garden with densely planted borders and many containers packed with traditional herbaceous and perennial cottage garden plants and shrubs. A herb garden, a shady area at the rear, and an experimental gravel area that is never watered. A water feature, a greenhouse, and a potting shed. Lots of spots to sit and think, chat, or doze. Some uneven ground. Local honey and bee-related products for sale.

86 UNDERHILL ROAD, SE22
East Dulwich, SE22 0QU. Claire & Rob Goldie. *Between Langton Rise & Melford Rd. Stn: Forest Hill. Buses: P13, 363, 63, 176, 185 & P4.* **Sun 24 May (2-6). Combined adm with 86A Underhill Road £9, chd free. Home-made teas. Open nearby 4 Piermont Green.**
A mature urban garden. An elegant slate terrace leads to a gravel garden, flanked by a small greenhouse and a living willow arbour, the perfect spot for a cuppa and a delicious piece of home-made cake. Vegetables are grown throughout the garden. Wind your way down to the shadier area, with cooler shades, foliage, and textures. The summerhouse has a beautiful floral mural to enjoy and inspire. The garden is near The Horniman Gardens, which are free to visit and within walking distance or a short bus ride away.

86A UNDERHILL ROAD, SE22
East Dulwich, SE22 0QU. Tony Edwards. *Between Langton Rise & Melford Rd. Stn: Forest Hill. Buses: P13, 363, 63, 176, 185 & P4.* **Sun 24 May (2-6). Combined adm with 86 Underhill Road £9, chd free. Home-made teas at 86 Underhill Road. Open nearby 4 Piermont Green.**
An evolving garden that changes as our child grows up and our dog calms down. It is divided into five parts: a deck nearest the house, a lawn with borders, a seating area under the shade of a large acer, a play area that adults are reclaiming, and a functional section with raised beds, a greenhouse, and a shed. Mature trees and shrubs surround the garden, providing a sense of privacy. The garden is near The Horniman Gardens, which is free to visit and within walking distance or a short bus ride away.

152A VICTORIA RISE, SW4
Clapham, SW4 0NW. Benn Storey, www.instagram.com/thenorthsouthgarden. *South West London. Entry via basement flat. Closest tube Clapham Common. Bus 77, 87, 137, 156, 345, 452.* **Sun 7 June (11-5). Adm £5, chd free. Tea, coffee & cake. Open nearby 51 The Chase.**
Featured on Gardeners' World in August 2024, this terraced garden is 21 metres long by 8 metres wide. Planting ranges from the lush greens of the courtyard to the perennial, insect friendly plants of the main level, to the espalier fruit trees and flowers of the productive levels. A copper beech hedge hides a secluded arbour seat and fire pit at the top of the plot, hidden from surrounding neighbours.

13 WAITE DAVIES ROAD, SE12
Lee, SE12 0NE. Janet Pugh. *Just off the A205 South Circular. Lee Train Stn, 11 min walk. Hither Green & Grove Park Stns, 20 min walk. Bus route 261 stops nearby. Buses 202 & 160 also stop close by. Usually free roadside parking.* **Sun 24 May (2.30-5.30). Combined adm with 15 Waite Davies Road £5, chd free. Cream teas. Open nearby 41 Southbrook Road.**
A colourful and welcoming front garden leads you down steps to a bright and peaceful, gently maturing space. The soft sound of a discreet water feature adds to the calm atmosphere, with attractive massed planting in a palette of pinks, purples, and creams. A rich selection of cream cakes adds to the charm.

15 WAITE DAVIES ROAD, SE12
Lee, SE12 0NE. Will Jennings. *Just off the A205 South Circular. Lee Train Stn, 11 min walk. Hither Green & Grove Park Stns, 20 min walk. Bus route 261 stops nearby. Buses 202 & 160 also stop close by. Usually roadside parking.* **Sun 24 May (2.30-5.30). Combined adm with 13 Waite Davies Road £5, chd free. Home-made teas at 13 Waite Davies Road. Open nearby 41 Southbrook Road.**
As featured in The English Garden magazine. Behind a Victorian terrace lies a beautifully kept, pocket sized garden. Rosa 'Malvern Hills' gently billows through the branches of a crabapple tree, its feet softened by foxgloves and lily of the valley. Nearby, the blush-pink flowers of climbing rose 'The Generous Gardener' bow gracefully over a stone patio, framed by lush box hedging. Plants for sale!

The National Garden Scheme funded six Macmillan Nurses in their roles across England, Wales and Northern Ireland in 2025.

West Lodge Park

GROUP OPENING
WANSTEAD GARDENS, E11
Wanstead, E11 2RS. *From Voluntary Pl, turn L into Greenstone Mews. Follow the cul-de-sac around to the R to reach the garage of 17 Greenstone Mews. The path beside the garage gives access to No. 21 & 22. Enter 32 Voluntary Pl via the back gate.* **Sun 31 May (2-5). Combined adm £5. Tea, coffee & cake.**

17 GREENSTONE MEWS
Mrs T Farnham.
NEW 21 GREENSTONE MEWS
Ms Carol Burgess.
NEW 22 GREENSTONE MEWS
E Grove.
32 VOLUNTARY PLACE
Derek Kelly.

Combined admission to four small town gardens, each very different in design and concept. 17 Greenstone Mews is planted with evergreen clothed fences with a raised bed and border of perennials, vegetables, and fruit. The bog garden houses newts and is overhung by a mature strawberry tree with a 'Graham Thomas' honeysuckle climber attached. 32 Voluntary Place is a newly designed, one yr old garden, already showcasing exuberantly planted, low maintenance flower beds alongside generous entertaining space. Numbers 21 and 22 are great examples of small lawned and courtyard gardens, with pretty planting and entertaining areas.

WARREN MEWS, W1
Fitzrovia, W1T 5NQ. Rebecca Hossack. *2 mins from Warren Street Tube Stn. Entrance to garden on Warren St, W1T 5NQ.* **Sun 21 June (12-4). Adm by donation. Tea, coffee & cake.**
Tucked away behind the bustling Tottenham Court Road is the enchanting garden of Warren Mews. At first glance, it is impossible to tell that the plants in this verdant garden have no access to the earth. Warren Mews is a place where pots of paradise flowers, window boxes bursting with geraniums, and containers of olive trees rule the street. Eclectic container planting with an Australian influence. The Rebecca Hossack Art Gallery is a 5 min walk away. The Mews is fully accessible and entirely cobbled.

9 WARWICK CLOSE, TW12
Hampton, TW12 2TY. Chris Churchman. *2m W of Twickenham, 2m N of Hampton Court, overlooking Bushy Park. 100 metres from Hampton Open Air Swimming Pool.* **Sun 16 Aug (10.30-5). Adm £5, chd free. Tea, coffee & cake.**
A small suburban garden in South West London, divided into four distinct spaces. The front garden features espaliered American lime trees, roses, lavender, and stipa. The shade garden inc rare ferns and herbaceous plants. The formal rear garden has a rain-fed canal water feature and a rectangular lawn with prairie style planting crossed with subtropical species. On the garage roof sits an allotment (the garotment). Sculptures in the garden inc superhero chairs.

THE WATERGARDENS, KT2
Warren Road, Kingston upon Thames, KT2 7LF. The Residents' Association. *1m E of Kingston. From Kingston, take A308 (Kingston Hill) towards London. After approx ½ m, turn R into Warren Rd. Take No. 57 bus along Coombe Lane West, alight at Warren Rd. Roadside parking only.* **Sun 26 Apr (1.30-4.30); Sun 25 Oct (1-4). Adm £5, chd free.**
A Japanese themed landscaped garden, originally part of Coombe Wood Nursery, planted by the Veitch family in the 1860s. Covering approx 9 acres, it features ponds, streams, and waterfalls. The garden contains many rare trees that provide stunning colour in spring and autumn. A must-see for tree lovers, the gardens are also attractive to wildlife. Major renovation and restoration have taken place over the past years, revealing a hitherto lost lake and waterfall. Restoration works ongoing. Unsuitable for those unsteady on their feet.

•))

WEST LODGE PARK, EN4
Cockfosters Road, Hadley Wood, EN4 0PY. Beales Hotels, 020 8216 3904, janegray@bealeshotels.co.uk, www.bealeshotels.co.uk/westlodgepark. *1m S of Potters Bar. On A111. J24 from M25 signed Cockfosters.* **Sun 17 May (2-5); Sun 25 Oct (1-4). Adm £7.50, chd free. Light refreshments. Pre-booking preferred or cash only on the day. Visits also by arrangement 26 Mar to 3 Nov.**
Open for the NGS for over 40 yrs, the 35 acre Beale Arboretum consists of over 800 varieties of trees and shrubs inc National Collections of hornbeam cultivars *Carpinus betulus*, Indian bean tree *Catalpa bignonioid*, and swamp cypress *Taxodium distichum*. Network of paths through good selection of conifers, oaks, maples and mountain ash, all specimens labelled. Stunning collection within the M25. Guided tours available. Breakfasts, morning coffee and biscuits, afternoon tea, restaurant lunches, light lunches, and dinner, all served in the hotel. Please see website for details.

31 WEST PARK ROAD, TW9
Kew, Richmond, TW9 4DA. Anna Anderson. *Close to the E side of Kew Gardens Stn. From Richmond bound exit from Kew Gardens Stn, West Park Rd is straight ahead & No.31 is the 2nd house on the LHS.* **Sun 12 July (2-5.30). Adm £4, chd free. Open nearby 119 Mortlake Road.**
Modern botanical garden with an oriental twist. Emphasis on foliage and an eclectic mix of unusual plants, a reflecting pool and willow screens. Planting inc tree ferns, pseudopanax, tetrapanax, arisaemas, saromatum and lots of ferns. Shady beds, mature trees and a private paved dining area with dappled light and shade.

NEW 47A WHEATLEY ROAD, TW7
Isleworth, TW7 6JJ. Kristina Alexander. *By train: Isleworth Stn, approx 10 min walk. By bus: 267, alight at Gumley School, then 8 min walk. By car: off-street parking available. Look for white gates at the end of shared drive.* **Sat 1 Aug (12.30-5). Adm £5, chd free. Tea, coffee & cake.**
Now in its fifth year, this urban jungle garden blends tropical plants with native ferns to create a lush, immersive space. Dense borders of palms, fatsias, tree ferns, tetrapanax and bamboo. A moon arch framed by acers and tree ferns open into the main part of garden where you will find palms and an eclectic mix

of plants with a tropical character to create a unique and evolving sanctuary.

116 WHITTON ROAD, TW3
Hounslow, TW3 2EP. Colin Powe. *5 mins from Twickenham Rugby Ground. Hounslow Overground Stn is a 3 min walk. 281 bus passes outside. Unrestricted parking on local roads.* **Sun 24 May (1-5). Combined adm with Sussex Cottage £8, chd free. Home-made teas at Sussex Cottage.**
A small, romantic, traditional garden inspired by Edwardian country gardens. It is approx 85ft long, with a manicured, striped lawn. Planting inc peonies, myrtle, clematis, old roses, fennel, lavender, and crab apples. The lawn is cut using a Ransomes Ajax (one is on display at The Garden Museum). Hazel features at the end of the garden and was planted in 1900; the house is called Hazeldene.

61 WOLSEY ROAD, KT8
East Molesey, KT8 9EW. Jan & Ken Heath. *10 min walk from Hampton Court Palace & station, located at the far end of Wolsey Rd. Very easy to find, with plenty of free street parking.* **Sun 7 June (2-6). Adm £6, chd free. Tea, coffee & cake.**
A romantic, secluded, and peaceful garden of two halves, designed and maintained by the owners. One part is shaded by a large copper beech tree with woodland planting and a fernery; the other is sunnier and accessed through a beech arch, featuring cottage garden planting and a large wildlife pond. An octagonal gazebo and an oak framed summerhouse, both designed and built by the owners, overlook the pond. There is extensive seating throughout the garden to sit quietly and enjoy your tea and cake.

39 WOOD VALE, SE23
Forest Hill, SE23 3DS. Nigel Crawley. *Entrance through Thistle Gates, 48 Melford Rd. Train stns: Forest Hill & Honor Oak Park. From Victoria Stn to West Dulwich, then take bus P4. Buses: 363 Elephant & Castle to Wood Vale/Melford Rd, 176, 185 & 197 to Lordship Ln/Wood Vale.* **Sun 12 Apr (1-5). Home-made teas. Evening opening Wed 15 Apr (5-7). Wine. Adm £5, chd free.**
Diverse garden dominated by a gigantic perry pear, part of one of the East Dulwich orchards. View our displays of auricula and pulsatilla. The emphasis in the garden is on its inhabitants: white comfrey and pear blossom keep the bees busy in spring. Clumps of narcissi around the old apple tree, and pots of hyacinths, fritillaries, early tulips, Semponium, and other succulents. A surprising green oasis in Forest Hill, close to Sydenham Woods, Horniman Gardens, and Camberwell Old Cemetery. Level wheelchair access, but the lane has rough terrain.

7 WOODBINES AVENUE, KT1
Kingston upon Thames, KT1 2AZ. Mr Tony Sharples & Mr Paul Cuthbert. *5 mins from Kingston town centre. Take K2, K3, 71 or 281 bus. From Surbiton, walk or bus stop outside Waitrose & exit bus at Kingston University stop. From Kingston, walk or K2, K3, 71 or 281 bus from Eden St (opp Heals).* **Sun 14 June (12-5). Combined adm with 15 Catherine Road £8, chd free. Home-made teas.**
We have created a winding path through our 70ft garden, with trees, evergreen structure, perennial flowers, and grasses. Wide herbaceous borders, an ancient grapevine, a box hedge topiary garden, large silver birches, and a hot summer terrace provide contrast.

NEW WOODLANDS, SE9
Mottingham Lane, Mottingham, SE9 4RW. *SE London. Mottingham Ln is off the A20. 'Woodlands' is opp Cedar Mount & next to The Chantry. Street parking. Mottingham Stn (20 min walk). Buses 124, 126, & 161 stop at Mottingham Rd/Court Rd (10 min walk).* **Sun 2 Aug (2-5). Adm £5, chd free.**
A long, narrow, south facing London garden with informal planting. There are a large number of plants in pots, inc acers and hostas. Year-round interest begins with geraniums, foxgloves, and euphorbia, culminating in a profusion of dahlias. The end of the garden is a working area, dedicated to growing vegetables and providing a nursery for young plants.

28A WORCESTER ROAD, E17
Walthamstow, E17 5QR. Mark & Emma Luggie, 07970 920019, pipinleshrew@hotmail.com. *12 min walk from Blackhorse Road tube stn. Just off Blackhorse Ln. On street parking.* **Visits by arrangement 31 July to 1 Oct for groups of up to 15. Adm £4, chd free.**
A typical London terraced back garden has been transformed into a lush oasis of foliage. Rare and exotic plants, mixed with more familiar varieties, create a calming retreat in the midst of the city. Varying leaf textures and forms intermix to provide year-round visual interest. A small stream leads from the patio to the pond seating area. Picnics are welcome; however, beware of our hungry Beagle, who loves food!

1 YORK CLOSE, W7
Hanwell, W7 3JB. Tony Hulme & Eddy Fergusson. *Access by road only. Entrance to York Cl via Church Rd. Nearest stn: Hanwell. Bus routes: E3, 195, 207.* **Sat 22, Sun 23 Aug (2-6). Adm £5, chd free.**
A tiny, quirky, prize-winning garden, extensively planted with an eclectic mix, inc a hosta collection and many unusual tropical plants. A plantaholic's paradise, full of surprises in this unique and very personal garden.

ZEN GARDEN AT JAPANESE BUDDHIST CENTRE, W3
Three Wheels, 55 Carbery Avenue, Acton, W3 9AB. London Shogyoji Trust, www.threewheels.org.uk/zen-garden. *Tube: Acton Town, 5 min walk. 200yds off A406.* **Sat 6, Sun 7, Sat 20, Sun 21 June (2-5). Adm £4, chd free. Matcha tea £4.**
Pure Japanese Zen garden (so no flowers) with 12 large and small rocks of various colours and textures, set in islands of moss and surrounded by a sea of grey granite gravel raked in a stylised wave pattern. Garden surrounded by trees and bushes outside a cob wall. Oak framed wattle and daub shelter with Norfolk reed thatched roof. Talk on the Zen garden. Buddha Room open to public.

NORFOLK

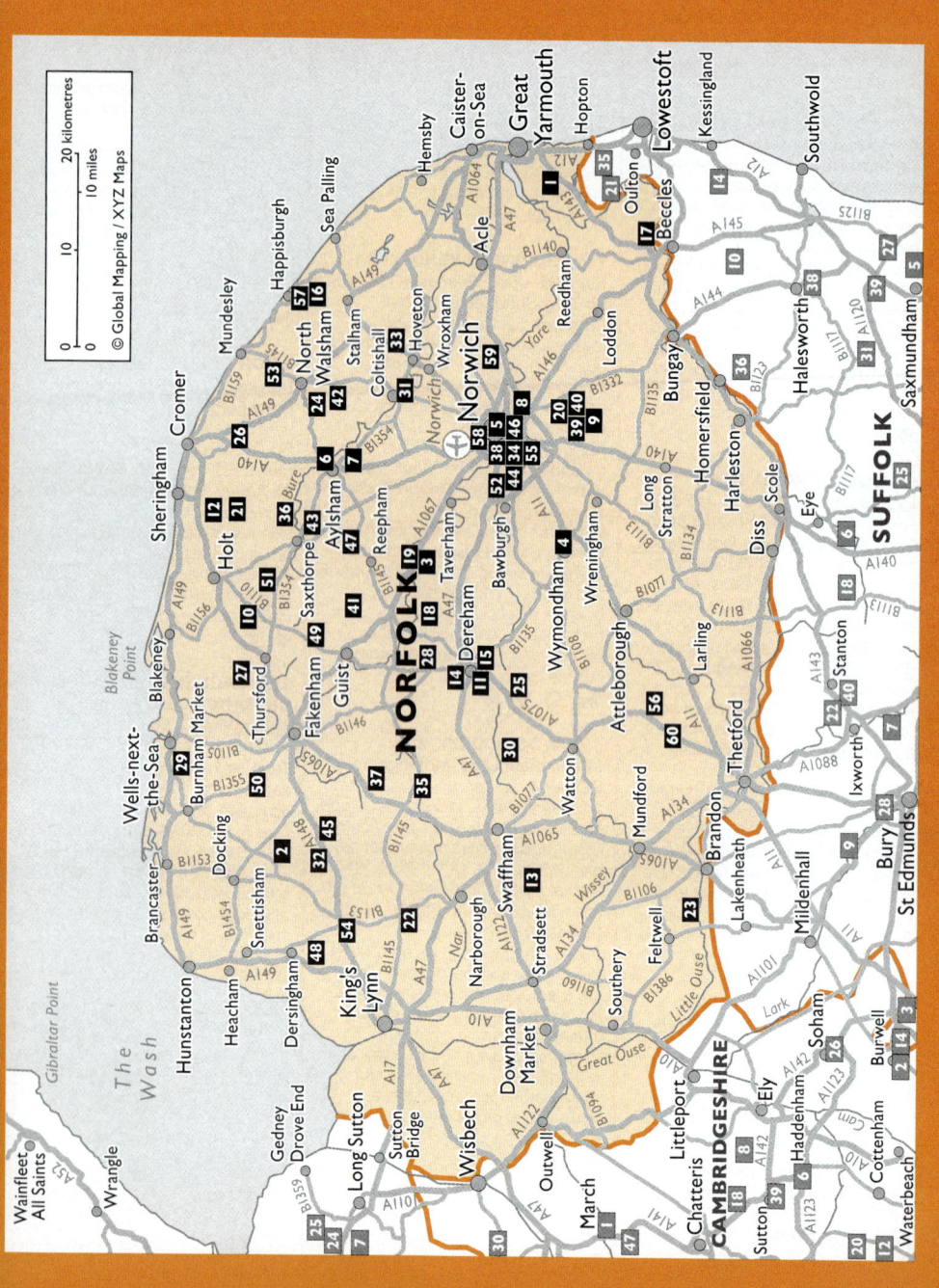

NORFOLK 371

VOLUNTEERS

County Organiser
Retty Wace 07876 648543
retty.wace@ngs.org.uk

Graham Watts 07534 681596
graham.watts@ngs.org.uk

County Treasurer
Andrew Stephens OBE
07595 939769
andrew.stephens@ngs.org.uk

Publicity & Social Media
Amanda McCallum 07769 883537
amanda.mccallum@ngs.org.uk

Photographer
Stew Flint 07958 165242
stewart.flint@ngs.org.uk

Booklet Co-ordinator
Juliet Collier 07986 607170
juliet.collier@ngs.org.uk

New Gardens Organiser
Fiona Black 07774 599911
fiona.black@ngs.org.uk

**Booklet Distribution,
Talks & Visits**
Graham Watts
(as above)

Talks
Julia Stafford Allen 07778 169775
julia.staffordallen@ngs.org.uk

Volunteer Co-ordinator
Gill Cook 07841 569003
gill.cook@ngs.org.uk

Assistant County Organisers
Jenny Clarke 07748 655815
jenny.clarke@ngs.org.uk

Nick Collier 07733 108443
nick.collier@ngs.org.uk

Gill Cook
(As above)

Sue Roe 07931 328484
sueroe8@icloud.com

Julia Stafford-Allen
(As above)

@ngsnorfolk
@norfolkngs

OPENING DATES

All entries subject to change.
For latest information check
www.ngs.org.uk
Map locator numbers are
shown to the right of each
garden name.

January

Sunday 25th
Chestnut Farm 12

February

Snowdrop Openings

Sunday 8th
Lexham Hall 35

Saturday 14th
Horstead House 31

Sunday 15th
NEW Brinton Hall 10
Lexham Hall 35

Sunday 22nd
Bagthorpe Hall 2
Chestnut Farm 12

April

Sunday 12th
Gayton Hall 22

Friday 17th
◆ Holkham Hall Garden 29

Saturday 18th
◆ East Ruston Old Vicarage 16

Sunday 19th
The Elms 17

Sunday 26th
Wretham Lodge 60

May

Thursday 7th
◆ Stody Lodge 51

Saturday 9th
NEW Heath Farm Barn 24

Sunday 10th
NEW Heath Farm Barn 24

Sunday 17th
Blickling Lodge 6

Sunday 24th
20 Le Strange Close 34
Lexham Hall 35
NEW The Sunken Garden at
The Children's Garden 52
NEW 1F Upton Road 55

Saturday 30th
NEW Priscilla Bacon Lodge
Gardens 44

Sunday 31st
Holme Hale Hall 30
NEW Old Common Wood 41

June

Saturday 6th
◆ Mannington Estate 36

Sunday 7th
Bolwick Hall 7
Elsing Hall Gardens 18
Ferndale 20
Greenacre Farmhouse 23
High House Gardens 25
Oulton Hall 43
The Rudhams 45

Saturday 13th
47 Norwich Road 39
51 Norwich Road 40
Swafield Hall 53

Sunday 14th
Bracondale Gardens 8
47 Norwich Road 39
51 Norwich Road 40
Swafield Hall 53
Tapping House 54

Sunday 21st
Manor House Farm, Wellington ... 37
Walcott House 57

Friday 26th
Old Manor Farmhouse 42

Saturday 27th
Old Manor Farmhouse 42

Sunday 28th
Old Manor Farmhouse 42

July

Friday 3rd
◆ Hoveton Hall Gardens 33

Sunday 5th
Bishop's House 5

Wednesday 15th
Lexham Hall 35
The Walled Garden, Little Plumstead 59

Sunday 19th
North Lodge 38
St Stephens Square 46
Salle Park 47

Saturday 25th
NEW 19 Bellrope Lane 4

Sunday 26th
NEW 19 Bellrope Lane 4
Ferndale 20
North Lodge 38
33 Waldemar Avenue 58

August

Sunday 2nd
Brick Kiln House 9
Fiddian's Follies 21

Sunday 9th
84 Fakenham Road 19
Severals Grange 49
33 Waldemar Avenue 58

Sunday 16th
Acre Meadow 1

Monday 17th
Acre Meadow 1

Sunday 23rd
Cobweb Cottage 13
33 Waldemar Avenue 58

September

Sunday 6th
Holme Hale Hall 30

Sunday 13th
High House Gardens 25

October

Saturday 17th
◆ East Ruston Old Vicarage 16

Sunday 18th
◆ Hindringham Hall 27

By Arrangement

Arrange a personalised garden visit with your club, or group of friends, on a date to suit you. See individual garden entries for full details.

Beck House 3
Blickling Lodge 6
Bolwick Hall 7
Brick Kiln House 9
Broadway Farm 11
Chestnut Farm 12
Cobweb Cottage 13
Dale Farm 14
Dunbheagan 15
Highview House 26
Hoe Hall 28
Holme Hale Hall 30
Horstead House 31
Manor House Farm, Wellingham 37
Old Manor Farmhouse 42
NEW Southgate Barn 50
Vicarage House 56
Walcott House 57

Old Common Wood

THE GARDENS

1 ACRE MEADOW
New Road, Bradwell, Great Yarmouth, NR31 9DU. Mr Keith Knights, www.acremeadow.co.uk. *Between Bradwell & Belton in arable surroundings. At Bradwell r'about on A143 take Belton/ Burgh Castle turn (New Road). Entrance 400yds on R. Please use NR31 9JW for SatNav. What3words app: verge. tasks.dynamics.* **Sun 16, Mon 17 Aug (10-3). Adm £5, chd free. Pre-booking essential, please visit www.ngs.org.uk for information & booking. Tea, coffee & cake.** A dramatic, intensely planted, hidden garden with a lawn free, richly colourful mix of exotic and other late season plants inc many cannas, large grasses, brugmansia, late season perennials, several unusual and uncommon plants and is alive with insects on sunny days. Separate areas inc tea garden, traditional conservatory and wildlife pond. Paths are gravel. Regret, no mobility scooters allowed in the main garden.

2 BAGTHORPE HALL
Bagthorpe, Bircham, King's Lynn, PE31 6QY. Mr & Mrs D Morton. *3½ m N of East Rudham, off A148. Take turn opp The Crown in East Rudham. Look for white gates in trees, slightly set back from road.* **Sun 22 Feb (11-4). Adm £6, chd free. Tea, coffee & cake.** Surrounded by farmland, this is a delightful circular walk which meanders through a stunning display of snowdrops naturally carpeting a woodland floor, and then returning through a walled garden.

3 BECK HOUSE
Lyng Easthaugh Road, Weston Longville, Norwich, NR9 5LP. Chris & Wendy Fitch, 07843 250840, fitch1001@gmail.com. *11m NW of Norwich, near Lenwade (Gt Witchingham). From either A47 at Honingham or A1067 at Lenwade, turn onto the B1535. Follow this road until you reach Lyng Easthaugh Rd. Follow until you reach Beck House.* **Visits by arrangement Mar to Oct for groups of 10+. Home-made teas.** A ¾ acre garden surrounded by countryside, tirelessly updated over the past five years by the current owners. Bordered by shallow becks which feed a large natural pond with Japanese inspired planting. Many different border styles inc Mediterranean, woodland, country cottage, rose and kitchen garden. Large patio areas with seating and lots of vertical interest with pergolas and specimen trees. Garden is fairly level and mainly grassed with gravel area at entrance.

4 NEW 19 BELLROPE LANE
Wymondham, NR18 0QX. Michael & Thomas Piggott. *10m SW of Norwich. From Norwich- on arrival to Wymondham turn to Norwich Rd, then to Folly Rd. Bellrope Ln is 1st turn on R. On street parking only.* **Sat 25, Sun 26 July (10-5). Adm £5, chd free. Pre-booking essential, please visit www.ngs.org.uk for information & booking. Tea, coffee & cake.** A town garden created from blank canvas over six years. This is a garden densely planted by keen plant enthusiasts, in a mix of styles with exotic elements. Narrow (sometimes wobbly) paths will lead you to a dry garden, pond area, dahlia borders, vegetable garden and mixed borders. Every nook and cranny filled with unusual plants and shrubs.

5 BISHOP'S HOUSE
Bishopgate, Norwich, NR3 1SB. The Bishop of Norwich, www.dioceseofnorwich.org/gardens. *Located in the city centre near the Law Courts & The Adam & Eve Pub. Parking available at town centre car parks inc one by the Adam & Eve pub.* **Sun 5 July (1-4). Adm £5, chd free. Refreshments provided by the Priscilla Bacon Hospice.** A four acre walled garden dating back to the C12. Extensive lawns with specimen trees. Borders with many rare and unusual shrubs. Spectacular herbaceous borders flanked by yew hedges. Rose beds underplanted with hostas. A meadow labyrinth, organic kitchen garden, herb garden and bamboo walk. Popular plant sales. Wheelchair access over gravel paths and some slopes.

6 BLICKLING LODGE
Blickling, Norwich, NR11 6PS. Michael & Henrietta Lindsell, nicky@lindsell.co.uk. *½ m N of Aylsham. Leave Aylsham on Old Cromer Rd towards Ingworth, over hump back bridge & house is on your R.* **Sun 17 May (12-5). Adm £6, chd free. Home-made teas.** **Visits also by arrangement 1 June to 2 Oct for groups of 10 to 40.** Georgian house (not open) set in 17 acres of parkland. Extensive gardens that inc cricket pitch, beautiful mixed borders, walled kitchen garden, yew garden, woodland, dovecotes and water garden.

7 BOLWICK HALL
Marsham, NR10 5PU. Dr C Fisher, 01263 732131, carolineofbolwick@gmail.com, www.carolinefisherprojects.org. *8m N of Norwich off A140. From Norwich, heading N on A140, just past Marsham take 1st R after Plough Pub, signed 'By Road' then next R onto private drive to front of Hall.* **Sun 7 June (1-5). Adm £6, chd free. Light refreshments.** **Visits also by arrangement in July for groups of 10 to 30. See website for further openings www.carolinefisherprojects.org/bolwick.** Landscaped gardens and park surrounding a late Georgian hall. The original garden design is attributed to Humphry Repton. The landscaping and borders have been rejuvenated, a gravel garden and formal area planted, and the walls of the house clad in old roses. Enjoy a woodland walk around the lake and a stroll through the working vegetable and the fruit garden with its double herbaceous border. A working kitchen garden and double herbaceous border, designed to provide year-round interest. Lakeside walks abounding with wildlife. A formal, walled area, shrub border and gravel garden. A collection of mature rhododendrons and roses that clamber up the old walls of the house. Most of the paths are gravel.

GROUP OPENING

8 BRACONDALE GARDENS
Norwich, NR1 2BB. *Park at County Hall & walk up Bracondale. Number 72 is on L opp King St. Return to Bracondale, cont up hill taking 1st L for 14 Conesford Dr & 1 Woodside Cottages.* **Sun 14 June (10-4). Combined adm £9, chd free. Home-made teas by Priscilla Bacon Hospice on the green at 1 Woodside Cottages.**

NEW 72 BRACONDALE
Mrs Geraldine Varley.

14 CONESFORD DRIVE
Mr Andrew Sankey.

1 WOODSIDE COTTAGES
Mr Wayne Waith.

A warm welcome awaits you at these three attractive compact town gardens a short walk apart and each with a different character. 1 Woodside Cottages: A very pretty, small cottage garden packed with colourful plants both ornamental and edible and even the resident chickens are decorative. Fruit trees and vegetables grow side by side with perennial and annual flowers and a small pond supports a multitude of frogs each spring. 14 Conesford Drive: Lush planting of shrubs, ferns and flowers greet you at the side of this 1960s modernist house leading to a densely planted cottage garden of carefully selected perennials and climbers. 72 Bracondale: a tranquil mature city garden hidden behind a Georgian townhouse. A grand copper beech tree with a wildflower meadow and yew hedge frames the space. A sunken area with box, yew, flint, and old walls reflects its history. Borders feature roses, salvia, irises, and geraniums, while patios with bay-filled pots complete the garden.

9 BRICK KILN HOUSE
Priory Lane, Shotesham, Norwich, NR15 1UJ. Jim & Jenny Clarke, 07748 655815, jennyclarke985@gmail.com. *6m S of Norwich. From Shotesham All Saints church Priory Ln is 200m on R on Saxlingham Rd.* **Sun 2 Aug (10-4). Adm £6, chd free. Home-made teas. Visits also by arrangement 22 June to 12 Sept for groups of 10 to 40.**

Two acre country garden with a large terrace, lawns and colourful herbaceous borders. There is a contemporary designed pergola garden, sculptures and a stream running through a diversely planted wood. Easy access for wheelchair users.

10 NEW BRINTON HALL
Stody Road, Brinton, Melton Constable, NR24 2QH. Mr & Mrs J Bagnall-Oakeley. *Turn off A148 to Sharrington & drive through village. Turn R at T-junc, ½m into Brinton. Hall is on L opp church. Parking on the road. What3words app: satin. repeating.skylights.* **Sun 15 Feb (10.30-3). Adm £15, chd free. Pre-booking essential, please visit www.ngs.org.uk for information & booking. Home-made teas at St Andrew's Church.**

A guided walk with the owners in the historic garden developed over 40 years. Begin with looking at the many snowdrop cultivars, the walk

1F Upton Road

then crosses over a meadow to the lake, where there are specimen trees and shrubs planted for winter interest and scent. Paths lead up the hillside through woods with large drifts of snowdrops returning downhill towards the house.

11 BROADWAY FARM
The Broadway, Scarning, Dereham, NR19 2LQ. Michael & Corinne Steward, 07881 691899, corinneasteward@gmail.com. *16m W of Norwich. 12m E of Swaffham. From A47 W take a R into Fen Rd, opp Drayton Hall Ln. From A47 E take L into Fen Rd, then immed L at T-junc, immed R into The Broadway.* **Visits by arrangement June & July for groups of 15 to 35.**
A ½ acre cottage garden surrounding a C14 clapboard farmhouse. Colourful herbaceous borders with a wide range of perennial and woody plants and a well planted pond, providing habitat for wildlife. A plantswoman's garden.

12 CHESTNUT FARM
Church Road, West Beckham, Holt, NR25 6NX. Mr & Mrs John McNeil Wilson, 01263 822241, judywilson100@gmail.com. *2½m S of Sheringham. From A148 opp Sheringham Park entrance. Take the road signed 'By way To West Beckham', about ¾m to the garden by village sign. N.B. SatNav will take you to the pub.* **Sun 25 Jan, Sun 22 Feb (11-4). Adm £6, chd free. Light refreshments inc gluten free options. Visits also by arrangement 25 Jan to 27 Sept for groups of 6 to 30.**
Mature three acre garden developed over 60 years with collections of many rare and unusual plants. The year commences with a good show of aconites, 100+ varieties of snowdrops, drifts of crocus with seasonal flowering shrubs. Later, wood anemones, fritillary meadow, wildflower walk, pond, small arboretum and colourful herbaceous borders.

13 COBWEB COTTAGE
51 Shingham, Beachamwell, Swaffham, PE37 8AY. Sue Bunting, 01366 328428, susannahbunting@btinternet.com. *5m from Swaffham. Shingham is next to Beachamwell. The cottage is 1st on L after the Shingham village sign.* **Sun 23**

Aug (11-4). Adm £5, chd free. Tea, coffee & cake. Visits also by arrangement 1 May to 30 Aug for groups of up to 40. Max 20 parking spaces.
A cottage garden on the edge of the village with mixed borders, a sunken greenhouse, pergola, and a wildlife pond. There is also a large productive ornamental kitchen garden with bees, chickens, treehouse, prairie planting and fruit cage. This is a wildlife friendly garden. There are uneven areas and narrow gravel paths.

14 DALE FARM
Sandy Lane, Dereham, NR19 2EA. Graham & Sally Watts, 07534 681596, graham.watts@ngs.org.uk. *16m W of Norwich. 12m E of Swaffham. From A47 take B1146 signed to Fakenham, turn R at T-junc, ½m turn L into Sandy Ln (before pelican X-ing).* **Visits by arrangement June & July for groups of 15 to 40. Adm inc home-made teas. Adm £12, chd free.**
A two acre plant lovers' garden with a large spring-fed pond. Over 1000 plant varieties in exuberantly planted borders with sculptures. Also, gravel, vegetable, nature and waterside gardens. Collection of 150 hydrangeas. Some grass paths and gravel drive. Wide choice of plants for sale.

15 DUNBHEAGAN
Dereham Road, Westfield, NR19 1QF. Jean & John Walton, 01362 696163, jandjwalton@btinternet.com. *2m S of Dereham. From Dereham turn L off A1075 into Westfield Rd by the Vauxhall garage/Premier food store. Straight ahead at Xrds into lane which becomes Dereham Rd. Garden on L.* **Visits by arrangement in July for groups of 20+. Discuss refreshments when booking. Adm £5, chd free. Home-made teas.**
Relax and enjoy the garden where the rare and unusual rub shoulders with the more recognisable plants in densely planted beds and borders in this ever-changing plantsman's garden. Lots of paths to explore. A riot of colour all summer. Lots of seating. Wheelchair access via gravel driveway.

16 ♦ EAST RUSTON OLD VICARAGE
East Ruston, Norwich, NR12 9HN. Alan Gray, 01692 650432, office@eastrustonoldvicarage.co.uk, www.eastrustonoldvicarage.co.uk. *3m N of Stalham. Turn off A149 onto B1159 signed Bacton, Happisburgh. After 2m turn R 200yds N of East Ruston Church (ignore sign to East Ruston).* **For NGS: Sat 18 Apr, Sat 17 Oct (12-5.30). Adm £15.50, chd £2. Light refreshments in the restaurant.** For other opening times and information, please phone, email or visit garden website.
Large garden with traditional borders and modern landscapes. Discover various types of gardens inc walled, rose and exotic gardens, topiary and box parterres. We have water features, Mediterranean garden, fruit cage and containers to die for in spring and summer. Cornfield and meadows, vegetable and cutting gardens, parkland and heritage orchard, in all 32 acres. Rare and unusual plants abound.

17 THE ELMS
Elms Road, Toft Monks, Beccles, NR34 0EJ. Mr & Mrs Andrew Freeland, www.elmsbarnweddings.co.uk. *Follow grey signs off A143 to 'Elms Barn'. Past the pond, L to main house. Follow signs for wedding traffic to the car park.* **Sun 19 Apr (10-4). Adm £5, chd free. Pre-booking essential, please visit www.ngs.org.uk for information & booking. Tea, coffee & cake in the marquee.**
Gardens are set around a beautiful moated Queen Anne house. Discover our extensive spring bulb display as well as the stunning herbaceous borders. Wander through the formal rose garden with rose arch and take in the view of the ponds. arboretum and year-round interest. Good wheelchair access.

Our donation in 2025 has enabled Parkinson's UK to fund 2 new nursing posts this year directly supporting people with Parkinson's.

18 ELSING HALL GARDENS
Elsing Hall, Hall Road, Elsing, NR20 3DX. Patrick Lines & Han Yang Yap. *6km NW of Dereham. From A47 take the N Tuddenham exit. From A1067 take the turning to Elsing opp the Bawdeswell Garden Centre.* **Sun 7 June (10-4). Adm £8, chd free. Tea, coffee & cake. Picnics allowed in the car park.**
C15 fortified manor house (not open) with working moat. 10 acre gardens and 10 acre park surrounding the house. Significant collection of old roses, walled garden, formal garden, marginal planting, ginkgo avenue, viewing mound, moongate, interesting pinetum and terraced garden. NB: Very limited WC facilities available.

19 84 FAKENHAM ROAD
Great Witchingham, Norwich, NR9 5AE. Trevor King. *Lenwade (B1067) towards Fakenham: Look for chip shop on L. The garden is opp, by the bus shelter. Please park in the shop forecourt.* **Sun 9 Aug (10-4). Adm £5, chd free. Pre-booking essential, please visit www.ngs.org.uk for information & booking. Light refreshments inc teas, coffee, cold drinks, biscuits & cake.**
This is a garden for keen plant enthusiasts, especially if you've an interest in exotics. Boundaries disappear behind dense planting, and narrow paths lead you round the garden. Space is at a premium. Even so, you will also see exotic pigeons, pheasants and parakeets among the plants. The owner is a firm believer in reuse and recycle and many of the garden structures reflect this ethos.

20 FERNDALE
14 Poringland Road, Upper Stoke Holy Cross, Norwich, NR14 8NL. Dr Alan & Mrs Sheila Sissons. *4m S of Norwich. From Norwich or Poringland on B1332, take Stoke Rd at Railway Tavern r'about. Ferndale is 0.7m on L. Parking on road.* **Sun 7 June, Sun 26 July (11-4). Adm £4, chd free. Light refreshments.**
⅓ acre garden, paved area with seating surrounded by borders of shrubs and flowers. A pond with water feature. In a second area is more seating plus apple trees, soft fruit, vegetable plot, greenhouse, herb bed. Shingled area with water feature, rose arbour, semi-circular wall planted with flowers. If dry, there will be an accordionist playing French music, plants for sale and a craft stall. Wheelchair access via 1 metre wide passageway.

21 FIDDIAN'S FOLLIES
Upwood Farm, North Barningham, Norwich, NR11 7LA. Dick & Debbie Fiddian, www.fiddiansfollies.uk. *North Barningham. Follow SatNav. Gardens will be signed from North Barningham & Baconsthorpe What3words app: laminate.placed.combining.* **Sun 2 Aug (10.30-5). Adm £7, chd free. Tea, coffee & cake.**
The garden at Upwood Farm (affectionately known as Fiddian's Follies), has been described as quirky, full of surprises and generally very different to usual herbaceous borders, rose beds and sweeping lawns. There are several follies, lovingly created with brick and stone elements, in and around what was once an old quarry. The garden, set in three acres, boasts wonderful unspoilt views.

22 GAYTON HALL
Gayton, King's Lynn, PE32 1PL. David & Katherine Marsham. *6m E of King's Lynn. Off the B1145. At village sign take 2nd exit off Back St to entrance.* **Sun 12 Apr (11-4). Adm £6, chd free. Tea, coffee & cake.**
This rambling semi-wild garden, has over two miles of paths which meander through lawn, streams, bridges and woodland. Primulas, astilbes, *Lysichiton*, hostas and gunnera grow along the waters edge. There is a good display of spring bulbs and a variety of unusual trees and shrubs, many labelled which have been planted over the years. Wheelchair access to most areas via gravel and grass paths.

23 GREENACRE FARMHOUSE
Nursery Lane, Hockwold, Thetford, IP26 4ND. Reverend Ray & Mrs Victoria Burman. *Drive along Main St, Hockwold-cum-Wilton & turn into Nursery Ln, follow NGS yellow signs to car park further down Nursery Ln.* **Sun 7 June (11-4). Adm £5, chd free. Tea, coffee & cake.**
A very pretty traditional cottage garden on the edge of the village. With mature trees, this garden, adjacent to C18 farmhouse is crammed with colour, roses, shrubs, flowers, pond and gravel dry garden, with beehives. Free beekeeping talk/demonstration. Wheelchair access but some gravel and small steps so will require help. Parking in meadow short walk from garden. Local honey for sale.

24 HEATH FARM BARN
Skeyton Road, North Walsham, NR28 0LU. Mark & Helen Webster. *Take Skeyton Rd from N Walsham for 1m, signed turn R, just before N Walsham wood. From Skeyton direction through N Walsham wood, signed turn L* **Sat 9, Sun 10 May (11-5). Adm £6, chd free. Tea, coffee & cake.**
Surrounding two newly converted dwellings; the area of the garden in close proximity to the houses is flower displays and a vegetable garden. Further away are large displays of bulbs, shrubs and trees extending out into 25 acres of grassland which has wild orchid collections, ponds and a bluebell wood with specimen tree planting and two memorials.

25 HIGH HOUSE GARDENS
Blackmoor Row, Shipdham, Thetford, IP25 7PU. Sue & Fred Nickerson. *6m SW of Dereham. Take the airfield or Cranworth Rd off A1075 in Shipdham. Blackmoor Row is signed.* **Sun 7 June, Sun 13 Sept (12-5). Adm £6, chd free. Home-made teas.**
Three acre plantsman's garden developed and maintained by the current owners, over the last 40 years. Garden consists of colour themed herbaceous borders with an extensive range of perennials, box edged rose and shrub borders, woodland garden, pond and bog area, orchard and small arboretum. Plus large vegetable garden. Wheelchair access via gravel paths.

26 HIGHVIEW HOUSE
Norwich Road, Roughton, Norwich, NR11 8NA. Graham & Sarah Last, 07976 066896, grahamrc.last@gmail.com. *Located on A140, approx ½m N of Roughton. Village mini r'abouts on R after layby. What3words app: warriors.town.shielding.* **Visits by arrangement July to Oct for groups of 20 to 80. Adm £12, chd**

Heath Farm Barn

free. Tea, coffee & cake.
Two acre garden designed and maintained by the current owners over the last 20 years. Large range of perennial plants, bulbs and shrubs. More than 200 salvia varieties feature through the planting of over12,000 plants to encourage wildlife. Acer trees, interesting garden structures, water feature. Home of the National Collection on *Salvia microphylla cvs.* and relatives. Wheelchair access: park on the main driveway. Some slopes will need to be accommodated.

27 ♦ HINDRINGHAM HALL
Blacksmiths Lane, Hindringham, NR21 0QA. Mr & Mrs Charles Tucker, 01328 878226, info@hindringhamhall.org, www.hindringhamhall.org. *7m from Holt/ Fakenham/ Wells. Turn off A148 at Crawfish Pub towards Hindringham. Drive 2m. Enter village of Hindringham. Turn L into Blacksmiths Ln after village hall.* **For NGS: Sun 18 Oct (10-4). Adm £10, chd free. Home-made teas & hot soup. For other opening times and information, please phone, email or visit garden website.**
Listed Medieval moat and fishponds surrounding the Grade II listed Tudor Hall. Discover the working walled vegetable garden and Victorian nut walk. Wander along formal beds, bog and stream gardens. Something of interest throughout the year, continuing well into autumn. History and horticulture combine in this special place. Wheelchair access via gravel paths.

28 HOE HALL
Hall Road, Hoe, Dereham, NR20 4BD. Mr & Mrs James Keith, 01362 693169, vrkeith@hoehall.co.uk. *The garden is situated next to Hoe church.* **Visits by arrangement 15 May to 30 June for groups of 10 to 50. Adm £10, chd free. Tea, coffee & cake.**
The main visual is a walled garden featuring a long white wisteria walk. This is set in the grounds of a Georgian rectory surrounded by parkland. The garden was redesigned in 1990 to incorporate climbers and herbaceous plants, with box parterres replacing the kitchen garden. There are espaliered fruit trees, and an old swimming pool with water lilies. Seating area and WC available in the walled garden.

In 2025, National Garden Scheme funding helped Perennial support 950 unique callers to their helpline looking for advice and information.

29 ◆ HOLKHAM HALL GARDEN
Holkham Hall, Wells-next-the-Sea, NR23 1AB. Holkham Estate, 01328 713111, info@holkham.co.uk, www.holkham.co.uk. *Drive through the main visitor entrance to Holkham Park car park. Guided Tours(Approx 1hr duration) start from outside the visitor reception, adjacent to the courtyard cafe.* **For NGS: Fri 17 Apr (10.30-4). Adm £20, chd free. Pre-booking essential, please visit www.ngs.org.uk for information & booking. Refreshments in the Lady Elizabeth Wing. Adm inc refreshments.** For other opening times and information, please phone, email or visit garden website.
Arboretum and Private Terraces Guided Tour. Discover the hidden corners of Holkham, not usually open to the public. Stroll through the arboretum, home to rare, majestic trees from around the world with historic features inc a shell garden and former rose garden. Step onto the terraces designed by W.A. Nestfield, with an impressive fountain, parterres with breathtaking parkland views.

30 HOLME HALE HALL
Holme Hale, Swaffham, IP25 7ED. Mr & Mrs Simon Broke, 07702 317272, simon.broke@hotmail.co.uk, www.instagram.com/holmehalehallgarden. *2m S of Necton off A47. 1m E of Holme Hale village on Bradenham Rd.* **Sun 31 May, Sun 6 Sept (12-4). Adm £8, chd free. Light refreshments served all day inc light lunches, teas & cakes.** Visits also by arrangement 6 Apr to 11 Oct. Discuss refreshments when booking.
Walled kitchen garden designed by Arne Maynard, replanted in 2016. Soft palette of herbaceous plants, some unusual varieties which provide a long season of interest. Greenhouse, vegetables, trained fruits, roses and topiary. 130 year old wisteria. Wildlife friendly with wildflower meadow and renovated island pond. Historic buildings with a dry garden formed from crushed concrete, rubble and sand. The hidden gem of Norfolk. Wheelchair access to most areas.

31 HORSTEAD HOUSE
Mill Road, Horstead, Norwich, NR12 7AU. Mr & Mrs Matthew Fleming, 07771 655637, horsteadsnowdrops@gmail.com. *6m NE of Norwich. Down Mill Rd opp the Recruiting Sergeant pub.* **Sat 14 Feb (11-4). Adm £6, chd free. Tea, coffee & cake.** Visits also by arrangement 8 Feb to 21 Feb.
Stunning display of beautiful snowdrops carpet the woodland setting with winter flowering shrubs. Another beautiful feature is the dogwoods growing on a small island in the River Bure, which flows through the garden. There is also a small walled garden. Wheelchair access to main snowdrop area.

32 ◆ HOUGHTON HALL WALLED GARDEN
Bircham Road, Houghton, King's Lynn, PE31 6TY. The Cholmondeley Gardens Trust, 01485 528569, info@houghtonhall.com, www.houghtonhall.com. *11m W of Fakenham. 13m E of King's Lynn. Signed from A148.* For opening times and information, please phone, email or visit garden website.
The award-winning, five acre walled garden, beautifully divided into different areas designed by the Bannermans, inc a kitchen garden with espalier fruit trees, glasshouses, a Mediterranean garden, rose parterre, wisteria pergola and a spectacular double-sided herbaceous border. Many antique statues, fountains and contemporary sculptures. Gravel and grass paths. Electric buggies available in the walled garden.

33 ◆ HOVETON HALL GARDENS
Hoveton Hall Estate, Hoveton, Norwich, NR12 8RJ. Harry & Rachel Buxton, 01603 784297, office@hovetonhallestate.co.uk, www.hovetonhallestate.co.uk. *8m N of Norwich. 1m N of Wroxham Bridge. Off A1151 Stalham Rd. Follow brown tourist signs.* **For NGS: Fri 3 July (10.30-5). Adm £10, chd £5.** For other opening times and information, please phone, email or visit garden website.
Explore the 15 acre gardens and woodlands taking you through the seasons. Enjoy this beautiful haven of mature walled herbaceous and kitchen gardens. Wander through informal woodlands and discover lakeside walks. Nature spy activity trail for our younger visitors. A varied events programme runs throughout the season. Light lunches and afternoon tea from our on site Garden Kitchen Cafe. Picnics are allowed for garden patrons only. The gardens are predominantly accessible to wheelchair users.

34 20 LE STRANGE CLOSE
Norwich, NR2 3PW. Rajul Shah, www.instagram.com/rajulshahgardendesign. *Le Strange Close is off Christchurch Rd. On-street parking available.* **Sun 24 May (10-4). Adm £6, chd free. Tea, coffee & cake. Open nearby 1F Upton Road.**
A modern cottage garden in the city, plant-filled and wildlife-friendly, with unusual materials and structures. The front garden is a mini allotment with crab apple arches framing the path. Designed and planted by the owner, garden designer, Rajul Shah. Level access to back garden is possible via driveway and paved path. A very gentle slope leads to the rear. The front path has one step.

35 LEXHAM HALL
nr Litcham, PE32 2QJ. www.lexhamestate.co.uk. *6m N of Swaffham off B1145. 2m W of Litcham.* **Sun 8, Sun 15 Feb (11-4). Adm £6, chd free. Sun 24 May, Wed 15 July (11-5). Adm £8, chd free. Light refreshments.** Donation to East Lexham Church (Feb only).
Parkland with lake and river walks surround C17 Hall (not open). Formal garden with terraces, roses and mixed borders. Traditional working kitchen garden with crinkle-crankle wall. Year-round interest; woods and borders carpeted with snowdrops in February, rhododendrons, azaleas, camellias and magnolias in the three acre woodland garden in May, and July sees the walled garden borders at their peak.

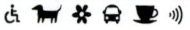

36 ♦ MANNINGTON ESTATE
Mannington, Norwich,
NR11 7BB. 01263 493275,
info@mannington.co.uk,
www.mannington.co.uk. *18m NW of Norwich. 2m N of Saxthorpe via B1149 towards Holt. At Saxthorpe/Corpusty follow signs to Mannington.* **For NGS: Sat 6 June (10-4). Adm £8, chd free. Light refreshments in the Garden Tearooms. Enjoy artisan coffee, pastries & sourdough from Bread Source, a much-loved Norfolk bakery, served fresh at Mannington. For other opening times and information, please phone, email or visit garden website.**
Explore 20 acres of beautiful gardens, lakes and woodlands surrounding a Medieval moated manor. Wander through wildflower meadows and tree-lined trails alive with birdsong. With historic follies, a Saxon church and miles of countryside walks, Mannington is a magical Norfolk gem for nature lovers. Wheelchair access via gravel paths. One steep slope.

37 MANOR HOUSE FARM, WELLINGHAM
Fakenham, King's Lynn,
PE32 2TH. Robin & Elisabeth Ellis, 01328 838227,
libbyelliswellingham@gmail.com,
www.manor-house-farm.co.uk.
½ m off A1065. 7m W from Fakenham & 8m E of Swaffham. **Sun 21 June (11-5). Adm £7, chd free. Tea, coffee & cake.** Visits also by arrangement 15 May to 15 July for groups of 15 to 40.
Charming four acre country garden surrounds an attractive farmhouse. Traditional and relaxed planting. Grasses and gravel, formal quadrants small arboretum, pleached lime walk, vegetable parterre and rose tunnel. Unusual walled 'Taj' garden with old-fashioned roses, tree peonies, lilies and formal pond. A variety of herbaceous plants. Small herd of Formosan Sika deer.

38 NORTH LODGE
51 Bowthorpe Road, Norwich,
NR2 3TN. Bruce Bentley & Peter Wilson. *1½ m W of Norwich City Centre. Turn into Bowthorpe Rd off Dereham Rd, garden 150m on L. By bus: 21, 22, 23, & 24 from city centre, Old Catton, Heartsease, Thorpe & most of W Norwich. Parking available outside & room for bikes.* **Sun 19, Sun 26 July (11-5). Adm £5, chd free. Home-made teas. Gluten-free & vegan cakes available.**
Magical town garden surrounding Victorian Gothic Cemetery Lodge. Strong structure and vistas inc a classical temple, oriental water gardens, formal ponds linked with winding pathways with a surprise around every corner. Original 25m-deep well. Predominantly herbaceous planting. Carnivorous and succulent collection in hand-built conservatory. Wheelchair access possible but difficult. Sloping gravel drive followed by steep, narrow ramp.

39 47 NORWICH ROAD
Stoke Holy Cross, Norwich,
NR14 8AB. Anna & Alistair Lipp.
4m S of Norwich. Head S through Stoke Holy Cross on Norwich Rd. Garden on R down private drive. Parking at sports ground car park on L of Long Ln; 500 yds to garden. **Sat 13, Sun 14 June (11-5). Combined adm with 51 Norwich Road £6, chd free. Home-made teas.**
A west-facing garden with views over Tas Valley and water meadows lovingly developed over 25 years. Wander beneath a rose and vine covered pergola, past gravel beds and raised terraces shaded by magnolias. Discover a greenhouse with exotic plants, a wildflower meadow, and an informal pond. Majority of garden accessible for wheelchair users.

40 51 NORWICH ROAD
Stoke Holy Cross, Norwich,
NR14 8AB. Mrs Vivian Carrington.
5m S of Norwich. Heading S through Stoke Holy Cross on Norwich Rd, garden on R down private drive. No parking at property. Parking at sports ground car park on L of Long Ln, 500yds to garden. **Sat 13, Sun 14 June (11-5). Combined adm with 47 Norwich Road £6, chd free.**
The garden has a variety of perennials, roses and annuals at the front with an asparagus bed and vegetables to the side and rear. There are cold frames and a small greenhouse. Behind the house there are further flower beds and a small lawn. Wheelchair access at the front and rear of garden.

41 NEW OLD COMMON WOOD
Reepham Road, Foulsham,
Dereham, NR20 5PP. Charles & Judy Levien. *Old Common Wood is 1m E from Foulsham on Reepham Rd. Pass Manor farm barns on R. Drive is on R after Manor House Farm. What3words app: ringers.grin.bump.* **Sun 31 May (10-4). Adm £6, chd free. Pre-booking essential, please visit www.ngs.org.uk for information & booking. Home-made teas.**
Protected conservation area, originally an intensively farmed seven acre field, that was once part of Thelmelthorpe common. A wood created in 1991 with 1000 native trees, diversified by local woodland plants, inc rare Black Poplars grown from cuttings of an ancient specimen. Colourful flower meadow with mown paths leading to wetland area and ponds where orchids flourish in summer.

42 OLD MANOR FARMHOUSE
The Hill, Swanton Abbott,
Norwich, NR10 5EA. Drs Paul & Sian Everden, 07768 376621,
info@hostebarn.com,
www.hostebarn.com. *N Norfolk Coast. From Swanton Abbott, take Long Common Ln until you see the car park sign on the bend of The Hill. The garden is 100m along the lane or 20 from the top paddock. What3words app: coolest.word.plot.* **Fri 26 June (1-5.30); Sat 27, Sun 28 June (9-5.30). Adm £6, chd free. Home-made teas.** Visits also by arrangement 1 May to 19 Sept.
Originally a field surrounding the derelict C17 listed farmhouse winning the Graham Allen Conservation Award in 1991 when the garden structure, sympathetic to the Dutch style of the house was laid down. Knot garden of box surrounded by pleached hornbeam, pollarded plane trees, beech and yew hedges flank herbaceous borders and lawns, clematis and rose walk to potager and spiral wildflower meadow.

43 OULTON HALL

Oulton, Aylsham, NR11 6NU. Bolton Agnew. *4m NW of Aylsham. From Aylsham: take B1354. After 4m turn L for Oulton Chapel. Hall ½m on R. From B1149 (Norwich/Holt Rd): take B1354, next R, Hall ½m on R.* **Sun 7 June (1.30-5). Adm £6, chd free. Home-made teas.**

C18 manor house (not open) and clocktower set in six acre garden with lake and woodland walks. Chelsea designer's own garden-herbaceous, Italian, bog, water, wild, verdant, sunken and parterre gardens all flowing from one tempting vista to another. Developed over 25 years with emphasis on structure, height and texture, with a lot of recent replanting in the contemporary manner.

44 NEW PRISCILLA BACON LODGE GARDENS

Century Place, Colney, Norwich, NR4 7YA. www.priscillabaconhospice.org.uk. *We are located opp the Inpatients wing of the Norfolk & Norwich University Hospital. Free parking a short walk away and disabled parking available on site.* **Sat 30 May (11-3). Adm £4.50, chd free. Light refreshments in the café.**

Designed by James Alexander-Sinclair, and opened in 2023, Priscilla Bacon Lodge gardens are a flamboyant mix of ornamental borders and expansive wildflower meadow. The planting focusses on year-round interest for patients, with a curated mix of herbaceous perennials, roses, grasses, and bulbs. Set on eight acres of Norfolk farmland, the gardens are managed by Head Gardener and a team of volunteers. Full wheelchair access to the café and main areas of the garden. Grass path access to wildflower meadows.

GROUP OPENING

45 THE RUDHAMS

East & West Rudham, PE31 8TD. *6m W of Fakenham straddling A148. Several car parks available.* **Sun 7 June (11-5). Combined adm £10, chd free. Sweet & savoury refreshments available at Wensum House with plentiful seating.**

DRAGONFLY COTTAGE
Nick & Liz Akers.

WENSUM FARMHOUSE
Julian & Cici Romney.

WENSUM HOUSE
Mr & Mrs A Dessent.

THE WHITE COTTAGE
Mr & Mrs I McCallum.

East and West Rudham are adjoining villages surrounded by countryside with Anglo Saxon origins. Easily accessible from Kings Lynn and

19 Bellrope Lane

Fakenham. The four gardens are very varied in history, design and planting providing inspiration and enjoyment for visitors. Georgian Wensum House with historic royal connections has a two acre garden alongside a winding stream with large herbaceous borders, rose arches and statuary. C18 Dragonfly Cottage has a ½ acre plot with colourful herbaceous borders, ponds, wildflower areas and small vegetable and cutting garden. Wensum Farmhouse sits on two acres with a small walled cottage style garden and adjoining wild meadow with ponds, meandering paths and restored shepherd's hut. Close by, The White Cottage is a naturalistic and pollinator friendly cottage garden with colourful borders and courtyard. A local art exhibition will also be available at Wensum Farmhouse.

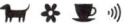

GROUP OPENING

46 ST STEPHENS SQUARE
Norwich, NR1 3SS. *Norwich City Centre. St Stephens Sq is off St Stephen's r'about by The Champion pub In Norwich City Centre. Paid parking if needed in Chantry Place or NCP next to the bus stn.* **Sun 19 July (11-4.30). Combined adm £6, chd free. Home-made teas.**

3 ST STEPHENS SQUARE
11A ST STEPHENS SQUARE
15 ST STEPHENS SQUARE
NEW SAINT STEPHENS SQUARE COMMUNITY GARDEN
35 ST STEPHENS SQUARE
37 ST STEPHENS SQUARE
39 ST STEPHENS SQUARE

A group of city centre front gardens and a vibrant community garden on a charming historic street of late Georgian terraced houses. Starting at the top of the square there is the community garden which is in full sun and packed with plants. It boasts colour throughout the year. As you move along the street you go from sun loving plants in the sunny gardens of nos. 3, 11A and 15 to shade loving plants under overarching trees in gardens 35, 37 and 39 at the end of the street. Each garden is individual and accurately reflects its owner. A charming group of wonderfully planted gardens. All gardens face onto the street and have level access (one with a slight slope) into each garden.

47 SALLE PARK
Salle, Reepham, NR10 4SF. Sir John White, www.sallepark.co.uk. *1m NE of Reepham. Off B1145, between Cawston & Reepham.* **Sun 19 July (10-4). Adm £6, chd free. Home-made teas in The Orangery.**
Explore a fully productive Victorian kitchen garden with original vine houses, beautiful double herbaceous borders, ice house, and Norfolk Heritage fruit orchard. Wander through formal Georgian pleasure gardens with yew topiary, rose gardens and lawns. Don't miss the freshly planted Orangery. This is the third year of no-dig in the garden. Wheelchair access via some bark chip paths.

48 ♦ SANDRINGHAM GARDENS
Sandringham Estate, Sandringham, PE35 6EH. Their Majesties King Charles III & Queen Camilla, 01485 522283, sally.porter@sandringhamestate.co.uk, www.sandringhamestate.co.uk. *Sandringham is 6m NE of King's Lynn. Signposted from the A148 Fakenham Rd and the A149 Hunstanton Rd. The Royal Park's postcode for SatNav is PE35 6AB.* **For opening times and information, please phone, email or visit garden website.**
Set in 25 hectares (60 acres) and enjoyed by the British Royal Family and their guests when in residence, the more formal gardens are open from April- October. The grounds have been developed in turn by each Monarch since 1863 when King Edward VII and Queen Alexandra purchased the Estate. Enjoy the Topiary Garden, Cottage Garden and Historic Trees, the Maze and Sundial Garden. Gravel paths are not deep, cover long distances. Please contact us or visit the website for an Accessibility Guide.

49 SEVERALS GRANGE
Holt Road, Wood Norton, NR20 5BL. Jane Lister, 01362 684206, hoecroft@hotmail.co.uk. *8m S of Holt, 6m E of Fakenham. 2m N of Guist on L of B1110. Guist is 5m SE of Fakenham on A1067 Norwich Rd.* **Sun 9 Aug (1-5). Adm £6, chd free. Home-made teas.**
The gardens surrounding Severals Grange are a perfect example of how colour, shape and form can be created by the use of foliage plants, from large shrubs to small alpines. Movement and lightness are achieved by interspersing these plants with a wide range of ornamental grasses, which are at their best in late summer. Splashes of additional colour are provided by a variety of herbaceous plants. Wheelchair access via some gravel paths.

50 NEW SOUTHGATE BARN
Southgate Road, South Creake, Fakenham, NR21 9PA. Nick & Jackie Sandford, 07811 916309, sandfordj63@gmail.com. *South Creake. Off B1355, approx 4m N Fakenham. Turn into Southgate Ln, Southgate Barn is the 1st house on the L. What3words app: original.page.mentioned.* **Visits by arrangement May & June for groups of 6 to 12. Limited parking for max 6 cars or minibus. Adm £12, chd free. Tea, coffee & cake. Discuss refreshments when booking.**
A 1¼ acre garden full of interest and a borrowed view. Woodland area with specimen trees, pond, gravel garden, wisteria arch, large terrace with box balls. Yew, hornbeam and beech hedging. Colourful herbaceous borders. Designed and planted from scratch by Tim Lees in 1980, restored from 2019 (in the current owners style) after being rented out for many years. Wheelchair access is possible around most of the garden, there are gravel paths.

The National Garden Scheme donated £3,875,596 to our nursing and health beneficiaries from money raised at gardens open in 2025.

51 ◆ STODY LODGE
Melton Constable,
NR24 2ER. Mr & Mrs Charles MacNicol, 01263 860572, gardens@stodyestate.co.uk, www.stodyestate.co.uk/stody-lodge-gardens. *16m NW of Norwich, 3m S of Holt. Off B1354. Signed from Melton Constable on Holt Rd. Gardens signed as you approach.* **For NGS: Thur 7 May (1-5). Adm £10, chd free. Home-made teas. Refreshments provided by selected charities. For other opening times and information, please phone, email or visit garden website.**

Spectacular gardens with one of the largest concentrations of rhododendrons and azaleas in East Anglia. Created in the 1920s, the gardens also feature magnolias, camellias, a variety of ornamental and specimen trees, late daffodils and bluebells. Expansive lawns and magnificent yew hedges. Woodland walks and four acre water garden filled with over 2,000 vividly-coloured azalea mollis. Wheelchair access to most areas of the garden. Some gravel paths with uneven ground.

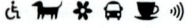

52 NEW THE SUNKEN GARDEN AT THE CHILDREN'S GARDEN
Watton Road, Norwich, NR4 7YB.
Ed & Claire Kenyon. *Grounds adjacent to car park opp private property: Colney Hall. Turning off Watton Rd.* **Sun 24 May (10-4). Adm £5, chd free. Light refreshments.**

A contemporary garden design with innovative and sustainable landscaping solutions with children being the predominant focus and occupants. Planting is relaxed and considerate of a changing climate, and conscious of the importance of pollinators. Garden can be viewed via boardwalk. Wheelchair access to lower levels and shepherds hut not possible.

53 SWAFIELD HALL
Knapton Road, Swafield, North Walsham, NR28 0RP. Tim Payne & Boris Konoshenko, 01692 402624, timpayne@mac.com, www.swafieldhall.co.uk. *Approx ½m along Knapton Rd from its start in the village of Swafield. Disabled parking is available at the Hall. There is a paddock nearby for general parking.* **Sat 13, Sun 14 June**

(10-4). Adm £6, chd free. Light refreshments.

C16 Manor House with Georgian additions (not open) set within four acres of gardens. Discover our parterre and various rooms inc a summer garden, orchard, cutting garden, pear tunnel and secret oriental garden (with nine flower beds based on a Persian carpet). Don't miss the Apollo Promenade of theatrical serpentine hedging. There is also a duck pond and walks through the woodland.

54 TAPPING HOUSE
Wheatfields, Hillington,
King's Lynn, PE31 6BH.
www.tappinghouse.org.uk.
Wheatfields is in Hillington off Station Rd, B1153. From the A148, take the turning into Station Rd, B1153 towards Grimston. Wheatfields is 1st turning on the R. The Hospice is located straight ahead at the end of the road. **Sun 14 June (10-2). Adm £4.50, chd free. Light refreshments.**

The Hospice garden has been created and maintained by a team of volunteers. The site was purpose built and formally opened in 2016. The gardens are still being developed but many areas are well established and provide a peaceful and tranquil backdrop to patients, visitors and staff alike. Set in grounds of approx two acres there is a variety of cottage garden plants, perennials and shrubs. There is a vegetable plot, the produce of which is used by the kitchen team and wildlife area with pond. Full wheelchair access means that our garden space is available for all to enjoy.

55 NEW 1F UPTON ROAD
Norwich, NR4 7PA. Anne & John Farrow. *Between Newmarket Rd & Unthank Rd Norwich. Upton Rd is 2nd road on R, on the A11 (Newmarket Rd) after the Daniels Rd r'about heading out of the city. The property is accessed via a long gravel drive.* **Sun 24 May (10-4). Adm £5, chd free. Tea, coffee & cake. Open nearby 20 Le Strange Close.**

A quiet and secluded garden with gravel paths between the large beds which are densely planted with a variety of trees, shrubs and herbaceous perennials. There is also a small greenhouse, pergola, pond,

and many containers with a wide variety of scented leaf pelargoniums.

56 VICARAGE HOUSE
Vicarage Road, Great Hockham, Thetford, IP24 1PE. Richard & Katie Darby, 07976 814450, info@vicaragehousenorfolk.com, www.vicaragehousenorfolk.com. *7m NE of Thetford, 6m S of Watton. L off A11,onto A1075 towards Watton. R into Great Hockham, L at village green and L into Vicarage Rd. Penultimate house on R.* **Visits by arrangement May to Sept for groups of 10 to 40. Adm £7.50, chd free. Light refreshments. Discuss refreshments when booking.**

Six acres with walled garden, gravel garden, sunken garden, cutting garden and small arboretum. Further cottage style long borders around house and pool house. Pool House garden with box edged beds and fruit trees. Avenue of yew drums with trained white hornbeam. Semi-circle of yew. Garden has developed over the last 35 years.

57 WALCOTT HOUSE
Walcott Green, Walcott, Norwich, NR12 0NU. Nick & Juliet Collier, 07986 607170, julietcollier1@gmail.com. *3m N of Stalham. Off the Stalham to Walcott Rd (B1159).* **Sun 21 June (11-5). Adm £6, chd free. Home-made teas. Visits also by arrangement in July for groups of 10 to 30.**

A 12 acre site with over an acre of formal gardens based on model C19 Norfolk farm buildings. Woodland and damp gardens, arboretum, vistas with tree lined avenues, woodland walks. Wheelchair access is limited.

58 33 WALDEMAR AVENUE
Hellesdon, Norwich, NR6 6TB.
Sonja Gaffer & Alan Beal,
www.facebook.com/hellesdontropicalgarden. *Near Norwich Airport. Waldemar Ave is situated approx 400yds off Norwich ring road towards Cromer, on A140.* **Sun 26 July (10-4). Sun 9 Aug (10-4). Pre-booking essential, please phone 07798 522380 or email sonjagaffer@gmail.com for information & booking. Sun 23 Aug (10-4). Adm £5, chd free. Tea, coffee & cake. Sausage**

rolls and cheese straws also available.

A surprising and large suburban garden of many parts with an exciting mix of exotic and tropical plants combined with unusual perennials. A quirky palm thatched Tiki hut is an eye catching feature. There is a wonderful treehouse draped in plants. You can sit by the pond which is brimming with wildlife and rare plants. A large collection of succulents will be on show and there will be plants to buy. This garden is about big leaves and foliage textures and colours. A wildlife pond snuggles beneath the big leaves. Good wheelchair access. Surfaces are mostly of lawn and concrete and are on one level.

59 THE WALLED GARDEN, LITTLE PLUMSTEAD

Old Hall Road, Little Plumstead, Norwich, NR13 5FA. Little Plumstead Walled Garden Community Shop & Cafe, www.thewalledgardenshop.co.uk. *6m E of Norwich. On arriving in Little Plumstead follow signs to The Walled Garden.* **Evening opening Wed 15 July (6-8). Adm £10, chd free. Pre-booking essential, please visit www.ngs.org.uk for information & booking. Light refreshments in the cafe.**

Richard Hobbs will be taking two guided walks around the recently restored Victorian walled garden with heritage apples and pears on beautifully restored brick walls. There are cutting beds, herbaceous and shrub areas together with a Victorian style glasshouse. There is a newly planted alpine area, a stumpery a range of herbs and some rare and unusual plants. Good wheelchair access throughout.

60 WRETHAM LODGE

East Wretham, IP24 1RL. Mr Gordon Alexander & Mr Ian Salter. *6m NE of Thetford. A11 E from Thetford, L up A1075, L by village sign, R at X-roads then bear L.* **Sun 26 Apr (11-5). Adm £7, chd free. Home-made teas at local church.**

A 10 acre garden surrounding former Georgian rectory (not open). In spring masses of species tulips, hellebores, fritillaries, daffodils and narcissi; bluebell walk and small woodland walk. Topiary pyramids and yew hedging lead to double herbaceous borders. Shrub borders and rose beds (home of the Wretham Rose). Traditionally maintained walled garden with fruit, vegetables and perennials.

> *Our donation to the Army Benevolent Fund supported 776 individuals with horticultural related grants in 2025.*

East Ruston Old Vicarage

NORTH EAST

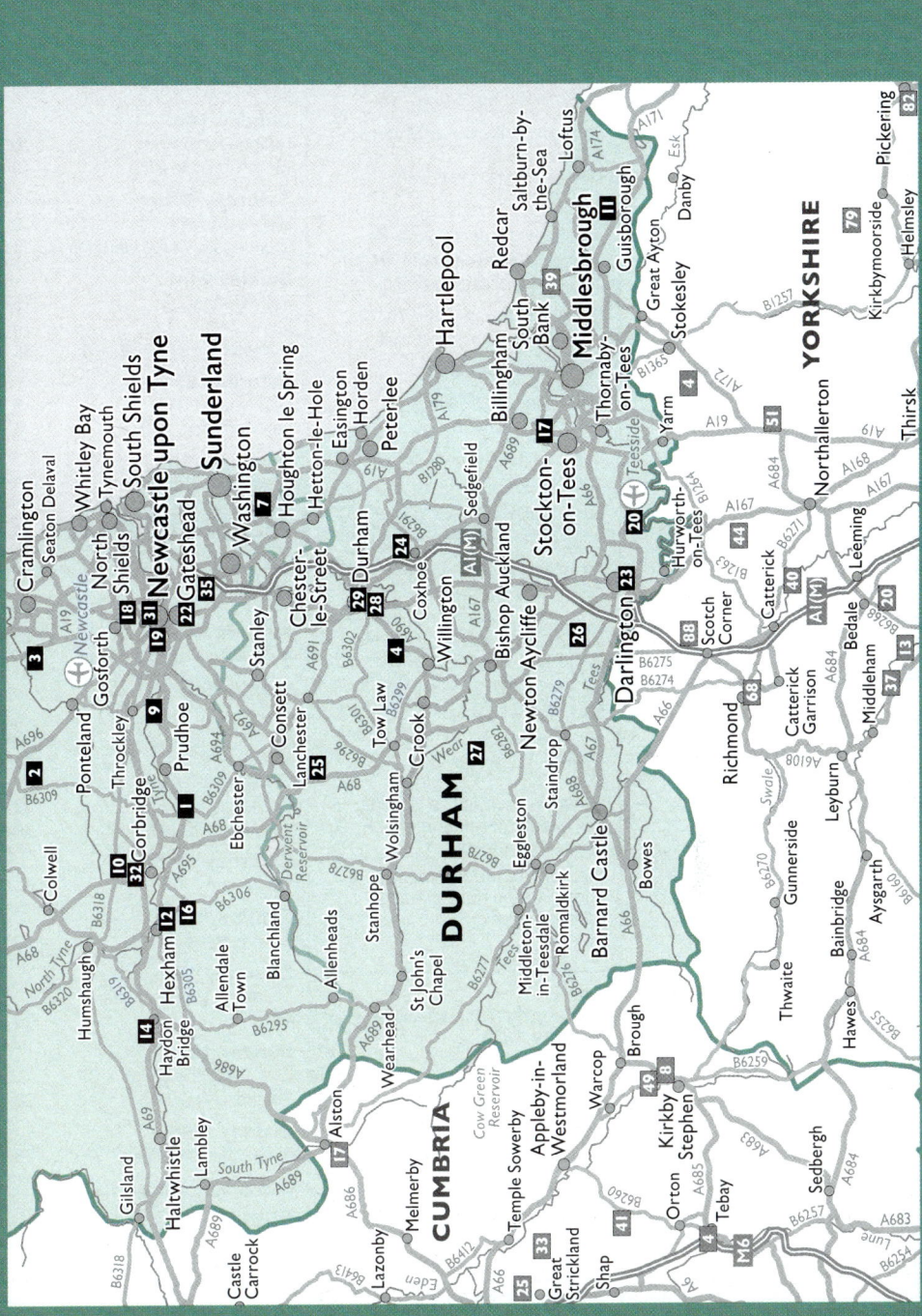

VOLUNTEERS

County Durham

County Organiser
Aileen Little
01325 356691
aileen.little@ngs.org.uk

County Treasurer
Monica Spencer
01325 286215
monica.spencer@ngs.org.uk

Publicity
Margaret Stamper
01325 488911
margaretstamper@tiscali.co.uk

Booklet Co-ordinator
Sue Walker
07849 451079
walker.sdl@gmail.com

Assistant County Organisers
Iain Anderson
01325 778446
iain.anderson@ngs.org.uk

Sarah Garbutt
sarah.garbutt@ngs.org.uk

Helen Jackson
helen.jackson@ngs.org.uk

Gill Naisby
01325 381324
gillnaisby@gmail.com

Margaret Stamper (see above)

Sue Walker (see above)

@gardensopenforcharity
@ngsnorthumber
@ngscountydurham

Northumberland & Tyne and Wear County Organiser & Booklet Coordinator
Maxine Eaton 077154 60038
maxine.eaton@ngs.org.uk

County Treasurer
David Oakley 07941 077594
david.oakley@ngs.org.uk

Publicity, Talks Co-ordinator & Social Media
Liz Reid 01914 165981
liz.reid@ngs.org.uk

Assistant County Organisers
Maureen Kesteven 01914 135937
maureen.kesteven@ngs.org.uk

Natasha McEwen 07917 754155
natashamcewengd@aol.co.uk

Liz Reid (see above)

Tina Snowball 07788 426006
tina.snowball@ngs.org.uk

Helen White 07485 432006
helen.white@ngs.org.uk

Susie White 07941 077594
susie@susie-white.co.uk

David Young 01434 600699
david.young@ngs.org.uk

OPENING DATES

All entries subject to change.
For latest information check
www.ngs.org.uk
Map locator numbers are shown to the right of each garden name.

April

Sunday 12th
High Trees   12

May

Sunday 24th
Blagdon   3

Saturday 30th
NEW Stagshaw House   32

Sunday 31st
Ferndene House   9

June

Saturday 6th
◆ Shieldfield Art Works   31

Sunday 7th
High Trees   12
Oliver Ford Garden   25

Sunday 14th
Halton Castle   10
Marie Curie Hospice   19

Saturday 20th
Bichfield Tower   2
Brancepeth Village Gardens   4

Sunday 21st
Kirky Cottage   15
Lambshield   16
◆ Mindrum House Garden   21

Saturday 27th
Capheaton Hall   5
Fallodon Hall   8

Sunday 28th
Capheaton Hall   5
13 Durham Road   7
Old Quarrington Gardens   24

July

Saturday 4th
◆ Whalton Manor Gardens   34

Sunday 5th
◆ Cresswell Pele Tower Walled Garden   6
NEW 9 Highmoor   13
St Margaret's Allotments, Church, Churchyard & Centre   29
NEW 42 St Mary's Field   30

Saturday 11th
Maggie's   18

Sunday 12th
NEW Trewhitt Hall   33

Saturday 18th
Middleton Hall Retirement Village   20

Sunday 19th
NEW Oakdene Lodge & 37 Southend Avenue   23

Sunday 26th
St Cuthbert's Hospice   28

August

Sunday 2nd
Heather Holm   11

By Arrangement

Arrange a personalised garden visit with your club, or group of friends, on a date to suit you. See individual garden entries for full details.

The Beacon	1
Fallodon Hall	8
Ferndene House	9
High Trees	12

NEW 9 Highmoor	13
Hill House	14
Kirky Cottage	15
NEW 13 Lapwing Lane	17
Old Quarrington Gardens	24
Quarry End	26
Ravensford Farm	27
Woodlands	35

78,000 people affected by cancer were reached by Maggie's centres supported by the National Garden Scheme over the last 12 months.

42 St Mary's Field

THE GARDENS

1 THE BEACON
10 Crabtree Road, Stocksfield, NE43 7NX. Derek & Patricia Hodgson OBE, 07765 862374, patandderek@btinternet.com. *12m W of Newcastle. From A69 follow signs into village. Stn & cricket ground on L. Turn R into Cadehill Rd then 1st R into Crabtree Rd (cul-de-sac) Park on Cadehill. Train to Stocksfield or Bus 10, 10A/10B.* **Visits by arrangement 1 June to 1 Sept. Piano recital and comedy available on request at garden. Adm £7, chd free. Home-made teas.**
This garden illustrates how to make a cottage garden on a steep site with loads of interest at different levels. Planted with acers, roses and a variety of cottage garden and formal plants. Water runs gently through it and there are tranquil places to sit and talk or just reflect. Stunning colour and plant combinations. Wildlife friendly with numerous birds, frogs, newts and hedgehogs. Haven for butterflies and bees. Owner available for entertaining group talks.

2 BICHFIELD TOWER
Belsay, Newcastle Upon Tyne, NE20 0JP. Lesley & Stewart Manners, 07511 439606, lesleymanners@gmail.com. *Private road off B6309, 4m N of Stamfordham & SW of Belsay village.* **Sat 20 June (1-4). Adm £8, chd free. Tea, coffee & cake in the carriage house and garden.**
A 6 acre mature garden set around a Medieval Pele Tower. There is an impressive stone water feature, large trout lake, mature woodland, pear orchard, and 2 walled gardens. Extensive herbaceous borders, rose borders and contemporary grass borders.

3 BLAGDON
Seaton Burn, NE13 6DE. Viscount Ridley, www.blagdonestate.co.uk. *5m S of Morpeth on A1. 8m N of Newcastle on A1, N on B1318, L at r'about (Holiday Inn) & follow signs to Blagdon. Entrance to parking area signed. Bus No.44.* **Sun 24 May (1-4). Adm £8, chd free. Home-made teas.**
Unique 27 acre garden encompassing formal garden with Lutyens designed 'canal', Lutyens structures and walled kitchen garden. Valley with stream and various follies, quarry garden and woodland walks. Masses of daffodils in spring. Large numbers of ornamental trees and shrubs planted over many generations. National Collections of Acer, Alnus and Sorbus. Partial wheelchair access.

4 BRANCEPETH VILLAGE GARDENS
Brancepeth, Durham, DH7 8EN. Alison Young. *5m W of Durham City on A690. Take A690 to Brancepeth. Turn to golf club and enter gates to castle where parking is arranged.* **Sat 20 June (10-4.30). Adm £6, chd free. Home-made teas.**
A variety of village gardens spread out over ½ mile in a picturesque historic setting. Refreshments will be available in the Village Hall. Parking courtesy of Brancepeth Castle. Dogs on leads please.

5 CAPHEATON HALL
Capheaton, Newcastle Upon Tyne, NE19 2AB. William & Eliza Browne-Swinburne, 01913 758152, estateoffice@capheatonhall.co.uk, www.capheatonhall.co.uk. *Off A696 24m N of Newcastle. From S turn L off A696 onto Silver Hill Rd signed Capheaton. From N, past Wallington/Kirkharle junc, turn R. Bus X74 then 1.3m walk. What3words app: guardian.blueberry.traps.* **Sat 27, Sun 28 June (10-4). Adm £10, chd free. Tea, coffee & cake.**
Set in parkland, Capheaton Hall has magnificent views over the Northumberland countryside. Formal ponds sit south of the house which has C19 conservatory and a walk to a Georgian folly of a chapel. The outstanding feature is the very productive walled kitchen garden, mixing colourful vegetables, espaliered fruit with annual and perennial flowering borders.

6 ♦ CRESSWELL PELE TOWER WALLED GARDEN
Cresswell Road, Cresswell, Morpeth, NE61 5JU. Mr Steve Lowe, 07941 734736, steve. lowe@cresswellpeletower.org. uk, www.cresswellpeletower. org.uk. *10m E of Morpeth. W of Cresswell Pele Tower, accessed through double gate. No parking on the village green. Public parking on seafront nearby. Arriva Bus1 Blyth to Amble.* **For NGS: Sun 5 July (1-4). Adm £3, chd free. Light refreshments inc home-made cakes and beverages. For other opening times and information, please phone, email or visit garden website.**
A newly restored C18 walled garden which was part of Cresswell Hall kitchen gardens, abandoned in the 1930's when the main house was demolished. With a grant from Heritage Lottery in 2022, the garden has been restored to inc borders, orchard, gazebo, wildlife pond and greenhouse. Work to increase plantings is underway. The garden is managed by volunteers. Features inc Medieval Orchard and cordoned fruit, raised beds for food growing, diverse floral borders, fern border, re-enactments, interpretation History book in print and beehives. Short slope on lightly gravelled path initially, then level paths to Tower and Garden, which is fully accessible.

&

7 13 DURHAM ROAD
East Herrington, Sunderland, SR3 3NR. Mr & Mrs A C Winfield. *3m SW of Sunderland city centre. 700yds from A19/A690 junc, direction Sunderland, considerate parking in side streets or designated at St Chad's Church, 200yds (signposted). Drop off possible. Buses from Sunderland and Durham.* **Sun 28 June (1.30-4.30). Adm £7, chd free. Home-made teas.**
A beautiful hidden gem that surprises visitors when they enter. The mature planting is varied, exuberant and full of colour with mixed perennial and herbaceous borders and traditional rose beds, a vegetable garden and a large selection of mature trees. The site, just under an acre, has numerous paths providing access to various levels. An interesting urban oasis - an inspiration for gardeners. Access is from a busy road, drop off possible. Various levels but paths provide wheelchair access - steep paths.

8 FALLODON HALL
Alnwick, NE66 3HF. Mark and Lucia Bridgeman, 07765 296197, luciabridgeman@gmail.com, www.brunton cottages.co.uk. *5m*

Middleton Hall Retirement Village

N of Alnwick, 2m off A1. From the A1 turn R onto the B6347 signed Christon Bank & Seahouses. Turn into the Fallodon gates after exactly 2m, at Xrds. Follow drive for 1m. **Sat 27 June (2-5). Adm £8, chd free. Home-made teas. Visits also by arrangement 30 Apr to 15 Oct for groups of 5 to 20.**
Part of Northumberland's history. Extensive, well established garden, with a hot greenhouse beside the bog garden. The late C17 kitchen garden walls surround cutting and vegetable borders and the fruit greenhouse. Natasha McEwen replanted the sunken garden (from 1898) and her redesigned 30 metres border was planted in 2019. Woodlands, pond and arboretum with over 10 acres to explore. Grave of Sir Edward Grey, Foreign Secretary during WW1, famous ornithologist and fly fisherman, is in the woods near the pond and arboretum. The walls of the kitchen garden contain a fireplace built to heat the fruit trees of the Salkeld family, renowned for their gardening expertise in the C17. Partial wheelchair access.

9 FERNDENE HOUSE
2 Holburn Lane Court, Holburn Lane, Ryton, NE40 3PN. Maureen Kesteven, maureen.kesteven@ ngs.org.uk, www.facebook.com/ northeastgardenopenforcharity.
In Ryton Old Village, 8m W of Gateshead. Off B6317, on Holburn Ln. Park on street or in Co-op car park on High St, cross road through Ferndene Park following yellow signs. Bus 10 10A/10B. **Sun 31 May (12.30-4.30). Adm £6, chd free. Home-made teas. Pizza (wood fired) & prosecco. Visits also by arrangement 6 Apr to 16 Aug for groups of 12+.**
¾ acre garden surrounded by trees. Informal areas of herbaceous perennials, formal box bordered area, wildlife pond, gravel and bog gardens (with boardwalk). Willow work. Early interest - hellebores, snowdrops, daffodils, bluebells and tulips. Summer interest from wide range of flowering perennials. 1½ acre mixed broadleaf wood with beck running through. Driveway, from which main borders can be seen, is wheelchair accessible but phone if assistance required.

10 HALTON CASTLE
Corbridge, NE45 5PH. Hugh & Anna Blackett. 2m N of Corbridge. 2m N of Corbridge turn E off the A68 onto the B6318 (Military Rd) towards Newcastle. Turn R onto drive through stone pillars after ¼ m. Or train to Hexham then Bus 74 to (Matfen). **Sun 14 June (11.30-4.30). Adm £7, chd free. Home-made teas. Light lunches and cream teas from 12pm.**
The terraced garden has stunning views over the Tyne Valley. Massive beech hedges give protection for herbaceous borders, lawns and shrubs. A box parterre is filled with fruit, vegetables and picking flowers. Paths lead through a wildflower meadow garden. The Castle (not open) is a C14 Pele tower with Jacobean manor house attached beside a charming chapel with Norman origins. Partial wheelchair access.

11 HEATHER HOLM
Stanghow Road, Stanghow, Saltburn-by-the-Sea, TS12 3JU. Arthur & June Murray. *Stanghow is 3.1m E of Guisborough on A171. Turn L at Lockwood Beck (signed Stanghow) Heather Holm is on the R past the Xrds.* **Sun 2 Aug (11-4). Adm £5, chd free. Tea, coffee & cake.**
Divided into several rooms, this is a garden of different aspects, formal, floral and architectural. The owners have a philosophy of colour throughout the year having hundreds of lilies flowering from March to October. Sheltered by mature hedges, acers, hostas, hydrangeas and agapanthus thrive. There are fruit trees, soft fruit bushes, a greenhouse, summerhouse and a large pond attracting wildlife.

12 HIGH TREES
South Park, Hexham, NE46 1BT. John and Sheila Richards, 07811 367902, hightreesgarden@btinternet.com. *½ m S of Hexham town centre (train and bus stations and Wentworth car park). Take B6306 S, fork L at 500yds. No parking at garden. Park in National Park Office car park on L or on the street beyond South Park which is 400yds on L. Garden entrance 1st on L down lane.* **Sun 12 Apr, Sun 7 June (1-5). Adm £5, chd free. Visits also by arrangement Mar to June for groups of 8 to 30.**
Specialist ½ acre plantsman's garden, with unusual plants; alpines, shrubs, small trees, woodland plants, herbaceous. Many grown from Alpine Garden Society seed; some new introductions. Much botanical interest- small rock gardens, troughs, tiny meadow, magnolias, rhododendrons, Himalayan poppies. Terrace: sun loving plants, annuals. Wildlife friendly.

13 9 HIGHMOOR
Morpeth, NE61 2AL. Mr & Mrs David and Dot Patterson, 07794 114892. *SatNav will bring to Highmoor (House No. 9) Please park considerately.* **Sun 5 July (10-4). Combined adm with 42 St Mary's Field £8, chd free. Pre-booking essential, please visit www.ngs.org.uk for information & booking. Tea, coffee & cake. Visits also by arrangement 19 June to 31 Aug for groups of 5 to 30.**
An ongoing six year project by a pair of plantaholics. This suburban garden features an ever increasing range of plants, including close to a hundred Hostas brought from the owner's previous garden. Keen propagators, many plants have been produced from seed or cuttings. Herbaceous borders, small pond, nearly fifty containers/planters, small greenhouse and vegetable patch.

14 HILL HOUSE
Haydon Bridge, Hexham, NE47 6HL. John and Mary Milford, 07850 464509, jmilford749@btinternet.com. *1½ m NW of Haydon Bridge. SatNav will bring visitors to the car park. Preferred route is via Haydon Village, rather than the single track lane from the A69 at Lipwood.* **Visits by arrangement 5 June to 5 Sept for groups of 15 to 50. Adm £8, chd free.**
Unusual double Walled Garden, generously planted in Cottage Garden style. Circle of box hedges, yew square and topiary; aquilegia and lupins in early June and dahlias, roscoeas and annuals in early September provide much colour. The old orchard, with wildflowers, gives access to a mown walk through a sheep grazed meadow to a woodland

Ferndene House

area, affording good views across South Tyne valley.

15 KIRKY COTTAGE
12 Mindrum Farm Cottages, Mindrum, TD12 4QN. Mrs Ginny Fairfax, 01890 850246, ginny@mindrumgarden.co.uk, www.mindrumestate.co.uk/kirky-garden. *6m SW of Coldstream. 9m NW of Wooler on B6352. 4m N of Yetholm village.* **Sun 21 June (12-5). Combined adm with Mindrum House Garden £10, chd free. Light refreshments at Mindrum House Garden and Plant stall at Kirky Cottage. Visits also by arrangement May to Sept. Refreshments upon request for by arrangement visits.**
Kirky Cottage Garden has been lovingly created by the garden owner in the beautiful Bowmont Valley, nestled and sheltered by the Border Hills. A gravel garden in cottage garden style, old roses, violas and others jostle with favourites from Mindrum. A lovely, abundant garden, ever evolving thanks to the owner's new and creative ideas. All plants are propagated directly from the garden itself.

16 LAMBSHIELD
Hexham, NE46 1SF. David Young. *2m S of Hexham. Take the B6306 from Hexham. After 1.6m turn R at chevron sign. Lambshield drive is 2nd on L after 0.6m.* **Sun 21 June (12.30-4.30). Adm £7, chd free. Home-made teas.**
3½ acre country garden begun in 2010 with strong structure and exciting plant combinations. Distinct areas and styles with formal herbaceous, grasses, contemporary planting, cottage garden, pool and orchard. Cloud hedging, pleached trees, and topiary combine with colourful and exuberant planting. Modern sculpture. Oak building and fencing by local craftsmen. Woodland garden.

17 NEW 13 LAPWING LANE
Stockton-On-Tees, TS20 1LT. Jennifer Pinder, 07741 845005, pinderjen2@gmail.com. *Just off the A19.* **Visits by arrangement 1 June to 13 Sept for groups of 5 to 15. Adm £5, chd free. Light refreshments.**

Norton is pretty with a village duckpond, fountain, green and Saxon Church. Garden on the small side with interest in hanging baskets, tree fern greenery and colour, not forgetting the delightful Nellie the Elephant crafted with a hedge trimmer. Colour and interest throughout the year. Solar dome greenhouse which is used to sit in and enjoy the bird. Mini pond with waterfall.

18 MAGGIE'S
Melville Grove, Newcastle Upon Tyne, NE7 7NU. www.maggies.org/our-centres/maggies-newcastle. *Driving into the grounds of the Freeman Hospital, Maggie's opp entrance to Northern Centre for Cancer Care. Nearest parking the Freeman Hospital multi-storey. Bus X63, 37 and 38.* **Sat 11 July (1-4). Adm by donation. Tea, coffee & cake.**
The garden (recently enlarged), by Chelsea medal winner, Sarah Price, is a sheltered sun trap. Banked wildflower beds and multiple planters, with seasonal displays, at ground level, plus two roof gardens. This gives a choice of outside spaces for visitors to enjoy. Copper beech, cherry blossom, crocus, bulbs, wildflowers and herbs give a colourful seasonal planting palette. A tranquil oasis. Gardener available to give a brief explanation of the garden and its design. Partial wheelchair access, gravel in the garden and roof garden, but the main section can be accessed.

19 MARIE CURIE HOSPICE
Marie Curie Drive, Newcastle Upon Tyne, NE4 6SS. www.mariecurie.org.uk/help/hospice-care/hospices/newcastle/about. *In W Newcastle just off Elswick Rd. At bottom of housing estate. Turning is between MA Brothers & Dallas Carpets. Bus numbers 30 and 31.* **Sun 14 June (2-4.30). Adm by donation. Light refreshments in garden Café.**
The landscaped garden of the purpose-built Marie Curie Hospice overlooks the Tyne and Gateshead and offers a beautiful, tranquil place for patients and visitors to sit and chat. Rooms open onto a patio garden with gazebo and fountain. There are climbing roses, evergreens and herbaceous perennials. The garden is well maintained by

volunteers. Come and see the work NGS funding helps make possible. Hospice and gardens are wheelchair accessible.

20 MIDDLETON HALL RETIREMENT VILLAGE
Middleton St George, Darlington, DL2 1HA. Middleton Hall Retirement Village, www.middletonhallretirementvillage.co.uk. *From A67 D'ton/Yarm, turn at r'about signed to Middleton St George. Turn L at the mini r'about & immediately R after the railway bridge, signed Low Middleton. Main entrance is ¼m on L.* **Sat 18 July (11-4). Adm £5, chd free. Light refreshments.**
Main features are natural woodland and parkland walks within the 45 acre estate. There is a Japanese themed garden, alongside wetland, ponds, a bird hide, fernery, a ceramic garden and allotments. There is also a Putting Green and Golf course. For more information please visit our website. Most routes are wheelchair accessible and linked by a series of woodland walks. Site map can be provided.

21 ♦ MINDRUM HOUSE GARDEN
Mindrum, TD12 4QN. Mr & Mrs T Fairfax, 01890 850634, info@mindrumpartnership.com, www.mindrumestate.co.uk. *6m SW of Coldstream, 9m NW of Wooler off B6352. Parking is available at both gardens (Mindrum and Kirky Cottage) with disabled parking What3words app: waters.presenter.dragonfly.* **For NGS: Sun 21 June (12-5). Combined adm with Kirky Cottage £10, chd free. Light refreshments at Mindrum House. Plant Stall at Kirky Cottage. For other opening times and information, please phone, email or visit garden website.**
A magical combination of old-fashioned roses, hardy perennials and wildlife gardens in a natural setting. Lawns surround the house with borders of climbing roses, mature shrubs and trees throughout. Mindrum House's more extensive gardens inc a rose garden, limestone rock garden (steep slope), fish ponds with terraced walk, and woodland walk with mature pines.

22 ♦ NGS BUZZING GARDEN
Saltwell Park, East Park Road, Gateshead, NE9 5AX. Gateshead Council, maureen.kesteven@ngs.org.uk, www.gateshead.gov.uk/article/11548/Growing-Gateshead-The-Buzzing-Garden. *Between Pets' Corner & Saltwell Towers from E Park Rd/car park in Joicey Rd. In 55 acre Saltwell Park, 'The People's Park'. Bus number 53 or 54.* **For opening times and information, please email or visit garden website.**
Unique collaboration between the National Garden Scheme North East, Trädgårdsresan, Region Västra Götaland and Gateshead Council. Opened 2019, it was funded by sponsorship and is a tribute to the importance of international friendship. The Swedish design reflects the landscape of West Sweden, with coast, meadow and woodland areas. Many of the plant species grow wild in Sweden, providing a welcoming vision for visitors and a feast for pollinators. Donate at www.justgiving.com/ngs. Refreshments at Saltwell Towers Café; and Prism Cafe, Almond Pavilion. Wide tarmac path around the garden and mown grass paths through the meadow, but much of the garden is loose gravel.

& 🐕 🚌

23 NEW OAKDENE LODGE & 37 SOUTHEND AVENUE
Oakdene Avenue, Darlington, DL3 7HR. Tony Inglis & Frances Herschel. *Pedestrian access only from Oakdene Ave. Find No.1 Oakdene Avenue & walk 40 metres down adjacent alleyway.* **Sun 19 July (1-5). Adm £7, chd free. Tea, coffee & cake.**
Garden established from 2008 and is bordered by large mature trees within neighbouring Green Park. The garden was developed to complement the house (circa 1825), which was originally the boat lodge for a Pease family mansion. Planting includes trees, shrubs and herbaceous borders. Alongside this garden, 37 Southend Avenue will also be opening their rear garden with access from the same back lane. Access to the garden is via a cobbled back lane. Paths surrounding the garden are all reasonably level and wheelchair accessible.

& ☕ 🔊

GROUP OPENING

24 OLD QUARRINGTON GARDENS
The Stables, Old Quarrington, Durham, DH6 5NN. John Little, 07967 267864, johndlittle10@gmail.com. *1m from J61 of A1(M). All vehicle access from Crow Trees Ln, Bowburn. SatNav may be misleading.* **Sun 28 June (10-5). Combined adm £6, chd free. Tea, coffee & cake at The Stables - also picnics and WC. Visits also by arrangement 1 May to 1 Oct for groups of 12+.**

ORCHARD COTTAGE
Chrissy and Steve Skinner.

ROSE COTTAGE
Mr Richard Cowen.

THE STABLES
John & Claire Little, www.facebook.com/thestablesOQ.

Three very distinct gardens in the hamlet of Old Quarrington. The Stables is a large family garden full of hidden surprises and extensive views. The main garden is about an acre inc gravel garden, orchard, play area, lawn and woodland gardens. There is a further 4 acres to explore which inc wildlife ponds, woodlands, meadows, hens, ducks and alpacas. The main garden at Rose Cottage is planted with wildlife friendly flowers and a pond that attracts 2 species of newts. To the rear there is a Mediterranean area and a woodland garden with stream beyond. Orchard Cottage has a strong focus on self sufficiency, re use and recycling, with a large vegetable plot growing a wide range of interesting edibles.

& 🐕 ☕ 🧺 🔊

25 OLIVER FORD GARDEN
Longedge Lane, Rowley, Consett, DH8 9HG. Bob & Bev Tridgett, www.gardensanctuaries.co.uk. *5m NW of Lanchester. Signed from A68 in Rowley. From Lanchester take road towards Sately. Garden will be signed as you pass Woodlea Manor.* **Sun 7 June (1-5). Adm £5, chd free. Tea, coffee & cake.**
A peaceful, contemplative 3 acre garden developed and planted by the owner and BBC Gardener of the Year as a space for quiet reflection. Arboretum specialising in bark, stream, wildlife pond and bog garden.

Semi-shaded Japanese maple and dwarf rhododendron garden. Rock garden and scree bed. Insect nectar area, orchard and $1\frac{1}{2}$ acre meadow. David Austin rose bed. Terrace and ornamental herb garden. The garden is managed to maximise wildlife and there are a number of sculptures around the garden.

🐕 ☕ 🧺

26 QUARRY END
Walworth, Darlington, DL2 2LY. Iain & Margaret Anderson, 07584 048368, quarryend@btinternet.com. *Approx 5m W of Darlington on A68 or ½m E of Piercebridge on A67. Follow brown signs to Walworth Castle Hotel. Just up the hill from the Castle entrance, follow NGS yellow signs down private track.* **Visits by arrangement Apr to Sept for groups of 8 to 25. Tea or coffee, scones and cakes will be provided for an additional charge of £4.00pp.**
Woodland garden in an ancient quarry setting. Redeveloped over 25 yrs the garden has a C18 ice house, a wide variety of trees, shrubs and perennials, a fernery and ornamental vegetable plot. Spectacular late summer display but something of interest throughout the year inc an acre of reclaimed naturalised woodland in the adjacent quarry. Extensive views over South Durham. Only partial wheelchair access to woodland area especially if wet. Main garden has flat grass areas but includes some rough steps and gravel paths.

& 🐕 ❄ 🚌 ☕ 🔊

27 RAVENSFORD FARM
Hamsterley, Bishop Auckland, DL13 3NH. Jonathan & Caroline Peacock, 01388 488305, caroline@ravensfordfarm.co.uk. *7m W of Bishop Auckland. From A68 between Witton-le-Wear & Toft Hill, turn W to Hamsterley. The postcode will bring you here, but garden is the older farm set back from the road, not the similarly named one on the roadside.* **Visits by arrangement Mar to Sept. Tea, coffee and biscuits on request. Adm £5, chd free. A voluntary donation for refreshments will be much appreciated.**
In 1984 Ravensford Farm was a ruin in a field full of weeds, with one tree. Today it is surrounded by a richly varied garden, a wood, two

Bichfield Tower

ponds, orchard, rhododendron dell and extensive flower beds. This is a garden of year-round interest and variety. The focus is on colour in all seasons, and on hardy plants, some of which are rare and which survive in this sometimes challenging north-east area. Unusual shrubs and trees, and working towards a national collection of Osmanthus. Some gravel, so assistance will be needed for wheelchairs.

28 ST CUTHBERT'S HOSPICE
Park House Road, Durham, DH1 3QF. St Cuthbert's Hospice, www.stcuthbertshospice.com. *1m SW of Durham City on A167. Turn into Park House Rd, the hospice is on L after the Merryoaks Community Hub building and play park. Parking available.* **Sun 26 July (10-4). Adm** £5, chd free. Tea, coffee & cake. Café open 10am-4pm for light refreshment (cash or card).

5 acres of mature gardens surround the Hospice. In development since 1988, the gardens are cared for by volunteers inc a Victorian-style greenhouse and large vegetable, fruit and cut flower area. Lawns surround smaller scale specialist planting, and areas for patients and visitors to relax. Woodland area with walks, sensory garden, and an 'In Memory' garden with stream. Opening in summer 2026, a newly planted Garden of Compassion, designed by Tom Hoblyn which appeared at Chelsea in 2025. Almost all areas are accessible for wheelchairs.

Our 2025 donation to the Queen's Institute of Community Nursing now helps support over 3,500 Queen's Nurses working in the community in England, Wales, Northern Ireland, the Channel Islands and the Isle of Man.

29 ST MARGARET'S ALLOTMENTS, CHURCH, CHURCHYARD & CENTRE

Margery Lane, Durham City, DH1 4QU. St Margaret's Allotments Association, www.stmargaretsallotments.com. *Close to Durham City Centre, S side; limited on-street parking; car parks in city centre. From A1(M), take A690 to City Centre/Crook; straight ahead at T-lights after 4th r'about. From A167, turn R along A690, and R at next T-lights. 10mins walk from bus / rail stn.* **Sun 5 July (11-5). Adm £5, chd free. Light refreshments at Old School Cafe in St Margaret's Centre, adjacent to allotments.** Almost 100 allotments against the spectacular backdrop of Durham Cathedral, with the chance to speak to gardeners, many using organic methods. Six acre churchyard rich in nature and history, with 500 gravestones plus Commonwealth war graves. Norman church open to visitors. St Margaret's Centre is open to visitors to showcase work supporting mental health and wellbeing, inc a community cafe. There will be self-guided tours, a scarecrow competition, musical programme and talks. Wildlife activities, crafts and trails for children. History and archaeology. Crafts and produce will also be on sale.

Oakdene Lodge

30 42 ST MARY'S FIELD [NEW]
Morpeth, NE61 2QF. Rebecca Wootton. *From A1 N take B1137 Great North Rd to Morpeth, after 1.4 m take L before The Sun Inn pub onto St Mary's Field. Follow St Mary's road around for 500yds to playing field car park. After parking head back on yourself, No. 42 has an Orange door.* **Sun 5 July (10-4). Combined adm with 9 Highmoor £8, chd free. Pre-booking essential, please visit www.ngs.org.uk for information & booking. Tea, coffee & cake at 9 Highmoor.**
In the historic market town of Morpeth lies Rebecca and Jean's garden. Set in the shadow of St Mary's church, this garden is a hidden gem. Step through the gate and immerse yourself in this plantsperson's paradise. Wander paths through packed borders flourishing with Roses, Perennials, Annuals, Fruits and Vegetables. Rebecca and Jean's commitment to permaculture is evident at every turn. A stunning small town garden bursting with wildlife.

31 ♦ SHIELDFIELD ART WORKS
1 Clarence Street, Newcastle Upon Tyne, NE2 1YH. Shieldfield Art Works, www.saw-newcastle.org/shieldfield-grows. *What3words app: indeed.frogs.known. 1m E of Newcastle city centre. SatNav will take visitors to car park. Metro to Manors or Bus No.22.* **For NGS: Sat 6 June (11-3). Adm £4, chd free. Tea, coffee & cake. Refreshments proceeds to SAW. For other opening times and information, please visit garden website.**
An urban community garden promoting sustainable food production, fair land usage and flourishing community. Enjoy exploring the vegetable garden, mown labyrinth, bustling wildflower and fruit tree banks, children's sensory play space, pergola, rotating art poster gallery and the famous chair made from a bath. Garden on one level with different surfaces inc paved areas, grass and a hoggin path. Level access to/from the car park and building.

32 STAGSHAW HOUSE [NEW]
Corbridge, NE45 5PG. Guy and Birdie Burnell, 07767 446006, birdie@btinternet.com, www.Stagshawhouse.com. *2 m N of Corbridge. The entrance to Stagshaw House is from the A68 1 m N of the A68 junc with the A69.* **Sat 30 May (12-5). Adm £7, chd free. Home-made teas.**
An historic Northumberland estate with extensive gardens and grounds surrounding a listed country house. Formal terraced garden with herbaceous and shrub planting and magnificent views over its park and the Tyne valley. Outstanding rhododendron and woodland garden with listed C19 private chapel. Walled gardens and partially restored glasshouses and vegetable garden.

33 TREWHITT HALL [NEW]
Thropton, Morpeth, NE65 7ET. James and Catarina Leigh-Pemberton. *5.4m N of Rothbury. From Rothbury through Thropton to Snitter. Follow signs from Snitter. 1m on L.* **Sun 12 July (12-4). Adm £10, chd free. Home-made teas.**
Fabulous views to the south (Simonside) and west. The garden, surrounding the hall, is a mix of formal, pastoral and woodland. Walled garden with large greenhouse, pond and voluminous herbaceous planting. Vegetable beds and espaliered fruit trees. Woodland walks. A beautiful garden in a rural setting.

34 ♦ WHALTON MANOR GARDENS
Whalton, Morpeth, NE61 3UT. Mr T R P S Norton, 07881 938080, pn@whaltonmanor.com, www.whaltonmanor.co.uk. *5m W of Morpeth. On the B6524, at E end of the village (signed). Public transport - Bus/train to Morpeth then taxi.* **For NGS: Sat 4 July (11-4). Adm £9, chd free. Home-made teas in the Game Larder. Teas provided by Whalton School (PAWS). For other opening times and information, please phone, email or visit garden website.**
The historic Whalton Manor, altered by Sir Edwin Lutyens in 1908, is surrounded by 3 acres of magnificent walled gardens, designed by Lutyens with the help of Gertrude Jekyll. The gardens, developed by the Norton family since the 1920s inc extensive herbaceous borders, spring bulbs, 30 yd peony border, rose garden, listed summerhouses, pergolas and walls festooned with rambling roses and clematis. Partial wheelchair access to main area but otherwise stone steps and gravel paths.

35 WOODLANDS
Pearteth Hall Road, Springwell Village, Gateshead, NE9 7NT. Liz Reid, 07719 875750, liz.reid@ngs.org.uk, www.facebook.com/visitgarden. *3½ m N Washington Galleries. 4m S Gateshead town centre. On B1288 turn opp Guide Post pub (NE9 7RR) onto Peareth Hall Rd. Continue for ½ m passing 2 bus stops on L. 3rd drive on L past Highbury Ave. Bus 56 Newcastle – Sunderland. Stop Heugh Hill.* **Visits by arrangement June & July for groups of 10 to 30. Adm £8, chd free. Tea, coffee & cake. Beer & wine also available.**
Mature garden on a site of approx 1/7 of an acre - quirky, with tropical themed planting and Caribbean inspired bar. Also an area of cottage garden planting. A fun garden with colour year-round, interesting plants, informal beds and borders and pond area. Display of mature tree ferns and palms. wildlife pond and water feature as well as significant area of well established cottage style planting.

Our donation to Marie Curie this year is equivalent to 17,521 hours of hospice at home care.

NORTHAMPTONSHIRE

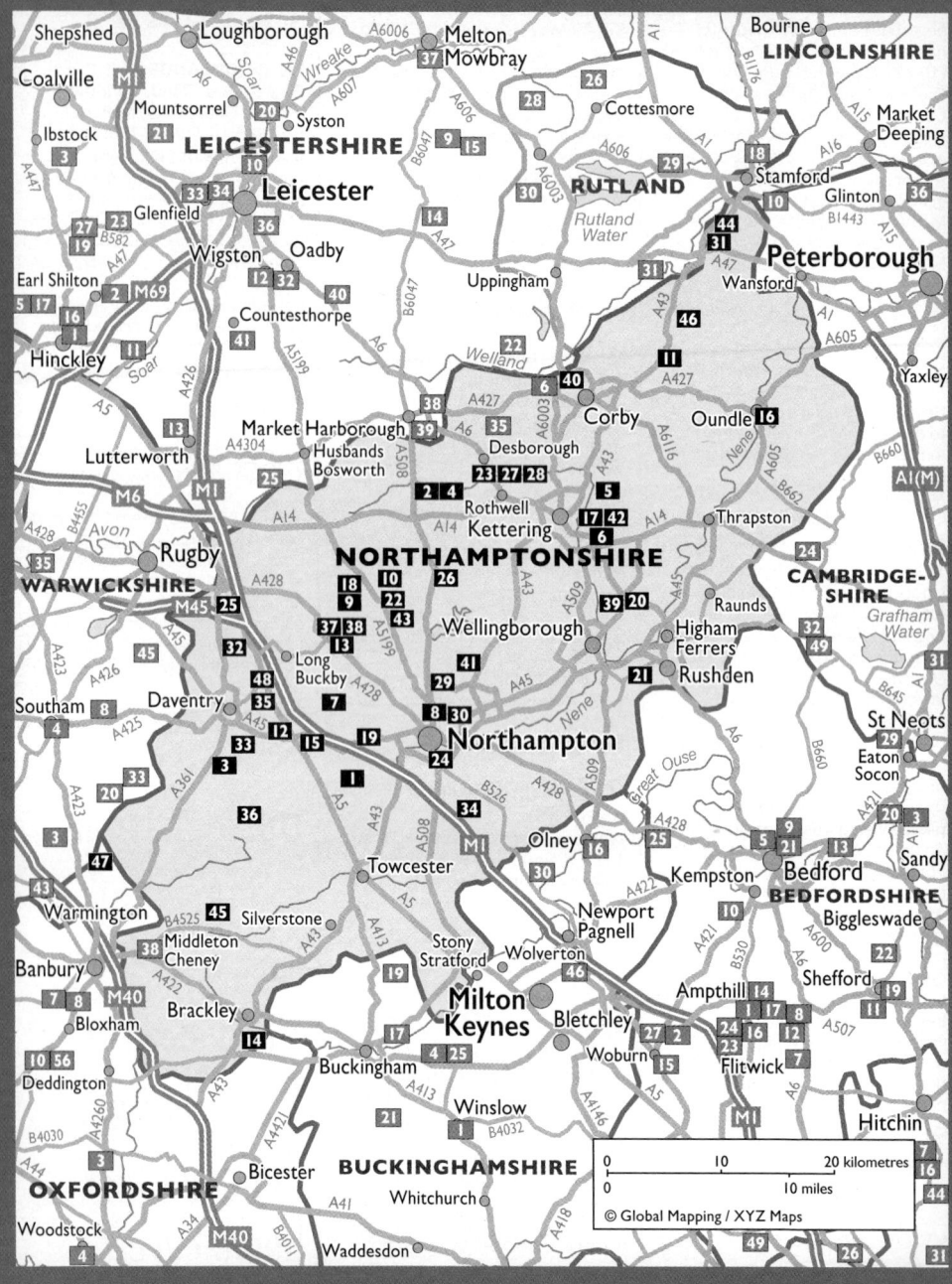

NORTHAMPTONSHIRE

VOLUNTEERS

County Organisers
David Abbott
01933 680363
david.abbott@ngs.org.uk

Gay Webster
01604 740203
gay.webster@ngs.org.uk

County Treasurer
David Abbott (as above)

Publicity
David Abbott (as above)

Photographer
Snowy Ellson
07508 218320
snowyellson@googlemail.com

Booklet Coordinator
William Portch
01536 522169
william.portch@ngs.org.uk

Talks
Elaine & William Portch
01536 522169
elaine@ngs.org.uk

Assistant County Organisers
Amanda Bell
01327 860651
amanda.bell@ngs.org.uk

Philippa Heumann
01327 860142
pmheumann@gmail.com

Tom Higginson
01327 349434
tom.higginson@ngs.org.uk

Elaine & William Portch
(as above)

@Northants Ngs
@NorthantsNGS
@northantsngs

OPENING DATES

All entries subject to change. For latest information check www.ngs.org.uk
Map locator numbers are shown to the right of each garden name.

February

Snowdrop Openings

Friday 13th
136 High Street 21
Saturday 14th
136 High Street 21
Sunday 15th
136 High Street 21
17 Lynton Avenue 29
Sunday 22nd
◆ Boughton House 5
67-69 High Street 20
The Old Vicarage 35

March

Monday 2nd
◆ Sulgrave Manor 45
Sunday 15th
The Old Vicarage 35
Sunday 22nd
Woodcote Villa 48
Sunday 29th
136 High Street 21

April

Sunday 5th
83 Main Road 31
Sunday 12th
Flore Gardens 15
Sunday 19th
Briarwood 6
Rosi's Taverna 42
Sunday 26th
◆ Cottesbrooke Hall Gardens 10
◆ Holdenby House & Gardens 22

May

Friday 1st
◆ Sulgrave Manor 45
Sunday 3rd
Guilsborough Gardens 18
Friday 8th
Ravensthorpe Nursery 38
Saturday 9th
◆ Evenley Wood Garden 14
Ravensthorpe Nursery 38
Sunday 10th
NEW The Manor House 32
Ravensthorpe Nursery 38
Sunday 17th
Badby Gardens 3
The Bringtons 7
Sunday 24th
Lynton Avenue Gardens 30
Newnham Gardens 33
Monday 25th
East Haddon Gardens 13
Sunday 31st
Walnut House 47

June

Sunday 7th
◆ Deene Park 11
Foxtail Lilly 16
Harpole Gardens 19
Old Rectory, Quinton 34
Rosearie-de-la-Nymph 41
Sunday 14th
Arthingworth Open Gardens 2
Hostellarie 23
14 Leys Avenue 27
16 Leys Avenue 28
Rosearie-de-la-Nymph 41
Spratton Gardens 43
Friday 19th
Ravensthorpe Nursery 38
Saturday 20th
Flore Gardens 15
◆ Lamport Hall 26
Ravensthorpe Nursery 38
Sunday 21st
Flore Gardens 15
Kilsby Gardens 25
Ravensthorpe Gardens 37
Tuesday 23rd
◆ Rockingham Castle 40

Saturday 27th
C2C Grows - Community
Allotment Garden 8

Sunday 28th
Dodford Gardens 12
NEW Springfield House,
Collyweston 44

July

Sunday 12th
The Green Patch 17

Sunday 19th
136 High Street 21
The Walled Garden,
Blatherwycke Estate 46

Sunday 26th
Woodcote Villa 48

August

Sunday 2nd
NEW 24 Regent Street 39

Sunday 30th
Joe & Linda's Tropical Water
Garden 24

September

Friday 4th
♦ Sulgrave Manor 45

Sunday 6th
Woodcote Villa 48

Friday 11th
Ravensthorpe Nursery 38

Saturday 12th
♦ Coton Manor Garden 9
Ravensthorpe Nursery 38

Sunday 13th
Ravensthorpe Nursery 38

October

Sunday 11th
♦ Boughton House 5

February 2027

Friday 12th
136 High Street 21

Saturday 13th
136 High Street 21

Sunday 14th
136 High Street 21

By Arrangement

Arrange a personalised garden visit with your club, or group of friends, on a date to suit you. See individual garden entries for full details.

16 Ace Lane 1
Bosworth House 4
Briarwood 6
Foxtail Lilly 16
67-69 High Street 20
136 High Street 21
Hostellarie 23
Joe & Linda's Tropical Water
Garden 24
14 Leys Avenue 27
16 Leys Avenue 28
83 Main Road 31
Old West Farm 36
Ravensthorpe Nursery 38
NEW Springfield House,
Collyweston 44

Vale View, Spratton Gardens

THE GARDENS

1 16 ACE LANE
Bugbrooke, Northampton, NN7 3PQ. Steve & Kate, 01280 860811, kate@qdl.co.uk, www.katewhitearchitects.co.uk/portfolio/our-garden. Located 1m E of the A5, 3m S of M1 J16. Parking at church car park nearby, SatNav for parking NN7 3RG. **Visits by arrangement 15 May to 15 Sept for groups of 15 to 30. Adm £10, chd free. Tea, coffee & cake.**
Over the last 15 yrs we have evolved our enclosed garden from what was previously extensively laid to lawn with traditional borders, to a varied characterful garden structured by hedges, paths and herbaceous borders. Topiary, creative planting and water features give emphasis and contrast with the lavender rill, pyramid and globe gardens. The lawn has gradually disappeared!

GROUP OPENING

2 ARTHINGWORTH OPEN GARDENS
Arthingworth, nr Market Harborough, LE16 8LA. *6m S of Market Harborough. From Market Harborough via A508, after 4m take L to Arthingworth. From Northampton, A508 turn R just after Kelmarsh. Park cars in Arthingworth village & tickets for sale in the village hall.* **Sun 14 June (1.30-6). Combined adm £7, chd free. Home-made teas at Bosworth House & village hall.**

Arthingworth features a Grade II* listed St Andrew's Church, a friendly pub, and a scenic setting by the River Ise, which you can cross via a small bridge. The village offers a variety of open gardens, ranging from small to park-like. Visitors are welcome to explore up to 8 gardens, inc hidden ones and Bosworth House, which has taken 25 yrs to develop. St Andrew's Church will be open. The village is also next to the national cycle path. Wheelchair access to some gardens.
&

GROUP OPENING

3 BADBY GARDENS
Badby, Daventry, NN11 3AR. *3m S of Daventry on E-side of A361.* **Sun 17 May (1-5). Combined adm £6, chd free. Home-made teas in St Mary's Church.**

CORNER HOUSE
Philip Turvil.

SHAKESPEARES COTTAGE
Jocelyn Hartland-Swann & Pen Keyte.

SOUTHVIEW COTTAGE
Alan & Karen Brown.

SPRINGFIELD HOUSE
Chris & Linda Lofts.

NEW WESTERING
Martyn & Jacqui Parratt.

A delightful hilly village with attractive old houses built from golden coloured Hornton stone, set around a C14 church and two village greens (no through traffic). Five gardens of differing sizes and styles will be open: a wisteria-clad thatched cottage with a sloping garden and modern sculptures; an elevated garden with views over the village and beyond; a ¼ acre garden with mature planting and new landscaping, with countryside views; a garden remodelled over the past three yrs, with lawns, herbaceous beds, a pond, and a small vegetable and soft fruit area; a recently redeveloped garden, opening for the first time, which inc a large wildlife pond and a small wooded area, all in keeping with a natural theme. We look forward to welcoming you to our lovely village!

4 BOSWORTH HOUSE
Oxendon Road, Arthingworth, nr Market Harborough, LE16 8LA. Mr & Mrs C E Irving-Swift, 01858 525202, cirvingswift@gmail.com. *When in Oxendon Rd, take the little lane with no name, 2nd to the R.* **Visits by arrangement May to July for groups of 10 to 20. Adm £12.**
For 26 yrs, the Bosworth House garden has matured, just like us. Spanning 3 acres, the garden is organic and features herbaceous borders, over 120 roses, an orchard, hedges, and paddocks. In 2024, we made our first mulberry jam, tried making medlar and quince jelly, harvested grapes, and carried out the first trimming of our stunning Wellingtonia. Partial wheelchair access.

5 ♦ BOUGHTON HOUSE
Geddington, Kettering, NN14 1BJ. Duke of Buccleuch & Queensberry, KT, www.boughtonhouse.co.uk. *3m NE of Kettering. From A14, 2m along A43 Kettering to Stamford, turn R into Geddington, house entrance 1½m on R. What3words app: crispier.sensible.maps.* **For NGS: Sun 22 Feb, Sun 11 Oct (1-4). Adm £8, chd £4. Pre-booking essential, please phone 01536 515731, email info@boughtonhouse.co.uk or visit www.boughtonhouse.co.uk for information & booking. Light refreshments.** For other opening times and information, please phone, email or visit garden website.
The Northamptonshire home of the Duke of Buccleuch. The garden opening inc opportunities to see the historic walled garden and herbaceous border, and the sensory and wildlife gardens. The wilderness woodland will open for visitors to view the spring flowers or the autumn colours. As a special treat the garden originally created by Sir David Scott (cousin of the Duke of Buccleuch) will also be open. Designated disabled parking. Gravel around house, please see our accessibility document for further information.

The National Garden Scheme donated £3,875,596 to our nursing and health beneficiaries from money raised at gardens open in 2025.

6 BRIARWOOD
4 Poplars Farm Road, Barton Seagrave, Kettering, NN15 5AF. William & Elaine Portch, 01536 522169, elaine@ngs.org.uk, www.instagram.com/elaineportch. 1½m SE of Kettering town centre. J10 off A14 turn onto Barton Rd (A6) towards Wicksteed Pk. R into Warkton Ln, after 200 metres R into Poplars Farm Rd. What3words app: finds.fully.bikes. **Sun 19 Apr (10-4). Combined adm with Rosi's Taverna £6.50, chd free. Light lunches & refreshments.** Visits also by arrangement 14 Apr to 31 May for groups of 10 to 30. Tea, coffee & home-made cake inc.

A garden for all seasons with quirky original sculptures and many faces. Firstly, a south aspect lawn and borders containing bulbs, shrubs, roses and rare trees with year-round interest; hedging, palms, climbers, a wildlife, fish and lily pond, terrace with potted bulbs and unusual plants in odd containers. Secondly, a secret garden with garden room, small orchard, raised bed potager and greenhouse. Good use of recycled and repurposed materials throughout the garden, inc a unique self-build garden cabin, sculpture and planters.

GROUP OPENING

7 THE BRINGTONS
Little and Great Brington, NN7 4HS. 6m N of Northampton & 5m S of Rugby, just off M1 J16 or J18. What3words app: lectured.decorate.worker. Signed parking on Folly Ln, Little Brington & on cricket pitch, Back Ln, Great Brington. Tickets for sale & map for all gardens available at ticket booth in Little Brington & at Folly House in Great Brington. **Sun 17 May (10.30-5.30). Combined adm £10, chd free. Tea, coffee & cake.**

ASHFIELD HOUSE
Alastair & Debbie Smith.

1 FERMOY COURT
Hilary & Chris Moore.

FOLLY HOUSE
Sarah & Joe Sacarello.

IVY COTTAGE
Mr David & Dirk Toulmin-Van Sittert.

MANOR COTTAGE
Derek & Carol Bull.

MANOR FARM HOUSE
Rob Shardlow.

NEW NEW LEAF COTTAGE
Carl & Julie Hollingworth.

6 PINE COURT
Stephan Beeusaert.

14 PINE COURT
Chris & Judy Peck.

2 THE POUND
Mrs Sue Saunders.

3 THE POUND
Robert Sneddon.

RIDLEY LODGE
Richard & Anne Wright.

ROCHE COTTAGE
Malcolm & Susan Uttley.

ROSE COTTAGE
David Green & Elaine MacKenzie.

THE STABLES
Mrs J George.

STONECROFT
Peter & Jenny Holman.

SUNDERLAND HOUSE
Mrs Margaret Rubython.

THE WICK
Ray & Sandy Crossan.

The Bunker, East Haddon Gardens

A collection of gardens opening across Little and Great Brington. Ten gardens will open in Little Brington and eight more in Great Brington. Some are large and formal, while others are smaller but no less interesting. All are set in rolling countryside and within two of the most attractive villages in the county. We also hope to provide a courtesy shuttle bus service between the two villages, adding a little extra fun. Or, if you prefer, there is a lovely one-mile walk between the villages across the fields. Two lovely pubs serving great food, the Althorp Coaching Inn in Great Brington and The Saracens Head in Little Brington, best to book ahead!

8 C2C GROWS - COMMUNITY ALLOTMENT GARDEN
Kingsthorpe Park Allotments, off Tollgate Close, Northampton, NN2 6RP. www.c2csocialaction.com/c2cgrows. *Off Mill Ln, towards Kingsthorpe. On arrival into Tollgate Cl, bear L at the T-junction & continue to the free car park. Cross the grass in the park, following the line of wooden bollards up to the*

metal allotment gate. **Sat 27 June (1-5). Adm £7, chd £1. Pre-booking essential, please visit www.ngs.org.uk for information & booking. A selection of refreshments will be available.**
C2C Grows is a community allotment project run by the charity C2C Social Action. The project offers social and therapeutic horticultural sessions for women referred to the project who may be experiencing poor health and social disadvantage. The project takes place on a triple sized allotment with several polytunnels, a greenhouse, fruit cages, raised beds and a peaceful wildlife area with pond. Artwork displayed. Allotment site is next to Thornton Park. The garden is accessible; for further details, contact the garden on 07885 685781.

& ✿ ☕))

9 ♦ COTON MANOR GARDEN
Coton, Northampton, NN6 8RQ. Mr & Mrs Ian Pasley-Tyler, 01604 740219, pasleytyler@cotonmanor.co.uk, www.cotonmanor.co.uk. *10m N of Northampton, 11m SE of Rugby. From A428 & A5199 follow tourist signs.* **For NGS: Sat 12 Sept (12-5). Adm £12.50, chd £5. Light refreshments & home-made teas at Stableyard Café. For other opening times and information, please phone, email or visit garden website.**
10 acre garden set in peaceful countryside with old yew and holly hedges and extensive herbaceous borders, containing many unusual plants. One of Britain's finest throughout the season, the garden is at its most magnificent in September and is an inspiration as to what can be achieved in late summer. Adjacent specialist nursery with over 1000 plant varieties propagated from the garden. This garden was proud to provide plants for the National Garden Scheme's Show Garden at Chelsea Flower Show 2024. Partial wheelchair access as some paths are narrow and the site is on a slope.

10 ♦ COTTESBROOKE HALL GARDENS
Cottesbrooke, Northampton, NN6 8PF. Mr & Mrs A R Macdonald-Buchanan, 01604 505808, welcome@cottesbrooke.co.uk, www.cottesbrooke.co.uk. *Cottesbrooke Hall is 3m off A14,*

J1. *Follow brown signs S towards Northampton & in Creaton turn L onto Violet Ln. What3words app: expand.allow.curly.* **For NGS: Sun 26 Apr (2-5.30). Adm £14, chd £5 (chd 13 yrs old & under free). Home-made teas. Please visit www.cottesbrooke.co.uk to pre-book tickets. For other opening times and information, please phone, email or visit garden website. Donation to All Saints Church, Cottesbrooke.**
Award-winning gardens by Geoffrey Jellicoe, Dame Sylvia Crowe, and more recently Arne Maynard and Angel Collins. Formal gardens and terraces surround Queen Anne house with extensive vistas onto the lake and C18 parkland containing many mature trees. Wild and woodland gardens, a short distance from the formal areas, are exceptional in spring. Partial wheelchair access as paths are grass, stone and gravel, please call ahead to discuss. Access map identifies best route.

& ✿ 🚗 ☕))

11 ♦ DEENE PARK
Deene, Corby, NN17 3EW. Mr Robert & Mrs Charlotte Brudenell, 01780 450278, admin@deenepark.com, www.deenepark.com. *6m N of Corby. Deene Park is located 12m SW of Stamford off the A43. Use postcode NN17 3EG for Porters Lodge entrance & follow blue estate signs. What3words app: sings.waistcoat.irony.* **For NGS: Sun 7 June (12-4). Adm £11, chd free. Tea, coffee & cake in the Old Kitchen Tea Room. For other opening times and information, please phone, email or visit garden website.**
Tranquil garden set in beautiful rolling parkland. Features inc box hedge parterre with teapot topiary designed by David Hicks echoing the C16 decoration on the porch stonework, long mixed borders, old-fashioned roses, Tudor courtyard, the White Garden and Golden Garden, and Victorian summerhouse. Lake and waterside walks with rare mature trees in a natural garden. Wheelchair access to main features of the garden with grass, gravel, and stone pathways.

& ✿ 🚗 ☕ 🪑))

GROUP OPENING

12 DODFORD GARDENS
Dodford House, Dodford, Northampton, NN7 4SX. *Off the A5 or A45, nr Weedon. The garden of Dodford House is located at the lower end of the village on a no through road.* **Sun 28 June (11-4). Combined adm £7.50, chd free. Home-made cakes & refreshments.**

DODFORD HOUSE
Paul & Stephanie Russell.

NEW THE HOLLIES
Jennifer Fuller & Steve Moore.

RUSHBROOKE
Michele & Simon Langhorn.

Dodford is a charming small village in a very peaceful location. This new and evolving group is centred around the beautiful 1½ acre garden at Dodford House, which inc a productive kitchen and cut flower garden, rose walkway, long borders, formal lawns, topiary, and a box parterre. Several gardens of contrasting types and styles will be open on the day, for more information closer to the open day, please visit www.ngs.org.uk. There will be something to delight everyone, from children, who can meet the lovely alpacas and join in the duck race along the stream that runs through the village, to adults exploring the beautiful gardens and enjoying the craft fair.

✿ ☕))

In 2025, our donations to Carers Trust helped them support over 1 million unpaid carers across the UK, as part of their network of local carer centres.

GROUP OPENING

13 EAST HADDON GARDENS
East Haddon, Northampton, NN6 8BT. *A few hundred yds off the A428 (signed), between M1 J18 (8m) & Northampton (8m). On-road parking. Strictly no parking in Priestwell Court, St Andrews Rd, or on the properties.* **Mon 25 May (1-5). Combined adm £9, chd free. Tea, coffee & cake at St Mary's Church.**

BRAEBURN HOUSE
Judy Darby.

NEW THE BUNKER
Kim Carne.

NEW BUTLER'S COTTAGE
Mrs Julie Steele.

♦ HADDONSTONE, THE JUBLIEE GARDENS
Haddonstone Ltd, 01604 770711, info@haddonstone.co.uk, www.haddonstone.com/en-gb/visit-haddonstone.

LIMETREES
Barry & Sally Hennessey.

9 PRIESTWELL COURT
Emma Forbes.

SADDLER'S COTTAGE
Val Longley.

THARFIELD
Julia Farnsworth.

TOWER COTTAGE
John Benson.

The pretty village of East Haddon dates back to the Norman invasion. The oldest surviving building is St Mary's, a C12 church. The village features many thatched cottages built from the local honey-coloured ironstone. A thatched village pump and former fire station, once housing a hand drawn pump, now serving as the bus shelter. The nine gardens opening this yr are a mixture of small to medium sized mature gardens, some offering beautiful views across rolling hills. They are bursting with rare and unusual plants, a variety of shrubs, climbers, roses, and perennials, along with borders, vegetable beds, espaliered fruit trees, and woodland areas. Tickets and refreshments will be available at the church. Plants propagated from the gardens and raised from seed, inc some rarities, will be on sale at Limetrees. The village is less than 10 mins from Coton Manor Gardens.
❋ ☕ 🔊

14 ♦ EVENLEY WOOD GARDEN
Evenley, Brackley, NN13 5SH. Whiteley Family, 07788 207428, info@evenleywoodgarden.co.uk, www.evenleywoodgarden.co.uk. *1m outside Brackley. Turn off at Evenley r'about on A43 & follow signs within the village to the garden which is situated off the Evenley & Mixbury road.* **For NGS: Sat 9 May (10-4). Adm £9.50, chd £2. Light refreshments.** For other opening times and information, please phone, email or visit garden website.
Set among the beautiful Northamptonshire countryside, our unique 60 acre private woodland garden has a large and notable collection of plants, trees, and shrubs. As May ushers in warmer weather, around 100 magnolias put on a magnificent display, complemented by azaleas and rhododendrons. The garden fills with delightful sights and scents. In previous yrs, we have let some of our areas grow wilder, leaving the grass longer and allowing wild flowers to bloom, which helps support our insect and bird population. Enjoy nature unfolding by taking a leisurely stroll through the garden, relaxing on one of our many benches, or simply soaking up the peaceful atmosphere. Morning tea or coffee, lunch with a glass of wine and home-made cakes available in the café. Please take care as all paths are grass or woodchip.

GROUP OPENING

15 FLORE GARDENS
Flore, Northampton, NN7 4LS. *Situated between the towns of Daventry & Northampton. 2m from J16 of the M1. Signs will direct you from the High St to the car park at Brodie Lodge Playing Fields. What3words app: mere.geology.aviators.* **Sun 12 Apr (2-6). Combined adm £7, chd free. Sat 20 June (11-6); Sun 21 June (11-5). Combined adm £10, chd free. Home-made teas in Chapel School Room (Apr). Morning coffee & teas in Church & light lunches & teas in Chapel School Room (June).** Donation to All Saints Church & United Reform Church, Flore (June).

THE CROFT
John & Dorothy Boast.
Open on all dates

25 LARBOURNE PARK ROAD
Jaqui Hoyle & Julian Hendon.
Open on Sat 20, Sun 21 June

THE OLD BAKERY
John Amos & Karl Jones.
Open on all dates

PRIVATE GARDEN OF BLISS LANE NURSERY
Christine & Geoffrey Littlewood.
Open on all dates

ROCK SPRINGS
Tom Higginson & David Foster.
Open on all dates

RUSSELL HOUSE
Peter Pickering & Stephen George, 01327 341734, peterandstephen@btinternet.com.
Open on all dates
🛏

64 SUTTON STREET
Heather & Andy Anderson.
Open on Sun 12 Apr

THREE CORNERS
Marg & Fabian Blamires.
Open on Sat 20, Sun 21 June

1 YEW TREE GARDENS
Mr & Mrs Martin Millard.
Open on Sat 20, Sun 21 June

Flore gardens have welcomed visitors since 1963 as part of the Flore Flower Festival, partnering with the NGS since 1992 with openings every yr. Flore is a picturesque village with views overlooking the Upper Nene Valley. We have a varied mix of large and small gardens, each developed by friendly, enthusiastic owners who will be in their garden on the day. From traditional to eccentric, the gardens offer year-round interest, with features such as greenhouses, gazebos, summerhouses, water features, and seating areas to rest while enjoying the gardens. The June opening coincides with the long running Flore Flower Festival, featuring themed floral displays in the church and chapel. Garden tickets are valid for both days in June. Most gardens offer partial wheelchair access; some assistance may be required, especially on gravel drives.

16 FOXTAIL LILLY
41 South Road, Oundle, PE8 4BP. Tracey Mathieson, 01832 274593, foxtaillilly41@gmail.com. *1m from Oundle town centre. From A605 at Barnwell Xrds take Barnwell Rd, 1st R to South Rd.* **Sun 7 June (11-5). Adm £5, chd free. Tea & cakes.**

Visits also by arrangement May to July for groups of 10 to 50.
A cottage garden where perennials and grasses are grouped creatively together amongst gravel paths, complementing one another to create a natural look. Some unusual plants and quirky oddities create a different and colourful informal garden. Lots of flowers for cutting and a gift shop in the barn. New meadow pasture turned into new cutting garden.

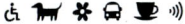

17 THE GREEN PATCH
Valley Walk, Kettering, NN16 0LU. www.facebook.com/ TheGreenPatchKettering. *NE of Kettering town centre. Signed from A4300 Stamford Rd, on the junction of Valley Walk & Margaret Rd.* **Sun 12 July (10-3). Adm £5, chd free. Tea, coffee, biscuits & cake.**
The Green Patch is a 2½ acre, Green Flag award-winning community garden, nestled in the heart of England. We have hens, ducks, beehives, ponds, children's play area, orchard and so much more. We rely on our wonderful volunteers to make our friendly and magical garden the warm and welcoming place it is. Run by the environmental charity Groundwork Northamptonshire. Vegetable seedlings, herbs, and apple trees for sale. Bring a blanket for a picnic. Wheelchair access and disabled WC.

GROUP OPENING

18 GUILSBOROUGH GARDENS
Guilsborough, NN6 8PT. www. instagram.com/gardenatfouracres. *10m NW of Northampton. 10m E of Rugby. Between A5199 & A428. Exit J1 off A14. Parking in field on Cold Ashby Rd, NN6 8QN. Please park in car park to avoid congestion in the village centre. If wet, ticket sales in village hall.* **Sun 3 May (2-6). Combined adm £10, chd free. Home-made teas in the village hall.**

BORSDANE HOUSE
John & Victoria Hall.

BRAMSTEAD HOUSE
Aubyn De Lisle, 07768 646962, Freddie@delisle.co.uk.

FOUR ACRES
Mark & Gay Webster.

THE GATE HOUSE
Mike & Sarah Edwards.

HOLLY COTTAGE
Mark & Beverley Brennan.

IVY HOUSE
Alistair & Diana Herschell.

THE OLD HOUSE
Vanessa Berry.

THE OLD VICARAGE
John & Christine Benbow.

ROSE COTTAGE
Ian & Amanda Miller.

Enjoy a warm welcome in this village with its very attractive rural setting of rolling hills and reservoirs. A group of contrasting gardens awaits your visit, with several recent additions, inc a 1⅓ acre garden undergoing a complete rebirth. Most of us grow fruit and vegetables in various settings, such as a walled kitchen garden and raised beds in cottage gardens. We aim for an abundance of spring flowers from bulbs (badgers permitting), shrubs, and blossom. No wheelchair access at Holly Cottage, Rose Cottage or The Gate House.

GROUP OPENING

19 HARPOLE GARDENS
Harpole, NN7 4BX. *On A45, 4m W of Northampton towards Weedon. Turn R at The Turnpike Hotel into Harpole. Village maps given to all visitors.* **Sun 7 June (1-6). Combined adm £7, chd free. Home-made teas at The Close.**

CEDAR COTTAGE
Spencer & Joanne Hannam.

THE CLOSE
Michael Orton-Jones.

KINGSLEY HOUSE
Gregory Hearne & Caroline Fisermanis.

1 LARKHALL LANE
Helen & Peter Fish.

19 MANOR CLOSE
Caroline & Eamonn Kemshed.

THE OLD DAIRY
David & Di Ballard.

Harpole is an attractive village nestling at the foot of Harpole Hills with many houses built of local sandstone. Visit us and delight in a wide variety of gardens of all shapes, sizes and content. You will see luxuriant lawns, mixed borders with plants for sun and shade, mature trees, shrubs, herbs, alpines, water features and tropical planting. We have interesting and quirky artifacts dotted around, garden structures and plenty of seating for the weary. Wheelchair access at Kingsley House, The Close, and The Old Dairy.

20 67-69 HIGH STREET
Finedon, NN9 5JN. Mary & Stuart Hendry, 01933 680414, sh_archt@hotmail.com. *6m SE Kettering. Garden signed from A6 & A510 junction.* **Sun 22 Feb (11-3). Adm £4, chd free. Soup & roll inc. Visits also by arrangement Feb to Sept. Refreshments to be discussed when booking.**
⅓ acre rear garden of C17 cottage (not open). Early spring garden with snowdrops and hellebores, summer and autumn mixed borders, many obelisks and containers, kitchen garden, herb bed, rambling roses and at least 60 different hostas. All giving varied interest from Feb through to Oct. Large selection of home-raised plants for sale (all proceeds to NGS).

21 136 HIGH STREET
Irchester, NN29 7AB. Ade & Jane Parker, jane692@btinternet.com. *200yds past the church on the bend as you leave the village going towards the A45. Please park on High St. Disabled parking only in driveway.* **Fri 13, Sat 14, Sun 15 Feb (12-3). Tea, coffee & cake. Sun 29 Mar, Sun 19 July (11-4). Light refreshments. Adm £5, chd free. 2027: Fri 12, Sat 13, Sun 14 Feb. Visits also by arrangement 16 Feb to 14 Aug for groups of 10+.**
Large garden developed by the current owners over the past 25 yrs. Features varied planting habitats, inc areas designed for shade, sun, and pollinator friendly sites. A wildlife pond attracts a wide range of birds, insects, and other creatures into the garden. Alpine houses, planted stone sinks, raised beds, and seasonally planted tubs for bold summer colour. Wildflower meadow. WC available. Wheelchair access mainly over grass with some gravel pathways.

22 ◆ HOLDENBY HOUSE & GARDENS

Holdenby House, Holdenby, Northampton, NN6 8DJ. Mr & Mrs James Lowther, 01604 770074, office@holdenby.com, www.holdenby.com. *7m NW of Northampton. Off A5199 or A428 between East Haddon & Spratton.* **For NGS: Sun 26 Apr (10-4). Adm £12, chd £6. Adm subject to change, please check website. Home-made teas & light refreshments.** For other opening times and information, please phone, email or visit garden website.

Holdenby has a historic Grade I listed garden. The inner garden inc Rosemary Verey's renowned Elizabethan Garden and Rupert Golby's Pond Garden and long borders. There is also a delightful walled kitchen garden. Away from the formal gardens, the terraces of the original Elizabethan Garden are still visible, one of the best preserved examples of their kind. Home-made cakes, light refreshments, tea and coffee available. For afternoon teas, pre-booking preferred, please contact our tearoom on 07484 196027. Accessible, but contact garden for further details. Assistance dogs only.

23 HOSTELLARIE

78 Breakleys Road, Desborough, NN14 2PT. Stella Freeman, 01536 760124, stelstan78@outlook.com. *6m N of Kettering. 5m S of Market Harborough. From church & war memorial turn R into Dunkirk Ave, then 3rd R. From cemetery L into Dunkirk Ave, then 4th L.* **Sun 14 June (2-5). Combined adm with 14 Leys Avenue & 16 Leys Avenue £5, chd free. Home-made teas & a gluten-free option.** Visits also by arrangement June & July for groups of 10 to 25.

Hostellarie is a long town garden divided into rooms. Lawns and grass paths lead you through varied colour borders, ponds, and water features. A courtyard garden, shaded by an old clematis, contains over 40 different hostas, with even more mature specimen hostas in the north facing bed and other shady spots. Roses, clematis, cottage and gravel borders, and a welcoming, relaxing atmosphere.

24 JOE & LINDA'S TROPICAL WATER GARDEN

3 Pilgrims Place, Delapre, Northampton, NN4 8NX. Joe & Linda Pemberton, 07572 158883, joeppemberton@gmail.com, www.facebook.com/joeandlindastropicalwatergarden. *1½m from Northampton town centre. From the r'about at Mere Way/A45 junction, exit onto A508 toward Delapre. After ½m turn L onto Queen Eleanor Rd & immed L into Pilgrims Pl.* **Sun 30 Aug (11-6). Adm £5, chd free. Pre-booking essential, please visit www.ngs.org.uk for information & booking. Tea, coffee & cake.** Visits also by arrangement 1 Mar to 30 Oct.

Escape the town and visit a small tropical rainforest in a water garden oasis. A wonderful example of what is possible in an urban space, featuring a pond, waterfalls, curved bridge, fire pit and many more surprises. The jungle feel is enhanced by large leaved plants underplanted with ferns, hostas, mosses and bright pops of colour. Plenty of ideas and plants to take home.

Shakespeare's Cottage, Badby Gardens

GROUP OPENING

25 KILSBY GARDENS
Rugby Road, Kilsby, Rugby, CV23 8XX. *5m SE of Rugby. 6m N of Daventry on A361. Kilsby Village Hall is located on the edge of the village with onsite parking & easy access from the A5 & M1 J18.* **Sun 21 June (1-5.30). Combined adm £7, chd free. Tea & home-made cakes at Kilsby Village Hall (1-5).**

Kilsby's name has long been associated with Stephenson's famous railway tunnel and an early skirmish in the Civil War. The houses and gardens of the village offer a mixture of sizes and styles, which reflect its development through time. Expect a warm welcome and delicious teas. Card payment at village hall. Sunday lunches served 12–4pm at The Red Lion with garden and parking. Best to book ahead! Some gardens are wheelchair accessible.

26 ♦ LAMPORT HALL
Lamport, Northampton, NN6 9HD. Lamport Hall Preservation Trust, 01604 686272, house@lamporthall.co.uk, www.lamporthall.co.uk. *For SatNav please use postcode NN6 9EZ. Exit J2 of the A14. Entry through the gate flanked by swans off the A508. What3words app: miracles. unusable.botanists.* **For NGS: Sat 20 June (10-4). Adm £8, chd £4. Light refreshments in The Stables Café.** *For other opening times and information, please phone, email or visit garden website.*

Home of the Isham family for over 400 yrs, the extensive herbaceous borders complement the Elizabethan bowling lawns, together with topiary from the 1700s. The 2 acre walled garden is full of colour, with 250 rows of perennials. Another highlight is the famous Lamport rockery, among the earliest in England, which was extensively refurbished in 2024. Wheelchair access on gravel paths within the gardens.

27 14 LEYS AVENUE
Desborough, Kettering, NN14 2PY. Dave & Linda Pascan, 07896 360309, davidpascan@gmail.com. *6m N of Kettering. 5m S of Market Harborough. From church & War Memorial turn R into Dunkirk Ave & 5th R into Leys Ave.* **Sun 14 June (2-5). Adm £5, chd free. Combined adm with 16 Leys Avenue & Hostellarie. Tea at 16 Leys Avenue.** Visits also by arrangement July to Sept for groups of 10 to 30.

Town garden with patio, two lawns bordered by curved pathway and a rockery with 'lion's head' waterfall feature. Mature trees give structure to herbaceous borders planted with flowering shrubs, lupins, clematis, primulas and more. Brick pillars and climbing plants provide the entrance through to a small orchard, greenhouse and log cabin.

28 16 LEYS AVENUE
Desborough, NN14 2PY. Keith & Beryl Norman, 01536 760950, bcn@stainer16.plus.com. *6m N of Kettering. 5m S of Market Harborough. From church & War Memorial turn R into Dunkirk Ave & 5th R into Leys Ave.* **Sun 14 June (2-5). Combined adm with 14 Leys Avenue & Hostellarie £5, chd free. Tea.** Visits also by arrangement July to Sept for groups of 10 to 30. Refreshments provided on request.

A town garden with two water features, plus a stream and a pond flanked by a 12ft clinker-built boat. There are six raised beds, two of which are planted with acers and one with sweet peas and dahlias. A patio lined with acers has two steps down to a gravel garden with paved paths. Mature trees and acers give the garden year-round structure and interest. Wheelchair access with two steps from patio to main garden.

29 17 LYNTON AVENUE
Lynton Avenue, Northampton, NN2 8LX. Stuart & Anita Smart. *Off the A508, Lynton Ave is opp The Whitehills pub.* **Sun 15 Feb (1-4). Adm £5, chd free. Opening with Lynton Avenue Gardens on Sun 24 May.**

A plantsman's garden with an eclectic range of unusual plants and water features in a constant state of flux. The latest project is a new pond. The Feb opening features over 70 varieties of snowdrops. Stuart's favourites inc Wendy's Gold, Green Tip and Green Tears. There will also be hellebores, crocus and other winter delights.

GROUP OPENING

30 LYNTON AVENUE GARDENS
Northampton, NN2 8LX. *Off the A508, Lynton Ave is opp The Whitehills pub.* **Sun 24 May (1-5). Combined adm £5, chd free. Tea, coffee & cake at 18 Lynton Avenue.**

2 LYNTON AVENUE
Josie Cuccia.

17 LYNTON AVENUE
Stuart & Anita Smart.
(See separate entry)

18 LYNTON AVENUE
Sianne Castle.

A group of varied gardens set in a suburban location that is surprisingly green. Some gardens are situated on steeply sloping sites, which present their own challenges. Two of the gardens are owned by horticultural professionals, so this is the place to come for expert advice on making the most of the size of garden that most of us have.

31 83 MAIN ROAD
Collyweston, Stamford, PE9 3PQ. Rosemary & Robert Fromm, rrfromm@msn.com. *On A43, 3½m SW of Stamford. 1m from A43/A47 r'about. Three doors from The Collyweston Slater pub.* **Sun 5 Apr (1-5). Adm £5, chd free. Tea, coffee & cake inc gluten free option.** Visits also by arrangement 2 Mar to 30 Sept for groups of 5 to 10.

Wildlife friendly garden with many small trees, bushes, and perennials. We aim to have something flowering every month of the yr to support insect life. Gravel paths and stone steps provide access to the sloping site, which is just under ¼ acre. The garden is in the process of being made even more wildlife friendly, with many more plants being added to feed bees, moths, and butterflies. Seating available on the patio and in the garden room. Plants for sale.

32 NEW THE MANOR HOUSE
Main Street, Ashby St Ledgers, Rugby, CV23 8UN. Nova Guest, 07946 343383, guest@ashbymanorhouse.com, www.ashbymanorhouse.com. Between Rugby & Daventry. What3words app: soups.branch.cascaded. **Sun 10 May (11-5). Adm £10, chd £3.50. Tea, coffee & cake.** Ashby Manor House is located at the far end of the pretty village of Ashby St Ledgers in Northamptonshire. Famed for being the home of Robert Catesby of Gunpowder plot notoriety, its beautifully landscaped gardens are the work of Edwin Lutyens at the turn of the century. New owners have restored the ancient walled garden with the help of talented designer Daniel Combes.

GROUP OPENING

33 NEWNHAM GARDENS
Newnham, Daventry, NN11 3HF. 2m S of Daventry on B4037 between the A361 & A45. Continue to the centre of the village & follow signs for the car park, just off the main village green. **Sun 24 May (11-5). Combined adm £6, chd free. Light refreshments in village hall.**

THE BANKS
Sue & Geoff Chester.

HILLTOP
Mercy Messenger.

WREN COTTAGE
Mr & Mrs Judith Dorkins.

You are so welcome to Newnham. Three plant-lovers' gardens all set in our beautiful old village nestled in the unspoilt Northamptonshire Uplands. The gardens are packed with spring colour, horticultural delights, lots of inspiration and lovely views. There is something to delight everyone. Spend the day with us enjoying and relaxing in the gardens, buying at our plant sales, strolling around the village lanes and visiting our C14 church. Treat yourself to a tasty light lunch and delicious cakes and refreshments in the village hall (several times!). We look forward to seeing you. The old village is hilly in parts. Most gardens are, at least, partially accessible for wheelchairs but may have steps or narrow paths.

34 OLD RECTORY, QUINTON
Preston Deanery Road, Quinton, Northampton, NN7 2ED. Alan Kennedy & Emma Wise, www.garden4good.co.uk. M1 J15, 1m from Wootton towards Salcey Forest. House is next to the church. On-road parking in village. Please note parking on village green is prohibited. **Sun 7 June (10-4). Adm £10, chd free. Pre-booking essential, please visit www.ngs.org.uk for information & booking. Light refreshments. Entry times at 10am, 12pm & 2pm.**
A contemporary 3 acre rectory garden by award-winning designer Anoushka Feiler. Inspired by the Old Rectory's C18 history and religious setting, the main garden is divided into six areas: kitchen garden, glasshouse and flower garden, woodland menagerie, pleasure garden, park, and orchard. Elements of C18 design such as formal structures, parterres, topiary, long walks, occasional seating areas and traditional craft work have been introduced, but with a distinctly C21 twist through the inclusion of living walls, modern materials and abstract installations. Hot and cold drinks, home-made cakes, scones, and savouries, inc vegan and gluten-free. Pop-up shop selling plants, garden produce, local honey, home-made bread, and organic gifts. Wheelchair access with gravel paths.

35 THE OLD VICARAGE
Daventry Road, Norton, Daventry, NN11 2ND. Barry & Andrea Coleman. Norton is approx 2m E of Daventry, 11m W of Northampton. From Daventry follow signs to Norton for 1m. On A5 N from Weedon follow road for 3m, take L turn signed Norton. On A5 S take R at Xrds signed Norton. Garden is R of All Saints Church. **Sun 22 Feb (12-3); Sun 15 Mar (1-4). Adm £7, chd free. Soup & bread in orangery inc in adm.**
The vicarage garden was once the centre of village life. Fifty yrs on, garden life is different with unexpected trees, bulbs, shrubs, perennials bursting out year-round with birdlife, wildlife and life in general. A warm welcome awaits both at the winter opening and in March. The interesting and beautiful C14 Church of All Saints will be open to visitors.

36 OLD WEST FARM
Little Preston, Daventry, NN11 3TF. Mr & Mrs G Hoare, caghoare@gmail.com. 7m SW Daventry, 8m W Towcester, 13m NE Banbury. ¾m E of Preston Capes on road to Maidford. Last house on R in Little Preston with white flagpole. Beware, the postcode applies to all houses in Little Preston. Off road parking. **Visits by arrangement May & June. Adm £7, chd free. Tea, coffee & cake.**
Large rural garden lovingly developed over the past 43 yrs on a very exposed site, planted with hedges and shelter for wildlife and birds. Roses, shrubs, and borders aiming for year-round interest. Particularly attractive in May and June. A peaceful place to sit and listen to birdsong. Home-made teas served on the terrace (weather permitting). Partial wheelchair access over grass.

GROUP OPENING

37 RAVENSTHORPE GARDENS
Ravensthorpe, NN6 8ES. 7m NW of Northampton. Please start & purchase tickets at Ravensthorpe Nursery which is the 1st property on the L when entering the village from the A428 via Long Ln. What3words app: edits.dispensed.shifting. **Sun 21 June (1.30-5.30). Combined adm £7.50, chd free. Tea, coffee & cake in village hall.**

1 CHURCH GARDENS
Tricia & Chris Freeman.

CORNERSTONE
Lorna Jones.

RAVENSTHORPE NURSERY
Mr & Mrs Richard Wiseman. (See separate entry)

TREETOPS
Ros Smith.

NEW UPPINGSTONE HOUSE
Patrick Given.

Attractive village in Northamptonshire uplands near to Ravensthorpe reservoir and Top Ardles Wood, Woodland Trust which have bird watching and picnic opportunities. Established and developing gardens set in beautiful countryside displaying a wide range of plants, many available from the nursery that now only opens on NGS open days. Offering inspirational planting, quiet contemplation, beautiful views, water

The Walled Garden, Blatherwycke Estate

features and gardens encouraging wildlife. N.B. Not all gardens welcome dogs. Disabled WC in village hall.

38 RAVENSTHORPE NURSERY
6 East Haddon Road, Ravensthorpe, NN6 8ES. **Mr & Mrs Richard Wiseman, 01604 770548, ravensthorpenursery@hotmail. com.** *7m NW of Northampton. 1st property on L approaching from A428 via Long Ln.* **Fri 8, Sat 9, Sun 10 May, Fri 19, Sat 20 June, Fri 11, Sat 12, Sun 13 Sept (11-5). Adm £6, chd free. Tea, coffee & cake. Opening with Ravensthorpe Gardens on Sun 21 June. Visits also by arrangement Apr to Sept for groups of 10 to 40.**
Over an acre of garden wrapped around the former nursery with beautiful views. Planted with many unusual shrubs and herbaceous perennials over the last 30+ yrs to reflect the wide range of plants produced, inc seven large island beds planted mainly with herbaceous perennials. In addition, our wildflower meadow is in its second yr, and a woodland path features shade loving plants. Plants for sale. Wheelchair access with a gradual slope.

39 NEW 24 REGENT STREET
Finedon, Wellingborough, NN9 5NB. **Neil Forster & Jonathan Canty.** *From A14 J10, take A6 to Finedon. From Wellingborough, follow A510; from Higham Ferrers, take A6. In Finedon, follow yellow signs off Wellingborough Rd, Bell Hill to Regent St.* **Sun 2 Aug (11-4). Adm £4.50, chd free. Tea, coffee & home-made cake.**
Charming ¼ acre garden features a summerhouse with views overlooking the lawn. This outdoor space inc patios, a small fish pond, and a larger wildlife pond. Located behind a historic Northamptonshire stone cottage c1800, once a butcher's shop, the garden has been a social hub for over 20 yrs. As the family grows, the garden adapts to support wildlife while remaining a welcoming area for relaxation.

40 ◆ ROCKINGHAM CASTLE
Rockingham Castle Estate, Rockingham, Market Harborough, LE16 8TH. **01536 770240, estateoffice@rockinghamcastle. com, www.rockinghamcastle.com.** *Located off the A6003, 1m N of Corby.* **For NGS: Tue 23 June (11-3.30). Adm £10, chd £3.50. For other opening times and information, please phone, email or visit garden website.**
Rockingham Castle was built on the orders of William the Conqueror, and features spectacular views over the Welland Valley. Its Motte and Bailey design influences the sweeping formal gardens you see today. Spread across 13 acres, divided into The Terrace, The Cross, The Rose Garden (planted with David Austin roses), Jewel Borders and dramatic Wild Garden, the gardens inc a wealth of roses from hybrid teas to climbers. Lunches, cream teas, home-made cakes, coffee and wine in Walker's House Tearoom. Tickets can be booked online in advance through castle website or purchased on arrival at the ticket office. Disabled parking. Ramps provided. Accessible WC.

41 ROSEARIE-DE-LA-NYMPH

55 The Grove, Moulton, Northampton, NN3 7UE. Peter Hughes, Mary Morris, Irene Kay, Steven & Netta Hughes. *N of Northampton town. Turn off A43 at small r'about to Overstone Rd. Follow NGS signs in village. The garden is on the Holcot Rd out of Moulton.* **Sun 7, Sun 14 June (11-4). Adm £5, chd free. Tea, coffee & cake.**

We have been developing this romantic garden for about 20 yrs and now have over 1800 English and French roses. There are over 120 tree ferns some up to 8ft high. Many unusual water features and specimen trees. Roses, scramblers and ramblers climb into trees, over arbours and arches. Collection of 100 Japanese maples. Mostly flat wheelchair access via a standard width doorway.

42 ROSI'S TAVERNA

20 St Francis Close, Barton Seagrave, Kettering, NN15 5DT. Rosi & David Labrum, www.instagram.com/rositaverna. *Approx 2m from J10 of the A14. Head towards Barton Seagrave, going through 3 sets of T-lights. At the 4th set turn R onto Warkton Ln. At the r'about turn L & take the next 2 R turns into St Francis Cl.* **Sun 19 Apr (10-4). Combined adm with Briarwood £6.50, chd free. Tea, coffee & cake at Briarwood.**

An established medium south facing town garden. Kitchen garden intermingles with flowers, shrubs, plenty of fruit trees, soft fruits and vegetables in raised beds. Cacti and succulents are in the new greenhouse. A new archway is under construction. A bog garden and a pyramid water feature. A unique taverna with mosaic flooring offers perfect shelter from sun, wind and drizzle.

Springfield House, Collyweston

GROUP OPENING

43 SPRATTON GARDENS
Smith Street, Spratton, NN6 8HP. 6½m NNW of Northampton. Parking in Spratton Hall School car park, please follow yellow NGS signs from outskirts of village from A5199 or Brixworth Rd. **Sun 14 June (11-5). Combined adm £8, chd free. Light refreshments.**

THE COTTAGE
Mrs Judith Elliott.

28 GORSE ROAD
Lee Miller.

11 HIGH STREET
Philip & Frances Roseblade.

MULBERRY COTTAGE
Kerry Herd.

OLD HOUSE FARM
Susie Marchant.

THE SHEILING
Jane & William Marshall.

STONE HOUSE
John Forbear.

VALE VIEW
John Hunt.

WALTHAM COTTAGE
Norma & Allan Simons.

As well as attractive cottage gardens alongside old Northampton stone houses, Spratton also has unusual gardens. These inc those showing good use of a small area, those dedicated to encouraging wildlife with views of the surrounding countryside, renovated gardens and those with new planting. You will also find a courtyard garden, a gravel garden with sculpture, and mature gardens with fruit trees and herbaceous borders. Refreshments in the Norman St Andrew's Church. The King's Head pub will be open, lunch reservations recommended. Well behaved dogs on short leads. Full or partial wheelchair access to most gardens, but some do have gravel and steps.

44 NEW SPRINGFIELD HOUSE, COLLYWESTON
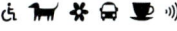
17 Main Road, Collyweston, Stamford, PE9 3PF. John & Anne Barratt, 07786 341459, anne@jwbarratt.com. *3m S of Stamford. On A43 between Easton-on-the-Hill & Collyweston. From Stamford LHS after Collyweston sign. What3words app: delighted. fixed.asterisk. Parking in nearby laybys.* **Sun 28 June (12-4). Adm £7, chd free. Home-made teas. Visits also by arrangement for groups of 10+.**
Springfield House is set within 3 acres, featuring formal garden areas, mature trees, a woodland walk, a wildflower meadow, and productive vegetable gardens. Recently redeveloped by the owners following a plan drawn up by Adam Frost, the garden seamlessly blends established planting with newly introduced formal beds. There is an extensive and interesting range of plants, reflecting the owners' deep love of plants. The garden is mostly accessible, with disabled parking available on the drive.

45 ♦ SULGRAVE MANOR
Manor Road, Sulgrave, Banbury, OX17 2SD. The Sulgrave Manor Trust, sulgravemanor.org.uk. *Please use our car park on Manor Rd, follow signed HS2 diversion signs.* **For NGS: Mon 2 Mar, Fri 1 May, Fri 4 Sept (10.30-3). Adm £5, chd free. Tea, coffee & cake.** For other opening times and information, please visit garden website.
Our garden was designed in the early 1900s by Sir Reginald Blomfield architect, garden designer and author. Yew hedges divide the garden into rooms, each one with its own atmosphere. Topiary peacocks welcome visitors at the front door and densely planted borders ensure botanical interest from spring through to autumn. Please Note: the house will not be open. Sulgrave Manor is a rural site with some uneven ground and gravel paths throughout the grounds.

46 THE WALLED GARDEN, BLATHERWYCKE ESTATE
Blatherwycke, Peterborough, PE8 6YW. Mr M George. *Blatherwycke is signed off the A43 between Stamford & Corby. Follow road through village; the garden entrance is located next to the large river bridge.* **Sun 19 July (11-4). Adm £6, chd free. Tea, coffee & cake.**
Blatherwycke Hall was demolished in the 1940s, and its gardens were lost. In 2011, renovation of the derelict 2 acre walled garden began. A kitchen garden, fruit trees, extensive herbaceous borders, wildflower meadows, tropical bed, shrub borders, and large arboretum have been planted. Restoration of the crinkle-crankle wall and ice house has been completed, and new central steps and gates created. Wheelchair access over grass and gravel paths, with some slopes and steps.

47 WALNUT HOUSE
Main Street, Charlton, Banbury, OX17 3DR. Sir Paul & Lady Hayter. *In Main St, Charlton between Banbury & Brackley.* **Sun 31 May (2-5). Adm £5, chd free. Home-made teas.**
Large garden behind C17 farmhouse (not open). Colour themed borders and separate small gardens with beech and yew hedges, each with their own character. Orchard with wild flowers and an old-fashioned vegetable garden. Wilderness (in C18 sense) and arboretum. Garden started in 1992 with new hot and gravel garden created in 2011. Wheelchair access to garden with gravel paths.

48 WOODCOTE VILLA
Old Watling Street, Long Buckby Wharf, Long Buckby, Northampton, NN6 7EW. Sue & Geoff Woodward. *2m NE of Daventry, just off A5. From M1 J16, take Flore bypass, turn R at A5 r'about for approx 3m. From Daventry, follow signs to Long Buckby, but turn L at A5 Xrds. From M1 J18 signed Kilsby, follow A5 S for approx 6m.* **Sun 22 Mar (11.30-4); Sun 26 July, Sun 6 Sept (11-4.30). Adm £4, chd free. Home-made teas & gluten free cake.**
In a much admired location, this stunning canalside garden has a large variety of plants, styles, structures and unusual bygones. Bulbs and hellebores abound in March, colourful planting in July/September, many well-stocked pots, all set against a backdrop of trees and shrubs in themed areas. Visitors comment on the many different bird species evident during their visit. Great choice of home-made cakes and beverages. Plants for sale (cash only). Sorry, no WC. Wheelchair access via ramp at entrance to garden.
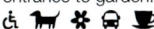

NOTTINGHAMSHIRE

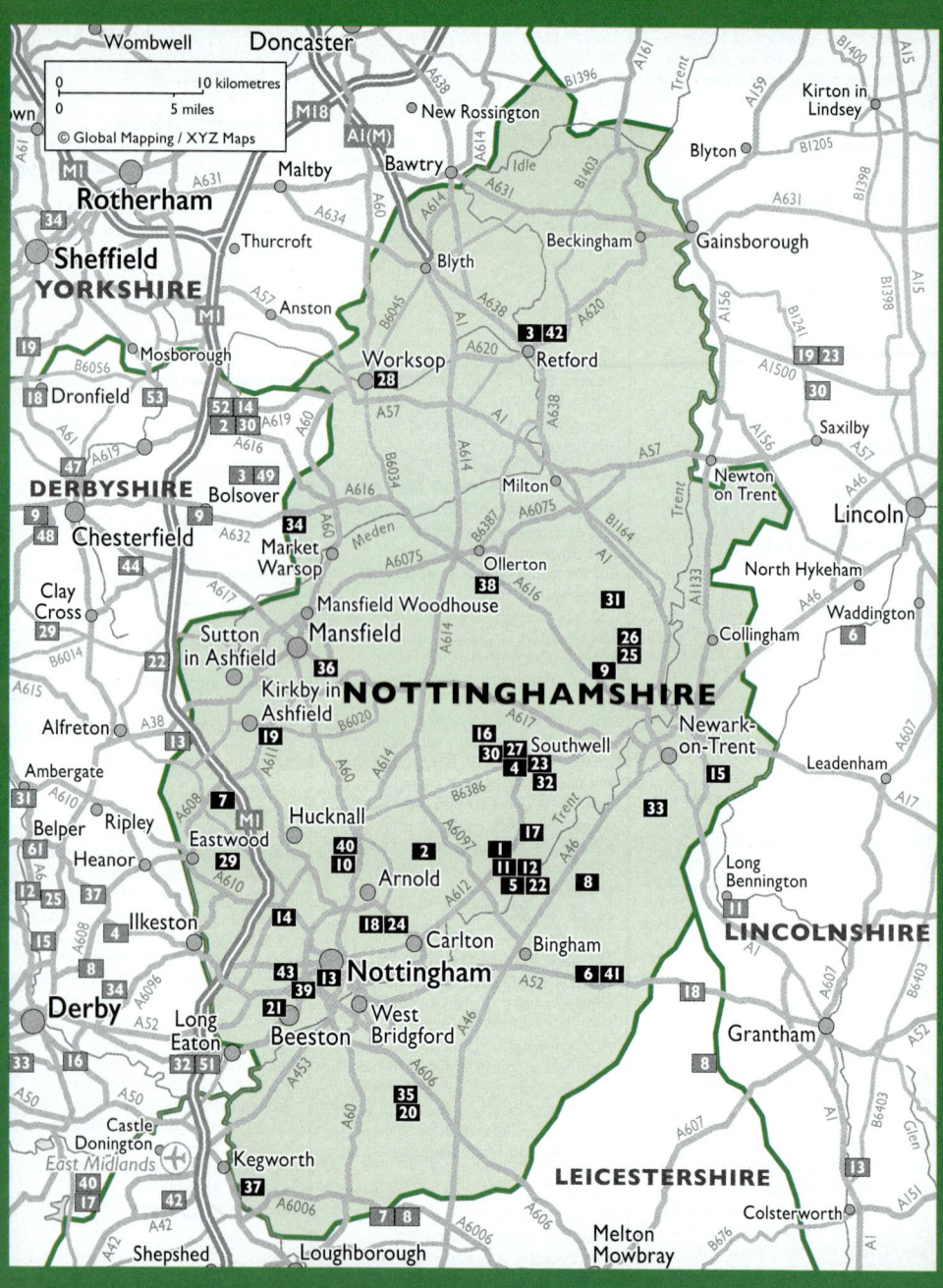

VOLUNTEERS

County Organiser
Andrew Young
01623 863327
andrew.young@ngs.org.uk

County Treasurer
Ian Brownhill
07970 126318
ian.brownhill@ngs.org.uk

Publicity
Smita Jobling
07966 298180
smita.jobling@ngs.org.uk

Social Media
Malcolm Turner
01159 222831
malcolm.turner14@btinternet.com

Booklet Co-ordinator
Martyn Faulconbridge
01949 850942
mjfaulconbridge@gmail.com

Assistant County Organisers
Ian Brownhill
07970 126318
ian.brownhill@ngs.org.uk

Michael Hirschl
07971 083869
michael.hirschl@ngs.org.uk

Beverley Perks
01636 812181
perks.family@talk21.com

Mary Thomas
01509 672056
nursery@piecemealplants.co.uk

@National Garden Scheme Nottinghamshire
@ngs_nottinghamshire

OPENING DATES

All entries subject to change. For latest information check www.ngs.org.uk

Map locator numbers are shown to the right of each garden name.

February

Snowdrop Openings

Sunday 1st
1 Highfield Road 14

Sunday 15th
1 Highfield Road 14

Sunday 22nd
Norwood Park 27

April

Saturday 4th
Oasis Community Gardens 28

Saturday 18th
Capability Barn 5

Sunday 19th
Capability Barn 5
◆ Felley Priory 7

May

Sunday 3rd
160 Southwell Road West 36

Sunday 10th
Cedarwood 6
Flintham Hall Gardens 8

Saturday 16th
The Old Vicarage 30

Sunday 17th
6 Hope Street 21
◆ Norwell Nurseries 26

Sunday 24th
Glebe Steading 11
Mapperley Gardens 24

Monday 25th
Glebe Steading 11

Saturday 30th
Sutton Bonington Gardens 37

Sunday 31st
Brook Cottage 4
20 Kirklington Road 23
Sutton Bonington Gardens 37

June

Sunday 7th
Home Farm House,
  17 Main Street 20
Hoveringham Gardens 22
The Poplars 33
Rose Cottage 35

Saturday 13th
Hill's Farm 16
The Old Vicarage 30

Sunday 14th
Hollinside 19
NEW The Old Stables 29

Thursday 18th
Rhubarb Farm 34

Saturday 20th
78 Hilton Road 18

Sunday 21st
78 Hilton Road 18
Ossington House 31

Saturday 27th
Park Farm 32

Sunday 28th
NEW 1 Hill Top Cottages 17
Norwell Gardens 25

July

Wednesday 1st
Norwell Gardens 25

Sunday 5th
Whatton Gardens 41

Saturday 11th
NEW Alpaca Farm 2

Sunday 12th
NEW Alpaca Farm 2

Thursday 16th
Rhubarb Farm 34

Sunday 19th
The Old Vicarage 30

Saturday 25th
Floral Media 9

Sunday 26th
10 Harlaxton Drive 13

August

Saturday 1st
NEW Alpaca Farm 2

Sunday 2nd
NEW Alpaca Farm 2
NEW 1 Hill Top Cottages 17

Saturday 8th
University Park Gardens 39

Sunday 9th
The Poplars 33

Sunday 16th
NEW Hill Top Farm 15
NEW ◆ Wollaton Hall Walled Garden 43

Thursday 20th
Rhubarb Farm 34

Sunday 23rd
The Old Vicarage 30

Saturday 29th
Allington 1

Sunday 30th
Allington 1

Monday 31st
Whatton Gardens 41

September

Sunday 6th
Brook Cottage 4
20 Kirklington Road 23

Sunday 27th
◆ Norwell Nurseries 26

By Arrangement

Arrange a personalised garden visit with your club, or group of friends, on a date to suit you. See individual garden entries for full details.

Allington 1
Bolham Manor 3
Cedarwood 6
Gaunts Hill 10
Glebe Steading 11
Hall Farmhouse 12
10 Harlaxton Drive 13
Home Farm House, 17 Main Street 20
6 Hope Street 21
Oasis Community Gardens 28
The Old Vicarage 30
Park Farm 32
The Poplars 33
Rose Cottage 35
160 Southwell Road West 36
Tithe Barn 38
Waxwings & Goldcrest 40
Whatton Gardens 41
NEW The Willows 42

Highfield House, Hoveringham Gardens

NOTTINGHAMSHIRE 413

THE GARDENS

1 ALLINGTON
Gonalston, Nottingham,
NG14 7JA. Mrs Catharine Bailey,
catharine.bailey@outlook.com,
www.hortusbaileyana.co.uk. NE
of Lowdham. From Lowdham, take
A612 to Southwell and take 2nd L
into the village, then follow the NGS
signs for Parking. As directed from
there with NGS signage. **Sat 29,
Sun 30 Aug (1-5). Adm £5, chd
free. Tea, coffee & cake.** Visits
also by arrangement 22 Feb to 23
Aug for groups of 10 to 25.
An invitation to visit a tranquil front
garden leading onto a Rose Garden
reminiscent of Victorian times. The
colour theories of Gertrude Jekyll are
brought to life in the Long Border
and you can taste ripe Mulberries in
the knot garden. The productive side
of the garden inc a potager, a small
orchard and a decorative greenhouse.

2 NEW **ALPACA FARM**
Park Avenue, Woodborough,
Nottingham, NG14 6EB.
Jane Masters,
www.oaktreealpacas.co.uk. 6m
N of Nottingham. From Nottingham
(A614) turn down Bank Hill, then
R onto Main St. From the A6097
take Lowdham Ln, Shelt Hill or go
through Calverton and follow Bonner
Hill and Foxwood Ln to Main St and
Park Ave. **Sat 11, Sun 12 July, Sat
1, Sun 2 Aug (11-5). Adm £8, chd
free. Home-made teas inc cake
and botanical ice cream made
from garden ingredients, with hot
or cold herb infusions.**
The Herb and Edible Flower garden
rests on agricultural land, nestling
between alpaca fields and ancient
woodland. As gardeners and artists,
the owners have focused on the
shape, colour and fibre of the plants
as well as nutritional and medicinal
value. Born from the creativity and
determination of a group of women,
and nourished by alpaca manure, it
embodies a balance of productivity
and beauty. Guests can say hello to
the Alpacas and watch spinning and
felting of the fleece. Fresh or dried
herbs and flowers for tea, cooking
and confetti are available.

3 BOLHAM MANOR
Bolham Way, Bolham, Retford,
DN22 9JG. Pam & Butch
Barnsdale, 07790 896022,
pamandbutch@hotmail.co.uk. 1m
from Retford. A620 Gainsborough
Rd from Retford, turn L onto Tiln Ln,
signed 'A620 avoiding low bridge'.
At sharp R bend, take road to
Tiln then L Bolham Way. **Visits by
arrangement 8 Feb to 14 Sept for
groups of 5 to 24. Adm £5, chd
free. Tea, coffee & cake.**
This 3 acre mature garden provides
year-round interest. In February,
swathes of snowdrops greet you,
followed by daffodils and other spring
bulbs. Topiary features and sculptures
guide you through the different areas
of the garden, with its mixed planted
terraces and herbaceous borders,
ponds, orchard and wildflower areas.
Partial wheelchair access to parts of
garden.

&♿ ✱ ☕ 🔊

4 BROOK COTTAGE
41 Church Street, Southwell,
NG25 0HQ. Mr Alastair Murray.
In Southwell 200 metres E of The
Minster. What3words app: lemmings.
octagonal.offline. Past Southwell
Minster around L bend - on L side.
Car Parking available opp Southwell
Minster/street parking. **Sun 31 May,
Sun 6 Sept (1-5). Combined adm
with 20 Kirklington Road £7, chd
free. Tea, coffee & cake.**
A peaceful spot to enjoy tea and
cake! 2 contrasting gardens. This
delightful ⅓ acre cottage garden,
located within walking distance
of Southwell Minster, showcases
stunning displays of climbing roses/
wisteria and clematis in early summer.
Secluded areas at the back and
sides, framed by an arbour and birch
trees, offer a surprise with diverse
plantings, topiary, and espaliered
fruit trees. Wheelchairs will be able
to access the majority of the garden
across the lawn.

&♿ ✱ ☕ 🔊

5 CAPABILITY BARN
Gonalston Lane, Hoveringham,
NG14 7JH. Malcolm & Wendy
Fisher, www.capabilitybarn.com.
8m NE of Nottingham. A612 from
Nottingham through Lowdham. Take
1st R into Gonalston Ln. Garden
is 1m on L. **Sat 18, Sun 19 Apr
(11-4.30). Adm £5, chd free.
Home-made teas. Opening with
Hoveringham Gardens on Sun 7
June.**

Imaginatively planted large country
garden with something new
each year. April brings displays
of daffodils, hyacinths and tulips
along with erythroniums, brunneras
and primulas. Wisteria, magnolia,
rhododendrons and apple blossom
greet May/June. Established trees,
shrubs and shady paths. Large
vegetable/fruit gardens with orchard
and flower meadow completes the
picture. Last year of opening for the
NGS.

✱ ☕

6 CEDARWOOD
Burton Lane, Whatton in the Vale,
NG13 9EQ. Louise Bateman,
01949 850227, louise.bateman@
hotmail.co.uk. 3m E of Bingham off
A52. Cedar-clad bungalow situated
in the old part of Whatton in the Vale
just around the corner from local
church diagonally opp 5 Burton Ln.
**Sun 10 May (12-4.30). Adm £4,
chd free. Home-made teas at 5
Burton Lane opposite. Opening
with Whatton Gardens on Sun 5
July.** Visits also by arrangement
8 May to 30 Sept for groups of 10
to 25.
A 1,240m² plantswoman's garden
developed over the last 20 yrs,
planted for year-round colour. Plants
are chosen for their attractiveness
to wildlife as well as people. It inc
various mixed borders, a pond, alpine
crevice garden and woodland planting
(no lawn). Primula and Sempervivium
collection. Many species of bees live
here due to the variety of habitats
and flower type. Live music in the
afternoon.

✱ ☕

Our donation to the Army Benevolent Fund supported 776 individuals with horticultural related grants in 2025.

7 ◆ FELLEY PRIORY

Underwood, NG16 5FJ. The Brudenell Family, 01773 810230, michelle@felleypriory.co.uk, www.felleypriory.co.uk. *8m SW of Mansfield. Off A608 ½ m W M1 J27.* **For NGS: Sun 19 Apr (10-4). Adm £5, chd free. Light refreshments.** For other opening times and information, please phone, email or visit garden website.

Garden for all seasons with yew hedges and topiary, snowdrops, hellebores, herbaceous borders and rose garden. There are pergolas, a white garden, small arboretum and borders filled with unusual trees, shrubs, plants and bulbs. The grass edged pond is planted with primulas, bamboo, iris, roses and Eucomis. Bluebell woodland walk (depending on the weather). Orchard with extremely rare daffodils.

8 FLINTHAM HALL GARDENS

Flintham, Newark, NG23 5LE. Sir Robert & Lady Hildyard. *5m SW of Newark. Flintham is signposted off A46. Follow twisting road past cricket ground & sch. At next bend turn R towards church for ample parking.* **Sun 10 May (12-5). Adm £7.50, chd free. Tea in the village hall adjacent to the gardens.**

C18 walled gardens with rose borders and espaliered fruit trees. Lewis Wyatt aviary/folly. Range of trees and shrubs with a profusion of shrub and rambling roses. Views of Grade I listed house impressively remodelled in 1850s by TC Hine in the Italianate style with an adjoining conservatory said to be the finest of its type in England. Balustraded terrace with views across park and lake. A place of true romance. Please note neither the house nor the conservatory is open.

9 FLORAL MEDIA

Norwell Road, Caunton, Newark, NG23 6AQ. Mr & Mrs Steve Routledge, 07811 399113, info@floralmedia.co.uk, www.floralmedia.co.uk. *Take Norwell Rd from Caunton. Approx ½ m from Caunton on L.* **Sat 25 July (10-4). Adm £5, chd free. Tea, coffee & cake.**

A beautifully maintained country garden. Beds overflowing with a variety of roses, shrubs and flowers. A gravel/oriental garden, cutting gardens, vegetable beds, Flower Farm supplying British grown stems to florists/farm shops. Long sweeping borders surrounding the main lawn leading to the wildflower meadows where you will find an interesting garden retreat. A horticulturalist's haven. Often live music in the garden from a local folk group of musicians. A good range of plants available for sale. Full wheelchair access inc disabled WC.

Flintham Hall Gardens

10 GAUNTS HILL
Bestwood Lodge, Arnold, NG5 8NF. Nigel & Penny Lymn Rose, 07778 028010, penny@lymn.co.uk. *5m N of Nottingham. Take Bestwood Lodge Dr up to the Bestwood Lodge Hotel, then turn R & continue until you see a sign saying vehicle access to stables only. Then turn R down the drive through the gates.* **Visits by arrangement. Adm £5, chd free.** An historic Victorian kitchen garden with listed brick walls. Featuring roses, dahlias, a tropical border and a small orchard. Features also inc original Victorian circular pond, French fountain, two gazebos and a large greenhouse. Some gravel paths and lawns. There are some steps but these can be avoided.

11 GLEBE STEADING
Gonalston, Nottingham, NG14 7JA. Smita and Craig Jobling, 07966 298180. *1st R off A612 from Southwell into village, 1st house on R. Green outbuildings and barn conversion. Signs on Gate post and by roadside turn off. What3words app: sundial.unlimited. tramps.* **Sun 24, Mon 25 May (2-5). Adm £5, chd free. Home-made teas. Visits also by arrangement for groups of 10 to 20.**
Welcome to an award winning garden designed around a small natural pool with full brightly coloured borders and plants, mingled with grasses for a looser feel. Flowering perennials attract pollinators and are left standing tall. A hillside of 35 trees with coppice/orchard and small kitchen garden. A small stream runs down the slope with a botanical medicinal border. Small natural pool with a summerhouse.

12 HALL FARMHOUSE
Gonalston, Nottingham, NG14 7JA. Helen Pusey, 07963 343564, helenpusey377@gmail.com. *What3words app: stall.fountain. mankind. From Southwell A612 take 1st R sign for Gonalston, Garden 500yds on R or from Nottingham take A612 L into Gonalston at Xrds. Follow road round L bend, take R after the post box, Garden 100yds on L.* **Visits by arrangement 18 May to 23 Aug. Adm £5, chd free. Tea, coffee & cake.**
Recently acquired established Cottage Garden with 3 distinct areas.  Spring sees wisteria, rhododendron, iris, allium, ceanothus, bluebells and a range of bulbs. Summer brings colour from roses, echinacea and rudbeckia. There are herbaceous borders and mature trees inc paulownia tomentosa, magnolia, ancient yew and varieties of apple. An historic pond is being re-developed to attract wildlife. Wheelchair access to two areas with ramp available for third.

13 10 HARLAXTON DRIVE
Lenton, Nottingham, NG7 1JA. Jan Brazier, 07968 420046, jan-28b@hotmail.com. *W of Nottingham city centre. From Nottingham centre, follow Derby Rd signs (A52), past St Barnabas Cathedral & just after Canning Circus, take 3rd L. From M1 J25, take A52 Nottingham & after 7m, 5th R after Savoy cinema.* **Sun 26 July (11-4.30). Adm £5, chd free. Home-made teas. Prosecco and beer also available. Visits also by arrangement 18 May to 31 Aug for groups of 15 to 25.**
City centre oasis, a short walk from the centre of Nottingham. Garden presented on three levels, separated by steep steps with handrails. The top terrace overlooks a large koi pond surrounded by bog plants, marginals and herbaceous perennials. Seating areas on second terrace under mature beech trees. On third level, a summerhouse as well as a small pond and densely-planted borders. Free on-street parking on Sundays.

14 1 HIGHFIELD ROAD
Nuthall, Nottingham, NG16 1BQ. Richard & Sue Bold. *4 mins from J26 M1. 4m NW of Nottingham City. From J26 M1 take the A610 towards Notts. R lane at r'about, take turn-off to Horsendale. Follow road to Woodland Dr, then 2nd R is Highfield Rd.* **Sun 1, Sun 15 Feb (10-3.30). Adm £5, chd free. Light refreshments inc tea, coffee, fruit teas & squash. Bacon rolls, sausage rolls & home-made cakes will be available inc a gluten free option.**
Visit in Feb to see the collection of 700+ snowdrop varieties, with 300 varieties in the garden and many more in show benches. The spring garden has lots of colour with many rare and unusual plants - miniature narcissus, acers, aconites and hellebores A good selection of unusual pots and garden ornaments. Many snowdrop varieties and other plants available for sale.

15 NEW HILL TOP FARM
Balderton Lane, Coddington, Newark, NG24 2QE. Mr Peter Robinson. *Look out for a row of poplars on Balderton Ln ½ way between Balderton and Coddington. Leave A1 at Coddington exit near Newark onto A17 Eastwards. After 500yds go R onto Brownlow's Hill then R after 150yds onto Balderton Ln. Drive ½m to find Hill Top Farm.* **Sun 16 Aug (12.30-4.30). Adm £5, chd free. Tea, coffee & cake.**
Diversely planted garden taking advantage of a vista towards Lincolnshire hills, originally designed by a Chelsea Gold Award winner. Contains koi pond and bog garden within seasonally planted brick raised beds. Also a summer tropically inspired 'room', a winter garden, a newly planted apple orchard and fruit cage, a Victorian-style greenhouse, a Finnish barbecue Hut, arboretum, and fairy woodland. The forecourt is gravelled and there are two steps down onto a flat lawn, leading to a gently sloping back garden. A ramp can be made available.

16 HILL'S FARM
Edingley, NG22 8BU. John & Margaret Hill. *Short drive of 1m towards Edingley from The Old Vicarage turn R at brow of the hill as signed; tarmac farmyard parking. Adm tickets at The Old Vicarage in Halam.* **Sat 13 June (1-4.30). Combined adm with The Old Vicarage £7, chd free. Home-made teas at The Old Vicarage in Halam (next door village).**
Created with passion to produce a delightful walk. 6 acres of Nottinghamshire hay meadow carpeted with colourful wildflowers; ragged robin, yellow rattle, pyramidal orchids. 40+ acres of this mixed organic farm were taken out of arable production 2006 to create traditional hay meadows - hay taken in July is fed to the native beef shorthorn cattle. See some of the cows in adjoining fields. Talk from John Hill for his organic passion. Meat sold at Farm Shop.

17 **NEW** **1 HILL TOP COTTAGES**
Southwell Road, Thurgarton, Nottingham, NG14 7GP. Zoe & Gary Richmond-Dixon. *3.3m S of Southwell, located on N edge of village. Situated on main A612 Nottingham-Southwell Rd. Located just as you enter Thurgaton RHS from Southwell direction. Park at the edge of the village.* **Sun 28 June, Sun 2 Aug (12-4). Adm £4, chd free. Tea, coffee & cake.**
Long, narrow, exuberant cottage style garden, developed over the past 30+yrs. Many unusual and interesting plants, which have left no place for a lawn! Relaxing seating areas to take in this densely planted retreat. Topiary front garden, with contrasting cottage garden plants. Recently developed small 'secret' white garden - a real treat.

18 **78 HILTON ROAD**
Nottingham, NG3 6AP. Julie Pinches. *What3words app: silk.lamps.lion. From Nottingham turn R at the junc of B684 Woodborough Rd onto Porchester Rd then 3rd L to Hilton Rd. No.78 is located 300yds on R.* **Sat 20, Sun 21 June (1-5). Adm £5, chd free. Tea, coffee & cake.**
This steep contemporary garden, is set on a hill in leafy Mapperley, on the edge of Nottingham. The style of the garden echoes the clean lines of the 1960's house which is built in a split-level design. It has a series of angular raised beds with white retaining walls of various heights softened by the planting which is now established since the owners started the garden in 2012.

19 **HOLLINSIDE**
252 Diamond Avenue, Kirkby-in-Ashfield, Nottingham, NG17 7NA. Sue & Bob Chalkley. *1m E of Kirkby in Ashfield at the Xrds of the A611 & B6020. Please park away from the busy junction.* **Sun 14 June (1.30-4.30). Adm £4, chd free. Home-made teas.**
A garden filled with lovely flowering borders packed with mixed planting and a sense of abundance. Topiary and formal hedges contrast well with a wildflower meadow and pond. A Victorian style glasshouse is at the centre of the garden. There are secluded spots to sit and enjoy the numerous fragrant plants. The garden evolves each year so there's always something new to see. Majority of garden is suitable for wheelchairs. Disabled parking near house by prior arrangement - tel: 07901 954073

20 **HOME FARM HOUSE, 17 MAIN STREET**
Keyworth, Nottingham, NG12 5AA. Graham & Pippa Tinsley, 07780 672196, Graham_Tinsley@yahoo.co.uk, www.homefarmgarden.wordpress.com. *7m S of Nottingham. Follow signs for Keyworth from A60 or A606 & head for church. Garden about 50yds down Main St. Parking on the street or at Village Hall or Bunny Ln car parks.* **Sun 7 June (12-5). Combined adm with Rose Cottage £5, chd free. Home-made teas. Visits also by arrangement May to July for groups of up to 25.**
Large garden near village centre. The old farm garden has rose pergolas, mixed borders, 'Green Man' pond, rose garden and an orchard. The old paddock is now an ornamental wilderness of unmown grass with perennials and shrubs, a turf mound and wildlife ponds. Maturing oaks, cedars, beech and limes along with clipped hedges of laurel, yew and beech make this a garden of hidden places to explore. Interesting and unusual plants for sale by Piecemeal Plants (nursery@piecemealplants.co.uk).

21 **6 HOPE STREET**
Beeston, Nottingham, NG9 1DR. Elaine Liquorish, 07425 167080, eliquorish@outlook.com. *3m S of Nottingham. From M1 J25, A52 for Nottingham. After 2 r'abouts, turn R for Beeston at The Nurseryman (B6006). Beyond hill, turn R into Bramcote Dr. 3rd turn on L into Bramcote Rd, then immed R into Hope St.* **Sun 17 May (1.30-5). Adm £4, chd free. Tea, coffee & cake inc gluten or dairy free options. Visits also by arrangement 26 May to 4 July for groups of 6 to 20.**
A small garden packed with a wide variety of plants providing flower and foliage colour year-round. Collections of alpines, bulbs, mini, small and medium size hostas (60+), ferns, grasses, carnivorous plants, succulents, perennials, shrubs and trees. A pond and a greenhouse with subtropical plants. Troughs and pots. Home-made crafts. Shallow step into garden, into greenhouse and at rear.

GROUP OPENING

22 **HOVERINGHAM GARDENS**
Hoveringham, NG14 7JP. *Between Nottingham and Southwell. S of A612, 2m E Lowdham. All gardens marked. 3 entry roads. Park in village or signed field and walk (Tickets purchased at any garden - please retain for all separate entry checks).* **Sun 7 June (12-4.30). Combined adm £7, chd free. Tea, coffee & cake in the Village Hall. Pimms served at Hoveringham Hall (not Village Hall) 10% income given to NGS.**

CAPABILITY BARN
Malcolm & Wendy Fisher.
(See separate entry)

CHURCH HOUSE
Alex & Sue Allan.

NEW **HIGHFIELD HOUSE**
Mr T & Mrs S Wright.

HOVERINGHAM HALL
Helen and Edward Nall.

MYRTLE COTTAGE
Mrs Val Parker.

ROSE BANK
Nicholas and Clare Litherland.

WATER'S EDGE
Chris and Pauline Bulpitt.

Hoveringham is a pretty village by the River Trent which inc a church, a pub and Village Hall, where teas will be served. There are seven gardens, one of which contrasts well with an established beautiful NGS garden which opens in April separately. The two small group gardens are exquisitely planted and one inc a Bonsai collection. The three larger traditional gardens inc the rambling grounds of the Hall where Pimms will be served under elegant mature trees on the lawn, with sweeping views and a riverside property which boasts a rose garden and Orchid house - the large gardens inc herbaceous borders, rock gardens, ornamental trees, growing areas and greenhouses. There will be a plant stall and clog dancing arranged for 2.15pm and 3.30pm. Look out for the Victorian Orchard, Water Tower, Greenhouse, and possibly Nottinghamshire's oldest swing.

23 20 KIRKLINGTON ROAD
Southwell, NG25 0AY. Mr & Mrs George and Margaret Sharman. *9m W of Newark-on-Trent. Limited parking on Kirklington Rd. Car parks in Southwell are a 10 min walk away at most.* **Sun 31 May, Sun 6 Sept (1-5). Combined adm with Brook Cottage £7, chd free. Tea, coffee & cake at Brook Cottage.**
Developed over recent years, incorporating existing mature fruit trees, the garden contains a wide variety of mainly ornamental varieties of flowers and shrubs - intended and planned to provide a year-round display of vibrant colour for the observer from different viewing points. Lovingly tended by skillful owners, the garden is described as "beautiful" by all who see it. A number of seating areas and hard surfaces are incorporated for leisurely enjoyment of the wildlife-friendly environment. Afternoon tutorials on 'How to Take Cuttings at No Cost' available to those who'd be interested.

GROUP OPENING

24 MAPPERLEY GARDENS
147 Kenrick Road, Nottingham, NG3 6EY. Mr Alex Purdon. *Please park with consideration for residents. Additional parking is available at Mapperley Day Nursery on Westdale Ln NG3 6ES.* **Sun 24 May (10-4). Combined adm £7, chd free. Tea, coffee & cake at 147 Kenrick Road.**

147 KENRICK ROAD
Mr Alex Purdon.

30 NORTHCLIFFE AVENUE
Sallie Cooper.

46 NORTHCLIFFE AVENUE
Lesley Ings.

3 gardens which are open on Kenrick Road and Northcliffe Avenue. They show achievable ideas and projects for the average amateur gardener with a small plot. Garden owners will be on hand to discuss how they have developed their garden and a range of homegrown plants and home-made cakes will be available in support of the NGS. Additional parking is available at Mapperley Day Nursery on Westdale Lane. The organisers hope the event will grow annually, so if you live nearby and would like to get involved in the future, please speak to one of the garden owners.

GROUP OPENING

25 NORWELL GARDENS
Newark, NG23 6JX. *6m N of Newark. ½ way between Newark & Southwell. Off A1 at Cromwell turning, take Norwell Rd at bus shelter. Or off A616 take Caunton turn. Field parking on 28th at Foxhall Cl (opp pub) if dry.* **Sun 28 June (1-5). Evening opening Wed 1 July (6-8.30). Combined adm £6.50, chd free. Home-made teas in Village Hall (28 June) and Norwell Nurseries (1 July).**

ASH HOUSE
Fiona and Geoff Mountford.

NEW BRAMBLE BARN
Mr & Mrs John and Pauline Hobson.

CHERRY TREE HOUSE
Simon & Caroline Wyatt.

NEW IVY COTTAGE
Mr Colin Wright.

NEW NORTHWELL HOUSE
Liz Welsh and Chris Garnett.

NORWELL ALLOTMENTS / PARISH GARDENS
Norwell Parish Council.

◆ NORWELL NURSERIES
Andrew & Helen Ward.
(See separate entry)

PINFOLD COTTAGE
Mrs Pat Foulds.

ROSE COTTAGE
Mr Iain & Mrs Ann Gibson.

WILLOUGHBY HOUSE
Mrs Suzannah Edward-Jones.

This is the 30th year that Norwell has opened a range of different, very appealing gardens all making superb use of the beautiful backdrop of a quintessentially English countryside village. Inc a garden and nursery of national renown. To top it all there are a plethora of breathtaking village gardens showing the diversity that is achieved under the umbrella of a cottage garden description. WCs at hall, church and nurseries. The beautiful medieval church will feature a display of weddings past and present, its peaceful churchyard will be open for quiet contemplation. In celebration of the 30th opening, the village will have a scarecrow trail and gardening themed displays.

26 ◆ NORWELL NURSERIES
Woodhouse Road, Norwell, NG23 6JX. Andrew & Helen Ward, 01636 636337, wardha@aol.com, www.norwellnurseries.co.uk. *6m N of Newark ½ way between Newark & Southwell. Off A1 at Cromwell turning, take road to Norwell at bus stop. Or from A616 take Caunton turn.* **For NGS: Sun 17 May, Sun 27 Sept (2-5). Adm £4.50, chd free. Home-made teas. Opening with Norwell Gardens on Sun 28 June, Wed 1 July.** For other opening times and information, please phone, email or visit garden website.
Jewel box of over 3,000 different, beautiful and unusual plants sumptuously set out in a 1 acre plantsman's garden inc shady garden with woodland gems, cottage garden borders, alpine and scree areas. Pond with opulently planted margins. Extensive herbaceous borders and effervescent colour themed beds. Sand beds showcase Mediterranean, North American and alpine plants. Nationally renowned nursery open with over 2,000 different rare plants for sale. Autumn opening features UK's largest collection of hardy chrysanthemums for sale and the National Collection of Hardy Chrysanthemums. New borders inc the National Collection of Astrantias. Innovative sand beds. Grass paths, no wheelchair access to woodland paths.

27 NORWOOD PARK
Halam Road, Southwell, NG25 0PF. Sir John Starkey, 01636 302099, events@norwoodpark.co.uk, www.norwoodpark.co.uk. *NW edge of Southwell. From Southwell follow brown signs to Norwood Park & yellow NGS arrows.* **Sun 22 Feb (10-3). Adm £7, chd free. Tea, coffee & cake in the golf clubhouse.**
The grounds of Norwood Park date back to medieval times when they were part of a series of deer parks. A new garden on the south front of the C18 house was created in 2021 to showcase plants for all seasons. To the west a lime avenue lined with snowdrops and daffodils leads on to Mrs. Delaney's Path to the ornamental temple.

28 OASIS COMMUNITY GARDENS
2a Longfellow Drive, Kilton Estate, Worksop, S81 0DE. Steve Williams, 07795 194957, Stevemark126@hotmail.com, www.oasiscommunitycentre.org. Nottinghamshire. From Kilton Hill (leading to the Worksop hospital), take 1st exit to R (up hill) onto Kilton Cres, then 1st exit on R Longfellow Dr. Car Park off Dickens Rd (1st R). **Sat 4 Apr (10-3). Adm £4, chd free. Tea, coffee & cake in Oasis Garden Cafe. Visits also by arrangement 1 Mar to 1 Oct for groups of up to 30.**
Oasis Gardens is a community project transformed from abandoned field to an award winning garden. Managed by volunteers the gardens boast over 30 project areas and hosts many community events. Take a look in the Cactus Kingdom, the Liquorice Garden, the Aviaries, Pre-school play village, Wildlife Wonderland and the wonderful variety of trees, plants, seasonal flowers and shrubs. The Oasis Gardens hosts the first Liquorice Garden in Worksop for 100 yrs. The site hosts the 'Flowers for Life' project which is a therapeutic gardening project growing and selling cut flowers and floristry. There is disabled access from Longfellow Dr. From the town end there is a driveway after the 1st fence on the right next to house No.2.

29 NEW THE OLD STABLES
1a Church Road, Moorgreen, Nottingham, NG16 2AB. Sue & Stephen Rainford. *Approx 5m from M1 J26 or J27. From M1 J26, B600 to Moorgreen. Park in St Mary's Church car park or adjoining lay-by, then follow NGS signs to garden (approx 300 metres). Please do not park in adjacent Horse & Groom pub car park.* **Sun 14 June (12-5). Adm £5, chd free. Tea, coffee & cake.**
Four parts to the garden. Sunken seating area with steps and gravel path leading to lawn and beds of perennials, shrubs, trees, hostas, ferns, roses and box hedging. A gravel courtyard with grasses, climbing roses and perennials leading to the 'rose' garden with hellebores, cyclamens, hydrangeas, shrubs. The largely walled garden has raised beds, sunken greenhouse, cold frames and ornamental pond.

30 THE OLD VICARAGE
Halam Hill, Halam, NG22 8AX. Mrs Beverley Perks, 01636 812181, 07977 920833, perks.family@talk21.com. *1m W of Southwell, 1st house on L as entering Halam village. Please park diagonally into beech hedge on verge with speed interactive sign or in village. Please enter through top entrance. Building works - no admittance bottom entrance.* **Sat 16 May (1-4.30). Adm £6, chd free. Sat 13 June (1-4.30). Combined adm with Hill's Farm £7, chd free. Sun 19 July, Sun 23 Aug (1-4.30). Adm £6, chd free. Home-made teas at The Old Vicarage inc combined opening with Hill's Farm. Visits also by arrangement 18 May to 14 Aug for groups of 15+. Contact by phone.**
Visit this much-admired gem in probably, the last year of opening. Complementing the natural landscape, this 2 acre organic, hillside garden was designed with an artful eye for texture, colour, height, love of unusual plants and trees. Beautiful backdrop of woodland and open field. Bottom garden of 4 yrs, contrasts with sunken contemporary PassivHaus - (build in progress). Pond attracts diverse wildlife. Beautiful C12 St Michael's Church open 9-5pm is only a short walk across open field through attractively planted churchyard with rare C14 stained glass window. Top entrance gravel drive. Undulating levels as on a hillside. Plenty of help available.

31 OSSINGTON HOUSE
Moorhouse Road, Ossington, Newark, NG23 6LD. Georgina Denison. *10m N of Newark, 2m off A1. From A1 N take exit marked Carlton, Sutton-on-Trent, Weston etc. At T-junc turn L to Kneesall. Drive 2m to Ossington. Roadside parking on Main St and Moorhouse Rd.* **Sun 21 June (2-5). Adm £6, chd free. Home-made teas in The Hut, Ossington.**
Vicarage garden redesigned in 1960 and again in 2014. Chestnuts, lawns, formal beds, woodland walk, poolside planting, orchard. Terraces, yews, grasses. Ferns, herbaceous perennials, roses and kitchen garden. Disabled parking available in drive to Ossington House.

32 PARK FARM
Crink Lane, Southwell, NG25 0TJ. Ian & Vanessa Johnston, 01636 812195, v.johnston100@gmail.com. *1m SE of Southwell. From Southwell town centre go down Church St, turn R on to Fiskerton Rd & 200yds up hill turn R into Crink Ln. Park Farm is on 2nd bend.* **Sat 27 June (1-4.30). Adm £6, chd free. Tea, coffee & cake. Visits also by arrangement 27 Apr to 3 July for groups of 10+. Guided tours £1 extra pp. Groups welcome to bring their own refreshments.**
3 acres developed over 40 yrs, with a huge variety of trees, shrubs and perennials, many rare or unusual. Much maturity but lots of new planting. Long vibrant borders, rose arches, alpine area, wildflower meadow, pond, and woodland garden. Plant labelling adds interest for both experienced and new gardeners. The spectacular view of the Minster is one of the sights of Nottinghamshire.

33 THE POPLARS
Cotham Lane, Hawton, Newark, NG24 3RL. Ian Brownhill & Michael Hirschl, 07970 126318, ian@staghill.co.uk. *Hawton village is approx 2m S of Newark-on-Trent. Parking in All Saints' church car park (What3words app: single.rejoins. beaters). House is 2nd turning on the L past All Saints' church in Hawton village.* **Sun 7 June, Sun 9 Aug (2-5). Adm £5, chd free. Tea, coffee & cake. Visits also by arrangement 8 June to 31 July for groups of 10 to 25.**
Discover 1.3 acres of vibrant, reimagined gardens blending modern design with cottage charm. Wander through a series of distinct areas bursting with seasonal interest, ornamental grasses, roses, herbaceous perennials and fragrant Mediterranean herbs. Relax on the patio among olive trees and lavender while bees and butterflies dance around you. Highlights inc a rare Wollemi pine. The garden is wheelchair accessible (driveways, lawned areas) apart from the gravel patio.

NOTTINGHAMSHIRE 419

Wollaton Hall Walled Garden

34 RHUBARB FARM
Hardwick Street, Langwith, Mansfield, NG20 9DR. Rhubarb Farm, www.rhubarbfarm.co.uk. On NW border of Nottinghamshire in village of Nether Langwith. From A632 in Langwith, by bridge (single file traffic) turn up steep Devonshire Dr. Take 2nd L into Hardwick St. Rhubarb Farm at end. Parking on grass area to R of gates. **Thur 18 June, Thur 16 July, Thur 20 Aug (10-3). Adm £3, chd free.** Light refreshments in on-site café, made by Rhubarb Farm staff and team members.
Rhubarb Farm is a 2 acre horticultural charity and social enterprise supporting adults with various needs, inc those with learning disabilities, mental and physical health challenges, and individuals recovering from substance misuse. Features inc polytunnels, keder house, free-range hens, pigs, a donkey, and a Shetland pony - all contributing to a vibrant, inclusive environment. Meet and chat with farm staff and team members. The main path suitable for wheelchairs but bumpy. Not all the site is fully accessible. The cafe and one composting toilet is wheelchair accessible.

35 ROSE COTTAGE
81 Nottingham Road, Keyworth, Nottingham, NG12 5GS. Richard & Julie Fowkes, 01159 376489, richardfowkes@yahoo.co.uk. 7m S of Nottingham. Follow signs for Keyworth from A606. Garden (white cottage) on R 100yds after Sainsburys. From A60, follow Keyworth signs & turn L at church, garden is 400yds on L. **Sun 7 June (12-5). Combined adm with Home Farm House, 17 Main Street £5, chd free.** Visits also by arrangement 11 May to 17 Aug for groups of 8 to 30.
As featured in Garden News magazine, and described as "A heavily planted heaven", with colourful, wildlife-friendly plants. This is a small cottage garden with features such as a sedum roof, decked seating area, summerhouse and a new chicken run. A stream meanders down between ponds and bog areas. Art studio open. Paintings and crafts by Julie will be on sale. Plants available from local nurseryman.

36 160 SOUTHWELL ROAD WEST
Mansfield, NG18 4HB. Barrie & Lynne Jackson, 01623 750466, landbjackson@gmail.com. Approx $\frac{1}{2}$ way between Mansfield & Rainworth on A1691. From A60 towards Mansfield, turn R at T-lights up Berry Hill Ln. At the T-junc turn L. We are on the service road on the L. No parking on the service road. **Sun 3 May (1-4.30). Adm £4, chd free.** Home-made teas. Visits also by arrangement 27 Apr to 31 May for groups of 10+.
The $\frac{1}{3}$ acre garden was started from scratch in spring 2018. We have a range of growing environments inc a woodland garden, a border designed to cope with sun, large island beds, a vegetable garden and a wide range of climbers growing up a variety of structures. Our particular interests are Agapanthus, woodland plants inc Trillium, plus fruit and vegetables. A sloping site which is accessible with assistance. Some grass paths.

NOTTINGHAMSHIRE

GROUP OPENING

37 SUTTON BONINGTON GARDENS
Main Street, Sutton Bonington, Loughborough, LE12 5PE. *2m SE of Kegworth (M1 J24). 6m NW of Loughborough. From A6 Kegworth, past University of Nottingham Sutton Bonington campus. From Loughborough, A6 then A6006. From Nottingham, A60 then A6006.* **Sat 30, Sun 31 May (2-6). Combined adm £7, chd free. Tea, coffee & cake at Forge Cottage and 118 Main Street.**

FORGE COTTAGE
Judith & David Franklin.

118 MAIN STREET
Alistair Cameron & Shelley Nicholls.

PIECEMEAL
Mary Thomas.

All 3 gardens are located at the north end of the village, near St Michael's Church and just a few minutes' walk apart. Piecemeal has a tiny walled garden featuring a wide range of unusual shrubs, most in terracotta pots bordering narrow paths. Also climbers, perennials and even a few trees! Focus is on distinctive form, foliage shape and colour combination. Half-hardy and tender plants fill the conservatory. Forge Cottage garden, a little larger and reclaimed from a blacksmith's yard, has vibrant, curved herbaceous borders extending into a woodland path. 118 Main Street is a large garden with well established trees and varied planting as well as an orchard/wildflower meadow. Varied features inc Japanese-inspired seating area, redesigned patio with water feature, as well as more traditional established borders surrounding lawn and pond. Attractive greenhouse.

38 TITHE BARN
Potter Lane, Wellow, Newark, NG22 0EB. Andrew & Carrie Young, 01623 863327, andrew.young@ngs.org.uk. *12m NW of Newark on A616 about 1m SE from Ollerton on A616. Potter Ln is 1st L after the 30mph limit from Newark or 50yd past Maypole hotel on R from Ollerton, Tithe Barn is the long drive on R after churchyard and Lodge Farm Bungalow.* **Visits by arrangement 1 May to 10 July for groups of 15 to 30. Adm £5, chd free. Home-made teas.**

The grass-lined approach to this garden between yew hedges sets the tone to the wide sweeps of lawn and generous terrace. Herbaceous beds, irises, roses and rambling roses scrambling into fruit trees. The mature planting of shrubs and weeping trees enhances this pretty barn conversion on the edge of the Wellow Dyke. Woodland garden along the edge of Wellow Dyke open. Patio not accessible by wheelchair without assistance. Woodland path not wheelchair accessible.

39 UNIVERSITY PARK GARDENS
Nottingham, NG7 2RD. University of Nottingham, www.nottingham.ac.uk/estates/grounds. *Approx 4m SW of Nottingham city centre & opp Queens Medical Centre. Purchase adm tickets online or on arrival in the Millennium Garden (in centre of campus), signed from N & W entrances to University Park & within internal road network.* **Sat 8 Aug (12-3). Adm £5, chd free. Light refreshments in Pavilion Café in the Lakeside Arts Centre. Also light refreshments**

Rose Cottage

adjacent to Millennium Garden in Monica Partridge Building (& WC facilities). University Park has many beautiful gardens inc the award-winning Millennium Garden with its dazzling flower gardens, timed fountains and turf maze. Also the huge Lenton Firs rock garden, and the Jekyll garden. For the NGS, the Walled Garden is also open and alive with exotic plantings. In total, 300 acres of landscape and gardens. Newly-added in 2024 is a Memorial Woodland Walk. Picnic area, café, walking tours, information desk, workshop, accessible minibus within the campus takes visitors to feature gardens. Car parking next to the Millennium Garden where tickets and plants are for sale. Some gravel paths and steep slopes.

40 WAXWINGS & GOLDCREST
Lamins Lane, Bestwood Village, Nottingham, NG6 8WS. Rob & Jill Carlyle, 07495 934449, jill.carlyle@outlook.com, www.sustainablegarden.co.uk. *A60 N of Redhill r'about. Take Lamins Ln. Single track road, limited visibility & passing places. The properties are 1m along lane on L.* **Visits by arrangement 6 July to 19 July. Adm £8, chd free. Home-made teas.**
Two architect-designed eco-homes within six acres of stunning, tranquil gardens developed with biodiversity in mind inc meadows, orchard, woodland and vegetable gardens. Mature trees, lawns, ponds and stumpery. Home to a rich diversity of pollinators, birds and habitats. A haven for humans and wildlife. Gravel drive and paths which may be uneven and soft.

GROUP OPENING

41 WHATTON GARDENS
Whatton, Nottingham, NG13 9EQ. 01949 850942, jpfaulconbridge@hotmail.co.uk. *3m E of Bingham. The gardens are within a few mins walk of each other and close to church. Tickets will be for sale at 5 Burton Ln only. Follow NGS signs from A52.* **Sun 5 July (11-4). Combined adm £10, chd free. Mon 31 Aug (11-4). Combined adm £8, chd free. Light refreshments inc options for special dietary requirements.**

Visits also by arrangement for groups of 10 to 25. Bookings can be arranged to visit the gardens combined or individually.

5 BURTON LANE
Julia Faulconbridge
www.ayearinthegardenblog.wordpress.com
Open on all dates

CEDARWOOD
Louise Bateman.
Open on Sun 5 July
(See separate entry)

THE COTTAGE
Toni Aplin
Open on all dates

 LABURNUM COTTAGE
Mrs Hannah Bembridge.
Open on all dates

5 Burton Lane: Organic cottage garden which is productive, highly decorative and wildlife friendly. Full of colour and scent from Spring to Autumn. Large beds filled with over 600 varieties of plants with paths through. Also features kitchen garden, seating, gravel garden, pond, shade planting, pergola with grapevine, wildflower lawn. Cedarwood: A 1,240m^2 plantswoman's garden developed over the last 20 yrs. Planted for year-round colour and attractiveness to wildlife as well as people. Various mixed borders, pond, alpine crevice bed and woodland planting. The Cottage: Walled cottage garden with generous herbaceous borders, vine covered pergola, herb area, patios, vegetable patch, rose arbour. Laburnum Cottage: cottage garden with roses over the arbour and colourful perennials at the front. At the back, a serene white-themed courtyard features anemones, hydrangeas, and roses, leading to flower-filled borders, cutting beds, and raised vegetable beds. On site pottery and shop.

42 NEW **THE WILLOWS**
Smeath Road, Bolham, Retford, DN22 9JJ. Mr & Mrs Joanna Underdown, 07508 548635, thegathererflorist@outlook.com. *1m from Retford. A620 Gainsborough Rd from Retford, turn L onto Tiln Ln, signed 'A620 avoiding low bridge'. At sharp R bend, turn R onto Smeath Rd, 1st house on L, gravel drive.* **Visits by arrangement 4 May to 28 Sept for groups of up to 24. Adm £5, chd free. Tea, coffee & cake.**
1 acre perennial packed Cutting Garden with British blooms alongside, an established foliage border, supplying flower farm customers. Stepping through the rose arch find 'Blooming fields' a 2 acre plot with yet more perennials and seasonal annual varieties, available from spring onwards. Also home to Giddy Kippers Plants Nursery, selling an extensive range of perennials. Member of Flowers from the Farm Tallulah Rose trained florist.

43 NEW ◆ **WOLLATON HALL WALLED GARDEN**
Wollaton Road, Wollaton, Nottingham, NG8 2AD. Nottingham City Council, www.friendsofwollatonpark.org.uk/walled-garden. *4m W of Nottingham Wollaton Rd to Wollaton Hall & Deer Park, Wollaton, NG8 2AE. Enter via black door opp lower main car park. Parking charges apply. See www.wollatonhall.org.uk/visit for details.. What3words app: from.length.moon.* **For NGS: Sun 16 Aug (11-4). Adm £5, chd free. Home-made teas in Courtyard.** For other opening times and information, please visit garden website.
Tours of Wollaton Hall's Walled Garden near Nottingham give visitors an opportunity to see the restored 4 acre site with 12ft high walls and Head Gardener's Cottage built between 1783 and 1788. The Hall is an Elizabethan country house of the 1580s standing on a hill in Wollaton Park. The surrounding parkland has a herd of deer, and is regularly used for large-scale outdoor events. Evidence of C18 heated walls. Original bothies and potting sheds under renovation. Some uneven ground.

OXFORDSHIRE

VOLUNTEERS

County Organiser
Marina Hamilton-Baillie
07748 158765
marina.hamilton-baillie@ngs.org.uk

Treasurer
Tom Hamilton-Baillie
07973 571065
tom.hamilton-baillie@ngs.org.uk

Talks Co-Ordinator
Priscilla Frost 01608 811818
info@oxconf.co.uk

Dr David Edwards
07973 129473
drdavidedwards@hotmail.co.uk

Social Media- Instagram
Dr Jill Edwards 07971 201352
jill.edwards@ngs.org.uk

Social Media & Marketing
John Fleming 07710 578174
john.fleming@ngs.org.uk

Assistant County Organisers
Lynn Baldwin 01608 642754
elynnbaldwin@gmail.com

Dr David Edwards (as above)

Dr Jill Edwards (as above)

Sarah Fernback 07500 009313
sarah.fernback@ngs.org.uk

Viccy Fleming 07943 253075
viccy.fleming@ngs.org.uk

Claire & Dave Parker 07971 621270
claire.parker@ngs.org.uk

Lyn Sanders 01865 739486
sandersc4@hotmail.com

Paul Youngson 07946 273902
paulyoungson48@gmail.com

@NGSOxfordshire
@ngs_oxfordshire

OPENING DATES

All entries subject to change.
For latest information check
www.ngs.org.uk
Map locator numbers are
shown to the right of each
garden name.

February

Snowdrop Openings
Sunday 8th
23 Hid's Copse Road 27
6 High Street 28
Sunday 15th
Lime Close 33

March
Saturday 28th
Claridges Barn 14
Sunday 29th
Ashbrook House 1
Claridges Barn 14

April
Friday 3rd
Sarsden Glebe 54
Monday 6th
Kencot Gardens 30
Sunday 12th
3 Halliday Lane 25
Magdalen College 35
50-52 North Hinksey Lane 42
Saturday 25th
Central North Oxford Gardens 11
Sunday 26th
♦ Broughton Grange 8
Central North Oxford Gardens 11

May
Friday 1st
Midsummer House 39
Sunday 3rd
Bolters Farm 5
Kings Cottage 31
Monday 4th
Bolters Farm 5

Kings Cottage 31
Saturday 9th
Claridges Barn 14
Sunday 10th
♦ Blenheim Palace 4
Claridges Barn 14
Sunday 17th
Broughton Poggs & Filkins
Gardens 9
Lime Close 33
The Manor Garden 36
The Priory, Charlbury 49
Friday 22nd
61 Cornish Road 15
Sunday 24th
Barton Abbey 3
Old Boars Hill Gardens 44
Upper Bolney House 61
Sunday 31st
Failford 20
NEW The Old Rectory, Churchill 46
116 Oxford Road 47
Wheatley Manor 66

June
Thursday 4th
♦ Stonor Park 57
Friday 5th
Claridges Barn 14
Midsummer House 39
Sandys House 53
Saturday 6th
Claridges Barn 14
Sandys House 53
Sunday 7th
Claridges Barn 14
Cumnor Village Gardens 16
Friars Court 22
Middleton Cheney Gardens 38
Mill House Garden 41
9 Rawlinson Road 50
11 Rawlinson Road 51
Sandys House 53
Tythe Barn 60
West Oxford Gardens 64
Sunday 14th
Brize Norton Gardens 6
Langford Gardens 32
Sibford Gardens 55
NEW Vernon Cottage 62
Friday 19th
61 Cornish Road 15

Saturday 20th
Stow Cottage Arboretum &
Garden 58

Sunday 21st
♦ Broughton Castle 7
♦ Broughton Grange 8
Whitehill Farm 67

Sunday 28th
NEW 93 Church Road 13

July

Sunday 5th
Midsummer House 39
North Moreton Gardens 43
Woolstone Mill House 68

Friday 17th
61 Cornish Road 15

Sunday 26th
♦ Broughton Grange 8
Merton College Oxford Fellows'
Garden 37

August

Sunday 2nd
Lincoln College 34
Trinity College 59

Friday 7th
Midsummer House 39

Sunday 16th
♦ Broughton Castle 7

Friday 21st
61 Cornish Road 15

Saturday 22nd
Aston Pottery 2

Sunday 23rd
Aston Pottery 2

September

Friday 4th
Midsummer House 39
Woolstone Mill House 68

Sunday 6th
Ham Court 26

Sunday 27th
50 Plantation Road 48

October

Friday 2nd
Midsummer House 39

November

Thursday 5th
♦ Waterperry Gardens 63

Thursday 12th
♦ Waterperry Gardens 63

By Arrangement

Arrange a personalised garden visit with your club, or group of friends, on a date to suit you. See individual garden entries for full details.

Bolters Farm 5
Bush House 10
Carter's Yard (Sibford Gardens) 55
Chivel Farm 12
Claridges Barn 14
61 Cornish Road 15
Dean Manor 17
103 Dene Road 18
Denton House 19
Failford 20
Foxington 21
The Grange 23
Greenfield Farm 24
Home Close, Garsington 29
Home Close, Sibford Ferris (Sibford Gardens) 55
Kings Cottage 31
Lime Close 33
Mill Barn 40
The Old Rectory, Albury 45
116 Oxford Road 47
9 Rawlinson Road 50
Rectory Farmhouse 52
South Newington House 56
Uplands (Old Boars Hill Gardens) 44
Westwell Manor 65
Whitehill Farm 67

Broughton Grange

THE GARDENS

1 ASHBROOK HOUSE
Westbrook Street, Blewbury, OX11 9QA. Mr & Mrs S A Barrett. *4m SE of Didcot. Turn off A417 in Blewbury into Westbrook St. 1st house on R. Follow yellow signs for parking in Boham's Rd at W entrance to the village.* **Sun 29 May (2-5.30). Adm £5, chd free. Home-made teas.**
The garden where Kenneth Grahame read Wind in the Willows to local children and where he took inspiration for his description of the oak doors to Badger's House. Come and see, you may catch a glimpse of Toad and friends in this 3½ acre chalk and water garden, in a beautiful spring line village. In spring the banks are a mass of daffodils and other bulbs.

2 ASTON POTTERY
Bampton Road, Aston, Bampton, OX18 2BT. Mr Stephen Baughan, www.astonpottery.co.uk. *4m S of Witney. On the B4449 between Bampton & Standlake.* **Sat 22 Aug (9.30-5); Sun 23 Aug (10.30-5). Adm £5, chd free.**
6 stunning borders set around Aston Pottery. 72 metre double hornbeam border full of riotous perennials. 80 metre long hot bank of alstroemeria, salvias, echinacea and kniphofia. Quadruple dahlia border with over 600 dahlias, grasses and asters. Tropical garden with bananas, cannas and ricinus. Finally, 80 metres of 120 different annuals planted in four giant successive waves of over 6000 plants. The gardens are fully accessible for wheelchair users. Please note that the paths consist of a mixture of paving, tarmac and grass.

3 BARTON ABBEY
Steeple Barton, OX25 4QS. Mr & Mrs P Fleming. *8m E of Chipping Norton. On B4030, ½ m from junc of A4260 & B4030.* **Sun 24 May (2-5). Adm £5, chd free. Tea, coffee & cake.**
15 acre garden with views from house (not open) across sweeping lawns and picturesque lake. Walled garden with colourful herbaceous borders, separated by established yew hedges and espalier fruit, contrasts with more informal woodland garden paths

with vistas of specimen trees and meadows. Working glasshouses and fine display of fruit and vegetables.

4 ◆ BLENHEIM PALACE
Woodstock, OX20 1UL. His Grace the Duke of Marlborough, 01993 810530, customerservice@blenheimpalace.com, www.blenheimpalace.com. *8m N of Oxford. Busses: Stagecoach S3 and 7 from Oxford city centre. S3 leaves from Oxford train stn. S3 & Bus 7 both pick up on Magdalen St. Timetables www.stagecoachbus.com.* **For NGS: Sun 10 May (10-4). Adm £10, chd £7.** For other opening times and information, please phone, email or visit garden website.
Created over the centuries by esteemed garden designers such as Henry Wise and Achille Duchêne, the Formal Gardens reflect a journey through the styles of the ages. Explore the majestic Water Terraces, the Duke's Private Italian Garden, the tranquil Secret Garden, the Churchill Memorial Garden, and the beautifully delicate Rose Garden. Admire Vanbrugh's Grand Bridge, the focal point of over 2,000 acres of landscaped parkland. Ride the miniature train to the Walled Garden where you will find the Marlborough Maze, Butterfly House, and Blenheim Palace Adventure Play. Wheelchair access with some gravel paths, uneven terrain and slopes. Dogs permitted on short leads in the Parkland and East Courtyard only.

5 BOLTERS FARM
Pudlicote Lane, Chilson, Chipping Norton, OX7 3HU. Robert & Mandy Cooper, 07778 476517, art@amandacooper.co.uk. *Centre of Chilson village. On arrival in the hamlet of Chilson, coming off the B4437, last in an old row of cottages on R. Please drive past following directions to signposted field (free parking on What3words app: lonely.fonts.piglets).* **Sun 3, Mon 4 May (1-5). Combined adm with Kings Cottage £8, chd free. Tea, coffee & cake inc gluten free options.** Visits also by arrangement Mar to Sept for groups of 10 to 50. Donation to Action Syria.
A cherished old cottage garden restored over the last 18 yrs. Tumbly moss covered walls and sloping lawns down to a stream with natural

planting and quirky characterful moments. Please park in the signposted village field. Running water, weeping willows, sloping lawns, wild area, some unusual planting and an enormous sense of peace.

GROUP OPENING

6 BRIZE NORTON GARDENS
Brize Norton, OX18 3LY. www.bncommunity.org/ngs. *3m SW of Witney. Brize Norton Village, S of A40, between Witney & Burford. Parking at Elderbank Hall. Coaches welcome with plenty of parking nearby. Tickets & maps available at Elderbank Hall & at each garden.* **Sun 14 June (1-6). Combined adm £7.50, chd free. Tea, coffee & cake in Elderbank Village Hall.**

BARNSTABLE HOUSE
Mr & Mrs P Butcher.

17 CHICHESTER PLACE
Mr & Mrs D Howard.

CLUMBER
Mr & Mrs S Hawkins.

2 ELM GROVE
Rod and Sonja Coles.

MILLSTONE
Bev & Phil Tyrell.

PAINSWICK HOUSE
Mr & Mrs T Gush.

PILGRIMS
Paul and Pamela Butler.

ROSE COTTAGE
Brenda & Brian Trott.

95 STATION ROAD
Mr & Mrs P A Timms.

STONE COTTAGE
Mr & Mrs K Humphris.

Brize Norton is a lovely Domesday village on the edge of the Cotswolds and by opening its gardens you have an opportunity to wander around this village from garden to garden. Plenty of gardens for you to walk around in with many seating areas to sit and relax and enjoy the gardens and the village. Each garden is different and has its own unique diversity; some with water features, others with their own vegetable gardens, but all of them have much to enjoy and maybe you'll take away an idea or two for your own garden. Come along and see for yourself. Enjoy tea and cake at the Elderbank Hall where there is ample parking for you to visit the gardens around the village. Plants for sale at individual gardens. A Flower Festival will take place in the Brize Norton St Britius Church. Partial wheelchair access to some gardens.

7 ♦ BROUGHTON CASTLE
Banbury, OX15 5EB. Martin Fiennes, 01295 276070, info@broughtoncastle.com, www.broughtoncastle.com. 2½ m SW of Banbury. On Shipston-on-Stour road (B4035). **For NGS: Sun 21 June (1.30-5), open nearby Broughton Grange. Sun 16 Aug (1.30-5). Adm £8, chd £8. Tea Room open 1.30-5pm.** For other opening times and information, please phone, email or visit garden website.
1 acre; shrubs, herbaceous borders, walled garden, roses, climbers seen against background of C14-C16 castle surrounded by moat in open parkland. House also open (additional charge).

8 ♦ BROUGHTON GRANGE
Wykham Lane, Broughton, Banbury, OX15 5DS. Sir Stephen Hester, 07791 747371, enquiries@broughtongrange.com, www.broughtongrange.com. ¼ m out of village. From Banbury take B4035 to Broughton. Turn L at Saye & Sele Arms Pub up Wykham Ln (one way). Follow road out of village for ¼ m. Entrance on R. **For NGS: Sun 26 Apr, Sun 21 June, Sun 26 July (10-4.30). Adm £14, chd free.** For other opening times and information, please phone, email or visit garden website.
An impressive 25 acres of gardens and light woodland in an attractive Oxfordshire setting. The centrepiece is a large terraced walled garden created by Tom Stuart-Smith in 2001. Vision has been used to blend the gardens into the countryside. Good early displays of bulbs followed by outstanding herbaceous planting in summer. Formal and informal areas combine to make this a special site inc newly laid arboretum with many ongoing projects.

GROUP OPENING

9 BROUGHTON POGGS & FILKINS GARDENS
Filkins, nr Lechlade, GL7 3JH. www.filkins.org.uk. *3m N of Lechlade. 5m S of Burford. Just off A361 between Burford & Lechlade on the B4477.* **Sun 17 May (2-6). Combined adm £10, chd free. Tea, coffee & cake at Filkins Village Hall.**

ANSTRUTHER
Nicky & Stephen Evans.
BROUGHTON POGGS MILL
Charlie & Avril Payne.
THE CORN BARN
Ms Alexis Thompson.
THE FIELD HOUSE
Peter & Sheila Gray.
FILKINS ALLOTMENTS
FILKINS HALL
LITTLE PEACOCKS
Colvin & Moggridge.
MERCHANTS COTTAGE
Paul & Corina Floyd.

Tythe Barn

PEACOCK FARMHOUSE
Pauline & Peter Care.

PIGEON COTTAGE
Rupert Waterson.

PIP COTTAGE
G B Woodin.

THE TALLOT
Ms M Swann & Mr D Stowell.

TAYLOR COTTAGE
Mrs Ronnie Bailey.

12 gardens and flourishing allotments in these beautiful and vibrant Cotswold stone twin villages. Scale and character vary from the grand landscape setting of Filkins Hall, to the small but action packed Pigeon Cottage, Taylor Cottage and Corn Barn. Broughton Poggs Mill has a rushing mill stream with an exciting bridge; Pip Cottage combines topiary, box hedges and a fine rural view. In these and the other equally exciting and varied gardens horticultural interest abounds. Features inc Swinford Museum of Cotswolds tools and artefacts, and Cotswold Woollen Weavers and Saxon church will be open. Many gardens have gravel driveways, but most are suitable for wheelchair access. Most gardens welcome dogs on leads.

10 BUSH HOUSE
Wigginton Road, South Newington, Banbury, OX15 4JR.
Mr John Ainley, 07503 361050,
rojoainley@btinternet.com. *In S Newington on A361 from Banbury to Chipping Norton, take 1st R to Wigginton, Bush House 1st house on the L in Wigginton Rd.* **Visits by arrangement Mar to Sept. Adm inc visits to South Newington House and Bush House with refreshments. Adm £12, chd free. Light refreshments at South Newington House.**
Set in eight acres, over 13 years, a two acre garden has emerged. Herbaceous borders partner dual level ponds and stream. The terrace leads to a walled parterre framed by roses and wisteria. The 'wildflower meadow' (sown 2021) orchard is screened by rose and vine covered wrought iron trellis. Kitchen gardens, greenhouses and fruit cage provide organically grown produce. Stream and interconnecting ponds. Walled parterre and knot garden. 1000 native broadleaved trees planted 2006, 2011 and 2014. Gravel drive, a few

small steps, and two gentle grass slopes on either side of the garden.

GROUP OPENING

11 CENTRAL NORTH OXFORD GARDENS
50 Plantation Road, Oxford, OX2 6HY. *City gardens situated in parallel streets: Leckford Rd & Plantation Rd. Access from Kingston Rd or Woodstock Rd. Parking in Leckford Rd, Warnborough Rd & Farndon Rd.* **Sat 25 Apr (2-5). Combined adm £8, chd free. Sun 26 Apr (2-5). Combined adm £9, chd free. Tea, coffee & cake at 38 Leckford Rd with plant sale.**

38 LECKFORD ROAD
Dinah Adams.
Open on Sun 26 Apr

41 LECKFORD ROAD
Liz & Mark Jennings.
Open on all dates

50 PLANTATION ROAD
Philippa Scoones.
Open on all dates
(See separate entry)

Three very different town gardens. 50 Plantation Road is a surprisingly wide and deep garden in two parts: lovely trees and planting, lots of pots, many varieties of tulips, an unusual water feature and stepping stones. 41 Leckford Road is an exquisitely designed garden for entertaining and relaxing. Hedge of pleached hornbeams is a foreground for lovely spring planting. Every area has vegetation suited to its microclimate. 38 Leckford Road is a protected long walled garden with varying levels of shade and many unusual and rare plants and mature trees.

12 CHIVEL FARM
Heythrop, OX7 5TR. John & Rosalind Sword, 01608 683227, rosalind.sword@btinternet.com.
4m E of Chipping Norton. Off A361 or A44. Parking at Chivel Farm.
Visits by arrangement 12 Jan to 28 Sept for groups of 10+. Light refreshments.
Beautifully designed country garden with extensive views, designed for continuous interest that is always evolving. Colour schemed borders with many unusual trees, shrubs and herbaceous plants. Small formal white garden and a conservatory.

13  93 CHURCH ROAD
Sandford-on-Thames, Oxford, OX4 4YA. Julie Anderson & Matthew Wilkinson. *S of Oxford City in village off the A4074. Just past the Kings Arms pub at Sandford-on-Thames lock at end of Church Rd. Ignore private road sign. Parking (to pay unless also pub customer) in pub car park nearby or visitor parking areas.* **Sun 28 June (2-5.30). Adm £6, chd free. Tea, coffee & cake. Cold drinks.**
Large garden with different areas. A formal garden set to lawn with mixed shrub and perennial borders, a pond, fruit and vegetable areas, chicken coop, natural woodland area beyond the formal garden leading to bog gardens and a wooden walkway to steps up a short but steep terraced bank to an open area with fruit trees and a further vegetable garden. Wheelchair access in formal gardens and woodland.

---

70 inpatients and their families are being supported at the newly opened Horatio's Garden Northern Ireland, thanks to the National Garden Scheme donations.

4 CLARIDGES BARN
Charlbury Road, Chipping Norton, OX7 5XG. Drs David & Jill Edwards, 07973 129473, drdavidedwards@hotmail.co.uk. *3m SE of Chipping Norton. Take B4026 from Chipping Norton to Charlbury after 3m turn R to Dean, 200 metres on the R. Please park on the verge.* **Sat 28, Sun 29 Mar, Sat 9, Sun 10 May (11-5). Adm £6, chd free. Fri 5, Sat 6, Sun 7 June (11-5). Combined adm with Sandys House £8, chd free. Light refreshments inc coffee & light lunches.** Visits also by arrangement. Full size coaches welcome. Discuss refreshments when booking.

3½ acres of family garden, wood and meadow hewn from a barley field on limestone brash. Situated on top of the Cotswolds, it is open to all weathers, but rewarding views and dog walking opportunities on hand. Large vegetable, fruit and cutting garden, wildlife pond and seven cedar greenhouses, using organic principles wherever possible, all loved by rabbits, deer and squirrel. Herbaceous borders and woodland gardens with gravel and flagged paths, divided by stone walls. Claridges Barn dates back to the 1600s, the cottage 1860s, converted about 36 yrs ago. Seven cedar greenhouses, wildlife pond and garden. Mainly level site with flagstone and gravel paths, flat lawns and some uneven steps. The gravel driveway can be hard work for wheelchair users.

5 61 CORNISH ROAD
Chipping Norton, OX7 5JX. Matthias Gentet, darcydante@gmail.com. *Towards Churchill on the B4450, take last L before leaving Chipping Norton. Go up on Hailey Rd then 1st R turn into Cornish Rd then down 500 metres. Garden is on the RHS.* **Fri 22 May, Fri 19 June, Fri 17 July, Fri 21 Aug (10-1). Adm £4, chd free. Pre-booking essential, please visit www.ngs.org.uk for information & booking.** Visits also by arrangement 22 May to 21 Aug for groups of up to 6.

Small residential garden created from scratch, consisting of shrubs, herbaceous/perennials and rose beds and borders with over 60 roses (shrubs, standards and climbers), wisteria, soft fruits and fruit trees,

raised beds, all of which with the aim of accommodating as many varieties of plants as possible; composting bins and a lean-to greenhouse.

»))

GROUP OPENING

6 CUMNOR VILLAGE GARDENS
Cumnor, Oxford, OX2 9QF. *4m W of central Oxford. From A420, exit for Cumnor & follow B4017 into the village. Parking on road & side roads, behind PO or behind village hall in Leys Rd.* **Sun 7 June (2-6). Combined adm £5, chd free. Home-made teas in United Reformed Church Hall, Leys Road.**

6 HIGH STREET
Dr Dianne & Prof Keith Gull.
(See separate entry)

19 HIGH STREET
Janet Cross.

10 LEYS ROAD
Penny & Nick Bingham.

Three contrasting gardens. 10 Leys Rd is a long, narrow, mature garden with four distinct areas, many unusual shrubs, perennials, grasses, ferns and exotics plus two small adjoining allotments. 19 High Street is a courtyard garden, cleverly planted for extremes of light and shade. 6 High Street is a thatched cottage with surrounding gardens overlooking meadows. It has old apple trees underplanted with ferns, a wildlife pond and many unusual plants.

7 DEAN MANOR
Dean, Chipping Norton, OX7 3LD. Mr & Mrs Johnny Hornby, pippa.hornby@gmail.com. *In Dean, 3m SE of Chipping Norton. Leaving Chipping Norton follow the B4026 for 2m. At the sharp bend, take the 2nd turning on R to Dean (there is no road sign). Follow the lane for 1m, Dean Manor is R at the next junction.* **Visits by arrangement.**

The gardens at Dean Manor cover approx six acres. Stone walls are home to an abundant and varied selection of climbing/rambling roses, clematis and hydrangeas. The formal gardens inc complex yew hedging and herbaceous borders, kitchen and cutting garden, areas

of wildflower meadow, an orchard and water gardens make up areas around the house. A spectacular new kitchen and cutting garden designed by Frances Rasch complete with new large glasshouse is currently in development, offering the opportunity to witness the beginnings of a major new chapter in the garden's rich history.

8 103 DENE ROAD
Headington, Oxford, OX3 7EQ. Steve & Mary Woolliams, 07778 617616, stevewoolliams@gmail.com. *S Headington, nr Nuffield. Dene Rd accessed from The Slade from the N, or from Hollow Way from the S. Both access roads are B4495. Garden on sharp bend.* **Visits by arrangement 11 Apr to 12 Sept for groups of up to 12. Adm £5, chd free. Tea, coffee & cake.**

A surprising eco-friendly garden with borrowed view over the Lye Valley Nature Reserve. Lawns, a wildflower meadow, pond and large kitchen garden are inc in a downhill sloping 60ft x 120ft site. Fruit trees, soft fruit and mixed borders of shrubs, hardy perennials, grasses and bulbs, designed for seasonal colour. This garden has been noted for its wealth of wildlife inc a variety of birds, butterflies and other insects such as the rare Brown Hairstreak butterfly, the rare Currant Clearwing moth and the Grizzled Skipper.

9 DENTON HOUSE
Denton, Oxford, OX44 9JF. Mr & Mrs Luke, 01865 874440, waveneyluke28@gmail.com. *Nr Oxford. In a valley between Garsington & Cuddesdon.* **Visits by arrangement Feb to Oct for groups of up to 30. Adm £6, chd free. Home-made teas.**

Large walled garden surrounds a Georgian mansion (not open) with shaded areas, walks, topiary and many interesting mature trees, large lawns, herbaceous borders and rose beds. The windows in the wall were taken in 1864 from Brasenose College Chapel and Library. Wild garden and a further walled fruit garden.

20 FAILFORD
118 Oxford Road, Abingdon, OX14 2AG. Miss R Aylward, 01235 523925, aylwardsdooz@hotmail.co.uk. *North Abingdon. Entrance is via 116 Oxford Rd. No. 118 is on LHS of Oxford Rd after Picklers Hill when coming from Abingdon Town, or on RHS when approaching from the A34 Abingdon N.* **Sun 31 May (11-4.30). Combined adm with 116 Oxford Road £6, chd free. Home-made teas.** Visits also by arrangement in June for groups of 10+. Afternoon and evening visits are available, with optional refreshments.

This town garden is divided into rooms both formal and informal. It changes every year. Features inc walkways through shaded areas, arches, a beach, grasses, fernery, roses, topiaries, acers, hostas and heucheras. Be inspired by the wide variety of planting, many unusual and quirky features, all within an area 570sq ft.

21 FOXINGTON
Britwell Salome, Watlington, OX49 5LG. Mrs Mary Roadnight, 01491 612418, mary@foxington.co.uk. *1m from Watlington. What3words app: initiates.goodness.restored. On B4009 at Red Lion Pub take turning to Britwell Hill. After 350yds turn into drive on L.* **Visits by arrangement May to Oct for groups of 10 to 30. Adm £11, chd free. Home-made teas inc in adm price. Special dietary options by prior request.**

Stunning views to the Chiltern Hills provide a wonderful setting for this impressive garden remodelled in 2009. Patio, heather and gravel gardens enjoy this view, whilst the back and vegetable gardens are more enclosed. A very large apple tree blew down in the spring of 2022 and has been replaced by a summerhouse. This has resulted in a major revision of the planting. There is a flock of white doves. Well behaved dogs are welcome but they must be kept on a lead at all times as there are many wild animals in the garden. Wildflower meadow, wood and neighbouring fields. Wheelchair access throughout the garden on level paths with no steps.

22 FRIARS COURT
Clanfield, OX18 2SU. Charles Willmer, www.friarscourt.com. *4m N of Faringdon. On A4095 Faringdon to Witney road. ½m S of Clanfield. What3words app: burst.courts.from.* **Sun 7 June (2-5). Adm £4, chd free. Cream teas.**

Three acres of formal and informal gardens, enclosed by the remaining arms of a C16 moat, surround the C17 Cotswold stone house. Features inc bridges, lawns, rose garden, water-lily and reed ponds, living willow tunnels, a newly created Labyrinth Garden. The gardens are level, a path goes around part of the grounds. Access to the museum is over gravel.

The Old School, Langford Gardens

23 THE GRANGE
1 Berrick Road, Chalgrove, OX44 7RQ. **Mrs Vicky Farren**, 07976 806161, vickyfarren@mac.com, www.thegrangegardener.com. *12m E of Oxford & 4m from Watlington, off B480. The entrance to The Grange is on Monument Rd, at the grass triangle between Berrick Rd & Monument Rd, by the pedestrian crossing. GPS is not reliable in the final 200yds.* **Visits by arrangement 8 June to 16 Oct for groups of 12 to 35. Tea, coffee & cake on request at booking.**
11 acres of gardens inc herbaceous borders and a large expanse of prairie with many grasses and a wildflower meadow. There is a lake with bridges and a planted island, a dry river bed and a labyrinth. A brook runs through the garden with a further pond, arboretum, old orchard and partly walled vegetable garden. Partial wheelchair access on many grass paths.

24 GREENFIELD FARM
Christmas Common, nr Watlington, OX49 5HG. **Andrew & Jane Ingram**, 01491 612434, andrew@andrewbingram.com. *4m from J5 M40, 7m from Henley. J5 M40, A40 towards Oxford for ½m, turn L signed Christmas Common. ¾m past Fox & Hounds Pub, turn L at Tree Barn sign.* **Visits by arrangement 5 May to 20 Sept for groups of 5 to 30. Adm £5, chd free.**
10 acre wildflower meadow surrounded by woodland, established 29 yrs ago under the Countryside Stewardship Scheme. Traditional Chiltern chalkland meadow in beautiful peaceful setting with over 100 species of perennial wildflowers, grasses and ten species of orchids. ½ mile walk from parking area to meadow. Opportunity to return via typical Chiltern beechwood.

25 3 HALLIDAY LANE
Oxford, OX2 0FG. **John and Viccy Fleming.** *Off North Hinksey Ln. Take Botley Interchange off A34. At McDonald's t-lights turn R then L into N Hinksey Ln. On street parking further down. (Halliday Ln is private with No Parking).* **Sun 12 Apr (2-5.30). Combined adm with 50-52 North Hinksey Lane £5, chd free. Home-made teas.**
Small town garden of a new house (not open) recently laid out on the site of old riding stables. Crevice garden at the front planted with more than 400 different alpine plants, a rear garden planted with a rich collection of bulbs, shrubs and perennials for year-round interest, and a narrow strip at the side with ferns, fruit, vegetables and a greenhouse for propagation.

26 HAM COURT
Ham Court Farm, Weald, Bampton, OX18 2HG. **Matthew Rice.** *Drive through the village towards Clanfield. The drive is on the R, exactly opp Weald St.* **Sun 6 Sept (11-4). Adm £7.50, chd free. Home-made teas.**
Several acres of garden, orchard and paddock surround the last gatehouse fragment of the medieval Bampton Castle, partially moated with walled kitchen garden, a productive greenhouse and farmyard with a variety of farm animals. This project begun by Emma Bridgewater and Matthew Rice is 14 yrs old so now 'bearing fruit' but will always be in a state of permanent change. Delicious teas and vintage tractors.

27 23 HID'S COPSE ROAD
Oxford, OX2 9JJ. **Blair Eldridge.** *W of central Oxford, ½ way up Cumnor Hill. Turn into Hid's Copse Rd from Cumnor Hill. Last house on the R, before the road's 'T-junction'.* **Sun 8 Feb (2-5). Combined adm with 6 High Street £5, chd free.**
The garden surrounds a house built in the early 1930s (not open) on a ½ acre plot. Designed to be wildlife friendly, it has a kitchen garden, two ponds with frogs and newts, a wildflower meadow and woodland areas under many trees. Small winding paths lead to areas to sit and contemplate. The planting is dependent on the area within the garden, and a special treat are the snowdrops in early spring. Some areas of the garden are wheelchair-accessible, and the main features are viewable.

28 6 HIGH STREET
Cumnor, Oxford, OX2 9PE. **Dr Dianne & Prof Keith Gull.** *4m from central Oxford. Exit to Cumnor from the A420. In centre of village opp Post Office. Parking at back of Post Office.* **Sun 8 Feb (2-5). Combined adm with 23 Hid's Copse Road £5, chd free. Opening with Cumnor Village Gardens on Sun 7 June.**
Front, side and rear garden of a thatched cottage. Front is partly gravelled and side courtyard has many pots. Rear garden overlooks meadows with old apple trees underplanted with ferns, wildlife pond, unusual plants, many with black or bronze foliage, planted in drifts and repeated throughout the garden. Planting has mild Japanese influence; rounded, clipped shapes interspersed with verticals. There are two pubs in the village serving food; The Bear & Ragged Staff and The Vine, the former has accommodation. Wheelchair access to garden via gravel drive.

29 HOME CLOSE, GARSINGTON
29 Southend, Garsington, OX44 9DH. **Mrs M Waud & Dr P Giangrande**, 01865 361394, m.waud@btinternet.com. *3m SE of Oxford. N of B480, opp Garsington Manor.* **Visits by arrangement May to Sept for groups of 10+. Adm £6, chd free. Tea, coffee & cake on request.**
Two acre garden with listed house (not open), listed granary and one acre mixed tree plantation. Unusual trees and shrubs planted for year-round effect. Terraces, stone walls and hedges divide the garden and the planting, which inc topiary, reflects a Mediterranean interest. Vegetable garden, orchard and woodland garden. Countryside views to the south of the garden.

GROUP OPENING

30 KENCOT GARDENS
Kencot, Lechlade, GL7 3QT. *5m NE of Lechlade. E of A361 between Burford & Lechlade.* **Mon 6 Apr (2-6). Combined adm £6, chd free. Tea, coffee & cake at village hall.**

THE ALLOTMENTS
Amelia Carter Charity.

BELHAM HAYES
Mr Joseph Jones.

IVY NOOK
Gill & Wally Cox.

MANOR FARM
Henry & Kate Fyson.

OXFORDSHIRE

QUENTON HOUSE
Henny and Rupert Haworth-Booth.

WELL HOUSE
Janet & Richard Wheeler.

Kencot group consists of five gardens plus allotments which are tended by ten people, growing a variety of vegetables, flowers and fruit. Belham Hayes, mature cottage garden, mixed herbaceous borders, two old fruit trees, vegetables. Emphasis on scent and colour coordination. Manor Farm, two acre walled garden Grade II C17 house (not open) bulbs, wood anemones, fritillaries, mature orchards, pleached limewalk, clipped 130 yr old yew balls, revolving summerhouse. Greenhouse with ancient Black Hamburg vine. Chickens. Well House, ⅓ acre garden, mature trees, hedges, miniature woodland glade, brook with waterfall. Spring bulbs, rockeries. Ivy Nook, Medium sized garden, mixed borders, spring bulbs, vegetable garden, greenhouse, small pond, magnolia tree. Quenton House. New garden, fourth season. Wildflowers, bulbs in woodland. Pleached crab apple, yew hedge, gravel garden, ornamental pond. Rear of the property a mixture of herbaceous borders, shaded and wildflower areas. Free range bantams. Wheelchair access to The Allotments is difficult due to step entrance and narrow paths. Other gardens maybe difficult due to gravel and uneven paths.

31 KINGS COTTAGE
Pudlicote Lane, Chilson, Chipping Norton, OX7 3HU. Mr Michael Anderson and Mr Ralph Mountford, 07771 861928, michaelfanderson66@outlook.com. *S end of Chilson village. Entering Chilson from the S, off the B4437, 1st house on L. Please drive past & follow directions to park in the signed field (free parking and What3words app: lonely.fonts.piglets).* **Sun 3, Mon 4 May (1-5). Combined adm with Bolters Farm £8, chd free. Tea, coffee & cake inc gluten free options.** Visits also by arrangement Mar to Sept for groups of 10 to 50.
An old row of cottages with mature trees, yew hedging and orchard. Interestingly laid out perennial and seasonal beds. Over the last 10 yrs a design and planting scheme has been worked on. This year a new garden room and vegetable area has been completed. Please park in the signposted field. Partial wheelchair access via gravel drive and grass paths. Moderate slopes, grass and some sections of garden only accessible via steps.

GROUP OPENING

32 LANGFORD GARDENS
Lechlade, GL7 3LF. *6m S of Burford A361 towards Lechlade. 1½ m E of Filkins. Large free car park in village. Map of gardens available.* **Sun 14 June (1-5). Combined adm £10, chd free. Tea, coffee & cake at Pember House & village hall.**

BAKERY COTTAGE
Mr & Mrs R Robinson.

BAY TREE COTTAGE
Mr & Mrs R Parsons.

CORNER COTTAGE
Ian Burrows.

COTSWOLD COTTAGE
Mr & Mrs Tom Marshall.

THE CROWN
Mr & Mrs D Evans.

DUNFORD HOUSE
Ms Claire Yates.

FAIRCROFT
Penny Gould & Andy Krouwel.

THE GRANGE
Mr & Mrs J Johnston.

KEMPS YARD
Mr & Mrs R Kemp.

LIME TREE COTTAGE
Diane & Michael Schultz.

MEADOW VIEW
Linda Moore and Derek Grimsley.

THE OLD SCHOOL
David Freeman.

PEMBER COTTAGE
Mrs Jo Edwards.

PEMBER HOUSE
Mr & Mrs J Potter.

RIVENDELL
Mr Mark Skinner.

ROSEFERN COTTAGE
Mrs D Lowden.

SPRINGFIELD
Mr & Mrs M Harris.

STONECROFT
Christine Apperley.

THREEWAYS
Claire & James Mulligan.

THE VICARAGE
Mr & Mrs C Smith.

WELLBANK
Sir Brian & Lady Pomeroy.

WELLBANK HOUSE
Mr Robert Hill and Emma Hallinan.

Langford is a charming small Cotswold village with both the important Grade I listed St Matthew's Church and a splendid pub, The Bell Inn where lunch is available. 22 gardens will be open with a delightful mix from large formal to small cottage gardens. Ancient Cotswold stone walls provide a backdrop for many old variety roses. The plant stall has a large range of local plants and shrubs.

33 LIME CLOSE
35 Henleys Lane, Drayton, Abingdon, OX14 4HU. M C de Laubarede, mail@mclgardendesign.com, www.mclgardendesign.com. *2m S of Abingdon. Henleys Ln is off main road through Drayton. When visiting Lime Cl, please respect local residents & park considerately.* **Sun 15 Feb, Sun 17 May (2-5). Adm £6, chd free. Home-made teas.** Visits also by arrangement 14 Feb to 1 July for groups of 10+. Donation to International Dendrology Society.
5 acre plantsman's garden with rare trees, shrubs, roses and bulbs. Mixed borders, raised beds, pergola, topiary and shade borders. Herb garden by Rosemary Verey. C16 house (not open). Cottage garden by MCL Garden Design, planted for colour, an iris garden with 100 varieties. Winter bulbs. Arboretum with rare trees and shrubs from Asia and America and new field planted by continents. The garden is flat and mostly grass with gravel drive and paths.

In 2025 we awarded over £288,800 in Community Garden Grants, supporting 114 community garden projects.

34 LINCOLN COLLEGE
Turl Street, Oxford, OX1 3DR. *100 metres N on Turl St from High St or 120 metres S on Turl St from Broad St.* **Sun 2 Aug (11-3). Adm £6, chd free. Tea at Trinity College.**
Lincoln is one the University of Oxford's oldest colleges, founded in 1427. The gardens offer formal lawns, mixed borders in traditional and contemporary styles, container displays, climbing plants and mature trees. The gardens are laid out in the classic quadrangle style, where each passageway leads into a different 'room', creating a uniquely varied horticultural and architectural experience.
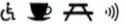

35 MAGDALEN COLLEGE
Oxford, OX1 4AU. Magdalen College, www.magd.ox.ac.uk. *Oxford. Entrance in High St.* **Sun 12 Apr (10-5). Adm £10, chd £9. Light refreshments.**
60 acres inc deer park, college lawns, numerous trees 150-200 yrs old; notable herbaceous and shrub plantings. Magdalen meadow where purple and white snake's head fritillaries can be found is surrounded by Addison's Walk, a tree lined circuit by the River Cherwell developed since the late C18. Ancient herd of 60 deer. Press bell at the lodge for porter to provide wheelchair access.

36 THE MANOR GARDEN
The Manor House, Berry Lane, Blewbury, OX11 9QJ. *4m SE of Didcot. In the middle of the Berry Ln. Black metal grid gates. Parking at the village hall (2 min walk). 3 disabled parking spaces by the house.* **Sun 17 May (10.30-4.30). Adm £5, chd free. Tea, coffee & cake in the barn and courtyard. Provided by the local WI.**
A 10 acre blend of formal and informal landscapes. Within this small yet diverse space, you'll find herbaceous borders neatly framed by box hedging, an organic kitchen garden flanked by greenhouses, and a wooden arch draped in roses and wisteria. A gravel garden is enclosed by a hornbeam alleyway, creating a picturesque escape. As you move further from the house, the grounds take on a more natural feel, with streams, a pond, and a woodland area inviting leisurely strolls. Moat, lake, streams, dial garden, wild beehives, wildlife supporting initiatives, organic gardening, formal and wild gardens.

37 MERTON COLLEGE OXFORD FELLOWS' GARDEN
Merton Street, Oxford, OX1 4JD. Merton College, 01865 276310, www.facebook.com/MertonGardens. *Merton St runs parallel to High St about ½ way down.* **Sun 26 July (10-5). Adm £8, chd free.**
Ancient mulberry, said to have associations with James I. Specimen trees, long mixed border, recently established herbaceous bed. View of Christ Church meadow.

Lime Close

© Andrew Lawson

GROUP OPENING

38 MIDDLETON CHENEY GARDENS
Middleton Cheney, Banbury, OX17 2ST. *3m E of Banbury. Parking on Main Rd between primary sch & library (OX17 2PD) for access to Upper & Lower Middleton. Open garden maps available at library.* **Sun 7 June (1-6). Combined adm £8, chd free. Home-made teas at Peartree House.**

5 CENTENARY ROAD
Kim Woodlock.

CROFT HOUSE
Richard & Sandy Walmsley.

LEXTON HOUSE
Matthew & Diane Tims.

63 MAIN ROAD
Ruth & Martin Edwards.

38 MIDWAY
Margaret & David Finch.

PEARTREE HOUSE
Roger & Barbara Charlesworth.

2A RECTORY LANE
Debbie Evans.

Large village with C13 church (open) with renowned pre-Raphaelite stained glass. Seven open gardens with a variety of sizes, styles and maturity. Of the smaller gardens, a modern garden contrasts formal features with colour-filled borders and exotic plants. A mature small front and back garden is planted profusely with a feel of an intimate haven. A new-build garden provides a peaceful setting whilst inc many features - rockery, topiary, pond with waterfall, borders. A stately garden inc a formal terrace is surrounded by hedges and fig trees with steps down to secluded lower space and small vegetable garden. A large garden has colourful cottage planting and vegetable garden. Another has an air of mystery with hidden corners and an extensive water feature weaving its way throughout the garden. A mature walled garden flourishes on the challenge of a mostly dry shade site and inc conservatory, pond and secret garden.

39 MIDSUMMER HOUSE
Woolstone, Faringdon, SN7 7QL. Penny Spink. *7m W & 7m S of Faringdon. Woolstone is a small village off B4507, below Uffington White Horse Hill. Take road towards Uffington from the White Horse Pub.* **Fri 1 May, Fri 5 June (2-5). Adm £5, chd free. Home-made teas. Sun 5 July (2-5). Combined adm with Woolstone Mill House £10, chd free. Tea, coffee & cake. Fri 7 Aug (2-5). Adm £5, chd free. Home-made teas. Fri 4 Sept (2-5). Combined adm with Woolstone Mill House £10, chd free. Tea, coffee & cake. Fri 2 Oct (2-5). Adm £5, chd free. Home-made teas.**
Midsummer Garden was designed by Justin Spink for his parents, Anthony and Penny Spink, in 2015. In 2018 Mike and Ann Collins continued designing and planting the garden. Over the road there is a newly planted arboretum and nature reserve established 2019, with spectacular views of the Uffington White Horse. Rare and unusual plants. Picnics welcome in the field opp. Wheelchair access over short gravel drive at entrance.

40 MILL BARN
25 Mill Lane, Chalgrove, OX44 7SL. Pat Hougham, 01865 890020, Gmec@outlook.com. *12m E of Oxford. Chalgrove is 4m from Watlington off B480. Mill Barn is in Mill Ln, W of Chalgrove, 300yds S of Lamb Pub.* **Visits by arrangement 1 May to 21 Sept for groups of 6 to 30. Adm £4, chd free. Cream teas.**
Mill Barn is an informal cottage garden set in a millstream landscape. It has 10 herbaceous borders with displays of flowers throughout the seasons that inc a variety of roses. A pergola covered in grape vines and roses lead to a vegetable plot surrounded by a cordon of fruit trees. A variety of fruit trees throughout the garden inc mulberry, medlar and quince.

41 MILL HOUSE GARDEN
Fernham Road, Uffington, Faringdon, SN7 7RD. Rupert & Julia Lycett Green. *Turn into Fernham Rd by the Tom Brown Museum. After 100 metres, turn into the private road marked 'Grounds Farm', Mill House is the 1st open gate on L.* **Sun 7 June (12.30-5). Adm £5, chd free. Light refreshments inc tea, lemonade and cakes.**
Wonderful setting overlooking the Uffington White Horse and wide views of the Downs. 1 acre garden divided into seasonal rooms connecting around the house. A walled garden leads into a lawned room of box-edged beds and follows into a spring garden and out to a wild growing bank and a rill following the course of the old mill race. Lastly, a vegetable garden with roses and cutting beds. Wheelchair access to central garden and then sloping grass paths to top garden. Exit possible through top stable yard.

42 50-52 NORTH HINKSEY LANE
Oxford, OX2 0LY. John & Mary Lines. *From Botley Rd at McDonald's follow NGS sign turning into North Hinksey Ln. Continue along lane past Halliday Ln, Yarnells Rd and 50-52 is situated on the service road on R.* **Sun 12 Apr (2-5.30). Combined adm with 3 Halliday Lane £5, chd free.**
This wider than average town garden is on a sloping site with mature fruit trees. The garden is laid out on different levels with lawns and mixed beds containing spring bulbs, perennial planting and annuals inc fuchsias, penstemons and salvias with mature shrubs. The garden has steep and uneven paths.

310,000 people are cared for each year who are approaching the end of life or diagnosed with a terminal illness through the hospice network supported by National Garden Scheme funding.

GROUP OPENING

43 NORTH MORETON GARDENS
Nr Didcot, OX11 9AT. *3m SE of Didcot. Off A4130 (Didcot-Wallingford Rd). Follow signs for car park.* **Sun 5 July (2-4). Combined adm £6, chd free. Tea, coffee & cake in C17 barn at North Moreton House.**

THE FILBERTS
Mr & Mrs Prescott.

MOUNT PLEASANT
Mr & Mrs Elliot.

NEW STAPLETONS CHANTRY
Dr & Mrs M A Parker.

Charming village with listed buildings and a Grade I Medieval church featuring C13 stained glass. Three gardens open for the NGS this year. Filberts: 1 acre garden featuring a formal garden with lily and fish ponds, parterre with lavender and penstemons, informal pond, mixed borders, island beds, architectural foliage, secluded areas and many clematis. Vegetable garden, fruit cage and orchard. Mount Pleasant: Just under ½ an acre on 2 levels with a high bank and rockery. Lower level with gravel garden and parterre. Upper level with lawn with flower beds and wildflower meadow. Stapleton's Chantry: C15 Grade II listed building with 2 acre garden and pony paddock. Flower beds along driveway, car park, and main garden. Four gates lead to beds beside lawns, yew and beech hedges, ancient apple trees, pond with rushes and lilies. Visiting mallards and coots nest amongst the reeds. Wheelchair access possible via steps. Some narrow and slippery paths. Partial access to Mount Pleasant (lower garden).

GROUP OPENING

44 OLD BOARS HILL GARDENS
Jarn Way, Boars Hill, Oxford, OX1 5JF. *3m S of Oxford. From S ring road towards A34 at r'about follow signs to Wootton & Boars Hill. Up Hinksey Hill take R fork. 1m R into Berkley Rd to Old Boars Hill.* **Sun 24 May (2-5.30). Combined adm £8, chd free. Home-made teas.**

HEDDERLY HOUSE
Mrs Julia Bennett.

UPLANDS
Lyn Sanders, 01865 739486, sandersc4@hotmail.com.
Visits also by arrangement.

YEW COTTAGE
OX1 5JJ. Michael Edwards.

Hedderly House built in Victorian times (house not open) has large patios with flower-filled terraces looking over a wide panorama of countryside and sky. Down the meadow slopes walk to the ponds and look back through pine trees to the rest of the garden. Uplands is a hidden cottage garden with tree lined borders supporting shade loving plants. A large sloped lawn is surrounded by many beds of perennial flowering plants and annuals to offer colour throughout the seasons. Yew Cottage has a grand magnolia tree with lovely cottage planting and a lawn to give shade in the afternoon. A special treat is the display of the owner's vintage cars. Some sloping lawns in Uplands and partial wheelchair access in Hedderley House due to steps.

45 THE OLD RECTORY, ALBURY
Albury, Thame, OX9 2LP.
Mr & Mrs J Nowell-Smith, 01844 339650, 07703 498609, Moonowellsmith@gmail.com.
Off A418 Wheatley to Thame road, 5m from Thame. What3words app: fonts.cowboy.motive. From Tiddington, turn R onto single track road signed Albury Church. **Visits by arrangement 16 Feb to 30 Sept for groups of up to 30. Adm £5, chd free. Home-made teas.**
5 acres of extensive herbaceous borders, rose avenue, woodland and lake walk, kitchen and cutting gardens. Surrounded by orchards and the glebe land with some beautiful mature trees with close access to Fernhill Wood, famous for bluebells. There is extensive planting of snowdrops and early bulbs, followed by perpetual roses, and continual herbaceous and annual planting. Sculptures by Andy Goldsworth and Tom Stogdon. Gravel drive and quite sloped garden but main borders and tea terrace quite accessible. Wheelchair accessible WC.

46 NEW THE OLD RECTORY, CHURCHILL
Sarsden Road, Churchill, Chipping Norton, OX7 6NU. Sarah and William Allardice. *3m SW of Chipping Norton. From Churchill church head down hill on Sarsden Rd, 1st house on L after 40mph sign.* **Sun 31 May (12-5). Adm £5, chd free. Home-made teas.**
One acre family garden with outstanding views across a Cotswold valley. Inc a natural swimming pond, gravel garden, herbaceous borders, orchard and vegetable patch. The garden has many places to sit and enjoy the views, a terrace and newly planted sunken rose garden. Most of the garden is accessible by wheelchair.

47 116 OXFORD ROAD
Abingdon, OX14 2AG. Mr & Mrs P Aylward, 01235 523925, aylwardsdooz@hotmail.co.uk. *North Abingdon. On RHS if coming from A34 North Abingdon exit, or on LHS after the Picklers Hill turn if approaching from Abingdon town centre.* **Sun 31 May (11-4.30). Combined adm with Failford £6, chd free. Home-made teas. Visits also by arrangement in June for groups of 10+. Afternoon or evening visits can be accommodated.**
This town garden brings alive the imagination of its creators. It will inspire both the enthusiast and the beginner. Use of recycled materials, lots of colour and architectural plants. A folly, fairy home, are just a couple of many quirky features. Raised beds, rockeries, specimen plants, beds of roses and hostas. There is something for everyone and there are changes every year.

48 50 PLANTATION ROAD
Oxford, OX2 6JE. Philippa Scoones. *Central Oxford. N on Woodstock Rd take 2nd L. Coming into Oxford on Woodstock Rd turn R after Leckford Rd. Best to park on Leckford Rd. No disabled parking near house.* **Sun 27 Sept (2-5). Adm £4, chd free. Home-made teas. Opening with Central North Oxford Gardens on Sat 25, Sun 26 Apr.**
Surprisingly spacious city garden designed in specific sections. North facing front garden, side alley filled

OXFORDSHIRE

with shade loving climbers. South facing rear garden with hundreds of tulips in spring, salvias, tithonias and dahlias in autumn, unusual trees inc Mount Etna Broom, conservatory, terraced area and secluded water garden with woodland plants and alpines. Good design ideas for small town garden and 100s of pots that add to the overall atmosphere.

49 THE PRIORY, CHARLBURY
Church Lane, Charlbury, OX7 3PX. Dr D El Kabir & Colleagues. *6m SE of Chipping Norton. Large Cotswold village on B4022 Witney-Enstone Rd, near St Mary's Church.* **Sun 17 May (2-5). Adm £6, chd free.** 1½ acre of formal terraced topiary gardens with Italianate features. Foliage colour schemes, shrubs, parterres with fragrant plants, old roses, water features, sculpture and inscriptions aim to produce a poetic, wistful atmosphere. Formal vegetable and herb garden. Arboretum of over three acres borders the River Evenlode and inc wildlife garden and pond. Partial wheelchair access.

50 9 RAWLINSON ROAD
Oxford, OX2 6UE. Ramnique Lall, 07803 607112, ranilall@hotmail.com. *¾m N of Oxford City Centre. Rawlinson Rd runs between Banbury & Woodstock roads midway between Oxford City Centre & Summertown shops.* **Sun 7 June (2-5). Combined adm with 11 Rawlinson Road £8, chd free. Tea at 11 Rawlinson Road.** Visits also by arrangement 14 Mar to 14 Oct for groups of up to 15. Townhouse garden with structured disarray of roses. Terrace of stone inlaid with brick and enclosed by Chinese fretwork balustrade, chunky brick and oak pergola covered with roses, wisteria and clematis; potted topiary. Until autumn the garden is delightfully replete with aconites, lobelias, phloxes, daisies and meandering clematis.

51 11 RAWLINSON ROAD
Oxford, OX2 6UE. Emma Chamberlain. *Central N Oxford. ½ way between Central Oxford & Summertown, off Banbury Rd.* **Sun 7 June (2-5). Combined adm with 9 Rawlinson Road £8, chd free. Tea.** A south facing 120ft walled Victorian town garden created from scratch since 2010. Interesting mix of herbaceous and shrubs with particular interest in late tulips, and unusual plants. Great emphasis on colour and succession planting with paths running through the beds. Constantly changing as owner is restless. Some sculptures. Pond sculptures and colour. There are wide paths through the garden and it is level.

52 RECTORY FARMHOUSE
Church Enstone, Chipping Norton, OX7 4NN. Andrew Hornung & Sally Coles, 01608 677374, giussanese@yahoo.co.uk. *N from Oxford on the A44. Turn R in Enstone to Church Enstone. Parking is on the Little Tew Rd by the church. Proceed through the churchyard, turn R and down the hill. Entrance on unmade road behind The Crown Inn.* **Visits by arrangement 6 June to 5 July. Adm £7, chd free. Home-made teas.** A large and very varied garden with a rich mix of formal and informal planting inc fruit trees, soft fruit and vegetable garden. About 100 varieties of rose, particularly big climbers; many unusual, some rare plants. The garden inc many different settings, ranging from gravel areas to fruit trees and pondside plantings. More recently developed areas alongside well established plantings. Garden slopes - assistance will be required for wheelchair user.

53 SANDYS HOUSE
Bull Hill, Chadlington, Chipping Norton, OX7 3ND. Jane Bell. *Centre of Chadlington village accessible via A361 (Burford-Chipping Norton) or A44 (Oxford). At Xrds turn down Bull Hill & enter garden on L through wooden gates. Parking on surrounding streets but not at property.* **Fri 5, Sat 6, Sun 7 June (11-5). Combined adm with Claridges Barn £8, chd free.** Bulbs, perennials and shrubs create a colourful mix in this informal cottage style garden to the rear of the former Sandys Arms pub featuring wildlife-friendly, drought tolerant planting. A series of small ponds and wildflower areas encourage bio-diversity. The garden inc a mature summer-flowering Magnolia Grandiflora against the house and tender annuals are displayed in the main greenhouse.

54 SARSDEN GLEBE
Churchill, Chipping Norton, OX7 6PH. Mr & Mrs Rupert Ponsonby. *Situated between Sarsden and Churchill. ¼m S of Churchill on the road to Sarsden. Turn in to the drive by a small lodge.* **Fri 3 Apr (12.30-5). Adm £7.50, chd free. Home-made teas.** A Rectory garden and park designed by Humphrey Repton and his son George. Formal terraced garden around the house; woodland garden full of spring bulbs, mature oaks and many other ornamental trees. Old orchard now home to three pigs. Walled garden with espaliered fruit trees, tulip pots and greenhouse. Wild garden with a sea of blue and white anemone blanda interspersed with fritillaries and daffodils in spring. Most of the garden can be accessed in a wheelchair.

GROUP OPENING

55 SIBFORD GARDENS
Sibford Ferris, OX15 5RE. *7m W of Banbury. Near the Warwickshire border, S of B4035, in centre of Sibford Ferris village at T-junc & additional gardens near the Xrds & Wykham Arms Pub in Sibford Gower. Parking in both villages.* **Sun 14 June (2-6). Combined adm £7, chd free. Home-made teas at Sibford Gower Village Hall (opp the church).**

CARTER'S YARD
Sue Bannister, 01295 780365, sebannister@gmail.com.
Visits also by arrangement 3 May to 4 Oct for groups of 5 to 25.

HOME CLOSE, SIBFORD FERRIS
Graham & Carolyn White, 07711 897902, carolyn@familywhites.co.uk, www.homecloseflowers.co.uk.
Visits also by arrangement 22 May to 4 July for groups of 10 to 25.

SHRUBBERY COTTAGE
Nic Durrant.

Two charming small villages of Sibford Gower and Sibford Ferris, off the beaten track with thatched stone cottages. 3 contrasting gardens comprising a truly traditional plants woman's cottage garden, an Artists garden with planting designed to inspire her works and lastly the gardens of an early C20 Arts and Crafts house. A fantastic collection bursting with bloom, structural intrigue, interesting planting and some rather unusual plants. Parking is available in both villages and a map will be provided on the day. Home Close - access from the rear via grass and stone paths and Shrubbery Cottage, gravel and grass paths but not Carters Yard.

56 SOUTH NEWINGTON HOUSE
South Newington, OX15 4JW. Mr & Mrs David Swan, 07711 720135, claire_ainley@hotmail.com. *6m SW of Banbury. South Newington is between Banbury & Chipping Norton. Take Barford Rd off A361, 1st L after 100yds in between oak bollards. For SatNav use OX15 4JL.* **Visits by arrangement Mar to Sept. Adm £12, chd free. Light refreshments.**
A tree lined drive leads to a garden of interest. Herbaceous borders designed for year-round colour. Organic kitchen garden with established beds, rotation and companion planting. Orchard of fruit trees with a pond for wildlife and hydration for the hives. Walled parterre planted for seasonal colour. A family garden, designed to blend seamlessly into the environment; a warm welcome awaits you. Some gravel paths, otherwise full wheelchair access.

57 ♦ STONOR PARK
Stonor, Henley-on-Thames, RG9 6HF. Lord and Lady Camoys, 01491 638587, administrator@stonor.com, www.stonor.com. *4m from Henley on Thames. Located between the M4 (J8/J9) & the M40 (J6) on the B480 Henley-on-Thames to Watlington road. If approaching Stonor on the M40 from the E, please exit at J6 only.* **For NGS: Thur 4 June (10.30-4.30). Adm £9, chd free. Home-made teas inc cakes and scones.** For other opening times and information, please phone, email or visit garden website.
Nestled within a hidden valley and ancient deer park, you will find the gardens at Stonor, which date back to Medieval times. Visitors love the serenity of our C17 walled, Italianate

Pleasure Garden and Old Kitchen Garden beyond. In the four acre walled gardens you'll find a 400ft long herbaceous border, topiary, ancient yews, ponds with water lilies, and beautiful park land views. Huge Rosa 'Kiftsgate' which hangs from a vast yew. Stunning parkland views Shrubbery.

58 STOW COTTAGE ARBORETUM & GARDEN
Junction Road, Churchill, Chipping Norton, OX7 6NP. Tom Heywood-Lonsdale. *2½m SW of Chipping Norton, off the B4450. Use postcode OX7 6NP & parking will be sign posted from William Smith Cl.* **Sat 20 June (1-5.30). Adm £5, chd free. Tea, coffee & cake. Donation to International Dendrological Society.**
The Arboretum and Garden cover approx 15 acres with extensive views towards Stow-on-the-Wold and beyond. The arboretum began in 2009 and has been extensively developed over the years. There is an array of 750 different trees, in particular 200 different oaks as well as many sorbus, limes, magnolias, dogwoods, walnuts, birches and liquidambars.

59 TRINITY COLLEGE
Broad Street, Oxford, OX1 3BH. Kate Burtonwood, Head Gardener, www.trinity.ox.ac.uk. *Central Oxford. Entrance in Broad St (Opp Turl St) Purchase tickets from Trinity College, Broad St, OX1 3BH.* **Sun 2 Aug (11-3). Adm £8.50, chd free. Open nearby Lincoln College.**
Iconic Oxford college site with listed gardens dating back to C13. 120 metre border by garden designer Chris Beardshaw reflecting the college's famed Baroque architecture. Quadrangles contain mature specimen trees and seasonal pot displays. Sustainable plantings have been created by Head Gardener Kate Burtonwood and the Garden Team in the Woodland, Fellows Garden and Library Quad following extensive redevelopment of college in recent years. The private walled gardens - the President's Garden and Fellows' Garden - will be open for viewing. Please note that this opening is cashless payments only. Restored gardens and dining hall. A focus on sustainable plantings. Most of site is accessible for wheelchair users. Some uneven paths and gravel

at points. Accessible facilities are provided.

60 TYTHE BARN
Guydens Hamlet, Oxford Road, Garsington, Oxford, OX44 9AZ. Claire and Dave Parker. *Beyond Oxford ring road to the E, after Unipart, at the edge of Garsington. Parking available at Unipart car park, about 150 metres along road from postcode: OX4 2PG. Disabled parking, and passenger drop-off at house.* **Sun 7 June (1.30-5). Adm £5, chd free. Home-made teas. Our own local honey and home-made preserves for sale.**
½ acre garden, designed by RHS Chelsea award winner Sarah Naybour. Bee friendly planting in the formal garden leads to woodland area. Oak pergola with roses overlooks the wildlife pond with orchard. Raised vegetable beds behind a mature beech hedge with vintage doorway. 2½ acre wildflower meadow with apiary. Children's wildlife quiz available, guided walks in the wildflower meadow may be available. Garden is flat and designed to be accessible to wheelchairs. Disabled parking adjacent to the house.

61 UPPER BOLNEY HOUSE
Upper Bolney Road, Harpsden, Henley-on-Thames, RG9 4AQ. Anna and Richard Wilson. *2m S of Henley on Thames, between Shiplake and Harpsden. Upper Bolney Rd can be accessed from Woodlands Rd. Only use the postcode in Google Maps.* **Sun 24 May (11-4). Adm £7, chd £3. Tea, coffee & cake inc cold drinks.**
The four acre garden has been extensively developed over the last 15 yrs. There are lawns with herbaceous borders. Terraces around the house inc planted areas and yew topiary. Various interesting areas lie beyond; a rose garden, wildflower meadow, rhododendron bed, tropical area, Victorian style stumpery, kitchen garden and greenhouse. New South African garden. Historic racing cars on display.

Broughton Castle

Chivel Farm

OXFORDSHIRE

62 VERNON COTTAGE
2 Weston Road, Lewknor, Watlington, OX49 5TU. Kevin and Emma Mears. *Located behind the Leathern Bottle pub in Lewknor, close to M40 J6.* **Sun 14 June (1.30-5). Adm £5, chd free. Home-made teas.**
Hidden ⅓ acre cottage garden with colourful borders full of perennials, leading down to a chalk stream. Productive Victorian style greenhouse, potager 'no dig' cut flower/vegetable garden, raised beds. Pretty patio area with small water feature, hydrangeas, hostas and acers. Large variety of succulents enjoying sunny areas. Mature and young fruit trees. Productive compost area. Majority of the garden is flat with no steps so ideal for wheelchairs and push chairs.

63 ◆ WATERPERRY GARDENS
Waterperry, Wheatley, OX33 1JZ. The School of Philosophy and Economic Science, 01844 339254, office@waterperrygardens.co.uk, www.waterperrygardens.co.uk. *7½ m from Oxford city centre. From E M40 J8, from N M40 J8a. Follow brown tourist signs. For SatNav please use OX33 1LA.* **For NGS: Thur 5, Thur 12 Nov (10-5). Adm £9.50, chd free.** For other opening times and information, please phone, email or visit garden website.
Twenty acres of beautifully landscaped ornamental gardens featuring a spectacular 200ft herbaceous border. Established as a School of Horticulture for Ladies by Beatrix Havergal in 1932, it is now also home to a quality plant centre, garden shop, art gallery, gift barn, museum, teashop and Saxon Church. Newly redesigned walled garden, river walk, statues and pear orchard. Riverside walk may be inaccessible to wheelchair users if it is very wet.

GROUP OPENING

64 WEST OXFORD GARDENS
Cumnor Hill, Oxford, OX2 9HH. *Take Botley interchange off A34 from N or S. Follow signs for Oxford & then turn R at Botley T-lights opp McDonald's & follow NGS yellow signs. Street parking.* **Sun 7 June (1-5). Combined adm £7, chd free. Home-made teas at 10 Eynsham Road.**

10 EYNSHAM ROAD
Jon Harker.

7 THE GARTH
Mrs Silvana Losito.

NEW 9 THE GARTH
Mr Trevor & Mrs Hilary Jones.

4 HALLIDAY LANE
Mr Nathaniel Ward.

86 HURST RISE ROAD
Ms P Guy & Mr L Harris.

New for 2026: 9 The Garth - a medium sized town garden with mature shrubs and borders, water features and a secret garden. 7 The Garth - a medium sized mature natural town garden with a mix of flower beds, trees, shrubs, vegetables and meadow flowers. 86 Hurst Rise Road - a small garden abounding in perennials, roses, small trees and shrubs displayed at different levels around a circular lawn and path with sculptural features. 10 Eynsham Road a New Zealander's take on an English-style garden inc many rose varieties, white garden, herbaceous borders and pond. 4 Halliday Lane is a professionally designed family garden with both planted beds and a meadow area. Pebble path 86 Hurst Rise Rd. Gravel driveway and narrow pathway 7 The Garth. Steep driveway/ partial access 9 The Garth.

65 WESTWELL MANOR
Westwell, nr Burford, OX18 4JT. Mr Thomas Gibson, 02074 998572, annabel@tgfineart.com. *2m SW of Burford. From A40 Burford-Cheltenham, turn L ½ m after Burford r'about signed Westwell. After 1½ m at T-junc, turn R & Manor is 2nd house on L.* **Visits by arrangement Apr to Aug. Donation to Aspire.**
7 acres surrounding old Cotswold manor house (not open) with knot garden, potager, shrub roses, herbaceous borders, topiary, earth works, moonlight garden, auricula ladder, rills and water garden.

66 WHEATLEY MANOR
26 High Street, Wheatley, OX33 1XX. Mark and Juliet Byford. *5m E of Oxford. Off A40, follow signs to Wheatley. The Manor House is at the Western End of the High St. What3words app: trout.hotdog. glimmers.* **Sun 31 May (2-6). Adm £5, chd free. Tea, coffee & cake.**
1½ acre garden of Elizabethan manor house (not open). Formal walk with herbaceous borders; many mature and unusual trees, herb garden and secret garden, lily pond surrounded by espaliered fruit trees, orchard with an ancient Mulberry tree and other fruit trees inc a Medlar, a shrubbery with lilacs and old roses and a separate kitchen garden. Plenty of places to sit down and enjoy the view.

67 WHITEHILL FARM
Widford, Burford, OX18 4DT. Mr & Mrs Paul Youngson, 01993 822894, paulyoungson48@gmail.com. *1m E of Burford and 100 metres N of A40. From A40 take road signed Widford. Turn R at bottom of hill, 1st house on R with ample car parking.* **Sun 21 June (1-5). Adm £5, chd free. Home-made teas.** Visits also by arrangement 1 June to 1 Sept for groups of 10+.
2 acres of hillside gardens and woodland with spectacular views overlooking Burford and Windrush valley. Informal plantsman's garden built up by the owners over 25 yrs. Herbaceous and shrub borders, ponds and bog area, old fashioned roses, ground cover, ornamental grasses, bamboos and hardy geraniums. Wildflower meadow with specimen trees. Features inc large cascade water feature, pretty tea patio and wonderful Cotswold views.

68 WOOLSTONE MILL HOUSE
Woolstone, Faringdon, SN7 7QL. Mr & Mrs Justin Spink. *7m W of Wantage. 7m S of Faringdon. Woolstone is a small village off B4507, below Uffington White Horse Hill.* **Sun 5 July, Fri 4 Sept (2-5). Combined adm with Midsummer House £10, chd free. Tea, coffee & cake at Midsummer House.**
Redesigned by new owner, garden designer Justin Spink in 2020, this 1½ acre garden has large mixed perennial beds, and small gravel, cutting, kitchen and bog gardens. Topiary, medlars and old fashioned roses. Treehouse with spectacular views to Uffington White Horse and White Horse Hill. C18 millhouse and barn (not open). Partial wheelchair access.

SHROPSHIRE

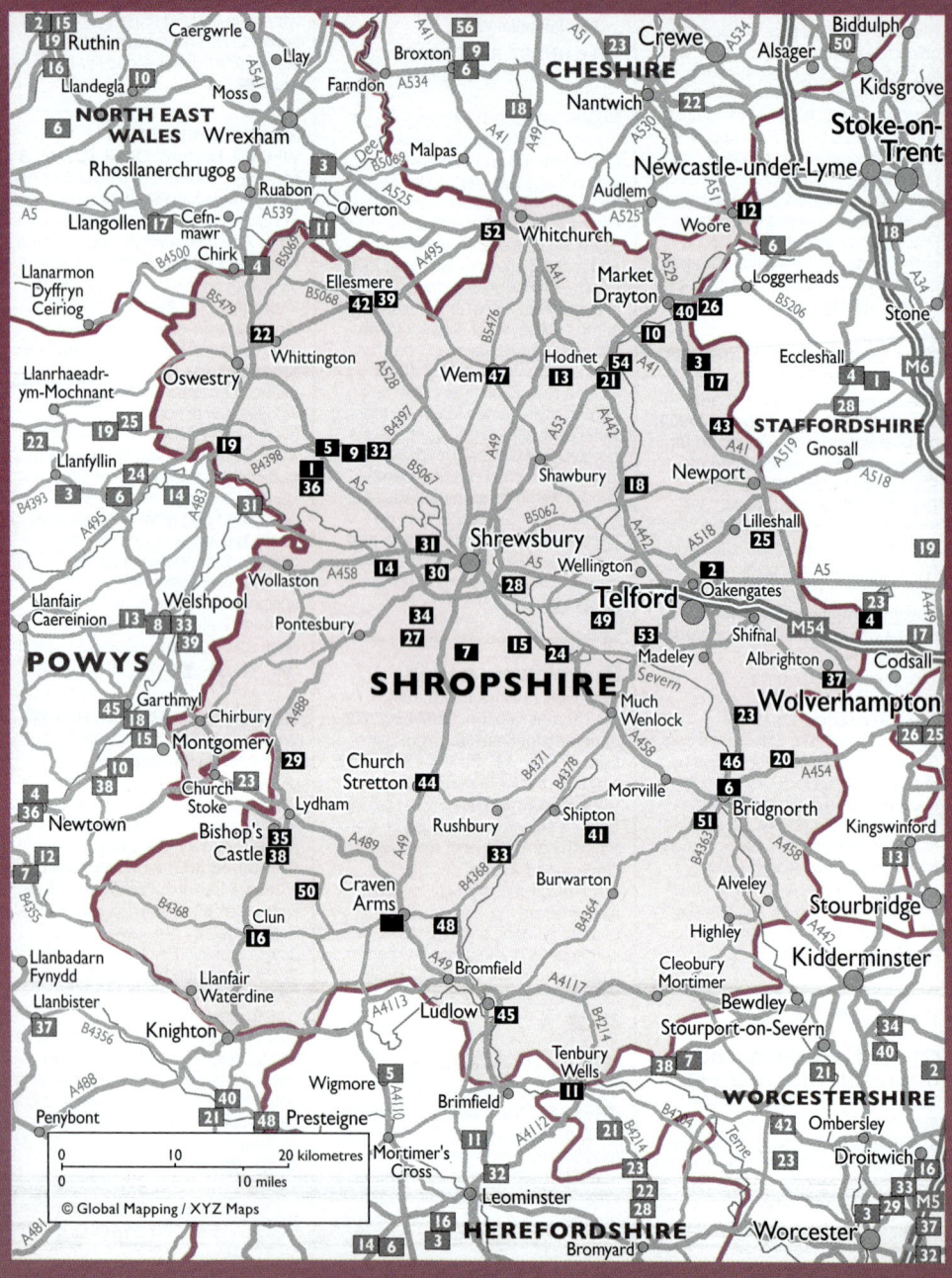

SHROPSHIRE   441

VOLUNTEERS

County Organiser
Andy Chatting
07546 560615
andy.chatting@ngs.org.uk

Treasurer
Elaine Jones 01588 650323
elaine.jones@ngs.org.uk

Volunteers Co-ordinator
Sheila Jones 01743 244108
smaryjones@icloud.com

Publicity
Douglas Wood 07704 683095
douglas.woods@ngs.org.uk

Facebook/Twitter
Della Chatting
della.chatting@ngs.org.uk

Instagram
John Butcher 07817 443837
butchinoz@hotmail.com

Booklet Co-ordinator
Martin Clifford-Jones
07506 140434
martin.jones@ngs.org.uk

Assistant County Organisers
Fiona Chancellor
01952 507675
fiona.chancellor@ngs.org.uk

Stella Clifford-Jones
07484 327979
stellaandmartin@ngs.org.uk

Jane Wood 01691 839564
jane.liz.wood@gmail.com

Angela Woolrich
angelawoolrich@hotmail.co.uk

@Shropshire NGS
@shropshirengs

OPENING DATES

All entries subject to change.
For latest information check
www.ngs.org.uk
Map locator numbers are
shown to the right of each
garden name.

April

Saturday 4th
Cherry Tree Arboretum   12
Upper Farm Garden   49

Sunday 5th
Upper Farm Garden   49

Saturday 18th
Horatio's Garden   22

Sunday 19th
Buntingsdale Park Gardens   10
◆ Burford House Gardens   11
NEW Hill View Hardy Plants   20

Sunday 26th
Sunningdale   47
Westwood House   51

May

Sunday 3rd
The Bramleys   7

Monday 4th
Oteley   39
Ruthall Manor   41

Wednesday 6th
Hundred House Hotel   23

Saturday 9th
Cherry Tree Arboretum   12

Sunday 10th
The Ferns   16
Longden Manor   27

Wednesday 13th
NEW The Citadel   13
◆ Goldstone Hall Gardens   17

Sunday 17th
Longner Hall   28
Riverside   40

Saturday 23rd
Beaufort   2
◆ Burford House Gardens   11

Sunday 24th
Beaufort   2
◆ Burford House Gardens   11
Ruthall Manor   41
◆ Walcot Hall   50

Monday 25th
Ruthall Manor   41
◆ Walcot Hall   50

Saturday 30th
Upper Farm Garden   49

Sunday 31st
Stanley Hall Gardens   46
Upper Farm Garden   49

June

Friday 5th
Lilleshall Home Farm   25

Saturday 6th
NEW Little Heath Green Cottage   26
Windy Ridge   53

Sunday 7th
Eaton Mascott Hall   15
The Mill House   32
Sunningdale   47
Windy Ridge   53

Wednesday 10th
◆ Goldstone Hall Gardens   17

Sunday 14th
NEW The Berringtons Farm   3
Bramble Ridge   6

Wednesday 17th
Hundred House Hotel   23

Thursday 18th
NEW ◆ Boscobel House and the
  Royal Oak   4

Saturday 20th
Ruthall Manor   41
NEW St Mary's Garden Trail   42
The Secret Gardens at
  Steventon Terrace   45

Sunday 21st
The Old Vicarage, Bishops
  Castle   38
Ruthall Manor   41

Saturday 27th
Grooms Cottage   18
1 Scotsmansfield   44

Sunday 28th
Grooms Cottage   18

July

Sunday 5th
◆ Hodnet Hall Gardens 21
Sambrook Manor 43

Saturday 11th
Grooms Cottage 18

Sunday 12th
Grooms Cottage 18

Wednesday 15th
◆ Goldstone Hall Gardens 17
Hundred House Hotel 23

Thursday 16th
Appledore 1
Offcot 36

Friday 17th
Appledore 1
Offcot 36

Saturday 18th
Appledore 1
Offcot 36
Ruthall Manor 41

Sunday 19th
Appledore 1
Buntingsdale Park Gardens 10
Offcot 36
Ruthall Manor 41

Saturday 25th
Lower Brookshill 29
Upper Farm Garden 49

Sunday 26th
Lower Brookshill 29
Riverside 40
Upper Farm Garden 49

August

Sunday 9th
The Ferns 16
Moat Hall 34

Wednesday 12th
◆ Goldstone Hall Gardens 17

September

Wednesday 2nd
◆ Wollerton Old Hall 54

Wednesday 9th
◆ Goldstone Hall Gardens 17

Saturday 19th
Upper Farm Garden 49

Sunday 20th
Buntingsdale Park Gardens 10
Upper Farm Garden 49

Saturday 26th
◆ Burford House Gardens 11

Sunday 27th
◆ Burford House Gardens 11

October

Saturday 3rd
Cherry Tree Arboretum 12

Friday 9th
Appledore 1
Offcot 36

Saturday 10th
Appledore 1
Offcot 36

Sunday 11th
Appledore 1
Millichope Park 33
Offcot 36

Saturday 17th
The Leasowes Garden & Arboretum 24

By Arrangement

Arrange a personalised garden visit with your club, or group of friends, on a date to suit you. See individual garden entries for full details.

NEW The Berringtons Farm 3
Bramble Cottage 5
48 Bramble Ridge (Bramble Ridge) 6
Brooches House 8
Brownhill House 9
Cruckfield House 14
The Ferns 16
Grooms Cottage 18
Gwynt Newydd 19
Hundred House Hotel 23
The Leasowes Garden & Arboretum 24
107 Meadowbout Way 30
Merton 31
Moat Hall 34
17 Mortimer Road (Buntingsdale Park Gardens) 10
The Mount 35
NEW The Old Farmhouse 37
Riverside 40
Ruthall Manor 41
Sambrook Manor 43
1 Scotsmansfield 44
Sunningdale 47
Tower House 48
Upper Farm Garden 49
The White House 52

Burford House Gardens

THE GARDENS

1 APPLEDORE
Kynaston, Kinnerley, Oswestry, SY10 8EF. Lionel Parker. *Just off A5 on Wolfshead r'about (at Oswestry end of Nesscliffe bypass) towards Knockin. Then1st L towards Kinnerley. Follow NGS signs from this road.* **Thur 16, Fri 17, Sat 18, Sun 19 July, Fri 9, Sat 10, Sun 11 Oct (10-5). Combined adm with Offcot £7, chd free. Tea, coffee & cake.**
Appledore adjoins neighbouring garden Offcot. It has gone through extensive changes and is managed by Tom Pountney from Offcot. Both gardens are opening together this year so that visitors can see a developing 'edible garden' with six large beds for a wide range of fruit and vegetables, all grown organically. To encourage pollinators, the garden also has a wildlife pond and a small wildflower meadow.

2 BEAUFORT
Coppice Drive, Moss Road, Wrockwardine Wood, Telford, TF2 7BP. Mike King, www.carnivorousplants.uk.com. *Approx 2m N from Telford town centre. From Asda Donnington, turn L at lights on Moss Rd, ⅓m, turn L into Coppice Dr. 4th Bungalow on L with solar panels.* **Sat 23, Sun 24 May (1-5). Adm £5, chd free. Tea, coffee & cake.** Donation to Plant Heritage.
If carnivorous plants are your thing, then come and visit our National Collection of *Sarracenia* (pitcher plants); also over 100 different Venus flytrap clones (*Dionaea muscipula*), Sundews (*Drosera*) and Butterworts (*Pinguicula*) - over 6000 plants in total. Large greenhouses at Telford's first carbon negative house; a great place to visit - kids will love it. Regret, greenhouses are not wheelchair accessible.

3 NEW THE BERRINGTONS FARM
Woodseaves, Market Drayton, TF9 2AU. Glyn Gratton, 07970 039361, ggratton@btinternet.com. *On the A529 midway between Market Drayton & Hinstock. From Market Drayton follow A529 through Woodseaves. Garden is 1.2m from Four Alls Public House. From the A41/A529 junc at Hinstock, garden is 2½m.* **Sun 14 June (12-4). Adm £5, chd free. Home-made teas. Visits also by arrangement 1 May to 30 Aug for groups of 10+.**
Relaxed two acre country garden developed by the owner over 20 years. Mature trees and more recent additions provide interest and habitat for birds and wildlife. Thoughtful planting provides year-round interest from winter flowering shrubs and spring bulbs through to the rich colours and fruits of autumn. Gravel courtyard with summer roses, hydrangeas, exotics, and many potted hostas. Gravel courtyard and several small steps where additional help may be required. Grass paths.

4 NEW ♦ BOSCOBEL HOUSE AND THE ROYAL OAK
Boscobel Lane, Bishops Wood, Stafford, ST19 9AR. English Heritage, www.english-heritage.org.uk/visit/places/boscobel-house-and-the-royal-oak. *8m NW of W'ton. The site is on a minor road off A41 Whitchurch Rd, N of M54 J3. Turn R at The Bell Inn, after 3m turn R at Bishop's Wood Village Hall.* **For NGS: Evening opening Thur 18 June (5.30-7). Adm £20, chd free. Pre-booking essential, please email fundraising@english-heritage.org.uk or visit www.english-heritage.org.uk/visit/places/boscobel-house-and-the-royal-oak for information & booking. Light refreshments. For other opening times and information, please email or visit garden website.**
Boscobel House's Royal Oak tree became a refuge for Charles II when he was fleeing for his life after his Civil War defeat at the Battle of Worcester in 1651. Discover a charming period garden complete with a winding willow tunnel. This delightful outdoor space invites visitors to meander through living features that echo the site's heritage and family life.

5 BRAMBLE COTTAGE
Shotatton, Ruyton XI Towns, Shrewsbury, SY4 1JG. Brigette & Adam Wilson, 07739 182315, brigette.wilson14@gmail.com, www.instagram.com/our.english.topiarygarden. *1m W of Ruyton Village towards Shotatton.* **Visits by arrangement Apr to Oct. Guided tours with the owners. Adm £5, chd free.**
Bramble Cottage is a topiary garden created and maintained by us for 28 years. We have box parterres, a formal rose garden and yew and box topiary. It is a ¾ acre site in rural Shropshire with lots of box balls and new topiary in development. There are also herbaceous borders with cottage style planting.

GROUP OPENING

6 BRAMBLE RIDGE
Bramble Ridge, Bridgnorth, WV16 4SQ. *From Bridgnorth N on B4373 signed Broseley: 1st on R, Stanley Ln then 1st on R. From Broseley S on B4373: L into Stanley Ln & 1st R.* **Sun 14 June (11-5). Combined adm £6, chd free. Home-made teas.**

NEW 16 BRAMBLE RIDGE
Rob & Wendy Barker.

NEW 25 BRAMBLE RIDGE
Elizabeth Stoll.

48 BRAMBLE RIDGE
Heather Frances, 07572 706706, heatherfran48@gmail.com.
Visits also by arrangement Apr to Oct.

Three unique cottage style gardens. Explore a steep garden with many steps; part wild, part cultivated, terraced in places and overlooking the Severn Valley with views to High Rock and Queens Parlour. A woodland adventure awaits with steps all the way up from bottom to top with amazing views. Then a wide gravel garden on different levels with raised beds and a waterfall. Interestingly planted with shrubs, herbaceous and climbers, some unusual. Lastly, developed over 20 years, the garden comprises a mixture of terraces and border along with a productive greenhouse, polytunnel and fruit cages. Also incorporating fern border, woodland, and rose border with established perennials and shrubs. All the garden owners are very much looking forward to sharing their gardens with visitors.

7 THE BRAMLEYS
Condover, Shrewsbury, SY5 7BH. Toby & Julie Shaw. *3m S of Shrewsbury. Through Condover towards Dorrington. Pass village hall follow road round, cross the bridge, in approx 100 metres there is a drive on L. Parking limited, please park at sch & walk to garden.* **Sun 3 May (11-5). Adm £6, chd free. Home-made teas.**

A large country garden extending to two acres with a variety of trees and shrubs, herbaceous borders and a woodland with the Cound Brook flowing through. A courtyard oasis welcomes you as you enter the garden with far-reaching views over open countryside. Wheelchair access around most of the garden, although not for the woodland area.

8 BROOCHES HOUSE
Park Lane, Craven Arms, SY7 9AB. Anthony & Julia Wood, 07971 020941, anthony@woodshropshire.co.uk. *1m from Craven Arms. From Craven Arms take B4368 towards Clun, as you leave the town turn L to Rowton, go under railway bridge & take R turn. Follow signs up grass track to parking.* **Visits by arrangement May to Aug for groups of 5 to 30. Adm £7.50, chd free. Home-made teas.**

The house and gardens have been created by the present owners over 40 years. A traditional layout with mixed herbaceous borders, rose beds, lawns and terraces with beautiful views towards the Stretton Hills. Further five acres recently acquired with kitchen and soft fruit sections, wildlife pools, and large areas of wildflower meadows with grassland walks. Majority of the gardens can be accessed by wheelchairs but some gravel paths.

9 BROWNHILL HOUSE
Ruyton XI Towns, SY4 1LR. Roger & Yoland Brown, 01939 261121, brownhill@eleventowns.co.uk, www.eleventowns.co.uk. *9m NW of Shrewsbury on B4397. On the B4397 in the village of Ruyton XI Towns.* **Visits by arrangement May & June. Adm £5, chd free. Home-made teas.**

A unique two acre hillside garden with many steps and levels bordering River Perry. Visitors can enjoy a wide variety of plants and styles from formal terraces to woodland paths. The Good Garden Guide said 'It has to be seen to be believed'. The lower areas are for the sure-footed while the upper levels with a large kitchen garden and glasshouses have many places to sit and enjoy the views.

GROUP OPENING

10 BUNTINGSDALE PARK GARDENS
Buntingsdale, Market Drayton, TF9 2EP. *Access only via Tern Hill A41. N on A41. Enter Tern Hill take 1st R onto Hedley Way, or going S turn L onto Hedley Way after Nationwide Caravans sales. What3words app: undivided.orbited. apprehend.* **Sun 19 Apr (1-4); Sun 19 July (2-5); Sun 20 Sept (1-4). Combined adm £6, chd free. Home-made teas at 17 Mortimer Rd.**

17 MORTIMER ROAD
Martin & Stella Clifford-Jones, 07484 327979, pomona_scj@hotmail.com.
Open on all dates
Visits also by arrangement 20 Apr to 4 Oct.

18 MORTIMER ROAD
Michael & Christine Simpson.
Open on all dates

10 OTTLEY WAY
Jean & Steve Carter.
Open on Sun 19 July

Buntingsdale Park is a hidden gem comprised of former RAF officers' houses built during World War II. Three very different gardens will open this year with features inc an orchard, vegetable plots, meadow, ponds and roses, plus rare and interesting plants inc orchids. There is an emphasis on encouraging wildlife through the planting of native species, habitat provision and avoidance of chemicals. Parking, WC, plant sale and refreshments are available at 17 Mortimer Road where there are a dozen different seating areas from which to choose. Wheelchair access to most areas of the gardens with one small step between some areas.

11 ♦ BURFORD HOUSE GARDENS
Burford House, Burford, Tenbury Wells, WR15 8HQ. British Garden Centres, 01584 810177, pbenson@britishgardencentres.com, www.britishgardencentres.com/burford-house-garden-centre. *1m W of Tenbury Wells on A456. Follow signs for Burford House Garden Centre off the A456 & the A49 at Wooferton.* **For NGS: Sun 19 Apr, Sat 23, Sun 24 May, Sat 26, Sun 27 Sept (10-4). Adm £5, chd free. Tea, coffee & cake in Burford House. Restaurant open nearby on site for breakfast, lunch & teas.** For other opening times and information, please phone, email or visit garden website.

The garden is being restored by the Garden Angels (volunteers) under the leadership of the newly appointed Head Gardener. Four acres of sweeping lawns bordered by the River Teme, and serpentine borders, set in the beautiful Teme Valley, around an elegant Georgian House (open for teas). Designed by the late, great plantsman, John Treasure and featuring over 100 varieties of clematis in addition to a myriad of plants in wonderful combinations and colours. Garden centre offers a comprehensive range of plants, gifts and outdoor leisure. Well behaved dogs on lead welcomed.

12 CHERRY TREE ARBORETUM
Cherry Tree Lane, Woore, CW3 9SR. John & Liz Ravenscroft, www.cherrytreearboretum.org. *½ m N of Woore on the Nantwich Rd. Off the A51 Nantwich Rd in Woore (just N of the village centre). Signs directing you along Cherry Tree Ln to its end.* **Sat 4 Apr, Sat 9 May, Sat 3 Oct (10.30-4). Adm £10, chd free. Light refreshments.**

Created in 2006 on 50 acres of unspoilt, pastureland scattered with mature oaks by John and Liz Ravenscroft. Located on a hilly area overlooking the Cheshire plain with views to the Pennines in the north, the Peckforton Hills to the northwest and the Breiddons to the southwest. It is a showcase of specimen trees with magnolias, peonies, dahlias, lilacs, deciduous azaleas and North American oaks. April is an avenue of white magnolias in many varieties. The earliest of the cherries will also be opening. A series of trails and paths run between meadows and native

Longner Hall

wildflowers in the arboretum. It also contains 19 of England's Champion Trees. Autumn colour is amazing.

13 NEW THE CITADEL
Weston-under-Redcastle, SY4 5JY. Beverley & Sylvia Griffiths, 07734 544617, hello@thecitadelweston.co.uk. *12m N of Shrewsbury on A49. At Xrds turn for Hawkstone Park, through village of Weston-under-Redcastle, ¼m on R beyond village.* **Wed 13 May (2-5). Adm £6, chd free. Home-made teas.**
Imposing castellated house (not open) stands in four acres. Mature garden, with fine trees, rhododendrons, azaleas, acers and camellias. Herbaceous borders; walled potager and Victorian thatched summerhouse provide added interest. Paths meander around and over sandstone outcrop at centre. First opened for the National Garden Scheme in 1927.

14 CRUCKFIELD HOUSE
Shoothill, Ford, SY5 9NR. Geoffrey Cobley, 01743 850222, geoffcobley541@btinternet.com. *5m W of Shrewsbury. A458 from Shrewsbury, turn L towards Shoothill.* **Visits by arrangement 31 May to 2 Aug. Adm £10, chd free. Tea & cakes only available to larger groups.**
An artist's romantic three acre garden, formally designed, informally and intensively planted with a great variety of unusual herbaceous plants. Nick's garden, with many species' trees, shrubs and wildflower meadow, surrounds a lake with bog and moisture-loving plants. Ornamental kitchen garden. Rose and peony walk. Courtyard fountain garden, large shrubbery and extensive clematis collection. Extensive topiary, and lily pond.

15 EATON MASCOTT HALL
Eaton Mascott, Cross Houses, Shrewsbury, SY5 6HG. The Gentilomo Family. *7m S of Shrewsbury. On A458 2nd R past Cross Houses, thereafter follow signs.* **Sun 7 June (10.30-4.30). Adm £5, chd free. Tea, coffee & cake.**
A beautiful six acre garden consisting of 1½ acre walled garden with extensive rose collection. Emphasis on symmetry with pergolas, water features and cross views. Bamboo walk and acer collection, specimen trees. Wander through the woodland garden and view glimpses of parkland and surrounding countryside, plus ferns, azaleas and rhododendrons. Wheelchair access possible if accompanied by helper.

16 THE FERNS
Newport Street, Clun, SY7 8JZ. Andrew Dobbin, 01588 640064, andrew.clun@outlook.com. *Enter Clun from Craven Arms. Take 2nd R signed into Ford St. At T-junc turn R for parking in the Memorial Hall car park (100 yds). Retrace steps to T-junc. The Ferns is on L.* **Sun 10 May, Sun 9 Aug (12-6). Adm £5, chd free. Visits also by arrangement 18 Apr to 11 Oct.**
A formal village garden of ¾ acre, approached via a drive lined with crab apple and pear trees. On the right is the autumn garden, giving fine views of the surrounding hills. From the front courtyard garden a path leads through double herbaceous borders full of late summer colour, to further rooms, of yew, beech and box. There is also a rear courtyard with tender exotics and a greenhouse. Lily pond and statuary. Yew and silver birch avenues.

17 ◆ GOLDSTONE HALL GARDENS
Goldstone, Market Drayton, TF9 2NA. John Cushing, 01630 661202, enquiries@goldstonehall.uk, www.goldstonehall.com. *5m N of Newport on A41. From Shrewsbury A53, R for A41 Hinstock & follow brown signs & yellow NGS signs What3words app: stirs.describes. mute.* **For NGS: Wed 13 May, Wed 10 June, Wed 15 July, Wed 12 Aug, Wed 9 Sept (12-5). Adm £9, chd free. Tea, coffee & cake. Hotel restaurant open for lunches. Pre-bookings only. For other opening times and information, please phone, email or visit garden website.**
Spanning five acres with productive kitchen garden inc unusual vegetables, fruits, spices and herb garden, all underpinning the award-winning hotel restaurant. Visitors enjoy roses in the Walled Garden from May, double-tiered herbaceous borders in July and late-season colour. Extensive kitchen garden, living box sign, colourful herbaceous borders, unusual plants and extensive well maintained lawns. Winner of the prestigious Good Hotel Guide's Editor's Choice Award for Gardens. Majority of garden is wheelchair accessible on gravel and lawns.

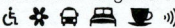

18 GROOMS COTTAGE
Waters Upton, Telford, TF6 6NP. Joanne & Andi Butler, 07484 236893, groomscottagegarden@gmail.com. *Parking available on the verge opp the church or in the village hall car park. Regret, no parking at the property due to restricted access.* **Sat 27, Sun 28 June, Sat 11, Sun 12 July (11-4). Adm £6, chd free. Tea, coffee & cake. Visits also by arrangement 22 June to 19 July for groups of 10 to 40.**
Be prepared to be surprised at what lies behind the garden gate. A cottage garden, around ½ an acre in size comprising mixed herbaceous borders and an abundance of English roses. Highlights inc home-made water features, raised beds and pergolas, oriental garden, hosta gardens and a productive fruit and vegetable garden and greenhouse. Travel inspired garden set out as different garden rooms. Some gravel areas not accessible for wheelchair users.

19 GWYNT NEWYDD
3 Penygarreg Rise, Pant, Oswestry, SY10 8JR. Douglas & Jane Wood, 07967 283721, douglas.woods@ngs.org.uk. *5m S of Oswestry. A483 S from Oswestry towards Welshpool. Follow signs when in Pant Village, turn opp shop in to Penygarreg Ln, then 1st R into Penygarreg Rise, No 3 on R.* **Visits by arrangement 1 Aug to 16 Aug for groups of up to 15. Parking on drive is limited, so car share if possible. Adm £5, chd free. Tea, coffee & cake.**
Much to discover in this average size garden to the side and rear of detached bungalow in a quiet close. Acer trees, borders with mixed herbaceous perennials, cannas, large hosta collection, ferns, phlox, greenhouse with succulents. Small area with productive raised vegetable beds. Fruit trees and ornamental trees.

20 NEW HILL VIEW HARDY PLANTS
Worfield, Bridgnorth, WV15 5NT. Mr John & Mrs Ingrid Millington, www.hillviewhardyplants.com. *1½m from Worfield. 300yds from B4176 Chesterton Golf course x-roads. From A454 turn R by Wheel pub & R after 15yds. 1½m turn L. Brown signs from both directions.* **Sun 19 Apr (10-4). Adm £5, chd free. Tea, coffee & cake.**
A small plant nursery specialising in auriculas with over a 1000 varieties flowering in the stock tunnel; this is most likely the largest collection in UK together with other primulas. In addition there are borders with mainly herbaceous plants, together with a pool and damp area covered in primulas. We also hold the National Collection of acanthus.

Stanley Hall Gardens

SHROPSHIRE 447

21 ♦ HODNET HALL GARDENS
Hodnet, Market Drayton, TF9 3NN. Sir Algernon & The Hon Lady Heber-Percy, 01630 685786, secretary@hodnethall.com, www.hodnethallgardens.org. 5½m SW of Market Drayton. 12m NE Shrewsbury. At junc of A53 & A442. Tickets available to purchase online or on the gate on the day. What3words app: footpath.shortens.challenge. **For NGS: Sun 5 July (10-5). Adm £10, chd £1. Light refreshments in the Garden Restaurant.** For other opening times and information, please phone, email or visit garden website.
The 60+ acres of Hodnet Hall Gardens are amongst the finest in the country. There has been a park and gardens at Hodnet for many hundreds of years. Magnificent forest trees, ornamental shrubs and flowers planted to give interest and colour from early spring to late autumn. Woodland walks alongside pools and lakes, home to abundant wildlife. Productive walled kitchen garden and historic dovecot. Maps are available to show access for our less mobile visitors.
& ⚐ ⊝ NPC ☕

22 HORATIO'S GARDEN
The Robert Jones & Agnes Hunt Orthopaedic Hospital, Gobowen, Oswestry, SY10 7AG. Horatio's Garden, www.horatiosgarden.org.uk. *From A5 follow signs to Orthopaedic Hospital & park in visitor car park (pay & display). Follow yellow NGS signs along Twmpath Ln to entrance gate. Free parking for National Garden Scheme visitors on the open day.* **Sat 18 Apr (12-3). Adm £6, chd free. Tea, coffee & cake.**
Beautifully designed by Bunny Guinness and delightfully planted, Horatio's Garden Midlands opened to great acclaim in September 2019. Partly funded by the National Garden Scheme, the garden offers a stunning sanctuary for patients, their families and NHS staff spending time in the Midland Centre for Spinal Injuries. Featuring social spaces and sheltered areas, raised beds, beautiful planting, garden room, glasshouse and serpentine rill, this is a horticultural and therapeutic delight like no other. Very good wheelchair access throughout.
& ✿ ☕

23 HUNDRED HOUSE HOTEL
Bridgnorth Road, Norton, Telford, TF11 9EE. Henry Phillips, 01952 580240, reservations@hundredhouse.co.uk, www.hundredhouse.co.uk. *10 mins from Ironbridge. Situated on the A442 in the village of Norton. Midway between Bridgnorth & Telford.* **Wed 6 May, Wed 17 June, Wed 15 July (11-4). Adm £5, chd free. Coffee, cakes & 3 menus on offer in our restaurant. Please see our website for details.** Visits also by arrangement for groups of 10 to 50.
An acre of gardens crafted over 35+ years, complete with sculptures, stonework and working herb and kitchen garden. From March onwards, you will find over 5000 bulb flowers inc tulips, hyacinths, daffodils, alliums, blossoming trees and dancing pond flowers. Summer brings a variety of flowers, inc David Austin roses, giant agapanthus, dahlias, clary, foxgloves, fuchsias and arum lilies. Please see website for restaurant booking and information.
⚐ ⊝ 🏠 ☕

24 THE LEASOWES GARDEN & ARBORETUM
Cound, Shrewsbury, SY5 6AF. Robert & Tricia Bland, 07802 667636, rjbbland1@outlook.com. *7m SE of Shrewsbury. On the A458 SE of Shrewsbury, 500m to the E of the Riverside Inn on Cressage Straight.* **Sat 17 Oct (10-4.30). Adm £7, chd free. Tea, coffee & cake.** Visits also by arrangement 1 Apr to 15 Nov for groups of 15 to 25. Donation to International Dendrology Society.
Within the super structure of mature larches and interconnected ponds, a wide range of rhododendrons and azaleas have been planted as well as shade appreciating trees and shrubs over 10 acres. A large offering of roses of all descriptions provide colour throughout the formal gardens.
& ⚐ ☕

25 LILLESHALL HOME FARM
The Incline, Lilleshall, Newport, TF10 9AP. Connie Sansom. *Follow signs for Lilleshall National Sports Centre. Our entrance is off the sports centre drive, which will be signposted.* **Fri 5 June (10-4). Adm £5, chd free. Tea, coffee & cake.**
A beautiful country farmhouse garden with far-reaching views across the Shropshire countryside. The garden is split into several areas for you to explore inc formal herbaceous borders with rose beds, a tennis court lined with hydrangeas, pergola and more. Discover our croquet lawn, pond, orchard, greenhouse and vegetable patch. The farm is also home to horses, sheep, chickens, ducks and two pigs. There will be plants and garden ornaments for sale. There is a wheelchair accessible route around the garden over areas of grass and gravel.
& ⚐ ✿ ☕ 🔊

26 NEW LITTLE HEATH GREEN COTTAGE
Little Heath Green, Almington, Market Drayton, TF9 2PW. David & Catherine Machin. *Off the A53 between Market Drayton & Loggerheads. Turn of A53 by thatched cottage. Go ¼m down lane & turn at grass triangle down single track: a dead end lane. What3words app: dance.assist.honeybees.* **Sat 6 June (11-4). Adm £5, chd free. Home-made teas.**
An English cottage style garden with a pond and colourful mixed borders as well as a courtyard and small wooded area. We have a variety of hostas, peonies, geraniums, dahlias and other planting. Explore the small orchard and take a seat at some covered areas. A wheelchair can access the main lawn and seating spots via a ramp.
& ✿ ☕

27 LONGDEN MANOR
Pontesbury, Shrewsbury, SY5 0XL. Karen Lovegrove. *5m S of Shrewsbury. From Shrewsbury take C150 Longden Road & on entering Longden Village, turn R opp The Tankerville Pub & Longden Stores.* **Sun 10 May (10-4). Adm £5, chd free. Home-made teas.**
Large estate garden with lots of character and interest: wander through woodland walks and on grass paths. Discover our humorous topiary, wide variety of specimen trees and rhododendrons and azaleas. We also have wildflowers, a water garden, holly garden and Fairy Trail. Relax and take in the panoramic vistas of surrounding countryside. A great place for all the family to visit. Topiary Trail for children.
✿ ☕ 🔊

28 LONGNER HALL
Atcham, Shrewsbury, SY4 4TG. Mr & Mrs R L Burton, www.longner.co.uk. *4m SE of Shrewsbury. From M54 follow A5 to Shrewsbury, then B4380 to Atcham. From Atcham take Uffington Rd, entrance ¼m on L. What3words app: brilliant.overtime.plugged.* **Sun 17 May (2-5). Adm £6, chd free. Home-made teas.**
A long drive approach through parkland designed by Humphry Repton. Walks lined with golden yew through extensive lawns, with views over the Severn Valley. Borders containing roses and herbaceous shrubs, also an ancient yew wood. Enclosed one acre walled garden open to National Garden Scheme visitors. Mixed planting, garden buildings, tower and game larder.

29 LOWER BROOKSHILL
Nind, nr Lydham, SY5 0JW. Patricia & Robin Oldfield, 01588 650137, robin.oldfield@live.com. *3m N of Lydham on A488. Take signed turn to Nind & after ½m sharp L & follow narrow road for another ¾m.* **Sat 25, Sun 26 July (1-5). Adm £6, chd free. Cream teas.**
Ten acres of hillside garden and woods at 950ft within the AONB. Begun in 2010 from a derelict and overgrown site, cultivated areas now rub shoulders with the natural landscape using fine borrowed views over and down a valley. Inc brook side walks, a 'pocket' park, four ponds (inc a Monet lily pond), mixed borders and lawns, cottage garden and wildflowers. Lovely picnic spots. Cash only at gate.

30 107 MEADOWBOUT WAY
Bowbrook, Shrewsbury, SY5 8QB. Sue & Mark Smith, 07736 837427, sue1706@outlook.com. *2m S of Shrewsbury. On the estate follow Squinter Pip Way until you see Meadowbout Way on R. You will see the NGS sign at the end of the straight section.* **Visits by arrangement 4 July to 9 Aug for groups of up to 14. Adm £6, chd free. Tea, coffee & cake.**
Our oasis is a small town garden completed in a tropical style. There are several examples of plants native to other shores but which are happy in the space we have created. With over 200 plants inc tree ferns, bananas, palm trees and cottage garden plants arranged around a variety of seating areas, our visitors have a perpetual sense of being on holiday. Direct access to the garden via a side gate.

31 MERTON
Shepherds Lane, Bicton, Shrewsbury, SY3 8BT. David & Jessica Pannett, 01743 850773, jessicapannett@hotmail.co.uk. *3m W of Shrewsbury. Follow B4380 from Shrewsbury past Shelton for 1m. Shepherd's Ln turn L garden signed on R. Or from A5 bypass at Churncote r'about, turn towards Shrewsbury, 2nd turn L is Shepherds Ln.* **Visits by arrangement 1 June to 27 Sept for groups of up to 25. Adm £5, chd free. Tea.**
Mature ½ acre botanical garden with a rich collection of trees and shrubs inc unusual conifers from around the world. Hardy perennial borders with seasonal flowers and grasses plus an award winning collection of hosta varieties in a woodland setting. Outstanding gunneras in a waterside setting with moisture loving plants. Wheelchair access over level paths and lawns.

32 THE MILL HOUSE
Mill Lane, Ruyton XI Towns, Shrewsbury, SY4 1LR. Debbie Sargent & Jeffrey Ewin. *SE of Ruyton X1Towns. Mill Ln can be found on leaving the village just before Platt Bridge. Parking in Mill Ln, 7mins walk from garden. Disabled parking at the house.* **Sun 7 June (2-5). Adm £5, chd free. Tea, coffee & cake.**
Four acre garden situated alongside the River Perry. Discover herbaceous borders with roses, peonies and climbers. Explore the terrace, sloping lawns, and unusual trees in a naturalised woodland as well as an ancient mill pond. We also have a vegetable garden and strive to be wildlife friendly. Uneven ground and some sloping pathways. Adjacent to arboretum with National Collection of *Betula*.

33 MILLICHOPE PARK
Munslow, SY7 9HA. Mr & Mrs Frank Bury, www.millichopepark.com. *8m NE of Craven Arms. Off B4368 Craven Arms to Bridgnorth Rd. Nr Munslow then follow yellow signs.* **Sun 11 Oct (2-5). Adm £6, chd free. Tea, coffee & cake.**
Historic landscape gardens covering 14 acres with lakes and cascades dating from C18, formal terraces, woodland walks and wildflowers. Spectacular display of autumnal colours in October. Please note, we regret the Walled Garden and Wildegoose Nursery will not be opening jointly on these National Garden Scheme days.

34 MOAT HALL
Annscroft, Shrewsbury, SY5 8AZ. Martin & Helen Davies, 01743 860216, helenatthefarm@hotmail.co.uk. *3m S of Shrewsbury. Take the Longden Rd from Shrewsbury to Hook a Gate. Our lane is 2nd on R after Hook a Gate & before Annscroft. Single track lane with passing places for ½m.* **Sun 9 Aug (2-5.30). Adm £6, chd free. Tea, coffee & cake. Visits also by arrangement Apr to Sept.**
An acre garden around an old farmhouse within a dry moat. Well organised and extensive kitchen garden, fruit garden and orchard for self-sufficiency. Colourful herbaceous borders; stumpery; raised cut flower borders; ⅔ acre pond nearby with oak gazebo; many interesting stone items inc troughs, cheese weights, staddle stones some uncovered in the garden. Plenty of seating areas on the lawns for enjoying the garden. Wheelchair access: mostly lawn with one grass and one concrete ramp; kitchen garden has 2' wide paved paths. Paved path to the pond and gazebo.

35 THE MOUNT
Bull Lane, Bishops Castle, SY9 5DA. Heather Willis, 07779 314609, adamheather@btopenworld.com. *Off A488 Shrewsbury to Knighton Rd. At top of the town, 130 metres up Bull Ln on R. No parking at property. Free parking in Bishops Castle.* **Visits by arrangement 13 Apr to 30 Sept for groups of 5+. Tea, coffee & cake.**
An acre of garden that has evolved over 24 years, with four lawns, a rose bed in the middle of the drive with pink and white English roses, and herbaceous and mixed shrub borders. There are roses planted throughout

the garden and in the spring daffodils and tulips abound. Two large beech trees frame the garden with a view that sweeps down the valley over fields and then up to the Long Mynd. Wheelchair access easy to most parts of the garden, but not to WC.

Buntingsdale Park Gardens

36 OFFCOT
Kynaston, Kinnerley, SY10 8EF. Tom Pountney. *Just off A5 on Wolfshead r'about (Oswestry end of Nesscliffe bypass) towards Knockin. Then take the 1st L towards Kinnerley. Follow NGS signs from this road.* **Thur 16, Fri 17, Sat 18, Sun 19 July, Fri 9, Sat 10, Sun 11 Oct (10-5). Combined adm with Appledore £7, chd free. Tea, coffee & cake.** A cottage garden with lots of winding pathways leading to different focal points. The garden is packed with a wide range of evergreen and deciduous trees and shrubs and underplanted with herbaceous perennials. There is a natural looking pond with a running stream feeding into it. A haven for wildlife. So many different areas to see and enjoy inc the garden bar.

37 NEW THE OLD FARMHOUSE
Church Lane, Boningale, Albrighton, WV7 3BY. Dipika & Nick Price, 07768 834695, dipika.price@gmail.com. *1m S of Albrighton. Off the A464. The house faces the 'No Entry' lane off Church Ln.* **Visits by arrangement May to Sept for groups of 10+. Adm £10, chd free. Tea, coffee & cake.** An acre cottage garden complementing a C17 timber-framed house in a rural hamlet. Planting reflects the house's character with lots of colour, a vegetable and cutting garden and cobbled paths. A local first-prize winner. Also open are Nick's wood, wetland meadow and replanted hedgerows, 11 acres of native planting from 1999, now a thriving ecosystem of orchids and wildflowers.

38 THE OLD VICARAGE, BISHOPS CASTLE
Church Lane, Bishops Castle, SY9 5AF. Helen & Jerry Robinson. *Nr the junc of Church St & Kerry Ln, directly behind St John's Church. Pedestrian access through the main gate on Church Ln or through the garden gate to the rear of St John's churchyard.* **Sun 21 June (12-7). Adm £6, chd free. Tea, coffee & cake.** Extending to just over 1½ acres, the gardens inc lawns surrounded by perennial beds and mature shrubs, a pond, orchard, rose garden and a romantic ruin, remains of the lost C13 church. Tending toward the wild, the garden is full of colour; foxgloves, roses, wisteria, rhododendron, alliums and ornamental trees. Sales by local artists and craftsmen throughout the garden.

39 OTELEY
Ellesmere, SY12 0PB. Mr Robert Mainwaring, www.oteley.com. *1m SE of Ellesmere. Entrance out of Ellesmere past Mere, opp Convent nr to A528/495 junc.* **Mon 4 May (10-4). Adm £6, chd free. Light refreshments.** Explore 10 acres running down to The Mere with stunning views. Walled kitchen garden, architectural features, many old interesting trees. Rhododendrons, azaleas, woodland walk and views across Mere to Ellesmere. First opened in 1927 when the National Garden Scheme started.

40 RIVERSIDE
Berrisford Road, Market Drayton, TF9 1JH. Eric & Susan Harrison, 01630 655678, riversidegardensuk@yahoo.co.uk. *Market Drayton. Enter Market Drayton on Newcastle Rd & turn into Great Hales St. Then take L into Berrisford Rd.* **Sun 17 May, Sun 26 July (1-5). Adm £5, chd free. Tea, coffee & cake. Visits also by arrangement 3 May to 30 Aug.** The garden is ¾ acre, with different planting areas. We have hydrangeas, hostas, woodland walk, hot garden and herbaceous borders with white garden with loggia. Plus an old and large wisteria and a very old climbing rose. Wheelchair access over gravel drive but mainly level paths.

41 RUTHALL MANOR
Ditton Priors, Bridgnorth, WV16 6TN. Mr & Mrs G T Clarke, 07791 099620, clrk608@btinternet.com. *7m SW of Bridgnorth. At Ditton Priors Church take road signed Bridgnorth, then 2nd L. Garden 1m. On 4th May ONLY please come to Ditton from the B4368 due to road closures.* **Mon 4, Sun 24, Mon 25 May, Sat 20, Sun 21 June, Sat 18, Sun 19 July (12.30-5). Adm £7, chd free. Home-made teas. Visits also by arrangement Apr to Oct.**
Offset by a mature collection of specimen trees, the garden is divided into intimate sections, carefully linked by winding paths. The front lawn flanked by striking borders, extends to a gravel, art garden and ha-ha. Clematis and roses scramble through an eclectic collection of wrought-iron work, unique pottery and secluded seating. Designed and planted by present owners since 1960. A stunning horse pond with primulas, iris and bog plants. Jigsaw puzzle sale. Wheelchair access to most areas of garden.

GROUP OPENING

42 NEW ST MARY'S GARDEN TRAIL
St Johns Hill, Ellesmere, SY12 0HA. Mr David Reffell. *From the centre of Ellesmere, at Cross St or The Mere, follow signs to St John's Hill or St Mary's Church.* **Sat 20 June (2-5). Combined adm £5, chd free. Home-made teas.**
A cluster of gardens surrounding the beautiful St Mary's Church in the oldest part of Ellesmere. Some 'hidden', some with views of the famous Mere and a real variety; inc newly designed gardens, traditional cottage gardens and others all situated a short walk from the centre of town.

43 SAMBROOK MANOR
Sambrook, TF10 8AL. Mrs E Mitchell, 01952 550256. *Between Newport & Tern Hill, 1m off A41.* **Sun 5 July (12-5). Adm £6, chd free. Home-made teas. Visits also by arrangement for groups of 10+.**
Deep, colourful, well-planted borders offset by sweeping lawns surrounding an early C18 manor house (not open).

Wide ranging herbaceous planting with plenty of roses to enjoy; the arboretum below the garden, with views across the river, has been further extended with new trees. The waterfall and Japanese garden are now linked by a pretty rill. Lovely garden to visit for all the family. Wheelchair access to most areas. Woodland area may be difficult.

44 1 SCOTSMANSFIELD
Burway Road, Church Stretton, SY6 6DP. Peter Vickers & Hilary Taylor, 07979 866695, hilary-taylor@htla.co.uk. *Scotsmansfield is on L, c.200m up Burway Rd (quite steep). Approach Church Stretton from A49. At Sandford Rd/ High St jct, turn R & then L, up Burway Rd. No parking. Easthope Rd car park (near Co-op) available SY6 6BL. Shuttle bus running from here.* **Sat 27 June (11-5). Adm £6, chd free. Light refreshments. Visits also by arrangement 4 Apr to 11 July for groups of 10 to 25.**
Terraced garden of ¾ acre, renewed over a decade after long neglect. Attached to east wing of 'Scotsmansfield' (not open), built 1908. Celebration of favourite plants, with colour, shape, texture, scent, light, shade and plentiful wildlife. Trees, fernery, lily pond, mixed borders, yew hedges, lavish roses. Areas of tranquillity and intimacy, occasions of drama and long views of surrounding woods and hills. Partial access via steep gravelled paths to some areas. Wheelchair users will need support from an assistant.

GROUP OPENING

45 THE SECRET GARDENS AT STEVENTON TERRACE
Steventon Terrace, Steventon New Road, Ludlow, SY8 1JZ. Kevin & Carolyn Wood. *Easily accessible from A49; on-street parking; Park & Ride stops outside the garden. Gardens are located behind row of terraced cottages.* **Sat 20 June (1-5). Combined adm £5, chd free. Tea, coffee & cake. Ice cream also available.**

Discover some very secret gardens hidden behind a row of Victorian terraced cottages in Ludlow. A ½ acre south facing garden that has

been developed over 30 years. It has been divided into different sections which inc a rose garden, herbaceous borders, koi fish, chickens, polytunnel and greenhouse and a Mediterranean garden.

46 STANLEY HALL GARDENS
Bridgnorth, WV16 4SP. Mr & Mrs M J Thompson. *½m N of Bridgnorth. Leave Bridgnorth by N gate B4373; turn R at Stanley Ln. Pass Golf Course Club House on L & turn L at Lodge.* **Sun 31 May (2-5.30). Adm £5, chd free. Home-made teas.**
Regency landscaped garden with rhododendrons, woodland walks, fish ponds and fine trees in parkland setting. Dower House (Mr and Mrs C Wells): four acres of specimen trees, contemporary sculpture and walled vegetable garden South Lodge (Mr Tim Warren): Hillside cottage garden. Wheelchair access to the main gardens.

47 SUNNINGDALE
9 Mill Street, Wem, SY4 5ED. Mrs Susan Griffiths, 07760 663730, sue.griffiths@btinternet. com, www.facebook.com/ SunningdaleGardenWem. *Wem is on B5476. Parking in car park at Barnard St. Garden is opp the purple house below the church. Some on-street parking on High St. Coaches can drop off at the main gate.* **Sun 26 Apr (11-2); Sun 7 June (11-3). Adm £4, chd free. Tea, coffee & cake. Visits also by arrangement 2 Mar to 9 Nov for groups of 6 to 60. Discuss refreshments when booking.**
Explore this half an acre town garden; a wildlife haven for a variety of birds inc nesting Goldcrests. A profusion of excellent nectar rich plants means that butterflies and other pollinators are in abundance. Interesting planting with carefully collected rare plants and unusual annuals means there is always something new to see. Large perennial borders, with exotic climbers, designed as an year-round garden. Discover the koi pond and natural stone waterfall rockery. There are antique and modern sculptures. Gravel garden and beautiful seating areas many of which are under cover. Sound break yew walkway. Wheelchair access the garden is on the level but with several steps mostly around the pond area; paths are

48 TOWER HOUSE
Bache, Craven Arms, SY7 9LN. Lady Spicer, 01584 861692, nicspicer@yahoo.com. *6m NW of Ludlow. B4365: Ludlow to Much Wenlock. Turn L after 3m (Bache, Burley), garden at top of hill after 1½m. B4368: Craven Arms to Bridgnorth. 2m R at Xrds. L after 200yds. 1m fork L. garden after 200yds.* **Visits by arrangement 14 Mar to 26 July. Adm £8, chd free. Tea, coffee & cake.**
A folly built circa 1838 with a two acre garden created by the present owner of over 50 years. On a perfect site with views over the Corvedale, with veg, herbaceous borders, a small parterre and pond.

49 UPPER FARM GARDEN
Rushton, Shrewsbury, TF6 5AG. Pete & Paul Turpin-Ottley, 07523 438802, upperfarm@icloud.com. *3m from M54 J7 Wellington. Exit 7 M54 take Little Wenlock/Wrekin turn. In 1m at bollards R for Uppington. In 2m at junc, turn L for Eaton Constantine. In ½m R for Charlton Hill. See NGS signs on L for garden & parking.* **Sat 4, Sun 5 Apr, Sat 30, Sun 31 May, Sat 25, Sun 26 July, Sat 19, Sun 20 Sept (11-4). Adm £6, chd free. Tea, coffee & cake. Visits also by arrangement 6 Apr to 13 Sept for groups of 15 to 55. Adm inc refreshments.**
Farmhouse Garden with views of the Wrekin and the Stretton Hills. Comprising several garden 'rooms' connected by gravelled walkways interspersed with ample seating opportunities. Unusual features inc a raised scree terrace, a rose pergola and bed with 40 varieties of English shrub roses, a two sided herbaceous walk, an elevated viewing deck, a cactus house and self-sufficient allotment beds.

50 ♦ WALCOT HALL
Lydbury North, SY7 8AZ. Mr & Mrs C R W Parish, 01588 680570, enquiries@walcothall.com, www.walcothall.com. *4m SE of Bishop's Castle. B4385 Craven Arms to Bishop's Castle, turn L by The Powis Arms in Lydbury North.* **For NGS: Sun 24, Mon 25 May (1.30-**

5). Adm £7, chd free. Home-made teas in the ballroom. For other opening times and information, please phone, email or visit garden website.
Arboretum planted by Lord Clive of India's son, Edward in1800. Cascades of rhododendrons and azaleas amongst specimen trees and pools. Fine views of Sir William Chambers' Clock Towers, with lake and hills beyond. Walled kitchen garden, dovecote, meat safe, ice house and mile long lakes. Russian wooden church, grotto and fountain, tin chapel. Relaxed borders and rare shrubs. Lakeside replanted and water garden at western end reestablished.

51 WESTWOOD HOUSE
Oldbury, Bridgnorth, WV16 5LP. Hugh & Carolyn Trevor-Jones. *Take the Ludlow Rd (B4364) out of Bridgnorth, after the Punch Bowl Inn turn 1st L, Westwood House signed on R. What3words app: berated. swerves.refrained.* **Sun 26 Apr (2-5). Adm £6, chd free. Home-made teas.**
A country garden, well designed and planted around the house, particularly known for its tulips and use of colour. Sweeping lawns offset by deeply planted mixed borders; pool garden and lawn tennis court; kitchen and cutting garden, with everything designed to attract wildlife for organic growth. Woodland walks with far-reaching views of this delightful corner of the county. Reasonable wheelchair access but there are gravel paths and some steps.

52 THE WHITE HOUSE
Redbrook Maelor, Whitchurch, SY13 3AD. Claire & James Hennie, 07795 573205, clairehennie1@gmail.com. *2m W of Whitchurch. From Chester: Take A41 towards Whitchurch, (from Shrewsbury take A49 towards Whitchurch, then A41). At McDonalds r'about take A525 towards Wrexham. Garden approx 2m on L.* **Visits by arrangement 2 May to 20 Sept for groups of up to 12. Adm £10, chd free. Light refreshments.**
Created over the past 18 years by current owners from open sloping lawn, into garden 'rooms'. ⅕ acre garden on the site of a former smithy

dating back to the 1700's. Cottage garden: roses, perennials, evergreen shrubs. Vegetable garden: raised beds, asparagus border, central pergola, pretty potting shed. Yew garden: topiary, 'castle wall' hedge. Front garden parterre and water features.

53 WINDY RIDGE
Church Lane, Little Wenlock, TF6 5BB. George & Fiona Chancellor. *2m S of Wellington. Follow signs for Little Wenlock from N (J7, M54) or E (off A5223 at Horsehay). Parking signed. Do not rely on SatNav.* **Sat 6, Sun 7 June (12-5). Adm £7, chd free. Home-made teas.**
Universally admired for its structure, inspirational planting and balance of texture, form and all season colour, the garden more than lives up to its award winning record. Developed over 40 years, 'open plan' garden rooms display over 1000 species (mostly labelled) in a range of colour-themed planting styles, beautifully set off by well-tended lawns, plenty of water and fascinating sculpture. Wheelchair access via some gravel paths but help available.

54 ♦ WOLLERTON OLD HALL
Wollerton, Market Drayton, TF9 3NA. Lesley & John Jenkins, 01630 685760, admin@wollertonoldhallgarden.com, www.wollertonoldhallgarden.com. *4m SW of Market Drayton. On A53 between Hodnet & A53-A41 junction at Tern Hill. Follow brown signs.* **For NGS: Wed 2 Sept (11-5). Adm £10, chd free. Light lunches available from 12pm. Afternoon & cream teas from 2pm. For other opening times and information, please phone, email or visit garden website.**
Four acre garden created around C16 house (not open). Formal structure creates variety of gardens each with own colour theme and character. Planting is mainly of perennials many in their late summer and early autumn hues, particularly the asters. Ongoing lectures by gardening personalities, designers and technical experts. Winter Workshops. See website for updated information.

SOMERSET & BRISTOL

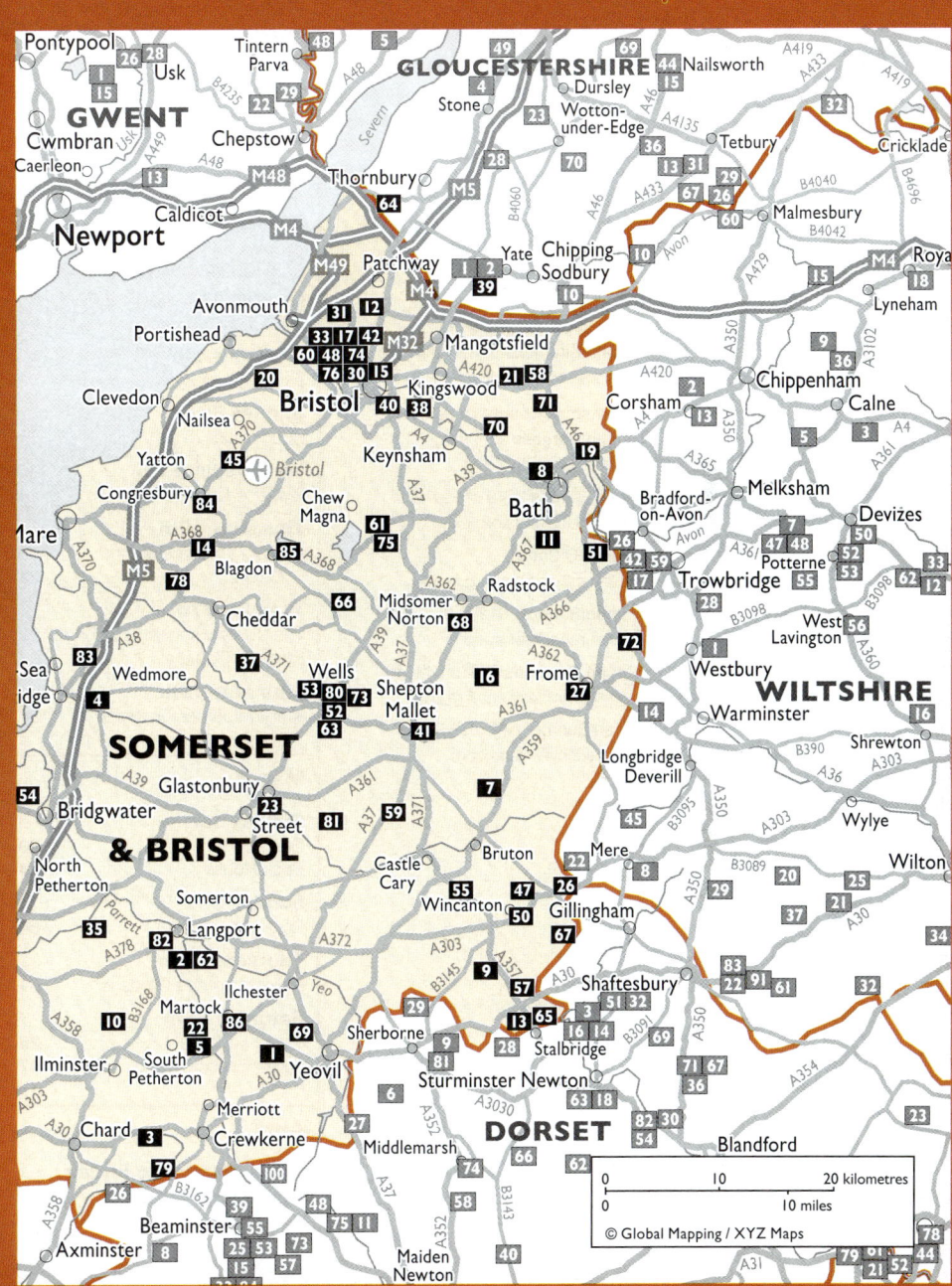

SOMERSET VOLUNTEERS

County Organiser
Laura Howard 01460 282911
laura.howard@ngs.org.uk

County Treasurer
Jill Wardle 07702 274492
jill.wardle@ngs.org.uk

Publicity
Roger Peacock
roger.peacock@ngs.org.uk

Social Media
Lisa Prior 07773 440147
lisa.prior@ngs.org.uk

Presentations
Dave & Prue Moon
01373 473381
davidmoon202@btinternet.com

Booklet Co-ordinator
John Simmons 07855 944049
john.simmons@ngs.org.uk

Booklet Distributor
Laura Howard (see above)

Assistant County Organisers
Jo Beaumont 07534 777278
jo.beaumont@ngs.org.uk

Marsha Casely 07854 882616
marsha.casely@ngs.org.uk

Patricia Davies-Gilbert
01823 412187
pdaviesgilbert@gmail.com

Alyson Holland 07729 059382
alyson.holland@btinternet.com

Janet Jones 01749 850509
janet.jones@ngs.org.uk

Sue Lewis 07885 369280
sue.lewis@ngs.org.uk

Lisa Prior (see above)

Judith Stanford 01761 233045
judith.stanford@ngs.org.uk

- @NGSSomerset
- @National Garden Scheme Bristol
- @ngssomerset
- @ngs_bristol_bath

BRISTOL AREA VOLUNTEERS

County Organiser
Roxanne Ismail 07966 474966,
roxanne.ismail@ngs.org.uk

County Treasurer
Harsha Parmar 07889 201185
harsha.parmar@ngs.org.uk

Publicity
Sheena Johnson 07712 043020
sheena.johnson@ngs.org.uk

Social Media
Harsha Parmar (see above)

Booklet Co-ordinator
John Simmons 07855 944049
john.simmons@ngs.org.uk

Assistant County Organisers
John Burgess 07795 466513
jb@chh.org.uk

Neil Jefferis 07792 539146
neil.jefferis@ngs.org.uk

Eilish O'Shea
eilish.oshea@ngs.org.uk

Irene Randow 01275 857208
irene.randow@sky.com

John Simmons 07855 944049
john.simmons@ngs.org.uk

Karl Suchy 07873 588540
karl.suchy@icloud.com

OPENING DATES

All entries subject to change.
For latest information check
www.ngs.org.uk
Map locator numbers are shown to the right of each garden name.
Extended openings are shown at the beginning of the month.

February

Snowdrop Openings

Sunday 1st	
Rock House	64
Thursday 5th	
Elworthy Cottage	24
Sunday 8th	
Rock House	64
Wednesday 11th	
Elworthy Cottage	24
Thursday 12th	
◆ East Lambrook Manor Gardens	22
Tuesday 17th	
The Downs Preparatory School	20
Elworthy Cottage	24
Thursday 19th	
◆ Hestercombe Gardens	34

March

Sunday 1st	
Greystones	30
Rock House	64
Sunday 8th	
Rock House	64
Thursday 19th	
◆ Hestercombe Gardens	34
Saturday 28th	
Forest Lodge	26
Lower Shalford Farm	47

April

Every Monday to Friday from Monday 13th
◆ Model Farm   54

SOMERSET & BRISTOL 455

Tuesday 7th	
Elworthy Cottage	24
Wednesday 8th	
Caisson Gardens	11
Thursday 9th	
◆ The Yeo Valley Organic Garden at Holt Farm	85
Sunday 12th	
Fairfield	25
Watcombe	78
Tuesday 14th	
◆ Greencombe Gardens	29
Saturday 18th	
Shanks House	67
Westbrook House	81
Tuesday 21st	
Elworthy Cottage	24
Saturday 25th	
Skool Beanz Children's Allotment	69
◆ The Walled Gardens of Cannington	77
Sunday 26th	
Greystones	30
4 Haytor Park	33
Lucombe House	48
◆ The Walled Gardens of Cannington	77

May

Every Monday to Friday to Friday 22nd	
◆ Model Farm	54
Saturday 2nd	
Forest Lodge	26
Lower Shalford Farm	47
The Manor	50
Sunday 3rd	
Court View	19
Little Yarford Farmhouse	46
The Manor	50
Monday 4th	
Little Yarford Farmhouse	46
Sunday 10th	
Stoke Bishop Gardens	74
NEW Yeo Meads	84
Tuesday 12th	
Elworthy Cottage	24
Thursday 14th	
Barford House	6

Saturday 16th	
◆ East Lambrook Manor Gardens	22
Sunday 17th	
Court House	18
Watcombe	78
Saturday 23rd	
Wick Farm	82
Sunday 24th	
Mellowstones	51
Wick Farm	82
Monday 25th	
Elworthy Cottage	24
Saturday 30th	
Japanese Garden Bristol	38
NEW Willow Bend	83
Sunday 31st	
81 Coombe Lane	17
◆ Milton Lodge	53
Wayford Manor	79

June

Every Monday to Friday	
◆ Model Farm	54
Saturday 6th	
NEW 9 Codrington Road	15
87 Hallen Road	31
30 Kingsholm Road	42
Sunday 7th	
Coleford House	16
87 Hallen Road	31
Kingsland	43
Lydeard House	49
Pennard House	59
Watcombe	78
Friday 12th	
◆ Kilver Court Gardens	41
Saturday 13th	
Batcombe House	7
Cherry Bolbery Farm	13
◆ East Lambrook Manor Gardens	22
John's Corner	40
Rose Cottage	65
Standerwick Court	72
◆ Stoberry Garden	73
Sunday 14th	
NEW Bath Priory Hotel	8
Cherry Bolbery Farm	13
Frome Gardens	27
John's Corner	40
Penny Brohn UK	60
Rose Cottage	65
◆ Stoberry Garden	73

Monday 15th	
NEW Bath Priory Hotel	8
Thursday 18th	
◆ Special Plants	71
Saturday 20th	
NEW Church View	14
The Old Rectory, Doynton	58
Shanks House	67
Sunday 21st	
NEW Church View	14
Tuesday 23rd	
Elworthy Cottage	24
Sunday 28th	
Court House	18
Doynton House	21
Hangeridge Farmhouse	32
◆ Milton Lodge	53
Nynehead Court	56
42 Silver Street	68

July

Every Monday to Friday to Friday 3rd	
◆ Model Farm	54
Sunday 5th	
NEW Charlton Road Allotments	12
◆ University of Bristol Botanic Garden	76
Yews Farm	86
Tuesday 7th	
Elworthy Cottage	24
Saturday 11th	
Babbs Farm	4
◆ East Lambrook Manor Gardens	22
Sunday 12th	
Babbs Farm	4
NEW Bath Priory Hotel	8
Monday 13th	
NEW Bath Priory Hotel	8
Tuesday 14th	
◆ Greencombe Gardens	29
Pennard House	59
Thursday 16th	
◆ Special Plants	71
Sunday 19th	
Stowey Gardens	75
Tuesday 21st	
Elworthy Cottage	24
Saturday 25th	
Babbs Farm	4
Goathurst Gardens	28
The Rib	63

Sunday 26th
Babbs Farm 4
Goathurst Gardens 28
Hangeridge Farmhouse 32

Wednesday 29th
The Downs Preparatory School 20

August

Saturday 1st
NEW The Blooming Wild Plant Nursery 9
NEW The Old Coach House 57

Saturday 8th
NEW Almonry Barn 2
NEW The Priest's House 62

Tuesday 11th
The Pony 61

Thursday 20th
◆ Special Plants 71

Saturday 29th
Westbrook House 81

Monday 31st
◆ Model Farm 54

September

Every Monday to Friday
◆ Model Farm 54

Saturday 5th
Skool Beanz Children's Allotment 69

Sunday 6th
NEW The Old Coach House 57
Yews Farm 86

Wednesday 9th
◆ The Newt in Somerset 55

Friday 11th
◆ Kilver Court Gardens 41

Saturday 12th
Batcombe House 7
South Kelding 70
◆ Stoberry Garden 73

Sunday 13th
◆ Stoberry Garden 73

Thursday 17th
◆ Special Plants 71

Saturday 19th
◆ The Walled Gardens of Cannington 77

Sunday 20th
◆ The Walled Gardens of Cannington 77

October

Every Monday to Friday to Friday 16th
◆ Model Farm 54

Thursday 15th
◆ Special Plants 71

Sunday 18th
NEW Japanese Garden, Frampton Cotterell 39

January 2027

Sunday 31st
Rock House 64

February 2027

Sunday 7th
Rock House 64

By Arrangement

Arrange a personalised garden visit with your club, or group of friends, on a date to suit you. See individual garden entries for full details.

Abbey Farm 1
Avalon 3
Barcroft Hall 5
Bradon Farm 10
Cherry Bolberry Farm 13
NEW Church View 14
81 Coombe Lane 17
Doynton House 21
NEW Elmcroft 23
Elworthy Cottage 24
Forest Lodge 26
Hangeridge Farmhouse 32
4 Haytor Park 33
Hillcrest 35
Hollam House 36
Honeyhurst Farm 37
Knoll Cottage 44
Little Bucklers 45
Little Yarford Farmhouse 46
Lucombe House 48
NEW 35 Millers Gardens 52
Pennard House 59
Penny Brohn UK 60
Rock House 64
Rose Cottage 65
Rose Cottage 66
42 Silver Street 68
South Kelding 70
Watcombe 78
Wellfield Barn 80
Westbrook House 81
Wick Farm 82
NEW Yeo Meads 84

The Old Coach House

THE GARDENS

1 ABBEY FARM
Montacute, TA15 6UA. Elizabeth McFarlane, 07769 116843, abbey.farm64@gmail.com. *4m from Yeovil. Follow A3088, take slip rd to Montacute, turn L at T-junction into village. Turn R between church & King's Arms (no through rd).* **Visits by arrangement 18 May to 26 June for groups of 10 to 30. Adm £10, chd free. Home-made teas. Details on request.**
A country house garden and wider historic landscape setting the scene for the Cluniac Priory gatehouse. Old ham stone walls together with a strong green structure gently restrain the exuberant planting. Towards the top of the garden a small arboretum has been planted with a view looking down on the ancient pastures.

2 NEW ALMONRY BARN
Law Lane, Muchelney, Langport, TA10 0DQ. Mr Neil & Mrs Romily Davies. *1m S of Langport, at the top of Law Lane on opp side to church. Large car park at property. What3words app: topic.shelving. decking.* **Sat 8 Aug (12-5). Combined adm with The Priest's House £7, chd £3. Tea, coffee & cake.**
A 2 acre garden on the edge of the Somerset Levels, surrounding a C13 barn, once part of Muchelney Abbey (now a wedding venue). Features inc an ancient cider orchard, walled garden, kitchen garden parterre and courtyard. Mixed borders offer year-round colour with varied seating areas inviting relaxation and views throughout.

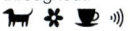

3 AVALON
Moor Lane, Higher Chillington, Ilminster, TA19 0PT. Dee & Tony Brook, 07506 688191, dee1jones@hotmail.com. *Just off the A30 between Crewkerne & Chard. From A30 turning signed to Chillington opp Swandown Lodges. Take 2nd L down Coley Ln & 1st L Moor Ln. Avalon is the large pink house. Parking limited so please car share. What3words app: dozed. peach.noise.* **Visits by arrangement June & July for groups of up to 40. Adm £7.50, chd £2. Home-made** teas. Gluten & dairy free cakes available if requested in advance.
Secluded hillside garden with wonderful views as far as Wales. The lower garden has large herbaceous borders, a sizeable wildlife pond and 2 greenhouses filled with RSA succulents. The middle garden has mixed borders, wild spotted orchids on the lawn, allotment area and a small orchard. The upper garden has a spring fed watercourse with ponds, and many terraces with different planting schemes. Partial wheelchair access across lower lawns & side paths. Steep slope & gravel paths. Wheelchairs will require to be pushed & attended at all times.

4 BABBS FARM
Westhill Lane, Bason Bridge, Highbridge, TA9 4RF. Sue & Richard O'Brien. *1½ m E of Highbridge, 1½ m SSE of M5 exit 22. Turn into Westhill Ln off B3141 (Church Rd), 100yds S of where it joins B3139 (Wells-Highbridge road).* **Sat 11, Sun 12, Sat 25, Sun 26 July (2-5). Adm £10, chd free. Tea, coffee & cake.**
A 1½ acre plantsman's garden on Somerset Levels, gradually created out of fields surrounding old farmhouse over last 30 yrs. Trees, shrubs and herbaceous perennials have been planted with an eye for form, foliage and shape in big flowing borders. The garden now consists of several interconnected areas, to suit a range of plants with diverse requirements, and is still being developed. Plants for sale if circumstances allow. Many unusual Salvias, especially in late summer. A garden with a restful atmosphere and attractive vistas.

5 BARCROFT HALL
North Street, South Petherton, TA13 5DA. Richard & Tracey Killen, 07702 128483, richard.killen02@gmail.com. *N side of S Petherton. From A303 drive to centre of S Petherton, through village, R at fork with Methodist Church into North St (St James St), R into Barcroft Ln, follow signs.* **Visits by arrangement Apr to Sept for groups of 10 to 40. Adm £10, chd free. Tea, coffee & cake.**
A lovely 10 acre garden with glorious views over the surrounding countryside. The garden has many features of interest inc formal planting, water and wildlife areas, a kitchen garden and greenhouse, soft fruits and large orchard. Over 1000 trees all set within the extensive lawns and 7 lakes and ponds. Seating areas throughout the gardens and on the beautiful terraces. There is some disabled parking by the main house plus drop off. Some gravel paths and slopes may only be accessible by motorised mobility vehicles.

6 BARFORD HOUSE
Spaxton, Bridgwater, TA5 1AG. Donald & Bee Rice. *4½ m W of Bridgwater. Midway between Enmore & Spaxton.* **Thur 14 May (2-5). Adm £7, chd free. Home-made teas.**
Secluded walled garden contains wide borders, kitchen garden beds, shrubs and fruit trees. Lawns lead to a 6 acre woodland garden of camellias, rhododendrons, azaleas and magnolias. Stream-side gardens feature candelabra primulas, ferns, foxgloves and lily-of-the-valley among veteran pines and oaks, and some rarer trees. Partial wheelchair access though some areas of the woodland garden inaccessible.

7 BATCOMBE HOUSE
Gold Hill, Batcombe, Shepton Mallet, BA4 6HF. Libby Russell, www.mazzullorusselllandscapedesign.com/batcombe_house. *In centre of Batcombe, 3m from Bruton. Parking between Batcombe House & church at centre of village will be clearly marked.* **Sat 13 June (12-5.30); Sat 12 Sept (2-5.30). Adm £8.50, chd free. Cream teas.**
Plantswoman and designer's garden of two parts – one a riot of colour through kitchen terraces, potager leading to wildflower orchard; the other a calm contemporary amphitheatre with large herbaceous borders and interesting trees and shrubs. Always changing. Dogs are welcome on a lead. On 13 June Somerset Hardy Plant Society are holding a Plant Fair with many top nurseries selling interesting plants. Pls contact Libby for private group visits (not for NGS), libby@mazzullorussell.com.

8 NEW BATH PRIORY HOTEL
Weston Rd, Bath, BA1 2XT. Tom Morel, Head Gardener, 01225 331922, garden@thebathpriory.co.uk, www.thebathpriory.co.uk. *Close to centre of Bath. Metered parking in Royal Victoria Park. No 4, 14, 39 and 37 buses from City centre. Please note disabled parking only in Hotel grounds.* **Sun 14, Mon 15 June, Sun 12, Mon 13 July (12-5). Adm £8, chd free. Tea, coffee & cake in the Hotel (not for NGS).**
Discover 3 acres of mature walled gardens. Quintessentially English, the garden has billowing borders, croquet lawn and boules pitch, wildflower meadow and ancient specimen trees. Roses abound in early summer and perennials and tender plants provide summer highlights while the kitchen garden supplies herbs, fruit and vegetables to the restaurant. Gravel paths and some steps.

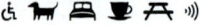

9 NEW THE BLOOMING WILD PLANT NURSERY
Cabbage Lane, Horsington, Templecombe, BA8 0DA. Steven & Lindsay Lister, www.plantwild.co.uk. *10mins from Wincanton & the A303. What3words app: fidget.agreement.expel.* **Sat 1 Aug (10-4). Adm £5, chd free. Tea, coffee & cake.**
Discover our nursery's range of herbaceous perennials, ornamental grasses, and wildflowers; perfect for wildlife friendly, and low maintenance planting in any outdoor space. Visit our demonstration area planted with a selection of perennials and grasses or explore our 3 pocket gardens by local designers, each showcasing plants that offer year-round interest and support biodiversity. Meet the designers of the pocket gardens during the course of the day. There will also be a small selection of stalls from other local producers with artisan food and beverages available to purchase.

10 BRADON FARM
Bradon Farm, Isle Abbotts, Taunton, TA3 6RX. Mr & Mrs Thomas Jones, deborahjstanley@hotmail.com. *Take turning to Ilton off A358. Bradon Farm is 1½ m out of Ilton on Bradon Lane.* **Visits by arrangement 18 May to 21 Aug for groups of 10+. Home-made teas.**
Classic formal garden demonstrating the effective use of structure with parterre, knot garden, pleached lime walk, formal pond, herbaceous borders, orchard and wildflower planting.

11 CAISSON GARDENS
Caisson House, Combe Hay, Bath, BA2 7EF. Amanda & Phil Honey, info@caissongardens.com, www.caissongardens.com. *3m S of Bath. Take A367 from centre of Bath towards Radstock, at 2nd r'about take 1st exit, follow signs to Combe Hay. 1st L after Wheatsheaf pub, marked No Through Rd. Entrance 1st on R.* **Wed 8 Apr (10-4). Adm £17, chd £6. Pre-booking essential, please visit www.ngs.org.uk for information & booking. Tea, coffee & cake.**
This is a wonderfully eclectic and romantic garden set in the most beautiful English countryside around a Georgian house built in 1815. It is a mix of herbaceous borders, topiaries, ponds and rills, a walled garden with fruit trees, greenhouses, flower and vegetable beds.There are wildflower meadows surrounding the garden and the disused Somerset Coal Canal runs through the property. Great variety of species and biodiversity, inc native orchids, kitchen walled garden, ponds and rills.

12 NEW CHARLTON ROAD ALLOTMENTS
Charlton Road, Brentry, Bristol, BS10 6JZ. Guy Manchester, www.facebook.com/ALIVEgardening. *N Bristol, on the border with S Glos. Opp 332 Charlton Rd. The entrance is through a gap in the hedge line. We're the 1st plot on the R when you come through the main gates.* **Sun 5 July (12-4). Adm £4, chd free. Tea, coffee & cake.**
A community allotment with a specific remit to be a safe, fully-accessible, engaging and stimulating space for people living with dementia, and their carers, to continue experiencing the therapeutic benefits of gardening into later life. Local charity, Alive Activities, designed and built the allotment from the ground up and continues to deliver weekly sessions here throughout the year. We are Bristol's flagship accessible growing space, aiming to inspire others to make their gardens more accessible/dementia-friendly. We are keen gardeners, using permaculture principles and are passionate about soil health, sustainability and biodiversity in our productive space. Fully wheelchair accessible, including the compost WC.

13 CHERRY BOLBERRY FARM
Furge Lane, Henstridge, BA8 0RN. Mrs Jenny Raymond, 01963 362177, cherrybolberryfarm@tiscali.co.uk. *6m E of Sherborne. In centre of Henstridge, R at small Xrds signed Furge Ln. Continue straight up lane, over 2 cattle grids, garden at top of lane on R.* **Sat 13, Sun 14 June (2-5.30). Combined adm with Rose Cottage £8, chd free. Home-made teas.** Visits also by arrangement 1 June to 21 June for groups of 10 to 20.
Designed and maintained by the owner, this 50 yr-old award winning 1 acre garden has been planted for year-round interest with wildlife in mind. Colour themed island beds, shrub and herbaceous borders, unusual perennials, shrubs, old roses and an area of specimen trees. Lots of hidden areas, brilliant for hide and seek! Vegetable and flower cutting garden, greenhouses, nature ponds. Wonderful extensive views. Garden surrounded by our dairy farm which has been in the family for over 100 yrs.

14 NEW CHURCH VIEW
Front Street, Churchill, Winscombe, BS25 5NB. John Simmons & Jill Maycock, 07855 944049, john.simmons@ngs.org.uk. *What3words app: adjuster.rolled. costs Turn R at the clock-tower on the A368, located 200 metres W of the A38 Churchill T-lights.* **Sat 20, Sun 21 June (2-5). Adm £5, chd free. Tea, coffee & cake.** Visits also by arrangement 15 June to 30 Aug for groups of 5 to 15. Adm £10 inc tea & cake.
The one-third acre plot at Church View has been evolving under new ownership since 2013. It includes mixed borders, vegetable beds (including a hugelkultur bed), pond, greenhouse, polytunnel, and sculptures. New additions are a little Little Karoo and a tropical rainforest. There are some steps but nearly all areas of the garden are accessible to wheelchairs.

Bath Priory Hotel

15 NEW 9 CODRINGTON ROAD
Bishopston, Bristol, BS7 8ET.
Chris Askew. *Buses from Centre go to Sommerville Rd stop (Bishopston library). Then a short walk via Berkeley Rd & Broadway Rd. There is limited street parking. It is a 10 min drive between gardens or there are regular buses.* **Sat 6 June (1-5). Combined adm with 30 Kingsholm Road £6, chd free. Pre-booking essential, please visit www.ngs.org.uk for information & booking. Tea, coffee & cake.**
This very small urban garden demonstrates what is possible by working with the characteristics of the garden. The space was transformed by doing away with the lawn, renewing the garden around permeable finishes, coupled with lush planting for wildlife with largely native species. It has resulted in a quiet haven within the city, full of nooks and crannies, frequented by bees and small birds. Level access from the street to most of the garden. Paved access narrow in places. Steps to decking area.
&

16 COLEFORD HOUSE
Underhill, Coleford, Radstock, BA3 5LU. **Mr James Alexandroff.** *5m from Frome. Coleford House is opp Kings Head pub in Lower Coleford with black wrought iron gates just before bridge over river. Parking in field 100 metres away.* **Sun 7 June (10-4.30). Adm £7.50, chd free. Home-made teas.**
The River Mells flows through this picturesque garden with large lawns, wildflower planting, ornamental pond, woodland, substantial herbaceous borders, walled garden, arboretum/orchard, kitchen garden, vegetable garden, bat house and orangery. The owner's private collection of twelve vintage Aston Martins will be displayed on the main lawn. Most of garden is wheelchair friendly.
&

The National Garden Scheme funded six Macmillan Nurses in their roles across England, Wales and Northern Ireland in 2025.

17 81 COOMBE LANE
Stoke Bishop, Bristol, BS9 2AT. Karl Suchy, 07873 588540, karl.suchy@icloud.com. *4m from Bristol city centre. J17 of M5, then follow A4018, direction Bristol for approx 2m. Turn R onto Canford Lane A4162. After 0.8m turn L onto Coombe Lane. Destination on R.* **Sun 31 May (12-5). Adm £6, chd free. Home-made teas.** Visits also by arrangement 17 May to 31 July for groups of 15 to 30. Seating for up to 30.
Hidden Victorian walled garden. Substantial mixed borders contain traditional and contemporary planting. Large lawns, numerous seating areas, summerhouse and French inspired patio with coppiced lime trees. Parterre and large raised Koi pond surrounded by bananas and tree ferns. Access to parterre and Koi pond might be difficult for wheelchair due to narrow gravel path, main part of garden is accessible.

18 COURT HOUSE
East Quantoxhead, TA5 1EJ. Mr & Mrs Hugh Luttrell. *12m W of Bridgwater. Off A39, house at end of village past duck pond. Enter by Frog St (Bridgwater/Kilve side from A39).* Car park £1 in aid of church. **Sun 17 May, Sun 28 June (2-5). Adm £7, chd free. Home-made teas in the Village Hall.**
Lovely 5 acre garden, trees, shrubs (many rare and tender), herbaceous and 3 acre woodland garden with spring interest and late summer borders. Views to sea and Quantocks. Gravel, stone and some mown grass paths.

19 COURT VIEW
Solsbury Lane, Batheaston, Bath, BA1 7HB. Maria & Jeremy Heffer, www.thebathgreenhouse.com. *3m E of Bath. In Batheaston High St take turning on L signed Northend, St Catherine. At top of rise L into Solsbury Lane. Court View is 2nd driveway on L. Drop off access only. Public car park in the village.* **Sun 3 May (10-4.30). Adm £6, chd free. Home-made teas. Donation to Plant Heritage.**
2 acre, south-facing garden featuring a colourful mix of trees, shrubs, annuals, perennials and over 100 geums inc the National Collection of *Geum coccinea* and *Geum rivale* cvs. The garden offers spectacular views from terraced lawns, a box parterre, a small orchard, a productive cutting garden and a meadow area. The National Collection of *Geum coccinea* and *Geum rivale* cvs were exhibited at RHS Chelsea Flower Show 2025 as part of Plant Heritage's display - 'Beauty of the National Plant Collections'.

20 THE DOWNS PREPARATORY SCHOOL
Charlton Drive, Wraxall, Bristol, BS48 1PF. The Downs Preparatory School, thedownsschool.co.uk. *4.3m from J19 of the M5 or 8.3m from the centre of Bristol. Follow signs for Noahs Ark Zoo Farm from motorway or centre of Bristol.* **Tue 17 Feb, Wed 29 July (11-3.30). Adm £6, chd free. Tea, coffee & cake.**
65 acres wrap around the Grade II listed Charlton House, once part of a wider estate inc the well known Tyntesfield NT property. Historic garden features inc stumpery, pond and greenhouse. In addition there are well presented annual bedding displays framed by beautiful views across open parkland with specimen trees dotted around the estate. Gravel paths and some steps. Majority of garden is wheelchair accessible.

Cherry Bolberry Farm

21 DOYNTON HOUSE
Bury Lane, Doynton, Bristol, BS30 5SR. Frances & Matthew Lindsey-Clark, franceslc11@gmail.com. *5m S of M4 J18, 6m N of Bath, 8m E of Bristol. Doynton is NE of Wick (turn off A420 opp Bath Rd) & SW of Dyrham (signed from A46). Doynton House is at S end of Doynton village, opp Culleysgate/Horsepool Lane. Park in signed field.* **Sun 28 June (2-6). Adm £8, chd free. Tea, coffee & cake.** Visits also by arrangement 9 Apr to 30 Sept for groups of 10 to 30.
A variety of garden areas separated by old walls and hedges. Mixed borders, lawns, wall planting, parterre, rill garden, walled vegetable garden, cottage beds, pool garden, dry gardens, peach house and greenhouse. Bees, chickens and meadow. Some rejuvenated planting for 2026. We can recommend our local pub, the Cross House, just a short stroll across our parking field. Paths are of hoggin, stone and gravel. The grade of the gravel makes it a hard push in places, but all areas are just about wheelchair accessible.

22 ♦ EAST LAMBROOK MANOR GARDENS
Silver Street, East Lambrook, TA13 5HH. Andrew & Alison Johnson, www.eastlambrook.com. *2m N of South Petherton. Follow brown tourist signs from A303 South Petherton r'about or B3165 Xrds with lights N of Martock. What3words app: motivations. minivans.earmarked.* **For NGS: Thur 12 Feb (10-4); Sat 16 May, Sat 13 June, Sat 11 July (10-5). Adm £8.50, chd free. Tea, coffee & cake.** For other opening times and information, please visit garden website.
The quintessential English cottage garden created by C20 gardening legend Margery Fish. Plantsman's paradise with contemporary and old-fashioned plants grown in a relaxed and informal manner to create a remarkable garden of great beauty and charm. With noted collections of snowdrops, hellebores and geraniums and the excellent specialist Margery Fish Plant Nursery Margery Fish's 1956 first book 'We Made A Garden' was republished June 2024.

23 NEW ELMCROFT
11 The Roman Way, Glastonbury, BA6 8AB. Mrs Joanna Cobb, 01458 832178, joannawohlfarth@gmail.com. *3 min by car from central Glastonbury or 15 mins walk (0.7m). On A39 towards Glastonbury, pass r'about nr Clarks Village, 1st R onto The Roman Way. Continue until you near the top. Elmcroft clearly marked on R. From Glastonbury take A361 up Fishers Hill towards Shepton Mallet, at bend turn R Butleigh Rd, immed R onto Tor View Ave then Roman Way. Elmcroft on L.* **Visits by arrangement 30 Mar to 31 July for groups of up to 20. Adm £5, chd free. Teas can be provided.**
Situated on legendary Wearyall Hill with far-reaching views of adjacent meadows, this once neglected garden has been transformed by art historian Joanna into an intriguing series of colourful 'rooms'. Incorporating all the elements and senses, here is space for exploration, inspiration, conversation, contemplation. Many exotic and rare plants and shrubs. Former winner of Glastonbury in Bloom, including Special Award. Artists, photographers and writers welcome. Bookings can be made for whole or half days. Picnics welcome. Basic kitchen equipment available at garden level including small fridge, kettle, coffee maker.

24 ELWORTHY COTTAGE
Elworthy, Taunton, TA4 3PX. Mike & Jenny Spiller, 01984 656427, mike@elworthy-cottage.co.uk, www.elworthy-cottage.co.uk. *12m NW of Taunton. On B3188 between Wiveliscombe & Watchet. What3words app: hazelnuts.stormy. sprinter.* **Thur 5, Wed 11, Tue 17 Feb, Tue 7, Tue 21 Apr, Tue 12, Mon 25 May, Tue 23 June, Tue 7, Tue 21 July (11-4.30). Adm £5, chd free. Tea, coffee & cake.** Visits also by arrangement Feb to Sept.
One acre plantsman's garden in tranquil setting. Island beds, scented plants, unusual perennials and ornamental trees and shrubs provide year-round interest. In spring, pulmonarias, hellebores and more than 350 varieties of snowdrops. Planted to encourage birds, bees and butterflies. Lots of birdsong, wildflower areas and developing wildflower meadow, decorative vegetable garden, living willow screen. Seats for visitors to enjoy views of the surrounding countryside. Garden attached to plantsman's nursery, open at the same time.

25 FAIRFIELD
Stogursey, Bridgwater, TA5 1PU. Lady Acland Hood Gass. *7m E of Williton. 11m W of Bridgwater. From A39 Bridgwater to Minehead road turn N. Garden 1½ m W of Stogursey on Stringston road. No coaches.* **Sun 12 Apr (2-4.30). Adm £7, chd free. Home-made teas.**
Woodland garden with many interesting bulbs inc naturalised anemones, fritillaria with roses, shrubs and fine trees. Paved maze. Views of Quantocks. The ground is flat and should be accessible, around half the paths are grass so may be more difficult when wet.

26 FOREST LODGE
Pen Selwood, BA9 8LL. James & Lucy Nelson, 07974 701427, lucillanelson@gmail.com, forestlodgegardens.co.uk. *1½ m N of A303, 3m E of Wincanton. Leave A303 at B3081 (Wincanton to Gillingham road), up hill to Pen Selwood, L towards church. ½ m, garden on L - low curved wall & yellow NGS signs. What3words app: relating.dummy.eggs.* **Sat 28 Mar, Sat 2 May (11-4). Combined adm with Lower Shalford Farm £10, chd free. Tea, coffee & cake. Lavender blue famous carrot cake, brownies & flapjacks.** Visits also by arrangement 16 Mar to 14 Sept for groups of 10 to 30.
3 acre mature garden with beautiful lake, full of bulbs and flowering trees. Many camellias and rhododendrons from March till May. Lovely views towards Blackmore Vale. Part formal with pleached hornbeam allée and rill, part water garden. Wonderful roses in June. Unusual spring flowering trees such as paulownia, *Davidia involucrata* and many beautiful cornus. Interesting garden sculpture. Good plant interest year-round due to acidic greensand soil (hamamelis, Daphne, magnolia, lovely rhododendrons, camellias and flowering trees in the spring) and south west facing slope. Beautiful in all seasons and good structure which underpins the planting. Wheelchair access to front garden only, however much of garden viewable from there.

GROUP OPENING

27 FROME GARDENS
Sancerre, 89A Weymouth Road, Frome, BA11 1HJ. Penny Lines. *15m S of Bath. Turn up Weymouth Rd from junction Badcox/Christchurch St West. 2nd entrance on L through light green wooden gate.* **Sun 14 June (12-5). Combined adm £8, chd free. Tea, coffee & cake at Sancerre, cash only. Card & cash for admission.**

61 NUNNEY ROAD
BA11 4LA. Mrs Caroline Toll.

SANCERRE, 89A WEYMOUTH ROAD
BA11 1HJ. Penny & Richard Lines.

1 TUCKER CLOSE
BA11 5LS. Bev Revie.

Three contrasting and exciting secret town gardens with unusual and interesting styles of design and planting complementing each other. All are returning gardens; Sancerre, a large mature garden with a newly landscaped courtyard garden formerly a swimming pool; 61 Nunney Rd, a well-cared for garden, has been redesigned from 2020 by a new owner who considers herself an untidy planter as she falls for plants and then finds the right place for them! Finally, 1 Tucker Close, a small walled town garden of unusual design planted by the owner with wildlife in mind. Its borders are set with decking and slate rather than grass. Most of Sancerre is accessible, mix of gravel & stone paths. Small step onto lawn at 61 Nunney Road, 1 Tucker Close, viewing from paths.

GROUP OPENING

28 GOATHURST GARDENS
Goathurst, Bridgwater, TA5 2DF. *4m SW of Bridgwater, 2½ m W of N Petherton. Parking at Halswell House & near the Temple of Pan. Disabled parking only at the Temple of Pan.* **Sat 25, Sun 26 July (2-5). Combined adm £7.50, chd free. Home-made teas.**

HALSWELL HOUSE
Mrs Oksana Kadatskaya.

THE TEMPLE OF PAN
Peter Strivens & Tessa Shaw.

Two gardens in the picturesque village of Goathurst on the edge of the Quantock Hills linked by a common history. The gardens at Halswell Park are a history of garden design in England, with a knot garden created to reflect an original C16 design, a walled garden and Georgian pleasure gardens with follies, bridges and ponds. The garden of the Temple of Pan surrounds an C18 baroque folly built as part of Halswell Park's Georgian pleasure gardens, now with herbaceous borders, lawns, ponds and woodland gardens. Halswell knot gardens has wheelchair access to most areas. Some but not all of the gardens at The Temple of Pan are wheelchair accessible.

29 ♦ GREENCOMBE GARDENS
Porlock, Minehead, TA24 8NU. Greencombe Garden Trust, 01643 862363, info@greencombe.org, www.greencombe.org. *W of Porlock below the wooded slopes of Exmoor. Take A39 to west end of Porlock & turn onto B3225 to Porlock Weir. Drive ½ m, turn L at Greencombe Gardens sign. Go up drive; parking signed.* **For NGS: Tue 14 Apr, Tue 14 July (2-6). Adm £7, chd £1. Cream teas. For other opening times and information, please phone, email or visit garden website. Donation to Plant Heritage.**

Organic woodland garden of international renown, Greencombe stretches along a sheltered hillside and offers outstanding views over Porlock Bay. Moss-covered paths meander through a collection of ornamental plants that flourish beneath a canopy of oaks, hollies, conifers and chestnuts. Camellias, rhododendrons, azaleas, lilies, roses, clematis, and hydrangeas blossom among 4 National Collections. Champion English Holly tree (*Ilex aquifolium*), one of the largest and oldest in the UK. Giant rhododendrons species and exceptionally large camellias. A millennium chapel hides in the mossy banks of the wood. A moon arch leads into a walled garden.

30 GREYSTONES
Hollybush Lane, Bristol, BS9 1JB. Mrs Pam Townsend. *2m N of Bristol city centre, close to Durdham Down,* backing onto the Botanic Garden. A4018 Westbury Rd, L at White Tree r'about, L into Saville Rd, Hollybush Lane 2nd on R. Narrow lane, parking limited, recommended to park in Saville Rd. **Sun 1 Mar (11-4). Home-made teas. Sun 26 Apr (11-4). Adm £5, chd free. Light lunches, tea, coffee and cakes.**

Peaceful garden with places to sit and enjoy a quiet corner of Bristol. Interesting courtyard, raised beds, large variety of conifers and shrubs leads to secluded garden of contrasts - sunny beds with olive tree and brightly coloured flowers to shady spots, with acers, hostas and ferns. Snowdrops, hellebores, spring bulbs, naturalised daffodils. Small orchard, espaliered pears. Paved footpath provides level access to all areas.

31 87 HALLEN ROAD
Henbury, Bristol, BS10 7RA. Andrew Hockey & Janet Hunt. *½ m from Blaise Castle Estate, nr Bristol/S Glos border. From Henbury to Hallen (Avonmouth Way becomes Hallen Rd), semi-detached on L (opp end of school field) before Windmill Lane. What3words app: late.clown. into. Park on side roads, not main road.* **Sat 6, Sun 7 June (2-5). Adm £4, chd free. Pre-booking essential, please visit www.ngs.org.uk for information & booking. Tea, coffee & cake.**

125 foot plantaholic's garden divided into different beds with unusual plants giving year-round interest. Almost 1000 different types inc many hardy Geraniums, heucheras, ferns, grasses, alpines and geums, plus several pots, troughs, 2 small ponds and an ancient, large Bramley apple tree. Some steps and uneven paths. Unsuitable for wheelchairs.

32 HANGERIDGE FARMHOUSE
Wrangway, Wellington, TA21 9QG. Mr & Mrs R E Chave & Mrs J Dobson, 07896 134920, treborchaver1978@gmail.com. *2m S of Wellington. Off A38 Wellington bypass signed Wrangway. 1st L towards Wellington monument, over motorway bridge 1st R.* **Sun 28 June, Sun 26 July (2-5). Adm £4, chd free. Tea, coffee & cake. Visits also by arrangement June to Aug.**

Nestled between the Blackdown & Quantock hills, sits this stunning 1 acre plantsman's garden. Rural

Charlton Road Allotments

countryside surrounds the garden, and with a cottage feel you will find a plethora of different plants to suit all tastes, island beds with unusual perennials, shrubs, old roses and specimen trees. There is somewhere for all to just sit back and relax, and let the tranquillity infiltrate your senses.

&

33 4 HAYTOR PARK
Bristol, BS9 2LR. **Mr C & Mrs P Prior, 07779 203626, p.l.prior@gmail.com.** *3m NW of Bristol city centre. From A4162 Inner Ring Rd take turning into Coombe Bridge Ave, Haytor Park is 1st on L. Please park responsibly.* **Sun 26 Apr (1-5). Adm £4, chd free. Open nearby Lucombe House. Opening with Stoke Bishop Gardens on Sun 10 May. Visits also by arrangement May to Aug for groups of 10 to 30.**
A secret space, lovingly cultivated for almost 40 years. Hiding behind a 30s semi and packed with gorgeous plants. Up trees, in pots, around ponds and on a green roof. Linger awhile in this peaceful spot on the many seats surrounded by scents. Seek out dragons, follow paths through spaces created by wacky screens.

34 ♦ HESTERCOMBE GARDENS
Cheddon Fitzpaine, Taunton, TA2 8LG. **Hestercombe Gardens Trust, 01823 413923, info@hestercombe.com, www.hestercombe.com.** *3m N of Taunton, less than 6m from J25 of M5. Follow brown daisy signs. SatNav postcode TA2 8LQ. What3words app: fancy.arena.* **For NGS: Thur 19 Feb, Thur 19 Mar (10-4.30). Adm £16.90, chd free. Light refreshments. Discount/prepaid vouchers not valid on the National Garden**
Scheme charity day. **For other opening times and information, please phone, email or visit garden website.**
Magnificent Georgian landscape garden designed by artist Coplestone Warre Bampfylde, a contemporary of Gainsborough and Henry Hoare of Stourhead. Victorian terrace and shrubbery and an exquisite example of a Lutyens/Jeykll designed formal garden. Enjoy 50 acres of woodland walks, temples, terraces, pergolas, lakes and cascades. Hestercombe House contains various Gertrude Jekyll exhibits including her own gardening trowel, along with many other treasures from the estate's rich history. Restored watermill and barn, fabulous bookshop, plant sales and cafe. Gravel paths, steep slopes, steps. An all-access route is shown on the guide map and visitors can pre-book an all-terrain tramper vehicle.

Avalon

35 HILLCREST
Curload, Stoke St Gregory, Taunton, TA3 6JA. Charles & Charlotte Sundquist, 01823 490852, chazfix@gmail.com. At top of Curload. From A358 take A378, L to & through North Curry, L ½ m after Willows & Wetlands centre. Hillcrest on R (parking directions). From A361 turn S at Burrowbridge Xrds. Then 1st R follow NGS signs. **Visits by arrangement Apr to June for groups of 5 to 30. Home-made teas inc in adm price. Adm £10, chd free. Gluten free catered for by prior arrangement.**
Boasting stunning views of the Somerset Levels, Burrow Mump and Glastonbury Tor this 6 acre garden offers plenty of interest, inc a standing stone. Enjoy woodland walks, varied borders, flowering meadow and several ponds. There are greenhouses, orchards, a new produce garden and newly built large gravel garden. Garden is mostly level with gentle sloping paths down through meadow. Cash only for refreshments and plants. Gravel around refreshment area.

36 HOLLAM HOUSE
Dulverton, TA22 9JH. Annie Prebensen, 01398 323445, annie@hollam.co.uk. *From Dulverton Bridge, go straight & bear R at the chemist. At the garage, Hollam Ln is the 2nd L turning immed after the garage, it is between a cottage & music shop.* **Visits by arrangement 1 Apr to 1 July for groups of 10+. Adm £7. Home-made teas.**
Extending over 5 acres, this sloping Exmoor garden inc ponds, a water garden, woodland planting, borders and meadow areas. There are magnificent mature trees and old rhododendrons. Spring highlights are the thousands of tulips and other bulbs as well as flowering shrubs and trees; magnolia, cornus and viburnum among others. Not suitable for those of limited mobility or small children. Regret no dogs.

37 HONEYHURST FARM
Honeyhurst Lane, Rodney Stoke, Cheddar, BS27 3UJ. Don & Kathy Longhurst, 01749 870322, donlonghurst@btinternet.com, www.ciderbarrelcottage.co.uk. *4m E of Cheddar. 6m W of Wells. From Wells (A371) turn L into Rodney Stoke signed Wedmore. Pass church on L & continue for almost 1m. From Cheddar (A371) turn R signed Wedmore, through Draycott. Turn L signed Rodney Stoke.* **Visits by arrangement 1 May to 1 Sept for groups of 10 to 40. Parking for numerous cars. Coaches welcome. Adm £5, chd free. Home-made teas.**
⅔ acre part walled rural garden with babbling brook and 4 acre traditional cider orchard, with views. Specimen hollies, copper beech, paulownia, yew and poplar. Pergolas, arbour and numerous seats. Mixed informal shrub and perennial beds with many unusual plants. Many pots planted with shrubs, hardy and half-hardy perennials. Level, grass and some shingle.

38 JAPANESE GARDEN BRISTOL
13 Glenarm Walk, Brislington, Bristol, BS4 4LS. Martin Fitton, www.japanesegardenbristol.com. *A4 Bristol to Bath. A4 Brislington, at Texaco Garage at bottom of Bristol Hill turn into School Rd & immed R into Church Parade. Car park 1st turn on R or proceed to Glenarm Walk.* **Sat 30 May (12-5). Adm £7, chd £3. Pre-booking essential, please visit www.ngs.org.uk for information & booking. Home-

made teas.
As you walk through the gate you will be welcomed by Japanese Koi. Then take a step to another level to the relaxing Japanese garden room and tea house surrounded by acers and cloud trees. Walk past Buddha corner into the Bonsai and Zen water feature area. Continue to a Japanese courtyard through a gate to a peaceful Japanese tea garden. There you will find seating to enjoy the serene atmosphere. Please note steps to different levels means the garden is unsuitable for disabled access.

39 NEW JAPANESE GARDEN, FRAMPTON COTTERELL
Star Cottage, 310 Badminton Road, Frampton Cotterell, Bristol, BS36 2NR. Dave & Star Lee, www.japanesegardenframptonbristol.com. *We are located next to & on the same side as the New Inn pub on the main A432 Badminton Road in Frampton Cotterell.* **Sun 18 Oct (12-5). Adm £7.50, chd £3. Pre-booking essential, please visit www.ngs.org.uk for information & booking.**
A four season Japanese inspired garden with winding path and seating areas. With authentic features highlighting the beauty of the Japanese culture.

40 JOHN'S CORNER
2 Fitzgerald Road, Bedminster, Bristol, BS3 5DD. John Hodge. *3m from city centre. South Bristol, off St. John's Lane, Totterdown end. 1st house on R entrance at side of house. On number 91 bus route. Parking in residential street.* **Sat 13, Sun 14 June (12-5). Adm £5, chd free. Home-made teas.**
Unusual and interesting city garden with a mixture of exciting plants and features. Ponds, rills, ferns and much more. Eden project style greenhouse with collection of cacti. Not all areas accessible by wheelchair.

41 ♦ KILVER COURT GARDENS
Kilver Street, Shepton Mallet, BA4 5NF. The Showering Family, 01749 705279, enquiries@kilvercourt.com, www.kilvercourt.com. *30 mins drive from Bristol & Bath on the A37. Opp Showerings factory on Kilver St. Disabled parking in lower car park.* **For NGS: Fri 12 June, Fri 11 Sept (9.30-4.30). Adm £7.50, chd £5. Discount/Prepaid vouchers**

not valid on the above NGS open days. **For other opening times and information, please phone, email or visit garden website.**
Visitors can wander by the millpond, explore the formal and informal gardens and enjoy a replica of the splendid Chelsea Flower Show Gold Medal winning rockery where a gushing recirculated stream flows from pool to pool and waterfalls into the lake. All this set against the stunning backdrop of Charlton Viaduct with the 100m herbaceous flower border beyond. Seek out the famous Babycham whilst here! Please note, on site payment is card only. Some slopes, rockery not accessible for wheelchairs but can be viewed from garden.

42 30 KINGSHOLM ROAD
Southmead, Bristol, BS10 5LH. Ms Emma Nelder, www.instagram.com/second_bassoon. *Turning is at the Bear & Rugged Staff T-lights on Southmead Rd. Pedestrian access from Kendon Drive & Kelston Rd. Kingsholm Rd is a no-through road & parking is limited. It is a 10 min drive between gardens or there are regular buses.* **Sat 6 June (1-5). Combined adm with 9 Codrington Road £6, chd free. Pre-booking essential, please visit www.ngs.org.uk for information & booking. Tea, coffee & cake.**
170ft urban garden developed since 2020 and divided into ornamental and productive areas. Herbaceous border, cutting beds, greenhouse, pond, and water features, along with a productive kitchen garden and resident flock of hens. Collections of pelargoniums, citrus trees, succulents, and hostas.

43 KINGSLAND
North Street, Milverton, Taunton, TA4 1LG. Mrs Mary-Anne Robb. *Entering Milverton from B3227, pass the sawmill & turn R into North St. From Wellington, pass the village shop, turn L up the hill, past the church graveyard, turn R into North St.* **Sun 7 June (2-5). Adm £7.50, chd £2.50. Light refreshments in the side garden.**
A plantsman's walled village garden, of approx 1 acre, laid out in 3 sections; the main garden bordered by herbaceous planting, a sunken gravel garden, and the third tier landscaped and planted with new trees and grasses. A walled

passageway walk transformed with climbers and roses leads to a small central courtyard. All areas are accessible by wheelchair, although gravel paths do make this difficult.

44 KNOLL COTTAGE
Stogumber, Taunton, TA4 3TN. Elaine & John Leech, 01984 656689, john@Leech45.com, www.knoll-cottage.co.uk. *3m SE of Williton. From A358 follow signs to Stogumber. After 2½ m, at T-junction, turn R towards Williton. After ⅓ m turn R up narrow lane. Knoll Cottage on L after 100yds.* **Visits by arrangement 15 June to 31 July for groups of up to 20. Adm £6, chd free. Home-made teas.**
Four acre garden started from fields in 1998. Extensive mixed beds with shrubs, perennials and annuals. Over 80 different roses, and many salvias and dahlias later in the season. Small arboretum area inc many different cornus, rowans, hawthorns, oaks and birches. Pond, large vegetable and fruit areas.

45 LITTLE BUCKLERS
Brockley Hall, Brockley Lane, Brockley, Bristol, BS48 3AZ. Carol & Peter Parfrey, 07526 874 067, p.parfrey111@gmail.com. *10m S of Bristol. Little Bucklers is in the grounds of Brockley Hall, just off the A370 Bristol to Weston-Super-Mare road at the bottom of Brockley Coombe. What3words app: perfumed.trombone.chip.* **Visits by arrangement May to Sept for groups of 10 to 25. If required groups can be given a guided tour. Adm £7, chd free. Home-made cakes, tea, coffee & soft drinks.**
¾ acre garden with countryside views. The garden has been developed gradually over the last 40 yrs. Mixed colour themed borders, herbaceous perennials, gravel gardens, 2 small ponds, path leading to small woodland area and onward to vegetable plot and greenhouse. Mature trees and lots of seating areas make the garden a delight to work and be in. The garden is mainly flat. Easy access to the front garden and rear patio. Access to the rear garden via 2 shallow steps.

46 LITTLE YARFORD FARMHOUSE
Kingston St Mary, Taunton, TA2 8AN. Mrs D Bradley, 01823 451350, dilly.bradley@gmail.com. 1½m W of Hestercombe, 3½m N of Taunton. From Taunton on Kingston St Mary road. At 30mph sign turn L at Parsonage Ln. Continue 1¼m W, to Yarford sign. Continue 400yds. Turn R up concrete road. If Kingston road is closed take Cheddon road & turn L just before Hestercombe. Continue to Mill Xroads, go straight across to Parsonage Ln. **Sun 3 May (2-5); Mon 4 May (11-4). Adm £7, chd free. Light refreshments.** Visits also by arrangement Apr to Oct. Guided tours limited to 10-12 participants at any one time. Refreshments.
Unusual 5 acre garden embracing C17 house (not open) Natural pond and 90ft water lily pond. A plantsman's garden notable for the aesthetics of its planting especially its 300+ rare and unusual tree cultivars: the best collection of broad leaf and conifer specimens in Western Somerset (link to full list can be found under Extended Description on NGS website); those trees not available to Bampfylde Warre at Hestercombe in C18. There will be a brief guided tree tour at 2.30 and 3.30pm. An exercise in landscaping, contrast planting and creating views both within the garden and without to the vale and the Quantock Hills. Mostly wheelchair accessible.

47 LOWER SHALFORD FARM
Shalford Lane, Charlton Musgrove, Wincanton, BA9 8HE. Mr & Mrs David Posnett. *Lower Shalford is 2m NE of Wincanton. Leave A303 at Wincanton go N on B3081 towards Bruton. Just beyond Otter Garden Centre turn R Shalford Lane, garden is ½m on L. Parking opp house.* **Sat 28 Mar (10-3); Sat 2 May (10-4.30). Combined adm with Forest Lodge £10, chd free. Home-made teas.**
Fairly large open garden with extensive lawns and wooded surroundings with drifts of daffodils in spring. Small winterbourne stream running through with several stone bridges. Walled rose/parterre garden, hedged herbaceous garden, mature wisterias in all their glory and several ornamental ponds.

48 LUCOMBE HOUSE
12 Druid Stoke Ave, Stoke Bishop, Bristol, BS9 1DD. Malcolm Ravenscroft, 01179 682494, famrave@gmail.com. *4m NW of Bristol centre. At top of Druid Hill. Turn in Druid Stoke Ave. Garden on R 300m from junction.* **Sun 26 Apr (1-5). Adm £4, chd free. Home-made teas. Open nearby 4 Haytor Park. Teas & home-made cakes provided by local scout group.** Visits also by arrangement 12 Apr to 13 Sept. Pls contact owner at least 2 weeks before planned visit.
For tree lovers of all ages! As well as a 260 yr old Lucombe Oak - one of the most significant trees in the UK - there are over 30 mature English trees planted to create an urban woodland underplanted with various native ferns. An Arts & Crafts garden has now been completed in the front and a woodland path provides a behind the scenes look at the woodland. A trio of recorder players will entertain visitors. Rough paths in woodland area and steps to patio.

49 LYDEARD HOUSE
West Street, Bishops Lydeard, Taunton, TA4 3AU. Mrs Vaun Wilkins. *5m NW of Taunton. A358 Taunton to Minehead, do not take 1st 3 R turnings to Bishops Lydeard but 4th signed to Cedar Falls. Follow signs to Lydeard House.* **Sun 7 June (2-5). Adm £6, chd free. Tea, coffee & cake.**
4 acre garden with C18 origins and many later additions. Sweeping lawns, lake overhung with willows, canal running parallel to Victorian rose-covered pergola, along with box parterre, chinoiserie-style garden, recent temple folly and walled vegetable garden plus wonderful mature trees. Plants for sale. Children must be supervised because of very deep water. Deep gravel paths and steps may cause difficulty for wheelchairs but most features are accessible by lawn and parking will be available.

50 THE MANOR
South Street, Wincanton, BA9 9DL. Anna Hughes. *On the R of South St on the one-way system in central Wincanton, opp Our Lady's Primary School. Parking on the High St or in the Memorial Hall car park. The garden is also known as 'The Dogs'.* **Sat 2, Sun 3 May (10.30-5). Adm £7.50, chd free. Tea, coffee & cake.**
Hidden and unexpected large walled garden in town centre around C17 manor house. Developed by the current owners over the last 25 yrs. Yew hedges provide good structure and divide the garden into distinct areas. Formal pond garden. Vegetable garden with box edging. Orchard. Tiny 'lockdown' garden created in 2020. A small number of parking places by the house for disabled use. Wheelchair access is available to the main upper part of the garden.

51 MELLOWSTONES
Staples Hill, Freshford, Bath, BA2 7WL. Mrs Jackie Kennedy. *5m S of Bath. A36 Bath/Warminster road. Take exit to Freshford; past pub over bridge up Staples Hill to top. Mellowstones is on the R. Parking at Downside Nurseries, 1st L after property (a 15 min walk).* **Sun 24 May (11-4). Adm £6, chd free. Tea, coffee & home-made cakes.**
Developed over the last 5 yrs, this 1 acre south facing hillside terraced garden is set in woodland, with wonderful views across the Frome valley. The upper level has cottage garden plants and yew hedges, a quarry kitchen and a grass path through wild flowers to the summerhouse. The Mediterranean terrace has olive trees, a gravel planting area with stepping stones across a corten steel pond. The lower terrace is a formal garden leading to a grass path which extends through the sloping wildflower orchard. Woodland and valley walks. Short distance from the canal.

52 NEW 35 MILLERS GARDENS
Wells, BA5 2TW. Judith O'Hagan, 07711 378292, judith@ohagan.me. *Last house on L at end of cul-de-sac.* **Visits by arrangement May to Sept for groups of 10 to 30. Adm £5, chd free.**
Plenty of interest in this small city garden, taking full advantage of south facing slope to grow Mediterranean

and tender plants. Living wall, pleached crab apples and birch glade at the front with lovely borders full of interesting and unusual plants, a gravel path, olive tree, greenhouse and views beyond at the back. Terrace with pots, greenhouse for propagating. Started in 2022 with ongoing improvements. No refreshments available but a wide range of cafes are within a 5 min walk. Partial wheelchair access.

53 ♦ MILTON LODGE
Old Bristol Road, Wells, BA5 3AQ. Simon Tudway Quilter, 01749 679341, www.miltonlodgegardens.co.uk. ½ m N of Wells. From A39 Bristol-Wells, turn N up Old Bristol Rd; car park 1st gate on L signed. **For NGS: Sun 31 May, Sun 28 June (2-5). Adm £6, chd free. Home-made teas. Teas & plants cash only. Children 14 & under free entry. Discount/ membership/prepaid vouchers not accepted on our 2 NGS charity days.** For other opening times and information, please phone or visit garden website.
This garden is a must for garden lovers and well worth a visit. Land was transformed into architectural terraces capitalising on views of Wells Cathedral and the Vale of Avalon. The Grade II terraced garden was restored to its former glory by the owner's parents, who moved here in 1960, replacing the orchard with a collection of ornamental trees, specimen trees and yew hedges. A serene, relaxing atmosphere within the garden succeeds the ravages of two World Wars. Cross over Old Bristol Rd to our 7 acre woodland garden, 'The Combe', open on NGS days, a natural peaceful contrast to the formal garden of Milton Lodge. Cash only for teas and plants, card or cash for admission.

54 ♦ MODEL FARM
Perry Green, Wembdon, Bridgwater, TA5 2BA. Dave & Roz Young, 01278 429953, dave@modelfarm.com, www.modelfarm.com. *4m from J23 of M5. Follow Brown signs from r'about on A39 2m W of Bridgwater.* **For NGS: Every Mon to Fri 13 Apr to 22 May (10-4). Every Mon to Fri 1 June to 3 July (10-4). Tea. Every Mon to Fri 31 Aug to 16 Oct (10-4). Adm £5, chd free. Tea, coffee**

& use of a large gas BBQ can be arranged on request. For other opening times and information, please phone, email or visit garden website.
Four acres of flat gardens to south of Victorian country house. Created from a field in last 16 yrs and still being developed. A dozen large mixed flower beds planted in cottage garden style with wildlife in mind. Wooded areas, mixed orchard, lawns, wildflower meadows and wildlife ponds. Plenty of seating throughout the gardens which are open on weekdays in term time from Easter. Swimming pond available to use.

SPECIAL EVENT

55 ♦ THE NEWT IN SOMERSET
Hadspen, Bruton, BA7 7NG. 01963 577750, enquiries@thenewtinsomerset.com, thenewtinsomerset.com/garden. *Located on the A359 between Bruton & Castle Cary, follow the brown tourist signs to the estate entrance. Upon entry, follow the 'Gardens' sign for the visitor car park.* **For NGS: Wed 9 Sept (10-5). Adm £30. Pre-booking essential, please visit www.ngs.org.uk for information & booking. Light refreshments.** For other opening times and information, please phone, email or visit garden website.
A limited number of tickets have been made available for this special 1 day event, kindly hosted by The Newt on behalf of The National Garden Scheme. It includes a talk from one of our lead gardeners on the gardens and more recent developments, with an emphasis on the Kitchen Garden. They will also provide further detail on what is growing in the garden currently and what are the main highlights of the gardens throughout the seasons. Light refreshments will be served at the Cyder Bar on arrival before walking down into the Kitchen Garden through the Parabola. For the morning visit this will inc tea or coffee and a cinnamon bun. For the afternoon a glass of cyder or apple juice and sausage roll. All refreshments are made on site and from produce produced within the kitchen garden and orchards.

56 NYNEHEAD COURT
Nynehead, Wellington, TA21 0BN. Nynehead Care Ltd, 01823 662481, admin@nyneheadcourt.co.uk, www.nyneheadcourt.co.uk. *1½ m N of Wellington. M5 J26 B3187 towards Wellington. R at Lidl r'about marked Nynehead & Poole, follow lane for 1½ m, take Milverton turning at fork, turning L into Chipley Rd. Enter through stone pillars 850 yards ahead.* **Sun 28 June (2-4.30). Adm £5, chd free. Tea, coffee & cake in Orangery.**
Nynehead Court was the home of the Sandford family from 1590-1902. The 14 acres of gardens are noted for specimen trees, and there will be a garden tour with the Head Gardener at 2.15pm (pls wear suitable footwear). Nynehead is now a private residential care home. The garden combines Victorian formality with natural style promoting wildlife further into the parkland in a managed grassland Park. A Historic England garden of national importance, Nynehead won a landscape heritage award in 2007 from the former Taunton Deane Borough Council.

57  THE OLD COACH HOUSE
The Empire Farm, Throop Road, Templecombe, BA8 0HR. Mrs Sally Morgan, www.empirefarm.co.uk. *4m S of Wincanton & A303. From A303 at Wincanton take A357 S to Templecombe, do not go under railway bridge, turn L before lights and immed R into Throop Rd, entrance 400m on L. By rail: station is 8 mins walk.* **Sat 1 Aug (12-5), open nearby The Blooming Wild Plant Nursery. Sun 6 Sept (12-5). Adm £8, chd free. Tea, coffee & cake.**
Walled garden with an orchard, potager, clover lawn, extensive ornamental borders, salvias and greenhouse. Managed organically with biodiversity at its core, the owner trials climate-resilient ideas: rainwater is channelled through ponds and rills, a dipping pond supplies water to the potager, plus aggregate beds, unusual vegetables, half hardy ornamentals and a separate perennial vegetable garden. Mostly level garden although some paths in the kitchen garden are deep wood chip.

58 THE OLD RECTORY, DOYNTON
18 Toghill Lane, Doynton, Bristol, BS30 5SY. Edwina & Clive Humby, www.tumblr.com/doyntongardens. *At heart of village of Doynton, between Bath & Bristol. Car parking is signed. Parking is restricted to designated areas.* **Sat 20 June (11-5). Adm £6, chd free. Cream teas.**
Doynton's Grade II listed Georgian Rectory's walled garden and extended 15 acre estate has been renovated over 12 yrs and sits within AONB. The garden has a diversity of modern and traditional elements, fused to create an atmospheric series of garden rooms. Large landscaped kitchen garden with canal, vegetable plots, fruit cages and treehouse. Bees and a woodland area are also features for a longer stroll.

59 PENNARD HOUSE
East Pennard, Shepton Mallet, BA4 6TP. Martin Dearden, 07802 243569, martin@pennardcottage.co.uk. *On the A37 approx 5m S of Shepton Mallet, turn R at the top of the hill by a little lodge house. Coming from the S, turn L at the bottom of the steep hill. Follow signs.* **Sun 7 June, Tue 14 July (11-5). Adm £7, chd free. Light lunches, teas, coffee & cakes.** Visits also by arrangement Apr to Sept for groups of 10 to 50.
Two delightful separate gardens, both with extensive lawns, mature trees, rose beds, rustic topiary, a Victorian spring fed swimming pool and ponds. Garden layout dates from 1835 when the Napier family enlarged the main house and acquired the house next door. Next door, Pennard Plants, will also open for plant purchasing. On offer is a selection of edible plants, fruit trees, herbs and seeds. The gardens are on a slope, but accessible with assistance.

60 PENNY BROHN UK
Chapel Pill Lane, Pill, BS20 0HH. Penny Brohn UK, 0303 3000118, fundraising@pennybrohn.org.uk, www.pennybrohn.org.uk. *4m W of Bristol. Off A369 Clifton Suspension Bridge to M5 (J19 Gordano Services). Follow signs to Penny Brohn UK & to Pill/Ham Green (5 mins).* **Sun 14 June (10-4). Adm £7, chd free. Tea, coffee, home-made cakes and cream teas.** Visits also by arrangement 1 Feb to 1 Dec for groups of 5 to 30.
3½ acre tranquil garden surrounds Georgian mansion with many mature trees, wildflower meadow, flower garden and cedar summerhouse. Fine views from historic gazebo overlooking the River Avon. Courtyard gardens with water features. Garden is maintained by volunteers and plays an active role in the charity's personalised cancer care approach. Plants, teas, music and plenty of space to enjoy a picnic. Tours of centre to find out more about the work of Penny Brohn UK. Some gravel and grass paths.

61 THE PONY
Moorledge Road, Newtown, Chew Magna, Bristol, BS40 8TQ. Josh & Holly Eggleton, theponychewvalley.co.uk. *2m E of Chew Magna. Turn off the A386 onto Moorledge Rd between Stanton Wick & Bishop Sutton. Or if coming through Chew Magna, turn off High St onto Tunbridge Rd which then becomes Moorledge Rd.* **Tue 11 Aug (10-2.30). Adm £7, chd free. Tea, coffee & cake. 20% of proceeds from teas will go to the NGS.**
Designed by RHS Chelsea Garden Show designer Jon Wheatley and his daughter Lizzy, the garden embraces the gentle slopes of the Chew Valley. Planted with an eye to the often changing weather patterns that move through the valley, the pub garden offers year-round interest and edible delights to serve the pub. The 'no dig' kitchen garden is in the adjoining field. Features inc fabulous views, unusual vegetables and polytunnel growing. There are gravelled paths in the main garden and grassed paths in the kitchen garden. The garden is sloped. Accessible toilets available.

62 NEW THE PRIEST'S HOUSE
Muchelney, Langport, TA10 0DQ. Alan & Jill du Monceau de Bergendal. *1m S of Langport. A National Trust House directly opp St Peter & Paul's Church in Muchelney. What3words app: curbed.deals.eggshell.* **Sat 8 Aug (12-5). Combined adm with Almonry Barn £7, chd £3. Home-made teas at Almonry Barn.**
A unique setting surrounding a C14 Priest's House this cottage garden reflects the owner's love of colour and form. Some areas have been planned juxtaposed with self seeders. The orchard's main feature is an ancient Mulberry tree. For 5 years nature has been allowed to take its course here, producing 28 species of native wild flowers, inc 45 orchids and 18 different grasses.

63 THE RIB
St Andrew Street, Wells, BA5 2UR. Paul Dickinson & David Morgan-Hewitt. *Wells City Centre, adjacent to east end of Wells Cathedral & opp Vicars Close. There is absolutely no parking at or very near this city garden. Visitors should use one of the 5 public car parks and enjoy the 10-15 minutes stroll through the city to The Rib.* **Sat 25 July (12-5). Adm £6, chd free.**
The Rib is one of the few houses in England that can boast a cathedral and a sacred well in its garden. Whilst the garden is compact, it delivers a unique architectural and historical punch. Long established trees, interesting shrubs and more recently planted mixed borders frame the view in the main garden. Ancient walled orchard and traditionally planted cottage garden. Lunch, tea and WC facilities available in the nearby Bishop's Palace, Wells marketplace or Wells Cathedral. Slightly bumpy but short gravel drive and uneven path to main rear garden. 2-3 steps up to orchard and cottage gardens. Grass areas uneven in places.

64 ROCK HOUSE
Elberton, BS35 4AQ. Mr & Mrs John Gunnery, 01454 413225, cmgunnery@googlemail.com. *10m N of Bristol. What3words app: stint.woes.plans. B4461 Severn Bridge to Alveston, turn into the Littleton road & immed R. BS35 4AQ starts at top of village, come down the hill, R to Littleton and R again.* **Sun 1, Sun 8 Feb, Sun 1, Sun 8 Mar (11-4). Adm £5, chd free. 2027: Sun 31 Jan, Sun 7 Feb.** Visits also by arrangement.
A 2 acre garden with woodland vistas with swathes of snowdrops in Feb and carpets of daffodils in March, some unusual. Spring flowers, cottage garden plants and climbing roses in season. Old yew tree, maturing cedar tree, pond.

65 ROSE COTTAGE
Church Street, Henstridge, BA8 0QE. Carol Perrett, 01963 363338. *6m E of Sherborne just off the A30. At T-lights turn into Henstridge, take 2nd R into Church St.* **Sat 13, Sun 14 June (2-5.30). Combined adm with Cherry Bolberry Farm £8, chd free. Home-made teas at Cherry Bolberry Farm.** Visits also by arrangement 1 June to 21 June for groups of 10 to 20.

¼ acre plantswoman's cottage garden on the site of the former village millpond, exuberantly planted to create a romantic atmosphere with emphasis on scent, colour, form and texture creating a wildlife haven. The garden is enthusiastically maintained by the owner on three levels, with a bog garden on the lower level, planted with bold waterside architectural perennials.

66 ROSE COTTAGE
Smithams Hill, East Harptree, Bristol, BS40 6BY. Bev & Jenny Cruse, 01761 221627, bandjcruse@gmail.com. *5m N of Wells, 15m S of Bristol. From B3114 turn into High St in EH. L at Clock Tower & immed R into Middle St, up hill for 1m. From B3134 take EH road opp Castle of Comfort, continue 1½m. Off road car parking on R (not SatNav).* **Visits by arrangement in Apr for groups of up to 30. Adm £5.50, chd free. Home-made teas.**

Organically gardened and planted to encourage wildlife. Bordered by a stream and mixed hedges, our acre of hillside cottage garden is carpeted with seasonal bulbs, primroses and hellebores and magnolias add to the spring colour. Plenty of seating areas to enjoy the panoramic views over Chew Valley. Full of spring colour.

67 SHANKS HOUSE
Long Lane, Cucklington, Wincanton, BA9 9QL. Mr Stephen Herrington, Head Gardener. *Just on the outskirts of Cucklington village, 5m from Wincanton & 4m from Gillingham. Parking is on the L as you enter the estate.* **Sat 18 Apr, Sat 20 June (10-4). Adm £8, chd free. Tea, coffee & cake.**

Beautiful 5 acre formal gardens set in 100 acres of parkland and wildflower meadows. The gardens were originally designed by Tom Stuart-Smith. The gardens are a collection of rooms with a walled garden, cut flowers, vegetable garden, bulb meadows, large pot displays and a glasshouse. A long lime avenue and apple orchards surround the elegant house which sits in the middle of the gardens. On 18th April Somerset Hardy Plant Society will hold their Spring Plant Fair in the garden.

68 42 SILVER STREET
Midsomer Norton, Radstock, BA3 2EY. Andrew King & Kevin Joint, kingandrew@talk21.com. *For our NGS open day only, parking is at Norton Hill School, Charlton Rd, BA3 4AD. From town centre, follow the B3355 Silver St for 0.4m, turn L into Charlton Rd, School car park is 100m on R.* **Sun 28 June (11-4). Adm £6, chd free. Home-made teas.** Visits also by arrangement 1 June to 19 July for groups of 10 to 30. Pls enquire about refreshments when booking.

Half acre plantsman's garden divided into 7 zones, developed from scratch by the owners over the last 15 yrs. Features inc a gravel garden with formal rill and pond, mixed/ herbaceous borders in cool colours, Iris garden (historic bearded irises), elliptical lawn with hot colour planting, informal area with woodland character and experimental bank with intermingled mixed herbaceous planting. The herbaceous planting on the bank was inspired by the Merton Borders at Oxford Botanic Gardens. The garden includes various structures made from green oak, an arbour and a pergola incorporating timbers from an old bus shelter. Level wheelchair access to most of the garden, enter via separate side entrance - pls ask at main entrance at the front of the house on arrival.

69 SKOOL BEANZ CHILDREN'S ALLOTMENT
Little Sammons Allotments, Chilthorne Domer, BA22 8RB. South Somerset County Council, www.skoolbeanzcic.com. *Near Yeovil. The garden is situated between Villa Verde Restaurant & the village school adjacent to Tintinhull road. Parking is a short walk away at The Rec just off Main Street.* **Sat 25 Apr, Sat 5 Sept (12-5). Adm £3, chd free. Home-made teas.**

Skool Beanz is a Children's Gardening Club run from their very own award winning No-Dig Children's Allotment which has dahlia beds, vegetable area, fruit trees, rainwater collecting station, 'Muddy Buddy' compost heap, quiet wildlife garden with tiny pond, secret den, polytunnel, upcycled sculptures, compost toilet and plenty of seating to sit and enjoy the garden. Lara contributed to Charles Dowding's No-Dig Children's Gardening Book sharing tips she has learnt from Skool Beanz on teaching the joys of gardening to children. Wheelchair access on the main path through the allotments. The woodchip paths may be soft depending on weather.

70 SOUTH KELDING
Brewery Hill, Upton Cheyney, Bristol, BS30 6LY. Barry & Wendy Smale, 07463 920222, wendy.smale@yahoo.com. *Halfway between Bristol & Bath. ½m up Brewery Hill off A431 just outside Bitton. Go past 2 rows of cottages on R. As road bends take tarmac lane on R, just below turrety stone wall. NGS sign at turning. Follow lane to end & cross gravel area to house. Postcode for SatNav BS30 6LY.* **Sat 12 Sept (10.30-4). Adm £12, chd free. Pre-booking essential, please visit www.ngs.org.uk for information & booking. Tea, coffee & cake. Adm inc refreshments & tour.** Visits also by arrangement 2 Mar to 23 Oct for groups of up to 30.

7 acre hillside garden offering panoramic views from its upper levels, with herbaceous and shrub beds, prairie-style scree beds, orchard, native copses and small, labelled arboretum grouped by continents. Large wildlife pond, boundary stream and wooded area featuring shade and moisture-loving plants. Due to slopes and uneven terrain this garden is unsuitable for disabled access.

Our donation to Marie Curie this year is equivalent to 17,521 hours of hospice at home care.

71 ♦ SPECIAL PLANTS
Greenways Lane, Cold Ashton, Chippenham, SN14 8LA. Derry Watkins, 01225 891686, derry@specialplants.net, www.specialplants.net. *6m N of Bath. From Bath on A46, turn L into Greenways Lane just before r'about with A420.* **For NGS: Thur 18 June, Thur 16 July, Thur 20 Aug, Thur 17 Sept, Thur 15 Oct (10.30-5). Adm £7, chd free. Home-made teas.** For other opening times and information, please phone, email or visit garden website.
Architect-designed ¾ acre hillside garden with stunning views. Started autumn 1996. Exotic plants. Gravel gardens for borderline hardy plants. Black and white (purple and silver) garden. Vegetable garden and orchard. Hot border. Lemon and lime bank. Annual, biennial and tender plants for late summer colour. Spring fed ponds. Bog garden. Woodland walk. Allium alley. Free list of plants in garden.

72 STANDERWICK COURT
Standerwick, Frome, BA11 2PP. Mr Guy Monson & Lady Rose Monson. *3m from Frome, 12m from Bath to Beckington. Follow A36 to Beckington r'about. Take turning to White Row Farm Shop. Follow lane in front of farm shop to end, pass gatehouse, entrance to garden on L, through black gates, parking signed.* **Sat 13 June (11-4). Adm £10, chd free. Tea, coffee & cake at the back of the house in the courtyard, or if wet in The Woolhouse.**
A hidden gem near the Somerset/Wilts border. With far-reaching views over the White Horse and Cley Hill lies a stunning Queen Anne House nestled in 76 acres of parkland. Ha-ha and woodland partially surround the formal gardens recently redesigned by Mark Lutyens and Catherine Fitzgerald to include an Italian inspired terrace, walled garden with tiki hut, tennis court, greenhouse and pool garden. Over the past 8 yrs the surrounding grounds have developed into a mix of contemporary cottage garden, formal hedging and lawns throughout. Do take an enjoyable stroll up the lime avenue to the folly, where deer, hares, rabbits and squirrels gather. Please supervise children at all times. Dogs on leads.

73 ♦ STOBERRY GARDEN
Stoberry Park, Wells, BA5 3LD. Frances & Tim Young, 01749 672906, stay@stoberry-park.co.uk, www.stoberryparkgarden.co.uk. *½ m N of Wells. From Bristol - Wells on A39, L into College Rd & immed L through Stoberry Park, signed.* **For NGS: Sat 13, Sun 14 June (12-4.30). Adm £6, chd free. Tea, coffee & cake. Sat 12, Sun 13 Sept (10.30-4.30). Adm £8, chd free. Light refreshments inc quiche & salad. Discount/prepaid vouchers not valid on NGS charity days.** For other opening times and information, please phone, email or visit garden website.
With breathtaking views over Wells Cathedral, this 5 acre family garden is planted sympathetically within its landscape providing stunning combinations of vistas accented with wildlife ponds, sculptures and water features. The 1½ acre walled garden is full of interesting planting. Colour and interest for every season; spring bulbs, irises, salvias, newly planted wildflower area, and modern rockery. Stoberry is hosting a sculpture exhibition in September which will have over 100 sculptures and art works integrated on the property- please visit our website for more details. Sorry, no dogs allowed

GROUP OPENING

74 STOKE BISHOP GARDENS
Stoke Bishop, Bristol, BS9 1DD. *All gardens are within the BS9 postal code area of Bristol. 1 Sunnyside & Oak Lodge are within a 5 min walk of each other. Haytor Park is a 20 min walk away or very short drive.* **Sun 10 May (1-5). Combined adm £7.50, chd free. Home-made teas at Oak Lodge.**

4 HAYTOR PARK
Mr C & Mrs P Prior.
(See separate entry)

OAK LODGE, 44 STOKE HILL
BS9 1EX. Jo Pople.

1 SUNNYSIDE
BS9 1BQ. Mrs Magda Goss.

Three very different gardens all within ½ m of each other. 4 Haytor Park has been lovingly created over almost 40 yrs. Wildlife in abundance with a pond and insect friendly plants. A totally peaceful haven in spite of being in a city suburb. Plenty of places to sit awhile and reflect, while spotting myriad plants for all seasons. Many arches lead to secret places, quirky features inc a bicycle wheel trellis. Oak Lodge is a country garden in an urban setting. On entering, the garden reveals its ½ acre size within a Georgian stone wall. It has herbaceous borders, hedging, mixed beds, privet trees, courtyard with potted plants, tennis court and lawns. A weeping silver birch provides a focal point whilst a shepherd's hut offers a quiet retreat. Sunnyside is an artist's C17 cottage in the heart of Stoke Bishop with part walled, cottage style front garden. Garden sculptures dominated by large magnolia, perennials, roses and spring bulbs. Courtyard garden with open studio at rear.

GROUP OPENING

75 STOWEY GARDENS
Stowey, Bishop Sutton, Bristol, BS39 5TL. *10m W of Bath. Stowey Village on A368 between Bishop Sutton & Chelwood. From Chelwood r'about take A368 to Weston-s-Mare. At Stowey Xrds turn R to car park, 150yds down lane, ample off road parking opp Dormers. Limited disabled parking at each garden which will be signed.* **Sun 19 July (2-6). Combined adm £7, chd free. Home-made teas at Stowey Mead (cash only for refreshments & plants).**

DORMERS
Mr & Mrs G Nicol.

STOWEY MEAD
Mr Victor Pritchard.

These gardens continue to attract visitors from near and far, and offer a broad spectrum of interest, styles and developments each year. The visitor's senses are aroused by the sights, scents and wide diversity of the gardens in this tiny, ancient village. There are abundant collections of mature trees and shrubs and ample seating within tranquil areas of the gardens, often with glorious views. Visitors enjoy the flower-packed borders and pots, roses, topiary, hydrangeas, exotic garden, many unusual trees and shrubs, orchards, vegetables, ponds, specialist sweet peas, a display of succulents, lawns and a ha-ha. There is something of interest for everyone, all within a few minutes walk of the car park at Dormers. Plant sales at Dormers. Teas at Stowey Mead. Well behaved dogs on short leads welcome. Wheelchair access restricted in places, many grassed areas in both gardens.

76 ♦ UNIVERSITY OF BRISTOL BOTANIC GARDEN

Stoke Park Road, Stoke Bishop, Bristol, BS9 1JG. 01174 282041, botanic-gardens@bristol.ac.uk, botanic-garden.bristol.ac.uk. *Located in Stoke Bishop ¼ m W of Durdham Downs & 1m from city centre. After crossing the Downs to Stoke Hill, Stoke Park Rd is 1st on R.* **For NGS: Sun 5 July (10-4.30). Adm £9, chd free. Light refreshments provided by local deli.** For other opening times and information, please phone, email or visit garden website. Donation to University of Bristol Botanic Garden.

Exciting and contemporary Botanic Garden with dramatic collections illustrating plant evolution on land, Mediterranean flora, rare native and useful plants (inc European and Chinese Medicinal herbs). New Guangzhou Garden, winner of Chelsea gold medal and coveted 'Best in Show' in 2021, now rebuilt and open. Glasshouses home to Amazon water lily, tropical fruit, exotic plants, orchids, cacti and unique sacred lotus. The Guangzhou Garden features a Chinese plant collection with many unusual and unique plants. Wheelchair available to borrow from Welcome Lodge on request. Wheelchair friendly primary route through garden inc glasshouses, accessible WCs.

77 ♦ THE WALLED GARDENS OF CANNINGTON

Church Street, Cannington, TA5 2HA. UCS College Group, 01278 655042, walledgardens@btc.ac.uk, www.btc.ac.uk/the-college/open-to-the-public/the-walled-gardens-of-cannington. *Cannington village centre nr Cannington Court & church. On A39 Bridgwater-Minehead road, at 1st r'about in Cannington 2nd exit, through village. War memorial, 1st L into Church St then 1st L.* **For NGS: Sat 25, Sun 26 Apr, Sat 19, Sun 20 Sept (10-4). Adm £7, chd free. Cakes, sandwiches, hot & cold drinks, ice-cream.** For other opening times and information, please phone, email or visit garden website.

Within the grounds of a medieval priory, the Walled Gardens of Cannington are a gem waiting to be discovered! Classic and contemporary features inc hot herbaceous border, blue garden, rose walk, sub-tropical walk and Victorian style fernery, amongst others. Botanical glasshouse where arid, sub-tropical and tropical plants can be seen. Tearoom, plant nursery, gift shop, also events throughout the year (open air theatre...). Gravel paths.

Court View

78 WATCOMBE
92 Church Road, Winscombe, BS25 1BP. **Peter & Ann Owen, 01934 842666, peterowen449@btinternet.com.** *12m SW of Bristol, 3m N of Axbridge. 100 yds after yellow signs on A38 turn L, (from S), or R (from N) into Winscombe Hill. After 1m reach The Square. Watcombe is on L after 150yds.* **Sun 12 Apr, Sun 17 May, Sun 7 June (2-5). Adm £5, chd free. Tea, coffee & cake. Gluten-free available. Visits also by arrangement 12 Apr to 7 June for groups of 10 to 30.**
¾ acre mature Edwardian garden with colour-themed, informally planted herbaceous borders. Strong framework separating several different areas; pergola with varied wisteria, unusual topiary, box hedging, lime walk, pleached hornbeams, cordon fruit trees, 2 small formal ponds and growing collection of clematis. Many unusual trees and shrubs. Small vegetable plot. Some steps but most areas accessible by wheelchair with minimal assistance.

79 WAYFORD MANOR
Wayford, Crewkerne, TA18 8QG. **Wayford Manor.** *3m SW of Crewkerne. Turn N off B3165 at Clapton, signed Wayford or S off A30 Chard to Crewkerne road, signed Wayford.* **Sun 31 May (2-5). Adm £7, chd £3. Tea, coffee & cake.**
The mainly Elizabethan manor (not open) mentioned in C17 for its 'fair and pleasant' garden was redesigned by Harold Peto in 1902. Formal terraces with yew hedges and topiary have fine views over W Dorset. Steps down between spring-fed ponds past mature and new plantings of magnolia, rhododendron, maples, cornus and, in season, spring bulbs, cyclamen and giant echium. Primula candelabra, arum lily and gunnera around lower ponds.

80 WELLFIELD BARN
Walcombe Lane, Wells, BA5 3AG. **Virginia Nasmyth, 01749 675129.** *½m N of Wells. From A39 Bristol to Wells road turn R at 30 mph sign into the narrow Walcombe Lane. Entrance at 1st cottage on R, parking signed.* **Visits by arrangement June & July for groups of 10 to 30. Adm £6, chd free. Please bring your own picnic.**

The Blooming Wild Plant Nursery

Our garden is a haven for wildlife. 29 yrs ago, a once bustling concrete farmyard grew into a tranquil ½ acre garden. Planned, created and still evolving today to provide enjoyment of colour and form for year-round enjoyment. Structured design integrates house, lawn and garden with the landscape. Wonderful views, ha-ha, specimen trees, mixed borders, hydrangea bed, hardy geraniums and roses. Formal sunken garden, grass walks with interesting young and semi-mature trees for each season. Now tranquillity, sheep as neighbours, perfect peace. Our collection of hardy geraniums was featured on BBC Gardeners' World with Carol Klein. Moderate slopes in places, an abundance of grass with some gravel paths.

81 WESTBROOK HOUSE
West Bradley, BA6 8LS. Keith Anderson & David Mendel, 07971 805560, westbrookgarden@icloud.com, www.instagram.com/keithbfanderson. *4m E of Glastonbury; 8m W of Castle Cary. From A361 at W Pennard follow signs to W Bradley (2m). From A37 at Wraxall Hill follow signs to W Bradley (2m).* **Sat 18 Apr, Sat 29 Aug (11-5). Adm £6, chd free.** Visits also by arrangement 1 May to 4 Sept for groups of 10+. Donation to West Bradley Church.
Layout and planting began in 2003 by a garden designer and a painter. 4 acres comprising 3 distinct gardens around house with exuberant mixed herbaceous and shrub borders leading to a meadow and orchard with wild flowers, masses of spring bulbs, species roses and lilacs.

82 WICK FARM
Wick, TA10 0NL. Mrs Penny Horne, 07923 984660, awakeningsatwick@gmail.com, www.awakeningsatwick.com. *Nr Langport. From Langport towards Curry Rivel, take R after Hurds Hill. Drive for ¾ m & Wick Farm is on L before sharp R bend.* **Sat 23, Sun 24 May (11-5). Adm £5, chd free. Tea, coffee & cake.** Visits also by arrangement 1 Apr to 1 Oct.
Nestled into 22 acres of land, Wick Farm is a colourful sanctuary offering curiosity and wonder. Expect tulips, alliums, a beautiful lime tree avenue, peonies and a kitchen garden full of spring delights. Sit and listen to the birds and soak in the serenity. Expect surprises. Playfully quaint. Regret no dogs.

83 NEW WILLOW BEND
2 Manor Ride, Brent Knoll, Highbridge, TA9 4DY. Helen & John Norris. *From J22 off the M5, go N on the A38 for approx ½ m. Turn L onto Brent St. Manor Ride is the 3rd on R, after approx ¾ m. (Brent Knoll school is 150 yds past the turning) Disabled parking on the drive.* **Sat 30 May (1-5.30). Adm £4, chd free. Light lunches, cream teas & cakes (gluten free available). Cash only.**
Newly established small garden, with late spring and early summer flowering, in the style of a plantswoman's cottage garden. Late spring tulips, iris, lupins, geum and phlox. Early summer salvia, roses, peonies and dianthus. With a summerhouse and lawns and an archway of roses. Regret no dogs. Combine your visit with a stroll up Brent Knoll hill and visit the local historic village church. Suitable for wheelchairs. Level surfaces, no steps.

84 NEW YEO MEADS
High Street, Congresbury, BS49 5JA. Debbie Fortune & Mark Hayward, debbie@debbiefortune.co.uk. *150yds along High St from Congresbury Arms pub on L. Park in Congresbury Arms public car park, (charges apply). No parking restrictions on the road. What3words app: mainland.landscape.minimums.* **Sun 10 May (11-4). Adm £5, chd free.** Visits also by arrangement 1 May to 14 Sept for groups of 5 to 25.
1¼ acres, formally laid out in C17 inc 350 yr-old cedar of Lebanon tree which fell in 2007 but is now a living feature, and a 150 yr-old lime, which is now a folly with a seat inside the base. Other trees inc acacia, ginkgo, cypresses and beech. Lead-lined pond with rill, large pond with 5 tier waterfalls, stone clapper bridge, Victorian pond, thatched summerhouse, kitchen garden, 2 greenhouses, folly, shed, orchard, herbaceous borders, rockeries.

85 ◆ THE YEO VALLEY ORGANIC GARDEN AT HOLT FARM
Bath Road, Blagdon, BS40 7SQ. Mr & Mrs Tim Mead, 01761 462798, visit@yeovalleyfarms.co.uk, www.yeovalley.co.uk. *12m S of Bristol. Off A368. Entrance approx ½ mile outside Blagdon towards Bath, on L, then follow garden signs past dairy.* **For NGS: Thur 9 Apr (10-5). Adm £8, chd £2. Light refreshments in the cafe.** For other opening times and information, please phone, email or visit garden website.
One of only a handful of ornamental gardens that is Soil Association accredited, 6½ acres of contemporary planting, quirky sculptures, bulbs in their thousands, purple palace, glorious meadow and posh vegetable patch. Great views, green ideas. Events, workshops and exhibitions held throughout the year - see website for further details. Level access to café. Around garden there are some grass paths and some uneven bark and gravel paths. Accessibility map available at ticket office.

86 YEWS FARM
East Street, Martock, TA12 6NF. Louise & Fergus Dowding. *What3words app: tweed.verbs.snap. Turn off Church St at Market House onto East St. Drive past White Hart & PO on R. Yews Farm 150 yds on R, opp Foldhill Lane.* **Sun 5 July, Sun 6 Sept (1.30-5). Adm £8, chd free. Home-made teas.**
Theatrical planting in large south facing walled garden, plants selected for height, form, leaf and texture. Prolific box topiary. Low maintenance perennials. High maintenance pots. Vegetables and cut flowers grown together. Self seeding hugely encouraged. Working organic kitchen garden. Greenhouses bursting with summer vegetables. Organic orchard with local cultivars. Free roaming hens. Cider making. Flowers for cutting. Exuberant perennials.

STAFFORDSHIRE
& West Midlands

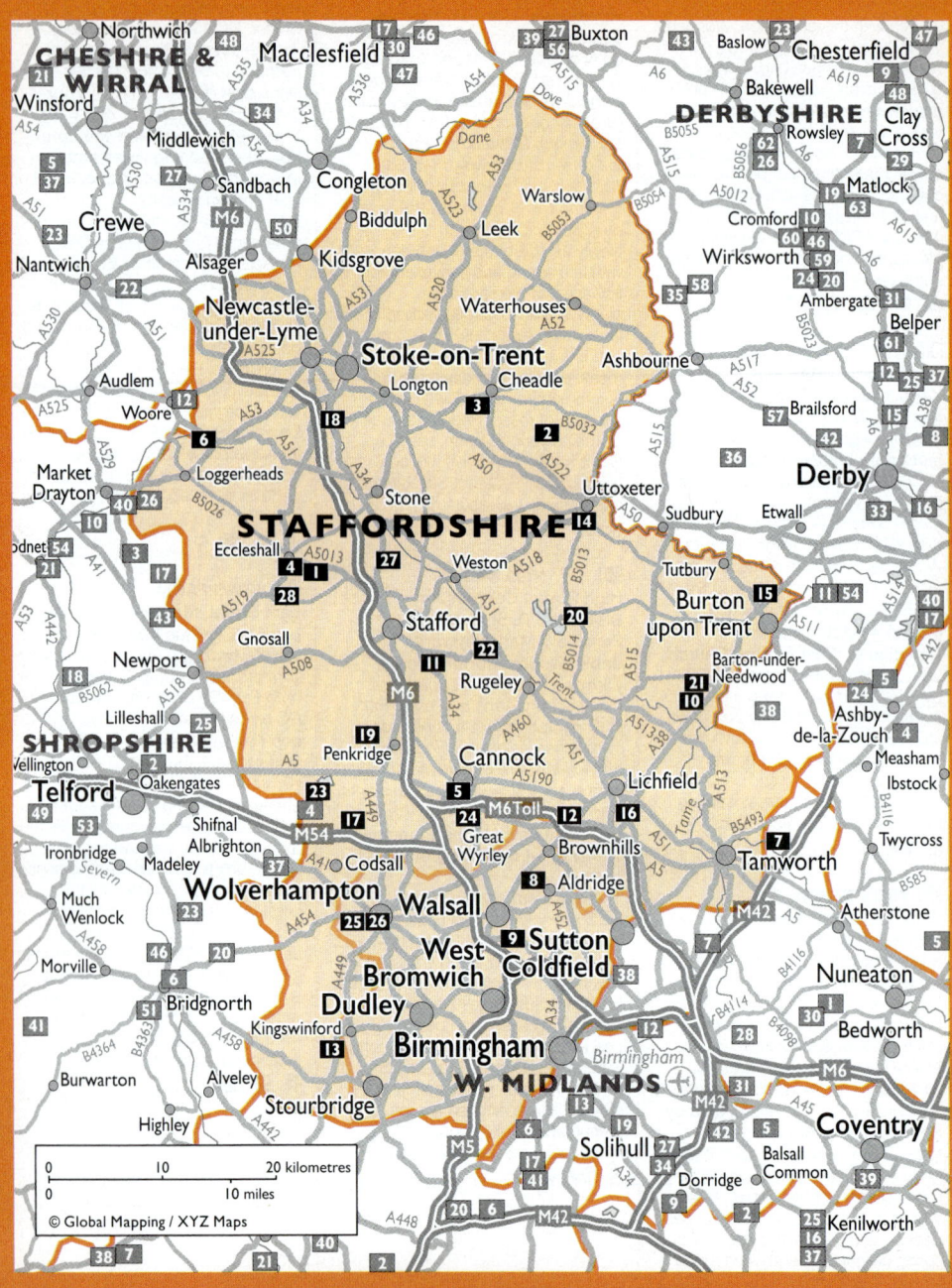

VOLUNTEERS

County Organiser
Anita & David Wright
01889 441049
davidandanita@ngs.org.uk

County Treasurer
Brian Bailey
01902 424867
brian.bailey@ngs.org.uk

Publicity
Ruth & Clive Plant
07591 886925
ruthandcliveplant@ngs.org.uk

Booklet Co-ordinator
Ruth Plant
07591 886925
ruthandcliveplant@ngs.org.uk

Assistant County Organisers
Fiona Horwath
07908 918181
fiona.horwath@ngs.org.uk

Alison & Peter Jordan
01785 660819
alisonandpeterjordan@ngs.org.uk

Ken & Joy Sutton
07791 041189
kenandjoysutton@ngs.org.uk

@ National Garden Scheme Staffordshire

OPENING DATES

All entries subject to change.
For latest information check
www.ngs.org.uk

Map locator numbers are shown to the right of each garden name.

February

Snowdrop Opening

Friday 6th
'John's Garden' at Ashwood Nurseries   13

Sunday 15th
5 East View Cottages   7

March

Sunday 8th
Millennium Garden   16

Sunday 22nd
The Old Mission   19

April

Sunday 5th
'John's Garden' at Ashwood Nurseries   13

Sunday 19th
Millennium Garden   16

May

Sunday 10th
115 Dartmouth Ave   5

Sunday 17th
10 Paget Rise   20

Thursday 21st
The Secret Garden   22

Saturday 30th
The Old Dairy House   18

Sunday 31st
The Old Dairy House   18
12 Waterdale   25
19 Waterdale   26

June

Friday 5th
The Secret Garden   22

Saturday 6th
14 Longbow Close   15
The Old Mission   19

Sunday 7th
Ashcroft   1
The Bungalow, Wood Farm   2
26 Claremont Road   4

Sunday 14th
33 Gorway Road   9
Monarchs Way   17

Saturday 20th
Fifty Shades of Green   8
Hammerwich House Farm   12
NEW 62 Park Road   21

Sunday 21st
Fifty Shades of Green   8
Hammerwich House Farm   12
NEW 62 Park Road   21

Wednesday 24th
5 East View Cottages   7

Friday 26th
The Secret Garden   22
Yarlet House   27

Saturday 27th
Yew Trees   28

Sunday 28th
115 Dartmouth Ave   5
5 East View Cottages   7
12 Waterdale   25
19 Waterdale   26
Yew Trees   28

July

Sunday 5th
The Bungalow, Wood Farm   2
Grafton Cottage   10

Sunday 12th
Cheadle Allotments   3

Thursday 16th
Grafton Cottage   10

Saturday 18th
Springfield Cottage   23

Sunday 19th
Grafton Cottage   10

Friday 24th
NEW 62 Park Road   21

STAFFORDSHIRE & WEST MIDLANDS

Sunday 26th
115 Dartmouth Ave — 5

August

Sunday 2nd
Grafton Cottage — 10

Saturday 8th
Yew Trees — 28

Sunday 9th
Yew Trees — 28

Saturday 29th
Fifty Shades of Green — 8

Sunday 30th
Fifty Shades of Green — 8

Monday 31st
Fifty Shades of Green — 8

September

Thursday 24th
'John's Garden' at Ashwood Nurseries — 13

October

Sunday 25th
◆ Dorothy Clive Garden — 6

February 2027

Sunday 14th
5 East View Cottages — 7

By Arrangement

Arrange a personalised garden visit with your club, or group of friends, on a date to suit you. See individual garden entries for full details.

115 Dartmouth Ave — 5
5 East View Cottages — 7
Fifty Shades of Green — 8
Grafton Cottage — 10
22 Greenfield Road — 11
NEW 33 Kingstone Road — 14
Monarchs Way — 17
The Old Mission — 19
The Secret Garden — 22
76 Station Street — 24
19 Waterdale — 26
Yew Trees — 28

The Secret Garden

THE GARDENS

1 ASHCROFT
1 Stafford Road, Eccleshall, ST21 6JP. Gillian Bertram. *7m W of Stafford. M6 J14 Take A5013 to Eccleshall. Ashcroft is 100 metres before junc with A518.* **Sun 7 June (2-5). Combined adm with 26 Claremont Road £5, chd free. Tea, coffee & cake.**
Tranquillity descends as you enter this one acre wildlife friendly garden. Pass the pond into a covered courtyard. Rooms flow seamlessly around the Edwardian house. Sunken herb bed, treillage, Victorian style greenhouse with raised beds. A topiary peacock struts in the gravel bed. In the woodland area a goblin lurks in the steps of the ruin. Look for the stone carvings and stained glass sculpture.

2 THE BUNGALOW, WOOD FARM
Great Gate, Nr Tean, Stoke-on-Trent, ST10 4HF. Mrs Dorothy Hurst. *Arrive in Great Gate & follow yellow signs.* **Sun 7 June, Sun 5 July (11-5). Adm £5, chd free. Tea, coffee & cake inc gluten free, vegan and dairy free cakes.**
Unique 1 acre country cottage garden with stunning views of the Weaver Hills surrounded by farmland. The garden inc a Thai theme underground temple with water feature, a relaxing Japanese area, also an area with a New Zealand and Mediterranean vibe, all with varied planting. As you wander around you will find plenty of quiet and tranquil seating. It is an experience that will lift your spirits. Most areas are wheelchair accessible with some assistance.

3 CHEADLE ALLOTMENTS
Delphouse Road, Cheadle, Stoke-on-Trent, ST10 2NN. Cheadle Allotment Association. *On the A521, 1m to W of Cheadle town centre.* **Sun 12 July (1-5). Adm £5, chd free. Tea, coffee & cake.**
The allotments, which were opened in 2015, are located on the western edge of Cheadle. There are 29 plots growing a variety of vegetables, fruits and flowers. A new addition in 2019 was a community area, with an adjacent wildlife area. A small orchard is currently being developed.
&

4 26 CLAREMONT ROAD
Eccleshall, Stafford, ST21 6DP. Maria Edwards. *7m W of Stafford. J14 M6. At Eccleshall end of A5013 the garden is 100 metres before junction with A519. On street parking nearby. Note: Some SatNavs give wrong directions.* **Sun 7 June (2-5). Combined adm with Ashcroft £5, chd free. Tea, coffee & cake.**
Relatively small town garden design based on Feng Shui principles. Lovingly manicured and constantly evolving herbaceous borders with shrubs, perennials and annuals to maintain colour and interest throughout the year. An artist with an artist's eye has blurred the boundaries of this Italianate-influenced garden, watched over by a large stone lion.

5 115 DARTMOUTH AVE
Cannock, WS11 1EQ. June and Ian Clayton, 07814 396588, junewclayton@hotmail.co.uk. *½ m from Cannock town centre. From A5 at Longford Island turn onto A4601 to Cannock. At next island take 1st exit- Longford Rd bearing L. Take next R Dartmouth Ave. Garden on R 200yds. What3words app: sleep. pokers.zealous.* **Sun 10 May, Sun 28 June, Sun 26 July (11.30-4). Adm £4, chd free. Tea, coffee & cake. Visits also by arrangement May to July for groups of 10 to 35. Adm price inc cream tea.**
Under ⅓ acre, this garden surrounds the bungalow. The front and back garden are full of herbaceous perennials, grasses, bulbs, ferns and shrubs, inc hosta, iris, allium, dierama and much more. With stand alone plants - cardoon, helenium, giant rudbeckia, scabious and sea kale. Sit in the beech hut or under the grapevine in the greenhouse. Admire the acers, cercis and snowdrop tree. New for 2026: an additional space displaying banana and larger leaf specimen plants.

6 ◆ DOROTHY CLIVE GARDEN
Willoughbridge, Market Drayton, TF9 4EU. Willoughbridge Garden Trust, 01630 647237, info@dorothyclivegarden.co.uk, www.dorothyclivegarden.co.uk. *3m SE of Bridgemere Garden World. From M6 J15 take A53 W, then A51 N. Midway between Nantwich & Stone, near Woore.* **For NGS: Sun 25 Oct (10-3.30). Adm £8, chd £2. Light refreshments in the Tearooms. Afternoon Tea can be pre-booked. For other opening times and information, please phone, email or visit garden website.**
12 informal acres, inc superb woodland garden, alpine scree, gravel garden, fine collection of trees and spectacular flower borders. Renowned in May when woodland quarry is brilliant with rhododendrons. Waterfall and woodland planting. Large Glasshouse. Spectacular autumn colour. Much to see, whatever the season. The Dorothy Clive Tearooms will be open Thursday, Friday, Saturday and Sunday during winter for refreshments, lunch and afternoon tea. Open all week in summer. Plant sales, gift room, picnic area and children's activities for a wide age range. Wheelchairs (+ electric) are available to book through garden website. Disabled parking available. WC on both upper and lower car parks.

7 5 EAST VIEW COTTAGES
School Lane, Shuttington, nr Tamworth, B79 0DX. Cathy Lyon-Green, 01827 892244, cathyatcorrabhan@hotmail.com, www.ramblinginthegarden.wordpress.com. *2m NE of Tamworth. From Tamworth, Amington Rd or Ashby Rd to Shuttington. From M42 J11, B5493 for Seckington & Tamworth. Pink house nr top of School Ln. Parking signed, overspill at Wolferstan Arms.* **Sun 15 Feb, Wed 24 June (12-4); Sun 28 June (1-5). Adm £5, chd free. Tea, coffee & cake. 2027: Sun 14 Feb. Visits also by arrangement Feb & June for groups of 12 to 30. Refreshments at extra cost, by arrangement.**
Deceptive, quirky plantlover's garden, full of surprises and always something new. Informally planted themed borders, cutting beds, woodland and woodland edge, stream, water features, sitooterie, folly, greenhouses and many artefacts. Roses, clematis, perennials, potted hostas. Snowdrops and witch hazels in Feb. Seating areas for contemplation and enjoying home-made cake. 'Wonderful hour's wander'.

8 FIFTY SHADES OF GREEN
20 Bevan Close, Shelfield, Walsall, WS4 1AB. Annmarie & Andrew Swift, 07963 041402, annmarie.1963@hotmail.co.uk, www.facebook.com/50SOGTheSwifts. *Parking in Broad Ln, as garden is in cul-de-sac. M6 J10 A454 to Walsall for 1.6m L at Lichfield St for ⅓ m L to A461 Lichfield Rd for 2m at Coop T-lights turn L to Mill Rd. Follow yellow signs. Also on Google maps.* **Sat 20, Sun 21 June, Sat 29, Sun 30 Aug (11-5). Tea, coffee & cake. Evening opening Mon 31 Aug (4-9). Light refreshments. Adm £3.50, chd free.** Visits also by arrangement 22 May to 30 Oct for groups of up to 30.
An award winning garden that has taken many years to create and landscape. Distinctive areas inc 2 ponds, stream, stone waterfalls, unique water features, places to sit, watch and relax. Wildlife encouraged and welcomed. Planting style is varied inc architectural plants, unusual foliage and textures, over 70+ trees and plant collections. Calm garden full of surprises, intrigue and discovery. A one off special illuminated evening on Bank Holiday Monday 31st August. Refreshments will inc hot sausage or veggie rolls as well as hot drinks and home-made cakes.
✤ ☕))

9 33 GORWAY ROAD
Walsall, WS1 3BE. Gillian Brooks. *M6 J9 turn N onto Bescot Rd, at r'about take Wallows L (A4148), in 2m at r'about, 1st exit Birmingham Rd, L to Jesson Rd, L to Gorway Rd.* **Sun 14 June (10.30-3). Adm £3.50, chd free. Home-made teas.**
Cottage style Edwardian house garden. Late spring bulbs and roses. Willow tunnel, pond and rockery. Garden viewing is over flat grass and paths. Wheelchair access through garage.

10 GRAFTON COTTAGE
Bar Lane, Barton-under-Needwood, DE13 8AL. Margaret & Peter Hargreaves, 01283 713639, marpeter1@btinternet.com. *6m N of Lichfield. Leave A38 for Catholme S of Barton, follow sign to Barton Green, L at Royal Oak, ¼ m.* **Sun 5, Thur 16, Sun 19 July, Sun 2 Aug (12.30-4.30). Adm £5, chd free. Home-made teas inc cream teas.** Visits also by arrangement 20 June to 20 Aug. Min group adm £100 if less than 20 visitors. Donation to Alzheimer's Research UK.
Described as a real treasure full of colour, texture and hidden corners. Viticella clematis and roses cover trellis, Hollyhocks adorn front of cottage, many dahlias, salvias and unusual perennials. Colour themed borders with scent, amphitheater, stream, parterre and more, has attracted visitors for over 30 yrs. Oak seating in extension with clematis and bed with hot colours, vegetable garden. Wheelchair access around garage to oak outdoor seating area.
& 🚗 ☕

11 22 GREENFIELD ROAD
Stafford, ST17 0PU. Alison & Peter Jordan, 01785 660819, alisonandpeterjordan@ngs.org.uk. *3m S of Stafford. Follow the A34 out of Stafford towards Cannock. 2nd L onto Overhill Rd.1st R into Greenfield Rd.* **Visits by arrangement 19 Apr to 12 July for groups of up to 25. Cream teas.**
Suburban garden, working towards year-round interest. In spring bulbs and stunning azaleas and rhododendrons. June onwards perennials and grasses. A garden that shows being diagnosed with Parkinson's needn't stop you creating a peaceful place to sit and enjoy. Two revamped areas this year. You might be able to catch a glimpse of Pete's model railway running. Flat garden but with some gravelled areas.
& 🐕 ✤ ☕

12 HAMMERWICH HOUSE FARM
Hall Lane, Hammerwich, Burntwood, WS7 0JP. Donna Harvey-Bailye. *3m from Lichfield Staffordshire. Follow Hall Ln from Muckley corner for 1½ m, gateway is just after church Ln on L. Continue through gate and parking is on L past house.* **Sat 20 June (11.30-4.30). Cream teas. Sun 21 June (11.30-4.30). Adm £8, chd free.**
Gardens in the grounds of an 1807 Staffordshire Farmhouse inc a large wildlife pond and an extensive collection of Roses. The garden has a greenhouse and vegetable garden to explore along with open fields overlooking Hammerwich Church to picnic in.
🐕

13 'JOHN'S GARDEN' AT ASHWOOD NURSERIES
Ashwood Lower Lane, Ashwood, nr Kingswinford, DY6 0AE. John Massey, www.ashwoodnurseries.com. *9m S of Wolverhampton. 1m past Wall Heath on A449 turn R to Ashwood along Doctor's Ln. At T-junc turn L. Garden entrance off main car park at Ashwood Nurseries.* **Fri 6 Feb (10-3); Sun 5 Apr, Thur 24 Sept (10-4). Adm £8, chd free.**
A stunning private garden adjacent to Ashwood Nurseries, it has a huge plant collection and many innovative design features in a beautiful canal-side setting. There are informal beds, woodland dells, herbaceous borders, a rock garden, unique ruin garden, an *Anemone pavonina* meadow and wildlife garden. Fine displays of snowdrops, spring-flowering plants and a notable collection of Malus. Tearoom, garden centre and gift shop at adjacent Ashwood Nurseries. Coaches are welcome by appointment only. Disabled access difficult if very wet. Sorry, no disabled access to the wildlife garden.
& ✤ NPC ☕))

14 33 KINGSTONE ROAD
Uttoxeter, ST14 8WH. Ken & Joy Sutton, 07791 041189, suttonjoy2@gmail.com. *Off A518. L turn after The Plough Inn. 1st exit at r'about then 1st L.* **Visits by arrangement June & July for groups of up to 15. Tea, coffee and biscuits inc in adm. Adm £5.**
A new garden developed by the owners with themed borders and an emphasis on colour from an electric mix of perennials, annuals, shrubs and roses etc. Lots of covered seating areas for refreshments while spending time relaxing for a while with the soothing sound of water from the fish pond feature.
✤

15 14 LONGBOW CLOSE
Stretton, Burton upon Trent, DE13 0XY. Debbie & Gavin Richards. *3m NW of Burton upon Trent in the village of Stretton. From A38 turn off at A5121 (Burton N) Follow signs to Stretton turning into Claymills Rd, then L to Church Rd, R into Bridge St & R into Athelstan Way. Please park on Athelstan Way.* **Sat 6 June (11-4). Adm £4, chd free. Home-made teas.**
A plantwoman's garden with exotic evergreens, gorgeous smelling roses,

a flower-filled sunny patio where refreshments can be enjoyed and a welcoming front garden. Its design features planting of herbaceous perennials, climbers and evergreen trees with a mauve, pink and purple colour theme. There is good level access to most of the garden with one shallow step.

✿ ☕))

16 MILLENNIUM GARDEN
London Road, Lichfield, WS14 9RB. Carol Cooper. *1m S of Lichfield. Off A38 along A5206 towards Lichfield ¼ m past A38 island towards Lichfield. Park in field on L. Yellow signs on field post.* **Sun 8 Mar, Sun 19 Apr (1-5). Adm £4, chd free. Light refreshments.**
Two acre garden with mixed spring bulbs in the woodland garden. In May the laburnum walk and wisteria arch are in full bloom in this English country garden. Designed with a naturalistic edge and with the environment in mind. A relaxed approach creates a garden of quiet sanctuary with the millennium bridge sitting comfortably, with surroundings of lush planting and mature trees. Well-stocked borders give shots of colour to lift the spirit and the air fills with the scent of wisterias and climbing roses. A stress free environment awaits you at the Millennium Garden. Park in field then follow the footpath round garden. Some uneven surfaces.

17 MONARCHS WAY
Park Lane, Coven, Wolverhampton, WV9 5BQ. Eileen & Bill Johnson, 07785 934085, snappy_eileen@hotmail.com, www.monarchsway-garden.co.uk. *Near Chillington Hall, Brewood. From Port Ln (main road between Codsall & Brewood) turn E onto Park Ln. Monarchs Way is on the sharp bend on Park Ln. Limited parking, (further parking is available at other end of Park Ln).* **Sun 14 June (11-4). Adm £6, chd free. Cream teas.** Visits also by arrangement 17 June to 28 Aug for groups of 8 to 20. Adm inc scones, unlimited tea & coffee for arranged visits.
The owners bought a 1¾ acre bare, treeless blank canvas in 2010 with grass around 3ft high! Since then they have designed a Tudor folly and jungle hut, built a pergola, excavated a lily pond with bog garden, created a cottage garden, orchard and vegetable garden. They have planted hundreds of conifer, evergreen, fruit and flowering trees, roses, hydrangeas, perennials and designed numerous flower beds. Wheelchair access is easy for most of the garden, on arrival request side gate for access. Minibuses can be accepted.

18 THE OLD DAIRY HOUSE
Trentham Park, Stoke-on-Trent, ST4 8AE. Philip & Michelle Moore. *S edge of Stoke-on-Trent. Next to Trentham Gardens. Off Whitmore Rd. Please follow NGS signs or signs for Trentham Park Golf Club. Parking in church car park.* **Sat 30, Sun 31 May (1.30-5.30). Adm £5, chd free. Tea, coffee & cake.**
Grade II listed house which originally formed part of the Trentham Estate, forms backdrop to this 2 acre garden in parkland setting. Shaded area for rhododendrons, azaleas and expanding hosta and fern collection. Mature trees, 'cottage garden', long borders and stumpery. Narrow brick paths in vegetable plot. Large courtyard area for teas. Some gravel paths but lawns are an option for wheelchairs.

✿ ☕))

![Yew Trees]

19 THE OLD MISSION
Bickford Road, Whiston, Penkridge, ST19 5QH. Mr Jason & Mrs Laura Beet, 07496 168161, jasonbeet@hotmail.com. *Postcode accurate for SatNav.* **Sun 22 Mar, Sat 6 June (10-4.30). Adm £5, chd free. Tea, coffee & cake.** Visits also by arrangement Mar to Oct.
The old Mission is situated amongst farmland in the small hamlet of Whiston. The one acre garden boasts an ancient giant oak, many shrub and flower borders, statues, carvings and other artistic ornaments. An amazing swimming pool with seating and an outdoor kitchen completes the scene. There are many shrub and climbing roses plus an orchard, kitchen garden and soft fruit cages.

20 10 PAGET RISE
Paget Rise, Abbots Bromley, Rugeley, WS15 3EF. Mr Arthur Tindle. *4m W of Rugeley 6m S of Uttoxeter & 12m N of Lichfield. From Rugeley: B5013 E. At T-junc turn R on B5014. From Uttoxeter take the B5013 S then B5014. From Lichfield take A515 N then turn L on B5234. In Abbots Bromley follow NGS yellow signs.* **Sun 17 May (11-4). Adm £3, chd free. Tea, coffee & cake.**
This medium sized split level garden has a strong Japanese influence. Rhododendrons and a wide range of flowering shrubs. Many bonsai-style Acer trees in shallow bowls occupy a central gravel area with stepping stones. The rear of the garden has a woodland feel with a fairy dell under the pine tree. A gem of a garden. Arthur hopes visitors will be inspired with ideas to use in their own garden. Arthur is a watercolour artist and will be displaying a selection of his paintings and framed prints, which will be for sale.

21 NEW 62 PARK ROAD
Barton Under Needwood, Burton-On-Trent, DE13 8DB. Mr Chris & Mrs Helen Charlton. *6m N of Lichfield. Leave A38 at Barton Turn, into village, past co-op on R take 2nd L into Park Rd.* **Sat 20, Sun 21 June (11.30-5.30). Light refreshments. Evening opening Fri 24 July (6.30-9). Wine. Adm £4, chd free.**
Overlooking farmland to the rear. A mature garden, fernery, herbaceous perennials, kalmias, crinodendron, myrtle, grevillea, and giant lilies, numerous clematis and sweet peas adorn the trellis. Pergola with hanging baskets, small bonsai garden and tubs full of colour.

'John's Garden' at Ashwood Nurseries

22 THE SECRET GARDEN
3 Banktop Cottages, Little Haywood, ST18 0UL. Derek Higgott & David Aston, 07843 505271, davidaston1065@yahoo.co.uk. *5m SE of Stafford. A51 from Rugeley or Weston signed Little Haywood A513 Stafford Coley Ln, Back Ln R into Coley Gr. Entrance 50 metres on L.* **Thur 21 May, Fri 5, Fri 26 June (11-4). Adm £5, chd free. Tea, coffee & cake.** Visits also by arrangement May to July for groups of 12 to 30. Daytime and evening visits welcome.
Wander past other gardens and through the evergreen arch to a fantasy for the eyes and soul. Stunning garden approx ½ acre, created over the last 45 yrs. Strong colour theme of trees and shrubs, underplanted with perennials and 1000 bulbs. Laced with clematis, roses and a laburnum tunnel. Other features inc water and a warm bothy for inclement days.

23 SPRINGFIELD COTTAGE
Kiddemore Green Road, Bishops Wood, Stafford, ST19 9AA. Mrs Rachel Glover. *A5 to Telford from Gailey Island. Turn L at sign for Boscobel House. Follow Ivetsey Bank Rd to Bishop's Wood. Turn 1st L Old Coach Rd past church 2nd white cottage on L.* **Sat 18 July (11-4). Adm £4, chd free. Tea, coffee & cake inc vegan options.**
6 yr old designed and landscaped plant enthusiasts cottage garden with unusual planting in areas, tropical area inc gunnera, canna, hedychium and palms, rose garden, herb garden and an established vegetable garden with large greenhouse. Fantastic views of the south Staffordshire countryside from all sides of the garden. Disabled parking for two cars, flat garden area and WC facilities.

24 76 STATION STREET
Cheslyn Hay, Walsall, WS6 7EE. Mr Paul Husselbee, 07522 208599, paulhusselbee@hotmail.co.uk. *Located on B4156. Limited on road parking.* **Visits by arrangement 31 May to 30 Aug for groups of 15 to 30. Light refreshments.**
40 yrs of gardening on this site has produced a hosta filled courtyard which leads to a Mediterranean patio, steps down to small area with folly, formal gardens area with stream, gated courtyard then finally find the secret garden. A quirky garden with a surprise round every corner.

25 12 WATERDALE
Compton, Wolverhampton, WV3 9DY. Colin & Clair Bennett. *1½ m W of Wolverhampton city centre. From Wolverhampton ring road take A454 towards Bridgnorth for 1m. Waterdale is on the L off A454 Compton Rd West.* **Sun 31 May, Sun 28 June (11.30-4.30). Combined adm with 19 Waterdale £6, chd free.**
A riot of colour welcomes visitors to this quintessentially English garden. The wide central circular bed and side borders overflow with classic summer flowers, inc the tall spires of delphiniums, lupins, irises, campanula, poppies and roses. Clematis tumble over the edge of the decked terrace, where visitors can sit among pots of begonias and geraniums to admire the view over the garden.

26 19 WATERDALE
Compton, Wolverhampton, WV3 9DY. Anne & Brian Bailey, 01902 424867, m.bailey1234@btinternet.com. *1½ m W of Wolverhampton city centre. From Wolverhampton ring road take A454 towards Bridgnorth for 1m. Waterdale is on L off A454 Compton Rd West.* **Sun 31 May, Sun 28 June (11.30-4.30). Combined adm with 12 Waterdale £6, chd free. Home-made teas.** Visits also by arrangement 3 June to 29 July for groups of 10 to 35. Inc visit to No.12 Waterdale garden.
A romantic garden of surprises, which gradually reveals itself on a journey through deep, lush planting, full of unusual plants. From the sunny, flower filled terrace, a ruined folly emerges from a luxuriant fernery and leads into an oriental garden, complete with tea house. Towering bamboos hide the way to the gothic summerhouse and mysterious shell grotto.

27 YARLET HOUSE
Yarlet, Stafford, ST18 9SD. Mr & Mrs Nikolas Tarling. *2m S of Stone. Take A34 from Stone towards Stafford, turn L into Yarlet School & L again into car park.* **Fri 26 June (10-1). Adm £5, chd free. Tea, coffee & cake.** Donation to Staffordshire Wildlife Trust.
Four acre garden with extensive lawns, walks, lengthy herbaceous borders and traditional Victorian box hedge. Peaceful Japanese water garden with fountain and rare lilies. Sweeping views from south walk across Trent Valley to Sandon. Victorian School Chapel and War Memorial. Garden chessboard and boules pitch. Gravel paths.

28 YEW TREES
Whitley Eaves, Ecclleshall, Stafford, ST21 6HR. Mrs Teresa Hancock, 07973 432077, hancockteresa@gmail.com. *7m from J14 M6. Situated on A519 between Eccleshall (2.2m) & Woodseaves, (1m). Traffic cones & signs will highlight the entrance.* **Sat 27, Sun 28 June, Sat 8, Sun 9 Aug (10-4). Adm £4, chd free. Pre-booking essential, please visit www.ngs.org.uk for information & booking. Home-made teas.** Visits also by arrangement 1 June to 1 Sept for groups of up to 30.
One acre garden divided into rooms by mature hedging, shrubs and trees enjoying views over the surrounding countryside. Large patio area with containers and seating. Other features inc pond, topiary, vegetable plot, hen run and wildlife area - always adding lots of new features, and lots of new plants. During June and July there are 8 acres of natural wildflower meadow to enjoy before it is cut for hay. Most of the garden can be accessed by wheelchair or mobility scooter, help is always on hand for anyone who may need it.

78,000 people affected by cancer were reached by Maggie's centres supported by the National Garden Scheme over the last 12 months.

SUFFOLK

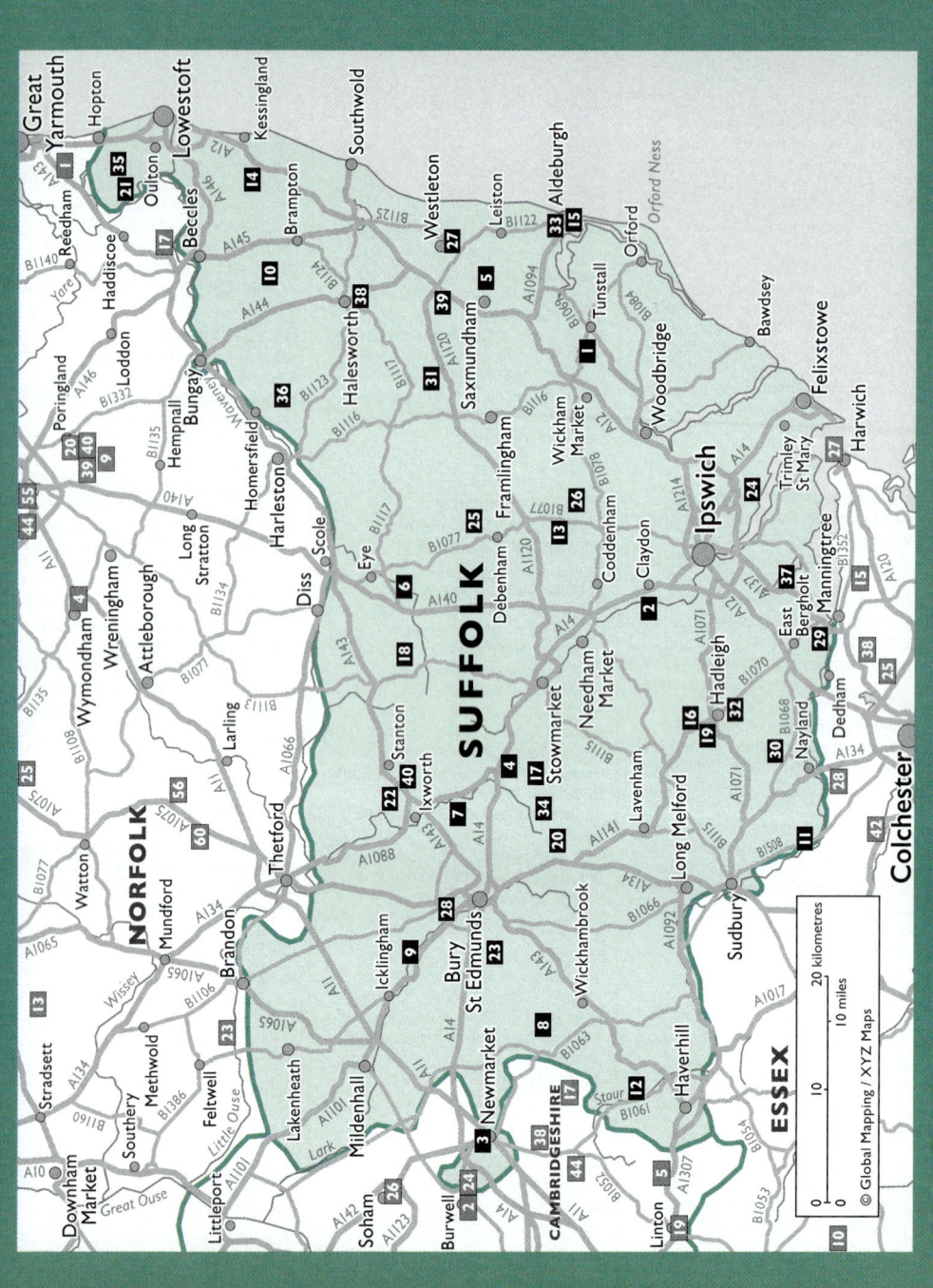

SUFFOLK

VOLUNTEERS

County Organiser
Jenny Reeve
01638 715289
jenny.reeve@ngs.org.uk

County Treasurer
Julian Cusack
01728 649060
julian.cusack@ngs.org.uk

Publicity
Jenny Reeve
(as above)

Social Media
Barbara Segall
01787 312046
barbara.segall@ngs.org.uk

Booklet Co-ordinator
Michael Cole
07899 994307
michael.cole@ngs.org.uk

Assistant County Organisers
John Ball
07770 378373
john.ball@ngs.org.uk

Michael Cole
(as above)

Tom Hoblyn
thomas@thomashoblyn.co.uk

Laura Maxim
07967 816550
laura.maxim@ngs.org.uk

Barbara Segall
(as above)

Peter Simpson
01787 249845
peter.simpson@ngs.org.uk

Marysa Norris
07855 284816
marysa.norris@ngs.org.uk

@SuffolkNGS
@suffolkngs
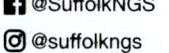

OPENING DATES

All entries subject to change.
For latest information check
www.ngs.org.uk
Map locator numbers are
shown to the right of each
garden name.

February

Snowdrop Openings

Sunday 8th
◆ Blakenham Woodland Garden   2

Sunday 15th
Gable House   10

Sunday 22nd
Great Thurlow Hall   12

April

Sunday 12th
◆ Blakenham Woodland Garden   2
Great Thurlow Hall   12
◆ The Place for Plants, East
  Bergholt Place Garden   29

Sunday 26th
The Old Rectory, Nacton   24

May

Sunday 3rd
◆ Fullers Mill Garden   9

Monday 25th
Mansard House   22

Saturday 30th
Smallwood Farmhouse   34

Sunday 31st
Wenhaston Grange   38

June

Wednesday 3rd
◆ Somerleyton Hall Gardens   35

Friday 5th
Helmingham Hall   13

Sunday 7th
Ashe Park   1
Great Bevills   11
Great Thurlow Hall   12
Holm House   17

Lillesley Barn   19
Manor House Farm   21
The Old Rectory, Nacton   24
5 Parklands Green   28

Sunday 14th
Church Cottage   6
Otley Hall   26

Wednesday 17th
◆ The Red House   33

Sunday 21st
Hillside   16
The Old Vicarage   25

Thursday 25th
Brampton Manor Care Home   3

Sunday 28th
Squires Barn   36
NEW Tattingstone Place   37

July

Saturday 4th
◆ Wyken Hall   40

Sunday 5th
◆ Wyken Hall   40

Sunday 12th
NEW Tattingstone Place   37

Sunday 19th
Heron House   15
Paget House   27

August

Sunday 2nd
The Lodge   20

Saturday 8th
Ivy Chimneys   18

Sunday 9th
Ivy Chimneys   18

Sunday 23rd
Henstead Exotic Garden   14

Sunday 30th
Bridges   4
The Priory, Laxfield Road   31

September

Sunday 6th
Wolsey Farmhouse   39

October

Sunday 4th
◆ Fullers Mill Garden   9

By Arrangement

Arrange a personalised garden visit with your club, or group of friends, on a date to suit you. See individual garden entries for full details.

By the Crossways	5
Church Cottage	7
Dip-on-the-Hill	8
Helmingham Hall	13
Heron House	15
The Lodge	20
Manor House Farm	21
Moat House	23
The Old Rectory, Nacton	24
The Old Vicarage	25
Paget House	27
5 Parklands Green	28
Polstead Mill	30
18 Raven Way	32

Our donation in 2025 has enabled Parkinson's UK to fund 2 new nursing posts this year directly supporting people with Parkinson's.

Blakenham Woodland Garden

© Marcus Harpur

THE GARDENS

1 ASHE PARK
Ivy Lodge Road, Campsea Ashe, Woodbridge, IP13 0QB. Mr Richard Keeling. Drive through entrance signed Ashe Park, past the gate cottage on L & follow signs to car park. **Sun 7 June (10-4.30). Adm £8, chd free.**
Explore an old 12 acre garden, planted in ruins of old house, comprised of different areas inc a large yew hedge, ancient cedars of Lebanon, canal and other water features. Walk through our walled garden and wild areas. Partial wheelchair access, some gravel paths and steps.

2 ◆ BLAKENHAM WOODLAND GARDEN
Little Blakenham, Ipswich, IP8 4LZ. M Blakenham, 07917 612355, info@blakenhamfarms.com, www.blakenhamwoodlandgarden.org.uk. 4m NW of Ipswich. Follow signs at Little Blakenham, 1m off B1113. **For NGS: Sun 8 Feb, Sun 12 Apr (10-4). Adm £7, chd £3. Tea, coffee & cake. Toatilly Granola shop will be open.** For other opening times and information, please phone, email or visit garden website.
Beautiful six acre woodland garden with variety of rare trees and shrubs, Chinese rocks and a landscape spiral form. Lovely in spring with snowdrops, daffodils and camellias followed by magnolias and bluebells.

3 BRAMPTON MANOR CARE HOME
Fordham Road, Newmarket, CB8 7AQ. Mr Carl Roberts, www.boutiquecarehomes.co.uk/care-homes-suffolk/brampton-manor. 1m S of J37 on A14 or ½ m N of Newmarket High St. **Thur 25 June (1.30-4). Adm £4, chd free. Home-made teas.**
Brampton Manor Care Home's gardens are focused on health and wellbeing of residents living with dementia and residential care needs. With sweeping accessible pathway and a variety of interesting horticultural features the garden inc mature trees, a resident run allotment,

beautiful lawn, bedding plants and raised planters. The gardens are lovingly maintained by residents and the team. Also a community event with a variety of activities and entertainment to enjoy. Fully accessible garden with step free access.

4 BRIDGES
The Street, Woolpit, Bury St Edmunds, IP30 9SA. Stanley Bates & Michael Elles. Off A14, halfway between Stowmarket & Bury St Edmunds. From A14 take slip road to Woolpit, follow signs to centre of village. Road curves to R. Bridges is on L & covered in Wisteria, opp Co-op. **Sun 30 Aug (11-5). Adm £5, chd free. Home-made teas.**
C15 Grade II terraced house in the centre of a C12 Suffolk village with walled garden to the rear of the property. Additional land was acquired 20 years ago, and this garden was developed into formal and informal planting. The main formal feature is the Shakespeare Garden featuring the bust of Shakespeare, and the 'Umbrella' a recently constructed pavillion in an Italianate design. Usually a wind quintet playing in the main garden. Paths wide enough for wheelchair users; however they will need to navigate one step up and two downs.

5 BY THE CROSSWAYS
Kelsale, Saxmundham, IP17 2PL. Mr & Mrs William Kendall, miranda@bythecrossways.co.uk. 2m NE of Saxmundham, just off Clayhills Rd. ½ m N of town centre, turn R to Theberton on Clayhills Rd. After 1½ m, 1st L to Kelsale, turn L immed after white cottage. **Visits by arrangement 1 Sept to 1 Oct for groups of 5 to 10. Adm £5, chd free. Light refreshments.**
A three acre wildlife garden designed as a garden within a working organic farm where wilderness areas lie next to productive beds. Large semi-walled vegetable and cutting garden and a spectacular crinkle-crankle wall. Extensive perennial planting, grasses and wild and uneven areas. The garden is mostly flat, with paved or gravel pathways around the main house, a few low steps and extensive grass paths and lawns.

6 CHURCH COTTAGE
Braiseworth Lane, Braiseworth, IP23 7DT. Mr Rajat Jindal. Enter from A140 on 1m single track road or through Eye. For parking, What3words app: stiffly.tearfully.solids. **Sun 14 June (10-5.30). Adm £7.50, chd free. Pre-booking essential, please visit www.ngs.org.uk for information & booking. Tea, coffee & cake.**
A naturalistic garden set in 2½ acres and developed from scratch over the last 14 years. A combination of formal and informal features inc a parterre, cottage garden surrounding an C18 thatched cottage, ponds, large prairie style beds, wildflower meadow, Hornbeam cubes, two copses, pleached limes, raised vegetable beds, willow dome and specimen trees.

7 CHURCH COTTAGE
Church Lane, Troston, Bury St Edmunds, IP31 1EX. Graeme & Marysa Norris, 07855 284816, marysanorris@gmail.com. 5m NE of Bury St Edmunds. From the A143 turn at the Bunbury Arms, signed Troston & Gt Livermere. Follow the road through Gt Livermere, signed to Troston. **Visits by arrangement 1 May to 14 June. Discuss refreshments when booking. Adm £8, chd free.**
A ¾ acre cottage garden. A central yew allee opens to a view of farmland. Mixed borders of grasses, perennials and fruit trees and a pond lie on one side. On the other is a small area of woodland plants, trees and shrubs, a kitchen/cutting garden and two greenhouses. Around the cottage are a gravel garden, small alpine beds and a patio with many planted containers. Church Cottage is opposite St Mary's Church, famous for its Medieval wall paintings. There is an excellent pub,'The Bull', in the village with has a well regarded restaurant. Open Wednesday to Sunday. Steps and a change of levels. Manageable with a robust wheelchair.

In 2025 we awarded over £288,800 in Community Garden Grants, supporting 114 community garden projects.

8 DIP-ON-THE-HILL
Ousden, Newmarket, CB8 8TW. **Geoffrey & Christine Ingham**, 07947 309900, gki1000@cam.ac.uk. *5m E of Newmarket; 7m W of Bury St Edmunds. From Newmarket: 1m from junc of B1063 & B1085. From Bury St Edmunds follow signs for Hargrave. Parking at village hall. Follow yellow NGS sign at the end of the lane.* **Visits by arrangement for groups of up to 12. Adm £6, chd free. Light refreshments.**
Approx an acre in a dip on a south facing hill based on a wide range of architectural/sculptural evergreen trees, shrubs and groundcover: pines; grove of *Phillyrea latifolia*; 'cloud pruned' hedges; palms; large bamboo; ferns; range of *Kniphofia* and *Croscosmia*. Visitors may wish to make an appointment when visiting gardens nearby.

9 ♦ FULLERS MILL GARDEN
West Stow, IP28 6HD. **Perennial**, 01284 728888, fullersmillgarden@perennial.org.uk, www.fullersmill.org.uk. *6m NW of Bury St Edmunds. Turn off the A1101 (Bury to Mildenhall Rd) signposted West Stow Anglo Saxon Village. Cont for 1½m and the entrance is clearly marked. Follow yellow signs on all major routes.* **For NGS: Sun 3 May, Sun 4 Oct (11-5). Adm £10, chd £4. Tea, coffee & cake.** For other opening times and information, please phone, email or visit garden website.
This award-winning seven acre garden is a tranquil, peaceful and enchanting waterside oasis set in the heart of Suffolk. It combines dappled woodland with a plantsman's collection of shrubs, perennials, lilies and marginal plants to create a year-round garden. Views of its fantastic displays of form and colour reflect off its mill pond, the River Lark and Culford Stream throughout the seasons. Some uneven surfaces, grassed areas, proximity to water and sloping ground limit disabled access to some areas.

&. ❋ 🚗 ☕

10 GABLE HOUSE
Halesworth Road, Redisham, Beccles, NR34 8NE. **Brenda Foster.** *5m S of Beccles. Signed from A144 Bungay/Halesworth Rd.* **Sun 15 Feb (11-4). Adm £5, chd free. Light refreshments inc soup lunches, tea & cakes.**

We have a large collection of snowdrops, cyclamen, hellebores and other flowering plants for our opening in February for you to discover. Many bulbs and plants will be for sale. The greenhouses contain rare bulbs and tender plants. We have a wide range of unusual trees, shrubs, perennials and bulbs collected over the last 50 years. The main garden is wheelchair accessible.

&. ❋ ☕

11 GREAT BEVILLS
Sudbury Road, Bures, CO8 5JW. **Mr & Mrs G T C Probert.** *4m S of Sudbury. N of Bures on the Sudbury Rd (B1508).* **Sun 7 June (2-5.30). Adm £6, chd free. Home-made teas.**
Overlooking the Stour Valley the gardens surrounding an Elizabethan manor house (not open) are formal and Italianate with Irish yews and mature specimen trees. Terraces, borders, ponds and woodland walks. A short drive away from Great Bevills visitors may wish to also see the C13 St Stephen's Chapel with wonderful views of the Old Bures Dragon recently re-created by the owner. Woodland walks give lovely views over the Stour Valley. There is also a recently created wildflower meadow with mown paths. Wheelchair access via gravel paths.

&. 🐕 ☕

12 GREAT THURLOW HALL
Great Thurlow, Haverhill, CB9 7LF. **Mr & Mrs George Vestey.** *12m S of Bury St Edmunds, 4m N of Haverhill. Great Thurlow village on B1061 from Newmarket; 3½ m N of junc with A143 Haverhill/Bury St Edmunds rd.* **Sun 22 Feb (2-4.30). Sun 12 Apr, Sun 7 June (2-5). Tea, coffee & cake in the church. Adm £7, chd free.**
13 acres of beautiful gardens set around the River Stour. Masses of snowdrops in late winter followed by daffodils and blossom around the riverside walk in spring. Herbaceous borders, rose garden and extensive borders come alive with colour from late spring onwards, arboretum with many mature trees. A yew parterre has recently been planted and the walled kitchen garden is undergoing redevelopment. The Curwen Print Study Centre, Art Studios and Gallery, located adjacent to Great Thurlow Hall will also be open to all garden visitors. Artists will be demonstrating fine art printmaking skills. Many paths

are gravel and there is some uneven terrain.

&. 🐕 ☕

13 HELMINGHAM HALL
Helmingham, Stowmarket, IP14 6EF. **Helmingham Events**, 01473 890799, info@helmingham.com, www.helmingham.com. *From A14 take J51 onto A140. Take 1st R onto Needham Rd (B1078). After 1½m, turn L onto Church Rd then R onto High St. R turn on Stonewall Hill towards Gosbeck. At end of Gosbeck Rd, turn L. Garden on L.* **Fri 5 June (10-5). Adm £10, chd £5. Visits also by arrangement 3 May to 30 Sept.**
It is hard to exaggerate the effect this beautiful park, with red deer and spectacular moated Hall in mellow patterned red brick with its famous gardens will have on the visitor. The whole combines to give an extraordinary impression of beauty and tranquillity. A classic parterre flanked by hybrid musk roses lies before a stunning walled kitchen garden with exquisite herbaceous borders and beds of vegetables interspersed by tunnels of sweet peas, runner beans and gourds. On the other side lies a herb and knot garden behind which is a rose garden of unsurpassable beauty. Gardens are accessible by wheelchair but mobility scooter is recommended due to challenging terrain and slope leading to the gardens.

14 HENSTEAD EXOTIC GARDEN
Church Road, Henstead, Beccles, NR34 7LD. **Andrew Brogan**, www.hensteadexoticgarden.co.uk. *Between Beccles & Southwold. 1m from A12 turn after Wrentham (signed Henstead). Close to B1127.* **Sun 23 Aug (11-5). Adm £6, chd £1. Tea, coffee & cake. Also available are home-made cheese scones & various savouries.**
Explore this two acre exotic garden featuring 100 large palms, over 20 bananas and giant bamboo; some of biggest in the UK. Discover streams and a 20ft tiered walkway leading to a Thai style wooden covered pavilion. Mediterranean and jungle plants around three large ponds with fish. Unique garden buildings, waterfalls, rock walkways, different levels and a Victorian grotto. Wheelchair access to parts of garden.

Church Cottage, Braiseworth

15 HERON HOUSE
Priors Hill Road, Aldeburgh, IP15 5EP. Mr & Mrs Jonathan Hale, 07968 906715, jonathanrhhale@aol.com. *At the SE junc of Priors Hill Rd & Park Rd. Last house on Priors Hill Rd on S side, at the junc where it rejoins Park Rd. Please note, entrance to Park Rd from SE is generally closed at weekends.* **Sun 19 July (2-5). Adm £6, chd free. Tea, coffee & cake. Visits also by arrangement Apr to Oct.**
Two acres with superb views over the North Sea, River Alde and marshes. Unusual trees, herbaceous beds, shrubs and ponds with a waterfall in large rock garden, and a stream and bog garden. Some half hardy plants in the coastal microclimate. Partial wheelchair access.

& ❦ ☕ ⋅))

16 HILLSIDE
Union Hill, Semer, Ipswich, IP7 6HN. Mr & Mrs Neil Mordey. *2½ m N of Hadleigh. Head NW on B1070. Turn R onto Calais St &* cont to Aldham MI Hl. Turn L onto A1071 & after 500 metres turn R onto Stone St. Follow for 1½ m. Car park through field gate. **Sun 21 June (11-4). Adm £6, chd free. Light refreshments.**
This garden, in its historic setting of 10½ acres, has sweeping lawns running down to a spring fed pond. The formal garden has island beds of mixed planting for a long season of interest. The wild area of meadow has been landscaped with extensive tree planting to complement the existing woodland. There is also a small walled kitchen garden and raised beds in the stable yard. Most areas are wheelchair accessible. Kitchen garden access over deep gravel drive.

& ❦ ☕ ⋅))

17 HOLM HOUSE
Garden House Lane, Drinkstone, Bury St Edmunds, IP30 9FJ. Mrs Rebecca Shelley. *7m SE of Bury St Edmunds. From E, exit A14 at J47. From W J46. Follow signs to Drinkstone, then Drinkstone Green. Turn into Rattlesden Rd & look for* Garden House Ln on L. 1st house on L. **Sun 7 June (9.30-4.30). Adm £7, chd free. Tea, coffee & cake. Savoury snacks.**
Approx 10 acres inc orchard, lawns, mature trees and clipped holm oaks. Formal garden with topiary, parterre and rose garden. Walk along the lake set in a wildflower meadow and discover the cut-flower garden with a greenhouse, kitchen garden with impressive greenhouse and Mediterranean courtyard with mature olive tree. Walk in the woodland with hellebores, camellias, rhododendrons and bulbs. Lake created in 2017 Kitchen garden. Much of the garden is wheelchair accessible. Regret, kitchen garden not suitable for wheelchairs.

& ❦ ☕ ⋅))

Moat House

18 IVY CHIMNEYS
Mill Street, Gislingham, Eye, IP23 8JT. Iris & Alan Stanley. *4m W of Eye, 3m W of A140, 9m N of Stowmarket & 8m S of Diss. A pale pink house in Mill St, ¼m from the village hall.* **Sat 8, Sun 9 Aug (11-4.30). Adm £5, chd free. Tea, coffee & cake. Savouries, gluten free cake, cordials & fruit teas also available.**
A garden planted for year-round interest and late summer colour. Ornamental trees, topiary, exotic border and fish pond set in an area of Japanese style; wisteria draped pergola supports a productive vine. A custom built planter fills a difficult corner and a large terrace gives views over the whole garden. Discover a secluded ornamental vegetable garden at the side of the house. Wheelchair access via low step to flat lawn.

19 LILLESLEY BARN
The Street, Kersey, Ipswich, IP7 6ED. Karl & Bridget Allen. *In village of Kersey, 2m NW Hadleigh. Driveway is 200m above 'The Bell' pub. Lillesley Barn is situated behind 'The Ancient Houses'. Parking is on street only.* **Sun 7 June (11-5). Adm £5, chd £2.50. Home-made teas.**
Dry gravel garden (inspired by the Beth Chatto Garden) inc variety of Mediterranean plants, ornamental grasses and herbs. Large herbaceous borders, pleached hornbeam hedge, rose arbours and small orchard. The garden contains various species of trees inc birch, amelanchier and willow in less than an acre of garden bordered on two sides by fields. Large collection of David Austin Roses.

20 THE LODGE
Bury Road, Bradfield St Clare, Bury St Edmunds, IP30 0ED. Christian & Alice Ward-Thomas, 07768 347595, alice.baring@btinternet.com, www.instagram.com/alicewardthomas. *4m S of Bury St Edmunds. From N: turn L up Water Ln off A134, at Xrds, turn R & go exactly 1m on R. From S: turn R up Ixer Ln, R at T-junc, ½m on R. Before post box on R & next door to Lodge Farm.* **Sun 2 Aug (12-5). Adm £7.50, chd free. Visits also by arrangement 1 May to 4 Oct for groups of up to 30. Discuss refreshments when booking.**
Recently filmed for Gardeners' World, this three acre naturalistic garden set in parkland is constantly changing throughout the year and there's usually plenty to see. Explore the gravel garden, large perennial garden and the courtyard rose garden. We have herbaceous borders and nursery beds, meadows and long sedum hedge. Minimal watering and experimental planting with climate resilience in mind. Wheelchair access over uneven ground. Please contact for more information.

21 MANOR HOUSE FARM
St Olaves Road, Herringfleet, Lowestoft, NR32 5QS. Mr Tommaso del Buono, 07889 131588, tommasodb@icloud.com, www.tdbstudio.co.uk. *Manor Farm sits next to the Somerleyton Estate Office & is accessed through a farm gate next to a very large brick & flint thatched barn.* **Sun 7 June (12-4.30). Adm £7.50, chd free. Tea, coffee & cake. Visits also by arrangement.**
Surrounding a Grade II listed 1655 house with a distinctive Dutch Gable, the garden at Manor Farm is being redeveloped by its landscape designer owner since 2020. Existing elements inc a Medieval wall. Tall Taxus hedges have been retained and incorporated within a framework that inc a new courtyard at the front, vegetable and cut flower gardens and more naturalistic areas. Separately listed Medieval brick and flint walled garden, bee orchids in the wildflower meadow.

22 MANSARD HOUSE
Low Street, Bardwell, Bury St Edmunds, IP31 1AR. Tom Hoblyn, www.thomashoblyn.co.uk. *From N: Go towards Bardwell (A1430). Mansard House is approx ¼m from the church on the R. From S: Take A1088 to Thetford. Follow signs to Bardwell. Mansard House is on the L approx ¼m after Knox Ln.* **Mon 25 May (11-5). Adm £6, chd free. Tea, coffee & cake.**
Chelsea gold medallist Thomas Hoblyn's naturalistic 2½ acre garden

surrounded by water meadows and wet woodland. Woodland planting, wildflower meadows, Benton End iris and peony beds lead to a crinkle-crankle walled kitchen garden and new climate resilient gravel garden in Suffolk's driest county. Partial wheelchair access.
& ❋ D ☕))

23 MOAT HOUSE
Little Saxham, Bury St Edmunds, IP29 5LE. Mr & Mrs Richard Mason, 01284 810941, suzannem207@gmail.com. *2m SW of Bury St Edmunds. A14 J42: leave r'about towards Westley. Through Westley village at Xroads. R towards Barrow/Saxham. After 1.3m turn L down track and follow signs. Garden is ½m from church.* **Visits by arrangement June & July for groups of 15 to 150. Cream teas. All refreshments are home-made.**
Set in a two acre historic and partially moated site. This tranquil, mature garden has been developed over 20 years. Bordered by mature trees the garden has various sections inc a sunken garden, rose and clematis arbours, herbaceous borders with hydrangeas and alliums, small arboretum. A Hartley Botanic greenhouse erected and parterre have been created. Secluded and peaceful setting and wonderful fencing. Each year the owners enjoy new garden projects.
& 🐎 ❋ 🚗 ☕

24 THE OLD RECTORY, NACTON
Nacton, IP10 0HY. Tizy & James Wellesley Wesley, 01473 659673, tizyww@gmail.com. *3m from Ipswich close to N side of the Orwell Estuary. On road to Nacton from 1st A14 turn after Orwell bridge going SE. Parking on Church Rd, by the church, 300m from Old Rectory gate.* **Sun 26 Apr, Sun 7 June (10.30-4.30). Adm by donation. Home-made teas in garden studio. Visits also by arrangement 18 Apr to 10 Oct for groups of 15 to 34. We also welcome visits for couples. Discuss refreshments when booking.**
Just under two acres of garden divided into areas for different seasons: mature trees and herbaceous borders, ample spring bulbs and blossom. Light soil so many self sown flowers. A lot of work done in 2025 to divert stream and create more extensive planting in the damp area of the garden. We have created a small pond with new marginal planting. Awaiting arrival of frogs, newts and toads. Most areas are wheelchair accessible, however grassy slopes and changes in levels.
& 🐎 ❋ ☕))

25 THE OLD VICARAGE
Church Lane, Kenton, Stowmarket, IP14 6JH. Mr Vic Woodgate, 01728 861118, vicwoodgate@winterbrook.co.uk. *Take Rishangles Rd out of Debenham. ½m on R turn into Bellwell Ln. Follow road for 1m. Car Park on L Kenton Field & Old Vicarage 200metres on R.* **Sun 21 June (10-5). Adm £6, chd free. Tea, coffee & cake. Visits also by arrangement 14 June to 13 Sept for groups of 10+.**
A beautiful garden with ample parking in the village. For 30 years the garden has been developed to inc a wild walk, concealed garden, specimen trees and shrubs, formal beds, garden statuary and a delightful orangery.
& 🐎 ☕))

26 OTLEY HALL
Hall Lane, Otley, Ipswich, IP6 9PA. Steve Southgate, www.otleyhall.co.uk. *Take Chapel Rd past the Otley village Post Office. After 250 yds take 1st L onto Hall Ln.* **Sun 14 June (11-4). Adm £6, chd free. Tea, coffee & cake at Marthas Barn Cafe.**
Discover 10 acres of both formal and informal gardens at Otley Hall which are managed with an eye to nature. There are stew ponds and woodland to explore. The garden features three Elizabethan garden recreations by Sylvia Landsberg.
& 🐎 🚗 ☕))

27 PAGET HOUSE
Back Road, Middleton, Saxmundham, IP17 3NY. Julian & Fiona Cusack, 07887 475299, julian.cusack@btinternet.com. *3m from RSPB Minsmere. From A12 at Yoxford take B1122 towards Leiston. Turn L after 1.2m at Middleton Moor. After 1m enter Middleton & drive straight ahead into Back Rd. Turn 1st R on Fletchers Ln for car park.* **Sun 19 July (10.30-5). Adm £6, chd free. Visits also by arrangement 19 Apr to 30 Aug for groups of 5 to 25.**
The 1½ acre garden is designed to be wildlife friendly with wild areas meeting formal planting. There is an orchard and a vegetable plot to explore. Walk through areas of woodland and see laid hedges and a pond supporting amphibians and dragonflies. There is also an abstract garden sculpture by local artist Paul Richardson. We are making changes designed to increase our resilience to drought. We have recorded over 40 bird species and a good showing of butterflies, dragonflies and wildflowers inc orchids. Wheelchair access: gravel drive and mown paths. Parking on drive by prior arrangement.
& 🐎 ❋ D ☕))

28 5 PARKLANDS GREEN
Fornham St Genevieve, Bury St Edmunds, IP28 6UH. Mrs Jane Newton, newton.jane@talktalk.net. *2m NW of Bury St Edmunds off B1106. Plenty of parking on the green.* **Sun 7 June (11-4). Adm £6, chd free. Home-made teas. Visits also by arrangement 2 Apr to 30 Sept for groups of 15 to 50. Adm inc refreshments.**
1½ acres of gardens developed since the 1980s for all year interest. There are mature and unusual trees and shrubs and riotous herbaceous borders. Explore the maze of paths to find four informal ponds, a treehouse, the sunken garden, greenhouses and woodland walks. Beautiful water garden.
🐎 ❋ 🚗 ☕

29 ♦ THE PLACE FOR PLANTS, EAST BERGHOLT PLACE GARDEN
East Bergholt, CO7 6UP. Mr & Mrs Rupert Eley, 01206 299224, sales@placeforplants.co.uk, www.placeforplants.co.uk. *2m E of A12, 7m S of Ipswich. On B1070 towards Manningtree, 2m E of A12. Situated on the edge of E Bergholt.* **For NGS: Sun 12 Apr (12-5). Adm £9, chd free. Home-made teas. For other opening times and information, please email or visit garden website.**
A 20 acre woodland garden originally laid out at the turn of the last century by the present owner's great grandfather. Full of many fine trees and shrubs, many seldom seen in East Anglia. A fine collection of camellias, magnolias and rhododendrons, topiary, and the National Collection of deciduous Euonymus. Partial wheelchair access in dry conditions. Advisable to call before visiting.
& 🚗 NPC ☕

30 POLSTEAD MILL
Mill Lane, Polstead, Colchester, CO6 5AB. Mrs Lucinda Bartlett, 07711 720418, lucyofleisure@hotmail.com, www.instagram.com/polsteadmill. *Between Stoke by Nayland & Polstead on the River Box. From Stoke by Nayland take road to Polstead. Mill Ln is 1st on L & garden is 1st on R.* Visits by arrangement 18 May to 30 Sept for groups of 10 to 40. Adm £7, chd free. Light refreshments. Discuss refreshments when booking.
The garden has been developed since 2002, it has formal and informal areas, a wildflower meadow and a large productive kitchen garden. The River Box runs through the garden and there is a mill pond, which gives opportunity for damp gardening, while the rest of the garden is arid and is planted to minimise the need for watering. Partial wheelchair access.

31 THE PRIORY, LAXFIELD ROAD
Badingham, IP13 8LS. Mr Nick Smith, www.priorybarn.co.uk. *A1120 to Badingham. At White Horse pub, turn in Low St. ¼ m R into Mill Rd. Uphill for ¾ m. L at post box onto Laxfield Rd. ½ m past Priory Cottage, follow yellow NGS signs.* Sun 30 Aug (11-5). Adm £6, chd free. Home-made teas.
Designed by Frederic Whyte, Chelsea Gold Medal winner, we wanted to create a garden with a contemporary feel, clear structure and focused on a refined palette of plants. A kitchen garden with raised vegetable beds, a rose garden, perennial borders and grasses interspersed with persicaria and gaura. At the front, a half moon lawn is framed by flowering trees, ornamental grasses and box. Live music and classic cars on display. A few steps in the garden. There are grass and gravel paths to negotiate.

32 18 RAVEN WAY
Hadleigh, Ipswich, IP7 5AX. Mrs Angela Wild, 01473 790141, wild123@talktalk.net. *A12 J31. Follow signs for Hadleigh. In Benton St, take 2nd R. From A1071 via Hight St, cont to Benton St, then 2nd R. What3words app: grow.fulfilled.cove.* Visits by arrangement Apr to July for groups of up to 20. Adm £5, chd free. Tea, coffee & cake. Please discuss refreshments & dietary requirements when booking.
A cottage garden with lush herbaceous beds, mature trees, ferns, roses, hostas, and an extensive variety of plants. Enjoy a peaceful pond with a rock water feature, a greenhouse, and a small vegetable patch. Admire a stunning 59-year-old acer, silver birches, and relax in shaded seating areas throughout. Access via a firm gravel driveway with one small step down onto the main garden.

33 ♦ THE RED HOUSE
Golf Lane, Aldeburgh, IP15 5PZ. Britten Pears Arts, 01728 451700, redhouse@brittenpearsarts.org, www.brittenpearsarts.org/visit-us/the-red-house. *Top of Aldeburgh, approx. 1m from the sea. From A12, take A1094 to Aldeburgh. Follow the brown sign directing you towards the r'about, take 1st exit: B1122 Leiston Rd. Golf Ln is 2nd L, follow sign to 'The Red House'.* For NGS: Wed 3 June (10.30-4.30). Adm £11, chd free. Light refreshments. For other opening times and information, please phone, email or visit garden website.
The former home of the British composer Benjamin Britten and his partner, the singer Peter Pears. The five acre garden provides an atmospheric setting for the house they shared and contain many plants loved by the couple. Inc mixed herbaceous borders, kitchen garden, meadows, contemporary planting and mature trees. The Red House and the collections left by Britten and Pears offers an extraordinary wealth of material documenting their lives. The garden offers a peaceful setting to this beautiful corner of Suffolk. Wheelchair access: brick, concrete, gravel paths and grass. Some areas are uneven. Wheelchair available on request.

34 SMALLWOOD FARMHOUSE
Smallwood Green, Bradfield St George, Bury St Edmunds, IP30 0AJ. Mr & Mrs P Doe. *S of A14, E of A134 on Bradfield St George to Felsham Rd. Disregard sign to Smallwood Green & follow the NGS yellow signage. Property is located on an unnamed road leading to/from Hessett.* Sat 30 May (11-4). Adm £6, chd free. Light refreshments.
The garden is a combination of traditional cottage planting and contemporary styles. At its heart, a C16 farmhouse provides the backdrop to a number of old English roses, a profusion of clematis and honeysuckle, and a variety of perennials. There are two natural ponds, a Mediterranean garden and a kitchen garden (currently under development), whilst paths meander through an area of ancient meadow. Partially wheelchair accessible, although not suitable in damp or wet weather.

35 ♦ SOMERLEYTON HALL GARDENS
Somerleyton, NR32 5QQ. Lord Somerleyton, www.somerleyton.co.uk. *5m NW of Lowestoft. From Norwich take the B1074, 7m SE of Great Yarmouth (A143). Coaches should follow signs to the rear W gate entrance.* For NGS: Wed 3 June (11-3). Adm £10.95, chd free. Light refreshments at The Greenhouse Cafe. For other opening times and information, please visit garden website.
Beautiful gardens of 12 acres contain a wide variety of magnificent specimen trees, shrubs, borders and plants providing colour and interest throughout the year. Sweeping lawns and formal gardens combine with majestic statuary and original Victorian ornamentation. Highlights inc the Paxton glasshouses, pergola, walled garden and yew hedge maze. House and gardens remodelled in 1840s by Sir Morton Peto. Most areas of the gardens are wheelchair accessible. Path surfaces are gravel, stone and can be difficult in places.

36 SQUIRES BARN
St Cross South Elmham, Harleston, IP20 0PA. Stephen & Ann Mulligan. *6m W of Halesworth, 6m E of Harleston & 7m S of Bungay. On New Rd between St Cross & St James. Parking in field opp. Yellow signs from A143 & other local roads.* Sun 28 June (10.30-4). Adm £5, chd free. Tea, coffee & cake inc gluten free, vegan options & ice creams. All cakes are home-made.
A country garden of three acres with a variety of beds planted with trees, shrubs, herbaceous and perennial planting. In addition there are two ponds, a wildflower mound, a mature orchard and a small vegetable area.

A recent addition is the swimming pool garden. A small copse of mixed planting is maturing. Plant stall, small local art exhibition, whilst a brass band will play between 12- 2pm. The garden is largely grass with some slight slopes. Seating is available across the garden. One single flight of steps can be bypassed.

& ✱ ☕

37 NEW TATTINGSTONE PLACE
Tattingstone Lane, Tattingstone, Ipswich, IP9 2FP. **Mr & Mrs Wills.** *6m from Ipswich. If using SatNav, IP9 2FP takes you to the entrance. Don't use black metal gates, use the large entrance a little further on.* **Sun 28 June, Sun 12 July (11.30-4). Adm £8, chd free. Home-made teas.** Beautiful garden around a historic property, features to inc a vibrant and productive kitchen garden, avenue of lime trees, two ponds and roses in both formal and informal settings. There is also a wonderful wildflower meadow to wander through and stone and gravel gardens which inc a wide variety of herbaceous plants. Grade II listed Georgian country house set in parkland overlooking Alton Water. Visitors can explore the different areas of the garden that frame the historic house. Partial wheelchair access to all parts of the garden.

& ✱ ☕))

38 WENHASTON GRANGE
Wenhaston, Halesworth, IP19 9HJ. **Mr & Mrs Bill Barlow.** *S of Halesworth. Turn SW from A144 between Bramfield & Halesworth. Take the single track road (signed Walpole 2). Wenhaston Grange is approx ½m, at the bottom of the hill on L.* **Sun 31 May (11-4). Adm £7, chd free. Home-made teas.** Over three acres of varied gardens on a long established site which has been extensively landscaped and enhanced over the last 20 years. Long herbaceous borders, old established trees and a series of garden rooms created by beech hedges. Levels and sight lines have been carefully planned. The vegetable garden is now coming on nicely and there is also a wildflower meadow and woodland garden.

🐕 ☕))

39 WOLSEY FARMHOUSE
Hog Hill Lane, Yoxford, Saxmundham, IP17 3JF. **Mrs Marion Anthony.** *1m out of Yoxford. In the village, turn into Strickland Manor Hill & cont to the fork in the road. Take the L fork & cont to Wolsey Farm House. What3words app: workroom.cattle. swanky.* **Sun 6 Sept (11-4). Adm £6, chd free. Tea, coffee & cake.** A large country garden with recently created wildflower meadow and prairie garden. Discover an established walled garden with shrub borders and rose beds surrounded by box hedging. Explore an orchard, a pond planted with marginal plants for wildlife and a moat with two bridges. The pond and moat are unfenced; children take care. Well behaved dogs on leads are welcome. The garden is generally level with areas of mown grass. There are some steps close to the house.

& 🐕 D ☕))

40 ♦ WYKEN HALL
Stanton, IP31 2DW. **Sir Kenneth & Lady Carlisle,** 01359 250262, shop@wykenvineyards.co.uk, www.wykenvineyards.co.uk. *9m NE of Bury St Edmunds. Along A143. Follow signs to Wyken Vineyards on A143 between Ixworth & Stanton.* **For NGS: Sat 4, Sun 5 July (10-5). Adm £6, chd free. Light refreshments at cafe and restaurant on site.** For other opening times and information, please phone, email or visit garden website.
Four acres around the old manor. The gardens inc knot and herb gardens, old-fashioned rose garden, kitchen and wild garden, nuttery, pond, gazebo and maze; herbaceous borders and old orchard. Enjoy a woodland walk and visit the vineyard nearby. Restaurant (booking 01359 250287), shop and vineyard.

& ✱ ☕

Lillesley Barn

SURREY

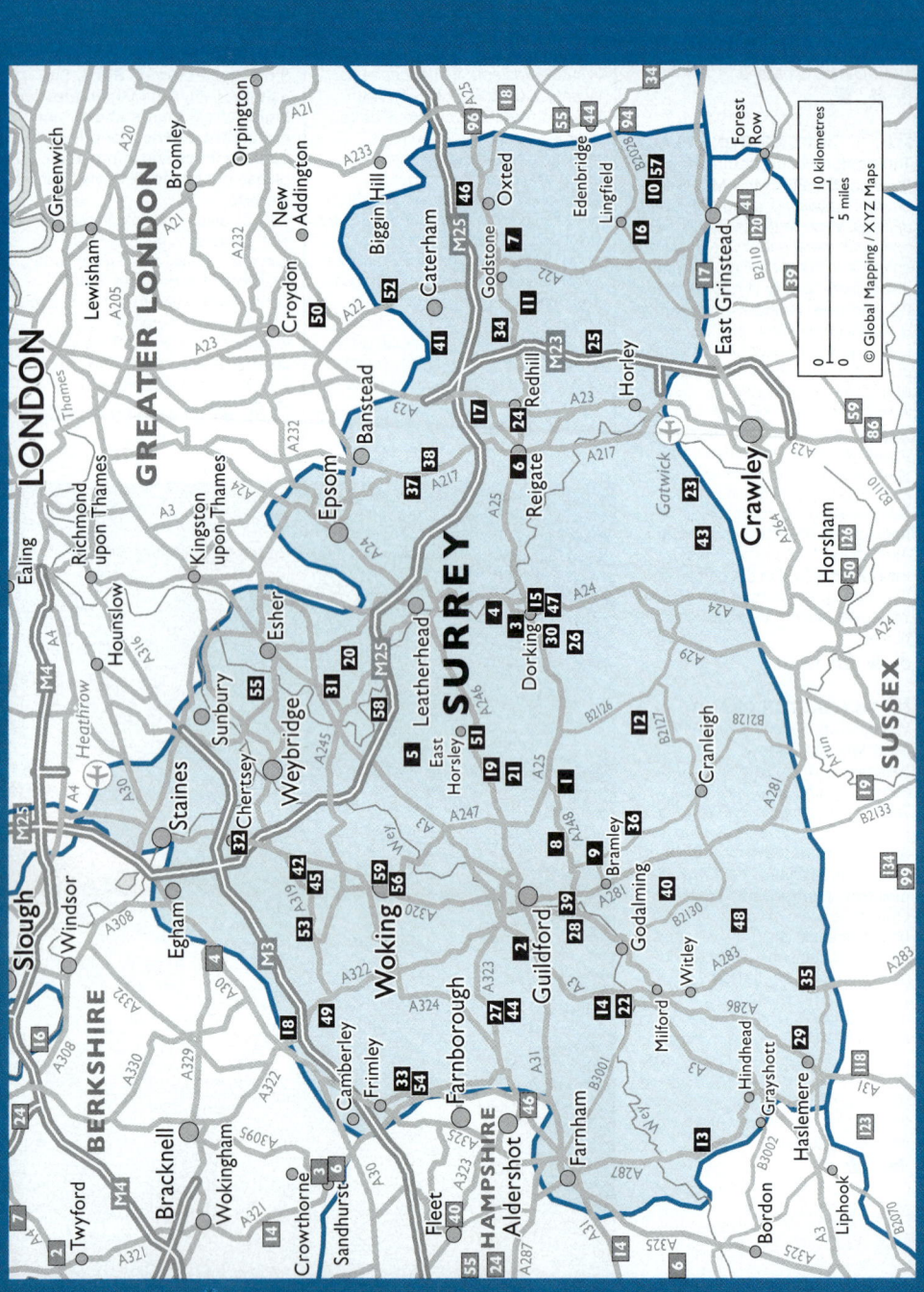

VOLUNTEERS

County Organiser
Clare Bevan
07956 307546
clare.bevan@ngs.org.uk

County Treasurer
Nigel Brandon
020 8643 8686
nbrandon@ngs.org.uk

Booklet Co-ordinator
Annabel Alford-Warren
01483 203330
annabel.alford-warren@ngs.org.uk

Booklet Distributor
Jānis Raubiška 07478 025184
janis.raubiska@ngs.org.uk

Publicity
Sarah Wilson
07932 445868
sarah.wilson@ngs.org.uk

Social Media
Annette Warren
07790 045354
annette.warren@ngs.org.uk

Assistant County Organisers
Jane Allison 07790 476394
jane.allison@ngs.org.uk

Jan Brandon 020 8643 8686
janmbrandon@outlook.com

Angela Gilchrist 01306 884613
ar.gilchrist@btinternet.com

Susie Gent 07831 585501
susanjmgent@gmail.com

Annie Keighley 01252 838660
annie.keighley12@btinternet.com

Jānis Raubiška (as above)

Robin Redmile-Gordon
07710 045647
robin.redmile-gordon@ngs.org.uk

Kate Smith 07788 746719
kate.smith@ngs.org.uk

Sarah Wilson (as above)

 @surreyngs
 @surreyngs

OPENING DATES

All entries subject to change.
For latest information check
www.ngs.org.uk
Extended openings are shown
at the beginning of the month.

Map locator numbers are
shown to the right of each
garden name.

January

Thursday 8th
Timber Hill 45

Thursday 22nd
Timber Hill 45

February

Snowdrop Openings

Sunday 8th
♦ Gatton Park 17

Thursday 12th
Timber Hill 45

Sunday 22nd
Shieling 38

Thursday 26th
Timber Hill 45

March

Every day from Monday 23rd to Saturday 28th
♦ Vann 48

Thursday 12th
Timber Hill 45

Sunday 22nd
Albury Park 1

Thursday 26th
Timber Hill 45

Sunday 29th
♦ Vann 48

April

Every Sunday from Sunday 12th
Coverwood Lakes 12

Thursday 9th
Timber Hill 45

Saturday 11th
11 West Hill 50

Sunday 12th
11 West Hill 50

Thursday 23rd
Timber Hill 45

Sunday 26th
♦ Hatchlands Park 19
Waterer's Garden 49

Thursday 30th
Crosswater Farm 13

May

Every Thursday, Friday and Saturday to Saturday 23rd
Crosswater Farm 13

Saturday 2nd
NEW Downs Solicitors 15

Sunday 3rd
Coverwood Lakes 12
The Garth Pleasure Grounds 16

Thursday 7th
Timber Hill 45

Friday 8th
Chauffeur's Flat 7

Saturday 9th
Chauffeur's Flat 7
Hall Grove School 18

Sunday 10th
Chauffeur's Flat 7
The Garth Pleasure Grounds 16
NEW 10 Upper Rose Hill 47
West Horsley Place 51
Westways Farm 53

Wednesday 13th
Claridge House 10

Friday 15th
♦ Ramster 35

Sunday 17th
Slades Farm 40
The Therapy Garden 44

Thursday 21st
Timber Hill 45

Friday 22nd
Little Orchards 25

Saturday 23rd
Monks Lantern 32

Sunday 24th
Chilworth Manor 8
Little Orchards 25
57 Westhall Road 52

Monday 25th
Shieling 38
57 Westhall Road 52

Saturday 30th
Hall Grove School 18
NEW Home Farm 22
NEW Johnston House 24

Sunday 31st
NEW Home Farm 22
◆ Titsey Place Gardens 46

June

Saturday 6th
NEW Yellowstones 59

Sunday 7th
The Manor House 29
Milton Way House 30
The Old Rectory 34
Wildwood 54
NEW Yellowstones 59

Friday 12th
Ashleigh Grange 4

Sunday 14th
Ashleigh Grange 4
◆ Loseley Park 28

Thursday 18th
Timber Hill 45

Saturday 20th
Hall Grove School 18

Sunday 21st
NEW Ashcombe Cottage 3

Saturday 27th
Bridge End Cottage 5
NEW Downs Solicitors 15

Sunday 28th
◆ Titsey Place Gardens 46
63 Wolsey Drive 55

July

Sunday 5th
High Clandon Estate Vineyard 21

Saturday 11th
NEW Woods Folly 57

Sunday 12th
Ichi-Coo Park 23

Sunday 19th
South Wind 41

Sunday 26th
◆ Titsey Place Gardens 46

August

Sunday 2nd
Shooting Star Children's Hospices, Christopher's 39

Sunday 16th
Shieling 38

Sunday 30th
◆ Titsey Place Gardens 46
Woodpeckers 56

September

Sunday 6th
Woodpeckers 56

Sunday 13th
West Horsley Place 51

Sunday 20th
The Therapy Garden 44

Saturday 26th
Hall Grove School 18

October

Saturday 3rd
NEW Johnston House 24

Sunday 4th
Albury Park 1

Thursday 15th
Timber Hill 45

Sunday 18th
Coverwood Lakes 12

Thursday 29th
Timber Hill 45

November

Sunday 1st
The Garth Pleasure Grounds 16

Thursday 5th
Timber Hill 45

By Arrangement

Arrange a personalised garden visit with your club, or group of friends, on a date to suit you. See individual garden entries for full details.

29 Applegarth Avenue 2
Ashleigh Grange 4
Bridge End Cottage 5
Caxton House 6
2 Chinthurst Lodge 9
Claridge House 10
Coldharbour House 11
Crosswater Farm 13
NEW Dolphin House 14
Heathside 20
Logmore Place 26
Longer End Cottage 27
Moleshill House 31
Monks Lantern 32
The Nutrition Garden 33
Shamley Wood Estate 36
41 Shelvers Way 37
Shieling 38
South Wind 41
NEW Tanglewood Cottage 42
Tanhouse Farm 43
Waterer's Garden 49
Westways Farm 53
Wrens' Nest Cottage 58

Hatchlands Park

THE GARDENS

1 ALBURY PARK
Albury, GU5 9BH. Trustees of Albury Estate. *5m SE of Guildford. From A25 take A248 towards Albury for ¼ m, then turn up New Rd. Entrance to Albury Park is immed on L.* **Sun 22 Mar, Sun 4 Oct (2-5). Adm £6, chd free. Home-made teas.**
The 14 acre pleasure grounds were laid out in the 1670s by John Evelyn for Henry Howard, who would later become the 6th Duke of Norfolk. The grounds inc a ¼ mile of terraces, a fine collection of trees, a lake, and a river. Wheelchair access via a gravel path with a gentle slope.

2 29 APPLEGARTH AVENUE
Guildford, GU2 8LX. Mr Robert Avenell, robavenell@outlook.com. *Just off the A3 at Guildford. Follow directions for The Royal Surrey Hospital from the A3 along Egerton Rd. Turn L at the r'about by Kings College & Applegarth Ave is opp the shops on Park Barn Estate.* **Visits by arrangement in June for groups of up to 10. Adm £6, chd free. Cream teas.**
Though not a large garden, this is somewhere to escape to and relax. The owner's love of vibrant colours is reflected in the garden, which is filled with cherished plants, glorious blooms, and attractive scents. As you walk through a series of outdoor rooms, you will discover a mix of trees, shrubs, herbaceous perennials, and roses. Winner of the 'Best Wildlife Garden' in Guildford and overall winner of Guildford in Bloom 2025.

3 NEW ASHCOMBE COTTAGE
Private lane off Ranmore Common Road, Ranmore Common, Dorking, RH5 6SP. *2m from Dorking. From Dorking/Horsley, turn off Ranmore Common Rd at the Old Post Office & continue straight for 1m, passing St Barnabas Church. What3words app: global.angel.jams.* **Sun 21 June (11-4). Adm £5, chd free. Tea, coffee & cake at St Barnabas Church (¾ mile away).**
Reopening after a 25 yr hiatus! Wander through ⅔ of an acre of flint-edged borders, overflowing with a carnival of colour, and ending with a tranquil respite in the secluded white garden. Rose bushes perfume the air, while the vegetable beds and glasshouse showcase the seasonal bounty. A chain of wildlife ponds provides the murmur of trickling water, and the Victorian cistern offers a modern twist.

4 ASHLEIGH GRANGE
Off Chapel Lane, Westhumble, RH5 6AY. Angela & Clive Gilchrist, 01306 884613, ar.gilchrist@btinternet.com. *2m N of Dorking. From A24 at Boxhill/Burford Bridge, follow signs to Westhumble. Continue through village & turn L up drive by ruined chapel (1m from A24). Sorry, no access for coaches.* **Evening opening Fri 12 June (5.30-8). Adm £10, chd free. Wine. Sun 14 June (2-5). Adm £5, chd free. Home-made teas. Visits also by arrangement 15 May to 18 July.**
A plantswoman's country garden set on a 3½ acre sloping chalk site in a charming rural setting with delightful views. Many areas of interest inc a rockery with water feature, raised ericaceous bed, prairie style bank, foliage plants, woodland walk, fernery, and folly. Large mixed herbaceous and shrub borders are planted for dry, alkaline soil and widespread interest.

5 BRIDGE END COTTAGE
Ockham Lane, Ockham, GU23 6NR. Clare & Peter Bevan, 07956 307546, clare.bevan@ngs.org.uk, bridgeendcottage.co.uk. *Nr RHS Garden Wisley. At Wisley r'about turn L onto B2039 to Ockham/Horsley. After ½ m turn L into Ockham Ln. House ½ m on R. From Cobham go to Blackswan Xrds.* **Sat 27 June (11-4). Adm £8, chd free. Tea, coffee & cake in the garden room. Visits also by arrangement 4 May to 13 July for groups of 10 to 25.**
A 4 acre country garden lovingly created over 20 yrs. Formal planting close to the house, less so across a rough lawn and mown paths in 2 acre wildflower meadow. A vibrant vegetable patch with interesting produce, and in good weather years, there is water in the pond. Sustainability and biodiversity are all important. Awarded Gold in the Nature Champion category by Guildford in Bloom in 2025.

6 CAXTON HOUSE
67 West Street, Reigate, RH2 9DA. Bob Bushby, 07836 201740, bushbybob@gmail.com. *On A25 towards Dorking, approx ¼ m W of Reigate. No parking on West St. Parking on road or past Black Horse on Flanchford Rd.* **Visits by arrangement Apr to June for groups of 10 to 30. Adm £10, chd free. Light refreshments.**
A lovely, large spring garden with an arboretum, two well-stocked ponds, and a large collection of hellebores and spring flowers. Pots are planted with colourful displays. A small Gothic folly, built by the owner. Herbaceous borders filled with grasses, perennials, and spring bulbs, along with a parterre, a bed of wild daffodils, prairie style planting in summer, and a new wildflower garden. Wheelchair access to most parts of the garden. Dogs on leads please.
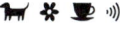

7 CHAUFFEUR'S FLAT
Tandridge Lane, Tandridge, RH8 9NJ. Mr & Mrs Richins. *2m E of Godstone. 2m W of Oxted. Turn off A25 at r'about for Tandridge. Take 2nd drive on L past church. Follow arrows to circular courtyard. Do not use Jackass Ln even if your SatNav tells you to do so.* **Fri 8, Sat 9, Sun 10 May (10-5). Adm £5, chd free. Home-made teas (cash only).**
Enter a 1½ acre tapestry of magical secret gardens with magnificent views. Touching the senses, all sure footed visitors may explore the many surprises on this constantly evolving, exuberant escape from reality. Imaginative use of recycled materials creates an inspired variety of ideas, while wild and specimen plants reveal an ecological haven.

Our 2025 donation to the Queen's Institute of Community Nursing now helps support over 3,500 Queen's Nurses working in the community in England, Wales, Northern Ireland, the Channel Islands and the Isle of Man.

8 CHILWORTH MANOR
Halfpenny Lane, Chilworth, Guildford, GU4 8NN. Mia & Graham Wrigley, www.chilworthmanorsurrey.com. 3½m SE of Guildford. From centre of Chilworth village turn into Blacksmith Ln. 1st drive on R on Halfpenny Ln. **Sun 24 May (11-5). Adm £8, chd free. Pre-booking essential, please visit www.ngs.org.uk for information & booking. Home-made teas. Chilworth Manor Vineyard sparkling & rosé wine for sale by the glass & bottle.**
The grounds of the C17 Chilworth Manor create a wonderful tapestry, a jewel of an C18 terraced walled garden, topiary, herbaceous borders, sculptures, mature trees and stew ponds that date back a 1000 yrs. A fabulous, peaceful garden for all the family to wander and explore or just to relax and enjoy! Perhaps our many visitors describe it best, 'Magical', 'a sheer delight', 'elegant and tranquil', 'a little piece of heaven', 'spiffing!'. Garden or tree talk at 12.15pm, 1.15pm and 3.15pm. Sorry, dogs are not allowed.

9 2 CHINTHURST LODGE
Wonersh Common, Wonersh, Guildford, GU5 0PR. Mr & Mrs M R Goodridge, 01483 535108, michaelgoodridge@ymail.com. 4m S of Guildford. From A281 at Shalford, turn E onto B2128 towards Wonersh. Just after Waverley sign & before village, garden on R, via stable entrance opp Little Tangley. No on-site parking for coaches. **Visits by arrangement May to July for groups of 12 to 40. Adm £10, chd free. Home-made teas.**
A 1 acre enthusiast's atmospheric and tranquil garden, divided into rooms with year-round interest. Features inc herbaceous borders, a dramatic white garden, specimen trees and shrubs, a gravel garden with water feature, a small kitchen garden, fruit cage, two wells, ornamental ponds, a herb parterre, and the Millennium rose, iris, and hollyhock garden. Wheelchair access with some avoidable gravel paths.

10 CLARIDGE HOUSE
Dormans Road, Dormansland, Lingfield, RH7 6QH. Meredith Wood, 01342 832150, welcome@claridgehouse.org.uk, www.claridgehouse.org.uk. *1m from Lingfield stn. From Racecourse Rd, veer R onto Dormans Rd, & follow yellow signs. Claridge House is clearly signed.* **Wed 13 May (10.30-4.30). Adm £7.50, chd free. Tea, coffee & cake. Visits also by arrangement 14 May to 15 May for groups of 5 to 15.**
An established two acre woodland garden with a variety of specimen trees and a woodland walk. Two wildflower meadows as well as more formal beds, with many benches to pause and enjoy the surroundings. We are as sustainable as possible, using compost created from Retreat food waste and no pesticides to support nature. We have beehives, bats, hedgehogs, and butterflies. Our natural pond has dragonflies, mayflies, and newts. Children must be accompanied and supervised. Dogs on leads only. Partial wheelchair access on paths to the formal garden.

11 COLDHARBOUR HOUSE
Coldharbour Lane, Bletchingley, Redhill, RH1 4NA. Mr Tony Elias, 01883 742685, eliastony@hotmail.com. *Coldharbour Ln, off Rabies Heath Rd, ½m from A25 at Bletchingley & 1m from Tilburstow Hill Rd. Parking at the house for up to 20 cars.* **Visits by arrangement Apr to Oct for groups of 10+. Adm £10, chd free. Coffee or tea & a slice of something sweet inc.**
This 1½ acre garden offers breathtaking views to the South Downs. Originally planted in the 1920s, it has since been adapted and enhanced. Several mature trees and shrubs inc a copper beech, a Canadian maple, magnolias, azaleas, rhododendrons, camellias, wisterias, *Berberis* 'Georgei', *Vitex agnus-castus*, fuchsias, hibiscus, potentillas, mahonias, a fig tree and a walnut tree.

12 COVERWOOD LAKES
Peaslake Road, Ewhurst, GU6 7NT. The Metson Family, www.coverwoodlakes.co.uk. *7m SW of Dorking. From the A25, follow signs for Peaslake. The garden is located ½m beyond Peaslake on Ewhurst Rd.* **Every Sun 12 Apr to 3 May, Sun 18 Oct (11-4). Adm £7.50, chd free. Light refreshments.**
14 acre landscaped garden in stunning position high in the Surrey Hills with four lakes and bog garden. Extensive rhododendrons, azaleas, and fine trees. 3½ acre lakeside arboretum. Marked trail leads through the 180 acre working farm, with Hereford cows and calves, sheep, and horses, all with views of the surrounding hills. Light refreshments inc home produced beef and lamb burgers, gourmet coffee and cakes from The Fillet & Bean (Airstream). Sorry, dogs are not allowed.

13 CROSSWATER FARM
Crosswater Lane, Churt, Farnham, GU10 2JN. David & Susanna Millais, 07771 558397, crosswaterfarmoffice@gmail.com. *6m S of Farnham, 6m NW of Haslemere. From A287 turn E into Jumps Rd, ½m N of Churt village centre. After ¼m turn acute L into Crosswater Ln & follow signs to Millais Nurseries, Crosswater Farm.* **Every Thur, Fri and Sat 30 Apr to 23 May (11-4). Adm £6, chd free. Tea, coffee & cake. Visits also by arrangement 20 Apr to 23 May for groups of 10+.**
Idyllic 5 acre woodland garden. Plantsman's collection of rhododendrons and azaleas inc rare species collected in the Himalayas and hybrids raised by the family. Everything from alpine dwarfs to architectural large leaved trees. Ponds, stream and companion plantings inc sorbus, magnolias and Japanese acers, and many recent new plantings. A specialist collection of rhododendrons and azaleas. Grass paths may be difficult for wheelchairs after rain.

14 NEW DOLPHIN HOUSE
Shackleford, GU8 6AH. Mr & Mrs C Bell, 01483 810257, Christineinnesbell@gmail.com. *5m SW of Guillford. Off A3 at the junction signed Shackleford, in centre of Shackleford village. Dolphin House is opp the junction of Lombard St & The Street.* **Visits by arrangement 14 June to 30 Aug for groups of 10 to 25. Adm £10, chd free. Home-made teas inc.**
The great feature of this 2 acre traditional country garden is its remarkable 200 yr old serpentine walls. Once designed to shelter tender plants, they now serve as the perfect backdrop for vibrant planting. The current owners have set out to create a peaceful, tranquil garden that inc large herbaceous borders, an

Tanglewood Cottage

orchard, gravel planting, and a variety of attractive trees. Access from the road is via steps, and the garden inc many gravel paths.

15 NEW DOWNS SOLICITORS
150-156 High Street, Dorking, RH4 1BQ. Christopher Millar.
Access to garden via Downs Solicitors located on High St. From M25 J9 take A24 to Dorking, turn R at A24/A25, or from J10 follow A25 to Dorking. Pay & display nearby. Stns: Dorking (main) & Dorking Deepdene. Bus stop: The White Horse. **Sat 2 May, Sat 27 June (10-4). Adm £5, chd free. Tea, coffee & cake.**
Hidden behind the Downs Solicitors offices on Dorking High Street is a small but beautiful walled garden, which has been lovingly restored over the past 3 yrs. The garden has been brought back to life with care and creativity, blending history, colour, community and calm in the heart of Dorking town centre. Wheelchair access via the office, on the High Street.

16 THE GARTH PLEASURE GROUNDS
The Garth, Newchapel Road, Lingfield, RH7 6BJ. Mr Sherlock & Mrs Stanley, hello@thegarth.info, www.thegarth.info. *Western edge of Lingfield. From A22 take B2028 by the Mormon Temple to Lingfield. The Garth is on the L after 1½m, opp Barge Tiles shop. Parking: Gun Pit Rd in Lingfield & limited space for disabled at Barge Tiles.* **Sun 3, Sun 10 May, Sun 1 Nov (1-5). Adm £10, chd free. Tea, coffee & cake.**
Mature 9 acre Pleasure Grounds, created by Walter Godfrey in 1919, offer an idyllic setting surrounding the former parish workhouse, restored in Edwardian style. Formal gardens, a nuttery, a spinney with many mature trees inc an ancient oak, and a pond to attract wildlife. Enjoy spring bluebells in May, autumn's Pumpkin Quest on 1 Nov, the woodland gardens, and beautiful borders full of colour and fragrance for year-round pleasure. Wheelchair access to most areas of the garden.

17 ◆ GATTON PARK

Reigate, RH2 0TW. Royal Alexandra & Albert School. *3m NE of Reigate. Entrance off Rocky Ln at main gate of Royal Alexandra & Albert School. What3words app: wool.jets.from.* **For NGS: Sun 8 Feb (12-5). Adm £9, chd free. Pre-booking preferred, please visit www.gattonpark.co.uk, email events@gatton-park.org.uk or phone 01737 649068 for information & booking. Tea, coffee & cake.** For other opening times and information, please phone, email or visit garden website.

Historic 260 acre estate in the Surrey Hills AONB. Capability Brown parkland with ancient oaks. Discover the Japanese garden, Victorian parterre and breathtaking views over the lake. Seasonal highlights inc displays of snowdrops and aconites in Feb. Ongoing restoration projects by the Gatton Trust. Bird hide open to see herons nesting. Free guided tours. A selection of hot and cold drinks, cakes and snacks. Plants for winter interest for sale. Adm: Adults £7 pre-book tickets (£9 on the day).

18 HALL GROVE SCHOOL

London Road (A30), Bagshot, GU19 5HZ. Mr & Mrs Graham. *6m SW of Egham. M3 J3, follow A322 for 1m until sign for Sunningdale A30. 1m E of Bagshot, opp Longacres Garden Centre. Entrance at footbridge. Ample car parking.* **Sat 9, Sat 30 May, Sat 20 June, Sat 26 Sept (2-5). Adm £5, chd free. Home-made teas.**

Formerly a small Georgian country estate, now a co-educational preparatory school. The Grade II listed house (not open). The grounds feature mature parkland with specimen trees, a historic ice house, and a walled kitchen garden with flowers, fruit, and children's vegetable plots. A lake, woodland walks, rhododendrons, azaleas, and acers. On 9 May and 26 Sept there will be live music at 3pm. On 30 May and 20 June, access to the walled garden only.

19 ◆ HATCHLANDS PARK

East Clandon, Guildford, GU4 7RT. National Trust, 01483 222482, hatchlands@nationaltrust.org.uk, www.nationaltrust.org.uk/hatchlands-park. *4m E of Guildford. Follow brown signs to Hatchlands Park (NT).* **For NGS: Sun 26 Apr (10-4.30). Adm £13, chd £6.50. Adm charges subject to change.**

Yellowstones

For other opening times and information, please phone, email or visit garden website.
Garden and park designed by Repton in 1800. Follow one of the park walks to the stunning bluebell wood in spring (2½ km round walk over rough and sometimes muddy ground). Partial wheelchair access to parkland with rough and undulating terrain, tracks and cobbled courtyard. Mobility scooter booking essential.

20 HEATHSIDE
10 Links Green Way, Cobham, KT11 2QH. Miss Margaret Arnott & Mr Terry Bartholomew, 07927 136308, m.a.arnott@btinternet.com. 1½ m E of Cobham. Through Cobham A245, 4th L after Esso garage into Fairmile Ln. Straight on into Water Ln. Links Green Way 3rd turning on L. **Visits by arrangement May to July. Morning coffee, afternoon tea, or wine & canapés.**
Terraced plants persons garden designed for year-round interest. Gorgeous planting all set off by harmonious landscaping. Many urns and pots give seasonal displays. Several water features add tranquil sound. Stunning colour combinations excite. Dahlias and begonias a favourite. Beautiful Griffin Glasshouse housing the exotic. Many inspirational ideas. Situated 5 miles from RHS Garden Wisley.

21 HIGH CLANDON ESTATE VINEYARD
High Clandon, East Clandon, GU4 7RP. Sibylla & Bruce Tindale, www.highclandon.co.uk. *A3/Wisley junction. Take L exit for Ockham/Horsley & continue for 2m to A246. Turn R for Guildford for 2m. Then 100yds past Hatchlands NT, turn L into Blakes Ln, straight uphill, through gates of High Clandon, to vineyard entrance. Extensive parking in our woodland area.* **Sun 5 July (11-4.30). Adm £7.50, chd free. Pre-booking preferred. Cream teas & home-made cakes. Gold awarded English sparkling wine for sale by the glass & bottle.**
Multi-gold award-winning English sparkling wine vineyard featuring gardens, a 2 acre wildflower meadow home to rare butterflies, water features, a Japanese garden, a truffle orchard, an apiary, and sculptures. Set in 12 acres of beautiful Surrey Hills AONB, with sweeping vistas across the Surrey Hills National Landscape and panoramic views to London. Exhibition of some 500 works of art and sculptures on show. During this season, the main wildlife pond often attracts wild Mallard ducks and their ducklings and the wildflower meadows are alive with butterflies and birdlife. Access is good; all garden paths are grassed lawns laid over firm ground with a hard, chalky substrate.

22  HOME FARM
Peper Harow, Elstead, Godalming, GU8 6BQ. Mrs Alison Fuller. *5m SW of Guildford, 2m W of Godalming, 1m E of Elstead, ½ m S of Shackleford. Turn off A3 at B3001 signed Elstead. Home Farm is situated on Park Avenue Rd (What3words app: trio.daredevil.bubbles). Park opp St Nicholas Church (What3words app: horses.cashew.buying).* **Sat 30, Sun 31 May (10.30-4.30). Adm £7.50, chd free. Tea, coffee & cake.**
A traditional Surrey cottage garden dating back to 1609, contained within a bargate stone wall. It features two mixed herbaceous borders with views across the surrounding fields, a mixed rose garden, and separate cutting and vegetable areas, with a greenhouse. Designed to maximise colour throughout the year. Step-free access via the front of the house by the greenhouse, not through the garden entrance. Please note that the lawn has varying levels.

23 ICHI-COO PARK
Russ Hill Farm, Russ Hill, Charlwood, RH6 0EL. Robin Redmile-Gordon, www.ichicoopark.net. *5m E of Gatwick Airport. From A23 N from Gatwick, or A23 S from Horley, or A217 S from Reigate, arrive at Longbridge r'about. Take exit heading E, signed Charlwood. Stay on road all the way.* **Sun 12 July (11-4). Adm £20, chd free. Teas, coffee, cake, wine & beer.**
Ichi-Coo Park is unlike any garden you've ever visited. With 16 acres to explore, allow at least 2 hrs, bring a picnic, and stay all day. Glorious shapes and shades of green, painted onto the natural background of the Sussex Weald. The park is an eclectic collection of plants, trees, water, spaces, forms, vistas, and habitats. It's a place for reflection, for relaxation, oh, and a plane spotter's dream! With assistance, there are ample level routes, but we are on a 1:10 hill. If you descend to the bottom, we will need to get you back up again!

24  JOHNSTON HOUSE
20 Hatchlands Road, Redhill, RH1 1BG. *From Redhill town center, head S on London Rd (A25) for 5m. At r'about, continue straight to stay on A25 for 2m. Turn R at Redhill Baptist Church, parking on the R. What3words app: almost.call.zealous.* **Sat 30 May, Sat 3 Oct (12-5). Adm £8, chd £4. Tea, coffee & cake.**
A garden with year-round interest, featuring open lawns and mature trees, inc copper beeches, Irish yews, and a redwood 'Wellingtonia'. The grassed areas are punctuated by borders packed with ornamental grasses and perennials, offering a rich tapestry of colour, texture, and movement. Wheelchair access to most areas of garden over a pebble path.

25 LITTLE ORCHARDS
Prince Of Wales Road, Outwood, Redhill, RH1 5QU. Nic Howard, www.instagram.com/nichoward. *A few hundred metres N of The Dog & Duck pub.* **Fri 22, Sun 24 May (12-4). Adm £6, chd £3. Tea, coffee & cake.**
A magical, artistic plantsman's paradise, planted for year-round interest using a tapestry of foliage as well as floral interest. The garden is arranged as a series of connected areas that flow between two properties: the old gardener's cottage and the old stables. Often compared to a mini Petersham Nursery by our visitors, we have a gift shop selling garden paraphernalia and a lovely café area.

The National Garden Scheme donated £3,875,596 to our nursing and health beneficiaries from money raised at gardens open in 2025.

26 LOGMORE PLACE
Logmore Lane, Westcott, Dorking, RH4 3JN. Jane Clarke, 07770 781317, jane@logmoreplace.co.uk. *In between Westcott & Coldharbour. From A25 past the church, turn L into Logmore Ln & Logmore Place is approx ½m on the R next to Florents Farm. Off road parking in sloping field. Disabled parking in front of house only.* **Visits by arrangement 15 June to 10 July for groups of 10 to 50. Light refreshments.** Established trees, rhododendrons, and yew hedges create a framework for the far-reaching views of the Surrey Hills. Small Japanese garden, walled flower garden, orchard, and two formal lawns featuring Piet Oudolf inspired beds. Walks on the estate inc field tracks, a lake with bridges, quiet ancient woodland, and stunning views towards Ranmore from the trig point. Wheelchair access to terrace and views only. Gravel paths, steps, and sloping grass paths to rest of site.

27 LONGER END COTTAGE
Normandy Common Lane, Normandy, Guildford, GU3 2AP. Mrs Caroline Lenton, 07443 044305, greatoutdoorsdesign@outlook.com. *4m W of Guildford on A323. From War Memorial Xrds in Normandy turn into Hunts Hill Rd, then R into Normandy Common Ln. Longer End Cottage is 3rd property on L. Parking at Hunts Hill Rd car parks. Limited parking along lane.* **Visits by arrangement 1 June to 28 Aug for groups of up to 25. Adm £7, chd free. Tea, coffee & cake.** A 1½ acre garden, gradually being remodelled by its current owner, a garden designer. It is divided into different areas surrounding a historic cottage, each with its own function and type of planting. Features inc mixed borders, meadows, a wildlife pond, gravel planting, grass borders, fruit and vegetables, and an exotic area. The garden is designed to maximise beauty, biodiversity, and sustainability.

28 ♦ LOSELEY PARK
Guildford, GU3 1HS. Mr & Mrs A G More-Molyneux, 01483 304440, 01483 405112, pa@loseleypark.co.uk, www.loseleypark.co.uk. *4m SW of Guildford. For SatNav please use GU3 1HS, Stakescorner Ln.* **For NGS: Sun 14 June (10.30-4.30). Adm by donation. Light refreshments in the tea hut in the White Garden. For other opening times and information, please phone, email or visit garden website.** Delightful 2½ acre walled garden. Award-winning rose garden with over 1000 bushes, mainly old-fashioned varieties, extensive herb garden, fruit and flower garden, white garden with fountain, and a spectacular organic vegetable garden. Magnificent vine walk, herbaceous borders, moat walk, ancient wisteria and mulberry trees.

29 THE MANOR HOUSE
Three Gates Lane, Haslemere, GU27 2ES. Mr & Mrs Gerard Ralfe. *NE of Haslemere. From Haslemere centre take A286 towards Milford. Turn R after museum into Three Gates Ln. At T-Junction turn R into Holdfast Ln. Car park on R.* **Sun 7 June (10-5). Adm £8, chd free. Tea, coffee & cake.** Described by Country Life as 'The Hanging Gardens of Haslemere', the well established Manor House gardens are tucked away in a valley of the Surrey Hills. Set within 6 acres, it was one of Surrey's inaugural NGS gardens, offering fine views, an impressive show of azaleas, wisteria, beautiful trees underplanted with bulbs, enchanting water gardens, and a magnificent rose garden.

30 MILTON WAY HOUSE
Guildford Road, Westcott, Dorking, RH4 3PZ. Ingrid Andree Wiltens. *2m E of Dorking. Access to & from the site is from the A25. The lane is assisted by CCTV to provide visibility around a blind corner. On exit L turns only are recommended. Parking is limited.* **Sun 7 June (11-4.30). Adm £5.50, chd free. Pre-booking essential, please visit www.ngs.org.uk for information & booking. Home-made teas. Timed slots at 11am, 1pm or 3pm.** Set in the beautiful Surrey Hills on a sloping site surrounded by mature trees, this small country garden, just shy of an acre, features a lush, green walled garden and a social area where teas will be available. There is also a vegetable garden, woodland area, and an informal wildflower lawn, all surrounded by mixed borders of perennials, grasses, and shrubs.

31 MOLESHILL HOUSE
The Fairmile, Cobham, KT11 1BG. Penny Snell, pennysnellflowers@btinternet.com, www.pennysnellflowers.co.uk. *2m NE of Cobham. On A307 Esher to Cobham Rd next to free car park by A3 bridge, at entrance to Waterford Cl.* **Visits by arrangement Apr to Sept for groups of 10+.** Romantic disarray. A naturalistic garden on the wild side, featuring many mature and interesting trees. A short path leads through woodland to a dovecote. Informal planting contrasts with formal topiary, box, and garlanded cisterns. Colourful courtyard, conservatory, pond with fountain, whitebeam avenue, circular gravel garden, gipsy caravan garden, green wall, and stumpery. Espaliered crab apples. Garden 5 mins from Claremont Landscape Garden, Painshill Park and RHS Garden Wisley.

32 MONKS LANTERN
Ruxbury Road, Chertsey, KT16 9NH. Mr & Mrs J Granell, 07840 098386, janicegranell@hotmail.com. *1m NW from Chertsey. M25 J11, signed A320/Woking. At r'about, take 2nd exit A320/Staines, then straight over next r'about. L on Holloway Hill, R Hardwick Ln. ½m, R over motorway bridge, onto Almners Rd, then Ruxbury Rd.* **Sat 23 May (2-5). Adm £5, chd free. Tea, coffee & cake. Visits also by arrangement 15 June to 14 Aug for groups of 10 to 30.** A delightful garden with borders arranged with colour in mind: silvers and white, olive trees blend with nicotiana and senecio. A weeping silver birch leads to the oranges and yellows of a tropical bed with large bottle brush, hardy palms, and *Fatsia japonica*. Large rockery and an informal pond. There is a display of hostas, *Cytisus battandieri*, and a selection of grasses in an island bed. An aviary with exotic birds. Workshop with a display of handmade guitars. Wheelchairs welcome; two reserved parking spaces at entrance to garden as gravel drive is not easy.

33 THE NUTRITION GARDEN
156A Frimley Green Road, Frimley Green, Camberley, GU16 6NA. Dr Trevor George RNutr, 07914 911410, t-george@hotmail.co.uk. *2m (5 mins) from J4 of the M3. From M3, follow signs for A331 towards Farnborough, then follow signs to Frimley Green (B3411). The garden is down a long drive with telegraph poles at each end, almost opp the recreation ground.* **Visits by arrangement July & Aug for groups of 6 to 20. Adm £10, chd free. Guided tour & refreshments made with plants from the garden inc.**
A garden designed by a registered nutritionist to produce and display a wide variety of edible plants, inc fruits, vegetables, herbs, and plants used for infusions. There are trees, shrubs, tubers, perennials, and annuals. Over 100 types of edible species and more than 200 varieties are grown throughout the year. These inc unusual food plants, as well as heritage and unusual coloured varieties. Wheelchair access on paved paths around fruit and vegetable beds. Other areas are step free on uneven grass.

& ✿ ☕))

34 THE OLD RECTORY
Sandy Lane, Brewer Street, Bletchingley, RH1 4QW. Mr & Mrs A Procter. *Top of village nr The Red Lion pub, turn R into Little Common Ln, then R at Cross Rd into Sandy Ln. Parking nr house, disabled parking in courtyard.* **Sun 7 June (11-4). Adm £5, chd free. Home-made teas.**
Georgian Manor House (not open). Quintessential Italianate topiary garden, statuary, box parterres, courtyard with columns, water features and antique terracotta pots. Much of the 4 acre garden is the subject of ongoing reclamation inc the ancient moat and woodland with fine specimen trees and one of the largest tulip trees in the country. New sunken water garden and tropical garden. Wheelchair access with gravel paths.

& 🐕 ☕))

Ashleigh Grange

© Matthew Bruce

35 ♦ RAMSTER

Chiddingfold, GU8 4SN. Mrs Rosie Glaister, 01428 654167, office@ramsterhall.com, www.ramsterevents.com. *12m S of Guildford. Ramster is on A283, 1½m S of Chiddingfold. Enter via large iron gates, signed from the main road. Ample free car parking. What3words app: coast.unto.immediate.* **For NGS: Fri 15 May (10-5). Adm £10, chd £3. Light refreshments. For other opening times and information, please phone, email or visit garden website.**
A stunning, mature woodland garden set in 25 acres, famous for its rhododendrone and azalea collection, and its carpets of bluebells in spring. Explore the bog garden with its stepping stones or relax in the tranquil, enclosed tennis court garden. Ramster has been opening for the NGS since the beginning in 1927 and proudly continues to support the scheme. The tea house by the entrance to the garden is open every day when the garden is open, serving roasted coffee, cakes, sandwiches, quiches, and soup. On the NGS day, proceeds from refreshments remain with Ramster. A lovely Sculpture Exhibition is held in the garden in May. Wheelchair access to the tea house and some paths in the garden.

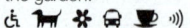

36 SHAMLEY WOOD ESTATE

Woodhill Lane, Shamley Green, Guildford, GU5 0SP. Mrs Claire Merriman, 07595 693132, claire@merriman.co.uk. *5m S of Guildford in village of Shamley Green. Entrance is approx ¼m up Woodhill Ln from centre of Shamley Green. What3words app: ideas.instincts.explain.* **Visits by arrangement 2 Mar to 30 Oct for groups of 10+. Adm £10, chd free. Teas with gluten free options.**
A garden that is worth visiting for its setting alone. Sitting high on the North Downs, it enjoys beautiful views of the South Downs and is approached through a 10 acre deer park. Set within approx 3 acres, the garden features a large pond and an established rose garden. Recent additions inc fire pits, vegetable patch, stream, tropical pergola, and a terraced wildflower lawn. Wheelchair access to most of garden. Step to access ground level WC.

37 41 SHELVERS WAY

Tadworth, KT20 5QJ. Keith & Elizabeth Lewis, 01737 210707, kandelewis@ntlworld.com. *6m S of Sutton off A217. 1st turning on R after Burgh Heath T-lights heading S on A217. 400yds down Shelvers Way on L.* **Visits by arrangement Apr to Aug for groups of 5+. Adm £10, chd free. Tea, coffee & cake.**
In spring a myriad of small bulbs, specialist daffodils and an assortment of many pots of tulips. In May azaleas and *Iris sibirica*. Choice perennials follow together with annuals to ensure colour until Sept. Plenty of seating plus a large conservatory to seat fourteen. A garden for all seasons.

38 SHIELING

The Warren, Kingswood, Tadworth, KT20 6PQ. Drs Sarah & Robin Wilson, 07932 445868, sarahwilson@doctors.org.uk. *Kingswood Warren Estate. Off A217, gated entrance just before church on S-bound side of dual carriageway, after Tadworth r'about. ¾m walk from station. Parking on The Warren or by church on A217.* **Sun 22 Feb (11-3); Mon 25 May, Sun 16 Aug (12-4). Adm £5, chd free. Home-made teas. Visits also by arrangement 23 Feb to 31 Mar & 1 Aug to 15 Aug for groups of 10 to 20. Wine & snacks for evening visits.**
1 acre garden restored to its original 1920s design. Formal front garden with island beds and shrub borders. Unusual large rock garden and mixed borders with collection of beautiful, slug-free hostas, uncommon woodland perennials, and acid loving plants. A new shrub border and a stumpery. There is lots for children to enjoy, inc a play area, Wendy house, and an amazing treehouse. A plant list is provided for visitors. Wheelchair access over resin drive, grass and paths. Some narrow paths in back garden.

39 SHOOTING STAR CHILDREN'S HOSPICES, CHRISTOPHER'S

Old Portsmouth Road, Artington, Guildford, GU3 1LP. Lucy Hooper. *Located next to Artington Park & Ride, with Christopher's signage visible at the entrance. From Guildford, take 1st exit at the r'about. From Peasmarsh, take 3rd exit at the r'about.* **Sun 2 Aug (12-4). Adm £5, chd free. Tea, coffee & cake.**
The gardens at the Guildford Hospice are enjoyed by families throughout the year and have been specifically designed with the needs of children in mind. They feature adapted play equipment, sensory trails, and tranquil open areas for remembrance and reflection. The gardens are maintained by a dedicated team of volunteer gardeners. Accessible pathway running throughout the garden. Accessible WC on site.

40 SLADES FARM

Thorncombe Street, Bramley, Guildford, GU5 0LT. Edward & Lulu Hutley. *Take the A281 to Bramley. At the r'about, turn into Snowdenham Ln; Slades Farm is 2½m ahead. Follow NGS signs.* **Sun 17 May (12-5). Adm £8, chd free. Tea, coffee & cake.**
Slades Farm gardens is predominantly a woodland garden, featuring an abundance of azaleas, camellias, rhododendrons, and gunnera glades. There are many different species of trees, home to a variety of birds and wildlife. Bridges cross beautiful lakes and streams, but please take care, as the ground can be uneven and ensure children are supervised.

41 SOUTH WIND

23 Doctors Lane, Chaldon, Caterham, CR3 5AE. Mrs Catherine Jones, opengardenchaldon@gmail.com. *2½m W of Caterham. Head W on Rook Ln past Surrey National Golf Club. After 1m turn R onto Doctors Ln. Limited parking on Doctors Ln, additional parking on Leazes Ave (2 min walk), & Rook Ln (5 min walk).* **Sun 19 July (1-5.30). Adm £5, chd free. Pre-booking essential, please visit www.ngs.org.uk for information & booking. Timed slots at 1pm, 2.30pm & 4pm. Home-made teas (cash only). Visits also by arrangement 29 June to 27 July for groups of 10 to 35.**
Delightful 1⅓ acre peaceful haven with a cottage garden feel. A multi-roomed garden maintaining constant interest with its different areas. Visitors can meander along gravel paths to the mixed herbaceous borders, vegetable beds, and orchard. The oak gazebo with fire pit is a perfect place to sit whilst listening to the birds in the woodland. Sorry, no dogs.

42 NEW TANGLEWOOD COTTAGE

29 Ottershaw Park, Ottershaw, Chertsey, KT16 0QG. Mrs Barbara Sampson, 07951 992886, wearegardenmad@gmail.com. *Park in car park opp Ottershaw Church, Guildford Rd, KT16 OPB. Cross the A320, turn R, take Cross Ln on the L. L at lodge into Ottershaw Chase Woodland, Tanglewood is ¼ m walk. Discuss disabled parking on booking.* Visits by arrangement 2 Feb to 30 Oct for groups of up to 20. Small parties & individuals are very welcome. Adm £7, chd free. Please discuss refreshments when booking.

Forty-three years in the making, this is a true plant lover's garden with a collection of unusual trees and shrubs, herbaceous plants, and bulbs. Two ponds are nestled within 5 acres of ancient oak woodland, creating a wildlife paradise. Please be aware that paths and grassy areas may become muddy and slippery in wet weather.

43 TANHOUSE FARM

Rusper Road, Newdigate, RH5 5BX. Mrs N Fries, 01306 631334. *8m S of Dorking. On A24 turn L at r'about at Beare Green. Turn R at T-junction in Newdigate. The farm is the 1st on the R, approx ⅔ m ahead, signed Tanhouse Farm Shop.* Visits by arrangement May to Sept. Adm £5, chd free.

A country garden created by the owners since 1987. 1 acre of charming, rambling gardens surrounds a C16 house (not open). Herbaceous borders and a stream with ducks and geese. Orchard with a wild garden, and plentiful seats and benches to stop for contemplation. Wheelchair access to level garden.

44 THE THERAPY GARDEN

Manor Fruit Farm, Glaziers Lane, Normandy, Guildford, GU3 2DT. The Therapy Garden General Manager, www.thetherapygarden.org. *SW of Guildford. Take A323 travelling from Guildford towards Aldershot, turn L into Glaziers Ln in centre of Normandy village, opp War Memorial. The Therapy Garden is 200yds on L.* Sun 17 May, Sun 20 Sept (10-4). Adm £5, chd free. Teas, coffee & home-made cakes.

BBQ & light lunches.
The Therapy Garden is a horticulture and education charity that uses gardening to have a positive and significant impact on the lives of people facing challenges in life. In our beautiful and tranquil 2 acre garden we work to change lives for the better and we do this by creating a safe place to enjoy the power of gardening and to connect with nature. We are a working garden full of innovation with an on site shop selling plants and produce. There will be a selection of fun family garden related activities to take part in. Wheelchair access over paved pathways throughout most of garden, many with substantial handrails.

45 TIMBER HILL

Chertsey Road, Chobham, GU24 8JF. Lavinia Sealy, 01932 873875, 07747 024695, lavinia@chobham.net, www.timberhillgarden.com. *A319 E of Chobham, & nr Woking, Chertsey, Sunningdale & Camberley. 2m from J11 M25. 1⅓ m from Ottershaw r'about, 2⅓ m from Chobham on side of A319, 400yds from Fairoaks airport. Lookout for large yellow sign!* Thur 8, Thur 22 Jan, Thur 12, Thur 26 Feb, Thur 12, Thur 26 Mar, Thur 9, Thur 23 Apr, Thur 7, Thur 21 May, Thur 18 June, Thur 15, Thur 29 Oct, Thur 5 Nov (11.30-2.30). Adm £7, chd £1. Pre-booking essential, please visit www.ngs.org.uk for information & booking. Tea, coffee & home-made cake in The Barn.

Welcome to 16 acres of informal garden, park, and woodland, with enticing views of the Surrey Hills from the hilltop. Enjoy winter and spring walks among witch-hazel, winter honeysuckle, crocuses, snowdrops, daffodils, narcissi, and other spring flowers, followed by gorgeous bluebells, azaleas, and fleeting cherry blossom. A large camellia collection in the woodland from Jan/Feb, and peaking in Mar/Apr. *Camellia sasanqua,* accompanied by maples in Oct/Nov. Additional dates planned in June, Oct and Nov. For further information, please telephone, email or visit garden website. No wheelchair access to the wood when ground is soft/wet unless electric-powered.

46 ◆ TITSEY PLACE GARDENS

Pitchfont Lodge, Water Lane, Titsey, Oxted, RH8 0SA. The Trustees of the Titsey Foundation, 07889 052461, office@titsey.org, www.titsey.org. *3m N of Oxted. A25 between Oxted & Westerham. Follow brown heritage signs to Titsey Estate from A25 at Limpsfield or see website for directions. Please enter via Water Ln & the Pitchfont car park (not Titsey Hill).* For NGS: Sun 31 May, Sun 28 June, Sun 26 July, Sun 30 Aug (1-5). Adm £7.50, chd £2. Light refreshments. For other opening times and information, please phone, email or visit garden website.

One of the largest surviving historic estates in Surrey. Magnificent ancestral home and gardens of the Gresham family since 1534. Walled kitchen garden and Golden Jubilee rose garden. Etruscan summerhouse adjoining picturesque lakes and fountain bed. 15 acres of formal and informal gardens. Titsey is in the English landscaped garden style. Pedigree herd of Sussex Cattle roam the park. Walks through the estate woodlands are open year-round. Tearoom serving home-made cakes and selling local produce from 12-5pm. Last admission to gardens at 4pm. Guide dogs only.

47 NEW 10 UPPER ROSE HILL

Dorking, RH4 2EB. Mr Michael & Mrs Kristina Shanahan. *Central Dorking. Garden will be signed from South St.* Sun 10 May (12-4). Adm £5, chd free. Tea, coffee & cake.

An urban garden tucked away behind a row of 1920s houses and surrounded by mature trees. Visitors are surprised by the different rooms and zones that help break up the steep slope in this south facing garden. We are planting more pollinators to help honey production from our four beehives. Somehow, we have squeezed in a greenhouse, a home office, a vegetable patch, and a tiny pond.

In 2025 we awarded over £288,800 in Community Garden Grants, supporting 114 community garden projects.

29 Applegarth Avenue

A hidden gem tucked away. A beautiful country cottage style garden set in ½ acre, designed by Sam Aldridge of Eden Restored. The garden flows through pathways, lawn, vegetable and play areas. Flower beds showcase outstanding tulips, and informal seating areas throughout the garden allow you to absorb the wonderful garden, whilst observing our ex battery chickens and rescue rabbits!

51 WEST HORSLEY PLACE
Epsom Road, West Horsley, Leatherhead, KT24 6AN. West Horsley Place Trust, www.westhorsleyplace.org. *5m E of Guildford. West Horsley Place is off the A246 between Guildford & Leatherhead. A 10 min drive from the A3/M25 intersection. Leave the A3 at J10.* **Sun 10 May, Sun 13 Sept (10-4). Adm £10, chd free. Light refreshments in the Place Farm Barn courtyard.**
West Horsley Place is set within a 380 acre estate. The garden adjacent to the Manor House dates back to the C15 and is approx 5 acres, completely surrounded by a wall over 300 yrs old. It has an ancient orchard, rose garden, interestingly striped formal lawns, an historic box hedge, many herbaceous borders, a magnificent white wisteria over 60ft tall and many wildflower areas. Recently opened new sensory garden in formerly neglected paddock. Accessible via a step-free route. Unpaved and the main surface is turf. Wheelchair accessible ground floor WC.

48 ♦ VANN
Hambledon, Godalming, GU8 4EF. Caroe Family, 01428 683413, info@vanngarden.co.uk, www.vanngarden.co.uk. *6m S of Godalming. A283 to Lane End, Hambledon, & follow yellow Vann signs for 2m. Please park in the field as signed, not on road. On most days there may not be anyone to greet you, so make your way into the garden.* **For NGS: Daily Mon 23 Mar to Sat 28 Mar, Sun 29 Mar (10-4). Adm £10, chd free. Pre-booking essential, please visit www.ngs.org.uk for information & booking. No refreshments Mon-Sat. Teas, coffee & cake on Sun 29 March (cash only). For other opening times and information, please phone, email or visit garden website.**
5 acre, 2* registered garden surrounding house dating from 1542 with Arts and Crafts additions by W D Caröe inc Bargate stone pergola. At the front, brick paved cottage garden; to the rear a lake, yew walk with rill. Gertrude Jekyll water garden. Snowdrops and hellebores, spring bulbs, and spectacular fritillaria. Island beds, crinkle crankle wall, orchard with wild flowers. Limited accessibility; please call for guidance. Also open for by arrangement visits for individuals or groups (not for NGS).

49 WATERER'S GARDEN
43 Ambleside Road, Lightwater, GU18 5TA. Alison & Trevor Millard, 01276 473343, alison@thehaloworks.com. *In the village of Lightwater in NW Surrey. Enter Lightwater via the A322, head to the r'about with estate agent on the corner. Waterer's Garden is located 200 metres on the LHS of Ambleside Rd.* **Sun 26 Apr (11-4). Adm £5, chd £4. Pre-booking essential, please visit www.ngs.org.uk for information & booking. Home-made teas. Visits also by arrangement 18 Apr to 1 Sept.**
A ⅓ acre plot within the village of Lightwater, hidden away behind the house built for George Waterer and his family in 1931. Garden designed and laid out in the 1930s by the Waterer family, who were nursery owners and now own Crocus. Restored and gardened by Trevor and Alison Millard since 1997.

50 11 WEST HILL
Sanderstead, CR2 0SB. Rachel & Edward Parsons. *M25 J6, A22, 3m r'about 4th exit to Succombs Hill, R to Westhall Rd, at r'about 2nd exit to Limpsfield Rd, r'about 2nd exit on Sanderstead Hill 1m, sharp R on West Hill. Please park on West Hill.* **Sat 11, Sun 12 Apr (2-5). Adm £5, chd free. Home-made teas.**

52 57 WESTHALL ROAD
Warlingham, CR6 9BG. Rob & Wendy Baston. *3m N of M25. From M25, J6, take A22 towards London. At Whyteleafe r'about, take 3rd R, go under railway bridge, & turn immed R into Westhall Rd.* **Sun 24, Mon 25 May (2-5). Adm £5, chd free. Tea, coffee & cake. Donation to Warlingham Methodist Church.**
A reward for the sure footed: many steps lead to three levels! Mature kiwi and grape vines. Mixed borders and raised vegetable beds. Bay, cork oak, and yew topiaries. An amphitheatre of potted plants lines the lower steps, while the top garden offers stunning views of Caterham and Whyteleafe. An olive tree floats on a circular pond

of white and pink flowers. Features inc flint walls, vegetable borders, summerhouse, apple tree with child swing, and gravel garden.

53 WESTWAYS FARM
Gracious Pond Road, Chobham, GU24 8HH. Paul & Nicky Biddle, 01276 856163, nicolabiddle@rocketmail.com. *4m N of Woking. From Chobham Church, proceed over r'about towards Sunningdale. At 1st Xrds, turn R into Red Lion Rd & continue to junction with Mincing Ln. Ample parking, inc coaches.* **Sun 10 May (10.30-5). Adm £8, chd free. Home-made teas. Visits also by arrangement 20 Apr to 19 June for groups of 10 to 50.**
6 acre garden surrounded by woodlands planted in 1930s with mature and rare rhododendrons, azaleas, camellias and magnolias, underplanted with bluebells, lilies and dogwood. Extensive lawns and sunken pond garden. Working stables and sand school. Lovely Queen Anne House (not open) covered with listed *Magnolia grandiflora*. Victorian design glasshouse, and new planting round garden room. This is our 26th year of opening for the National Garden Scheme so a cause for celebration!

54 WILDWOOD
34 The Hatches, Frimley Green, Camberley, GU16 6HE. Annie & Richard Keighley. *3m S of Camberley. M3 J4 follow A325 to Frimley Centre, towards Frimley Green for 1m. Turn R by the green, R into The Hatches for on-street parking. 10 min walk from Farnborough North train stn.* **Sun 7 June (12-5). Adm £5, chd free. Pre-booking essential, please visit www.ngs.org.uk for information & booking. Home-made teas.**

This romantic cottage garden is loved for its hidden surprises. Enjoy the tumbling roses, topiary and scented *Magnolia grandiflora*. Explore a haven of sun and shade with wildlife pond, hidden dell, fernery, sheltered loggia and secret summerhouse. Cutting garden with topiary birds, raised beds, vegetables, herbs, fruit trees and potting shed patio. Display of garden paintings.

55 63 WOLSEY DRIVE
Walton-on-Thames, KT12 3BB. Carl & Pamela Fisher. *1m from Walton-on-Thames centre. Wolsey Dr is off Rydens Rd (accessed from Tudor Dr). Turn L from Tudor Dr & follow road for approx 500 metres. No. 63 is located on LHS. On-street parking. Nearest stns: Hersham & Walton-on-Thames.* **Sun 28 June (11-5). Adm £5, chd free. Tea, coffee & cake.**
Our aim has always been to attract pollinators and wildlife to the garden. Over the past 10 yrs, we have transformed the space using our horticultural and design backgrounds, evolving the garden bit by bit. Large planting beds, gravel paths, and a raised bridge through the centre lead to a pergola at the far end. Scented plants and a colour palette of purple, orange, white, and green envelop you.

56 WOODPECKERS
Poplar Grove, Woking, GU22 7SD. Mr Janis Raubiška, www.instagram.com/grandiflorus.co.uk. *Next to Woking Leisure Centre. Please use Woking Leisure Centre car park (GU22 9BA) & follow signs for garden entrance. Coach parking available.* **Sun 30 Aug, Sun 6 Sept (11-4). Adm £6, chd free. Cream teas.**
A journey through a horticultural designer's own garden, where plants take centre stage in succession, providing year-round colour and interest. The garden is divided into three rooms, each with a different planting style and purpose: vibrant colours in the jewel's amphitheatre, leafy textures and pastels in the social room, and a productive area featuring a glasshouse and 'grow your own' space. Created in 2022, the garden has sustainability at its heart. Wheelchair access via a slight slope at the entrance gate, with assistance provided.

57 NEW WOODS FOLLY
Ford Manor Road, Dormansland, Lingfield, RH7 6NZ. Mrs Rosemary & Mr Richard Williams. *1½m SE of Lingfield. After turning off the B2028 from Lingfield into Ford Manor Rd, Woods Folly is 200 metres ahead on the R.* **Sat 11 July (10.30-4.30). Adm £7, chd free. Pre-booking essential, please visit www.ngs.org.uk for information & booking. Tea, coffee & cake.**

A colourful perennial lover's garden features mature trees and a lawn edged by flower beds, grasses, roses, and hydrangeas. There are two enclosed courtyards, one with a bubbling water feature surrounded by potted plants. A miniature railway borders the garden. Please note unfenced swimming pool and steps. Wheelchair access to courtyards only, with views overlooking the main garden.

58 WRENS' NEST COTTAGE
Ockham Lane, Cobham, KT11 1PG. Mrs Patty Robertson & Mr Fil Towers, 07957 495934, pattyrobertson45@gmail.com. *1½m from Cobham High St. From Wisley r'about turn L onto B2039 to Ockham/Horsley. After ½m, turn L into Ockham Ln. House 2m on R. From Cobham take Downside Bridge Rd, turn R into Chilbrook Rd, then turn R. Garden on R.* **Visits by arrangement Apr to July for groups of 6 to 20.**
1½ acre country garden with island beds of perennials and ancient bluebell wood. Wildlife friendly with a butterfly corner, a stream running the length of the garden, and many beautiful mature trees. Front garden with many pots and courtyard. Sunny sitting areas to enjoy a cup of tea and a slice of cake. 2 miles from RHS Garden Wisley. Wheelchair access to most of garden.

59 NEW YELLOWSTONES
37A Heathside Road, Woking, GU22 7EY. Mr Ollie & Mrs Ruth Whiddett. *10 min walk from Woking town centre. Ample local parking.* **Sat 6, Sun 7 June (11-4). Adm £6, chd free. Tea, coffee & cake.**
A recently redesigned family garden blending activity and calm. It features space for teenagers, a stylish garden room, and inviting areas to relax or gather with friends. Abundant planting supports pollinators and wildlife, while thoughtful design balances energy, nature, and calm for a healthy outdoor lifestyle.

SUSSEX

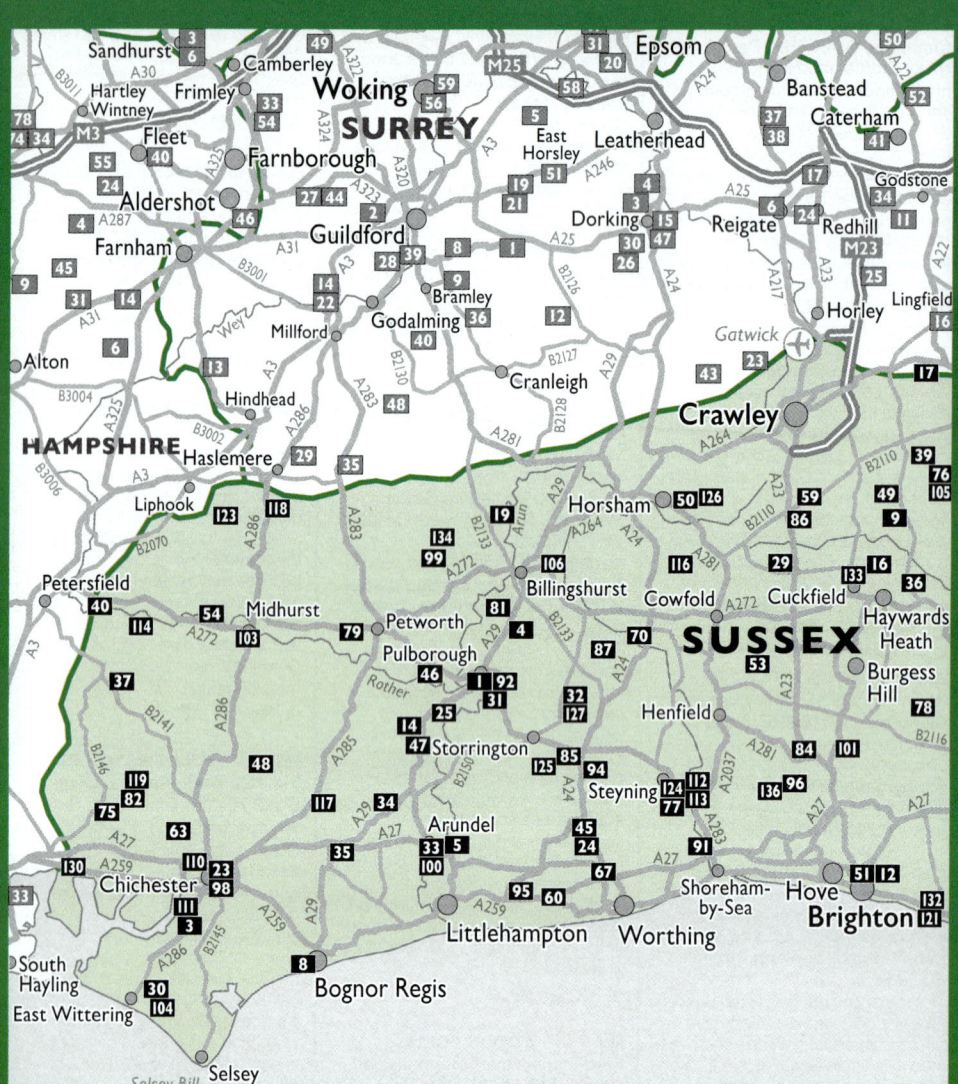

SUSSEX 507

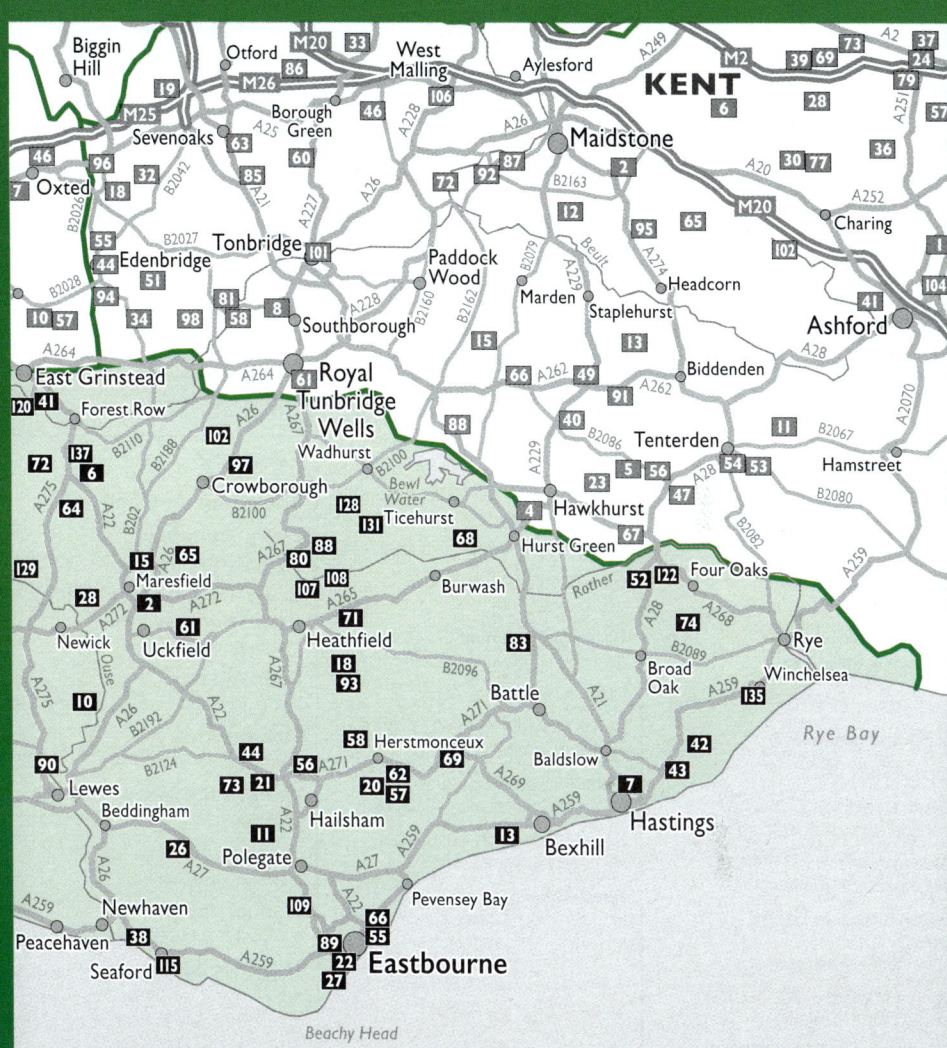

EAST & MID SUSSEX VOLUNTEERS

County Organiser, Booklet & Advertising Co-ordinator
Irene Eltringham-Willson 01323 833770
irene.willson@btinternet.com

County Treasurer
Andrew Ratcliffe 01435 873310
andrew.ratcliffe@ngs.org.uk

Publicity
Geoff Stonebanks 01323 899296
sussexeastpublicity@ngs.org.uk

Social Media
Nicki Crabb 07720 640761
nicki.crabb@ngs.org.uk

Social Media & Photographer
Kelly Whitaker Hughes
07920 402677
kelly.whitakerhughes@ngs.org.uk

Assistant County Organisers
Joan Ball
07976 349000
joanball53@gmail.com

Michael & Linda Belton
01797 252984
belton.northiam@gmail.com

Shirley Carman-Martin
01444 473520
shirley.carmanmartin@ngs.org.uk

Isabella & Steve Cass
07908 123524
oaktreebarn@hotmail.co.uk

Nicki Crabb (as above)

Linda Field

Diane Gould 01825 750300
lavenderdgould@gmail.com

Aideen Jones 01323 899452
sweetpeasa52@gmail.com

Susan & Richard Laing
01892 770168
splaing@btinternet.com

Jennie Maillard 07730 480308
jennie@maillard.me.uk

Sarah Ratcliffe 01435 873310
sarah.ratcliffe@ngs.org.uk

Dianna Tennant 01892 752029
tennantdd@gmail.com

@SussexNGSEast
@SussexNGS
@ngseastsussex

WEST SUSSEX VOLUNTEERS

County Organiser, Booklet & Advertising Co-ordinator
Maggi Hooper 07793 159304
maggi.hooper@ngs.org.uk

County Treasurer
Philip Duly 07789 050964
philipduly@tiscali.co.uk

Publicity
Kate Harrison 01798 817489
kate.harrison@ngs.org.uk

Social Media
Claudia Hawkes 07985 648216
claudiapearce17@gmail.com

Talks
Philip Duly (as above)

Booklet Distribution
Lesley Chamberlain 07950 105966
chamberlain_lesley@hotmail.com

Assistant County Organisers
Teresa Barttelot 01798 865690
tbarttelot@gmail.com

Emma Broda 07739 516178
emma.broda@gmail.com

Lesley Chamberlain (as above)

Diane Cotes 07789 565094
dirose8@me.com

Gillian de Beaumont 07746 408989
gdebeaumont@yahoo.co.uk

Claudia Hawkes (as above)

Carrie McArdle 01403 820272
carrie.mcardle@btinternet.com

Fiona Phillips 07884 398704
fiona.h.phillips@btinternet.com

Susan Pinder 07814 916949
nasus.rednip@gmail.com

Teresa Roccia 07867 383753
teresa.m.roccia@gmail.com

@Sussexwestngs
@sussexwestngs

OPENING DATES

All entries subject to change. For latest information check **www.ngs.org.uk**

Extended openings are shown at the beginning of the month.

Map locator numbers are shown to the right of each garden name.

January

Monday 26th
5 Whitemans Close　　　　133

Wednesday 28th
5 Whitemans Close　　　　133

Friday 30th
5 Whitemans Close　　　　133

February

Snowdrop Openings

Every Thursday
The Old Vicarage　　　　94

Every Thursday and Friday from Thursday 12th
Pembury House　　　　101

Sunday 1st
Manor of Dean　　　　79

Monday 2nd
5 Whitemans Close　　　　133

Wednesday 4th
5 Whitemans Close　　　　133

Tuesday 10th
5 Whitemans Close　　　　133

Wednesday 11th
◆ Highdown Gardens　　　　60

Thursday 12th
◆ Highdown Gardens　　　　60
5 Whitemans Close　　　　133

Saturday 14th
5 Whitemans Close　　　　133

Sunday 15th
Sandhill Farm House　　　　114

Monday 16th
◆ Denmans Garden　　　　35

Tuesday 17th
5 Whitemans Close　　　　133

SUSSEX

Wednesday 18th
5 Whitemans Close 133

March

Every Thursday
The Old Vicarage 94

Every Thursday and Friday to Friday 6th
Pembury House 101

Saturday 21st
◆ King John's Nursery 68
◆ Nymans 86

Sunday 22nd
◆ Bates Green Garden 11
47 Denmans Lane 36
Manor of Dean 79

Friday 27th
Butlers Farmhouse 20
The Garden House 51

Saturday 28th
Butlers Farmhouse 20
Down Place 37

Sunday 29th
Down Place 37
The Garden House 51
Penns in the Rocks 102

April

Every Wednesday from Wednesday 22nd
Fittleworth House 46

Every Thursday
The Old Vicarage 94

Saturday 4th
Peelers Retreat 100

Sunday 5th
47 Denmans Lane 36

Monday 6th
47 Denmans Lane 36
The Old Vicarage 94

Saturday 11th
NEW Quarry Wood Farm & Tilsmore Vineyard 107
Rymans 111

Sunday 12th
Rymans 111

Saturday 18th
Chalk Farm Flowers 24
Limekiln Farm 73
The Oast 88
Peelers Retreat 100

Sunday 19th
Chalk Farm Flowers 24
Limekiln Farm 73
The Oast 88

Thursday 23rd
The Old Rectory, Warbleton 93

Saturday 25th
Banks Farm 10
NEW 53 Cedar Drive 23
Duckyls 39
Judy's Cottage Garden 67
Kotimaki 71
NEW 25 Parklands Road 98

Sunday 26th
Banks Farm 10
NEW 53 Cedar Drive 23
Duckyls 39
Manor of Dean 79
Newtimber Place 84
NEW 25 Parklands Road 98

Monday 27th
◆ Denmans Garden 35

Tuesday 28th
Peelers Retreat 100

Wednesday 29th
◆ Highdown Gardens 60

Thursday 30th
◆ Highdown Gardens 60

May

Every Wednesday to Wednesday 13th
Fittleworth House 46

Every Thursday
The Old Vicarage 94

Saturday 2nd
96 Ashford Road 7

Sunday 3rd
47 Denmans Lane 36
Stanley Farm 123

Monday 4th
47 Denmans Lane 36

Saturday 9th
96 Ashford Road 7
Forest Ridge 49

Sunday 10th
Champs Hill 25
Forest Ridge 49
Hammerwood House 54
Mountfield Court 83
Sienna Wood 120

Tuesday 12th
Bignor Park 14
◆ Borde Hill Garden 16

Wednesday 13th
NEW Rapkyns Nursery 108

Saturday 16th
96 Ashford Road 7
Bumble Farm 19
Cookscroft 30
Kotimaki 71
Pigeon Mead House 104

Sunday 17th
Ashdown Park Hotel 6
Bumble Farm 19
Meadow Farm 81
Penns in the Rocks 102
Pigeon Mead House 104

Wednesday 20th
Balcombe Gardens 9

Saturday 23rd
The Cottage 31
Grovelands 53
◆ King John's Nursery 68
Peelers Retreat 100
◆ The Priest House 105

Sunday 24th
Foxglove Cottage 50
Grovelands 53
4 Hillside Cottages 63
9 Puttock Way 106
Shalford House 118

Tuesday 26th
Peelers Retreat 100

Thursday 28th
Wych Warren House 137

Friday 29th
Orchard Cottage 97
1 Pest Cottage 103

Saturday 30th
Orchard Cottage 97
Skyscape 121

Sunday 31st
51 Carlisle Road 22
Chelmsford Lodge 27
Hollymount 65
Orchard Cottage 97
1 Pest Cottage 103
Seaford Gardens 115
Skyscape 121

June

Every Thursday
The Old Vicarage 94

Tuesday 2nd
Peelers Retreat 100

Friday 5th
Apuldram Roses 3

Saturday 6th
Bumble Farm 19
Durford Abbey Barn 40
Highlands 61
Kitchenham Farm 69
◆ Knepp Castle 70
Kotimaki 71
Lordington House 75
Peelers Retreat 100
Swallow Lodge 126

Sunday 7th
Bumble Farm 19
Durford Abbey Barn 40
Fairlight Hall 43
Hellingly Parish Trail 56
◆ High Beeches Woodland and
    Water Garden 59
4 Hillside Cottages 63
Lordington House 75
Offham House 90
Town Place 129

Tuesday 9th
Butlers Farmhouse 20

Wednesday 10th
Butlers Farmhouse 20

Thursday 11th
◆ Clinton Lodge 28
The Orchard 96
Woodlands 136

Friday 12th
◆ Charleston 26
Parsonage Farm 99
Wadhurst Park 131

Saturday 13th
The Old Rectory, Pulborough 92
NEW Quarry Wood Farm &
    Tilsmore Vineyard 107
Swallow Lodge 126
Wadhurst Park 131

Sunday 14th
The Old Rectory, Pulborough 92
Rymans 111
Seaford Gardens 115
Town Place 129

Tuesday 16th
Bignor Park 14
Peelers Retreat 100

Wednesday 17th
Town Place 129

Friday 19th
NEW Nutbourne Village Gardens 85

Saturday 20th
Alderbury 1
Bexhill-on-Sea Trail 13
◆ Farleys Sculpture Garden 44
NEW Nutbourne Village Gardens 85
Steyning Gardens 124

Sunday 21st
Alderbury 1
NEW The Aviary Garden 8
Down Place 37
East Grinstead Gardens 41
Foxglove Cottage 50
Steyning Gardens 124
Whithurst Park 134

Monday 22nd
Down Place 37

Tuesday 23rd
NEW The Aviary Garden 8
NEW Little Gate Flowers 74

Wednesday 24th
Oaklands Farm 87
Town Place 129

Thursday 25th
Foxglove Cottage 50

Friday 26th
◆ St Mary's House Gardens 113

Saturday 27th
Balcombe Gardens 9
Judy's Cottage Garden 67
◆ King John's Nursery 68
Luctons 76
◆ The Priest House 105
◆ St Mary's House Gardens 113

Sunday 28th
Balcombe Gardens 9
The Folly 48
16 Hardy Drive 55
Herstmonceux Parish Trail 58
Hollymount 65
36 Jellicoe Close 66
Luctons 76
◆ The Priest House 105
Seaford Gardens 115
Town Place 129

July

**Every Wednesday from
Wednesday 22nd**
Fittleworth House 46

Every Thursday
The Old Vicarage 94

Friday 3rd
Apuldram Roses 3

Sunday 5th
Hill House 62
Lynwood 77
Old Well Cottage 95
Rose Cottage 109
Saffrons 112
Seaford Gardens 115
Town Place 129

Tuesday 7th
Peelers Retreat 100
Sullington Old Rectory 125

Wednesday 8th
Sullington Old Rectory 125

Friday 10th
Lynwood 77
Saffrons 112

Saturday 11th
Peelers Retreat 100

Friday 17th
Five Oaks Cottage 47

Saturday 18th
NEW 53 Cedar Drive 23
D & S Haus 33
Five Oaks Cottage 47
Kotimaki 71
NEW 25 Parklands Road 98
Wanderdown 132
Winchelsea's Secret Gardens 135

Sunday 19th
NEW The Aviary Garden 8
NEW 53 Cedar Drive 23
D & S Haus 33
4 Hillside Cottages 63
NEW 25 Parklands Road 98
Wanderdown 132

Tuesday 21st
NEW The Aviary Garden 8
Peelers Retreat 100

Wednesday 22nd
◆ Herstmonceux Castle Estate 57

Thursday 23rd
Cumberland House 32
NEW Little Gate Flowers 74
Thakeham Place Farm 127

Sunday 26th
Architectural Plants 4
Cumberland House 32
The Folly 48
Hollymount 65
Penns in the Rocks 102
Thakeham Place Farm 127

August

Every Thursday
The Old Vicarage 94

Saturday 1st
Mayfield Gardens 80

Sunday 2nd
Mayfield Gardens 80
Shalford House 118

Wednesday 5th
Fittleworth House 46

Thursday 6th
Bourne Botanicals 17

Saturday 8th
Chalk Farm Flowers 24
Kitchenham Farm 69

Sunday 9th
NEW 1 Belton Close 12
Chalk Farm Flowers 24
Champs Hill 25

Saturday 15th
Bourne Botanicals 17
Holly House 64
Tuppenny Barn 130

Sunday 16th
4 Hillside Cottages 63
Holly House 64

Thursday 20th
D & S Haus 33

Saturday 22nd
Butlers Farmhouse 20

Sunday 23rd
NEW 1 Belton Close 12
Butlers Farmhouse 20
Findon Place 45
The Folly 48

Saturday 29th
Limekiln Farm 73

Sunday 30th
Limekiln Farm 73

Monday 31st
The Old Vicarage 94

September

Every Thursday
The Old Vicarage 94

Saturday 5th
The Cottage 31
Judy's Cottage Garden 67
Kotimaki 71

Sunday 6th
East Grinstead Gardens 41
Parsonage Farm 99

Wednesday 9th
NEW Rapkyns Nursery 108

Friday 11th
NEW Black Shed Studios
Garden 15

Saturday 12th
NEW Black Shed Studios
Garden 15
♦ King John's Nursery 68

Sunday 13th
Ashdown Park Hotel 6
NEW Black Shed Studios
Garden 15
Rymans 111

Sunday 20th
Tidebrook Manor 128

Tuesday 22nd
Bignor Park 14

Sunday 27th
♦ High Beeches Woodland and
Water Garden 59

October

Thursday 1st
The Old Vicarage 94

Saturday 3rd
Kotimaki 71

Sunday 4th
♦ Bates Green Garden 11

Monday 26th
♦ Denmans Garden 35

By Arrangement

Arrange a personalised garden visit with your club, or group of friends, on a date to suit you. See individual garden entries for full details.

Alpines 2
NEW The Aviary Garden 8
Bourne Botanicals 17
Brightling Down Farm 18
Butlers Farmhouse 20
Camberlot Hall 21
Champs Hill 25
Colwood House 29
Cookscroft 30
Cosy Cottage (Seaford
Gardens) 115
The Cottage 31

Cupani Garden (Seaford
Gardens) 115
Dale Park House 34
47 Denmans Lane 36
Down Place 37
Driftwood 38
Fairlight End 42
Findon Place 45
Fittleworth House 46
The Folly 48
Foxglove Cottage 50
The Garden House 51
4 Hillside Cottages 63
Holly House 64
Hollymount 65
Legsheath Farm 72
Lordington House 75
Luctons 76
Lynwood 77
Malthouse Farm 78
Manor of Dean 79
Meadow Farm 81
Mitchmere Farm 82
Oaklands Farm 87
Ocklynge Manor 89
Old Erringham Cottage 91
The Old Manor (Nutbourne
Village Gardens) 85
The Old Vicarage 94
Orchard Cottage 97
NEW 25 Parklands Road 98
Penns in the Rocks 102
8 Rushy Mead 110
Rymans 111
Saffrons 112
Sedgwick Park House 116
Selhurst Park 117
Shalford House 118
Shepherds Cottage 119
Sienna Wood 120
South Grange 122
Town Place 129
Winterfield (Balcombe Gardens) 9

In 2025, National Garden Scheme funding helped Perennial support 950 unique callers to their helpline looking for advice and information.

Tidebrook Manor

THE GARDENS

1 ALDERBURY
Church Hill, Pulborough, RH20 1AB. John & Marianne Dixon. *From A283 Lower St, Pulborough, exit r'about onto A29 towards Billingshurst. After 200 metres, turn R onto Old Rectory Ln (Chequers Hotel on corner). Immed after turning, park in East Glebe Field on R. Walk down slope, across field, following the signs.* **Sat 20, Sun 21 June (11-5). Adm £7, chd free. Tea, coffee & cake.**
A garden of just under 2 acres adjoins East Glebe Field in the village. It is divided into a series of distinct rooms, inc a large vegetable garden, both large and small greenhouses, an orchard, a duck pond, a lawn area with ornamental beds, parterres with seasonal flowers, and herb beds. There is also a large and unusual tree sculpture.

2 ALPINES
High Street, Maresfield, Uckfield, TN22 2EG. Ian & Cathy Shaw, 07887 825032, Info@shaw.buzz. 1½ m N of Uckfield. *Garden approx 150 metres N of Budletts r'about towards Maresfield. Parking at garden for pre-arranged groups, check when booking.* **Visits by arrangement 25 May to 16 Aug for groups of 5 to 16. Tea, coffee & home-made cake.**
A largely level, 1 acre garden incorporating the ornamental and the edible. It offers a riot of colour and scent over many months, especially in early summer, with large and rampant mixed borders, many scented roses, a small mixed orchard, wildflower meadow, fruit cage and vegetable garden, and shade, cottage and white borders. A wildlife pond, bog garden, a pretty Victorian style greenhouse, and plenty of seating. Wheelchair access over wide sweeps of lawn and gravel drive areas. Two steps down to greenhouse.

3 APULDRAM ROSES
Crouchers Farm, Birdham Road, Chichester, PO20 7EQ. Elizabeth Sawday, 01243 785769, support@apuldramroses.co.uk, www.apuldramroses.co.uk. *2m S of Chichester. Located exactly opp the Dell Quay Rd on the L when travelling S. What3words app: nightcap.bumpy.laughs. Please arrive promptly for the talk at 2pm.* **Fri 5 June, Fri 3 July (2-3.30). Adm £12.50. Pre-booking essential, please visit www.ngs.org.uk for information & booking. Tea, coffee & cake.**
Spend a delightful afternoon listening to an informative talk on keeping your roses thriving. You will then have time to explore the rose garden, a summer paradise, especially from June to August when the roses are in full bloom. The garden transforms into a vibrant display of colours and fragrances during these months. The roses, meticulously cared for, showcase a stunning array of varieties, each with its unique charm and beauty. Plants for sale on site.

4 ARCHITECTURAL PLANTS
Stane Street, North Heath, Pulborough, RH20 1DJ. Mr Guy Watts, www.architecturalplants.com. *What3words app: jogged.fabric.land. Black & white bollards outside the front entrance, diagonally opp Hepworth Brewery.* **Sun 26 July (10-4). Adm £15, chd free. Tea, coffee & cake. Guided tours on the hour.**
Architectural Plants is home to an ensemble of captivating garden spaces designed to inspire you. Explore the Mediterranean lake garden and surrounding bankside walk tended by Head Gardener Colin and his apprentices. Italian cypress, olives, pines, hardy palms, spiky plants, and bamboo grove. The guided tour inc the large Acer house, the greenhouse of exciting and rare exotics, and a specialist Niwaki Production Zone. Prepare to enter exotica. The best cake in Sussex, so we hear. Hourly horticultural tours and some clipping demonstrations. Wheelchair access to the garden and lake view via grass lawns, and the plant nursery spans over a flat site.

5 ◆ ARUNDEL CASTLE & GARDENS
Arundel, BN18 9AB. Arundel Castle Trustees Ltd, 01903 882173, visits@arundelcastle.org, www.arundelcastle.org. *In the centre of Arundel, N of A27.* For opening times and information, please phone, email or visit garden website.
Ancient castle, family home of the Duke of Norfolk. 40 acres of grounds and gardens which inc hot subtropical borders, English herbaceous borders, stumpery, two glasshouses, walled flower and organic kitchen gardens, and Fitzalan Chapel white garden.

6 ASHDOWN PARK HOTEL
Wych Cross, East Grinstead, RH18 5JR. Mr Kevin Sweet, 01342 824988, reservations@ashdownpark.co.uk, www.ashdownpark.com. *6m S of East Grinstead. Take A22 towards Wych Cross. At T-lights turn onto Colemans Hatch Rd, passing garden centre. In approx 1m, take 2nd turning R & enter Ashdown Park through main entrance, follow NGS signs to car parks.* **Sun 17 May, Sun 13 Sept (1-4). Adm £7, chd free. Tea, coffee & cake.**
Ashdown Park spans 186 acres of woodland, grazing land, parkland, an 18-hole golf course, and ornamental gardens. The Walled Garden features perennials, shrubs, fruit trees, and seasonal blooms. To the east lies the tranquil Secret Garden with flowing water amongst trees. Mature specimen trees grace the rolling lawns that lead to the main lake, perfect for peaceful exploration.

7 96 ASHFORD ROAD
Hastings, TN34 2HZ. Lynda & Andrew Hayler. *Nr Alexander Park. From A21 (Sedlescombe Rd N) towards Hastings, take 1st exit on r'about A2101, then 3rd on L (approx 1m).* **Sat 2, Sat 9, Sat 16 May (1-4.30). Adm £4, chd free.**
Small (100ft x 52ft) Japanese inspired front and back garden. Full of interesting planting with many acers, azaleas and bamboos. Over 100 different hostas, many miniature ones. The garden also features an attractive Japanese Tea House and courtyard with a fish pond, as well as a Japanese bridge and pond in the lower garden.

Our donation to the Army Benevolent Fund supported 776 individuals with horticultural related grants in 2025.

8 NEW **THE AVIARY GARDEN**
111 Aldwick Road, Bognor Regis, PO21 2NY. Mr Ian Easterbrook & Mr Matthew Edwards, ianre64@hotmail.com. *300 metres from Aldwick seafront. Aviary Garden on B2166, ¼ m from Martlets r'about on R heading to Bognor Regis. On street parking on Aldwick Rd & nearby roads. Paid parking on seafront, then walk through Marine Park Gardens.* **Sun 21, Tue 23 June, Sun 19, Tue 21 July (10-4). Adm £6, chd free. Pre-booking essential, please visit www.ngs.org.uk for information & booking. Tea, coffee, cake & cream teas. Visits also by arrangement 1 June to 24 July for groups of 10 to 20.**
A south facing garden, just 300 metres from the sea. An exotic garden giving a tropical, jungle feel. Gravel paths with stepping stones are interspersed with planting to soften the journey. Large leaved plants, statues, seating, a 12ft giraffe, an Indonesian elephant, and a well-stocked aviary are amongst the surprises that await as you amble through the garden.
❋ ☕ 🔊

GROUP OPENING

9 BALCOMBE GARDENS
3m N of Cuckfield on B2036, 3m S of J10A on M23. Just N of Balcombe stn, turn R into Newlands Rd, which leads to Oldlands Ave. What3words app: tastings.estimate.inflating. **Wed 20 May, Sat 27, Sun 28 June (12-5). Combined adm £7.50, chd free. Tea, coffee & cake at Stumlet.**

THE COPPICE
Oldlands Avenue, RH17 6LP.
Carol & Sandy Jarvest-Chen.

STUMLET
Oldlands Avenue, RH17 6LW.
Max & Nicola Preston Bell.

WINTERFIELD
Oldlands Avenue, RH17 6LP. Sarah & Ian Lamaletie, 07977 201637, sarah.lamaletie@yahoo.co.uk.
Visits also by arrangement 20 May to 30 June for groups of up to 30.

Three quite different, adjacent gardens on an easy walking trail. Winterfield is a long-established plantsman's garden, full of uncommon shrubs and trees, herbaceous borders, a pond, and a wildlife area. Stumlet has evolved from a 'work in progress' garden into a restful and special space, with places to sit and enjoy a little peace, scent, colour, and interesting planting. The Coppice is a garden to watch as it develops over the coming years, transforming from a newly designed and partially planted area into an inspirational space. The areas near the house are already planted, offering a glimpse of the promise to come.
🐕 ❋ ☕ 🔊

10 BANKS FARM
Boast Lane, Barcombe, Lewes, BN8 5DY. Nick & Lucy Addyman. *6m N of Lewes. From Barcombe Cross, follow signs to Spithurst & Newick. Take 1st road on R into Boast Ln towards the Anchor pub. At sharp bend, continue into Banks Farm.* **Sat 25, Sun 26 Apr (10.30-4). Adm £5, chd free. Tea, coffee & cake.**
9 acre garden set in rural countryside. Extensive lawns and shrub beds merge with the more naturalistic woodland garden set around the lake. An orchard, vegetable garden, ponds and a wide variety of plant species add to an interesting and very tranquil garden. Refreshments served outside, so may be limited during bad weather. Wheelchair access to the upper part of garden. Sloping grass paths in the lower area.
♿ 🐕 ☕ 🍴 🔊

11 ♦ **BATES GREEN GARDEN**
Tye Hill Road, Arlington, BN26 6SH. John McCutchan, 01323 485151, john@bluebellwalk.co.uk, www.batesgreengarden.co.uk. *3½ m SW of Hailsham & A22. Midway between the A22 & A27, 2m S of Michelham Priory. Bates Green is in Tye Hill Rd (N of Arlington village), 350yds S of Old Oak Inn. Ample parking on hard-standing verges.* **For NGS: Sun 22 Mar, Sun 4 Oct (10.30-3.30). Adm £8, chd £4. Home-made soup, cakes, scones, & light lunches in large insulated Bluebell Barn. For other opening times and information, please phone, email or visit garden website.**
This plantswoman's tranquil garden provides interest through the seasons. Woodland garden created around a majestic oak tree. Colour themed middle garden. Courtyard gardens with seasonal container displays. Front garden a spring and autumn joy with narcissi, primroses, violets then coloured stems and leaves of cornus and salix. Wildlife pond and wildflower meadow. Spring visitors walk through a wild daffodil glade leading to the 24 acre ancient oak and hornbeam wood, home of the Arlington Bluebell Walk. Beatons Wood is managed for conservation and diversity and autumn guests can enjoy spotting the abundant fungi within. Dogs not in garden but allowed in barn and wood. Wheelchair access to most areas. Mobility scooters for experienced users to borrow free of charge. Accessible WC.
♿ ❋ 🐕 ☕ 🍴 🔊

12 NEW **1 BELTON CLOSE**
Brighton, BN2 3RY. Steve Bustin & John Williams. *Round Hill area within Brighton. Alley between 7 & 9 Belton Rd (no parking in close). Nearest paid parking on Princes Crescent, 2 min walk away. Buses 26, 46 & 50, stop at Princes Crescent. London Road train stn, 6 min walk.* **Sun 9, Sun 23 Aug (11-5). Adm £5, chd free. Pre-booking essential, please visit www.ngs.org.uk for information & booking. Tea, coffee & cake.**
This compact city garden packs texture and colour into a small space. Designed 5 yrs ago around a bold extension, the garden inc sitting/dining areas, an outdoor kitchen, a rill and ponds, a kitchen garden, and both sun-baked and shaded beds. It comes into its own in late summer, with planting that inc grasses, dahlias, perennials, annuals, aeoniums, and climbers.
❋ ☕ 🔊

In 2025, our donations to Carers Trust helped them support over 1 million unpaid carers across the UK, as part of their network of local carer centres.

Aldebury

GROUP OPENING

13 BEXHILL-ON-SEA TRAIL
Bexhill & Little Common. Follow NGS signs to gardens from main roads. Tickets & maps available at each garden. All gardens are close to Bexhill & Little Common, except for Chez Nous on Ninfield Rd. **Sat 20 June (11-4). Combined adm £7, chd free. Tea, coffee & cake.**

NEW 1 BROOKLANDS ROAD
Little Common, TN39 4FQ.
Pam & Peter Cooper.

NEW CHEZ NOUS
Ninfield Road, TN39 5JJ.
Rachel & Andy Castle.

THE CLINCHES
Collington Lane East, TN39 3RJ.
Val Kemm.

64 COLLINGTON AVENUE
TN39 3RA. Dr Roger & Ruth Elias.

DE WILP
Collington Lane East, TN39 3RJ.
Stuart & Hazel Wood.

SHAMBLES
202 Cooden Drive, TN39 3AH.
Sylvia & John Brady.

NEW 1 STOWE DRIVE
Little Common, TN39 4GL.
Joan Ball.

This beautiful trail evolves every year. The gardens vary in size and feature well-designed borders with specimen plants, shrubs, and trees. Most have ponds with wildlife and fish, as well as vegetable beds and fruit trees. One garden has beautiful sculptures and a Gothic folly while another has a modern designed front garden with a rill. Chickens can also be seen at Chez Nous. There is a mix of town, country, cottage, and coastal styles, with a wide variety of trees, roses, and mixed planting, all focused on attracting wildlife and offering excellent ideas for your own garden. 1 Stowe Drive and Chez Nous will offer refreshments. Some gardens will be selling a variety of plants, and artwork will be for sale at Chez Nous. Enjoy the Ukrainian Culbaba (Dandelion) dance at The Clinches and live music at 1 Stowe Drive. WC available at The Clinches, Chez Nous, 1 Stowe Drive, and Brooklands. Wheelchair access or partial access to most gardens.

14 BIGNOR PARK
Pulborough, RH20 1HG. The Mersey Family, www.bignorpark.co.uk. 5m S of Petworth & Pulborough. Well signed from B2138. Nearest villages Sutton, Bignor & West Burton. Approach from the E, directions & map available on website. **Tue 12 May, Tue 16 June, Tue 22 Sept (2-5). Adm £7, chd free. Home-made teas.**

11 acres of peaceful garden to explore with magnificent views of the South Downs. Interesting trees, shrubs and wildflower areas. The walled garden has been replanted with herbaceous borders and the Dutch garden has a new central obelisk and planting inc climbing roses, salvias and echinaceas. Temple, Greek loggia, Zen pond and unusual sculptures. Former home of romantic poet Charlotte Smith, whose sonnets were inspired by Bignor Park. Spectacular cedar of Lebanon and rare Lucombe oak. Wheelchair access to shrubbery and croquet lawn. Gravel paths in rest of garden and steps in stables quadrangle.

15 NEW BLACK SHED STUDIOS GARDEN
Sunnyview, Nursery Lane, Fairwarp, Uckfield, TN22 3BD. Sandy Infield. What3words app: expect.butterfly.point. From B2026 turn at Fairwarp (signed Foresters Arms), then turn at 1st signed track on R for disabled access only. Parking at Fairwarp Village Hall, then follow signs to garden. Do not use postcode. **Fri 11, Sat 12, Sun 13 Sept (10-6). Adm £5, chd free. Pre-booking essential, please email blackshedstudios@gmail.com or visit www.blackshedstudios.com for information & booking. Tea, coffee & cake.**

Set in the Ashdown Forest, this unique 3 acre garden blends formal structure with naturalistic planting. Designed by an artist, it features sculpture, painting, ceramics, and glass art throughout. Explore a wildlife pond, meadow, and a small wetland, all offering tranquillity and inspiration in a relaxed, welcoming setting. The artists' studios will be open during visit. Conservation zoologist Dr Mark Infield will give talks at 1pm on Saturday and Sunday. Many of the garden paths and studios are wheelchair accessible when conditions are dry.

16 ♦ BORDE HILL GARDEN
Borde Hill Lane, Haywards Heath, RH16 1XP. Borde Hill Garden, 01444 450326, info@bordehill.co.uk, www.bordehill.co.uk. 1½m N of Haywards Heath. 20 mins N of Brighton or S of Gatwick on the A23. Take exit 10a via Balcombe; after approx 3m, the garden is on the R as you enter Haywards Heath. **For NGS: Tue 12 May (10-5). Adm £14, chd £9. Light refreshments.** For other opening times and information, please phone, email or visit garden website.

Tranquil and picturesque, Borde Hill has been planted with passion by five generations of the Stephenson Clarke family. With rare and fine rhododendrons, magnolias, rose borders, and champion trees, exploring the thirteen outdoor rooms is like travelling around the world in one garden. Wheelchair access to 17 acres of formal garden.

17 BOURNE BOTANICALS
The Bourne, Chesterfield Close, Furnace Wood, Felbridge, East Grinstead, RH19 2PY. Jackie & Andy Doherty, 07785 562558, bournebotanic@outlook.com. A264 between Copthorne & Felbridge. 1⅙m from Felbridge. Parking in layby RH19 2QF on W bound A264 signed to Furnace Wood. Metrobus 400. Enter Furnace Wood via footpath R of barrier, 8 min walk to Bourne Botanicals. **Thur 6, Sat 15 Aug (11-5). Adm £8. Tea, coffee & cake.** Visits also by arrangement 1 Aug to 24 Aug for groups of 15+.

Yes, we have some bananas!! But that's not all. There's giant gunnera, spiky agave and yucca, tetrapanax, bamboo, palm trees, and so many more unusual plants. Featuring 'Our Folly', a sunken garden with figs, peaches, canna, colocasia and many frogs! All set in a lush one acre garden with many quirky touches. A very different garden, miss it if you dare! National Collection holder. Parking at property for disabled badge holders and those with mobility issues only, please phone 07785 562558 to go through barrier.

18 BRIGHTLING DOWN FARM

Observatory Road, Dallington, TN21 9LN. Val & Pete Stephens, 07770 807060, valstephens@icloud.com. *1m from Woods Corner. At Swan Pub, Woods Corner, take road opp to Brightling. Take 1st L to Burwash & almost immed, turn into 1st driveway on L.* **Visits by arrangement 1 May to 25 Sept for groups of 12 to 35. Preferred days Mon or Fri. Adm £14, chd free. Home-made teas inc.**

The garden has several different areas inc a Zen garden, water garden, walled vegetable garden with two large greenhouses, herb garden, herbaceous borders and a woodland walk. The garden makes clever use of grasses and is set amongst woodland with stunning countryside views. Winner of the Society of Garden Designers award. Most areas of garden can be accessed with the use of temporary ramps.

19 BUMBLE FARM

Drungewick Lane, Loxwood, Billinghurst, RH14 0RS. Will Carver. *Very well signed in the middle of Drungewick Ln.* **Sat 16, Sun 17 May, Sat 6, Sun 7 June (2-5). Adm £6, chd free. Home-made teas.**

A delightful large country garden, passionately and imaginatively created by an enthusiastic owner over the past 20 yrs. The garden features a series of circular lawns, surrounded by borders filled with mass drift and repeat planting of harmonious perennials, roses, shrubs, and more. A newly developed white garden, a wisteria covered pergola, a kitchen and cutting garden, fountains, and various seating areas.

In 2025 we awarded over £288,800 in Community Garden Grants, supporting 114 community garden projects.

1 Belton Close

20 BUTLERS FARMHOUSE
Butlers Lane, Herstmonceux, BN27 1QH. Irene Eltringham-Willson, 01323 833770, irene.willson@btinternet.com, www.butlersfarmhouse.co.uk. 3m E of Hailsham. Take A271 from Hailsham, go through village of Herstmonceux, turn R signed Church Rd, then approx 1m turn R. Do not use SatNav! **Fri 27, Sat 28 Mar, Tue 9, Wed 10 June (2-5). Adm £5, chd free. Sat 22, Sun 23 Aug (2-5). Adm £8, chd free. Home-made teas. Live jazz in Aug only.** Visits also by arrangement 26 Mar to 12 Oct. Please phone to discuss refreshments.

'Quirky and fun' are two words that pop up in visitors' comments - come and see our 1 acre country garden for yourself! Enjoy the secret jungle garden, Cornish inspired beach corners, rainbow border, and the poison garden. Set around a C16 farmhouse in 6 acres of rural Sussex with the South Downs in the distance; mainly a traditionally managed wildflower meadow with a few orchids, enjoy a walk in June. The garden is pretty in the spring, awash in primroses and violets. Picnics welcome in June and Aug. Most of garden accessible by wheelchair.

21 CAMBERLOT HALL
Camberlot Road, Lower Dicker, Hailsham, BN27 3RH. Nicky & Paul Kinghorn, 07710 566453, nickykinghorn@hotmail.com. *500yds S of A22 at Lower Dicker, 4½m N of A27 Drusillas r'about. From A27 Drusillas r'about, through Berwick Stn to Upper Dicker. Turn L into Camberlot Rd after The Plough pub, we are 1m on L. From A22, we are 500yds down Camberlot Rd on R.* **Visits by arrangement 15 June to 4 Sept for groups of 8 to 25. Adm £14, chd free. Tea & cake inc.**
A 3 acre country garden with a lovely view across fields and hills to the South Downs. Created from scratch over the past 12 yrs, with all design, planting, and maintenance by the owner. Features inc a lavender-lined carriage driveway, naturalistic border, vegetable garden, shady garden, a 30 metre white border, dahlia garden, part-walled garden, and summerhouse. Wheelchair access over gravel drive and some uneven ground.

22 51 CARLISLE ROAD
Eastbourne, BN21 4JR. Elaine & Nigel Fraser-Gausden, the3growbags.com. *200yds inland from seafront (Wish Tower), close to Congress Theatre.* **Sun 31 May (1-5). Combined adm with Chelmsford Lodge £5, chd free. Tea, coffee & cake.**
A secluded, award-winning, 75' x 65' garden, with glorious early summer colour from an abundance of old roses, perennials, mixed beds, and diverse planting. There is a small pond, and areas for plants that love shade or sun. Special plants, inc abutilon and *Euphorbia mellifera*, that enjoy the relatively mild microclimate of this below street level space, very close to the south coast. Refreshments enjoyed in the garden and the adjoining communal garden.

The Old Rectory, Pulborough

SUSSEX 519

23 NEW 53 CEDAR DRIVE
Chichester, PO19 3EH. Felicity Fox. *Parklands. What3words app: bind.invest.easy.* **Sat 25, Sun 26 Apr, Sat 18, Sun 19 July (10.30-5). Combined adm with 25 Parklands Road £7, chd free. Tea, coffee & cake.**
This garden behind a 1937 semi plays host to a venerable Bramley. Other trees, such as Tibetan birch and *Photinia* 'Red Robin', were chosen for their colour, which is carried through the seasons by tulips, Geum, Alstroemeria, dahlias, cannas, roses, and penstemon. Cotinus and Heuchera enrich the palette. Hard landscaping and a potting shed, added in 2022, helped to pull the plant collection into a cohesive design.

24 CHALK FARM FLOWERS
Rogers Lane, Findon, Worthing, BN14 0RE. chalkfarmflowers.com. *4m N of Worthing. On A24, just S of Findon village. Turn onto Rogers Ln directly at entrance to Findon Vale Garden Centre. We are located by the 1st farm gate on the L. Parking at farm, limited spaces at garden centre.* **Sat 18 Apr (9-5.30); Sun 19 Apr (10-4.30); Sat 8 Aug (9-5.30); Sun 9 Aug (10-4.30). Adm £6, chd free. Pre-booking essential, please visit www.ngs.org.uk for information & booking. Light refreshments.**
A sustainable working flower farm, run by two young horticulturalists with a passion for the environment. Our mission is to spread the word about British-grown flowers and share our story with visitors. We grow a wide range of flowers across a 1 acre site, where fresh, chemical-free bunches are available. You can also enjoy refreshments with a beautiful view of the flower field. Wheelchair access over gentle slopes and wide grassy and bark paths alongside the flower farm growing beds.

25 CHAMPS HILL
Waltham Park Road, Coldwaltham, Pulborough, RH20 1LY. Mrs Mary Bowerman, 01798 831205, info@thebct.org.uk, www.thebct.org.uk. *3m S of Pulborough. On the A29, turn R towards Fittleworth onto Waltham Park Rd. The garden is 400 metres on R. What3words app: call.lakeside.*

fellow. **Sun 10 May (11-5); Sun 9 Aug (2-5). Adm £7, chd free. Home-made teas.** Visits also by arrangement 2 Mar to 4 Sept for groups of 10+. Adm inc tea, coffee & biscuits.
A natural landscape, the garden has been developed around three disused sand quarries with far-reaching views across the Amberley Wildbrooks to the South Downs. A woodland walk in spring leads you past beautiful sculptures, against a backdrop of colourful rhododendrons and azaleas. In summer the garden is a colourful tapestry of heathers, well-known for their abundance and variety. The travelling exhibition 'Art of the Newlyn School' can be viewed in the Music Room on Sun 10 May prior to its two year UK tour. Optional combined garden and art exhibition entry £10 (pay on the day only).

26 ♦ CHARLESTON
Firle, Lewes, BN8 6LL. The Charleston Trust, 01323 811626, press@charleston.org.uk, www.charleston.org.uk. *Charleston is on the A27 signed halfway between Brighton & Eastbourne. From A27 follow narrow lane with deep ditches either side. Parking 200 metres from house entrance. Blue badge parking only 50 metres from house. Please arrive promptly for tour & talk to start.* **For NGS: Fri 12 June (10-12). Adm £12.50, chd free. Pre-booking essential, please visit www.ngs.org.uk for information & booking. Tour & talk about the garden at 10am & 11am with Head Gardener. For other opening times and information, please phone, email or visit garden website.**
Created in 1918 by Roger Fry, Charleston's walled garden became a painter's paradise and sanctuary for artists Vanessa Bell and Duncan Grant. Alive with colour from spring bulbs to summer roses, autumn dahlias to daisies, it brims with creativity and cottage charm. Still artistically tended, it offers inspiration year-round and hosts Festival of the Garden in July. Featuring a variety of sculpture, mosaics and tiled pools, orchard and tranquil pond. Refreshments available to purchase at on site café. Garden and grounds partially accessible. Gravel pathways, some uneven and narrow.

27 CHELMSFORD LODGE
12 Granville Road, Eastbourne, BN20 7HE. Jane Stevens. *500yds from seafront (Wish Tower). From Congress Theatre, take Carlisle Rd. Turn L at Granville Rd Xrds, then continue for 100yds. Chelmsford Lodge is on the R. Easy on-street parking.* **Sun 31 May (1-5). Combined adm with 51 Carlisle Road £5, chd free.**
A beautiful ¾ acre garden with winding pathways, continuing to develop each year. It features a magnificent collection of unusual and mature trees, herbaceous beds, a rose garden, shrubs, formal beds around a pond, a rockery, fruit trees, and a soft fruit area. Within this space are smaller gardens, making it a lovely place to stroll. The owner has created an informative map identifying the many different trees.

28 ♦ CLINTON LODGE
Fletching, TN22 3ST. Lady Collum, 01825 722952, garden@clintonlodge.com, www.clintonlodgegardens.co.uk. *4m NW of Uckfield. Clinton Lodge is situated in Fletching High St, N of The Griffin Inn. Off road parking provided, weather permitting. It is important visitors do not park in street. Parking available from 11am.* **For NGS: Thur 11 June (11-5). Adm £8, chd free. Home-made teas from 12pm. No lunches. Cash only on the day. For other opening times and information, please phone, email or visit garden website. Donation to local charities.**
6 acre formal and romantic garden overlooking parkland with old roses, William Pye water feature, double white and blue herbaceous borders, yew hedges, pleached lime walks, medieval style potager, vine and rose allée, wildflower garden, small knot garden and orchard. Caroline and Georgian house (not open).

The National Garden Scheme funded six Macmillan Nurses in their roles across England, Wales and Northern Ireland in 2025.

29 COLWOOD HOUSE
Cuckfield Lane, Warninglid, RH17 5SP. **Mrs Rosy Brenan**, 01444 461352, rbrenan@me.com. *6m W of Haywards Heath, 6m SE of Horsham. Entrance on B2115 Cuckfield Ln. From E, N & S, turn W off A23 towards Warninglid for ¾ m. From W, enter through Warninglid village.* **Visits by arrangement 14 May to 27 Aug for groups of 10 to 40. Adm £8, chd free. Groups can bring their own refreshments & picnics.**
12 acres of garden featuring mature and specimen trees dating from the late 1800s, with lawns and a woodland edge. Formal parterre, rose and herb gardens. A 100ft terrace and herbaceous border overlook a flower rimmed croquet lawn. Cut turf labyrinth and a forsythia tunnel. Water features, statues, and gazebos. Pets' cemetery. Giant chessboard. Lake with island and temple. Wheelchair access with gravel paths and some slopes.
& 🐕 🎋 ᵛ⁾

30 COOKSCROFT
Bookers Lane, Earnley, Chichester, PO20 7JG. **Mr J Williams**, 01243 513671, john@cookscroft.co.uk, www.cookscroft.co.uk. *6m S of Chichester. At end of Birdham Straight (A286) from Chichester, take L fork onto the B2198 to East Wittering. After 1m, on sharp bend, turn L into Bookers Ln, then 2nd house on L. Parking available.* **Sat 16 May (11-4). Adm £6, chd free. Light refreshments. Visits also by arrangement 1 May to 6 Sept for groups of up to 25.**
A garden for all seasons which delights the visitor. Started in 1988, it features cottage, woodland and Japanese style gardens, water features and borders of perennials with a particular emphasis on southern hemisphere plants. Unusual plants for the plantsman to enjoy, many grown from seed. The differing styles of the garden flow together making it easy to wander anywhere. Wheelchair access over grass, bark paths and unfenced ponds.
& 🐕 ❀ 🚗 ☕ ᵛ⁾

31 THE COTTAGE
Potts Lane, Pulborough, RH20 2BT. **Claire Denman**, 07739 820712, Claire.denman1@yahoo.co.uk. *Potts Ln is a pedestrian lane off Lower St (A283) in Pulborough. The entrance is between two houses, next to T-lights. Parking in Lower St public car park, almost opp Potts Ln.* **Sat 23 May, Sat 5 Sept (10-4). Adm £6, chd free. Home-made teas. Visits also by arrangement 20 May to 4 Sept for groups of 6 to 20.**
A quintessential English cottage garden, packed with a mix of perennials and bulbs, set on a potentially challenging, multi-layered site. Comprising four distinct rooms, inc a small roof terrace, a top terrace sitting above the house garden, and a vegetable garden built in what was once a small swimming pool. Every square inch has been used.
❀ ☕ ᵛ⁾

32 CUMBERLAND HOUSE
Cray's Lane, Thakeham, Pulborough, RH20 3ER. **George & Jane Blunden**. *At junction of Cray's Ln & The Street, nr St Mary's Church. Park at Thakeham Place Farm, a 1 min walk away.* **Thur 23, Sun 26 July (2-5). Combined adm with Thakeham Place Farm £10, chd free. Home-made teas at Thakeham Place Farm.**
A Georgian village house (not open) next to a C12 church, with a beautiful, mature ¾ acre English country garden. The garden comprises a walled area laid out as a series of rooms with well-stocked flower beds, two rare ginkgo trees, and yew topiary. This leads to an informal garden with vegetable, herb, and fruit areas, pleached limes, and a lawn shaded by a copper beech tree. Wheelchair access through gate at right-hand side of house.
& 🐕 ☕ ᵛ⁾

33 D & S HAUS
41 Torton Hill Road, Arundel, BN18 9HF. **Darrell Gale & Simon Rose**. *1m SW of Arundel town square. From A27 Ford Rd/Chichester Rd r'about, take exit to Ford & immed turn R into Torton Hill Rd. Continue uphill, & at large oak tree, keep L. Garden on L as you go down the hill.* **Sat 18, Sun 19 July (12-5). Home-made teas. Evening opening Thur 20 Aug (7-10). Light refreshments. Adm £7, chd free.**
A lush rainforest/jungle garden, which we have planted from scratch over the past 12 yrs. Both front and rear gardens contain a mass of palms, bananas, bamboos, and all manner of spiky, luxuriant foliage. Normal rules are not followed! Surreal sculptures and new features to delight. A visitor commented: 'It is more spectacular than I have ever seen with the National Garden Scheme'. Tropical planting with lots of unusual plants, quirky sculptures and features.
🚗 ᵛ⁾

34 DALE PARK HOUSE
Madehurst, Arundel, BN18 0NP. **Robert & Jane Green**, 01243 814260, robertgreenfarming@gmail.com. *4m W of Arundel. Take A27 E from Chichester or W from Arundel, then A29 (London) for 2m, turn L to Madehurst & follow red arrows.* **Visits by arrangement 25 May to 30 June for groups of 10+. Adm £6, chd free. Tea, coffee & cake.**
Set in parkland, enjoying magnificent views of the sea. Come and relax in the large walled garden, which features an impressive 200ft herbaceous border. There is also a sunken gravel garden, mixed borders, a small rose garden, dreamy rose and clematis arches, an interesting collection of hostas, foliage plants and shrubs, along with an orchard and kitchen garden.
🚗 🎋 ☕

35 ♦ DENMANS GARDEN
Denmans Lane, Fontwell, BN18 0SU. **Gwendolyn van Paasschen**. *5m from Chichester & Arundel. Off A27, ½ m W of Fontwell r'about.* **For NGS: Mon 16 Feb, Mon 27 Apr, Mon 26 Oct (9.30-4). Adm £10, chd £8. Pre-booking essential, please phone 01243 278950, email office@denmans.org or visit www.denmans.org for information & booking. Light refreshments. For other opening times and information, please phone, email or visit garden website.**
Award-winning Grade II registered tranquil contemporary garden, created by gravel gardening pioneer Joyce Robinson and developed by renowned landscape designer John Brookes MBE. Known for its curvilinear layout and complex planting, features inc year-round colour, unusual plants, structure and fragrance in the gravel gardens, dry riverbeds, ponds, walled garden, and conservatory. Plant Nursery with specially selected and unusual shrubs, grasses, ferns, and herbaceous perennials. The Gift Shop has beautifully curated gifts

and locally made products. Midpens Café serves breakfast, lunch, and afternoon tea.

&. 🐎 ✻ ☕ ☕ ♫))

36 47 DENMANS LANE
Lindfield, Haywards Heath, RH16 2JN. Sue & Jim Stockwell, 01444 459363, jamesastockwell@aol.com, www.lindfield-gardens.co.uk/47denmans-lane. Approx 1½m NE of Haywards Heath town centre. From Haywards Heath train stn follow B2028 signed Lindfield & Ardingly for 1m. At T-lights turn L into Hickmans Ln, then after 100 metres take 1st R into Denmans Ln. **Sun 22 Mar, Sun 5, Mon 6 Apr, Sun 3, Mon 4 May (11-4). Adm £7, chd free. Tea, coffee & cake. Visits also by arrangement 1 Mar to 20 Sept for groups of 5 to 50.**
This beautiful and tranquil 1 acre garden was described by Sussex Life as 'a garden where plants star'. Created by the owners over the past 20 yrs, it is planted for interest throughout the year. Spring bulbs are followed by azaleas, rhododendrons, roses, and herbaceous perennials. The garden also has ponds, vegetable and fruit gardens. An extensive choice of plants and home-made jams for sale. Most of the garden accessible by wheelchair with some steep slopes.

&. ✻ 🚗 ☕ ♫))

37 DOWN PLACE
Hill Lane, South Harting, Petersfield, GU31 5PN. Mrs David Thistleton-Smith, 01730 825374, selina@downplace.co.uk. 1m SE of South Harting. From B2141 to Chichester, turn L down unmarked lane below the top of the hill. From Chichester on B2141, take the R turn just after the South Downs Way crosses the road. **Sat 28, Sun 29 Mar, Sun 21, Mon 22 June (1.30-5.30). Adm £6, chd free. Tea, coffee, home-made cakes & cream teas. Visits also by arrangement 1 Mar to 26 July for groups of 15 to 45. Talk on the house & garden, followed by a guided tour.**
Set high in the South Downs with sweeping views of rolling woodland, this garden blends beautifully into its natural surroundings. Rose and herbaceous borders contour the slopes, while a productive vegetable garden and shaded beech walks lead to a vibrant wildflower meadow. In spring, it bursts with wild daffodils and cowslips, followed by six native orchid varieties and other wildflowers from late May to early July. Seeds from the meadow help restore damaged areas across the South Downs National Park, making this garden a haven for both beauty and biodiversity.

✻ ☕ ♫))

38 DRIFTWOOD
4 Marine Drive, Bishopstone, Seaford, BN25 2RS. Geoff Stonebanks & Mark Glassman, 01323 899296, visitdriftwood@gmail.com, www.driftwoodbysea.co.uk. A259 between Seaford & Newhaven. From Seaford, turn R into Bishopstone Rd, immed L into Marine Dr, then take 2nd on R. Please park on the same side as the house only, not on the bend beyond the drive. **Visits by arrangement 1 June to 2 Aug for groups of up to 25. Singles & groups welcome. Optional £3 for garden talk. Adm £7, chd free. Tea, coffee & cake.**
Introduced by Monty Don on BBC Gardeners' World in 2016 and again in 2024. In 2024, The Sunday Times said 'visit this rejigged award-winning plot'. Featured on Channel 4's George Clarke's Beautiful Builds in 2025, where research led them to Driftwood as the perfect inspiration for a seaside garden design. A perfect paradise made up of different gardens, each with individuality and creativity. Check out the 260 5-star reviews on TripAdvisor, with three successive Certificates of Excellence and five consecutive Travellers' Choice Awards. Enjoy a selection of Geoff's home-made cakes, all served on vintage china, on trays, in the garden. No WC.

🐎 🚗 ☕ ♫))

39 DUCKYLS
Selsfield Road, East Grinstead, RH19 4LP. Gia & Richard Thompson. Mid-way between Turner's Hill & West Hoathly. Duckyls entrance on Selsfield Rd (L from Turners Hill), set back from road, follow yellow NGS signs. What3words app: facelift.available.firms. A one-way system in place, exit via Vowels Ln only. **Sat 25, Sun 26 Apr (11-4). Adm £8, chd free. Pre-booking essential, please visit www.ngs.org.uk for information & booking. Tea, coffee & cake. Two hour timed slots at 11am & 2pm.**

A recently renovated 15 acre garden with wonderful views across Sussex. Consisting of a rhododendron woodland, a newly planted orchard, ponds and a more formal secret garden. Mostly laid out in the 1920s and 30s by a dedicated plant collector and orchid breeder. Delight in the blazes of spring colour to be seen. Please note this garden inc steep slopes and many climbs. Suitable footwear is required. Regret, no dogs allowed.

✻ ☕ 🪑 ♫))

40 DURFORD ABBEY BARN
Petersfield, GU31 5AU. Mr & Mrs Lund. 3m from Petersfield. Situated on the S side of the A272 between Petersfield & Rogate, 1m from the junction with B2072. **Sat 6, Sun 7 June (1-5.30). Adm £6, chd free. Home-made teas.**
A 1 acre plot with areas styled with cottage garden, prairie and shady borders set in the South Downs National Park with views of the Downs. Plants for sale. Partial wheelchair access due to quite steep grass slopes.

&. 🐎 ✻ ☕ ♫))

GROUP OPENING

41 EAST GRINSTEAD GARDENS
7m E of Crawley on A264 & 14m N of Uckfield on A22. For Allotments park at Imberhorne Lane Car Park, disabled parking on site. For 5 Nightingale Cl & 7 Nightingale Cl park on Hurst Farm Rd. Roadside parking at 35 Blount Ave & Cherry Cottage. **Sun 21 June, Sun 6 Sept (1-5). Combined adm £6, chd free. Tea, coffee & cake at 5 Nightingale Close (June) & 7 Nightingale Close (Sept).**

35 BLOUNT AVENUE
RH19 1JJ. Nicki Crabb.
Open on all dates

NEW CHERRY COTTAGE
Furzefield Road, RH19 2JN. Sue & John Robinson.
Open on Sun 21 June

IMBERHORNE ALLOTMENTS
RH19 1QX. Imberhorne Allotment Association, www.imberhorneallotments.org.
Open on Sun 6 Sept

5 NIGHTINGALE CLOSE
RH19 4DG. Carole & Terry Heather.
Open on all dates

7 NIGHTINGALE CLOSE
RH19 4DG. Gail & Andy Peel.
Open on all dates

Come and enjoy a variety of gardens, each offering its own unique inspiration. New this year: Cherry Cottage, a ½ acre cottage garden featuring a wide range of plants (opening in June only). Imberhorne Allotments with 80 thriving plots filled with grapevines, vegetables, fruits, and flowers. Perfect for anyone interested in growing their own (opening Sept only). 35 Blount Avenue, a contemporary design with south facing borders alive with tropical plants, while vibrant dahlias and roses bring the front garden to life. 5 Nightingale Close, beautifully landscaped gardens spread across two levels, inc lush planting, herbaceous beds, roses, and elegant topiary trees. 7 Nightingale Avenue, roses and flowering plants cascade down to a stream. This enchanting garden also inc a potager and a wonderful collection of bonsai. Plant sales at 35 Blount Avenue and 5 Nightingale Close. Kindly note: No dogs allowed. The Town Council hanging baskets and planting in the High Street are not to be missed and have achieved a Gold Medal from South and South East in Bloom. For steam train fans, the Bluebell Railway starts nearby.

42 FAIRLIGHT END
Pett Road, Pett, Hastings, TN35 4HB. Chris & Robin Hutt, 07774 863750, chrishutt@fairlightend.co.uk, www.fairlightend.co.uk. *4m E of Hastings. From Hastings take A259 to Rye. At White Hart Beefeater turn R into Friars Hill. Descend into Pett village.* **Visits by arrangement May & June for groups of 12+. Home-made teas.** Donation to Pett Village Hall.

Gardens Illustrated said 'The 18th century house is at the highest point in the garden with views down the slope over abundant borders and velvety lawns that are punctuated by clusters of specimen trees and shrubs. Beyond and below are the wildflower meadows and the ponds with a backdrop of the gloriously unspoilt Wealden landscape'.

43 FAIRLIGHT HALL
Martineau Lane, Hastings, TN35 5DR. Mr & Mrs David Kowitz, www.fairlighthall.co.uk. *2m E of Hastings. A259 from Hastings towards Dover & Rye, after 2m, turn R into Martineau Ln. Entrance approx 650yds on L.* **Sun 7 June (10-4). Adm £10, chd free. Pre-booking preferred. Light refreshments at pop-up café (10-3).**

A restored stunning garden in East Sussex. The formal gardens extend over 9 acres and surround the Victorian Gothic mansion (not open). Features semitropical woodland avenues, a huge contemporary walled garden with amphitheatre and two 110 metre perennial borders above and below ha-ha with far-reaching views across Rye Bay. Home-made preserves, vegetables, and cut flowers for sale. Most of the garden can be viewed by wheelchair. Please inform us on arrival, so we can direct you to disabled parking.

Banks Farm

44 ♦ FARLEYS SCULPTURE GARDEN

Muddles Green, Chiddingly, nr Lewes, BN8 6HW. Farleys House & Gallery Ltd, 01825 872856, Galleries@leemiller.co.uk, www.farleyshouseandgallery.co.uk/sculpture-garden. *9m from Lewes, off A22. Turn L off A22 towards Eastbourne at BP garage at Golden Cross. After 1m turn R at T- junction. Farleys is on R. Free car park.* **For NGS: Sat 20 June (10-4.30). Adm £6, chd free. Locally baked cake, light salads, soup & refreshments.** For other opening times and information, please phone, email or visit website.

Designed as different themed rooms for sculpture, Farleys garden presents our permanent collection of works chosen by photographer Lee Miller and surrealist artist Roland Penrose alongside works by contemporary guest sculptors. Over the years, giants, goddesses, mythical creatures and Roland's own work has populated the garden in the company of work by their artist friends. The visit also inc access to Farleys Gallery with two different exhibitions to enjoy. You may recognise part of the garden as having been featured as the view through the window in the movie 'Lee' starring Kate Winslet.

45 FINDON PLACE

Findon, Worthing, BN14 0RF. Miss Caroline Hill, 01903 877085, hello@findonplace.com, www.findonplace.com. *Directly off A24 N of Worthing. Follow signs to Findon Parish Church & park through the 1st driveway on LHS.* **Sun 23 Aug (2-5). Adm £8, chd £4. Pre-booking essential, please visit www.ngs.org.uk for information & booking. Cream teas.** Visits also by arrangement Apr to Sept for groups of 15 to 40.

Stunning grounds and gardens surrounding a Grade II listed Georgian country house (not open), nestled at the foot of the South Downs. The most glorious setting for a tapestry of perennial borders set off by Sussex flint walls. The many charms inc a yew allée, cloud pruned trees, espaliered fruit trees, a productive ornamental kitchen garden, rose arbours and arches, and a cutting garden.

🐕 ✱ 🚗 ☕ 🍽️

46 FITTLEWORTH HOUSE

Bedham Lane, Fittleworth, Pulborough, RH20 1JH. Edward & Isabel Braham, 07738 013523, marksaunders66.com@gmail.com, www.racingandgreen.com. *2m E, SE of Petworth. Midway between Petworth & Pulborough on the A283 in Fittleworth, turn into lane signed Bedham, just off sharp bend. The garden is 50yds along on the L. Plenty of car parking available.* **Every Wed 22 Apr to 13 May, 22 July to 5 Aug (2-5). Adm £6, chd free. Home-made teas.** Visits also by arrangement 23 Apr to 6 Aug for groups of 5 to 40. Parking for a coach available.

A tranquil, romantic 3 acre country garden with a redesigned walled kitchen garden growing fruit, vegetables, and flowers inc a large collection of dahlias. A large glasshouse, an old potting shed, mixed flower borders, roses, rhododendrons, and lawns. A magnificent cedar tree overlooks the wisteria-covered, Grade II listed Georgian house (not open). A wild garden with long grass and a 70 metre naturalised stream with ferns and hydrangeas. The garden sits on a gentle slope but is mostly accessible for wheelchairs and buggies.

🐕 ✱ ☕

47 FIVE OAKS COTTAGE

Petworth, RH20 1HD. Jean & Steve Jackman. *5m S of Pulborough. SatNav does not work! To ensure best route, we provide printed directions, please email jeanjackman@hotmail.com or call 07939 272443.* **Fri 17, Sat 18 July (2-4.30). Adm £7, chd free. Pre-booking essential, please visit www.ngs.org.uk for information & booking. Home-made teas (cash only).**

An acre of delicate jungle surrounds an Arts and Crafts style cottage (not open), with stunning views of the South Downs. Our unconventional garden is designed to encourage maximum wildlife, featuring a knapweed and hogweed meadow on clay that attracts clouds of butterflies, along with two small ponds and plenty of seating. An award-winning, organic garden with a magical atmosphere.

☕

48 THE FOLLY

Charlton, Chichester, PO18 0HU. Joan Burnett, 01243 811307, joankeirburnett@gmail.com, www.thefollycharlton.com. *7m N of Chichester & S of Midhurst, off A286 at Singleton, follow signs to Charlton. Follow NGS parking signs. No parking in lane, drop off only. Parking nr the Fox Goes Free pub.* **Sun 28 June, Sun 26 July, Sun 23 Aug (2-4.30). Adm £6, chd free. Home-made teas.** Visits also by arrangement 22 June to 26 Aug for groups of 12 to 30.

Colourful cottage garden surrounding a C16 period house (not open), set in the pretty downland village of Charlton, close to Levin Down Nature Reserve. Herbaceous borders are well-stocked with a wide range of plants. A variety of perennials, grasses, annuals, and shrubs provide a long season of colour and interest. The garden also features an old well, busy bees, and an art studio open to visitors. Partial wheelchair access with steps from patio to lawn. Visitors with mobility issues can be dropped off at the gate.

♿ 🐕 ✱ 🛏️ ☕ 🍽️

49 FOREST RIDGE

Paddockhurst Lane, Balcombe, RH17 6QZ. Philip & Rosie Wiltshire, 07900 621838, rosiem.wiltshire@btinternet.com. *3m from M23 J10a. From M23 J10a take B2036 to Balcombe. After ⅔m take 1st L onto B2110. After Worth School turn R into Back Ln, that becomes Paddockhurst Ln. Forest Ridge on R. Ignore SatNav. Follow signs to parking.* **Sat 9, Sun 10 May (2-5.30). Adm £6.50, chd free. Home-made teas.**

A charming 4½ acre Victorian garden with far-reaching views, boasting the oldest Atlantic cedar in Sussex. The owners themselves are undertaking a major restoration: felling, planting, and redesigning areas. The garden features both formal and informal planting, a woodland dell, and a mini arboretum. Azaleas, rhododendrons, and camellias abound, inc rare and unusual species. This is a garden to watch in the coming years as new plantings mature and redesigned areas flourish. A garden to explore! Please note: There is one deep water pond. Wheelchair access via wide gravel paths to some parts of the garden. Disabled parking only on the owner's drive.

♿ 🐕 🛏️ ☕ 🍽️

50 FOXGLOVE COTTAGE
29 Orchard Road, Horsham, RH13 5NF. Peter & Terri Lefevre, 01403 256002, teresalefevre@outlook.com. *East Horsham. At Horsham stn, over bridge, at r'about 3rd exit (Crawley), 1st R Stirling Way, at end turn L, 1st R Orchard Rd. From A281, take Clarence Rd, at end turn R, at end turn L Orchard Rd. Street parking.* **Sun 24 May, Sun 21, Thur 25 June (1-5). Adm £6, chd free. Home-made teas inc vegan, gluten & dairy free cake. Visits also by arrangement 26 May to 5 July for groups of 12 to 30. Individuals can ask to be added to an existing group visit.**
An unexpected ¼ acre cottage garden. There's no lawn, but gravel and bark paths divide colour-packed mixed borders, unusual containers, and quirky salvaged items hidden throughout. Water features encourage wildlife. Sit and enjoy vignettes from a wide variety of seating. At the end of the garden, you'll find climbers, drought tolerant plants, and a plant nursery. Plenty of ideas to take home. A gravel garden with a large, rusty metal arbour, called the Dome! Members of the Hardy Plant Society. A large selection of unusual plants for sale.

51 THE GARDEN HOUSE
5 Warleigh Road, Brighton, BN1 4NT. Bridgette Saunders & Graham Lee, 07729 037182, contact@gardenhousebrighton.co.uk, www.gardenhousebrighton.co.uk. *1½ m N of Brighton Pier, Garden House is 1st L after Xrds, past the Open Market. Paid street parking. London Road stn nearby. Buses 26 & 46 stopping at Bromley Rd.* **Fri 27, Sun 29 Mar (12-6). Adm £6, chd free. Home-made teas. Visits also by arrangement 16 Mar to 31 Oct for groups of 10 to 20.**
One of Brighton's secret gardens. We aim to provide year-round interest with trees, shrubs, herbaceous borders and annuals, fruit and vegetables, two glasshouses, a pond and rockery. A friendly garden, always changing with a touch of magic to delight visitors, above all it is a slice of the country in the midst of a bustling city. Plants for sale.

52 ♦ GREAT DIXTER HOUSE, GARDENS & NURSERIES
Northiam, TN31 6PH. Great Dixter Charitable Trust, 01797 253107, www.greatdixter.co.uk. *8m N of Rye. Off A28 in Northiam, follow brown signs.* **For opening times and information, please phone or visit garden website.**
A vibrant, daring, and immersive garden with a C15 house restored by Sir Edwin Lutyens. Leading the way in ornamental gardening, gardening for biodiversity, and horticultural education. Created by the great gardener and garden writer Christopher Lloyd, OBE, VMH. Please see garden website for accessibility information.

53 GROVELANDS
Wineham Lane, Wineham, Henfield, BN5 9AW. Mrs Amanda Houston. *8m SW Haywards Heath. From Haywards Heath: Take A272 W for approx 6m, then L into Wineham Ln. House 1¾ m on L, after The Royal Oak pub. 3m NE Henfield: N on A281, R onto B2116 Wheatsheaf Rd, L into Wineham Ln. House ½ m on R.* **Sat 23, Sun 24 May (10-4.30). Adm £8, chd free. Tea, coffee & cake.**
A South Downs view welcomes you to this rural garden set in over an acre in the hamlet of Wineham. Created and developed by local landscape designer Sue McLaughlin and the owners, it is designed to delight throughout the seasons. Features inc mixed borders, mature shrubs and orchard. A vegetable garden with a greenhouse and a pond hides behind a tall, clipped hornbeam hedge.

54 HAMMERWOOD HOUSE
Iping, Midhurst, GU29 0PF. Mr & Mrs M Lakin. *3m W of Midhurst. Take A272 from Midhurst. Approx 2m outside Midhurst, turn R for Iping. Over bridge, uphill to a grassy junction, then turn R. From A3, take exit for Liphook, & follow B2070. Turn L for Milland & Iping.* **Sun 10 May (1-5). Adm £7, chd free. Home-made teas.**
A large south facing garden with many mature shrubs, inc camellias, rhododendrons, and azaleas. An arboretum with a variety of flowering and fruit trees. Old yew and beech hedges give a certain amount of formality to this traditional English garden. Tea on the terrace is a must, with the most beautiful view of the South Downs. For the more energetic, there is a woodland walk. Partial wheelchair access as garden is set on a slope.

55 16 HARDY DRIVE
Eastbourne, BN23 6ED. Deb Cornford. *Near the Sovereign Centre. Between Sovereign & Langley r'abouts. Going N turn R into Beatty Rd, in 300yds turn R into Hardy Dr.* **Sun 28 June (1-5). Combined adm with 36 Jellicoe Close £5, chd free. Tea, coffee & home-made cakes.**
A small coastal town garden, made private by strategic planting and plenty of work. Filled with perennials, shrubs and climbers to give privacy and colour. Central to the garden is a magnificent 37 yr old Canary palm. The garden is well designed with lots of interest. An excellent example of what can be accomplished in a small garden, resulting in an oasis of peacefulness and calm! Lovely home-made cakes accompanied by a cup of tea or coffee awaits you!

GROUP OPENING

56 HELLINGLY PARISH TRAIL
What3words app: forks.standing.snowstorm. From A267 turn into B2104 & immed L into village, follow signs to gardens. Parking opp church green & in field by Brook Cottage & Cuckoo Trail. All gardens within walking distance. **Sun 7 June (11-5). Combined adm £8, chd free. Lunch & home-made teas at Brook Cottage. Ice-creams at Globe Place.**

BROAD VIEW
Church Road, BN27 4EX. Gill Riches.

BROOK COTTAGE
Mill Lane, BN27 4HD. Dr Colin Tourle MBE & Mrs Jane Tourle.

GLOBE COTTAGE
Mill Lane, BN27 4EY. Veronica Lee.

GLOBE PLACE
Mill Lane, BN27 4EY. Emma & Simon Freedman.

MAY HOUSE
7 The Martlets, BN27 4FA. Lynda & David Stewart.

POND COTTAGE
Mill Lane, BN27 4EY. Gill Nichols.

PRIORS COTTAGE
6 Church Path, BN27 4EZ.
Pat Booth.

Seven gardens are opening in the delightful Sussex village of Hellingly. Visitors can enjoy a pretty walled cottage garden with a summerhouse and sunny terrace. A garden entered via a bridge over a large pond, perfect for wildlife, with countryside views. There's also a charming cottage garden overlooking the C12 Church of St Peter and St Paul. Another garden, located in the heart of the village, is extensive and still in development, with beautiful trees and roses, with ice creams for sale. On the other side of the village, a unique garden, where lunches and teas will be served, incorporates the River Cuckmere, a sluice gate, and a lush mix of perennials and mature trees. On the outskirts, an inspiring new-build garden offers areas for sun and shade, climbers, and fruit trees, all amid the sounds of trickling water. Tickets and maps available on the green near the church, at May House, and Brook Cottage. The historic church will also be open. Wheelchair access to some gardens. Dogs on short leads.

57 ◆ HERSTMONCEUX CASTLE ESTATE
Wartling Road, Hailsham, BN27 1RN. Bader College, Queen's University (Canada), 01323 833816, bc.events@queensu.ca, www.herstmonceux-castle.com. *9m NE of Eastbourne. Located between Herstmonceux & Pevensey on Wartling Rd. From Herstmonceux take A271 towards Bexhill. Turn R after Windmill Hill. If using SatNav enter Wartling Rd instead of postcode.* **For NGS: Wed 22 July (10-6). Adm £12, chd £6.50. Light refreshments in our farm shop. For other opening times and information, please phone, email or visit garden website.**
The Herstmonceux Castle Estate has formal gardens, woodland trails, meadows and lakes set around a majestic C15 moated castle. The gardens and grounds first opened for the NGS in 1927. Partial wheelchair access to formal gardens. A map showing an accessible route around the gardens is available from the ticket office.

Selhurst Park

GROUP OPENING

58 HERSTMONCEUX PARISH TRAIL

3m E of Hailsham. Follow yellow NGS signs. Tickets & maps available at each garden. Ticket covers all gardens. Please note: this is not a walking trail. **Sun 28 June (11-5). Combined adm £7, chd free. Home-made teas at Hill House (12-5). Teas (12-5) & BBQ lunch (12-2) at The Windmill.**

FLITTERBROOK FLOWER FARM
West End, BN27 4NZ. Georgina Bollen, www.flitterbrookflowerfarm.co.uk.

HILL HOUSE
Maureen Madden & Terry Harland. (See separate entry)

KERPSES
Trolliloes Lane, Cowbeech, BN27 4JG. Lynn & Peter Maguire.

MERRIE HARRIERS BARN
Cowbeech, BN27 4JQ. Lee Henderson.

THE WINDMILL
BN27 4RT. Windmill Hill Windmill Trust, windmillhillwindmill.org.

Five gardens, inc a historic windmill. In Cowbeech, there are two gardens: Merrie Harriers Barn is a garden with sweeping lawn and open countryside, colourful herbaceous planting, and a large pond with seating areas to enjoy the view. Kerpses is a delightful mix of mature trees, shrubs, herbaceous borders, a vegetable garden, ponds, and a meadow. Flitterbrook Flower Farm in Herstmonceux has an impressive collection of flowers grown for the retail market. Hill House in Windmill Hill has abundant roses, trees, shrubs, and varied perennials, along with a greenhouse and a wildlife pond with water lilies. There are plenty of seating areas to sit, reflect, and enjoy tea. The historic Windmill is well worth a visit, where you can enjoy a BBQ lunch or tea.

59 ◆ HIGH BEECHES WOODLAND AND WATER GARDEN

High Beeches Lane, Handcross, Haywards Heath, RH17 6HQ. High Beeches Gardens Conservation Trust, 01444 400589, gardens@highbeeches.com, www.highbeeches.com. 5m NW of Cuckfield. On B2110, 1m E of A23 at Handcross. **For NGS: Sun 7 June, Sun 27 Sept (1-5). Adm £12, chd £5. Tea, coffee & cake.** For other opening times and information, please phone, email or visit garden website.
25 acres of enchanting, landscaped woodland and water gardens, featuring spring daffodils, bluebells and azalea walks, many rare and beautiful plants, an ancient wildflower meadow and glorious autumn colours. Picnic area. National Collection of Stewartias.

60 ◆ HIGHDOWN GARDENS

33 Highdown Rise, Littlehampton Road, Goring-by-Sea, Worthing, BN12 6FB. Highdown Tower Garden & Pleasure Ground Trust, highdown.gardens@adur-worthing.gov.uk, www.highdowngardens.co.uk. What3words app: quiet.stages.camera. Off the A259 Littlehampton Rd heading E towards Worthing. Turn L up Highdown Rise. Nearest train stn: Goring-by-Sea. **For NGS: Wed 11, Thur 12 Feb (10-4.30); Wed 29, Thur 30 Apr (10-7). Adm by donation.** For other opening times and information, please email or visit garden website.
Highdown Gardens were created by Sir Frederick Stern. They are home to rare plants and trees, many grown from seed collected by Wilson, Farrer and Kingdon-Ward. A fully equipped glasshouse enables the propagation of this National Plant Collection. A visitor centre shares stories of the plants and people behind the gardens. An accessible path leads to a sensory garden with a secret sea view. Highdown is also offering Snowdrop Identification tours on 11 and 12 Feb and Peony Identification tours on 29 and 30 April (not for NGS), for more information and booking, see garden website. Accessible top pathway and lift to visitor centre, see garden website accessibility page for full details.

61 HIGHLANDS

Etchingwood Lane, Framfield, Uckfield, TN22 5SA. Matthew Johnson, Head Gardener. 1½ m E of Uckfield. Leave Uckfield on B2102 (Framfield Rd). Bear L onto Sandy Ln. Turn L at Xrds with Etchingwood Ln. Entrance via field gate in 100 metres on R. Do not use postcode for SatNav, use Highlands. **Sat 6 June (10-4.30). Adm £9, chd free. Pre-booking essential, please visit www.ngs.org.uk for information & booking. Home-made teas.**
An 8 acre garden set around a house with C15 origins (not open), amid pasture and woodland. Intensively gardened beds near the house inc hot and pink beds and a white garden, are kept vibrant through waves of annuals planted through the perennials. These give way to meadow, orchard, ponds and woodland plantings.

62 HILL HOUSE

Windmill Hill, Herstmonceux, BN27 4RU. Maureen Madden & Terry Harland. 4m NE of Hailsham. Opp Windmill Hill PO. Parking for about 6 cars; additional parking can be found in adjacent streets. **Sun 5 July (12-5). Adm £5, chd free. Home-made teas. Opening with Herstmonceux Parish Trail on Sun 28 June.**
10 yrs ago, the garden consisted of lawn and a pond. The pond now is a wildlife pond with water lilies. The garden is divided into three sections by a pergola and two arches with climbing roses and honeysuckle. Trees, shrubs, and as many perennials as the flower beds can hold have been planted, and roses abound in the rose bed. It's a garden that's easy to walk around, with plenty of seating areas to sit and reflect. Wheelchair access through side gate. No steps in main garden, but steps (not steep) at end of garden leading to the greenhouse and vegetable patch.

63 4 HILLSIDE COTTAGES

Downs Road, West Stoke, Chichester, PO18 9BL. Heather & Chris Lock, 07876 227933, candhlock@gmail.com. 3m NW of Chichester. From A286 at Lavant, head W for 1½ m, nr Kingley Vale. **Sun 24 May, Sun 7 June, Sun 19 July, Sun 16 Aug (2-5). Adm £5, chd free. Home-made teas. Visits also by arrangement 24 May to 16 Aug.**
In a rural setting, this stunning garden is densely planted with mixed borders and shrubs. It features a large collection of roses, clematis, fuchsias, and dahlias, creating a profusion of colour and scent in a well maintained

SUSSEX

garden. Please visit www.ngs.org.uk for pop-up openings in June, July, and August. Please note: there are seven steps to access the garden.

64 HOLLY HOUSE
Beaconsfield Road, Chelwood Gate, Haywards Heath, RH17 7LF. Mrs Deirdre Birchill, 01825 740484, db@hollyhousebnb.co.uk, www.hollyhousebnb.co.uk. *7m E of Haywards Heath. From Nutley village on the A22, turn off at Hathi Restaurant, signed Chelwood Gate 2m. Chelwood Gate Village Hall is on R; Holly House is opp.* **Sat 15, Sun 16 Aug (2-5). Adm £7, chd free. Home-made teas. Visits also by arrangement 10 May to 30 Aug.**
An acre of English garden providing views and cameos of plants and trees round every corner with many different areas giving constant interest. A fish pond and a wildlife pond beside a grassy area with many shrubs and flower beds. Among the trees and winding paths there is a cottage garden which is a profusion of colour and peace. Exhibition of paintings and cards by owner. Garden accessible by wheelchair in good weather, though it is not easy.

65 HOLLYMOUNT
Burnt Oak Road, High Hurstwood, Uckfield, TN22 4AE. Jonathan Hughes-Morgan, 07968 848418, jonnyhughesmorgan@gmail.com. *Exactly halfway between Uckfield & Crowborough, just off the A26. From A26 S of Crowborough or A272 between Uckfield & Buxted, follow signs to High Hurstwood. From N approx 2m down Chillies Ln, take 1st L. From S, 1½m up Hurstwood Rd, take 3rd R. Garden is ½m on L.* **Sun 31 May, Sun 28 June, Sun 26 July (12-5). Adm £8, chd free. Home-made teas. Visits also by arrangement 30 Apr to 30 Sept for groups of 10+.**
A beautiful 7 acre garden centred around water. Streams run down the hill, through waterfalls into ponds flanked by luscious planting. A huge variety of plants creates interest from May through to Oct. Thick jungle borders flank the top garden, while the beds further down are filled with rhododendrons, acers, irises, day lilies, and roses. There are pigs, alpacas, chickens, and ducks. The secret garden is a must-see.

66 36 JELLICOE CLOSE
Eastbourne, BN23 6DD. Amanda Haines. *E of Eastbourne, nr the Marina. Between Sovereign & Langley r'abouts. Going N turn R into Beatty Rd, in 300yds turn R into Hardy Dr, then 1st L into Jellicoe Cl. No.36 is at the top on RHS.* **Sun 28 June (1-5). Combined adm with 16 Hardy Drive £5, chd free.**
An artist's and plantswoman's garden, with colourful mixed borders of perennials, exotics, and overflowing pots. The meandering paths, well-planted borders, and seating areas demonstrate what can be achieved in a smaller garden. It was described by The Sunday Times as a 'sub-tropical paradise.' The owner's pottery studio is open for viewing and sales, and there is an excellent variety of plants for sale.

67 JUDY'S COTTAGE GARDEN
33 The Plantation, Worthing, BN13 2AE. Mrs Judy Gordon. *Salvington. A24 meets A27 at Offington r'about, turn into Offington Ln, 1st R into The Plantation.* **Sat 25 Apr, Sat 27 June, Sat 5 Sept (10.30-3). Adm £5, chd free. Home-made teas.**
A beautiful medium sized cottage garden with something of interest all year-round. The garden has several mature trees creating a feeling of seclusion. The informal beds contain a mixture of shrubs, perennials, cottage garden plants and spring bulbs. There are little hidden areas to enjoy, a small fish pond and other water features. There is also a raised, pretty log cabin overlooking the garden.

68 ♦ KING JOHN'S NURSERY
Sheepstreet Lane, Etchingham, TN19 7AZ. Harry Cunningham, 01580 819220, harry@kingjohnsnursery.co.uk, www.kingjohnsnursery.co.uk. *2m W of Hurst Green. Off A265 nr Etchingham. From Burwash, turn L before Etchingham Church, from Hurst Green, turn R after church, into Church Ln, which leads into Sheepstreet Ln after ½m, then turn L after 1m.* **For NGS: Sat 21 Mar, Sat 23 May, Sat 27 June, Sat 12 Sept (10-5). Adm £5, chd free. Light refreshments.** For other opening times and information, please phone, email or visit garden website.

Garden developed alongside the nursery, a romantic pond garden, gravel garden, long border, meadows and cutting garden. A garden of wild flowers and full of ideas. The garden is mostly flat, with stepped areas generally accessible from other parts of the garden. Disabled WC.

69 KITCHENHAM FARM
Kitchenham Road, Ashburnham, Battle, TN33 9NP. Amanda & Monty Worssam. *5m S of Battle. S of Ashburnham Place from A271 Herstmonceux to Bexhill road, take L turn 500 metres after Boreham St. Kitchenham Farm is 500 metres on L.* **Sat 6 June, Sat 8 Aug (2-5). Adm £6, chd free. Home-made teas.**
1 acre country house garden set amongst traditional farm buildings with stunning views over the Sussex countryside. Series of borders around the house and Oast House (not open). Lawns and mixed herbaceous borders inc roses and delphiniums. A ha-ha separates the garden from the fields and sheep. The garden adjoins a working farm. Wheelchair access to the garden. One step to WC.

70 ♦ KNEPP CASTLE
The Apple Store, nr Knepp Castle, off Pound Lane, West Grinstead, Horsham, RH13 8LJ. Sir Charles & Lady Burrell, www.knepp.co.uk. *8m S of Horsham. Entrance off Pound Ln, following NGS signage. Parking in field nr the garden (200 metre walk).* **For NGS: Sat 6 June (10-5). Adm £15, chd free. Pre-booking essential, please visit www.ngs.org.uk for information & booking. Timed slots at 10am, 11.30am & 2pm.** For other opening times and information, please visit garden website.
The Walled Garden at Knepp has been transformed into a garden for biodiversity. With designers Tom Stuart-Smith and James Hitchmough, we have applied some of the principles we've learned from rewilding the wider landscape to this small, confined space to create a mosaic of dynamic habitats for wildlife. The croquet lawn is now a riot of humps and hollows, hosting almost 1000 species of plants. Lunches available at Knepp Wilding Kitchen, RH13 8NQ.

71 KOTIMAKI

Tottingworth Park, Broad Oak, Heathfield, TN21 8UH. Mark Riches & John Jenkins. *Lane off A265 between Broad Oak & Burwash Common. The lane is located 1m outside Broad Oak, nr Swife Ln, on opp side of A265. A telegraph pole next to lane marked with NGS sign, then follow NGS signs down lane. SatNav may direct you to the wrong lane.* **Sat 25 Apr, Sat 16 May, Sat 6 June, Sat 18 July, Sat 5 Sept, Sat 3 Oct (10-12). Adm £12, chd £6. Pre-booking essential, please visit www.ngs.org.uk for information & booking. Tea, coffee & cake inc. Talk about the garden at 10:30am.**

Large, creatively planted gardens featuring a long double border enclosed by yew hedging, along with a rockery, shade garden, exotic garden, pot garden, wildflower meadows, and a kitchen garden. Emphasis on continuity of interest through imaginative mixed plantings of shrubs, climbers, perennials, bulbs, annuals, and self-sowers. The garden also inc a varied collection of wisterias, trained as shrubs, on trellis work, and on a pergola.

72 LEGSHEATH FARM

Legsheath Lane, nr Forest Row, RH19 4JN. Mr & Mrs Michael Neal, 07973 679538, legsheath@btinternet.com. *4m S of East Grinstead. 2m W of Forest Row. 1m S of Weirwood Reservoir.* **Visits by arrangement. Home-made teas. Donation to Holy Trinity Church, Forest Row.**

Legsheath was first mentioned in Duchy of Lancaster records in 1545. It was associated with the role of Master of the Ashdown Forest. Set high in the Weald, with far-reaching views of East Grinstead and Weirwood Reservoir. The garden covers 11 acres, with a spring-fed stream feeding ponds. There is a magnificent davidia, rare shrubs, embothrium, and many different varieties of meconopsis and abutilon.

73 LIMEKILN FARM

Chalvington Road, Chalvington, Hailsham, BN27 3TA. Dr J Hester & Mr M Royle. *10m N of Eastbourne. Nr Hailsham. Turn S off A22 at Golden Cross & follow the Chalvington Rd for 1m. The entrance has white gates on LHS. Disabled parking spaces close to house, other parking 100 metres further along road.* **Sat 18, Sun 19 Apr, Sat 29, Sun 30 Aug (2-5). Adm £8, chd free. Home-made teas in the Oast House. Talk at 3pm.**

The garden was designed in the 1930s when the house was owned by Charles Stewart Taylor, MP for Eastbourne. It has not changed in basic layout since then. The planting aims to reflect the age of the C17 property (not open) and original garden design. The house and garden are mentioned in Virginia Woolf's diaries of 1929, depicting a particular charm and peace that still exists today. Flint walls enclose the main lawn, herbaceous borders and rose garden. Nepeta lined courtyard. Informal pond and specimen trees inc a very ancient oak. Many spring flowers and tree blossom. New prairie style garden with grasses and perennials. Physic garden with talk at 3pm about medicinal plants. Mostly flat access with two steps up to main lawn and herbaceous borders.

74 NEW LITTLE GATE FLOWERS

Little Gate Farm, Horseshoe Lane, Beckley, Rye, TN31 6RZ. Hannah Whitham, www.littlegate.org.uk. *Between A28 at Broad Oak & Beckley village. On A28, ⅓m N of Broad Oak Xrds, follow Furnace Ln. After 1¼m, turn L into Horseshoe Ln. Horseshoe Ln can be followed from Beckley village, about 2m. What3words app: facelift.quarrel.removes.* **Tue 23 June, Thur 23 July (11-3). Adm £6, chd free. Pre-booking essential, please visit www.ngs.org.uk for information & booking. Timed slots at 11am & 1.30pm. Light refreshments.**

Based at Little Gate Farm in Beckley near Rye, Little Gate Flowers is a cut flower garden with a difference! Working with autistic and learning disabled adults we run a Social Enterprise teaching transferable work skills ready for paid employment. Our trainees grow a mix of annual and perennials in this colourful, quirky and unique working garden which is a haven for social change and inclusion. Uneven ground in some areas and partial wheelchair access to certain parts of the garden.

75 LORDINGTON HOUSE

Lordington, Chichester, PO18 9DX. Mr & Mrs John Hamilton, 01243 375862, hamiltonjanda@btinternet.com. *7m W of Chichester. On W side of B2146, ½m S of Walderton, 6m S of South Harting. Enter through white railings on bend.* **Sat 6, Sun 7 June (2-5). Adm £7, chd free. Tea, coffee & cake. Visits also by arrangement 8 June to 5 Sept for groups of up to 30. Optional guided tour.**

Early C17 house (not open) and walled gardens in South Downs National Park. Clipped yew, lawns, borders and fine views. Informal sunken garden. Vegetables, fruit and poultry in kitchen garden. Over 100 roses planted since 2008. Trees both mature and young. Lime avenue planted in 1973 to replace elms. Wildflower meadow outside walls, accessible from garden. Gardens overlook Ems Valley, farmland and wooded slopes of South Downs, all in AONB. Wheelchair access is possible but may be difficult with gravel paths, uneven paving, and slopes. WC facilities are limited. No disabled WC.

76 LUCTONS

North Lane, West Hoathly, East Grinstead, RH19 4PP. Drs Hans & Ingrid Sethi, 07787 523510, ingrid@sethis.co.uk. *4m SW of East Grinstead, 6m E of Crawley. In the centre of West Hoathly village, nr the church, The Cat Inn, & Priest House. Car parks in the village.* **Sat 27, Sun 28 June (1.30-4.30). Adm £6, chd free. Open nearby The Priest House. Home-made teas at Priest House on 27 June & Luctons on 28 June. Visits also by arrangement June to Aug for groups of 10 to 30.**

'A garden with everything', 'lots of unusual plants', and 'stunning herbaceous borders' are comments from NGS and overseas garden tour visitors. Set within 2 acres, this Gertrude Jekyll style garden features herbaceous borders, a wildflower orchard, swathes of spotted orchids, a pond, roses, vegetables, a herb garden, vine house, greenhouses, croquet lawn, and shrubberies. WC facilities.

77 LYNWOOD
Holland Road, Steyning, BN44 3GJ. Debbie Chalmers. 6m NE of Worthing. Exit r'about on A283 at S end of Steyning bypass into Clays Hill Rd. 1st R into Goring Rd, 4th L into Holland Rd. What3words app: surpasses.winner.evolution. **Sun 5, Fri 10 July (1-5). Combined adm with Saffrons £8, chd free. Tea, coffee & cake at Saffrons.** Visits also by arrangement 15 June to 31 July for groups of 8 to 30. To book, contact Tim Melton at Saffrons (07850 343516).
Medium sized garden with three distinct areas around an Edwardian house. Recently replanted, the garden features colour-themed mixed borders of perennials and annuals, inc flowers for cutting, eating, and scent. Two lawned areas and two pot-filled patios, plus a cedarwood greenhouse where many of the plants are raised from seed. Wheelchair access over gravel and grass.

78 MALTHOUSE FARM
Streat Lane, Streat, Hassocks, BN6 8SA. Richard & Helen Keys, 01273 890356, helen.k.keys@btinternet.com. 2m SE of Burgess Hill. From r'about between B2113 & B2112, take Folders Ln & Middleton Common Ln E (away from Burgess Hill). After 1m, turn R into Streat Ln; the garden is ½m on R. Please park carefully as signed. **Visits by arrangement 1 June to 20 Sept for groups of 10 to 40. Home-made teas.**
A rural 5 acre garden with stunning views of the South Downs. The garden is divided into separate rooms, featuring a box parterre and borders with glass sculpture, herbaceous and shrub borders, and a mixed border for seasonal colour. An orchard with wild flowers leads to partitioned areas with grass walks, a snail mound, birch maze, and willow tunnel. A wildlife farm pond is surrounded by planting. Partial wheelchair access across grassed areas, though some gravel paths and steps may limit access to certain parts.

79 MANOR OF DEAN
Tillington, Petworth, GU28 9AP. Mr & Mrs James Mitford, 07887 992349, emma@mitford.uk.com. 3m W of Petworth, just off A272. Car park accessed via New Rd. What3words app: unique.only.novels. **Sun 1 Feb (2-4); Sun 22 Mar, Sun 26 Apr (2-5). Adm £6, chd free. Tea, coffee & cake.** Visits also by arrangement 2 Feb to 19 June for groups of 20+.
Approx 3 acres of traditional English garden with extensive views of the South Downs. Herbaceous borders, early spring bulbs, bluebell woodland walk, walled kitchen garden with fruit, vegetables and cutting flowers. NB under long term programme of restoration, some parts of the garden may be affected.

GROUP OPENING

80 MAYFIELD GARDENS
Mayfield, TN20 6AB. 10m S of Tunbridge Wells. Turn off A267 into Mayfield. Parking in the village, TN20 6BE. A detailed map available at each garden. **Sat 1, Sun 2 Aug (11-5). Combined adm £7, chd free. Home-made teas.**

AIRLIE COTTAGE
Robert & Claire Montagu.

THE OAST
Mike & Tessa Crowe.
(See separate entry)

SOUTH STREET PLOTS
Val Buddle.

Mayfield is a beautiful Wealden village with tearooms, an old pub and many interesting historical connections. The gardens to visit are all within walking distance of the village centre. They vary in size and style with a wide range of shrubs, herbaceous and annual planting and inc wildflower meadows, fruit and vegetable plots, mature trees and colourful pot displays. There are far-reaching, panoramic views over the beautiful High Weald.

81 MEADOW FARM
Blackgate Lane, Pulborough, RH20 1DF. Charlie & Ness Langdale, nesslangdale@icloud.com. 3m N of Pulborough. From Pulborough take A29 N. Turn L into Blackgate Ln signed to Toat. After 1½m, pass Scrase Farms sign & keep going straight. Parking signed on R. What3words app: bordering.vowel.youngest. **Sun 17 May (1.30-5.30).**
Adm £7, chd free. Home-made teas. Visits also by arrangement 18 May to 25 June for groups of 12 to 25. Adm inc home-made teas.
A 2 acre garden with wildflower meadows, designed and planted from scratch by the current owners. Features inc colour themed beds, double borders, a formal pond, gravel garden, and white garden. A pleached hornbeam avenue with views of the Sussex countryside. The walled garden provides fruit, cut flowers, and vegetables. There is an orchard with a hazelnut walk, a wildlife swimming pond with a bog garden, and a newly planted prairie bed.

82 MITCHMERE FARM
Stoughton, Chichester, PO18 9JW. Neil & Sue Edden, 02392 631456, sue@mitchmere.co.uk. 5½m NW of Chichester. Turn off the B2146 at Walderton towards Stoughton. The farm is ¾m on L, ¼m beyond the turning to Upmarden. Please do not park on verge, follow signs for parking. **Visits by arrangement 10 Feb to 31 Oct. Adm £6, chd free. Min group charge £60. Tea, coffee & biscuits.**
A 1½ acre garden in a lovely downland position, with a stream flowing through most years when the Winterbourne rises. The garden features an orchard and unusual trees and shrubs, providing year-round colour and interest. Large areas of bulbs, inc special snowdrops, a wildlife pond, a 'ruin' with a mosaic floor, terraces enclosed by yew hedges, and summer colour with roses and clematis. Optional 10 min walk: down the long field beside the river, across the sleeper bridge, take the path through the copse with snowdrops, up the steps into the new wood, then into the meadow and back to the garden. Wellies advisable. Dogs on short leads. Wheelchair access over gravel and grass.

The National Garden Scheme donated £3,875,596 to our nursing and health beneficiaries from money raised at gardens open in 2025.

83 MOUNTFIELD COURT
Robertsbridge, TN32 5JP. Mr & Mrs Simon Fraser. *3m N of Battle. On the A21 London-Hastings road, approx ½ m NW of Johns Cross.* Sun 10 May (2-5). Adm £7, chd free. Home-made teas.
3 acre wild woodland garden with bluebell lined walkways through exceptional rhododendrons, azaleas, camellias, and other flowering shrubs. Fine trees and outstanding views. Stunning paved herb garden.

84 NEWTIMBER PLACE
Newtimber, BN6 9BU. Andrew & Carol Clay, 07795 346974, andy@newtimberholidaycottages.co.uk, www.newtimberplace.co.uk. *7m N of Brighton. From A23, take A281 towards Henfield. After approx ½ m, turn R at small Xrds signed Newtimber. Go down Church Ln; garden is on L at end of lane.* Sun 26 Apr (2-5.30). Adm £7, chd free. Home-made teas.
Beautiful C17 moated house (not open). Gardens and woods full of bulbs and wild flowers in spring. Herbaceous border and lawns. Moat flanked by water plants. Mature trees, wild garden, and ducks. Wheelchair access across lawn to parts of garden, tearoom and WC.

GROUP OPENING

85 NEW NUTBOURNE VILLAGE GARDENS
The Street, Nutbourne, Pulborough, RH20 2HE. *2m E of Pulborough. Take A283 from Pulborough towards Storrington. Turn L onto West Chiltington Rd, then L onto Nutbourne Rd. Go along The Street, pass The Rising Sun pub. Follow parking directions by a volunteer.* Fri 19, Sat 20 June (11-5). Combined adm £10, chd free. Home-made teas.

NEW HOBBS
Mr Brian & Mrs Lynne White.

NEW MILL HOUSE
Robert & Jane Allison.

THE OLD MANOR
Mr Frank & Mrs Erica Riddle, 01798 813484, edra263@icloud.com.
Visits also by arrangement May to Oct for groups of 5 to 10. Home-made teas inc.

SHORTS FARM
Sarah & John Browne.

Nutbourne is a beautiful, tranquil, and friendly hamlet near Pulborough. It boasts a thousand years of history dating back before the Norman conquest and has spectacular views across the South Downs. This is a wonderful opportunity to meander through the village and visit four very different gardens, all within a short walking distance of each other. The gardens can be visited in any order, and tickets will be on sale at a central location. Hobbs is a small cottage style garden with a fabulous wisteria covered pergola. The Old Manor is a fascinating Victorian allotment style kitchen garden. Next, wander down to the Mill House and explore the contrast of rose and herb gardens, with an enchanting mill stream running along the bottom of the garden. Finally, enjoy a drink on the lawn beneath the Indian bean tree at the beautiful Shorts Farm, a classic cottage style country garden.

Bourne Botanicals

SUSSEX

86 ◆ NYMANS
Staplefield Road, Handcross, RH17 6EB. National Trust, 01444 405250, nymans@nationaltrust.org.uk, www.nationaltrust.org.uk/nymans. *4m S of Crawley. On B2114 at Handcross signed off M23/A23 London-Brighton road. Metrobus 271 & 273 stop nearby.* **For NGS: Sat 21 Mar (10-5). Adm £23, chd £11.50. Adm subject to change. Light refreshments.** For other opening times and information, please phone, email or visit garden website. Donation to Plant Heritage.
One of NT's premier gardens with rare and unusual plant collections of national significance. In spring see blossom, bulbs and a stunning collection of subtly fragranced magnolias. The comfortable yet elegant house, a partial ruin, reflects the personalities of the creative Messel family. Some level pathways. See full access statement on Nymans website.

87 OAKLANDS FARM
Hooklands Lane, Shipley, Horsham, RH13 8PX. Zsa & Stephen Roggendorff, 01403 741270, zedrog@roggendorff.co.uk. *S of Shipley village. Off the A272 towards Shipley, R at Countryman pub, follow yellow signs. Or N of A24 Ashington, off Billingshurst Rd, 1st R signed Shipley, garden 2m up the lane.* **Wed 24 June (11-5). Adm £6, chd free. Home-made teas. Visits also by arrangement 4 Apr to 5 Sept for groups of 5 to 25.**
Country garden designed by Nigel Philips in 2010. Oak lined drive leading to the house (not open) and farm opens out to an enclosed courtyard with pleached hornbeam and yew. The herbaceous borders are colourful throughout the year. Vegetable garden with raised beds and greenhouse with white peach and vine. Wild meadow leading to orchard and views across the fields, full of sheep and poultry. Mature trees. Wheelchair access over gravel and brick paths, large lawn area and grassy paths.

88 THE OAST
Fletching Street, Mayfield, TN20 6TN. Mike & Tessa Crowe. *10m S of Tunbridge Wells. Turn off A267 into Mayfield. Parking along East St & in the village public car parks. Please do not park outside The Oast in Fletching St as it is very narrow.* **Sat 18, Sun 19 Apr (11-5). Adm £6, chd free. Home-made teas. Opening with Mayfield Gardens on Sat 1, Sun 2 Aug.**
A 1 acre garden in an idyllic High Weald setting with a beautiful view. Year-round interest, with highlights in spring and late summer/autumn. In April, over 4000 tulips and other spring bulbs bloom, while later in summer, dahlias, salvias, grasses, and asters are interplanted with colourful annuals. A ½ acre wildflower meadow with old roses and an orchard. Woodland-edge walk, wildlife pond, vegetables and soft fruit. Quality homegrown plants for sale.

89 OCKLYNGE MANOR
Mill Road, Eastbourne, BN21 2PG. Wendy & David Dugdill, 01323 734121, ocklyngemanor@hotmail.com, www.ocklyngemanor.co.uk. *Take A22 (Willingdon Rd) towards Old Town, then turn L into Mill Rd by the Hurst Arms pub.* **Visits by arrangement 14 Apr to 14 May for groups of up to 20. Garden tours on Tues & Suns, (2–3.30) only.**
This beautiful garden is a hidden oasis behind an ancient flint wall, with both sunny and shaded places to sit. Informal and tranquil, this ½ acre chalk garden features architectural and unusual trees, with rhododendrons, azaleas, and acers in raised beds. Evolving over 20 yrs, it is maintained by the owners. The Georgian house (not open) was once the home of Mabel Lucie Attwell. Wheelchair access via a short gravel path before entering the garden, with a brick path running around the perimeter.

90 OFFHAM HOUSE
The Street, Offham, Lewes, BN7 3QE. Mr & Mrs P Carminger & Mr S Goodman. *2m N of Lewes on A275. Offham House is on the main road (A275) through Offham between the filling station & Blacksmiths Arms. On road parking, off the main road, down by the church. Limited parking at the house.* **Sun 7 June (1-5). Adm £8, chd free. Home-made teas.**
A romantic garden featuring fountains, flowering trees, and an established arboretum. Stroll along the double herbaceous border and the long peony bed, explore the herb and walled kitchen gardens with glasshouses and cold frames, then relax with tea and home-made cakes. Pelargoniums and other plants available to buy.

91 OLD ERRINGHAM COTTAGE
Steyning Road, Shoreham-By-Sea, BN43 5FD. Fiona & Martin Phillips, 07884 398704, fiona.h.phillips@btinternet.com. *2m N of Shoreham-By-Sea. From A27 Shoreham flyover, take A283 towards Steyning. Take 2nd R into private lane. Follow sharp LH-bend at the top; house on L.* **Visits by arrangement 28 May to 30 June for groups of 10 to 25. Home-made teas.**
Plantsman's garden set high on the South Downs with panoramic views overlooking the Adur valley. 1⅓ acres with stream bed and ponds, formal and informal planting areas with over 600 varieties of plants. Very productive fruit and vegetable garden with glasshouses. Many plants grown from seed and coastal climate gives success with tender plants.

92 THE OLD RECTORY, PULBOROUGH
Old Rectory Lane, Pulborough, RH20 2AF. Claire Roscoe. *From A29, 200 metres from r'about to A283, enter Old Rectory Ln (Chequers Hotel on the corner). Pass the signboard listing all houses in the lane. The Old Rectory is the 1st house on your L.* **Sat 13, Sun 14 June (11-5). Adm £7, chd free. Home-made teas.**
A formal front garden with a sunken centrepiece and rose and flower beds, approx ½ acre in size. The large rear garden consists of a small wood, a croquet lawn with beds, a natural swimming pond, and a large summerhouse. There is also a small orchard and meadow, along with a walled area by the pickleball court. Many interesting trees, inc a 500 yr old sweet chestnut.

93 THE OLD RECTORY, WARBLETON

Kingsley Hill, Warbleton, TN21 9PT. Lord Barker Of Battle & George Prassas, www.instagram.com/theoldrectorygarden. *5m S of Heathfield town centre. What3words app: glow.funky.ritual takes you to the property's white front gate. Parking in the lane, or by the church a 9 min walk away. Please be considerate of neighbours' access.* **Thur 23 Apr (10-3). Adm £10, chd free. Pre-booking essential, please visit www.ngs.org.uk for information & booking. Tea, coffee & cake.**
Nestled in the High Weald AONB, The Old Rectory garden was re-imagined by renowned designer Arne Maynard. His vision blends formal elements like yew and beech topiary, a knot garden, and herbaceous borders with wild flowers and rambling roses. A stream separates the formal garden from an orchard interplanted with roses and wild flowers. Over 10,000 tulips bloom in spring. Other features inc cutting garden, pond, copse, meadows, pot displays, and gravel garden.

94 THE OLD VICARAGE

The Street, Washington, RH20 4AS. Lady Walters, 07766 761926, meryl.walters@me.com, www.instagram.com/the_old_vicarage_washington. *2½ m E of Storrington, 4m W of Steyning. From Washington r'about on A24, take A283 to Steyning. After 500yds, turn R to Washington. Pass Frankland Arms pub, then turn R to St Mary's Church. Car park available, but no large coaches.* **Every Thur 5 Feb to 1 Oct (10-4). Adm £10, chd free. Pre-booking essential, please visit www.ngs.org.uk for information & booking. Self service light refreshments on Thurs (cash only) & picnics welcome. Mon 6 Apr, Mon 31 Aug (10-5). Adm £10, chd free. Home-made teas. Purchase ticket in advance or at the gate on the day. Visits also by arrangement 16 Mar to 1 Oct for groups of 10 to 30. No private group visits on Thursdays.**
A truly creative garden, nurtured over 35 yrs to become a visitor favourite. Spanning 3½ acres, it features formal topiary, seasonal borders, a contemporary water sculpture, an Italianate gazebo, specimen and mature trees, a Japanese garden with waterfall and tea house, a large copse with a stream, a stumpery and treehouse, and a kitchen garden with fruit trees. With 4000 tulips and bulbs planted annually, the garden also opens in Feb for snowdrops. WC available. Wheelchair access to front garden; rear garden is on a slope.

95 OLD WELL COTTAGE

High Street, Angmering, Littlehampton, BN16 4AG. Mr N Waters. *Situated nr Angmering Manor Hotel & almost adjacent to the top of Weavers Hill in the High St. Look for the 'mushroom' shape tree! On road parking only, please be mindful of residents.* **Sun 5 July (11-4). Adm £5, chd free. Tea, coffee & cake.**
A ⅓ acre walled garden surrounding a C16–C18 cottage (not open) in Angmering Conservation Area. Formal areas, perennial borders and topiary create structure, with splendid holm oak and bay, espalier apple trees and a small kitchen garden. Rich in purples, whites and pinks, this is a harmonious mix of formality, productivity and seasonal colour.

96 THE ORCHARD

Dyke Lane, Poynings, Brighton, BN45 7AA. Ms Nigs Digby. *Take the A281 off the A23 towards Henfield. About 0.6m along, you will see signs for Poynings. Continue into the village & look for signs to the garden. Street parking only. Very short drive to the other garden opening.* **Thur 11 June (11-5). Combined adm with Woodlands £7, chd free. Pre-booking essential, please visit www.ngs.org.uk for information & booking. Home-made teas. Two hour timed slots at 11am, 1pm & 3pm.**
This is a new garden, planted in autumn 2023 following the completion of a new build on site. At the front, there is soft prairie style planting, while around the back you will find a rambling, informal cottage garden with a cutting bed, soft fruit, vegetables, and a small natural pond. The garden enjoys stunning views of the South Downs.

97 ORCHARD COTTAGE

Boars Head Road, Boarshead, Crowborough, TN6 3GR. Jane & Ray Collins, 07910 521573, collinsjane1@hotmail.co.uk. *6m S of Tunbridge Wells, off A26. Turn off A26 signed Boarshead. At T-junction, do not follow SatNav. Instead, turn L down dead end. Orchard Cottage is at the bottom of the hill on LHS.* **Fri 29, Sat 30, Sun 31 May (10-4). Adm £7, chd free. Tea, coffee & cake. Visits also by arrangement 1 Apr to 12 June.**
A mature 1½ acre plantaholic's garden with a large variety of trees, shrubs, perennials, and bulbs, many unusual. Gardened organically, with mainly colour themed beds planted informally. A small woodland, meadow, and deep pond to encourage wildlife, along with a kitchen garden with raised beds. Member of the Hardy Plant Society. Classic cars will be on display on Saturday. Access via gravel drive with wide, gently sloping grass paths suitable for wheelchairs and mobility scooters. Drop-off in drive by prior arrangement.

98 NEW 25 PARKLANDS ROAD

Chichester, PO19 3DX. Mrs Fiona Bell Currie, 07773 529031, fionabellcurrie@gmail.com. *From West St to r'about with The Crate & Apple pub on R, continue down Westgate, then turn R into Parklands Rd.* **Sat 25, Sun 26 Apr, Sat 18, Sun 19 July (10.30-5). Combined adm with 53 Cedar Drive £7, chd free. Tea, coffee & cake. Visits also by arrangement 18 Apr to 7 July for groups of up to 6.**
Developed from rough grass in 2020, this exuberant gravel garden was created by its artist owner. Contrasting foliage, less common plants, and effervescent flowers linger long. Many plants self-seed, increasing a natural look. This west facing town garden is loosely divided into three sections, with a fine greenhouse housing fascinating cacti and succulents.

99 PARSONAGE FARM

Kirdford, nr Billingshurst, RH14 0NH. David & Victoria Thomas. *5m NE of Petworth. Located between Petworth & Wisborough Green in the village of Kirdford. Opp side of the road from the turn to Plaistow. Use postcode*

SUSSEX

RH14 0NG to reach Plaistow turning. **Fri 12 June, Sun 6 Sept (2-6). Adm £10, chd free. Home-made teas.** Major garden in beautiful setting developed over 30 yrs with fruit theme and many unusual plants. Formally laid out on grand scale with long vistas. C18 walled garden with borders in apricot, orange, scarlet and crimson. Topiary walk, pleached lime allée, tulip tree avenue, rose borders and vegetable garden with trained fruit. Turf amphitheatre, autumn shrubbery, yew cloisters and jungle walk. Wheelchair access to the whole garden with one step that can be avoided. Accessible WC.

100 PEELERS RETREAT
70 Ford Road, Arundel, BN18 9EX. Tony & Lizzie Gilks. *1m S of Arundel. At Chichester r'about take exit to Ford & Bognor Regis onto Ford Rd. We are situated just before Maxwell Rd on the RHS.* **Sat 4, Sat 18, Tue 28 Apr, Sat 23, Tue 26 May, Sat 2, Sat 6, Tue 16 June, Tue 7, Sat 11, Tue 21 July (2-5). Adm £5, chd free. Home-made teas.**
This inspirational space is a delight with permanent gazebos and comfortable seating to sit and relax, enjoying delicious teas. When cold we light the fire for our guests. Interlocking beds packed with year-round colour and scent, shaded by specimen trees, inventive water features and a range of quirky woodland sculptures.

101 PEMBURY HOUSE
Ditchling Road, Clayton, BN6 9PH. Nick & Jane Baker, www.pemburyhouse.co.uk. *6m N of Brighton, off A23. No parking at house. Car park opp church on Underhill Ln off A273 (height restrictor). Follow signs across playing field to footpath to back gate. Good public transport. Use safety pedestrian refuges.* **Every Thur and Fri 12 Feb to 6 Mar (10.30-3.30). Adm £12, chd free. Home-made teas inc. Pre-booking essential, please visit www.ngs.org.uk for information & booking. Timed slots at 10.30am & 2pm.**
Depending on the vagaries of the season, hellebores and snowdrops are at their best in February and March. It is a country garden, tidy but not manicured. New borders and features. Winding paths give a choice of walks through 3 acres of garden, which is in and enjoys views of the South Downs National Park. Suitable footwear, macs and winter woollies advised. A German visitor observed 'this is the perfect woodland garden'. Year-round interest. Plants for sale. Cash only.

102 PENNS IN THE ROCKS
Groombridge, Tunbridge Wells, TN3 9PA. Mr & Mrs Hugh Gibson, 01892 864244, www.pennsintherocks.co.uk. *7m SW of Tunbridge Wells. On B2188 Groombridge to Crowborough road, just S of Xrd to Withyham. For SatNav use TN6 1UX which takes you to the white drive gates, through which you should enter the property.* **Sun 29 Mar, Sun 17 May, Sun 26 July (2-6). Adm £7.50, chd free. Home-made teas. Cash only on the day.** Visits also by arrangement Apr to July for groups of 10+.
A large garden with a spectacular outcrop of rocks, 140 million yrs old. The grounds inc a lake, C18 and C20 temples, and woods. Daffodils, bluebells, azaleas, and magnolias. An old walled garden with herbaceous borders, roses, and shrubs. A 1928 pool and pond gardens. Part C18 house (not open) once owned by William Penn of Pennsylvania. Restricted wheelchair access. No disabled WC.

103 1 PEST COTTAGE
Carron Lane, Midhurst, GU29 9LF. Jennifer Lewin. *W edge of Midhurst, behind Carron Lane Cemetery. Free parking at recreation ground at top of Carron Ln. Short walk along woodland track to garden, please follow signs.* **Fri 29 May (2-5); Sun 31 May (1-5). Adm £5, chd free.**
This edge of woodland architect's garden, of approx ¾ acre, sits on a sloping sandy site. Designed to support biodiversity, a series of outdoor spaces connected with informal paths through lightly managed areas, creates a secret world tucked into the surrounding common land. The chosen planting palette is being adapted in response to changing weather patterns. Exhibition of architect's projects.

104 PIGEON MEAD HOUSE
Earnley Manor Close, Earnley, Chichester, PO20 7JQ. Mr Adrian & Mrs Rachel Dadds. *5½m SE of Chichester. A 2 min walk from C13 Earnley Church & 5 min walk from RSPB Medmerry Reserve. What3words app: jots.gadget. toasted.* **Sat 16, Sun 17 May (11-4). Adm £6, chd free. Pre-booking essential, please visit www.ngs.org.uk for information & booking. Tea, coffee & cake.**
A ⅓ acre plot about ¾ mile from the coast. The south facing rear garden with a formal structure and informal mixed planting. Features inc a greenhouse, a formal lawn surrounded by beds and espaliered crab apples, a small labyrinth, and a shaded area. It's a family friendly space with places to sit and enjoy the garden. The front garden inc a wildlife pond, a small meadow area, and a lovely, established magnolia tree.

105 ♦ THE PRIEST HOUSE
North Lane, West Hoathly, RH19 4PP. Sussex Archaeological Society, 01342 810479, priest@sussexpast.co.uk, www.sussexpast.co.uk. *4m SW of East Grinstead, 6m E of Crawley. In the centre of West Hoathly village, nr the church & The Cat Inn. Car parks in the village.* **For NGS: Sat 23 May (10.30-5). Sat 27 June (10.30-5); Sun 28 June (12-5), open nearby Luctons. Adm £4, chd free. Home-made teas at Priest House on 23 May & 27 June, at Luctons on 28 June.** For other opening times and information, please phone, email or visit garden website.
A C15 timber framed farmhouse with a cottage garden on acid clay. A large collection of culinary and medicinal herbs in a small formal herb garden and mixed with perennials and shrubs in exuberant borders. Long established yew topiary and espalier apple trees provide structural elements. A traditional fernery and stumpery, recently enlarged with a small, secluded shrubbery and gravel garden. Be sure to visit the fascinating Priest House Museum, adm £1 for NGS visitors.

Shorts Farm, Nutbourne Village Gardens

106 9 PUTTOCK WAY
Billingshurst, RH14 9ZJ. Emma & Simon Parker. *7m SW of Horsham. From the Hilland r'about to the N of Billingshurst, head E along the A272 (Hilland Rd) & take the 1st R turning into the estate (Rhodes Way). Take 2nd R onto Puttock Way.* **Sun 24 May (11-4). Adm £5, chd free. Pre-booking essential, please visit www.ngs.org.uk for information & booking. Home-made teas.**

A very small, sloping, new build garden which has been transformed from bare heavy clay into a series of spaces with interesting hard landscaping features. An unexpected cacophony of architectural shapes and textures greets you as you walk through the gate, a true plant lover's paradise. This space shows what can be achieved in a short space of time through hard work and passion. Awarded gold for Best Pollinator Garden and Best Large Front Garden, and overall Pollinator Category winner at the 2025 Billingshurst in Bloom Front Garden competition.

107 NEW QUARRY WOOD FARM & TILSMORE VINEYARD
Newick Lane, Mayfield, TN20 6RQ. Richard Bysouth, Head Gardener. *2m S of A267 Mayfield r'about. 3m N of Heathfield. The driveway is off a sharp bend, approx halfway along Newick Ln. Follow the newly laid tarmac all the way to the black gates at the top. What3words app: obtain. views.learns.* **Sat 11 Apr (10.30-3.30). Adm £6, chd free. Sat 13 June (11-5). Adm £8, chd free. Home-made teas.**

A 2 acre organic garden set in a beautiful valley, surrounded by wildflower meadows and mature woodland. It features extensive spring bulbs and flowering shrubs, mixed herbaceous borders, and colourful pots. There is a Mediterranean garden, as well as vegetable and cut flower gardens with raised beds. Woodland walks, a vineyard, and an orchard. Wine tasting in the vineyard (not for NGS). Wheelchair access to most of the garden, with packed gravel paths and gentle slopes.

108 NEW RAPKYNS NURSERY
Street End Lane, Broad Oak, Heathfield, TN21 8UB. Morag Hockin. *From Broad Oak, Heathfield, turn into Street End Ln & drive for 2m. From Mayfield, turn into Fletching St, then R at the Rose & Crown & drive for 2m. Large gravel car park onsite. What3words app: cheese.purely.irrigated.* **Wed 13 May, Wed 9 Sept (11-4). Adm £15, chd free. Pre-booking essential, please visit www.ngs.org.uk for information & booking. Light refreshments inc.Two hour timed slots at 11am & 2pm.**

We have been growing plants in an idyllic country setting for over 30 yrs, and during that time have amassed an extensive range, inc a large collection of salvias. Join us for a talk about the nursery and discover more about how we grow and propagate our beautiful plants, with a chance to learn some of our secrets. There will also be an opportunity to ask questions about all things gardening.

109 ROSE COTTAGE
50 Wannock Lane, Willingdon, Eastbourne, BN20 9SD. Chris & Nick Ireland. *Between Eastbourne & Polegate on the A2270. From Eastbourne (A2270), turn L into Gorringe Valley Rd, at give way turn R. From Polegate, turn R into Gorringe Valley Rd.* **Sun 5 July (12.30-4.30). Adm £5, chd free.**
The 1930s cottage nestles at the foot of the South Downs, with the 1066 trail starting nearby. This beautiful west facing, 200ft by 55ft rear garden, has a wide selection of shrubs, herbaceous plants, perennials, and trees. There are two small fish ponds, a vegetable plot, and greenhouses. Little nooks and seating areas add interest, with a surprise at the end of the garden for any model railway enthusiast. Local cafés nearby.
❀

110 8 RUSHY MEAD
West Broyle, Chichester, PO19 3FW. Heather Millican, 07732 397756, heather.millican@btinternet.com. *1m N of Chichester. Off B2178 at r'about onto Drovers Ln, then R to High Meadow & L to Rushy Mead.* **Visits by arrangement 1 May to 15 Aug for groups of 6 to 20. Adm £7. Home-made teas.**
Created from scratch on a new build development, this space has been transformed into a haven for bees, butterflies, and birds. Once an uninspiring turfed area, it is now full of colour and interest. After attending a garden design course at nearby West Dean College, the owners created their own landscaping and planting plans. Within just three yrs, they have seen a remarkable transformation. No steps to access the garden. While some paths are shingle and may be difficult, most of the garden can be enjoyed from the paved patio.
♿ ❀ ☕))

111 RYMANS
Appledram Lane South, Apuldram, Chichester, PO20 7EG. Zarina Chatwin, rymans.garden@gmail.com. *1m S of Chichester. If coming from A27, exit at Fishbourne r'about & follow signs to Fishbourne. Take 1st L onto Appledram Lane South, the house is 1m S.* **Sat 11, Sun 12 Apr, Sun 14 June, Sun 13 Sept (2-5). Adm £8, chd free. Visits also by arrangement 11 Apr to 25 Sept for groups of 10 to 30.**
Walled and other gardens surround a C15 stone house (not open). Featuring bulbs, flowering shrubs, roses, ponds, a potager, and many unusual and rare trees and shrubs. In late spring, the wisterias are spectacular. Hybrid musk roses fill the walled garden in June, and in late summer, the garden is filled with dahlias, sedums, late roses, sages, and Japanese anemones.
🐕 ❀ ☕))

112 SAFFRONS
Holland Road, Steyning, BN44 3GJ. Tim Melton & Bernardean Carey, 07850 343516, tim.melton@btinternet.com, www.thetransplantedgardener.co.uk. *6m NE of Worthing. Exit r'about on A283 at S end of Steyning bypass into Clays Hill Rd. Take 1st R into Goring Rd, then 4th L into Holland Rd. Park on Goring Rd or Holland Rd.* **Sun 5, Fri 10 July (1-5). Combined adm with Lynwood £8, chd free. Home-made teas. Visits also by arrangement 15 June to 31 July for groups of 8 to 30. Combined visit with Lynwood may be possible.**
Planted with an artist's eye for contrast and complementary colours. Vibrant late summer flower beds filled with salvias, eryngiums, agapanthus, grasses, and lilies that attract bees and butterflies. A broad lawn is surrounded by borders containing maples, rhododendrons, hydrangeas, and mature trees, interspersed with ferns and grasses. The large fruit cage and vegetable beds comprise the productive area of the garden. Level garden with good access, except in very wet conditions.
♿ 🐕 ❀ ☕))

113 ♦ ST MARY'S HOUSE GARDENS
Bramber, BN44 3WE. Roger Linton & Peter Thorogood, 01903 816205, info@stmarysbramber.co.uk, www.stmarysbramber.co.uk. *1m E of Steyning. 10m NW of Brighton in Bramber village, off A283.* **For NGS: Fri 26, Sat 27 June (2-6). Adm £11, chd free. Light refreshments.** For other opening times and information, please phone, email or visit garden website.
5 acres inc formal topiary, a large prehistoric *Ginkgo biloba*, and a magnificent *Magnolia grandiflora* around an enchanting timber-framed medieval house (not open for NGS). Victorian Secret Gardens inc a splendid 140ft fruit wall with pineapple pits, Terracotta Garden, Jubilee Rose Garden, King's Garden, and a circular Poetry Garden. Woodland walk and a Landscape Water Garden. In the heart of the South Downs National Park. WC facilities. Wheelchair access with level ground throughout.
♿ ❀ 🚌 ☕))

114 SANDHILL FARM HOUSE
Nyewood Road, Rogate, Petersfield, GU31 5HU. Rosemary Alexander. *4m SE of Petersfield. From A272 Xrds in Rogate, take road S signed to Nyewood & Harting. Follow road for approx 1m, over a small bridge. Sandhill Farm House is on R, just after the cattle grid.* **Sun 15 Feb (12-4). Adm £10, chd free. Home-made teas.**
The front and rear gardens are broken up into garden rooms, inc a small kitchen garden. The front garden features a small woodland area planted with early spring flowering shrubs, ferns, and bulbs. There is also a white and green garden, a large leaf border, and a terraced area. The rear garden has rose borders, a small decorative vegetable garden, a red border, and a grasses border. Snowdrop day on Sun 15 Feb. Home of author and principal of The English Gardening School. Dogs on leads.
🐕 ❀ D ☕))

310,000 people are cared for each year who are approaching the end of life or diagnosed with a terminal illness through the hospice network supported by National Garden Scheme funding.

Forest Ridge

GROUP OPENING

115 SEAFORD GARDENS
Signed from the A259, gardens are located N and S of this road. Free parking outside most gardens, and several accessible by bus from Brighton & Eastbourne, or by train to Seaford. NB Not a walking trail although some gardens are close to each other. **Sun 31 May (12-5). Combined adm £6, chd free. Sun 14 June (12-5). Combined adm £8, chd free. Sun 28 June (12-5). Combined adm £7, chd free. Sun 5 July (12-5). Combined adm £8, chd free. Tea, coffee & cake.**

BURFORD
Cuckmere Road, BN25 4DE.
Chris Kilsby.
Open on Sun 14, Sun 28 June

34 CHYNGTON ROAD
BN25 4HP. Maggie Wearmouth & Richard Morland.
Open on Sun 31 May, Sun 14 June

5 CLEMENTINE AVENUE
BN25 2UU. Joanne Davis.
Open on Sun 5 July

101 CLEMENTINE AVENUE
BN25 2XG. John & Ness Kelly.
Open on Sun 5 July

COSY COTTAGE
69 Firle Road, BN25 2JA. Ernie & Carol Arnold, 07763 196343, ernie.whitecrane@gmail.com, www.facebook.com/CosyCottage69Garden.
Open on Sun 31 May, Sun 5 July
Visits also by arrangement 17 Apr to 28 June for groups of up to 16.

CUPANI GARDEN
8 Sandgate Close, BN25 3LL.
Dr Denis Jones & Ms Aideen Jones OBE, 01323 899452, sweetpeasa52@gmail.com, www.cupanigarden.com.
Open on Sun 14, Sun 28 June, Sun 5 July
Visits also by arrangement 1 June to 15 July for groups of 6 to 14. Not a group of 6? Please call, we may be able to fit you in.

8 DOWNS ROAD
BN25 4QL.
Mr Phil & Mrs Julie Avery.
Open on Sun 14, Sun 28 June

LAVENDER COTTAGE
69 Steyne Road, BN25 1QH.
Christina & Steve Machan.
Open on Sun 31 May, Sun 14 June

MADEHURST
67 Firle Road, BN25 2JA.
Martin & Palo.
Open on Sun 28 June, Sun 5 July

129 PRINCESS DRIVE
BN25 2QT. Sue & Darrel Topp.
Open on Sun 31 May, Sun 5 July

SEAFORD ALLOTMENTS
Sutton Drove, BN25 3NQ.
Peter Sudell.
Open on Sun 5 July

SEAFORD COMMUNITY GARDEN
East Street, BN25 1AD.
Seaford Community Garden, renaturingseaford.org/seaford-community-garden.
Open on Sun 14 June

53 SOUTHDOWN ROAD
BN25 4PG.
Eileen & Julian Counsell.
Open on Sun 14, Sun 28 June

WHITEHOUSE
130 Firle Road, BN25 2JD.
Jayne & Fred Bass.
Open on Sun 31 May, Sun 28 June

Discover fourteen beautiful gardens across Seaford on four dates! 31 May (5 gardens), 14 June (7 gardens), 28 June (6 gardens), 5 July (7 gardens), all open from 12–5pm. Each garden offers its own unique charm, with a huge range of different planting styles, making this a truly inspiring group of gardens to visit. Enjoy tea, ice cream, plants, and artwork for sale at various gardens. Tickets and maps are available from any participating garden on the day. For full garden descriptions and details, visit www.ngs.org.uk.

116 SEDGWICK PARK HOUSE
Sedgwick Park, Horsham, RH13 6QQ. Clare Davison, 01403 734930, clare@sedgwickpark.com, www.sedgwickpark.co.uk. *1m S of Horsham off A281. A281 to Cowfold. Pass Hillier Garden Center on R, then 1st R into Sedgwick Ln. At end of lane, enter north gates of Sedgwick Park, or west gate via Broadwater Ln from Copsale or Southwater, off A24.* **Visits by arrangement Apr to June for groups of 10+. Home-made teas.**
Set in the grounds of Grade II listed Ernest George mansion (not open), there are amazing views of South Downs, Chanctonbury Ring and Lancing College. Formal gardens by Harold Peto featuring 20 interlocking ponds, impressive water garden known as The White Sea. Large Horsham stone terraces and lawns look out onto clipped yew hedging and specimen trees. Herbaceous area and turf labyrinth. Some areas have been left to nature. Garden has uneven paving, which can be slippery when wet, as well as unfenced ponds and swimming pool.

117 SELHURST PARK
Halnaker, Chichester, PO18 0LZ. Richard & Sarah Green, 01243 839310, sjg@selhurstparkhouse.co.uk. *8m S of Petworth. 4m N of Chichester on A285.* **Visits by arrangement 25 May to 9 Aug for groups of 10 to 30. Adm £8, chd free. Home-made teas.**
Come and explore the varied gardens surrounding a beautiful Georgian flint house (not open), approached by a chestnut avenue. The flint walled garden has a mature 160ft herbaceous border with unusual planting, along with rose, hellebore, and hydrangea beds. Pool garden with exotic palms and grasses is divided from a formal knot and herb garden by espaliered apples. Kitchen and walled fruit garden. Wheelchair access to walled garden, partial access to other areas.

70 inpatients and their families are being supported at the newly opened Horatio's Garden Northern Ireland, thanks to the National Garden Scheme donations.

118 SHALFORD HOUSE
Square Drive, Kingsley Green, GU27 3LW. Mr Paul Morrow & Mr Robert Beard, Paulmorrow@talktalk.net. *2m S of Haslemere. A sharp narrow turning directly off from A286 (please take care). Heading S, Square Dr is at brow of hill to the L. Turn L again after ¼ m & follow road to R at bottom of hill.* **Sun 24 May, Sun 2 Aug (12-5). Adm £10, chd free. Pre-booking essential, please visit www.ngs. org.uk for information & booking. Home-made teas. Visits also by arrangement 18 May to 31 Aug for groups of 40 to 60.**
A garden designer and plantsman's garden, set in 40 acres, with 10 acres of well maintained gardens created over 30 yrs. Featuring various herbaceous borders, ponds, a waterfall lake, and a 120 metre rill. Walled garden with large Alitex greenhouse with interesting plants inc acers, hostas, *Cornus kousa* and hydrangeas, all within a beautiful setting. A further 30 acres with arboretum and lake is perfect for picnics. Flat gravel areas with York stone terrace around the house with access to the main sloping lawns via gently sloping paths. Disabled WC.
& ⛾ 🚗 »)

119 SHEPHERDS COTTAGE
Milberry Lane, Stoughton, Chichester, PO18 9JJ. Jackie & Alan Sherling, 07795 388047, milberrylane@gmail.com, www. instagram.com/drjackieblackman. *9⅛ m NW Chichester. Off the B2146, in the next village after Walderton. Shepherds Cottage is nr the telephone box & beside St Mary's Church. No parking in the lane beside the house.* **Visits by arrangement Apr to Aug for groups of 10 to 35. Adm £15, chd free. Adm inc home-made teas.**
A compact terraced garden that borrows the landscape of Kingley Vale in the South Downs. The south facing flint stone cottage (not open) is surrounded by a Purbeck stone terrace and numerous individually planted and styled seating areas throughout the garden to enjoy the views. A small orchard underplanted with meadow, lawns, topiary yew hedges, Amelanchier, Cercis, and drifts of wind grass provides structure and year-round interest. The garden features many novel design ideas and unusual perennial combinations, all suitable for a small space.
✿ D ⛾

120 SIENNA WOOD
Coombe Hill Road, East Grinstead, RH19 4LY. Belinda & Brian Quarendon, 07970 707015, belinda222@hotmail.com. *1m W of East Grinstead. Off B2110 East Grinstead to Turners Hill. Garden is ½ m down Coombe Hill Rd on L.* **Sun 10 May (1-4.30). Adm £7, chd free. Tea, coffee & cake. Visits also by arrangement Apr to Sept for groups of 15+.**
Explore our beautiful 4½ acre garden, picturesque lakeside walk and 6 acre ancient woodland. Start at the herbaceous borders surrounding the croquet lawn, through the formal rose garden to the lawns and summer borders stopping at the new Italian terrace, through the arboretum to the lake and waterfall and back past the exotic border, orchard and vegetable garden. Many unusual trees and shrubs. Possible sighting of wild deer inc white deer. Many interesting statues. Partial wheelchair access to many parts of the garden.
& ⛾ »)

121 SKYSCAPE
46 Ainsworth Avenue, Ovingdean, Brighton, BN2 7BG. Lorna & John Davies. *From Brighton take A259 coast road E, passing Roedean School on L. Take 1st L at r'about to Greenways & 2nd R into Ainsworth Ave. Skyscape at the top on R. No. 52 bus runs hourly to Ainsworth Ave.* **Sat 30, Sun 31 May (1-5). Adm £5, chd free. Tea, coffee & cake.**
A 250ft south facing rear garden on a sloping site with fantastic views of the South Downs and the sea. Garden created by the owners over the past 13 yrs and features an orchard, flower beds, wildlife ponds, and planting with bees and wildlife in mind. Full access to the site via a purpose-built sloping path (not suitable for mobility scooters).
& 🐕 ✿ 🚗 ⛾

122 SOUTH GRANGE
Quickbourne Lane, Northiam, Rye, TN31 6QY. Linda & Michael Belton, 01797 252984, belton.northiam@gmail.com. *Between A268 & A28, approx ½ m E of Northiam. From Northiam centre follow Beales Ln into Quickbourne Ln, or Quickbourne Ln leaves A286 approx ½ m S of A28 & A286 junction. Disabled parking at front of house.* **Visits by arrangement 1 Mar to 18 Oct. No limits on group sizes, large groups welcome. Adm £10, chd free. Tea, coffee & cake. Confirm**

refreshments at time of booking. Hardy Plant Society members' garden, tended with wildlife in mind for year-round interest. A wide variety of often unusual trees, shrubs, and fruit trees in a meadow setting, along with a wildwood, herbaceous borders, vegetables, and a wildlife pond. We try to maintain nectar and pollen supplies and varied habitats for most of the creatures that we share the garden with, hoping that this variety will keep the garden in good heart. Home propagated plants for sale. Wheelchair access over hard paths through much of the garden, with steps up to patio and WC.
& ✿ 🚗 🏠 ⛾

123 STANLEY FARM
Highfield Lane, Liphook, GU30 7LW. Bill & Emma Mills. *For SatNav please use GU30 7LN which takes you to Highfield Ln & then follow NGS signs. Track to Stanley Farm is 1m.* **Sun 3 May (12-5). Adm £6, chd free. Home-made teas.**
1 acre garden created over the last 15 yrs around an old West Sussex farmhouse (not open), sitting in the midst of its own fields and woods. The formal garden inc a kitchen garden with heated glasshouse, orchard, espaliered wall trained fruit, lawn with ha-ha and cutting garden. A motley assortment of animals inc sheep, donkeys, chickens, ducks and geese. Bluebells flourish in the woods, so feel free to bring dogs and a picnic, and take a walk after visiting the gardens. Wheelchair access via a ramp to view main part of the garden. Difficult access to woods due to muddy, uneven ground.
& 🐕 ✿ ⛾ »)

GROUP OPENING

124 STEYNING GARDENS
4m N of Shoreham by Sea. Tickets can be purchased at each garden & visited in any order. They will be signed on the day & detailed directions available on website. On-street parking. **Sat 20, Sun 21 June (10.30-5). Combined adm £10, chd free. Home-made teas at Nightingale House.**

BRAMBLETYE
25 Maudlyn Park Way, BN44 3PT. Nicola & Paul Middleton.

NIGHTINGALE HOUSE
Twittenside, BN44 3TW. Lynne Broome.

SUSSEX

15 PENLANDS RISE
BN44 3PJ. Patsy Walton.

Steyning is a lively market town on the edge of the South Downs, home to many artists and crafts people. The three gardens open are all very different. Brambletye is a south facing garden designed with a prairie effect to attract birds and pollinators. It is planted with bulbs, shrubs, herbaceous perennials, and roses, and a small sunken area with raised beds for vegetables and herbs. Nightingale House has a recently designed cottage style garden with both perennials and annuals. There is an attractive greenhouse and a bespoke metal screen covered in roses and clematis. 15 Penlands Rise is a small cottage garden that has evolved into a series of borders and island beds, with narrow paths in between. There are roses, clematis, many salvias and perennials, and a collection of over 100 pots, some with hydrangeas, but most filled with a colourful mix of annuals and tender plants.

25 SULLINGTON OLD RECTORY
Sullington Lane, Storrington, Pulborough, RH20 4AE. Jack Bryant, Head Gardener, jack@sullingtonoldrectory.com. *Travelling S on A24, take 3rd exit at Washington r'about. Continue to Xrds on A283 for Sullington Ln & Water Ln. Turn L onto Sullington Ln; the garden is located at the top.* **Tue 7, Wed 8 July (9.30-5). Adm £12, chd free. Pre-booking essential, please visit www.ngs.org.uk for information & booking. Home-made teas. Two hour timed slots at 9.30am,12pm & 2.30pm.** With a backdrop of stunning views of the South Downs, the naturalistic style of this beautiful country garden sits perfectly into the surrounding landscape. This rarely opened garden inc a potager, orchard, herb garden, mature trees and shrubs, a South African themed border, newly extended large perennial borders, a profusion of grasses, and experimental planting in the moist meadows. A range of home-made cakes, biscuits and light snacks, along with fresh coffee, a variety of teas, and home-made apple juice. The Head Gardener will be available for any Q&As. Wheelchair access to most areas.

26 SWALLOW LODGE
St Leonard's Park, Horsham, RH13 6EG. Kathryn Shackleton. *E side of Horsham. What3words app: officials.spirit.chill. Swallow Lodge is on R at the very end of Hampers Ln.* **Sat 6, Sat 13 June (2-6). Adm £5, chd free. Home-made teas.** Small rural and charming garden surrounded by fields, focusing on roses and delphiniums with a large cottage border and vegetable garden.

27 THAKEHAM PLACE FARM
The Street, Thakeham, Pulborough, RH20 3EP. Mr & Mrs T Binnington. *3m N of Storrington. The farm is at the E end of The Street, where it turns into Crays Ln. Follow signs down farm drive to Thakeham Place.* **Thur 23, Sun 26 July (2-5). Combined adm with Cumberland House £10, chd free. Home-made teas.** Set in the middle of a working dairy farm, the garden has evolved over the last 35 yrs. Taking advantage of its sunny position on free draining greensand, the borders are full of sun loving plants and grasses with a more formal area surrounding the farmhouse (not open). In 2024 a new natural pond was created in the wilder area of the garden to encourage wildlife.

28 TIDEBROOK MANOR
Tidebrook, Wadhurst, TN5 6PD. Edward Flint, Head Gardener. *Between Wadhurst & Mayfield. From Wadhurst: Take B2100 towards Mark Cross, L at Best Beech Ln, past church on R, then take drive on L. From Mayfield: Take Coggins Mill Ln for 2½ m to Tidebrook, then take drive on R. Please Note: Narrow access; traffic control may be in place, please be patient.* **Sun 20 Sept (11-4). Adm £8, chd free.** A beautiful 4 acre country garden developed over the last 20 yrs with outstanding views of the Sussex countryside. In the Arts and Crafts tradition, the garden features large mixed borders, intimate courtyards, meadows, hydrangea walk, kitchen garden with raised beds, a willow plat and a wild woodland garden. A lively and stimulating garden throughout the year, with a real emphasis on autumn interest from annuals, grasses, meadow bulbs and late season perennials.

29 TOWN PLACE
Ketches Lane, Freshfield, Sheffield Park, RH17 7NR. Anthony & Maggie McGrath, 01825 790221, mcgrathsussex@hotmail.com, www.townplacegarden.org.uk. *5m E of Haywards Heath. From A275, turn W at Sheffield Green onto Ketches Ln toward Lindfield. Town Place is 1¾ m on L.* **Sun 7, Sun 14, Wed 17, Wed 24, Sun 28 June, Sun 5 July (2-5). Adm £10, chd free.** Visits also by arrangement 1 June to 4 July for groups of 15+. A stunning 3 acre garden with a growing international reputation for the quality of its design, planting and gardening. Set round a C17 Sussex farmhouse (not open), the garden has over 400 roses, herbaceous borders, herb garden, white garden, topiary inspired by the sculptures of Henry Moore, an 800 yr old oak, potager, and a unique ruined Priory Church and Cloisters in hornbeam. Sorry, no dogs allowed, and no refreshments available. Picnics welcome. Although there are steps on-site, all areas can be viewed from a wheelchair.

30 TUPPENNY BARN
Main Road, Southbourne, PO10 8EZ. Maggie Haynes, www.tuppennybarn.co.uk. *6m W of Chichester, 1m E of Emsworth. On Main Rd A259, corner of Tuppenny Ln. Disabled parking.* **Sat 15 Aug (12-4). Adm £6, chd free. Light refreshments. Food intolerances & allergies catered for.** An iconic, organic smallholding used as an outdoor classroom to teach children about the environment, sustainability and healthy food. 2½ acres featuring a wildlife pond, an orchard with heritage top fruit varieties, two solar polytunnels, fruit cages, and raised beds for vegetables, herbs and cut flowers. Willow provides natural arches and wind breaks. Bug hotel and beehives support vital pollinators. Most of the grounds are accessible for wheelchairs, though undulated areas are more difficult.

131 WADHURST PARK
Riseden Road, Wadhurst, TN5 6NT. Nicky Browne, wadhurstpark.co.uk. *6m SE of Tunbridge Wells. Turn R along Mayfield Ln, off B2099 at NW end of Wadhurst. Then turn L onto Tidebrook Rd, & L again onto Riseden Rd.* **Fri 12, Sat 13 June** (10-4). Adm £7, chd free. Home-made teas inc vegan & gluten-free cakes.

Naturalistic gardens designed by Tom Stuart-Smith, recently updated by Hortus Collective. A C19 site within an 800 hectare estate, managed organically to enhance wildlife, cultural heritage and beauty. The gardens invite the wider landscape in with native woodland flora, meadows and hedgerows, framing views to hills and lake. We strive to garden with a greater respect for the natural world. Features inc restored Victorian orangery, naturalistic gardens planted with mainly native species, meadows, potager and brownfield site. Due to uneven paths, please wear sensible shoes. Sorry no dogs. Wheelchair access to main garden features. Some uneven surfaces over grass, cobbles and steps.

132 WANDERDOWN
2 Wanderdown Way, Ovingdean, Brighton, BN2 7BX. John Conlon & Chris Judge. *Located in Ovingdean village, E of Brighton, approx 5m from the city centre. By car A259 (E) from Brighton, or B2123 (Falmer Rd) from the A27. Bus No. 52 from Brighton alighting Ovingdean Stores, or No. 2 from Brighton alighting Ovingdean Rd.* **Sat 18, Sun 19 July** (12-5). Adm £5, chd free. Tea, coffee & cake.

Created almost from scratch six seasons ago, Wanderdown is adjacent to the South Downs National Park with wonderful views of the Downs to the sea. Primarily a coastal chalk garden, the planting reflects the location with cultivated and wild flowers set against a backdrop of subtropical plants and garden sculptures.

133 5 WHITEMANS CLOSE
Cuckfield, Haywards Heath, RH17 5DE. Shirley Carman-Martin. *1m N of Cuckfield. On B2036 signed Balcombe, Whitemans Cl is 250yds from r'about on LHS. No parking in Whitemans Cl. Buses stop at Whitemans Green, where there is also a large free car park.* **Mon 26, Wed 28, Fri 30 Jan, Mon 2, Wed 4, Tue 10, Thur 12, Sat 14, Tue 17, Wed 18 Feb** (10.30-3.30). Adm £9, chd free. Pre-booking essential, please phone 01444 473520 or email shirley.carmanmartin@ngs.org.uk for information & booking. Home-made teas inc.

This garden shows that winter need not be dull as there is much to see and enjoy in the depths of winter. Here in my garden I have collected many single and double snowdrops, hellebores, bulbs and other winter treasures, some not widely known. As it is a sheltered garden, yes, there are flowers to enjoy in January and early February. Come and see the enormous *Daphne bholua* that scents the garden for weeks on end at this time of year. Sorry, no WC.

Cumberland House

SUSSEX 541

134 WHITHURST PARK
Plaistow Road, Kirdford, nr Billingshurst, RH14 0JW. Mr Richard Taylor & Mr Rick Englert, www.whithurst.com. *7m NW of Billingshurst. Take A272 to Wisborough Green, follow signs to Kirdford, turn R at 1st T-junction through village, then turn R again onto Plaistow Rd. Look for white Whithurst Park sign at roadside.* **Sun 21 June (10-5). Adm £7, chd free. Home-made teas.**
14 yr old walled kitchen garden with many espaliered fruit trees. Herb beds, vegetable beds, flower borders and cutting beds. Central greenhouse and potting shed with interesting support buildings behind the wall inc extensive compost area close to beehives. Sustainability through permaculture principles. Plants for sale in courtyard at the front of house, with teas available on the adjacent lawn. The open lawns around the walled garden and house are ideal for picnics, and woodland footpaths surround the house and lake. Wheelchair access via ramp over 10cm step onto garden paths.

GROUP OPENING

135 WINCHELSEA'S SECRET GARDENS
Winchelsea, TN36 4EN. *2m W of Rye, 8m E of Hastings. Follow A259 from Rye or Hastings. Follow signs for central card payment point or pay cash at any garden gate.* **Sat 18 July (11-5). Combined adm £10, chd free. Home-made teas at Winchelsea New Hall.**

NEW **1 BARRACK SQUARE**
John & Lyn Davidson.

NEW **2 BARRACK SQUARE**
Terry & Penny Fuller.

NEW **CLEVELAND HOUSE**
Nicholas Shiren & Eric Rowe.

CLEVELAND PLACE
Sally & Graham Rhodda.

GILES POINT
Ant Parker & Tom Ashmore.

KENT CLOSE COMMUNAL GARDEN
Kent Close Residents.

KING'S LEAP
Philip Kent.

LOOKOUT COTTAGE
Anne Magee & David Richards.

2 MARITEAU HOUSE
Mary & Roger Tidyman.

THE ORCHARDS
Brenda & Ralph Courtenay.

PERITEAU HOUSE
Simon & Maxine Kemp.

1 ST GILES CLOSE
Charlotte & Paul Praeger.

WHITE COTTAGE
Caroline & Jeremy Naylor.

Old favourites return with new owners, and the group expands to thirteen mostly cottage style gardens large and small. Set in the historic Cinque Port of Winchelsea with its picturesque townscape and long unspoiled sea and country views. Explore the town with its magnificent church. Check winchelsea.com for the latest information on tours of our famous medieval cellars. If you are bringing a coach please contact ryeview@gmail.com, 01797 226524. Eight of the thirteen gardens are wheelchair accessible, either fully or partially.

136 WOODLANDS
The Street, Fulking, Henfield, BN5 9LT. Carolyn & Roger Loveless. *What3words app: defrost.massaging.slot. Ignore SatNav. On E edge of Fulking, on sharp RH bend from Poynings. Black & white chevrons on wall, walk down bridlepath. Limited street parking. Off-road parking from Poynings & nr Shepherd & Dog pub, a short walk away. Very short drive to The Orchard.* **Thur 11 June (11-5). Combined adm with The Orchard £7, chd free. Pre-booking essential, please visit www.ngs.org.uk for information & booking. Home-made teas at The Orchard. Two hour timed slots at 11am, 1pm & 3pm.**
Quiet location at the foot of the South Downs, with lovely views and easy access for walking. East, south, and west facing garden with beautiful herbaceous perennials, alliums, shrubs, roses, and grasses set against lawn, gravel, and decking. A small pond, along with sculptures of a tree owl and glass flowers.

137 WYCH WARREN HOUSE
Wych Warren, Forest Row, RH18 5LF. Colin King & Mary Franck. *1m S of Forest Row. Proceed S on A22, track turning on L, 100 metres past 45mph warning triangle sign. Or 1m N of Wych Cross T-lights, track turning on R. Go 400 metres across golf course till the end.* **Thur 28 May (2-5). Adm £6, chd free. Tea, coffee & cake.**
6 acre garden in Ashdown Forest, AONB, much of it mixed woodland with a perimeter walk around property. A delightful and tranquil setting with plenty of space to roam, and various points of interest that provide a sensory and relaxing visit, ideal for forest bathing! Lovely stonework, specimen trees, three ponds, herbaceous borders, an exotic bed, a greenhouse, and always something new on the go. Plants for sale and a great range of chutney and jams. Dogs on leads and children welcome. Partial wheelchair access via tarmac track to the kitchen side gate.

78,000 people affected by cancer were reached by Maggie's centres supported by the National Garden Scheme over the last 12 months.

WARWICKSHIRE
& West Midlands

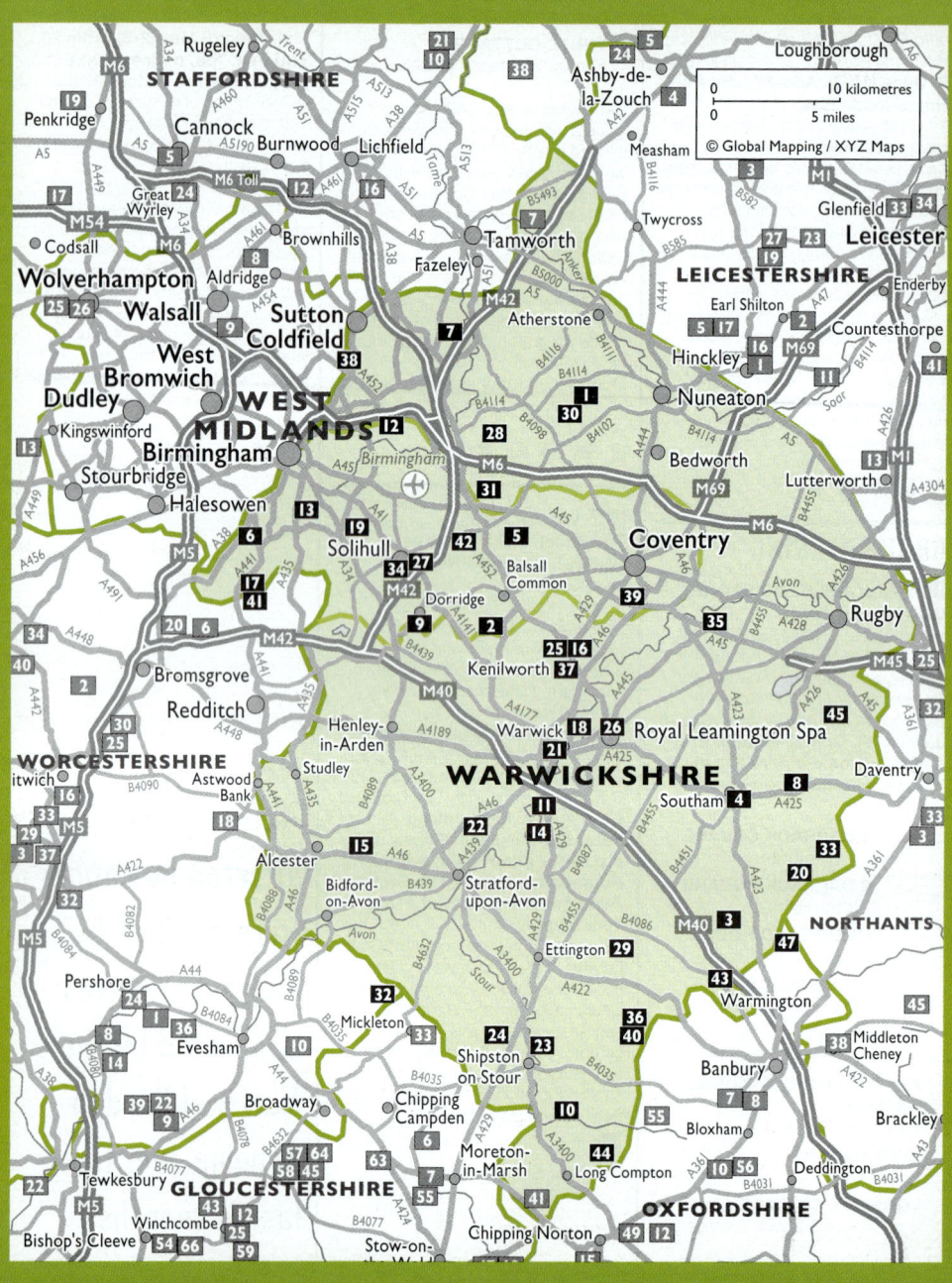

VOLUNTEERS

County Organiser
Liz Watson
01926 512307
liz.watson@ngs.org.uk

County Treasurer
Ian Roberts
01926 864181
ian.roberts@ngs.org.uk

Publicity
Lily Farrah
07545 560298
lily.farrah@ngs.org.uk

Social Media
Jenny Edwards
07884 177889
jenny.edwards@ngs.org.uk

Booklet Co-ordinator
Hazel Blenkinsop
07787 005290
hazel.blenkinsop@ngs.org.uk

Booklet Advertising
Hugh Thomas
01926 423063
hugh.thomas@ngs.org.uk

Photographer
Annie Casey 07555 448109
annie.casey@ngs.org.uk

Assistant County Organisers
Jane Cerone
01827 873205
jane.cerone@ngs.org.uk

Jane Redshaw
07803 234617
jane.redshaw@ngs.org.uk

Isobel Somers
07767 306673
ifas1010@aol.com

@WarwickshireNGS
@WarksNGS
@warwickshirengs

OPENING DATES

All entries subject to change.
For latest information check
www.ngs.org.uk

Extended openings are shown at the beginning of the month

Map locator numbers are shown to the right of each garden name.

February

Snowdrop Openings
Wednesday 11th
Woolscott Barn   45

Saturday 14th
◆ Hill Close Gardens   21

Sunday 15th
Fieldgate   16
2 St Nicholas Avenue   37

Wednesday 18th
Woolscott Barn   45

March

Sunday 15th
Woolscott Barn   45

April

Every Saturday and Sunday
◆ Bridge Nursery   8

Friday 3rd
◆ Bridge Nursery   8

Saturday 4th
NEW Safehaven   36

Sunday 5th
NEW Safehaven   36
Woolscott Barn   45

Monday 6th
◆ Bridge Nursery   8
Woolscott Barn   45

Saturday 11th
◆ Castle Bromwich Hall
Gardens   12

Saturday 18th
NEW Safehaven   36

Sunday 19th
NEW Safehaven   36

Saturday 25th
6 Canon Price Road   11

Sunday 26th
Broadacre   9
6 Canon Price Road   11

May

Every Saturday and Sunday
◆ Bridge Nursery   8

Saturday 2nd
NEW Safehaven   36

Sunday 3rd
NEW Safehaven   36

Monday 4th
◆ Bridge Nursery   8

Sunday 10th
Beech Hurst   4

Saturday 16th
6 Canon Price Road   11
NEW Safehaven   36

Sunday 17th
Beech Hurst   4
Burmington Grange   10
6 Canon Price Road   11
Cats Whiskers   13
Lillington Road Gardens   26
NEW Safehaven   36

Saturday 23rd
Ilmington Gardens   24

Sunday 24th
Ilmington Gardens   24
Pebworth Gardens   32

Monday 25th
Bridge House   7
◆ Bridge Nursery   8
Pebworth Gardens   32

Saturday 30th
Priors Marston Manor   33
NEW Safehaven   36

Sunday 31st
Hardwick Hill   20
8 Rectory Road   34
NEW Safehaven   36

June

Every Saturday and Sunday
◆ Bridge Nursery   8

Saturday 6th
6 Canon Price Road   11
Hall Green Gardens   19

Sunday 7th
6 Canon Price Road	11
Hall Green Gardens	19
Honington Gardens	23
Styvechale Gardens	39

Saturday 13th
NEW Safehaven	36

Sunday 14th
Ansley Gardens	1
Bournville Village	6
Maxstoke Castle	28
NEW Safehaven	36

Saturday 20th
Marie Curie Hospice Garden	27

Sunday 21st
Kenilworth Gardens	25
Warmington Gardens	43
Whichford & Ascott Gardens	44

Saturday 27th
Tysoe Gardens	40

Sunday 28th
Berkswell Gardens	5
Old Arley Gardens	30
8 Rectory Road	34
Tysoe Gardens	40

Tuesday 30th
Monksbridge	29

July

Every Saturday and Sunday
◆ Bridge Nursery	8

Wednesday 1st
NEW Walled Garden at Hampton Manor	42

Thursday 2nd
Monksbridge	29

Saturday 4th
6 Canon Price Road	11
Packington Hall	31

Sunday 5th
6 Canon Price Road	11

Tuesday 7th
Monksbridge	29

Wednesday 8th
NEW Walled Garden at Hampton Manor	42

Thursday 9th
Monksbridge	29

Saturday 11th
◆ Ryton Organic Gardens	35
NEW Safehaven	36

Sunday 12th
Avon Dassett Gardens	3
NEW Safehaven	36

Saturday 18th
128 Green Acres Road	17
48 Varlins Way	41

Sunday 19th
Guy's Cliffe Walled Garden	18

Saturday 25th
NEW Safehaven	36

Sunday 26th
NEW Safehaven	36

August

Every Saturday and Sunday
◆ Bridge Nursery	8

Saturday 8th
NEW Safehaven	36

Sunday 9th
NEW Safehaven	36

Saturday 22nd
NEW Safehaven	36

Sunday 23rd
NEW Safehaven	36

Sunday 30th
Cedar House	14

Monday 31st
◆ Bridge Nursery	8

September

Every Saturday and Sunday
◆ Bridge Nursery	8

Friday 4th
170 Station Road	38

Saturday 12th
◆ Ryton Organic Gardens	35
NEW Safehaven	36

Sunday 13th
NEW Safehaven	36

Saturday 26th
NEW Safehaven	36

Sunday 27th
NEW Safehaven	36

October

Saturday 24th
◆ Hill Close Gardens	21

By Arrangement

Arrange a personalised garden visit with your club, or group of friends, on a date to suit you. See individual garden entries for full details.

Avening	2
Beech Hurst	4
Bridge House	7
Broadacre	9
6 Canon Price Road	11
Cedar House	14
59 The Chesils (Styvechale Gardens)	39
The Croft House	15
36 Ferndale Road (Hall Green Gardens)	19
The Hill Cottage	22
8 Rectory Road	34
NEW Safehaven	36
Woolscott Barn	45

The Croft House

THE GARDENS

GROUP OPENING

1 ANSLEY GARDENS
Ansley, CV10 9PS. *Ansley is situated W of Nuneaton, adjacent to Arley. Ansley is directly off the B4114. Tickets are available from the car park or in individual gardens.* **Sun 14 June (1.30-5.30). Combined adm £6, chd free. Tea, coffee & cake.**

25 BIRMINGHAM ROAD
Pat & David Arrowsmith.

79 BIRMINGHAM ROAD
Stephen Shaw.

261 BIRMINGHAM ROAD
Mr & Mrs Caroline Round.

CHURCH FARM
Mrs Sally Goadby.

NEW **11 HATTERS WAY**
Ms Mel Ellis.

THE OLD POLICE HOUSE
Mike & Hilary Ward.

1 PARK COTTAGES
Janet & Andy Down.

Ansley is a small ex-mining village situated in north Warwickshire. In 2024 the village won Gold in the Britain in Bloom Competition so is well worth a visit. The seven gardens in and around the village that are opening are a selection of different styles and offerings and this year there are some new gardens opening. They range from a very small traditional cottage garden crammed with flowers and pots to larger gardens and those maximising the amazing views of the countryside. There are small cottage gardens, a beautiful farmhouse garden complete with ducks and guinea fowl, an amazing tropical garden as well as a country garden with mature plants and ancient roses - something to inspire everyone. Most of the gardens are in the village with the opportunity to walk across the fields on public footpaths to the others if you are able. (There is parking available if not). The local Norman church will be open and the Morris Dancing Group will be entertaining visitors during the day. The actual village is also a treat with over 15 beautifully planted tubs and areas as part of the Britain in Bloom entry.

✿ ☕))

2 AVENING
Oldwich Lane East, Kenilworth, CV8 1NR. Helen Jones, 07894 321919, hello@mygardenoasis.co.uk, www.mygardenoasis.co.uk. *8m SE of Solihull & 5m W of Kenilworth. At the end of College Ln, a short single-track lane off Oldwich Ln E which runs between Chadwick End and Fen End.* **Visits by arrangement Apr to Sept. Adm £5, chd free. Tea, coffee & cake.**
Designed in 2009, this is a ¾ acre garden oasis in the West Midlands. It has been designed to attract wildlife and has a typical cottage garden feel. Features inc 2 ponds joined by a waterfall, wildflower meadow, wide mixed shrub/herbaceous border with a stepping stone path running through it and small vegetable plot. There are no steps in the garden, although some of the paths are unsuitable for wheelchairs.

♿ ☕

GROUP OPENING

3 AVON DASSETT GARDENS
Avon Dassett, CV47 2AE. *7m N of Banbury. From M40 J12 turn L & L again onto the B4100, following signs to Herb Centre & Gaydon. Take 2nd L (signed) into bottom end of village. Please park in cemetery car park at top of hill, or where signed.* **Sun 12 July (2-6). Combined adm £7, chd free. Home-made teas.**

DASSETT HOUSE
Mrs Sarah Rutherford,
dassettdwelling@gmail.com.
🛏

THE EAST WING, AVON CARROW
Christine Fisher & Terry Gladwin.

HILL TOP FARM
Mr D Hicks.

THE OLD RECTORY
Lily Hope-Frost.

SINCLAIR WITH THE SNUG
Mrs Deb Watts.

Pretty Hornton stone village sheltering in the lee of the Burton Dassett hills. A wide variety of gardens inc cottage, stepped, formal and wildlife friendly, with The Old Rectory mentioned in the Domesday Book. A range of plants inc alpines, herbaceous, perennials, roses, climbers, shrubs and even a topiary elephant. The gardens are on or off the main road through the village which is set on a long and steep hill. We would be grateful if visitors could park in designated areas and not along this main road. Plant sales, home-made teas and an historic church open. Lunch available at The Yew Tree, a community-owned pub. Wheelchair access to most gardens, but parking is not available at individual gardens. The village is set on a long steep hill.

♿ 🐄 ✿ 🚗 ☕))

4 BEECH HURST
3 Warwick Road, Southam, CV47 0HN. Michael and Sharon Mitchell, 01926 817895, michael@fmmitchell.net. *On R, ¼ to ½ m down Warwick Rd from A425 from Leamington Spa.* **Sun 10, Sun 17 May (2-5). Adm £6, chd free.** Visits also by arrangement 1 Apr to 15 Sept for groups of 10 to 30. Teas on request for group visits only.
Regency House with an established 1¼ acre garden inc lawns, woodland areas, many mature and some historic trees, established shrubs, herbaceous borders and a recently added Japanese-inspired garden with a raked gravel bed and a variety of flowering cherries, acers, rhododendrons, azaleas and camellias. It also has a fine display of late winter and springtime bulbs. The property has a gravel drive.

♿))

Our donation to Marie Curie this year is equivalent to 17,521 hours of hospice at home care.

WARWICKSHIRE

GROUP OPENING

5 BERKSWELL GARDENS
Berkswell, Meriden, Coventry, CV7 7SU. Gordon Clark. *7m W of Coventry. A452 to Balsall Common & follow signs to Berkswell. Tickets & maps available at each garden. Car necessary to visit all gardens.* **Sun 28 June (11-6). Combined adm £6, chd free.**

27 BONNEVILLE CLOSE
Mrs Lilian McGrath.

1 MONS AVENUE
Mrs Tracy Vernum-Cooke.

SPENCER'S END
Gordon Clark & Nicola Content.

NEW 5 WASTE LANE
Mrs Jenny White.

Berkswell is a beautiful village dating back to Saxon times with a C12 Norman church and has several C16 and C17 buildings inc the pub. In 2014/15 the village was awarded Gold in the RHS Britain in Bloom campaign, plus a special RHS award in 2014 for the Best Large Village in the Heart of England. The gardens provide good variety with examples of small and large, formal and informal, wild, imaginatively planted herbaceous borders and productive vegetable gardens. Something for everyone and plenty of ideas to take home. The C12 Norman church and garden is also open to visitors. Cashless payment at Spencer's End.

GROUP OPENING

6 BOURNVILLE VILLAGE
Birmingham, B30 1QY. Bournville Village Trust, www.bvt.org.uk. *Gardens spread across 1,000 acre estate. Walks of up to 30 mins between some. Map available on the day with details of parking, WC and refreshments.* **Sun 14 June (11-5). Combined adm £7, chd free. Tea, coffee & cake.**

NEW 183 BEAUMONT ROAD
Mr Nick Bassett.

5 BLACKTHORN ROAD
Mr A & Mrs L Christie.

21 HIGH HEATH CLOSE
Dr Faint & Ms Dorward.

32 KNIGHTON ROAD

Mrs Anne Ellis & Mr Lawrence Newman.

NEW 37 LABURNUM ROAD
Mrs Frances Henderson.

NEW 258 MARYVALE ROAD
Mr & Mrs Becca Tigue.

SELLY MANOR MUSEUM
www.sellymanormuseum.org.uk.

Bournville Village is showcasing seven gardens. Bournville is famous for its large gardens, outstanding open spaces and of course its chocolate factory in a garden! We have a secret garden escape, a garden railway amongst bonsai, a small garden for easy maintenance, a little changed original style garden, a reimagined traditional garden, a modern take on a typical garden and a Tudor garden in a museum. Free information sheet/map available on the day. For those with a disability, full details of access are available on the NGS website. Visitors with particular concerns with regards to access are welcome to call Bournville Village Trust on 0300 333 6540 or email: Communityadmin@bvt.org.uk a map will be available to download from www.bvt.org.uk nearer to the date and will be available on the day. Refreshment and cake sale available across a number of sites. WCs at Selly Manor Museum.

7 BRIDGE HOUSE
Dog Lane, Bodymoor Heath, B76 9JD. Mr & Mrs J Cerone, 01827 873205, janecerone@btinternet.com. *5m S of Tamworth. From A446 at Belfry Island take A4091 to Tamworth, after 1m turn R onto Bodymoor Heath Ln & continue 1m into village, parking in field opp garden.* **Mon 25 May (2-5). Adm £5, chd free. Tea, coffee & cake. Visits also by arrangement 17 May to 30 Sept for groups of 6 to 25.**
One acre garden surrounding converted public house. Divided into smaller areas with a mix of shrub borders, azalea and fuchsia, herbaceous and bedding, orchard, kitchen garden with large greenhouse. Pergola walk, arch to formal garden with big fish pool, pond, bog garden and lawns. Some unusual carefully chosen trees. Kingsbury Water Park and RSPB Middleton Lakes Reserve located within a mile.

8 ◆ BRIDGE NURSERY
Tomlow Road, Napton, Southam, CV47 8HX. Christine Dakin, 01926 812737, chris.dakin25@yahoo.com, www.bridge-nursery.co.uk. *3m E of Southam. Brown tourist sign at Napton Xrds on A425 Southam to Daventry Rd.* **For NGS: Fri 3 Apr (10-4). Every Sat and Sun 4 Apr to 27 Sept (10-4). Mon 6 Apr, Mon 4, Mon 25 May, Mon 31 Aug (10-4). Adm £4, chd free. Light refreshments. For other opening times and information, please phone, email or visit garden website.**
Clay soil? It can be very challenging but here is an acre of garden with an exciting range of plants which thrive in hostile conditions. Grass paths lead you round borders filled with many unusual plants, a pond and bamboo grove complete with panda! A peaceful haven for wildlife and visitors. Comments are often made about the tranquillity of the garden. Group visits welcome. The ground can be unsuitable for wheelchairs after a lot of rain.

9 BROADACRE
Grange Road, Dorridge, Solihull, B93 8QA. John Woolman, 07818 082885, jw234567@gmail.com, www.broadacregarden.org. *Approx 3m SE of Solihull. On B4101 opp The Railway Inn. Plenty of parking.* **Sun 26 Apr (2-6). Adm £7, chd free. Tea, coffee & cake inc in adm price. All food is provided and served by Bentley Heath Country Market members. Visits also by arrangement.**
Broadacre is a landscaped garden of trees, pools and lawns surrounded by meadows and woodland managed for conservation and run organically with the focus on biodiversity and wildlife. The borders and lawns around the house are mostly left to grow wild and the vegetable garden, providing food and honey, is wild too but the result is a garden thriving with wildlife. It is a pleasure to walk around. Several native Orchid species are colonising, and foxes, badgers, Roe and Muntjac deer visit regularly, together with a wide variety of birds, moths and butterflies. It is a haven for flora and fauna and contains everything you would expect to see in wild, undisturbed countryside in the Midlands. Most areas are accessible over grass paths.

Walled Garden at Hampton Manor

10 BURMINGTON GRANGE
Cherington, Shipston-on-Stour, CV36 5HZ. **Mr & Mrs Patrick Ramsay.** *2m E of Shipston-on-Stour. Take Oxford Rd (A3400) from Shipston-on-Stour, after 2m turn L to Burmington, go through village & continue for 1m, turn L to Willington & Barcheston, on sharp L bend turn R over cattle grid.* **Sun 17 May (2-5.30). Adm £7.50, chd free. Tea, coffee & cake.**
Interesting plantsman's garden extending to about 1½ acres, set in the rolling hills of the North Cotswolds with wonderful views over unspoilt countryside. The garden is well developed considering it was planted 20 yrs ago. Small vegetable and picking garden, beautiful sunken rose garden with herbaceous and shrub borders. Orchard and tree walk with unusual trees.

11 6 CANON PRICE ROAD
Nursery Meadow, Barford, CV35 8EQ. **Mrs Marie-Jane Roberts,** 07775 584336, Mroberts897@btinternet.com. *1m from Warwick. From A429 turn into Barford. Park on Wellesbourne Rd & walk into Nursery Meadow by red phone box. No.6 is R in 1st close. Disabled parking by house.* **Sat 25,** **Sun 26 Apr (2-4.30). Adm £3, chd free. Sat 16, Sun 17 May, Sat 6, Sun 7 June, Sat 4, Sun 5 July (2-4.30). Adm £5, chd free. Tea, coffee & cake in the garden room or seating around the garden.** **Visits also by arrangement 25 Apr to 5 July. Discuss refreshments when booking.**
Unexpectedly large and mature garden with colour themed shrub and perennial plants immaculately grown. Separate areas for cut flowers, herbs, vegetables and 19 types of fruit, some fan trained. Lots of hardy perennials to buy throughout the garden. Spectacularly colourful patio pots, a small delightful rockery, pond and wildlife garden. There are many seating areas throughout. Cash only please. Access via a single slab path that joins a wide path through the garden.

12 ♦ CASTLE BROMWICH HALL GARDENS
Chester Road, Castle Bromwich, Birmingham, B36 9BT. **Castle Bromwich Hall & Gardens Trust,** 01217 494100, cbhallgardens@gmail.com, www.castlebromwichhallgardens.org.uk. *4m E of Birmingham centre. 1m J5 M6 (exit N only) What3words app: rated.cake.those.* **For NGS: Sat 11 Apr (10.30-4.30). Adm £6, chd £3. Light refreshments. For other opening times and information, please phone, email or visit garden website.**
10 acres of restored C17/18 walled gardens attached to a Jacobean manor (now a hotel), with a further 30 acres of historic parkland and nature reserve. Formal yew parterres, wilderness walks, summerhouses, holly maze, espaliered fruit and wild areas. Cream Tea in a Box, cafe and picnics all season. Play area for families Holly Maze. Paths are either lawn or rough hoggin - sometimes on a slope. Most areas generally accessible, rough areas outside the walls difficult when wet.

Our donation in 2025 has enabled Parkinson's UK to fund 2 new nursing posts this year directly supporting people with Parkinson's.

CATS WHISKERS
42 Amesbury Rd, Moseley, Birmingham, B13 8LE. Dr Alfred & Mrs Michele White. *Opp back of Moseley Hall Hospital. Past Edgbaston Cricket ground straight on at r'about & up Salisbury Rd. Amesbury Rd, 1st on R.* **Sun 17 May (12-5). Adm £5, chd free. Light refreshments inc cake, non-alcoholic wine & soft drinks.**
A terraced rear garden in the 1923 style, featuring many unusual and interesting trees, shrubs, and perennials collected by the owners over 40yrs of dedicated development. While some structures show signs of age and a few shrubs have become unruly, the garden remains attractive with plenty of special plants to interest visitors. Notably a new Arisaema bed is being developed in the hope of becoming a national collection.

CEDAR HOUSE
Wasperton, Warwick, CV35 8EB. Mr D Burbidge, 07836 532914, david.burbidge@burbidge.org.uk, www.cedarhousegardens.co.uk. *5m from Warwick. Turn off A429 into Wasperton. There is only 1 road in the village. Continue for approx ½ m. What3words app: wool.parsnips. trickles.* **Sun 30 Aug (1.30-5). Adm £10, chd free. Home-made teas at Wasperton Village Hall. Visits also by arrangement 5 May to 14 Oct for groups of 15 to 25.**
Six acre former vicarage gardens, mature and exciting. Extensive tulips and rhododendrons in spring - colourful herbaceous borders in summer - brilliant colour in autumn. Water meadow garden, woodland glade and walk with mix of young and mature specimen trees, inc two notable vintage trees, tranquil grass and bamboo area leading to the swimming pool garden. Lots of good seating areas. Interesting walks across the fields to the River Avon, Charlecote and Hampton Lucy. Cedar House is close to Warwick and Stratford upon Avon. Some gravel and woodchip paths.

THE CROFT HOUSE
Haselor, Alcester, B49 6LU. Isobel & Patrick Somers, 07767 306673, ifas1010@aol.com. *6m W of Stratford-upon-Avon, 2m E of Alcester, off A46. From A46 take Haselor turn. From Alcester take old Stratford Rd, turn L signed Haselor, then R at Xrds. Garden in centre of village. Please park considerately.* **Visits by arrangement May & June for groups of up to 30. Visits welcome at short notice. Adm £7, chd free. Tea, coffee & cake.**
Almost an acre of trees, shrubs and herbaceous borders densely planted with a designer's passion for colour and texture. Hidden areas invite you to linger. Gorgeous scented wisteria on 2 sides of the house. Organically managed, providing a haven for birds and other wildlife. Frog pond, treehouse, small vegetable plot and a few venerable old fruit trees from its days as a market garden.

FIELDGATE
Fieldgate Lane, Kenilworth, CV8 1BT. Liz & Bob Watson. *Fieldgate is at the very bottom of Fieldgate Ln, on the corner next to the T-lights. Parking available at Abbey Fields car park & limited street parking on High St & Fieldgate Ln.* **Sun 15 Feb (12-4). Adm £3, chd free. Home-made teas in St Nicholas Church from 1pm. Open nearby 2 St Nicholas Avenue. Combined adm £5. Opening with Kenilworth Gardens on Sun 21 June.**
¼ acre town garden with lawns, herbaceous borders and formal ponds. It was remodelled by the owners in 2002 and has matured nicely. The borders contain a wide variety of plants and are colourful throughout summer and late into September with asters and dahlias. A small woodland area was created in 2021 planted with shade lovers, ferns and many snowdrops some of which are unusual. Kenilworth Castle is close by and there are pleasant walks in Abbey Fields. The Millennium Walk,

Felly Lodge, Pebworth Gardens

starting at the castle is an hour's walk through the Warwickshire countryside around the shore of the now drained Kenilworth Castle mere.

17 128 GREEN ACRES ROAD
Kings Norton, Birmingham, B38 8NL. Mark & Karen Whitehouse. *From the M42 J2 take the A441 towards Birmingham take the 2nd exit at r'about continue along the A441 for 3m Green Acres Rd is on the R next to Spar.* **Sat 18 July (10-4.30). Combined adm with 48 Varlins Way £5, chd free. Tea, coffee & cake.**
A garden with lots of character full of interest and abundance of colour, inc various seating areas to enjoy different aspects and views. The garden has many different types of perennials, a large selection of dahlias, a fish pond, water feature, a wild flower garden, cut flower garden and a new tropical area. To access the garden, please follow signs to enter the garden from the rear.

18 GUY'S CLIFFE WALLED GARDEN
Coventry Road, Guy's Cliffe, Warwick, CV34 5FJ. Sarah Ridgeway, www.guyscliffewalledgarden.org.uk. *Behind Hintons Nursery in Guy's Cliffe. On the A429, between N Warwick & Leek Wootton.* **Sun 19 July (10.30-3.30). Adm £5, chd free. Tea, coffee & cake.**
A Grade II listed garden of special historic interest, having been the kitchen garden for Guy's Cliffe House. The garden dates back to the mid-1700s. Restoration work started 12 yrs ago using plans from the early C19. The garden layout has already been reinstated and the beds, once more, planted with fruit, flowers and vegetables inc many heritage varieties. Part of the Peach House is being restored. The sunken Melon house is visible but not yet restored so not accessible. Original C18 walls. Fernery. Exhibition of artefacts discovered during restoration. 'No Dig' approach to all gardening activities Lots of signs describe different parts of the garden. Access, inc wheelchairs, is through entrance of Hintons Nursery and paths through garden are accessible. WC with disabled access.

GROUP OPENING

19 HALL GREEN GARDENS
Hall Green, Birmingham, B28 8PH. *Off A34, 4m from city centre, 6m from M42, J4. Start at 65 Woodford Green Rd, B28 8PH.* **Sat 6, Sun 7 June (1.30-5.30). Combined adm £5, chd free. Tea, coffee & cake at 111 Southam Road.**

36 FERNDALE ROAD
Mrs E A Nicholson, 01217 774921.
Visits also by arrangement Apr to Sept. Prices and refreshments by prior arrangement with owner.

638 SHIRLEY ROAD
Dr & Mrs M Leigh.

111 SOUTHAM ROAD
Ms Val Townend & Mr Ian Bate.

65 WOODFORD GREEN ROAD
Mrs Maxine Chapman.

Four very different suburban gardens in leafy Hall Green with its beautiful mature trees and friendly residents. Visitors love the unique atmosphere in each garden. It is such a perfect way to share a relaxing early summer saunter and pause for refreshments served by the brilliant catering team. 36 Ferndale Rd: Florist's large suburban garden, ponds and waterfalls, and fruit garden. 111 Southam Rd: Mature garden with well defined areas inc ponds, white garden and a majestic cedar. 638 Shirley Rd: Large garden with herbaceous borders, cutting patch, vegetables and greenhouses. 65 Woodford Green Rd: Much loved, small garden abounding in charming old teapots, bottle edging, and worn-out hiking boots now used as planters.

20 HARDWICK HILL
Lower End, Priors Hardwick, Southam, CV47 7SP. Mrs Candida Kelly, www.candykelly.co.uk. *4½ m SE of Southam. What3words app: piled.ever.tasty. Turn off A23 to Wormleighton. Turn L after Wormleighton and 1½ m later after village sign drive on R before bend. Please check for HS2 road closures.* **Sun 31 May (2-5). Adm £7.50, chd free. Home-made teas.**
The main lawn ends in a ha-ha with views stretching to the Malvern Hills. A 5 acre garden replanted and landscaped 20 yrs ago. Full of mature trees inc Copper Beeches, Corsican Pine and two Mulberry trees. Long borders lined with espaliered Malus Robusta by an ornamental pond that leads to a summerhouse with small wildflower meadow and beehives. A vegetable garden. A variety of hedging from wild roses, willow, weeping pear to buckthorn and hornbeam.

21 ♦ HILL CLOSE GARDENS
Bread and Meat Close, Warwick, CV34 6HF. Hill Close Gardens Trust, 01926 493339, hello@hcgt.org.uk, www.hillclosegardens.com. *Town centre. Follow signs to Warwick racecourse. Entry from Friars St onto Bread & Meat Cl Car park is by entrance next to racecourse. 2hrs free parking. Disabled parking outside the gates. What3words app: chat.apple.cute.* **For NGS: Sat 14 Feb, Sat 24 Oct (11-4). Adm £8.50, chd £2. Tea, coffee & cake. For other opening times and information, please phone, email or visit garden website.**
Restored Grade II Victorian leisure gardens comprising 16 individual hedged gardens, 8 brick summerhouses. Herbaceous borders, heritage apple and pear trees, C19 daffodils, over 100 varieties of snowdrops, many varieties of asters and chrysanthemums. Heritage vegetables. Plant Heritage border, auricula theatre, and Victorian style glasshouse. Children's garden. Wheelchair available. Please phone to book in advance.

In 2025, National Garden Scheme funding helped Perennial support 950 unique callers to their helpline looking for advice and information.

22 THE HILL COTTAGE
Kings Lane, Snitterfield, Stratford-upon-Avon, CV37 0QA. Gillie & Paul Waldron, 07895 369387, info@thehillcottage.co.uk, www.thehillcottage.co.uk. 5 mins from M40, J15. Take A46 to Stratford. 1m take 2nd exit at r'about. 1m take L into Kings Ln, through S bends, house on R. Or from village, up White Horse Hill, R at T-junc, over A46, R into Kings Ln, 2nd on L. **Visits by arrangement Apr to Sept for groups of up to 20. Adm £6.50, chd free. Tea, coffee & cake at £3.50pp.**
Come and savour spectacular views from this 2¼ acre plantsman's garden with hot and exotic borders, shady island beds and mature bluebell woodland. Discover the romantic stone summerhouse by the oak circle and wildlife pond, a walled vegetable garden and glasshouse. Ongoing projects inc stone terracing, a gravel garden, chamomile lawn and knot garden. Access to all the upper areas inc walled kitchen garden and orchard through roadside gate on request.

GROUP OPENING

23 HONINGTON GARDENS
Honington, Shipston-on-Stour, CV36 5AA. 1½ m N of Shipston-on-Stour. Take A3400 from Shipston-on-Stour, towards Stratford-upon-Avon, then turn R signed Honington. What3Words app: universal.events.landmark. **Sun 7 June (1.30-5.30). Combined adm £6, chd free. Home-made teas on the Village Green within walking distance of car park, WC and the gardens.**

HOLTS COTTAGE
Mr & Mrs A Golding.

HONINGTON GLEBE
Mr and Mrs AMH Orchard.

HONINGTON HALL
B H E Wiggin.

THE OLD HOUSE
Mrs D Beaumont.

ORCHARD HOUSE
Mr & Mrs Monnington.

THE ORCHARD, HOME FARM
Mr Guy Winter.

C17 village, recorded in Domesday, entered by old toll gate. Ornamental stone bridge over the River Stour and interesting church with C13 tower and late C17 nave after Wren. 6 contrasting gardens inc a garden with extensive lawns and fine mature trees with river and garden monuments. A plantsman's garden with unusual trees and shrubs creating year-round interest. A traditional orchard with mown pathways and active beehives. A developing garden with a hint of Japan. A natural, wildlife-friendly cottage garden with pond and vegetable areas. A structured cottage garden formally laid out with box hedging. Entrance payments in advance or by cash or card at booths on site. Teas on the Village Green at Honington are a special feature of the afternoon. Classic Car display at Honington Hall added this year as special feature. Car parking is free, please follow signs and be guided by stewards to car park area. Some of the smaller gardens have only partial wheelchair access.

GROUP OPENING

24 ILMINGTON GARDENS
Ilmington, CV36 4LA. 8m S of Stratford-upon-Avon. 8m N of Moreton-in-Marsh. 4m NW of Shipston-on-Stour off A3400. 3m NE of Chipping Campden. **Sat 23, Sun 24 May (12.30-5.30). Combined adm £10, chd free. Home-made teas in Ilmington Community Shop, Upper Green on Sat, and at the Village Hall on Sun.** Donation to Shipston Home Nursing.

THE BEVINGTONS
Mr & Mrs N Tustain.

COMPTON SCORPION FARM
Mrs Karlsen.

THE DOWER HOUSE
Mr & Mrs M Tremellen.

FROG ORCHARD
Mr & Mrs Jeremy Snowden.

GRUMP COTTAGE
Martin Underwood & Anne Slowther.

ILMINGTON MANOR
Mr Martin Taylor.

MEADOW VIEW
Mr Geoff Davis.

OLD FOX HOUSE
Rob & Sarah Beebee.

NEW PUDDOCKS
Bill Buckley.

RAVENSCROFT
Mr & Mrs Clasper.

STUDIO COTTAGE
Sarah Hobson.

Ilmington is an ancient hillside Cotswold village 2 miles from the Fosse Way. Start at Ilmington Manor (next to the Red Lion Pub); wander the 3 acre gardens with many roses, much topiary and a fish pond. Next, go up Grump Street, above the Village Hall, to Ravenscroft's large, sculpture-filled garden with sloping vistas commanding the hilltop. Walk to nearby Frog Lane to view Puddocks, Frog Orchard's and The Studio's delightful gardens then down, via Old Fox House at the bottom of Foxcote Hill, to the Bevington's many-chambered cottage garden at the bottom of Valanders Lane. Finally visit the charming cottage gardens surrounding Meadow View and the large terraced garden of The Dower House in Back Street, overlooking the Manor ponds and Berry Orchard. The traditional Ilmington Morris Dancers will be performing in the village on Sunday. Cash only please.

GROUP OPENING

25 KENILWORTH GARDENS
Kenilworth, CV8 1BT. Fieldgate Ln, off A452. Parking available at Abbey Fields or in town. Street parking is available. Tickets & maps at all gardens. Transport is necessary to visit all the gardens. **Sun 21 June (12-5.30). Combined adm £8, chd free. Home-made teas in St Nicholas Parochial Hall from 1pm.**

BEEHIVE HILL ALLOTMENTS
Kenilworth Allotment Association.

NEW 22 BRIDGE STREET
Rev David & Mrs Linda Butterworth.

FIELDGATE
Liz & Bob Watson.
(See separate entry)

14C FIELDGATE LANE
Sandra Aulton.

KENILWORTH COMMUNITY GARDENS
Kenilworth Community Gardeners, www.facebook.com/kenilworthcommunitygardeners.

9 LAWRENCE GARDENS
Leo Lewis & Judith Masson.

23 LINDSEY CRESCENT
Mr John & Mrs Ruth Titley.

65 RANDALL ROAD
Mrs Jan Kenyon.

2 ST NICHOLAS AVENUE
Mr Ian Roberts.
(See separate entry)

1 SIDDELEY AVENUE
Clare Wightman.

69 SPRING LANE
Mr Chris Coton & Mr Nick Wood.

TREE TOPS
Joanna & George Illingworth.

Kenilworth was historically a very important town in Warwickshire. It has one of England's best castle ruins, Abbey Fields and plenty of pubs and good cafes. There are 10 gardens open this year around the town plus allotments and the community gardens near the town centre. There are small, medium and large gardens with lots of variety - formal, prairie and cottage styles with trees, shrubs, herbaceous borders, ponds, many wildlife friendly features plus plenty of vegetables. Several of the gardens have won Gold in the Kenilworth in Bloom garden competition. Abbey Fields is an attractive park in the old part of town close to Kenilworth Castle and the Millennium Walk, starting here is an hour's walk through the Warwickshire countryside around the now drained Kenilworth Castle mere.

GROUP OPENING

26 LILLINGTON ROAD GARDENS
Lillington Road, Leamington Spa, CV32 5YY. Mr Ian & Mrs Viv Roberts. *On the E side of Lillington Rd, S of the junc with Wathen Rd. On street parking available. What3words app: frame. storm.gross.* **Sun 17 May (1-5). Combined adm £5, chd free. Tea, coffee & cake.**

NEW 8 LILLINGTON ROAD
Ms Jo Strudwick and Mr Rob Bassil.

18 LILLINGTON ROAD
Mr Steve & Mrs Vicky Bell.

32 LILLINGTON ROAD
Mr Ian & Mrs Viv Roberts.

A great opportunity to see three different walled town gardens to the rear of a row of Victorian properties in the Lillington Road Conservation Area. The gardens feature flower filled, mixed herbaceous borders with trees and shrubs. Espaliered fruit trees and pleasant seating areas to enjoy the garden complete the picture and there is a signature Wollemi Pine at number 32. All the gardens are wheelchair accessible from the road.

27 MARIE CURIE HOSPICE GARDEN
Marsh Lane, Solihull, B91 2PQ. Mrs Do Connolly, www.mariecurie.org.uk/westmidlands. *Close to J5 M42 to E of Solihull Town Centre. M42 J5, travel towards Solihull on A41. Take slip toward Solihull to join B4025 & after island take 1st R onto Marsh Ln. Hospice on R. Some onsite parking - plenty for blue badge holders.* **Sat 20 June (11-4). Adm £5, chd free. Tea, coffee & cake.**
The gardens contain two large, formally laid out patients' gardens, indoor courtyards, a long border adjoining the car park and a wildlife area with fairy garden and pond area. Children's games. The volunteer gardening team hope that the gardens provide a peaceful and comforting place for patients, their visitors and staff. The path to the fairy garden has a woodchip surface and may not be suitable for all wheelchair access.

28 MAXSTOKE CASTLE
Castle Lane, Coleshill, B46 2RD. Mr G M Fetherston-Dilke. *Located in between Birmingham and Coventry. 2½ m E of Coleshill. The Castle drive is on Castle Ln (adjacent to the golf course).* **Sun 14 June (11-5). Adm £12, chd £8. Pre-booking essential, please email events@maxstokecastle.com for information & booking. Tea, coffee & cake inc gluten and lactose free options.** Donation to other charities.
Five acres of garden and grounds with roses, herbaceous plants, shrubs and trees in the courtyard and immediate surroundings of this C14 moated castle. Plant and gift stalls.

128 Green Acres Road

Packington Hall

29 MONKSBRIDGE
Butlers Marston, Warwick, CV35 0NA. Mr & Mrs Piercey.
Within the village of Butlers Marston (near Kineton), take lane signposted "Parish Church". Car park is next to church. What3words app: flamed.longingly.mime. **Tue 30 June, Thur 2, Tue 7, Thur 9 July (9-3). Adm £8, chd free. Tea, coffee & cake at the local church.**
Monksbridge is a former vicarage, built in 1838 on the foundations of a much older dwelling. The redeveloped Victorian gardens inc herbaceous borders, parterre, kitchen garden, stone circle, Japanese garden and wildflower walks, all designed with sensitivity to the surrounding landscape.

GROUP OPENING

30 OLD ARLEY GARDENS
Coventry, CV7 8FT. *Enter Ansley Ln via B'ham Rd or Rectory Rd. Parking at the Arc School. Transport may be required to visit all gardens.* **Sun 28 June (2-6). Combined adm £5, chd free. Tea, coffee & cake in Methodist Hall.**

1 ELM GROVE
Ms Jane Taylor.

NEW **18 ROWLAND COURT**
Mr John & Mrs Kim Burton.

35 ST WILFREDS COTTAGES
Mrs Justine Clee.

THE SCHOOL HOUSE
Mrs Pauline McAleese.

17 SPINNEY CLOSE
Mr David Cox.

Old Arley is an ancient village which appears in the Domesday book. More recently it was a small mining community and St Wilfreds Cottages were built in 1907 to accommodate the mine's supervisors and their families. The gardens around the village vary in style and size and the planting is varied, ranging from traditional cottage to more contemporary styles. Walking the route is 1½ miles so transport may be necessary.

31 PACKINGTON HALL
Meriden, nr Coventry, CV7 7HF. Lord & Lady Guernsey, www.packingtonestate.co.uk. *Midway between Coventry & B'ham on A45. Main entrance is 400yds from Stonebridge r'about heading towards Coventry. What3words app: dreamers.mandolin.portfolio as SatNav often takes you to the wrong location.* **Sat 4 July (11-5). Adm £7.50, chd free. Tea, coffee & cake on the terrace or in the Pompeiian Room if wet.**
Packington Hall is the setting for an elegant Capability Brown landscape. Designed from 1751, the gardens inc a serpentine lake, impressive Cedars of Lebanon, Wellingtonias and a 1762 Japanese bridge. There are also wildflower meadows, mixed terrace borders, and a recently restored walled garden. Wheelchair access is possible but please note there are no paths in the garden. The gravelled terrace, where teas are served, is easily accessible.

The National Garden Scheme donated £3,875,596 to our nursing and health beneficiaries from money raised at gardens open in 2025.

WARWICKSHIRE

GROUP OPENING

32 PEBWORTH GARDENS
Pebworth, Stratford-upon-Avon, CV37 8XN. www.pebworth.org/pebworth-open-gardens---national-garden-scheme. *7m SW of Stratford-upon-Avon. For parking & SatNav please use CV37 8XN.* **Sun 24, Mon 25 May (12-5). Combined adm £7, chd free. Home-made teas at Pebworth Village Hall.**

FELLY LODGE
Maz & Barrie Clatworthy.

ICKNIELD BARN
Sheila Davies.

IVYBANK
Mr & Mrs R Davis.

JASMINE COTTAGE
Ted & Veronica Watson.

THE KNOLL
Mr & Mrs K Wood.

NEW LUTON COTTAGE
Mr & Mrs Rob and Sandra Lewis.

MAPLE BARN
Richard & Wendi Weller.

MARTINS
Tony and Galina Espley.

MEON COTTAGE
David & Sally Donnison.

THE OLD BARN
Mike Finlay and Lucy Metcalfe.

Pebworth is a picturesque village, home to charming thatched cottages, alongside houses both old and new. Visitors can explore an array of beautiful gardens, from classic cottage planting to stylish walled and terraced designs. Overlooking the village stands St Peter's Church, distinguished by its remarkable ring of ten bells, a rare treasure in a rural parish. This year, 10 gardens will be open to visitors, offering plenty of inspiration and variety. In the village hall, the Pebworth WI will be serving delicious teas and cakes. Adding to the day's attractions, the Messerschmitt car Museum will be open, giving a glimpse into its fascinating history, while St Peter's Church invites you to try your hand at bell ringing in its famous tower. Its churchyard won 2nd place in Worcestershire's Best Kept Churchyard. Only partial wheelchair access in some gardens. Ramp available for village hall.

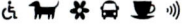

33 PRIORS MARSTON MANOR
The Green, Priors Marston, CV47 7RH. Dr & Mrs Mark Cecil. *8m SW of Daventry. Off the A361 between Daventry & Banbury at Charwelton. Follow signs to Priors Marston, approx 2m. Arrive at T-junc with a war memorial on R. The manor will be on your L.* **Sat 30 May (10-6). Adm £8, chd free. Tea, coffee & cake.**
Arrive in Priors Marston village and explore the manor gardens. Greatly enhanced by the present owners to relate back to a Georgian manor garden and pleasure grounds. Wonderful walled kitchen garden provides seasonal produce and cut flowers for the house. Herbaceous flower beds and a sunken terrace with water feature by William Pye. Lawns lead down to the lake and estate around which you can walk amongst the trees and wildlife with stunning views up to the house. Partial wheelchair access. Entrance through gravel courtyard.

34 8 RECTORY ROAD
Solihull, B91 3RP. Nigel & Daphne Carter, 07527 475759, npcarter@blueyonder.co.uk. *Solihull Town Centre. Located in the town centre: off Church Hill Rd, turn into Rectory Rd, bear L down the road, house on the R 100 metres down.* **Sun 31 May (2.30-7); Sun 28 June (11-6). Adm £4, chd free. Home-made teas. Visits also by arrangement 1 May to 1 Sept for groups of up to 20.**
Stunning town garden divided into areas with different features. A garden with unusual trees and intensively planted borders and an unusual folly. Walk to the end of the garden and step into a Japanese themed garden complete with pond, fish and traditional style bridge. Sit on the shaded decking area. A garden to attract bees and butterflies with plenty of places to relax. Japanese themed features, unusual folly with working fireplace and stunning moongate. Some steps; those with mobility issues may find access a little difficult; handrail is situated along side the steps.

35 ♦ RYTON ORGANIC GARDENS
Wolston Lane, Ryton on Dunsmore, Coventry, CV8 3LG. Garden Organic, 02476 303517, enquiry@gardenorganic.org.uk, www.gardenorganic.org.uk. *5m SE of Coventry. From A45 take the exit signed Wolston with brown tourist signs for Ryton Gardens.* **For NGS: Sat 11 July, Sat 12 Sept (1-5). Adm £5, chd free. Light refreshments. For other opening times and information, please phone, email or visit garden website.**
Garden Organic's inspirational and sustainable demonstration garden at Ryton contains a wonderful fruit and vegetable potager, together with several large ornamental flower beds. Packed full of ideas for gardens of all sizes, it features a large glasshouse, polytunnel, composting area, water features, no-dig and container gardens plus two National Plant Collections.

36 NEW SAFEHAVEN
5 Malletts Close, Tysoe, Warwick, CV35 0SY. Tarryn and Alec Henson, 07432 871517, henson69tarryn@icloud.com. *Please park on Oxhill Rd, then follow the signs to the garden.* **Sat 4, Sun 5, Sat 18, Sun 19 Apr, Sat 2, Sun 3, Sat 16, Sun 17, Sat 30, Sun 31 May, Sat 13, Sun 14 June, Sat 11, Sun 12, Sat 25, Sun 26 July, Sat 8, Sun 9, Sat 22, Sun 23 Aug, Sat 12, Sun 13, Sat 26, Sun 27 Sept (11-3). Adm £5, chd free. Tea, coffee & cake. Opening with Tysoe Gardens on Sat 27, Sun 28 June. Visits also by arrangement Apr to Sept for groups of up to 20.**
Safehaven has so far taken 5 years to create, and along that journey the garden owners have gained a real passion for anything green. There is a courtyard, two greenhouses, several borders, seating areas, large vegetable patch and rose garden. All the flowers and vegetables are grown from seed. The owners encourage as much wildlife as possible into the garden, inc a woodpecker which comes back each year. A whole garden experience. Produce grown in the garden available on a first come first served basis.

37 2 ST NICHOLAS AVENUE
Kenilworth, CV8 1JU. Mr Ian Roberts. **Sun 15 Feb (12-4). Adm £3, chd free. Home-made teas in St Nicholas Church from 1pm. Open nearby Fieldgate. Opening with Kenilworth Gardens on Sun 21 June.**
The garden has been developed over the past 30 yrs. It has been transformed from an overgrown uninteresting patch to a mature and varied garden containing a wide selection of plants inc a collection of Snowdrops. It contains many features inc mixed borders, ponds, rockery, structures, mature trees and shrubs. All areas are interconnected by paths so the garden can be enjoyed at leisure.

38 170 STATION ROAD
Sutton Coldfield, B73 5LE. Mrs Jenny Ratcliff. *Sutton Coldfield, to the NE of Birmingham. Location is easy to find just enter postcode B73 5LE into SatNav, or What3words app: tonic.drip.enter.* **Evening opening Fri 4 Sept (6-8.30). Adm £6, chd free. Wine inc in adm price. Additional drinks can be purchased by donation.**
A typical suburban garden that has seen many changes over 30 yrs. From football pitch and adventure playground to a garden with different spaces. Inc scruffy bits, wildlife pond, vegetable garden with raised beds, shady area with fernery and well-stocked herbaceous beds and borders. Naturalised bulbs in the spring through to autumn hot colours. The garden is flat and accessible, however the drive is gravel which can be challenging for wheelchair users.

GROUP OPENING

39 STYVECHALE GARDENS
Baginton Road, Coventry, CV3 5DE. *Located on the S side of Coventry close to A45. Tickets & map available on the day from Baginton Rd United Reform Church hall, CV3 6FP.* **Sun 7 June (12-6). Combined adm £5, chd free. Tea, coffee & cake.**

NEW 48 ASTHILL GROVE
John and Kate Purcell.

11 BAGINTON ROAD
Ken & Pauline Bond.

105 BAGINTON ROAD
Parmjit and Jas Dhugga.

164 BAGINTON ROAD
Fran & Jeff Gaught.

NEW 25 THE CHESILS
Louise and George Hills.

59 THE CHESILS
John Marron, johnmarron@btinternet.com. Visits also by arrangement 4 July to 30 Aug for groups of 10 to 25. Weekends only. Refreshments inc in adm price.

66 THE CHESILS
Ami Samra & Rodger Hope.

NEW 42 CLARENDON STREET
Liz Campbell and Denis Crowley.

NEW 48 CLARENDON STREET
Amanda Bicknell.

NEW 7 DAWLISH DRIVE
Asha Jutti.

NEW 9 DAWLISH DRIVE
Alistair McColm and Linda Powell.

16 DELAWARE ROAD
Val & Roy Howells.

40 HARTINGTON CRESCENT
Viv & George Buss.

50 KNOLL DRIVE
Anita & Barry Hallam.

NEW 13 LUPTON AVENUE
Mrs Loretta & Mr Paul Williams.

NEW 117 MANTILLA DRIVE
Lisa Daniels.

NEW ST THOMAS MORE CATHOLIC PRIMARY SCHOOL
Clare Staines.

23 SPENCER AVENUE
Susan & Keith Darwood.

27 SPENCER AVENUE
Helene Devane.

NEW 50 SPENCER AVENUE
Nicki Walmsley.

Explore an eclectic mix of suburban gardens in Styvechale and Earlsdon, from kitchen plots to exotic planting, restful retreats to vibrant borders. Expect roses, ponds, water features and shady corners. Each garden offers its own unique charm and inspiration promising a memorable experience and deserving of a place near the top of your visit shortlist.

GROUP OPENING

40 TYSOE GARDENS
Tysoe, Warwick, CV35 0TR. *W of A422, N of Banbury (9m). E of A3400 & Shipston-on-Stour (4m). N of A4035 & Brailes (3m). Please park on the village Recreation Ground beside the Old Fire Stn CV35 0FF. What3words app: ports.exotic.general.* **Sat 27, Sun 28 June (2-6). Combined adm £7.50, chd free. Tea, coffee & cake at the Village Hall.**

5 AVON AVENUE
Penny & Rob Varley.

NEW BYEWAYS
Ian & Annabel Kay.

NEW THE CHESTNUTS
Mrs Kayleigh Lewis.

GARDEN COTTAGE & WALLED KITCHEN GARDEN
Sue & Mike Sanderson, www.twkg.co.uk.

12 OXHILL ROAD
Mrs Christine Tuffin.

2 PEACOCK LANE
Julie and Martin Smart.

NEW SAFEHAVEN
Tarryn and Alec Henson.
(See separate entry)

Tysoe, an original Hornton stone village stands on the North East foothills of the Cotswolds below Edge Hill. Seven wonderful gardens open this year, two of which have never opened before. You can be sure that Tysoe will offer a happy atmosphere, some terrific teas at the village hall. Contactless payment available at the village hall and Garden Cottage for entrance tickets, cash payments can be made at all gardens. Cash and card payments for teas and cash only for plant sales. Bus available to help you see all the gardens.

41 48 VARLINS WAY
Kings Norton, Birmingham, B38 9UX. Mr David Fernie. *A441 Birmingham Redditch Rd. Through Kings Norton. L at "Man on Moon" L at Bracken Way then L to park in Longdales Rd.* **Sat 18 July (10.30-4.30). Combined adm with 128 Green Acres Road £5, chd free.**
Suburban garden with unusual collection of trees and shrubs with wildlife in mind. Colourful patio area, small pond, climbers, vegetables and fruit and hidden corners. Wheelchair access to lawn and main features.

WARWICKSHIRE

42 NEW WALLED GARDEN AT HAMPTON MANOR
Shadow Brook Lane, Hampton-In-Arden, Solihull, B92 0EN. 01675 446080, reservations@hamptonmanor.com, www.hamptonmanor.com/ethos. *5min drive from Birmingham Airport. M42 to Coventry Rd/A45 in Bickenhill. Take the exit from M42. Take A4545 and Shadowbrook Ln. On the estate, follow the sign to Grace & Savour car park. We'll welcome you at Grace & Savour reception.* **Wed 1, Wed 8 July (10-12). Adm £20. Pre-booking essential, please visit www.ngs.org.uk for information & booking. Tea, coffee & cake.** Nestled in 45 acre estate Hampton Manor, the Victorian walled garden is a delightful ornamental kitchen garden growing food for the kitchens. The guiding principle is biodiversity with soil health, no digging, organic growing and composting underpinning the produce. You'll be welcomed with hot drinks and a signature welcome cookie. Then join the gardeners for a private tour of the walled garden.

GROUP OPENING

43 WARMINGTON GARDENS
Banbury, OX17 1BU. *5m NW of Banbury. Take B4100 N from Banbury, after 5m turn R across short dual carriageway into Warmington. From N take J12 off M40 onto B4100.* **Sun 21 June (1-5). Combined adm £6, chd free. Home-made teas at Warmington Village Hall.**

GOURDON
Jenny Deeming.

GREENWAYS
Tim Stevens.

THE MANOR HOUSE
Mr & Mrs G Lewis.

THE ORCHARD
Mike Cable.

SPRINGFIELD HOUSE
Jenny & Rosemarie Handscombe, 01295 690286, jehandscombe@btinternet.com.

1 THE WHEELWRIGHTS
Ms E Bunn.

Warmington is a charming historic village, mentioned in the Domesday Book, situated at the NE edge of the Cotswolds in a designated AONB. There is a large village green with a pond overlooked by an Elizabethan Manor House (not open). There are other historic buildings inc St Michael's Church, The Plough Inn and Springfield House all dating from the C16 or before. There is a mixed and varied selection of gardens to enjoy during your visit to Warmington. These inc the formal knot gardens and topiary of The Manor House, cottage and courtyard gardens, terraced gardens on the slopes of Warmington Hill and orchards containing local varieties of apple trees. Some gardens will be selling homegrown plants. WC at village hall.

GROUP OPENING

44 WHICHFORD & ASCOTT GARDENS
Whichford & Ascott, Shipston-on-Stour, CV36 5PG. *6m SE of Shipston-on-Stour. For parking please use CV36 5PG, parking by the church. Parking also available at the roadside in Ascott.* **Sun 21 June (1.30-5). Combined adm £7.50, chd free. Home-made teas.**

ASCOTT LODGE
Charlotte Copley.

BELMONT HOUSE
Robert & Yoko Ward.

LENTICULARS
Mrs Diana Atkins.

MURTON COTTAGE
Hilary & David Blakemore.

THE OLD RECTORY
Peter & Caroline O'Kane.

NEW PEAR TREE COTTAGE
Mrs Fiona Robertson.

PLUM TREE COTTAGE
Janet Knight.

THE WHICHFORD POTTERY
Jim & Dominique Keeling, www.whichfordpottery.com.

The gardens in this group reflect many different styles. The 2 villages are in an AONB, nestled within a dramatic landscape of hills, pasture and woodland, which is used to picturesque effect by the garden owners. Fine lawns, mature shrubs and interesting planning will all enrich your visit to our beautiful gardens.

Many incorporate the inventive use of natural springs, forming ponds, pools and other water features. Classic cottage gardens contrast with larger and more classical gardens which adopt variations on the traditional English garden of herbaceous borders, climbing roses, yew hedges and walled enclosures. Partial wheelchair access as some gardens are on sloping sites and have steps.

45 WOOLSCOTT BARN
Woolscott, Rugby, CV23 8DB. Neil Higginson, 07836 511495, neilnrhigginson@btinternet.com. *2m from Dunchurch. Take the A45 S from Dunchurch towards Daventry until R turn for Grandborough. After 1m, go round a big bend & past manor house. Woolscott barn is 400m after manor house on L.* **Wed 11, Wed 18 Feb, Sun 15 Mar (10-4); Sun 5, Mon 6 Apr (10-5). Adm £6, chd free. Pre-booking essential, please visit www.ngs.org.uk for information & booking. Tea, coffee & cake. Visits also by arrangement 31 Jan to 17 Aug. Parking is limited, please contact the owner to confirm availability.** A plantsman's garden set in 1½ acres a great variety of plants. Large areas of shade plantings. Over 300 different snowdrops, Anemone nemorosa, Erythroniums, ferns and geraniums. A dwarf conifer rockery with a range of choice bulbs and herbaceous borders. Vegetable beds. Autumn brings mass plantings of Cyclamen to the party. There is a large area dedicated to propagation of more unusual plants.

Our 2025 donation to the Queen's Institute of Community Nursing now helps support over 3,500 Queen's Nurses working in the community in England, Wales, Northern Ireland, the Channel Islands and the Isle of Man.

WILTSHIRE

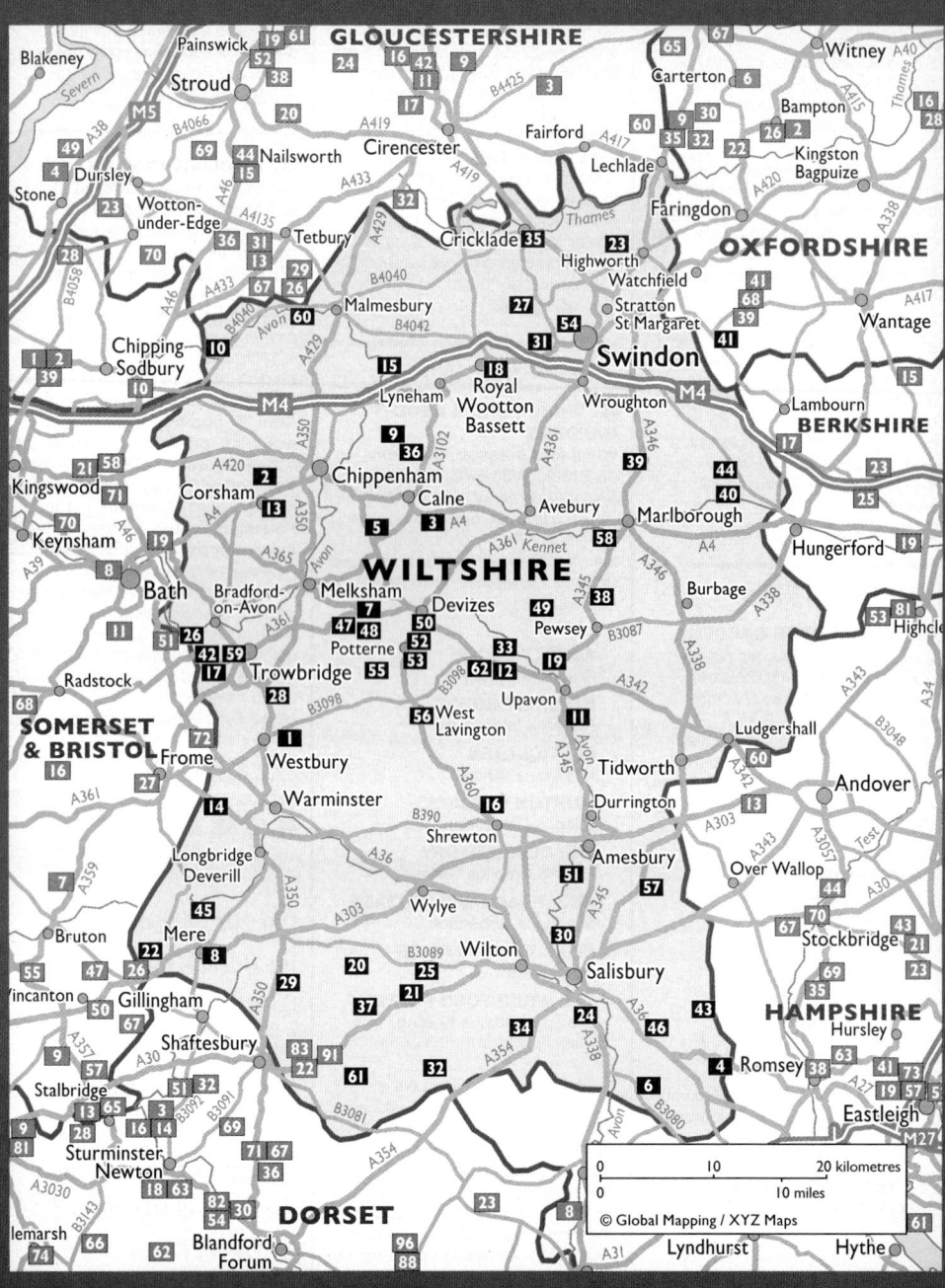

WILTSHIRE 557

VOLUNTEERS

County Organisers
Ros Ford 07717 135028
ros.ford@ngs.org.uk

Alex Graham 07906 146237
alex.graham@ngs.org.uk

County Treasurer
Tony Roper 01249 447436
tony.roper@ngs.org.uk

Booklet Co-ordinator & Publicity
Tricia Duncan 01672 810443
tricia.duncan@ngs.org.uk

Social Media
Maud Peters 07595 266299
maud.peters@ngs.org.uk

Assistant County Organisers
Sue Allen 07785 294153
sue.allen@ngs.org.uk

Sarah Coate 01722 782365
sarah.coate@ngs.org.uk

Andy Devey 07810 641595
andy.devey@ngs.org.uk

Jo Hankey 01722 742472
jo.hankey@ngs.org.uk

Julie Harding 07775 683163
julie.harding@ngs.org.uk

Sophie Malpas 07850 139200
sophie.malpas@ngs.org.uk

Jane Milligan 07771 901352
jane.milligan@ngs.org.uk

Alison Parker 07786 985741
alison.parker@ngs.org.uk

Amelia Tester 01672 520218
amelia.tester@ngs.org.uk

@WiltshireNGS
@Wiltshirengs

OPENING DATES

All entries subject to change.
For latest information check
www.ngs.org.uk

Map locator numbers are shown to the right of each garden name.

Extended openings are shown at the beginning of the month.

January

Every Thursday
Westcroft 57

Saturday 17th
Westcroft 57

Saturday 31st
Westcroft 57

February

Snowdrop Openings

Every Thursday
Westcroft 57

Sunday 1st
Westcroft 57

Friday 13th
Westcroft 57

Sunday 15th
Westcroft 57

Saturday 21st
Westcroft 57

Sunday 22nd
Westcroft 57

March

Every Thursday to Thursday 12th
Westcroft 57

Sunday 15th
◆ Corsham Court 13

Sunday 29th
◆ Corsham Court 13

April

Sunday 12th
Brow Cottage 7
Seend House 47

Saturday 18th
Wellaway 55

Sunday 19th
Wellaway 55

Saturday 25th
Conock Manor 12

Sunday 26th
Fonthill House 20

May

Saturday 9th
Horatio's Garden 24

Sunday 10th
Manor Farm House 33

Friday 15th
Biddestone Manor 2

Saturday 16th
Winkelbury House 61

Sunday 17th
Hyde's House 25
1 Southview 50
Trymnells 53
◆ Twigs Community Garden 54

Saturday 30th
Fovant House 21
Knoyle Place 29
The Old Vicarage 41

Sunday 31st
NEW Elmcroft 18
North Cottage 37
The Old Mill 40

June

Tuesday 2nd
NEW Manor Farm House 32

Thursday 4th
Cadenham Manor 9

Saturday 6th
Seend House 47
Seend Manor 48

Sunday 7th
Chisenbury Priory 11
Dauntsey Gardens 15
Hannington Village Gardens 23
NEW 2 Naish House 36
NEW Shell Cottage 49

Wednesday 10th
Whatley Manor 60

Saturday 13th
20 Jubilee Estate 27
◆ Lydiard Park Walled Garden 31
West Lavington Manor 56

558 WILTSHIRE

Sunday 14th
Burton Grange	8
Drax House	16
Gasper Cottage	22
20 Jubilee Estate	27
The Old Vicarage	42
4 Westwood Road	59

Sunday 21st
North Cottage	37
Rodmead Farm	45

Wednesday 24th
Preston Farm	44

Sunday 28th
Duck Pond Barn	17
Oare House	38

July

Sunday 12th
Little Durnford Manor	30

Sunday 19th
Cherry Orchard Barn	10
◆ Twigs Community Garden	54

Sunday 26th
Corsley House	14
NEW Mount House	35

August

Friday 14th
The Old Mill	40

Saturday 29th
Ogbourne Manor	39

September

Saturday 5th
Falkners Cottage	19
◆ Iford Manor Gardens	26

Sunday 6th
1 Southview	50

Saturday 12th
Wellaway	55

Sunday 13th
Wellaway	55

Wednesday 16th
Blackland House	3

By Arrangement

Arrange a personalised garden visit with your club, or group of friends, on a date to suit you. See individual garden entries for full details.

Beggars Knoll Chinese Garden	1
Bluebells	4
NEW Brampton	6
Cadenham Manor	9
Chisenbury Priory	11
Falkners Cottage	19
Gasper Cottage	22
Kettle Farm Cottage	28
Manor House, Stratford Tony	34
NEW Mount House	35
NEW 2 Naish House	36
NEW Pilgrims Croft	43
NEW Rowdens Farm	46
1 Southview	50
Teasel	51
Tristenagh House	52
West Lavington Manor	56
Westcroft	57
Westwind	58
Wudston House	62

Burton Grange

THE GARDENS

1 BEGGARS KNOLL CHINESE GARDEN
Newtown, Westbury, BA13 3ED.
Colin Little & Penny Stirling,
01373 823383, silkendalliance@
talktalk.net. *1m SE of Westbury.
Turn off B3098 at White Horse
Pottery, up hill towards the White
Horse for ¾ m. Parking at end
of drive for 10-12 cars.* **Visits by
arrangement June & July for
groups of 5 to 20. Adm inc tea,
coffee & cake, and a tour by the
owners. Adm £10, chd free.**
A series of Chinese style garden
rooms, separated by elaborate
gateways inc moongate, with mosaic
paths winding past pavilions, ponds
and many rare Chinese trees, shrubs
and flowers. Relatively new, a tranquil
Islamic style tiled garden influenced
by NW China. Potager full of flowers
and vegetables. Spectacular views to
the Mendips

2 BIDDESTONE MANOR
Chippenham Lane, Biddestone,
SN14 7DJ. Ina Astrup. *On A4
between Chippenham & Corsham
turn N from A420, 5m W of
Chippenham, turn S.* **Fri 15 May
(10.30-4). Adm £8, chd free.
Home-made teas & cakes.**
Cotswold stone C17 manor house
(not open) with 5 acres of garden
to enjoy. Lake, ponds, streams,
arboretum, Chinese trees, vegetable and cutting
gardens and orchard. Formal front
garden featuring box and yew topiary.

3 BLACKLAND HOUSE
Quemerford, Calne, SN11 8UQ.
Polly & Edward Nicholson,
www.bayntunflowers.co.uk. *Foot of
the Marlborough Downs, just outside
Calne. Situated just off A4. Use
Google Maps. Enter the grounds
through the side entrance signed
St. Peter's Church & Blackland Park
Deliveries. Opp The Willows on
Quemerford.* **Wed 16 Sept (2-5).
Adm £10, chd free. Pre-booking
essential, please visit www.ngs.
org.uk for information & booking.
Home-made teas. Vegan & gluten
free cakes. Tea & cakes charged
at £5. Donation to Dorothy House
Hospice.**
A wonderfully varied 6 acre garden

adjacent to the River Marden that
juxtaposes ornamental plantings
with wilder areas. Formal walled
productive and cutting garden,
traditional glasshouses, rose garden
and wide herbaceous borders.
Interesting topiary, trained fruit
trees, historic tulips (inc the National
Collection of historic tulips). Certified
organic with the Soil Association.
Hand-tied bunches of seasonal
flowers and copies of Polly's book
'The Tulip Garden' by Polly Nicholson,
Phaidon 2024, will be for sale. Partial
wheelchair access, steps, grass
and cobbles, wooden bridges, deep
water.

4 BLUEBELLS
Cowesfield, Whiteparish,
Salisbury, SP5 2RB. Hilary
Mathison, 07709 205589,
hilary.mathison@icloud.com. *SW
of Salisbury. On main A27 road
from Salisbury to Romsey. 1½m SE
of Whiteparish, on A27, 100-200
metres inside Wilts county boundary.
What3words app: centuries.baths.
herbs.* **Visits by arrangement 20
Apr to 20 Sept for groups of 6 to
35. Cars on site10 ideal, 12 max.
Adm £5, chd free. Cream teas £4.
Wine & savoury bites for evening
visits £5. Please bring cash for
refreshments.**
Rural 1½ acre garden with small
woodland which has carpets of
bluebells in season. Themed borders
inc grasses and coneflowers, hostas
and other shade lovers, winter
garden. South facing rear garden
with perennials, some unusual. Many
tulips in spring with mainly perennials
and shrubs Large vegetable area, fruit
trees, inc espalier trees, 'stepovers'
and 2 ponds. A garden with lots
of design ideas. Partial wheelchair
access.

5 ♦ BOWOOD WOODLAND GARDEN
Calne, SN11 9PG. The Marquis
of Lansdowne, 01249 812102,
houseandgardens@bowood.org,
www.bowood.org. *3½ m SE of
Chippenham. Located off J17 M4
nr Bath & Chippenham. Entrance
off A342 between Sandy Lane &
Derry Hill Villages. Follow brown
tourist signs.* **For opening times and
information, please phone, email or
visit garden website.**
A separate attraction on the Bowood
Estate, the Woodland Garden is only

open for 6 weeks during the flowering
season (mid April to early June).
Covering over 30 acres, there are just
over 2 miles of meandering paths
intersecting the Woodland Garden
with an oasis of azaleas, bluebells,
magnolias and rhododendrons.
From the individual flowers to the
breathtaking sweep of colour, this is a
garden not to be missed, with hidden
treasures at every corner.

6 NEW BRAMPTON
The Row, Redlynch,
Salisbury, SP5 2JT. Dr
Anita Green, 07969 577431,
anitagreen@me.com. *8m SE of
Salisbury. Brampton is a white house
approx 100 metres along The Row,
set back on R. The Kings Head pub
can be seen as you approach The
Row.* **Visits by arrangement in
June for groups of 10 to 30. Adm
£5, chd free. Home-made teas.
We are a vegetarian home and
can cater for vegans and gluten
free diets with home-made
cakes.**
Brampton is a medium sized garden
created over the last 2 years from
an undeveloped plot. The garden
inc young trees, cottage garden
style borders, a potager area with
raised beds and a small greenhouse,
2 water features, small orchard
with meadow and sitting areas, inc
secluded walled fire pit space with
woodland planting. The garden needs
to be appreciated as a new, evolving
garden the owners are still developing
and keen to share with visitors at this
early stage.

Our donation to the Army Benevolent Fund supported 776 individuals with horticultural related grants in 2025.

WILTSHIRE

7 BROW COTTAGE
Seend Hill, Seend, Melksham, SN12 6RU. Alexandra & James Gray, www.alexandragray.com. *2m W of Devizes on A361. Garden on L when coming from E, at top of Inmarsh Lane. Parking on green in village centre. Footpath via fields as marked by yellow signs.* Sun 12 Apr (1-5). Combined adm with Seend House £8, chd free. Home-made teas.
A ½ acre contemporary cottage garden owned by a garden designer and created over the past 26 yrs. A garden of many harmonious parts inc lawns, well-stocked borders, topiary, potager, sunken pool garden, wildlife pond, short woodland walk, species bulb and wildflower lawn and canopied dining area. Open with Seend House and connected by a field footpath. Shuttle available. WC avail by the car park. Wheelchair access over gravel driveway.

8 BURTON GRANGE
Burton, Mere, BA12 6BR. Sue Phipps & Paddy Sumner, www.suephipps.com. *What3words app: closes.part.standards. Take lane, signed to Burton, on A303 just E of Mere bypass. After 400 yds follow road past pond & round to L. Go past wall on R. Burton Grange entrance is in laurel hedge on R.* Sun 14 June (11.30-5). Adm £5, chd free. Home-made teas.
1½ acre peaceful garden, created from scratch since 2014. Lawns, borders, large ornamental pond, some gravel planting, vegetable garden, cutting garden and pergola rose garden, together with a number of wonderful mature trees.

9 CADENHAM MANOR
Foxham, Chippenham, SN15 4NH. Victoria & Martin Nye, contact@cadenham.com, www.cadenham.com. *B4069 from Chippenham or M4 J17, turn R in Christian Malford & L in Foxham. On A3102 turn L from Calne or R from Lyneham at Xrds between Hilmarton & Goatacre. See map www.cadenham.com/contact.* Thur 4 June (2-6). Adm £10, chd free. Pre-booking essential, please visit www.ngs.org.uk for information & booking. Tea, coffee & cake. Visits also by arrangement 14 Apr to 30 Sept for groups of 15 to 40.
This glorious 4 acre garden surrounds a listed C17 manor house with moats and a C16 dovecote. Its many rooms are furnished with specimen trees, fountains and statues to focus the eye. Known for its stunning displays of old roses, it also has swathes of spring bulbs, wisteria, irises, a water garden in the old canal, and extensive vegetable and herb gardens. Plus a spectacular late summer garden. Wisteria and bearded irises in May, peonies in May/June and old roses in June. Vegetable and herb gardens and late summer borders in July, August and September.

10 CHERRY ORCHARD BARN
Luckington, SN14 6NZ. Paul Fletcher & Tim Guard. *Cherry Orchard Barn is ¾ m before the centre of SN14 6NZ at a T junction. Passing the Barn is ill-advised, as turning rapidly becomes difficult.* Sun 19 July (1-5). Adm £5, chd free. Tea, coffee & cake.
A charming one acre garden, created from the corner of a field, with open views of surrounding countryside. Containing seven rooms, three of which are densely planted with herbaceous perennials, each with individual identities and colour themes. The garden is described by visitors as a haven of tranquillity. Largely level access to all areas of garden. Some gravel paths.

11 CHISENBURY PRIORY
East Chisenbury, Pewsey, SN9 6AQ. Mr & Mrs John Manser, 07810 483984, peterjohnmanser@yahoo.com. *3m SW of Pewsey. Turn E from A345 at Enford then N to E Chisenbury, main gates 1m on R.* Sun 7 June (2-6). Adm £10, chd free. Home-made teas. Visits also by arrangement May & June for groups of 10 to 30.
Medieval Priory with Queen Anne face and early C17 rear (not open) in middle of 5 acre garden on chalk. Mature garden with fine trees within clump and flint walls, herbaceous borders, shrubs and roses. Moisture loving plants along mill leat, carp pond, orchard and wild garden, many unusual plants.

12 CONOCK MANOR
Conock, Devizes, SN10 3QQ. Justin Kennedy. *5m SE of Devizes. Conock lies just off the A342 between the turnings for Urchfont & Chirton. Conock Manor is on the R side of the lane. What3words app: flap.emeralds.cashiers.* Sat 25 Apr (2-4). Adm £8, chd free. Tea, coffee, cold drinks & cakes.
A relaxed family garden embracing C18 architecture (inc a rustic dairy) and defined by its long, south facing wall. There are lawns and wildflower meadows, mixed borders and climbers, a magnolia grove and a vegetable garden with greenhouse. Evolving under the stewardship of Pip Morrison, the garden utilises a ha-ha to sit comfortably in the surrounding wooded parkland with views out to the surrounding hills and the Alton Barnes chalk-horse. Soft lawn, some gravel paths.

13 ♦ CORSHAM COURT
Corsham, SN13 0BZ. Lord Methuen, 01249 701610, staterooms@corsham-court.co.uk, www.corsham-court.co.uk. *4m W of Chippenham. Signed off A4 at Corsham.* For NGS: Sun 15 Mar (2-4); Sun 29 Mar (2-5). Adm £12.50, chd £6. For other opening times and information, please phone, email or visit garden website.
Park and gardens laid out by Capability Brown and Repton. Large lawns with fine specimens of ornamental trees surround the Elizabethan mansion. C18 bath house hidden in the grounds. Spring bulbs, beautiful lily pond with Indian bean trees, young arboretum and stunning collection of magnolias. Wheelchair (not motorised) access to house, gravel paths in garden.

14 CORSLEY HOUSE
Corsley, Warminster, BA12 7QH. Glen Senk & Keith Johnson. *From Longleat on the A362 towards Frome turning 1st R on Deep Lane. Corsley House is ¼ m on R. The parkland entrance, where there is parking, is on R beyond the house.* Sun 26 July (11-5). Adm £10, chd free. Tea, coffee & cake.
Recently featured on Gardeners' World, this is a garden full of surprises to reflect the eclectic nature of a Georgian home with a secret Jacobean facade. A unique sculpted wave lawn and a truly exceptional walled garden. Many well preserved ancient outbuildings such as a potting and apple storage shed and a granary built on staddle stones. All gloriously overlooking the NT's Cley Hill.

WILTSHIRE

GROUP OPENING

15 DAUNTSEY GARDENS
Church Lane, Dauntsey, Malmesbury, SN15 4HT. **Mr & Mrs Christopher Jerram.** *5m SE of Malmesbury. Approach via Dauntsey Rd from Gt Somerford, 1¼m from Volunteer Inn Great Somerford.* **Sun 7 June (1-5). Combined adm £10, chd free. Home-made teas at Idover House. Cash only for admission & refreshments.**

THE COACH HOUSE
Mrs J Seddon-Brown.

DAUNTSEY PARK
Mr & Mrs Giovanni Amati,
01249 721777, enquiries@dauntseyparkhouse.co.uk.

THE GARDEN COTTAGE
Miss Ann Sturgis.

IDOVER HOUSE
Mr & Mrs Christopher Jerram.

THE OLD COACH HOUSE
Tony & Janette Yates.

THE OLD POND HOUSE
Mr & Mrs Stephen Love.

THE OLD RECTORY
Mr Christopher & Mrs Claire Mellor-Hill, hello@theoldrectorydauntsey.com,
www.theoldrectorydauntsey.com.

This group of 7 gardens, centred around the historic Dauntsey Park Estate, ranges from the Classical C18 country house setting of Dauntsey Park, with spacious lawns, old trees and views over the River Avon, to mature country house gardens and traditional walled gardens. Enjoy the formal rose garden in pink and white, old fashioned borders and duck ponds at Idover House, and the quiet seclusion of The Coach House with its thyme terrace and gazebos, climbing roses and clematis. Here, mop-headed pruned *Crataegus prunifolia* line the drive. The Garden Cottage has a traditional walled kitchen garden with organic vegetables, orchard, woodland walk and yew topiary. Meanwhile the 2 acres at The Old Pond House are both clipped and unclipped! Large pond with lilies and fat carp, and look out for the giraffe and turtle. The Old Coach House is a small garden with perennial plants, shrubs and climbers. The Old Rectory is a 2 acre garden adjoining the River Avon with mature trees, roses and shrubs.

16 DRAX HOUSE
Orcheston, Salisbury, SP3 4RL. **Mr & Mrs J Pugh.** *12 m NW of Salisbury, just N of Shrewton. Turn off the A360 towards Orcheston. At Xrds follow signs for parking & garden. Garden approx 80 metres walk from village hall. Follow signs.* **Sun 14 June (1.30-5.30). Adm £6, chd free. Home-made teas.** Relaxed informal farmhouse garden with herbaceous border, small wildlife pond and some wilder areas. Walled kitchen garden with raised beds filled with vegetables and cutting garden. Several seating areas, some narrow and uneven paths and steps. Garden has been lovingly reclaimed over last 12 yrs with areas awaiting further work. The garden is still evolving.

Beggars Knoll Chinese Garden

17 DUCK POND BARN
Church Lane, Wingfield, Trowbridge, BA14 9LW. Janet & Marc Berlin. *9m SW of Bath. On B3109 from Frome to Bradford on Avon, turn opp Poplars pub into Church Lane. Duck Pond Barn is at end of lane. Big field for parking next door. No parking on the Farm.* **Sun 28 June (10-5). Adm £5, chd free. Tea, coffee & cake.**
Garden of 2 acres with large duck pond, lawns, ericaceous beds, dry bed, orchard, vegetable garden, large greenhouse, wood and wild areas of grass and trees with many wild flowers. Large dry stone wall topped with flower beds with rose arbour. 3 ponds linked by a rill in flower garden and large pergola in orchard. Set in farmland and mainly flat. Many interesting and rare succulents. Tea and cakes served outside in covered farm area. Wheelchair access to nearly all areas.

18 NEW ELMCROFT
Glebe Road, Royal Wootton Bassett, SN4 7DU. Mrs Nicola Case. *6m W of Swindon. Parking in pay & display car park SN4 7AX. Elmcroft is a 6min walk from the car park. Walk down Station Rd, take the 2nd R onto Glebe Rd. Elmcroft is about 100 metres on the R.* **Sun 31 May (11-4). Adm £5, chd free. Tea, coffee, squash with a slice of cake £5.00.**
An ever evolving, organically managed garden with a mixture of planting inc woodland, drought resistant gravel gardens, free flowering and seeding plants and mixed hedging. All with a view to increase 'food chain' for nature. Irrigated when necessary using an underground 7500 litre rainwater harvesting tank.

19 FALKNERS COTTAGE
North Newnton, Pewsey, SN9 6LA. Anne & John Thompson-Ashby, 01980 630988, anne.thompsonashby@btinternet.com. *3m W Pewsey. SW from Pewsey on A345 direction Salisbury, exit 3 at Woodbridge r'about to Hilcott. Pass farm, next house on sharp L hand bend. Care turning R.* **Sat 5 Sept (2-5). Adm £7, chd free. Tea, coffee & cake. Visits also by arrangement 27 Apr to 7 Sept for groups of 10 to 35.**
This 5 acre site in formal garden with colourful borders, topiary and box framed parterre and courtyard 'rooms' with contemporary sculpture.

Behind the thatched barn lies a kitchen garden with hens. There is a meadow with ornamental trees, a small lake with a summerhouse on an island, a woodland, a wildlife pond and a bog garden. A short walk from the meadow is the C13 St James' Church.

20 FONTHILL HOUSE
Tisbury, SP3 5SA. The Lord Margadale of Islay, www.fonthill.co.uk/gardens. *13m W of Salisbury. Via B3089 in Fonthill Bishop. 3m N of Tisbury. Please use Fonthill Park entrance. What3words app: creamed. moderated.passwords.* **Sun 26 Apr (12-5). Adm £10, chd free. Light refreshments. Sandwiches, quiches, cakes, soft drinks, tea, coffee & wine.**
Wonderful woodland walks with daffodils, rhododendrons, azaleas, shrubs and bulbs. Magnificent views, formal gardens. The gardens have been extensively redeveloped under the direction of Tania Compton and Marie-Louise Agius. The formal gardens are being continuously improved with new designs, exciting trees, shrubs and plants. Gorgeous William Pye fountain and other sculptures. Partial wheelchair access.

21 FOVANT HOUSE
Church Lane, Fovant, Salisbury, SP3 5LA. Amanda & Noel Flint. *Approx 10m W of Salisbury. 6½m W of Wilton & 9.3m E of Shaftesbury. Take A30 to Fovant then head N through village and follow signs to St George's Church. Car parking at end of Church Lane.* **Sat 30 May (2-5). Adm £8, chd free. Home-made teas.**
Fovant House is a former Rectory set in about 3 acres of formal garden. In 2016 the garden was redesigned by Arabella Lennox Boyd. Garden inc 60 metre herbaceous border, terraces and parterre. A range of mature trees inc cedar, copper beech, oak and lime. Majority of garden has easy wheelchair access subject to ground conditions being dry.

22 GASPER COTTAGE
Gasper Street, Gasper Stourton, Warminster, BA12 6PY. Bella Hoare & Johnnie Gallop, 07812 555 883, bella.hoare@icloud.com, www.gaspercottage.com. *Nr*

Stourhead Gardens, 4m from Mere. Turn off A303 at B3092 Mere. Follow Stourhead signs. Go through Stourton. After 1m, turn R after phone box, signed Gasper. Parking before house on R, in field. House 2nd on R going up hill. **Sun 14 June (11-5). Adm £7, chd free. Visits also by arrangement 1 May to 18 Sept for groups of 10 to 30. Fridays only. £14 adm price inc refreshments. Strictly no coaches.**
Two acre garden, with stunning rural views. Luxuriously mixed planting of perennials and shrubs with numerous hardy and tender annuals. Orchard embedded in a forest garden with a wildlife pond and model steam powered railway. Artist's studio surrounded by colour balanced planting and formal pond. Several seating areas. Can accommodate max 12 seater minibus due to narrow lane. Cafe 1m away at Stourhead.

GROUP OPENING

23 HANNINGTON VILLAGE GARDENS
Hannington, Swindon, SN6 7RP. *Off B4019 Blunsdon to Highworth Rd by the Freke Arms. Park as directed by signs, in the street where possible, or opp Lushill House.* **Sun 7 June (11-5). Combined adm £10, chd free. Tea, coffee & cake in Hannington Village Hall.**

CHESTNUT HOUSE
Mary & Garry Marshall.

CHESTNUT VILLA
David Cornish.

GLEBE HOUSE
Charlie & Tory Barne.

LUSHILL HOUSE
John & Sasha Kennedy.

QUARRY BANK
Paul Minter & Michael Weldon.

22 QUEENS ROAD
Jan & Pete Willis.

NEW 24 QUEENS ROAD
Mr Les & Mrs Sue Marland.

ROSE COTTAGE
Mrs Ruth Scholes.

STEP COTTAGE
Mr & Mrs J Clarke.

THE BUTLER'S COTTAGE
Alan & Laura Felton.

YORKE HOUSE GARDEN
Mr Miles & Mrs Cath Bozeat.

Hannington has a dramatic hilltop position on a Cotswold ridge overlooking the Thames valley. A great variety of gardens, from large manor houses to small cottage gardens, many of which follow the brow of the hill and afford stunning views of the surrounding farmland. You will need lots of time to see all that is on offer in this beautiful historic village.

24 HORATIO'S GARDEN
Duke of Cornwall Spinal Treatment Centre, Salisbury Hospital NHS Foundation Trust, Odstock Road, Salisbury, SP2 8BJ. Horatio's Garden Charity, www.horatiosgarden.org.uk. *1m from centre of Salisbury. Follow signs for Salisbury District Hospital. Please park in car park 8, which will be free to NGS visitors on the day. Enter by gate next to the top zebra crossing. What3words app: sheep.nearly.frost.* **Sat 9 May (2-5). Adm £5, chd free. Tea & delicious cakes, made by Horatio's Garden volunteers, will be served in the Garden Room.**
Award winning hospital garden, opened in Sept 2012 and designed by Cleve West for patients with spinal cord injury at the Duke of Cornwall Spinal Treatment Centre. Built from donations given in memory of Horatio Chapple who was a volunteer at the centre in his school holidays. Low limestone walls, which represent the form of the spine, divide densely planted herbaceous beds. Everything in the garden is designed to benefit patients during their long stays in hospital. The garden is run by a Head Gardener and team of volunteers. Designer Cleve West has 9 RHS gold medals.

25 HYDE'S HOUSE
Dinton, SP3 5HH. Mr George Cruddas. *9m W of Salisbury. Off B3089 nr Dinton Church on St Mary's Rd. See signs & arrows.* **Sun 17 May (2-5). Adm £8, chd free. Home-made teas at Thatched Old School Room with outside tea tables.**
3 acres of wild and formal garden in beautiful situation with series of hedged garden rooms. Numerous shrubs, flowers and borders, all allowing tolerated wild flowers and preferred weeds, while others creep in. Large walled kitchen garden, herb garden and C13 dovecote (open). Charming C16/18 Grade I listed house (not open), with lovely courtyard. Every year varies. Free walks around park and lake. Steps, slopes, gravel paths and driveway.

26 ♦ IFORD MANOR GARDENS
Bradford-on-Avon, BA15 2BA. Mr Cartwright-Hignett, www.ifordmanor.co.uk. *7m S of Bath. Off A36, brown tourist sign to Iford 1m. From Bradford-on-Avon or Trowbridge via Lower Westwood Village (brown signs). Please note all approaches via narrow single track lanes with passing places.* **For NGS: Sat 5 Sept (11-4). Adm £12. Pre-booking essential, please phone 01225 863146, email info@ifordmanor.co.uk or visit www.ifordmanor.co.uk for information & booking. Light refreshments in Iford Manor's award winning restaurant, or adjacent café & bakery. Regret children under 10 will not be admitted to the garden. For other opening times and information, please phone, email or visit garden website.**
Harold Peto's former home, this 2½ acre terraced garden provides timeless inspiration. Influenced by his travels, particularly to Italy and Japan, Peto embellished the garden with a collection of classical statuary and architectural fragments. Steep steps link the terraces with pools, fountains, loggias, colonnades, urns and figures, with magnificent rural views across the Iford Valley.

27 20 JUBILEE ESTATE
Purton, Swindon, SN5 4EU. Gavin & Ellen James, www.facebook.com/JubileeEst. *NW of Swindon. From Station Rd, turn onto Witts Lane & follow this to Jubilee Estate on the L. Number 20 is on the R.* **Sat 13, Sun 14 June (10-4). Adm £6, chd free. Cream teas.**
Set in the picturesque village of Purton, this small cottage style garden is a hidden gem packed with roses and planted for wildlife. Divided into different areas, with shaded pergola, sunny lawn and wildlife pond. Home-made cream teas are served on the patio. Not fully accessible due to gravel paths. Parking is limited so please be considerate.

28 KETTLE FARM COTTAGE
Kettle Lane, West Ashton, Trowbridge, BA14 6AW. Tim & Jenny Woodall, 01225 753474, trwwoodall@outlook.com. *Kettle Lane is halfway between West Ashton T-lights & Yarnbrook r'about on S side of A350. Garden ½ m down end of lane. Limited car parking for up to 6 cars.* **Visits by arrangement 8 June to 21 Aug for groups of up to 15. Adm £12, chd free. Adm inc home-made teas.**
Previously of Priory House, Bradford on Avon, which was featured on Gardeners' World, we now have a cottage garden that was featured in the August 2024 edition of The English Garden. The garden is full of colour and style, flowering from June to August. Bring a loved one/friend to see the garden and have tea. One or two steps.

29 KNOYLE PLACE
Holloway, East Knoyle, Salisbury, SP3 6AF. Lizie de la Moriniere. *What3words app: theme.poets.gadget. Turn off A350 into E Knoyle & follow signs to parking at Lower Lye. Walk 5 mins to Knoyle Place through village following signs.* **Sat 30 May (2-5). Adm £10, chd free. Home-made teas.**
Very beautiful and elegant garden created over 60 yrs by previous and current owners. Above the house there are several acres of mature rhododendron and magnolia woodland planting. Among the many different areas in this 9 acre garden is a box parterre, rose garden, vegetable garden and, around the house, a recently planted formal garden designed by Dan Combes. Sloping lawns and woodland paths, stone terrace.

In 2025 we awarded over £288,800 in Community Garden Grants, supporting 114 community garden projects.

30 LITTLE DURNFORD MANOR
Little Durnford, Salisbury, SP4 6AH. **The Earl & Countess of Chichester.** *3m N of Salisbury. Just N beyond Stratford-sub-Castle. Remain to E of R Avon at road junction at Stratford Bridge & cont towards Salterton for ½m heading N. Entrance on L just past Little Durnford sign. What3words app: remark.collides.zones.* **Sun 12 July (2-5). Adm £5, chd free. Home-made teas in cricket pavilion within grounds.**
Extensive lawns with cedars, wildflower meadows, walled gardens, fruit trees, large vegetable garden, small knot and herb gardens. Terraces, borders, sunken garden, water garden, lake with islands, river walks, labyrinth walk. Little Durnford Manor is a substantial grade I listed, C18 private country residence (not open) built of an attractive mix of Chilmark stone and flint. Camels, alpacas, guanacos, llamas, pigs, pygmy goats, donkeys, horses, ponies and sheep are all grazing next to the gardens.

31 ♦ LYDIARD PARK WALLED GARDEN
Lydiard Tregoze, Swindon, SN5 3PA. **Swindon Borough Council**, 01793 464644, lydiardpark@swindon.gov.uk, www.lydiardpark.org.uk. *3m W Swindon, 1m from J16 M4. Follow brown signs from W Swindon.* **For NGS: Sat 13 June (11-4). Adm £3.15, chd £1.85. Light refreshments in Coach House Tea Rooms.** For other opening times and information, please phone, email or visit garden website.
Beautiful ornamental C18 walled garden. Trimmed shrubs alternating with individually planted flowers and bulbs inc rare daffodils and tulips, sweet peas, annuals and wall-trained fruit trees. Unique features inc a well and sundial. Wide level paths, no steps.

32 NEW MANOR FARM HOUSE
Quidham Street, Bowerchalke, Salisbury, SP5 5BU. **David & Caroline Floyd.** *10 SW of Salisbury. A30 to Fovant & head S to Bowerchalke. What3words app: reinforce.obscuring.remix. Parking in farmyard opp.* **Tue 2 June (2-5). Adm £8, chd free. Home-made teas.**
The garden contains interesting trees inc a large beehive shaped yew, a tulip tree and a catalpa. The rose covered veranda offers seating with glorious views of the Chalke Valley downs. The walled garden contains herbaceous and shrub borders and a pretty rose clad summerhouse to sit in. The ornamental fruit garden is edged with lavender and bee loving teucrium. Some gravel in driveway otherwise accessible.

33 MANOR FARM HOUSE
Manor Farm Lane, Patney, Devizes, SN10 3RB. **Mark & Tricia Alsop.** *Between Pewsey & Devizes. Take 3rd entrance on L going up Manor Farm Lane from village green. Parking available in paddock.* **Sun 10 May (2-5). Adm £6, chd free. Tea, coffee & cake.**
2 acre plantsman's garden originally designed by Michael Balston and updated by us over the past 14 yrs. Lawned areas with borders

Seend Manor

© Marcus Harpur

surrounded by hornbeams and yew hedging, long border and gravel garden by tennis court, formal vegetable garden with buxus parterres and meadow with spring bulbs, box mound and walkway through moisture loving plants. Regret no WC.

34 MANOR HOUSE, STRATFORD TONY
Stratford Tony, Salisbury, SP5 4AT. Mr & Mrs Hugh Cookson, 01722 718496, lc@stratfordtony.co.uk. *4m SW of Salisbury. Take minor road W off A354 at Coombe Bissett. Garden on S after 1m. Or take minor road off A3094 from Wilton signed Stratford Tony & racecourse. What3words app: belonged.haunt.smuggled.* **Visits by arrangement 1 May to 10 Sept. Adm £10, chd free.** Varied 4 acre garden with year-round interest. Formal and informal areas. Herbaceous borders, vegetable garden, parterre garden, orchard, shrubberies, roses, specimen trees, lakeside planting, winter colour and structure, many original contemporary features and places to sit and enjoy the downland views. Some gravel and uneven paving.

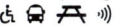

35 NEW MOUNT HOUSE
23 High Street, Cricklade, SN6 6AP. Yseult Ogilvie & Anthony Eyre, 07736 609789, yseult@yoarchitecture.com. *7m from Cirencester. Mount House is on the High St opp the Town Council offices. Limited parking available, but there is additional parking by the Town Hall nearby.* **Sun 26 July (11-5). Adm £10, chd free. Tea, coffee & cake. Visits also by arrangement 24 July to 31 Dec for groups of 12 to 50.**
Mount House occupies a ½ acre of walled gardens overlooked by St Sampson's Church. Architect designed, the gardens are undergoing a substantial restoration, having been neglected for many years. The designs includes herbaceous borders containing rare species in variety, grassed mounds, lawns, trees, shrubs, ferns, glasshouse, water-feature, and sculpture. It is very much a work in progress.

36 NEW 2 NAISH HOUSE
Spirthill, Calne, SN11 9HW. Mrs Sue Allen, 07787 536337, sue@microbz.co.uk, microbz.co.uk/pages/our-story. *4m S of Lyneham. Turn off A3102, turn L from Calne or R from Lyneham at Xrds between Hilmarton & Goatacre. Straight on to Spirthill & follow signs. What3words app: enjoys.drifting.puzzled.* **Sun 7 June (1-5). Adm £8, chd free. Tea, coffee & cake. Visits also by arrangement 6 June to 7 June for groups of up to 15. (any time on the 6th June & morning only on the 7th).**
A wild wellbeing garden of approx 8 acres inc meadow walks, labyrinth, ponds, courtyard garden, orchard and polytunnels. Over 20 yrs, we have lovingly developed this unconventional garden, also home to a probiotic brewery, which works with the invisible architects of life: soil-based microbes. Join a talk at 2pm or 4pm outlining the magic of microbial life in healthy soil. Accessible for off-road type mobility vehicles, plus accessible toilet.

37 NORTH COTTAGE
Tisbury Row, Tisbury, SP3 6RZ. Jacqueline & Robert Baker, 01747 870019, baker_jaci@icloud.com. *12m W of Salisbury. From A30 turn N through Ansty, L at T-junction, towards Tisbury. From Tisbury take Ansty road. Car park entrance nr junction signed Tisbury Row.* **Sun 31 May, Sun 21 June (11-5). Adm £5. Home-made light lunches & teas.**
Hard to encapsulate in a few words as each part of the garden and smallholding differs in style and appearance. Experience the intimacy of the garden around the cottage and afterwards walk through orchards, coppice woodland and fields. Cherry on top is the home-made lunches and teas. Metal sculptures and plant supports by Metal Menagerie. Ceramics and wood furniture made by the garden's owners. Please visit www.ngs.org.uk for details of extra pop-up open days.

38 OARE HOUSE
Rudge Lane, Oare, nr Pewsey, SN8 4JQ. Mr Ned Mackay. *2m N of Pewsey. On Marlborough Rd (A345).* **Sun 28 June (2-6). Adm £10, chd free. Light refreshments. Donation to The Order of St John.**
1740s mansion house later extended by Clough Williams Ellis in 1920s (not open). The original formal gardens around the house have been developed over the years to create a wonderful garden full of many unusual plants and a fine collection of rarities. Garden is undergoing a renaissance but still maintains split compartments each with its own individual charm; traditional walled garden with fine herbaceous borders, vegetable areas, trained fruit, roses and grand mixed borders surrounding formal lawns. The magnolia garden is wonderful in spring with some trees dating from 1920s, together with strong bulb plantings. Large arboretum and woodland with many unusual and champion trees. There is always something of interest, with the glorious Pewsey Vale as a backdrop. Partial wheelchair access.

39 OGBOURNE MANOR
Ogbourne St George, Marlborough, SN8 1SU. Mr Andrew Tuckey. *Please follow SatNav. The Manor is the most westerly house in the village beside the church.* **Sat 29 Aug (10-5). Adm £8, chd free. Home-made teas.**
The Manor House dates from 1619 and is built on the site of an ancient priory. The gardens have been extensively extended and improved by the present owners over the past 20 yrs and inc a parterre, swimming pool, tennis court, vegetable garden and stable block. Roses along the parterre walls and dahlias in the borders are particular features. Apart from a rich architectural history the house (not open) has more contemporary fame as the address from which the love letters were written as part of the successful WW2 deception featured in the book and film Operation Mincemeat.

40 THE OLD MILL
Ramsbury, SN8 2PN. Annabel & James Dallas. *8m NE of Marlborough. From Marlborough head to Ramsbury. At The Bell pub follow sign to Hungerford. Garden behind yew hedge on R 100yds beyond The Bell.* **Sun 31 May, Fri 14 Aug (2-5). Adm £8, chd free. Light refreshments.**
A beautiful and characterful garden on the banks of the River Kennet, with wild and cultivated areas, rich mature borders and a vegetable/cutting garden. Walk along mown paths by the river, through water meadows and view the downs beyond. Or stay near the house to enjoy the tranquil and inspirational quirkiness. A garden for all ages to enjoy and relax in. Partial wheelchair access as gravel paths and bridges, and very soft ground in places.
& 🍵 »)

41 THE OLD VICARAGE
Church Lane, Ashbury, Swindon, SN6 8LZ. Mr David Astor. *In the village of Ashbury, next to the church.* **Sat 30 May (10-3). Adm £5, chd free. Tea, coffee & cake.**
Within The Vale of the White Horse, Ashbury is a picturesque village with thatched cottages and a friendly atmosphere. Nestled between the village pub and St Mary's Church is the garden of The Old Vicarage. The garden surrounds the house and is made up of a floriferous walled garden, a wildflower meadow, an extensive kitchen garden, filled with flowers, as well as vegetables, plus more.
🍵 »)

42 THE OLD VICARAGE
Lower Westwood, Bradford-on-Avon, BA15 2AF. Mrs Elizabeth Triggs. *SW side of Bradford-On-Avon. Enter Lower Westwood, take turning opp the New Inn. 2nd house on R after the church. Parking outside the church, overflow parking in field.* **Sun 14 June (12-5). Adm £5, chd free. Refreshments in the Parish Rooms next door between 2-5pm.**
A large garden (²⁄₃ acre) with lovely views to open countryside. At its heart a landscaped family space created with wildlife in mind. Features include a formal Italianate area, fruit and vegetable patches, small orchard and wild meadow, and a large family area and treehouse hidden amongst prairie planting. Lunch available at the New Inn, 200 metres away, booking recommended. Flat with some areas of gravel.
& 🍵 »)

43 NEW PILGRIMS CROFT
West Dean, Salisbury, SP5 1JN. Sara Gruzelier, dandsgruzelier@gmail.com. *1m NE of West Dean. From West Dean village take the West Tytherley road. Leave village, L bend then R bend, entrance on L over cattle grid.* **Visits by arrangement 27 Feb to 13 June for groups of 8 to 30. Drop off for small coaches. Parking for coach ³⁄₄ m away. Adm £7.50, chd free.**
5 acres of garden created over the last 45 yrs around pretty early C18 farmhouse buildings and barns. A garden with year-round interest, inc wide range of herbaceous borders, shrubs, topiary and climbers. Pond with bog area, greenhouse and kitchen garden, hazel coppice and paddock planted in 1984 with a wide variety of trees. Not all areas are easily accessible, pls ask when booking.
& ⛱

44 PRESTON FARM
Preston, Marlborough, SN8 2HF. Shara Grylls. *1m SE of Aldbourne on B4192. Just beyond the small thatched toll cottage on L.* **Wed 24 June (12-4). Adm £8, chd free. Tea, coffee & cake.**
This glorious garden, with views over the surrounding countryside, has been created during the last 20 yrs with the help of designer Justin Spink and is divided into different areas. The parterre contains roses and magnolias, climbing roses tumble over arches, there are well-stocked herbaceous borders, a lawned area leading to the wildflower meadow and a small cutting garden, making this a wonderful garden to explore and enjoy. There is also a newly planted arboretum/pinetum.
& 🍵 »)

45 RODMEAD FARM
Rodmead, Maiden Bradley, Warminster, BA12 7HP. Angus & Sarah Neish. *8m SW of Warminster. Leave Maiden Bradley (with the church on your L) on the B3092. Drive 300m out of the village, and take the L fork to Rodmead Farm.* **Sun 21 June (2-5.30). Adm £6, chd free. Tea, coffee & cake.**
Set in the middle of a working farm, the garden has glorious views of surrounding downland. The extensive gardens have been created over the last 25 yrs and have many different areas to explore, from a spectacular new rill, a formal parterre, an old farm pond and a wildflower meadow, surrounded by traditional farm buildings all covered by a huge variety of climbing roses.
🐕 D 🍵 »)

46 NEW ROWDENS FARM
Grimstead Road, West Grimstead, Salisbury, SP5 3RF. Mr Garry & Mrs Allison Miller, 07843 840166, garry@figandbramble.co.uk. *What3words app: Stops.firelight.butterfly. From A36 turn off at the Alderbury junction, head towards West Grimstead. Rowdens Farm can be found approx 1m on L at the top of the hill.* **Visits by arrangement in June for groups of 10 to 30. Adm £5, chd free.**
A traditional cottage garden style, featuring beautiful herbaceous borders in the courtyard area. The rear garden boasts a lovely selection of flowers and additional herbaceous borders. We also have a small wildlife pond and over 140 pots, primarily filled with hostas. Furthermore, we grow a variety of cut flowers on site to support our daughter's wedding florist business. Please visit www.ngs.org.uk for details of pop-up opening
🐕 ✿ 🍵 »)

47 SEEND HOUSE
High Street, Seend, Melksham, SN12 6NR. Maud Peters, www.instagram.com/maud_seendgarden. *In Seend village. Nr church & opp PO. Parking on village green.* **Sun 12 Apr (1-5). Combined adm with Brow Cottage £8, chd free. Sat 6 June (1-5). Combined adm with Seend Manor £10, chd free. Home-made teas at Brow Cottage on 12 Apr and Seend House on 6 June.**
Seend House is a Georgian house with 6 acres of gardens and paddocks. Framed with yew and box. Highlights inc cloud and rose garden, stream lavender, view of knot garden from above, fountain with grass border, walled garden as well as formal borders. Amazing view across the valley to Salisbury Plain. There is a shuttle bus running between Seend House and Brow Cottage for the opening in April.
🐕 🍵 »)

WILTSHIRE

48 SEEND MANOR
High Street, Seend, Melksham, SN12 6NX. Stephen & Amanda Clark. *In centre of village, opp village green with car parking for garden visitors.* **Sat 6 June (1-5). Combined adm with Seend House £10, chd free. Home-made teas at Seend House.**
Created over 25 yrs, a stunning walled garden with 4 quadrants evoking important parts of the owners' lives in England, China, Africa and Italy. Extensive trelliage, hornbeam hedges on stilts, cottage orne, temple, Chinese ting, grotto, fern walk, fountains, parterres, stone loggia and more. Kitchen garden. Folly ruin in woods. Courtyard garden, and Garden Cottage Garden. Extensive walled gardens, water features, garden structures, topiary and hedging and one of the best views in Wiltshire. Many gravel paths, so only suitable for wheelchairs with thick tyres.

49 NEW SHELL COTTAGE
Alton Priors, Marlborough, SN8 4JX. Mr Josh & Mrs Hayley Carson, www.haymeadowflowers.co.uk. *3m W of Pewsey. Shell cottage on the L nr the bottom of Alton Rd coming from Pewsey. From Devizes take Horton road which leads to Alton Priors.* **Sun 7 June (1.30-5.30). Adm £7, chd free. Home-made teas.**
A charming cottage garden set within medieval thatch topped walls, which include beautifully planted and laid out herbaceous borders, orchard, pond and a glasshouse. Box and yew hedges define different areas. There is an extensive cutting flower garden.

50 1 SOUTHVIEW
Wick Lane, Devizes, SN10 5DR. Teresa Garraud, 07592 728570, tl.garraud@hotmail.co.uk. *From Devizes Market Place go S (Long St). At r'about go straight over, at mini r'about turn L into Wick Ln. Continue to end of Wick Ln. Park in road or roads nearby.* **Sun 17 May, Sun 6 Sept (1.30-4.30). Adm £5, chd free. Visits also by arrangement 19 May to 5 Sept for groups of up to 25. Tea or coffee with biscuits.**
An atmospheric and very long town garden, full of wonderful planting surprises at every turn. Densely planted with pots near the house and large borders further up, it houses a collection of beautiful and often unusual plants, shrubs and trees, many with striking foliage. Colour from seasonal flowers is interwoven within this textural tapestry. 'Truly inspirational' is often heard from visitors.

Knoyle Place

51 TEASEL
Wilsford, Amesbury, Salisbury, SP4 7BL. Ray Palmer, 07785 233155, Ray.Palmer@fierarealestate.com. *Between Stonehenge & Salisbury in the Woodford Valley. 2m SW of Amesbury on western banks of R Avon which runs through the gardens.* **Visits by arrangement Apr to Sept for groups of 10 to 17. Home-made teas.**
Extensively developed since 2020, Teasel's 11 acres inc long herbaceous borders, a lake and ½ m riverside walk. Recently added potager, shrub border, hoggin pathways through orchard to fruit store, Monet inspired bridge, duck house on small pond, water lilies, specimen trees, chess pavilion and croquet lawn. Enjoy teas on the upper terrace with magnificent views of the garden and river. Lovely lake and riverside walk. Goats, Indian Runner ducks and guinea fowl.

52 TRISTENAGH HOUSE
23 Devizes Road, Potterne, Devizes, SN10 5LW. Andrew & Ros Ford, ros.ford@ngs.org.uk. *1m S of Devizes towards Salisbury on A360. Entrance through open wooden gates. What3words app: drifting.defensive.mini.* **Visits by arrangement 1 May to 27 July for groups of 10+. Adm £10, chd free. Tea, coffee & cake.**
Garden of approx 2 acres, created over the past 20 yrs. Island beds with a mixture of herbaceous plants, bulbs, annuals and shrubs. Year-round structure provided by beech and yew hedges, box topiary and by mature beech trees. Small vegetable garden. Some gravelled areas with containers. Good views of valley from terrace. Wheelchair access to most parts of garden on grass paths. Partial access to terrace due to gravel. Some steps.

53 TRYMNELLS
1a Coxhill Lane, Potterne, Devizes, SN10 5PH. Linda Smith. *Coxhill Ln is opp George & Dragon pub. Trymnells is 2nd property on L & is at the top of a gravel drive. Parking at Potterne Village Hall, Some space on drive for those with limited mobility.* **Sun 17 May (1-5). Adm £5, chd free. Open nearby 1 Southview. Afternoon tea is available throughout the afternoon.**
Trymnells garden was started approx 9 yrs ago and has an interesting and challenging plot. It is now maturing and has many trees, shrubs, hedges and perennials. The garden is steep and slopes up from the property and reaches a bank at the very top. Sleepers, fences, walls and plants have imposed a sense of structure with bulbs and perennials providing wonderful colour.

54 ♦ TWIGS COMMUNITY GARDEN
Manor Garden Centre, Cheney Manor, Swindon, SN2 2QJ. TWIGS, 01793 523294, reception@therecoverytreecharity.org.uk, www.therecoverytreecharity.org.uk. *From Gt Western Way, under Bruce St Bridges onto Rodbourne Rd. 1st L at r'about, Cheney Manor Industrial Est. Through estate, 2nd exit at r'about. Opp Pitch & Putt. Signs on R to Manor Garden Centre.* **For NGS: Sun 17 May, Sun 19 July (12-4). Adm £3.50, chd free. Home-made teas.** For other opening times and information, please phone, email or visit garden website.
Delightful 2 acre community garden, created and maintained by volunteers. Features inc 7 individual display gardens, ornamental pond, plant nursery, Iron Age roundhouse, artwork, fitness trail, separate kitchen garden site, Swindon beekeepers and the haven, overflowing with wild flowers. Most areas wheelchair accessible. Disabled WC at TWIGS.

55 WELLAWAY
Close Lane, Marston, SN10 5SN. Mrs P Lewis. *5m SW of Devizes. From A360, Devizes to Salisbury, R in Potterne just before George & Dragon pub. Through Worton. L at end of village signed to Marston, Close Lane ½ m on L.* **Sat 18, Sun 19 Apr, Sat 12, Sun 13 Sept (1-5). Adm £6, chd free. Home-made teas.**
Two acre flower arranger's garden comprising herbaceous borders, orchard, vegetable garden, ornamental and wildlife ponds, lawns and naturalised areas. Planted since 1979 for year-round interest. Shrubberies and rose garden, other areas underplanted with bulbs or ground cover. Springtime particularly colourful with daffodils, tulips and hellebores. Extensive autumn colour.

56 WEST LAVINGTON MANOR
1 Church Street, West Lavington, SN10 4LA. Andrew Doman & Jordina Evins, 07768 773856, andrewdoman01@gmail.com, www.instagram.com/westlavingtonmanor. *6m S of Devizes, on A360. House opp White St, where parking is available.* **Sat 13 June (11-6). Adm £10, chd free. We offer an extended lunch & tea menu inc wines, beer & other beverages. Seating near to refreshment marquee. Visits also by arrangement 2 Jan to 24 Dec.** Donation to West Lavington Youth Club and Nestling Trust.
A C15 manor house with spectacular 5 acre walled garden, established by Sir John Danvers, who brought the Italianate garden to the UK. Delightful aspects inc a Laburnum walk, replanted herbaceous border, an authentic Japanese garden, new Mulberry rotunda, orchard with 25 different apple and pear species, an arboretum with outstanding specimen trees and lake with duck house. Many of our visitors comment on the peaceful nature of the gardens and the gentle undulations through the arboretum down to the stream and lake. The Japanese garden is frequently admired. Partial wheelchair access.

57 WESTCROFT
Boscombe Village, nr Salisbury, SP4 0AB. Lyn Miles, 07787 852756, lynmiles@icloud.com, www.westcroftgarden.co.uk. *7m NE Salisbury. On A338 from Salisbury, just past Boscombe & District Social Club. Park there or in field opp house, or where signed on day. Disabled parking only on drive.* **Every Thur 1 Jan to 12 Mar (11-4). Sat 17, Sat 31 Jan, Sun 1, Fri 13, Sun 15, Sat 21, Sun 22 Feb (11-4). Adm £4, chd free. Home-made soups & teas, outside or undercover. Visits also by arrangement 2 Jan to 9 July for groups of 15+.**
Whilst overflowing with roses in June, in Jan and Feb the bones of this ⅔ acre galanthophile's garden on chalk are on show. Brick and flint walls, terraces, rustic arches, gates and pond add character. Drifts of snowdrops carpet the floor whilst throughout is a growing collection of well over 500 named varieties. Many hellebores, pulmonarias, grasses and seedheads add interest. Snowdrops (weather dependent) and snowdrop

sundries for sale inc greetings cards, mugs, bags, serviettes, also chutneys and free range eggs.

58 WESTWIND
Manton Drove, Manton, Marlborough, SN8 4HL. Kate Stewart-Hilliar, 07738 180759, westwindmanton@gmail.com. *1m W of Marlborough off A4. In Manton, bear R past Oddfellows Arms, then after 180 metres go L into Manton Drove. House is up the hill on the R.* **Visits by arrangement 11 May to 14 June for groups of up to 15. Max 5 cars. Adm £7, chd free. Light refreshments.**
Working in harmony with nature, Westwind is a relaxed informal country garden set in 4 acres inc a 2½ acre meadow and woodland. It hosts the weekly outdoor learning for the village school and welcomes artists and photographers throughout the seasons. Westwind has an abundance of mature trees, beds full of herbaceous plants and 10 raised beds stuffed with colour from April to October.

59 4 WESTWOOD ROAD
Trowbridge, BA14 9BR. Mrs Helen Hewlett. *Northern edge of Trowbridge. Off Bradford-on-Avon Road. Plenty of parking in nearby residential roads, please be considerate to local residents.* **Sun 14 June (11-5). Adm £5, chd free. Home-made teas.**
New garden of approx 1 acre created over the last 5 yrs. Vegetable area with raised beds and espalier fruit trees and greenhouse. Small wildlife pond becoming established. Mixed herbaceous borders with many roses. Small woodland area. Eco friendly with use of water butts, and minimal chemicals. Level ground, but some uneven areas in the grass. No steps.

60 WHATLEY MANOR
Easton Grey, Malmesbury, SN16 0RB. Christian De Coulon & Alix Landolt, 01666 822888, reservations@whatleymanor.com, www.whatleymanor.com/gardens. *4m W of Malmesbury. From A429 at Malmesbury take B4040 signed Sherston. Manor 2m on L.* **Wed 10 June (2.30-5.30). Adm £9.50, chd free. Tea, coffee & cake in The Loggia Garden.**

12 acres of English country gardens with a strong theme based on colour, scent or style. Original 1920s Arts & Crafts plan inspired the design and combines classic style with more contemporary touches, inc specially commissioned sculpture. Dogs must be on a lead at all times. Casual dining menu, afternoon tea and dinner can be booked in advance in Grey's. See website for details.

61 WINKELBURY HOUSE
Berwick St John, Shaftesbury, SP7 0EY. Ian & Carrie Stewart. *5m E of Shaftesbury. From A30 follow sign to Berwick St John, after 1½m turn L into Woodlands Lane following Car Park signs.* **Sat 16 May (2-5). Adm £7.50, chd free. Home-made teas.**
1½ acres with glorious views of surrounding countryside. The garden has evolved over last 10 yrs to inc kitchen garden with bothy and greenhouse, mown paths through informal areas, wildflower meadow planted with spring bulbs, 30 metre iris border, ha-ha, wildlife pond and bee friendly planting.

62 WUDSTON HOUSE
High Street, Wedhampton, Devizes, SN10 3QE. David Morrison, 01380 840965, djm@piml.co.uk. *Wedhampton lies on N side of A342 approx 4m SE of Devizes. House is set back on East side of village street at end of drive lined with a beech hedge.* **Visits by arrangement 1 June to 11 Sept for groups of up to 50. light refreshments available at additional cost £5 per head. Adm £10, chd free.**
The garden was started in 2010, following completion of the house. It consists of formal gardens round the house, perennial meadow, pinetum and arboretum. Nick Macer & James Hitchmough, who have pioneered the concept of perennial meadows, have been extensively involved in aspects of the garden, which is still developing.

Corsley House

WORCESTERSHIRE

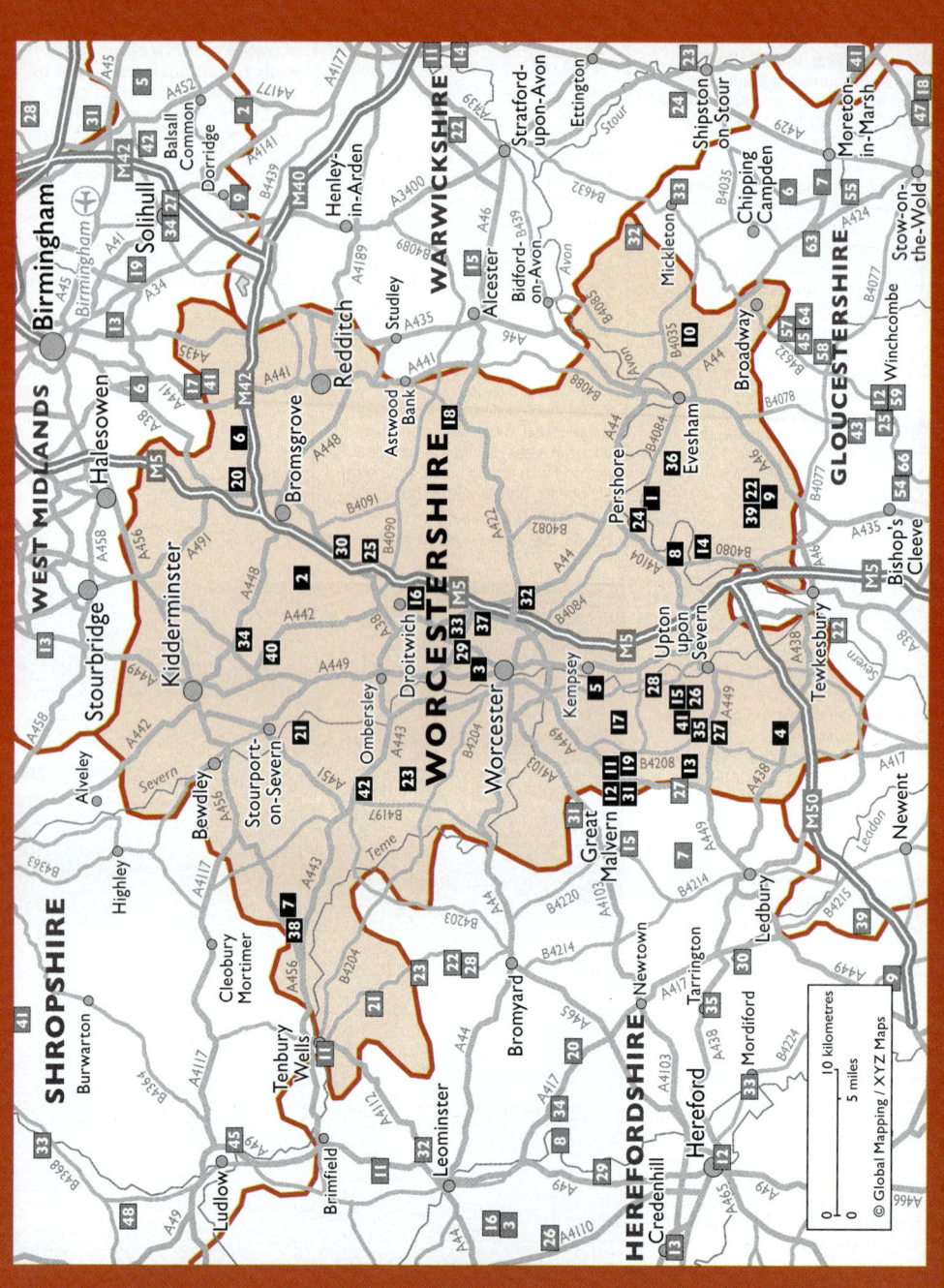

VOLUNTEERS

County Organiser
David Morgan 01214 453595
meandi@btinternet.com

County Treasurer
Doug Bright 01886 832200
doug.bright@ngs.org.uk

Publicity
Pamela Thompson 01886 888295
peartree.pam@gmail.com

Social Media
Brian Skeys 01684 311297
brian.skeys@ngs.org.uk

Booklet Co-ordinator
Steven Wilkinson & Linda Pritchard
07487 899179
steven.wilkinson48412@gmail.com

Assistant County Organisers
Andrea Bright 01886 832200
andrea.bright@ngs.org.uk

John and Leslie Bryant
johnlesbryant@btinternet.com
01905 840189

Malcolm & Anne Garner
anne.restharrow@gmail.com
01684 310503

Lynn Glaze 01386 751924
lynnglaze@cmail.co.uk

Philippa Lowe 01684 891340
philippa.lowe@ngs.org.uk

Stephanie & Chris Miall
0121 445 2038
stephaniemiall@hotmail.com

Rachel Pryke
rachelgpryke@btinternet.com

David & Sandra Traynor
traynor007@btinternet.com

 @WorcestershireNGS
 @WorcsNGS

OPENING DATES

All entries subject to change.
For latest information check
www.ngs.org.uk
Map locator numbers are shown to the right of each garden name.

February

Snowdrop Openings

Sunday 15th
Warndon Court 37

Wednesday 18th
Brockamin 5

Sunday 22nd
Brockamin 5

March

Wednesday 11th
♦ Cotswold Garden Flowers 10

Sunday 22nd
Brockamin 5

Sunday 29th
Overbury Court 22

April

Wednesday 8th
♦ Cotswold Garden Flowers 10

Sunday 12th
♦ Spetchley Park Gardens 32

Saturday 18th
♦ Whitlenge Gardens 40

Sunday 19th
Brockamin 5
♦ Whitlenge Gardens 40

May

Sunday 3rd
The Dell House 13
Nimrod, 35 Alexandra Road 19
Pear Tree Cottage 23

Monday 4th
The Dell House 13
Nimrod, 35 Alexandra Road 19

Saturday 9th
Conderton Manor 9
Eckington Gardens 14

Sunday 10th
Eckington Gardens 14

Wednesday 13th
♦ Cotswold Garden Flowers 10

Thursday 14th
Madresfield Court 17

Saturday 16th
Rothbury 31

Sunday 17th
Rothbury 31
Warndon Court 37
19 Winnington Gardens 41

Saturday 23rd
Ravelin 26

Sunday 24th
2 Brookwood Drive 6
1 Church Cottage 8
Ravelin 26
Rothbury 31

Monday 25th
1 Church Cottage 8
Ravelin 26
Rothbury 31
NEW 77 Station Road 33

June

Saturday 6th
Pershore Gardens 24

Sunday 7th
Birtsmorton Court 4
Pershore Gardens 24
Warndon Court 37

Wednesday 10th
♦ Cotswold Garden Flowers 10

Saturday 13th
Hanley Swan NGS Gardens 15

Sunday 14th
Hanley Swan NGS Gardens 15
Hiraeth 16
3 Oakhampton Road 21

Saturday 20th
Conderton Manor 9
Rest Harrow 27
The River School 29
NEW The Threshing Barn 35
Walnut Cottage 36
Wharf House 38
♦ Whitlenge Gardens 40

WORCESTERSHIRE

Sunday 21st
Rest Harrow 27
NEW The Threshing Barn 35
Walnut Cottage 36
Wharf House 38
◆ Whitlenge Gardens 40

Sunday 28th
Cowleigh Lodge 11
3 Oakhampton Road 21
NEW 77 Station Road 33

July

Saturday 4th
5 Beckett Drive 3

Sunday 5th
5 Beckett Drive 3
◆ Spetchley Park Gardens 32

Wednesday 8th
◆ Cotswold Garden Flowers 10

Sunday 12th
3 Oakhampton Road 21

Sunday 26th
3 Oakhampton Road 21

August

Saturday 8th
Nimrod, 35 Alexandra Road 19

Sunday 9th
Nimrod, 35 Alexandra Road 19

Wednesday 12th
◆ Cotswold Garden Flowers 10

Saturday 15th
NEW ◆ Witley Court and Gardens 42

Sunday 16th
3 Oakhampton Road 21

Saturday 22nd
◆ Morton Hall Gardens 18
Rest Harrow 27
◆ Whitlenge Gardens 40

Sunday 23rd
Rest Harrow 27
◆ Whitlenge Gardens 40

Saturday 29th
3 Oakhampton Road 21

Sunday 30th
Pear Tree Cottage 23

Monday 31st
3 Oakhampton Road 21

September

Wednesday 9th
◆ Cotswold Garden Flowers 10

Saturday 12th
Ravelin 26

Sunday 13th
Ravelin 26

Sunday 20th
Brockamin 5

Wednesday 23rd
Brockamin 5

October

Sunday 4th
19 Winnington Gardens 41

Saturday 10th
Ravelin 26

Sunday 11th
Ravelin 26

Wednesday 14th
◆ Cotswold Garden Flowers 10

Saturday 31st
The Dell House 13

November

Sunday 1st
The Dell House 13

By Arrangement

Arrange a personalised garden visit with your club, or group of friends, on a date to suit you. See individual garden entries for full details.

The Alpine Garden Society 1
Badge Court 2
5 Beckett Drive 3
Brockamin 5
Cherry Tree Barn 7
1 Church Cottage 8
Conderton Manor 9
Cowleigh Lodge 11
Cowleigh Park Farm 12
The Dell House 13
Hiraeth 16
Nimrod, 35 Alexandra Road 19
Oak Tree House 20
Overbury Court 22
Pear Tree Cottage 23
Rashwood Care Home 25
Ravelin 26
Rest Harrow 27
Rhydd Gardens 28
NEW 77 Station Road 33
Warndon Court 37
Wharf House 38
Whitcombe House 39
19 Winnington Gardens 41

Warndon Court

THE GARDENS

1 THE ALPINE GARDEN SOCIETY
Avon Bank, Wick, Pershore, WR10 3JP. The Alpine Garden Society, 01386 554790, ags@alpinegardensociety.net, www.alpinegardensociety.net. *Wick, ½m from Pershore town. Take the Evesham Rd from Pershore over the River Avon, cont for ½m & turn R for Pershore College, the garden is the 1st entrance on L.* **Visits by arrangement 6 Apr to 24 Sept for groups of 10+. Adm £5, chd free. Light refreshments.**
Inspirational small garden next to the Alpine Garden Society office. The garden shows a wide range of alpine plants that are easy to grow in contemporary gardens over a long season. Visitors can see different settings to grow alpines, inc rock and tufa, scree, a dry Mediterranean bed, shade and sunny areas, also a dedicated alpine house, and many pots and troughs with alpines and small bulbs. Information about the display garden and planting alpines in various settings will be available for group bookings. The garden slopes gently upwards with gravel paths which are accessible to wheelchairs with some assistance.

2 BADGE COURT
Purshull Green Lane, Elmbridge, Droitwich, WR9 0NJ. Stuart & Diana Glendenning, 01299 851216, dianaglendenning1@gmail.com. *5m N of Droitwich Spa. 2½m from J5 M5. Turn off A38 at Wychbold down side of the Swan Inn. Turn R into Berry Ln. Take next L into Cooksey Green Ln. Turn R into Purshull Green Ln. Garden is on L.* **Visits by arrangement June & July for groups of 6 to 30. Weekdays preferred. Adm £12, chd free. Home-made teas available at £3pp.**
The 2½ acre garden is set against the backdrop of a C16 house (not open). There is something for all gardeners inc mature specimen trees, huge range of clematis and roses, lake with waterfall, stumpery, topiary garden, walled garden, Mediterranean garden, specialist borders, long herbaceous border, large potager vegetable garden and Japanese Garden.

3 5 BECKETT DRIVE
Northwick, Worcester, WR3 7BZ. Jacki & Pete Ager, 07531 296655, agers@outlook.com. *1½m N of Worcester city centre. A cul-de-sac off the A449 Ombersley Rd. 1m S of the Claines r'about on A449.* **Sat 4, Sun 5 July (1-5). Adm £5, chd free. Home-made ice cream on sale.** Visits also by arrangement 16 May to 31 July for groups of 10 to 20.
An extraordinary town garden on the northern edge of Worcester packed with different plants and year-round interest guaranteed to give visitors ideas and inspiration for their own gardens. For more than 20 yrs visitors have enjoyed the unique and surprising features of this garden which has many planting schemes for a variety of situations.

4 BIRTSMORTON COURT
Birtsmorton, nr Malvern, WR13 6JS. Mr & Mrs N G K Dawes. *7m E of Ledbury. Off A438 Ledbury/Tewkesbury road.* **Sun 7 June (2-5.30). Adm £9, chd free. Tea, coffee & cake.**
10 acre garden surrounding beautiful medieval moated manor house (not open). White garden, built and planted in 1997 surrounded on all sides by old topiary. Potager, vegetable garden and working greenhouses, all beautifully maintained. Rare double working moat and waterways inc Westminster Pool laid down in Henry VII's reign to mark the consecration of the knave of Westminster Abbey. Ancient yew tree under which Cardinal Wolsey reputedly slept in the legend of the Shadow of the Ragged Stone.

5 BROCKAMIN
Old Hills, Callow End, Worcester, WR2 4TQ. Margaret Stone, 01905 830370, stone.brockamin@btinternet.com. *5m S of Worcester. ½m S of Callow End on the B4424, on an unfenced bend, turn R into the car park signed Old Hills. Walk towards the houses keeping R.* **Wed 18 Feb (1-4); Sun 22 Feb (11-4); Sun 22 Mar, Sun 19 Apr, Sun 20, Wed 23 Sept (1-4). Adm £5, chd free. Home-made teas.** Visits also by arrangement 15 Feb to 15 Oct for groups of 10+. Donation to Plant Heritage.
1½ acre plantsman's garden situated next to common land. Informal mixed borders with a wide variety of hardy perennials where plants are allowed to self seed. Large collection of snowdrops. Plant Heritage National Collections of Pulmonarias, *Symphyotrichum novae-angliae* and some hardy geraniums. Open for snowdrops in Feb, daffodils and pulmonarias in March and April, hardy geraniums in June and Michaelmas Daisies in September. Seasonal pond/bog garden. Teas with home-made cakes and unusual plants for sale. An access path reaches a large part of the garden.

6 2 BROOKWOOD DRIVE
Barnt Green, Birmingham, B45 8GG. Mr Mike & Mrs Liz Finlay. *5m N of Bromsgrove. Please park courteously in local roads or in village. Brookwood Dr is on R towards top of Fiery Hill Rd approx. ¼m from station. Press the access button to open security gates if closed.* **Sun 24 May (10-4). Adm £5, chd free. Tea, coffee & cake.**
A multi-themed mature garden with numerous water features and colourful borders. There is a formal white garden, wildlife pond and cutting garden surrounded by large rhododendrons which give a colourful display in late spring. Parking on Brookwood Drive for disabled only.

7 CHERRY TREE BARN
Southnett, Mamble, Kidderminster, DY14 9JT. Mr Ian & Mrs Julie Stackhouse, Stackhouse571@btinternet.com. *12m W of Kidderminster on the A456. Nearest motorway M5 J6. A456 from Kidderminster, past Mamble village approx 1m, garden on L up a track off main road. A456 from Tenbury Wells, past Broombank. Garden on R up a track off main road, follow signs.* **Visits by arrangement 1 July to 15 Aug for groups of 15 to 30. Refreshments inc in adm. Adm £10, chd £5. Home-made teas inc a selection of cakes will be available.**
The garden has been planted out with a wide variety of trees and shrubs providing year-round interest. The main event are the herbaceous beds filled with a riot of colour from May onwards. There are two ponds, a bog garden inc stumpery, a rose bed, gravel garden, two azalea beds and a small woodland area. The rear garden offers wonderful views of the surrounding countryside.

1 CHURCH COTTAGE

Church Road, Defford, Worcester, WR8 9BJ. John Taylor & Ann Sheppard, 01386 750863, ann98sheppard@btinternet.com. 3m SW of Pershore. A4104 Pershore to Upton Rd, turn into Harpley Rd, Defford. Don't go up Bluebell Ln as directed by SatNav, black & white cottage at side of church. Parking in village hall car park. **Sun 24, Mon 25 May (11-5). Adm £6, chd free. Home-made teas.** Visits also by arrangement 14 Feb to 31 Aug for groups of 10 to 25. Adm inc tea and cake for by arrangement visits.

True countryman's ⅓ acre cottage garden. Japanese style feature with 'dragons den'. Specimen trees, many rare and unusual plants and trees, water features, perennial garden, vegetable garden, poultry, stream side bog garden. Wheelchair access to most areas, narrow paths may restrict access to some parts.

CONDERTON MANOR

Conderton, nr Tewkesbury, GL20 7PR. Glyn and Kathleen Powell, 07585 400305, Kathleenandglyn@gmail.com. 5½m NE of Tewkesbury. From M5 - A46 to Beckford - L for Overbury/Conderton. From Tewkesbury B4079 to Bredon - then follow signs to Overbury. Conderton from B4077 follow A46 directions from Teddington r'about. **Sat 9 May, Sat 20 June (12-5). Adm £10, chd free. Pre-booking essential, please visit www.ngs.org. uk for information & booking. Tea, coffee & cake.** Visits also by arrangement 6 Apr to 2 Nov. Please contact Skip Baker on 07724 771239 if the owners are not available.

7 acre garden with flowering cherries and bulbs in spring. Formal terrace with clipped box parterre; huge rose and clematis arches, mixed borders of roses and herbaceous plants, bog bank and quarry garden. Many unusual trees and shrubs make this a garden for all seasons. Visitors are particularly encouraged to visit in spring and autumn when the trees are at their best. This is a garden/small arboretum of particular interest for tree lovers. The views towards the Cotswolds escarpment are spectacular and it provides a peaceful walk of about an hour. Some gravel paths and steps - no disabled WC.

◆ COTSWOLD GARDEN FLOWERS

Sands Lane, Badsey, Evesham, WR11 7EZ. Mr Bob Brown and Mr Edmund Brown, 01386 833849, info@cgf.net, www.cotswoldgardenflowers. co.uk. *Sands Ln is the last road on the L when leaving Badsey for Wickhamford. Garden is nearly ½m down lane.* **For NGS: Wed 11 Mar, Wed 8 Apr, Wed 13 May, Wed 10 June, Wed 8 July, Wed 12 Aug, Wed 9 Sept, Wed 14 Oct (11-4). Adm £5, chd free. Light refreshments.** For other opening times and information, please phone, email or visit garden website.

The garden consists of one acre of stockbeds with many thousands of kinds of plants many of which are unusual and rare. Guided tours are available on NGS open days. Please note this is a working nursery and not a traditional garden. This garden proudly provided plants for the National Garden Scheme's Show Garden at Chelsea Flower Show in 2024.

Witley Court and Gardens

1 COWLEIGH LODGE
16 Cowleigh Bank, Malvern,
WR14 1QP. Jane & Mic
Schuster, 07854 015065,
janeschuster700@gmail.com. *7m
SW from Worcester. From Hereford,
turn R after Storridge church, follow
road approx 2½m, then L onto
Cowleigh Bank. From Worcester R
at Link Top - Hornyold Rd, R onto St.
Peter's Rd, follow yellow signs.* **Sun
28 June (11-5). Adm £6, chd free.
Tea, coffee & cake inc home-
made sausage rolls. Visits also by
arrangement 25 May to 31 July for
groups of 10+.**
The now mature one acre 'quirky'
garden on the slopes of the Malvern
Hills has a formal rose garden, grass
beds, bamboo walk, colour themed
beds, nature path leading to a wildlife
pond, Acer bank and chickens. Large
vegetable plot and orchard with views
overlooking the Severn Valley. Explore
the polytunnel and then relax with
a cuppa and slice of home-made
cake served with a smile. This is the
11th year of opening this developing
and expanding garden. Visitors from
previous years will be able to see the
difference. Lots of added interest with
staddle stones, troughs, signs and
other interesting artefacts. The garden
is definitely now mature.

2 COWLEIGH PARK FARM
Cowleigh Road, Malvern,
WR13 5HJ. John & Ruth
Lucas, 01684 566750,
info@cowleighparkfarm.co.uk,
www.cowleighparkfarm.co.uk. *On
the edge of Malvern. Leaving Malvern
on the B4219 Cowleigh Park Farm
driveway is on the R just before
national speed limit sign. Coming from
A4103, driveway is on L just after the
30mph sign.* **Visits by arrangement
20 Mar to 26 Sept. Adm £6, chd
free. Tea, coffee & cake.**
The 1½ acre garden at Cowleigh
Park Farm surrounds a Grade II listed
timber framed former farmhouse
(not open). Whilst no longer a farm,
the property has views to adjacent
orchards and inc lawns, spring
fed ponds, a waterfall and stream.
The focus in established beds and
borders is to be wildlife and bee
friendly. The garden contains multiple
seating areas and a summerhouse.
The whole garden can be viewed
from wheelchair accessible places but
some parts have steep grassy slopes
that may not be accessible.

3 THE DELL HOUSE
2 Green Lane, Malvern
Wells, WR14 4HU. Kevin &
Elizabeth Rolph, 01684 564448,
kande@dellhousemalvern.uk,
www.dellhousemalvern.uk. *2m S
of Gt Malvern. Behind former church
on corner of Wells Rd & Green Ln.
Small car park for those pre-booked.
Approach downhill from Wells Rd.
Don't use postcode in SatNav.
What3words app: remember.shrub.
robot.* **Sun 3, Mon 4 May, Sat 31
Oct, Sun 1 Nov (11-5). Adm £5,
chd free. Pre-booking essential
only if arriving by car, please visit
www.ngs.org.uk for information
& booking. Light refreshments.
Visits also by arrangement Feb to
Nov. Individuals or small groups
welcome at short notice.**
Two acre wooded hillside garden.
Revived from a derelict state by
the current owners over ten years,
creating a mature garden natural
in style and rich in variety. A former
Victorian rectory garden containing
magnificent specimen trees and
historic garden buildings, and more
recent additions of tree carvings and a
model railway. Spectacular views from
the terrace. Garden tours at 11:15am.
Pre-booking is only essential if
you need a parking space. Partial
wheelchair access. Parking is on
gravel with level access to the paved
terrace with great views. Sloping bark
paths, some quite steep.

GROUP OPENING

4 ECKINGTON GARDENS
Willow Pond, Pass Street,
Eckington, WR10 3AX. Group
Coordinator James Field. *9m
SW of Worcester. A4104 from
Pershore to Upton & Defford, L turn
B4080 to Eckington. In centre, by
war memorial, turn L into New Rd.
Willow Pond (to purchase tickets),
Pass St is 2nd R off New Rd.* **Sat
9, Sun 10 May (11-5). Combined
adm £10, chd free. Home-made
teas at Mantoft on Saturday and
Quietways on Sunday. Picnics
welcome at Willow Pond.**

MANTOFT
Mrs Tupper.

NAFFORD HOUSE
George & Joanna Stylianou.

QUIETWAYS
Mr Russell & Mrs Jude Stracey.

WILLOW POND
James Field & Mike Washbourne,
07970 962842, james.field@
washbournefield.co.uk, www.
thedairyeckington.co.uk.

Four diverse gardens set in lovely
village of Eckington. Mantoft:
thatched cottage with 1½ acres of
gardens. Fishpond with koi, Cotswold
and red brick walls, large topiary,
treehouse with seating, summerhouse
and dovecote, pathways, vistas and
stone statues, urns and herbaceous
borders. Willow Pond: Listed black
and white cottage with 1 acre garden
for wildlife with lawn and long grass,
herbaceous borders, water features,
flower cutting patch, large pots
and lots of places to sit and relax.
Quietways: A mature and fun-filled
family garden with a grade II listed
cottage at its heart. There are tree
swings, garden buildings, sculptures,
wild areas, lawns, vegetable garden,
loose planting, containers and formal
herbaceous beds. Nafford House:
a natural garden of 6 acres, sloping
down to the Avon. Two formal
gardens, mature herbaceous borders
and plenty of seating. Views of
Bredon Hill, The Malverns and Vale of
Evesham.

The National Garden Scheme donated £3,875,596 to our nursing and health beneficiaries from money raised at gardens open in 2025.

GROUP OPENING

15 HANLEY SWAN NGS GARDENS
Hanley Swan, WR8 0DJ. Group Co-ordinator Brian Skeys, www.brimfields.com. 5m E of Malvern, 3m NW of Upton upon Severn, 9m S of Worcester. From the B4211 towards Great Malvern & Guarlford (Rhydd Rd) turn L to Hanley Swan continue to Orchard Side WR8 0EA for entrance tickets & maps. Or from the village cross roads. **Sat 13, Sun 14 June (1-5). Combined adm £7.50, chd free. Tea, coffee & cake at 19 Winnington Gardens.**

NEW ORCHARD HOUSE
Mr & Mrs T Feest.

ORCHARD SIDE
Mrs Gigi Verlander,
01684 310602,
gigiverlander@icloud.com.

THE PADDOCKS
Mr & Mrs N Fowler.

19 WINNINGTON GARDENS
Brian Skeys.
(See separate entry)

20 WINNINGTON GARDENS
Mr & Mrs Sauntson.

YEW TREE COTTAGE
Mr & Mrs Read.

6 gardens in the beautiful historic village of Hanley Swan all different in style and design. Entrance tickets and maps from Orchard Side. Wristbands valid for both days. Many wildlife features within the gardens with increasing environmental considerations, growing vegetables, fruit trees, herbs, perennials and exotics, cottage garden style plantings. C17 black and white cottage (not open) sits in one of the gardens. Gardens with plenty of places to sit. One new garden and one returning this year. New planting schemes within the group. 19 Winnington Gardens has wildlife photographs and vintage garden, blacksmith and carpentry tools on display. Here you can sit and enjoy your tea. Hanley Swan is in a beautiful setting in the shadow of the Malvern Hills close to the Three Counties Showground, home of the RHS Spring Show. It is home to a school, shop, pub and pond with ducks and occasional swans.

16 HIRAETH
30 Showell Road, Droitwich, WR9 8UY. Sue & John Fletcher, 07752 717243, sueandjohn99@yahoo.com. *1m S of Droitwich. On The Ridings estate. Turn off A38 r'about into Addyes Way, 2nd R into Showell Rd, 500yds on R - Follow the yellow signs.* **Sun 14 June (12-5). Adm £5, chd free. Tea, coffee & cake.** Visits also by arrangement 11 May to 31 Aug for groups of up to 30.
⅓ acre gardens. The front has three barrels of ericaceous plants. A conifer bed, hydrangeas and a 300+ yr old olive tree, monkey puzzle, acers, silver birch and shrubs. The centre features a piece of Forest of Dean rock. A rose arch at one entrance. The rear garden is an oasis of colour created by numerous trees inc acers, weeping purple beech and an unusual angelica, a roses, hosta bed and ferns. Various statues and metal sculptures on display containing a variety of animals inc an alligator or crocodile (we're not sure which). A local minister has described the garden as 'a haven on the way to heaven'! Partial wheelchair access.

17 MADRESFIELD COURT
Madresfield, Malvern, WR13 5AJ. Trustees of Lord Beauchamp's 1963 Settlement, 01684 573614, office@madresfield.co.uk, www.madresfield.co.uk. *2m E of Malvern. Entrance ½ m S of Madresfield village, just outside Malvern.* **Thur 14 May (12-4). Adm £10, chd £5. Tea, coffee & cake.**
Gardens mainly laid out in 1865, based on three avenues of oak, cedar and Lombardy poplar, within and around which are specimen trees and flowering shrubs. Meadows within the avenues covered in daffodils, and later, fritillaries, bluebells, cowslips etc. Recent rhododendron plantings. Holly hedge enclosure with 100m walk of peonies and irises, next to a crescent tunnel of pollarded limes. Overall a parkland garden of approx 60 acres. Tarmac main drive interspersed with gravel and grass paths. Accessible WC available.

18 ♦ MORTON HALL GARDENS
Morton Hall Lane, Holberrow Green, Redditch, B96 6SJ. Mrs A Olivieri. *13m W of Stratford-Upon-Avon. In centre of Holberrow Green, at a wooden bench around a tree, turn up Morton Hall Ln. Follow NGS signs to gate opp Morton Hall Farm.* **For NGS: Sat 22 Aug (10-5). Adm £12, chd free. Pre-booking essential, please phone 01386 791820, email morton.garden@mhcom.co.uk or visit www.mortonhallgardens.co.uk for information & booking. Light refreshments inc gluten free & vegetarian options.** For other opening times and information, please phone, email or visit garden website.
Secluded private garden full of drama and colour. Seven garden rooms with bold landscapes and exquisite planting schemes guarantee a unique visit. Late summer borders are glorious, with brilliant and inspiring combinations. The elegant Japanese Garden and majestic Rockery offer an exciting contrast. Grand views over the Vale of Evesham complete the enthralling experience. For the NGS Open Day, click on the yellow banner on the Morton Hall Gardens website homepage. Pre-booking closes at 10.00am on 22.08.26. Only the formal gardens are suitable for wheelchairs.

19 NIMROD, 35 ALEXANDRA ROAD
Malvern, WR14 1HE. Margaret & David Cross, 01684 569019, margaret@ssorco.co.uk. *From Worcester A449. From Malvern Link, pass train stn, ahead at T-lights, 1st R into Alexandra Rd. From Great Malvern, go through Link Top T-lights (junc with B4503), 1st L.* **Sun 3, Mon 4 May, Sat 8, Sun 9 Aug (10.30-5). Adm £5, chd free. Home-made teas.** Visits also by arrangement May to Sept.
Overlooked by the Malvern Hills, this peaceful garden is on two levels with mature trees, pond with stream, small wildflower meadow, shady woodland area, cottage garden, Japanese garden, rockeries, a New Zealand garden, all filled with a wide variety of plants. Elgar wrote some of the Enigma variations in a bell tent here. Colourful shrubs and trees in May and lots of flower colour in August. With help, the garden can be accessed by wheelchair, there are few steps but gravel paths and gradients. Closer parking can be made available - please contact garden owner.

WORCESTERSHIRE 577

20 OAK TREE HOUSE
504 Birmingham Road, Marlbrook, Bromsgrove, B61 0HS. Di & Dave Morgan, 01214 453595, meandi@btinternet.com. *On main A38 midway between M42 J1 & M5 J4. Park in old A38 - R fork 250 yds N of garden or small area in front of Miller & Carter Pub car park 200 yds S or local roads.* **Visits by arrangement May to July for groups of 6 to 40. Coach parties welcome but drop off only at garden as no coach parking area. Adm £4, chd free. Light refreshments.**
Plantswoman's cottage garden overflowing with plants, pots and interesting artifacts. Patio with spring colour, azaleas, rhododendrons and acers, small pond and waterfall. Plenty of seating, separate wildlife pond, water features, rear open vista. Scented plants, hostas, dahlias, alpines and lilies. Conservatory with art by owners. New Summerhouse for 2026. Also: 'Wynn's Patch' - part of next door's garden being maintained on behalf of the owner.

21 3 OAKHAMPTON ROAD
Stourport-on-Severn, DY13 0NR. Sandra & David Traynor. *Between Astley Cross Inn & Kings Arms. From Stourport take A451 Dunley Rd towards Worcester. In 1m turn L into Pearl Ln. 4th R into Red House Rd, past the Kings Arms Pub, & next L to Oakhampton Rd. Extra parking at Kings Arms Pub.* **Sun 14, Sun 28 June, Sun 12, Sun 26 July, Sun 16, Sat 29, Mon 31 Aug (10-5). Adm £5, chd free. Tea, coffee & cake.**
Beginning in March 2016 the plan was to create a garden with a decidedly tropical feel to inc palms from around the world, with tree ferns, bananas and many other strange and unusual plants from warmer climes that would normally be considered difficult to grow here as well as a pond and small waterfall. Not a large garden but you'll be surprised what can be done with a small space. Home-made cakes using eggs and honey from the neighbours whose bees visit the garden flowers.

22 OVERBURY COURT
Overbury, GL20 7NP. Sir Bruce Bossom & Penelope Bossom, 01386 725111, gardens@overburyenterprises.co.uk, www.overburyenterprises.co.uk. *5m NE of Tewkesbury. Overbury signed off A46. Turn off village road beside the church. Park by the gates & walk up the drive. What3words app: cars.blurs.crunches.* **Sun 29 Mar (11-4). Adm £5, chd free. Visits also by arrangement Apr to Sept for groups of 10 to 30.**
A 10 acre historic garden, at the centre of a picturesque Cotswold village, nestled amongst Capability Brown inspired Parkland. The garden compromises vast formal lawns skirted by a series of rills and ponds which reflect the ancient plane trees that are dotted throughout the garden. The south side of the house has a formal terrace with mixed borders and yew hedging, overlooking a formal lawn with a reflection pool and yew topiary. Running parallel to the pool is a long mixed border which repeats its colours of silver and gold down to the pool house. Some slopes, while all the garden can be viewed, parts are not accessible to wheelchairs.

Pear Tree Cottage

23 PEAR TREE COTTAGE
Witton Hill, Wichenford, WR6 6YX. Pamela & Alistair Thompson, 01886 888235, peartree.pam@gmail.com, www.peartreecottage.me. *13m NW of Worcester & 2m NE of Martley. From Martley, take B4197. Turn R into Horn Ln then 2nd L signed Witton Hill. Keep L & Pear Tree Cottage is on R at top of hill.* **Sun 3 May (12-5). Home-made teas. Sun 30 Aug (2-9). Adm £6, chd free. Sun 30 Aug - Twilight Garden by Candlelight. Wine and Pimm's will be served after 6pm.** Visits also by arrangement 1 May to 30 Aug. Max of 10 cars. Home-made teas require pre-booking.

A Grade II listed black and white cottage (not open) SW facing gardens with far-reaching views across orchards to Abberley Clock Tower. The ¾ acre garden comprises gently sloping lawns with mixed and woodland borders, shade and plenty of strategically placed seating. It not only exudes a quirky and humorous character but a thriving example the world's rarest tree! A built in reclaimed cast iron range with Victorian tiled surround complete with vintage kitchenalia provides an unusual take on an outdoor kitchen! On the 3rd May, the annual Plant Bonanza will take place at neighbouring garden 'Maranatha' in aid of the St Laurence Church. Barrels and Bells Clarinet Choir will be performing in Pear Tree Cottage Garden. Home to a mature specimen of a Wollemi Pine (*Wollemia nobilis*) - the world's rarest tree. Partial wheelchair access.

GROUP OPENING

24 PERSHORE GARDENS
Pershore, WR10 1BG. Group Co-ordinator Laura Lines, www.visitpershore.co.uk. *On B4084 between Worcester & Evesham, & 6m from J7 on M5. There is also a train stn to N of town.* **Sat 6, Sun 7 June (1-5). Combined adm £7.50, chd free. Light refreshments at selected gardens as indicated on the map/description sheet. Inc Holy Redeemer Primary School, Number 8 Community Arts Centre and 19 Whitcroft Rd.**

Most years about 15 gardens open in Pershore. This small town has been opening gardens as part of the NGS for 50 yrs, almost continuously. Some gardens are surprisingly large, well over an acre, while others are courtyard gardens. All have their individual appeal and present great variety. The Abbey and the River Avon are some of the many points of interest in this market town. Tickets, which take the form of a wristband, map and garden descriptions, are valid for both days. They can be purchased before the event at 19 Whitcroft Road, WR10 1EN or at the Town Hall. On the Sunday they can be bought at Number 8 Community Arts Centre in the High St and any open garden. Gardens are open all over the town inc Bridge St, Broad St, Newlands, Defford Rd, Station Rd, Priest Ln, Whitcroft Rd and Hunter Rise. Parking available in car parks off Queen Elizabeth Dr and Asda car park. Both free on Sunday only.

25 RASHWOOD CARE HOME
Rashwood, Droitwich, WR9 0BP. Mrs R Wilson, 01527 861258, enquiries.rashwood@elizabethfinn.co.uk, www.elizabethfinn.co.uk. *1m from J5 M5 follow signs for Droitwich. Sharp L after Robin Hood Pub. Rashwood Care Home is signposted at this turn. Drive to end of road.* **Visits by arrangement May to Sept for groups of up to 15. Adm £8, chd free. Tea, coffee & cake.**

A 6½ acre landscaped garden, surrounding a large Queen Anne period house, designed as wildlife friendly due to the thriving population of woodland animals with many seasonal flowering shrubs, mixed borders, sculptures, rose garden, mature trees inc redwoods, pine, beech and '*Davidia involucrata*' (dove or handkerchief tree) plus a 100 yr old wisteria. Plenty of seating. Rashwood operates as a Nursing and Residential care home providing care where people can flourish, as part of the Elizabeth Finn Homes group. Most areas are wheelchair accessible. Disabled toilets available.

26 RAVELIN
Gilberts End, Hanley Castle, WR8 0AS. Mrs Christine Peer, 01684 310215, caroline.peer@btinternet.com. *3m from Upton upon Severn, 5m from Malvern 2½ m from Welland. From Worcester/Callow End B4424 or from Upton B4211 to Hanley Castle. Then B4209 to Hanley Swan. From Malvern B4209 to Hanley Swan. At pond/Xrds turn to Welland. ½ m turn L opp Hall, to Gilberts End.* **Sat 23, Sun 24, Mon 25 May, Sat 12, Sun 13 Sept, Sat 10, Sun 11 Oct (1-5). Adm £6, chd free. Cream teas.** Visits also by arrangement Apr to Oct. Evening visits available.

Developed over 60 yrs, this ½ acre garden features unusual plants, hidden areas and plentiful seating. It flows through herbaceous borders, woodland and pond rooms, leading to a modern, lit paradise and courtyard. A treat for gardeners, plant lovers and flower arrangers, with seasonal colour from spring blooms, heucheras and hardy geraniums, to dahlias, asters, aconitum and a 55 yr old silver pear. Views across fields and Malverns. The garden also contains a summerhouse. A quiz for children. Thought to be built on medieval clay pottery works in the royal hunting forest. Largely flat, partial access for disabled - some access for small mobility scooters.

27 REST HARROW
California Lane, Welland, Malvern, WR13 6NQ. Mr Malcolm & Mrs Anne Garner, 01684 310503, anne.restharrow@gmail.com. *4.6m S of Gt Malvern in un-adopted California Ln off B4208 Worcester Rd. From Gt Malvern A449 towards Ledbury, L onto Hanley Rd/B4209 signed Upton. After about 1m R (Blackmore Park Rd/B4209). After 1m R onto B4208. After ⅓m R (California Ln). Garden 300 yds on L.* **Sat 20, Sun 21 June, Sat 22, Sun 23 Aug (1.30-5). Adm £6, chd free. Tea, coffee & cake.** Visits also by arrangement 15 June to 19 Aug for groups of 15 to 30. Parking for group visits available.

1½ acre garden plus five acre wildflower meadow, woodland and stunning borrowed views of Malvern Hills. Colourful and diverse flower beds, unusual plants, roses, alstroemeria, stocks and shrubs. Potager kitchen garden, fruit trees and rustic trellis made from our own pollarded trees. Sit, relax, enjoy the views or stroll through the wildflower meadow to the wetland border area. Wheelchair access in garden but unsuitable down in field.

WORCESTERSHIRE 579

28 RHYDD GARDENS
Worcester Road, Hanley Castle, Worcester, WR8 0AB. Bill Bell & Sue Brooks, 01684 311001, NGS@Rhyddgardens.co.uk, www.rhyddgardens.co.uk. *1.2m N of Hanley Castle. Gates 200 metres N of layby on B4211.* **Visits by arrangement. We are happy to try and accommodate visits at short notice. Adm £12, chd free. Tea, coffee & cake inc in adm price.**
Two walled gardens and a 60ft greenhouse from the early 1800s set in six acres with wonderful views of the entire length of the Malvern ridge. One Walled garden is set out with formal paths and borders bounded by box hedging. We have planted fruit trees in espaliers and cordons as they would have been when the garden was first set out and have a nature area with walks and some woodland. Teas and home-made cakes on the lawn, or in the greenhouse if inclement weather. Self-guided tour leaflets available. Wheelchair access to the main walled garden with grass and paving paths. Parking near gates can be arranged in advance.

29 THE RIVER SCHOOL
Oakfield House, Droitwich Road, Worcester, WR3 7ST. Worcester Christian Education Trust, www.riverschool.co.uk. *2.4m S of Worcester City Centre on A38 towards Droitwich. At J6 M5, take A449 signed for Kidderminster, turn off at 1st turning marked for Blackpole. Turn R to Fernhill Heath & at T-junc with A38 turn L. The school is ½m on R.* **Sat 20 June (10.30-3.30). Adm £5, chd free. Light refreshments in the Lewis Room near garden entrance.**
A former Horticultural College garden being brought back to life. For 35 years after WW2 it was known as Oakfield Teacher Training College for Horticulture. It now features a Forest School, apiary, wildlife pond, and children's vegetable plots within a walled garden. It has many uncommon trees and shrubs with others coming to light as the estate develops.

30 ♦ RIVERSIDE GARDENS AT WEBBS
Wychbold, Droitwich, WR9 0DG. Webbs of Wychbold, 01527 860000, customers@webbs.co.uk, www.webbsdirect.co.uk. *2m N of Droitwich Spa. 1m N of M5 J5 on A38. Follow tourism signs from M5 What3words app: regarding.clapper.cardinal.* **For opening times and information, please phone, email or visit garden website.**
Set on the banks of the River Salwarpe, there are themed gardens inc colour spectrum, tropical and dry garden, rose garden, vegetables, seaside garden, bamboozeleum and a shrubbery. Over the bridge is a more natural garden for wildlife and seasonal interest with grasses, perennials and a Hobbit House. Keep on the path to explore the Woodland Walk - watch out for the Troll. There are willow wigwams and wooden tepees made for the young at heart, bird hides, Trolls Head and a sleeping Miss Moss. Over The Bridge and Woodland Walk are also wheelchair accessible.
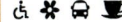

31 ROTHBURY
5 St Peter's Road, North Malvern, WR14 1QS. John Bryson & Philippa Lowe, www.facebook.com/RothburyNGS. *7m W of M5 J7 (Worcester). Turn off A449 Worcester to Ledbury Rd at B4503, signed Leigh Sinton. Almost immed take the middle road (Hornyold Rd). St Peter's Rd is ¼m uphill, 2nd R. What3words app: departure.repaid.trip.* **Sat 16, Sun 17, Sun 24, Mon 25 May (12-5.30). Adm £5, chd free. Home-made teas inc gluten free and vegan options.**
Set on slopes of Malvern Hills, ⅓ acre plant-lovers' garden surrounding Arts & Crafts house (not open), created by owners since 1999. Dense planting with herbaceous borders, rockery, pond, small orchard. Siberian irises in May. A series of hand-excavated terraces accessed by sloping paths and steps. Views and seats available. Partial wheelchair access. One very low step at entry, one standard step to main lawn and one to WC. Decking slope to top lawn. Dogs on leads please.

32 ♦ SPETCHLEY PARK GARDENS
The Estate Office, Spetchley Park, Worcester, WR5 1RS. Mr Henry Berkeley, 01905 345106, enquiries@spetchleyparkestate.co.uk, www.spetchleyparkestate.co.uk. *2m E of Worcester. On A44, follow brown signs.* **For NGS: Sun 12 Apr, Sun 5 July (10.30-5). Adm £11, chd £7. For other opening times and information, please phone, email or visit garden website.**
Surrounded by glorious countryside lays one of Britain's best kept secrets. Spetchley is a garden for all tastes and ages, containing one of the biggest private collections of plant varieties outside the major botanical gardens and weaving a magical trail for younger visitors. Spetchley is not a formal paradise of neatly manicured lawns or beds but rather a wondrous display of plants, shrubs and trees woven into a garden of many rooms and vistas. Features inc plant sales, gift shop and coffee shop serving home-made treats, and light lunches during the open season. Flat gravel paths, and grassed areas.

33 NEW 77 STATION ROAD
Fernhill Heath, Worcester, WR3 7UP. Mrs Pip & Mr Bob Wright, 07999 884471, pipnbob@yahoo.co.uk. *3½m N of Worcester. 3m S of Droitwich. Follow SatNav to WR3 7UP. What3words app: online.proven.trees. Please park considerately on the road.* **Mon 25 May, Sun 28 June (11-5). Adm £5, chd free. Tea, coffee & cake. Visits also by arrangement 16 Mar to 27 Sept for groups of 10 to 20.**
⅓ acre wildlife friendly garden (surprisingly tucked away behind a 1925 semi) inc an oval patio with feature gabion wall (or a giant bug house?), 2 wildlife ponds connected by a pretty stream, a cottage garden with rose covered obelisks, a vegetable garden enclosed by a brick pergola and a small orchard with wildflower meadow. We have used many repurposed materials when creating our garden and there are several artistic creations made by garden owner, Bob. There is a children's trail available and there is plenty of seating.

34 ◆ STONE HOUSE COTTAGE GARDENS
Church Lane, Stone, DY10 4BG. Louisa Arbuthnott, 07817 921146, louisa@shcn.co.uk, www.shcn.co.uk. *2m SE of Kidderminster. Via A448 towards Bromsgrove, next to church, turn up drive.* **For opening times and information, please phone, email or visit garden website.**
A beautiful and romantic walled garden adorned with unusual brick follies. This acclaimed garden is exuberantly planted and holds one of the largest collections of rare plants in the country. It acts as a shop window for the adjoining nursery. This garden was proud to provide plants for the National Garden Scheme's Show Garden at Chelsea Flower Show in 2024. Partial wheelchair access.
♿ ✿ 🚗

35 NEW THE THRESHING BARN
Lombard Tree Farm, Hanley Swan, Worcester, WR8 0EJ. Mr Mike & Mrs Liz Boxall. *6m from Great Malvern, 4m from Upton Upon Severn. Located down a private lane signed to Lombard Tree Cattery. What3words app: fewer.pavilions. pulsing for access to parking.* **Sat 20, Sun 21 June (10-5). Adm £5, chd free. Tea, coffee & cake.**
In 2020, when the owners moved in, the one acre garden consisted of two neglected beds, a poorly laid patio and an overgrown orchard. The owners took advantage of the blank canvas and commissioned a design from Rune Landscaping. Except for the patio, all the work has been carried out by the owners themselves - digging beds, removing hardcore, planting, pruning and hacking back the orchard jungle. The owners have built a cider press and shed. A quiet 1 acre garden with formal planting and views of open countryside. Whilst in parts the ground is uneven, the garden and orchard is spacious and all on flat ground with no steps or narrow paths.
♿ 🐕 ☕ 🪑))

36 WALNUT COTTAGE
Lower End, Bricklehampton, Pershore, WR10 3HL. Mr Richard & Mrs Janet Williams. *2½m S of Pershore on B4084, then R into Bricklehampton Ln to T-junc, then L. Cottage is on R.* **Sat 20, Sun 21 June (2-5). Adm £6, chd free. Glass of wine or soft drink inc in adm.**

1½ acre garden with views of Bredon Hill, designed into rooms, many created with high formal hedging of beech, hornbeam, copper beech and yew. There is a small 'front garden' with circular gravel path, well-stocked original garden area with wildlife pond and arches to the side of the house. Magnolia garden, mixed herbaceous beds and large area of unusual trees. Year-round interest and colour. Raised fish pond and stairway leading to roof-based viewing platform surrounded by roses. The garden continues to evolve with plenty of seating and interesting artefacts.
☕

37 WARNDON COURT
St Nicholas Lane, Worcester, WR4 0SL. Drs Rachel & David Pryke, 07944 854393, rachelgpryke@btinternet.com, www.facebook.com/rachelprykeartist. *½m from J6 of M5, Worcester N. St Nicholas Ln is off Hastings Dr.* **Sun 15 Feb (12-4). Adm £5, chd free. Sun 17 May, Sun 7 June (12-4). Adm £6, chd free. Home-made teas in St Nicholas Church Barn. For Feb snowdrop opening hot chocolate and Welsh cakes available. Visits also by arrangement 1 May to 12 June for groups of 12+. An introductory talk is offered on the garden's development.**
A two acre family garden surrounding a Grade II listed farmhouse (not open) featuring a circular route with formal rose gardens, terraces, two ponds, pergolas, topiary (inc a scruffy dragon), pretty summerhouse, a potager and woodland walk along the dry moat and through the secret garden. It has bee-friendly wildlife areas and is home to great-crested newts and slow worms. Grade I listed St Nicholas Church will also be open to visitors. There will be an exhibition of original paintings, cards for sale and display of vintage cars. The gardens around the house can be accessed over lawns and down a slight slope to the potager. Disabled parking by the house.
♿ 🐕 ✿ ☕))

38 WHARF HOUSE
Newnham Bridge, Tenbury Wells, WR15 8NY. Gareth Compton & Matthew Bartlett, 01584 781966, gco@no5.com, www.wharf-house-gardener.blog. *Off A456 in hamlet of Broombank, between Mamble & Newnham Bridge. Follow signs. Do not rely on SatNav.* **Sat 20, Sun 21 June (10-5). Adm £7, chd free. Home-made teas. Visits also by arrangement May to Sept.**
Two acre country garden, set around an C18 house and outbuildings (not open). Mixed herbaceous borders with colour theming: white garden, bright garden, spring garden, canal garden, long double borders, intimate courtyards, a scented border, stream with little bridge to an island, vegetable garden. The garden is on several levels, with some uneven paths and only partial wheelchair access.
🐕 ✿ ☕ 🪑))

39 WHITCOMBE HOUSE
Overbury, Tewkesbury, GL20 7NZ. Faith Hallett, 01386 725206, 07702 892791, faith.hallett1@gmail.com. *9m S of Evesham, 5m NE Tewkesbury. Leave A46 at Beckford to Overbury (2m). Or B4080 from Tewkesbury through Bredon/Kemerton (5m). Or small lane signed Overbury at r'about junc A46, A435 & B4077. Approx 5m from J9 M5.* **Visits by arrangement 1 Apr to 10 July. Refreshments available from May. Adm £5, chd free. Home-made teas inc coffee and cakes (am), wine and canapés (evenings).**
An acre of colour from April-Sept in a peaceful shrub and herbaceous garden with mature and young trees inc weeping beech and catalpa. This is not a formal garden but one where plants mostly do what they want! Spring fed stream bordered by primulas, hostas and astilbe. Lavender and well over 100 roses. Secret corners, arches, vines, figs, a vegetable parterre and lots of seats for relaxation. C18 Listed Cotswold stone house (not open). Lovely village of Overbury with St Faith's Church dating from Norman times. Wheelchair access possible up gravel path via usual garden entrance. Better access through double wooden gates at back of house by prior arrangement.
♿ 🐕 🚗 ☕))

40 ◆ WHITLENGE GARDENS
Whitlenge Lane, Hartlebury, DY10 4HD. Mr & Mrs K J Southall, 01299 250720, keith.southall@creativelandscapes.co.uk, www.whitlenge.co.uk. *5m S of Kidderminster, on A442. A449 Kidderminster to Worcester L at T-lights, A442 signed Droitwich, over*

island, ¼ m, 1st R into Whitlenge Ln. Follow brown signs. **For NGS: Sat 18, Sun 19 Apr, Sat 20, Sun 21 June, Sat 22, Sun 23 Aug (9.30-4.30). Adm £6.95, chd £3.95. Light refreshments in the tearooms.** For other opening times and information, please phone, email or visit garden website.

Three acre show garden of professional garden designer inc large variety of trees, shrubs etc. Features inc a twisted brick pillar pergola, 2½ metres diameter solid oak moongate set into reclaimed brickwork, and a four turreted, mini moated castle folly with vertical wall planter set between two water falls, then walk through giant gunnera leaves into the Fairy Garden. There is a full size standing stone circle, a 400 sq metre turf labyrinth and a children's play/pet corner. Extensive plant nursery, Gift shop and large tearoom. Wheelchair access on a mix of hard paths, gravel paths and lawn.

41 19 WINNINGTON GARDENS
Hanley Swan, Malvern, WR8 0DJ. Brian Skeys, 01684 311297, brimfields@icloud.com, www.brimfields.com. *5m E of Malvern, 3m NW of Upton upon Severn, 9m S of Worcester & M5. Yellow arrows from the village Xrds. What3words app: torso.directs.bonkers.* **Sun 17 May, Sun 4 Oct (1-5). Adm £4, chd free. Tea. Opening with Hanley Swan NGS Gardens on Sat 13, Sun 14 June. Visits also by arrangement 18 May to 3 Oct for groups of up to 20.**
A small wildlife-friendly garden planted in a series of garden rooms, for year-round interest from daffodils to dahlias. A green and white garden an oriental garden a mixed border with iris, asters, grasses hardy perennials, enclosed with shrubs, clematis and climbing roses. Fruit trees, developing more environmental drought tolerant planting. Pelargoniums and succulents. A no-dig garden, the owner has been experimenting with peat-free compost for four years and now testing reduced fertiliser inputs to help control plant disease. A growing iris collection. There are several seats in the garden to sit and enjoy the surroundings and observe the birds on the feeders.

42 NEW ◆ WITLEY COURT AND GARDENS
Worcester Road, Great Witley, Worcester, WR6 6JT. English Heritage. *10m N of Worcester on A443. What3words app: pumps.processes.decorated.* **For NGS: Evening opening Sat 15 Aug (5.30-7). Adm £20, chd free. Pre-booking essential, please email fundraising@english-heritage.org.uk or visit www.english-heritage.org.uk/visit/places/witley-court-and-gardens/events for information & booking. Light refreshments.** For other opening times and information, please email or visit garden website.
Meet the Head Gardener and members of their team for an exclusive evening tour of the gardens. Experience grandeur in the French parterre gardens with ornamental terraces, ornamental box hedges, and vibrant floral bedding in summer. Don't miss the monumental Perseus and Andromeda Fountain beside the Wilderness Gardens, where rhododendrons and wildflowers flourish in summer. Tickets must be purchased in advance and will be available from the English Heritage website from the 1st March 2026.

77 Station Road

In 2025, our donations to Carers Trust helped them support over 1 million unpaid carers across the UK, as part of their network of local carer centres.

YORKSHIRE

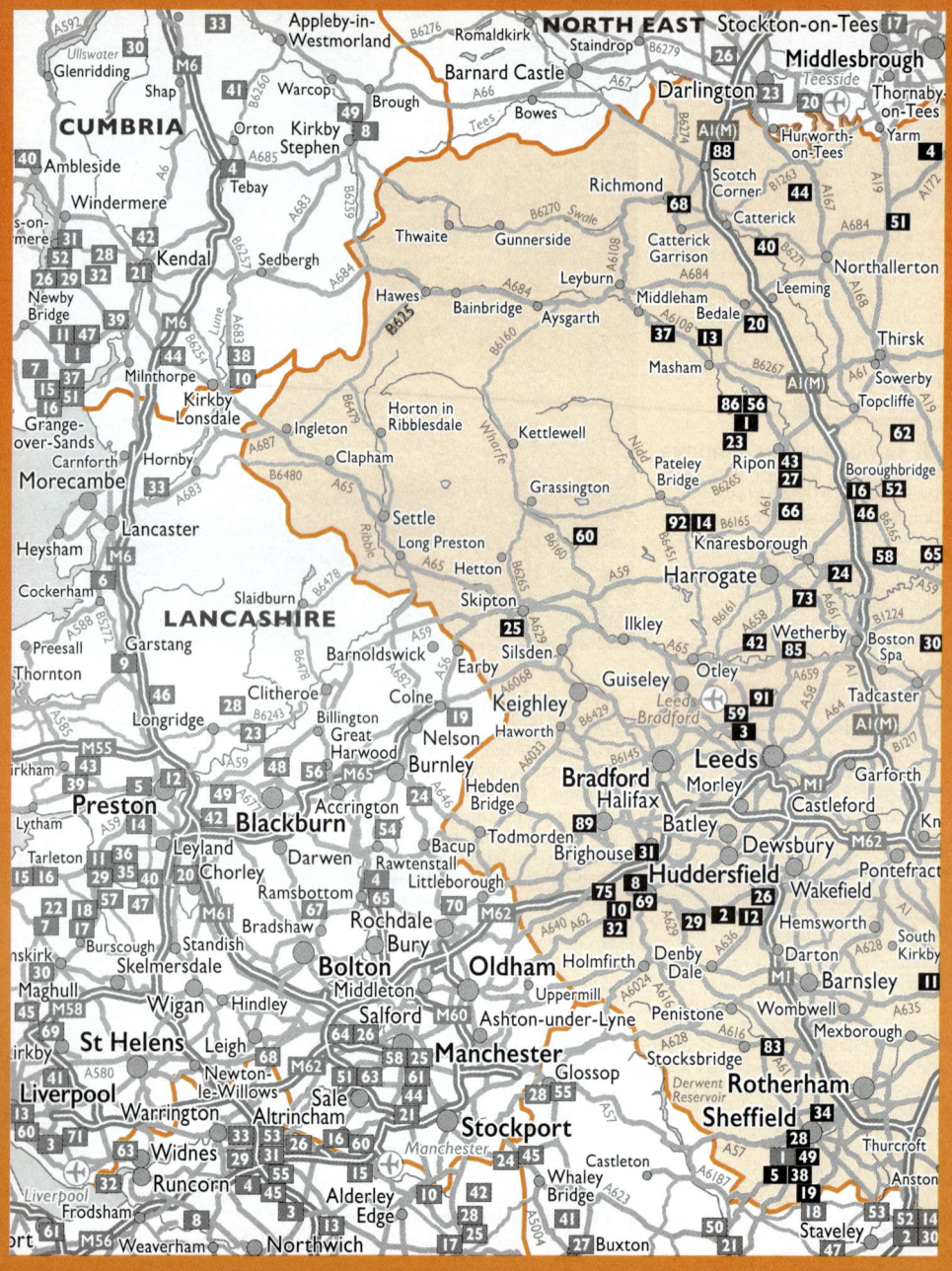

YORKSHIRE

VOLUNTEERS

County Organisers

East Yorks
Helen Marsden 07703 529112
helen.marsden@ngs.org.uk

North Yorks
Dee Venner 01765 690842
dee.venner@ngs.org.uk

South & West Yorks
Elizabeth & David Smith
01484 644320
elizabethanddavid.smith@ngs.org.uk

County Treasurer
Angela Pugh 01423 330256
angela.pugh@ngs.org.uk

Publicity & Social Media
Sally Roberts 01423 871419
sally.roberts@ngs.org.uk

Booklet Advertising
Sally Roberts (as above)

Group Visits Co-ordinator
Mandy Gordon 01423 331643
mandy.gordon@ngs.org.uk

Assistant County Organisers

East Yorks
Ian & Linda McGowan 01482 896492
ianandlinda.mcgowan@ngs.org.uk

Hazel Rowe 01430 861439
hazel.rowe@ngs.org.uk

Natalie Verow 01759 368444
natalieverow@aol.com

North Yorks
Annabel Alton 07803 907042
annabel.alton@ngs.org.uk

Jo Gaunt 07443 505291
jo.gaunt@ngs.org.uk

Susan Kerr 07952069419
susan.kerr@ngs.org.uk

South & West Yorks
Felicity Bowring 07773 647243
felicity.bowring@ngs.org.uk

Charlotte Cummins 07802 439051
charlotte.cummins@ngs.org.uk

Peter Lloyd 07958 928698
peter.lloyd@ngs.org.uk

@YorkshireNGS
@YorkshireNGS

OPENING DATES

All entries subject to change.
For latest information check
www.ngs.org.uk
Map locator numbers are
shown to the right of each
garden name.

February

Snowdrop Openings

Thursday 12th
Primrose Bank Garden and
    Nursery   64
Skipwith Hall   78

Friday 13th
Primrose Bank Garden and
    Nursery   64

Saturday 14th
Primrose Bank Garden and
    Nursery   64

Sunday 15th
Devonshire Mill   15

March

Sunday 22nd
Fawley House   17

Sunday 29th
Clifton Castle   13
Goldsborough Hall   24

April

Sunday 12th
NEW 9 Bedford View   3

Sunday 19th
Fern House, 5 Wold Road   18

Saturday 25th
249 Barnsley Road   2

Sunday 26th
249 Barnsley Road   2

Tuesday 28th
The Walled Garden at Middleton
    Lodge   88

May

Saturday 2nd
NEW 18-20 Hall Lane   29
NEW Station House   83

Sunday 3rd
The Orchard   59
The Ridings   70
Scape Lodge   75
Warley House Garden   89

Monday 4th
Saltmarshe Hall   74

Wednesday 6th
Warley House Garden   89

Friday 8th
◆ Shandy Hall Gardens   76

Saturday 9th
◆ York Gate   91

Sunday 10th
◆ Jackson's Wold   36
Scape Lodge   75
◆ Stillingfleet Lodge   84
NEW Tanfield Lodge   86

Wednesday 13th
High Dalby House   33
NEW Horatio's Garden Sheffield &
    East   34
Primrose Bank Garden and
    Nursery   64

Sunday 17th
NEW Broad Oak Barn   10
Galehouse Barn   22
The Poplars   63
Rudding Park   73

Tuesday 19th
NEW 148 Healey Wood Road   31

Wednesday 20th
NEW 148 Healey Wood Road   31

Thursday 21st
NEW 148 Healey Wood Road   31

Sunday 24th
NEW The Laurels   41
115 Millhouses Lane   49
Prospect House   66

Tuesday 26th
NEW 148 Healey Wood Road   31

Wednesday 27th
NEW 148 Healey Wood Road   31

Thursday 28th
NEW 148 Healey Wood Road   31

Saturday 30th
Old Sleningford Hall   56

The Poplars

Sunday 31st
NEW 9 Bedford View 3
Marton cum Grafton Gardens 46
Old Sleningford Hall 56

June

Saturday 6th
Frog Hall Barn 21
NEW The Limes 42
Shiptonthorpe Gardens 77

Sunday 7th
Firby Hall 20
Frog Hall Barn 21
The Old Vicarage 58
Shiptonthorpe Gardens 77

Wednesday 10th
The Priory, Nun Monkton 65

Thursday 11th
NEW ◆ Richmond Castle 68
Skipwith Hall 78

Friday 12th
◆ Shandy Hall Gardens 76

Saturday 13th
NEW Healaugh Old Hall 30

Sunday 14th
NEW Galphay Manor 23
NEW Huntington Grange 35
◆ Jackson's Wold 36
Penny Cottage 61
18 Riplingham Road 71
8 South Glebe 80

Saturday 20th
NEW The Triangle Gardens 87

Sunday 21st
Beverley Gardens 6
Yorke House & White Rose Cottage 92

Saturday 27th
NEW 18-20 Hall Lane 29
NEW ◆ Kirkleatham Walled Garden 39
◆ York Gate 91

Sunday 28th
Bilton Garth 7
Fern House, 5 Wold Road 18
Fernleigh 19
Marton cum Grafton Gardens 46
Myton Grange 52
Ness Hall 53

July

Wednesday 1st
◆ Mount Grace Priory 51

Saturday 4th
12 Brendon Drive 8
Welton Lodge 90

Sunday 5th
Littlethorpe Manor 43
The Ridings 70
Sleightholmedale Lodge 79

Wednesday 8th
The Grange 25
Mires Beck Nursery 50

Saturday 11th
33 Heights Drive 32

Sunday 12th
Dacre Banks Gardens 14

Wednesday 15th
◆ Brodsworth Hall 11

Sunday 19th
NEW 6 Melander Close 48
The Nursery 54
Standfield Hall Farm 82

Monday 20th
The Nursery 54

Tuesday 21st
The Nursery 54

Wednesday 22nd
Standfield Hall Farm 82

Friday 24th
High Dalby House 33

Saturday 25th
NEW Azerley Chase 1

Sunday 26th
Goldsborough Hall 24
The Old Vicarage 57
Ridgewood 69

August

Sunday 2nd
Fern House, 5 Wold Road 18
Greencroft 27
NEW Tanfield Lodge 86

Wednesday 5th
The Grange 25

Saturday 8th
Mansion Cottage 45

The Laurels

Sunday 9th
Great Cliff Exotic Garden 26
Mansion Cottage 45

Saturday 22nd
NEW Station House 83

Saturday 29th
Swindon House Farm 85

Sunday 30th
Fernleigh 19
138 Greystones Road 28

Monday 31st
Pilmoor Cottages 62

September

Friday 4th
Duncanne House 16

Sunday 6th
Clifton Castle 13
138 Greystones Road 28
Southwood Hall 81

Thursday 10th
◆ Parcevall Hall Gardens 60

Sunday 13th
◆ Stillingfleet Lodge 84

By Arrangement

Arrange a personalised garden visit with your club, or group of friends, on a date to suit you. See individual garden entries for full details.

NEW Bentley House 4
90 Bents Road 5
Bilton Garth 7
Bridge House 9
The Circles Garden 12
Devonshire Mill 15
Fawley House 17
Fern House, 5 Wold Road 18
Fernleigh 19
Frog Hall Barn 21
Galehouse Barn 22
NEW Galphay Manor 23
The Grange 25
Greencroft 27
NEW 18-20 Hall Lane 29
NEW Healaugh Old Hall 30
33 Heights Drive 32
High Dalby House 33
Jervaulx Hall 37
The Jungle Garden 38
Langdale End (Shipthorpe Gardens) 77

Langton Farm 40
NEW The Laurels 41
The Manor, Birkby 44
Mansion Cottage 45
Marton cum Grafton Gardens 46
NEW Meadow Croft 47
115 Millhouses Lane 49
The Nursery 54
The Old Priory 55
The Old Vicarage 58
Pilmoor Cottages 62
The Poplars 63
Prospect House 66
Rewela Cottage 67
Ridgewood 69
The Ridings 70
NEW Rose Dale 72
Saltmarshe Hall 74
Scape Lodge 75
Skipwith Hall 78
Southwood Hall 81
Standfield Hall Farm 82
Welton Lodge 90
NEW 1 Wilds Pasture (Beverley Gardens) 6
Yorke House & White Rose Cottage 92

THE GARDENS

1 NEW AZERLEY CHASE
Azerley, Ripon, HG4 3JJ. Mr & Mrs John and Cherry Dalton. *4m NW of Ripon. From Ripon, take the Kirby Malzeard road. Azerley Chase entrance is 4m on L by the white lodge.* Sat 25 July (2-5). Adm £7, chd free. Tea, coffee & cake in the studio.
A romantic setting amongst a mature and tranquil landscape. The artist owner has enhanced the gardens with unique architectural features. Wisteria, naturalised hollyhocks and roses add charm. Magnolia walk, birch copse and undulating lawns lead down to a river, lakes, woodland walks and folly.

2 249 BARNSLEY ROAD
Flockton, Wakefield, WF4 4AL. Nigel & Anne Marie Booth. *On A637 Barnsley Rd. M1 J38 or J39 follow signs for Huddersfield. Parking on local roads. Please park with consideration.* Sat 25, Sun 26 Apr (1-5). Adm £5, chd free. Tea, coffee & cake.
An elevated south facing garden with panoramic views. ⅓ of an acre garden packed with spring bulbs, perennials and shrubs. Large plant sale. Disabled drop-off point at the bottom of the drive.
&

3 NEW 9 BEDFORD VIEW
Leeds, LS16 6DL. Mr & Mrs Geoff and Clare King. *N W Leeds on the edge of the city. Leeds ring road A6120, head N on A660 Otley. Turn L Otley Old Rd, uphill L at T-lights to Tinsill Ln. Downhill 4th on L to Bedford Dr follow to 1st R Bedford View. Parking at Welcome In Centre.* Sun 12 Apr, Sun 31 May (1-4.30). Adm £5, chd free. Tea, coffee & cake. Donation to OPAL - Older People's Action in the Locality.
A suburban garden about 500ft above sea level, on a dry sandy soil, open to the south and west, sheltered from northerly winds. Courtyard to the front and 3 mixed borders to the rear (one predominantly spring interest). Wide range of shrubs, herbaceous and bedding plants. Wildlife pond and vegetable plot, fruit trees and greenhouse with frames.

4 NEW BENTLEY HOUSE
Skutterskelfe, Yarm, TS15 0JR. Dr Khalid & Mrs Adele Khan, adelekhan@icloud.com. *In between Stokesley and Hutton Rudby. From Stokesley High St, head SW for 2.7m to Hutton Rudby and house is on L. From Hutton Rudby head NE for 1.3m to Stokesley, house is on R.* Visits by arrangement 6 June to 6 Sept. Adm £8, chd free. Tea, coffee & cake.
A large rural Cottage garden inc a wildlife pond and small stream. The borders and smaller gardens are designed to represent "gardens from around the world" such as a Japanese walkway, Mediterranean terrace, Mexican Courtyard, Moon garden and an Anglo Indian scented garden. Most plants have been propagated in house and are carefully chosen to grow in the North Yorkshire climate. Refreshments and Art sale (on certain dates). Wheelchair access is available for chairs up to 90cm wide.
&

5 90 BENTS ROAD
Bents Green, Sheffield, S11 9RL. Mrs Hilary Hutson, 01142 258570, h.hutson@paradiseregained.net. *3m SW of Sheffield. From inner ring road nr Waitrose, follow A625 (Ecclesall Rd). Bents Rd approx 3m on R.* Visits by arrangement 25 July to 2 Aug for groups of up to 40. Adm £5, chd free. Light refreshments.
Plantswoman's north east facing garden with many unusual species. Patio with alpine troughs for year-round interest and pots of colourful tropical plants in summer. Conservatory with exotic plants. Mixed borders surround a lawn which leads to a second patio and mature trees underplanted with shade-loving plants. Many examples of maximum impact with minimal maintenance.

GROUP OPENING

6 BEVERLEY GARDENS
1 Wilds Pasture, Beverley, HU17 8SW. *Garden Lodge, Wylies Rd outside North Bar. 39 North Bar Without on L. 231 Grovehill Rd is near Flemingate Centre. 1 Wilds Pasture is off Minster Way.* Sun 21 June (10.30-4.30). Combined adm £8, chd free. Light refreshments at Garden Lodge and 231 Grovehill Rd.

GARDEN LODGE
Mr James Marritt.

NEW 231 GROVEHILL ROAD
Kaye Fraser.

39 NORTH BAR WITHOUT
Mr & Mrs C Ryan.

NEW 1 WILDS PASTURE
Andrew Jackson, ajacksonuk1985@gmail.com. Visits also by arrangement 30 Apr to 31 July for groups of 5 to 15.

Garden Lodge: Unexpected tranquillity hidden behind high town walls. Designed and created by the current owners, it makes good use of old walls. Modern features complement a mixture of shrubs, young fruit trees, vegetables, soft fruits, herbs and perennials. 231 Grovehill Rd: Created in 2022 from grass patches, an old pear tree and a few roses, now inc a mix of borders with fruit trees, wildflowers and cultivated species. New woodland area and wildlife pond. Managed on organic principles. 39 North Bar Without: Traditional townhouse garden with borders of roses and perennials. Beyond is wilder area of fruit trees and winding paths. Hidden plot for vegetables, cutting flowers and beehives. 1 Wilds Pasture: New-build garden, designed to demonstrate what can be achieved in 3 yrs. English cottage garden style with shrub borders mixed with perennials. Sculpture and living poetry installations around. Natural water feature. Seating areas at Garden Lodge and 231 Grovehill Rd.

---

70 inpatients and their families are being supported at the newly opened Horatio's Garden Northern Ireland, thanks to the National Garden Scheme donations.

7 BILTON GARTH
Back Street, Bainton, Driffield, YO25 9LL. Andrew Snee, Asnee@btinternet.com. *6m SW of Driffield. Off A164 on W side of village, behind Bainton Stop cafe/bistro. Additional parking available on large lay-by on Main St a short walk away.* **Sun 28 June (11-4). Adm £6, chd free. Visits also by arrangement 2 May to 31 July for groups of 10+.**
Current owner started the large garden in 2013 (a former ¾ acre pony paddock) by planting many young native trees and shrubs to provide basic structure and aspect. Over the years, borders and numerous island beds were created to provide a stunning layout of many plant species. Features inc a renovated vintage tractor and treehouse. Plenty of seating areas to enjoy the different views.

8 12 BRENDON DRIVE
Birkby, Huddersfield, HD2 2DF. *Off Birkby Rd.* **Sat 4 July (11-5). Adm £3.50, chd free. Pre-booking essential, please visit www.ngs.org.uk for information & booking. Tea, coffee & cake.**
The inspiration for the garden is to create a family space with an atmosphere of relaxation and sensory experiences. Relaxed and informal, the garden is packed with striking blooms, colour and interest. Meandering paths, a pond and idyllic views are complemented by the sound of water and wildlife attracted to the garden. Architectural plants and wide borders create colour, drama and variety.

9 BRIDGE HOUSE
Main Street, Elvington, York, YO41 4AA. Mrs W C Bundy, 07974 277792, wendy@bundy.co.uk. *6m E from York ring road (A64). On B1228 from York, last house on R before bridge.* **Visits by arrangement 26 May to 31 July for groups of up to 45. Adm £10, chd free. Tea, coffee & cake.**
Two acre garden carved out of the River Derwent's floodplain 40 yrs ago. It survives annual winter flooding of the river which can last up to many months. Formal rose garden, mixed borders, shrubbery, large pond surrounded by hostas and ferns. Productive kitchen garden and orchard. Various devices in kitchen garden used to keep above water level. Groups may book a talk about flooding with garden tour. Slopes to main garden are steep.

10 NEW BROAD OAK BARN
Broad Oak, Linthwaite, Huddersfield, HD7 5TE. Ben and Rachel Stirling. *3.2m W of Huddersfield. From Huddersfield ring road follow A62 Manchester Rd. After approx 2m fork R at Horse & Groom pub traffic lights up Cowlersley Ln. Parking on main road only, above Broad Oak Bowling Club.* **Sun 17 May (11-4). Adm £5, chd free. Home-made teas. Donation to Hospice UK.**
A plant lovers garden. Formal and informal sweeping paths and stepping-stones lead you on a journey through ever changing outdoor rooms. Unusual trees and shrubs, formally trained espalier and cordon fruit trees. Octagonal and wildlife water lily ponds, formal topiary, Rhododendron bed and alpine garden.

11 ♦ BRODSWORTH HALL
Brodsworth, Doncaster, DN5 7XJ. English Heritage. *In Brodsworth, 5m NW of Doncaster off A635 Barnsley Rd; from J37 of A1(M). Please follow brown tourist signs to Brodsworth, do not rely on SatNav directions.* **For NGS: Evening opening Wed 15 July (5.30-7). Adm £20, chd free. Pre-booking essential, please email fundraising@english-heritage.org.uk or visit www.english-heritage.org.uk/visit/places/brodsworth-hall-and-gardens/events for information & booking. Light refreshments. For other opening times and information, please email or visit garden website.**
Join our Head Gardener and expert gardens team for an exclusive evening tour. Brodsworth Hall is a Victorian country house, built in the 1860s. Admire the restored formal parterre gardens with geometric beds filled in spring with tulips and violas, and summer displays of pelargoniums, cannas, and banana plants.

12 THE CIRCLES GARDEN
8 Stocksmoor Road, Midgley, nr Wakefield, WF4 4JQ. Joan Gaunt, mandy.gordon@ngs.org.uk. *Equidistant from Huddersfield, Wakefield & Barnsley, W of M1. Turn off A637 in Midgley at the Black Bull Pub (sharp bend) onto B6117 Stocksmoor Rd. Park on road.* **Visits by arrangement 1 Apr to 28 Aug for groups of 5 to 25. Not open on Sunday. Adm £5, chd free. Home-made teas provided by St Austin's Choir, Wakefield.**
An organic and self-sustaining plantswoman's ½ acre garden on gently sloping site overlooking fields, woods and nature reserve opposite. Designed and maintained by owner. Herbaceous, bulb and shrub plantings linked by grass and gravel paths, woodland area with mature trees, meadows, fernery, greenhouse, fruit trees, viewing terrace with pots. About 100 hellebores propagated from owner's own plants. South African plants, hollies, and small bulbs of particular interest.

13 CLIFTON CASTLE
Ripon, HG4 4AB. Lord & Lady Downshire. *2m N of Masham. On road to Newton-le-Willows & Richmond. Gates on L just before turn to Charlcot. What3words app: salmon.kebab.falls.* **Sun 29 Mar, Sun 6 Sept (2-5). Adm £7, chd free. Home-made teas.**
Impressive gardens and parkland with fine views over lower Wensleydale. Formal walks through the wooded 'pleasure grounds' feature bridges and follies, cascades and abundant wild flowers. The walled kitchen garden is similar to how it was set out in the C19, abundant produce in the summer. Recent wildflower meadows have been laid out with modern sculptures. Gravel paths and steep slopes to river.

GROUP OPENING

14 DACRE BANKS GARDENS
Nidderdale, HG3 4EW. www.yorkehouse.co.uk. *4m SE Pateley Bridge, 10m NW Harrogate, 10m N Otley, on B6451. On-site parking at Yorke House and public car park opp the Royal Oak pub in Dacre Banks.* **Sun 12 July (12-4.30). Combined adm £8, chd free. Cream teas at Yorke House.**

Station House

ORCHARD HOUSE
Mrs G Spain.

YORKE HOUSE & WHITE ROSE COTTAGE
Pat, Mark & Amy Hutchinson. (See separate entry)

Dacre Banks Gardens are located in the beautiful countryside of Nidderdale and are designed to take advantage of the scenic Dales landscape. The gardens are linked by a short walk. The 2 acre garden at Orchard House contains perennial borders and attractive shrubs selected to attract a diverse wildlife population. Yorke House has extensive colour-themed borders, rambling roses and water features with beautiful waterside plantings. There are plentiful seating areas with attractive views. The adjacent garden at White Rose Cottage is specifically designed for wheelchair users and features a colourful cottage garden, woodland plantings and large collection of hostas. Picnic area in the orchard at Yorke House. Entrance fee for all gardens paid at Yorke House. White Rose Cottage has full wheelchair access. Orchard House and Yorke House offer access to main features. Reserved parking available at Yorke House.

Cash only for refreshments. Visitors are welcome to picnic in the orchard at Yorke House.

15 DEVONSHIRE MILL
Canal Lane, Pocklington, York, YO42 1NN. Sue & Chris Bond, 01759 302147, chris.bond.dm@btinternet.com, www.facebook.com/gardenatdevonshiremill. *1m S of Pocklington. Canal Ln, off A1079 on opp side of the road from the canal towards Pocklington.* **Sun 15 Feb (11-4.30). Adm £6, chd free. Home-made teas.** Visits also by arrangement.

Drifts of double snowdrops, hellebores and ferns surround the historic Grade II listed watermill (not open). Explore the two acre garden with mill stream, orchards, woodland, herbaceous borders, hen run and greenhouses. The old mill pond is now a vegetable garden with raised beds and polytunnel. Over the past 30 yrs the owners have developed the garden on organic principles to encourage wildlife.

16 DUNCANNE HOUSE
Roecliffe Lane, Boroughbridge, York, YO51 9LN. Colette & Tom Walker. *Off Roecliffe Ln leaving Boroughbridge, on L along small private drive, just before Boroughbridge Manor Care Home.* **Evening opening Fri 4 Sept (5.30-8.30). Adm £15, chd free. Pre-booking essential, please visit www.ngs.org.uk for information & booking. Wine and canapés.**

A secluded town garden, which borrows enclosure from surrounding gardens. From the front garden a birch glade leads to theatrical rear garden with water feature, sculptural grass bank, lawns, beds and two vistas terminated by an urn and rustic tea pavilion. The product of a landscape architect and garden tour operator team, who have lovingly developed the garden over the last 12 yrs. Wheelchair accessible via grass paths with some cross falls.

17 FAWLEY HOUSE
7 Nordham, North Cave, nr Brough, Hull, HU15 2LT. Mr & Mrs T Martin, 07951 745033, louisem200@hotmail.co.uk, www.nordhamcottages.co.uk. *15m W of Hull. Leave M62E at J38. L at '30' & signs: Wetlands & Polo. At L bend, turn R into Nordham, garden on RHS. From Beverley, B1230 to N Cave. R after church & over bridge on LHS.* **Sun 22 Mar (12-5). Adm £6, chd free. Home-made teas in beamed cottage tearoom with log burners. Visits also by arrangement 16 Feb to 12 June for groups of 25+. Min charge for 25 visitors. Adm inc tea and home-made shortbread.**
Tiered, 2½ acre formal garden with lawns, mature trees, hedging, gravel pathways. Lavender beds, mixed shrub and hot double herbaceous borders. Apple espaliers, pears, soft fruit, produce and herb gardens. Terrace with pergola and vines. Sunken garden with white border. Further woodland area with naturalistic planting and spring bulbs. Quaker well, stream and spring with bridges, ferns and hellebores near mill stream. Snowdrops and aconites early in year. Treasure hunt for children on open day. Wheelchairs welcome on pea gravelled terrace for garden views and teas. Tearoom/WC is not accessible due to narrow entrance and steps.

& 🐕 ✿ 🚗 🛏 ☕

18 FERN HOUSE, 5 WOLD ROAD
Nafferton, Driffield, YO25 4LB. Peter & Jennifer Baker, 01377 255224. *N Nafferton. Follow directions rather than SatNav. From Driffield bypass to Nafferton on A614. Then 1st L & 1st L on Wold Rd. Park on street.* **Sun 19 Apr (10-4). Sun 28 June (10-4), open nearby Bilton Garth. Sun 2 Aug (10-4). Adm £4, chd free. Visits also by arrangement 19 Apr to 6 Sept.**
Designed and developed by owners since 2019. This small garden feels spacious with over 50 varieties of fern amongst many other plants. Mixed planting in quirky containers, up trellises and walls. A pond, a living wall and 2 greenhouses, one entirely full of ferns and the other of house plants. Opening in April for tulips and other spring flowers. Plenty of seating. Camomile and flagstone walkway. New garden room and greenhouse.

19 FERNLEIGH
9 Meadowhead Avenue, Meadowhead, Sheffield, S8 7RT. Mr & Mrs C Littlewood, 07514 615099, littlewoodchristine@gmail.com. *4m S of Sheffield. From city centre. A61, A6102, B6054 r'about, exit B6054. 1st R Greenhill Ave, 2nd R. From M1 J33, A630 to A6102, then as above.* **Sun 28 June, Sun 30 Aug (11-5). Adm £4, chd free. Tea, coffee & cake. Visits also by arrangement 1 May to 16 Aug for groups of 10 to 30.**
Plantswoman's ⅓ acre cottage style suburban garden. Large variety of unusual plants set in different areas provide year-round interest. Several seats to view different aspects of garden. Auricula theatre, patio, gazebo and greenhouse. Miniature log cabin with living roof and cobbled area with unusual plants in pots. Sempervivum, alpine displays, collection of Epimedium and wildlife hotel. Over 30 varieties of peonies end of May into June. Wide selection of homegrown plants for sale. Animal Search for children.

✿

20 FIRBY HALL
Firby, Bedale, DL8 2PW. Mrs S Page. *½m along Masham Rd out of Bedale, follow sign to Firby. Hall gates on L after ½m. What3words app: waitress.cornering.recently.* **Sun 7 June (12-5). Adm £8, chd free. Light refreshments in the greenhouse set in the walled garden.**
The Hall sits in 4 acres with a walled garden to the north and 2 lakes to the south, the largest of which features a folly. The walled garden and greenhouse were restored in 2019. The main garden continues to undergo renovation: the ha-ha was restored during the 2020 lockdown as were the 110m long herbaceous beds. Ongoing work is now focused on the main west facing lawns. Some steps but most of the garden is wheelchair accessible.

& 🐕 ✿ ☕))

21 FROG HALL BARN
Breighton, Selby, YO8 6DH. Mr & Mrs Clarke, 07511 821353, sarahclarke100@icloud.com. *From Bubwith, pass sign for Breighton, 3rd house on R.* **Sat 6, Sun 7 June (10-4.30). Adm £4.50, chd free. Tea, coffee & cake. Visits also by arrangement 1 May to 8 June.**

Bee friendly flower and vegetable garden in ¾ acre around a converted threshing barn. At the front, a walled courtyard garden of perennials and annuals. To the rear, the garden reaches down to the Derwent Ings. Borders full of cottage garden flowers selected to encourage wildlife. A small meadow, fruit trees, and beehives. Kitchen garden with traditional greenhouse.

🐕 ✿ ☕ 🛏))

22 GALEHOUSE BARN
Bishopdyke Road, Cawood, Selby, YO8 3UB. Mr & Mrs P Lloyd and Mrs M Taylor, 07768 405642, junelloyd042@gmail.com. *On B1222 out of Cawood towards Sherburn-in-Elmet. On B1222 1m out of Cawood towards Sherburn in Elmet.* **Sun 17 May (12-5). Adm £4.50, chd free. Home-made teas. Visits also by arrangement 1 June to 2 Oct for groups of 5 to 20. Refreshments and price to be determined by agreement.**
The Barn: A plantaholic's informal cottage garden, created in 2015, to encourage birds and insects. Raised beds with tranquil seating area. The Farm: South facing, partly shaded varied herbaceous border. North facing exposed shaded border redeveloped 2017, ongoing for spring and autumn interest. Raised beds for vegetables. Paddock with mature trees. Partial wheelchair access. Help available.

& 🐕 ✿ ☕))

23 NEW GALPHAY MANOR
Galphay, Ripon, HG4 3NJ. Andrew & Bairbre Duncan, bairbreduncan@gmail.com. *5m W of Ripon. From Ripon, take B6265 W. Turn R after Tate's garden centre. Follow road for 4m to Galphay.* **Sun 14 June (2-5). Adm £7, chd free. Tea, coffee & cake. Visits also by arrangement June to Sept.**
3 acres of established grounds with sweeping lawns, an Edwardian pond and original rockery. Water garden feature, large greenhouse with gravelled garden. Multiple roses throughout the herbaceous borders. Lots of peaceful seating areas.

☕

24 GOLDSBOROUGH HALL
Church Street, Goldsborough, HG5 8NR. Mr & Mrs M Oglesby, 01423 867321, info@goldsboroughhall.com, www.goldsboroughhall.com. *2m SE of Knaresborough. 3m W of A1(M). Off J47 (A59 York-Harrogate). Spring: parking at Hall top car park. Summer: parking E of village in field off Midgley Ln. Disabled parking only at front of Hall.* **Sun 29 Mar, Sun 26 July (11-4). Adm £7.50, chd free. Light refreshments inc sandwiches, scones and cakes along with tea & coffee.** Donation to St Mary's Church, Goldsborough.
Historic 12 acre garden and formal landscaped grounds in parkland setting around Grade II, C17 house, former residence of HRH Princess Mary, daughter of George V and Queen Mary. Gertrude Jekyll inspired 120ft double herbaceous borders, rose garden and woodland walk. Large restored kitchen garden with rill, fountain and large glasshouse which produces fruit and vegetables for the Hall's commercial kitchens. ¼ mile lime tree walk planted by royalty in the 1920s, orchard and flower borders featuring 'Yorkshire Princess' rose, named after Princess Mary. Gravel paths and some steep slopes.
& 🐕 ✱ 🚗 ☕ 🔊

25 THE GRANGE
Carla Beck Lane, Carleton in Craven, Skipton, BD23 3BU. Mr & Mrs R N Wooler, 07740 639135, margaret.wooler@hotmail.com. *1½ m SW of Skipton. Turn off A56 (Skipton-Clitheroe) into Carleton. Keep L at Swan Pub, continue to end of village then R into Carla Beck Ln.* **Wed 8 July, Wed 5 Aug (11.30-4.30). Adm £7.50, chd free. Home-made teas. Visits also by arrangement July & Aug for groups of 20+.** Donation to Sue Ryder Care Manorlands Hospice.
Over 4 acres of wonderfully varied garden set in the grounds of Victorian house (not open) with mature trees and panoramic views towards The Gateway to the Dales. The garden has been restored and expanded by the owners over the past three decades. Bountiful herbaceous borders with many unusual species, rose walk, parterre, mini-meadows and water features. Topiary and large greenhouse. Extensive vegetable and cut flower beds. Oak seating placed throughout the garden invites quiet contemplation - a place to 'lift the spirits'. Gravel paths and steps in some areas.
& ✱ 🚗 ☕

26 GREAT CLIFF EXOTIC GARDEN
Cliff Drive, Crigglestone, Wakefield, WF4 3EN. Kristofer Swaine, www.greatcliffexoticgarden.co.uk. *1m from J39 M1. From M1 (J39) take A636 towards Denby Dale, past Cedar Court Hotel then L at British Oak pub onto Blacker Ln. Parking on Cliff Rd m'way bridge a 3 min walk from the garden.* **Sun 9 Aug (10.30-3). Adm £4, chd free. Pre-booking essential, please visit www.ngs.org.uk for information & booking. Tea, coffee & cake inc vegan options.**
An exotic garden on a long narrow plot. Possibly the largest collection of palm species planted out in Northern England inc a large Chilean wine palm. Large desert planting area with Yuccas, Agaves and Cacti. Jungle clearing area with large leaved tropical looking plants. Jungle hut, winding paths and a pond that traverses the full width of the garden.
✱ ☕ 🔊

27 GREENCROFT
Pottery Lane, Littlethorpe, Ripon, HG4 3LS. David & Sally Walden, 01765 602487, s-walden@outlook.com. *1½ m SE of Ripon town centre. Off A61 Ripon bypass, signs to Littlethorpe, R at church. From Bishop Monkton take Knaresborough Rd towards Ripon then R to Littlethorpe.* **Sun 2 Aug (12-4). Adm £5, chd free. Cream teas. Visits also by arrangement July & Aug for groups of 20+.**
½ acre country garden with long herbaceous borders packed with colourful late summer perennials, annuals and exotics. Circular garden with views through to large wildlife pond and surrounding countryside. Ornamental features inc gazebo, temple pavilions, formal pool, stone wall with mullions, gate to pergola and a water cascade.
& 🐕 ✱ 🚗 ☕ 🔊

28 138 GREYSTONES ROAD
Sheffield, S11 7BR. Mr Nick Hetherington. *From Sheffield inner Ring Rd, W on A625 (Ecclesall Rd) for 1.8m; R onto Greystones Rd.* **Sun 30 Aug, Sun 6 Sept (10-4). Adm £4, chd free. Tea, coffee & cake.**
This typical, small suburban plot has been developed into a lovely garden over 20 yrs. It features many trees and acers combined with stunning late tender perennials inc banana plants, Ricinus, Canna, Agapanthus, Colocasia and dahlias. Several sculptures created by the owner are displayed amongst the plants. The garden has a tropical feel with splashes of colour, mainly orange and purple.
✱ ☕ 🔊

29 NEW 18-20 HALL LANE
Kirkburton, Huddersfield, HD8 0QW. Helen Harrison and Simon Hirst, 07766 697894, hharrison1965@hotmail.com. *Highburton, Huddersfield. From Huddersfield take A629, turn L at White Swan pub onto Far Dene, then R by Smiths Arms. Pass garden on corner ahead, then L onto Highfield Rd where you can park.* **Sat 2 May, Sat 27 June (11-6). Adm £5, chd free. Cream teas inc vegan options. Vintage afternoon tea options with sandwiches. Visits also by arrangement 30 Apr to 30 June for groups of 5 to 30.**
Set in the grounds of a Victorian Yorkshire stone house, this garden is divided into sections. Cottage style planting leads to relaxed borders, seating areas, vegetable plot, cutting garden, and wooden greenhouse. Vintage items and pottery add quirk and charm. Only one small step leads into the garden, the rest is flat.
& 🐕 ✱ ☕ 🪑 🔊

310,000 people are cared for each year who are approaching the end of life or diagnosed with a terminal illness through the hospice network supported by National Garden Scheme funding.

30 HEALAUGH OLD HALL

Wighill Lane, Healaugh, Tadcaster, LS24 8DA. Mr Oliver & Mrs Priscilla Smith, 07592 414579, priscillahealaugh@gmail.com. *Between Wetherby & York. 5m N of Tadcaster.* **Sat 13 June (11-4). Adm £7, chd free. Light refreshments. Visits also by arrangement May & June for groups of up to 20.**
C17 manor house with 2 acre partly walled gardens on the edge of a pretty village. Mature yew hedges creating tranquil and contemplative rooms in which to sit and enjoy - the Secluded Garden with summer herbaceous and roses, a yew 'ruined chapel', potager with coppiced willow, lawn tennis court with extensive pastoral views, box parterre. Host for the Quiet Garden Movement - www.quietgarden.org. Some gravel paths.

31 148 HEALEY WOOD ROAD

Brighouse, HD6 3RR. Rich and Catherine Richardson. *½m from Brighouse town centre. A641 out of town, past railway stn & then take 2nd R into Aire St. Continue into Healey Wood Rd, up steep hill. No.148 is on the RHS near the top. 2 parking spaces are available in the drive.* **Tue 19, Wed 20, Thur 21, Tue 26, Wed 27, Thur 28 May (10.30-2.30). Adm £6, chd free. Pre-booking essential, please visit www.ngs.org.uk for information & booking.**
Developed over 20 yrs, this deceptively sized garden runs down to cliffs, with extensive views over the wooded hills beyond Rastrick. A series of hedges divide the garden into rooms, each containing a different mix of shrubs, herbaceous plants and grasses. A variety of fruit and ornamental trees add to the diverse colours and textures of the garden. Stone and gravel paths in some areas.

32 33 HEIGHTS DRIVE

Linthwaite, Huddersfield, HD7 5SU. Dawn & Roy Meakin, 07825 184919, roymeakin7@btinternet.com. *4m SW of Huddersfield. From Huddersfield on A62 Manchester Rd for about 2m then fork L at T-lights, Cowlersley Ln, then Gillroyd Ln, all one road for 2m, parking on main road by bus shelter opp Heights Dr.* **Sat 11 July (10-4). Adm £5, chd free. Tea, coffee & cake. Cash Only. Visits also by arrangement 4 May to 28 Sept for groups of 15+. Donation to Royal National Lifeboat Institute (RNLI).**

Goldsborough Hall

Situated on a Pennine hillside is a quirky garden overlooking the Colne Valley. The plot has been carefully designed with a flower arranger's eye and offers many handmade bespoke features. The meandering paths draw the visitor's eye around the garden, within a wide range of different room settings. The garden has a range of modern and quirky twists, with a wonderful nod to tradition. Bespoke handmade creations nestled around the garden complementing the colour schemes of the plants, creating traditional and contemporary settings. Flower arranging demonstrations could be offered, please ask for details.

33 HIGH DALBY HOUSE
Dalby, Pickering, YO18 7LP. Linda and Ian Robinson, 01751 460001, ian@highdalbyhouse.com, www.highdalbyhouse.com. *Dalby Forest, North York Moors National Park. Enter Dalby Forest via Thornton Dale entrance barriers. Proceed for 2.2m, house on L.* **Wed 13 May, Fri 24 July (11-4). Adm £6, chd free. Pre-booking essential, please visit www.ngs.org.uk for information & booking. Tea, coffee & cake.** Visits also by arrangement 7 Apr to 31 Dec for groups of 5 to 12.
Set in the heart of Dalby Forest, the garden comprises over six acres of a mix of woodland, small lake, wild areas, a cherry orchard, Labyrinth, formal borders inc an RHS Tatton award-winning border. Newly-developed unique Trinity Garden with lively beck running through, crossing bridges and surrounding specimen trees. There are many places to sit, reflect and enjoy its variety. Host for the Quiet Garden Movement - www.quietgarden.org.

34 HORATIO'S GARDEN SHEFFIELD & EAST
Princess Royal Spinal Injuries Unit, off Barnsley Road Drive, Northern General Hospital, Sheffield, S5 7AU. Ruth Calder, www.horatiosgarden.org.uk/the-gardens/horatios-garden-sheffield-east. *Head uphill on Barnsley Rd Dr, take the service road on R at end of wooded area. Continue until wooden gates. What3words app: tested.tunnel.clips. Street parking available on roads E of hospital.* **Wed 13 May (1-5).**

Adm £5, chd free. Pre-booking essential, please visit www.ngs.org.uk for information & booking. Tea, coffee & cake.
Horatio's Garden Sheffield & East began as a show garden which won Best in Show at the RHS Chelsea Flower Show 2023. Opened in April 2025, it supports people with spinal injury, their visitors, and NHS staff. Designed by Harris Bugg Studio, the garden is inspired by the history, geography and industry of Yorkshire. Spring is the perfect time to enjoy the naturalistic planting. The garden is fully wheelchair accessible. Please contact garden for information about accessible parking - 07471 002179.

35 NEW HUNTINGTON GRANGE
New Lane, Huntington, York, YO32 9NA. Jay Badenhorst and Darren O'Connor. *Opp Highthorn Rd. 2.2 m NE of York S off the A1237 ring road. Buses 1,5,5a,9 and 20 from York. What3words app: tree.snow.wicked.* **Sun 14 June (11-4). Adm £5, chd free. Tea, coffee & cake.**
A garden where formal elegance meets cottage charm. Over the last 3 yrs, the owners have created 'rooms' with unique vibes and serene spots around the farmhouse. Meandering paths reveal a rose garden, wildflower meadow, wildlife pond and productive fruit and vegetable areas. Moongates frame views, colourful borders extend the seasons, and seating areas offer peace and inspiration. Partial wheelchair access to certain areas.

36 ♦ JACKSON'S WOLD
Sherburn, Malton, YO17 8QJ. Mr & Mrs Richard Cundall, 07966 531995, jacksonswoldgarden@gmail.com, www.jacksonswoldgarden.com. *11m E of Malton, 10m SW of Scarborough. A64 E to Scarborough. R at T-lights in Sherburn. Take the Weatherhorpe Rd. After 100 metres R fork to Helperthorpe & Luttons. 1m to top of hill. Turn L at garden sign. Do not use SatNav.* **For NGS: Sun 10 May, Sun 14 June (12-5). Adm £5, chd free. Tea, coffee & cake.** For other opening times and information, please phone, email or visit garden website.
Spectacular two acre country garden. Many old shrub roses underplanted with unusual perennials in walled garden. Woodland paths lead to further shrub and perennial borders. Lime avenue with wildflower meadow. Traditional vegetable garden inc roses and flowers with a Victorian greenhouse. Small adjoining nursery. Tours by appointment.

37 JERVAULX HALL
Jervaulx, Ripon, HG4 4PH. Mr & Mrs Phillip Woodrow, phillip@nowtryus.net. *Parking by arrangement at Jervaulx Abbey tearooms.* **Visits by arrangement June to Sept for groups of 30+.**
Eight acre garden adjacent to ruins of Jervaulx Abbey and inc Abbey Mill ruins with views of River Ure. Mixed borders and beds, croquet lawn, parterre, glasshouse. A small vegetable garden and fernery. Magnificent older trees and woodland areas with choice trees and shrubs planted in last ten years, inc magnolia, acer, Sorbus and Betula. Growing collection of contemporary sculptures.

38 THE JUNGLE GARDEN
124 Dobcroft Road, Millhouses, Sheffield, S7 2LU. Dr Simon & Julie Olpin, 07710 559189, simonjolpin@blueyonder.co.uk. *3m SW of city centre. Dobcroft Rd runs between A625 & A621.* **Visits by arrangement 15 June to 30 Sept for groups of up to 25. Tea, coffee & cake is by request and additional cost. Adm £5, chd free. Donation to Sheffield Children's Hospital.**
Not a traditional garden, but a fascinating mature space of specialist interest using mainly hardy exotics creating a jungle effect. Long (250ft) narrow site, densely planted with mature trees and shrubs inc many Trachycarpus, European fan palms, large bamboos, several tree ferns, mature Eucalyptus and a number of species of mature Scheffleras. The planting has a South East Asian theme.

The National Garden Scheme funded six Macmillan Nurses in their roles across England, Wales and Northern Ireland in 2025.

39 NEW ♦ KIRKLEATHAM WALLED GARDEN
Plantation Road, Kirkleatham, Redcar, TS10 4AS. Head Gardener - Hazel Robinson, 01642 054125, hazel.robinson@elior.co.uk, www.facebook.com/KirkleathamWalledGarden. *Teesside, N Yorkshire. Follow signs to the Crematorium, not the Kirkleatham Museum, to find the correct roundabout on the A174. What3words app: panels.petal.locate.* **For NGS: Sat 27 June (9-4). Adm £5, chd free. Light refreshments at adjacent cafe.** For other opening times and information, please phone, email or visit garden website.
Grade II listed Walled Garden within the Kirkleatham Estate, built in the C17 by the Turner family. In 2021 the garden was carefully restored back to its former glory utilising much of it's original design. Beautiful formal and informal gardens with wide range of perennials and annuals particularly salvias. Children's splash area, bothy art gallery, glasshouse and cafe. The garden is beautifully planted with a wide range of perennials and annuals with Salvia's being a special favourite. Access across the site for wheelchairs. Pathways are wide and level with disabled parking in the car park beside the garden.

&♿ 🐕 🚗 ☕ »)

40 LANGTON FARM
Great Langton, Northallerton, DL7 0TA. Richard & Annabel Fife, annabelfife1661@gmail.com. *5m W of Northallerton. B6271 in Great Langton between Northallerton & Scotch Corner.* **Visits by arrangement May to Aug for groups of up to 25.**
Garden designer's organic garden created since 2000. Romantic flower garden with mixed borders, roses, poppies, Astrantias, delphiniums, white lilies and pebble pool. Formal and informal gravel areas, nuttery. Pear avenue underplanted with double helix of white daffodils.

♿ 🐕 ❀ 🚗

41 NEW THE LAURELS
Moor End, Acaster Malbis, York, YO23 2UQ. Jill and Jon Harris, 07772 107444, jillythelaurels@icloud.com. *5m S of York. Follow signs off the A64 for Acaster Malbis. NGS Signs will be positioned to guide you to the garden.* **Sun 24 May (11-4). Adm £5, chd free. Home-made teas.**

Visits also by arrangement 24 May to 31 Aug for groups of 5+.
An informal, sloping one acre cottage garden, evolved over 10 yrs, with flower borders, shrubs, topiary, seating areas, mature trees and arbours, planted to shelter and encourage wildlife. A shaded woodland area, opens out to reveal a small orchard. A bridge over a dyke gives access to a meadow and summerhouse on a west facing bank. Vegetable and cutting garden to the front of the house.

🐕 ❀ ☕ »)

42 NEW THE LIMES
Weeton Lane, Weeton, Leeds, LS17 0AN. Sarah and Johnny Pearson, www.thelimes.online. *Near Harrogate. What3words app: surprised.crescendo.raking.* **Sat 6 June (10-4). Adm £7, chd free. Tea, coffee & cake. Wine and Champagne available by the glass.**
Set against a beautiful house in open countryside surrounded by stunning views, The Limes gardens offer French-inspired "rooms" with distinct colours and character. Highlights inc prairie planting, gravel garden, wildflower meadow, woodland, orchard, croquet lawn, and pétanque pitch. Drought-tolerant planting, mature trees and Pete Carling's sculptures enrich the setting. Art gallery and café for refreshments.

❀ ☕ »)

43 LITTLETHORPE MANOR
Littlethorpe Road, Littlethorpe, Ripon, HG4 3LG. Mrs M C Thackray, www.littlethorpemanor.com. *Outskirts of Ripon nr racecourse. Ripon bypass A61. Follow Littlethorpe Rd from Dallamires Ln r'about to stable block with clock tower. Parking in adjacent field. See map on website.* **Sun 5 July (1.30-5). Adm £8, chd free. Home-made teas in marquee.**
11 acres. Walled garden with perennials, roses and gazebo. Sunken garden with ornamental plants and herbs. Brick pergola with wisteria, blue and yellow borders. Formal lawn with fountain pool, hornbeam towers, yew hedging. Box-headed hornbeam drive with Aqualens. Large pond with classical pavilion and boardwalk. Contemporary Physic garden with rill, raised beds, medicinal plants. Winter garden. Gravel paths and some steep steps.

♿ ❀ ☕ »)

44 THE MANOR, BIRKBY
Birkby Lane, Birkby, Northallerton, DL7 0EF. Ginny and Jonathan McCloy, 07903 757250, ginny.lloyd@me.com. *7m NNW of Northallerton. On A167, 5½m N of Northallerton turn L into Birkby Ln. ½m along lane garden is immed after St Peter's Church.* **Visits by arrangement 19 May to 31 July for groups of 10 to 30. Adm inc hot drink and cake. Adm £10, chd free.**
C18 manor (not open) former rectory to adjacent church. 2½ acre gardens surrounded by mature trees. Lawns remodelled late 2025, mixed shrub and flower borders. Current owners have added new features inc specimen trees, glasshouse, planned rose gazebo, and an elliptical shaped orchard with Corten steel planters for flowers and vegetables. Meandering woodland path with curiosities for the observant. WC access for wheelchair users.

♿ 🐕 ☕ »)

45 MANSION COTTAGE
8 Gillus Lane, Bempton, Bridlington, YO15 1HW. Polly & Chris Myers, 07749 776746, chrismyers0807@gmail.com. *2m NE of Bridlington. From Bridlington take B1255 to Flamborough. 1st L at T-lights - Bempton Ln, continue through r'about and next R into Short Ln then L at end. L fork at church.* **Sat 8, Sun 9 Aug (10-4). Adm £5, chd free. Light refreshments inc home-made savoury and sweet small plates served from the conservatory.** Visits also by arrangement 25 May to 3 Aug for groups of 10 to 40.
A truly hidden, private and secret garden with exuberant, packed, vibrant borders. Visitors' book says 'a veritable oasis', 'the garden is inspirational', with a surprise around every corner. Japanese influenced area, mini hosta walk, 100ft border, summerhouse and art studio. Vegetable plot, cuttery, late summer borders with planting for pollinators, large sweeping deck and lawns. Produce, plants and home-made soaps for sale.

🐕 ❀ 🚗 ☕

GROUP OPENING

46 MARTON CUM GRAFTON GARDENS
Marton cum Grafton, York, YO51 9QJ. Mrs Glen Garnett, 07901 592768, gwg01@talktalk.net. 2½ m S of Boroughbridge. Turn off the A168 or B6265 to Marton or Grafton, S of Boroughbridge. Parking in Grafton. **Sun 31 May, Sun 28 June (1-5). Combined adm £7.50, chd free.** Visits also by arrangement May & June for groups of 10 to 30.

ORCHARD HOUSE
Mr Rob & Mrs Lizzie Shepherd.

PADDOCK HOUSE
Tim & Jill Smith.

WELL HOUSE
Glen Garnett.

Three gardens in two adjacent rural villages within walking distance of each other. In Marton, Paddock House is on an elevated site with extensive views and sloping lawn to a wildlife pond. The house is encircled by a profusion of pots combing cottage garden and Mediterranean styles. A terrace of Yorkshire stone and steps using gravel and wood sleepers leads to seating areas and cutting garden with small greenhouse. Orchard House is a contemporary village garden with an abundance of features inc gravel garden, raised beds and extensive views across an alpaca paddock and wildflower meadow. Well House in Grafton nestles under the hillside. A traditional English cottage garden with herbaceous borders, climbing roses and ornamental shrubs with a variety of interesting species. Paths meander through the borders to an orchard with chickens.

47 NEW MEADOW CROFT
East End, Ampleforth, York, YO62 4DA. Messrs Robert Scott & Jarrod Marsden, 07900 003538, rdsjsm@gmail.com. *4m SW of Helmsley. Park on Main St. Meadow Croft is situated E of the village. What3words app: studio.clinic.realm.* **Visits by arrangement 16 Mar to 31 Oct for groups of 5 to 12. Tea, coffee & cake available, weather permitting (no indoor seating).** Redesigned in 2024, the garden features a series of garden rooms. The front garden inc shade-loving plants, small parterre, fruit/vegetable garden, lean-to glasshouse, gravel area and pots. The rear formal garden has stone paving on 3 levels, seating, pond and a stream. Arch to lawn, herbaceous perennials, shrubs and trees. Gravel area with feature dry stone wall and views of the Howardian Hills.

Our donation to Marie Curie this year is equivalent to 17,521 hours of hospice at home care.

Rewela Cottage

48 NEW 6 MELANDER CLOSE
York, YO26 5RP. Mr Peter & Mrs Linda Nicholson. *From A1237 take B1224 towards Acomb. At r'about turn L (Beckfield Ln). 3rd turning on L.* **Sun 19 July (1-6). Combined adm with The Nursery £7, chd free. Tea.**
Evolved since 1987 this 50x18 metre urban garden has been created for year-round interest with clipped evergreen shrubs and topiary. There are two small wildlife ponds, gravelled areas, a greenhouse and vegetable plots.

49 115 MILLHOUSES LANE
Sheffield, S7 2HD. Sue & Phil Stockdale, 07941 513306, phil.stockdale@gmail.com. *4m SW of Sheffield city centre nr Derbyshire border. From city, follow A625 Castleton/Dore Rd, 4th L after Prince of Wales pub, 2nd L. Otherwise, take A621 Baslow Rd. After Tesco garage take 2nd R, then 1st L.* **Sun 24 May (11-4.30). Adm £5, chd free. Light refreshments. Visits also by arrangement 16 May to 29 Aug for groups of 5 to 30.**
Plantswoman's 1/3 acre south facing level cottage style garden with many choice and unusual perennials and bulbs, providing year-round colour and interest. A large collection of over 70 hostas, roses, peonies, irises and clematis alongside many tender and exotic plants inc aeoniums, echeverias, aloes, bananas, colocasia and echiums. Seating areas around the garden. Many home-propagated plants for sale. Most of the garden is accessible for wheelchairs.

50 MIRES BECK NURSERY
Low Mill Lane, North Cave, Brough, HU15 2NR. www.miresbeck.co.uk. *Between N & S Cave. Do not follow SatNav if entering North Cave from the A63/ M62. Through village, take S Cave Rd & reset SatNav. What3words app: amount.occupations.spades.* **Wed 8 July (10-4). Adm £5, chd free. Tea, coffee & cake.**
Charity that provides horticultural work experience for adults with learning disabilities. 14 acre site features herbaceous borders, vegetable beds, dementia garden and Hull's official Garden of Sanctuary. We grow 500 herbaceous perennials, 50 herbs, 100 wild flowers for regional garden centres and heritage sites. Exclusive to NGS Visitors - Woodland walk, planting and history of the charity talks. Tarmac main paths, and compressed gravel side paths.

51 ♦ MOUNT GRACE PRIORY
Staddlebridge, Northallerton, DL6 3JG. English Heritage. *12m N of Thirsk and 6m NE of Northallerton, nr A19. Take care when turning off the dual carriageway. Look out for brown English Heritage direction signs 1/2 m before the turning.* **For NGS: Evening opening Wed 1 July (5.30-7). Adm £20, chd free. Pre-booking essential, please email fundraising@english-heritage.org.uk or visit www.english-heritage.org.uk/visit/places/mount-grace-priory/events for information & booking. Light refreshments. For other opening times and information, please email or visit garden website.**
Meet the Head Gardener and members of their team for an exclusive evening tour of the gardens. Mount Grace Priory was the last of the great Yorkshire monasteries, founded in 1398. Wander the arts-and-crafts terraced gardens restored by Sir Lowthian Bell in the early C20, featuring rich, mature borders on the terraces and a stroll to the peaceful Monks' Pond through a wildflower meadow.

52 MYTON GRANGE
Myton On Swale, York, YO61 2QU. Nick & Annie Ramsden. *15m N of York. From the N go through Helperby on York Rd. After 1/2 m follow yellow signs towards Myton. From the S leave A19 through Tollerton & Flawith. Turn L at Xrds.* **Sun 28 June (1-5). Adm £8, chd free. Home-made teas.**
This garden, attached to a Victorian farmhouse, once formed part of the Myton Estate. Size 3/4 acre and adjacent to the River Swale. Inc a paved terrace garden, formal parterre, circular garden with mixed shrub and herbaceous border, lawn with topiary borders and new gravel garden. There will be a talk about the restored Victorian Stud Farm buildings, and history of the Myton Estate at 3pm.

53 NESS HALL
East Ness, Nunnington, YO62 5XD. Mr Richard & the Hon Mrs Harriette Murray Wells, www.nesshall.com/garden. *6m E of Helmsley, 22m N of York. From B1257 Helmsley-Malton road turn L at Slingsby signed Kirkbymoorside, 3m to Ness What3Words app: workroom.snail.oblige.* **Sun 28 June (12-4). Adm £7, chd free. Tea, coffee & cake.**
Ness is a romantic English flower garden created by three generations of keen gardeners. Surrounded by parkland it has views to the North Yorkshire Moors. A 2 1/2 acre walled garden with mixed and herbaceous borders as well as self seeding beds, and a water garden, vegetable, cutting garden, rockery, rose, woodland area set in an extended garden totalling 6 acres. There are steps and slopes in the walled garden although some of the garden is accessible for wheelchairs.

54 THE NURSERY
15 Knapton Lane, Acomb, York, YO26 5PX. Tony Chalcraft & Jane Thurlow, 01904 781691, janeandtonyatthenursery@hotmail.co.uk. *2 1/2 m W of York. From A1237 take B1224 towards Acomb. At r'about turn L (Beckfield Ln). After 150 metres turn L.* **Sun 19 July (1-6). Combined adm with 6 Melander Close £7, chd free. Mon 20, Tue 21 July (1-6). Adm £5, chd free. Home-made teas. Visits also by arrangement June to Aug for groups of 10+.**
A former suburban commercial nursery, now an attractive and productive one acre organic, private garden. Over 100 fruit trees, many in trained form. Many different vegetables grown both outside and under cover in a 20 metre greenhouse. Productive areas interspersed with informal ornamental plantings and cut flower areas to provide colour and habitat for wildlife.

55 THE OLD PRIORY
Everingham, YO42 4JD. Dr J D & Mrs H J Marsden, 07703 529112, helen.marsden@ngs.org.uk. *15m SE of York, 6m from Pocklington. 2m S of A1079. On E side of village. What3words app: foggy.headache. imparting.* **Visits by arrangement 24 May to 28 June. Adm £10, chd free. Tea, coffee & cake.**

2 acre rural garden. Created in 1990s to enable self-sufficiency in vegetables, meat, fruit, logs and timber. Walled vegetable garden (not dug) and greenhouse. Borders planted to cope with sandy loam. Garden slopes down to natural bog garden. Dove tree, variegated tulip tree and various willows. Beyond garden roughly mown pathway through woodland, along ponds, lake and lightly grazed pasture. Plenty wild flora and fauna.

56 OLD SLENINGFORD HALL
Mickley, nr Ripon, HG4 3JD. Jane & Tom Ramsden. *5m NW of Ripon. Off A6108. After N Stainley turn L, follow signs to Mickley. Gates on R after 1½m opp cottage.* **Sat 30, Sun 31 May (12-4). Adm £7.50, chd free. Home-made teas.** Donation to other charities.
A large English country garden and award winning now rewilding permaculture forest garden. Early C19 house (not open) and garden with original layout. Wonderful mature trees, woodland walk and Victorian fernery, romantic lake with islands, watermill, walled kitchen garden, beautiful long herbaceous border, yew and huge beech hedges. Several plant and other stalls. Picnics around the mill pond very welcome. Of particular interest to anyone interested in permaculture. Reasonable wheelchair access to most parts of garden. Disabled WC at Old Sleningford Farm next to the garden.

57 THE OLD VICARAGE
North Frodingham, Driffield, YO25 8JT. Professor Ann Mortimer. *From Driffield take B1249 E for approx 6m, garden on R opp church. Entrance at T-junc of road to Emmotland & B1249. From N Frodingham take B1249 W for ½m. Park in farmyard 50yds E opp side B1249.* **Sun 26 July (10.30-4.30). Adm £6, chd free. Home-made teas inc sandwiches, hot and cold drinks, home-made cakes and cream teas.**
1½ acre plantsman's garden inc rose garden, jungle, desert, nuttery, orchard, turf maze, winter, fountain, scented, kitchen gardens and glasshouses. Mini grass garden and grouse moor. Classic and modern statues, unusual trees and shrubs, large and small ponds. Children's interest: 'Jungle Book', dinosaurs, wild animal statues. Neo-Jacobean revival house, built 1837, mentioned in Pevsner (not open). The land occupied by the house and garden was historically owned by the family of William Wilberforce.

58 THE OLD VICARAGE
Church Street, Whixley, YO26 8AR. Mr & Mrs Roger Marshall, 01423 330474, biddymarshall@icloud.com. *8m W of York, 8m E of Harrogate, 6m N of Wetherby. Off A59 3m E of A1(M) J47 (Postcode not for SatNav).* **Sun 7 June (11-4). Adm £6, chd free. Home-made teas.** Visits also by arrangement 1 Mar to 1 July for groups of up to 40.
The walls, house and various structures within this village garden are festooned with climbers. Mixed borders, old roses, hardy and half-hardy perennials, topiary, bulbs and many hellebores give interest all year. Gravel and old brick paths lead to hidden seating areas creating the atmosphere of a romantic English garden. Partial access for wheelchairs - some gravel and small steps.

59 THE ORCHARD
4a Blackwood Rise, Cookridge, Leeds, LS16 7BG. Carol & Michael Abbott. *5m N of Leeds centre, 5 mins from York Gate garden. Off A660 (Leeds-Otley) N of A6120 Ring Rd. Turn L up Otley Old Rd. At top of hill turn L at T-lights (Tinshill Ln). Please park in Tinshill Ln.* **Sun 3 May (12.30-4.30). Adm £5, chd free. Tea, coffee & cake.**
⅓ acre plantswoman's hidden oasis. A wrap around garden of differing levels made by owners using stone found on site, planted for year-round interest. Extensive rockery, unusual fruit tree arbour, oriental style seating area and tea house, linked by grass paths, lawns and steps. Mixed perennials, hostas, ferns, shrubs, bulbs and pots amongst paved and pebbled areas.

60 ◆ PARCEVALL HALL GARDENS
Skyreholme, Skipton, BD23 6DE. Walsingham College, 01756 720311, parcevallhallgarden@gmail.com, www.parcevallhallgardens.co.uk. *9m N of Skipton. Signs from B6160 Bolton Abbey-Burnsall road or off B6265 Grassington-Pateley Bridge & at A59 Bolton Abbey r'about.* **For NGS: Thur 10 Sept (10-4.30). Adm £10, chd free. Light refreshments.** For other opening times and information, please phone, email or visit garden website.
The only garden open daily in the Yorkshire Dales National Park. 24 acres on a sloping south facing hillside in Wharfedale sheltered by mixed woodland. Terrace garden, rose garden, rock garden and ponds. Mixed borders, spring bulbs, tender shrubs and autumn colour.

61 PENNY COTTAGE
Thorpe, Lockington, Driffield, YO25 9SR. Mr John & Mrs Sue Rowson. *7m N of Beverley. 300yds from 8 South Glebe.* **Sun 14 June (11-5). Combined adm with 8 South Glebe £6, chd free. Home-made teas at Lockington Village Hall.**
An interesting example of how to make best use a small garden. Raised vegetable plot, fruit trees, path leads through planted shady area. Folly with garden crammed with plants built by current owner, scree wadi through evergreens. Extensive collection of Hostas and Irises. A complete contrast of style with our companion garden. Partial access with good views of the garden.

62 PILMOOR COTTAGES
Pilmoor, nr Helperby, YO61 2QQ. Wendy & Chris Jakeman, 01845 501848, cnjakeman@outlook.com. *20m N of York. From A1M J48. From B'bridge follow road towards Easingwold. From A19 follow signs to Hutton Sessay then Helperby. Garden next to mainline railway.* **Mon 31 Aug (11-4.30). Adm £5, chd free. Light refreshments.** Visits also by arrangement May to Sept. Coach parking ¼ mile away & transfers available for disabled visitors.
A year-round garden for rail enthusiasts and garden visitors alike. A ride on the 7¼' gauge railway runs through two acres of gardens and gives you the opportunity to view the garden from a different perspective. The journey takes you across water, through a little woodland area, past flower filled borders, and through a tunnel behind the rockery and water cascade. 1½ acre wildflower meadow and pond. Featuring a Clock-golf putting green.

63 THE POPLARS
Main Street, Newton upon Derwent, York, YO41 4DA. Peter & Christina Young, young.at.poplars@gmail.com. 9m E of York. From A1079 at Wilberfoss, turn S towards Sutton upon Derwent. After ¾m, turn R into Newton, then L. Garden on R past pub. **Sun 17 May (1-5). Adm £5, chd free. Tea, coffee & cake in the nearby chapel. Visits also by arrangement May & June for groups of 5 to 40.**
A plant lover's paradise. Over 100 different trees and shrubs around a Victorian house and barns provide structure and shelter for a succession of flowers through the seasons. Many unusual plants. Glasshouses full of tender plants that spill out into the gardens in summer. Meadow walk leads to two acre arboretum with over 200 woody species around a wildlife pond. Ceramics on display and for sale.

64 PRIMROSE BANK GARDEN AND NURSERY
Dauby Lane, Kexby, York, YO41 5LH. Sue Goodwill & Terry Marran. 4m E of York. At junc of A64 & A1079 take road to Hull. After 3m, on entering Kexby, turn R to Dauby Ln, towards Elvington. From E on A1079 to York. Turn L in Kexby. **Thur 12, Fri 13, Sat 14 Feb (12-4). Light refreshments. Wed 13 May (12-5). Home-made teas. Adm £6, chd free. Soup and savouries at February opening.**
Two acres of rare and unusual plants, shrubs and trees. Bulbs, hellebores and Spring flowering shrubs. Followed by planting for year-round interest. Courtyard garden, mixed borders, summerhouse and pond. Contemporary rock garden, woodland garden with pond and stumpery. New sand beds. Ongoing restoration of 1902 carriage. New Magnolia walk. New Hydrangea and pollinator area. Award-winning nursery. Poultry and Hebridean sheep. Dogs allowed on a short lead in car park and at designated tables outside the tearoom. Most areas of the garden are level and are easily accessible for wheelchairs. Accessible WC available.

65 THE PRIORY, NUN MONKTON
York, YO26 8ES. Mrs Kate Harpin. 9m W of York, 12m E of Harrogate. E of A1M J47 off A59 signed Nun Monkton. **Wed 10 June (11-4). Adm £7.50, chd free. Tea, coffee & cake in the greenhouse. Pop-up tearoom in the swimming pool garden, run by the staff and pupils of the village school.**
Large and varied country garden surrounding Grade II William and Mary house (not open) at the confluence of the Rivers Nidd and Ouse. Featuring species trees, calm swathes of lawn, clipped yew, beech and box, formal rose garden, mixed borders, kitchen garden and informal parkland. Gravel paths.

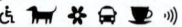

66 PROSPECT HOUSE
Scarah Lane, Burton Leonard, Harrogate, HG3 3RS. Cathy Kitchingman, 07989 195773, cathyrk@icloud.com, www.abrightprospect.co.uk. 5m S of Ripon 5½m from A1, J48. Exit A61 signed Burton Leonard. Parking marshals on Station Ln. Drop off only for those with mobility issues outside Prospect House. **Sun 24 May (12.30-4.30). Adm £5, chd free. Visits also by arrangement 17 May to 13 Sept for groups of 10 to 40.**
One acre walled garden with mixed herbaceous borders, ornamental pond and cutting garden beds. Continuous new planting since 2019. Colour-themed borders, physic bed, woodland area. Also mature hedging, trees and seasonal interest throughout. A renovated outhouse converted into a pretty potting area used for garden workshops.

67 REWELA COTTAGE
Skewsby, YO61 4SG. John Plant & Daphne Ellis, 07711 555665, 07539 428892, rewelacottage@gmail.com, www.rewelahostas.com. 4m N of Sheriff Hutton, 15m N of York. After Sheriff Hutton, towards Terrington, turn L towards Whenby & Brandsby. Turn R just past Whenby to Skewsby. Turn L into village. 500yds on R. **Visits by arrangement 17 May to 30 Aug for groups of 10+. Adm £10, chd free. Tea, coffee & cake inc in adm price.**
Situated in a lovely quiet country village, Rewela Cottage was designed from an empty paddock, to be a labour saving, shade garden, using unusual trees and shrubs for year-round interest. Their foliage, bark and berries enhance the well-designed structure of the garden. The garden owner now specialises in growing and selling Hostas. Over 900 varieties of Hosta in the garden.

68 NEW ♦ RICHMOND CASTLE
Tower Street, Richmond, DL10 4QW. English Heritage. In Richmond, just off the marketplace. What3words app: collects.instructs. afflicted. **For NGS: Evening opening Thur 11 June (5.30-6.30). Adm £20, chd free. Pre-booking essential, please email fundraising@english-heritage.org.uk or visit www.english-heritage.org.uk/visit/places/richmond-castle/events for information & booking. Light refreshments.** For other opening times and information, please email or visit garden website.
Explore Richmond Castle's dramatic Contemporary Heritage Garden, designed in 2000 by Neil Swanson. Walled and contemplative, the garden features a parterre of sixteen topiary yews marking the imprisoned conscientious objectors of WWI, herbaceous borders with bold perennials like Echinacea and Helianthus, and fragrant climbers framed against sweeping views of the countryside beyond.

69 RIDGEWOOD
7 Park Drive South, Greenhead, Huddersfield, HD1 4HT. Mr Steve Cale and Ms Shireen Joshi, 07962 125084, ridgewoodgardens@btinternet.com. ½m N of Huddersfield Town Centre. 3m from J23 M62. From M62 J23 take A640 towards Huddersfield Town Centre. Turn R onto Park Ave then R again onto Park Drive South. From Huddersfield ring road take the 'Rochdale A640' turn off then L onto Park Ave. **Sun 26 July (12-4). Adm £5, chd free. Tea, coffee & cake. Visits also by arrangement May to Sept.**
South facing elevated garden with panoramic views. Originally designed in 1953 with stone tiered beds and terrace, the garden has been refreshed in recent years with a range of perennials, annuals, trees, and shrubs inc dahlias, salvias, agapanthus, grasses, and acers. Inc fruit and vegetable garden, paths, hens and wildlife friendly area.

YORKSHIRE 599

70 THE RIDINGS
South Street, Burton Fleming, Driffield, YO25 3PE. Roy & Ruth Allerston, 01262 470489. *11m NE of Driffield. 11m SW of Scarborough. From Driffield B1249, before Foxholes turn R to Burton Fleming. From Scarborough A165 turn R to Burton Fleming.* **Sun 3 May, Sun 5 July (12-4). Adm £4, chd free. Home-made teas. Visits also by arrangement Apr to July.**
Secluded cottage garden with colour-themed borders surrounding neat lawns. Grass and paved paths lead to formal and informal areas through rose and clematis covered pergolas and arbours. Box hedging defines well-stocked borders with roses, herbaceous plants and trees. Seating in sun and shade offers vistas and views. Greenhouse and summerhouse. Terrace with water feature. Indoor model railway. Terrace, tea area and main lawn accessible via ramp.

71 18 RIPLINGHAM ROAD
Skidby, Cottingham, HU16 5TR. **Mrs Mary Caldwell.** *Between Beverley and Hull. From Humber Br A164 to Beverley L at Skidby r'about. From Beverley A164 to Humber Br R at Skidby r'about. Follow Main St past church then sch on L. Riplingham Rd straight ahead.* **Sun 14 June (1.30-5.30). Adm £5, chd free. Tea, coffee & cake.**
A small garden created by owner. The front has colour themed borders and many pots. At the rear planting creates a feeling of seclusion. From an octagonal lily pond paths radiate outwards under arches festooned in clematis leading to hidden corners. Borders overflow with trees, flowering shrubs, perennials, dozens of roses, hidden statues. Greenhouse, soft fruit. Seating areas. Rear garden can be viewed in part from lower patio. Front garden accessible.

72 NEW ROSE DALE
Willitoft, Goole, DN14 7NX. **Mrs Brenda Mallinson, 07748 056060, bmallinson6@gmail.com.** *3m N of Howden. From Howden take Station Rd, B1248. 2m past Howden train stn turn R at Xrds, Wood Ln. Property approx 200 metres on R.* **Visits by arrangement 15 May to 5 July for groups of 6 to 20. Adm £8, chd free. Tea, coffee & cake.**
A highly productive ¼ acre garden started from scratch in 2002. Features 2 greenhouses, vegetable garden and soft fruit in cages. Meandering gravel paths wind through tightly packed beds of mixed Heuchera and other plants. A Fremontodendron, trees, shrubs and many types of fruit trees linked by paths. Interesting topiary. Gravel mound. Seating areas and whole garden accessible by gravel or paved paths.

73 RUDDING PARK
Follifoot, Harrogate, HG3 1JH. **Mr & Mrs Simon Mackaness, www.ruddingpark.co.uk.** *3m S of Harrogate off the southern bypass A658. Follow brown tourist signs. Use hotel entrance. What3words app: invent.grand.social.* **Sun 17 May (12.30-4). Adm £6, chd free. Tea, coffee & cake.**
20 acres of attractive formal gardens, extensive kitchen garden and lawns around a Grade I Regency House extended and now used as an hotel. Humphry Repton parkland. Formal gardens designed by Jim Russell with extensive rhododendron and azalea planting. Recent designs by Matthew Wilson featuring grasses and perennials.

78,000 people affected by cancer were reached by Maggie's centres supported by the National Garden Scheme over the last 12 months.

Skipwith Hall

74 SALTMARSHE HALL
Saltmarshe, Howden, DN14 7RX.
Andrew Dunkley, 01430 434920, info@saltmarshehall.com, www.saltmarshehall.com. *6m E of Goole. From Howden (M62, J37) follow signs to Howdendyke & Saltmarshe.* **Mon 4 May (9-5). Adm £5, chd free. Light refreshments available outside. Afternoon teas in Hall and picnic hampers available via pre-booking on garden website. Visits also by arrangement 2 Jan to 27 Mar. Refreshments additional cost for by arrangement visits.**
Sits in 17 acres. Parkland, woodland and 5 acres of ornamental gardens created by previous owners. Their design has been adhered to by subsequent gardeners. Victorian-style pond, high walls with borders planted for all year interest. Mature shrubs and trees. Vegetables and herbs grown for chef. Orchard. Lime avenue. Enjoy a pre-booked afternoon tea in the River Garden with its white floral palette On site Head Gardener will be available. Wheelchair to the house via a ramp. Garden is accessed via gravel paths, narrow walkways and shallow steps.

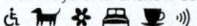

75 SCAPE LODGE
11 Grand Stand, Scapegoat Hill, Golcar, Huddersfield, HD7 4NQ. Elizabeth & David Smith, 01484 644320, elizabethanddavid.smith@ngs.org.uk. *5m W of Huddersfield. From J23 or J24 M62, follow signs to Rochdale. From Outlane village, 1st L. At top of hill, 2nd L. Park at Scapegoat Hill Baptist Church (HD7 4NU) or in village. 5 min walk to garden. 303/304 bus.* **Sun 3, Sun 10 May (1.30-4.30). Adm £5, chd free. Home-made teas. Visits also by arrangement 4 May to 31 Aug. Donation to Mayor of Kirklees Charity Appeal.**
$\frac{1}{3}$ acre contemporary country garden at 1000ft in the Pennines on a steeply sloping site with far-reaching views. Gravel paths lead between mixed borders on many levels. Colour-themed informal planting sits comfortably in the landscape and gives year-round interest. Steps lead to a terraced kitchen and cutting garden. Gazebo, pond, shade garden, large collection of pots and tender plants.

76 ♦ SHANDY HALL GARDENS
Thirsk Bank, Coxwold, York, YO61 4AD. The Laurence Sterne Trust, 01347 868465, info@laurencesternetrust.org.uk, www.laurencesternetrust.org.uk. *N of York. From A19, 7m from both Easingwold & Thirsk, turn E signed Coxwold. Park on road.* **For NGS: Evening opening Fri 8 May, Fri 12 June (6.30-8). Adm £5, chd free. For other opening times and information, please phone, email or visit garden website.**
Home of C18 author Laurence Sterne. Two walled gardens, one acre of unusual perennials interplanted with tulips and old roses in low walled beds. In old quarry another acre of trees, shrubs, bulbs, climbers and wild flowers encouraging wildlife, inc over 450 recorded species of moths. Features inc moth trapping demonstration. Partial wheelchair access. Gravel car park, steps down to Wild Garden.

GROUP OPENING

77 SHIPTONTHORPE GARDENS
Shiptonthorpe, York, YO43 3PQ. *2m NW of Market Weighton. All 4 gardens are in main village on N side of A1079.* **Sat 6, Sun 7 June (11-5). Combined adm £10, chd free. Tea, coffee & cake in the village hall.**

LANGDALE END
Di Thompson, di.thompson2@nhs.net.
Visits also by arrangement 1 May to 19 July for groups of up to 20.

ORANMORE COTTAGE
Susan & Paul Kraus.

WAYSIDE
Susan Sellars.

YORK HOUSE
Tracey Baty.

Four contrasting gardens with different gardening styles, two of which survived and have thrived since being under flood water in 2023. Langdale End is an eclectic maze-like garden with a mix of contemporary and cottage garden styles, featuring tropical plants, an Asian inspired garden, water features and a pond. Wayside has artistically planted areas providing a variety of styles. Ever changing vegetable and fruit garden. Interesting old

Bridge House

farm and garden implements. Pond and surroundings made for wildlife. Oranmore Cottage is a surprising 'hidden garden' divided into two distinct areas featuring decorative architectural plants and carefully chosen herbaceous perennials. York House has a gravel bed, a shaded border, newly designed circular bed, raised vegetable beds, fruit and chattering hens. Partial wheelchair access in Langdale End.

78 SKIPWITH HALL
Skipwith, Selby, YO8 5SQ. Sir Charles and Lady Forbes Adam, 07976 821903, rosalind@escrick.com, www.escrick.com. *9m S of York, 6m N of Selby. From York A19 Selby, L in Escrick, 4 m to Skipwith. From Selby A19 York, R onto A163 to Market Weighton, then L after 2m to Skipwith.* **Thur 12 Feb (11-2). Light refreshments. Thur 11 June (1-4). Home-made teas. Adm £7, chd free. Visits also by arrangement in June for groups of 10 to 50.**
4 acre walled garden of Queen Anne house. Mixture of historic formal gardens, some designed by Cecil Pinsent (worked largely in Italy in 1st half of the C20) and informal planting for wildlife. Woodland with variety of specimen trees and meadows woven to create a wood meadow. No-dig kitchen garden with maze and pool, Italian garden, gravel garden, many roses. Orchard with trained fruit on walls. Gravel paths.

79 SLEIGHTHOLMEDALE LODGE
Fadmoor, YO62 7JG. Patrick & Natasha James. *6m NE of Helmsley. Parking limited in wet weather. Garden is 1st property in Sleightholmedale, 1m from Fadmoor.* **Sun 5 July (1-5). Adm £8, chd free. Home-made teas.**
A glorious south facing, three acre hillside garden with views over a peaceful valley in the North York Moors. Cultivated for over 100 yrs, wide herbaceous borders and descending terraces lead down the valley with beautiful, informal planting within the formal structure of walls and paths. The garden features roses, delphiniums and other classic English country garden perennials. In 2024, Sleightholmedale Lodge was awarded a commemorative plaque in recognition of its 75 years of opening for the National Garden Scheme.

80 8 SOUTH GLEBE
Lockington, Driffield, YO25 9ST. Ms Stephanie Taylor. *Off Church Ln. What3words app: chess.nitrate. chariots.* **Sun 14 June (11-5). Combined adm with Penny Cottage £6, chd free. Home-made teas at Lockington Village Hall.**
A contemporary East Yorkshire garden designed in 2013 by award-winning garden designer Matt Haddon. A modern garden created to be both easy to maintain and a pleasure to enjoy from every room in the house. Both the house and the garden have evolved together over the past decade, with thoughtful planting and design choices that ensure the space continues to thrive.

81 SOUTHWOOD HALL
Burton Road, Cottingham, HU16 5AJ. Kevin and Janet Barnes, 07976 605669, kevingasbarnes@icloud.com. *Burton Rd on street parking only. Drop off for disabled visitors at back of the hall. Please use postcode: HU16 5EB.* **Sun 6 Sept (10-4). Adm £6, chd free. Light refreshments. Visits also by arrangement Apr to Sept for groups of 10+.**
Explore nearly 2 acres of secluded grounds surrounding this historic property. Spot the Alice in Wonderland sculptures in the Secret Walled Garden around a dipping pool and fountain. Enjoy teas in the formal front garden and parterre. View extensive driveway flower beds. Meander through the hidden dell garden, pottering garden, greenhouse and raised beds and marvel at the extensive composting area. Wheelchair access possible in the grounds with assistance, all paths are gravel/grass, ramp available to access walled garden (2 steps).

82 STANDFIELD HALL FARM
Westgate Carr Road, Pickering, YO18 8LX. Mike and Pam Sellers, 01751 477853, mike@standfieldhall.co.uk. *W of Pickering. From Helmsley on A170, through Middleton after Middleton Garage, 2nd R onto Westgate Carr Rd. From Pickering on A170 after A169 junction, 1m L after* bungalows. **Sun 19, Wed 22 July (11-4). Adm £6, chd free. Tea, coffee & cake. Visits also by arrangement 15 June to 26 Aug for groups of 6 to 24.**
Soil Association Organic Hidden Garden, developed by retired organic market gardeners from a 2 acre field. Expansive lawn with large pond, margins planted for wildlife, inlet and outlet stream flowing under bridge. Herbaceous borders. Copse of choice pines, acers and conifers, nuttery, area with wild flowers, woodland walk and variety of fruit and ornamental trees. Raised vegetable beds. Most of the garden is covered in firm grass. WC is not wheelchair accessible or suitable for disabled users.

83 NEW STATION HOUSE
Finkle Street, Wortley, Sheffield, S35 7DH. Helena Davies, www.nurturenature.org.uk. *10m N of Sheffield. Enter S35 7DH into SatNav. Park in Trans Pennine Trail car park behind Wortley Wagyu. Station House is on Finkle St Ln approx 50 metres opp Wortley Wagyu. Signs will be in place.* **Sat 2 May, Sat 22 Aug (10-4). Adm £5, chd free. Tea, coffee & cake.**
The garden is planned as a healing garden. There are a number of discrete areas with terracing. The area nearest the house is the most curated with a hot bed, cool bed, spring bed and fern/grass bed as well as herbaceous borders. Elsewhere is naturalistic and inc a woodland garden, at its best in spring, and a culvert. There is a wide variety of species and interest throughout the year. There is flat access to the main part of the garden, with a ramp leading down to the lower area. Please note that the path is uneven in places.

Our donation in 2025 has enabled Parkinson's UK to fund 2 new nursing posts this year directly supporting people with Parkinson's.

84 ♦ STILLINGFLEET LODGE
Stewart Lane, Stillingfleet, York, YO19 6HP. Mr & Mrs J Cook, 01904 728506, vanessa.cook@stillingfleetlodgenurseries.co.uk, www.stillingfleetlodgenurseries.co.uk. *6m S of York. From A19 York-Selby take B1222 towards Sherburn in Elmet Ln village turn opp church.* **For NGS: Sun 10 May, Sun 13 Sept (1-5). Adm £7.50, chd free. Home-made teas.** For other opening times and information, please phone, email or visit garden website.
Organic, wildlife garden subdivided into smaller gardens, each based on a colour theme with emphasis on use of foliage plants. Wildflower meadow, natural pond, 55 yd double herbaceous borders and modern rill garden. Rare breeds of poultry wander freely in garden. Adjacent nursery. Garden courses run all summer (see garden website.) Art exhibitions in the café. Gravel paths and lawn. Ramp to café if needed. No disabled WC.
& ❀ 🚗 ☕ 🎵

85 SWINDON HOUSE FARM
Spring Lane, Kirkby Overblow, Harrogate, HG3 1HT. Penny Brook, 07770 916666, pennybrook65@gmail.com. *1m S of Kirkby Overblow village. From Spring Ln/Swindon Ln junction, the drive is exactly ½ m on the RHS.* **Sat 29 Aug (10-4). Adm £5, chd free. Tea, coffee & cake inc home-made cakes made with organic ingredients from the garden.**
An English country garden surrounded by farmland, with mixed perennial borders, a pond garden, orchard, roses, mature trees and native hedges, with wildlife at its heart. Wildflower areas have been created in the paddock together with re-wilding areas and paths mown through. A potager with espaliers, raised willow hurdle beds for vegetables and cut flowers, thyme path and small camomile lawn. Parking for wheelchair users so that all areas are accessible.
& ❀ ❀ 🛏 ☕ 🎵

86 NEW TANFIELD LODGE
West Tanfield, Ripon, HG4 5LE. Richard and Daphne Bourne-Arton. *Please follow the NGS yellow signs from West Tanfield.* **Sun 10 May, Sun 2 Aug (10-4). Adm £7, chd free. Light refreshments.**
Three lovely gardens, set between ancient woodland, the River Ure and vast lawns. William's garden, a woodland garden, walkways, hidden paths, enchanting dome and a stumpery. The wildflower walk, an easy springtime walk amongst an abundance of wild flowers. One acre working walled garden with vegetables, cut flowers, roses, fruit.
& 🐕 ❀ 🚗 ☕ 🎵 🎵

GROUP OPENING

87 NEW THE TRIANGLE GARDENS
The Triangle, North Ferriby, HU14 3AT. Fergus & Sally Aitken. *2m W from Humber Bridge. From Hull, A63 W from Humber Bridge. Junc for N Ferriby. At village X'rds S on Church Rd. At Parish Church turn R on New Walk and carry on for ½ m to The Triangle. What3words app: encloses.ripe.wash.* **Sat 20 June (11-4). Combined adm £10, chd free. Tea, coffee & cake.**

NEW 8 THE TRIANGLE
Garry & Helen Mason.

NEW 9 THE TRIANGLE
Duncan & Katherine Ross.

NEW 10 THE TRIANGLE
Alan & Paula Oliver.

NEW 23 THE TRIANGLE
Fergus & Sally Aitken.

NEW 25 THE TRIANGLE
Andrew & Susan Rowden.

A group of 5 traditional English gardens in The Triangle, an Edwardian Arts and Crafts development centred round a wooded green, described in Pevsner as typical of the Garden Suburb style. They are of a similar size and layout but offer different types of cultivation, plants, gardening methods and use of the available space. No.23 is divided in to distinct areas with a mature birch tree as its focal point. No.25 is well-manicured with attractive water features and unusual trees. No.8 has a fish pond and fountain in addition to a small rockery and ornamental succulent bed. No.9 includes a wildlife friendly area and a collection of tender exotic plants. No.10 is designed with family and friends in mind with a number of novelty items within the garden including a collection of teapots in the willow tree. Four of the five gardens are wheelchair accessible.
& ❀ ☕ 🎵

88 THE WALLED GARDEN AT MIDDLETON LODGE
Kneeton Lane, Middleton Tyas, Richmond, DL10 6NJ. events@middletonlodge.co.uk, www.middletonlodge.co.uk. *Near the Scotch Corner. Follow signage to Coach House then walk from Coach House car park along side of restaurant following the gravel path to walled gardens.* **Tue 28 Apr (11-4). Adm £7, chd free. Pre-booking essential, please visit www.ngs.org.uk for information & booking. Coach House Restaurant available to order coffee and cake or lunch. Pre-booking essential, please call 01325 377977.**
Magnificent 2 acre Georgian walled garden on the Middleton Lodge estate designed by renowned landscape designer Tom Stuart-Smith. Spring, Summer and Prairie borders provide a tapestry of colour and form throughout the seasons. The Fig House looks out over a formal lawn. Four large arbours trawl with pears, wisteria and white roses. An extensive kitchen garden provides produce for the estate kitchens. Gardeners will be on hand to guide and inform you. Gravel footpaths in gardens.
& ❀ 🅳 🚗 ☕

89 WARLEY HOUSE GARDEN
Stock Lane, Warley, Halifax, HX2 7RU. Mr & Mrs Cooke, www.warleyhousegardens.com. *2m W of Halifax. Take A646 (towards Burnley) from Halifax centre. Go through large intersection after approx 1m. Approx 1m, turn R up Windle Royd Ln. Disabled parking on site, for 4/5 vehicles.* **Sun 3, Wed 6 May (1.30-4.30). Adm £5, chd free. Home-made teas.**
Partly walled 2½ acre garden of demolished C18 House. Rocky paths and Japanese style planting lead to lawns and lovely south facing views. Alpine ravine planted with ferns and fine trees give structure to the woodland area. Drifts of shrubs, herbaceous plantings, wild flowers and heathers maintain constant seasonal interest. This is an historic garden, renovated after total neglect from 1945 to 1995. Spring planting is enhanced by many new rhododendrons and woodland. Most of the garden is accessible to wheelchairs. Lawns usually suitable unless very wet. Disabled access to WCs and tearoom.
& ☕ 🎵

90 WELTON LODGE
Dale Road, Welton, Brough, HU15 1PE. Brendon Swallow, 07792 345858, manager@weltonlodge.co.uk. *11m W of Hull nr A63. From A63 take exit for Welton, Elloughton & Brough. Immed turn R at junc. Straight through village, to Xrds and straight on. Garden on R after 10yds.* **Sat 4 July (12-3). Adm £6, chd free. Tea, coffee & cake. Visits also by arrangement 1 June to 12 July for groups of 10 to 50.**
Welton Lodge is a Grade II listed house with three themed gardens on 1½ acres. The top lawn features oriental Gazebo, roman pond, rose rotunda and statues. The mid level has Italian garden with pond, formal hedge and Mediterranean planting. The walled garden is in the mid-Victorian ornate style with espaliers of fruit trees and vines around formal lawns and flower beds and a 20m orangery. Since 2024, the grounds have undergone significant enhancements, inc the creation of a Chinoiserie-inspired oriental garden complete with a pavilion and pond. The Italian garden has been revitalised, and the Victorian gardens now feature newly added rose arches and ornamental urn. Block paved ramp leads to gravelled access to lower and upper gardens without steps. Steep upper garden access.

& 🐕 🚗 ☕ 📢

91 ♦ YORK GATE
Back Church Lane, Adel, Leeds, LS16 8DW. Perennial, 01132 678240, yorkgate@perennial.org.uk, www.yorkgate.org.uk. *5m N of Leeds. A660 to Adel, turn R at lights after the Co-op. L on to Church Ln. After church, R onto Back Church Ln. Garden on L.* **For NGS: Sat 9 May, Sat 27 June (10-3.30). Adm £10, chd £4. Light refreshments. The cafe serves home-made food, reflecting the seasons and promoting local produce. Open for breakfast, lunch and afternoon teas.** For other opening times and information, please phone, email or visit garden website.
This award-winning one acre garden near Leeds with Grade II National Heritage status is inspired by the Arts and Crafts movement. Diverse plant combinations show through a series of inspirational garden rooms. A palette of colour bursts to life in spring and summer with tulips, bulging borders, succulents and exotics and a meadow full of wildflowers and wildlife.

✽ 🚗 ☕ 📢

92 YORKE HOUSE & WHITE ROSE COTTAGE
Dacre Banks, Nidderdale, HG3 4EW. Pat, Mark & Amy Hutchinson, 01423 780456, 07592 600138, pat@yorkehouse.co.uk, www.yorkehouse.co.uk. *4m SE of Pateley Bridge, 10m NW of Harrogate, 10m N of Otley. On B6451 near centre of Dacre Banks. Car park on site.* **Sun 21 June (11-4.30). Adm £6, chd free. Cream teas. Visitors welcome to use picnic area in orchard. Cash only for refreshments. Opening with Dacre Banks Gardens on Sun 12 July.** Visits also by arrangement 15 June to 15 July for groups of 10+.
Award-winning English country garden in the heart of Nidderdale. A series of distinct areas flowing through two acres of ornamental garden. Colour-themed borders of herbaceous perennials, roses and shrubs. Natural pond and stream with delightful waterside plantings. Large collection of Hosta. Secluded seating areas and attractive views. Adjacent cottage garden designed for wheelchair access. All main features and car parking accessible to wheelchair users.

& 🐕 ✽ 🚗 ☕ 🪑 📢

Littlethorpe Manor

CHANNEL ISLANDS

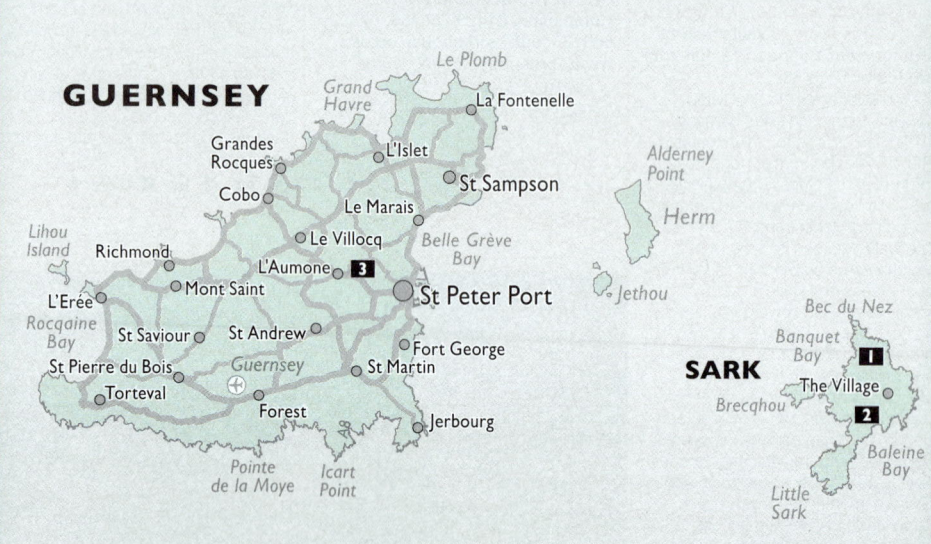

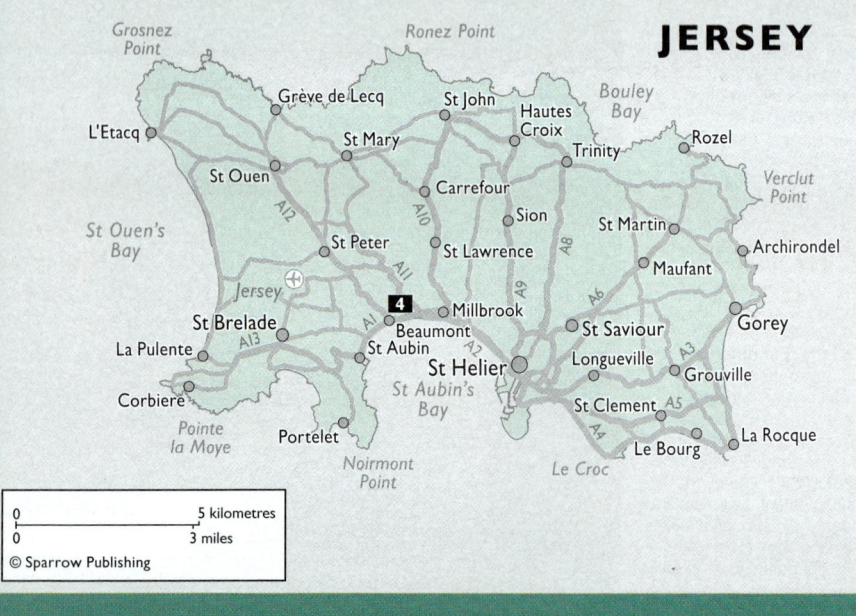

VOLUNTEERS

Area Organiser
Patricia McDermott
patricia.mcdermott@gov.gg

Publicity
Alison Carney
alison.carney@gov.gg

Booklet Coordinator
Ellie Phillips
ellie.phillips@gov.gg

Treasurer
Theresa Prince
07781 435372
theresa.prince@ngs.org.uk

OPENING DATES

All entries subject to change. For latest information check www.ngs.org.uk

Map locator numbers are shown to the right of each garden name.

June

Saturday 6th
◆ La Seigneurie   1
Le Grand Dixcart   2

Sunday 7th
Le Grand Dixcart   2
NEW Stuart Court   4

Saturday 13th
NEW Les Rocquettes   3

Sunday 14th
NEW Les Rocquettes   3

THE GARDENS

1 ◆ LA SEIGNEURIE
Sark, Guernsey, GY10 1SF. Sarah Beaumont, gardens@laseigneuriedesercq.uk, www.laseigneuriedesercq.uk. Follow signs to La Seigneurie, or ask any local for directions. **For NGS: Sat 6 June (10-5). Adm £8, chd £2. Lunch booking is advisable (01481 832233). For other opening times and information, please email or visit garden website.**
The gardens are a place to relax, unwind and find inspiration. There are 4 diverse acres to explore and an on site café and restaurant to enjoy. The Walled Garden is one of the finest of its kind in the Channel Islands and has regularly won awards for its planting schemes and diversity of flora.

2 LE GRAND DIXCART
Sark, Guernsey, GY10 1SD. Helen Magell, 01481 832943, helen@horse.gg, www.legranddixcart.com/gardens. Next to Stocks Hotel. Take the boat from Guernsey to Sark & follow the signs to Stocks Hotel. Once at the hotel continue up Dixcart Ln towards La Coupee & Le Grand Dixcart will be on your R. **Sat 6, Sun 7 June (11-3). Adm £6, chd £3. Tea, coffee & cake. Home-made jam.**
The gardens surround an old farmhouse and date from 1565. They are formed into five distinct areas over 2 acres and are cultivated for beauty, wildlife and food. There is a large mandala style permaculture area providing many different vegetables and cutting flowers alongside habitats for wildlife, ponds, lawns, herbaceous borders, two glasshouses, woodland, sculptures and an orchard. Wheelchair access around Sark can be difficult but once you are actually at the gardens there are just grassy slopes and paths.

3 NEW LES ROCQUETTES
Les Gravees, St Peter Port, Guernsey, GY1 1RN. Mrs Karel Harris, 01481 722146, lesrocquettesguernsey.com. On the outskirts of St Peter Port, opp St Stephen's Church. What3words app: muffin.participating.occulted. **Sat 13, Sun 14 June (11-4.30). Adm £5, chd free. Tea, coffee & cake.**
For other opening times and information, please phone or visit garden website.
Les Rocquettes hotel garden has been described as a well kept secret. There are lawns, fruit trees, including a very old mulberry tree, and a pond. Native and pollinator friendly planting encourages insect and bird life. A petanque court is available to use. There is ample seating and ramped access for visitors with limited mobility. Historical standing stones in the grounds.

4 NEW STUART COURT
La Rue De Haut, St Lawrence, Jersey, JE3 1JQ. Methodist Homes For The Aged, Jersey. What3words app: waveform.convection.framework. **Sun 7 June (10-4.30). Adm £5, chd free. Tea, coffee & cake.**
Stuart Court is a small not for profit care home run by Methodist Homes for the Aged. With spectacular sea views, our garden offers a serene, coastal environment designed to be a functional sensory space to meet the needs of our residents. An accessible patio provides a comfortable outdoor seating area to relax, while a strategically placed summerhouse offers a sheltered spot for relaxation, socializing, or quiet reflection with the sound and scent of the sea carried on the breeze. The garden is still very much a work in progress and we would welcome ideas from our garden visitors on the day. Tea, coffee, cakes and ice cream will be served.

La Seigneurie

NORTHERN IRELAND

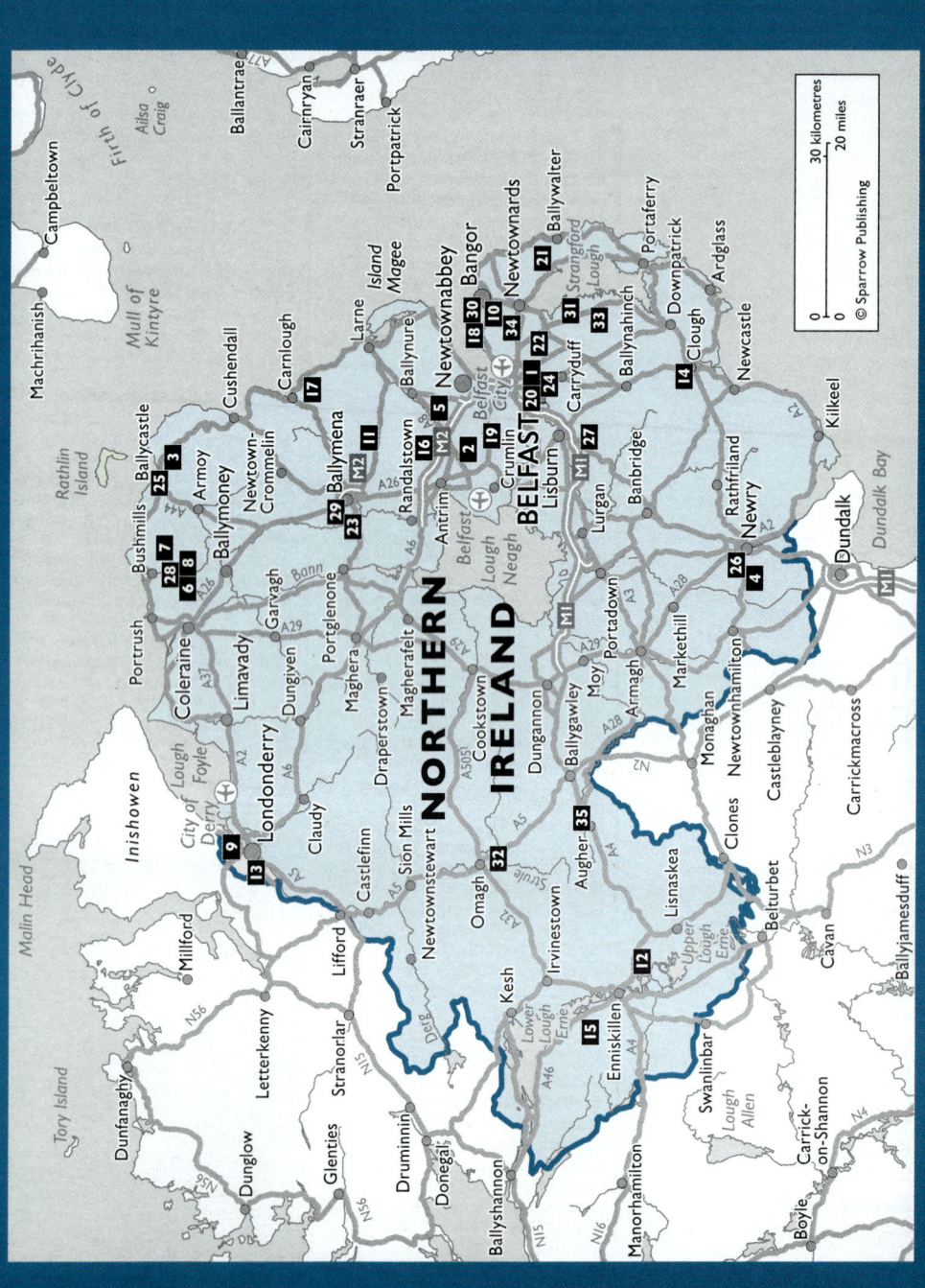

VOLUNTEERS

Area Organiser
Rosslind McGookin
02825 878848
rosslind.mcgookin@ngs.org.uk

Area Treasurer
Ann Fitzsimons
07706 110367
ann.fitzsimons@ngs.org.uk

Assistant Area Organisers
Pat Cameron
07866 706825
pat.cameron@ngs.org.uk

Kaye Campbell
07739 095840
kaye.campbell@ngs.org.uk

Patricia Clements
07470 474527
patricia.clements@ngs.org.uk

Patricia Corker
07808 926779
pat.corker@ngs.org.uk

Trevor Edwards
07860 231115
trevor.edwards@ngs.org.uk

Will Hamilton
02890 825967
will.hamilton@ngs.org.uk

Jackie Harte
07977 537842
jackie.harte@ngs.org.uk

Sally McGreevy
07871 427025
sally.mcgreevy@ngs.org.uk

Margaret Orr

Joy Parkinson
07792 801510
joy.parkinson@ngs.org.uk

@ngsnorthernireland
@ngsnorthernireland

OPENING DATES

All entries subject to change. For latest information check www.ngs.org.uk
Map locator numbers are shown to the right of each garden name.

February

Snowdrop Openings

Saturday 14th
Billy Old Rectory Peace Garden 7
Sunday 15th
Billy Old Rectory Peace Garden 7
Saturday 21st
Benvarden Gardens 6
Sunday 22nd
Benvarden Gardens 6

April

Saturday 11th
♦ Brook Hall Estate & Gardens 9
Sunday 12th
♦ Brook Hall Estate & Gardens 9
Saturday 25th
35 Sheridan Drive 30
Sunday 26th
35 Sheridan Drive 30
Tuesday 28th
NEW ♦ Glenarm Castle Walled Garden 17

May

Friday 15th
NEW Clendinning Cottage 12
Saturday 16th
NEW Clendinning Cottage 12
Saturday 23rd
Brockagh Wood 8
NEW Tuffley Lawn 34
Sunday 24th
Brockagh Wood 8
Clandeboye Estate 10
NEW Tuffley Lawn 34
Monday 25th
Clandeboye Estate 10

June

Saturday 13th
Holly House Garden 19
NEW 26 Leyland Park 25
Sunday 14th
Holly House Garden 19
NEW 26 Leyland Park 25
Saturday 20th
Billy Old Rectory Peace Garden 7
NEW L'Arche Village 24
Sunday 21st
Billy Old Rectory Peace Garden 7
Sunday 28th
♦ Ballyrobert Gardens 5

July

Saturday 18th
NEW Donegore Hill Garden 16
Sunday 19th
NEW Donegore Hill Garden 16
Saturday 25th
9 Devenish Church Road 15
NEW 46 Killane Road 23
Sunday 26th
9 Devenish Church Road 15
NEW 46 Killane Road 23

August

Saturday 8th
Horatio's Garden Northern Ireland 20
Friday 21st
Rustic Garden at 14 Woodgrove 29
Saturday 22nd
Rustic Garden at 14 Woodgrove 29
Sunday 23rd
Rustic Garden at 14 Woodgrove 29
Monday 24th
Rustic Garden at 14 Woodgrove 29
Saturday 29th
Helen's Bay Organic 18

February 2027

Saturday 13th
Billy Old Rectory Peace Garden 7
Sunday 14th
Billy Old Rectory Peace Garden 7

NORTHERN IRELAND

By Arrangement

Arrange a personalised garden visit with your club, or group of friends, on a date to suit you. See individual garden entries for full details.

Adrian Walsh Belfast Garden	1
NEW Alder Cottage	2
13 Ballynagard Road	3
NEW 4 Ballynalack Road	4
Brockagh Wood	8
Clayburn	11
Creevagh House	13
Cumran House	14
NEW Donegore Hill Garden	16
Iona Cottage Garden	21
Ivydene	22
The McKelvey Garden	26
Old Barrack House Garden	27
10 Riverside Road	28
35 The Straits, Lisbane	31
Tattykeel House Garden	32
NEW 85 Thornyhill Road	33
Tullybroom	35

Donegore Hill Garden

# THE GARDENS

1 ADRIAN WALSH BELFAST GARDEN
59 Richmond Park, Stranmillis, Belfast, BT9 5EF. Adrian Walsh, 07808 156856, www.facebook.com/belfast.garden. *From the r'about at Stranmillis College & going along the Stranmillis Rd towards Malone Rd, Richmond Park is the 2nd exit on the L. No 59 is on the L.* **Visits by arrangement June to Oct for groups of 5 to 20. Adm £5, chd free.**
Described by Shirley Lanigan, in 'The Open Gardens of Ireland', as a garden that 'has become a favourite horticultural destination', and 'a veritable sea of plants', this is an imaginatively designed naturalistic city garden that combines a vibrant mix of annuals, perennials, grasses, shrubs and trees set within a formal layout. Former winner of BBC UK TV 'Gardener of the Year' competition.

2 NEW ALDER COTTAGE
71 Printshop Road, Nutts Corner, Crumlin, BT29 4YN. Elizabeth & James Stothers, 07870 203459, estothers51@gmail.com. *Printshop Rd off 7m straight. Coming from Antrim join the 7m straight heading for Nutts Corner after large farm buildings on R, turn L into Printshop Rd take the 3rd laneway to the top.* **Visits by arrangement in May for groups of 6 to 20. Adm £5, chd free.**
A mature and natural habitat created for wildlife with a water rill pond containing Koi and a wildlife pond. Inc a small glade with ferns and grasses. The garden wraps around the one level house with mature shrubs and flower beds with priority given to wildlife and is organic. Two greenhouses and planters are used for family produce.

3 13 BALLYNAGARD ROAD
Ballyvoy, Ballycastle, BT54 6PW. Tom & Penny McNeill, 07754 190687, pennymcneill@yahoo.co.uk. *3m outside Ballycastle. Drive through Ballycastle, pass hotel on L, 2nd exit in r'about to Cushendall. From Ballyvoy drive ¾ m, Ballynagard Rd is on R. Drive ¾ m. Arrive at 1st bungalow on R.* **Visits by arrangement 12 June to 28 Aug for groups of up to 10. Adm £5, chd free.**
A challenging ½ acre site 400ft above sea level with stunning rural and sea views. Designed to meet prevailing environmental conditions and to protect each section from severe winds. Seasonal planting with mature shrubs and rockery on a terraced site create cosy contrasting rooms with seating area. Regret unsuitable for young children due to steep paths through rockery.

4 NEW 4 BALLYNALACK ROAD
Camlough, Newry, BT35 7HU. Martin & Sheila Darling, 07710 174752, martinjdarling@hotmail.co.uk. *From Newry, A25 through Camlough, after that L onto B30, Crossmaglen/Castleblaney, across the lake, L, same signs, from the lake up the hill, 1st L into Ballynalack Rd, 1st house on L.* **Visits by arrangement 28 Mar to 26 Sept for groups of up to 20. Adm £6, chd free.**
Nestled in the County Armagh countryside overlooking Camlough Lake (The Crooked lake) with lots of colour from Spring to Autumn. Borders with herbaceous perennials and a variety of colour. A selection of trees and shrubs adding to interest among the beds. Colour and texture right through the season. Room to relax and wander at leisure.
&

5 ◆ BALLYROBERT GARDENS
154 Ballyrobert Road, Ballyclare, BT39 9RT. Mr Maurice Parkinson, 02893 322952, maurice.parkinson@ballyrobertgardens.com, www.ballyrobertgardens.com. *At the northern edge of Ballyrobert Village, near Ballyclare, on the B56.* **For NGS: Sun 28 June (1-5). Adm £14, chd free. Pre-booking essential, please visit www.ngs.org.uk for information & booking. Light refreshments. For other opening times and information, please phone, email or visit garden website.**
Ballyrobert Gardens is a uniquely created Ulster Garden. The setting for the garden is a C17 landscape complete with the original cottage, barn and wilding area extending to 16 acres. Sensitively integrating the elements is a six acre garden containing an extensive collection of plants. Appeared on BBC TV's Breakfast programme as an exemplar naturalistic garden. There will be a guided tour at 1pm and 3pm. Traditional entrance, extensive plant collection, small lake/large pond, large spiral, concentric rings and Bridgid's Cross in the wilding area. Traditional buildings inc the cottage and nearby barn. Stream running through a glen. Access is available for key areas in the garden.
&

6 BENVARDEN GARDENS
36 Benvardin Road, Ballybogey, Ballymoney, BT53 6NN. Hugh Montgomery, www.benvarden.co.uk. *Between Ballybogy & Derrykeigan, N.Antrim. From Ballymoney head toward Portrush, in the village of Ballybogey turn R into the Benvardin Rd after ½ m (before the River Bush) the Gardens are on your R.* **Sat 21, Sun 22 Feb (12-4). Adm £7, chd free. Tea, coffee & cake in Stableyard Tearoom.**
The garden at Benvarden has been enclosed since the mid C17, most probably evolved from a semi-fortified Bawn. It is shown on a 1788 map soon after the neighbouring rhomboid cobbled courtyard was built. Bought by the Montgomery family in 1797, it was transformed into a modern walled garden with the bawn wall faced with brick and the height raised to the present 16ft, with paths and beds laid out. From the pond, paths lead to the banks of the River Bush, well-known as the river which leads to the Bushmills Distillery, the world's oldest whiskey, and here the river is spanned by a splendid bridge, built by Robert James Montgomery, who survived the charge of the Heavy Brigade in the Crimean war.

70 inpatients and their families are being supported at the newly opened Horatio's Garden Northern Ireland, thanks to the National Garden Scheme donations.

7 BILLY OLD RECTORY PEACE GARDEN
5 Cabragh Road, Castlecat, Bushmills, BT57 8YH. Mrs Meta Page. *Ballymoney bypass straight at Kilraughts Rd take 2nd R to B66 sign Dervock turn L (B66) sign Bushmills through Derrykeighan after 2.3m at Castlecat, Turn L sign Billy ½ m & L - Haw Rd at Church R-Cabragh Rd.* **Sat 14, Sun 15 Feb (1-4). Sat 20, Sun 21 June (1-5). Home-made teas on the lawn. Limited refreshments at snowdrop opening. Adm £7, chd free. 2027: Sat 13, Sun 14 Feb.**
A mature 3 acre garden on an historic site. Front of the Georgian Rectory is a lawn with shrubs, pond and summerhouse. Integrated into the garden are 20 small peace gardens. See guide for further information. There is the Old Orchard Nature Garden comprising of one acre.

8 BROCKAGH WOOD
47 Benvarden Road, Ballybogey, Ballymoney, BT53 6NN. Mr Shaun Boyd, 07973 682319, shaunboyd2020@gmail.com. *From Ballymoney take road to Portrush. At Ballybogey turn R onto Benvarden Rd. 1½ m on L.* **Sat 23, Sun 24 May (1-5). Adm £6, chd free. Light refreshments. Visits also by arrangement 25 May to 31 July for groups of 5+.**
Living better with nature. A rewilding habitat created during lockdown 2020. This 15 acre site inc a two acre pond, native wildflower meadows, marginal plants, water lilies, moorhens, mallard ducks and little grebes. The 1 mile undulating walk around the perimeter of Brockagh Wood will enrich our lives and help us to reconnect with Mother Nature. Key to a happy and healthy life. Wheelchair access is available to the main pond but not the perimeter walk around Brockagh Wood.

9 ◆ BROOK HALL ESTATE & GARDENS
65-67 Culmore Road, Londonderry, BT48 8JE. Mr Gilliland, 02871 358968, info@brookhall.co.uk, www.brookhall.co.uk. *3m N of Derry, Londonderry. From the Culmore r'about off the Foyle Bridge, take the exit towards Moville (A2). Continue on the Culmore Rd (A2) for 1m to the entrance on the R.* **For NGS: Sat 11, Sun 12 Apr**

(2-5). Adm £5, chd free. Light refreshments in the Visitors Centre. For other opening times and information, please phone, email or visit garden website.
Brook Hall Estate & Gardens is a C18 demesne, home to one of the finest private arboretums in the north west of Ireland with unique collections of conifers, rhododendrons, magnolias and camellias. The C17 walled garden on the edge of the River Foyle once used to feed the people of the City of Derry, now home to many of the gardens magnolia and camellia collections. Hard surface paths suitable for wheelchairs and prams through the arboretum and gardens. Please note that some paths may be quite steep.

10 CLANDEBOYE ESTATE
Bangor, BT19 1RN. Mrs Karen Kane, www.clandeboye.co.uk. *Main entrance is off the main Belfast to Bangor A2 circa 2m before Bangor.* **Sun 24, Mon 25 May (2-6). Adm £10, chd free. Pre-booking essential, please visit www.ngs.org.uk for information & booking. Tea, coffee & cake at the Banqueting Hall.**
A series of intimate walled gardens adjoin the courtyard and house. These inc the delightful Bee Garden, the Chapel Walk and the intimate Conservatory Garden. Refreshments are available to purchase in the Banqueting Hall each day.

11 CLAYBURN
30A Ballynulto Road, Glenwherry, Ballymena, BT42 4RJ. Judith & Hugh Jackson, 07539 712991. *What3words app: schematic. composers.remedy. From the A36 Ballymena to Larne Rd, ½ m E of its junc with B94, turn L onto Ballynulto Rd. The garden is 0.8m on the R.* **Visits by arrangement 13 June to 13 Sept for groups of up to 10. Refreshments available by request. Adm £6, chd free.**
Clayburn has been transformed from an exposed site in the shadow of Slemish Mountain to become a low maintenance prairie style garden. Shrubs, grasses and insect attracting perennials along with traditional hedging and many dry stone walls. Also incorporated are numerous trees providing both windbreaks and habitat for many bird species.

12 NEW CLENDINNING COTTAGE
71 Cloghcor Road, Lisbellaw, BT94 5BH. Mr I & Mrs J Black. *¼ m from village of Lisbellaw. Approaching Lisbellaw from the A4 Belfast Rd turn L onto Faughard Rd, B140. After 0.3m turn L onto Cloghcor Rd and the garden is ½ m along on R.* **Fri 15, Sat 16 May (2-5). Adm £5, chd free. Cream teas.**
This is an established garden on an ancient site incorporating a bronze age stone circle. The elevated position affords extensive views towards Cuilcagh World Heritage Park which encompasses one of the largest expanses of blanket bog in Northern Ireland. Extensive herbaceous planting is enhanced by clipped box hedging and topiary. In addition an antique and garden business adjoins.

13 CREEVAGH HOUSE
63 Letterkenny Road, Londonderry, BT48 9XQ. Mr William & Mrs Elma Lynn, 07771 608084, wlynn_geology@hotmail.com. *3m S of Derry-Londonderry. On Letterkenny Rd (N40). From lower deck Craigavon Bridge turn L to Letterkenny. Pass settlement at Nixon's Corner then ½ m with entrance on R (white gates) through black iron gates and cattle grid.* **Visits by arrangement 27 Apr to 30 May for groups of up to 20. Adm £7.**
A mature garden set in 2½ acres of woodland surrounding a Georgian house c1780 (not open). Variety of trees and shrubs most notably a collection of rhododendrons, camellias and azaleas with mature trees, some dating from the construction of the house. Easy access with a network of level gravel or grass paths with a profusion of bluebells in late April/early May. Some remnants of United States naval hospital in the grounds from 1943 to 1945. Owner can be available for short introductory talk to groups. Wheelchair access to main features.

14 CUMRAN HOUSE
231, Newcastle Road, Seaforde, Downpatrick, BT30 8SQ. Mrs Polly Hughes, 02844 811217. *Between Seaforde and Clough, Co Down. Access is via a long (700 metres)*

lane from the Newcastle Rd. From Seaforde turn R after 750 metres. From Clough turn L after 500 metres. **Visits by arrangement Mar to Aug for groups of up to 15. Adm £5, chd free.**
A mature garden planted with colourful herbaceous plants and shrubs, surrounding a charming house built in 1840. Stunning views of the Mournes enhance the drifts of snowdrops and daffodils at the start of the year followed by Eucryphia displays in August.

15 9 DEVENISH CHURCH ROAD
Monea, Enniskillen, BT74 8GE. J and G Thompson. 5½m NW of Enniskillen. From Enniskillen take A46 to Belleek, after approx 1m turn L (B81 to Derrygonnelly) After 5m, just before Monea, turn R onto Devenish Church Rd. No 9 is last bungalow on L. **Sat 25, Sun 26 July (2-5). Adm £5, chd free. Cream teas.**
Just 17 yrs on from a neglected site with poor soil, this delightful small garden now contains sunny sitting areas and many flowering plants. Bulbs, perennials and climbers, intermingled with roses and shrubs are planted to provide all year colour. Annuals grown in a cutting bed are used to fill gaps when the perennials finish and a glut of salads and vegetable are produced in raised beds. Bouquets of garden flowers available to buy from near neighbour.

16 NEW DONEGORE HILL GARDEN
24 Donegore Hill, Muckamore, Antrim, BT41 2HW. Kaye Campbell, 07739 095840, kayeonthehill@hotmail.co.uk. J5 of M2 / Templepatrick. From Templepatrick, follow signs for Donegore. From the B95, follow signs for Donegore. Up the steep hill, pass The Moat Inn and take the 2nd entrance on L. **Sat 18, Sun 19 July (1-5). Adm £6, chd free. Light refreshments.** Visits also by arrangement 1 Apr to 1 July for groups of 10 to 50.
Well established garden nestled beside the historic Donegore Moat. 2 acres of very colourful gardens with mature shrubs, herbaceous borders, roses and hydrangeas in abundance. 5 acres of semi mature woodland. Gravel paths. Unique opportunity to climb Donegore Moat for panoramic views to the Sperrins and Lough Neagh (steep steps).

17 NEW ♦ GLENARM CASTLE WALLED GARDEN
Glenarm, Ballymena, BT44 0BQ. The Earl and Countess of Antrim, 02828 841203, events@glenarmcastle.com, www.glenarmcastle.com. Located close to Glenarm village. Travelling from Belfast, head N on M2, then take the Causeway Coastal Route from Larne to Glenarm. Travelling from Ballymena, head E towards Broughshane and follow the signs for Glenarm. **For NGS: Tue 28 Apr (10-5). Adm £10, chd £5. Light refreshments at onsite tearoom.** For other opening times and information, please phone, email or visit garden website.
Wander through the Walled Garden where thousands of vibrant tulips burst into bloom as part of the Glenarm Castle Tulip Festival, creating a truly magical display. Enjoy delightful herbaceous borders, a soothing water feature and kitchen garden. Located at the top of the Walled Garden, our Woodland Walk offers a tranquil green retreat with sweeping views across the garden and the estate beyond. NGS opening will be part of the Pre-Show week for Glenarm Castle Tulip Festival: 2nd-4th May 2026. All areas accessible to disabled visitors. Designated parking provided.

Glenarm Castle Walled Garden

46 Killane Road

NORTHERN IRELAND

18 HELEN'S BAY ORGANIC
Coastguard Avenue, Helen's Bay, BT19 1JY. Mr John McCormick, www.helensbayorganic.com. *Off Craigdarragh Rd. Coming from A2 (Main Belfast-Bangor road). Drive 200 metres past the railway bridge on Craigdarragh Rd then turn L onto Coastguard Ave. Go over 2 speed bumps & enter 1st farm gate on L.* **Sat 29 Aug (2-5). Adm £6, chd free. Light refreshments in the garden provided by Community Garden Volunteers.**
An urban market garden, established in 1991, producing over 50 varieties of organic vegetables for direct retailing. Also hosts a community garden and allotments which inc an extensive range of fruit and vegetables. An ideal space to get ideas to combine flowers, fruit, food and biodiversity in your garden.

19 HOLLY HOUSE GARDEN
3 Ballyutoag Hill, Nutts Corner, Crumlin, BT29 4UH.
Mr Will Hamilton,
www.hollyhousegardens.com.
In the hills over looking W Belfast. Crumlin Rd, following signs for Crumlin/Int Airport (A52). After 3m Horseshoe bend, 4m turn L onto Ballyutoag Hill & the garden is the 1st entrance on the R. **Sat 13, Sun 14 June (2-5). Adm £6, chd free. Tea.**
Holly House Gardens has been created over the last 25 yrs from former farmland. It comprises several contrasting but complementary garden styles inc traditional herbaceous borders, alpine beds, water elements, mature woodland and shrub areas, an Iris Garden and a 'modern' garden. The owner is currently developing a stumpery and a large new wildlife pond. Partially wheelchair friendly.

20 HORATIO'S GARDEN NORTHERN IRELAND
Musgrave Park Hospital, Stockmans Way, Belfast, BT9 7JB. Mr Matthew Lee, www.horatiosgarden.org.uk/the-gardens/horatios-garden-northern-ireland. *Off Stockmans Ln, Balmoral. Off Stockmans Ln turn into Stockmans Way - signed Musgrave Park Hospital the garden is to the rear of the Withers Orthopaedic Centre.* **Sat 8 Aug (1-5). Adm £5, chd free. Tea, coffee & cake.**
Horatio's Garden Northern Ireland is a beautiful, accessible, restorative garden located at the heart of the Spinal Cord Injuries Unit (SCIU) at Musgrave Park Hospital in Belfast. Designed by nine-time RHS Chelsea Gold Medal winner Andy Sturgeon, the garden supports people adjusting to life-changing spinal injuries from across the entirety of Northern Ireland. Designed for patients, their friends and families, and NHS staff spending time at the Spinal Cord Injuries Unit (SCIU) at Musgrave Park Hospital in Belfast. Full wheelchair access throughout the garden.

21 IONA COTTAGE GARDEN
14C Cardy Road, Greyabbey, Newtownards, BT22 2LS.
Mr Darren & Mrs Victoria Colville, 07793 672653, victoria.colville@googlemail.com. *From North Ards 4m down Portaferry Rd, turn L onto Mount Stewart Rd. After 3m, sharp R turn onto Cardy Rd. Sharp R turn down concrete lane. Go over 3 speed bumps to 2nd lane, 14C on R.* **Visits by arrangement. Available on 27 & 28 June and 4, 5, 18 & 19 July. Adm £5, chd free.**
A relaxed, environmentally friendly country cottage garden which has been under development for the past 11 yrs. The garden, which inc herbaceous borders, kitchen garden and cut flower garden is pesticide free with wildlife friendly habitats such as pond, log piles, bird boxes and meadow. Some natural exposed rock areas and slightly uneven terrain. Fantail doves fly freely. Most of the garden has wheelchair access.

22 IVYDENE
64 Ballystockart Road, Comber, Newtownards, BT23 5QY. Mr Robert Russell, robertrussellbally@gmail.com. *Located between Dundonald and Comber. From Dundonald, take A22 (Comber Rd). After approx 2m, turn R at Hill Head Rd, then 200yds turn L to Ballystockart Rd. Drive ½m, garden is on L after the quarry.* **Visits by arrangement in July for groups of up to 10. Adm £10, chd free.**
A charming plant lover's garden surrounding an Irish farmhouse dating from 1850 (not open). Consists of 1½ acres of gardens arranged into rooms together with a 2 acre wildflower meadow with mowed pathway. An inspiring selection of herbaceous plants and over a hundred old and new varieties of roses, also a wide variety of trees from native to specimen.

23 NEW 46 KILLANE ROAD
Ahoghill, Ballymena, BT42 1JB. Mrs Kay Rainey. *½m from Ahoghill Village. From Galgorm Rd, turn R at Graham's MAXOL ⅓m 1st bungalow on L. From Portglenone Rd travel through village, turn L at Graham's MAXOL ⅓m bungalow on L.* **Sat 25, Sun 26 July (2-5). Adm £7. Light refreshments.**
A bee and butterfly haven, this recently extended garden has deep herbaceous borders. Generously repeated pops of colour delight the eye and create a sense of rhythm. At the rear a wildlife pond and stone folly add interest and mature trees provide shade. Ornamental plants, tomatoes, vegetables and cut flowers are grown from seed. Stone path encircling the garden area is accessible with caution.

Our 2025 donation to the Queen's Institute of Community Nursing now helps support over 3,500 Queen's Nurses working in the community in England, Wales, Northern Ireland, the Channel Islands and the Isle of Man.

24 L'ARCHE VILLAGE
36B Manse Road, Belfast, BT8 6SA. L'Arche Village, www.larchebelfast.org.uk. *Beside Lagan College Belfast. From Four Winds r'about, head along the Manse Rd to Lagan College on R, pass Lagan College and proceed down the hill, L'Arche Village is next on R.* **Sat 20 June (12-4). Adm £5, chd free. Tea, coffee & cake.** The two acre site is a former tree nursery. Now named 'The Village', it has been developed with a community garden space, two polytunnels, a greenhouse, several working spaces and kitchens. The biodiverse planting is naturalistic, sustainable and attracts wildlife. It inc shrubs for green structure, grasses, herbaceous and annuals to provide cut flowers, along with seasonal vegetables. Most of the main areas in the garden are accessible.

25 26 LEYLAND PARK
Ballycastle, BT54 6DL. Mr Gregory Baptie. *Arriving on the B67 or A44 into Coleraine Rd. L into Leyland Rd. Across the r'about and 1st R into Leyland Park to No 26 on RHS.* **Sat 13, Sun 14 June (12-5). Adm £7, chd free.**
Attractive bijou setting with garden rooms and topiary; home-made hurdle fencing, trained privet arch, pleached willow, 2 water features inc fish. Roses, clematis, geraniums, alliums, flower arrangers' shrubs. Stunning views of Knocklayde Mountain from this town garden.

26 THE MCKELVEY GARDEN
7 Mount Charles North, Bessbrook, Newry, BT35 7DW. Mr William & Mrs Hilary McKelvey, 02830 838006, www.facebook.com/themodelgarden. *In the village of Bessbrook. Enter village from Millvale Rd. Turn L at Morrow's Garage. 300yds up hill past terraced houses turn L through gate.* **Visits by arrangement 2 May to 31 Aug for groups of up to 50. Adm £5, chd free.**
A connoisseurs garden situated in a village setting containing snowdrops, alpine crevice beds, salvias and a large collection of clematis planted among herbaceous and shrub borders. Wheelchair access via side entrance.

27 OLD BARRACK HOUSE GARDEN
7 Main Street, Hillsborough, BT26 6AE. Ken & Dawn McEntee, 07711 617585. *Situated at the bottom of Main St in Royal Hillsborough, opp the Parish Church.* **Visits by arrangement in June. Adm £5, chd free. Refreshments not in aid of NGS.**
Old Barrack House garden is in essence a secret garden, hidden behind the Grade I listed house. Venturing down the alley between the houses you reach the yard and barn, subtly changed and improved to create charming pebbled terraces and garden areas. Dawn's creative instinct is much in evidence. Plants and flowers are chosen for height, form and leaf colour in relation to the ambiance of each area.

28 10 RIVERSIDE ROAD
Bushmills, BT57 8TP. Mrs Pam Traill, 07927 956720, pmtraill@gmail.com. *1½ m from Bushmills on Riverside Rd, off the B66. Turn L by Drum Lodge, 100yds further on R beware ramps.* **Visits by arrangement 15 Jan to 30 June for groups of up to 30. Adm £7, chd free.**
Rambling cottage garden with unusual shrubs, deep borders, spring garden with aconites, snowdrops and scillas, rockery and arboretum.

29 RUSTIC GARDEN AT 14 WOODGROVE
14 Woodgrove, Ballymena, BT43 5JQ. Colin & Gill Agnew. *1½ m N of B'mena on the B'money Rd At r'about turn L onto the Carnburn Rd. Turn R onto the Carniny Rd then L onto the Woodtown Rd. Woodgrove is the 1st cul-de-sac on R.* **Fri 21, Sat 22, Sun 23, Mon 24 Aug (10-8). Adm £10. Pre-booking essential, please phone 07710 577732 for information & booking. Light refreshments.**
The Rustic Garden is a suburban garden bordered to the north by the Antrim countryside. Features inc a small pond and stream with marginal planting and a modest collection of hydrangea species. Well established trees help to create a natural canopy under which a sunken fernery has been developed. Ornamental grasses and agapanthus thrive in the south facing aspect of the garden. There are water features, mature ornamental trees and quirky recycling artwork. Garden visit inc tour.

30 35 SHERIDAN DRIVE
Helen's Bay, Bangor, BT19 1LB. Prof Desmond and Mrs Amy Archer. *Located between Bangor and Holywood, Co. Down. A2 to Craigdarragh Rd, Helen's Bay, and 2nd L to Sheridan Dr. The garden is on the sea side.* **Sat 25, Sun 26 Apr (2-5). Adm £6, chd free.**
Two acre garden along Belfast Lough. Developed over 50 yrs from a challenging site with a stream, small pond and steep inclines. The garden features Japanese maples, magnolias, azaleas, hydrangeas, unusual trees inc *Cornus controversa* 'Variegata', *Cercidiphyllum japonicum*, *Magnolia campbellii* and *Parrotia persica*.

31 35 THE STRAITS, LISBANE
Comber, Newtownards, BT23 6AQ. Mrs Olwen Sheridan, 07721 880137, olwensheridan@hotmail.co.uk. *4m S of Comber towards Killinchy on A22. In the village of Lisbane, turn into The Straits (opp The Old Post Office Tea Shop). No.35 is situated on R after ½ m. Garden entrance on L at top of a long lane.* **Visits by arrangement 1 June to 10 July for groups of up to 30. Adm £5, chd free.**
Nestled in the Co Down countryside with wrap-around views of Strangford Lough and Scrabo Tower, this 8 yr old garden of approx 1 acre comprises well-stocked and herbaceous shrub borders. A delightful Bothy Garden complete with pond and potting shed provides an enchanting foil for an impressive display of pots and window boxes. In development is a vegetable garden. Wheelchair access to most parts of the garden.

32 TATTYKEEL HOUSE GARDEN
115 Doogary Road, Omagh, BT79 0BN. Mr Hugh & Mrs Kathleen Ward, 02882 249801, tattykeelhouse@hotmail.com, www.tattykeelhouse.com/gardens. *Approx 2½ m from Omagh on the S side of the A5 Omagh to Ballygawley Rd. There's a sign outside the entrance Tattykeel House & Studio.*

Visits by arrangement May to Aug for groups of 5 to 30. Adm £7, chd free. Refreshment to be arranged at booking.
'Borders brimming with blossom and lush planting are seamlessly offset by sweeps of well tended lawn in the carefully choreographed garden at Tattykeel House' as described by Conrad McCormick (Irish Garden Magazine Aug 2024). The garden features in 'The Open Gardens of Ireland' by Shirley Lanigan. The 1$\frac{1}{2}$ acres inc sheltered seating areas, a Japanese inspired area, and many climbers. Partially suitable for wheelchairs.

33 NEW 85 THORNYHILL ROAD
Killinchy, Newtownards, BT23 6SG. Mrs Inge Ferguson, 07889 854711, ingeferguson@outlook.com. *Between Killinchy and Raffrey. From Comber S to Balloo. 0.2m after Balloo House, turn R to Thornyhill Rd. 2m then No.85 is on R. From Raffrey take B'gowan/Carrickmannon Rd. After 0.1m take R to Thornyhill Rd, 1m, No.85 is on L.* **Visits by arrangement** in May for groups of up to 30. Adm £5, chd free.
An eco-friendly cottage garden of roughly an acre, in picturesque drumlin country. The garden has diverse mature trees, a labyrinth, a walk to a flax pond once used in the linen industry, wildflower meadows and a gravel garden. It features land art made from locally sourced materials and there is a gallery/exhibition space promoting the celebration and conservation of nature.

34 NEW TUFFLEY LAWN
14 Ballyrogan Park, Newtownards, BT23 4SD. Doreen and Ivan Wilson. *3m W of Newtownards. From Dundonald, travelling along dual carriageway to Newtownards turn L into Belfast Rd. After 0.9m turn R into Ballyrogan Rd then 1st L into Ballyrogan Park.* **Sat 23, Sun 24 May (2-5). Adm £7, chd free.** Light refreshments.
A one acre, organic plantsman's garden containing many exotic and rare plants which has been developed over 45 yrs. Azaleas, rhododendrons, herbaceous plants, fruit trees and vegetables in abundance while the small pond is surrounded by rodgersia, primulas and hostas. Most of the garden is wheelchair accessible.

35 TULLYBROOM
48 Tullybroom Road, Clogher, BT76 0UW. Mr Alan Beatty, 07713 851777, alanwbeatty@gmail.com. *Do not rely on SatNav. Road signs are Corick Rd. Access via the A4. $\frac{1}{2}$ way between Augher & Clogher. At sign for Corick House Hotel turn L (from Clogher), R (from Augher). Pass hotel and at the Xrds go straight over. Garden $\frac{1}{4}$m on R.* **Visits by arrangement** 1 June to 20 Sept for groups of 8 to 25. Adm £6, chd free.
$\frac{1}{2}$ acre intensively planted garden developed over the last 30 yrs in rural setting with borrowed landscape of green-fields and surrounding hills, inc Knockmany, burial site of Queen Anya, an ancient Queen of Ireland. Plantspersons/flower arrangers garden featuring mostly shrubs and herbaceous - many unusual. Features inc borders, small courtyard, gravel area and stone troughs. Most of the garden is accessible to wheelchair users.

In 2025, National Garden Scheme funding helped Perennial support 950 unique callers to their helpline looking for advice and information.

35 The Straits, Lisbane

WALES · CYMRU

CARMARTHENSHIRE & PEMBROKESHIRE

VOLUNTEERS

County Organisers
Jackie Batty
01437 741115
jackie.batty@ngs.org.uk

Mary-Ann Nossent
07985 077022
maryann.nossent@ngs.org.uk

County Treasurer
Graeme Halls
07484 775553
graeme.halls@ngs.org.uk

Assistant County Organisers
Elena Gilliatt
01558 685321
elenamgilliatt@hotmail.com

Gayle Mounsey
07900 432993
gayle.mounsey@gmail.com

Liz and Paul O'Neill
01994 240717
lizpaulfarm@yahoo.co.uk

Social Media
Paula Davies
07967 125881
paula.davies@ngs.org.uk

Fran Rumbelow
07862 736341
fran.rumbelow@ngs.org.uk

@CarmsandPembsNGS
carmsandpembsngs

OPENING DATES

All entries subject to change.
For latest information check
www.ngs.org.uk

Extended openings are shown
at the beginning of the month.

Map locator numbers are
shown to the right of each
garden name.

February

Saturday 21st
Gelli Uchaf 10

Sunday 22nd
Gelli Uchaf 10

March

Every Sunday
Annwyn Arboretum 1

Saturday 21st
Gelli Uchaf 10

Sunday 22nd
Gelli Uchaf 10

Sunday 29th
Treffgarne Hall 28

April

Every Sunday
Annwyn Arboretum 1

Every Tuesday and Sunday
Moelfryn 15

Monday 6th
Moelfryn 15

Saturday 11th
Gelli Uchaf 10

Sunday 12th
Gelli Uchaf 10

May

Every Sunday
Annwyn Arboretum 1

Every Tuesday and Sunday
Moelfryn 15

Saturday 2nd
NEW Pentywyn 21

Sunday 3rd
Pentresite 20
Treffgarne Hall 28

Monday 4th
Moelfryn 15

Saturday 9th
NEW Laswern Farm 13

Sunday 10th
NEW Laswern Farm 13

Wednesday 13th
Cold Comfort Farm 4

Saturday 16th
Cae Bach 3
Cornerstone House 5
Gelli Uchaf 10

Sunday 17th
Cae Bach 3
Cornerstone House 5
Gelli Uchaf 10

Wednesday 20th
Cold Comfort Farm 4

Saturday 23rd
Cornerstone House 5
Dwynant 6

Sunday 24th
Dwynant 6
Dyffryn Mill 8

Monday 25th
Dwynant 6
Dyffryn Mill 8
Moelfryn 15

Friday 29th
NEW Tynewydd 29

Saturday 30th
NEW Froghall Barn 9
NEW Tynewydd 29

Sunday 31st
Cold Comfort Farm 4
Pont Trecynny 22

June

Every Sunday
Annwyn Arboretum 1

**Every Tuesday and Sunday
to Tuesday 23rd**
Moelfryn 15

Wednesday 3rd
Cold Comfort Farm 4

Saturday 6th
Skanda Vale Hospice Garden 25

CARMARTHENSHIRE & PEMBROKESHIRE

Sunday 7th
◆ Dyffryn Fernant ... 7
Norchard ... 18

Wednesday 10th
Cold Comfort Farm ... 4
Pont Trecynny ... 22
◆ Upton Castle Gardens ... 31

Saturday 13th
NEW Tenby Gardens ... 27

Sunday 14th
House On Stilts ... 12
NEW Tenby Gardens ... 27

Saturday 20th
Gelli Uchaf ... 10
Pantybara ... 19
West Wales Willows ... 32

Sunday 21st
Gelli Uchaf ... 10
Pantybara ... 19

Friday 26th
NEW Tynewydd ... 29

Saturday 27th
NEW Tynewydd ... 29

July

Every Sunday
Annwyn Arboretum ... 1

Every Tuesday and Sunday
Moelfryn ... 15

Saturday 4th
◆ Scolton Manor ... 23

Sunday 5th
Pentresite ... 20
Pont Trecynny ... 22
◆ Scolton Manor ... 23

Saturday 18th
NEW Laswern Farm ... 13

Sunday 19th
NEW Laswern Farm ... 13

Saturday 25th
Dwynant ... 6
Neuadd y Felin ... 17

Sunday 26th
Dwynant ... 6
Neuadd y Felin ... 17
Pont Trecynny ... 22

August

Every Sunday
Annwyn Arboretum ... 1

Every Tuesday and Sunday
Moelfryn ... 15

Saturday 15th
NEW Laswern Farm ... 13

Sunday 16th
NEW Laswern Farm ... 13
Pont Trecynny ... 22

Monday 31st
Moelfryn ... 15

September

Every Tuesday and Sunday to Sunday 13th
Moelfryn ... 15

Wednesday 2nd
NEW Froghall Barn ... 9

Saturday 5th
NEW Froghall Barn ... 9
◆ Scolton Manor ... 23

Sunday 6th
◆ Dyffryn Fernant ... 7
◆ Scolton Manor ... 23

October

Saturday 3rd
NEW Froghall Barn ... 9

By Arrangement

Arrange a personalised garden visit with your club, or group of friends, on a date to suit you. See individual garden entries for full details.

Annwyn Arboretum ... 1
NEW Bryn Teg ... 2
Cae Bach ... 3
Cold Comfort Farm ... 4
Dwynant ... 6
NEW Froghall Barn ... 9
Gelli Uchaf ... 10
Grove of Narberth ... 11
House On Stilts ... 12
Llwyngarreg ... 14
Moelfryn ... 15
Pantybara ... 19
Pentresite ... 20
NEW Pentywyn ... 21
Pont Trecynny ... 22
Shoals Hook Farm ... 24
Stable Cottage ... 26
Treffgarne Hall ... 28
Ty'r Maes ... 30

Tynewydd

THE GARDENS

1 ANNWYN ARBORETUM
Four Seasons Health Club, Nantgaredig, SA32 7NY. Mr William Berry, 01267 590011, enquiries@annwyn.co.uk, www.annwyn.co.uk. *7m E of Carmarthen. At x-rds of A40 & B4310 in Nantgaredig, head N for ½ m & follow signs for 'Four Seasons'. Go up drive, turn L & park where indicated. What3words app: shadows.eradicate.carbon.* **Every Sun 1 Mar to 1 Sept (10-4). Adm £5, chd free. Visits also by arrangement 1 Mar to 31 Aug for groups of 5 to 30.**
A 10 acre Arboretum (formerly a 9 hole golf course), planted 40 years ago with an extensive collection of common and unusual trees. These inc redwoods, southern beeches, limes, handkerchief tree and *Magnolia macrophylla*. Beautiful views over the Tywi valley with lots of fun things to explore inc a treasure hunt. Some uneven paths, so good footwear recommended.

2 NEW BRYN TEG
Capel Iwan, Newcastle Emlyn, SA38 9LT. Colin & Kath McKane, 07483 119456, kath@pressurewasherservices.co.uk. *3m from Newcastle Emlyn. On A484 towards Cenarth bypassing Newcastle Emlyn take L for sch then L for Capel Iwan. Stay on main road for 3m to village square & go downhill past chapel & cemetery 200 metres. Drive on R.* **Visits by arrangement Apr to Sept for groups of up to 20. Discuss refreshments when booking. Adm £6, chd free.**
A stunning, beautifully presented five acre garden with beds, wide lawns and many unusual trees. Collections of peonies, clematis, hostas, lilliums etc; wind your way along paths bordered by mass planted beds and through specimen trees, stumpery, newly planted rose bed and avenue of acers. Further beds around house inc pond, pots, greenhouse, vegetable and fruit cages.

3 CAE BACH
Hermon, Glogue, nr Crymych, SA36 0DS. Liz & Will North, 01239 831663, elizabethmmnorth@gmail.com. *2m SE of Crymych. From Crymych take Hermon Rd at Ysgol Bro Preseli, at T-junc in Hermon, turn L. Cae Bach is 300 yds on R. Disabled only parking at house; parking signed in village. What3words app: accent.grace.vans.* **Sat 16, Sun 17 May (11-5). Adm £5, chd free. Tea, coffee & cake. Open nearby Cornerstone House. Visits also by arrangement in May for groups of up to 25. Discuss refreshments when booking.**
A 1½ acre newly established garden designed to attract wildlife, particularly bees and butterflies. Wander through the garden and discover herbaceous borders, ponds, grasses and our Japanese garden with rill. Our rose garden has 40 varieties. We also have a greenhouse, exotic area, conifers, heathers, and gravel garden, wildflower and meadow area, fruit and vegetables.

4 COLD COMFORT FARM
Wolfscastle, Haverfordwest, SA62 5PA. Judy & Paul Rumbelow, 07809 560409, judy.rumbelow@gmail.com, www.coldcomfortplants.com. *7m N of Haverfordwest. Signed off A40 at Wolfscastle. Turn towards Hayscastle at Wolfe Inn. 1m along lane on L. What3words app: pool.airliners.kickers.* **Wed 13, Wed 20, Sun 31 May, Wed 3, Wed 10 June (11-4). Adm £5, chd free. Home-made light lunches on Wed & Teas on Sun Visits also by arrangement 11 May to 19 July for groups of 6 to 50. Please discuss refreshments when booking.**
Five acres of wildflower meadow alongside wrap around farm garden and small plant nursery. Perennial beds, showcasing interesting perennials from nursery stock, rockery, gravel garden, raised beds, greenhouses, polytunnel and compost. Welcoming garden under development on sloping plot, full of planting ideas for windy and difficult conditions. Outstanding views of the Preseli Mountains.

5 CORNERSTONE HOUSE
Glandwr, Whitland, SA34 0XY. Ruth Swaffield. *3.8m S of Crymych. From Narberth, N on A478 for approx 11m, turn R at the sign for Glandwr. From Cardigan S on the A478 for approx 11 m turn L, 1m downhill turn R.* **Sat 16, Sun 17 May (11-5), open nearby Cae Bach. Sat 23 May (11-5). Adm £4, chd free. Tea, coffee & cake.**
A rural sloping garden of an acre which features a pond, small sunken garden and a gravel area, patio and seating areas, and view of hills. A path leads through a wisteria covered pergola and shrubbery to another pergola with hops and climbing roses leading to a sun house. The garden contains many rhododendrons and azaleas. Fruit trees and low hedges separate the fruit cage and vegetable gardens.

6 DWYNANT
Golden Grove, SA32 8LT. Mrs Sian Griffiths *14m E of Carmarthen, 3m from Llandeilo. Take B4300 Llandeilo to Carmarthen. Take L turn to Gelli Aur, pass church & vicarage then 1st R onto Old Coach Rd. Dwynant is approx ¼ m on R.* **Sat 23, Sun 24, Mon 25 May, Sat 25, Sun 26 July (11-6). Adm £5, chd free. Pre-booking essential, please phone 07502 539737 or email sian.41@btinternet.com for information & booking. Visits also by arrangement Apr to Sept. Discuss refreshments when booking.**
A ¾ acre garden set on a steep slope designed to sit comfortably within a verdant countryside environment with beautiful scenery and tranquil woodland setting. A garden with lily pond, selection of plants and shrubs inc azaleas, rhododendrons, hydrangeas, and rambling roses set amongst a carpet of bluebells. Seating in appropriate areas to enjoy the panoramic view and flowers.

7 ♦ DYFFRYN FERNANT
Llanychaer, Fishguard, SA65 9SP. Christina Shand & David Allum, 01348 811282, christina@dyffrynfernant.co.uk, www.dyffrynfernant.co.uk. *3m E of Fishguard. A487 E, 2m from Fishguard turn R towards Llanychaer. Follow lane for ½ m, entrance on L. Look for yellow garden signs. Disabled parking near house. Please*

Cae Bach

Pentywyn

note: gravel paths and steep slopes For NGS: Sun 7 June, Sun 6 Sept (12-5). Adm £10, chd free. For other opening times and information, please phone, email or visit garden website.
Magical 2.4 ha garden, evolving from wilderness and ancient rocky landscape. Distinctively planted areas leading down to marsh and woodland, against backdrop of the Preselis. Planting inc: tulips, primulas, *Camassias*, *Wisteria alba*, orchard fruit blossom, roses. Peonies and *Embothrium coccineum*, salvias, dahlias, *Hedychium*, *Canna*, *Colocasia*, *Ricinus*, and ornamental grasses. RHS Partner Garden and Member Great Gardens of West Wales.

8 DYFFRYN MILL
Llanmill, Narberth, SA67 8UE. Mrs Abigail Hart. 2½ m E of Narberth. Go past Narberth crematorium on L. ½ m downhill, signed parking on farmyard in Llanmill. 10 min walk to garden. Limited parking at house for disabled visitors. What3words app: rails.majoring.cult. **Sun 24, Mon 25 May (2-5). Adm £5, chd free. Tea, coffee & cake.**
A 'natural' garden which makes the most of its rural landscape. Rewilding on 10 acres with lake, ponds, boggy scrapes and woodland planted in 2019. Hostas, ferns, corydalis, astilbes, epimediums abound and giant water tanks turned into planters to soften old industrial mill building. Wisteria and rambling roses, shrubbery, orchard, 'hot' slate bed. Wander along the river and through woodland.

9 NEW FROGHALL BARN
Spittal, Haverfordwest, SA62 5RF. Mrs Sarah Higgon, 07899 404366. Located 1m past Scolton Manor Country Park on B4329 towards Cardigan. Turn R at a small farm x-roads denoted by a 'Froghall Farms' milk-stand. Go down lane into the trees. White stone barn on L. **Sat 30 May, Wed 2 Sept (11-4). Sat 5 Sept (10-5), open nearby Scolton Manor. Sat 3 Oct (11-4). Adm £3.50, chd free. Tea, coffee & cake.** Visits also by arrangement 1 Apr to 3 Oct for groups of 4+. Please discuss refreshments when booking.
A longstanding family farm undergoing an interesting rewilding project since 2014. Some 50 acres of broadleaf woodland and small pockets of spruce. A further 20 acres planned for winter 2025. When planting began in 2017 it was Wales' largest newly created woodland. Grass and wildflower meadows interspersed with green lanes and more ancient woodland with views to the Preselis. Guided tours.

10 GELLI UCHAF
Rhydcymerau, Llandeilo, SA19 7PY. Julian & Fiona Wormald. 5m SE of Llanybydder. 1m NW of Rhydcymerau. From the B4337 in Rhydcymerau take minor road opp bungalows. After 300yds turn R up track. Limited parking so essential to phone or email 1st. What3words app: grounded.passively.prone. **Sat 21, Sun 22 Feb, Sat 21, Sun 22 Mar, Sat 11, Sun 12 Apr, Sat 16, Sun 17 May, Sat 20, Sun 21 June (10.30-5.30). Adm £6, chd free. Pre-booking essential, please phone 01558 685119, email thegardenimpressionists@gmail.com or visit www.thegardenimpressionists.com/visiting-the-garden for information & booking.** Visits also by arrangement 14 Feb to 28 June for groups of 10 to 20. Please discuss refreshments when booking.
This 1½ acre garden complements our C17 Longhouse and 11 acre smallholding. In the garden trees and shrubs are underplanted with thousands of snowdrops, crocus, cyclamen, and daffodils, together with many rhododendrons, skimmias, clematis, rambling roses and hydrangeas. There are several wildflower hay meadows, wildlife ponds, stream and shepherd's hut to explore beyond the main garden. Extensive views and seats to enjoy them. Year-round flower interest with naturalistic plantings. Two ponds and stream.

11 GROVE OF NARBERTH
Molleston, Narberth, SA67 8BX. 01834 860915, events@grovenarberth.co.uk, www.grovenarberth.co.uk. 2m S of Narberth. From A40 between Whitland & Haverfordwest, take A4075 towards Tenby. Take L on the A4115 towards Templeton. L at brown sign for Grove. Follow for approx 2m. **Visits by arrangement 16 Jan to 31 Dec for groups of up to 20. Individuals & couples welcome. Cream teas bookable in advance (£14pp). Adm £7.**
The garden is framed by ancient oaks and towering beeches, and from our hillside glade you can enjoy views across the rolling Pembrokeshire countryside to the Preseli Hills. 26 acres of woodlands, meadows and gardens, inc an historic walled garden, kitchen garden, and cut flower garden. Extensive woodland walks through the grounds, which inc some steep slopes and undulating paths.

12 HOUSE ON STILTS
Rotten Pill Road, Ferryside, SA17 5TN. Paula & Iain Davies, 07967 125881, paulapdavies@gmail.com, www.instagram.com/houseonstilts_wales. 9m SW of Carmarthen. A484 to Kidwelly, R at Llandyfaelog junc to Ferryside, then NGS signs. House on Stilts on Google Maps or What3words app: windy.oldest.carpentry. Drop off only. Parking at rugby club (7 min walk). **Sun 14 June (1-6). Adm £6, chd free. Pre-booking essential, please visit www.ngs.org.uk for information & booking. Tea, coffee & cake.** Visits also by arrangement 1 May to 26 June. Discuss refreshments when booking.
A ⅓ acre garden surrounds a mid-century modern house resembling a bird hide nestled in a rural estuary setting. A garden designed with an artist's eye, subtle colour palette, form and texture. A mosaic of different habitats for wildlife, from a large pond at the rear to a dry cockle shell garden to the front. An emphasis on promoting biodiversity, whilst creating a relaxing space for people. Coastal front garden, wildlife pond with viewing deck, bog garden, native hedging, summerhouse (for sheltering from the rain), slopes planted with shrubs, perennials, wildflowers, bulbs and edibles, wild area with log pile etc. Potting shed and propagation area. Compost corner.

13 LASWERN FARM
Pontyberem, Llanelli, SA15 5BP. Chris & Ann Sambrook. 6½m SE of Carmarthen. Laswern is located on a sharp bend. Look for NGS signs & large rocks outside wooden gate. Please park on yard. No parking on road. What3words app: chains. simple.worms. **Sat 9, Sun 10 May, Sat 18, Sun 19 July, Sat 15, Sun 16 Aug (11-4). Adm £5, chd free. Tea, coffee & cake.**
A mature, herbaceous, wildlife friendly garden and pond in ⅓ acre on a smallholding currently being developed by new owners. Inc a herb garden and greenhouse. Additionally there is a vegetable garden with two polytunnels, a fruit cage and vegetable beds, all irrigated using gravity fed rainwater. There are also two fruit orchards and willow beds to visit plus several beehives. Only main garden is wheelchair accessible.

14 LLWYNGARREG
Llanfallteg, Whitland, SA34 0XH. Paul & Liz O'Neill, 01994 240717, lizpaulfarm@yahoo.co.uk, www.llwyngarreg.co.uk. 19m W of Carmarthen. A40 W from Carmarthen, turn L at Llandewi Velfry r'bout then R to Llanfallteg. Go through village, garden ½m further on: 2nd farm on R. Car park in bottom yard on R. What3words app: challenge.quality.redouble **Visits by arrangement Feb to Oct. Adm £8, chd free. Phone message to confirm daily opening.**
Llwyngarreg is always a work in progress, delighting plant lovers with its many rarities inc primulas, many huge bamboos with *Roscoeas, Hedychiums* and salvias extending the season through to autumn colour. Trees and rhododendrons are underplanted with perennials. The sunken garden and gravel gardens contain unusual exotics. Springs form a series of linked ponds across the main garden, providing colourful bog gardens. Fruit and vegetables, composting, numerous living willow structures, mobiles and quirky installations, swing, chickens, goldfish. Partial wheelchair access.

15 MOELFRYN
Llandeilo Road, Castell y Rhingyll, Gorslas, Llanelli, SA14 7LU. Elaine & Graeme Halls, 07484 775553, revelainehalls@gmail.com, www. instagram.com/the.moelfryn.garden. Between Crosshands & Llandeilo. On A476 N of Gorslas and S of Carmel. Yellow arrows at gate. What3words app: indeed.noise.hedgehog. **Every Tue and Sun 5 Apr to 23 June (10.30-4.30). Mon 6 Apr, Mon 4, Mon 25 May (10.30-4.30). Every Tue and Sun 5 July to 13 Sept (10.30-4.30). Mon 31 Aug (10.30-4.30). Adm £5, chd free. Tea, coffee & cake. Gluten & dairy free cakes also available. Visits also by arrangement Apr to Sept for groups of up to 20. Individuals also welcome.**
A ⅓ acre taking account of its Welsh hillside. Aesthetically pleasing, this organic eco-friendly garden has much to discover. From herbs, fruit and vegetable to shrubs and perennials, trees, and orchard. Plants to note inc cranesbills, hydrangeas, clematis and wisteria. An array of cold frames, wormery, hot bin, pond, stumpery, enclosure for hens and a propagation area. Grassy and slate chipping paths lead you on, with something to attract and inspire both new and well-seasoned gardeners. Lots of quirky areas and every twist and turn reveals something more. A tranquil, life-affirming and inspiring space.

16 ♦ NATIONAL BOTANIC GARDEN OF WALES
Middleton Hall, Llanarthne, SA32 8HN. 01558 667149, www.botanicgarden.wales. Between Cross Hands & Carmarthen. From Carmarthen take A48 E, after 8m take slip road

11 St David's Close, Tenby Gardens

signed B4310 to Nantgaredig. Follow brown signs. **For opening times and information, please phone or visit garden website.**
Dedicated to conservation, horticulture, science, education, leisure and the arts, the National Botanic Garden of Wales features the Great Glasshouse, Tropical House, Walled Garden, a working farm, Waun Las Nature Reserve and British Bird of Prey Centre. Set in a historical Regency landscape of over 500 acres, it hosts a programme of events and activities throughout the year.

17 NEUADD Y FELIN
Neuadd Road, Garnant, Ammanford, SA18 1UF. Terry & Sara Knight. *On A474, 5m W of Pontardawe, 5m E of Ammanford. Access to garden from Nant Gwinau Rd. Turn R as you enter Garnant on A474 from Pontardawe. From Ammanford, turn L just before you leave Garnant on A474.* **Sat 25, Sun 26 July (10.30-4). Adm £5, chd free. Tea, coffee & cake.**
A mature two acre smallholding with many different areas. A large garden with sloping perennial beds, large dahlia display, mature shrubs and shaded planted areas. 40 foot white wisteria climbing up a pergola, wildlife and fish ponds. Wander through the meadow, bog garden, large ornamental grass beds, wildflower beds, a walk through 600 willow trees, and woodland garden leading to river seating area. Located on the site of an old C14 watermill.

18 NORCHARD
The Ridgeway, Manorbier, Tenby, SA70 8LD. Ms H Davies. *4m W of Tenby. From Tenby, take A4139 for Pembroke. ½m after Lydstep, take R at Xrds. Proceed down lane for ¾m. Norchard on R.* **Sun 7 June (1-5). Adm £8, chd free. Tea, coffee & cake.**
Historic gardens at a Medieval hall nestled in tranquil location and sheltered by an ancient oak woodland. Strong structure with formal and informal areas. Early walled gardens, restored Elizabethan parterre, ornamental kitchen garden, subtropical planting and orangery. 1½ acre orchard of old (many local) varieties. Young arboretum and meadow looking towards grist mill. Extensive collections of roses, daffodils and tulips. Millpond with moorhens and ducks. Partial wheelchair access.

Access to lower level of the kitchen garden via steps only.

19 PANTYBARA
Velindre, Llandysul, SA44 5XT. Mrs Helen Maxwell, 07816 673743, helen@rural-office.co.uk, www.instagram.com/rural_creator. *4m S of Newcastle Emlyn. From Newcastle Emlyn take B4333 towards Cynwyl Elfed. After 4m turn sharp L on unmarked road. Garden is 0.7m down this lane on R. What3words app: skater.target.massaging.* **Sat 20, Sun 21 June (12-4.30). Adm £5, chd free. Home-made teas.** Visits also by arrangement 16 May to 26 July. No coaches but minibuses are fine. Discuss refreshments when booking.
An acre of garden on a sloping south facing hillside 250m high and terraced on several levels with dry stone walls. Designed to provide year-round interest, to benefit wildlife, provide food and as a setting for our home. The garden consists of a pond, bog garden, rockeries, perennial beds, mixed borders, dry stone walls and vegetable gardens. The garden is designed to join seamlessly with the wilder areas of the smallholding, with stone walls being used to separate the scrub from the more cultivated areas (please be aware of some steep steps and narrow paths).

20 PENTRESITE
Rhydargaeau Road, SA32 7AJ. Gayle & Ron Mounsey, 07900 432993, gayle.mounsey@gmail.com. *4m N of Carmarthen. Take A485 heading N out of Carmarthen, once out of Peniel take 1st R to Horeb & cont for 1m. Turn R at NGS sign, 2nd house down lane.* **Sun 3 May, Sun 5 July (11-5). Adm £6, chd free. Home-made teas.** Visits also by arrangement 26 Apr to 20 Sept.
Approx two acre garden developed over the last 19 years with extensive lawns, colour filled herbaceous and mixed borders, on several levels, a bog garden and magnificent views of the surrounding countryside. There are many unusual trees, shrubs and herbaceous plants, with an interesting collection of hydrangeas. This garden is south facing and catches the south westerly winds from the sea. The garden features statuary by James Doran-Webb.

21 NEW PENTYWYN
Cwmale, Croesyceiliog, SA32 8DT. Anne & John Roberts-Harry, j.roberts_harry@btinternet.com. *3m S of Carmarthen. From Carmarthen, S on A484. Follow signs Ysgol Bro Myrddin & Croesyceiliog. Through village, up hill. After village & 40mph sign, take L for Cwmale. Single lane, 200yds along, 2 white gate pillars.* **Sat 2 May (11-4). Adm £5, chd free. Tea, coffee & cake.** Visits also by arrangement 4 May to 9 May for groups of up to 20. Please discuss refreshments when booking.
Nestling on the slopes of a shallow valley, with lovely views over adjacent pasture and woodland, this garden has been developed over 20 years with mixed, informal, cottage style planting. Follow gravel paths as they cross between borders with acers, white birch and gunnera. Patio, orchard, vegetables, wildflower meadow and dry stone walls. Ranked 2nd in Llandyfaelog Community Council flower garden competition. Wheelchair access to front of house, partial whelchair access to rear garden.

22 PONT TRECYNNY
Garn Gelli Hill, Fishguard, SA65 9SR. Wendy Kinver *1½m N of Fishguard. Driving up the hill from Fishguard to Dinas turn R halfway up the road & follow signs. SatNav will take you to a lay-by opp the garden, please ignore as we are on the other side.* **Sun 31 May, Wed 10 June, Sun 5, Sun 26 July, Sun 16 Aug (1-4). Adm £5, chd free. Pre-booking essential, please phone 07722 105655 or email wendykinver@icloud.com for information & booking.** Visits also by arrangement 31 May to 30 Aug for groups of 10+.
A diverse garden of 3½ acres. Meander through the meadow planted with native trees, pass the pond and over a bridge which takes you along a path, through an arboretum, orchard and gravel garden and into the formal garden full of cloud trees, exotic plants and pots,which then leads you to the stream and vegetable garden.

23 ◆ SCOLTON MANOR

Bethlehem, Haverfordwest, SA62 5QL. 01437 731328, scolton.enq@pembrokeshire.gov.uk, www.scoltonmanor.co.uk. *6m outside Haverfordwest. On B4302 Cardigan Rd, brown-signed off A40 from both Haverfordwest & Fishguard.* **For NGS: Sat 4, Sun 5 July (10-4). Sat 5 Sept (10-4), open nearby Froghall Barn. Sun 6 Sept (10-4). Adm £5, chd free. Free parking near Manor on NGS days. For other opening times and information, please phone, email or visit garden website.**

The Welsh collection of salvias, with over 60 fabulous varieties, is displayed as a formal labelled group but some are also planted within the walled garden's herbaceous borders. The on site nursery provides many of these for sale. The walled garden also features organic produce and flowers, willow arch, pineapple house, perennial borders and arboretum. Scolton Manor comprises 60 acres of park and woodland surrounding a Victorian Manor House, with a Welcome Centre, Bee-keeping Centre, sculpture trail, tearoom, play areas and gift shop. A Tree Nursery has endangered native trees from West Wales, grown from seed for local groups to plant. Wheelchair access in Walled Garden and majority of grounds, some restrictions in Manor House. Disabled toilets and baby-changing facilities available.

24 SHOALS HOOK FARM

Shoals Hook Lane, Haverfordwest, SA61 2XN. Karen & Robert Hordley, 07712 268899, shoalshook@icloud.com, www.shoalshook.com. *On the outskirts of Haverfordwest. From A40 take B4329 to H/west town centre (Prendergast). Before fork with Fishguard Rd, turn L into Back Ln, turn L to Shoals Hook Ln. 1m, property on L. What3words app: clips.november.samplers.* **Visits by arrangement 20 Apr to 17 Sept for groups of up to 15. Visits from Mon-Thurs only. Please discuss refreshments when booking. Adm £5, chd free.**

Approx six acre garden on our smallholding. Designed and made by ourselves over 30 years. Inc flower borders, vegetable garden, fruit trees, woodland walk, lake garden and specimen trees. Planted for the different seasons and to encourage wildlife. Many spring bulbs at the start of the year, ending with a late summer prairie style grass garden area.

25 SKANDA VALE HOSPICE GARDEN

Saron, Llandysul, SA44 5DY. www.skandavalehospice.org. *Between Carmarthen & Cardigan. On A484, in village of Saron.* **Sat 6 June (11-4.30). Adm £3.50, chd free. Home-made teas.**

Tranquil garden of approx one acre, built for therapy, relaxation and fun. Maintained by volunteers, lawns and glades link garden buildings with willow spiral, wildlife pond, borders, sculptures and stained glass. Blue and gold planting at entrance inspires calm and confidence, leading to brighter red, orange and white. Hospice facilities open for viewing. A garden for quiet contemplation, wheelchair friendly, with lots of small interesting features. For accommodation please visit www.skanda-hafan.com/en/.

26 STABLE COTTAGE

Rhoslanog, Mathry, Haverfordwest, SA62 5HG. Michael & Jane Bayliss, 01348 837712, michaelandjane1954@michaelandjane.plus.com. *Between Fishguard & St David's. Heading W on A487, turn R at Square & Compass sign. ½m, at hairpin take track L. Stable Cottage on L with block paved drive.* **Visits by arrangement 1 May to 12 July for groups of up to 12. Discuss refreshments when booking. Adm £4, chd free.**

Garden extends to approx ⅓ of an acre. It is divided into several smaller garden types, with a seaside garden, small orchard and wildlife area, scented garden, small kitchen garden, and two Japanese areas - a stroll garden and courtyard area.

GROUP OPENING

27 NEW TENBY GARDENS

Tenby, SA70 8HE. *Head S from A40 on A478 or E from Pembroke on A4139. See map on NGS website for convenient public car parks. Tickets & maps at Zion House, SA70 8AH & 11St David's Close, SA70 8BT.* **Sat 13, Sun 14 June (2-5). Combined adm £10, chd free. Home-made teas at The Coach House & 11 St David's Close.**

NEW   THE COACH HOUSE
Mrs H Arentz.
Open on all dates

NEW   5 ROCKY PARK
Michelle James.
Open on all dates

NEW   11 ST DAVIDS CLOSE
Roland & Lucy Lewis.
Open on all dates

NEW   6 TRAFALGAR ROAD
Annie Webster.
Open on Sun 14 June

NEW   21 TRAFALGAR ROAD
Sally McHardy.
Open on all dates

NEW   ZION HOUSE
Judith Hughes.
Open on all dates

Six town gardens in the popular coastal town of Tenby, showcasing a variety of styles: The Coach House - a colourful, spacious, urban courtyard garden with pots and containers of many sizes and types, and different display areas; 21 Trafalgar Rd- a jungly urban town garden providing a green oasis of wildlife friendly plants and shrubs (plants and preserves for sale); 6 Trafalgar Rd - a tiny walled garden filled to the brim with plants, making a quiet secluded spot for birds and owner alike (botanical-themed craftwork for sale); 5 Rocky Park - small stone walled garden on 2 levels with raised beds and containers featuring olive trees, alliums, libertia, hellebores, agapanthus, etc: Zion House - a walled garden not visible from the road, set on different levels with many shrubs, roses and annuals (steep paths and steps); and 11 St David's Close - an edge of town garden with lawn and colour-themed borders, front and rear gardens, split level, raised borders, greenhouse and patio with pots. Tickets valid for both days.

28 TREFFGARNE HALL

Treffgarne, Haverfordwest, SA62 5PJ. Martin & Jackie Batty, 07884 410753, jmv.batty@gmail.com, www.instagram.com/battyplanting2. *7m N of Haverfordwest, signed off A40. Go up through village & follow road round sharply to L, Hall ¼m further on L. What3words app:doubt.thrones.*

awesome. **Sun 29 Mar, Sun 3 May (1-5). Adm £6, chd free. Home-made teas.** Visits also by arrangement Mar to Sept. Please discuss refreshments when booking.
Stunning hilltop location with panoramic views: Grade II listed Georgian house (not open) provides formal backdrop to garden of four acres with wild lawns and themed beds. A walled garden, with double rill and pergolas, planted with a multitude of borderline hardy exotics. Summer border, gravel garden, heather bed, stumpery. woodland area and rose garden. Planted for year-round interest. The planting schemes seek to challenge the boundaries of what can be grown in Pembrokeshire. Gravel paths not wheel-friendly. Some steps.

29 NEW TYNEWYDD
Pengelli, Gwynfe, Llangadog, SA19 9PE. Jessica & Nick Allen. *6m S of Llangadog off A4069. From Llangadog take A4069 to Pontadawe. Black Mountain sign after 4m. Turn L up lane (no through road). Follow Tynewydd sign through farm onto mountain track.* **Fri 29, Sat 30 May, Fri 26, Sat 27 June (1.30-6.30). Adm £5, chd free. Pre-booking essential, please phone 01550 740340 or email jsrallen@btinternet.com for information &** booking. **Discuss refreshments when booking.**
A 20 acre relaxed rural garden in an off grid small holding high on the Black Mountain with wild ponds, orchard, soft fruit and vegetable garden, stone bed, compost bins, Polycrub, small ancient woodland and 360 degree views. Strong shoes needed to walk through fields and rough terrain.

30 TY'R MAES
Tyr Maes, Farmers, Llanwrda, SA19 8JP. John & Helen Brooks, 01558 650541, johnhelen140@gmail.com. *7m SE of Lampeter. 8m NW of Llanwrda. From Llanwrda 1m N of Pumsaint on A482. 1st L after Ffarmers turn. From Lampeter 1st R after Springwater Lakes. 30yds down lane. Please use postcode SA19 8DP (SatNav). What3words app: eminent.notch.dunk.* **Visits by arrangement Mar to Oct. Adm £6, chd free. Discuss refreshments when booking.**
A four acre garden with splendid views. Herbaceous and shrub beds, full of cottage garden favourites and many unusual plants. Wildlife and lily ponds; arboretum with many rare trees; masses of rhododendron, magnolia and hydrangea cultivars. Gloriously colourful from early spring till late autumn. Guided tours available. Look out for autumn plant sale Some gravel paths.

31 ♦ UPTON CASTLE GARDENS
Cosheston, Pembroke Dock, SA72 4SE. Prue & Stephen Barlow, 01646 689996, info@uptoncastle.com, www.uptoncastlegardens.com. *4m E of Pembroke Dock. 2m N of A477 between Carew & Pembroke Dock. Follow brown signs to Upton Castle Gardens through Cosheston.* **For NGS: Wed 10 June (10-4.30). Adm £9.50, chd free. Tea. For other opening times and information, please phone, email or visit garden website.**
Privately owned, listed, historic gardens and arboretum of 35 acres surround C13 castle (not open). Terraces of herbaceous borders and formal rose garden with over 150 roses provide constant summer interest. Walled productive kitchen garden, chapel garden with millennial yew. Rare magnolias, rhododendrons, camellias, and new hydrangea beds. Woodland with rare and champion trees. Walk on the Wild Side: Woodland walks funded by C.C.W. and Welsh Assembly Government. Medieval chapel as featured on Time Team. Partial wheelchair access.

32 WEST WALES WILLOWS
The Mill, Gwernogle, Brechfa, SA32 7SA. Justine & Alan Burgess, www.facebook.com/WestWalesWillows. *3m from Brechfa. On A40 at Nantgaredig, take B4310 to Brechfa. ½m after Brechfa, turn L towards Gwernogle. After 2½m pass Chapel on R, up steep hill & bear R. Take 1st R & The Mill is on R.* **Sat 20 June (10-4). Adm £4.50, chd free. Tea, coffee & cake.**
Located in a scenic valley, halfway up a mountain, the National Plant Collection of *Salix* (willow) is set in a sloping field with grass pathways. Approx 260 varieties are on show, inc varieties for pollinators, autumn colour, bio fuel, hedging and windbreaks. The field also has sample living willow structures on display inc domes, tepee, tunnel, hedges and a new arbour.

Treffgarne Hall

CEREDIGION

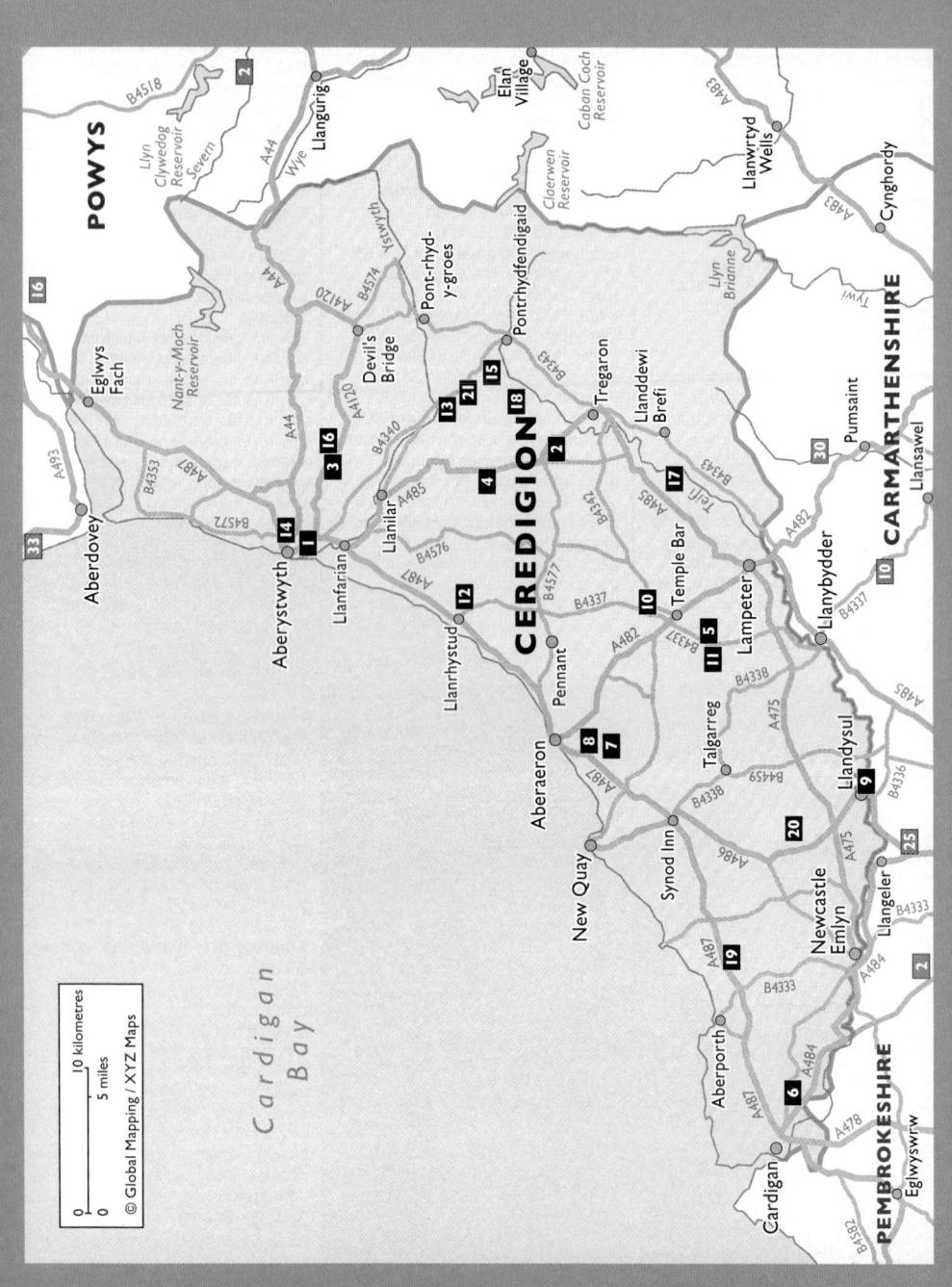

CEREDIGION

VOLUNTEERS

County Organiser
Stuart Bradley
07757 799553
stustart53@outlook.com

County Treasurer
Elaine Grande
01974 261196
elaine.grande@ngs.org.uk

Publicity
Shelagh Yeomans
07796 285003
shelaghyeo@hotmail.com

Social Media
Samantha Wynne-Rhydderch
07899 911483
samantha.wynne-rhydderch@ngs.org.uk

Assistant County Organisers
Gay Acres
01974 251559
gayacres@aol.com

Joanna Kennaugh
07872 451821
joanna.kennaugh@ngs.org.uk

@Ceredigion Gardens
@ceredigion_ngs

OPENING DATES

All entries subject to change.
For latest information check
www.ngs.org.uk
Map locator numbers are shown to the right of each garden name.

April

Saturday 18th
Bryngwyn 3

Sunday 19th
The Hidden Garden 9

May

Sunday 3rd
Plas Penglais 14

Sunday 10th
Llanllyr 10

Saturday 16th
Y Felin 21

Sunday 17th
Rhos Villa 17
Y Felin 21

June

Saturday 6th
Bryngwyn 3
Temple Bar Farm 19

Sunday 7th
Temple Bar Farm 19

Thursday 11th
Bryngwyn 3

Sunday 14th
Ffynnon Las 8

Sunday 21st
Llanllyr 10

Sunday 28th
Rhos Villa 17

July

Saturday 4th
Penybont 13

Sunday 5th
◆ Cae Hir Gardens 5
Penybont 13

Sunday 12th
Penelton 12

Sunday 19th
Aberystwyth Allotments 1

Sunday 26th
Felinfach House 7

August

Saturday 1st
NEW Troed y Rhiw 20

Sunday 2nd
NEW Troed y Rhiw 20

Sunday 16th
NEW Purple Trees 15

Sunday 23rd
The Hidden Garden 9

By Arrangement

Arrange a personalised garden visit with your club, or group of friends, on a date to suit you. See individual garden entries for full details.

NEW Bryn Hebog 2
Bwlch y Geufforcd Gardens 4
Cilbronnau Mansion 6
Ffynnon Las 8
Llanllyr 10
NEW The Old Woollen Mill 11
Penybont 13
NEW Rhos Eithin 16
Tanffordd 18
Temple Bar Farm 19
Y Felin 21

The National Garden Scheme donated £3,875,596 to our nursing and health beneficiaries from money raised at gardens open in 2025.

THE GARDENS

1 ABERYSTWYTH ALLOTMENTS
5th Avenue, Penparcau, Aberystwyth, SY23 1QT. Aberystwyth Town Council. On S side of R.Rheidol on Aberystwyth by-pass. From N or E, take A4120 between Llanbadarn & Penparcau. Cross bridge then take 1st R into Minyddol. Allotments ¼ m on R. **Sun 19 July (1-5). Adm £5, chd free. Home-made teas.**
There are 47 plots in total on two sites just a few yards from each other. The allotments are situated in a lovely setting alongside River Rheidol close to Aberystwyth. Wide variety of produce grown, vegetables, soft fruit, top fruit, flowers, herbs and a newly created wildlife pond. There will be surplus plants and produce for sale, with donations gratefully received. Refreshments will be provided by the local Scout Group. Grass and gravel paths throughout. For more information contact Brian Heath 01970 617112.

2 NEW BRYN HEBOG
Tynreithin, Tregaron, SY25 6LN. Mike & Julia Roberts, 01974 209233, robertsmike2005@aol.com. *3m NW of Tregaron, halfway between Aberystwyth & Lampeter, on the A485. From Tregaron 3m up the hill until you see the signs/layby on R. From Aberystwyth, A485 for14m, bear L in Tyncelyn, cont on, then park in lay-by, by house on L after Swyddffynnon turn.* **Visits by arrangement May to Sept for groups of up to 15. Adm £5, chd £2.50. Light refreshments.**
Approx one acre hillside plantsman's newish garden with many uncommon and rare shrubs, trees and herbaceous borders. It is comprised of two distinct areas: one in full sun, which is grassy with lawned paths and views of plentiful farmland and mountains. The other is more steep with sloping grass paths leading to a small wooded area.

3 BRYNGWYN
Capel Seion, Aberystwyth, SY23 4EE. Terry & Sue Reeves. *5m E of Aberystwyth on A4120. On the A4120 between the villages of Capel Seion & Pant y Crug. Parking for up to 15 cars available on site. What3words app: elephant. sunflower.forks.* **Sat 18 Apr, Sat 6, Thur 11 June (2-5). Adm £5, chd free. Home-made teas.**
Managing our land for wildlife is at the heart of all we do. As a result of conservation work and tree planting, habitat has been restored to such, that numbers and diversity of wildflowers and wildlife have increased. Explore along mown paths through traditional wildflower-rich hay meadows. Small orchard containing Welsh heritage apples and pears. Wildflower seeds are available for sale.

4 BWLCH Y GEUFFORDD GARDENS
Bronant, Aberystwyth, SY23 4JD. Mr & Mrs J Acres, 01974 251559, gayacres@aol.com, bwlch-y-geuffordd-gardens.myfreesites.net. *12m SE of Aberystwyth, 6m NW of Tregaron off A485. Take turning opp village sch in Bronant for 1½ m then L up ½ m uneven track.* **Visits by arrangement. Adm £6, chd £3.50. Tea.**
1000ft high, three acre, constantly evolving wildlife and water garden. An adventure and fantasy garden for children (and the young at heart). Themed gardens inc Mediterranean, cottage garden, woodland, Oriental, memorial and jungle. Plenty of seating. Unique home crafted garden sculptures and buildings. Fantasy, music and adventure. Garden is wildlife rich, particularly insects and birds.

Troed y Rhiw

CEREDIGION 631

5 ♦ CAE HIR GARDENS
Cribyn, Lampeter,
SA48 7NG. Julie & Stuart
Akkermans, 07538 789180,
caehirgardens@gmail.com,
www.caehirgardens.com. *5m W of
Lampeter. Take A482 from Lampeter
towards Aberaeron. After 5m turn
S on B4337. Garden on N side of
village of Cribyn.* **For NGS: Sun 5
July (10-5). Adm £7.50, chd £2.50.
Light refreshments. Open nearby
Penybont.** **For other opening times
and information, please phone,
email or visit garden website.**
A Welsh garden with a Dutch history.
Cae Hir is a true family garden of
unassuming beauty, made tenable by
its innovative mix of ordinary garden
plants and wildflowers growing in
swathes of perceived abandonment.
At Cae Hir the natural meets the
formal and riotous planting meets
structure and form. A garden not
just for plant lovers, but also for
design enthusiasts. Five acres of fully
landscaped gardens. Tearoom serving
a selection of home-made cakes
and scones and a 'Soup of the Day'.
Partial wheelchair access.

6 CILBRONNAU MANSION
Llangoedmor, Cardigan,
SA43 2LP. Lyn & Roger
Bushell, 07817 944593,
bushellroger962@gmail.com.
*2m E of Cardigan. Situated on the
B4570, 2m from Cardigan. Turn
down track between the 2 lodge
houses & drive carefully- there are
ramps to help with drainage.* **Visits
by arrangement May to Sept for
groups of 6 to 20. Adm £5, chd
free. Home-made teas.**
The 2½ acre garden inc a courtyard
cottage garden, Mediterranean and
gravel gardens, vegetable plots,
lawns, beds and borders, all at
various stages of development. There
are a number of yews, ancient oaks,
beech and Wellingtonia. Most, areas
are accessible to wheelchair users in
dry conditions.

7 FELINFACH HOUSE
Oakford, Llanarth, SA47 0RP.
Andrew & Rachael McInnes.
*Between New Quay & Aberaeron.
Off the A487. Turn off A487 at
Llwyncelyn (near the Petrol Stn)
following signs towards Oakford.
After approx 1m turn R into car
park. What3words app: slept.towns.
sweetened.* **Sun 26 July (11-5).**

**Adm £5, chd free. Tea, coffee &
cake.**
Explore this acre of productive
country garden with a variety of
elements inc large lawned area,
vegetables, flower borders, fruit trees,
polytunnel and greenhouses. There is
a wildlife pond with water lilies leading
to a woodland walk and gentle
flowing stream. Poultry pen and a
variety of wild birds. A quiz sheet for
children. Wooded area is not suitable
for wheelchair access.

8 FFYNNON LAS
Ffosyffin, Aberaeron, SA46 0HB.
Liz Roberts, 01545 571687,
lizhomerent@hotmail.co.uk. *A
short distance off the A487. 1m S
of Aberaeron. Turn off A487 opp
Morrisons in Ffosyffin, 300m up the
road take the L turn at the T-junc.*
**Sun 14 June (12-5). Adm £5, chd
free. Home-made teas. Visits also
by arrangement 4 July to 31 July
for groups of 5 to 15. Donation to
Pancreatic Cancer Research.**
A two acre garden that has been
in the making for over 15 years,
Ffynnonlas is a beautiful area that
delivers on many different aspects
of gardening. There are large lawns,
several beds of mature shrubs and
flowers. A small lake and two smaller
ponds that are separated by a
Monet style bridge with lilies. There
is a wildflower meadow, a work in
progress that has spectacular wild
orchids in spring. A rockery with
water cascade, vegetable garden with
raised beds. For wheelchair users,
please note there are grass paths and
level ground.

9 THE HIDDEN GARDEN
Farmyard Farm, Dol Llan Road,
Llandysul, SA44 4RL. Mr Richard
Bramley, www.facebook.com/
FarmyardNurseries. *Approx 1m
from Llandysul. Head towards
Llandysul & find the petrol stn (Valley
Services). Follow brown signage to
Farmyard Nurseries. Approx 1m up
the road opp garage.* **Sun 19 Apr,
Sun 23 Aug (10-4). Adm £5, chd
free. Tea, coffee & cake.** Donation
to Plant Heritage.
A large, serene woodland garden with
extensive plantings to complement
the existing natural trees and shrubs.
Numerous paths lead to a small
lake with many ducks in residence,
the 'hobbit house' and adjoining
large stumpery, and acer grove.

Hydrangeas and hellebores are
widespread with masses of spring
bulbs. Great care has been taken to
give year-round interest.

10 LLANLLYR
Talsarn, Lampeter, SA48 8QB.
Loveday Gee & Patrick Gee,
01570 470900, lgllanllyr@aol.com.
*6m NW of Lampeter. On B4337
to Llanrhystud. From Lampeter,
entrance to garden on L, just before
village of Talsarn.* **Sun 10 May, Sun
21 June (2-6). Adm £5, chd free.
Tea, coffee & cake. Visits also by
arrangement Apr to Sept.**
Large early C19 garden on site of
Medieval nunnery, renovated and
replanted since 1989. Discover the
large pool and bog garden as well
as a formal water garden. There are
also rose and shrub borders, gravel
gardens, and a beautiful rose arbour.
Wander through the allegorical
labyrinth and mount, all exhibiting fine
plantsmanship. Year-round appeal,
interesting and unusual plants. Visit
our spectacular rose garden planted
with fragrant old fashioned shrub and
climbing roses. Specialist Plant Fair
by Ceredigion Growers Association.
Garden mostly flat for wheelchair
users.

**11 NEW THE OLD WOOLLEN
MILL**
Cribyn, Lampeter, SA48 7QH.
Terry & Cheryl Hill, 01570 471211,
hillsonthehill@hotmail.co.uk. *5m
NW of Lampeter. From Cribyn,
take steep L down by bus shelter/
monument. Bear R toward
Mydroilyn, 200yds L past Tan Y
Bryn at the top of our drive, park
at the bottom by the Mill.* **Visits by
arrangement for groups of up to
10. Limited parking for 4 vehicles.
Adm £5, chd free. Tea, coffee &
cake. Discuss refreshments when
booking.**
Terry and Cheryl run a permaculture
smallholding and would be delighted
to show you about low-impact
sustainable living. Do not expect
manicured lawns; everything is
allowed to flower and go to seed.
At The Old Woollen Mill diversity is
the name of the game, supporting
a huge array of wildlife, butterflies,
dragonflies, and 65 species of birds.
Special interests inc health, biochar,
compost toilets.

12 PENELTON
Llanrhystud, SY23 5BA. Mr Arthur Newman. ½ m from Llanrhystud in the village of Cwm Mabws. From Llanrhystud take the B4337. Take the 2nd L turn signed Cwm Mabws. The garden is approx ¼ m on the L with parking opp. **Sun 12 July (11-4.30). Adm £5, chd free. Tea, coffee & cake.**
A two acre garden recently recovered and replanted, benefitting from established large trees. Comprising of interesting herbaceous and shrub plantings in island beds, in addition to impressive borders beside a long, south facing stone garden wall. Highly productive vegetable garden, polytunnel and small orchard. Two small ponds add to the charm and tranquillity of an inspirational garden.

13 PENYBONT
Llanafan, Aberystwyth, SY23 4BJ. Norman & Brenda Jones, 07970 900960, tobrenorm@gmail.com. *Ystwyth Valley. 9m SE of Aberystwyth. On the Ystwyth Cycle Trail. B4340 between Trawscoed & Pontrhydfendigaid. Stone bridge. ¼ m up hill. Turn R along lane/Ystwyth Trail via Gwelystwyth. What3words app: bump.housework.supported.* **Sat 4, Sun 5 July (11-5). Adm £5, chd free. Home-made teas.** Visits also by arrangement 9 May to 30 Aug.
Carefully designed hillside country garden next to the Ystwyth Forest with views overlooking the valley. An acre of vistas with varied interest, colour and textures; from spring bulbs and bluebells, to a pond, rhododendrons, and azaleas throughout May. Roses bloom from June and the garden has a Mediterranean summer feel with swathes of lavender, grapevines and lots of brightly coloured hydrangeas. Oak seats with stunning views over fields, woodland, valley and hills. Bird life inc red kites and buzzards. Sloping lawns mean partial wheelchair access.

14 PLAS PENGLAIS
Penglais, Aberystwyth, SY23 3DF. Aberystwyth University. *NE of Aberystwyth. Parking at Aberystwyth Uni, across the road from gardens. Cross the A487 & enter past white lodge house. Walk down the lane. Regret, no parking at house.* **Sun 3 May (1-5). Adm £5, chd free. Home-made teas. Home-made cakes.**
Three acres of gardens, specimen trees, shrubs and a walled garden. The garden is being slowly restored and is very much a work in progress. The gardens consists of two main lawn areas with large specimen trees, inc many different types of firs, two Himalayan Hemlock trees, a variety of oaks, weeping cyprus, and a monkey puzzle tree. Views of the sea are possible from raised areas of the lawn. Large shrubs are all around the gardens, creating a wonderful walk around a very special space. Not all areas are wheelchair accessible.

15 NEW PURPLE TREES
Bryn Teifi, Ystrad Meurig, SY25 6AA. Alan Cookson & Angharad Edwards, www.purpletrees.co.uk. *7½ m N of Tregaron, 14m SE of Aberystwyth. The 'purple trees' nursery sign on the B4340 is in the middle of Ystrad Meurig, turn N at the junc of St Ioan's & the nursery. Parking is 50yds up the road on the R in adjacent field.* **Sun 16 Aug (12-8.30). Adm £2, chd free. Tea, coffee & cake.**
Our ¾ acre garden and tree nursery was established in 2022, incorporating a ornamental home garden with pond and newly planted borders and beds. A herb and apothecary garden styled around the 'golden ratio'. A native tree nursery and a Pumpkin Patch along with fruit cage and vegetable garden. A garden and plant fundraising auction will be held on the day and to begin at 6pm.

16 NEW RHOS EITHIN
Pant-Y-Crug, Capel Seion, Aberystwyth, SY23 4EF. Dr Peter Wootton-Beard, peter.woottonbeard@gmail.com. *Along the A4120 between Aberystwyth & Devil's Bridge. Approx 6m along A4120 from Aberystwyth towards Devil's Bridge. Through Moriah, & Capel Seion to Pant-Y-Crug. On the brow of the hill, with a large Monkey Puzzle tree in the field opp.* **Visits by arrangement 1 Apr to 19 July for groups of up to 20. Adm £5, chd free. Tea, coffee and cake available on request, by prior arrangement.**
A new garden started in 2020 which features very little hard landscaping, intentionally soft edges, and has an ethos of treading lightly to enhance ecological value. The owner also has a penchant for growing unusual and interesting woody shrubs and trees. The garden is designed to blend defined spaces for entertaining and relaxing with pathways that encourage visitors to wander.

17 RHOS VILLA
Llanddewi Brefi, Tregaron, SY25 6PA. Andrew & Sam Buchanan. *Between Olmarch & Llanddewi Brefi. From Lampeter, take the A485 towards Tregaron. After Llangybi turn R opp junc for Olmarch. The property can be found on the R after 1½ m.* **Sun 17 May, Sun 28 June (10.30-4). Adm £5, chd free. Home-made teas.**
A ¾ acre garden creatively utilising local materials. Secret pathways meander through sun and shade, dry and damp. A variety of perennials and shrubs are inter-planted to create interest at every turn and throughout the year. A productive vegetable and fruit garden with semi-formal structure contrasts the looser planting through the rest of the garden. Interesting and beautifully crafted pitch cobble paths and walls constructed from local stone.

18 TANFFORDD
Swyddffynnon, Ystrad Meurig, SY25 6AW. Jo Kennaugh & Stuart Bradley, 07872 451821, stustart53@outlook.com. *1m W of Ystrad Meurig. 5m E of Tregaron. Tanffordd is ¼ m from Swyddffynnon village on the road to Tregaron. Please do not follow SatNav.* **Visits by arrangement 1 May to 27 Sept for groups of up to 25. Refreshments £5. Adm £5, chd free. Tea, coffee & cake. Soft drinks also available.**
Wildlife garden, rich in biodiversity, set in a five acre smallholding with large pool. The garden inc a small woodland area and beds of shrubs and herbaceous planting containing more unusual plants. Vegetables, polytunnel and poultry enclosures with chickens and ducks. Wander along to meet the friendly donkeys and ponies who share a buttercup filled field in late spring and early summer.

Llanllyr

19 TEMPLE BAR FARM
Sarnau, Llandysul, SA44 6QU.
Jenny & Teifi Davies,
01239 811079,
jennydavies3@live.co.uk. *Located on A487 between villages of Sarnau & Tanygroes. Situated 8m N of Cardigan & 14m S of Aberaeron on A487. Turn into side road at junc. What3words app: measure.household.printing.* **Sat 6, Sun 7 June (11.30-4). Adm £5, chd free. Tea, coffee & cake. Visits also by arrangement 6 June to 18 July for groups of up to 10.**
A colourful garden on a farm. Planting areas wherever space allows. There's a bog garden featuring candelabra primulas, foxglove and tree lupin walk, mixed perennial beds with shrubs and many containers nestling in original farmyard. Also a herd of rare Ancient Cattle of Wales plus an important Iron Age Fort (Cadw) on the farm, with amazing views over Cardigan Bay and Ceredigion countryside.

20 NEW TROED Y RHIW
Tregroes, Llandysul, SA44 4NP.
Mr Justin Messenger. *6m N of Llandysul, tucked in a valley just off the A486. From Llandysul, head towards New Quay on the A486. After approx 6m turn R at Bwlchygroes x-roads, signposted to Tregroes.* **Sat 1, Sun 2 Aug (10-4). Adm £5, chd free. Pre-booking essential, please visit www.ngs.org.uk for information & booking. Tea, coffee & cake.**
A charming, semi wild garden, having been reclaimed from the brambles over the last four years. Still very much a work in progress with several areas inc a large nature pond and riverside setting. Wander through woodland gardens, orchard and wildflower meadow. There are herbaceous borders, new tree and shrub plantings, vegetable beds and polytunnel all tucked away in a Welsh valley.

21 Y FELIN
Tynygraig, Ystrad Meurig,
SY25 6AE. Brian & Hilary Malaws, 07779 801968, hilary.malaws@btinternet.com. *10m SE of Aberystwyth via B4340. Pass Tynygraig village sign, branch R signed Swyddffynnon. Turn R 70 metres before house Ty Chwarel. What3words app: positives.remembers.clown.* **Sat 16, Sun 17 May (12-5). Adm £5, chd free. Tea, coffee & cake. Visits also by arrangement 3 May to 14 June for groups of up to 15. Discuss refreshments when booking.**
A two acre garden set within a 14 acre wooded landscape with historic industrial features, inc a former corn mill and pond. From the garden, a view of Caradog Falls (100ft waterfall) can be seen. The garden inc masses of rhododendron, azalea, camellia and magnolia with many other unusual trees and shrubs. There are woodland walks although Storm Darragh has caused a significant loss of the woodland. Explore the mill pond and old mill with waterwheel. There is also an old mine, now a cave and disused railway tunnel.

GLAMORGAN

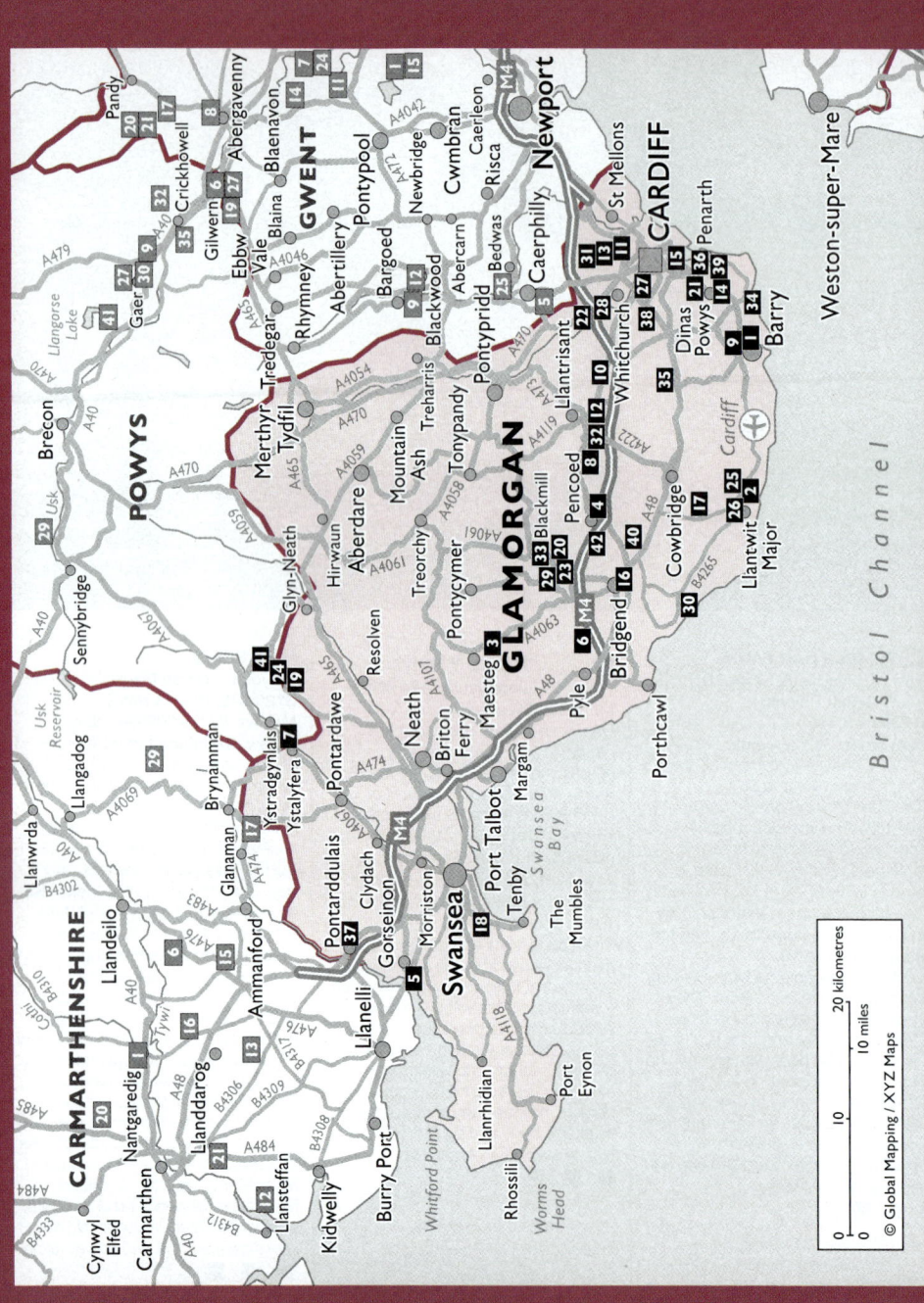

GLAMORGAN

VOLUNTEERS

County Organiser
Rosamund Davies 01656 880999
rosamund.davies@ngs.org.uk

Emma Berry 07733 328101
emma.berry@ngs.org.uk

County Treasurer
Steven Thomas 01446 772339
steven.thomas@ngs.org.uk

Publicity
Bernadette Nicholas 07815 449568
bernadette.nicholas@ngs.org.uk

Social Media
Sue Deary 01656 720833
suedeary888@gmail.com

Booklet Co-ordinator
Marie Robson
mariedrobson@gmail.com

Talks Co-ordinator
Derek Price 07717 462295
derekprice7@btinternet.com

Health and Gardens Co-ordinator
Miranda Workman 02920 766225
miranda.parsons@talktalk.net

Assistant County Organisers
Cheryl Bass 07969 499967
cheryl.bass@ngs.org.uk

Sol Blytt Jordens 01792 391676
sol.blyttjordens@ngs.org.uk

Frances Bowyer 02920 892264
frances.bowyer@ngs.org.uk

Pam Creed
pam.creed@ngs.org.uk

Janet Evans 07961 542452
janetevans54@me.com

Tony Leyshon 07896 799378
anthony.leyshon@icloud.com

Ceri Macfarlane 01792 404906
ceri@mikegravenor.plus.com

OPENING DATES

All entries subject to change.
For latest information check
www.ngs.org.uk
Map locator numbers are
shown to the right of each
garden name.

February

Sunday 15th
Slade — 30

April

Saturday 11th
NEW 333 Barry Road — 1

Sunday 12th
NEW 333 Barry Road — 1

Saturday 18th
Horatio's Garden Cardiff — 21

May

Sunday 10th
NEW Upper Mill Gardens — 37

Saturday 16th
NEW 74 Castle Street — 5

Sunday 17th
16 Hendy Close — 18
NEW Y Celyn — 41

Sunday 24th
Old Froglands — 25

Monday 25th
Uplands — 35

Friday 29th
100 Pendwyallt Road — 28

Saturday 30th
Dinas Powys — 14
17 Maes y Draenog — 22
NEW Old Place — 26
100 Pendwyallt Road — 28

Sunday 31st
Dinas Powys — 14
17 Maes y Draenog — 22

June

Saturday 6th
Bronygarn House — 3
Hafod y Fro — 17

Sunday 7th
Creigiau Village Gardens — 10
Hafod y Fro — 17

Friday 12th
V21 Community Garden — 38

Saturday 13th
Boverton House — 2
Heol Laethog — 20
NEW Ty Hafan Children's Hospice Garden — 34

Sunday 14th
22 Dan-y-Coed Road — 13

Saturday 20th
Tal-Y-Fan Farm — 33
NEW 21 Willow Close — 39

Sunday 21st
Tal-Y-Fan Farm — 33
NEW 21 Willow Close — 39

Saturday 27th
NEW 333 Barry Road — 1
38 South Rise — 31

Sunday 28th
NEW 333 Barry Road — 1
Cefn Cribwr Garden Club — 6
NEW 35 Danybryn — 12
NEW Grove Road Gardens — 16
38 South Rise — 31
12 Uplands Crescent — 36

July

Saturday 4th
NEW 116 Colcot Road — 9
NEW 107 Cyncoed Road — 11
NEW Willow Cottage — 40

Sunday 5th
NEW 33 Cae Talcen — 4
12 Uplands Crescent — 36

Sunday 12th
112 Heol Heddwch — 19
Maes-y-Wertha Farm — 23

Saturday 18th
NEW Yew Tree Cottage — 42

Sunday 19th
Rose Cottage — 29
NEW Yew Tree Cottage — 42

Saturday 25th
16 Hendy Close — 18

Sunday 26th
Swn y Coed — 32

August

Saturday 1st
NEW 30 Palace Avenue 27

Sunday 9th
12 Uplands Crescent 36

Sunday 16th
4 Clyngwyn Road 7

Sunday 23rd
112 Heol Heddwch 19
12 Uplands Crescent 36

September

Sunday 6th
Coed Cae Farm 8

Saturday 19th
NEW Grangetown Kitchen Garden 15

February 2027

Sunday 14th
Slade 30

By Arrangement

Arrange a personalised garden visit with your club, or group of friends, on a date to suit you. See individual garden entries for full details.

Bronygarn House 3
NEW 74 Castle Street 5
Coed Cae Farm 8
16 Hendy Close 18
17 Maes y Draenog 22
Maes-y-Wertha Farm 23
Nant Melyn Farm 24
Rose Cottage 29
Swn y Coed 32
12 Uplands Crescent 36

Nant Melyn Farm

… 637

THE GARDENS

1 **333 BARRY ROAD**
Barry, CF62 8HG. Mrs Jo Tanner. *Central Barry, 4m from Cardiff. Garden on Barry Rd, close to The Cherry Orchard public house. Follow NGS signs. What3words app: snap.cute.closer.* **Sat 11 Apr (12-5); Sun 12 Apr (12-4); Sat 27 June (12-5); Sun 28 June (11-3). Adm £5, chd free. Tea, coffee & cake.**
A newly designed and planted cottage garden (2024-25). Follow a winding path that leads you past borders filled with spring bulbs, perennials, roses, shrubs and some small trees. A pond and bug hotels together with bee-friendly plants encourage wildlife to the garden. Flat with a variety of spaces to sit and enjoy the space. Beyond the arbour is a greenhouse and raised beds.
✿ ☕ 🔊

2 BOVERTON HOUSE
Boverton, Llantwit Major, CF61 1UH. Mr John Wainwright. *Boverton, at the E end of Llantwit Major. Garden entrance is approx 50 metres E of the Boverton Post Office. Please follow yellow NGS signs.* **Sat 13 June (10-4). Adm £4.50, chd free. Tea, coffee & cake.**
A walled garden next to the River Hoddnant, recently brought back to use. Formerly an orchard and kitchen garden, the garden has a unique character and has been designed to create a beautiful garden space and encourage wildlife, whilst retaining its unique historic character. Discover a range of mature and espalier fruit trees, a wildlife pond and secluded bird hide. There is a raised kerb to enter from the road which may require assistance. Thereafter level grass throughout.
♿ 🐕 ☕ 🔊

3 BRONYGARN HOUSE
Station Street, Maesteg, CF34 9AL. Dr Noel Thomas & Alina Ascari, 01656 737358, nthomas@doctors.org.uk. *Please follow NGS yellow signs to Station St and Bronygarn House, trees over pavement and garden wall, with further signs to house.*  **Sat 6 June (12-5.30). Adm £5, chd free. Tea, coffee & cake. Visits also by arrangement 15 Apr to 30 Aug for groups of up to 8.**
Enjoyed by six generations of same family over 160 years. Many interesting mature trees, young fruit trees, rhododendrons, ponds, numerous roses and standards, and much else of interest, even in the wilder areas. Lawn used for tennis in last century, now smaller and left unmown in parts, wildflowers encouraged. We live and let live, encourage all wildlife, try to garden organically.
✿ ☕

4 **33 CAE TALCEN**
Pencoed, Bridgend, CF35 6RP. Mrs Margaret Holcombe. *E of Bridgend. M4 J35, Bridgend Rd towards Pencoed, go through 2 sets of t-lights & then follow yellow NGS signs.* **Sun 5 July (11-4). Adm £4.50, chd free. Tea, coffee & cake.**
A very small town garden, showing how to make it seem larger, and more interesting, with different 'rooms', filled with a variety of cottage garden flowers, a minute lawn, several sitting areas to enjoy the sun at all hours of the day. There are roses: tea, rambling, climbing and clematis, hydrangeas, dierama, honeysuckles, buddliea, cosmos, to carry you through the seasons.

5 **74 CASTLE STREET**
Loughor, Swansea, SA4 6TS. Mr Maurizio Brotto, 07948 799890, morrisbrotto13@gmail.com. *M4 J48 to Llanelli & then to Loughor. Follow National Garden Scheme signs.* **Sat 16 May (11-5). Adm £7, chd free. Tea, coffee & cake. Visits also by arrangement 23 May to 6 June.**
A beautifully landscaped terraced garden creating a classical and elegant atmosphere. The garden is divided into two sections; the upper section, connected to the Grade II listed house, the oldest part of the garden. The second section is at a lower level; with several ornate statues, stone urns and planters, here, the garden was created from scratch. Stunning views over the River Loughor. An ancient chapel, a pond, and a hedge maze surround a Grade II listed house that was home to the Knights Templar and the Knights Hospitaller, two significant military orders from the Crusades, giving the current house its name.
🐕 🏠 🚗 ☕ 🔊

GROUP OPENING

6 CEFN CRIBWR GARDEN CLUB
Cefn Cribwr, Bridgend, CF32 0AP. www.cefncribwrgardeningclub.com. *5m W of Bridgend on B4281.* **Sun 28 June (11-5). Combined adm £6, chd free. Tea, coffee & cake in the village hall. WC facilities also available and will have stalls selling plants and crafts.**

13 BEDFORD ROAD
Mr John Loveluck.

2 BRYN TERRACE
Alan & Tracy Birch.

CEFN CRIBWR GARDEN CLUB ALLOTMENTS
Cefn Cribwr Garden Club.

77 CEFN ROAD
Peter & Veronica Davies & Mr Fai Lee.

15 GREEN MEADOW
Tom & Helen.

6 TAI THORN
Mr Kevin Burnell.

3 TY-ISAF ROAD
Ryland & Claire Downs.

Cefn Cribwr is an old mining village atop a ridge with views of Swansea to the west, Somerset to the south and home to Bedford Park and the Cefn Cribwr Iron Works. The village hall is at the centre with teas, cakes and plants for sale. The allotments are to be found behind the hall. Children, art and relaxation are just some of the themes to be found in the gardens besides the flower beds and vegetables. There are also water features, fish ponds, wildlife ponds, summerhouses and hens adding to the diverse mix in the village. Themed colour borders, roses, greenhouses, recycling, composting and much more. Visitors may travel between gardens on a covered trailer behind a tractor, courtesy of the Bridgend County Vintage Club.
✿ ☕ 🔊

Our donation to the Army Benevolent Fund supported 776 individuals with horticultural related grants in 2025.

7 4 CLYNGWYN ROAD
Ystalyfera, Swansea, SA9 2AE. Paul Steer, www.artinacorner.blogspot.com. *A4067 from Swansea or Brecon, stay on A4067 until r'about to Tesco & take 3rd exit. Turn R up Commercial St, then 2nd R to Alltygrug Rd. Follow yellow signs to Clyngwyn Rd.* **Sun 16 Aug (11-3.30). Adm £4, chd free. Tea, coffee & cake.**
The Coal Tip Garden is a small personal space created to help us relax. Its main character is enclosure. It is not a flowery garden but is formed out of shrubs and trees- a tapestry with niches being cut in order to place sculpture and to produce a visual rhythm. A key philosophy is using native perennials and repetitive planting leading the eye through the space to the studio.

8 COED CAE FARM
Llanharan, Pontyclun, CF72 9NH. The Liley Family, 07967 580099, jeremy@farmtrack.wales. *M4 J34 or J35 on the A473. Turn off A473 at gates/stone pillars of Llanharan Manor House, approx. ½ m E of village of Llanharan. Farm track has passing places. What3words app: reputable.casino.shorthand.* **Sun 6 Sept (11-5). Adm £6, chd free. Home-made teas. Visits also by arrangement 15 May to 15 Sept for groups of up to 20.**
While it's the garden you come to view, your first instinct will be to stop and admire the panoramic views over the countryside. The gardens are laid out for all seasons, bulbs and herbaceous in shrub borders. Water features with cascades down to a pond, surrounded by mixed borders and trees, offering shade. A native woodland, with paths and pond offer a relaxation area. Accessible parking in yard.

9 NEW 116 COLCOT ROAD
Barry, CF62 8UH. Mrs Wendy Jones. *Directly opp Barry Hospital & Memorial Park. Please follow yellow National Garden Scheme signs.* **Sat 4 July (12-4). Adm £4, chd free. Home-made teas.**
A much loved and mature garden, that has been created over a 20 year period. You will take a meandering walk through several rooms, encouraging you to stop and enjoy the journey to the newly landscaped rear seating area.

The garden has a cottage feel, with mature shrubs and acers, encouraging wildlife, together with a small pond. Access to the top terrace only, with a partial view to the garden.

GROUP OPENING

10 CREIGIAU VILLAGE GARDENS
Maes Y Nant, Creigiau, CF15 9EJ. *W of Cardiff (J34 M4). From M4 J34 follow A4119 to T-lights, turn R by Castell Mynach Pub, pass through Groes Faen & turn L to Creigiau. Follow NGS signs.* **Sun 7 June (11-5). Combined adm £8, chd free. Tea, coffee & cake at 28 Maes y Nant.**

28 MAES Y NANT
Mike & Lesley Sherwood.

WAUNWYLLT
John Hughes & Richard Shaw.

Enjoy a warm welcome at Creigiau Village Gardens- two vibrant and innovative gardens. Each quite different, they combine some of the best characteristics of design and planting for modern town gardens as well as cottage gardens. Each has its own forte: Waunwyllt's ½ acre is divided into garden rooms and 28 Maes y Nant is where cottage garden planting reigns. Regret, cash only at gardens.

11 NEW 107 CYNCOED ROAD
Cardiff, CF23 6AD. Barney & Kamila Hawthorne. *Opp the entrance to Cardiff Met University on Cyncoed Rd. Come off the A48 at the Llanedeyrn turnoff, 1st exit off the r'about onto Llanedeyrn Rd. R at the top onto Cyncoed Rd. Garden is on the L, 3 houses after Cefn Coed Rd.* **Sat 4 July (11-5). Adm £5, chd free. Tea, coffee & cake.**
A spacious garden, with spring interest at the front camellias, azaleas and hellebores. The back garden is approached through a Japanese walkway, leading to a series of landscaped borders, inc herbaceous perennials, acers, a roped rose colonnade, and pond planting. A round bed containing a showstopper weeping pear with a heuchera clock. Overlooked by a sun terrace showcasing begonias.

12 NEW 35 DANYBRYN
Brynsadler, Pontyclun, CF72 9DH. Mrs Susan Jones. *E of Pencoed. S of Pontyclun. From Pontyclun on A4222: pass The Ivor Arms & take next R towards Llanharry, then 2nd R to Danybryn. NGS signs posted.* **Sun 28 June (10-4). Adm £5, chd free. Tea, coffee & cake.**
This garden is a labour of love. Through the years it has steadily evolved into a peaceful haven with seating and shaded areas. A stream runs through the garden past the summerhouse. The shaded areas of the garden have a variety of ferns and hostas, the remainder of the garden has an array of acers, herbaceous border, and and the garden is crowned by a large oak tree.

13 22 DAN-Y-COED ROAD
Cyncoed, Cardiff, CF23 6NA. Alan & Miranda Workman. *Dan y Coed Rd leads off Cyncoed Rd at the top & Rhydypenau Rd at the bottom. No 22 is at the bottom of Dan y Coed Rd. There is street parking & level access to the R of the property.* **Sun 14 June (11-5). Adm £5, chd free. Tea, coffee & cake.**
A medium sized, much loved garden. Owners share a passion for plants and structure, each year the lawn gets smaller to allow for the acquisition of new features. Hostas, ferns, acers and other trees form the central woodland theme as a backdrop is provided by the Nant Fawr woods. Year-round interest has been created for the owner's and visitor's greater pleasure. There is a wildlife pond, many climbing plants and a greenhouse with cacti, succulents and pelargoniums. There is wheelchair access to the garden patio area only.

GROUP OPENING

14 DINAS POWYS
Dinas Powys, CF64 4TS. *Approx 6m SW of Cardiff. Exit M4 J33, follow A4232 to Leckwith, onto B4267 & follow to Merry Harrier t-lights. Turn R & enter Dinas Powys. Follow yellow NGS signs.* **Sat 30, Sun 31 May (11-5). Combined adm £7, chd free. Tea, coffee & cake at Westcliffe. Prosecco & non-alcoholic cordial at 23 Cardiff Road. Donation to Dinas Powys Voluntary Concern.**

GLAMORGAN 639

21 CARDIFF ROAD
Rob & Pam Creed.

23 CARDIFF ROAD
Eoghan Conway & David Manfield.

NEW 1 ORCHARD CRESCENT
Mrs Shirley Willis.

THE POUND
Helen Parsons.

NEW 5 WELLWOOD DRIVE
Mr John Williams.

WEST CLIFF
Alan & Jackie Blakoe.

The six gardens in this friendly village demonstrate how different and personal a garden can be and will provide inspiration for visitors. From formal layouts to naturalistic planting, beautiful flowers to bold foliage, the gardens also inc ponds, chickens, specimen trees, terracing and raised beds for edibles. There are plenty of opportunities to sit and enjoy the gardens and to chat with their owners. Good wheelchair access to most gardens.

15 NEW GRANGETOWN KITCHEN GARDEN
Avondale Road, Cardiff, CF11 7DT. Grangetown Kitchen Garden, gkgcardiff.co.uk. *Behind Grangetown Nursery Sch. Exit A4243/Grangetown link road at junc with A4055 & follow IKEA signage. At IKEA r'about proceed along Ferry Rd, turning down Jim Driscoll Way. Garden is on R. What3words app: coach.nature.highs.* **Sat 19 Sept (11-5). Adm £5, chd free. Tea, coffee & cake.**
Thriving in the mild climate of Cardiff's bay area, the garden encompasses an orchard, raised as well as no-dig beds, a polytunnel and wildlife areas. Embedded in the local multicultural community, a wide array of vegetables and fruits grow. Expect pumpkins, hardy kiwi, lemongrass, tulsi, banana plants and sunflowers, amongst many others. The garden promotes wellbeing and sustainable living. The site is level with paved paths. Grassy paths between beds and within the polytunnel, which can be muddy.

In 2025, our donations to Carers Trust helped them support over 1 million unpaid carers across the UK, as part of their network of local carer centres.

74 Castle Street

Hafod y Fro

GLAMORGAN 641

GROUP OPENING

16 NEW **GROVE ROAD GARDENS**
Bridgend, CF31 3EF. *20m W of Cardiff & E of Swansea, M4 J35 from Cardiff & J37 from Swansea. Follow signs for Bridgend turn into B4265 Ewenny Rd & then Grove Rd. Gardens along both sides, payment at no 90 Grove Rd. What3words app: cards.gets.tinsel.* **Sun 28 June (11-4). Combined adm £6, chd free. Tea, coffee & cake.**

NEW **17 GROVE ROAD**
Ian & June Price.

NEW **39 GROVE ROAD**
Chris & Jane Hawkins.

NEW **60 GROVE ROAD**
Ms Christine Taylor.

NEW **88 GROVE ROAD**
Mrs Liz Maddocks.

90 GROVE ROAD
Claudia Scicluna & John Doran.

An interesting and varied group of town gardens on the south side of Bridgend each with its own distinctive character. Highlights inc walled gardens, lush herbaceous planting with cottage garden favourites, various species of magnolia, a succulent theatre, a garden devoted to growing flowers suitable for drying, wildlife ponds alive with birds dragon flies and newts, and hidden gardens.

✽ ☕

17 **HAFOD Y FRO**
Sigingstone, Cowbridge, CF71 7LP. Rhodri & Kathy Williams. *Garden ½ m N of the village. W on A48 past Cowbridge. L at Pentre Meyrick on B4268 (sign Sigingstone Llysworney/Llantwit Major). 1m after Llysworney turn L (Sigingstone/Victoria Inn). What3words app: runners.gratitude.wages.* **Sat 6, Sun 7 June (1.30-5). Adm £7, chd free. Tea, coffee & cake.**

For 30+ years, our 1½ acre garden has evolved from a farmyard and open fields. Sunny courtyard with wildlife pond, pergola and climbers. Enclosed cottage garden of geometric curves, architectural trees and shrubs, acers, roses and herbaceous borders giving contrasting vistas. Raised terrace with summerhouse and waterfall. Productive kitchen garden with orchard leading to open area and woodland.

☕ 🔊

18 **16 HENDY CLOSE**
Derwen Fawr, Swansea, SA2 8BB. Peter & Wendy Robinson, 07773 711973, robinsonpetel@hotmail.co.uk. *Approx 3m W of Swansea. A4067 Mumbles Rd follow sign for Singleton Hosp. Then R onto Sketty Ln at mini r'about. Turn L then 2nd R onto Saunders Way. Follow yellow NGS signs. Please park on Saunders Way if possible.* **Sun 17 May, Sat 25 July (2-5). Adm £6, chd free.** Visits also by arrangement 17 May to 13 Sept for groups of 10 to 20.
Originally the garden was covered with 40ft conifers. Cottage style, some unusual and mainly perennial plants which provide colour in spring, summer and autumn. The garden is an example of how to plan for all seasons. Visitors say it is like a secret garden because there are a number of hidden places. Plants to encourage all types of wildlife in to the garden.

☕

19 **112 HEOL HEDDWCH**
Seven Sisters, Neath, SA10 9AE. Sharon Preddy. *Approx 10m from Neath. From A465 take slip road to Blaendulais. 3rd exit on r'about to A4109. Follow yellow signs. From A4067 go R onto A4421, 2nd turn R after 2m. Turn R onto A4109. What3words app: explain.relishes.pound.* **Sun 12 July, Sun 23 Aug (11-4.30). Adm £4.50, chd free. Tea, coffee & cake.**
On the outskirts of Bannau Brycheiniog (Brecon Beacons). From the unassuming façade you enter into a secluded small front garden with a distinctive Balinese style. Densely planted with mature trees, palms and a vast array of lush plants, it hosts a plethora of Balinese features alongside a tropical hut and pond. This garden has been lovingly created using upcycled items and jungle style planting.

☕

GROUP OPENING

20 **HEOL LAETHOG**
Bryncethin, Bridgend, CF32 9JE. Ms Sue Deary. *Follow the common road from Bryncethin for approx 2m & approx 1m from Heol Y Cyw. What3words app: straying.* **scavenger.trial. Sat 13 June (11-5). Combined adm £5, chd free. Home-made cakes & savouries.**

NEW **2 RAILWAY TERRACE**
Mrs Carey Mills.

NEW **3 RAILWAY TERRACE**
Ross & Kelly Davies.

8 RAILWAY TERRACE
Jason & Tammy Cheung.

9 RAILWAY TERRACE
Ms Sue Deary.

10 RAILWAY TERRACE
William & Megan Gwilliam.

A row of former miners cottages on the common between Bryncethin and Heol Y Cyw, known as Heol Laethog or Tyn'Waun locally. All have uninterrupted views of the common with a large green in front with a park at the end. Five gardens opening, all typical cottage gardens with vegetables, fruit and flowers. Front south facing gardens and rear gardens accessed by a small lane at the back.

✽ ☕ 🔊

21 **HORATIO'S GARDEN CARDIFF**
University Hospital Llandough, Penlan Road, Llandough, CF64 2XX. Owen Griffiths, www.horatiosgarden.org.uk/the-gardens/horatios-garden-wales. *Turn into the University Hospital Llandough & keep going straight. The garden is raised, situated beside the spinal ward. What3words app: cubs.solved.stale.* **Sat 18 Apr (11-4). Adm £7, chd free. Pre-booking essential, please visit www.ngs.org.uk for information & booking. Light refreshments.**
Sarah Price's design was inspired by the Welsh landscape. The planting is naturalistic and gentle featuring valerian, poppies, field maple, and crab apples. The garden is adorned with climbers such as clematis, grapes, and roses. Circular openings within the perimeter fence frame the countryside and sea in the distance. It provides beneficiaries with a beautiful place to spend time in year-round. Fully wheelchair accessible.

♿ ✽ ☕ 🔊

22 17 MAES Y DRAENOG
Tongwynlais, Cardiff, CF15 7JL. Mr Derek Price, 07717 462295, derekprice7@btinternet.com. *From M4 J32, take A4054 into village. Turn R at Lewis Arms pub, up Mill Rd & take 2nd R into Catherine Dr. Parking in signed area (no parking in Maes y Draenog). Follow signs to garden.* **Sat 30, Sun 31 May (12-5). Adm £5, chd free. Tea, coffee & cake. Visits also by arrangement 1 June to 5 June for groups of 6 to 16.**
A hidden garden, in the shadow of Castell Coch, fed by a mountain stream, with a wooden footbridge to a naturalised, woodland area. There are wonderful late spring flower displays set against a woodland backdrop. Developed over many years with a wide variety of lavender beds and herbaceous borders, summerhouse, seating areas, greenhouse and vegetable area. A good variety of plants in different borders around house. Rear of house is set against woodland and fields, while front areas have mature roses and herbaceous plants, borders.

23 MAES-Y-WERTHA FARM
Bryncethin, CF32 9YJ. Stella & Tony Leyshon, 01656 721016, anthony.leyshon@icloud.com. *3m N Bridgend. Follow sign for Bryncethin, turn R at Masons Arms. Follow sign for Heol-y-Cyw, garden about 1m outside Bryncethin on R.* **Sun 12 July (11-7). Adm £7, chd free. Home-made teas. Visits also by arrangement Apr to Sept for groups of 5 to 50. Good parking available.**
A three acre hidden gem outside Bridgend. Entering the garden you find a small Japanese garden fed by a stream, this leads you to informal mixed beds and enclosed herbaceous borders. Ponds and rill are fed by a natural spring. A meadow with large lawns under new planting gives wonderful vistas over surrounding countryside new summerhouse with open views over the garden. Mural in the summerhouse by contemporary artist Daniel Llewelyn Hall. His work is represented in the Royal Collection and House of Lords. Fresh handmade sandwiches available and live music all afternoon.

24 NANT MELYN FARM
Seven Sisters, Neath, SA10 9BW. Mr Craig Pearce, cgpearce@hotmail.co.uk. *From M4 J43 take A465 towards Neath. Exit for Seven Sisters at r'about take 3rd exit, 6m for Seven Sisters you come to Pantyffordd sign, turn L under low bridge.* **Visits by arrangement 1 June to 30 Aug. Adm £6, chd free. Home-made teas.**
A spacious and interesting garden with many features which inc a stunning natural waterfall, a meandering woodland stream which is covered by a canopy of entwined trees, a picturesque Japanese garden and beautiful lawned areas with winding pathways.

25 OLD FROGLANDS
Llanmaes, Llantwit Major, CF61 2XY. Dorne & David Harris. *5m S of Cowbridge. Going E on B4265 turn L at t-lights into Eglwys Brewis Rd. Take 1st L. Old Froglands is 1st house on the R. Postcode takes you to village not house. What3words app: meaning.danger. barstool.* **Sun 24 May (1-5). Adm £5, chd free. Tea, coffee & cake.**
One acre farmhouse cottage garden with woodland and stream. 'Rooms' are linked by bridges and patios. Ponds and natural water features provide a playground for chickens to roam freely. Wetland areas provide a habitat for primula candelabras, ferns and hostas. Kitchen garden now productive. Wellies required if wet. Wheelchair access difficult on a wet day.

26 NEW OLD PLACE
Castle Street, Llantwit Major, CF61 1AP. Nick & Rebecca Lloyd James. *Ent near the junc of Castle St, Turkey St & Old West Rd in the old town. Parking is available a 5min walk away in public car parks at the Town Hall & near the stn.* **Sat 30 May (11-5). Adm £5, chd free. Tea, coffee & cake in the courtyard (which is wheelchair accessible). Picnicking is possible in the fields.**
Mature garden behind a 500 year old cottage. Distinct areas are separated by old walls and steps. At entrance level is a courtyard with climbers, pots and seating, leading to a circular lawn surrounded by mixed herbaceous borders. Steps lead up to an old apple tree with shrubs and cottage herbaceous planting. Beyond is a formal pond, with further borders leading to fields with trees and space.

27 NEW 30 PALACE AVENUE
Cardiff, CF5 2DW. Mrs Louise Thomas. *Last turn on R as you come down Cardiff Rd towards cathedral sch or 1st L turn as you come up Cardiff Rd pass cathedral sch.* **Sat 1 Aug (10-6). Adm £5, chd free. Light refreshments.**
Explore this tropical themed garden with a small courtyard. There are an eclectic variety of plants, trees and shrubs to discover.

28 100 PENDWYALLT ROAD
Whitchurch, Cardiff, CF14 7EH. *Near M4 J32. Cul-de-sac on opp side of road to Village Hotel. Take narrow road (opp side of road to Whitworth Sq.) Go uphill past blocks of flats (Odet Court and Greenmeadow Court).* **Fri 29, Sat 30 May (12-5). Adm £5, chd free.**
Intensive planting creates privacy with informal paths meandering through towering trees, *Eucryphia*, Japanese maples, shrubs, tree ferns, tree heathers and bamboos. A long pergola with clematis, wisteria, roses. Large ponds, one of which has windows to view large koi carp. Explore three areas, two in front and one behind the bungalow.

29 ROSE COTTAGE
32 Blackmill Road, Bryncethin, Bridgend, CF32 9YN. Maria & Anne Lalic, scarecrowcottagewales@gmail.com, www.instagram.com/scarecrowcottagewales. *1m N of M4 J36 on A4061. Follow A4061 to Bryncethin. Straight on at mini r'about for approx 400 metres. Just past used car garage, turn R & park on grass. Please do not block the track as farmer requires access.* **Sun 19 July (12-5). Adm £4, chd free. Tea, coffee & cake. Visits also by arrangement 31 May to 16 Aug for groups of up to 6.**
Rose Cottage is an old fashioned Welsh cottage garden with jumbled flower beds, a herb yard and lots of fruit and vegetables. We borrow ideas from permaculture, no-dig and companion planting but in many ways- apart from a lovely big polytunnel which allows year-round growing. The garden at Rose Cottage is the same now as it has always

Yew Tree Cottage

been: simple, sustainable, pretty and productive. Our pop-up tearoom sells tea, coffee and home-made cakes (inc vegan options). Main path and gateways suitable for wheelchairs. Some paths are loose stone or narrow and bark chipped. These are uneven and care should be taken.

30 SLADE
Southerndown, CF32 0RP. **Rosamund & Peter Davies,** rosamund.davies@ngs.org.uk, www.instagram.com/ sladewoodgarden. *5m S of Bridgend. M4 J35 Follow A473 to Bridgend. Take B4265 to St. Brides Major. Turn R in St. Brides Major for Southerndown, then follow yellow NGS signs.* **Sun 15 Feb (12-4). Adm £7, chd free. Home-made teas. 2027: Sun 14 Feb.**
Hidden away, Slade garden is an unexpected jewel to discover next to the sea with views overlooking the Bristol Channel. The garden tumbles down a valley protected by a belt of woodland. From terraced lawns great sweeps of grass stretch down the hill enlivened by snowdrops, hellebores and cyclamen. In front of the house are delightful formal areas a rose and clematis pergola and herbaceous borders. Partial wheelchair access.

31 38 SOUTH RISE
South Rise, Llanishen, Cardiff, CF14 0RH. **Dr Khalida Hasan.** *N of Cardiff. From Llanishen Village take Station Rd past train stn & go down The Rise to South Rise. Or from Lisvane Rd to South Rise directly. Following yellow signs.* **Sat 27, Sun 28 June (10-5). Adm £5, chd free. Tea, coffee & cake. South Asian savouries (e.g. samosa, chick pea chaat) available.**
An inner city garden backing on to Llanishen Reservoir gradually establishing with something of interest and colour all year-round. Herbaceous borders, vegetables and fruit plants surround central lawn. Wildlife friendly; variety of climbers and exotics. In front shrubs and herbaceous borders to a lawn. Stepping stones leading to children's play area and vegetable plot also at the back. Wheelchair access to rear from the side of the house.

32 SWN Y COED
Tyla Garw, Pontyclun, CF72 9HD. **Mair & Owen Hopkin,** 07434 096410, mair.hopkin@icloud.com. *From M4 J34: Onto A4119, r'about 1st exit to A473. Thru t-lights, L at r'about, at nxt r'about 2nd L follow yellow signs. From J35: Take A473 thru Llanharan, follow signs from r'about, 4th exit.* **Sun 26 July (11-4). Adm £6, chd free. Tea, coffee & cake inc gluten & dairy free options. Visits also by arrangement 1 July to 2 Aug.**
This family friendly garden started from a blank canvas nine years ago, initially laid to lawn. Raised vegetable beds were installed and a 75m natural hedge planted along the side boundary to encourage wildlife. This was supplemented with fruit trees, flower and herb borders to attract insects. The lawn provides a clearing to the surrounding forestry attracting a variety of birds. Large greenhouse. Disabled parking on drive. Ramped access to rear patio and WC. Path adjacent to herb border and lawn access in dry weather.

33 TAL-Y-FAN FARM
Blackmill, Bridgend, CF35 6UD. Suzanne, 07721 385633, skchurchill100@hotmail.co.uk. *Between Llangeinor & Blackmill. Accessed via A4093. Take turn opp hanging sign for the Llangeinor Arms & follow the yellow signs. Access is along a private gravel road crossing the common.* **Sat 20, Sun 21 June (10.30-5). Adm £6, chd free. Home-made teas.**
Elevated country garden with stunning 360 degree views over the Bristol Channel to the Devon coastline; situated in an isolated location. David Austin roses are the main attraction in the garden it has a parterre and rose arch, surrounded by 180 year old beech trees. Currently under development Japanese pond and bridge. There is a large seating area with glass balustrade to enjoy the views. We have pigs, alpaca, chickens, geese and turkeys. There is a small campsite and glamping in the adjacent paddock. Access onto terrace area with views over the garden and far reaching coastal views.

34 NEW TY HAFAN CHILDREN'S HOSPICE GARDEN
Hayes Road, Sully, Penarth, CF64 5XX. Ty Hafan Children's Hospice, www.tyhafan.org. *Travelling on Hayes Rd from Sully Village the entrance to Ty Hafan is on the L, just after the 20mph sign. Follow yellow signs.* **Sat 13 June (10-5). Adm £5, chd free. Pre-booking essential, please visit www.ngs.org.uk for information & booking. Tea, coffee & cake.**
A wonderful and accessible garden with stunning sea views. The large grounds welcome everyone and inc space for joy, reflection, therapy and fun for the families that use the hospice. Visitors will be delighted with the sensory garden, the woodland walk, trees and play areas. The planting is beautiful, inc roses, peonies, shrubs and fruit trees. Wildlife is encouraged everywhere.

35 UPLANDS
Gwern-y-Steeple, Peterston Super Ely, CF5 6LG. David Richmond. *12m W of Cardiff. From A48 between St Nicholas & Bonvilston, take the Peterston Super Ely turn & follow yellow arrow. Park at small green near Gwern-y-Steeple sign.* **Mon 25 May (12-5). Adm £4.50, chd free. Tea, coffee & cake.**
Uplands has an informal and multi-textured look within a cottage garden design. The front garden has flower, vegetables and fruit beds. The back was planted in 2019 and was once all grass. There are four main herbaceous borders, fruit trees, ornamental grasses, ferns, shrubs and roses, with many places to relax and enjoy the garden. Medium sized greenhouse and several sculptures located around the garden.

36  12 UPLANDS CRESCENT
Llandough, Penarth, CF64 2PR. Mr Dean Mears, 07910 638682, dean.mears@ntlworld.com. *Close to Llandough Hospital. Head for Llandough Hospital & at either of 2 junc turn E into the estate. Follow NGS signs & look for tall banana plants & weeping birch visible in the front garden.* **Sun 28 June, Sun 5 July, Sun 9, Sun 23 Aug (2-4). Adm £5, chd free. Visits also by arrangement 1 May to 27 Sept for groups of up to 12.**
An exotic small garden full of unusual and large plants and a pond. Banana plants, tree ferns, gunnera, *Tetrapanax* and a foxglove tree surround the garden. Ferns, *Phormium, Brunnera, Brugmansia, Cordyline* and giant reed add interest to the garden. An area of potted tropical plants, *Canna, Alocasia, Colocasia, Strelitzia* and palms add to the significant variety of exotic plants.

GROUP OPENING

37 NEW UPPER MILL GARDENS
Upper Mill, Pontarddulais, Swansea, SA4 8ND. Ms Jacqui Fowler. *8m NW of Swansea. At M4 J47 follow A48 for 3½ m towards Pontarddulais. R at t-lights (Co-op on L) onto Alltiago Rd. R onto Glynhir Rd. Ample parking on Glynhir Rd, with short walk to Upper Mill.* **Sun 10 May (11-4). Combined adm £6, chd free. Tea, coffee & cake.**

NEW CARTREF
John & Carol Voysey.

NEW LONGSIGHT
David & Manu Oromith.

NEW TY'R NANT
Idwal & Margaret Thomas.

NEW 1 UPPER MILL
Mrs Sue Rees.

NEW 2 UPPER MILL
Ms Tina Walker.

NEW 3 UPPER MILL
Jacqui Fowler & Phillipa Farrell.

Six nature loving neighbours welcome you into their individually unique gardens in the leafy, semi-rural, unadopted lane that is Upper Mill. The Dulais flows alongside the woodland edge bringing diversity of wildlife and a temperate climate to the historic neighbourhood once busy with woollen mills and blacksmiths. Today the sounds of the river and birdsong complement our colourful spaces. Wheelchair access is available within two gardens only, but with a small step or two to maneuver, inc the garden with refreshments.

38 V21 COMMUNITY GARDEN
Sbectrwm, Bwlch Road, Cardiff, CF5 3EF. Mr R Bailey, www.V21.org.uk. *3m W of central Cardiff. From the A48 turn R onto St Fagans Rd. Cont onto Norbury Rd leading to Finchley Rd & Bwlch Rd.* **Fri 12 June (10-4). Adm £5, chd free. Tea, coffee & cake at the on site café.**
The V21 Community Garden is developed and maintained by people with learning disabilities. The garden is designed to be an accessible learning environment. The garden has a newly developed herbaceous flower border, a spring garden, a wildlife pond, bog garden and areas for growing fruit and vegetables. There is also a large polytunnel and glasshouse to extend the growing season. Wheelchairs access via main paths.

39 NEW 21 WILLOW CLOSE
Penarth, CF64 3NG. Ms Viv Mumby. *2m off the B4267 (Redlands Rd) on way to Cosmeston Country Park. Follow yellow signs. Garden is at the end of the cul-de-sac & parking may be difficult. Recommend parking in surrounding roads approaching Willow Cl.* **Sat 20, Sun 21 June (11-5). Adm £4.50, chd free. Tea, coffee & cake.**
A surprise awaits behind this ordinary semi-detached house- a south west

facing garden with a wide variety of perennials and climbers in purples, creams and pinks and a rose and honeysuckle arch leading to a small meditation area with shade loving plants. Several seating areas to admire the garden at different times of the day. An unexpected gem. Side access wide enough for a wheelchair and small ramp provided into garden.

40 NEW WILLOW COTTAGE
Treoes, Bridgend, CF35 5DL. **Colin & Christine Anstee.** *S of M4, between Bridgend & Cowbridge. M4 J35, exit for Bridgend. L at next 3 r'abouts, arriving into Treoes. The Star Inn will be on R, head towards the car park behind. We are directly ahead.* **Sat 4 July (10.30-4.30). Adm £6, chd free. Tea, coffee & cake.**
One acre secluded garden, located in the Vale of Glamorgan. Designed and built by the owners who are landscape professionals. Nestled behind an award winning thatched village pub and high stone wall, all plants have been chosen to give year-round colour either with flowers or folia, and planted to attract the insects and butterflies. Disabled parking and wheelchair accessible. Mainly flat with one set of steps to the lawn. Lawn can be accessed by alternative route.

41 NEW Y CELYN
Heol Y Maes, Coelbren, Neath, SA10 9PT. **Mrs Claire Gorton.** *4m from Ystradgynlais. 6m from Glyneath. Signposted Coelbren from A4221. W end of village. Y-Celyn is situated at bottom of Llyncelyn Terrace, on Heol Y Maes. Parking at top on Cefnbyrle Rd. What3words app: fame.fail.nooks.* **Sun 17 May (1-5). Adm £4, chd free. Tea, coffee & cake.**
The front garden is lawn surrounded by an herbaceous border. The rear garden has panoramic views of the Brecon Beacons. A cottage garden with wildlife pond, climbing plants, small greenhouse and raised vegetable bed. Steps lead down to a Potager style garden where fruit vegetables herbs and flowers intermingle. The gardens are enhanced by several home-made wildlife sculptures.

42 NEW YEW TREE COTTAGE
Hendre Road, Pencoed, Bridgend, CF35 6PU. **Mrs Abbey Figg.** *1m w of Pencoed. From M4 J35 head to Pencoed Town Centre. At monument cross over railway, follow Hendre Rd to lane. House is 2nd on R before the bridge crossing over M4. What3words app: herb.rejoiced. youthful.* **Sat 18, Sun 19 July (10-4). Adm £6, chd free. Tea, coffee & cake.**
The main garden has been designed with colourful herbaceous borders, unusual shrubs and climbing plants. There is a large pond with bog and marginal planting. Winding gravel paths direct you to a hidden seated area. Decking areas are full of colourful salvias, dahlias and other tender perennials. A separate additional garden has winding grass paths through mixed herbaceous and shrub planting.

Old Place

GWENT

VOLUNTEERS

County Organiser
Debbie Field
01873 832752 / 07885 195304
wenalltisaf@gmail.com

County Treasurer
David Warren
01873 880031
david.warren@ngs.org.uk

Publicity
Penny Reeves
01873 880355
penny.reeves@ngs.org.uk

Social Media
Mike & Tina Booth
07921 128169
christinabooth@me.com

Roger Lloyd
01873 880030
droger.lloyd@btinternet.com

Booklet Co-Ordinator
Veronica Ruth
07967 157806 / 01873 859757
veronica.ruth@ngs.org.uk

Assistant County Organiser
Suzanne George
01443 837708
philandsuzannegeorge@gmail.com

Tim Haynes
07738 236899
tim.haynes@hotmail.co.uk

Jenny Lloyd
01873 880030 / 07850 949209
jenny.lloyd@ngs.org.uk

Veronica Ruth
(as above)

@gwentngs
@GwentNGS
@gwentngs

OPENING DATES

All entries subject to change.
For latest information check
www.ngs.org.uk
Map locator numbers are shown to the right of each garden name.

March

Sunday 29th
Llanover 14

April

Saturday 18th
Longhouse Farm 16
Sunday 19th
Longhouse Farm 16
Saturday 25th
Park House 22
Sunday 26th
High Glanau Manor 10

May

Sunday 3rd
NEW The Pant 21
Monday 4th
NEW The Pant 21
Saturday 9th
Glebe House 7
Sunday 10th
Glebe House 7
Sunday 17th
Monmouth Gardens 18
Saturday 23rd
Hillcrest 12
Sunday 24th
Baileau 2
Hillcrest 12
Monday 25th
Hillcrest 12

June

Thursday 4th
◆ Wyndcliffe Court 29
Saturday 6th
Long Owl Barn 15

Sunday 7th
Rockfield Park 23
Sunday 14th
Highfield Farm 11
Sunday 21st
The Caerphilly Miners Community
   Centre - Climate Change Garden 5
Mione 17
Saturday 27th
Usk Open Gardens 26
Sunday 28th
The Growing Space Garden 8
Usk Open Gardens 26

July

Sunday 5th
Hillcrest 12
Mione 17
Sunday 12th
Birch Tree Well 3
Highfield Farm 11
Saturday 18th
14 Gwerthonor Lane 9
Sunday 19th
14 Gwerthonor Lane 9
Woodbine House 28
Saturday 25th
Ty Isaf Farm 25
Sunday 26th
Ty Isaf Farm 25

August

Sunday 2nd
Hillcrest 12
Sunday 9th
Highfield Farm 11
Sunday 16th
Neuadd Stone Barn 19
Sunday 23rd
April House 1
Sunday 30th
Wenallt Isaf 27

September

Saturday 5th
Little Caerlicyn 13
Sunday 6th
Little Caerlicyn 13
Sunday 13th
Highfield Farm 11

By Arrangement

Arrange a personalised garden visit with your club, or group of friends, on a date to suit you. See individual garden entries for full details.

Birch Tree Well	3
Bryngwyn Manor	4
NEW Dan-y-Warren	6
Glebe House	7
Highfield Farm	11
Hillcrest	12
Little Caerlicyn	13
Llanover	14
Long Owl Barn	15
NEW New Inn Farm	20
Rockfield Park	23
Trostrey Lodge	24
Wenallt Isaf	27

The National Garden Scheme donated £3,875,596 to our nursing and health beneficiaries from money raised at gardens open in 2025.

New Inn Farm

THE GARDENS

1 APRIL HOUSE
Llanbadoc, Usk, NP15 1PT. **Charlotte Fleming.** *2m W of Usk. From Usk bridge go S towards Caerleon. Take 1st R towards Coed y Paen & go uphill for 1.9m. Garden is on L. SatNav gets you here. What3words app: enormous.eliminate.civic.* **Sun 23 Aug (11-5). Adm £7, chd free. Home-made teas.**
One acre site with glorious views over the Usk Valley and Wentwood Forest. Garden developed over past 20 years from bramble thicket and dairy pasture. Large herbaceous border, bog and shrub borders, wildlife pond. Fruit and vegetables. Regret, no WC facilities

2 BAILEAU
Llantilio Crossenny, Abergavenny, NP7 8TA. **Sue Wilson & Seb Gwyther.** *Between Llantilio Crossenny & Treadam. Please follow the yellow NGS signs. What3words app: dislikes.piglet.views.* **Sun 24 May (11-4). Adm £6, chd free. Tea, coffee & cake. Light lunches also available.**
A mature cottage style garden around an ancient farmhouse (not open). Packed with fruit and vegetables, the garden inc a rose walk, a crab apple walk, herbaceous borders, a circular ornamental vegetable garden and an old orchard. Activities for children and dogs welcome. Plenty of spots for a picnic. Views to Blorenge and Sugarloaf Mountains. Baked goods, light lunches, drinks and treats for sale, making creative use of abundant produce from the garden.
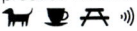

3 BIRCH TREE WELL
Upper Ferry Road, Penallt, Monmouth, NP25 4AN. **Jill Bourchier,** 01600 775327, gillian.bourchier@btinternet.com. *4m SW of Monmouth. From Monmouth on B4293, turn L (Penallt/Trelleck). After 2m turn L to Penallt. In village turn L at Xrds & follow yellow signs. Lanes are single track & steep. What3words app: alerting.dramatic.blues.* **Sun 12 July (2-5). Adm £5, chd free. Home-made teas.** Visits also by arrangement May to Sept for groups of 5 to 25.

Situated in the heart of the Lower Wye Valley, amongst the ancient habitat of woodland, rocks and streams. The garden features bluebells, specialist hydrangeas as well as unusual plants and trees attracting butterflies, bees and insects. The rock and woodland area has narrow, cumbersome paths with fallen trees attracting wildlife, for nimble footed only.

4 BRYNGWYN MANOR
Bryngwyn, Raglan, NP15 2JH. **Peter & Louise Maunder,** 07860 922324, louiseviola@live.co.uk. *2m W of Raglan. SatNav unreliable. Take B4598 (old Abergavenny- Raglan Rd signed Clytha). Turn S between the 2 garden centres. House ¼m up lane on L. What3words app: fond.haggle.like.* Visits by arrangement 1 Jan to 10 July for groups of 15+. **Adm £12.50, chd free. Cream teas. All refreshments are home-made.**
A relaxed three acre garden featuring snowdrops, daffodil walk, mature trees, walled parterre garden, mixed borders, lawns, ponds and shrubbery. Family friendly afternoon out, with children's activities, loads of space to run about, and scrumptious teas. Ground is uneven and mainly grass paths. Most areas are accessible without needing to use steps. Please contact owner with any concerns or questions.

5 THE CAERPHILLY MINERS COMMUNITY CENTRE - CLIMATE CHANGE GARDEN
Watford Road, Caerphilly, CF83 1BJ. www.caerphillyminerscentre.co.uk. *From Ystrad Mynach: A469 to Caerphilly then exit onto St Cenydd Rd. From Newport: M4 J32 take A470, Cardiff(N)/Merthyr Tydfil A468 then A469 turn onto Watford Rd. What3words app: often.hunter.occupy.* **Sun 21 June (11-4). Adm £5, chd free. Tea, coffee & cake.**
A climate change garden promoting carbon reduction, biodiversity, health and wellbeing. Discover the stumpery, wildlife pond and children's wildlife and play area in the wildflower meadow. We also have a drought resistant garden, borders planted to demonstrate sustainability in all weathers, attract pollinators and local fauna alongside a border which aims

to show how easy it is to grow cut flowers in our climate. Wheelchair accessible paths at top of the front garden. Accessible slope to the rear garden.

6 NEW DAN-Y-WARREN
Crickhowell Road, Gilwern, Abergavenny, NP7 0EH. **John & Olive Scurr,** 01873 830274, olive.scurr@gmx.com. *From centre of Gilwern, turn R for Crickhowell & Brecon. Proceed about 1½m. Entrance is on the R.* Visits by arrangement in Feb for groups of up to 10. **Adm by donation. Tea.**
Dan-y-Warren was originally part of the Dan-y-Parc Estate. It borders the River Usk and has large old oaks, a circle of redwoods and other interesting trees. The garden contains a variety of borders, an orchard, vegetable beds and a fruit cage. A woodland walk through a dell and newly planted valley goes down to the River Usk with drifts of snowdrops and spring blossoms. Regret, no wheelchair access to woodland walk.
&

7 GLEBE HOUSE
Llanvair Kilgeddin, Abergavenny, NP7 9BE. **Mr & Mrs Murray Kerr,** 01873 840422, joanna@amknet.com. *5m SW of Abergavenny. Midway between Abergavenny & Usk on B4598. What3words app: fortunes.spreading.reeling.* **Sat 9, Sun 10 May (2-6). Adm £7, chd free. Home-made teas.** Visits also by arrangement 15 Apr to 15 July for groups of up to 30.
Borders bursting with spring colour inc camassia, narcissi, smyrnium and alliums. South facing terrace with wisteria and honeysuckle, decorative vegetable garden and orchard densely underplanted with succession of bulbs. Some topiary and formal hedging in 1½ acre garden in wonderful setting of Usk valley AONB. St Mary's church, Llanfair Kilgeddin will also be open to view famous Victorian scraffito murals. Some gravel and gently sloping lawns.

GWENT

8 THE GROWING SPACE GARDEN
Mardy Park Resource Centre, Hereford Road, Mardy, Abergavenny, NP7 6HU. Jim Quinn. 1½m N of centre of Abergavenny, on the Hereford Rd opp the Crown & Sceptre public house. What3words app: create.shudders.knees. **Sun 28 June (9.30-4.30). Adm £5, chd free. Tea, coffee & cake.**
The gardens are laid out around disabled access paths, herbaceous borders, a prairie style border, and fruit and vegetable beds. There is also a tropical border and large raised beds. We have two polytunnels and a small craft and carpentry workshop. The gardens are tended by a hard working team of volunteers of mixed ability and ages from 18 to 96. Adjoining parkland is perfect for a picnic. Woodland and the River Gavenny. Good access for wheelchair users. There is a handrail as garden is on a slight slope.

9 14 GWERTHONOR LANE
Gilfach, Bargoed, CF81 8JT. Suzanne & Philip George. 8m of Caerphilly. A469 to Bargoed, through the T-lights next to sch & then L filter lane at next T-lights onto Cardiff Rd. 1st L into Gwerthonor Rd, 4th R into Gwerthonor Ln. What3words app: bless.input.famed. **Sat 18, Sun 19 July (11-5). Adm £5, chd free. Home-made teas.**
The garden has a beautiful panoramic view of the Rhymney Valley. A real plantswoman's garden with over 800 varieties of perennials, annuals, bulbs, shrubs and trees. There are numerous rare, unusual and tropical plants combined with traditional and well loved favourites (many available for sale). A small wildlife pond adds to the tranquil feel of the garden.

10 HIGH GLANAU MANOR
Lydart, Monmouth, NP25 4AD. Mr & Mrs Hilary Gerrish, 07966 809204, helenagerrish@gmail.com, www.highglanaugardens.com. 4m SW of Monmouth. Situated on B4293 between Monmouth & Chepstow. Turn R into private road, ¼m after Craig-y-Dorth turn on B4293. **Sun 26 Apr (2-5.30). Adm £7, chd free. Home-made teas.** Listed Arts and Crafts garden laid out by H Avray Tipping 100 years ago. Original features inc impressive stone terraces with far-reaching views over the Vale of Usk to Blorenge, Skirrid, Sugar Loaf and Brecon Beacons. Pergola, herbaceous borders, Edwardian glasshouse, rhododendrons, azaleas, tulips, orchard with wildflowers. Originally open for the National Garden Scheme in 1927. Garden guidebook by owner, Helena Gerrish, available to purchase. Garden lovers cottage to rent.

11 HIGHFIELD FARM
Penperlleni, Goytre, NP4 0AA. Dr Roger & Mrs Jenny Lloyd, 01873 880030, jenny.plants@btinternet.com, www.highfieldfarmgarden.co.uk. 4m W of Usk, 6m S of Abergavenny. Turn off the A4042 at Goytre Arms, over railway bridge, bear L. Garden ½m on R. From Usk off B4598, turn L after Chain Bridge, then L at Xrds. Garden 1m on L. What3words app: loaders.motoring.arriving. **Sun 14 June, Sun 12 July, Sun 9 Aug, Sun 13 Sept (11-4). Adm £7, chd free. Home-made teas.** Visits also by arrangement 18 May to 25 Sept for groups of 10 to 40.
Highfield Farm Garden is a celebration of plants. There are over 1400 cultivars, with many rarities, densely planted over three acres and set within the majestic Monmouthshire landscape. It offers an exuberant display across the seasons, providing an intimate, immersive experience with a diverse array of herbaceous, shrubs and trees. Huge sale of plants from the garden. Live music. Access to almost all garden without steps.

12 HILLCREST
Waunborfa Road, Cefn Fforest, Blackwood, NP12 3LB. Mr M O'Leary, 01443 837029, olearymichael18@gmail.com. 3m W of Newbridge. B4254/A469: T-junc turn L to B'wood. At x-road take lane ahead. 1st L at top of hill. A4048/B4251: cross Chartist Bridge, 2nd exit on 2 r'bouts. End of road turn L & immed R onto Waunborfa. What3words app: view.fall.brush. **Sat 23, Sun 24, Mon 25 May, Sun 5 July, Sun 2 Aug (11-6). Adm £5, chd free. Light refreshments.** Visits also by arrangement Apr to Sept.
A cascade of secluded gardens of distinct character with 1½ acres with a naturalistic approach in some areas. Magnificent, unusual trees, interesting shrubs, perennials and annuals. Choices at every turn, visitors are well rewarded as hidden delights and surprises are revealed. Well placed seats encourage a relaxed pace to fully appreciate the garden's treasures. Tulips in April, glorious blooms of the Chilean firebushes, handkerchief tree and cornuses in May and many unusual trees and many different vistas. Lowest parts of garden not accessible to wheelchairs.

13 LITTLE CAERLICYN
Caerlicyn Lane, Langstone, Newport, NP18 2JZ. Mrs Katharine Notley, 07793 122936, lc.flowerfarm@gmail.com, www.lcflowerfarm.co.uk. Off the A48 from Newport towards Penhow/Chepstow. Just over 2m from the Coldra r'about (M4 J24). Please follow yellow signs up Caerlicken Ln. What3words app: builds.encloses.tickling. **Sat 5, Sun 6 Sept (11-4). Adm £5, chd free. Home-made teas.** Visits also by arrangement Apr to Oct for groups of 6+. Adm inc refreshments & a farm tour.
Small flower farm and gardens around renovated Tudor cottage and barn, situated on a steep hillside. Four distinct areas, perennials, roses, dahlias, grape vines and wildflower areas and an ancient mulberry tree plus bees and woodland walk. Protecting and promoting of wildlife is central to this garden whose owners follow a no dig approach. Amazing views over the Severn Estuary.

14 LLANOVER
Abergavenny, NP7 9EF. Mr & Mrs M R Murray, 07753 423635, elizabeth@llanover.com, www.llanovergarden.co.uk. 4m S of Abergavenny, 15m N of Newport, 20m SW Hereford. Garden is off the A4042 in Llanover, opp the bus stop. What3words app: flash.ready.limits. **Sun 29 Mar (2-5). Adm £8, chd free. Home-made teas. Picnics welcome in the field.** Visits also by arrangement for groups of up to 5.
Benjamin Waddington, the direct ancestor of the current owners, purchased the house and land in 1792. Subsequently he created a series of ponds, cascades and rills which form the backbone of the 15 acre garden as the stream winds its way from its source in the Black Mountains to the River Usk. There are

The Pant

herbaceous borders, a drive lined with *Narcissi*, spring bulbs, wildflowers, a water garden, champion trees and two arboreta. The house (not open) is the birthplace of Augusta Waddington, Lady Llanover, C19 patriot, supporter of the Welsh language and traditions. Gravel and grass paths and lawns. No disabled WC.

5 LONG OWL BARN
Coedypaen, Pontypool, NP4 0TB. Mike & Tina Booth, 07486 579317, michaelbooth891@gmail.com, www.instagram.com/michaelbooth1963. *2m W of Usk. 1m from Llandegveth reservoir. Take turn to Coed-y-paen from Llanbadoc or Llangybi; follow yellow signs. From Cwmbran Crem take Tre-Herbert Ln towards Llangybi & turn to Coed-y-Paen. What3words app: crispier.racing.achieving.* **Sat 6 June (11-5). Adm £5, chd free. Tea, coffee & cake.** Visits also by arrangement 1 July to 30 Aug for groups of 5 to 20.

In a rural setting with extensive views, there are meandering paths, colourful borders and wildlife areas with plenty to explore in a little over an acre. Small orchard, ponds, a vegetable plot and greenhouse. Extensive perennial beds full of colour. Sloping ground makes some areas inaccessible. Uneven steps and loose surface paths throughout.

6 LONGHOUSE FARM
Penrhos, Raglan, NP15 2DE. Mr & Mrs M H C Anderson. *Midway between Monmouth & Abergavenny. 4m from Raglan. Off Old Raglan/Abergavenny rd signed Clytha. At Bryngwyn/Great Oak Xrds turn towards Great Oak- follow yellow NGS signs from red phone box down narrow lane. What3words app: cake.audibly.oxidation.* **Sat 18, Sun 19 Apr (2-5.30). Adm £6, chd free. Light refreshments.**

Spacious two acre country garden with colourful borders, interesting trees, shrubs and productive vegetable garden. Discover the natural pond, house and barns covered with roses and vines. A roundabout with un-named ancient Perry Pear tree surrounded by bulbs and seasonal plants. Woodland walk around a series of spring fed ponds with wonderful views of hidden parts of Monmouthshire.

7 MIONE
Old Hereford Road, Llanvihangel Crucorney, Abergavenny, NP7 7LB. John O'Neil. *5m N of Abergavenny. From Abergavenny take A465 to Hereford. After 4.8m turn L - signed Pantygelli. Mione is ½m on L.* **Sun 21 June, Sun 5 July (10.30-5). Adm £5, chd free. Tea, coffee & cake.**

Reopening in memory of Yvonne who originally designed the garden. Her husband, John, is continuing to develop her plan for this beautiful garden. There are a wide variety of established plants, many rare and unusual. A pergola with climbing roses and clematis numerous containers with a diverse range of planting plus a wildlife pond with many newts, insects and frogs.

GROUP OPENING

8 MONMOUTH GARDENS
Monnow Street, Monmouth, NP25 3EN. *Central Monmouth. Parking at Monnow St Car Park. Please follow signage throughout Monmouth to the gardens. What3words app: rejoin.shape.hindering.* **Sun 17 May (11.30-5.30). Combined adm £10, chd free. Home-made teas at North Parade House & St Johns.**

CORNWALL HOUSE, 58 MONNOW STREET
Jane Harvey & John Wheelock, www.historichouses.org/house/cornwall-house/visit.

NEW THE GABLES
Patrick & Stefanie Toms.

THE NELSON GARDEN
The Nelson Garden Monmouth, www.nelsongarden.org.uk.

NORTH PARADE HOUSE
Tim Haynes & Lisa O'Neill.

ST JOHNS
Simon & Hilary Hargreaves.

Five very different town gardens open under the banner of Monmouth Gardens. The Nelson Garden dates back to Roman times, and as the name suggests has links with Lord Nelson. St Johns, in Glendower St is a charming walled garden which has undergone extensive restoration with a sunken central lawn and deep herbaceous borders. Entrance to both these gardens is via Chippenham Fields. Cornwall House has a beautiful walled garden and productive kitchen garden dating from the C17. North Parade House is a hidden gem with a surprisingly large and secluded walled garden with mature specimen trees, herbaceous borders and a kitchen garden. The Gables is a terraced garden surrounding a beautiful Arts and Crafts house. The garden leads down to the River Monnow and has beautiful herbaceous borders. Range of different gardening styles in town gardens. Plant sales at the Nelson Garden. Tickets available at each garden along with maps to aid visitors.

9 NEUADD STONE BARN
Church Road, Gilwern, Abergavenny, NP7 0HF. Mrs Katherine Franklin, www.brambleandbombus.co.uk. *From the middle of Gilwern, follow Church Rd, past the Church on the R & follow yellow signs. What3words app: compress.envelope.sparrows.* **Sun 16 Aug (11-5). Adm £5, chd free. Tea, coffee & cake.**

Newly established flower farm which is part of a working farm. The site is in an AONB and has breathtaking views of the three hills surrounding Abergavenny. A huge array of perennial and annual flowers are grown for cutting and sale.

In 2025 we awarded over £288,800 in Community Garden Grants, supporting 114 community garden projects.

Usk Open Gardens

20 NEW NEW INN FARM
Forest Coal Pit, Abergavenny, NP7 7LT. Stephen & Judith Anderton, stephenanderton95@btinternet.com. *6m N of Abergavenny. From Llanvihangel Crucorney follow signs to Llanthony. 1m turn L to Forest Coalpit. At 5 Ways x-rds, turn R. Garden ½m on L. What3words app: crouches.river.among.* **Visits by arrangement July to Sept for groups of 12 to 32. Adm inc refreshments & and tour with owners. Adm £20, chd free. Tea, coffee & cake.**
Enclosed flower garden is a lush mix of modern and traditional perennials interspersed with clipped evergreens. Specialities inc ferns, succulents and South African plants. Simple green terraces retained by sculpted hedges offer valley and mountain views. A scented garden of shrubs, bulbs and meadow grass adjoins a small orchard. A steep 15 acre, riverside oak woodland is maintained for its carpet of mosses. Don't miss the ancient woodland moss garden and cloud pruning.

21 NEW THE PANT
Fforest Coal Pit, Abergavenny, NP7 7LT. Mrs Jeremy Swift. *5m N of Abergavenny. From A465 Llanv Crucorney, direction Llanthony, then L to Fforest Coal Pit. At Five ways X-rd turn 1st sharp R before grey telephone box.* **Sun 3, Mon 4 May (12-6). Adm £8, chd free. Home-made teas.**
An extraordinary garden set in secluded, spectacular Black Mountains scenery with 25 acres of landscaped woodland, orchard, checkerboard herb garden, walled garden, Islamic garden and green theatre. Large dry stone turtle, ruined village, curious whale shaped lake, all with wonderful views.

22 PARK HOUSE
School Lane, Itton, Chepstow, NP16 6BZ. Professor Bruce & Dr Cynthia Matthews. *From M48: take A466 towards Tintern. At 2nd r'about turn L (B4293). After blue sign turn R & Park House is at end of lane. Parking 200metres before house. From Devauden: B4293 1st L in Itton.* **Sat 25 Apr (10-5). Adm £5, chd free.**
Approximately one acre garden with large vegetable areas and many mature trees, rhododendrons, azaleas, camellias in a woodland setting. Bordering on Chepstow Park Wood. Magnificent views over open country.

23 ROCKFIELD PARK
Rockfield, Monmouth, NP25 5QB. Mark & Melanie Molyneux, 07803 952027, melmolyneux@yahoo.co.uk. *On arriving in Rockfield village from Monmouth, turn R by phone box. After approx 400yds, church on L. Entrance to Rockfield Park on R, opp church, via private bridge over river. What3words app: blueberry.cabin.bind.* **Sun 7 June (10-5). Adm £7, chd free. Home-made teas on the terrace. Visits also by arrangement May to July.**
Rockfield Park dates from C17 and is situated in the heart of the Monmouthshire countryside on the banks of the River Monnow. The extensive grounds comprise formal gardens, meadows and orchard, complemented by riverside and woodland walks. Possible to picnic on riverside walks. Main part of gardens are wheelchair accessible, but not steep garden leading to river.

Hillcrest

GWENT 655

24 TROSTREY LODGE
Bettws Newydd, Usk, NP15 1JT. Frances Pemberton, trostrey@googlemail.com. *4m W of Raglan. 7m E of Abergavenny. Off old A40 (B4598) Abergavenny-Raglan. 1m S of Clytha Gates & 1½m N of Bettws Newydd. What3words app: blip.ants.operated.* **Visits by arrangement 1 May to 1 July for groups of up to 12. Light refreshments.**
Wander over the ha-ha and through the C18 listed iron gate which leads to the tall tulip tree, you will find a delightful walled garden full of colour and imagination. Poppies, herbs, vines, roses and honeysuckle thread through the box topiary all attractive to bees and insect life. Home artworks and packets of flower seeds available, all to help the bees. Artworks and packets of seeds for sale.

25 TY ISAF FARM
Pandy Mawr Road, Bedwas, Caerphilly, CF83 8EQ. Mrs Linda Davies. *3m N of Caerphilly. From A468 at Caerphilly head towards Bedwas & then Pandy-Mawr Rd. Follow NGS yellow signs. What3words app: clash.swims.down.* **Sat 25, Sun 26 July (11-4). Adm £5, chd free. Tea, coffee & cake.**
This garden, on a working farm, surrounds the Grade II listed sub-Medieval farmhouse and barn. The garden is being revitalised with the renovation of beds and development of areas such as the wildlife pond. The ancient yew is a magnificent feature as are the stone walls surrounding areas of the garden. A naturalistic approach to planting and spectacular far-reaching views.

GROUP OPENING

26 USK OPEN GARDENS
Maryport Street, Usk, NP15 1BH. www.uskopengardens.uk. *Main car park postcode is NP15 1AD. From M4 J24 take A449 for 8m N to Usk exit. Signposts to free parking around town. Blue badge parking in main car parks. Map of gardens provided with ticket.* **Sat 27, Sun 28 June (10-5). Combined adm £10, chd free.** Donation to local charities.

Usk's floral public displays are a wonderful backdrop to the gardens. Around 15 to 20 private gardens opening. Gardeners' Market with interesting plants. Lovely day out for all the family with lots of places to eat and drink inc places to picnic. Wheelchair accessible gardens and gardens allowing well-behaved dogs on leads are noted on map. Available from the ticket desks on the day at the free car park at Usk Memorial Hall (NP15 1AD).

27 WENALLT ISAF
Twyn Wenallt, Gilwern, Abergavenny, NP7 0HP. Tim & Debbie Field, 07885 195304, wenalltisaf@gmail.com. *3m W of Abergavenny. Between Abergavenny & Brynmawr. Leave the A465 at Gilwern & follow yellow NGS signs through the village. Do not follow SatNav. What3words app: sensibly.gone.connects.* **Sun 30 Aug (1-5). Adm £6, chd free. Tea, coffee & cake. Home-made cakes (gluten free & lactose free cakes available). Visits also by arrangement 6 Apr to 30 Sept for groups of 8+. Tour by the owner inc talk about the history of the garden.**
A hidden gem of nearly three acres owner designed in sympathy with its surroundings and the challenges of being 650ft up on a north facing hillside. Far-reaching views of the magnificent Black Mountains, mature trees, rhododendrons, viburnum, spectacular hydrangeas, herbaceous borders, vegetable garden, small polytunnel, orchard, chickens, bees. Child friendly with plenty of space to run about. Stone circle. Amazing views of the Black Mountains.

28 WOODBINE HOUSE
Monmouth Road, Usk, NP15 1QY. Mr Jonathan Stephens FLS. *From Usk, take the Monmouth Rd. At t-lights take L fork signed Gwehelog. After the one-way, in 50yds turn R into Cwrt Bryn Derwen. Kerbside parking on Monmouth Rd. What3words app: dairy.went.requiring.* **Sun 19 July (11-5.30). Adm £5, chd free. Tea, coffee & cake.**
A hidden naturalistic garden extending to about 2½ acres. Woodland walks with quirky features at every turn.

A lake, dug and landscaped by the owners with an island, a boathouse, well established gunnera, and ferns. Quite an amazing area developed over a number of years, a children's paradise, not a traditional garden.

29 ◆ WYNDCLIFFE COURT
St Arvans, NP16 6EY. Mr & Mrs Anthony Clay, 07710 138972, sarah@wyndcliffecourt.com, www.wyndcliffecourt.com. *3m N of Chepstow. Off A466, turn at Wyndcliffe signpost coming from the Chepstow direction. What3words app: merely.piano.healers.* **For NGS: Thur 4 June (1-5). Adm £10, chd free. Pre-booking essential, please visit www.ngs.org.uk for information & booking. Home-made teas.** For other opening times and information, please phone, email or visit garden website.
Exceptional and unaltered garden designed by H. Avray Tipping in 1922. Explore the Arts and Crafts 'Italianate' style garden inc stone summerhouse, terracing and ponds. Yew hedging and topiary, sunken garden, rose garden, bowling green and woodland. Walled garden new in 2023 for Charles III coronation. Renaissance mural and vine shaded arbour. Rose garden designed by Sarah Price.

---

70 inpatients and their families are being supported at the newly opened Horatio's Garden Northern Ireland, thanks to the National Garden Scheme donations.

GWYNEDD & ANGLESEY
GWYNEDD A MÔN

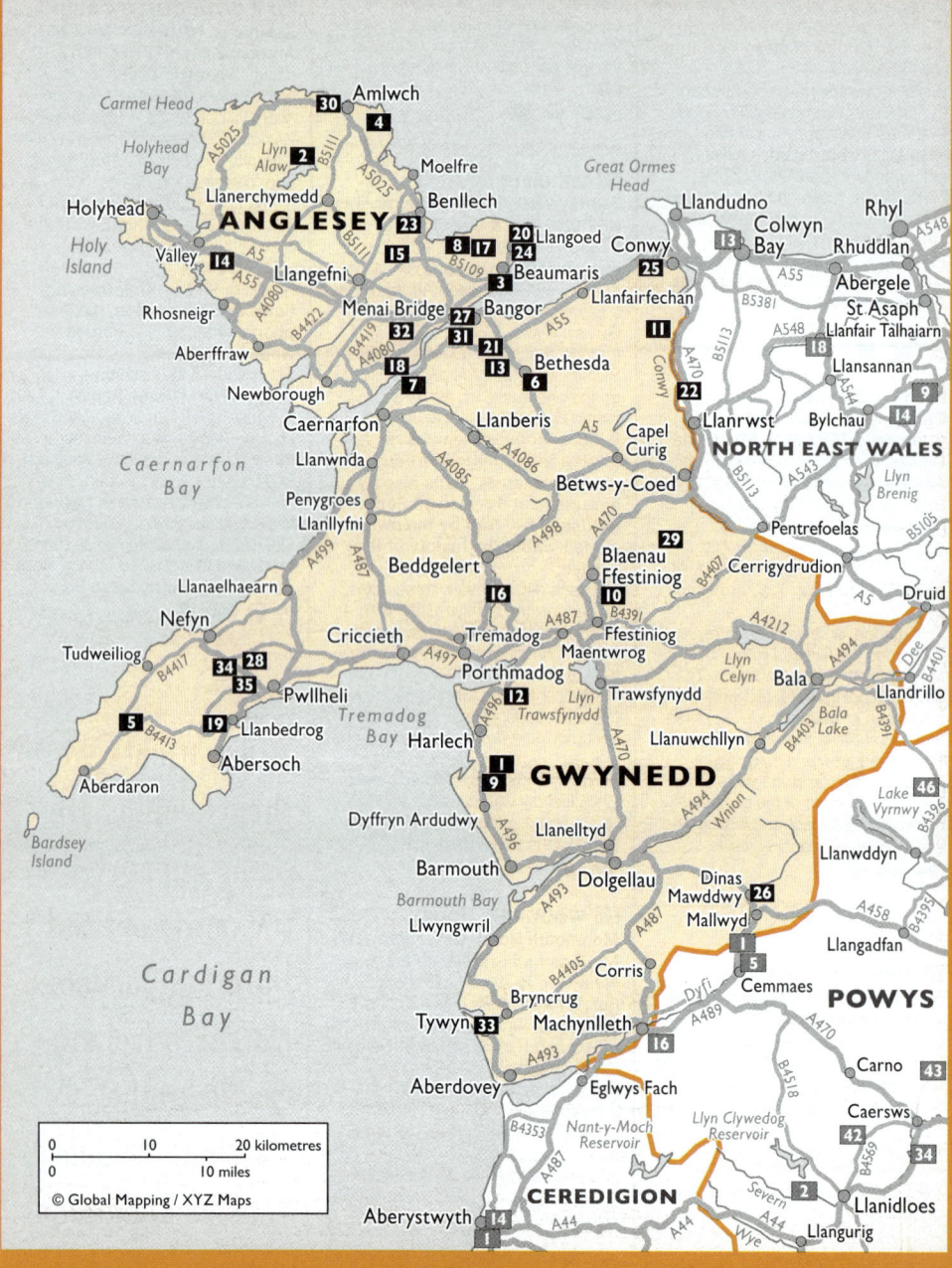

VOLUNTEERS

County Organiser
Kay Laurie
07971 083361
kay.laurie@ngs.org.uk

Heather Broughton
07747 737237
heather.broughton@ngs.org.uk

County Treasurer
Brenda Simpson
01248 810144
brenda.simpson@ngs.org.uk

Publicity
Lowri Haf
lowri.haf@ngs.org.uk

Booklet Co-Ordinator
Heather Broughton
(as above)

Photographer
Gary Phillips
07742 892743
gaphll@aol.com

Social Media
Lili Evans
lili.evans@ngs.org.uk

Assistant County Organisers
Hazel Bond
07378 844295
hazelcaenewydd@gmail.com

Janet Jones
01758 740296
janetcoron@hotmail.co.uk

Delia Lanceley
01286 650517
delia@lanceley.com

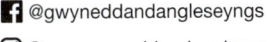
@gwyneddandangleseyngs
@ngs.gwyneddandanglesey

OPENING DATES

All entries subject to change. For latest information check
www.ngs.org.uk

Map locator numbers are shown to the right of each garden name.

March

Every Saturday and Sunday from Saturday 28th
Coed Ty Mawr 5

April

Every Saturday and Sunday from Saturday 7th
Coed Ty Mawr 5

Sunday 19th
The Granary 13

Sunday 26th
Maenan Hall 22

Wednesday 29th
♦ Plas Cadnant Hidden Gardens 27

May

Saturday 2nd
Coed Ty Mawr 5
Llanidan Hall 18

Sunday 3rd
Coed Ty Mawr 5
NEW Glyn Cywrach 12

Saturday 9th
Plas Pont y Cribyn 28

Saturday 16th
Tyn Y Pant 34

Sunday 17th
Cyplau 9
Gwaelod Mawr 14

Thursday 21st
Castle Court 3

Friday 22nd
Castle Court 3

Sunday 24th
NEW Hafod Garegog 16

Tuesday 26th
NEW Glyn Cywrach 12

June

Saturday 13th
♦ Crûg Farm 7
NEW Gerddi 'Stiniog 10

Sunday 14th
♦ Pensychnant 25

Thursday 18th
NEW Aber Artro Hall 1

Saturday 20th
Llanidan Hall 18

Sunday 21st
NEW Aber Artro Hall 1

Saturday 27th
Llwydiarth 19

Sunday 28th
Llwydiarth 19

July

Saturday 4th
Caswallon 4
Llanidan Hall 18
Ty Cadfan Sant 33
Y Felin Rhyd Hir 35

Sunday 5th
Ty Cadfan Sant 33
Y Felin Rhyd Hir 35

Saturday 11th
Llanddona Village Gardens 17

Sunday 12th
♦ Pensychnant 25

Saturday 18th
Tyn Y Pant 34

Sunday 19th
♦ Crûg Farm 7

Saturday 25th
Coed Ty Mawr 5

Sunday 26th
Coed Ty Mawr 5
Maenan Hall 22

August

Sunday 2nd
Plas Pont y Cribyn 28

Sunday 16th
The Granary 13

September

Saturday 5th
Treborth Botanic Garden, Bangor University   31

Sunday 6th
◆ Plannwch y Plas   26

Sunday 13th
NEW Craig Ogwen   6

By Arrangement

Arrange a personalised garden visit with your club, or group of friends, on a date to suit you. See individual garden entries for full details.

Cae Newydd	2
Caswallon	4
Coed Ty Mawr	5
Cuddfan	8
Gilfach	11
Gwenfro Uchaf	15
Llwyn Onn	20
Llys-y-Gwynt	21
Mynydd, Cors Goch	23
The Old School	24
Plasglasgwm	29
Sunningdale	30
Trefnant Bach	32
Ty Cadfan Sant	33
Tyn Y Pant	34

THE GARDENS

1 NEW **ABER ARTRO HALL**
Llanbedr, LL45 2PA. *1m from Llanbedr. From Dyffryn: turn R off A496 by The Victoria Inn in Llanbedr (L if from Harlech). After 1m turn R at sign for Cwm Nantcol then follow signs. What3words app: breaches. flicked.winded.* **Thur 18, Sun 21 June (9.30-5.30). Adm £6, chd free. Pre-booking essential, please visit www.ngs.org.uk for information & booking. Tea, coffee & cake.**
Six acres of beautiful gardens surrounding the Arts and Crafts mansion built in 1910 by C. E. Bateman. Hillside rock and wild gardens lead to ancient woodland, and lawns with ponds, fountains and managed flower beds lead to two magnificent terraces. Large kitchen garden with huge fruit pergola, orchard and peach-house, adjoin the separate Italian and Japanese gardens, with a lovely riverside walk. Partial wheelchair access; one steep slope.

2 **CAE NEWYDD**
Rhosgoch, Amlwch, LL66 0BG. Hazel & Nigel Bond, 07378 844295, nigel@cae-newydd.co.uk. *3m SW of Amlwch. A5025 from Benllech to Amlwch, follow signs for leisure centre & Lastra Farm. Follow yellow NGS signs (approx 3m), car park on L.* **Visits by arrangement 14 Feb to 30 Aug. Small coaches only due to access. Adm £5, chd free. Tea, coffee & cake.**
Once a field with views of Llyn Alaw and Eryri (Snowdonia), after more than 20 years, now an informal country garden of 2½ acres. Lots of paths to explore the varied planting and roses, birds to hear, seats to sit on and soak up the peaceful atmosphere. Good variety of shrubs and trees and large wildlife pond. The lower garden has areas of long grass; wander the cut paths to a small woodland. Hay meadow with cut paths, beehives, visit in February and March to see snowdrops and hellebores, colourful herbaceous planting attracts bees and butterflies in summer. Productive polytunnel and a collection of cacti. Garden area closest to house suitable for wheelchairs.

3 **CASTLE COURT**
Beaumaris, LL58 8AL. Janine and Stephen Walters. *Castle Court is next to Beaumaris Castle in the town centre. Public parking on The Green or at The Canolfan. No parking at the garden.* **Thur 21, Fri 22 May (11-4). Adm £5, chd free.**
Castle Court is a 200+ year old walled garden set in a plot of approx ⅓ acre. It is immediately adjacent to Beaumaris Castle in the beautiful town of Beaumaris. Entrance is at the rear through a contemporary double garage. A 3m high Grade II listed wall conceals a surprisingly large garden with an expansive lawn opening onto deep herbaceous borders, a "Hedge Shed" and a front courtyard. No refreshments at garden. Lots of cafes in Beaumaris.

4 **CASWALLON**
Llaneilian, Amlwch, LL68 9NN. Julian & Gillian Sandbach, gillian.sandbach@mac.com. *Mynydd Eilian. From the A5025 take the turn to Pengorffwysfa near Amlwch. The garden will be signed from village. It is a single track lane. Plenty of parking.* **Sat 4 July (10-4.30). Adm £5, chd free. Tea, coffee & cake.** Visits also by arrangement Apr to Sept.
Large historic garden which had been under years of undergrowth. We have discovered formal gardens, an ancient well, crumbling dry stone walls and steps carved into bedrock. Take one of our meandering paths and explore small woodland dells and a walled garden. Everyday is an adventure as there is always more to discover.

5 **COED TY MAWR**
Ty Mawr, Bryncroes, Pwllheli, LL53 8EH. Nonni & David Goadby, 07799 877590, nonni@goadby.net, www.coed-ty-mawr.co.uk. *12m W of Pwllheli. Take B4413 Llanbedrog to Aberdaron. 1¾m past Sarn Meyllteyrn. Turn R at Pengroeslon sign. From Nefyn take B4417, at x-roads with B4413 turn L. What3words app: extra.lump. spillage.* **Every Sat and Sun 28 Mar to 3 May (11-1.30). Pre-booking essential, please visit www.ngs.org.uk for information & booking. Sat 25, Sun 26 July (10-5). Adm £5, chd free. Tea, coffee & cake.** Visits also by arrangement 28 Mar to 25 Oct for groups of up to 50. For parties of 10+ a guided tour is available.
A five acre woodland and parkland garden created from wilderness and situated among beautiful scenery with year-round interest. Over 3,000 trees and shrubs inc growing collections of magnolia, rhododendron, hydrangea, Cornus and many unusual trees and shrubs. Also, a large pond, an orchard, a fernery and sea view gardens. Sit on the raised deck, take in the sea views and enjoy a home-made tea. Wheelchair access via grass paths.

6 NEW CRAIG OGWEN

Ogwen Terrace, High Street, Bethesda, LL57 3AY. Dan & Sarah Bristow, www.studiobristow.com. *Down the lane behind the Douglas Arms Hotel, off Bethesda High St. What3words app: beams.sunflower.jumpy.* **Sun 13 Sept (11-4). Adm £5, chd free. Tea, coffee & cake.** Small, impactful garden- home to RHS Chelsea gold medal winning garden designer Dan Bristow. Featuring bold planting with rare and unusual species informed by his many plant hunting travels. Innovative bespoke landscaping elements abound, inc a 'floating' cast bench nestled into the bedrock. The garden is set against a rushing river. Beyond lies ancient woodland, visually framing the garden. RHS Chelsea gold medal winning garden designer opens his private garden for the first time.

7 ◆ CRÛG FARM

Griffiths Crossing, Caernarfon, LL55 1TU. Bleddyn & Sue Wynn-Jones, 01248 670232, sue@crug-farm.co.uk, www.crug-farm.co.uk. *2m NE of Caernarfon. Main A487 Caernarfon to Bangor road. Do not join new by-pass At r'about follow signs for local traffic. Brown tourist sign Crûg Farm Plants.* **For NGS: Sat 13 June, Sun 19 July (11-4). Adm £5, chd free. Tea, coffee & cake. Refreshments in aid of Parkinson's Cymru on Sat 13 June & in aid of NGS on Sun 19 July.** For other opening times and information, please phone, email or visit garden website.

Sue and Bleddyn Wynn-Jones travelled the world hunting for plants. Many you will see are new, not seen in cultivation before. Wander into the ruin garden, up to the mound garden, then the walled garden and woodland everywhere wonderful collections grow. Don't worry if you do not recognise them, help is at hand, Sue and Bleddyn have yet to meet any visitor who can recognise everything they see. Partial wheelchair access.

8 CUDDFAN

Llanddona, Beaumaris, LL58 8TR. Mrs Jacquie Blakeley, 07836 549361, jacquine.blakeley@btinternet.com. *From Beaumaris, turn L signposted Pentraeth. Head towards Wern y Wylan for 1m (single track with passing places). Enter village & after ⅕m Cuddfan is on R. What3words app: echo.animate.lilac.* **Visits by arrangement 1 Apr to 30 Oct for groups of up to 12. Very limited parking; please car share. No coach turning place. Adm £10. Light refreshments.**

Cuddfan, a garden in the Japanese style features a range of mature cloud pruned pine, acer, ginko and other trees with rocks, ponds and meandering paths. The design with its constrained palette has colour bursts from azaleas in season. It connects with nature incorporating symbolic Japanese aesthetics highlighting the natural landscape.

9 CYPLAU

Llanbedr, LL45 2ND. Ms Jacqueline Gilleland. *7m NW Barmouth. From Barmouth A496 direct to Llanbedr. From Harlech 3m on A496 to Llanbedr.* **Sun 17 May (11-4.30). Adm £5, chd free. Tea, coffee & cake. Soft drinks & choice of cakes inc gluten free.**

Under an acre of intensely planted hillside garden created over 25 years. Twisting pathways with steps lead to small garden areas, topiary, cloud pruned yew, tsunami heather hedge, multi stemmed and shaped shrubs, ornaments and sculptures. Superb sea views in hillside garden. Vegetable potager, modern greenhouse, fruits. This garden is a way of living to encourage nature and enjoy peace. Relax and listen to a choir in the garden.

Aber Artro Hall

10 NEW GERDDI 'STINIOG
Llan Ffestiniog, LL41 4AB. Mrs Sioned Lewis, www.serencyf.org. *Located behind Gwesty Seren Hotel (LL41 4NS). From Porthmadog: come up Alltgoch, pass hotel on L, after bend entrance to cemetary is on L, go through cemetery. What3words app: teach.altering. reprints.* **Sat 13 June (10-4). Adm by donation. Tea, coffee & cake.**
Established in 1997, Gerddi 'Stiniog Gardens is a three acre social and therapeutic horticulture site which is based at Llan Ffestiniog with spectacular views of the Moelwyn Mountains. The garden is a haven for wildlife with our chickens, a nature pond, beehives and a wildlife observation space. Discover our raised beds, productive polytunnels and pergola. There is wheelchair access to the gardens, but the paths are gravel.

11 GILFACH
Rowen, Conwy, LL32 8TS. James & Isoline Greenhalgh, 01492 650216, isolinegreenhalgh@btinternet.com. *4m S of Conwy. At X-rds 100yds E of Rowen, S towards Llanrwst, past Rowen Sch on L, turn up 2nd drive on L.* **Visits by arrangement 19 Apr to 30 Aug. Adm £4, chd free. Discuss refreshments when booking.**
An acre of country garden on south facing slope with magnificent views of the River Conwy and mountains; set in 35 acres of farm and woodland. Discover the collection of mature shrubs which is added to yearly, the woodland garden, herbaceous border and small pool. Spectacular panoramic view of the Conwy Valley and the mountain range of the Carneddau.

12 NEW GLYN CYWRACH
Talsarnau, LL47 6TE. Ms Joanne Mart, 01766 780338, info@glynestate.co.uk, www.glyncywarch.co.uk . *2½m N of Harlech on A496. Turn R onto B4573. 8m from Maentwrog on A496 straight on to B4573. 3½m from Penrhyndeudraeth on A496 straight on to B4573. What3words app: typically.donates.flipper.* **Sun 3, Tue 26 May (11-4). Adm £5, chd free. Cream teas.**
With a revolutionary nod to C17 planting, the yew walk leading into a bluebell glade, nut and fruit trees planted in a wildflower meadow in the walled garden, a fernery of slate and moss in the shadow of the Hall and a hydrangea walk leading to the Gatehouse. The rose garden with a sluice of running water from the waterfall.

13 THE GRANARY
Felin Hen Road, Bangor, LL57 4BB. Dr Maya Nedeva. *Between Bangor & Tregarth. Leave A55 J11 & take A4424 (services). Turn L onto B4409. Garden on L. Drop off only at garden. Parking at Moelyci, a 10-15 mins walk down Lon Las Ogwen.* **Sun 19 Apr, Sun 16 Aug (11-4). Adm £5, chd free. Tea, coffee & cake.**
A 2½ acre garden with a lot of rare and unusual plants from around the world, many grown from seed with a special interest in Australasian and xeric plants. This would not be a Welsh garden without many ferns, inc tree ferns. Discover a large pond in the front garden and many palms, yuccas and a rockery in the back garden. Partial wheelchair access as part of the garden is on a slope.

14 GWAELOD MAWR
Caergeiliog, LL65 3YL. Tricia Coates. *6m E of Holyhead. ½m E of Caergeiliog. From A55 J4: R'about 2nd exit signed Caergeiliog. 300yds, Gwaelod Mawr is 1st house on L.* **Sun 17 May (11-4). Adm £5, chd free. Tea, coffee & cake.**
A two acre garden created by owners over 30 years with lake, large rock outcrops and palm tree area. Spanish style patio and wonderful laburnum arch in May which leads to sunken garden and wooden bridge over lily pond with fountain and waterfall. Peaceful Chinese garden offering contemplation. Separate koi carp pond. Abundant seating throughout. Garden is mainly flat, with gravel and stone paths. No wheelchair access to sunken lily pond area.

15 GWENFRO UCHAF
Lon Gwenfro, Talwrn, Llangefni, LL77 8JD. Ms Karen Hillyer, gwenfrouchaf@yahoo.com. *4m NE from Llangefni towards Llanbedrgoch & Red Wharf Bay. From Bridge take A5025 towards Amlwch; go through Pentraeth, turn L to Llanbedrgoch after layby; Take 2nd L onto Lon Gwenfro, follow signs for 1m. Limited parking.* **Visits by arrangement for groups of up to 10. Adm £5, chd free. Light refreshments inc home-made soup, teas & cakes using garden produce.**
Discover 2½ acres of formal and informal areas with encroaching nature and great views; with wild meadow walks, trees, hedgerows and stream; a kitchen garden, lean-to greenhouse, orchard and apiary, divided by hedges and stonewall terracing with steps. All paths are mown, with one slate path down slope to house and lawn, teas, seating and fire pit. Food and nature focused. A collection of 15 apple and pear tree varieties. Honey from the apiary for sale and possibly other garden produce (herbs, juice, fruit) depending on availability. Parking may be restricted.

16 NEW HAFOD GAREGOG
Nantmor, Caernarfon, LL55 4YN. Dr B.A Martin. *3m S Beddgelert, 2⅗m N of Garreg on the A4085. From Beddgelert: Head S on A498 towards Nantmor. After 1½m turn L onto A4085. After 1½m turn R. What3words app: digestion.aviators. learning.* **Sun 24 May (11-4). Adm £5, chd free. Tea, coffee & cake. Home-made cakes, hot and cold drinks available.**
One acre mature garden with three seasons of interest bordering the Nanmor river and national nature reserve. Garden surrounds the part C17 house, rebuilt in 1622 from the C14 home of the poet Rhys Goch Eryri, whose poetry survives. Upper and lower water gardens, walled and pleasure gardens with beautiful views of Yr Wyddfa (Snowdon), Cnicht, Moel Hebog and Eryri (Snowdonia). Majority of garden is wheelchair accessible.

The National Garden Scheme funded six Macmillan Nurses in their roles across England, Wales and Northern Ireland in 2025.

The Granary

Hafod Garegog

GROUP OPENING

17 LLANDDONA VILLAGE GARDENS
Beaumaris, LL58 8TU. *3m from Beaumaris. From Beaumaris take B5109 for 1m turn R at T-junc. 2 m to Llanddona.* **Sat 11 July (11-4). Combined adm £6, chd free. Home-made teas at Cefn Farm and Village Hall all day. Lunches at Owain Glyndwr Pub (pre-booking advised 01248 810710).**
Llanddona is one of the highest villages in Anglesey and sits between Red Wharf Bay and the Menai Strait. Some of the gardens need shelter from strong winds but many plants do well. There are 10 gardens to visit this year inc three new ones. You can visit a Georgian farmhouse, a former Chapel built in c.1840, both with gardens being restored, and a working farm. Many gardens have spectacular sea, countryside or mountain views and range from small to very large, with a variety of features from woodland and orchard to raised vegetable beds and greenhouses. Most gardens are within a short walk of each other but transport between gardens will be available. Plants for sale. Dogs welcome on lead. Adm tickets are sold at the Owain Glyndwr Pub where visitors will be given a map showing the location of the gardens.

18 LLANIDAN HALL
Brynsiencyn, Llanfairpwllgwyngyll, LL61 6HJ. *5m E of Llanfair Pwll. From LlanfairPG follow A4080 towards Brynsiencyn for 4m. After Hooton's farm shop on R take next L, follow lane to gardens.* **Sat 2 May, Sat 20 June, Sat 4 July (11-4). Adm £6, chd free. Donation to RSPCA.**
Walled garden of 1¾ acres with physic and herb gardens as well as an ornamental vegetable garden. Discover the herbaceous borders, water features and spring bulb display. There are many varieties of old roses in June and well established summer perennials. Sheep, rabbits and hens to see. Llanidan Old Church will be open for viewing. Regret, no dogs or refreshments. Hard gravel paths and gentle slopes.

19 LLWYDIARTH
Mynytho, Pwllheli, LL53 7RW. **David & Anne Mitchell.** *Garden on main road through Mynytho village. 5½m from Pwllheli 3½m from Abersoch.* **Sat 27, Sun 28 June (11-5). Adm £5, chd free. Teas, coffees and a selection of home-made cakes and scones with jam and clotted cream.**
In 2020 we bought the small field next door to extend our garden. The lawned areas in this cottage style garden are studded with beautiful rose beds. The meandering gravel paths lead you through borders with imaginative and colourful planting of shrubs, herbaceous plants, grasses and trees to the wildlife pond. A Mediterranean style backyard is the perfect place to relax and have tea and cakes.

20 LLWYN ONN
Penmon, nr Beaumaris, LL58 8SG. **Paul Richardson & Pauline Williams, 07917 060324, paulinemwilliams@btinternet.com.** *3m NE of Beaumaris. Pass Beaumaris Castle on coast road. After 1.7m turn R to Penmon & follow yellow signs.* **Visits by arrangement Mar to June for groups of 15+. Demo of biochar making. If available, can be combined with visit to neighbour garden, The Old School. Adm £15, chd free. Tea, coffee & cake.**
The garden benefits from coastal and mountain views with approx three acres of deciduous woodland, originally planted in the C19, mostly with beech. We have protected the remaining old trees, encouraged natural regeneration, and enriched the woodland with some plantings. The garden we created inc lawns, herbaceous borders, and a small wildlife pond. Bio-char demo on trial on wildflower plots.

21 LLYS-Y-GWYNT
Pentir Road, Llandygai, Bangor, LL57 4BG. **Jennifer Rickards, 07799 893418, mjrickards@gmail.com.** *3m S of Bangor. 300yds from Llandygai r'about at J11, A5 & A55, just off A4244. Follow signs for Services (Gwasanaethau). Turn off at No Through Rd sign, 50yds beyond. Do not use SatNav.* **Visits by arrangement. Adm £5, chd free. Tea, coffee and biscuits.**
Interesting, harmonious and very varied two acre garden inc magnificent views of Eryri (Snowdonia). An exposed site inc Bronze Age burial cairn. Winding paths, varied levels planted to create shelter, year-round interest, microclimates and varied rooms. Ponds, bridge and other features use local materials and craftspeople. Wildlife encouraged, well organised compost. Good family garden with visiting peacocks, garden designed for easy maintenance in later years. Most of the garden is wheelchair accessible.

22 MAENAN HALL
Maenan, Llanrwst, LL26 0UL. **Mrs Mclaren & Family.** *2m N of Llanrwst. On E side of A470, ¼m S of Maenan Abbey Hotel.* **Sun 26 Apr, Sun 26 July (10.30-4.30). Adm £5, chd free. Light refreshments inc light lunches and afternoon tea. Catering for dietary needs.**
Superbly beautiful four hectares on the slopes of the Conwy Valley. Dramatic views of Eryri (Snowdonia), set amongst mature hardwoods. Both the upper part, with sweeping lawns, ornamental ponds and retaining walls, and the bluebell carpeted woodland dell contain copious specimen shrubs and trees, many originating at Bodnant. Magnolias, rhododendrons, camellias, pieris, cherries and hydrangeas, amongst many others, make a breathtaking display. Upper part of garden accessible but with fairly steep slopes.

23 MYNYDD, CORS GOCH
Llanbedrgoch, LL76 8TZ. **Wyn & Ann Williams, 01248 853269, gardenannwyn@gmail.com.** *2m N of Pentraeth, ½ m N of Llanbedrgoch next to Cors Goch nature reserve. From Pentraeth take L to Llanbedrgoch & go through village. Parking is on L after ½m. From B5108 turn at sign for Llanbedrgoch, parking on R.* **Visits by arrangement May to July for groups of 12 to 30. Adm £12, chd free. Adm inc home-made tea and cakes.**
An acre garden planted with trees, mature shrubs, perennials, heathers and bulbs. Another three acres devoted to wildlife inc a pond and a copse. Wildflower meadow with a good show of wild orchids end of June early July. The garden is adjacent to Cors Goch nature reserve.

24 THE OLD SCHOOL
Penmon Village, nr Beaumaris, LL58 8RU. Kay Laurie, 07971 083361, kay.laurie@ngs.org.uk. *3m NE of Beaumaris. Pass Beaumaris Castle on coast road, after 1.7m turn R to Penmon & follow yellow signs.* **Visits by arrangement Mar to June for groups of 15+. If available, can be combined with visit to neighbour garden, Llwyn Onn. Adm £15, chd free. Tea, coffee & cake.**
Created from brambly wilderness since 2015, the garden is on unforgiving rocky remains of quarried stone from building the Old School. South facing, views of Menai Strait. Sheltered from westerly winds dry, free draining soil suits agapanthus; ginger lilies; salvias and enormous echiums. Winding paths, steep in parts, mean accessibility is limited. Biomass heated greenhouse: An ongoing project. Sea and mountain views. Historic Old School. Use of recycled materials for structures.

25 ◆ PENSYCHNANT
Sychnant Pass, Conwy, LL32 8BJ. Pensychnant Foundation; Warden Julian Thompson, 01492 592595, jpt.pensychnant@btinternet.com, www.facebook.com/pensychnant. *2½m W of Conwy at top of Sychnant Pass. From Conwy: L at Lancaster Sq into Upper Gate St; after 2½m, Pensychnant's drive signed on R. From Penmaenmawr: fork R by shops, up Sychnant Pass; after walls at top of Pass, U turn L into drive.* **For NGS: Sun 14 June, Sun 12 July (11-5). Adm £4, chd free. Tea, coffee & cake.** For other opening times and information, please phone, email or visit garden website.
Wildlife garden with diverse herbaceous cottage garden borders surrounded by mature shrubs, banks of rhododendrons, ancient and Victorian woodlands. 12 acre woodland walks with views of Conwy Mountain and Sychnant. Listen out for woodland birds. Picnic tables, archaeological trail on mountain. Peaceful little gem. Large Victorian Arts and Crafts house (open), wildlife art exhibition. Sorry no dogs. Partial wheelchair access, please phone for advice.

26 ◆ PLANNWCH Y PLAS
Dinas Mawddwy, Machynlleth, SY20 9JB. Mr Michael Hennessy, plannwchyplas@gmail.com, www.facebook.com/people/Plannwch-Y-Plas. *From Mallwyd: pass through village, at the Llew Coch Pub go straight 200yds to garden. From Dolgellau: turn into village, take 1st L. What3words app: powder.frail.makes.* **For NGS: Sun 6 Sept (10-4). Adm by donation. Tea, coffee & cake.** For other opening times and information, please email or visit garden website.
A community garden, woodland and wildlife pond, created to provide a growing and communal space where people can grow, chat and relax. A garden for production of food and to connect with nature with raised beds and a space for wildflowers. The area is haven for wildlife packed with native and non-native species of trees and shrubs. History of the Plas Dinas site and woodland tours are available. There is a walk through the woodland and pond area. Historical guided tours available throughout the day.

27 ◆ PLAS CADNANT HIDDEN GARDENS
Cadnant Road, Menai Bridge, LL59 5NH. Mr Anthony Tavernor, 01248 717174, plascadnantgardens@gmail.com, www.plascadnantgardens.co.uk. *½m E of Menai Bridge. Take A545 & leave Menai Bridge heading for Beaumaris, then follow brown tourist information signs. SatNav not always reliable.* **For NGS: Wed 29 Apr (12-5). Adm £10.50, chd free.** For other opening times and information, please phone, email or visit garden website. Donation to Wales Air Ambulance.
Early C19 picturesque garden undergoing restoration since 1996. Valley gardens with waterfalls, large ornamental walled garden, woodland and early pit house. Also Alpheus water feature and Ceunant (Ravine) which gives visitors a more interesting walk featuring unusual moisture loving alpines. Recently voted one of the nation's favourite gardens. Guidebook available. Visitor centre with historic photos, before original restoration, and showing how well garden has recovered 10 years following terrible flood damage. Partial wheelchair access. Steps, gravel paths and slopes. Access statement available. Accessible Tea Room and WC.

28 PLAS PONT Y CRIBYN
Llannor, Pwllheli, LL53 8LZ. Ralph Martin & Xiaoqing Li. *3m NW of Pwllheli. Go N out of Llannor village. Keep L at fork, where the main road bends R. Our drive is the 1st drive on the L. What3words app: branched.releases.dose.* **Sat 9 May, Sun 2 Aug (10.30-4). Adm £5, chd free. Pre-booking essential, please visit www.ngs.org.uk for information & booking. Tea, coffee & cake.**
A stunning two acre mixed garden with flower beds, fruit trees, a productive vegetable garden and a large greenhouse filled with a vast collection of cacti and succulents. Follow the paths and wander through the woodland. May is the ideal time to see cacti flowers, and August is best for the garden flowers.

29 PLASGLASGWM
Penmachno, Betws-Y-Coed, LL24 0PU. Peter & Tamsyn Gallimore, 01690 760181, office@plasglasgwm.co.uk, www.plasglasgwm.co.uk. *5m from Betws y Coed. Turn off the A5 at Conwy Falls Cafe onto the B4406 to Penmachno. Once in Penmachno, please follow the brown tourism signs for Plasglasgwm for 1m out of the village.* **Visits by arrangement 3 Apr to 30 Sept for groups of up to 18. Adm £5, chd free. Tea.**
Discover a hidden place tucked away in the foothills of Eryri (Snowdonia). Five acres of gardens and grounds created by the owners over 30 years at this historic mountain farm. Hedges of yew, box and beech complement mixed and herbaceous borders, a re-introduced orchard, natural woodland and natural areas. Wander along the pathways to discover all the secret corners of this C16 farm holding. Yew and box hedging, box parterre, orchard, woodland walks, stream, bridges, seating areas and cafe.

30 SUNNINGDALE
Bull Bay Road, Bull Bay, Amlwch, LL68 9SD. Mike & Gill Cross, 01407 830753, mikeatbb@aol.com. *1½m NW of Amlwch. On A5025 through Amlwch towards Cemaes. Go past the Trecastel Hotel. It is 5 houses past. Regret, no parking at house.* **Visits by arrangement 3 May to 30 June for groups of 8+. Discuss refreshments when booking. Adm £5.**

Located on a headland overlooking the Irish sea, there are spectacular views, wildflowers and sheer drops with seating. The garden has many paths to take; discover raised fishpond and wildlife ponds, with plants jostling together and constantly evolving. Wander through the woodland but don't miss the hosta area with rill, raised vegetable beds complete with compost area and arches with climbers. Access to private headland and a completely different atmosphere in the rear garden. A 70 year old laburnum surrounded by lots of plants, different rooms and many paths and surprises to be found. Ideas for other gardeners with smaller spaces. Wheelchair access to front garden only.

31 TREBORTH BOTANIC GARDEN, BANGOR UNIVERSITY
Treborth, Bangor, LL57 2RQ. Natalie Chivers-Cross, www.treborth.bangor.ac.uk. *On the outskirts of Bangor towards Anglesey. Approach Menai Bridge from Upper Bangor on A5 or A55 J9 & travel towards Bangor for 2m. At Antelope Inn r'bout turn L before entering the Menai Bridge. What3words app: cleanest.flocking.witless.* **Sat 5 Sept (11-3). Adm £4, chd free. Tea, coffee & cake.**
Owned by Bangor University and used as a resource for teaching, research, public education and enjoyment. Treborth comprises planted borders, species rich natural grassland, ponds, arboretum, Chinese and Welsh herbal gardens, ancient woodland, and a rocky shoreline habitat. Six glasshouses provide specialised environments for tropical, temperate, orchid and carnivorous plant collections. Partnered with National Botanic Garden of Wales to champion Welsh horticulture, protect wildlife and extol the virtues of growing plants for food, fun, health and wellbeing. National Collection of Welsh Native Ferns Wheelchair access to some glasshouses and part of the garden. Woodland path is surfaced but most of the borders only accessed over grass.

32 TREFNANT BACH
Anglesey Bees, Llanddaniel Fab, Gaerwen, LL60 6ET. Dafydd & Dawn Jones, 07816 188573, dafydd@angleseybees.co.uk, www.angleseybees.co.uk. ⅖m *from the centre of Llanddaniel Fab. A5 from LlanfairPG, 1½ km W, turn L for Llanddaniel. Village centre, by bus shelter follow signs down farm track. Parking onsite. Alternatively park in village & 10 min walk.* **Visits by arrangement in Apr. Adm £5, chd free. Tea, coffee & cake. Discuss refreshments when booking.**
An eight acre smallholding which is a pollinator and wildlife sanctuary. Discover our spring-fed pond with islands and honeybee friendly woodland and lakeside walks. Spring bulbs and honeybee specific herbaceous borders as well as an apiary. Wander through the orchard with soft fruit and raised vegetable bed. Meadows grazed with Shropshire tree-friendly sheep. Beekeeping training and experiences. Local award-winning honey for sale. Very gentle slopes, short-mowed grassed or hard paths. Refreshment area accessible with hard surface. Regret WC unsuitable for wheelchair access.

33 TY CADFAN SANT
National Street, Tywyn, LL36 9DD. Mrs Katie Pearce, 07816 604851, katie@tycadfansant.co.uk. *3m from Aberdovey. A493 going S & W: Turn L into one way, garden ahead. Bear R, parking on 2nd L. A493 going N: 1st R in 30mph zone, L at bottom by garden, parking 2nd L.* **Sat 4 July (1.30-5.30). Cream teas. Sun 5 July (11.30-4). Light refreshments. Adm £5, chd free. Pulled pork baps on Sunday lunchtime. Drinks and home-made cakes.** Visits also by arrangement 14 Mar to 1 Nov. Discuss refreshments when booking. Please text or email to book visit.
Large eco friendly garden with much to discover. In the front garden you will find shrubbery, mixed flower beds and roses that surround a mature copper beech. Six steps lead to the largely productive back garden which has an apiary in the orchard, fruit, vegetables, flowers and a polytunnel. Plenty of seating throughout to sit and enjoy the garden. Seasonal produce available, honey and preserves, plants. Bee keeper present, information on environmentally friendly gardening. Partial wheelchair access due to steps to rear garden.

34 TYN Y PANT
Boduan, Pwllheli, LL53 6DT. Mrs Elizabeth Broadbent, 07925 888356, royandlizbroadbent@hotmail.co.uk. *Off the A497 between Pwllheli & Nefyn. On the A497 travelling from Pwllheli, turn L opp St Buan's Church, (from Nefyn R) after approx 500 metres. Sharp R into our driveway which has the house name clearly displayed.* **Sat 16 May, Sat 18 July (11-4.30). Adm £5, chd free. Tea, coffee & cake.** Visits also by arrangement 29 May to 18 Sept for groups of up to 20.
A rural garden developing around mature trees, shrubs and ponds. We are constantly adding to the planting, recycling, reusing and repurposing materials and growing plants from seeds, cuttings and division. There are plenty of places to sit and relax. A productive organic vegetable garden includes a polytunnel and raised beds. Around five years old the garden is maturing and changing almost daily. There are a number of quirky art installations and structures throughout the garden made by repurposing items normally bound for landfill. A craft studio has been created from a derelict piggery. Wooden boardwalks provide access to damp areas all year round. There are lots of places to sit. The main garden is wheelchair accessible. There are areas of gravel and paths that may not be suitable.

35 Y FELIN RHYD HIR
Efailnewydd, Pwllheli, LL53 8TN. Adrian & Carol Priest, 07756 115138, adrian.priest2908@gmail.com, www.facebook.com/p/Y-Felin-Rhyd-Hir. *Situated on the B4415 between Efailnewydd & Rhydyclafdy. What3words app: refreshed.windy.braked.* **Sat 4, Sun 5 July (11-3.30). Adm £5, chd free. Tea, coffee & cake.**
Y Felin Rhyd Hir (Melin Bodfel) is a stone built water-powered corn mill. The composite overshot waterwheel with cast iron shrouds has been renovated. The extensive grounds inc newly landscaped garden, Victorian style glasshouse, vegetable beds and orchard. A viewing cabin on stilts overlooks a lake which provides a habitat for wildlife and there is a walk beside a woodland of native species.

NORTH EAST WALES

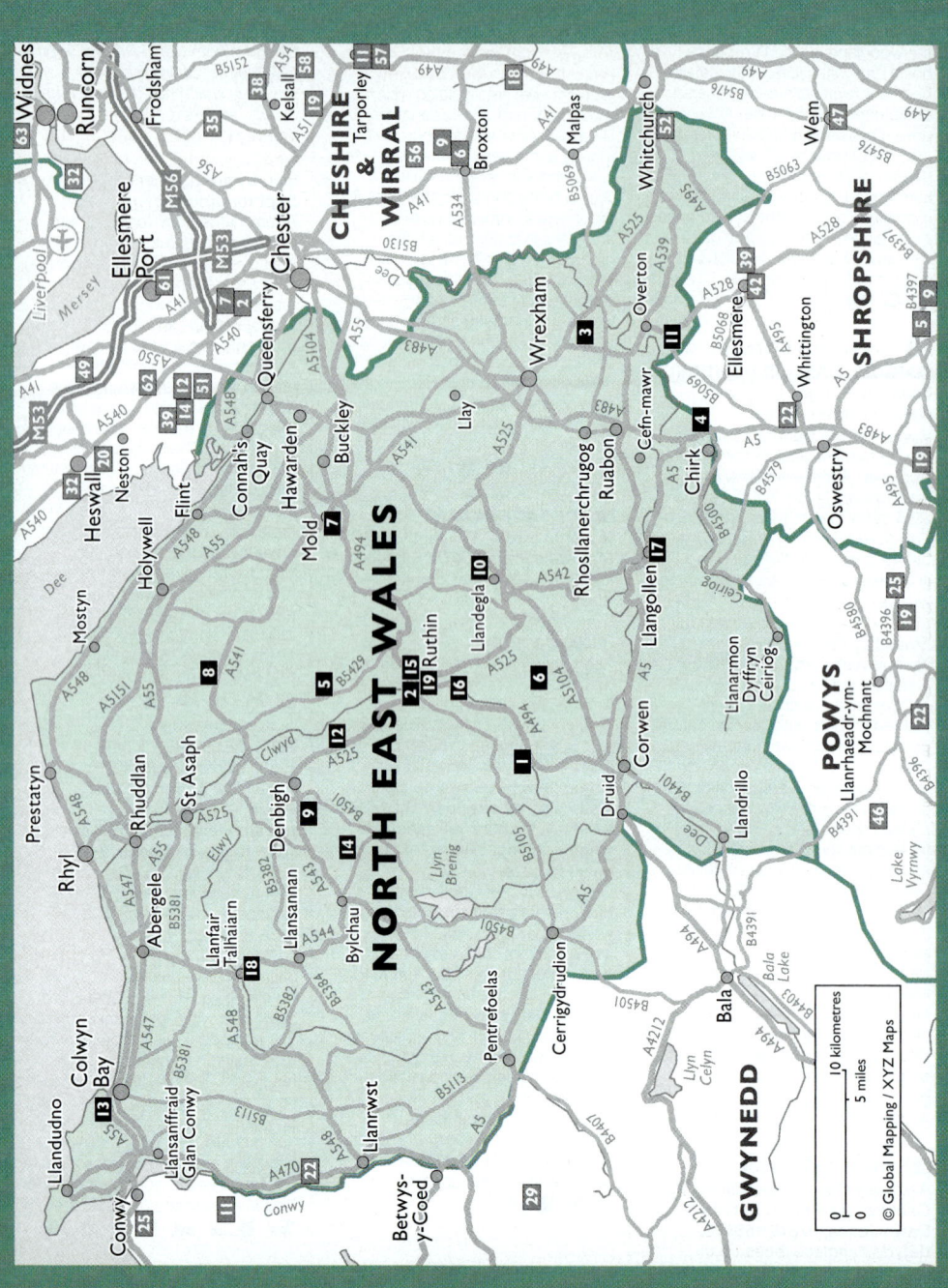

NORTH EAST WALES

VOLUNTEERS

County Organiser
Deborah Vogwell
07788 645094
deborah.vogwell@ngs.org.uk

County Treasurer
Vera Bluhm
07437 688339
vera.bluhm@ngs.org.uk

Booklet Co-ordinator
Heather Broughton
07747 737237
heather.broughton@ngs.org.uk

Talks
Shelagh Williams
shelagh.williams@ngs.org.uk

Publicity
Sharon Blanchard
07930 077105
sharon.blanchard@ngs.org.uk

Assistant County Organisers
Fiona Bell
07813 087797
bell_fab@hotmail.com

Iris Dobbie
01745 886730
iris.dobbie@ngs.org.uk

Jane Moore
07769 046317
jane.moore@ngs.org.uk

Elizabeth Thorburn
07502 610916
elizabeth.thorburn@ngs.org.uk

@North East Wales NGS
@north_east_wales_ngs

OPENING DATES

All entries subject to change. For latest information check www.ngs.org.uk
Map locator numbers are shown to the right of each garden name.

February

Snowdrop Openings

Wednesday 4th
Aberclwyd Manor   1

Wednesday 18th
Aberclwyd Manor   1

March

Wednesday 4th
Aberclwyd Manor   1

Wednesday 18th
Aberclwyd Manor   1

April

Wednesday 1st
Aberclwyd Manor   1

Wednesday 15th
Aberclwyd Manor   1

Wednesday 29th
Aberclwyd Manor   1

May

Monday 4th
Dibleys Nurseries   6

Wednesday 13th
Aberclwyd Manor   1

Sunday 17th
Brynkinalt Hall   4

Wednesday 27th
Aberclwyd Manor   1

Sunday 31st
Bron y Gaer   2
Nantclwyd y Dre   15

June

Saturday 6th
Knolton Hall   11
Scott House   19

Sunday 7th
Scott House   19

Wednesday 10th
Aberclwyd Manor   1

Sunday 21st
Gwaenynog   9
NEW Helen's Garden   10

Wednesday 24th
Aberclwyd Manor   1

Friday 26th
◆ Plas Newydd   17

Saturday 27th
NEW Bryn Afon Hall   3
Mysevin   14

Sunday 28th
NEW Bryn Afon Hall   3
Mysevin   14

July

Thursday 2nd
NEW Llys Euryn Cottage 13

Wednesday 8th
Aberclwyd Manor   1

Saturday 11th
The Laundry   12

Sunday 12th
The Laundry   12

Wednesday 22nd
Aberclwyd Manor   1

Sunday 26th
NEW Helen's Garden   10

August

Wednesday 5th
Aberclwyd Manor   1

Wednesday 19th
Aberclwyd Manor   1

Saturday 29th
Glasfryn Hall   8

Sunday 30th
Glasfryn Hall   8

Monday 31st
Glasfryn Hall   8

September

Wednesday 2nd
Aberclwyd Manor 1

Wednesday 16th
Aberclwyd Manor 1

Wednesday 30th
Aberclwyd Manor 1

By Arrangement

Arrange a personalised garden visit with your club, or group of friends, on a date to suit you. See individual garden entries for full details.

Aberclwyd Manor 1
NEW Bryn Afon Hall 3
NEW Castanwydden 5
Fron Haul 7
NEW Llys Euryn Cottage 13
NEW Penymynydd 16
Primrose Cottage 18

THE GARDENS

1 ABERCLWYD MANOR
Derwen, Corwen, LL21 9SF. Mr & Mrs G Sparvoli, 01824 750431, aberclwydgarden@outlook.com. *7m from Ruthin. Travelling on A494 from Ruthin to Corwen. At Bryn SM Service Stn turn R, follow sign to Derwen. Aberclwyd gates on L before Derwen. Do not follow SatNav directions.* Wed 4, Wed 18 Feb, Wed 4, Wed 18 Mar, Wed 1, Wed 15, Wed 29 Apr, Wed 13, Wed 27 May, Wed 10, Wed 24 June, Wed 8, Wed 22 July, Wed 5, Wed 19 Aug, Wed 2, Wed 16, Wed 30 Sept (11-4). Adm £5, chd free. Cream teas. **Visits also by arrangement 4 Feb to 30 Dec for groups of 10+. Parking for small coaches.**

A four acre garden on a sloping hillside overlooking the Upper Clwyd Valley. The garden has mature trees with snowdrops, fritillaries and cyclamen. An Italianate garden of box hedging lies below the house ponds, perennials, roses and an orchard are also to be enjoyed within this cleverly structured area. Mass of cyclamen in September and spring flowers a must visit in April. Mostly flat with some steps and slopes.

2 BRON Y GAER
Castle Street, Ruthin, LL15 1DP. Mr Richard Chamberlain. *120yd up Castle St from the Square on the R.* Sun 31 May (11-4). **Combined adm with Nantclwyd y Dre £7, chd free.**

A real secret garden. Hidden from the bustle of town, and nestled next door to Nantclwyd y Dre. This garden has beautiful cottage garden planting, a small collection of medicinal herbs and seating by a quiet reflective pool. Good wheelchair access, but please be aware that the garden has two low steps.

Helen's Garden

3 NEW BRYN AFON HALL

Kiln Lane, Cross Lanes, Wrexham, LL13 0TA. Julia & Stephen Whitby, 07710 251644, jmwhitby@gmail.com. *4m S of Wrexham. Situated on Kiln Ln (B5130). From Wrexham take the A525 towards Whitchurch. At the T-lights at Cross Lanes turn R. The main drive is ¾m on R. What3words app: indicated.compound.ankle.* **Sat 27, Sun 28 June (11-4). Adm £6, chd free. Tea, coffee & cake.** Visits also by arrangement 29 June to 1 Sept for groups of 5 to 15.

A seven acre garden parts date back to the early C19 with mature trees inc oaks, wellingtonia, *Acacia robinia* and an orchard. Since 2020 the owners have bought back and cleared an area neglected for decades which would have been part of a formal garden. There are herbaceous borders, rose parterre, summerhouse and ponds leading on to a wildlife area where over a 100 trees have been planted.

Penymynydd

4 BRYNKINALT HALL

Brynkinalt, Chirk, Wrexham, LL14 5NS. Iain & Kate Hill-Trevor, www.brynkinalt.co.uk. *6m N of Oswestry, 10m S of Wrexham. Come off A5/A483 & take B5070 into Chirk village. Turn into Trevor Rd (beside St Mary's Church). Cont past houses on R. Turn R on bend into Estate Gates. N.B. Do not use postcode with SatNav.* **Sun 17 May (11-4). Adm £6, chd free. Tea, coffee & cake.**

A five acre ornamental woodland shrubbery, overgrown until recently, now cleared and replanted, rhododendron walk, historic ponds, well, grottos, ha-ha and battlements, new stumpery, ancient redwoods and yews. Also two acre garden beside Grade II* house, with modern rose and formal beds, deep herbaceous borders, pond with shrub, mixed beds, pleached limes and hedge patterns. Home of the first Duke of Wellington's grandmother and Sir John Trevor, Speaker of House of Commons. Stunning rhododendrons and formal West Garden. Major film location for Lady Chatterley's Lover.

5 NEW CASTANWYDDEN

Fforddlas, Llandyrnog, LL16 4LR. Mr A M Burrows, 01824 790404. *4m E of Denbigh. Take road from Denbigh due E to Llandyrnog approx 4m. From Ruthin take B5429 due N to Llandyrnog.* Visits by arrangement for groups of up to 15. Adm £5, chd free.

An acre garden, overflowing with unusual cottage garden plants. Discover the sunken patio garden with stone troughs as well as a newly replanted rock garden and gravel bed with grasses. Trellises covered in roses and clematis delight visitors. Some unusual trees and wonderful colour means there is interest all summer. We also have late flowering salvias and autumn cyclamen.

6 DIBLEYS NURSERIES

Cefn Rhydd, Llanelidan, Ruthin, LL15 2LG. Lynne Dibley, www.dibleys.com. *7m S of Ruthin. Follow brown signs off A525 nr Llysfasi College. What3Words app: screaming.topples.submits.* **Mon 4 May (10-4). Adm £6, chd free. Tea, coffee & cake.** Donation to Plant Heritage.

An eight acre woodland garden with a wide selection of rare and unusual trees set in beautiful countryside. In late spring there is a lovely display of rhododendrons, magnolias, cherries and camellias. Much of our grassland promotes native wildflowers. Our ¾ acre commercial glasshouses are open showing a display of *Streptocarpus* and other rare houseplants. Houseplant shop. Partial wheelchair access to glasshouses, uneven ground and steep paths in arboretum and elsewhere.

7 FRON HAUL

Denbigh Road, Mold, CH7 1BL. David & Hilary Preece, 07966 080032, dglynnep@gmail.com. *We are a yellow house, opp the entrance to Bailey Hill. For SatNav use 'Shire View, Mold' instead of the postcode. The house is not in Shire View but adjoins the entrance to that estate.* Visits by arrangement 1 Apr to 20 Sept for groups of 5 to 20. Adm £5, chd free. Tea, coffee & cake.

Approximately ⅔ acre garden created around 1870, possibly under Edward Kemp's guidance, and may be considered the oldest 'domestic' garden in Mold. The general layout and many original features remain. It comprises herbaceous borders, a small orchard, lawns, a pond and a wisteria covered walkway. There is also a wooded area with a number of old yew trees dating back to Victorian times. Disabled parking available, please call in advance. Access to garden via terraced area, the garden is on a slope and some paths are uneven.

8 GLASFRYN HALL

South Street, Caerwys, Mold, CH7 5AF. Mrs Lise Roberts, www.orielglasfryn.com. *Nr Caerwys town centre. Follow signs for Caerwys from the A55 N Wales expressway or the A541 Mold/ Denbigh Rd. Garden is at Oriel Glasfryn Gallery, which is clearly signed at the S end of the town.* **Sat 29, Sun 30, Mon 31 Aug (10.30-3.30). Adm £6, chd free. Tea, coffee & cake in the Horsebox cafe. Ice-cream & alcoholic beverages also available. Seating is outdoors. Regret, no picnics.**
Victorian villa set in three acres of gardens with an interesting variety of mature trees, beds, tea house, pond and parterre. Horsebox café serving on the croquet lawn with its stunning views of the Clwydian hills. The property is also home to Oriel Glasfryn Gallery, featuring work by leading Welsh artists. The 2025 open gardens coincide with the spring exhibition meaning the house will be open. The gardens are on level ground and most areas can be accessed by wheelchair.

& 🐾 ☕ 🔊

9 GWAENYNOG

Denbigh, LL16 5NU. Major & Mrs Tom Smith. *1m W of Denbigh. On A543, Lodge on L, ¼m drive.* **Sun 21 June (2-5.30). Adm £5, chd free. Home-made teas.**
Two acres inc the restored walled garden where Beatrix Potter wrote and illustrated the Tale of the Flopsy Bunnies; also a small exhibition of some of her work. Long herbaceous borders and island beds, some recently replanted, espalier fruit trees, rose pergola and vegetable area. C16 house (not open) visited by Dr Samuel Johnson during his Tour of Wales. Wheelchair users will need to negotiate grass paths.

& ❀ ☕

10 NEW HELEN'S GARDEN

Plas yn Coed, Llandegla, LL11 3AL. Fraser Robertson. *½m outside Llandegla. Postcode for SatNav: LL11 3AW. Follow yellow NGS signs. What3words app: users. fever.inviting.* **Sun 21 June, Sun 26 July (11-4.30). Adm £5, chd free. Tea, coffee & cake. Home-made cakes, tea, coffee & squash.**
This one acre garden is maturing well with a good show of many herbaceous perennials, shrubs and trees giving year-round interest and has fabulous views over the Horseshoe Pass and beyond. A productive vegetable plot, soft fruit cage, greenhouse and orchard give extra interest for the visitors. Also a pond and areas are set aside for attracting wildlife. Partial wheelchair access in areas. Some steep slopes and gravel paths.

& 🐾 ☕ 🔊

11 KNOLTON HALL

Oswestry Road, Overton, Wrexham, LL13 0LG. Mr & Mrs Edward Chantler. *5m N of Ellsemere, 8m S of Wrexham. Take B5069 towards Oswestry. Pass Knolton cheese farm & do not turn R down the unmade road. Driveway on R by black & white gate lodge. What3words app: starring.bounding. orbit.* **Sat 6 June (10-4.30). Adm £5, chd free. Tea, coffee & cake.**
Situated on the banks of the Shellbrook and the River Dee this five acre garden has beautiful views of the Lower Dee Valley. The garden has many mature trees underplanted with snowdrops, fritillaries and bluebells. A tiered Italianate garden of box hedging lies below the house and shrubs, ponds, perennials and roses. Abundance of spring flowers, rhododendrons and magnolia. wheelchair access to top of the garden. There are changes in levels and small steps.

& ☕ 🔊

12 THE LAUNDRY

Llanrhaeadr, Denbigh, LL8 4NL. Mr & Mrs T Williams, 07841 422497, jenny@thelaundrygarden.co.uk, www.thelaundryretreat.co.uk. *3m SE of Denbigh. Entrance off A525 Denbigh to Ruthin Rd.* **Sat 11, Sun 12 July (11-4). Adm £7, chd free. Home-made teas.**
A chance to see a new garden evolving within an old setting. Terraced courtyard garden, developed since 2009, surrounded by old stone walls enclosing cottage style planting and formal hedging. 12 years ago, work started on the old kitchen walled garden with a view to incorporating it within the whole garden plan. Woodland walk, roses, pleached limes, peonies and herbaceous planting. Some deep gravel areas, may prove difficult for wheelchair users.

& ❀ 🚗 🛏 ☕ 🔊

13 NEW LLYS EURYN COTTAGE

Tan Y Bryn Road, Rhos On Sea, Colwyn Bay, LL28 4AA. Mr & Mrs D Kitson, 07747 721059, dav1dck1ts0n@yahoo.co.uk. *2m W of Colwyn Bay. J20 A55. B5115 towards Llandrillo yn Rhos. L at t-lights onto Rhos Rd. At T-junc with Tan y Bryn Rd (LL28 4TT) go straight over to Bryn Euryn Nat. Res. car park. Take 300m track or steps to garden.* **Thur 2 July (2-7). Adm £7, chd free. Tea, coffee & cake.** Visits also by arrangement Apr to Aug for groups of 15 to 30. Discuss refreshments when booking.
More than an acre of garden set in woodland with sea views. Discover inner walled area with small trees, shrubs and herbaceous perennials. Hostas are a feature. Terraces planted with drought tolerant plants. Outer garden has a vegetable area, greenhouses, and shrub and herbaceous perennial borders. A steep grassy slope is planted with unusual small trees and shrubs. Sensible footwear is advised.

❀ ☕ 🔊

14 MYSEVIN

Nantglyn, Denbigh, LL16 5PG. Ms Alex Kerr-Wilson. *4½m SW of Denbigh. From Denbigh B4501 to Nantglyn. Mysevin entrance on R opp footpath sign. Stone gate pillars to 8ft wide drive & bridge. What3words app: stay.denoting.hips.* **Sat 27, Sun 28 June (2-5). Adm £6, chd free. Tea, coffee & cake.**
Situated on a wooded hillside over looking lawned gardens, a little rose garden, meadows and interesting herbaceous borders running down to the River Ystrad. To the rear of the house is a green bank inc white garden and ornamental woodland garden. The garden is the essence of peace and serenity, with rare plants and a shell house by Blott Kerr-Wilson. Wheelchair access to front garden on gravel paths.

& ❀ ☕ 🔊

15 NANTCLWYD Y DRE

Castle Street, Ruthin, LL15 1DP. Denbighshire County Council, www.denbighshire.gov.uk/nantclwyd-y-dre-ruthin. *100yd along Castle St from the square on the R. Access via alleyway to side of house. Nearest parking Market St or Dog Ln car park.* **Sun 31 May (11-4). Combined adm with Bron y**

Gaer £7, chd free. Cream teas at Nantclwyd y Dre. Gluten free and non dairy options available.

With far-reaching views over Ruthin and the Clwydian Range, this Grade II listed walled garden was the former kitchen garden for Ruthin Castle. The garden features elements from three distinct periods; Medieval aspects inc an orchard with wildflowers, hedges, a nuttery, and vegetable beds representative of the C17 and C19 additions such as a glasshouse and herbaceous borders. One of the oldest timber framed town houses in Wales and the Lord's Garden first mentioned in 1282 is thought to pre-date the structure, C17 summerhouse. Most of the garden is wheelchair accessible but with gravel paths.

16 NEW **PENYMYNYDD**
Pwllglas, Ruthin, LL15 2PD. Gill & Sandy Toogood, 07818 200959, gill.toogood@me.com. *3m out of Ruthin on A494. On entering Pwllglas take 2nd R turn, go up the hill behind the houses. After 300 yards you will reach small x-roads, proceed straight on. Penymynydd is the last drive on R.* **Visits by arrangement 23 May to 26 June for groups of 5 to 25. Adm £5, chd free. Tea, coffee & cake.**
Set in about an acre of ground is a new garden and work in progress. Divided into small areas around a limestone outcrop the garden has herbaceous borders, water features, seating areas, mature trees, and a woodland walk. The garden is accessible but there are steps and slopes. The woodland path is uneven. Special features inc limestone ridges, tree carving, and a bridged water flow. Garden is accessed by a short single track lane.

17 ♦ **PLAS NEWYDD**
Llangollen, LL20 8AW. Denbighshire County Council, 01978 862834, plasnewydd@ denbighshire.gov.uk, www. instagram.com/plasnewyddllan. *Follow brown sign from A5 in Llangollen. Hill St is steep.* **For NGS: Fri 26 June (8.30-4). Adm by donation. For other opening times and information, please phone, email or visit garden website.**
Home to the famous Ladies of Llangollen (1780-1831), boasts a picturesque Grade II* garden with a formal parterre, intricate topiary, and a

Gorsedd stone circle (C19). A serene woodland walk follows the Cyflymen stream. The garden features a stunning rose collection, inc varieties cherished by the Ladies, offering a blend of history and natural beauty.

18 PRIMROSE COTTAGE
Water Street, Llanfairtalhaiarn, Abergele, LL22 8SB. Mrs Elizabeth Thorburn, 07502 610916, elizabethprimrose@icloud.com. *6m from Abergele on A548. From Swan Sq, with post office on R, walk & look L for a wide footpath. Primrose Cottage can be found halfway up hill to L & before the handrail. What3words app: firewall.deflect.insects.* **Visits by arrangement 1 May to 28 June for groups of 5 to 20. Adm £6.50, chd free. Tea, coffee & cake.**
Small cottage garden on a south west facing sloped site. There is stone wall terracing and steps that lead to different areas inc a wildlife pond, raised ponds, gravel planting, small herbaceous borders, lawn area, mini orchard, Japanese style courtyard and seating areas. Lovingly developed over the years, still making mistakes and still a work in progress.

19 SCOTT HOUSE
Corwen Road, Ruthin, LL15 2NP. Scott House Residents. *Park in town, then walk from town square onto Castle St. Garden 300m beyond Ruthin Castle Hotel, entrance on R. Disabled parking at garden.* **Sat 6, Sun 7 June (11-4). Adm £5, chd free. Cream teas.**
Redesigned 2½ acre shared garden surrounding a fine 1930s Arts and Crafts house former nurses home to Ruthin Castle hospital. Breathtaking open views of the Vale of Clwyd. Avenue of limes and a magnificent cedar of Lebanon stands sentinel over a newly planted arboretum. Long herbaceous borders planted for summer long interest. New highly scented rose garden and recently constructed vegetable plot. Partial wheelchair access due to steps and terraces.

Bryn Afon Hall

POWYS

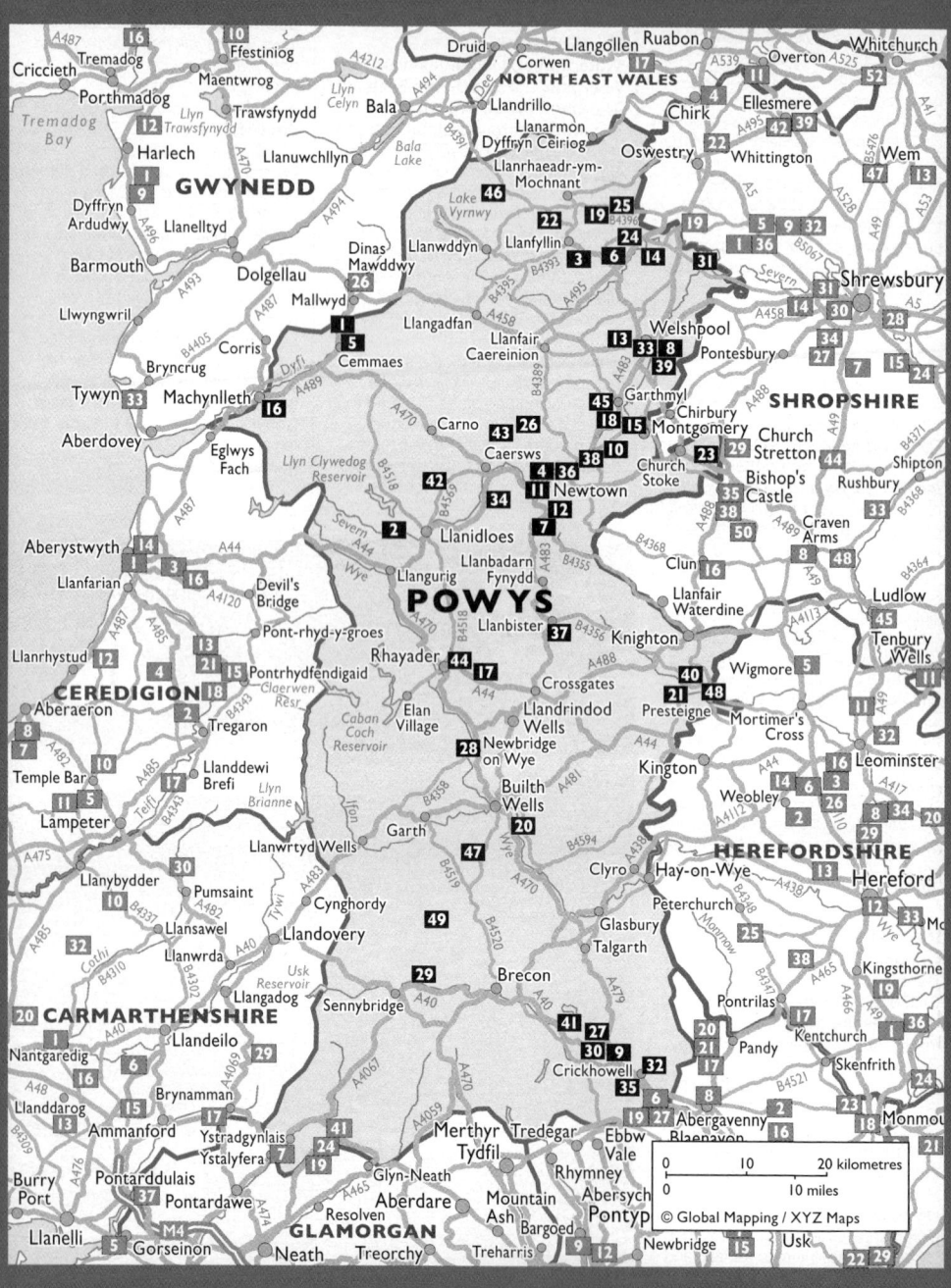

POWYS

VOLUNTEERS

North Powys County Organiser
Susan Paynton 01686 650531
susan.paynton@ngs.org.uk

County Treasurer
Jude Boutle 07702 061623
jude.boutle@ngs.org.uk

Publicity
Jill Hill
jill.hill@ngs.org.uk

Sue McKillop 07753 289701
sue.mckillop@ngs.org.uk

Simon Quin 07958 915120
simon.quin@ngs.org.uk

Talks
Helen Anthony 07986 061051
helen.anthony@ngs.org.uk

Social Media
Rebecca Taylor 07554 152667
rebecca.taylor@ngs.org.uk

Booklet Co-ordinator
Position Vacant

Assistant County Organisers
Simon Cain 07958 915115
simon.cain@ngs.org.uk

Jane Cliff 07709 236531
jane.cliff@ngs.org.uk

Gill Powell 07968 250364
gill.powell@ngs.org.uk

South Powys County Organiser
Dr Alison Kemp 07791 361305
alison.kemp@ngs.org.uk

Temporary County Treasurer
Jude Boutle 07702 061623
jude.boutle@ngs.org.uk

Publicity Officer and Talks
Gail Jones 07974 103692
gail.jones@ngs.org.uk

Photographer
Laura Shepherd
laura.shepherd@ngs.org.uk

@powysngs
@powysngs

OPENING DATES

All entries subject to change. For latest information check
www.ngs.org.uk

Extended openings are shown at the beginning of each month

Map locator numbers are shown to the right of each garden name.

March

Sunday 29th
Llangedwyn Hall 25
Oak Cottage 33

April

Monday 6th
Oak Cottage 33

Sunday 19th
Oak Cottage 33

May

Sunday 3rd
Treberfydd House 41

Monday 4th
Oak Cottage 33

Saturday 9th
◆ Dingle Nurseries & Garden 13
Garregllwyd 17

Sunday 10th
◆ Dingle Nurseries & Garden 13
Garregllwyd 17

Sunday 17th
Glanwye 20

Saturday 23rd
Bachie Uchaf 3

Sunday 24th
Bachie Uchaf 3
Llysdinam 28

June

Saturday 6th
Plum Tree Cottage 35
The Rock House 37

Sunday 7th
Hurdley Hall 23
Llwynau Mawr Farm 27
Maes Llechau 30
The Neuadd 32
The Rock House 37

Wednesday 10th
Fairdene Gallery Garden 15

Sunday 14th
Cwm-Weeg 12

Saturday 20th
Lower Wernfigin Barns 29
14 St Mary's Place 39

Sunday 21st
NEW Clywd Dwyrain 9
Hurdley Hall 23
Lower Wernfigin Barns 29
14 St Mary's Place 39

Wednesday 24th
Vaynor Park 45

Saturday 27th
Ash and Elm Horticulture 2
Forge Village Gardens 16
NEW Hafotty Ganol 22
NEW Upper Bwlch Farm 44

Sunday 28th
Ash and Elm Horticulture 2
Forge Village Gardens 16
NEW Hafotty Ganol 22
NEW Upper Bwlch Farm 44

July

Saturday 4th
1 Church Bank 8
NEW Vicarage Farm 46

Sunday 5th
1 Church Bank 8
NEW Trefeglwys Gardens 42
NEW Vicarage Farm 46

Saturday 11th
NEW Bryn Uchel Caravan Park 5

Sunday 12th
NEW Bryn Uchel Caravan Park 5
Eve's Garden 14

Wednesday 15th
Fairdene Gallery Garden 15

Saturday 18th
Cultivate Community Garden 11

Sunday 19th
Willowbrook 48
NEW Yscirfechan 49

Thursday 23rd
- Welsh Lavender — 47

Friday 24th
- Welsh Lavender — 47

Saturday 25th
- Bryn Teg — 4
- Ponthafren — 36
- Welsh Lavender — 47

Sunday 26th
- Bryn Teg — 4
- NEW Llanfechain Gardens — 24
- Ponthafren — 36
- Welsh Lavender — 47

August

Saturday 1st
- NEW Caelydan Bungalow — 7

Sunday 2nd
- Bryngwyn Hall — 6
- NEW Caelydan Bungalow — 7

Saturday 8th
- Aberangell Village Gardens — 1

Sunday 9th
- Aberangell Village Gardens — 1
- NEW Yscirfechan — 49

Sunday 30th
- Llwyn — 26
- NEW Yscirfechan — 49

Monday 31st
- Garthmyl Hall — 18

October

Saturday 10th
- Dingle Nurseries & Garden — 13

Sunday 11th
- Dingle Nurseries & Garden — 13

By Arrangement

Arrange a personalised garden visit with your club, or group of friends, on a date to suit you. See individual garden entries for full details.

- Bryn Teg — 4
- 1 Church Bank — 8
- Cuckoo Hall — 10
- Eve's Garden — 14
- Garregllwyd — 17
- Glan Yr Afon — 19
- The Grove — 21
- The Malthouse — 31
- The Neuadd — 32
- Plas Dinam — 34
- Ponthafren — 36
- Rock Mill — 38
- Tranquility Haven — 40
- Tyn-y-Graig — 43
- NEW Vicarage Farm — 46

Vicarage Farm

THE GARDENS

GROUP OPENING

1 ABERANGELL VILLAGE GARDENS
Aberangell, Machynlleth, SY20 9ND. *On A470 midway beween Dolgellau & Machynlleth. From Mallwyd r'about to Cemmaes Rd turn R at Aberangell sign. From Machynlleth, come through Cemmaes & Cwm Llinau, turn L at Aberangell sign.* **Sat 8, Sun 9 Aug (11-5). Combined adm £7, chd free. Home-made teas at Ger Y Llyn & Pen Pentre.**

BETHANIA CHAPEL
John Linden.
GER Y LLYN
Janet Twigg.
NEW NANT Y CYFF
Ant and Cathy Brown.
THE OLD COACH HOUSE
Sue McKillop.
PEN PENTRE
Jacqueline Parsons.
NEW SWN YR AFON
Mrs Jan Williams.
TY HEBRON
Linda Rogers.

The beautiful village of Aberangell is on the River Angell on edge of Eryri National Park (Snowdonia) with forest tracks and mountains providing backdrop. Seven very different gardens: Ger y Llyn, designed and thoughtfully developed garden, beautiful borders, vegetable plot, originally designed water feature, wild area. Ty Hebron terraced garden built into steep hillside with viewpoint, raised beds and innovative ideas. Pen Pentre on site of old station, many railway artefacts displayed in original waiting room and cottage garden style planting with vegetable plot. Slate steps lead to seating area by river. Bethania Chapel is full of salvaged and upcycled artefacts used to provide planters and interest, espaliered fruit trees grow along chapel walls. Nant y Cyf is a large garden with interesting features and planting, vegetable beds, wide borders. Swn yr Afon, a rewilded garden on the riverbank, transformed from wasteland. The Old Coach House has cottage style garden with shrubs, perennials and vegetables. Free transport around the village and to The Old Coach House. WC facilities in village hall, Pen Pentre, The Old Coach House and Nant y Cyff.

2 ASH AND ELM HORTICULTURE
Cae Felyn, Old Hall, Llanidloes, SY18 6PW. Emma Maxwell, www.ashandelm.co.uk. *3m from Llanidloes. At Llanidloes Market Hall turn R on Shortbridge St over river & stay on this road for 3m. Garden on L.* **Sat 27, Sun 28 June (11-3.30). Adm £5, chd free. Light refreshments. Range of cakes, seasonal fruit & home-made elderflower cordial.**

Diverse five acre market garden; flowers, vegetables, fruit, nuts and plants grown using agroecological techniques that nurture nature. Enjoy wandering through the extensive cut flower garden or explore the one acre orchard, home to a family of barn owls. See beehives and a wide range of seasonal vegetables growing in the polytunnels, glasshouse and in the field or just relax by one of the wildlife pools.

3 BACHIE UCHAF
Bachie Road, Llanfyllin, SY22 5NF. Glyn & Glenys Lloyd. *S of Llanfyllin. Going towards Welshpool on A490 turn R onto Bachie Rd after Llanfyllin primary sch. Keep straight for ⅘ m. Take drive R uphill at cottage on L.* **Sat 23, Sun 24 May (12-5). Adm £6, chd free. Home-made teas.**

Inspiring and colourful hillside country garden. Gravel paths meander around extensive planting and over streams cascading into ponds. Specimen trees, shrubs, rhododendrons and azaleas aplenty and a vegetable garden. Enjoy the wonderful views from one of the many seats; your senses will be rewarded.

4 BRYN TEG
Bryn Lane, Newtown, SY16 2DP. Novlet Childs, 01686 624549, mikeanddolly@talktalk.net, www.instagram.com/dollys_jamaican_garden. *From centre Newtown, turn L on B4568 at t-lights then R on Llanfair Caereinion Rd. Turn L Bryn Ln signed Hospital.* **Sat 25, Sun 26 July (11-4.30). Adm £4, chd free. Tea, coffee & cake at Ponthafren. Open nearby Ponthafren. Visits also by arrangement 1 June to 17 July for groups of 6 to 20.**

Amazing exotic, secret Caribbean garden in centre of Newtown planted to remind me of my childhood in Jamaica and an exciting walk through the jungle. High above the head are banana leaves and colourful climbers. A winding path takes you on a journey through a moongate into another land. Sounds of water fill the air; explosion of colourful intermingling flowers and plants. A huge number of plants on many levels. All shapes, sizes and colours mixed together as found in tropical jungles. Feel transported to another continent. Even in the rain you will get that jungle experience.

5 NEW BRYN UCHEL CARAVAN PARK
Cwmllinau, Machynlleth, SY20 9PE. Mr Gwynant Davies, www.brynuchel.co.uk. *9m NW of Machynlleth next to the A470. From Machynlleth, follow A489 for 6m. At r'about, L to A 470 for 3m to Cwm Llinau, turn R. From Welshpool A458 W to Mallwyd r'about, turn L on A 470 for 3m, turn L at Cwm Llinau. ½ m to Caravan Park.* **Sat 11, Sun 12 July (11-4). Adm £6, chd free. Tea, coffee & cake in the reception building.**

Discover the blossoming beauty nestled in the heart of the Dyfi Valley, Bryn Uchel Caravan Park has been a beloved retreat since its establishment in 1965. In 2017, we took a significant step to enhance our green spaces by hiring a skilled landscape gardener. This decision transformed our gardens, resulting in a stunning array of hundreds of varieties of flowers, shrubs, and bushes. Partial wheelchair access; the top level may be too steep for wheelchairs.

Our donation to Marie Curie this year is equivalent to 17,521 hours of hospice at home care.

6 BRYNGWYN HALL
Bwlch-y-Cibau, Llanfyllin, SY22 5LJ. Auriol Marchioness of Linlithgow, www.bryngwyn.com. *3m SE Llanfyllin. From Llanfyllin take A490 towards Welshpool for 3m turn L up drive just before Bwlch-y-Cibau.* **Sun 2 Aug (11.30-4.30). Adm £8, chd free. Home-made teas. For other opening times and information, please visit garden website.**
Stunning Grade II* listed nine acre garden with 60 acres parkland design inspired by William Emes. Woodland garden, shrubbery, rose garden, restored herbaceous borders, meadows and serpentine lake. Unusual trees, shrubs and unique Poison Garden.

7 NEW CAELYDAN BUNGALOW
Dolfor, Newtown, SY16 4AL. Sarah & Dave Beauchamp. *3m S Newtown. Take A483 S toward Llandrindod Wells, 1st R at end of 30mph zone in Dolfor- from Llandrindod Wells, L down lane, ¼m before Dolfor, start of 30mph zone. What3words app: tricky.desktops. commit.* **Sat 1, Sun 2 Aug (12-5). Adm £5, chd free. Tea, coffee & cake.**
A ⅓ acre garden at 1000ft encouraging wildlife and diversity. Started in 2020 from grazing land, discover many features inc perennial beds, pond and gazebo, raised vegetable beds and bog garden. Wander through a heritage orchard and wildflower meadow with many native species. Take a seat to soak up the views (Cadair Idris)– the garden is evolving and adapting as our own gardening skills develop.

8 1 CHURCH BANK
Welshpool, SY21 7DR. Mel & Heather Parkes, 01938 559112, melandheather@live.co.uk. *Centre of Welshpool. Church Bank leads onto Salop Rd from Church St. Follow one way system, use main car park then short walk. Follow yellow NGS signs.* **Sat 4, Sun 5 July (12-5). Adm £4, chd free. Tea, coffee & cake. Visits also by arrangement Apr to Sept for groups of 5 to 30.**
An intimate jewel in the town with many interesting plants and unusual features where the sounds of water fill the air. Densely planted garden with Gothic arch and zig zag path leading to shell grotto, bonsai garden and fernery. Explore the ground floor of this C17 barrelmakers cottage and museum of tools and memorabilia.

9 NEW CLYWD DWYRAIN
Tretower, Crickhowell, NP8 1RF. Kathryn & Howard Toplis. *2m N of Crickhowell on A40. Turn R at the Nantyffin Cider Mill onto the A479. After 1m turn L signposted Tretower Court & Castle. Clwyd Dwyrain, pink house before village hall.* **Sun 21 June (12-4.30). Adm £5, chd free. Tea, coffee & cake in the village hall.**
South facing garden adjacent to Tretower Court. In four years, the garden has been transformed from a gravel patch with little biodiversity into a cottage garden featuring wildlife friendly perennials, fruit trees, pond, vegetable patch and cascades of climbers. Partial wheelchair access.

10 CUCKOO HALL
Abermule, Montgomery, SY15 6LD. Gill & Cliff Plowes, 01686 630209, gillian.plowes@gmail.com. *3m W of Montgomery. From Newtown A483 N approx 3m, turn R B4386 signposted Abermule/ Clun/ Montgomery. At r'bout take L (B4385) to Montgomery, after 0.2m over bridge immed R to Llandyssil. Follow yellow signs.* **Visits by arrangement 16 May to 30 June for groups of 25 to 40. Adm inc tea, coffee & cake. Adm £11, chd free.**
A 1½ acre garden developed and designed by retired nursery owners and RHS gold medallists. Semi mature trees with island beds, mature grasses with shrubs give permanent structure: three wildlife ponds, streamside garden, rose pergola, herbaceous borders inc Robert's bed, inspired by a young boy who left a legacy of love. Colour co-ordination foremost in mind during the design. New Potager garden and Japanese style garden. Lots of unusual plants for sale.

11 CULTIVATE COMMUNITY GARDEN
Pendinas, Llanidloes Road, Newtown, SY16 4HX. www.cultivate.uk.com. *A489 W from centre Newtown adjacent to Newtown College & Theatre Hafren.* **Sat 18 July (10.30-3). Adm £4.50, chd free. Tea, coffee & cake.**
Thriving two acre community garden run by local food hub, Cultivate. Extensive range of vegetables, herbs and fruit growing on communal plots and 'micro-allotments'. Lawns to relax on and wildlife area with pond. Managed by Cultivate with the help of a team of volunteers. Look out for the turf-roofed roundhouse, amazing colourful mural, and trained apple trees and our no-dig vegetable beds. Polytunnels and lots of compost heaps Awarded a Community Gardens Grant. Wheelchair access to main parts of garden. Accessible compost toilet.

12 CWM-WEEG
Dolfor, Newtown, SY16 4AT. Dr W Schaefer & Mr K D George, 01686 628992, wolfgang@cwmweeg.co.uk, www.cwmweeg.co.uk. *4½m SE of Newtown. Off bypass, take A489 E from Newtown for 1½m, turn R towards Dolfor. After 2m turn L down asphalted farm track (signposted). Do not follow SatNav, we are on Google Maps (Cwm Weeg Gardens).* **Sun 14 June (2-5). Adm £6, chd free. Cream teas & home-made cakes available.**
A 2½ acre garden set within 35 acres of wildflower meadows and bluebell woodland with stream centred around C15 farmhouse. Formal garden in English landscape tradition with vistas, grottos, sculptures, stumpery, lawns and extensive borders terraced with stone walls. Translates older garden vocabulary into an innovative C21 concept. Grotto. Covered seating area in the large pavilion. Extensive woodland walks along stream with several bridges. The tower/mausoleum under construction. Partial wheelchair access.

13 ♦ DINGLE NURSERIES & GARDEN
Welshpool, SY21 9JD. Mr & Mrs D Hamer, 01938 555145, info@dinglenurseriesandgarden.co.uk, www.dinglenurseryandgarden.co.uk. *2m NW of Welshpool. From Welshpool take A490 towards Llanfyllin & Guilsfield. After 1m turn L at sign for Dingle Nurseries & Garden. Follow signs & enter the Garden from adjacent plant centre.* **For NGS: Sat 9, Sun 10 May, Sat 10, Sun 11 Oct (9-5). Adm £3.50, chd free. Tea & coffee available. For other opening times and**

information, please phone, email or visit garden website.
A 4½ acre internationally acclaimed RHS partner garden on south facing site, sloping down to lakes. Huge variety of rare and unusual trees, ornamental shrubs and herbaceous plants give year-round interest. Set in the hills of mid Wales this beautiful well known garden attracts visitors from Britain and abroad. Plant collector's paradise.

14 EVE'S GARDEN
The Old Stackyard, Cefn-Y-Coed, Llansantffraid, SY22 6TB. Emyr Wigley, 01691 828360. *2m S Llansantffraid. Across bridge out of Llansantffraid on B4393 in direction of Shrewsbury. Turn R for Deuddwr & follow signs to garden.* **Sun 12 July (11-5). Adm £5, chd free. Home-made teas. Visits also by arrangement July to Sept for groups of 5 to 99.**
Deep borders filled with roses, fuschias, pelargoniums, annuals and flowering shrubs surround the house which is itself adorned with pots, hanging baskets and climbing roses. At the back there is a lawn with Japanese maples and a kitchen garden for vegetables, fruit and cut flowers. A home-made greenhouse with tomatoes completes this vibrant garden made in memory of the owner's wife. Level paths throughout the garden for wheelchair access.

SPECIAL EVENT

15 FAIRDENE GALLERY GARDEN
Caerhowel Meadows, Montgomery, SY15 6HE. Frieda Hughes, www.friedahughes.com. *2.3m NW Montgomery. From Montgomery take B4385 N for 2m & turn R signed Caerhowel, after ⅕m take 1st tarmac turn on L (Caerhowel Meadows), keep R onto gravel, turn L at red brick wall – gateway to car park is on the R, at the end of the wall.* **Wed 10 June, Wed 15 July (2-4.30). Adm £25. Pre-booking essential, please visit www.ngs.org.uk for information & booking. Adm inc home-made teas in the gallery.**
A private garden and gallery evolved over 20 years designed and planted by its artist owner and reflects her idiosyncratic style, love of co-ordinated colour, enthusiasm for rock placement, and joy in designing extraordinary metalwork. A limited number of tickets have been made available for these two special one-day events kindly hosted by Frieda Hughes. Introductory talk by Frieda on her garden and art followed by tour of garden and gallery.

&.

GROUP OPENING

16 FORGE VILLAGE GARDENS
Forge, Machynlleth, SY20 8RN. *1½m E Machynlleth. From Machynlleth: A489 E for 0.3m. Turn R on Forge Rd for 1.1m. Car parking just over the bridge on L.* **Sat 27, Sun 28 June (11-4). Combined adm £6, chd free. Home-made teas at Glanyrafon.**

BRONAWEL
Mrs M Sadler.

BRYNGLAS
Mrs J Kirby.

BWTHYN CYMRAEG
Mrs J Hibbert.

GLAN Y PANDY
Neil & Jane Griffin.

GLANYRAFON
Jane & Colin Lees.

Five delightful gardens in the hamlet of Forge adjacent to the River Dulas. Four established riverside gardens with shrubs, borders and raised beds, one newly developed garden on a small and challenging plot. Gardens overlooking the river have historical interest having once been an area with many working mills. Wheelchair access to most areas of some of the riverside gardens. Refreshments at Glanyrafon. Children's garden trail.

17 GARREGLLWYD
Nantmel, Rhayader, LD6 5PE. Stephanie Morgan, 07425 358550, samorgan100@hotmail.com. *5m E of Rhayader. From Rhayader take A44 E for 3½m to Nantmel. Turn L by Dolau Chapel signed Abbeycwmhir. Follow lane for 1½m then turn R by red warning triangle signed Garregllwyd. Follow track for ½m.* **Sat 9, Sun 10 May (12-5). Adm £5, chd free. Light refreshments. Visits also by arrangement Apr to Sept for** groups of up to 99.
A three acre landscaped garden at 1000' with stunning panoramic views of mid Wales. Restored gardens and features inc large ponds with abundance of wildlife, specimen trees, daffodils, bluebells, rhododendrons and raised vegetable beds and greenhouses growing seasonal produce. Designed to cope with exposed altitude, changing weather conditions with minimal maintenance and to encourage wildlife. Variety of seating areas to enjoy the panoramic views and ever changing weather conditions.

18 GARTHMYL HALL
Garthmyl, Montgomery, SY15 6RS. Julia Pugh, 01686 639401, hello@garthmylhall.co.uk, www.garthmylhall.co.uk. *On A483 midway between Welshpool & Newtown (both 8m). Turn R 200yds S of Nag's Head Pub.* **Mon 31 Aug (1-5). Adm £5, chd free. Tea, coffee & cake.**
Grade II listed Georgian manor house (not open) surrounded by five acres of grounds. 100 metre herbaceous borders, newly restored one acre walled garden with gazebo, circular flower beds, lavender beds, wildflower meadow, pond, two fire pits and gravel paths. Fountain, three magnificent cedar of Lebanon and giant redwood. Partial wheelchair access. Accessible WC.

19 GLAN YR AFON
Llangedwyn, Oswestry, SY10 9LQ. Nick & Gill Powell, 07968 250364, gill.powell@ngs.org.uk. *10m W of Oswestry. From Llynclys x-roads (A483) follow B4396 towards Llanrhaeadr YM. After approx 5m turn L at T-junc by Llangedwyn Sch. Over river bridge, take next R: cottage is 4th property on L.* **Visits by arrangement May to Aug for groups of 5 to 20. Limited parking for 6 cars. Adm £5, chd free. Home-made teas.**
500 year old cottage in an acre sloping plot overlooking the Tanat Valley. Large decked area with pergola and arbour. Pond with cascade, productive orchard, raised beds and greenhouse. Steep steps to summerhouse with far-reaching views. Extensive shrub and perennial plantings. Small paddock bordered by natural wooded stream.

20 GLANWYE
Builth Wells, LD2 3YP. **Mr & Mrs H Kidston.** *2m SE Builth Wells. From Builth Wells on A470, after 2m R at Lodge Gate. From Llyswen on A470, after 6m L at Lodge Gate. Will be signposted. Suggest not using SatNav as unreliable.* **Sun 17 May (2-5). Adm £6, chd free. Tea, coffee & cake.**
Large Victorian garden with spectacular rhododendrons and azaleas. Discover herbaceous borders, extensive yew hedges and lawns. Enjoy one of our long woodland walk with bluebells and other woodland flowers. Magnificent views of upper Wye Valley.

21 THE GROVE
Presteigne, LD8 2NS. grovegarden82@gmail.com. *3m W of Presteigne on the B4357, between Evenjobb (2m) and Whitton. (1.3m) What3words app: back.juggler.tumblers.* **Visits by arrangement 1 June to 16 Aug for groups of 10 to 45. Teas, coffee & cakes can be provided (£3). Discuss when booking. Adm £10.**
Stunning seven acre garden divided into large defined areas, each with its own mood and planting style. Beautiful walled garden, courtyard garden, stunning grass garden, very productive vegetable plot and greenhouse. Arboretum with 200+ varieties of tree. Riverside walk and unique sculptures complement the planting. Around every corner there are surprises and delights to discover. For groups at a convenient date before any visit, a 1hr well illustrated presentation 'The Evolution of Grove Garden: One Step at a Time' can be delivered. Discuss when booking if presentation is required.

22 NEW HAFOTTY GANOL
Pen-Y-Garnedd, Llanfyllin, Oswestry, SY10 0AW. **William Denne, 01691 860548, willdenne@icloud.com.** *3m W of Llanfyllin. From Llanfyllin head W on A490/B4391. Take 2nd L after turn for Rhos Y Brithdir. Drop off at Hafotty Ganol. Car Park at What3words app: awake.oxidation.initiated.* **Sat 27, Sun 28 June (11-5). Adm £5, chd free. Tea, coffee & cake.**
A wild, hilltop, wooded three acre garden, 950ft above the Tanat Valley. Unimproved upland wildflower meadows, extensive paved vegetable garden, beehives, fruit, nut and berry orchard forest with naturally regenerating boundaries providing varied wildlife habitats. A nationally significant stand of butterfly orchids is in bloom from mid-June to early July over-stood by champion western red cedars and larch.

23 HURDLEY HALL
Hurdley, Churchstoke, SY15 6DY. **Simon Cain & Simon Quin.** *2m from Churchstoke. Take turning for Hurdley off A489, 1m E of Churchstoke. Garden is a further 1m up the lane.* **Sun 7, Sun 21 June (11-5). Adm £6.50, chd free. Home-made teas.**
'A glorious Welsh Garden' (Country Life) set in a stunning location. 25 acres to explore with topiary, large and colourful herbaceous and mixed borders, ponds and kitchen garden leading to the county of Montgomery's Coronation Meadows with wildflowers inc hundreds of orchids, an orchard with 76 mixed fruit trees, beehives and streamside walk through ancient woodland.

GROUP OPENING

24 NEW LLANFECHAIN GARDENS
Llanfechain, SY22 6UQ. *10m SW Oswestry. From Oswestry take A483 S. R turn at Llynclys then A495 through Llansantffraid. Take R for Llanfyllin, proceed 2½ m to Llanfechain. Turn R for village centre & parking is 100yds on L.* **Sun 26 July (11-4). Combined adm £6, chd free. Home-made teas at Community Centre.**

NEW FRONGOCH
Mr & Mrs Morgan.
NEW LLANFECHAIN SCHOOL COMMUNITY GARDEN
NEW 13 MAES MECHAIN
Warren & Lorraine Green.
NEW 29 MAES MECHAIN
Eric Holmes & Michelle Cooper.
NEW 30 MAES MECHAIN
Anne Trommelen.
NEW 7 MAES YR YSGOL
Nita & Alan Duff.
NEW THE OLD SCHOOL ROOM
Vennetta & Wayne Smith.

Beautiful historic village in glorious setting on River Cain with otters and a myriad of bird life. Motte and bailey fort Domen Gastell; church of St Garmon dating back to 1603 and a C17 pub. Seven gardens: a school community garden, two carefully tended bungalow gardens, a delightful hidden garden with a rill, two small terraced gardens showing what can be achieved with a small plot, and a large garden with productive vegetable and fruit area and beehives designed to encourage wildlife approx 10-15 mins walk from the village centre.

25 LLANGEDWYN HALL
Llangedwyn, Oswestry, SY10 9JW. **Nicholas Williams-Wynn, www.llangedwyn.co.uk.** *8m SW of Oswestry. From Oswestry, A483 S for 3½ m, turn R at Llynclys x-roads, continue W on to the B4396 towards Llanrhaeadr-ym-Mochnant.* **Sun 29 Mar (12-4). Adm £6, chd free. Home-made teas in Llangedwyn Village Hall.**
Beautiful four acre formal terraced garden on three levels, designed and laid out in late C17 and early C18. Fabulous spring colour with banks of daffodils and early flowering shrubs. Unusual herbaceous plants, sunken rose garden, small water garden, walled kitchen garden. Fantastic views over the surrounding countryside with the C18 Cadw listed octagonal Stallion House. Woodland walks, summerhouse, formal ponds and newly planted arboretum.

26 LLWYN
Tregynon, Newtown, SY16 3PP. **Bob & Liz Davies.** *6m N Newtown. In Tregynon from S: L after sch. In Tregynon from N: 1st R, then L at church. Llwyn ¾ m on R. From Bwlch y Ffridd, L up hill. After 1m 1st R towards Tregynon. Llwyn 1m on L.* **Sun 30 Aug (1-5). Adm £4, chd free. Home-made teas.**
This small, colourful garden is packed with interest for the inquisitive visitor, inc pond, paths, hidden places and productive kitchen garden. New uses have been found for basic materials (logs, roots, sacks, old containers, golf clubs) and the compost heaps are nurtured as much as the flower beds. Many plants are available for sale. The practical workings of the garden are visible.

Caelydan Bungalow

27 LLWYNAU MAWR FARM
Cwmdu, Crickhowell, NP8 1RS.
Dr Pauline Ruth. *N of Tretower on edge of Cwmdu. Travelling N on A479 turn L at the Farmers Arms pub in Cwmdu. Through village following signs to Llwynaumawr. Llwynaumawr Farm is the 300 year old barn. Parking will be signposted.* **Sun 7 June (12-5). Combined adm with Maes Llechau £10, chd free. Tea, coffee & cake. Savouries & apple juice.**
Old barn beautifully located on Beacons Way facing south with fantastic views of Black Mountains. Since October 2022, Pauline has been working on an established garden with productive vegetable plot, two acre orchard of rare apples, pears, plums, damsons, cherry, crabapple and walnut. Woodland walks. Climbing roses, fig and vine. Borders and wildflower area. Multiple seating areas to enjoy. Stream, mown paths, dry stone walling, arbour, greenhouses, ancient pears, wildflowers and pollinators.

28 LLYSDINAM
Newbridge-on-Wye, LD1 6NB. **Sir John & Lady Venables-Llewelyn & Llysdinam Charitable Trust,** www.llysdinamgardens.org. *5m SW of Llandrindod Wells. Turn W off A470 at Newbridge-on-Wye; turn R immed after x-ing River Wye. Entrance is up the hill.* **Sun 24 May (2-5). Adm £5, chd free. Cream teas.**
Llysdinam Gardens are among the loveliest in mid Wales. Covering six acres, they command sweeping views down the Wye Valley. The family have developed the gardens over 150 years to inc woodland with specimen trees, herbaceous borders and a water garden provide colourful planting. The Victorian walled kitchen garden and greenhouses grow a variety of vegetables, fruit and exotic plants. The gardens are noted for a magnificent display of rhododendrons and azaleas in May. Wheelchair access via gravel paths.

29 LOWER WERNFIGIN BARNS
Trallong, Brecon, LD3 8HW. **Mark Collins & Alan Loze.** *A40 W from Brecon: 2nd signpost to Trallong (R). Down, over river, up to Trallong Common then follow yellow signs. A40 E from Sennybridge: take 1st sign to Trallong then the same.* **Sat 20, Sun 21 June (12-5). Adm £6, chd free. Tea, coffee & cake. Squash & cream scones available.**
A terraced south facing garden with dense planting of herbaceous perennials and shrubs. Rear garden planted with hydrangeas, azaleas and rhododendrons. A newly planted area of woodland and field walk. A small orchard, vegetable and fruit garden, all managed, like the flower garden without chemicals. In front of the house is a large courtyard with formal rill, fishpond and seating areas.

30 MAES LLECHAU
Cwmdu, Crickhowell, NP8 1SB.
Drs Douglas & Alison Paton.
5m NW of Crickhowell. A40 from Crickhowell, at 4½m turn R. Follow to T-junc & turn L. Maes Llechau is on R. From Brecon, 1st L off A40 after Bwlch, to Maes Llechau after 1m. **Sun 7 June (12-5). Combined adm with Llwynau Mawr Farm £10, chd free. Tea, coffee & cake. Savoury options available.**
We moved to Maes Llechau in 2016. Developed from barren farmland, the 1½ acre garden inc colour coordinated perennial borders, meadows, orchard, new woodland and vegetable garden. Maes Llechau draws from the borrowed landscape of the Black Mountains.

31 THE MALTHOUSE
Llandrinio, Llanymynech, SY22 6SG. Veronica & Alec White, 01691 831473, veronica@llandrinio.com. *B4393 between the Punchbowl Pub & Llandrinio Church. Turn into drive for Llandrinio Hall, then immed fork R & follow the drive for the Malthouse. Accessible parking by house.* **Visits by arrangement Apr to July for groups of 6 to 24. Adm £6, chd free. Home-made teas. Discuss refreshments when booking.**
Walled kitchen garden dating from the C17, adjacent to Llandrinio Hall (Grade II listed building). Restored and planted by present owners over the last 20 years. A long herbaceous border, vegetable parterres, interesting range of C17 pig sties, fruit trees, beehives, long view to the Breidden Hills. A leaflet explaining the history of the house and garden will be available. In April and May, there is a variety of spring blossom, followed by several wisteria. June welcomes a display of wall trained roses followed by Magnolia Grandiflora in July. Box parterres potager, greenhouse, beehives, small pond. Extensive views inc Rodney's Pillar. Garden is flat and wheelchair accessible.

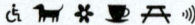

32 THE NEUADD
Llanbedr, Crickhowell, NP8 1SP. James Hooper, 07970 034535, jamescwhooper@gmail.com. *1m NE of Crickhowell. Leave Crickhowell by Llanbedr Rd. At junc with Great Oak Rd bear L, cont up hill for approx 1m, garden on L. Ample parking.* **Sun 7 June (2-6). Adm £6.50, chd free. Home-made teas in the courtyard. Visits also by arrangement 8 June to 31 July for groups of 6 to 12.**
The late Robin Herbert and his wife Philippa started work on the garden at The Neuadd in 1999 and planted many unusual trees and shrubs in the dramatic setting of the Bannau Brycheiniog National Park. One of the major features is the walled garden, with both traditional and decorative planting of fruit, vegetables and flowers. Circuit walks of the garden. Spectacular views, water feature, rare trees and shrubs and a great plant stall. Most of the garden is accessible for wheelchair users, but some steep paths.

33 OAK COTTAGE
23 High Street, Welshpool, SY21 7JP. Tony & Margaret Harvey. *Centre of Welshpool. From High St turn R on Jehu Rd by fish & chip shop & immed L on Bowling Green Ln. Enter from back of house.* **Sun 29 Mar, Mon 6, Sun 19 Apr, Mon 4 May (2-5). Adm £4, chd free. Tea, coffee & cake.**
Intimate garden continues to be developed but is still an oasis of green in the town centre. Gravel paths and stepping stones meander through a wide variety of plants, inc unusual species, and make the garden seem much larger than it is. Alpines are still a favourite as are the insectivorous plants. Modern representation of a Wardian cabinet, with hepaticas. Places to sit and enjoy garden views. Gravel paths with steps and steep slope at entrance.

The Old School Room, Llanfechain Gardens

34 PLAS DINAM
Llandinam, Newtown, SY17 5DQ. Eldrydd Lamp, 01686 248890, info@plasdinam.co.uk, www.plasdinamcountryhouse.co.uk. 7½m SW Newtown on A470. Entrance on L. **Visits by arrangement Mar to Nov for groups of 15+. Mon-Thurs only. Adm £6, chd free. Tea, coffee & cake.**
Discover 12 acres of parkland, gardens, lawns and woodland set at the foot of rolling hills with spectacular views across the Severn Valley. A host of daffodils followed by one of the best wildflower meadows in Montgomeryshire with 36 species of flowers and grasses inc hundreds of wild orchids; Glorious autumn colour with *Parrotias, Liriodendrons, Cotinus* etc. Millennium wood. Explore the new Remarkable Tree Walk which inc eight champion trees. From 1884 the home of Lord Davies and still owned by his descendants. (House not open). Paths are wheelchair accessible.

35 PLUM TREE COTTAGE
Ffawyddog, Crickhowell, NP8 1PY. Mr & Mrs Bennett. *1m S of Crickhowell. From Crickhowell cross river & turn R by Vine Tree. Head into Llangattock & take 1st R after the Horseshoe pub. Follow yellow signs up hill to Ffawyddog common.* **Sat 6 June (12-5). Adm £6, chd free. Tea, coffee & cake.**
This large cottage garden in the heart of the Brecon Beacons National Park is around ¾ acre and comprises a shaded area, herbaceous borders, vegetable beds and wild areas. Wild orchids grow freely in unmown grass along with other wildflowers. The garden is organic and free of herbicides and pesticides. Borders have wide range of traditional and unusual plants. Uncultivated areas have been allowed to encourage wildlife. Large greenhouse for raising and growing plants. Adjacent to Ffawyddog Common, an AONB.

36 PONTHAFREN
Long Bridge Street, Newtown, SY16 2DY. Ponthafren, 01686 621586, admin@ponthafren.org.uk, www.ponthafren.org.uk. *Park in bus stn car park in town centre, 5 mins walk. Turn L out of car park, turn L over bridge, garden on L. Limited disabled parking, please phone for details.* **Sat 25 July (11-4). Sun 26 July (11-4.30), open nearby Bryn Teg. Adm by donation. Tea, coffee & cake. Visits also by arrangement Apr to Sept for groups of 5 to 20.**
Ponthafren is a registered charity that provides a caring community to promote positive mental health and wellbeing for all. Open door policy so everyone is welcome. Interesting community garden on banks of River Severn run and maintained totally by volunteers: sensory garden with long grasses, herbs, scented plants and shrubs, quirky objects. Productive vegetable plot. Lots of plants for sale. Covered seating areas positioned around the garden to enjoy the views. We received a Community Garden Grant in 2023. Partial wheelchair access.

37 THE ROCK HOUSE
Llanbister, LD1 6TN. Jude Boutle & Sue Cox. *10m N of Llandrindod Wells. Off B4356 just above Llanbister village. What3words app: jousting.radically.iron.* **Sat 6, Sun 7 June (12-5). Adm £5.50, chd free. Home-made teas. Gluten free & vegan cakes available.**
About an acre of informal mature hillside garden, with views over the Radnorshire Hills. Over 30 years we have created wildlife ponds, a bluebell meadow, laburnum arch and a vegetable garden with a greenhouse and polytunnel. An example of what can be achieved 1000ft up a Welsh hillside.

38 ROCK MILL
Abermule, Montgomery, SY15 6NN. Rufus & Cherry Fairweather, 01686 630664, fairweathers66@btinternet.com. *1m S of Abermule on the Kerry Rd (B4368) on L. Best approached from the village as there is an angled entrance into field for parking.* **Visits by arrangement in May for groups of 10 to 30. Adm £10, chd free. Home-made cream tea & guided tour inc in adm.**
A river runs through this magical three acre award-winning garden in a beautiful wooded valley. Discover colourful borders and shrubberies, specimen trees and terraces. Take a stroll along woodland walks, bridges and extensive lawns. You'll find fishponds, an orchard, herb and vegetable beds, roundhouse and remnants of industrial past (corn mill and railway line). There is much to explore.

39 14 ST MARY'S PLACE
Union Street, Welshpool, SY21 7PF. Jill Rock. *Centre of Welshpool below St Mary's Church. Car park behind town hall, cross road & turn R. House is past cafe on L. Follow yellow NGS signs.* **Sat 20, Sun 21 June (11-5). Adm £4, chd free.**
Interesting secret town garden on two levels behind house. Steep steps to first level with paved area made from floors of older houses once on the site. Large acers, potted hostas and studio with wisteria and jasmine growing up it. Steps to side of studio to higher level with views of Welshpool. Borders mainly planted with perennials. Seating areas. Unusual varieties of plants and interesting pots. Very steep steps sturdy footwear required.

40 TRANQUILITY HAVEN
7 Lords Land, Whitton, Knighton, LD7 1NJ. Val Brown, 01547 560070, valerie.brown1502@gmail.com. *Approx 3m from Knighton & 5m Presteigne. From Knighton take B4355 after approx. 2m turn R on B4357 to Whitton. Car park on L by yellow NGS signs.* **Visits by arrangement Apr to Sept for groups of up to 30. Adm £5, chd free.**
Amazing Japanese inspired garden with borrowed views to Offa's Dyke. Winding paths pass small pools and lead to Japanese bridges over natural stream with dippers and kingfishers. Sounds of water fill the air. Enjoy peace and tranquillity from one of the seats or the Japanese Tea House. Dense oriental planting with *Cornus kousa* 'Satomi', acers, azaleas, unusual bamboos and wonderful cloud pruning.

310,000 people are cared for each year who are approaching the end of life or diagnosed with a terminal illness through the hospice network supported by National Garden Scheme funding.

41 TREBERFYDD HOUSE
Llangasty, Bwlch, Brecon, LD3 7PX. Sally Raikes, 07748 155484, sally@treberfydd.com, www.treberfydd.com. *6m E of Brecon. From Abergavenny on A40, turn R in Bwlch on B5460. Take 1st L towards Pennorth & cont 2m along lane. From Brecon, turn L off A40 in Llanhamlach towards Pennorth. Go through Pennorth, 1m on L.* **Sun 3 May (12.30-5.30). Adm £6.50, chd free. Cream teas. Home-made cakes & scones, tea & coffee available.**

Grade I-listed Victorian Gothic house with 10 acres of grounds designed by W A Nesfield. Magnificent cedar of Lebanon, towering Atlantic cedars and other notable historic trees. A Victorian rockery, herbaceous border and manicured lawns are ideal for a picnic. Wonderful views of the Black Mountains. Plants available from commercial nursery in grounds - the Walled Garden Treberfydd. Easy wheelchair access to most areas around the house.

GROUP OPENING

42 NEW TREFEGLWYS GARDENS
Trefeglwys, Caersws, SY17 5PH. Susan Paynton. *4.6m SW Caersws. From Caersws turn L B4569. Car Park & Adm Tickets at The Memorial Hall. All within walking distance of car park.* **Sun 5 July (12-5). Combined adm £7, chd free. Home-made teas in The Memorial Hall.**

NEW THE DINGLE
Ann & Anthony Hirst.

NEW 3 GLANTRANNON
Chris Penfold.

NEW LLWYN CELYN
Caroline Rowlands.

NEW LLWYNDERW
Lisa & Darrin Stead, 01686 430930, lisa.danycoed@btinternet.com.

NEW THE SMITHY
Emlyn Jones.

NEW TANGNEFEDD
Marion Brench.

Six delightful gardens set in the village of Trefeglyws in the beautiful Trannon Valley with church dating back to C12 and C18 pub. Cottage gardens, very productive vegetable gardens, streamside and wildlife gardens buzzing with insects showing what can be achieved in small spaces. Displays by the local Swift Conservation Group and the Wildlife Trust.

43 TYN-Y-GRAIG
Bwlch y Ffridd, Newtown, SY16 3JB. Simon & Georgina Newson, 07989 855925, simon.newson@yahoo.com. *4m N Caersws. B4568 from Newtown: Turn R after Aberhafesp. At fork bear L past community centre, then at x-roads turn R. At next fork bear L. Go over cattle grid take 1st R onto rough track.* **Visits by arrangement May & June for groups of up to 18. Adm inc tea, coffee & cake. Adm £12.**

Plant-person's garden at 300m elevation with views of surrounding hills. Varied borders and hectare of indigenous wildflower meadow managed for biodiversity sits around a large pond and woodland. Garden planted to achieve different moods inc a herb area, bright, white and pastel borders, rose garden, farmyard borders, fernery, fruit trees and vegetable beds. Partial wheelchair access. Grass paths, some steps, most can be avoided. Wheelchair users may be dropped off at house.

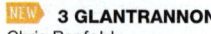

44 NEW UPPER BWLCH FARM
Rhayader, LD6 5NT. Ian & Ruth Rees. *2m NE Rhayader. From Rhayader take the 'Abbeycwmhir' road. Drive 2m & our farm gateway is on your R with a stone engraved with 'Upper Bwlch'. What3words app: thighs.chip.dries.* **Sat 27, Sun 28 June (2-5). Adm £5, chd free. Tea, coffee & cake.**

Small cottage garden on a working farm, created and featured on BBC Garden Rescue and designed by Charlie Dimmock. The team turned Ian and Ruth's rural plot into a country garden which was created in 2019 over 2 days with a revisit filmed in 2024. Interesting story of before and after creation which hosts are happy to share with you. Traditional cottage planting, stumpery, peaceful and rural. There is a short steep incline of 3 metres to gateway of garden.

SPECIAL EVENT

45 VAYNOR PARK
Berriew, Welshpool, SY21 8QE. Mr & Mrs William Corbett-Winder. *5m S Welshpool. Leave Berriew going over bridge & straight up the hill on the Bettws Rd. Entrance to Vaynor Park is on R ¼m from speed derestriction sign.* **Wed 24 June (2-4.30). Adm £25, chd free. Pre-booking essential, please visit www.ngs.org.uk for information & booking. Adm inc home-made teas.**

Spectacular five acre garden set in parkland with medieval oaks. In June the herbaceous borders are at their peak, planted with perennials. Stately cardoons and *Crambe Cordifolia* are underplanted with *Centaurea*, poppies, roses, alliums, *Circium*, *Tradescantia* and flowering shrubs. Roses bloom in the box edged parterre and these formal plantings contrast with the natural grasses that have been encouraged for the summer in the long Victorian archery lawn on the terrace. A limited number of tickets have been made available for this special one-day event kindly hosted by William and Kate Corbett-Winder. Meet in the courtyard for an introductory talk by Kate, followed by a guided tour accompanied by Kate and her gardener Rupert Redway.

46 NEW VICARAGE FARM
Llangynog, Oswestry, SY10 0HG. Sarah Chambers & Shaun Hurlow, 01691 860622, sarah@vicaragefarm.net. *9m NW Llanfyllin, 17m W Oswestry. From Llanfyllin follow B4391 (for Bala) approx 7m through Penybontfawr to Llangynog. Turn L at The New Inn, 1m towards Pennant Melangell. What3words app: topic.songs.directors.* **Sat 4, Sun 5 July (11-4). Adm £5, chd free. Home-made teas. Visits by arrangement 15 June to 27 Aug for groups of 5 to 20. Limited parking. Car sharing recommended.**

Whether it be the stunning views surrounding Vicarage Farm, the large flower borders, the vegetable patch, the rose border, the variety of fruit grown, the large rhubarb area, the beehives, the thyme lawn or the small secret garden - there is something of interest for everyone. This large acre of land has been converted

47 ◆ WELSH LAVENDER
Cefnperfedd Uchaf, Maesmynis, Builth Wells, LD2 3HU. Nancy Durham, 01982 552467, farmers@welshlavender.com, www.welshlavender.com. *Approx 4½m S of Builth Wells & 13m N from Brecon Cathedral off B4520. The farm is 1⅓m from turn signed Farmers' Welsh Lavender.* **For NGS: Thur 23, Fri 24, Sat 25, Sun 26 July (10-4). Adm £5, chd free. Pre-booking essential, please visit www.ngs.org.uk for information & booking. Tea, coffee & cake.** For other opening times and information, please phone, email or visit garden website.
The farm, situated at 1100ft high in the hills of mid Wales, offers spectacular views in all directions. Jeni Macfarlane's stylish wild planting of the steep bank above the ever popular wild swimming pond is a riot of colour. Walk through the fields of blue lavender at their peak. The farm is a bumblebee haven with its wildflower area, orchards and a vegetable garden. Learn how the distillation process works, and visit the farm shop to try body creams and balms made with lavender oil distilled on the farm. Swim in the pond before enjoying coffee, tea and light refreshments or go the whole hog and book the sauna online at welshlavender.com before you visit. Partial wheelchair access. Large paved area adjacent to shop area.

48 WILLOWBROOK
Knighton Road, Presteigne, LD8 2ET. Fiona Collins & David Beech. *Outskirts of Presteigne on B4355 towards Knighton. Turn L just before the bridge.* **Sun 19 July (11-5). Adm £5, chd free. Tea, coffee & cake.**
Arts and Crafts inspired level garden, with yew hedging creating garden 'rooms' and vistas. Discover the pergola cottage garden planted with a wisteria and climbing roses, a formal 'Italian' style pond garden and a double 'hot' summer border. Hydrangeas add to the summer colour, whilst the productive vegetable plot has raised beds, polytunnel and fruit trees.

49 NEW YSCIRFECHAN
Merthyr Cynog, Brecon, LD3 9SB. Rebecca & Sean Davies, www.rivermeadowflowerfarm.co.uk. *9m N of Brecon. Take B4520 from Brecon. Turn L at sign for Cradoc Golf Club. R at the junc towards Battle. Go through Battle & Pontfaen. What3words app: danger.observes.chestnuts.* **Sun 19 July, Sun 9, Sun 30 Aug (12-5). Adm £6, chd free. Tea, coffee & cake.**
A unique opportunity to enjoy a sneak peek behind the scenes of a working cut flower farm. River Meadow Flower Farm extends to over an acre, encompassing cut flower beds, herbaceous borders and PYO beds. Nestled in the peaceful Yscir Valley and flanked by the River Yscir, this is a secluded flower-filled haven. Glorious bunches of homegrown cut flowers will be for sale.

Yscirfechan

More than sixty gardens that open for the National Garden Scheme are holders of a Plant Heritage National Plant Collection. These gardens carry the [NPC] symbol. Through the National Collections, Plant Heritage members are safeguarding 95,000 different plants for the future by growing them, recording them and sharing them. Find out more: www.plantheritage.org.uk.

Acanthus
Hill View Hardy Plants, Shropshire

Acer (excl. palmatum cvs.)
Blagdon, North East

Ajuga spp. & cvs.
59 Ashburton Avenue, London

Alnus
Blagdon, North East

Aster & related genera (autumn flowering)
The Picton Garden, Herefordshire

Astrantia
Norwell Nurseries, Norwell Gardens, Nottinghamshire

Buddleja (hardy spp. & cvs.)
Longstock Park Water Garden, Hampshire

Calendula spp.
Ryton Organic Gardens, Warwickshire

Camellia (autumn & winter flowering)
Green Island, Essex

Camellia & Rhododendron (introduced to Heligan pre 1920)
The Lost Gardens of Heligan, Cornwall

Carpinus
Sir Harold Hillier Gardens, Hampshire

Carpinus betulus cvs.
West Lodge Park, London

Catalpa
West Lodge Park, London

Ceanothus
Eccleston Square, London

Cercidiphyllum
Sir Harold Hillier Gardens, Hampshire
Hodnet Hall Gardens, Shropshire

Chrysanthemum (hardy)
Norwell Nurseries, Norwell Gardens, Nottinghamshire
Hill Close Gardens, Warwickshire

Citrus
Shortgrove Manor Farm, Hertfordshire

Clematis viticella
Roseland House, Cornwall

Codonopsis & related genera
Woodlands, Lincolnshire

Colchicum
East Ruston Old Vicarage, Norfolk

Convallaria
Kingston Lacy, Dorset

Cornus
Sir Harold Hillier Gardens, Hampshire

Corylus
Sir Harold Hillier Gardens, Hampshire

Cotoneaster
Sir Harold Hillier Gardens, Hampshire

Cyclamen (excl. persicum cvs.)
Higher Cherubeer, Devon

Dionaea
Beaufort, Shropshire

Echium spp. & cvs. from the Macaronesian Islands
Renishaw Hall & Gardens, Derbyshire

Erica & Calluna (Sussex heather cvs.)
Nymans, Sussex

Erythronium
Greencombe Gardens, Somerset & Bristol

Eucalyptus spp.
The World Garden at Lullingstone Castle, Kent

Eucryphia
Whitstone Farm, Devon

Euonymus (deciduous)
The Place for Plants, East Bergholt Place Garden, Suffolk

Ferns (Polypodiopsida) Native Welsh species
Treborth Botanic Garden, Bangor University, Gwynedd

Ficaria verna cvs.
The Hidden Garden, Ceredigion

Gaultheria (incl Pernettya)
Greencombe Gardens, Somerset & Bristol

Geranium phaeum cvs. & primary hybrids
The New Barn, Leicestershire & Rutland

Geranium sanguineum, macrorrhizum & x cantabrigiense
Brockamin, Worcestershire

Geum cvs.
1 Brickwall Cottages, Kent

Geum coccineum & G. rivale cvs.
Court View, Somerset & Bristol

Hamamelis
Sir Harold Hillier Gardens, Hampshire

Hamamelis cvs.
Green Island, Essex

Heritage Seed Library (vegetable)
Ryton Organic Gardens, Warwickshire

Hilliers (plants raised by)
Sir Harold Hillier Gardens, Hampshire

Hoheria
Abbotsbury Subtropical Gardens, Dorset

Hypericum sect. Androsaemum & Ascyreia spp.
Holme for Gardens, Dorset

Hypericum spp. & cvs.
Sir Harold Hillier Gardens, Hampshire

Jovibarba
Fir Croft, Derbyshire

Juglans
Upton Wold, Gloucestershire

Lantana
Hampton Court Palace, London

Lapageria rosea (& named cvs.)
Roseland House, Cornwall

Lewisia
'John's Garden' at Ashwood Nurseries, Staffordshire, Birmingham & West Midlands

Ligustrum
Sir Harold Hillier Gardens, Hampshire

Lithocarpus
Sir Harold Hillier Gardens, Hampshire

Malus (ornamental)
Barnards Farm, Essex

Metasequoia
Sir Harold Hillier Gardens, Hampshire

Narcissus cvs. (bred & introduced by Noel Burr)
Bourne Botanicals, Sussex

National Comfrey Collection (Symphytum)
Ryton Organic Gardens, Warwickshire

Nymphaea
Bennetts Water Gardens, Dorset

Pennisetum spp. & cvs. (hardy)
Knoll Gardens, Dorset

Peperomia cvs.
Meveril Lodge, Derbyshire

Photinia
Sir Harold Hillier Gardens, Hampshire

Pinus
Sir Harold Hillier Gardens, Hampshire

Polystichum
Greencombe Gardens, Somerset & Bristol

Primula auricula (Alpine)
Hill View Hardy Plants, Shropshire

Primula auricula hort. (doubles)
Hill View Hardy Plants, Shropshire

Primula sieboldii
The Hidden Garden, Ceredigion

Pterocarya
Upton Wold, Gloucestershire

Pulmonaria cvs.
Brockamin, Worcestershire

Quercus
Chevithorne Barton, Devon
Sir Harold Hillier Gardens, Hampshire

Quercus (Sir Bernard Lovell collection)
The Lovell Quinta Arboretum, Cheshire

Rhododendron (Colonel Stephenson Clarke's collection at Borde Hill)
Borde Hill Garden, Sussex

Rhus
The Place for Plants, East Bergholt Place Garden, Suffolk

Rosa (Hybrid Musk intro by Pemberton & Bentall 1912-1939)
Dutton Hall, Lancashire

Rosa (rambling)
Moor Wood, Gloucestershire

Rubus spp.
Sir Harold Hillier Gardens, Hampshire

Salix
West Wales Willows, Carmarthenshire & Pembrokeshire

Salvia (microphylla & relatives)
Highview House, Norfolk

Salvia (tender)
Kingston Maurward Gardens and Animal Park, Dorset

Salvia rosmarinus cvs.
Great Comp Garden, Kent

Sambucus
Cotswold Garden Flowers, Worcestershire

Sarracenia
Beaufort, Shropshire

Sarracenia spp. & cvs. (incl. Adrian Slack hybrids)
The Hidden Garden, Ceredigion

Saxifraga sect. Ligulatae spp. & cvs.
Waterperry Gardens, Oxfordshire

Saxifraga sect. Porphyrion subsect. Porophyllum
Waterperry Gardens, Oxfordshire

Sempervivum
Fir Croft, Derbyshire

Sorbus
Ness Botanic Gardens, Cheshire
Blagdon, North East

Stewartia
High Beeches Woodland and Water Garden, Sussex

Streptocarpus
Dibleys Nurseries, North East Wales

Strobilanthes
The Hidden Garden, Ceredigion

Symphyotrichum (Aster) novae-angliae
Brockamin, Worcestershire

Symphytum
Ryton Organic Gardens, Warwickshire

Taxodium spp. & cvs.
West Lodge Park, London

Toxicodendron
The Place for Plants, East Bergholt Place Garden, Suffolk

Tulbaghia spp. & cvs.
1 Beeches Farm Cottages, Kent

Tulipa (historic tulips)
Blackland House, Wiltshire

Vaccinium
Greencombe Gardens, Somerset & Bristol

Yucca
Spring View, Burwell Village Gardens, Cambridgeshire
Renishaw Hall & Gardens, Derbyshire

Visit Scottish gardens open for charity

Explore nearly 400 secret gardens in beautiful Scotland in 2026, from tiny urban oases to grand Scottish estates and castle gardens.

scotlandsgardens.org   SC049866

Pictured: Foulis Castle Garden © Tim Winterburn

Acknowledgements

Each year the National Garden Scheme receives fantastic support from the community of garden photographers who donate and make available images of gardens: sincere thanks to them all. Our thanks also to our wonderful garden owners who kindly submit images of their gardens.

Unless otherwise stated, photographs are kindly reproduced by permission of the garden owner.

The 2026 Production Team: Dr Richard Claxton, Vicky Flynn, Louise Grainger, Vince Hagan, Sarah Hosker, Isabelle Osborne, Kay Palmer, Christina Plowman, Helena Pretorius, George Plumptre, Laura Steel, Catherine Swan, Georgina Waters, Anna Wili.

The moral right of the author has been asserted. All rights reserved. No part of this publication may be reproduced, stored in a retrieval system, or transmitted, in any form, or by any means, without the prior permission in writing of the publisher, nor be otherwise circulated in any form of binding or cover other than that in which it is published and without a similar condition including this condition being imposed on the subsequent purchaser.

A CIP catalogue record for this book is available from the British Library.

ISBN: 978-1-0369-3565-8

Designed by Level Partnership
Cover designed by lydiafee.co.uk
Maps by Mary Spence © Global Mapping and XYZ Maps
Printed and bound in the United Kingdom by PCP Ltd

www.carbonbalancedpaper.com
CBP021465

HERITAGE HANDMADE
— GARDEN COLLECTIONS —

2026 CATALOGUE AVAILABLE
01386 584414   www.heritagegardencollections.co.uk   office@hhgc.co.uk

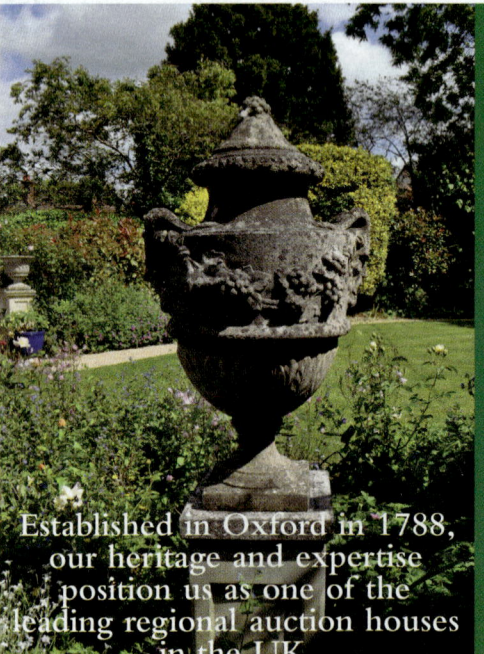

Established in Oxford in 1788, our heritage and expertise position us as one of the leading regional auction houses in the UK.

Mallams
1788

Offering a wide range of sales across our three branches, we offer unique antiques and decorative items for your home & garden.

If you are considering selling an item or a collection, please contact us for a free and confidential valuation.

Visit our website, www.mallams.co.uk for full details of all our sales in 2026 or contact your local branch on the numbers below.

OXFORD	ABINGDON	CHELTENHAM
01865 241358	01235 462840	01242 235712